The Second Coming Bible Commentary

The Complete Text
of Every Scripture Passage
Concerned with the Second Coming of Christ
plus Commentary on Each Verse

William E. Biederwolf

BAKER BOOK HOUSE
Grand Rapids, Michigan 49506

Reprinted 1985 by
Baker Book House Company
from the original printing
made in 1924

Cover art: Albercht Dürer (1471-1528)
Seven Angels with Trumpets, woodcut
The Cleveland Museum of Art
Gift of the Print Club of Cleveland
Used with permission

The Bible text used
in this work is the
American Standard Version

Previously published under the titles: *The Millennium Bible* and
The Second Coming Bible

ISBN: 0-8010-0887-5

Printed in the United States of America

BY WAY OF INTRODUCTION

This volume is not designed, and will prove uninteresting, as mere cursory reading. It is intended the rather, as indicated on its title page, as a help to those who desire to study for themselves as to what the Scriptures really do testify concerning the important event known as the Second Coming of the Lord.

The volume is neither a Pre-millennial, nor a Post-millennial, nor a Non-millennial one. It is an impartial study from the standpoint of pure exegesis of such parts of the Old and New Testaments as deal with the glorious appearing of our Lord and Saviour Jesus Christ. It has been born out of the author's own experience and has consumed by far the larger part of ten years of his time in the course of its preparation.

The author confesses to a ministry of twenty years without a single reference to the coming of the Lord. Other lines of study and his own ignorance of Scripture testimony as to the theme now under investigation furnished him with an excuse of seemingly sufficient validity, in those days, for his mental reserve as to this matter, which he has later found to be so highly important and so extremely vital.

A series of doctrinal sermons were prepared and the nature of the volume demanded that the Second Coming of Christ should find a place in it. But the writer, better than anyone else, of course, knew how shallow his knowledge of the subject really was, and at that time was formed the determination not to speak until at least he could speak with something of an authority born out of an honest and thorough investigation of the matter at issue.

The study was undertaken with no thought of committing the manuscript to the printer. But as the volume of the work, its intricacy and ofttimes its perplexity began to assert themselves, there came the conviction that the character of the volume, regardless of any merit the author's own conclusions might have, would be helpful to others who were desirous of more than the usual superficial knowledge of the subject, but who might not have the necessary time for independent investigation nor the privilege of dealing in the original text of the Word. We have been encouraged in this by a very large number of ministerial and lay friends.

The work has been prepared not so much with the view of setting forth the author's own conclusions, although this, as a rule, as been done; but with the view of setting forth in popular, plain and concise style the arguments on each side of any portion of Scripture bearing upon the subject in hand, where difference of opinion as to its meaning exists, and thus make it possible for every interested reader to intelligently *form his own conclusions* as to what such Scriptures doubtless teach.

We have included in our study the ancient covenants and the promises made by Jehovah to Israel and the many prophecies concerning Israel's future only because they are closely related in the minds of so many to the events connected with the coming again of our Lord.

The volume has been not a little reduced from its original draft, and an endeavor has been made at all times to avoid unnecessary technicality. While the work is presented as a study and cannot therefore at times avoid being somewhat difficult because of the nature of the subject, the author has earnestly tried to keep in view a style and a content such as the average mind can with conscientious application appreciate.

There is always great satisfaction in knowing what the various scholarly interpreters have held concerning any Scripture testimony at issue, and one's own belief is naturally confirmed and strengthened when he knows how large a number of the keenest expositors stand with him in his views. For this reason we have quoted freely and referred copiously to some five hundred or more authorities throughout the work. The mention and repetition of these names, if written in full, would too largely encumber the volume and we have therefore used the briefest possible abbreviation of these names. For the convenience of the student we have placed these abbreviations with the names they represent in alphabetical order at the end of the volume. Whenever the expression, "our text", is used the reference is, of course, to the text employed throughout the entire work, being that of the American Revised Version, used with its accompanying notes through the courtesy of Thomas Nelson and Sons.

Some may wonder why so many verses not dealing directly with the subject in hand have been interpreted along the way. Our answer is that we have given a running comment to the entire passage containing such reference as may be pertinent to the subject, in order that the student may the easier understand the setting of the reference in question, inasmuch as this is as a rule essential to an intelligent grasp of the subject matter under discussion.

The work has been a source of keen satisfaction to the author. It has been at times difficult and laborious, but it has proven so richly remunerative that he has been already more than repaid. If now this humble effort to magnify the grace of God, so richly bestowed upon those who love His appearing, shall prove to be equally helpful to others, it will make him doubly grateful for the rare opportunity and the high privilege of giving himself to so sacred a task and for His precious approval, thus attested, we earnestly pray as this volume is released to those who may find comfort and inspiration in its study.

WILLIAM EDWARD BIEDERWOLF.

THE OLD AND NEW TESTAMENT BOOKS

ARRANGED IN THEIR CUSTOMARY ORDER

THE BOOKS OF THE OLD TESTAMENT

GENESIS	I. Kings	Ecclesiastes	Obadiah
Exodus	II. Kings	Song of Solomon	Jonah
Leviticus	I. Chronicles	Isaiah	Micah
Numbers	II. Chronicles	Jeremiah	Nahum
Deuteronomy	Ezra	Lamentations	Habakkuk
Joshua	Nehemiah	Ezekiel	Zephaniah
Judges	Esther	Daniel	Haggai
Ruth	Job	Hosea	Zechariah
I. Samuel	Psalms	Joel	Malachi
II. Samuel	Proverbs	Amos	

THE BOOKS OF THE NEW TESTAMENT

ST. MATTHEW	II. Corinthians	I. Timothy	II. Peter
St. Mark	Galatians	II. Timothy	I. John
St. Luke	Ephesians	Titus	II. John
St. John	Philippians	Philemon	III. John
The Acts	Colossians	Hebrews	Jude
Romans	I. Thessalonians	James	Revelation
I. Corinthians	II. Thessalonians	I. Peter	

NAMES OF THE OLD AND NEW TESTAMENT BOOKS

ALPHABETICALLY ARRANGED

ACTS	Habakkuk	Kings (I.)	Proverbs
Amos	Haggai	Kings (II.)	Psalms
Chronicles (I.)	Hebrews	Lamentations	Revelation
Chronicles (II.)	Hosea	Leviticus	Romans
Colossians	Isaiah	Luke	Ruth
Corinthians (I.)	James	Malachi	Samuel (I.)
Corinthians (II.)	Jeremiah	Mark	Samuel (II.)
Daniel	Job	Matthew	Song of Solomon
Deuteronomy	Joel	Micah	Thessalonians (I.)
Ecclesiastes	John	Nahum	Thessalonians (II.)
Ephesians	John (I.)	Nehemiah	Timothy (I.)
Esther	John (II.)	Numbers	Timothy (II.)
Exodus	John (III.)	Obadiah	Titus
Ezekiel	Jonah	Peter (I.)	Zechariah
Ezra	Joshua	Peter (II.)	Zephaniah
Galatians	Jude	Philemon	
Genesis	Judges	Philippians	

THE BOOK OF

GENESIS

(←———B. C. 1689)

CHAPTER TWELVE

Now Jehovah said unto Abram, Get thee out of thy country, and from thy kindred, and from thy father's house. unto the land that I will show thee: 2 and I will make of thee a great nation, and I will bless thee, and make thy name great; and be thou a blessing: 3 and I will bless them that bless thee, and him that curseth thee will I curse: and in thee shall all the families of the earth be blessed.

Vers. 1-3. THE ABRAHAMIC COVENANT FORMED.

"I will bless them that bless thee, and him that curseth thee will I curse." This seems to have been wonderfully fulfilled in the history of the dispersion. It has invariably fared ill with the people who have persecuted the Jews, and the favor of God seems to have been with those who have given the Jews protection. Will the future still more remarkably fulfill this prediction? (Deut. 30.7; Isa. 14.1,2; Joel 3.1-8; Matt. 25.40, 45.)

CHAPTER THIRTEEN

14 And Jehovah said unto Abram, after that Lot was separated from him, Lift up now thine eyes, and look from the place where thou art, northward and southward and eastward and westward: 15 for all the land which thou seest, to thee will I give it, and to thy seed for ever. 16 And I will make thy seed as the dust of the earth: so that if a man can number the dust of the earth, then may thy seed also be numbered. 17 Arise, walk through the land in the length of it and in the breadth of it: for unto thee will I give it. 18 And Abram moved his tent, and came and dwelt by the oaks of Mamre, which are in Hebron, and built there an altar unto Jehovah.

Vers. 14-18. THE ABRAHAMIC COVENANT CONFIRMED.

Ver. 15. *"for all the land which thou seest, to thee will I give it, and to thy seed forever."* Does the latter part of this promise pertain to Abraham's literal seed or to his spiritual seed?

Says Keil, "The possession of the land is promised forever. The promise of God is unchangeable. As the seed of Abraham was to exist before God forever, so Canaan was to be its everlasting possession. But this applied not to the lineal posterity of Abraham, to his seed according to the flesh, but to the true spiritual seed, which embraced the promise in faith and held it in pure, believing heart. The promise therefore neither prevented the expulsion of the unbelieving seed from the land of Canaan, nor guaranteed to existing Jews a return to the earthly Palestine after their conversion to Christ."

Scofield, on the other hand, remarks, "The gift of the land is modified by prophecies of three dispossessions and restorations (Gen. 15.13, 14, 16;

9

Jer. 25.11,12; Deut. 28.62-65; 30.1-3). Two dispossessions and restorations have been accomplished. Israel is now in the third dispersion, from which she, the literal seed of Abraham, will be restored to Palestine at the Second Coming of the Lord as King under the Davidic Covenant (Deut. 33.3; Jer. 23.5-8; Ezk. 37.21-25; Lu. 1.30-33; Acts 15.14-17)."

Ver. 16. *"I will make thy seed as the dust of the earth"*,—To Abram, accustomed to the petty tribes that then roamed over the pastures of Mesopatamia and Palestine, a people who should fill the land of Canaan would seem innumerable.

CHAPTER TWENTY-TWO

15 And the angel of Jehovah called unto Abraham a second time out of heaven, 16 and said, By myself have I sworn, saith Jehovah, because thou hast done this thing, and hast not withheld thy son, thine only son, 17 that in blessing I will bless thee, and in multiplying I will multiply thy seed as the stars of the heavens, and as the sand which is upon the sea-shore; and thy seed shall possess the gate of his enemies; 18 and in thy seed shall all the nations of the earth be blessed; because thou hast obeyed my voice.

Vers. 15-18. THE ABRAHAMIC COVENANT AGAIN CONFIRMED.

Ver. 17. *"thy seed shall possess the gate of his enemies"*,—i. e., be masters and rulers of their cities and territories. (K. Mu.)

Lange says, "But the *gate* here points to a deeper meaning. The hostile world has a gate or gates in its susceptibilities through which the believing Israel should enter (Ps. 24.7-9), and the following words prove that this is the sense here."

Ver. 18. *"and in thy seed shall all the nations of the earth be blessed"*,—This great promise was first given without reference to his character (Chap. 12.3); now it is confirmed to him because he has proven himself to be actually righteous after the inward man.

Campbell Morgan says, "This prophecy has never been realized, except to some extent in the first advent of Christ, but it awaits complete and very literal fulfillment in the Millennium age. All Gentile nations are to come into a place of blessing as a result of this restored nationality of Israel. The same truth is taught in Isa. 56.6,7."

"The conquests of the seed of Abraham", says Gerlach, "are those of the Christian Church", and, says Jacobus, "the multiplying of the seed looks beyond mere natural posterity to spiritual progeny".

Again it is a question of literal or spiritual fulfillment.

CHAPTER TWENTY-FOUR

By many Isaac is taken as a type of the Bridegroom (Christ) who goes out to meet and receive His Bride (verse 63 and I Thess. 4.14-16), the Church; and the servant is a type of the Spirit bringing the Bride to the meeting with the Bridegroom. (I Thess. 4.14-16.)

CHAPTER TWENTY-SIX

3 sojourn in this land, and I will be with thee, and will bless thee; for unto thee, and unto thy seed, I will give all these lands, and I will establish the oath which I sware unto Abraham thy father; 4 and I will multiply thy seed as the stars of heaven, and will give unto thy seed all these lands; and in thy seed shall all the nations of the earth be blessed;

23 And he went up from thence to Beer-Sheba. 24 And Jehovah appeared unto him the same night, and said, I am the God of Abraham thy father; fear not, for I am with thee, and will bless thee, and multiply thy seed for my servant Abraham's sake.

Vers. 3, 4, 23, 24. THE ABRAHAMIC COVENANT CONFIRMED TO ISAAC.

CHAPTER TWENTY-EIGHT

13 And, behold, Jehovah stood [1]above it, and said, I am Jehovah, the God of Abraham thy father, and the God of Isaac: the land whereon thou liest, to thee will I give it, and to thy seed; 14 and thy seed shall be as the

[1]Or, *beside him.*

dust of the earth, and thou shalt [2]spread abroad to the west, and to the east, and to the north, and to the south; and in thee and in thy seed shall all the families of the earth be blessed.

[2]Heb., *break forth.*

Vers. 13, 14. THE ABRAHAMIC COVENANT CONFIRMED TO JACOB.

CHAPTER THIRTY-FIVE

9 And God appeared unto Jacob again, when he came from Paddanaram, and blessed him. 10 And God said unto him, Thy name is Jacob: thy name shall not be called any more Jacob, but Israel shall be thy name: and he called his name Israel. 11 And God said unto him, I am God Al-

mighty: be fruitful and multiply; a nation and a company of nations shall be of thee, and kings shall come out of thy loins; 12 and the land which I gave unto Abraham and Isaac, to thee I will give it, and to thy seed after thee will I give the land.

Vers. 9-12. THE ABRAHAMIC COVENANT CONFIRMED AGAIN TO JACOB.

THE BOOK OF

LEVITICUS

(B. C. 1491)

CHAPTER TWO

11 No meal-offering, which ye shall offer unto Jehovah, shall be made with leaven; for ye shall burn no leaven, nor any honey, as an offering made by fire unto Jehovah.

Ver. 11. LEAVEN, THE APT SYMBOL OF CORRUPTION.

Some think the reason why leaven and honey were excluded from the offerings unto the Lord is that they were used in the idolatrous rites of the heathen. The chief, and perhaps the sole reason, however, is undoubtedly their fermenting quality. Honey was anciently used in the preparation of vinegar. Fermentation has ever been recognized as "an apt symbol of the working of corruption in the human heart," as Adam Clark says, both in Scripture (Lu. 12.1; I Cor. 5.8; Gal. 5.9), and among the ancients generally, and hence was unsuitable for the altar of Jehovah.

The leavened bread of Chap. 7.13 was simply used for the sacrificial meal and was not placed upon the altar at all, and so there is no conflict there with the prohibition of our verse and of Ex. 23.18 and 34.25. Leavened bread was common at feasts and was offered with the peace-offering besides the usual accompaniments of the other sacrifices. Christ is our peace-offering, and in Chap. 7.12 we have this in type, and so leaven is of course excluded, as in Him there is no sin; but in verse 13 of this same chapter the one bringing the peace-offering is giving thanks for his participation in it, and so may it not be that leaven seems here to fitly signify, that though having peace with God through the work of the Sinless One, there is still sin in him who presents the offering. (Amos. 4.5.)

CHAPTER SIXTEEN

18 And he shall go out unto the altar that is before Jehovah, and make atonement for it.

Ver. 18. THE COMING FROM THE HEAVENLY SANCTUARY SET FORTH IN TYPE.

This verse, and in fact the whole chapter, should be read in connection with Hebrews 9.

Scofield says, "Dispensationally, for Israel, this is yet future; the High Priest is still in the Holiest. When He comes out to His ancient people they will be converted and restored (Rom. 11.23-27; Zech. 12.10, 12; 13.1; Rev. 1.7). Meantime, believers of this dispensation, as priests (I Pet. 2.9), enter into the holiest where He is (Heb. 10.19-22). It will be at His second coming that He will come forth, the Great High Priest returning unto His people as Lord of lords and King of kings."

CHAPTER TWENTY-THREE

34 Speak unto the children of Israel, saying, On the fifteenth day of this seventh month is the feast of ¹tabernacles for seven days unto Jehovah.
¹Heb., *booths*

Ver. 34. THE KINGDOM-SABBATH SET FORTH IN TYPE.

Just as the Lord's Supper for the Church is both memorial and prophetic ("in remembrance of me," and "ye do show forth the Lord's death until He come"), so likewise is the feast of tabernacles a memorial as to redemption of Israel out of Egypt (verse 43), and, says Scofield, "it is prophetic as to the kingdom-rest of Israel after her regathering and restoration, when the feast again becomes memorial, not for Israel alone, but for all nations (Zech. 14.16-21)."

CHAPTER TWENTY-SIX

Vers. 14-39. The Curse for Apostacy and Contempt of the Law.

The divine threats contained in this chapter embrace the whole of Israel's history. They are not to be thought of as in historical or temporal succession; they were not to multiply continuously, but were in each case to correspond to the amount of the sin. The subject is the general apostacy of the nation and not the sins of individuals. "There are five degrees," says Gerlach, "in the ever seven times more severe punishment."

14 But if ye will not hearken unto me, and will not do all these commandments; 15 and if ye shall reject my statutes, and if your soul abhor mine ordinances, so that ye will not do all my commandments, but break my covenant; 16 I also will do this unto you: I will appoint terror over you, even consumption and fever, that shall consume the eyes, and make the soul to pine away; and ye shall sow your seed in vain, for your enemies shall eat it. 17 And I will set my face against you, and ye shall be smitten before your enemies; they that hate you shall rule over you; and ye shall flee when none pursueth you.

Vers. 14-17. The Punishment in the First Degree.

If Israel gave herself up to ungodliness, then Jehovah would appoint over them "terror," a general notion particularized in verses 16 and 17 by disease, famine and defeat.

18 And if ye will not yet for these things hearken unto me, then I will chastise you seven times more for your sins. 19 And I will break the pride of your power: and I will make your heaven as iron, and your earth as brass; 20 and your strength shall be spent in vain; for your land shall not yield its increase, neither shall the trees of the land yield their fruit.

Vers. 18-20. The Punishment in the Second Degree.

If the punishments already mentioned did not cause the nation to keep the statutes of the Lord, then they would be punished still more severely, even with a sevenfold measure.

"*seven times*",—Seven is at once the number of perfection, indicating the full strength of the visitation, and also the Sabbatical number, reminding the people of the broken covenant.

In the verses before us the sevenfold punishment consists in the barrenness of the land. The earth was to be hard and dry as metal and not a drop of rain was to fall from heaven to moisten it.

21 And if ye walk contrary unto me, and will not hearken unto me, I will bring seven times more plagues upon you according to your sins. 22 And I will send the beast of the field among you, which shall rob you of your children, and destroy your cattle, and make you few in number; and your ways shall become desolate.

Vers. 21-22. The Punishment in the Third Degree.

By beasts of prey Jehovah would destroy their cattle and by barrenness the nation would become small so that the highways would be deserted. "This is an exact picture of the present state of the Holy Land," says Jamieson, "which has long lain in a state of desolation, brought on by the sins of the ancient Jews." (See Isa. 33.8 and Zeph. 3.6.)

23 And if by these things ye will not be reformed ¹unto me, but will walk contrary unto me; 24 then will I also walk contrary unto you; and I will smite you, even I, seven times for your sins. 25 And I will bring a sword upon you, that shall execute the vengeance of the covenant; and ye shall be gathered together within your cities: and I will send the pestilence among you; and ye shall be delivered into the hand of the enemy. 26 When I break your staff of bread, ten women shall bake your bread in one oven, and they shall deliver your bread again by weight: and ye shall eat, and not be satisfied.

¹Or, *by*

Vers. 23-26. The Punishment in the Fourth Degree.

If they still rose up in hostility to the Lord they were to be punished sevenfold with war, plague, and hunger.

By *"the vengeance of the covenant"* is meant the punishment inflicted for a breach of the same, the severity of which, says Keil, "corresponded to the greatness of the covenant blessings forfeited by a faithless apostacy."

The means of sustenance would become so scarce that ten women could bake their bread in a single oven, whereas in ordinary times every woman required an oven for her self.

27 And if ye will not for all this hearken unto me, but walk contrary unto me; 28 then I will walk contrary unto you in wrath; and I also will chastise you seven times for your sins. 29 And ye shall eat the flesh of your sons, and the flesh of your daughters shall ye eat. 30 And I will destroy your high places, and cut down your sun-images, and cast your dead bodies upon the bodies of your idols; and my soul shall abhor you. 31 And I will make your cities a waste, and will bring your sanctuaries unto desolation, and I will not smell the savor of your sweet odors. 32 And I will bring the land into desolation; and your enemies that dwell therein shall be astonished at it. 33 And you will I scatter among the nations, and I will draw out the sword after you: and your land shall be a desolation, and your cities shall be a waste.

Vers. 27-33. The Punishment in the Fifth and Severest Degree.

Verse 29 refers to a fact which literally occurred in Samaria during the period of the Syrians (II Kings 6.28,29), and in Jerusalem during the time of the Chaldeans (Lam. 2.20; 4.10), and in the most appalling manner during the siege of Jerusalem by Titus in A. D. 70.

The judgment is then more minutely described in four leading features: the idolatrous abominations were to be overthrown (verse 30), the towns and sanctuaries were to be destroyed (verse 31), the land was to be devastated (verse 32), and the people were to be dispersed among the heathen (verse 33).

The cities of Israel were made waste (verse 31) by the forced removal of the people during and long after the captivity. It is realized to even a far greater extent now.

Jehovah, in verse 33, says He will draw out a sword after them; i. e., He will drive them away with a drawn sword, and scatter them to all the winds of heaven. For the story of these deportations look at Jewish history all the way from Alexander to Hadrian.

34 Then shall the land enjoy its sabbaths, as long as it lieth desolate, and ye are in your enemies' land; even then shall the land rest, and enjoy its sabbaths. 35 As long as it lieth desolate it shall have rest, even the rest which it had not in your sabbaths, when ye dwelt upon it. 36 And as for them that are left of you, I will send a faintness into their heart in the lands of their enemies; and the sound of a driven leaf shall chase them; and they shall flee, as

14

one fleeth from the sword; and they shall fall when none pursueth. 37 And they shall stumble one upon another, as it were before the sword, when none pursueth; and ye shall have no power to stand before your enemies. 38 And ye shall perish among the nations, and the land of your enemies shall eat you up. 39 And they that are left of you shall pine away in their iniquity in your enemies' lands; and also in the iniquities of their fathers shall they pine away with them.

Vers. 34-39. THE EFFECT OF THESE PUNITIVE VISITATIONS.

Verses 34 and 35 express the restorative effect upon the land. It would enjoy the sabbaths of which it had been deprived by the avarice and apostacy of the people—weekly and yearly. It would be allowed now to rest throughout the duration of the captivity, seventy years, in fact.

Verses 36 and 39 describe in fearful terms the effect upon the remnant who should escape immediate destruction. (See Num. 13.32 and Ezek. 36.13.)

40 And they shall confess their iniquity, and the iniquity of their fathers, in their trespass which they trespassed against me, and also that, because they walked contrary unto me, 41 I also walked contrary unto them, and brought them into the land of their enemies: if then their uncircumcised heart be humbled, and they then accept of the punishment of their iniquity; 42 then will I remember my covenant with Jacob; and also my covenant with Isaac, and also my covenant with Abraham will I remember; and I will remember the land. 43 The land also shall be left by them, and shall enjoy its sabbaths, while it lieth desolate without them; and they shall accept of the punishment of their iniquity; because, even because they rejected mine ordinances, and their soul abhorred my statutes. 44 And yet for all that, when they are in the land of their enemies, I will not reject them, neither will I abhor them, to destroy them utterly, and to break my covenant with them; for I am Jehovah their God; 45 but I will for their sakes remember the covenant of their ancestors, whom I brought forth out of the land of Egypt in the sight of the nations, that I might be their God: I am Jehovah. 46 These are the statutes and ordinances and laws, which Jehovah made between him and the children of Israel in mount Sinai by Moses.

Vers. 40-46. THE ABRAHAMIC COVENANT STILL ENDURES.

Upon repentance and obedience He would renew again this Covenant and gather them again out of the heathen and adopt them as His nation.

THE BOOK OF

NUMBERS

(B. C. 1490—B. C. 1451)

CHAPTER TWENTY-FOUR

14 And now, behold, I go unto my people: come, *and* I will advertise thee what this people shall do to thy people in the latter days.

15 And he took up his parable, and said,

Balaam the son of Beor saith,
And the man whose eye[1] was closed saith;
16 He saith, who heareth the words of God,

[1] Or, *is opened*

And knoweth the knowledge of the Most High,
Who seeth the vision of the Almighty,
Falling down, and having his eyes open:

17 I see him, but not now;
I behold him, but not nigh:
There shall come forth a star out of Jacob,
And a scepter shall rise out of Israel,
And shall smite through the corners of Moab,
And break down all the sons of tumult.

18 And Edom shall be a possession,
Seir also shall be a possession, *who were* his enemies;
While Israel doeth valiantly.

19 And out of Jacob shall one have dominion,
And shall destroy the remnant from the city.

23 And he took up his parable and said,
Alas, who shall live when God doeth this?

24 But ships shall come from the coast of Kittim,
And they shall afflict Asshur, and shall afflict Eber;
And he also shall come to destruction.

Vers. 14-19. THE VICTORIOUS SUPREMACY OF ISRAEL'S MESSIANIC DAYS FORETOLD.

Balaam's fourth prophecy is distinguished from the previous ones by the fact that according to verse 14 it is occupied exclusively with the future and foretells the victorious supremacy of Israel over all her foes and the destruction of all the powers of the world.

The Jews always held that this prophecy received its preliminary fulfillment in David but that it pointed farther on to the Messiah in whom the kingdom was to reach perfection and who was to destroy all the enemies of Israel.

Ver. 17. The prophecy commences with a picture from *"the latter days"* (verse 14), which rises up before the mental eye of the seer. Says Gosman, " *'The latter days'* for Moses and Balaam could only be when the strifes and hindrances should be removed, the enemies overcome. These days for them began with the line of David. The prophecy then received its preliminary and partial fulfillment. But that fulfillment was only relatively perfect, since the entire opposing powers to the people of God were not yet destroyed. There remained yet a future and a wider fulfillment. The *'latter days'* were not yet complete."

"I see",—A prophetic insight like that of Abraham.

"him",—We think Jamieson is wrong in referring this pronoun to Israel. The sentence extends rather in its typical significance to the time of the kings of Israel, but still farther on to the time of the ideal king.

"but not now",—i. e., not as having already appeared.

"but not nigh",—i. e., not to appear immediately, but to come forth out of Israel in the far distant future.

"a star out of Jacob",—This refers, says Jamieson, primarily to David, but secondarily and pre-eminently to the Messiah.

"If there could be any doubt," says Keil, "that the rising star represented the appearance of a glorious ruler or king, this doubt would be entirely removed by the parallel, 'a sceptre shall arise out of Israel'." This ruler would destroy all the enemies of Israel.

"corners of Moab",—This expression is equivalent to the two sides of Moab, i. e., Moab from one end to the other. It is an expression that is often put for the whole country.

16

"all the sons of tumult",—i. e., those rising up tumultuously against Israel, like the Moabites who were men of wild, warlike confusion.

Ver. 18.   Edom and Seir are to be taken by this ruler who is to arise. They were to become his possession, and Israel's through him, by reason of which possession Israel shall become empowered and do valiantly.   Edom is the name of the people and Seir the name of the country.   The fulfillment of this prophecy began with the subjugation of the Edomites by David, but it will not be completed until the *"latter days,"* when all the enemies of God and his Church will be made the footstool of Christ.   Keil remarks, "Edom, as the leading foe of the kingdom of God, will only be utterly destroyed when the victory of the latter over the hostile powers of the world has been fully and finally secured."

Ver. 19.   The subject of this verse is indefinite and is to be supplied from the verb, but it is quite evident from the sense of the words that we have to think of the ruler foretold as a star and a sceptre.

"the remnant from the city",—Out of every city in which there is left a remnant of Edom it shall be destroyed.   Jamieson thinks the reference is to those who flee from the fields to the fortified cities, but we prefer, with Lange, to think of the fugitives fleeing from the captured cities.   The explanation of Ewald which refers the city to Jerusalem is forced and cannot be sustained from the parallelism.

The prophecy closes with single sentences foretelling the general destruction of all heathen powers.

Ver. 23.   This is the fourth division of the prophecy, all introduced by the words, *"he took up his parable"*, the first relating to Edom and Moab (verses 17-19), the second to Amalek, the arch enemy of Israel (verse 20), the third to the Kenites, who were allied to Israel (verses 21, 22); while in the fourth (verses 23,24) the overthrow of the great powers of the world is predicted.

"when God doeth this?"—Keil regards the lamentation as introductory to the prophecy concerning Asshur (Assyria), Balaam's own people. Lange and Knoble, however, with perhaps better reason, think that Balaam is still bewailing the future of Israel and explain this particular expression as meaning, "when God appoints, establishes (see margin) Asshur to do this", i. e., to so afflict Israel.   This disjunctive particle "But" in verse 24, and that the fact that the judgment upon the naval power from Chittim is not introduced with a new parable, favor the latter view.

Ver. 24.   At last the universal ruin of the nations of the world appears in the vision.   The nations that were to come to humble Assyria are not mentioned by name because this lay beyond the range of the prophet's vision, but the reference is without doubt to the Greek and the Roman empires.

"and he also shall come to destruction",—The reference is not to Asshur and Eber, but to their conquerors.

"Whatever powers might rise up in the world of peoples," says Hofmann, "the heathen prophet of Jehovah sees them all fall, one through another, and one after another; but at last he loses in the distance the power to discern whence it is that the last which he sees rise up is to receive its fatal blow."

17

"The overthrow of this last power of the world, concerning which the prophet Daniel was the first to receive and proclaim new revelations," says Keil, "belongs to 'the end of the days' in which the star out of Jacob is to arise upon Israel as a 'bright morning star' (Rev. 22.16), and by the 'end of the days', both here and everywhere else, we are to understand the Messianic era, and that not merely at its commencement, but in its entire development, until the final completion of the kingdom of God at the return of our Lord to judgment."

THE BOOK OF

DEUTERONOMY

(B. C. 1451)

CHAPTER FOUR

26 I call heaven and earth to witness against you this day, that ye shall soon utterly perish from off the land whereunto ye go over the Jordan to possess it; ye shall not prolong your days upon it, but shall utterly be destroyed. 27 And Jehovah will scatter you among the peoples, and ye shall be left few in number among the nations, whither Jehovah shall lead you away. 28 And there ye shall serve gods, the work of men's hands, wood and stone, which neither see, nor hear, nor eat, nor smell. 29 But from thence ye shall seek Jehovah thy God, and thou shalt find him, when thou searchest after him with all thy heart and with all thy soul. 30 When thou art in tribulation, and all these things are come upon thee,[1] in the latter days thou shalt return to Jehovah thy God, and hearken unto his voice: 31 for Jehovah thy God is a merciful God; he will not fail thee, neither destroy thee, nor forget the covenant of thy fathers which he sware unto them.

[1]Or, *if in the latter days thou return*

Vers. 26-31.   THE FUTURE DISPERSIONS OF ISRAEL FORETOLD.

Ver. 26.   The dispersion was of course conditioned on their own forgetfulness of God.

"*heaven and earth*",—These are hardly to be taken as the rational beings dwelling in them, but they are the rather personified and represented as capable of thought and speech.   It was and is a solemn and common form of adjuration.   They were to be witness, to rise up against Israel, not to proclaim vengeance but to bear witness that God was just in punishing them, because He had warned them and had set before them the choice of life and death.

Ver. 27.   For the thing intended see Lev. 26.33,36,38,39; and Deut. 28.64.   From these passages it is evident that the author had in mind not any particular dispersion; not, "the fate of the nation in the time of the Assyrians," as Knobel says; but rather, as Keil says, "all the dispersions which would come upon the rebellious nation in future times, even down to the dispersion under the Romans which still continues; so that Moses contemplated the punishment in its fullest extent."

"*and ye shall be left few in number among the nations*",—This is hardly "*few*" as compared with the number of the heathen, as Schroeder says, but rather, as Keil says, "because they should so far perish through want, persecution and suffering."

The word scatter here is in a form that denotes a driving, urgent pressure.

Ver. 29.   Necessity will lead the holy seed, the remnant to prayer.

Ver. 30.   *"in the latter days thou shalt return to Jehovah"*,—Says Schroeder, "In the kingdom of God last times are ever times of need.   The expression has, indeed, a more or less Messianic form."

The literal of the expression is, "at the end of the days," and does not therefore refer merely to some future time, but the rather to the end in contrast with the beginning; hence not the future generally, but the last future (Hen.), the Messianic age of consummation. (II Pet. 3.3; Heb. 1.2; Acts 2.17; II Tim. 3.1.)   The main reference therefore is to the age of the Messiah, which is commonly called *"the latter days"*, when the scattered tribes of Israel shall be converted to the Gospel of Christ.   This does not mean, however, that a preliminary fulfillment is not to be found in the destined close of their captivities.

Ver. 31.   The Lord is always found by those who earnestly seek Him.

"the covenant of thy fathers",—(See Lev. 26.42-45; Gen. 17 and 26.3,4.)

CHAPTER TWENTY-EIGHT

64 And Jehovah will scatter thee among all peoples, from the one end of the earth even unto the other end of the earth; and there thou shalt serve other gods, which thou hast not known, thou nor thy fathers, even wood and stone. 65 And among these nations shalt thou find no ease, and there shall be no rest for the sole of thy foot: but Jehovah will give thee there a trembling heart, and failing of eyes, and pining of soul; 66 and thy life shall hang in doubt before thee; and thou shalt fear night and day, and shalt have no assurance of thy life. 67 In the morning thou shalt say, Would it were even! and at even thou shalt say, Would it were morning! for the fear of thy heart which thou shalt fear, and for the sight of thine eyes which thou shalt see. 68 And Jehovah will bring thee into Egypt again with ships, by the way whereof I said unto thee, Thou shalt see it no more again: and there ye shall sell yourselves unto your enemies for bondmen and for bondwomen, and no man shall buy you.

Vers. 64-68.   THE FUTURE DISPERSIONS OF ISRAEL FORETOLD.

Ver. 64.   There is perhaps not a country in the world where Jews are not to be found.   The Jews have not, however, served gods of wood and stone among the nations where they are scattered today, nor have they so done since the Assyrian and Babylonian captivity; therefore the reference to this in the verse shows that these earlier dispersions were also, and perhaps primarily, included in the words of the author.

Ver. 65.   When banished among these nations Israel could find no place where it could quietly set its foot and be at peace; even a trembling heart, a failing of the eyes (the going out of the lamp of life) and a pining of soul was to be their heritage.

Ver. 66. *"and thy life shall hang in doubt before thee"*,—"It will be", says Knobel, "like some valued object, hanging by a thin thread before thine eyes, which any moment might tear down." It will be ever hanging in the greatest danger.

On these verses Scofield says, "How wonderfully, and with what exact literalness, this passage has been fulfilled. Written more than 3000 years ago, in the wilderness of Moab, before the tribes had gone into the promised land, before the nation had been constituted, these chapters contain in a prophetic form a synopsis of the entire history of the chosen people from that day to this—closing with such a prophecy as might be taken bodily for a description of the present-day Israel. In Russia with her 4,000,000 Jews, everywhere they are persecuted. Again, wherever the Jew is persecuted he is orthodox, believing that the prophecies will be literally fulfilled in him." It is a fact that as the Jew becomes wealthy and established in power he gradually ceases to believe in the literal fulfillment of the prophecies, and loses all desire, as is seen in the case of the Reformed Jew, to go back to the Holy Land or to have his national life reconstituted.

Ver. 67. They will say what is here announced because of perpetual dread of what each day or night might bring to them.

Ver. 68. The worst is mentioned last, their being taken back into Egypt to ignominious slavery.

"I said unto thee; thou shalt see it no more again",—God will cause them to take a way which they would never have seen again if they had been faithful in their loyalty to Him.

"in ships",—i. e., in violence, packed in slave ships and without any possibility of escape.

"and no man shall buy you",—Says Schroeder, "Even in the slave markets of Egypt, their look, the curse of God, would frighten the buyer away." The clause is one which indicates the utmost contempt.

Under Titus, according to Josephus, multitudes of Jews were transported in ships to Egypt and there sold into bondage, and also under Hadrian Jews without number were sold. "But the word of God is not so contracted. The curses were fulfilled in the time of the Romans in Egypt, but they were also fulfilled in a terrible manner during the middle ages, and are still in a course of fulfillment, though frequently less sensibly felt." (Schultz.)

CHAPTER TWENTY-NINE

The Covenant which God here makes with His people is not a new covenant besides the one He made with them in Horeb, but it is rather a renewed declaration of that same covenant. The conditions of the covenant they had violated, and Moses here rehearses these conditions and summons the people to enter again into the covenant which God was now once more making with them, in order that He might be their God and fulfill His promises concerning them (verses 10-15). Then comes in the closing verses the allusions to the punishments which threatened them in case of apostasy.

CHAPTER THIRTY

1 And it shall come to pass, when all these things are come upon thee, the blessing and the curse, which I have set before thee, and thou shalt call them to mind among all the nations, whither Jehovah thy God hath driven thee, 2 and shalt return unto Jehovah thy God, and shalt obey his voice according to all that I command thee this day, thou and thy children, with all thy heart, and with all thy soul; 3 that then Jehovah thy God will ¹ turn thy captivity, and have compassion upon thee, and will return and gather thee from all the peoples whither Jehovah thy God hath scattered thee. 4 If *any of* thine outcasts be in the uttermost parts of heaven, from thence will Jehovah thy God gather thee, and from thence will he fetch thee: 5 and Jehovah thy God will bring thee into the land which they fathers possessed, and thou shalt possess it; and he will do thee good, and multiply thee above thy fathers. 6 And Jehovah thy God will circumcise thy heart, and the heart of thy seed, to love Jehovah thy God with all thy heart, and with all thy soul, that thou mayest live. 7 And Jehovah thy God will put all these curses upon thine enemies, and on them that hate thee, that persecuted thee. 8 And thou shalt return and obey the voice of Jehovah, and do all his commandments which I command thee this day. 9 And Jehovah thy God will make thee plenteous in all the work of thy hand, in the fruit of thy body, and in the fruit of thy cattle, and in the fruit of thy ground, for good: for Jehovah will again rejoice over thee for good, as he rejoiced over thy fathers; 10 if thou shalt obey the voice of Jehovah thy God, to keep his commandments and his statutes which are written in this book of the law; if thou turn unto Jehovah thy God with all thy heart, and with all thy soul.

¹Or, *return to*

Vers. 1-10. THE PROMISE OF RESTORATION DECLARED.

Ver. 1. *"the blessing and the curse"*,—i. e., the blessing for the obedient and the curse for the obdurate. Even in the direst times and deepest apostacy on the part of the nation there would always be a holy seed to which the blessings pertained, as well as the incorrigible majority upon whom the curse exhausted itself.

Ver. 2. (See Chap. 4.29.)

Ver. 3. *"will turn thy captivity"*,—This does not mean to bring back the captives (Kn. Ges. Mic.), in as much as this is said in what follows to be the consequence of the turning of their captivity; while furthermore the form of the verb will not permit this interpretation.

It must be taken either in a figurative sense, to turn the imprisonment, i. e., to put an end to the captivity (K. Mei.), or be taken, as Hengstenberg and Schroeder take it, in the sense of the marginal rendering of our text, "The return of the Lord to the captivity, from which, with the wretchedness of His people, He had hitherto concealed His face." This latter rendering seems to suit the connection and especially the parallelism with the "return" of the Lord in the following part of the verse. (See Jer. 29.14; 30.3,18.)

"and will return",—This return of Jehovah to His people seems to resume the thought of the first *"return"* and thus confirms somewhat the interpretation given above.

Vers. 4,5. "These words", says Keil, "do not furnish any proof that the Jews will ultimately be brought back to Palestine. The possession of earthly Canaan for all time is nowhere promised to the Israelitish nation in the law. The words 'multiply thee above thy fathers', while

21

they have some reference to the final redemption of Israel, are fatal to the view of any literal restoration. If there is to be an increase in the number of the Jews, when they are gathered out of their dispersion, above the number of their fathers, and therefore above the number in the time of Solomon and the first monarchs of the two kingdoms, Palestine will never furnish room enough for a nation multiplied like this."

There is little, if any force at all, in this objection, which is also voiced by Wordsworth and others. If the Lord pleased to make the land capable of sustaining larger numbers He could easily do so. The passage does seem to point to a national and local return. It has received partial fulfillment again and again in the history of the Jews, but whether, after the conversion of the Jews to Christ, they are to be literally restored to the earthly Canaan must be determined in keeping with the various other Scriptures on this matter.

Keil says, "The multiplication promised here will consist in the realization of the promise given to Abraham, that his seed should grow into nations, not of 'Israel according to the flesh,' but of 'Israel according to the spirit', whose land is not restricted to the boundaries of an earthly Palestine." (Schr. Wor. Gosman.)

Jamieson, on the other hand, contends that, "The promise was not fulfilled on the restoration of the Jews from Babylon, for Israel was not then scattered in the manner here described—'among all nations', 'unto the utmost parts of heaven' (verse 4); and when God recalled them from that bondage all the Israelites were not brought back, and they were not multiplied above their fathers (verse 5), nor were their hearts nor those of their children circumcised to love the Lord (verse 6). It is not, therefore, of the Babylonish captivity Moses is speaking in this passage; it must be of the dispersed state to which they have been doomed for 1800 years. This prediction may have been partially accomplished upon the return from Babylon; for, according to the structure and design of Scripture prophecy, it may have pointed to several similar eras in their national history. But undoubtedly it will receive its complete and full accomplishment in the conversion of the Jews to the Gospel of Christ, after which they will return and obey the voice of the Lord. The words may, therefore, be interpreted either wholly in a spiritual sense (John 11.51,52), or, as many think, in a literal sense also."

Scofield says, "Here, then, if there were no other passage, is a plain declaration of the purpose of God to plant again his ancient people in their own land."

Ver. 6. "The fulfillment of this promise," says Keil, "does not take place all at once. It commenced with small beginning at the deliverance from Babylonish exile, and in a still larger degree at the appearance of Christ in the case of all the Israelites who received Him then as their Saviour. Since then it has been carried on through all ages in the conversion of individual children of Abraham to Christ, and it will be realized in the future in a more glorious manner in the nation at large (Rom. 11.25)."

Ver. 7. The reverse side of these acts of grace, after the manner of Gen. 12.3.

Vers. 8-10. Now follows the general thought that the Israelites would come again into right relations with Jehovah, their God, would enter into true covenant relationship with Him and enjoy the blessings of the covenant under Him.

The *"fathers"* are not the patriarchs alone but all the pious ancestors of the people.

These verses Scofield calls "The Palestinian Covenant," and says that it "gives the conditions under which Israel entered the promised land. It is important to see that the nation has never yet taken the land under the unconditional Abrahamic Covenant, nor has it ever possessed the whole land. The Palestinian Covenant is in seven parts:

(1) Dispersion for disobedience, verse 1.
(2) The future repentance of Israel while in the dispersion, verse 2.
(3) The return of the Lord, verse 3.
(4) Restoration to the land, verse 5.
(5) National conversion, verse 6.
(6) The judgment of Israel's oppressors, verse 7.
(7) National prosperity, verse 9."

In verse 20 is set forth once more the condition of life, and of long life in the land promised to their fathers.

THE SECOND BOOK OF
SAMUEL
(B. C. 1056—B. C. 1017)

CHAPTER SEVEN

8 Now therefore thus shalt thou say unto my servant David, Thus saith Jehovah of hosts, I took thee from the ¹sheepcote, from following the sheep, that thou shouldest be ²prince over my people, over Israel; 9 and I have been with thee whithersoever thou wentest, and have cut off all thine enemies from before thee; and I will make thee a great name, like unto the name of the great ones that are in the earth. 10 And I will appoint a place for my people Israel, and will plant them, that they may dwell in their own place, and be moved no more; neither shall the children of wickedness afflict them any more, as at the first, 11 and as from the day that I commanded judges to be over my people Israel; and I ³will cause thee to rest from all thine enemies. Moreover Jehovah telleth thee that Jehovah will make thee a house. 12 When thy days are fulfilled, and thou shalt sleep with thy fathers, I will set up thy seed after thee, that shall proceed out of thy bowels, and I will establish his kingdom.

¹Or, *pasture*
²Or, *leader*
³Or, *have caused*

13 He shall build a house for my name, and I will establish the throne of his kingdom for ever. 14 I will be his father, and he shall be my son: if he commit iniquity, I will chasten him with the rod of men, and with the stripes of the children of men; 15 but my lovingkindness shall not depart from him, as I took it from Saul, whom I put away before thee. 16 And thy house and thy kingdom shall be made sure for ever before thee: thy throne shall be established for ever. 17 According to all these words, and according to all this vision, so did Nathan speak unto David.

24 And thou didst establish to thyself thy people Israel to be a people unto thee for ever; and thou, Jehovah, becamest their God.

29 now therefore ⁴let it please thee to bless the house of thy servant, that it may continue for ever before thee; for thou, O Lord Jehovah, hast spoken it: and with thy blessing let the house of thy servant be blessed for ever.

⁴Or, *begin and bless*

Vers. 8-17,24,29. THE COVENANT WITH DAVID.

Ver. 10. "The gradually advancing manifestations of the Lord's favor to David as set forth in verses 8 and 9 look to the well-being of the people of Israel." (Er.)

"*I will appoint a place*",—By subduing their enemies the Lord made room for a safe and unengendered expansion by the people of Israel in the promised land.

"*will plant them*",—This is the promise of a firm, deep-rooted national life.

"*dwell in their own place*",—i. e., within the limits secured for them by the Lord.

"*as at the first*",—This doubtless refers to the beginning of their history in Egypt.

The sense is, as W. J. Erdman says, that after all the manifestations of His favor in the past up to this time, the Lord will for the future assure His people a position and an existence wherein they shall no more experience the affliction and oppression that they formerly suffered from godless nations.

Ver. 11. "*and I will cause thee to rest*",—Some take the verb in the perfect tense as in the Authorized Version, resuming the thought from verse 9, but this is inadmissible because the discourse has already in the preceding words turned to the future, and such a retrogressive repetition would be intolerable considering especially the rapid advance in thought.

"*Jehovah will build thee a house*",—There is here no allusion to David's house of cedar, the building of the house being here naturally figurative of the bestowment of a blessed posterity, etc. (See I Chron. 17.25.)

Ver. 12. After David's death the promise was to be fulfilled.

"*thy seed*",—This does not refer to the whole posterity of David, as is clear from the explanatory words in I Chron. 17.11, "*thy seed that shall be of thy sons*"; nor is it merely a single individual, but a selection from the posterity, which will be appointed by God's favor to succeed David on the throne.

Ver. 13. "*for my name*",—The name stands for God Himself—not simply in His honor, or as a place to call on Him, but a place which should be the sign and pledge of His presence in Israel.

Ver. 14. "*the rod of men*",—This means with such punishment as men suffer for their sins and not merely "moderate punishments", as Clericus says.

Ver. 15. Hengstenberg finely remarks, "The contrast is that between the punishment of sin in individuals and the favor that remains permanently with the family, whereby the divine promise becomes an unconditional one."

"*before thee*",—i. e., before thy face.

Ver. 16. David, as ancestor and beginner of the line of kings, is conceived of as he who passes all his successors before him in vision, as Gerlach supposes, or as Keil says, "continues to exist in his descendants".

When David's earthly throne became extinct God raised up Christ as his seed to sit on his throne forever.

Ver. 24. The first clause does not refer merely to the liberation of Israel out of Egypt, nor hardly to the conquest of Canaan alone, as W. J. Erdman supposes, but rather as Keil says, "to all that the Lord had done for the establishment of Israel as the people of His possession, from the time of Moses till His promise of the eternal continuance of the throne of David."

"*establish*",—The thought is of the establishment of their dwellings, their possessions and their whole life.

"*to be a people unto thee forever*",—Gerlach says, "All nations are finally merged in this people, the divine Israel, the congregation of Jesus Christ." Again, as throughout the passage, it is a question of literal or spiritual interpretation.

Ver. 29. "*for thou, O Lord Jehovah, hast spoken it*",—This represents the content of verse 21 as the divine ground of the desired fulfillment of the promise.

"*with thy blessing*",—This is better rendered, "from thy blessing", as the source of all blessings. Then instead of the optative form of the Authorized Version and of our text, the future form of the last clause gives a richer sense and one more appropriate to the connection, i. e., God hath spoken it and it WILL be so. The sentence best reads, "And from thy blessing will the house of thy servant be blessed forever."

Says Scofield, "This Davidic covenant has but one condition: disobedience in the Davidic family is to be visited with chastisement, but *not* to the abrogation of the Covenant (II Sam. 7.15; Psa. 89.20-37; Isa. 24.5; 54.3). The chastisement fell; first in the division of the kingdom under Rehoboam, and, finally in the captivities (II Kings 25.1-7). Since that time but one King of the Davidic family has been crowned at Jerusalem and He was crowned with thorns. But the Davidic covenant confirmed to David by the oath of Jehovah, and renewed to Mary by the angel Gabriel, is immutable (Psa. 89.30-37), and the Lord God will yet give to that thorn-crowned One 'the throne of His father David' (Luke 1.31-33; Acts 2.29-32; 15.14-17)."

THE FIRST BOOK OF THE

CHRONICLES

(<———B. C. 1015)

CHAPTER SEVENTEEN

7 Now therefore thus shalt thou say unto my servant David, Thus saith Jehovah of hosts, I took thee from the [1]sheepcote, from following the sheep, that thou shouldst be [2]prince over my people Israel: 8 and I have been with thee whithersoever thou hast gone, and have cut off all thine enemies from be-

[1]Or, *pasture*

[2]Or, *leader*

fore thee; and I will make thee a name like unto the name of the great ones that are in the earth. 9 And I will appoint a place for my people Israel, and will plant them, that they may dwell in their own place and be moved no more; neither shall the children of wickedness waste them any more, as at the first, 10 and *as* from the day that I commanded judges to be over my people Israel; and I ³will subdue all thine enemies. Moreover I tell thee that Jehovah will build thee a house. 11 And it shall come to pass, when thy days are

³Or, *have subdued*

fulfilled that thou must go to be with thy fathers, that I will set up thy seed after thee, who shall be of thy sons; and I will establish his kingdom. 12 He shall build me a house, and I will establish his throne for ever. 13 I will be his father, and he shall be my son: and I will not take my lovingkindness away from him, as I took it from him that was before thee; 14 but I will settle him in my house and in my kingdom for ever; and his throne shall be established for ever. 15 According to all these words, and according to all this vision, so did Nathan speak unto David.

Vers. 7-15. THE DAVIDIC COVENANT.

(See II Samuel 7.8-17.)

"David is here," says Scofield, "as often, a type of his Son after the flesh (Matt. 1.1; Rom. 1.3), Jesus the Shepherd-King. At His first coming He took the shepherd's place, first in death (John 10.11), and now in resurrection power (Heb. 13.20). At His return He will take the place of "ruler over Israel" (Isa. 11.10-12; Jer. 23.5-8; Luke 1.32,33; Acts 15.14-17). This is the precise order of Psalms 22,23,24. In the first the Good Shepherd is giving His life for the sheep; in the second He is caring for the sheep; in the third He comes to reign as King in glory."

Ver. 9. *"I will appoint"*,—The perfects here are to be taken as future statements of that which God will further show to His people. Some would have the promises of future salvation begin only with verse 11.

"children of wickedness",—The Egyptians are doubtless chiefly intended.

Ver. 10. *"I tell thee"*,—It is inadmissible to give this a past meaning, as do some, and render, "I have told thee"; because we cannot discover that such an announcement was made before, in as much as our historical books nowhere mention it.

Ver. 11. *"who shall be of thy sons"*,—II Sam. 7.12 no doubt presents the original, "that shall proceed out of thy bowels".

Keil, Starke, and older commentators say that the writer here meant to designate not so much Solomon but the Messiah. But the first words of verse 12 seem to indicate that Solomon was meant, as in II Chron. 7.18 his person and not that of some future Messianic descendant is manifestly designated. Accordingly, as in II Sam. 7.12, so in Chronicles the Messianic element is limited essentially to the eternal duration that is promised to the kingdom of Solomon (verses 12-14).

Ver. 13. *"him that was before thee"*,—i. e., Saul.

Ver. 14. *"in my house and in my kingdom"*,—First in the Old Testament theocracy and then in the Messianic kingdom of the new covenant, the full glory of which is yet to come.

THE BOOK OF

JOB

(B. C. 1520)

CHAPTER NINETEEN

25 But as for me I know that my Redeemer liveth,
And at last he will stand up upon the earth;

26 And after my skin, even this body, is destroyed,
Then without my flesh shall I see God.

Ver. 25-26. JOB'S FAITH IN HIS FUTURE VINDICATION.

There is really some doubt as to whether this passage in Job can rightly be said to hold any reference to Christ, or to Job's resurrection or to any contemplated vision of the coming Lord.

The Hebrew word "Goel" may quite as properly be translated "Vindicator"; the words "day", "worms" and "body" are not in the text, and it is somewhat doubtful whether even the idea of death inheres in the passage. Many modern translators think Job meant to say no more than that even though his skin, that is, his body, waste away, yet *"in his flesh"*, that is, before he dies, he would see God interposing to vindicate his character, even as the concluding part of the poem shows to have been the case. While these expositors do not question that Job did believe in the immortality of the soul, they contend that it is a question whether at that early period he could have had any such well defined doctrine of the Resurrection. or would have used it in this connection if he had.

By far the majority of modern expositors, however, it is held that Job does refer to his resurrection, and that although no reference is made to his resurrection body, the hope is expressed of a future spiritual beholding of God as a glorified spirit. But, with Delitzsch, we do not believe this exhausts the meaning of Job's confession.

If the translation, "in my flesh", be retained, the reference, accordingly, must be to his resurrection body. The translation of our text, however, ("without my flesh") is much to be preferred and is held by practically all of our ablest commentators. It must further be noticed that Job says that not merely he, but his *eyes* shall behold God, and he must therefore have imagined his spirit clothed with a new spiritual body instead of the old decayed one, all of which points to a rather clear hope of a coming resurrection.

"And at last He will stand upon the earth",—In view of the foregoing it is certainly within the limits of sound interpretation to see in these words a prophecy of the Redeemer's Second Coming, or, as is often the case with the prophets, a double prophecy, viz., of the Redeemer's incarnation and His coming to judgment, the first necessary to the second and the second the compliment of the first. Certainly as thus taken, this magnificent passage is worthy, as one has said, to be "written in gems and gold".

THE PSALMS
(B. C. 1055)

PSALM ONE

> 5 Therefore the wicked shall not stand
> in the judgment, nor sinners in
> the congregation of the righteous.

Ver. 5. THE WICKED AND THE RIGHTEOUS IN JUDGMENT-TIME.

"the wicked shall not stand in the judgment",—We are reminded by certain scholars that it is not without significance that the Greek version reads here, "the wicked shall not *rise*", and for "sinners in the congregation of the righteous" it reads, "sinners in the *counsel* of the righteous", as if not only would the ungodly not rise at the same time with the righteous, but that the latter would be a congregation or a company to whom special judicial functions would belong. (Deut. 7.22 and Rev. 20.4.) Exegetical refinement of this character is, however, not to be relied upon.

PSALM TWO

The first three verses of this Psalm describe the conduct of the rebellious nations, the next three set forth God as replying to them by word and deed, while in the next three the Messiah, the Anointed Himself, speaks without being introduced and declares the divine decree in relation to Himself, and in the last three verses the Psalmist exhorts the nations to submission.

Scofield says this Psalm gives the order of the establishment of the Kingdom. He says, "It is in six parts. (1) The rage of the Gentiles, the vain imagination of the 'people' (the Jews), and the antagonism of the rulers against Jehovah's Anointed (verses 1-3). The inspired interpretation of this is in Acts 4.25-28, which asserts its fulfillment in the crucifixion of Christ. (2) The derision of Jehovah (verse 4) that men should suppose it possible to set aside His covenant (II Sam. 7.8-17), and oath (Psa. 89.34-37). (3) The vexation (verse 5) fulfilled, *first* in the Destruction of Jerusalem, A. D. 70; and in the final dispersion of the Jews at that time; and to be fulfilled more completely in the tribulation (Matt. 24.29) which immediately precedes the return of the King (Matt. 24.30). (4) The establishment of the rejected King upon Zion (verse 6). (5) The subjection of the earth to the King's rule (verses 7-9). (6) The present appeal to the world-powers (verses 10-12)."

1 Why do the nations [1]rage,
    And the peoples meditate a vain thing?
2 The kings of the earth set themselves,
    And the rulers take counsel together,

Against Jehovah, and against his anointed, *saying*
3 Let us break their bonds asunder,
    And cast away their cords from us.
4 He that sitteth in the heavens will laugh:
    The Lord will have them in derision.

[1]Or, *tumultuously assemble*

28

5 Then will he speak unto them in his
   wrath,
   And ²vex them in his sore displeasure:
6 Yet I have set my king
   Upon my holy hill of Zion.
7 I will tell of the decree:
   Jehovah said unto me, Thou art my
   son;
   This day have I begotten thee.
8 Ask of me, and I will give *thee* the
   nations for thine inheritance,
   And the uttermost parts of the earth
   for thy possession.

²Or, *trouble*

9 Thou shalt break them with a rod
   of iron;
   Thou shalt dash them in pieces like
   a potter's vessel.
10 Now therefore be wise, O ye kings:
   Be instructed, ye judges of the earth.
11 Serve Jehovah with fear,
   And rejoice with trembling.
12 Kiss the son, lest he be angry, and ye
   perish in the way,
   For his wrath ³will soon be kindled.
   ⁴Blessed are all they that take refuge
   in him.

³Or, *may*
⁴Or, *Happy*

Vers. 1-12.   THE REIGN OF JEHOVAH'S ANOINTED.

Ver. 5.   This verse Scofield thinks is to find its final and more complete fulfillment in the great tribulation just before Christ's coming in glory
and especially in the moment of that coming, while verse 6 he thinks refers
to the establishment of the rejected Messiah upon Mount Zion, and the
three following verses to the submission of the earth to His rule.   With
this we find those of the same school of interpretation in agreement.   There
is no question whatever as to the Messianic character of the Psalm, and in
so far as it has not as yet found fulfillment it must of course look still to
the future.

Says Alexander, "The same rash and hopeless opposition to the Lord
and His Anointed still continues, and is likely to continue until the kingdoms of this world become the kingdoms of our Lord and of His Christ."
These authorities, belonging to opposite schools of interpretation, contend, as will be noted, the one for a literal and the other for a spiritual
fulfillment of this prophetical Psalm.

Ver. 7.   *"I will tell the decree"*,—i. e., the statute, the organic law
or constitution of my kingdom.

"Jehovah said unto me",—i. e., at my inauguration or induction into
office.

"This day have I begotten thee",—The relation here described as
manifest in time rests upon one that is essential and eternal, and the interpretation of the passage as describing the inauguration of Christ as Mediatorial King by no means impugns the Eternal Sonship of His Divine nature.
It does not therefore, by implying something recent, exclude the eternal
reference any more than the universality of Christ's kingdom is excluded
by the local reference to Zion.   The phrase, "I have begotten thee", is
equivalent to saying "I have become thy Father."

Ver. 8.   Here Jehovah speaks to His Son.

"uttermost parts of the earth",—i. e., all that lies between the uttermost ends of the earth.   This is to be the Messiah's kingdom.   That He
has asked for this and received it as His heritage is implied in verses 2 and
3 where the nations are represented as in revolt against Him as their rightful sovereign.   This verse of course asserts the share of the Gentiles in the
blessings of the Messiah's rule yet not as heathen, but as submissive to the
Messianic kingdom.

Seiss remarks here that this Psalm and especially this verse is much upon the lips of those who expect the world's conversion, and a blessed Millenium *prior* to the return of Christ to judge the alien world. But he says, "This is a mistake. We have here the Father's covenant to the Son, and not to men in this world; and the time given for its fulfillment is the judgment time; the time when the confederated anti-christian powers are to be dashed to pieces like brittle pottery; the time when God shall enthrone His King on the holy hill of Zion. This Psalm synchronizes in its import with Dan. 2.44-45; 7.9-14 and Lu. 19.15-27."

Ver. 9. *"Thou shalt break them with a rod of iron"*,—The Messiah is thus represented also in Rev. 12.5 and 19.5. This utterly shatters the objection of De Wette to the Messianic interpretation. The Messiah's power is to be exercised in wrath as well as in mercy. The Septuagint and several older versions change some of the vowel points and make it read like Micah 7.14, "to rule", or "to feed with a rod of iron" (as a shepherd). This last figure is a common one to represent the exercise of regal power, and there may be an ironical allusion to this here.

"Thou shalt dash them in pieces like a potter's wheel",—A description of the easy and immediate destruction of a worthless vessel.

Blackstone remarks here, "He is coming to sit upon the throne of His glory (Matt. 25.31), and to be admired in all them that believe (II Thess. 1.10), and to rule, in judgment and equity, all the nations of the earth. His coming in His Kingdom and His coming in His glory are synonymous, and both are yet future."

PSALM EIGHT

4 What is man, that thou art mindful of him?
And the son of man, that thou visitest him?
5 For thou hast made him but little lower than [1]God,
And crownest him with glory and honor.

[1]Or, *the angels*. Heb. *Elohim*.

6 Thou makest him to have dominion over the works of thy hands;
Thou hast put all things under his feet:
7 All sheep and oxen,
Yea, and the beasts of the field,
·8 The birds of the heavens, and the fish of the sea,
Whatsoever passeth through the paths of the seas.

Vers. 4-8. CHRIST'S FUTURE DOMINION FORETOLD.

This Psalm is taken by many as next in order of the Messianic Psalms. That its main reference, however, is to the dignity of human nature, as it was at first and as it is to be restored in Christ, there can be no doubt. "It is very evident, however," says Jamieson, "by the Apostle's inspired expositions (Heb. 2. 6-8; I Cor. 15.27,28) that the language here employed finds its fulfillment only in the final exaltation of Christ's human nature."

In Psalm 2 Jehovah's rejected and crucified Son is yet to reign in Zion; here, though in His human nature made a little lower than the angels (verses 4-6), He is to have dominion over the redeemed creation. (See Heb. 2.6-11.)

Says Scofield, "Heb. 2.6-11, in connection with this Psalm and Rom. 8.17-21, shows that the 'many sons', whom He is bringing to glory, are joint heirs with Him in both the royal right of Psa. 2 and the human right of Heb. 2.''

PSALM SIXTEEN

9 Therefore my heart is glad, and my glory rejoiceth;
My flesh also shall dwell in ¹safety.
10 For thou wilt not leave my soul to Sheol;

¹Or, *confidently*

Neither wilt thou suffer ²thy holy one to see ³corruption.

²Or, *godly;* or *beloved.* Another reading is, *holy ones.*
³Or, *the pit*

Vers. 9,10.   CHRIST'S RESURRECTION FORETOLD.

This is the next in order of the Messianic Psalms.   According to Peter (Acts 2.25) and Paul (Acts 13.35), this Psalm relates to Christ, and expresses, as Jamieson says, ''the feelings of His human nature in view of His sufferings and victory over death and the grave, including His subsequent exaltation at the right hand of God.''

Vers. 9,10.   ''As a prophet'', says Scofield, ''David understood that, not at His first advent, but at some time subsequent to His death and resurrection Christ would assume the Davidic throne.''

PSALM TWENTY-TWO

This Psalm is next in order as Messianic.

28 For the kingdom is Jehovah's; and he is the ruler over the nations.
29 All the fat ones of the earth shall eat and worship:
All they that go down to the dust shall bow before him,
Even he that cannot keep his soul alive.

30 A seed shall serve him;
It shall be¹ told of the Lord unto the next generation.
31 They shall come and shall declare his righteousness
Unto a people that shall be born, that he hath done it.

¹Or, *counted unto the Lord for* his *generations*

Vers. 28-31.   THE LORD SHALL RULE THE NATIONS OF THE EARTH.

In verse 28 the kingdom is said to be Jehovah's, while in verse 30 the Lord is in view as ruling on behalf of Jehovah.

The great end and object of the rule of the Lord is the restoration of the kingdom to Jehovah (I Cor. 15.23,24).

The true meaning here of the word ''*seed*'' is ''posterity''.

PSALM TWENTY-FOUR

The Messianic reference of the Twenty-fourth Psalm (S. Hen. Mic. Schm.) is somewhat doubtful, but Alexander has well said of it, ''The sanctuary of the old economy was intended to symbolize God's special presence and residence among His people; and as this was realized in the advent of Christ, the Psalm before us may in a certain sense be described as Messianic.''

31

7 Lift up your heads, O ye gates;
  And be ye lifted up, ye [1]everlasting
    doors:
  And the King of glory will come in.
8 Who is the King of glory?
  Jehovah, strong and mighty,
  Jehovah, mighty in battle.

9 Lift up your heads, O ye gates;
  Yea, lift them up, ye [1]everlasting
    doors
  And the King of glory will come in.
10 Who is this King of glory?
   Jehovah of hosts,
   He is the King of glory.

[1]Or, *ancient*

Vers. 7-10. THE THRONE GIVEN TO THE KING OF GLORY.

The order of the Psalm is somewhat as follows: First, The declaration of Title, "the earth is the Lord's" (verses 1,2); Second, The Requirement of Holiness for rulership of the earth (verses 3-6); Third, The Ascension to the throne of the worthy One, the King of Glory.

"It is", says Scofield, "a question of worthiness, and no one is worthy but the Lamb, and thus the Lamb, the King of Glory, takes the throne of the earth."

PSALMS FORTY AND FORTY-ONE

These are the two next in order of the Messianic Psalms.

Psalm Forty speaks of Jehovah's Servant obedient unto death, while Psalm Forty-one relates to the betrayal of the Son of man, as Jesus Himself taught in the thirteenth chapter of John's Gospel.

PSALM FORTY-FIVE

1 My heart overfloweth with a goodly
    matter;
  [1]I speak the things which I have
    made touching the king:
  My tongue is the pen of a ready
    writer.
2 Thou art fairer than the children of
    men;
  Grace is poured [2]into thy lips:
  Therefore God hath blessed thee for
    ever.
3 Gird thy sword upon thy thigh, O
    mighty one,
  Thy glory and thy majesty.
4 And in thy majesty ride on prosper-
    ously,
  [3]Because of truth and meekness *and*
    righteousness:
  And [4]thy right hand shall teach thee
    terrible things.
5 Thine arrows are sharp;
  The peoples fall under thee;
  They are in the heart of the king's
    enemies.
6 [5]Thy throne, O God, is for ever and
    ever:

[1]Or, *I speak: my work is for a king*
[2]Or, *upon*
[3]Or, *In behalf of*
[4]Or, *let thy right hand teach*
[5]Or, *Thy throne is the throne of God &c.*

A sceptre of equity is the sceptre of
  thy kingdom.
7 Thou hast loved righteousness, and
  hated wickedness:
Therefore God, thy God, hath
  anointed thee
With the oil of gladness above thy
  fellows.
8 All thy garments *smell of* myrrh,
  and aloes, *and* cassia;
Out of ivory palaces stringed instruments have made thee glad.
9 Kings' daughters are among thy honorable women:
At thy right hand doth stand the
  queen in gold of Ophir.
10 Hearken, O daughter, and consider,
   and incline thine ear;
Forget also thine own people, and
  thy father's house:
11 So will the king desire thy beauty;
For he is thy lord; and reverence
  thou him.
12 And the daughter of Tyre *shall be
  there* with a gift;
The rich among the people shall entreat thy favor.

13 The king's daughter[6] within *the* palace is all glorious:
Her clothing is inwrought with gold.
14 She shall be led unto the king in broidered work:
The virgins her companions that follow her
Shall be brought unto thee.
15 With gladness and rejoicing shall they be led:

[6]Or, *in the inner part* of the palace

They shall enter into the king's palace.
16 Instead of thy fathers shall be thy children,
Whom thou shalt make princes in all the earth.
17 I will make thy name to be remembered in all generations:
Therefore shall the peoples give thee thanks for ever and ever.

Vers. 1-17. THE UNION AND GLORY OF CHRIST AND HIS TRIUMPHANT CHURCH DESCRIBED.

Next in order is the Forty-fifth Psalm, to which the Messianic sense is given by the oldest interpreters, both Jewish and Christian. Says Fausset, "Several Jewish monarchs, from Solomon to the wicked Ahab and various foreign princes, have been named as the hero of the song. But to none of them can the terms here used be shown to apply, and it is hardly probable that any mere nuptial song, especially of a heathen king, would be permitted a place in the sacred songs of the Jews." It is the union of Christ and the Church finally triumphant that is set forth. Scofield says, "This great Psalm of the King obviously looks forward to the advent in glory. The divisions are: (1) The supreme beauty of the King (verses 1,2); (2) the coming of the King in glory (verses 3-5). (Compare Rev. 19.11-21); (3) the Deity of the King and the character of His reign (verses 6,7); (4) as associated with Him in earthly rule, the queen is presented (verses 9-13); (5) the virgin companions of the queen, who would seem to be the Jewish remnant, are next seen (verses 14,15); and (6) the Psalm closes with a reference to the earthly fame of the King (verses 16,17)."

On the other hand some have sought to find in the bride the Jewish Church and in the companions of the bride, the Gentile Churches. But it is not necessary to find in the history of Christ and His Church exact parallels for every part of this splendid allegory, and it will not do to press the interpretation of the details in this manner.

Fausset remarks that, "As to the time in which the prophecy is to be fulfilled, it may be said that no periods of time are especially designated. The *characteristics* of the relation of Christ and His Church are indicated, and we may suppose that the whole process of His exaltation from the declaration of His Sonship, by His resurrection, to the grand catastrophe of the final judgment, with all the collateral blessings to the Church and to the world, lay before the vision of the inspired prophet."

PSALM FORTY-EIGHT

THE BEAUTY AND THE GLORY OF ZION.

This, some would have us believe, is next in order of the Messianic Psalms. Indeed the Jewish interpreters take it to be descriptive of Jerusalem in the Messianic times, after the victory over Gog and Magog. The Psalm was most probably written to commemorate the same event as does the one before it, namely, the victory of Jehosaphat over the Ammonites and the Edomites as recorded in the twentieth chapter of Second Chronicles, and the simpler method of interpretation is that it celebrates Jehovah and Jerusalem as His residence and sets forth the privileges and blessings of Jehovah's spiritual dominion as the terror of the wicked and the joy of the righteous. The older Christian expositors apply the Psalm to the eternal glory of the spiritual Zion.

PSALM SIXTY-EIGHT

THE KING IN TRIUMPHANT ASCENSION AND UNIVERSAL DOMINION.

This is next in order of the Messianic Psalms. Indeed the Fathers, most of the older theologians and some moderns (Mic.) take it as a direct prophecy of Christ, as to His advent, His saving doctrine, His triumphant ascension into heaven (Eph. 4.8) and His all-embracing sovereignty and divine glory; while Jamieson, Stier and others consider the Psalm to be typically Messianic.

21 But God will smite through the head of his enemies,
The hairy scalp of such a one as goeth on still in his guiltiness.
22 The Lord said, I will bring again from Bashan,
I will bring *them* again from the depths of the sea;
23 That thou mayest crush *them*, dipping thy foot in blood,
That the tongue of thy dogs may have its portion from *thine* enemies.
24 They have seen thy goings, O God, Even the goings of my God, my King, ¹into the sanctuary.
25 The singers went before, the minstrels followed after,
In the midst of the damsels playing with timbrels.
26 Bless ye God in the congregations, Even the Lord, *ye that are* of the fountain of Israel.
27 There is little Benjamin their ruler, The princes of Judah *and* their ²council,
The princes of Zebulun, the princes of Naphtali.
28 Thy God hath commanded thy strength:

¹Or, *in the sanctuary* Or, *in holiness*
²Or, *company*

³Strengthen, O God, that which thou ⁴has wrought for us.
29 Because of thy temple at Jerusalem Kings shall bring presents unto thee.
30 Rebuke the wild beast of the reeds, The multitude of the bulls, with the calves of the peoples,
⁵Trampling under foot the pieces of silver:
⁶He hath scattered the peoples that delight in war.
31 Princes shall come out of Egypt; ⁷Ethiopia shall haste to stretch out her hands unto God.
32 Sing unto God, ye kingdoms of the earth;
Oh sing praises unto the Lord:
[Selah
33 To him that rideth upon the heaven of heavens, which are of old;
Lo, he uttereth his voice, a mighty voice.
34 Ascribe ye strength unto God: His excellency is over Israel,
And his strength is in the skies.
35 O God, *thou art* terrible out of thy holy places:
The God of Israel, he giveth strength and power unto *his* people.
Blessed be God.

³Or, *Be strong, O God, thou that hast &c.*
⁴Or, *hast wrought for us out of thy temple.*
Unto Jerusalem &c.
⁵Or, *Every one submitting himself with pieces of silver*
⁶Or, as otherwise read, *Scatter thou*
⁷Heb. *Cush.*

"The entire Psalm," says Scofield, "is pervaded by the joy of Israel in the kingdom, but a stricter order of events begins with verse 18, which verse is quoted by Paul in the fourth chapter of Ephesians of Christ's ascension ministry. Verses 21-23 refer to the regathering of Israel, and the destruction of the Beast and his armies. Verses 24-35 are descriptive of full and universal kingdom blessing."

PSALM SIXTY-NINE

THE KING IN HUMILIATION.

Next in order of the Messianic Psalms is the Sixty-ninth. It is the Psalm of His humiliation and rejection. The quotations from it and the references to it in the New Testament show how far the older interpreters were justified in so construing it.

35 For God will save Zion, and build the cities of Judah;
And they shall abide there, and have it in possession.

36 The seed also of his servants shall inherit it;
And they that love his name shall dwell therein.

Vers. 35,36. JEHOVAH'S SERVANTS TO DWELL IN THE CITIES OF JUDAH.

Says Moll, "This does not expressly state a restoration of Zion and a repeopling of the cities of Judah. The words admit of being understood generally on the basis of the promise contained in the Law, of continuance and growth and of our supposing that there is a prophetic glance at the fate of the land and people in individual experience."

Alexander says, "As temporal and spiritual blessings were inseparably blended in the old dispensation, the promise of perpetual possession and abode in Palestine is merely the costume in which that of everlasting favor to the Church is clothed in the Old Testament."

Fausset says, "Though, as usual, the imagery is taken from terms used of Palestine, the whole tenor of the context indicates that the spiritual privileges and blessings of the Church are meant."

The reference here, however, to a literal restoration in the holy land is not to be easily brushed aside, as the words may quite as readily contain such reference, provided, of course, such interpretation harmonizes with the teaching of the Scriptures elsewhere, and if other prophetical passages do teach a literal restoration, then it would seem fitting to so interpret here.

PSALM SEVENTY-TWO

1 Give the king thy judgments, O God,
And thy righteousness unto the king's son.
2 He will judge thy people with righteousness,
And thy poor with justice.
3 The mountains shall bring peace to the people,
And the hills, in righteousness.
4 He will judge the poor of the people,
He will save the children of the needy,
And will break in pieces the oppressor.
5 They shall fear thee while the sun endureth,
And 'so long as the moon, throughout all generations.
'Heb. *before the moon*

6 He will come down like rain upon the mown grass,
As showers that water the earth.
7 In his days shall the righteous flourish,
And abundance of peace, till the moon shall be no more.
8 He shall have dominion also from sea to sea,
And from the River unto the ends of the earth.
9 They that dwell in the wilderness shall bow before him;
And his enemies shall lick the dust.
10 The kings of Tarshish and of the isles shall render tribute:
The kings of Sheba and Seba shall offer gifts.

11 Yea, all kings shall fall down before
   him;
   All nations shall serve him.
12 For he will deliver the needy when
   he crieth,
   And the poor, [2]that hath no helper.
13 He will have pity on the [3]poor and
   needy,
   And the souls of the needy he will
   save.
14 He will redeem their soul from [4]op-
   pression and violence;
   And precious will their blood be in
   his sight:
15 And [5]they shall live; and to him
   shall be given of the gold of
   Sheba:
   And men shall pray for him continually;
   [5]They shall bless him all the day
   long.

[2]Or, *and him that hath*
[3]Or, *weak*
[4]Or, *fraud*
[5]Or, *he*

16 There shall be [6]abundance of grain
   in the [7]earth upon the top of the
   mountains;
   The fruit thereof shall shake like
   Lebanon:
   And they of the city shall flourish
   like grass of the earth.
17 His name shall endure for ever;
   His name shall [8]be continued [9]as long
   as the sun;
   And men shall [10]be blessed in him;
   All nations shall call him happy.
18 Blessed be Jehovah God, the God of
   Israel,
   Who only doeth wondrous things:
19 And blessed be his glorious name for
   ever;
   And let the whole earth be filled with
   his glory.
   Amen, and Amen.
20 The prayers of David the son of
   Jesse are ended.

[6]Or, *a handful*
[7]Or, *land*
[8]Or, *have issue*
[9]Heb. *before the sun*
[10]Or, *bless themselves*

Vers. 1-20. THE REIGN OF THE RIGHTEOUS KING.

Next in order of the Messianic Psalms is the one before us. It is a
glowing description of the reign of the Messiah. His reign shall be a
righteous one (verses 1-7), a universal one (verses 8-11), a beneficent one
(verses 12-14) and a perpetual one (verses 15-17).

By the older Jewish and most modern Christian interpreters this
Psalm has been referred to Christ, whose reign, present and prospective, says
Fausset, alone corresponds with its statements.

While the one school of interpretation spiritualizes the picture and
makes it prophetic of Christ's present spiritual reign on earth, Morgan,
Seiss, Scofield, and others of their school, believe that the Psalm as a whole
forms a complete vision of the Millennium kingdom which is to be ushered
in with Christ's personal return to earth.

Says Scofield, "Verse 1 refers to the investiture of the King's Son with
the kingdom, of which investiture the formal description is given in Dan.
7.13,14; Rev. 5.5-10. Verses 2-7 and 12-14 give the character of the
kingdom, while verses 8-11 speak of its universality. Verse 16 hints at
the means by which universal blessing is to be brought in. Converted
Israel will be the 'handful of corn' (Amos 9.9), as the King Himself in
death and resurrection was the single grain, the 'corn of wheat' (John
12.24). 'To the Jew first' is the order alike of Church and kingdom. It
is through restored Israel that the kingdom is to be extended over the
earth."

"The sublime 72nd Psalm," says Seiss, "is also largely drawn upon
to adorn and sustain the theory of a universal peace and glory for this
world before the present dispensation ends. It is there recorded that the
Son of David 'shall have dominion from sea to sea and from the river to
the ends of the earth. Yea, all kings shall fall down before Him; all
nations shall serve Him'. Wonderful changes for the better, in the whole

government and condition of the world are thus foretold, which are too good not to be seized and appropriated to crown the outcome of human progress and effort. But notes of the time are not thus to be ignored. If we ask *when* all this is to be, the answer is given: 'When He shall judge the people'—when 'He shall come down'—when 'God shall give the King His judgments'—and hence not in the present course of things; not before the period of great consummation."

PSALM EIGHTY-FIVE

JEHOVAH'S RETURNING FAVOR UPON THE NATION.

Blackstone would have us believe that this Psalm is Messianic and that it refers, as seen especially in such verses as 10 and 11, to kingdom blessings. The Psalm is a description of God's returning favor, and as Fausset says, "The writer doubtless had in view that more glorious period, when Christ shall establish His government on God's reconciled justice and abounding mercy." This view of the Psalm is, however, not to be accepted without hesitation. The Psalm is a prayer for deliverance from present evils on the ground of former benefits. "It seems," says Alexander, "to be appropriate to every case in which the fulfillment of the promise in Lev. 26.3-13 was suspended or withheld." The older commentators, however, looked upon the Psalm as prophetic.

PSALM EIGHTY-NINE

1 I will sing of the lovingkindness of Jehovah for ever:
With my mouth will I make known thy faithfulness to all generations.

2 For I have said, Mercy shall be built up for ever;
Thy faithfulness wilt thou establish in the very heavens.

3 I have made a covenant with my chosen,
I have sworn unto David my servant:

4 Thy seed will I establish for ever,
And build up thy throne to all generations.   [Selah

5 And the heavens shall praise thy wonders, O Jehovah;
Thy faithfulness also in the assembly of the holy ones.

6 For who in the skies can be compared unto Jehovah?
Who among the ¹sons of the ²mighty is like unto Jehovah?

7 A God very terrible in the council of the holy ones,
And to be feared above all them that are round about him?

8 O Jehovah, God of hosts,

Who is a mighty one, like unto thee, O ³Jehovah?
And thy faithfulness is round about thee.

9 Thou rulest the pride of the sea:
When the waves thereof arise, thou stillest them.

10 Thou hast broken ⁴Rahab in pieces, as one that is slain;
Thou hast scattered thine enemies with the arm of thy strength.

11 The heavens are thine, the earth also is thine:
The world and the fullness thereof, thou hast founded them.

12 The north and the south, thou hast created them:
Tabor and Hermon rejoice in thy name.

13 Thou hast ⁵a mighty arm:
Strong is thy hand, and high is thy right hand.

14 Righteousness and justice are the foundation of thy throne:
Lovingkindness and truth go before thy face.

¹Or, sons of God
²Or, gods See Ps. 29. 1.

³Heb. Jah
⁴Or, Egypt
⁵Heb. an arm with might

15 Blessed is the people that know the
  [6]joyful sound:
  They walk, O Jehovah, in the light
    of thy countenance
16 In thy name do they rejoice all the
  day;
  And in thy righteousness are they
    exalted.
17 For thou art the glory of their
  strength;
  And in thy favor [7]our horn shall be
    exalted.
18 For our shield belongeth unto Jehovah;
  [8]And our king to the Holy One of
    Israel.
19 Then thou spakest in vision to thy
  [9]saints,
  And saidst, I have laid help upon
    one that is mighty;
  I have exalted one chosen out of the
    people.
20 I have found David my servant;
  With my holy oil have I anointed
    him:
21 With whom my hand shall be established;
  Mine arm also shall strengthen him.
22 The enemy shall not [10]exact from
  him,
  Nor the son of wickedness afflict him.
23 And I will beat down his adversaries
  before him,
  And smite them that hate him.
24 But my faithfulness and my lovingkindness shall be with him;
  And in my name shall his horn be
    exalted.
25 I will set his hand also on the sea,
  And his right hand on the rivers.
26 He shall cry unto me, Thou art my
  Father,
  My God, and the rock of my salva-
    tion.
27 I also will make him my firstborn,
  The highest of the kings of the
    earth.
28 My lovingkindness will I keep for
  him for evermore;
  And my covenant shall [11]stand fast
    with him.
29 His seed also will I make to endure
  for ever,
  And his throne as the days of heaven.
30 If his children forsake my law,
  And walk not in mine ordinances;
31 If they [12]break my statutes,
  And keep not my commandments;

32 Then will I visit their transgression
  with the rod,
  And their iniquity with stripes.
33 But my lovingkindness will I not
  utterly take from him,
  Nor suffer my faithfulness to fail.
34 My covenant will I not [12]break,
  Nor alter the thing that is gone out
    of my lips.
35 [13]Once have I sworn by my holiness:
  I will not lie unto David:
36 His seed shall endure for ever,
  And his throne as the sun before me.
37 [14]It shall be established for ever as
  the moon,
  [15]And as the faithful witness in the
    sky.   [Selah
38 But thou hast cast off and rejected,
  Thou hast been wroth with thine
    anointed.
39 Thou hast abhorred the covenant of
  thy servant:
  Thou hast profaned his crown by
    casting it to the ground.
40 Thou hast broken down all his
  hedges;
  Thou hast brought his strongholds
    to ruin.
41 All that pass by the way rob him:
  He is become a reproach to his neigh-
    bors.
42 Thou hast exalted the right hand of
  his adversaries;
  Thou hast made all his enemies to
    rejoice.
43 Yea, thou turnest back the edge of
  his sword,
  And hast not made him to stand in
    the battle.
44 Thou hast made his brightness to
  cease,
  And cast his throne down to the
    ground.
45 The days of his youth hast thou
  shortened:
  Thou hast covered him with shame.
                [Selah
46 How long, O Jehovah? wilt thou
  hide thyself for ever?
  How long shall thy wrath burn like
    fire?
47 Oh remember how short my time is:
  For what vanity hast thou created all
    the children of men!
48 What man is he that shall live and
  not see death,
  That shall deliver his soul from the
    [16]power of Sheol?   [Selah

[6]Or, trumpet sound
[7]Another reading is, thou shalt exalt our horn
[8]Or, Even to the Holy One of Israel our King
[9]Or, as otherwise read, saint
[10]Or, do him violence
[11]Or, be faithful
[12]Heb. profane

[13]Or, One thing
[14]Or, As the moon which is established for ever
[15]Or, And the witness in the sky is faithful
[16]Heb. hand

49 Lord, where are thy former loving-
kindnesses,
Which thou swarest unto David in
thy faithfulness?

50 Remember, Lord, the reproach of thy
servants;
How I do bear in my bosom *the*

reproach of all the [17]mighty
peoples,
51 Wherewith thine enemies have reproached, O Jehovah,
Wherewith they have reproached the
footsteps of thine anointed.
52 Blessed be Jehovah for evermore.
Amen, and Amen.

[17]Or, *many*

Vers. 1-52. THE COVENANT WITH DAVID CONFIRMED.

This Psalm Scofield thinks is next in order as Messianic. He says, "It is at once the confirmation and the exposition of the Davidic Covenant, and that the Covenant itself looks far beyond David and Solomon is sure from verse 27: 'Higher than the kings of earth' can only refer to King Immanuel." This same description, however, is applied elsewhere to Israel (Ex. 4.22), and to Ephraim (Jer. 31.9), and may with propriety be applied to David himself and successors as well as to Christ (Heb. 1.6), and therefore it will not do to rest the defense of the Messianic interpretation of this Psalm upon this ascription and promise alone.

The Psalm has, however, been applied prophetically to the suffering Messiah by the ancient and the older English commentators as well as by Wordsworth and others of the more recent times. Jewish commentators have applied it to the miseries of the Jews since the prevalence of Christianity, while Calvin, Stier and others apply it to the afflicted Church, inasmuch as Christ lives and suffers in His followers.

The Psalm, we think, has, as Moll says, a Messianic application only insofar as it was intended to set forth the necessary conflict which was to be waged before the great fundamental promise could be realized.

The particular promise insisted upon in this Psalm is that in II Sam. 7, "which", says Alexander, "constitutes the basis of all Messianic Psalms."

Scofield says, "The Psalm is in four parts: (1) The Covenant, though springing from the loving kindness of Jehovah, yet rests upon His oath (verses 1-4). (2) Jehovah is glorified for His power and goodness in connection with the Covenant (verses 5-18). (3) The response of Jehovah (verses 19-37). This is in two parts; (a) He confirms the Covenant (verses 19-29), but (b) He warns that disobedience in the royal posterity of David will be punished with chastenings (verses 30-32). Historically this chastening began in the division of the Davidic kingdom and culminated in the captivities and that subordination of Israel to the Gentiles which still continues. (4) The plea of the remnant, who urge the severity and long continuance of the chastening."

PSALMS NINETY-THREE TO NINETY-NINE

THE RULE OF JEHOVAH AND THE DESTRUCTION OF THE UNBELIEVING NATIONS.

These Psalms constitute a series which celebrate the coming of Jehovah as King. The Jewish and many of the older expositors took these Psalms as Messianic, and understood the past tenses as being employed prophetically, and as describing the end of the world and its final judgment. The same reason exists for taking one as Messianic as for taking them all in this sense. (See the opening and closing verse of Psalm 94; also Psalm 96.13, and the 97th Psalm, as well as Psalm 98.9.)

PSALM ONE HUNDRED TWO

1 Hear my prayer, O Jehovah,
And let my cry come unto thee.
2 Hide not thy face from me in the day of my distress:
Incline thine ear unto me;
In the day when I call answer me speedily.
3 For my days consume away ¹like smoke,
And my bones are burned ²as a firebrand.
4 My heart is smitten like grass, and withered;
For I forget to eat my bread.
5 By reason of the voice of my groaning
My bones cleave to my flesh.
6 I am like a pelican of the wilderness;
I am become as an owl of the waste places.
7 I watch, and am become like a sparrow
That is alone upon the housetop.
8 Mine enemies reproach me all the day;
They that are mad against me do curse by me.
9 For I have eaten ashes like bread,
And mingled my drink with weeping.
10 Because of thine indignation and thy wrath:
For thou hast taken me up, and cast me away.
11 My days are like a shadow that ³declineth;
And I am withered like grass.
12 But thou, O Jehovah, ⁴wilt abide for ever;
And thy memorial *name* unto all generations.
13 Thou wilt arise, and have mercy upon Zion;
For it is time to have pity upon her,
Yea, the set time is come.
14 For thy servants take pleasure in her stones.
And have pity upon her dust.

15 So the nations shall fear the name of Jehovah,
And all the kings of the earth thy glory.
16 For Jehovah hath built up Zion;
He hath appeared in his glory.
17 He hath regarded the prayer of the destitute,
And hath not despised their prayer.
18 This shall be written for the generation to come;
And a people which shall be created shall praise ⁵Jehovah.
19 For he hath looked down from the height of his sanctuary;
From heaven did Jehovah behold the earth;
20 To hear the sighing of the prisoner;
To loose ⁶those that are appointed to death;
21 That men may declare the name of Jehovah in Zion,
And his praise in Jerusalem;
22 When the peoples are gathered together,
And the kingdoms, to serve Jehovah.
23 He ⁷weakened my strength in the way;
He shortened my days.
24 I said, O my God, take me not away in the midst of my days:
Thy years are throughout all generations.
25 Of old didst thou lay the foundation of the earth;
And the heavens are the work of thy hands.
26 They shall perish, but thou shalt endure;
Yea, all of them shall wax old like a garment;
As a vesture shalt thou change them, and they shall be changed:
27 But thou art the same,
And thy years shall have no end.
28 The children of thy servants shall continue,
And their seed shall be established before thee.

¹Or, *in smoke*
²Or, *as a hearth*
³Or, *is stretched out*
⁴Or, *sittest* as Kings

⁵Heb. *Jah*
⁶Heb. *the children of death*
⁷Another reading is, *afflicted* me with *his strength*

Vers. 1-28. THE HUMILIATION AND THE COMING GLORY OF THE KING.

The only reason for considering this Psalm Messianic is that verses 25-27 are in Hebrews 1:11-12 referred to Christ, and consequently a reasonable ground is furnished for thinking that the preceding verses express for us the exercises of His holy soul in the days of his humiliation and rejection, together with certain prophetic statements of the glory awaiting Him in the time of the consummation of His kingdom.

Says Fausset, "Hebrews 1.10 quotes verses 25-27 as addressed to Christ in His divine nature. The scope of the Psalm, as already seen, so far from opposing, favors this view, especially by the sentiments of verses 12-15 (compare Isa. 60.1). The association of the Messiah with a day of future glory to the Church was very intimate in the minds of Old Testament writers, and with correct views of His nature it is very consistent that He should be addressed as the Lord and Head of His Church, who would bring about that glorious future on which they ever dwelt with fond and delightful anticipations."

Accordingly Seiss, Blackstone, Morgan, and others of the same school take verse 16, *For Jehovah hath built up Zion,* as a reference to the second coming of Christ. The Millennium or universal peace and righteousness, says Seiss, cannot take place before His second coming, but it is to begin when "He shall appear in His glory" "God does not restore Israel and rebuild Zion," says Blackstone, "until Christ appears in glory, nor does He build up Zion until He has taken out the Church" (Acts 15.13-17).

PSALM ONE HUNDRED TEN

1 Jehovah saith unto my Lord, sit thou at my right hand,
Until I make thine enemies thy footstool.

2 Jehovah will ¹send forth the ²rod of thy strength out of Zion:
Rule thou in the midst of thine enemies.

3 Thy people ³offer themselves willingly
In the day of thy ⁴power, ⁵in holy array:
Out of the womb of the morning
⁶Thou hast the dew of thy youth.

4 Jehovah hath sworn, and will not repent;
Thou art a priest for ever
After the ⁷order of Melchizedek.

5 The Lord at thy right hand
⁸Will strike through kings in the day of his wrath.

6 He will judge among the nations,
⁹He ¹⁰will fill *the places* with dead bodies;
He ⁸will strike through the head ¹¹in many countries.

7 He will drink of the brook in the way:
Therefore will he lift up the head.

¹Or, *stretch*
²Or, *sceptre*
³Heb. *are freewill-offerings*
⁴Or, *army*
⁵Or, *in the beauty of holiness*
⁶Or, *Thy youth are to thee* as *the dew*

⁷Or, *manner*
⁸Or, *Hath stricken*
⁹Or, *The places are full of &c.*
¹⁰Or, *hath filled*
¹¹Or, *over a wide land*

The explicit application of this Psalm to our Lord by Himself and the Apostles leave us in no doubt as to its purely Messianic character. As Fausset says, "The Psalm celebrates the exaltation of Christ to the throne of an eternal and increasing kingdom, and a perpetual priesthood, involving the subjugation of His enemies and the multiplication of His subjects."

Historically, the Psalm begins with the Ascension of Christ (verse 1); prophetically, it looks on to the time when Christ is to appear as the rod of Jehovah's strength, the Deliverer out of Zion (verse 2), to the conversion of Israel (verse 3) and on to the judgment upon the Gentile powers (verses 5,6).

41

Vers. 1-7. THE KINGDOM, WITH ITS POWER AND GLORY, GIVEN TO THE KING.

Ver. 1.   *"my Lord"*,—i. e., David's Lord.   The Messiah is meant; so recognized by the Jews of ancient times, and clear not only from their traditions, but from Matt. 22.46.   David is here not to be thought of merely as a private person, nor even as an individual king, but as representing his own royal race and the house of Israel over which it reigned.

"Sit thou at my right hand",—A seat at the right hand of a king implies a participation in his power.   The participation in the divine power thus ascribed to Christ is a special and an extraordinary one, having reference to the total subjugation of His enemies.   It does not imply inactivity while Jehovah conquered His foes for Him, but it is in and through the Messiah that Jehovah acts for the destruction of His enemies and for that very end He is vested with almighty power, as denoted by His sitting at the right hand of Jehovah.   This session is to last until the total subjugation of His enemies, and this special and extraordinary power of the Messiah is then to terminate, as Paul puts it in I Cor. 15.24-28, where the verse before us is distinctly referred to, though not expressly quoted.

Ver. 2.   David now addresses the Messiah directly.

"the rod",—i. e., of correction and chastisement.

"of thy strength",—The rod by means of which thy strength is to be exerted.

"rule thou in the midst of thine enemies",—The verb here used is one not applied to a peaceful rule, but to a coercive one over conquered enemies.

Ver. 3.   *"Thy people offer themselves willingly"*,—The reading of the Authorized Version is entirely inadmissible, since the word translated, "willingly", is a plural feminine substantive, and cannot agree with the singular noun, "people".   It is the word used to denote freewill offerings or spontaneous gifts under the law of Moses.   By supplying the correlative verb, "offer", the fine sense of our text is obtained, or as it might be rendered, "Thy people are freewill offerings."

"In the day of thy power",—The reference is to the day when His power is displayed in the subjugation of His enemies.

"in holy array",—The Authorized rendering is a more literal one, and it may have its obvious spiritual sense as in Psa. 29.2, or it may have the sense of "holy decorations", with an illusion to the sacerdotal dress which in Lev. 16.4 is expressly called *"garments of holiness"*.   This last we prefer with most modern commentators.   It then means that when the people make this solemn offering of themselves to Jehovah they appear clothed in sacerdotal vestments, as servants of a priestly King (verse 4), and themselves a *"kingdom of priests"* (Ex. 19.6.).

"womb of the morning",—This, says Alexander, is a very strong poetical description of the origin or source of the dew, and the sense of this word "dew" determines that of the whole clause.   Dew is a constant emblem of whatever is refreshing and strengthening.

Some think the expression refers to the multitude of people or warriors who devote themselves to the Messiah and who are described as no less numerous than the drops of dew born from the womb of the morning.

Others think the comparison refers to the beauty of Messiah's people. But neither of these figures are common or natural, and the latter is a combination not likely to occur to the mind of any writer.

Still others think, and doubtless more acceptably, that the clause relates to the perpetual succession of Messiah's people, the successive generations of which constantly renew His body even as the dew is engendered afresh daily from the womb of the morning, i. e., thy youth, thy body shall be constantly refreshed by successive accessions of people as dew from the early morning.

The Messiah, as leading His people, is represented as continually in the vigor of youth, refreshed and strengthened by the early dew of God's grace and Spirit.

Ver. 4. *"Jehovah hath sworn and will not repent"*,—There is no fear or even possibility of His breaking or retracting this engagement.

"a priest forever after the order of Melchizedek",—This likeness consists primarily in the union of the kingly and priestly office, such as was the case with Melchizedek.

Ver. 5. Some suppose this verse addressed to Jehovah and "the Lord" to mean the Messiah, on the ground that they could not both be on the right hand of the other. But the whole idea is a figurative one. On the right hand has the same meaning here as in Psa. 109.31, where it denotes the place of protection or assistance. In one sense therefore Christ is at the right hand of God and in another God is at the right hand of Christ. The day of Jehovah's wrath is coincident with the day of the Lord's strength, in verse 3. The strength of the Messiah as a conquerer is to be exerted in giving effect to Jehovah's wrath against His enemies.

Ver. 6. The Messiah is again spoken of here in the third person.

"He will judge among the nations",—This is another figure for the conquest just described.

"He will strike through the head in many countries",—The Authorized Version takes both nouns as collective,—"the heads over many countries". Others make only the first noun collective, "the heads over the earth"; while our text takes only the last noun collectively. The expression is obscure, but the general idea is clear enough; it is that of universal conquest on the part of the Messiah, striking down the head, the ruler in all earthly principalities and powers.

Ver. 7. *"He will drink of the brook in the way"*—The probable meaning of this clause is that He shall not be exhausted like those wandering in the desert, but refreshed and strengthened.

"Therefore will He lift up the head",—The raising of the head is a figure of exhilaration. Is this effect supposed to be produced in the conqueror himself or in others? The first clause of the verse favors the exhilaration of himself. In favor of the latter interpretation, however, is Psa. 3.4 and 27.6. The interpretations are not, says Alexander, incompatible or exclusive, and it is best to leave them side by side. The words doubtless suggested both ideas to the Hebrews.

THE BOOK OF

ISAIAH

(B. C. 760—B. C. 698)

The book of Isaiah falls into two chief divisions:

I. Chapters 1 to 39, looking toward the Assyrian Captivity.

II. Chapters 40 to 66, looking toward deliverance and future blessing.

THE FIRST CHIEF DIVISION OF THE BOOK

This division may be conveniently arranged in seven sections.

Section One.—The Growth of the Obduracy of the Mass of the People.

CHAPTERS 1 TO 6

CHAPTER ONE

> 9. Except Jehovah of hosts had left unto us a very small remnant, we should have been as Sodom, we should have been like unto Gomorrah.

Vers. 1-24.   JEHOVAH'S CASE AGAINST HIS REBELLIOUS AND UN-GRATEFUL PEOPLE.

Ver. 9.   *"a very small remnant",*—Alexander says, "The idea of a desolation almost total is expressed in other words, and with an intimation that the narrow escape was owing to God's favor for the remnant according to the election of grace, who still existed in the Jewish Church.   That the verse has reference to quality as well as quantity is evident from Romans 9.29 where Paul makes use of it, not as an illustration, but as an argument to show that mere connection with the Church could not save men from the wrath of God."

25 and I will ¹turn my hand upon thee, and ²thoroughly purge away thy dross, and will take away all thy ³tin; 26 and I will restore thy judges as at the first, and thy counsellors as at the beginning: afterward thou shalt be called The city of righteousness, a faithful town.   27 Zion shall be redeemed with justice, and ⁴her converts with righteousness.   28 But the ⁵destruction of transgressors and sinners shall be together, and they that forsake Jehovah shall be consumed.   29 For they shall be ashamed of the ⁶oaks which ye have desired, and ye shall be confounded for the gardens that ye have chosen.   30 For ye shall be as ⁷an oak whose leaf fadeth, and as a garden that hath no water. 31 And the strong shall be as tow, and his work as a spark; and they shall both burn together, and none shall quench them.

¹Or, *bring my hand again*
²Heb. *as with lye*
³Or, *alloy*
⁴Or, *they that return of her*
⁵Heb. *breaking*
⁶Or, *terebinths*
⁷Or, *a terebinth*

Vers. 25-31.   ZION TO BE PURGED AND REDEEMED.

Ver. 25.   *"turn my hand upon thee",*—This expression is sometimes used with the idea of punishment and sometimes with that of mercy. Here both are included, with the emphasis, however, upon the idea of mercy, that is, blessing through purging.

"thy dross . . . thy tin",—The reference is here not to sins but to sinful persons who are intermingled with the elect remnant of grace.

Ver. 26.   Nagelsbach says, "Regarding the fulfillment of this prophecy many have found in it a promise of a return of the days of the Judges, that is, the days of a Jephtha, a Gideon, a Samuel, etc.; others understand the language as referring to the return out of the Babylonian captivity under Zerubbabel, Joshua, Ezra and Nehemiah; others understood it of the restitution of the kingdom, while still others find its fulfillment in the days of the Messiah.   But all these explanations are evidently too narrow and one sided.   The fulfillment has its degrees.   And if Zerubbabel, Ezra and Nehemiah are justly regarded as the representatives of the first feeble beginnings of the great restitution of Israel; if further the Apostles are justly regarded as the founders of a new Zion on a higher plane, still by all this the prophecy is not at all fulfilled.   It will only then be fulfilled when the Lord comes 'into His kingdom'.   (Luke 23.42.)"

Ver. 27.   *"her converts"*,—This is literally, "they that return of her", and by many it is so rendered (C. Pe. Lut. Del. Sep.).   Others, however, and perhaps the majority (F. Al.) take the word in the spiritual sense as meaning those who return to God in true repentance.   This is doubtless to be preferred inasmuch as the exile has not yet been mentioned, although there is no objection to combining both views, as Nagelsbach does.

"Zion",—By this word the believing people of God are of course meant.

"justice . . . righteousness",—Whose justice and righteousness is meant?

(1) That of the acts themselves, i. e., the very same events by which the divine justice was to manifest itself in the destruction of the wicked should be the means of deliverance to the true people of God.   (Al.)

(2) That of the people, i. e., the practice of justice and righteousness on their part.   (Ges., the Rabbins especially, and most modern German authorities.)

(3) That of the judges and counselors mentioned in verse 26. (Na.)

(4) That of God, i. e., God's righteousness bestowed as a gift of grace on those who escape His punitive justice.   (C. F. Del.)

The first view seems to be the simplest and the most preferable.   This is of course God's justice and righteousness as well, although it is not here used in the New Testament sense as the last view would have us take it.

Ver. 29.   *"the oaks . . . the gardens"*,—i. e., the groves and enclosures for idolatrous worship.

"they",—This may be taken as a reference to men in general (Ges.), or to the Jews of future generations (V.), or it is perhaps better taken as a case of enallage so frequent in Hebrew, i. e., a change of person, and made to refer to the same people as *"ye"* in both this verse and the next one. (Al.)

This section Scofield calls "a renewal of the promise of the Palestinian Covenant of future restoration and exaltation".

CHAPTER TWO

Introducing the second prophecy, which continues to the end of chapter.

This prophecy is set forth in three parts:

1. Part one. Vers. 1-5.

1. The word that Isaiah the son of Amoz saw concerning Judah and Jerusalem.

2 And it shall come to pass in the latter days, that the mountain of Jehovah's house shall be established ¹on the top of the mountains, and shall be exalted above the hills; and all nations shall flow unto it. 3 And many peoples shall go and say, Come ye, and let us go up to the mountain of Jehovah, to the house of the God of

¹Or, at the head

Jacob; and he will teach us of his ways, and we will walk in his paths; for out of Zion shall go forth ²the law, and the word of Jehovah from Jerusalem. 4 And he will judge ³between the nations, and will decide concerning many peoples; and they shall beat their swords into plowshares, and their spears into pruning-hooks: nation shall not lift up sword against nation, neither shall they learn war any more. 5 O house of Jacob, come ye, and let us walk in the light of Jehovah.

²Or, instruction
³Or, among

Vers. 1-5. THE PROMISE FOR THE LAST DAYS.

For explanation of these verses see under Micah 4.1-3. Delitzsch says of verses 1-3 that all other fulfillments were but preludes to an end still to be executed, and forming their completion: for there is no fulfillment yet of what is predicted in verse 4.

Nagelsbach says, "As regards the fulfilling of our prophecy, the Prophet himself says that it shall follow in the last time. If it now began a long time ago; if especially the appearance of the Lord in the flesh, and the founding of His kingdom and the preaching of the Gospel among all nations be an element of that fulfillment, yet it is by no means a closed-up transaction. What it shall yet bring about we know not. If many, especially Jewish expositors, have taken the words too coarsely and outwardly, so, on the other hand, we must guard against a one-sided spiritualizing. Certainly the prophets do not think of heaven. Plows and pruning hooks have as little to do with heaven as swords and spears. And what has the high place of Mount Zion to do in heaven? Therefore our passage speaks for the view that one time, and that too, here on this earth, the Lord shall appropriate the kingdom, (Chap. 60.21 and Matt. 5.5), suppress the world kingdoms and bring about a condition of peace and glory. That then what is outward shall conform to what is inward, is certain, even though we must confess our ignorance in regard to the ways and means of the realization in particulars."

Seiss says, "The prophet is not describing a gradual evolution in the course of the present dispensation, but connects this happy condition with great convulsive changes—with awful judgment—with the manifest presence of the Lord Himself. Does not verse 10 and what follows signify the personal presence of the Judge? What is this but the *Dies irae,* of which Thomas of Celano so famously sang? It is the exact parallel of Rev. 6.12-17. And it is only in connection with the revelation of the Lord Jesus from heaven, 'with His mighty angels in flaming fire' that this blessed transformation and sanctification of society and the world is to be wrought."

2. Part two. Chap. 2.6 to Chap. 4.1, setting forth the actual condition of Israel and the judgment of the coming day of Jehovah.

10 Enter into the rock, and hide thee in the dust, from before the terror of Jehovah, and from the glory of his majesty. 11 The lofty looks of man shall be brought low, and the haughtiness of men shall be bowed down, and Jehovah alone shall be exalted in that day. 12 For [1]there shall be a day of Jehovah of hosts upon all that is proud and haughty, and upon all that is lifted up; and it shall be brought low; 13 and upon all the cedars of Lebanon, that are high and lifted up, and upon all the oaks of Bashan, 14 and upon all the high mountains, and upon all the hills that are lifted up, 15 and upon every lofty tower, and upon every fortified wall, 16 and upon all the ships of Tarshish, and upon all pleasant [2]imagery. 17 And the loftiness of man shall be bowed down, and the haughtiness of men shall be brought low; and Jehovah alone shall be exalted in that day. 18 And the idols shall utterly pass away. 19 And men shall go into the caves of the rocks, and into the holes of the earth, from before the terror of Jehovah, and from the glory of his majesty, when he ariseth to shake mightily the earth. 20 In that day men shall cast away their idols of silver, and their idols of gold, which have been made for them to worship, to the moles and to the bats; 21 to go into the caverns of the rocks, and into the clefts of the ragged rocks, from before the terror of Jehovah, and from the glory of his majesty, when he ariseth to shake mightily the earth. 22 Cease ye from man, whose breath is in his nostrils: for wherein is he to be accounted of?

[1]Or, *Jehovah of hosts hath a day*
[2]Or, *watch-towers*

Vers. 10-22. THE JUDGMENT OF THE COMING DAY OF JEHOVAH.

Vers. 10. Such being their sin and their guilt they have nothing to do in view of the terror of the judgment Jehovah has prepared for them but to seek a hiding place from His wrath, the day of Jehovah being pictured as already come or near at hand.

Ver. 11. *"in that day"*,—i. e., the day of Jehovah mentioned in the next verse. In this verse 11 is summed up the result of Jehovah's vindication of Himself "in that day" of coming judgment. The prophet has used for the first time in this verse the expression "in that day," which afterwards occurs so often. He points of course to the time which he had before designated as "the last days".

Ver. 12. *"the day of Jehovah"*,—"This day", says Nagelsbach, "is a day of judgment, as already even the older prophets portray it: (Joel 1.15; 2.1,2,11; 3.4; Amos 5.18,20)."

Fausset persists in thinking only or chiefly of the final period of judgment time. He says, "Man has many days; 'the day of Jehovah' shall come at last, beginning with judgment, a never-ending day in which God shall be 'all in all' (I Cor. 15.28; II Peter 3.10)."

"upon every thing",—The version "every one" (E-V. Jun. Sep.) limits the phrase too much to persons, which is but a part of the meaning as conveyed in the expression "everything". (F. V. Al. Na. Del. Ges.) The judgment was to come upon everything in which the nation prided itself.

Ver. 13. The prophet now begins to enumerate in pairs all the high things upon which the judgment falls.

The cedars and oaks are not to be taken as emblems of great men in general (V. Ges. Jer. Tar.), nor of the great men of Syria and Israel

(Gro.), nor are they to be applied to the buildings erected by Uzziah and Jotham out of the cedars and oaks grown in the places mentioned (Kn.). They are to be taken not as symbols at all, but as samples or specimens of their class. (Al. Na. Del.)

Ver. 14. *"the high mountains . . . the hills"*,—Not the fastnesses to which they had recourse in times of danger (F. Bar.), nor the fortresses erected by Jotham (Kn.), nor the mountaineers of Palestine (Oec.), nor states and governments (Lo.), nor the high places on which sacrifices were unlawfully offered (F.), but merely an additional specification of the general statement in verse 12. (Al.)

Nagelsbach says, "II Peter 3.10 seems to me to afford the best commentary of these last two verses, the high mountains and the hills being names only as representatives of the entire terrestial nature, as also afterwards the towers, the ships of Tarshish, etc., are only representative of human works, and thus also the productions of art."

Delitzsch says, "What the prophet predicts was already actually beginning to be fulfilled in the military inroads of the Assyrians, the cedar forests of Lebanon being unsparingly shorn", but he says, "This participation of the lower creation in the judgment of God will come into special prominence at the close of this world's history." He reminds us that Scripture assumes throughout that all nature is joined with man, and is under the influence of sin which proceeds from man and under the wrath and grace which proceed from God to man."

Ver. 15. *"upon every lofty tower and fortified wall"*,—A third class of objects with which the idea of strength and loftiness are usually associated. These are not symbols of military strength (Lo.), nor do they refer to the fortifications built by Jotham and Uzziah (Kn.), although these would doubtless come to mind.

Ver. 16. *"the ships of Tarshish"*,—Suggesting the idea of the largest class of vessels, justly included in this catalogue of lofty and imposing objects, says Alexander.

"upon all pleasant imagery",—This seems to be one comprehensive word for all that goes before; all attractive and majestic objects, and not to be limited to "pictures" (A-V), nor "statues" (Mic. Ros. Do.), nor "lofty images or obelisks" (Ew.), nor "tapestry" (C.), nor the gay flags of the vessels (Ges.).

Ver. 18. *"Fulfilled to the letter"*,—says Fausset, "after the return from the Babylonian captivity. For the future fulfillment, see Zech. 13.2 and Rev. 13.15; 19.20."

Ver. 19. The fulfillment answering exactly to the threat.

"to shake mightily the earth",—A figure of severe and universal judgments.

Ver. 20. *"to the moles and to the bats"*,—The idols are cast here not alone that the wicked might facilitate their flight, but because they belong there, to the gnawing beasts of night in all their unclean holes.

Ver. 22. An exhortation to renounce all trust in man, man who is to be "brought low" and who is accounted as of little value. This verse forms an appropriate transition to the following chapter.

CHAPTER THREE

1 For, behold, the Lord, Jehovah of hosts, doth take away from Jerusalem and from Judah stay and staff, the whole stay of bread, and the whole stay of water; 2 the mighty man, and the man of war; the judge, and the prophet, and the diviner, and the elder; 3 the captain of fifty, and the honorable man, and the counsellor, and the expert [1]artificer, and the skillful enchanter. 4 And I will give children to be their princes, and [2]babes shall rule over them. 5 And the people shall be oppressed, every one by another, and every one by his neighbor: the child shall behave himself proudly against the old man, and the base against the honorable. 6 When a man shall take hold of his brother in the house of his father, saying, Thou hast clothing, be thou our [3]ruler, and let this ruin be under thy hand; 7 in that day shall he lift up his voice, saying, I will not be [4]a healer; for in my house is neither bread nor clothing: ye shall not make me ruler of the people. 8 For Jerusalem is ruined, and Judah is fallen; because their tongue and their doings are against Jehovah, to provoke the eyes of his glory. 9 [5]The show of their countenance doth witness against them; and they declare their sin as Sodom, they hide it not. Woe unto their soul! for they have done evil unto themselves. 10 Say ye of the righteous, that it shall be well with him; for they shall eat the fruit of their doings. 11 Woe unto the wicked! it shall be ill with him; for what his hands have done shall be done unto him. 12 As for my people, children are their oppressors, and women rule over them. O my people,

they that lead thee cause thee to err, and [6]destroy the way of thy paths. 13 Jehovah standeth up to contend, and standeth to judge the [7]peoples. 14 Jehovah will enter into judgment with the elders of his people, and the princes thereof: It is ye that have eaten up the vineyard; the spoil of the poor is in your houses: 15 what mean ye that ye crush my people, and grind the face of the poor? saith the Lord, Jehovah of hosts.

16 Moreover Jehovah said, Because the daughters of Zion are haughty, and walk with out-stretched necks and wanton eyes, walking and mincing as they go, and making a tinkling with their feet; 17 therefore the Lord will smite with a scab the crown of the head of the daughters of Zion, and Jehovah will lay bare their secret parts. 18 In that day the Lord will take away the beauty of their anklets, and the [8]cauls, and the crescents; 19 the pendants, and the [9]bracelets, and the mufflers; 20 the headtires, and the ankle-chains, and the sashes, and the perfume-boxes, and the amulets; 21 the rings, and the nose-jewels; 22 the festival robes, and the mantles, and the shawls, and the satchels; 23 the hand-mirrors, and the fine linen, and the turbans, and the veils. 24 And it shall come to pass, that instead of sweet spices there shall be rottenness; and instead of a girdle, a rope; and instead of well set hair, baldness; and instead of a robe, a girding of sackcloth; branding instead of beauty. 25 Thy men shall fall by the sword, and thy [10]mighty in the war. 26 And her gates shall lament and mourn; and she shall be [11]desolate and sit upon the ground.

[1]Or, charmer
[2]Or, with childishness shall they rule over them
[3]Or, judge
[4]Heb. a binder up
[5]Or, Their respecting of persons doth &c.

[6]Heb. swallow up
[7]Or, people
[8]Or, networks
[9]Or, chains
[10]Heb. might
[11]Or, emptied

Vers. 1-26.   THE DAY OF JEHOVAH UPON JERUSALEM AND JUDAH.

The judgment of Jehovah, which in the previous chapter was proclaimed more especially in its universal character, is in this chapter referred more especially to Jerusalem and Judah on account of their prevailing iniquities.

Ver. 1.   The chapter opens with a general prediction of the loss of that in which they so much trusted, beginning in this first verse with the two indispensible conditions of life, bread and water. This was literally fulfilled in the siege under Nebuchadnezzar and afterwards by the siege of Titus in the days of the Roman empire.

Vers. 2-3.   Next the supports of the State are to be removed; public men, including civil, military and religious functionaries together with the practitioners of the black art upon whom they relied.

Ver. 4.   As a result of the judgment just announced the government falls into weak and incompetent hands.   The *"babes"* are mentioned not with respect to age but rather to character, i. e., little children in ability so far as governing capacity goes.

Ver. 5.   Anarchy, insubordination and confusion naturally result from the regime of such imbecile rulers.

Vers. 6-7.   At last the people would gladly make a ruler of anyone who in the least rises above the universal wretchedness, who has even so much as the semblance of a respectable garment, but not even such an one is willing to accept office.

Vers. 8-9.   All this disaster is but the result of their own sin and they have but themselves to blame, for "they have done evil unto themselves".

Vers. 10-11.   But God's judgments are not indiscriminate; it shall be well with the righteous but ill with the wicked.

Ver. 12.   Then comes a *resume,* the whole course of thought from verses 1 to 11 being comprehended again, while the prophet expresses wonder and concern at the result of the nation's unworthy and incapable rulers.

Ver. 13.   Here, says Delitzsch, "the judgment of the world comes anew before the prophet's mind."   With this agrees Nagelsbach, who says that "here we are introduced into quite another moment of time, the judgment of the nations, not, however, the judging of the nations generally, but only the judgment of the people of God as a part of the universal judgment, and then too not of the nation in its totality, but of the destroyers of this totality, the princes and the elders, as seen in the following verse."

"standeth up",—i. e., ready and prepared for instant execution of the judgment.

"to plead",—The word means to conduct a cause for another or for one's self, and is here to be taken in the sense of accuse.   God stands—the Accuser and Judge and Executioner in one Person.

Vers. 14-15.   In these verses the Lord's accusation turns especially upon the incompetent and faithless rulers who have become the spoilers of His vineyard instead of its guardians, and the oppressors of the people instead of their protectors.

Vers. 16-24.   The prophet breaks off in the midst of his description of the judgment-scene and threatens the women with punishment, privation and disgrace as one of the principal causes of the prevailing evils because of the pride of their hearts, their luxury and extravagant ornamentation and outward conduct.

Vers. 25-26, and Chap. 4.1.   Among the agencies in this retribution is a disastrous war by which the men of the land are so reduced in numbers that the unnatural state of things will be brought about wherein women will not be sought by men but the men by the women.

3. Part three. Chap. 4.2 to 6, reverting to the safe and glorious condition of the future kingdom.

CHAPTER FOUR

2 In that day shall the [1]branch of Jehovah be beautiful and glorious, and the fruit of the [2]land shall be [3]excellent and comely for them that are escaped of Israel. 3 And it shall come to pass, that he that is left in Zion, and he that remaineth in Jerusalem, shall be called holy, even every one that is written [4]among the living in Jerusalem; 4 when the Lord shall have washed away the filth of the daughters of Zion, and shall have purged the blood of Jerusalem from the midst thereof, by the [5]spirit of justice, and by the [5]spirit of burning. 5 And Jehovah will create over [6]the whole habitation of mount Zion, and over her assemblies, a cloud and smoke by day, and the shining of a flaming fire by night; for over all the glory *shall be spread* a covering. 6 And there shall be a pavilion for a shade in the daytime from the heat, and for a refuge and for a covert from storm and from rain.

[1]Or, *shoot*   Or, *sprout*
[2]Or, *earth*
[3]Or, *missing*
[4]Or, *unto life*

[5]Or, *blast*
[6]Or, *every dwelling place*

Vers. 2-6. THE GLORIOUS CONDITION OF THE FUTURE KINGDOM.

Ver. 2. The division of this and the previous chapter is plainly wrong, for verse 1 is the closing one of the prophecy against the women as found in the previous chapter.

"In that day",—This is the same day as that mentioned in verse 1 and refers back to "the last days" of Chap 2.2, as well as to the calamitous times between, on the ground of course that this is all one prophecy, which Alexander says is now universally accepted, even by the modern Germans.

Delitzsch says, "The prophet now proceeds to describe the one great day of God at the end of time in its leading features, as beginning with judgment but bringing deliverance.

There are those, however, who contend that these chapters contain a series of detached prophecies between the beginning and the closing sections, the latter part of Chap. 2 referring to the great judgment of the closings days, while Chap. 3, they maintain, refers to pre-Messianic times. (Na. Ei. Kop. Ber.)

"the branch of Jehovah" and *"the fruit of the land"*,—

1. These are doubtless two names for the Messiah, denoting perhaps His divine and human origin. (V. F. Al. La. Um. Ros. Dre. Cas. Ste. Del. Tar. Hen. Cha. Strac.)

2. Others say the two expressions are synonomous for the produce of the earth. (Ma. Ew. Hof. Hit.) But,

   (a) This is incongruous with the predicates, honorable, glorious, sublime, beautiful.

   (b) It is precluded by the addition of the name Jehovah.

   (c) The parallel breaks down because the relation between the branch and Jehovah must be the same as that between the fruit and the land.

   (d) It is quite unsuited for forming a contrast that would quite outshine the worldly glory hitherto prevailing.

3. Others say the first phrase means spiritual gifts of God in contrast or opposition to temporal and earthly gifts." (C. Ju. Na. Schl.)

    (a) But the last phrase means the offspring of the earth and so must the first one mean the offspring of Jehovah, and this expression can only be applied to persons.

"*them that are escaped of Israel*",—Fausset quite aptly remarks that this finds its fulfillment after the fashion of concentric circles, the reference being to the elect remnant (Rom. 11.5), (1) in the return from Babylon, (2) in the escape from Jerusalem's destruction under Titus, and (3) in the still future assault on Jerusalem and the deliverance of the "third part".

Ver. 3. "*he that is left in Zion . . . that remaineth in Jerusalem*",— i. e., the "*escaped of Israel*" of verse 2, the remnant of grace, says Delitzsch.

"*shall be called holy*",—He shall not only be holy but shall be recognized as such.

"*written among the living in Jerusalem*",—The marginal reading, we think, carries the idea somewhat better. The verb has in it the idea of "written as destined for", and there is always the presupposition of a divine "Book of Life." (C. V. D. Na. Al. Ju. Mi. Um. Ew. Lo. Lu. Del. Coc. Mic. Ges. Hen. Cle.) Fausset says it refers primarily to the register kept of the Jewish families and antitypically to the Book of Life, as in Phil. 4.3 and Rev. 3.5.

Ver. 4. "*daughters of Zion*",—The women before mentioned (F. Al. Del.), and not the other towns of Judah (Um. Ros. Hen.).

"*blood of Jerusalem*", i. e., the bloodguiltiness of Jerusalem, of the people in general, especially the rulers.

"*by the spirit*",—The word should be capitalized, the reference being to the Holy Spirit (C. Al. Ew. Del. Lut.), and not to "influence" (Ges. Hen.) nor to "breath" (Um.).

Ver. 5. The presence of God, here denoted by the ancient symbol of a fiery cloud, is promised to the Israelites of the final redemption-days.

"*over all the glory*",—i. e., that previously mentioned.

"*a covering*",—A promise of refuge and security. (Al. Um. Ew. Hen. Del.) Alexander looks for the complete fulfillment of this prophecy not, as he says, "in the literal Mount Zion or Jerusalem, but in those various assemblies or societies of true believers which now possess in common the privileges once exclusively enjoyed by the Holy City and the chosen race." But that there is as well a further and more remote reference in the prophecy, as the majority maintain, can scarcely be denied.

CHAPTER FIVE

ISRAEL TO REAP THE FRUIT OF HER DISOBEDIENCE.

A new prophecy, entire in itself, being the concluding discourse of the first cycle of prophecy and containing a description of the prevalent iniquities of Israel and the judgments which had been or were to be inflicted on the people in consequence.

Vers. 1-7. The prophet represents Israel as a vineyard from which the Lord had expected the fruits of righteousness, but it had brought forth bad fruit.

Vers. 8-24. What sort of bad fruit is seen in a sixfold woe which is pronounced upon the people.

Vers. 25-30. The devastation foretold is seen first in a figurative description of a violent stroke of God's hand, and then in the shape of an invading army before whom Israel disappears, as it were, in total darkness.

Nagelsbach says, "The prophecy finds its fulfillment in all the catastrophes that brought foreign powers against Israel, from the Assyrians to the Romans," and with this Delitzsch and practically all others are in agreement.

Nagelsbach furthermore refers the expression, *"in that day"* in verse 30 back to Chap. 2.11,17,20; 3.7,18; 4.1 and 4.2, and says, "that hereby is intimated that this prophecy too, shall be fulfilled in the 'last days'."

It should, however, by no means be thought necessary to always throw the reference in the expression, *"in that day"* to the end-time; in this particular instance it quite appropriately refers to the time in which the events of the immediately preceding verses are to take place, and the primary reference of these is without doubt to the besieging armies of the Assyrians.

CHAPTER SIX

The Inaugural Vision of the Prophet.

11 Then said I, Lord, how long? And he answered, Until cities be waste without inhabitant, and houses without man, and the land become utterly waste, 12 and Jehovah have removed men far away, and the forsaken places be many in the midst of the land. 13 [1]And if there be yet a tenth in it, it also shall in turn be [2]eaten up: as a terebinth, and as an oak, [3]whose [4]stock remaineth, when they [5]are felled; so the holy seed is the stock thereof.

[1]Or, *but yet in it shall be a tenth, and it shall return, and shall be eaten up*
[2]Or, *burnt*
[3]Or, *whose substance is in them*
[4]Or, *substance*
[5]Or, *cast* their leaves

Vers. 11-13. The Elect Remnant the Guarantee of a New Life and a New Glorious Future.

Ver. 11. *"Lord, how long"*,—Not how long must he be the bearer of this thankless message (Hit.), but how long shall the blindness of his people continue. (F. Al.)

"until cities be waste", etc.,—Grotius supposes the allusion is to Sennacherib's invasion, while Clericus and Kimchi think it is to that of Nebuchadnezzar; but as the foregoing description is repeatedly applied in the New Testament to the Jews who were contemporaneous with our Saviour, the threatening must be equally extensive and is equivalent to saying that the land shall be completely wasted not at one time but repeatedly, as Alexander says.

Ver. 12. *"the forsaken places be many",*—The literal rendering is, "great shall be that which is left in the land". The reference, however, is to the land itself (F. Al. Del.), and it does not mean therefore that "many ruins" shall be left (Ges.), nor a "great vacancy" (Ew.), nor that those left in the land shall be multiplied (Sep. Vul.).

Ver. 13. According to Isaiah not all Israel, but the elect remnant alone is destined to salvation.

"in turn",—This is better than "return" of the Authorized Version; the tenth left in the land could hardly, says Alexander, be described as returning to it.

"whose stock remaineth",—The word for "stock" is variously translated; "substance", i. e., vitality (Al.), "stump" (Na.), "sap" (Tar.), "root" (D.), "trunk" (Ges.), "germ" (Hit.), "stock" (F. Del.). The etymology of the word and the connection seem to favor "substance". The thought is the same. The stock of the tree when felled of course contains this substance, this vitality, etc.

"the holy seed is the stock thereof",—The remnant of the tenth is the stock or the substance from which the nation is to be renewed. "However frequently", says Alexander, "the people may seem to be destroyed, there shall still be a surviving remnant, a tenth, and however frequently this very remnant may appear to perish, there shall still be a remnant of the remnant left and this indestructible residuum shall be the holy seed, the elect remnant according to grace (Romans 11.5)."

"There is nothing tougher than the life of this everlasting Jew."

Section Two.   The Assyrian Oppression and the Coming Messiah.

CHAPTERS 7 TO 12.

Chapters 7 to 12 deal only with the deliverance of Judah from Syria and Israel; the subsequent subjection of Judah to Assyria and other foreign powers; the final destruction of Judah's enemies, and the advent of the Messianic kingdom.

CHAPTER EIGHT

> 9 [1]Make an uproar, O ye peoples, and be broken in pieces; and give ear, all ye of far countries; gird yourselves, and be broken in pieces; gird yourself and be broken in pieces.
> [1]Or, *Break, O ye*

Ver. 9.   THE ENEMIES OF JUDAH TO BE BROKEN IN PIECES.

The prophecy refers primarily to the attack of Rezin and Pekah. Fausset and Horsley think, "It probably looks on also to the final conspiracy of Antichrist and his supporters against the Heir of David's throne in the latter days and to their overthrow." There is, however, no sufficient reason for finding such a reference in connection with the passage under discussion.

CHAPTER NINE

The calamity predicted is not to be perpetual.

1 ¹But there shall be no gloom to her that was in anguish. In the former time he brought into contempt the land of Zebulun and the land of Naphtali; but in the latter time hath he made it glorious by the way of the sea, beyond the Jordan, ²Galilee of the nations. 2 The people that walked in darkness have seen a great light: they that dwelt in the land of the ³shadow of death, upon them hath the light shined. 3 Thou hast multiplied the nation, ⁴thou hast increased their joy: they joy before thee according to the joy in harvest, as men rejoice when they divide the spoil. 4 For the yoke of his burden, and the staff of his shoulder, the rod of his oppressor, thou hast broken as in the day of Midian. 5 For ⁵all the armor of the armed man in the tumult, and the garments rolled in blood, shall be for burning, for fuel of fire. 6 For unto us a child is born, unto us a son is given; and the government shall be upon his shoulder: and his name shall be called ⁶Wonderful, Counsellor Mighty God, ⁷Everlasting Father, Prince of Peace. 7 Of the increase of his government and of peace there shall be no end, upon the throne of David, and upon his kingdom, to establish it, and to uphold it with justice and with righteousness from henceforth even for ever. The zeal of Jehovah of hosts will perform this.

¹Or, *For*
²Or, *the district*
³Or, *deep darkness*
⁴Another reading is, *thou didst not increase the joy.*

⁵Or, *every boot of the booted warrior*
⁶Or, *Wonderful Counsellor*
⁷Heb. *Father of Eternity*

Vers. 1-7. THE BIRTH AND REIGN OF THE KING OF PEACE.

Ver. 1. *"her that was in anguish"*,—i. e., Judah.

"the land of", etc.,—The same region is described first by the tribes which occupied it, and then by its relative position with respect to the river Jordan and the sea, i. e., the sea of Galilee. The country formerly most debased was to receive peculiar honor, as explained in the next verse. *"But"*,—Some take the last verse of the preceding chapter as the beginning of the promise and so translate this word "For". (Al. Mi. Ma. Hit. Hen. Del.) It is, however, less abrupt to take the preceding words as a threat and translate with our text as *"But"*. (Na. Ew. Ros. Ges.) *"in the latter time"*,—i. e., in Messianic times.

Ver. 2. *"The people"*,—i. e., the Galileans just mentioned. (V. Al. Na. Ju. Mic. Hend.) The reference is not then to all Israel (Ma.), nor to Judah (C. Kim.), nor to the people of Jerusalem (Gro.), nor yet to the people of God, the spiritual Israel (Coc.). Of course the reference is extended to the whole of Israel. The light came by way of Galilee where Christ first and most publicly exercised His ministry. The verse is descriptive of a great change from ignorance and misery to illumination and enjoyment.

Ver. 3. *"Thou hast multiplied the nation"*,—The reference here is to Israel, i. e., to Israel in general, that had melted down to a small remnant after their return from captivity. (F. Na. Del. Hit.)

"they joy before thee",—This is to be taken as holy joy, in the sense of religious worship. (V. F. Al. Ew. Coc. Hit. Hen. Del.)

Ver. 4. The reason for this holy joy.

"thou hast broken",—The past is here used for the future in prophetic vision and expresses the certainty of the event.

"his",—Not the oppressor's (Bar. For.), but Israel's, the nation's.

"as in the day of Midian",—i. e., when Gideon overthrew Midian, suddenly, totally and with the miraculous help of heaven, the reference being to that wonderful display of divine power which took place in the same part of the land to which this prophecy refers.

That this prediction refers primarily to the times of the coming Messiah is evidenced beyond doubt by content of verse 6.

Alexander says, "This promise was not fulfilled in the deliverance of the Jews from Babylon (C.), nor in the destruction of Sennacherib's army (Gro.), nor in the destruction of Jerusalem by Titus (Mi.), but it was fulfilled in the glorious deliverance of the Gentiles (the first converts to Christianity) and of all who with them made up the true Israel, from the heavy burden of the covenant of works, the galling yoke of the Mosaic law, the service of the Devil, and the bondage of corruption."

Many authorities, on the other hand, think we are warranted in seeing with Fausset and others a reference in these verses to the days of the final Antichrist. Fausset says, "The deliverance referred to was not only that of Ahaz and Judah from the Assyrian tribute (II Kings 16.8) and of Israel (the ten tribes) from the oppressor (II Kings 15.19), but of the Jewish Christian Church from its last great enemy. As Gideon, with a handful of men conquered the Midian hosts, so Messiah and the small Israel under Him shall overthrow the mighty hosts of the Antichrist, containing the same contrast, and alluding also to the 'Assyrian', the then enemy of the Church, as here in Isaiah the type of the last great enemy."

Horsley says, "The prophet sees in a vision a shifting scene comprehending at one glance the history of the Christian Church to the remotest times—a land dark and thinly peopled—lit up by a sudden light—filled with new inhabitants—then struggling with difficulties and again delivered by the utter and final overthrow of their enemies."

Again we are confronted with the question of a spiritual or literal interpretation.

Ver. 5. *"rolled in blood"*,—Not merely dyed (Hit.), but stained with the blood of conflict.

"for fuel of fire",—Fire is mentioned merely as a powerful consuming agent to express the abolition of the implements of war. The complete fulfillment of the prediction, says Alexander, will only be when the lion and the lamb lie down together.

Ver. 6. The child here predicted refers of course to Christ. By many it is explained to be Hezekiah (Ja. Kim. Gro. Pau, Ges. Hens. Hend.). But this is exegetical helplessness of a pathetic sort, and the view is even rejected by such modern Germans as Eichorn, Umbreit, Ewald and Hitzig.

Ver. 7. *"peace"*,—The Hebrew word denotes not only peace as opposed to war, but welfare and prosperity. The angel choir proclaiming His birth sang of this peace and good will.

"there shall be no end",—i. e., it is to be both universal and eternal.

"upon the throne of David",—The Prince was to be a descendant of David.

"judgment",—i. e., righteous government.

"justice",—i. e., righteousness which He practices and transmits to the members of His kingdom.

CHAPTER TEN

Vers. 1-4.   The prophet first completes his picture of the prevailing iniquity of his people and then threatens as a punishment the death and deportation which is to come through the invasion of the Assyrian army.

Vers. 5-19.   The predicted judgment of Jehovah upon Assyria who has been but a rod in His hand for the chastisement of Israel.

Vers. 20-23.

20 And it shall come to pass in that day, that the remnant of Israel, and they that are escaped of the house of Jacob, shall no more again lean upon him that smote them, but shall lean upon Jehovah. The Holy One of Israel, in truth. 21 A remnant shall return, *even* the remnant of Jacob, unto the mighty God.   22 For though thy people, Israel, be as the sand of the sea, *only* a remnant [1]of them shall return: a destruction *is* determined, overflowing with righteousness. 23 For a full end, and that determined, will the Lord. Jehovah of hosts, make in the midst of all the [2]earth.

[1]Heb. *in it*
[2]Or, *land*

Vers. 20-23.   THE BELIEVING REMNANT RESTORED.

Ver. 20.   *"in that day"*,—i. e., in the day when the destruction of Assyria just foretold has taken place.   "The prediction, however," says Alexander, "although it began then to be fulfilled did not receive its final fulfillment before Christ's appearance."

Scofield refers the expression to "the day of the Lord," and says, "The prophecy here passes from the general to the particular, from historic and fulfilled judgments upon Assyria to the final destruction of *all* Gentile world-power at the return of the Lord in glory."   The vision here, he says, is that of the Jewish remnant in the great tribulation.

"the remnant of Israel",—The reference is to those who shall be left after the invasion of the Assyrian army, although in keeping with the idea of continuous fulfillment it must refer, as Alexander says, as well to those left after the Babylonian captivity and as well to the remnant according to the election of grace.   (Romans 11.5.)

Fausset says, "Fulfilled in part in the days of pious Hezekiah; but from the future aspect under which Paul in Romans 9.27,28 regards the prophecy, the 'remnant' who 'stay upon the Lord' probably will receive their fullest realization in the portion of the Jews left after the Antichrist shall have been overthrown, who shall 'return to the Lord'. (Zeph. 3.12; Zech. 12.9,10.)"

"lean upon him",—i. e., upon the Assyrian, who here stands also as the representative of foreign help in general.

Ver. 21.   *"The remnant shall return"*,—Fausset remarks, "As the Assyrians in the reign of Sennacherib *did not* carry Judah (the house of

Jacob) away captive, the returning remnant *cannot mainly* refer to this time.''

Alexander says, "It really means those who should survive God's judgments threatened in this prophecy, not merely the Assyrian invasion or the Babylonian captivity, but the whole series of remarkable events including the destruction and the dispersion of the nation by the Romans under Titus."

Ver. 22. *"For though thy people be"*,— (Lut. Ges. Bar.) Others prefer "shall be," as referring to the ancient promise of Gen. 13.16 (C. Lo. Al. Coc.), while still others (D. Ew. Um. Hit. Del. Aug. Hend.) render, "For even if thy people were".

"thy people",—The whole race, and neither Judah nor Israel alone.

"a destruction is determined",—i. e., of the majority of them.

"righteousness",—The meaning is not that of "piety" or "virtue" (C. Gro.), but rather that of retributive and punitive justice. (F. V. Al. Ma. Del.)

Ver. 23. *"a full end"*,—i. e., a thorough destruction or con-sumption.

"all the earth",—The judgment is to be a universal one of which that on Israel is a central constituent.

Vers. 24-27. Now comes a renewed prediction of severe judgment upon Assyria like that which came on Midian at Oreb and on Egypt at the Red Sea.

Vers. 28-32. Scofield would have us believe that these verses describe the approach of the Gentile hosts to the battle of Armageddon, but this appears as somewhat strained, and it is much simpler to take this section as describing the march of the Assyrians under Sennacherib against Jerusalem. (F. Na. Al. Del.) This latter may, however, serve as a type of the former.

Vers. 33-34. These verses relate doubtless to the destruction of Sennacherib's army, rather than to the destruction of the Gentile hosts under the Beast as described in Revelation 19.20, as Scofield would have us take it.

CHAPTER ELEVEN

1 And there shall come forth a shoot out of the stock of Jesse, and a branch out of his roots shall bear fruit. 2 And the Spirit of Jehovah shall rest upon him, the spirit of wisdom and understanding, the spirit of counsel and might, the spirit of knowledge and of the fear of Jehovah. 3 And [1]his [2]delight shall be in the fear of Jehovah; and he shall not judge after the sight of his eyes, neither decide after the hearing of his ears; 4 but with righteousness shall he judge the poor, and decide with equity for the meek of the [3]earth; and he shall smite the [3]earth with the rod of his mouth; and with the breath of his lips shall he slay the wicked. 5 And righteousness shall be the girdle of his waist, and faithfulness the girdle of his loins.

6 And the wolf shall dwell with the lamb, and the leopard shall lie down with the kid; and the calf and the young lion and the fatling together; and a

[1]Or, *he shall be of quick understanding*
[2]Heb. *scent*
[3]Or, *land*

little child shall lead them. 7 And the cow and the bear shall feed; their young ones shall lie down together; and the lion shall eat straw like the ox. 8 And the suckling child shall play on the hole of the asp, and the weaned child shall put his hand on the adder's den. 9 They shall not hurt nor destroy in all my holy mountain; for the earth shall be full of the knowledge of Jehovah, as the waters cover the sea.

10 And it shall come to pass in that day, that the root of Jesse, that standeth for an ensign of the peoples, unto him shall the nations seek; and his resting-place shall be [1]glorious.

11 And it shall come to pass in that day, that the Lord [2]will set his hand again the second time to [3]recover the remnant of his people, that shall remain, from Assyria, and from Egypt, and from Pathros, and from Cush, and from Elam, and from Shinar, and from Hamath, and from the [4]islands of the

sea. 12 And he will set up an ensign for the nations, and will assemble the outcasts of Israel, and gather together the dispersed of Judah from the four corners of the earth. 13 The envy also of Ephraim shall depart, and they that vex [5]Judah shall be cut off: Ephraim shall not envy Judah, and Judah shall not vex Ephraim. 14 And they shall fly down upon the shoulder of the Philistines on the west; together shall they despoil the children of the east: they shall put forth their hand upon Edom and Moab; and the children of Ammon shall obey them. 15 And Jehovah will [6]utterly destroy the tongue of the Egyptian sea; and with his scorching wind will he wave his hand over the River, and will smite it into seven streams, and cause men to march over dryshod. 16 And there shall be a highway for the remnant of his people, that shall remain, from Assyria; like as there was for Israel in the day that he came up out of the land of Egypt.

[1]Heb. *glory*
[2]Or, *will again the second time recover with his hand*
[3]Or, *purchase* See Ex. 15, 16.
[4]Or, *coast-lands*

[5]Or, *in Judah*
[6]Heb. *devote*

Vers. 1-16. The Kingdom of David and How It Will Be Established.

"This chapter," says Scofield, "is a prophetic picture of the glory of the future kingdom. This is the kingdom announced by John the Baptist as 'at hand'. It was then rejected, but will be set up when David's Son returns in glory. That nothing of this occurred at the first coming of Christ is evident from a comparison of the history of the times of Christ with this and all other parallel prophecies. So far from regathering dispersed Israel and establishing peace in the earth, His crucifixion was soon followed by the destruction of Jerusalem, and the utter scattering of the Palestinian Jews amongst the nations of the world."

Ver. 1. *"the stock of Jesse"*,—The reference is to the "stump" (F. Al. Del.), showing the depressed state of the house of David. It should not therefore be translated "seed" (Ab.), nor "root" (Sep.), nor "trunk" (Ges. Hit. Hend.). Jesse is used here instead of David to intimate perhaps that David's stock will be reduced to its rank previous to the time of David when it was only the stock of the obscure citizen of Bethlehem.

The reference is not to Hezekiah (Ab. Hend.), because he was already born, and his house was not in the condition here described. Nor is the reference to Zerubbabel, nor to the Maccabees, who were not even descendants of Jesse, nor to an ideal Messiah (D. Ei. Ew. Hit. Ges. Bau. Ros.), but to Jesus Christ.

Ver. 2. *"the Spirit of Jehovah"*,—The general designation of the self-same Spirit afterwards described in detail, He being the author of what

59

thus rests upon Christ. It is an old opinion that the seven Spirits of Revelation have reference to the seven Spirits of this verse.

Ver. 3. *"his delight"*,—The Hebrew word means to delight in the odor of a thing, literally to "scent", and the meaning is that the fear of the Lord is fragrance to Him.

"he shall not judge", etc.,—His decisions shall not rest upon mere external appearances or hearsay.

Ver. 4. *"the breath of his lips"*,—This has been taken to mean a sentence of death (Coc. Hit. Cle. Hend.), as a natural expression of anger (D. Ges.), as a secret influence producing conviction (V. Aba. Kim.), but the proper thought seems to be that a word of his mouth, or a mere breath, as something even less than a word, is sufficient to effect His purpose. (C. Al. Ew.)

Fausset says, "The everlasting deliverance under the Messiah's reign spoken of in this chapter refers not merely to His first coming but chiefly to His second coming. It implies that the earth will be very wicked when He shall come to judge and reign. His reign shall therefore be ushered in with judgments upon the apostates. He, as the word of God, comes to strike that blow which shall decide His claim to the kingdom, previously usurped by Satan and the Beast to whom Satan delegates his power. It will be a day of judgment to the Gentile dispensation as the first coming was to the Jews."

Alexander says, "Paul in I Thess. 2.8 applies these words with little change to the destruction of Antichrist at the second coming of Christ. It does not follow, however, that this is a specific and exclusive prophecy of that event, but only that it comprehends it, as it evidently does."

Ver. 6. This and the next two verses have been taken in three different ways:

1. As literal, but only a beautiful dream and wish never to be realized. Rationalistic interpreters.
2. "A literal change in the relation of animals to man and to each other, restoring the state in Eden, is the most likely interpretation." (F.)
3. As wholly metaphorical, describing the peace to be enjoyed by God's people under the new dispensation. (C. V. Al. Hen. Del. Lut. Schm., and the early Fathers.)

One of the advocates of this last view (Naylor) remarks, "Any one with physiological knowledge of the difference between the structure of herbivorous and carnivorous animals, or with any knowledge of dentistry, will at once see that the lion could no more eat straw like an ox than he could fly to the moon; even if his teeth were changed so that he could masticate the straw, it would prove fatal to him, since he could by no means digest or assimilate it. This is simply a figure of the peace that would come to humanity as a result of Christ's coming as a Saviour into the world. It is true now."

Campbell Morgan, however, remarks concerning these verses, "You cannot spiritualize that passage. It is a plain statement of the fact that, under the sway of the Redeemer, the ferocity of wild beasts shall depart, and nature itself shall feel the blessed influence of the reigning Prince of

Peace. I have been asked whether this Golden Age will be marked by dietetic abstinence from flesh. While I do not believe in vegetarianism for today, except under certain conditions, I may express the belief that nature itself will then be free from everything that savours of cruelty; for 'they shall not hurt nor destroy in all my holy mountain'. Certain it is that the lower animals will be vegetarians, for 'The lion shall eat straw like an ox'." (See Nagelsbach in Lange's Commentary on Isaiah, page 163.)

Ver. 8. *"the hole of the asp"*,—The word *"hole"* as well as the word *"den"* properly denotes a cavity admitting light and no doubt the reference in each case is to the beautiful eye of the serpent and the cockatrice.

Ver. 9. *"my holy mountain"*,—i. e., Mount Zion, and Jerusalem in particular.

"for",—i. e., because.

Ver. 10. *"a root of Jesse"*,—The literal is "root-sprout"; it is the root of Jesse, now under ground, as it were.

"the nations",—i. e., the Gentiles.

"his resting place shall be glorious",—The reference is not to the rest (A-V) which He gives to His people, but to His residence, the place where He resides, in which He dwells, i. e., His Kingdom.

Ver. 11. *"set his hand a second time to recover the remnant"*,— The remnant here refers to those living at the time the deliverance takes place, or more restrictedly to the remnant according to grace. (C. Al.)

"a second time",—"Therefore", says Fausset, "the coming restoration of the Jews is to be distinct from that after the Babylonian captivity, and yet to resemble it. The first restoration was literal; therefore shall the second be; the latter, however, to be much more universal as is here implied."

Thus also Blackstone who says, "In the first restoration only those who were minded came back from Babylon (Ezra 7.13); but in the future, or second restoration, not one will be left. (Deut. 30.4; Isa. 43.5-7; Ezek. 34.11-13; Ezek. 39.28-29.) In the first restoration it was members of the two tribes who returned; in the second, or future restoration it will be both the two and the ten tribes. (Jer. 3.18; Ezek. 36.10; 37.15-22.) At the first restoration they returned to be overthrown and driven out again; but in the second they shall return to remain, no more to go out. (Amos 9.15; Ezek. 34.28; Isa. 60.15,16; 49.22,23; Mic. 4.1,2; Zech. 8.20-23; 14.16.) In the first restoration, because of their blindness they rejected and crucified Jesus; but in the future restoration they shall repent of all this and have clean hearts and accept Christ who shall be their Saviour. (Zech. 12.10-14; Jer. 31.9,10,33; Ezek. 36.24-28; 37.23-27; 34.23,24; Jer. 23.3-6.)

Scofield remarks here, "Comment upon a passage so explicit should be superfluous. I will ask you only to note that the prophet declares the restoration here predicted to be the 'second'; that it cannot refer to the partial restoration under Ezra and Nehemiah, from the Babylonian captivity, because, first, it is not a deliverance from Assyria only, but the regathering of a world-wide dispersion, and, second, because both Israel (the ten tribes) and Judah are gathered. Ezra and Nehemiah, as is well known, led back only a remnant of Judah with a few Levites."

Alexander says, "It is not second in reference to the return from Babylon, but to the deliverance from Egypt. The complete fulfillment is to be expected only when all Israel shall be saved. The dispersion spoken of was not merely such as had taken place already at the date of the prediction (Ges.), but others still in the future (Hen.), including not only the Babylonian exile, but the present dispersion."

The countries mentioned are put for all in which the Jews should be scattered. The event prefigured is, according to Fausset, Keith and many others, the still future return of the Jews to Palestine, while by others (C. V. Hen.) it is their admission to Christ's kingdom on repentance and the reception of the Christian faith. Alexander thinks the prediction must be figuratively understood because the nations mentioned in this verse have long since ceased to exist.

Ver. 12. *"nations"*,—The Gentile nations, not especially those holding captive the Jews, as if calling them to release the captives and assist them in returning, but the call shall be to Gentile nations in general to come themselves.

"the outcasts of Israel",—The dispersed of the ten tribes are so called because they have been longer and more utterly cast away.

Ver. 13. *"they that vex Judah"*,—i. e., those in Ephraim.

"That this prediction was not fulfilled in the return from exile is sufficiently notorious: That it had not been fulfilled when Christ came is plain from the continued enmity between the Jews, the Samaritans and the Galileans. The only fulfillment it has ever had is in the abolition of all national and sectional distinctions in the Christian Church. Its full accomplishment is yet to come in the reunion of the tribes under Christ (Hos. 1.11)". (Al.)

Ver. 14. *"the children of the east"*,—i. e., the Arabians.

Ver. 15. *"the tongue of the Egyptian sea"*,—This is the narrow gulf in which the Red Sea terminates to the northwest near Suez through which the Israelites passed when they left Egypt.

"with his scorching wind",—Literally, "in the glowing puff of His breath."

"smite it into seven streams",—i. e., the River Euphrates to be divided into many smaller ones, as Cyrus divided the Gyndes, so as to be easily forded. Egypt and Assyria were the two greatest powers from which Israel had suffered and from which she was yet to be delivered; and the thought emphasized here is that all obstacles to return shall be removed, and this is set forth by strong figures drawn from the earliest history of the Israelites.

Ver. 16. The fulfillment of this and the other verses has been sought by some in the return from Babylon; by others in the general progress of the Gospel, and by others still in the future restoration of the Jews.

The return from Babylon was of course only a partial fulfillment, but against the last named view Alexander urges the figurative expressions of the destroying the tongue of the Red Sea, etc.

CHAPTER TWELVE

This is a Thanksgiving hymn of the restored and converted Jews. Scofield and many others think it belongs to the time of the Millennial kingdom, but this of course depends upon the view that one takes of the preceding chapter, as it is quite certain that the expression "in that day" makes it contemporaneous with the same expression in that chapter.

Section Three. Prophecies Concerning the Heathen; Their Judgment and Their Salvation.

CHAPTERS 13 TO 23

CHAPTER THIRTEEN

1 The [1]burden of Babylon, which Isaiah the son of Amoz did see.

2 Set ye up an ensign upon the bare mountain, lift up the voice unto them, wave the hand, that they may go into the gates of the nobles. 3 I have commanded my consecrated ones, yea, I have called my mighty men for mine anger, even [2]my proudly exulting ones. 4 The noise of a multitude in the mountains, as of a great people! the noise of a tumult of the kingdoms of the nations gathered together! Jehovah of hosts is mustering the host for the battle. 5 They come from a far country, from the uttermost part of heaven, even Jehovah, and the weapons of his indignation, to destroy the whole land.

6 Wail ye; for the day of Jehovah is at hand; as destruction from [3]the Almighty shall it come. 7 Therefore shall all hands be feeble, and every heart of man shall melt: 8 and they shall be dismayed; [4]pangs and sorrows shall take hold of them; they shall be in pain as a woman in travail: they shall look in amazement one at another; their faces shall be faces of flame. 9 Behold, the day of Jehovah cometh, cruel, with wrath and fierce anger; to make the land a desolation, and to destroy the sinners thereof out of it. 10 For the stars of heaven and the constellations thereof shall not give their light: the sun shall be darkened in its going forth, and the moon shall not cause its light to shine. 11 And I will punish the world for their evil, and the wicked for their iniquity: and I will cause the arrogancy of the proud to cease, and will lay low the haughtiness of the terrible. 12 I will make a man more rare than fine gold, even a man than the pure gold of Ophir. 13 Therefore I will make the heavens to tremble, and the earth shall be shaken out of its place, in the wrath of Jehovah of hosts, and in the day of his fierce anger. 14 And it shall come to pass, that as the chased [5]roe, and as sheep that no man gathereth, they shall turn every man to his own people, and shall flee every man to his own land. 15 Every one that is found shall be thrust through; and every one that is [6]taken shall fall by the sword. 16 Their infants also shall be dashed in pieces before their eyes; their houses shall be rifled, and their wives ravished.

17 Behold, I will stir up the Medes against them, who shall not regard silver, and as for gold, they shall not delight in it. 18 And *their* bows shall dash the young men in pieces; and they shall have no pity on the fruit of the womb; their eye shall not spare children. 19 And Babylon, the glory of kingdoms, the beauty of the Chaldeans' pride, shall be as when God overthrew Sodom and Gomorrah. 20 It shall never be inhabited, neither shall it be dwelt in from generation to generation: neither shall the Arabian pitch tent there; neither shall shepherds make their flocks to lie down there. 21 But wild beasts of the desert shall lie there; and their houses shall be full of doleful creatures; and ostriches shall dwell there, and wild goats shall dance there. 22 And [7]wolves shall [8]cry in their castles, and jackals in the pleasant palaces: and her time is near to come, and her days shall not be prolonged.

[1]Or, *oracle concerning*
[2]Or, *them that exult in my majesty*
[3]Heb. *Shaddai.* See Gen. 17.1.
[4]Or, *they shall take hold of pangs and sorrows.*

[5]Or, *gazelle*
[6]Or, *joined* thereunto
[7]Heb. *howling creatures*
[8]Or, *answer*

Vers. 1-22. THE JUDGMENT PRONOUNCED ON THE BABYLONIAN EM-
PIRE AND THE FINAL OVERTHROW AND DESTRUCTION
OF BABYLON HERSELF, THROUGH THE CONQUESTS OF
THE MEDES AND PERSIANS.

In speaking of the day of the Lord that is to come upon Babylon,
the prophet in verses 9 to 13 seems to use language, as Horsley says, which
can only primarily and partially apply to Babylon, but which applies more
fully and exhaustively to the judgments to come hereafter upon the whole
world.

Scofield remarks, "The *city*, Babylon, is not in view here, as the immediate context shows.   It is the political Babylon which is in view, literally as to the then existing city, and symbolically as to the times of the
Gentiles.   By political Babylon is meant the Gentile world-system.   In
Revelation religious Babylon, apostate Christianity, is destroyed by political
Babylon (Rev. 17.16), and political Babylon is destroyed by the coming
of the Lord in glory (Rev. 19.19-21).   Verses 12 to 16 of our chapter
look forward to the Apocalyptic judgments (Rev. 6-13).   Verses 17-22
have both a near and a far view.   They predict the destruction of literal
Babylon then existing and this has been literally fulfilled.   But the place
of this prediction in a great prophetic strain which looks forward to the
destruction of both politico-Babylon and ecclesio-Babylon in the time of
the Beast shows that the destruction of the actual Babylon typifies the
greater destruction yet to come upon the mystical Babylon."

That the chapter has such a typical reference we have no reason to
doubt, but there is less reason to doubt that its primary reference is to
the downfall of the literal Babylon existing in the days of the prophet.
Alexander puts the matter thus: "The truth, however, seems to be, first,
that the downfall of Babylon, an opponent and persecutor of the ancient
Church, affords a type of emblem of the destiny of all opposing powers
under the new Testament; and, secondly, that in consequence of this
analogy the Apocalyptic prophecies apply the name Babylon to the Antichristian power.   But these Apocalyptic prophecies are new ones, not
interpretations of the one before us."   But surely if it is a type of the one
it is equally a type of the other.

Nagelsbach says, "Isaiah regards the judgment against Babylon as
the germ-like beginning of 'the day of the Lord' in general."

Ver. 1.   *"burden"*,—i. e., a weighty or mournful prophecy, heavy
because the wrath of God is in it.

Ver. 2.   *"upon the bare mountain"*,—From such a height the banner
could be seen from afar to rally the people against Babylon.

"shake the hand",—i. e., beckon the nations on toward their march
against the city.

The pronoun *"them"* refers to the Medes and the Persians. while *"the
nobles"* refers to the Babylonians.

Ver. 3.   *"my consecrated ones"*,—The warriors are so called because
the war is a holy one.

Ver. 5.   *"from a far country"*,—i. e., from Media and Persia.

"from the end of heaven",—This is not perhaps a geographical

description, but a statement as to from what point he sees them coming, i. e., from the remotest point in sight, the boundary line of the horizon.

"the whole land",—i. e., of Babylonia.

Nagelsbach thinks it is quite improbable that by the expressions in this verse Isaiah would designate the Medes and Persians. With regard to the expression, "the whole land", he says, "The end that the Lord will accomplish by means of 'the weapons of His indignation' is to overturn 'the whole earth'. The whole *earth!* For this judgment on Babylon belongs to 'the day of the Lord'. It is thus an integral part of the world's judgment."

Ver. 6. *"the day of Jehovah"*,—i. e., the day of His vengeance on Babylon, and a type of the future "day of wrath."

Says Nagelsbach, "Here we see in verses 6 to 8 how plainly the prophet would represent the judgment on Babylon as a part of the world's judgment. For the traits that now follow are entirely taken from the descriptions of the world's judgments as we meet them already in the older Prophets, and as, on the other hand, the later New Testament descriptions of the great day of judgment connect with our present one."

Ver. 9. *"cruel with wrath and fierce anger"*,—i. e., unsparingly just; opposed to mercy.

"to lay the land desolate",—i. e., as in verse 5, the land of Babylonia, primarily of course. Some make it the earth without reservation. (Ew. Um. Sep.); while Knobel understands the term as an allusion to the universal sway of the Babylonian Empire.

Ver. 10. Here is the usual description or the usual Scriptural characteristics of the *"day of the Lord"*—any day of His judgment. Here it must be figurative for anarchy, distress and revolutions of kingdoms, "although," says Fausset, "there may be a literal fulfillment finally, shadowed forth under this imagery." (Rev. 21.1.)

Ver. 11. *"the world"*,—This is doubtless a poetical equivalent for Babylon as embracing most of the then known world, although the wider reference usual to the prophecy may also be included.

Ver. 12. Scofield would make this verse refer to the Jewish remnant in the great tribulation, and the next verse to that tribulation period itself. But this seems somewhat strained and arbitrary. The reference is doubtless to the scarcity of men in consequence of the slaughter of Babylon's defenders, while verse 13 is to be taken in the same sense as verse 10.

Ver. 17. Here we are made aware for the first time who are to be the executors of God's judgment against Babylon.

"shall not regard silver . . nor delight in gold",—"In vain", says Fausset, "will one try to buy his life from them for a ransom." "The Prophet intimates", says Nagelsbach, "that they are impelled by higher motives than common love of booty—perhaps a thirst for revenge (Del.), but they might also have their source in an impulse to fulfill some mission of which they were unconscious."

CHAPTER FOURTEEN

1 For Jehovah will have compassion on Jacob, and will yet choose Israel, and set them in their own land: and the sojourner shall join himself with them, and they shall cleave to the house of Jacob. 2 And the peoples shall take them, and bring them to their place; and the house of Israel shall possess them in the land of Jehovah for servants and for handmaids: and they shall take them captive whose captives they were; and they shall rule over their oppressors.

Vers. 1,2.   BABYLON'S DESTRUCTION AND ISRAEL'S RESTORATION AND EXALTATION.

Ver. 1.   *"will yet choose"*,—i. e., choose again; still treat them as His chosen, their restoration being grounded on their election.

"the strangers shall be joined with them",—The reference is here to the proselytes from the heathen who had joined themselves to Israel.   "An earnest", says Fausset, "of the future effect on the heathen world of the Jews' spiritual restoration."

Ver. 2.   The meaning is that the people of Babylon will bring the Jews back to their own land, i. e., to the land of the Jews, the "they" in the latter half of the verse referring to the Jews.

"shall possess them",—i. e., the Gentiles.

Cocceius, at one extreme, finds the whole fulfillment in the final deliverance of the Christian Church from persecution in the Roman empire, while Clericus, at the other, applies it to the number of foreign servants that the Jews brought back from exile.

Calvin and Fausset make the change predicted an altogether moral and spiritual one, the conquest of the true religion over those who were once its physical oppressors.

The fact is there is a twofold fulfillment, the lower physical one in the literal exchange of places, as between the Jews and their oppressors, which took place upon the return of the Jews from Babylonian captivity, and the higher spiritual one which is yet to be accomplished, but "not with respect to the Jews as a people", says Alexander, "for their pre-eminence has ceased forever, but with respect to the Church, including Jews and Gentiles, which has succeeded to the rights and privileges, promises and actual possessions of God's ancient people."

As to whether it is to have a still future literal fulfillment depends upon one's method of treating the whole line of such prophecies.

Vers. 4-23.   ISRAEL'S SONG OF TRIUMPH OVER HER FALLEN ENEMY.

Scofield, not without considerable strain in his exegesis, gives a future setting to the whole of the chapter; the first seven verses referring to the Millennial kingdom as set up; verses 7 and 8 to the joy of that kingdom; verses 9 to 11 to the mystical Babylon, the beast in hell; verses 12 to 17 to an address by the Beast to Satan in hell (to what purpose?); verses 18 to 23 to the judgment on mystical Babylon in the final world-battle.

These verses, however, in their entirety are with far greater simplicity and consistency referred to the king and people of Babylon, Lucifer, in verse 12, meaning merely "the shining one", "the bright star", "the morning star", which in Latin is called "lucifer", and there is therefore no occasion for the popular perversion of this beautiful name to signify the Devil. Fausset says, "The language is so framed as to apply to the Babylonian king primarily, and at the same time to shadow forth through him, the great final enemy, the man of sin, Antichrist, of Daniel, Saint Paul and Saint John; he alone shall fulfill exhaustively all the lineaments here given."

Blackstone says that in Lucifer the Antichrist is seen, of whom the king of Babylon was a type, and who weakens the nations, exalts his "throne above the stars of God, and sits upon the mount of the congregation."

Vers. 24-27.   A PROPHECY AGAINST THE ASSYRIAN HOST UNDER SENNACHERIB.

This was doubtless given, as Alexander says, as a sort of a pledge to accredit the prediction against Babylon, or for the purpose of assuring the people that while God had decreed their deliverance from remoter dangers (Babylonian oppression), He would also protect them from those near at hand.

Ver. 26.   *"purposed upon the whole earth"*,—"This universality", says Scofield, "is significant and marks the whole passage as referring, not merely to a near judgment upon Assyria, but in a yet larger sense to the final crash of the present world-system at the end of the age."

Fausset also here remarks, "This is a hint that the prophecy embraces the present world of all ages in its scope, of which the purpose concerning Babylon and Assyria, the then representatives of the world-power, is but a part."

Alexander says, "On the supposition that this prophecy relates to Assyria alone, we are obliged to understand 'the whole earth' and 'all nations' as describing the universal sway of this great power at that time in question."

Vers. 28-32.   A PROPHECY AGAINST PHILISTIA.

This prophecy is a warning to the Philistines who had also suffered from the Assyrian power and were disposed to exult unduly because of its overthrow, since they were yet to suffer greater bondage.   Fausset thinks it was given to comfort the Jews lest they should fear the Philistines.

CHAPTER FIFTEEN

This chapter, together with the following one form one prophecy concerning the downfall of Moab.

"This burden," says Scofield, "had a precursive fulfillment in Sennacherib's invasion, B. C. 704, three years after the prediction (Isa. 16.14), but the words have a breadth of meaning which includes also the final world-battle."

CHAPTER SIXTEEN

1 Send ye the lambs for the ruler of the land from ¹Selah to the wilderness, unto the mount of the daughter of Zion. 2 For it shall be that, as wandering birds, as a scattered nest, so shall the daughters of Moab be at the fords of the Arnon. 3 Give counsel, execute justice; make thy shade as the night in the midst of the noonday; hide the outcasts; betray not the fugitive. 4 Let mine outcasts dwell with thee; as for Moab, be thou a covert to him from the face of the destroyer. For ²the extortioner is brought to nought, destruction ceaseth, ³the oppressors are consumed out of the land. 5 And a throne shall be established in lovingkindness; and one shall sit thereon in truth, in the tent of David, judging, and seeking justice, and swift to do righteousness.

¹Or, *Petra*

²Or, *extortion*
³Heb. *the treaders down*

Vers. 1-5. THE DAVIDIC KINGDOM FORESEEN.

They are, in verse 1, exhorted to send tribute to Jerusalem for the reason set forth in verse 2.

Older writers maintain that these verses as well as the next ones are addressed by the prophet to Moab and they are exhorted to submit themselves to Israel and to show mercy to her in her affliction (Moab being one of the lands to which Israel is said to have fled when oppressed by Nebuchadnezzar—Jer. 40.11,12), thus preparing for the day of their own calamity when the Israelites will be in a position to assist them because (the reason being given in the last clause of verse 4 and in verse 5) the cessation of all violent oppression is near at hand and the dominion of the kingdom of God under one great line of David shall be set up. (V. Na. Bar.) The Prophet foresees that Moab will be too proud (verse 6) to pay the tribute or to conciliate Judah by sheltering its outcasts; therefore judgment shall be executed.

Others, however, (F. Ho. Ew. Ma. Del. Ges.) take verses 3 and 4 as the address of the suppliant Moab, asking Israel to show kindness to her; the outcasts in this case being those of Moab. Verse 5 is then taken as a promise to Israel if they shelter the outcasts of Moab.

There are difficulties attending either explanation, though not serious in either case. The latter explanation, which is in agreement with our text, is perhaps to be preferred, in which case it would seem better to take the first two verses with Alexander as a mutual exhortation of the Moabites to themselves in their confusion and distress.

Most interpreters, ancient and modern, take the verbs in the last clause of verse 4 in the future sense, as is often done in Hebrew, though they be in the past tense grammatically. This gives an appropriate sense whether the words be addressed to Israel or to Moab.

Fausset says, "By the time that Moab begins to beg Judah for shelter, Judah shall be in a condition to afford it, for the Assyrian oppressor shall have been 'consumed out of the land'."

Ver. 5. *"in truth"*,—One who is truthful and reliable. "A king", as Delitzsch says, "who makes truth the criterion of his actions."

"judging and seeking judgment and hasting righteousness",—"The language is so divinely framed as to apply to 'the latter days' under King Messiah when the Lord 'shall bring again the captivity of Moab'." (F.)

Says Alexander, "The words of verse 5 are intended to include a reference to all the good kings of the house of David, not excepting the last King of that race, to whom God was to give the throne of his father David, who was to reign over the house of Jacob forever and of whose kingdom there should be no end."

Scofield says that verses 1-5, which are a continuation of the prophecy against Moab, shows the "tabernacle of David" set up, the next event in order after the destruction of the Beast and his armies.

Says Nagelsbach, "Isaiah sees in spirit the end of the world-power, therefore the cessation of all violent oppression and the dominion of the kingdom of God under a great one of the line of David."

CHAPTER SEVENTEEN

A Prophecy of Desolation To the Kingdoms of Syria and Ephraim (verses 1-11), Closing with a General Threatening Against the Enemies of Judah (verses 12-14).

Here again Scofield says, "As in the burden of Moab, there was doubtless a near fulfillment in Sennacherib's approaching invasion, but verses 12 to 14 as evidently look forward to the final invasion and battle of Armageddon."

CHAPTER EIGHTEEN

1 Ah, the land [1]of the rustling of wings, which is beyond the rivers of [2]Ethiopia; 2 that sendeth ambassadors by the sea, [3]even in vessels of papyrus upon the waters, *saying*, Go, ye swift messengers, to a nation [4]tall and smooth, to a people terrible from their beginning onward, a nation [5]that meteth out and treadeth down, whose land the rivers [6]divide!

7 In that time shall a present be brought unto Jehovah of hosts *from* a people [4]tall and smooth, even from a people terrible from their beginning onward, a nation that meteth out and treadeth down, whose land the rivers divide, to the place of the name of Jehovah of hosts, the mount Zion.

[1]Or, *shadowing with wings*
[2]Heb. *Cush.*
[3]Or, *and*
[4]Or, *dragged away and peeled*
[5]Or, *meted out and trodden down* Heb. *of line, line, and of treading down.*
[6]Or, *have despoiled*

Vers. 1,2,7. The Danger and Deliverance of Ethiopia.

Ver. 1. The introductory particle in verse 1 is not one that carries in it the idea of a threat, but rather one of appeal, a particle of calling, and should not be rendered "Woe," as in the Authorized Version. (F. Al.)

Ver. 2. On the supposition that the people described in verses 2 and 7 are Ethiopians; the command to *"Go"* may be taken, as in our text, as a command of the Ethiopians to their own messengers to go and call the people to preparation for battle; or the word *"saying"* may be omitted, and the command be taken as that of the prophet (F. Al. Na. Del.) asking the messengers to carry to their own people announcement, either (1) that

God Himself would without their help undertake the destruction of the common enemy of Israel and Ethiopia (Al.) or (2) that they should gather themselves together for the battle. (Na. Del.)

Of the two explanations the latter in each case is to be preferred.

Ver. 7. The older view, and especially Jewish, was that the people described in this verse and verse 2 were the people of Israel, and that the prophecy relates to the restoration of the Jews. The language used is supposed to be descriptive of their degraded and oppressed condition. (F. Ho. Ew. Kn. Hof. Mei. Sco. Then.) The descriptive language as applied to the Ethiopians refers to their warlike qualities.

"present be brought unto Jehovah of hosts from a people", etc.,—Of those who refer the two verses in question to the Jews, some refer the present to the exiled Jews sent back to Jerusalem by the Ethiopians, while Horsley, Fausset and others refer the whole matter to the restoration of the Jews in the latter times.

Fausset says, "Horsley is probably right that the ultimate and fullest reference of the prophecy is to the restoration of the Jews in the Holy Land through the instrumentality of some distant people skilled in navigation, perhaps England, which may of course be included in the description of all remote lands 'beyond' the Nile's mouths."

Of those who refer the verses in question to the Ethiopians the present is the presentation of the Ethiopians with their gifts by themselves. The decision is not an easy one, but the latter one seems by far the better. The Ethiopians were then an earnest and partial fulfillment of what is still to take place in larger measure in the future.

This latter view is that of the older Christian writers and relates itself to the calling of the Gentiles. The prophecy as such has never yet come true but is being fulfilled throughout this dispensation while it waits for complete fulfillment in the latter days. (See Chap. 66.19.)

CHAPTER NINETEEN

This chapter falls easily into two parts, one of which (verses 1-17) contains a threatening against Egypt, and the other (verses 18-25) promises.

On the whole it is better to take these last verses in a sense similar to the last verses of the preceding chapter, as a prediction of the calling of the Gentiles, and to think that just as the prophet had described the downfall of Egypt in the first part under figures borrowed from the then actual condition of Egypt, so in the second part he describes the introduction of the true religion by figures drawn from the religious institutions of the old economy.

CHAPTER TWENTY

This chapter contains a continuation of the subject of the preceding one, but at a later date, and relates to the captivity of Egypt and Ethiopia.

CHAPTER TWENTY-ONE

This chapter relates to the conquest of Babylon by the Medes and Persians (verses 1-10); to the conquest of Edom, or the Arabian tribe Dumah (verses 11-12) and finally to that of Arabia herself (verses 13-17).

CHAPTER TWENTY-TWO

While the second part of this chapter is devoted to a prediction concerning an individual, Shebna, who is to be removed from office, the first part of the chapter is given to a prediction of the overthrow of Jerusalem by the armies of Sennacherib.

CHAPTER TWENTY-THREE

This chapter also consists of two parts. The first predicts the fall of Tyre, of which God is the author and the Chaldeans His instruments; the second part relates how Tyre shall be forsaken and forgotten for seventy years (verse 15), after which she shall be restored to her former flourishing condition (verses 16,17), and her wealth thereafter devoted to the Lord. This latter statement seems to be the more reasonable explanation of verse 18, because otherwise it would be hard to conceive how the Lord would restore a nation on which He had inflicted His vengeance, in order that it may begin again its old life of harlotry, and how the wages of this prostitution could be consecrated to the Lord, since in Deut. 23.18 it is expressly forbidden to bring the "hire of a whore" into the house of the Lord.

If verse 18 be taken in this sense it must be the mystical Tyre that is thought of in this verse, as it was the mystical Ethiopia in Chapter 18 and the mystical Egypt and Assyria in Chapter 19, but in either sense this part of the prophecy of course waits complete fulfillment in days yet to come.

Says Fausset, "Her traffic and her gains shall at last be consecrated to Jehovah. Jesus Christ visited the neighborhood of Tyre, Paul founded disciples there; it early became a Christian bishopric, but the full evangelization of that whole race, as of the Ethiopians themselves (Chap. 18) and of the Egyptians and Assyrians (Chap. 19) is yet to come (Chap. 60.5)."

Section Four. Prediction of Coming Desolation and Deliverance therefrom together with Songs and Thanksgiving.

CHAPTERS 24 TO 27.

It is by no means easy to determine the principal reference throughout this portion of the prophet's writing. There are two general views.

View 1. Delitzsch says, "The cycle of prophecy that begins here finds a counterpart in the Old Testament only perhaps in Zech. 9-14. Both of these sections are eschatological and apocalyptic in content."

Fausset says, "The prophet passes to the last times of the world at large and of Judah the representative and future head of the churches. The four chapters form one continuous poetical prophecy, descriptive of the dispersion and successive calamities of the Jews (Chap. 24.1-12); the preaching of the Gospel by the first Jewish converts throughout the world (verses 13-16); the judgments on the adversaries of the Church and its final triumph (verses 16-23); thanksgiving for the overthrow of the apostate faction (Chap. 25); establishment of the righteous in lasting peace (Chap. 26); judgment on leviathan and entire purgation of the Church (Chap. 27)."

Nägelsbach says, "The prophet transports himself in spirit to the end of all things. He describes the destruction of the world."

Blackstone says, "From these chapters an idea may be gained of the terrible character of the tribulation period, during which Antichrist will also be revealed. Some, especially from the remnant of Israel, will accept Christ and become His witnesses, and be slain by the Antichrist. These we call the tribulation saints, who are to be raised at the close of the great tribulation, as the gleanings of the great harvest of the first resurrection."

View 2. On the other hand Alexander, with others, maintains that the main reference of the prophecy is to the coming Babylonian conquest and its outcome, and that the land in question is Palestine.

There are questions most perplexing, and for which no solution altogether satisfactory has been found, connected with either view. The view of Alexander, at first thought, seems the simpler and more natural, especially if we may see in these prophecies a typical or secondary reference to final times.

CHAPTER TWENTY-FOUR

The Judgment upon the Earth Foretold.

1 Behold, Jehovah maketh the [1]earth empty, and maketh it waste, and turneth it upside down, and scattereth abroad the inhabitants thereof. 2 And it shall be, as with the people, so with the priest; as with the servant, so with his master; as with the maid, so with her mistress; as with the buyer, so with the seller; as with the creditor, so with the debtor; as with the taker of interest, so with the giver of interest to him. 3 The earth shall be utterly emptied, and utterly laid waste; for Jehovah hath spoken this word. 4 The earth mourneth and fadeth away, the world languisheth and fadeth away, [2]the lofty people of the earth do languish. 5 The earth also is polluted under the inhabitants thereof; because they have transgressed the laws, violated the statutes, broken the everlasting covenant. 6 Therefore hath the curse devoured the earth, and they that dwell therein are found guilty: therefore the inhabitants of the earth are burned, and few men left. 7 The new wine mourneth, the vine languisheth, all the merry-hearted do sigh. 8 The mirth of tabrets ceaseth, the noise of them that rejoice endeth, the joy of the harp ceaseth. 9 They shall not drink wine with a song; strong drink shall be bitter to them that drink it. 10 The waste city is broken down; every house is shut up, that no man may come in. 11 There is a crying in the streets because of the wine; all joy is darkened, the mirth of the land is [3]gone. 12 In the city is left desolation, and the gate is smitten with destruction.

[1]Or, *land* (and so in ver 3, 4, &c.)
[2]Or, *the high ones of the people*

[3]Heb. *gone into captivity*

Vers 1-12. THE BEGINNING OF THE JUDGMENT.

According to view one, the eschatological view, the judgment here is upon the *earth*. It is, as Delitzsch says, "universal, not merely within the borders of Palestine, but as regards the inhabitants of the *earth*, for the word here used means *earth*, and implies even the New Testament ethical idea of kosmos."

According to view two, that of Alexander and others, by earth is here meant Palestine, the word "earth" and "world" not to be taken in their widest sense, but as poetical descriptions of the land of Palestine.

According to view one the *"waste city"* of verse 10 is the city as the center of the world and its alienation from God, the city in general.

According to view two the reference is to Jerusalem.

Concerning verses 1 to 12 Nagelsbach says, "If I am to state what future events will correspond to this prophecy of the first act of the judgment of the world, it appears to me that the description of the prophet corresponds to what our Lord in His discourse on the last things says of the signs of His coming, and of *the beginning of sorrows* (Matt. 24.6-8; Mk. 13.7-8; Lu. 21.9). And the beginning of sorrows corresponds again to what the Revelation of John represents under the image of seven seals, seven trumpets and seven vials (Rev. 6. sqq.)."

13 For thus shall it be in the midst of the earth among the peoples, as the ¹shaking of an olive-tree, as the gleanings when the vintage is done.

14 These shall lift up their voice, they shall shout; for the majesty of Jehovah they cry aloud from the sea. 15 Wherefore glorify ye Jehovah in the ²east, even the name of Jehovah, the God of Israel, in the ³isles of the sea.

¹Heb. *beating*

²Or, *lights* Or, *fires*
³Or, *coast-lands*

Vers. 13-15. THE REMNANT AND THEIR SONG.

Ver. 13. *"as the shaking . . . as the gleanings"*,—These are figurative expressions for the remnant, the few left after the judgments foretold.

"in the midst of the earth",—Some authorities place a comma after *"earth"*, thus making *"among the peoples"* the place where the remnant is scattered, but our text emphasizes rather the extent of the desolation before described, and is perhaps the smoother reading.

Ver. 14. *"These"*,—Not the "nations" (Schel.), nor the Jews left in Palestine (Bar.), but the remnant, the dispersed survivors of these judgments.

"There will be", says Delitzsch, "as few men left in the great wide world as olives and grapes after the principal harvest in each case. Those who are saved belong especially, but not exclusively (Joel 3.5) to Israel: The place where they assemble is the land of Promise."

Alexander, according to view two, confines this remnant of course to the dispersed Jews after the Babylonian invasion and conquest.

"from the sea",—i. e., from the lands beyond the sea whither they have escaped.

Ver. 15. This verse is an exhortation by the prophet to the remnant (Al.), and not the song of the remnant continued, as Ewald thinks.

"in the east",—The literal is "fires". The weight of exegetical

authority favors the reading of our text, as against "fires" of the Authorized Version, the east being the region of sunrise or of dawning light. This corresponds well to the *"isles of the sea"*, the west.

16 From the uttermost part of the earth have we heard songs: Glory to the righteous.

But I said, [1]I pine away, I pine away, woe is me! the treacherous have dealt treacherously; yea, the treacherous have dealt very treacherously. 17 Fear, and the pit, and the snare, are upon thee, O inhabitant of the earth. 18 And it shall come to pass, that he who fleeth from the noise of the fear shall fall into the pit; and he that cometh up out of the midst of the pit shall be taken in the snare: for the windows on high are opened, and the foundations of the earth tremble. 19 The earth is utterly broken, the earth is rent asunder, the earth is shaken violently. 20 The earth shall stagger like a drunken man, and shall sway to and fro like a hammock; and the transgression thereof shall be heavy upon it, and it shall fall, and not rise again.

21 And it shall come to pass in that day that Jehovah will [2]punish the host of the [3]high ones on high, and the kings of the earth upon the earth. 22 And they shall be gathered together, as prisoners are gathered in the [4]pit, and shall be shut up in the prison; and after many days shall they be [5]visited. 23 Then the moon shall be confounded, and the sun ashamed; for Jehovah of hosts will reign in mount Zion, and in Jerusalem; and before his elders shall be glory.

[1]Heb. *Leanness to me.*

[2]Heb. *visit upon*
[3]Heb. *height*
[4]Or, *dungeon*
[5]Or, *punished*

Vers. 16-23. THE CONSUMMATION OF THE JUDGMENT.

Ver. 16. *"we heard songs"*,—The songs of the remnant in dispersion wafted toward Jerusalem as a distant chorus.

"glory to the righteous",—By *"righteous"* is here meant righteous men in general (F. Al. Na. Del.), and not God (Hend.).

Nagelsbach says, "From the first clause of this verse we perceive that the remnant, the elect of God, are hidden in a safe place, gathered on the holy mountain and there find protection (Chap. 4.5), but this is just the occasion for the signal to be given for the occurrence of the last and most frightful catastrophe, the judgment on the ungodly."

"But I said",—The prophet of course connects himself with the blessed experiences of the future, but at once becomes conscious of the sufferings that must first of all be experienced, and realizing that he cannot see these without also experiencing them, he connects himself with them. We hear promises and praise but our actual experience is misery.

"the treacherous",—i. e., the foreign nations that oppress Jerusalem.

Ver. 17. This verse explains the wretchedness spoken of in verse 16.

"Fear",—The Hebrew word denotes a feathered device which when fluttered in the air scares the beasts into the pit or the birds into the snares.

Ver. 18. The prophet is here threatening the guilty earth with instant vengeance.

"the windows on high are opened",—Either to produce a deluge, with manifest reference to Gen. 7.11 (Al. Del.), or that other weapons of his vengeance may descend, wind, fire, thunder, lightning, drought, pestilence, which also in a sense may be said to descend from heaven (F. Kn. Na.). Perhaps, in view of the promise that the earth should not again be destroyed by water (Gen. 9.11), the latter explanation is preferable, although even so the figure may be drawn from the passage in Genesis.

"the foundations of the earth tremble",—The reference here is manifestly to earthquakes. Thus, "the globe of the earth", says Nagelsbach, "is assailed from above and from beneath. The reference of the whole passage is not a local, but a universal one."

Ver. 19. Says Delitzsch, "The earth first gets fractured, then yawning chasms open, once more it sways to and fro, and falls."

Ver. 20. *"it shall fall and not rise again"*,—Nagelsbach says, "These words are clear proof that the total destruction of the globe of the earth in its present form is the subject treated of. In its *present* form! For the earth shall rise again in a higher, holier form beyond the range of sin and its consequence, death. For there is a new heaven and a new earth, wherein dwelleth righteousness."

Ver. 21. *"the host of the high ones on high"*,—

(1) The high earthly potentates. (C. Al. Lut. Hav. Tar.)
But this plainly destroys the antithesis which is evident in the verse.

(2) The starry host, the heavenly bodies, as in Chap. 34.4. (Sm. Um. Hof. Baud.)
But the idea of personality runs through the entire verse and the contrast between inanimate objects and earthly powers for the purpose noted, i. e., imprisonment, does not go well together.

(3) The wicked angels, invisible heads of the worldly powers, are no doubt intended. (F. Na. Kn. Ab. Del. Hit. Ros.)

Ver. 22. *"gathered together as prisoners"*,—The persons meant are of course the principalities and powers mentioned in the preceding verse.

"after many days they shall be visited",—This visitation may be in mercy (C. F. He. Pe. Ew. Kn. Hit. Luz. Kim.), or it may be in wrath (Al. Ho. Na. Ei. Um. Del. Ros. Ges. Sco. Mor. Bla. Tor. Hend.).

Fausset, who takes the visitation as one of mercy, says, "The 'shutting up' of the Jews in Jerusalem under Nebuchadnezzar, and again under Titus, was to be followed by a visitation of mercy *'after many days'*— seventy years in the case of the former—the time is not yet elapsed in the case of the latter."

Those who hold the reference of the prophecy to be to the times of the end think here of a visitation of wrath upon the ungodly Gentile world-powers. The *"pit"*, they say (Na. Del.), is used for Sheol, as oftentimes (Chap. 15.15,19; 38.18).

Nagelsbach says, "But not merely the binding of those angelic and worldly powers, their being *set loose* for a time is also announced by the prophet. Only by a brief, obscure word, probably not seen through by himself, does the prophet intimate this. Even we should not understand this word if the revelation of the New Testament, which is nearer the time of the fulfillment, did not throw light on this dark point. It declares expressly that after a thousand years Satan should be loosed out of his prison. Isaiah here uses the indefinite *'after many days'*. This visitation can be a gracious one, but it can also be a new stage in the visitation of judgment. The setting loose of Satan is only the prelude to his total destruction." With this Delitzsch and many others are in accord.

Ver. 23. Because Jehovah reigns all inferior luminaries were to be eclipsed. "The simple meaning of the verse," says Alexander, "appears to be that Jehovah's reign over His people shall be more august than that of any created sovereign." The elders, he maintains, are the rulers of Israel as the Church. Among the supporters of view one we find Scofield referring the content of this verse to the kingdom age, while Nagelsbach says, "The earth now becomes the common dwelling place of God and man; the heavenly Jerusalem now descends upon the renovated earth, and in this city where Jehovah reigns there is no need of sun or moon, for the Lord Himself is its light." Delitzsch says, "Then the Lord reigns with His own in the New Jerusalem in such glory that the silvery moon shame-facedly veils itself, and the glowing sun is confounded with shame, because in the presence of such glory the two great lights of heaven will be, according to a Jewish expression, like a lamp in the noontide sunshine. Then shall 'elders' after God's own heart be given to the Israel of the Jerusalem of the future."

It is evident after careful study that the difficulties attending the second view are greater than those of the first, and to this view we are inclined—that which takes the passage as foretelling last-time events—even though we may not be able to fully comprehend the prophetic words in all their detail. What the prophet has left indefinite we must not attempt to make specific.

CHAPTER TWENTY-FIVE

1 O Jehovah, thou are my God; I will exalt thee, I will praise thy name; for thou hast done wonderful things, *even* counsels of old, in faithfulness *and* truth. 2 For thou hast made of a city a heap, of a fortified city a ruin, a palace of strangers to be no city; it shall never be built. 3 Therefore shall a strong people glorify thee; a city of terrible nations shall fear thee. 4 For thou hast been a stronghold to the poor, a stronghold to the needy in his distress, a refuge from the storm, a shade from the heat, when the blast of the terrible ones is as a storm against the wall. 5 As the heat in a dry place wilt thou bring down the noise of strangers; as the heat by the shade of a cloud, the song of the terrible ones shall be brought low.

Vers. 1-5. THANKSGIVING FOR THE OVERTHROW OF THE OPPRESSORS.

In keeping with the two views under consideration, Delitzsch, representing the first one, says, "The prophet transported to the end of time celebrates in psalm and song what he saw, praising God for having destroyed the mighty city of the world and for having proved Himself the shield and defense of the hitherto oppressed community against the tyranny of the city of the world", while Alexander, representing the second view, says, "We have in these verses a thanksgiving to God for the destruction of Babylon and the deliverance of the Jews."

Ver. 2. *"made of a city a heap"*,—The *"city"* according to view one is to be taken as in Chap. 24.10, city in general; according to view two it is Babylon.

Ver. 3. *"a strong people"*,—Not the Jews, but other nations which were compelled to own Jehovah conqueror.

"The fall of the world-power", says Delitzsch, "is followed by the conversion of the heathen who submit to Jehovah with proper reverence."

Says Alexander, "The destruction of Babylon and the fulfillment of the prophecy thereby, shall lead even the boldest and wildest of the heathen to acknowledge Jehovah as true God. It may just as well denote a compulsory extorted homage, fear being taken in its proper sense, and the verse may then be taken as a description of the effect produced by Jehovah's overthrow of Babylon on the Babylonians themselves."

It is evident that if *"city"* in verse 2 be referred to Babylon, which is there spoken of as destroyed and never to be built, the *"city"* of this verse cannot refer to Babylon, which fact is an argument for the first view of the meaning of this word.

Ver. 4. *"the poor . . . the needy"*,—i. e., the Jews in dispersion. The nations shall reverence Jehovah, not merely as the destroyer of the oppressing power, but as the deliverer of His own people.

> 6 And in this mountain will Jehovah of hosts make unto all peoples a feast of fat things, a feast of wines on the lees, of fat things full of marrow, of wines on the lees well refined. 7 And he will [1]destroy in this mountain the face of the covering that covereth all peoples, and the veil that is spread over all nations. 8 He hath swallowed up death for ever; and the Lord Jehovah will wipe away tears from off all faces; and the reproach of his people will he take away from off all the earth: for Jehovah hath spoken it.
>
> 9 And it shall be said in that day, Lo, this is our God; we have waited for him, and he will save us; this is Jehovah; we have waited for him, we will be glad and rejoice in his salvation.
>
> [1]Heb. *swallow up*

Vers. 6-9.   THE FEAST IN ZION FOR ALL NATIONS.

Ver. 6.   Here begins again the eschatological prophecy, resuming the thread of the discourse interrupted at the end of the last chapter. (Na. Al. Del.)   The feast is a spiritual feast, says Nagelsbach and Delitzsch, of which not only Israel but *"all peoples"* are to partake, the feast being on earth, says Delitzsch, because the Old Testament knows nothing of a heaven where blessed men are gathered.

Nagelsbach says that in the New Testament it appears in Luke 14.16 as the Great Supper, in Matt. 22.1 as the Marriage of the King's Son, and in Rev. 19.7,9,17 as the Marriage of the Lamb, in which latter place the counterpart of this feast is set forth.

Alexander says, "There is nothing to indicate the time when the promise should be fulfilled, nor indeed to restrict it to any time in particular.   Jerusalem has always more or less fulfilled the office here ascribed to it."

Ver. 7.   The expressions here used are symbolical, not of grief and mourning, as many, if indeed not most interpreters take it, the veiling of the face being the sign of mourning; but it is a symbolical expression of spiritual blindness, as in II Cor. 3.15,16.   But while the chief reference is to the understanding, the thought of sorrow may be included, as indeed this is but the result of spiritual ignorance.

Ver. 8.   "Naturally," says Delitzsch, "this applies to the *ecclesia triumphans,* the prophet's vision of things having brought him to the same point as that reached by Paul in I Cor. 15.28, and by John on the last page of his Apocalypse."

Nagelsbach says, "John in Rev. 7.17 and 21.4 quotes our passage to prove that he regards the things which he saw as a fulfillment not only of his own prophecy but also of that spoken by Isaiah. The fulfillment is on the new earth, the dwelling place of God with man."

Alexander says that the true sense of the passage is that all misery and suffering comprehended under the generic name of death shall be completely done away with, the words being a promise to God's people of the final, perpetual, triumphant abolition of death, which in its highest sense may never be realized by any individual till after death.

Ver. 9. "The redeemed now *see* the Lord in whom they have hitherto only `believed." (Na.)

"we have waited",—"We have waited but He has come at last to vindicate His truth and our reliance upon him." (Al.)

10 For in this mountain will the hand of Jehovah rest; and Moab shall be trodden down in his place, even as straw is trodden down [1]in the water of the dunghill. 11 And he shall spread forth his hands in the midst [2]thereof as he that swimmeth spreadeth forth his hands to swim; but Jehovah will lay low [3]his pride [4]together with the craft of [5]his hands.

12 And the high fortress of thy walls [5]hath he brought down, laid low, and brought to the ground, even to the dust.

[1]Another reading is, *in the dunghill*
[2]Or, *of them*

[3]Or, *their*
[4]Or, *for all the craft*
[5]Or, *will he bring down, lay low, and bring, &c.*

Vers. 10-12. THE DISGRACEFUL RUIN OF MOAB THREATENED.

Ver. 10. While Israel is being protected the foe is being destroyed.

"For in this mountain will the hand of Jehovah rest",—i. e., as its permanent protector. The joy is to be everlasting.

Moab and Edom were two hereditary inveterate enemies of Israel, but quite often, as apparently here, both or either is taken as inclusive of Israel's enemies in general. Indeed Moab must be included in the *"all nations"*, and *"all faces"* of verses 6, 7 and 8, and must here be taken as the representative of all the ungodly of all nations. Alexander persists of course in identifying this mountain, Mount Zion, with the Church of New Testament times.

"even as straw", etc.,—Straw is cast into the filthy water of the dunghole that it may be saturated by it and rendered fitter for manure. Thus the Lord humbles the proud by making disgrace an element of their punishment.

Ver. 11. The subject of the first verb is without doubt Moab (Lo. Na. Al. Del. Hit. Gro.), and not Jehovah, as many have taken it. (F. C.) It is the person cast into the hole seeking to save himself. To make Jehovah the swimmer does violence to the context and is highly offensive. Those so construing it think of Jehovah as striking Moab here and there, in every part, as a swimmer strikes the waves in every direction. But this idea might have been expressed more clearly in a score of different ways.

Ver. 12. The figurative statement of verse 11 literally exemplified.

The reference is not to the city mentioned in the second verse, but to the cities of Moab in general.

CHAPTER TWENTY-SIX

ISRAEL AS RESTORED OR RAISED TO LIFE AGAIN.

1 In that day shall this song be sung in the land of Judah; We have a strong city; salvation will he appoint for walls and bulwarks.

2 Open ye the gates, that the righteous nation which keepeth faith may go in.

3 [1]Thou wilt keep him [2]in perfect peace whose [3]mind is stayed; because he trusteth in thee.

4 Trust ye in Jehovah for ever; for in Jehovah, even Jehovah, is an [4]everlasting rock.

5 For he hath brought down them that dwell on high, the lofty city: he layeth it low even to the ground; he bringeth it even to the dust.

6 The foot shall tread it down; even the foot of the poor, and the steps of the needy.

7 The way of the just is [5]uprightness; thou that art upright doth [6]direct the path of the just.

8 Yea, in the way of thy judgments, O Jehovah, have we waited for thee; to thy name, even to thy memorial name, is the desire of our soul.

9 With my soul have I desired thee in the night; yea, with my spirit within me will I see thee earnestly: for when thy judgments are in the earth, the inhabitants of the world learn righteousness.

10 Let favor be showed to the wicked, yet will he not learn righteousness; in the land of uprightness will he deal wrongfully, and will not behold the majesty of Jehovah.

11 Jehovah, thy hand is lifted up, yet they see not: but they shall see [7]thy zeal for the people, and be put to shame; yea [8]fire shall devour thine adversaries.

12 Jehovah, thou wilt ordain peace for us; for thou hast also wrought all our works for us.

13 O Jehovah our God, other lords besides thee have had dominion over us; but by thee only will we make mention of thy name.

14 [9]They are dead, they shall not live; they are [10]deceased, they shall not rise; therefore hast thou visited and destroyed them, and made all remembrance of them to perish.

15 Thou hast increased the nation, O Jehovah, thou hast increased the nation; thou art glorified; [11]thou hast enlarged all the borders of the land.

16 Jehovah, in trouble have they [12]visited thee: they poured out a [13]prayer when thy chastening was upon them.

17 Like as a woman with child, that draweth near the time of her delivery, is in pain and crieth out in her pangs; so we have been [14]before thee, O Jehovah.

18 We have been with child, we have been in pain, we have as it were brought forth wind; we have not wrought any deliverance in the earth; [15]neither have the inhabitants of the world fallen.

19 Thy dead shall live; my dead bodies shall arise. Awake and sing, ye that dwell in the dust: for thy dew is as the dew of [16]herbs, and the earth shall cast forth [17]the dead.

[1]Or, *a steadfast mind thou keepest in perfect peace, because it &c.*
[2]Heb. *peace, peace*
[3]Or, *imagination*
[4]Or, *a rock of ages*
[5]Or, *a right way; the path of the just thou directest aright.*
[6]Or, *level*
[7]Or, *and be put to shame, in their envy at the people*

[8]Or, *the fire of thine adversaries shall devour them*
[9]Or, *the dead live not. the deceased rise not*
[10]Or, *shades*
[11]Or, *thou hast removed it far unto all the ends of the earth*
[12]Or, *looked for*
[13]Heb. *whisper*
[14]Or, *at thy presence*
[15]Or, *neither have inhabitants of the world been born*
[16]Or, *light*
[17]Or, *the shades*

Vers. 1-19. THE WORSHIP AND TESTIMONY OF RESTORED ISRAEL.

Ver. 1. *"In that day"*,—Contemporaneous and homogeneous with *"in that day"* of Chap. 25.9-12. It is the day of deliverance just mentioned.

The *"land of Judah"* is plainly employed to form an antithesis to Moab of the preceding chapter.

The *"city"* mentioned is Jerusalem, and by *"he"* Jehovah is meant.

According to view one the prophet relates a hymn which he hears coming from the holy mountain and out of the holy city, the leading thought of which corresponds to II Pet. 3.13, it being the redeemed who sing the song. According to view two the singers are the Jews after their return from exile. Knobel contends that they are the Jews left by the Babylonians in the land of Judah; but this is entirely out of keeping with the context.

Ver. 2. The speakers are the same as in the preceding verse.

"The cry is a heavenly one", says Delitzsch, "and those who open the gates are angels." Alexander thinks of the returning exiles calling to the keepers of the gates of Jerusalem.

Ver. 3. This, says Alexander, is a general truth deduced from the experience of those who are supposed to be the speakers. To be resigned to God, to lean on Him, brings composure and peace.

Ver. 4. The same speakers addressing an exhortation to all who hear them to continue in the frame of mind just mentioned.

Ver. 5. *"the lofty city"*,— (See explanation under Chaps. 24.10-12 and 25.2.)

Ver. 6. The ruins of the conquered city to be trodden under foot by those who had before been trodden in the dust by the feet of the worldly power, the oppressor.

Ver. 8. *"waited for thee"*,—i. e., to see Thee come forth as a judge for the vindication of thy people and the destruction of their enemies. (Al. Ma. Na. Del.) Delitzsch, followed by Nagelsbach, says, "The Church of the last days tells how she, looking back into the past, waited longingly for the manifestation of Jehovah's righteousness which has now taken place."

Ver. 9. The faithful Jews here speak individually, says Fausset. Others (Na. Del.) think the prophet is here speaking for himself, especially attributing to himself in the night of his sorrow and trouble the desire that God would thus manifest Himself. The latter thought is without doubt the correct one.

Ver. 11. *"thy hand is lifted up"*,—i. e., to punish the foes of God's people.

"but they shall see",—Those who *will* not see shall be made to see; "a general truth," says Delitzsch, "which had then received its most splendid confirmation through the fall of the world city."

Ver. 12. "An expression of strong hope and confidence", says Alexander, "founded on what has already been experienced."

It is quite generally agreed that by *"our works"* are meant the works done for us by God Himself.

Ver. 13. Nagelsbach's unique and strange imagination gives us the view that beginning with this verse and continuing through verse 18 the speakers are the dwellers in Sheol and that the prophet brings into view the resurrection of the dead. In verse 14 the dead are speaking according to the prevailing opinion; in verse 16 we find, says he, that the longing for life and the hope of regaining it are not extinguished even in the realm of the dead, while verse 17 supposes the possibility of deliverance from Sheol, the hope of which is still alive in its occupants, and verse 18 shows that all efforts of their own to bring themselves to a new life are ineffectual like the bringing forth of wind on the part of a travailing woman. Then in verse 19 the prophet speaks, as the interpreter of Jehovah, words of consolation to the shades in Sheol, and in the spirit of prophecy utters the triumphant call to awake, which will one day be pronounced by a mightier voice that it may be fulfilled. There is nothing to commend Nagelsbach's view; this earth and not Sheol is the theater of what is described in verses 15 to 18, and it is either the Church Triumphant speaking on this redeemed earth, or the remnant of Israel after their return, according to which ever view is taken of the entire prophecy.

"other lords besides thee",—The somewhat current explanation of these lords is that they refer to the Chaldeans and the Babylonians, and to this we are inclined although Alexander gives strong reasons for referring them to the idols which the Jews served before the exile. Fausset includes both in his explanation.

Ver. 14. Most expositors, following Clericus, refer this verse to the Babylonians. Hitzig and Umbreit refer it to the forefathers of Israel who on account of their idolatry had perished. But this brings in a new subject not previously introduced. Alexander of course refers it to the idols, the lords of verse 13, with some allusion, however, to the idolatrous oppressors of Israel. Delitzsch refers it naturally to the oppressors of Israel who, like the king of Babylon, have fallen into the realm of the shades, from which they cannot now be brought back. The idea is that we are not to think of a self resusitation, and not that they are dead forever as if there were no resurrection of the dead, because Isaiah certainly knew that there was to be such a thing, as verse 19 shows. Hosea, an earlier prophet than Isaiah, also announced that death and Sheol should be deprived of their prey. (Hos. 13.14.) (See also Isa. 25.8.)

Ver. 15. When Israel has cause to praise God in this way it will again have become a numerous people and so larger territory will be needed. The verse is a grateful acknowledgment of what God had done for his suffering people.

Ver. 16. *"visited thee"*,—i. e., in the sense of supplication. The prayer, as in verses 8 and 9, seems to return to the night of sorrow which preceded their deliverance.

Ver. 18. By referring this verse to the resurrection we have the strange spectacle of the shades in Hades fruitlessly striving to resusitate themselves and to get back into the world with a view to blessing it with deliverance from evil and oppression. "Generous shades!" exclaims Dunlop Moore.

Ver. 19. To the ineffectual efforts of the people to save themselves is now opposed their actual deliverance by Jehovah Himself. They will rise because they are God's dead.

81

There is here of course a resurrection of some king predicted. To what does it refer?

(1) Not to an actual or possible event, but a passionate wish that the depopulated land might be replenished with inhabitants, the resurrection in this case referring to the Jews already dead and a wish that they might be made alive. But this gives a construction to the verb which is neither natural nor obvious, and besides it would be a most unnatural conclusion of this address to Jehovah.

(2) A spiritual resurrection or resusitation of the people of Israel, the reference being to the restoration of exiled Israel under the figure of a resurrection, i. e., raised from the dust of degradation. (Al. Reu. and doubtless most expositors.)

(3) The literal resurrection at the time of the end. Delitzsch says it is the language of the Church in the last days after it has turned to God. Through long-continued sufferings and chastisement it has melted away to a small remnant, and many of those who could really be numbered among its members were now lying in their graves. It is, however, only the righteous *"my dead bodies"* who shall arise, and it is the first resurrection of Rev. 20.4 which is here predicted.

Alexander thinks this is plainly out of place here, and that besides they needed to be comforted with the promise of an earlier resurrection just as Martha did who was not satisfied with the promise of the resurrection at the last day.

Scofield says, "The restoration and re-establishment of Israel as a nation is also spoken of as a resurrection (Ezek. 37.1-11), and many hold that no more than this is meant here. But since the first resurrection is unto participation in the kingdom (Rev. 20.4-6) it seems the better view that both meanings be found here." With this agree others (F. Ho.).

The decision must depend upon the general view one takes of the entire prophecy under discussion, but the view of the last quoted authorities harmonizes with either.

20 Come, my people, enter thou into thy chambers, and shut thy doors about thee: hide thyself for a little moment, until the indignation be overpast.

21 For, behold Jehovah cometh forth out of his place to punish the inhabitants of the earth for their iniquity: the earth also shall disclose her blood, and shall no more cover her slain.

Vers. 20-21. THE PUNISHMENT OF THE GOD-OPPOSED POWERS OF THE WORLD.

Ver. 20. The ingenious Nagelsbach says we are here transported into the time *after* the resurrection. He says the time during which they are to hide is during the "little season" while Satan is loosed just before the second resurrection. But surely the blessed dead could not be described, as they are here, as shades in misery who must hide after they have come forth in the first resurrection, even though this theory of the resurrection be a Scriptural one. The words of this verse cannot be addressed to those mentioned in the preceding verse, but are addressed to individuals in existence prior to that time.

Delitzsch says that no mention is made of the judgment which is to come upon the persecutors and oppressors of the Church until after the Church has been made up by the addition through the first resurrection of its members who had died, although this judgment in order actually precedes this resurrection and uniting of God's people. The "little moment", he says, is the period of judgment on the ungodly which is shortened for the elects' sake.

Alexander, on the other hand, says, "The people of God are here addressed as such, and warned to hide themselves until God's indignation *against them* is past. The relief from God's displeasure, which had just been promised, must be preceded by the experience of the displeasure itself, for the time of His indignation is not yet past."

Fausset says, "When God is about to take vengeance on the ungodly, the saints shall be shut in by Him in a place of safety, as Noah and his family were in the days of the flood; the saints are calmly and confidently to await the issue."

It must not be overlooked that the words of this verse may be addressed to those concerned in the preceding verse, in the sense that they are to remain in the grave until the time of this judgment be past. Such an interpretation is admissible both on the ground of a literal and of a figurative resurrection.

The "hiding" referred to is, according to Delitzsch and Nagelsbach as well, the shutting of the Church off from the world in the solitude of prayer.

Ver. 21. Some (Ros. Hit.) take the last clause as a prediction that the dead should actually come forth from their graves, but it is much more natural to understand the whole verse as a simple variation of the one before it.

CHAPTER TWENTY-SEVEN

An amplification of the last verse of the preceding chapter.

1 In that day Jehovah with his hard and great and strong sword will punish leviathan the [1]swift serpent, and leviathan the [2]crooked serpent; and he will slay the monster that is in the sea. 2 In that day: A vineyard of wine, sing ye [3]unto it. 3 I Jehovah am its keeper; I will water it every moment; lest any hurt it, I will keep it night and day. 4 Wrath is not in me: would that the briers and thorns were against me in battle! I would march upon them, I would burn them together. 5 Or else let him take hold of my strength, that he may make peace with me; *yea*, let him make peace with me. 6 [4]In days to come shall Jacob take root; Israel shall blossom and bud; and they shall fill the face of the world with fruit.

7 Hath he smitten them as he smote those that smote him? or are they slain according to the slaughter [5]of them that were slain by them? 8 [6]In measure, [7]when thou sendest them away, thou dost contend with them; he hath removed *them* with his rough blast in the day of the east wind. 9 Therefore by this shall the iniquity of Jacob be [8]forgiven, and this is all the fruit [9]of taking away his sin: that he maketh all the stones of the altar as chalkstones that are beaten in sunder, *so that* the Asherim and the sun-images shall rise no more. 10 For the fortified city is solitary, a

[1]Or, *gliding* Or, *fleeing*
[2]Or, *winding*
[3]Or, *of*
[4]Or, *In the generations that come*

[5]Or, *of their slain*
[6]The meaning of the Hebrew word is uncertain.
[7]Or, *by sending them away*
[8]Or, *expiated*
[9]Or, *to take away*

habitation deserted and forsaken, like the wilderness: there shall the calf feed, and there shall he lie down, and consume the branches thereof. 11 When the boughs thereof are withered, they shall be broken off; the women shall come, and set them on fire; for it is a people of no understanding; therefore he that made them will not have compassion upon them, and he that formed them will show them no favor.

Vers. 1-11. THE JUDGMENT UPON JEHOVAH'S ENEMIES CONTINUED.

Ver. 1. Jehovah's destruction of the enemies of His people is here foretold as the slaughter of three great sea monsters.

"*In that day*",—Indicating that what is introduced belongs to the same stage of the world's history as that which has gone before.

It has been much disputed as to whether the destruction here predicted is that of a single nation or of several, but the description seems to call for three. These monsters are most likely Egypt, Assyria and Babylonia, but it is impossible to wholly identify them. (Na. Del.)

Gill thinks the three are the Devil, the Beast and the False Prophet; while Fausset thinks the reference is to the great enemy of the Church, the Devil, the three expressions referring to the same individual.

Ver. 2. This verse does not belong to the song itself, containing as it does only the theme and the summons to celebrate it in song.

"*a vineyard of wine*".—The reference is to Israel, the Church, the people of God, elevated to high joy and honor while the worldly powers are annihilated. (F. Ma. Ho. Al. Na. Del.)

Ver. 4. There are two explanations of this verse:

(a) I am no longer angry with my people. Oh, that their enemies, as thorns and briers, would array themselves against me that I might rush upon them and consume them. (F. Al. Del.)

(b) It is not because I am angry that I thus afflict my people, but because she is a vineyard overrun by thorns and briers on account of which I must pass through her and consume her, i. e., burn the thorns and briers out of her.

The first explanation is rightly preferred by most writers.

Ver. 5. They must either be overcome by the storm of war just mentioned, or lay hold on the protection of God.

Ver. 6. The prophet says here in figurative language what Paul declares in Rom. 11.12, that when Israel is restored to favor as a nation she will become "the riches of the Gentiles".

Ver. 7. The thought runs thus: Did the Lord smite His people Israel as severely as He did the enemies whom He employed to chastise Israel, or is Israel slain according to the slaughter wherewith the enemy is slain? No, indeed!

Ver. 8. This verse expresses more distinctly the negation implied in the preceding verse. Israel was moderately punished, and for a time only, by being removed out of her place as if by a transient storm or blast of wind.

Ver. 9. *"Therefore",*—A conclusion drawn from the preceding *"in measure"*. God's punishment is remedial.

Ver. 10. *"the fortified city is solitary",*—Delitzsch and Fausset think the reference is to Jerusalem, while Nagelsbach says it cannot possibly be Jerusalem but is the great city of the world, the center of the worldly power to which the prophet has so repeatedly referred. There are good arguments on either side. Either, however, would be appropriate in this connection as the interpretation of the chapter would not be affected one way or the other.

In this verse and the following this city is depicted as a desolate, forsaken place, overgrown with bushes whose tender branches the calves eat off and whose withered twigs the women gather for fuel.

12 And it shall come to pass in that day, that Jehovah will ¹beat off *his fruit* from the flood of the River unto the brook of Egypt; and ye shall be ²gathered ³one by one, O ye children of Israel.

¹Or, *beat out* his grain
²Or, *gleaned*
³Or, *one to another*

13 And it shall come to pass in that day, that a great trumpet shall be blown; and they shall come that were ⁴ready to perish in the land of Assyria, and they that were outcasts in the land of Egypt; and they shall worship Jehovah in the holy mountain at Jerusalem.

⁴Or, *lost*

Vers. 12-13. ISRAEL RESTORED.

Ver. 12. To the downfall of the "fortified city" he now adds its most important consequences—the restoration of the Jews. The *"river"* is doubtless the Euphrates and the *"brook of Egypt"* is the Nile or perhaps the Wady Elarish, and the simple meaning of the whole expression is *from Assyria to Egypt.*

Gesenius says, "The kingdom will be repeopled to the fullest extent that had been promised, and that too, as rapidly and as numerous as if human beings were dropping like olives from the beaten trees." But the word rendered "beat off" is the one employed usually to indicate the beating out of those husked fruits which are too tender and valuable to be threshed, and the meaning therefore can hardly be that of a sudden streaming in of a great multitude, but refers the rather to the careful and complete ingathering of that which otherwise might be lost or left behind. Delitzsch contends that this verse does not relate to the gathering in of the Jews, but, with a somewhat far-fetched and strained exegesis, he says that what is meant is the resurrection from the grave of the dead Jews as set forth in the previous chapter, to which thought the prophet here returns. But this conclusion, we feel, is unwarranted. The boundaries mentioned are not meant as defining the limits of the promised land to which Israel was to be gathered, but the rather the regions whence they should return.

Ver. 13. This verse points to the same event as the one just before it, the gathering of Israel, only under a different figure.

Delitzsch, in keeping with his explanation of the previous verse, says, "To the risen Church there comes the *still living* scattered ones, gathered by divine signal, not alone from Assyria and Egypt, though especially named, but from all the lands of exile."

Alexander says, "The application of this verse to a future restoration

85

of the Jews can neither be established nor disproved. If such a restoration can be otherwise shown to be a subject of prophecy, this passage may be naturally understood as at least comprehending it. But in itself considered it appears to contain nothing which may not naturally be applied to events now long past or which has not found in those events an adequate fulfillment.

Section Five. The Ungodly Alliance with Assyria and Egypt.

CHAPTERS 28 TO 33.

These chapters relate altogether to events of the prophet's own day. Many writers see in the vivid descriptions of judgment pronounced and blessing promised a secondary reference to Jehovah's final judgment on the antichristian worldly powers and the kingdom blessings of Israel, as for instance Scofield, who says, "In these chapters the same blended meanings of near and far fulfillments are found—the near and far horizons blend—the near view being that of the Egyptian alliance and the Assyrian invasion while the far view is that of the end-time day of the Lord and the kingdom blessing to follow."

Of course all such prophecies may in a sense be said to be typical, and this secondary reference ought not perhaps to be denied to those who contend for its place in the prophet's words, yet we feel the need of caution lest this mode of exegesis be pressed too far. The expressions of the prophet, which may to some seem extravagant for merely local adaptation, may after all be thus understood in view of the highly picturesque and figurative language so peculiar to him throughout all his writings. The following are the passages under discussion:

CHAPTER TWENTY-EIGHT

14 Wherefore hear the word of Jehovah, ye scoffers, that rule this people that is in Jerusalem: 15 Because ye have said, We have made a covenant with death, and with Sheol are we at agreement; when the overflowing scourge shall pass through, it shall not come unto us; for we have made lies our refuge, and under falsehood have we hid ourselves: 16 therefore thus saith the Lord Jehovah, Behold, I [1]lay in Zion for a foundation a stone, a tried stone, a precious corner-*stone* of sure foundation: he that believeth shall not be in haste. 17 And I will make justice the line, and righteousness the plummet; and the hail shall sweep away the refuge of lies, and the waters shall overflow the hiding-place. 18 And your covenant with death shall be annulled and your agreement with Sheol shall not stand; when the overflowing scourge shall pass through, then ye shall be trodden down by it. 19 As often as it passeth through, it shall take you; for morning by morning shall it pass through, by day and by night: and it shall be nought but terror to understand the [2]message. 20 For the bed is shorter than that a man can stretch himself on it; and the covering narrower than that he can wrap himself in it. 21 For Jehovah will rise up as in mount Perazim, he will be wroth as in the valley of Gibeon; that he may do his work, his strange work, and bring to pass his act, his strange act. 22 Now therefore be ye not scoffers, lest your bonds be made strong; for [3]a decree of destruction have I heard from the Lord, Jehovah of hosts, upon the whole [4]earth.

[1]Or, *have laid*
[2]Or, *report*
[3]Heb. *destruction, and that decreed*
[4]Or, *land*

Vers. 14-22. THE FATE OF EPHRAIM A WARNING TO JUDAH.

Says Alexander, "To their confident assurance of safety God opposes, first, the only sure foundation which He Himself had laid, and then the utter destruction which was coming on their own chosen objects of reliance." By the art of falsehood, cunning policy and fine diplomacy they hope to be saved from death and hades, with which they imagine they have already formed an alliance. Assyria they compare to an overflowing scourge. By the "lies" and "falsehood" they doubtless mean a secret league with Egypt while they were professing loyalty to Assyria in the days of their dependence on Assyria into which Ahaz had brought them.

The *"tried stone"* of verse 16 is of course the Messiah. Says Fausset, "whether Isaiah understood the fullness or not, the Holy Spirit plainly contemplated its fulfillment in Christ alone."

Says Scofield, "There is in these verses a near reference to the Egyptian alliance ('we have made a covenant', etc.), while the reference to the stone in verse 16 carries the meaning forward to the end time, and the covenant of unbelieving Israel with the Beast (Dan. 9.27)."

Blackstone says, "The Antichrist will be received even by the Jews, who having returned to their own land and rebuilt their temple, will make a treaty with him, called by the Prophet Isaiah, 'a covenant with death and an agreement with hell'."

CHAPTER TWENTY-NINE

3 And I will encamp against thee round about, and will lay siege against thee with posted troops, and I will raise siege works against thee. 4 And thou shalt be brought down, and shalt speak out of the ground, and thy speech shall be low out of the dust; and thy voice shall be as of one that hath a familiar spirit, out of the ground, and thy speech shall [1]whisper out of the dust.

5 But the multitude of thy [2]foes shall be like small dust, and the multitude of the terrible ones as chaff that passeth away; yea, it shall be in an instant suddenly. 6 [3]She shall be visited of Jehovah of hosts with thunder, and with earthquake, and great noise, with whirlwind and tempest, and the flame of a devouring fire. 7 And the multitude of all the nations that fight against Ariel, even all that fight against her and her stronghold, and that distress her, shall be as a dream, a vision of the night. 8 And it shall be as when a hungry man dreameth, and, behold, he eateth; but he awaketh, and his soul is empty: or as when a thirsty man dreameth, and, behold, he drinketh; but he awaketh, and, behold, he is faint, and his soul hath appetite: so shall the multitude of all the nations be, that fight against mount Zion.

[1]Or, *chirp*
[2]Heb. *strangers*
[3]Or, *There shall be a visitation from Jehovah &c.*

Vers. 3-8. THE INVASION AND OVERTHROW OF THE ASSYRIAN HOST.

The city here mentioned is Jerusalem.

Scofield says, "The near view is that of Sennacherib's invasion and the destruction of the Assyrian host by the angel of the Lord; the far view is that of the final gathering of the Gentile hosts against Jerusalem at the end of the great tribulation, when a still greater deliverance will be wrought."

Fausset says, "This prediction was not fully realized under Sennacherib, but was under the Roman siege. It probably contemplates ultimately, besides the affliction and deliverance in Sennacherib's time, the destruction of Jerusalem by Rome, the dispersion of the Jews, their restoration, the destruction of the enemies that besiege the Holy City (Zech. 14.2) and the final glory of Israel, as seen in verses 17 to 24. The ulterior fulfillment of verse 6 in the case of the enemies of the Jews in the last days may be more literal."

17 Is it not yet a very little while, and Lebanon shall be turned into a fruitful field, and the fruitful field shall be esteemed as a forest? 18 And in that day shall the deaf hear the words of [1]the book, and the eyes of the blind shall see out of obscurity and out of darkness. 19 The meek also shall increase their joy in Jehovah, and the poor among men shall rejoice in the Holy One of Israel. 20 For the terrible one is brought to nought, and the scoffer ceaseth, and all they that watch for iniquity are cut off; 21 that [2]make a man an offender [3]in *his* cause, and lay a snare for him that reproveth in the gate, and turn aside the just with a thing of nought.

22 Therefore thus saith Jehovah, who redeemed Abraham, concerning the house of Jacob: Jacob shall not now be ashamed, neither shall his face now wax pale. 23 [4]But when he seeth his children, the work of my hands, in the midst of him, they shall sanctify my name; yea, they shall sanctify the Holy One of Jacob, and shall stand in awe of the God of Israel. 24 They also that err in spirit [5]shall come to understanding, and they that murmur shall receive instruction.

[1]Or, *a book* (or, *writing*)
[2]Or, *make men to offend by* their *words*
[3]Or, *for a word*

[4]Or, *But when his children see &c.*
[5]Heb. *shall know understanding*

Vers. 17-24. THE BLESSING OF ISRAEL AFTER DELIVERANCE.

The moral change in the Jewish nation is to be as great as if the wooded Lebanon were to become a fruitful field and vice versa.

Nagelsbach thinks the meaning is that the lofty Lebanon (Assyria) shall be brought low and the lowly field (Israel) shall be exalted. But the comparison seems to be between the cultivated and the wild rather than between the high and the low.

Delitzsch says there is a promise in both clauses and that the last clause means that what they now call a fruitful field shall then *be so much more so* that what they now esteem a fruitful field will seem as if it were a forest in comparison with itself in the days to come.

Fausset however takes the last clause as a threat, and says the meaning of the whole passage is that in the Messianic days men's hearts which were once a moral desert (the wooded Lebanon) are to be reclaimed so as to bear fruits of righteousness, whereas, vice versa, the ungodly who seem prosperous both in the moral and literal sense (the fruitful field) shall be exhibited in their real barrenness.

Scofield takes the words of this section as a type of the kingdom blessings which are to follow the days of tribulation.

Nagelsbach says, "The prospect of blessedness which the prophet here presents belongs also to the days of the Messiah, as we clearly perceive from verses 18 and 19; for in fact he here beholds along with the near view the time of the end, and in holding out the prospect of this reformation within a brief period he does so in the exercise of that prophetic manner of contemplation which reckons the times not according to a human but a divine measure."

Fausset says the reference contemplates the outpouring of the Spirit in the latter days, first on the Jews, which shall be followed by their national restoration, and then on the Gentiles.

CHAPTER THIRTY

23 And he will give the rain for thy seed, wherewith thou shalt sow the ground; and bread of the increase of the ground, and it shall be fat and plenteous. In that day shall thy cattle feed in large pastures; 24 the oxen likewise and the young asses that till the ground shall eat savory provender, which hath been winnowed with the shovel and with the fork. 25 And there shall be upon every lofty mountain, and upon every high hill, brooks and streams of waters, in the day of the great slaughter, when the towers fall. 26 Moreover the light of the moon shall be as the light of the sun, and the light of the sun shall be sevenfold, as the light of seven days, in the day that Jehovah bindeth up the hurt of his people, and healeth the stroke of their wound.

27 Behold, the name of Jehovah cometh from far, burning with his anger, and in thick rising smoke: his lips are full of indignation, and his tongue is as a devouring fire; 28 and his breath is as an overflowing stream, that reacheth even unto the neck, to sift the nations with the sieve of destruction: and a bridle that causeth to err shall be in the jaws of the peoples. 29 Ye shall have a song as in the night [1]when a holy feast is kept; and gladness of heart, as when one goeth with a pipe to come unto the mountain of Jehovah, to the Rock of Israel. 30 And Jehovah will cause his glorious voice to be heard, and will show the lightning down of his arm, with the indignation of his anger, and the flame of a devouring fire, with [2]a blast, and tempest, and hailstones. 31 For through the voice of Jehovah shall the Assyrian be dismayed; with his rod will he smite him. 32 And every [3]stroke of the [4]appointed staff, which Jehovah shall lay upon him, shall be with the sound of tabrets and harps; and in battles with the brandishing of his arm will he fight with them. 33 For a Topheth is prepared of old; yea, for the king it is made ready; he hath made it deep and large; the pile thereof is fire and much wood; the breath of Jehovah, like a stream of brimstone, doth kindle it.

[1]Or, when a feast is hallowed
[2]Or, crashing
[3]Heb. passing
[4]Or, staff of doom (Heb. foundation)

Vers. 23-33. THE BLESSINGS WHICH ARE TO FOLLOW ISRAEL'S DEVASTATION.

Here is a promise of increased prosperity after a dreadful period of war and devastation through which the Jews are to pass.

What Scofield calls "a foreshadowing of kingdom blessing" Rosenmuller designates as "a description of the Golden Age."

Says Nagelsbach, "The glorious time of the end lies beyond a dreadful period which first must be passed through. This latter he has described so often as to be able to suppose that these brief allusions would be quite well understood by his readers."

Ver. 25. Even the otherwise barren hills shall then flow with water, a common figure for a great change for the better.

Hitzig interprets the "towers" as living towers, i. e., the Assyrian chiefs. But as the slaughter pertains here chiefly to the Jews it would seem that the towers ought also to find their reference in Jewish association. Knobel refers them to the fortifications of the Jews which would no longer be needed in the happy times described, while Delitzsch thinks they refer to Jewish self-confidence and pride. Perhaps Nagelsbach is right when he says, "I find here simply an allusion to the great judgments which must fall on people and city before the day of redemption. The old theocratic Jerusalem with its towers and its temples is reduced to ruins while streams of blood have at the same time flown."

Gill refers the *"slaughter"* to that of the antichristian kings described in Rev. 19.17-21, and among other references Vitringa finds one to the seventh apocalyptic period.

Ver. 26.   The shining of the moon and the sun must of course here be taken in a figurative sense, an image from the heavenly bodies to express either, as Fausset says, "the increase of spiritual light and felicity", or as Alexander says, "some great revolution in the state of society".

"This verse", says Nagelsbach, "transports us into a time which lies beyond the present state of things, though not into the time of the new heavens and the new earth, for the present sun and the present moon still exist." He quotes Delitzsch as being certainly right in saying, "It is not the new heaven of which the prophet here speaks, but that glorification of nature promised both in the Old and the New Testament prophecy for the final period of the world's history". (Compare, says Nagelsbach, Rev. 20.1-4.)

Ver. 27.   "The imagery of verses 27 and 28 is cumulative. Judah is making an alliance with Egypt when she might be in league with Him whose judgment upon the world-powers will be like a terrible thunder-tempest (verse 27), turning streams into torrents neck-deep (verse 28, f. c.) ; who will sift the nations in their own sieve of vanity (or 'destruction'), and put His bridle into the jaws of the peoples." (Sco.)

"the name of Jehovah",—Many authorities take this expression as meaning Jehovah Himself (F. Del.) and this is no doubt its immediate reference.   Others would have us believe it refers to Him who is the Agent in every revelation of the Godhead, and accordingly He to whom the Father hath committed all judgment, the Messiah, and this may rightly be said to be its secondary reference, and Nagelsbach says, "He cometh to judgment from afar because He comes from heaven".

Ver. 28.   *"to sift the nations with the sieve of destruction"*,—Some say this is a sieve which lets only the light, useless grain fall through it to destruction; but it is a sieve of ruin, of emptiness, of falsehood, pointing out the issue of the process, and we believe those right who see here, as Gill does, that, "they were to be sifted not with a good and profitable sieve, which retains the corn and shakes out the chaff, but with a sieve that lets all through and so reduces to nothingness all who find themselves in it." (F. C. Al. Lo. Bar.)

"a bridle that causeth to err",—Most interpreters see here the specific sense of leading astray, causing to go in the wrong direction, the bridle put in their jaws compelling them to go from the way they had intended.

Ver. 29.   As in the Passover-night they celebrated with songs their deliverance from Egypt so shall they celebrate their deliverance from the bondage here under view, and the festal processions in which, accompanied with song and music, they used to go up to the temple is but a type of the joy that shall in that day be granted to Israel.

Ver. 31. Those who contend for the blending of the near and far fulfillments of this prophecy see of course in Assyria not only the then existing Gentile power but a type of the world-power at the end of this age, and even Alexander says, "The express mention of Assyria in this verse, although it does not prove it to have been from the beginning the specific subject of the prophecy, does show that it was a conspicuous object in Isaiah's view, as an example both of danger and of deliverance, and that at this point he concentrates his prophetic vision on this object *as a signal illustration* of the general truths which he has been announcing."

Ver. 32. "*shall be with the sound of tabrets and harps*", i. e., on the part of the people of Jerusalem who have only to look on and rejoice in the coming deliverance.

"*with the brandishing of his arm*",—The literal is "battles of swinging", or "battles of shaking", and the idea seems to be that it is not to be with darts or other weapons, but that with the incessant swinging of His arm He will smite Assyria.

Ver. 33. Tophet means a place of burning. The Tophet in the valley of Hinnon was a place of sacrifice dedicated to Moloch, and here the idea is only that of a Tophet-like place. The words contain a figurative representation of Assyria's temporal doom and a premonition of his doom hereafter.

CHAPTER THIRTY-ONE

Vers. 1 to 3 contain another warning against trusting in the chariots of Egypt through an alliance with that ungodly power.

Vers. 4 to 5 express Jehovah's determination and power to save those who put their trust in Him.

Vers. 6 to 9 invite the children of Israel to return to Jehovah, as they will be constrained to do with shame when they behold the judgment which He is about to bring upon their oppressors.

CHAPTER THIRTY-TWO

1 Behold, a king shall reign in righteousness, and princes shall rule in justice. 2 And a man shall be as a hiding-place from the wind, and a covert from the tempest, as streams of water in a dry place, as the shade of a great rock in a weary land. 3 And the eyes of them that see shall not be [1]dim, and the ears of them that hear shall hearken. 4 And the heart of the [2]rash shall understand knowledge, and the tongue of the stammerers shall be ready to speak plainly. 5 The fool shall be no more called noble, nor the [3]churl said to be bountiful. 6 For the fool will speak folly, and his heart will work iniquity, to practice profaneness, and to utter error against Jehovah, to make empty the soul of the hungry, and to cause the drink of the thirsty to fail. 7 And the instruments of the churl are evil; he deviseth wicked devices to destroy the [4]meek with lying words, even when the needy speaketh right. 8 But the noble deviseth noble things; and [5]in noble things shall he continue.

[1]Or, *closed*
[2]Heb. *hasty*
[3]Or, *crafty*
[4]Or, *poor*
[5]Or, *by liberal things shall he stand*

Vers. 1-8. THE PROMISE OF THE KING AND HIS RIGHTEOUS GOVERNMENT.

Scofield remarks here again that in this chapter and the three following the same blended meanings of near and far fulfillments are found, the near view being still of Sennacherib's invasion and the far view the day of the Lord and the kingdom blessing to follow.

These eight verses continue the promises of the foregoing text.

Ver. 1. *"a king"*,—The reference may be to Hezekiah's reign as at least a beginning and foretaste of what is here promised, but, as Fausset says, "If Hezekiah be meant at all it can only be as a type of Messiah, the King, to whom alone the language is fully applicable", for, as Nagelsbach says, "Only in Messianic times can the kind of a rule prophesied be true."

"princes shall rule in justice",—To whom these refer in the far view of the prophecy is not easy to determine unless, as Fausset says, "to all in authority under Christ in the coming kingdom on earth, e. g., the Apostles, etc., but this Alexander calls very forced and neither justified nor required by the context.

Ver. 2. *"a man shall be"*, etc.,—Most late interpreters give to *"man"* the sense of a distributive pronoun meaning death, i. e., each of the princes just mentioned. The word is, however, seldom so used except with a plural verb, and the meaning here is rather that there shall be a man on the throne who instead of oppressing will protect the helpless.

Ver. 3. The reference is to spiritual transformations and the verse applies to the people generally.

Ver. 4. It would seem best to understand these bodily defects as denoting others of an intellectual and spiritual nature.

Vers. 9-13. In these verses the prophet reverts to the prospect of coming disaster and addresses especially the proud women who by their luxurious habits contribute so largely to existing evils and for whom the coming invasion would be especially disastrous.

14 For the palace shall be forsaken; the populous city shall be deserted; the hill and the watch-tower shall be for dens for ever, a joy of wild asses, a pasture of flocks; 15 until the Spirit be poured upon us from on high, and the wilderness become a fruitful field, and the fruitful field be esteemed as a forest. 16 Then justice shall dwell in the wilderness; and righteousness shall abide in the fruitful field. 17 And the work of righteousness shall be peace; and the effect of righteousness, quietness and confidence for ever. 18 And my people shall abide in a peaceful habitation, and in safe dwellings, and in quiet resting-places. 19 But it shall hail in the downfall of the forest; and the city shall be utterly laid low. 20 Blessed are ye that sow beside all waters, that send forth the feet of the ox and the ass.

Vers. 14-20. THE FUTURE GLORY OF THE NATION.

Ver. 15. This verse tells how long the desolation is to last, i. e., until, etc. Nagelsbach calls the passage between this verse and the preceding one, "a bold bridge from the then present into the remote future". He says, "The prophet sets the glorious Messianic last time over against the pernicious then present time, yet in a way that overlaps the long intervening centuries, and sees the future directly behind the present. How far-reaching and comprehensive is the gaze of the prophet here!"

This can only partially apply to the spiritual revival in Hezekiah's time; its full accomplishment belongs to the Christian dispensation, first at Pentecost (Joel 2.28; Acts 2.17), perfectly in coming times (Zech. 12.10; Ezek. 36.26; 39.29), when the Spirit shall be poured on Israel, and through her on the Gentiles (Micah 5.7).

The desolation is to last, as Alexander says, "until by a special divine influence a total revolution shall take place in the character, and as a necessary consequence in the condition of the people. To attempt to restrict it to the return from exile, or to the day of Pentecost, or to some great effusion of the Spirit upon the Jews still future, perverts the passage by making that its whole meaning, which at most is but a part."

For explanation of the latter part of the verse see Chap. 29.17.

Ver. 16.   This verse does not apparently mean that both in the cultivation of the wilderness and the desolation of the field the righteousness of God shall be displayed; it means rather that what is now a wilderness and what is now a fruitful field shall both alike be the abode of justice and righteousness.

Ver. 19.   *"the downfall of the forest"*,—The *"forest"* we know to be an emblem of Assyria (Chap. 10.34), the Assyrian host dense as the trees of a forest.

"and the city shall be utterly laid low",—Some think this an instance of "prophetic recurrence from remoter promises to nearer threats", as if he had said, "Before these things come to pass the city must first be laid low", the subject therefore being the same as that in verse 13, i. e., Jerusalem, (Al. Kn. Del. Hit. Cas.)

Others take it, and as we think more properly, as a direct continuation according to which it must be taken as the downfall of some hostile city. Fausset thinks of Ninevah, as do probably the most. In a sense it is of course the *world-city*, as others take it. (Na. Dre. Ros.) Nagelsbach asks, "Why of a sudden this dark trait in the picture of light? Is not the abasement of Jerusalem sufficiently declared in verses 13 and 14? Why a repetition here? If the forest that falls under the hail-storm means the world-power generally, then the city must mean the world-city."

Ver. 20.   Delitzsch says here, "They sow wherever they please, by all waters that fertilize the soil, on fruitful land requiring little toil to cultivate it, and because everything is rich in abundance they can let oxen and asses roam at large." (Na. He.)

Some think the last clause refers to the custom of sending forth the oxen and asses to tread the ground before sowing (F. Lo.), while Ewald, with Alexander, explains the passage exclusively of moral cultivation, implying that none can expect to reap good without diligently sowing it.

CHAPTER THIRTY-THREE

1 Woe to thee that destroyest, and thou wast not destroyed; and dealest treacherously, and they dealt not treacherously with thee! When thou hast ceased to destroy, thou shalt be destroyed: and when thou hast made an end of dealing treacherously, they shall deal treacherously with thee. 2 O Jehovah, be gracious unto us; we have waited for thee; be thou ¹our arm every

¹Heb. *their*

morning, our salvation also in the time of trouble. 3 At the noise of the tumult the peoples are fled; at the lifting up of thyself the nations are scattered. 4 And your spoil shall be gathered as the caterpillar gathereth; as locusts leap shall men leap upon it. 5 Jehovah is exalted, for he dwelleth on high: he hath filled Zion with justice and righteousness. 6 [2]And there shall be stability in thy times, abundance of salvation, wisdom, and knowledge: the fear of Jehovah is [3]thy treasure.

7 Behold, their valiant ones cry without; the ambassadors of peace weep bitterly. 8 The highways lie waste, the wayfaring man ceaseth: [4]the enemy hath broken the covenant, he hath despised the cities, he regardeth not man. 9 The land mourneth and languisheth; Lebanon is confounded and withereth away; Sharon is like [5]a desert; and Bashan and Carmel shake off their leaves. 10 Now will I arise saith Jehovah; now will I lift up myself; now will I be exalted. 11 Ye shall conceive chaff, ye shall bring forth stubble; your breath is a fire that shall devour you. 12 And the peoples shall be as the burnings of lime, as thorns cut down, that are burned in the fire.

13 Hear, ye that are far off, what I have done; and, ye that are near, acknowledge my might. 14 The sinners in Zion are afraid; trembling hath seized the godless ones: Who among us can dwell with the devouring fire? who among us can dwell with everlasting burnings? 15 He that walketh right-

eously, and speaketh uprightly; he that despiseth the gain of [6]oppressions, that shaketh his hands from taking a bribe, that stoppeth his ears from hearing of blood, and shutteth his eyes from looking upon evil: 16 he shall dwell on high; his place of defence shall be the munitions of rocks; his bread shall be given him; his waters shall be sure.

17 Thine eyes shall see the king in his beauty; they shall behold [7]a land that reacheth afar. 18 Thy heart shall muse on the terror: Where is [8]he that counted, where is he that weighed the tribute? where is he that counted the towers? 19 Thou shalt not see the fierce people, a people of a deep speech that thou canst not comprehend, of a [9]strange tongue that thou canst not understand. 20 Look upon Zion, the city of our [10]solemnities; thine eyes shall see Jerusalem a quiet habitation, a tent that shall not be removed, the stakes whereof shall never be plucked up, neither shall any of the cords thereof be broken. 21 But there Jehovah will be with us in majesty, [11]a place of broad rivers and streams, wherein shall go no galley with oars, neither shall gallant ship pass thereby. 22 For Jehovah is our judge, Jehovah is our lawgiver, Jehovah is our king; he will save us. 23 Thy tacklings are loosed; they could not strengthen the foot of their mast, they could not spread the sail: then was the prey of a great spoil divided; the lame took the prey. 24 And the inhabitant shall not say, I am sick: the people that dwell therein shall be forgiven their iniquity.

[2]Or, And abundance of salvation, wisdom, and knowledge shall be the stability of thy times.
[3]Heb. his
[4]Heb. he
[5]Or, the Arabah
[6]Or, fraud
[7]Or, a land that is very far off Heb. a land of far distances.
[8]Or, the scribe
[9]Or, stammering
[10]Or, set feasts
[11]Or, but in the place .... streams there shall go, &c.

Vers. 1-24. THE WOE UPON ASSYRIA AND THE SALVATION OF JERUSALEM.

Ver. 1. The enemy addressed is rightly taken by the majority to be Assyria. The words are of course applicable to any oppressive and deceitful enemy. Some think that Nebuchadnezzar is meant either as an individual or as a representative of the Assyrian power. Vitringa thinks of Antiochus Epiphanes, Jerome of Satan, while Gill thinks by this enemy the Antichrist is meant.

The enemy is described as acting without provocation and as having never yet suffered reverses.

Ver. 3. "At the noise of the tumult".—"The approach of Jehovah", says Fausset, "is likened to an advancing thunder storm, which is

His voice causing *'the peoples'*, the Assyrians, to flee." He lets them hear a voice which, as it were, has no actual existence. The verse is addressed to Jehovah.

"the lifting up of thyself",—i. e., when, in order to strike, one rouses himself from a state of seeming inaction.

Ver. 4. The address is to the Assyrians. The prophet sees the Israelites plundering their camp and gathering the spoil as the caterpillars (the wingless locust) gather, that is, greedily and thoroughly, not leaving a field or a tree until they have stripped it.

"as locusts leap",—i. e. eagerly, voraciously, with a view to satisfying the appetite.

Ver. 6. The object of the address is most probably the people of Judah (K. Al. Na. Del.), and not Hezekiah, for which latter there is no reason, the same being true of the explanation which refers the object to the Messiah. The Hebrew for *"thy"* is *"his"*, but it either refers to the same object, i. e., Judah, by a change of person common in Hebrew poetry, and is therefore properly rendered *"thy"* in our text; or if *"his"* be retained it must be made to mean Jehovah's treasure which He bestows.

Ver. 7. From the vision of future glory the prophet returns to the disastrous present.

These *"valiant ones"* and the *"ambassadors"* of the next clause, apparently one and the same, are not those sent by Hezekiah to Isaiah, but they are the messengers sent to Sennacherib to treat for peace, the messengers sent by Hezekiah to the Assyrian king (II Kings 18.14-18). Their terms were accepted and the peace money handed over, after which the Assyrian commander would not retire but demanded the surrender of Jerusalem; hence the bitter weeping.

"cry without",—i. e., probably without the enemy's camp.

Ver. 8. The scene presented is that of the condition of Judah during the Assyrian invasion. Gilt thinks it is that of the Protestant cities seized by Antichrist and a stop put to their religious course and conversation.

Ver. 9. The most fertile and flourishing parts of the country are here described as desolate, the language being figurative of course, which may be inferred from the fact that none of the places mentioned are in Judah.

Ver. 11. *"chaff . . . stubble"*,—The common Scriptural figure for failure.

"breath",—Various renderings are "puffings" (Na.) "anger" (Gro.), "pride" (Cle.), "panting" (Del.) ; their rage against Jerusalem is the fire that shall consume them.

Ver. 12. *"the peoples"*,—i. e., primarily the races mingled in the Assyrian army, but in general all nations that defy God.

Gill refers this verse to the future destruction of antichristian Rome. (Rev. 17.16; 18.8.)

Ver. 13. *"ye that are afar off"* and *"ye that are near"* refer doubtless to all people without exception. (F. Al. Bar.) Hendewerk says they are the ten tribes and the two tribes; Junius and Nagelsbach say they are the Gentiles and the Jews, while Delitzsch says it refers to a farness and nearness to God of those who are in Jerusalem.

Ver. 14.   *"The sinners in Zion"*,—i. e., the impious Jews.

What follows is the language of the wicked Jews in Jerusalem and is expressive of their terror, alarm and desperation.   The *"devouring fire"* is therefore not the wrath of God as executed by the Assyrians (Gro. Pis.), but the wrath of God as executed on or against the Assyrians, and the thought is, If this be a specimen of God's vindicatory justice, what can we expect?   Who of us can dwell with this devouring fire?

Henderson, not without some reason, thinks the reference is to eternal punishment, and that the argument is from the less to the greater, namely, if these are God's temporal judgments what must His eternal wrath be; who of us can dwell with such devouring fire?

Ver. 15.   This is taken by many (F. Na. Del.) as an answer to the question of the preceding verse.   If this be proper, then that verse cannot refer to future punishment because the righteous are not supposed to endure that.   It may be so taken if the *"devouring fire"* refers only to God's judgments against the Assyrians, because the righteous man shall be secure in the midst of such devouring fire of Jehovah.

We believe it is best, however, to separate this verse from the preceding context, making it the beginning, as it were, of a new paragraph, because the sentence is plainly incomplete in this verse and finds its conclusion in the next.   (Al. He.)

Ver. 16.   *"dwell on high"*,—Not exalted position, but safety from enemies.   "Enclosed as within the impregnable walls of a rocky fortress on inaccessible heights."   (Del.)

Ver. 17. *"the king in his beauty"*,—Some refer this to Hezekiah exclusively.   (Al. Del. Ges.)   Delitzsch says, "The king of Judah hitherto deeply abased by tyrannous oppression and unfortunate wars, is then glorified by the victory of his God, and the nation, answering to the description of verses 15 and 16, shall behold him in his God-given beauty."

Calvin, Nagelsbach and others think of King Hezekiah as a type of the Christ, while Fausset and Abarbenel think only of the Messiah.   Fausset says, "Not as now, Hezekiah in sackcloth oppressed by the enemy, but King Messiah in His beauty."

"a land that reacheth afar",—i. e., a land of far stretching extent (Del.), a wide-extended land (Na.), the land in its remotest extent (F.). Luther thinks of the land as actually extended by conquered territory, while Hitzig says that they can see from Jerusalem far and wide because their view is no longer obstructed by fortresses, entrenchments and the presence of the enemy.   The Hebrew is *"a land of far distances"*.

Ver. 18.   They reflect on the terror that is now past.   The scribe, the collector of tribute, the weigher who tested the weight of the gold and silver paid in as tribute money, and the counter of the towers who drew up the plan of the city that was to be attacked—these are all vanished.

Ver. 19.   The Assyrians, a people of fierce, insolent bearing, of obscure, unintelligible ("*deep*") speech and obscure ("*stammering*" or "*strange*") tongue so perplexing to the Israelites, will have disappeared from the land.

Ver. 20. The beauty of the imagery lies in ascribing permanency to a tent which, from its very nature, is movable and undependable.

Ver. 21. Babylon, Ninevah and other great cities were usually defended by great rivers and river canals. Jerusalem had none such, but Jehovah, figuratively speaking, will be to her such river defenses, and neither oar-ship nor sail-ship (ships of war) shall be able to pass these mighty waters. Others contend that the collocation of words forbids this interpretation, and they read "But a glorious One dwells there for us, Jehovah" (Del.), or "But there shall Jehovah be mighty for us" (Al.),— then in consequence of His dwelling there Jerusalem shall be like a place of rivers, etc.

Ver. 23. A sudden apostrophe to the enemy considered as a ship.

"*they could not strengthen the foot of their mast*",—i. e., they could not hold firm the support, the socket of the mast.

By many these words are held as addressed to Jerusalem (Na. Or. Del. Dre. Che.). But the reasons adduced by Nagelsbach, who says we stand again in this verse in the period before the overthrow of the Assyrians, are not at all convincing, and it is better to take the address as being made to Assyria, as do the majority of writers. (F. Al. Ew. Bi. Reu. Luz. Bar.)

When Assyria is spoiled the lame will join in the pillage, by which statement the eagerness of the gathering in of the spoil is pictured.

Ver. 24. "*The inhabitants shall not say, I am sick*",—Either there shall be no sickness or those who are sick shall recover.

"*shall be forgiven their iniquity*",—Some interpret the sickness as a spiritual malady and so take this clause as meaning the same as the one that went before it. Others take it as explaining that bodily sickness is caused by sin (F. Na. Al.). The words really mean that all sickness shall cease with sin. "The words", says Alexander, "are strictly applicable only to a state of things still future, either upon earth or in heaven."

Section Six. The Eschatological Judgment of the Nations and the Redemption of Israel.

CHAPTERS 34 AND 35

CHAPTER THIRTY-FOUR

1 Come near, ye nations, to hear; and hearken, ye peoples: let the earth hear, and the fullness thereof; the world, and all things that come forth from it. 2 For Jehovah hath indignation against all the nations, and wrath against all their host: he hath [1]utterly destroyed them, he hath delivered them to the slaughter. 3 Their slain also shall be cast out, and the stench of their dead bodies shall come up; and the mountains shall be melted with their blood. 4 And all the host of heaven shall [2]be dissolved, and the heavens shall be rolled together as a scroll; and all their host shall fade away, as the leaf fadeth from off the vine, and as a fading *leaf* from the fig-tree.

[1]Heb. *devoted*

[2]Or, *moulder away*

Vers. 1-4. THE JUDGMENT ON THE WHOLE WORLD.

Some have applied this section as well as what follows to the desolation of Edom (Gro. Schi.), but there is little doubt but that it belongs to the judgment of the end-time because it takes place with the contemporaneous destruction of the present heaven and earth. (F. Na. Eu. Cy. Del.) Scofield says it is the battle of Armageddon.

Ver. 1. The summons goes forth to the whole of nature, impersonal as well as personal, because the former will have to share in this judgment. They are not invited to witness but to hear about this judgment.

Ver. 3. *"the mountains shall be melted with their blood"*,—i. e., as they are sometimes washed away by the rain.

Ver. 4. *"And all the host of heaven shall be dissolved"*,—The verb rendered *"dissolve"* is commonly applied to pining away through disease. In Psa. 38.6 it means to "run as a sore" and from this Gesenius, adopting the poetical notion of likening the stars to wax candles, gets the idea of melting. Maurer therefore quite aptly takes the expression as a statement that the heavenly bodies will pine away into sickly, dying lights. (V. Al.)

"rolled together as a scroll",—Pfeiffer has well said that as Jehovah is elsewhere said to have stretched out the heavens as a curtain, so their destruction or any total change in their appearance would be described as a rolling up of the expanse.

5 For my sword hath drunk its fill in heaven: behold, it shall come down upon Edom, and upon the people of my [1]curse, to judgment. 6 The sword of Jehovah is filled with blood, it is made fat with fatness, with the blood of lambs and goats, with the fat of the kidneys of rams; for Jehovah hath a sacrifice in Bozrah, and a great slaughter in the land of Edom. 7 And the wild-oxen shall come down with them, and the bullocks with the bulls: and their land shall be drunken with blood, and their dust made fat with fatness.

8 For Jehovah hath a day of vengeance, a year of recompense for the cause of Zion. 9 And the streams [2]of Edom shall be turned into pitch, and the dust thereof into brimstone, and the land thereof shall become burning pitch. 10 It shall not be quenched night nor day; the smoke thereof shall go up for ever; from generation to generation it shall lie waste; none shall pass through it for ever and ever. 11 But the pelican and the porcupine shall possess it; and the [3]owl and the raven shall dwell therein: and he will stretch over it the line of confusion, and the [4]plummet of emptiness. 12 [5]They shall call the nobles thereof to the kingdom, but none shall be there; and all its princes shall be nothing. 13 And thorns shall come up in its palaces, nettles and thistles in the fortresses thereof; and it shall be a habitation of jackals, a court of ostriches. 14 And the wild beasts of the desert shall meet with the [6]wolves, and the wild goat shall cry to his fellow; yea, [7]the night-monster shall settle there, and shall find her a place of rest. 15 There shall the dart-snake make her nest, and lay, and hatch, and gather under her shade; yea, there shall the kites be gathered, every one with her mate.

[1]Heb. *devoting,* or, *ban*
[2]Heb. *thereof*
[3]Or, *bittern*
[4]Heb. *stones*
[5]Or, *As for her nobles, none shall be there to proclaim the kingdom*
[6]Heb. *howling creatures*
[7]Heb. *Lilith*

Vers. 5-15. THE JUDGMENT ON EDOM AS REPRESENTING ALL HOSTILE WORLD-POWER.

Ver. 5. *"my sword hath drunk its fill in heaven"*,—God's sword is here described as drunk with wrath in heaven before it is drunk with wrath on earth. (Del. Ges.) The saying is one doubtless expressing divine fore-ordination: In the sight of God the sword, although not yet actually used, was already dripping with blood.

"people of my curse",—This expression is not to be extended to other nations (Ju.), but is a repetition pointing again to Edom as the people doomed to the curse of God.

Ver. 6. The Edomites are regarded as a sacrifice and here compared to sheep, goats and rams. Bozra is the chief city of Edom.

"made fat with fatness",—i. e., smeared with the fat and the blood as the animal substance offered in sacrifice.

Ver. 7. Some think the *"wild oxen"* or *"wild buffalo"* refers to malignant enemies, but it means rather that the wild as well as the tame animals will be included in the slaughter.

"shall come down with them",—i. e., either to the slaughter, or *"come down"*, meaning to fall or sink under the fatal stroke.

Ver. 9. Here is signified the completest destruction, as if her streams were turned to pitch, and her dust to sulphur.

Nagelsbach says, "When the streams are flowing with pitch and the dust is sulphur the whole land will become a place of fearful conflagration."

Gill applies the last clause to the future burning of Rome as in Rev. 17.16 and 18.8.

Ver. 10. "The inextinguishable fire and the eternally ascending smoke", says Delitzsch, "prove that the final end is referred to (Rev. 19.3)."

"It is", says Nagelsbach, "the flame of the last judgment and the burning continues forever and ever." (F.)

Alexander, on the other hand, remarks that while these images are copied in Rev. 14.10,11, it does not follow that the copy was intended to determine the sense of the original.

Ver. 11. As right building demands the measuring line and the plummet, so God will move deliberately and by rule in His work of destruction.

Ver. 12. In as much as *"nobles"* is a nominative absolute, it is far better here to read with the margin, *"As for her nobles, none shall be there to proclaim the kingdom. The nobles and princes have come to nothing."*

Vers. 14-15. The general sense of these two verses is that the human population shall be succeeded by wild and lonely animals, implying total and continued desolation, and there is no need to concern ourselves with the detailed discussion in the various commentaries as to the particular species of animal referred to in each case.

16 Seek ye out of the book of Jehovah, and read: no one of these shall be missing, none shall want her mate; for my mouth, it hath commanded, and his Spirit, it hath gathered them. 17 And he hath cast the lot for them, and his hand hath divided it unto them by line: they shall possess it for ever; from generation to generation shall they dwell therein.

Vers. 16, 17. A Summons to Compare the Prophecy with Its Fulfillment.

Ver. 16. The persons addressed are the future witnesses of the events here predicted. The prophet seems to take his stand at a point of time after the event.

"the book of Jehovah",—We prefer, with Kimchi and Alting, to refer this to the prophecy just delivered, although, as Alexander says, it may be referred to prophecy in general or to the entire Scriptures without material change of sense. Other explanations are His decrees (Ab.), His record of events (For.), that part of Genesis relating to unclean animals (Jar.), the law in general (C.) the book of Revelation (Gill).

The pronouns in this verse and the next refer to the *animals* aforementioned.

"my mouth . . . his Spirit",—The sudden change of persons has led to various explanations, but on the whole the explanation of Delitzsch is to be preferred. He renders, "my mouth and its breath", thus making God the speaker in both instances. Indeed it is not even necessary to change the form of the pronoun, for such changes of person are frequent in Hebrew poetry.

Ver. 17. As Canaan was divided by lot and measuring line to Israel, so Edom is allotted to these doleful creatures.

CHAPTER THIRTY-FIVE

1 The wilderness and the dry land shall be glad; and the desert shall rejoice, and blossom as the ¹rose. 2 It shall blossom abundantly, and rejoice even with joy and singing; the glory of Lebanon shall be given unto it, the excellency of Carmel and Sharon: they shall see the glory of Jehovah, the excellency of our God.

3 Strengthen ye the weak hands, and confirm the ²feeble knees. 4 Say to them that are of a ³fearful heart, Be strong, fear not: ⁴behold, your God will come *with* vengeance, *with* the recompense of God; he will come and save you.

5 Then the eyes of the blind shall be opened, and the ears of the deaf shall be unstopped. 6 Then shall the lame man leap as a hart, and the tongue of the dumb shall sing; for in the wilderness shall waters break out, and streams in the desert. 7 And the ⁵glowing sand shall become a pool, and the thirsty ground springs of water; in the habitation of jackals, where they lay, shall be ⁶grass with reeds and rushes. 8 And a highway shall be there, and a way, and it shall be called The way of holiness; the unclean shall not pass over it; but it shall be for ⁷*the redeemed*: the wayfaring men, yea fools, shall not err *therein.* 9 No lion shall be there, nor shall any ravenous beast go up thereon; they shall not be found there; but the redeemed shall walk *there*; 10 and the ransomed of Jehovah shall return, and come with singing unto Zion; and everlasting joy shall be upon their heads: they shall obtain gladness and joy, and sorrow and sighing shall flee away.

¹Or, *Autumn crocus*
²Or, *tottering*
³Heb. *hasty*
⁴Or, *behold, your God! Vengeance will come, even the recompense of God*
⁵Or, *mirage*
⁶Or, *a court for reeds, &c.*
⁷Heb. *t.°em*

Vers. 1-10. Israel's Redemption and Regathering.

Ver. 1. This and the following verse, as someone has well said, prepare the theater in general, as it were, for the return of Israel, which return is to be through the desert, a desert, however, which shall conform to the blessed people who wander through it,—it will change its nature; hitherto a place of cursing, the abode of demons, it will become a place of blessing, a paradise.

"blossom as the rose",—Perhaps crocus, or narcissus, or lily are nearer the original meaning, but the *"rose"* is true to poetry if not to botany, and is perhaps best retained as more familiar and as containing a more striking image of beauty.

Ver. 2.   Lebanon, Sharon and Carmel are here united as types of the most luxuriant and glorious vegetation.

"they shall see",—Some take this as referring to the house of Israel. (Al. Cle. Sep. Tar. Bred.)   Others refer it, and rightly, to the immediate antecedents (V. Na. Del.), declaring that the discourse only comes to the Judeans in the next verse.   Alexander says that if the immediate antecedents had been meant there would have been no need for the use of the pronoun, and it must have been introduced for the purpose of directing the attention to some other than the nominatives nearest.   This argument is, however, by no means conclusive.

Ver. 3.   Are they exhorted to do this for others or for themselves? Both thoughts are best included and there is no reason for the exclusion of either.   The reference is of course to self-encouragement and the encouragement of others.

Ver. 4.   *"fearful heart"*,—i. e., hasty of heart, the impatient, those who cannot wait for the fulfillment of God's promises (Al. Cle.), although it has been variously explained, "inconsiderate" (Ju.), "precipitate" (Coc.), "inconstant" (Vat.), "faint-hearted" (Lo.), "palpitating" (Ros.), "ready to flee" (Ges.).

The rendering of the margin, *"Behold, your God! vengeance will come,—even the recompense of God"*, is preferable to that of our text, as most later writers agree.   (V. Al. Ju. Na. Coc.)

Alexander says, "While Barnes denies that the phrase 'your God' refers at all to the Messiah, Calovius alleges that the name of Jesus is expressly mentioned, being included in the verb.   The words are really a promise to God's people of deliverance, and include, as the most important part of their contents, the unspeakable gift of Christ and His salvation."

Vers. 5,6.   The words are to be understood more in a spiritual sense than in a corporeal, although it is not impossible that the latter, in a conditional sense, may be included.   Perhaps, however, as Alexander says, the simple meaning of the passage is that there shall be such a wonderful change wrought in the condition of mankind, *as if* the blind were to receive their sight, the dumb to speak, the deaf to hear, the lame to walk, and deserts to be fertilized and blossom like the rose.

Ver. 7.   *"in the habitation"*,—This is to be connected neither with what precedes, *"springs of water in the habitation"*, etc. (Al.), nor with what follows, *"in the habitation, etc., there shall be a highway"* (Ew.), both of which constructions allow no promise to be found in the last clause of this verse.   Our text is certainly right in seeing here a promise that what was once the haunt of jackals is to become fit for a resting place, a place where grass and reed and cane can grow because of the moisture, or a *"court for reeds and rushes"*, as in the margin.

By the *"glowing sand"* is meant the "mirage" which shall become an actual pool or lake of water.

Ver. 8. *"a highway shall there be"*,—Not a faint track in the desert, but a solid artificial highway.

"and a way",—This is merely a heniadys, a highway and a way for a highway.

"the unclean shall not pass over it",—This means that the people of Jehovah shall be holy. It is not an "effusion of national hatred" (Kn.), nor "a trace of later Judaism" (Hit.) excluding the heathen generally.

"but it shall be for the redeemed (them)",—It means merely for them for whose sake it was made, the redeemed of course. Hence it is needless to specify, "the blind whose eyes are opened" (Ju.), "Israel" (Kim.), "the exiles" (Hit.), "those redeemed from idolatry" (He.), "those redeemed by suffering" (Kn.).

"the wayfaring man",—The traveler.

"yea, fools",—This is explanatory and emphatic. Only moral impurity, but not ignorance nor weakness shall exclude men from this highway. Whoever goes upon it must be sanctified and such an one will be under Jehovah's protecting care.

Ver. 9. Nothing can go on this highway that may in any wise be occasion for alarm or fear. The way is so high that no beast can leap up.

Ver. 10. *"upon their heads"*,—Joy is manifest in the face and countenance.

Says Alexander, "With respect to the subject of this chapter there has been such diversity of opinion. It has been explained with equal confidence as a description of Judah under Hezekiah (Gro.), of the return from exile (Cle.), of the state of Judah after that event (Ros.), of that state and the times of the New Testament together (Mi.), of the calling of the Gentiles (Coc.), of the Christian dispensation (C. Lut.), of the state of the Church after the fall of Antichrist (V.), of the state of Palestine at some future period (Mic.), and of a future state of blessedness (Gill). These arbitrary hypotheses refute each other. The best description of the chapter is that given by Augusti in the title to his version of it, where he represents it as the description of a happy condition of the Church after a period of suffering. This is no doubt its true import, and when thus explained it may be considered as including various particulars, none of which may be regarded as its specific or exclusive subject. Gesenius says this prophecy was of course never fulfilled; but so far is this from being true, that it has rather been fulfilled again and again. Without any change of its essential meaning it may be applied to the restoration of the Jews from Babylon, to the vocation of the Gentiles, to the whole Christian dispensation, to the course of every individual believer, and to the blessedness of heaven."

Scofield, on the other hand and representing the opposite school of interpretation, says the chapter points to the kingdom blessing and the regathering of Israel.

Section Seven.   The Conclusion of the Assyrian and the Preparation for the Babylonian Period.

CHAPTERS 36 TO 39.

CHAPTERS THIRTY-SIX AND THIRTY-SEVEN

THE ATTEMPT OF ASSYRIA TO COMPEL THE SURRENDER OF JERUSALEM.

Chap. 37.31,32.   The king of Assyria had taken all the fenced cities of Judah, but into the city of Jerusalem Jehovah had said to the king of Assyria that he should not come (verse 33), and the remnant here refers to the inhabitants of Jerusalem and those who had fled there for safety.

CHAPTERS THIRTY-EIGHT AND THIRTY-NINE

HEZEKIAH'S SICKNESS AND RECOVERY AND THE EMBASSY FROM BABYLON OCCASIONED BY IT.

THE SECOND PRINCIPAL DIVISION OF THE BOOK

The twenty-seven chapters which compose this second division of the writings of Isaiah subdivide into three parts containing each nine chapters; Chaps. 40 to 48—49 to 57—58 to 66.   Each of these parts in turn contain three addresses.

The general theme of this division is the Redemption of Israel beginning with the return from Babylonian exile and ending with the creation of a new heaven and a new earth.

CHAPTER FORTY

This chapter, after a general introduction (verses 1-11) to the entire twenty-seven chapters as well as to the subsequent parts of this chapter itself, contains a presentation of the absolute power and wisdom of God as the objective basis of the redemption in view.

CHAPTER FORTY-ONE

This chapter both introduces the redeemer from the east (Cyrus) and sets forth the redeemed "servant of Jehovah", the people Israel, whom God promises to make strong unto victory, upon which is based an argument for the sole divinity of Jehovah and the nothingness of idols.

CHAPTER FORTY-TWO

This chapter introduces the Messiah who as the personal representative of a new covenant will mediate for all nations, and then occupies itself with a call to all nations, and especially Israel, to rejoice in promised deliverance.

Scofield, Fausset and others see in this chapter, as well as in others, a twofold account of the coming of Christ, His first in mercy to the penitent and His second in judgment on His enemies. Such verses as 13 and 14 they think set forth the judicial aspect of the Gospel which shall be consummated victoriously only at His second coming. But even though the general truth advanced by these writers be admitted, great caution should be used in drawing it out of passages of doubtful reference. Insofar as the name Jehovah in verse 13, and in Chap. 40.10, as referred to by Scofield, may be referred to Christ there is reasonable ground for the position taken by these authorities. It is doubtless true, as Delitzsch says of verses 13 and 14, that "The defeat which Jehovah here inflicts on heathendom is the final and decisive one. The deliverance of Israel, now nearing its accomplishment, is deliverance both from the punishment of exile and all the misery of sin. The post-exilian and the New Testament period flow into one."

CHAPTER FORTY-THREE

In this chapter the redemption itself is described as one that shall come to pass in spite of all difficulties, even though the heathen must be sacrificed for the sake of it. It is to be all-comprehending, bringing Israel back from out of *all* lands of the earth. This restoration, which finds its beginning in the return from Babylon, is described in such language as contains without doubt a reference to the more distant Messianic salvation, set forth under the usual figures of transformed nature.

Under verse 18 Fausset remarks that "plainly the still future restoration of Israel is the event ultimately meant."

CHAPTER FORTY-FOUR

In this chapter a new pledge of deliverance is given and a new exhortation to trust in Jehovah is set forth, the wisdom and glory of the latter being set forth in comparison with the wretchedness of impotent idols and their worshippers.

CHAPTER FORTY-FIVE

In this chapter is set forth the deeds of Cyrus as the instrument in the initial ushering in of the salvation promised to Israel, assurance of this being set forth in the fact that, beside the northern world-power directly ruled by Cyrus, even the southern world-power, Egypt, with the lands of its dominion, shall join itself to the people of Jehovah, as a result of which Israel shall at last and definitely abjure its idols.

The "coming over unto Israel" (verse 14) of Egypt, Ethiopia and Sabea Fausset says "mainly and fully describes the gathering in of the Gentiles unto Israel, especially at Israel's future restoration."

CHAPTER FORTY-SIX

In this chapter Israel is exhorted to remember the power of Jehovah and the impotence of idols that are carried by beasts of burden into captivity.

CHAPTER FORTY-SEVEN

This chapter is occupied wholly with the downfall of Babylon. It exposes the reasons for this judgment which came upon them and sets forth the uselessness of all the means employed to rescue the nation thus sentenced by the decree of Jehovah.

CHAPTER FORTY-EIGHT

In this chapter the prophet points Israel to the fulfillment of the old prophecies in order to move them to faith in the new, after which the chief content of the new prophecy is repeated, promising again the restoration of Jehovah's people and reminding them of the promise.

The evident reference to redemption from the bondage of Egypt found in verse 21 leads Fausset to say that the blending of this deliverance with that from Babylon shows that the language cannot be wholly and exclusively referred to either one of them, but that it points mainly to the mystical deliverance of man under the Messiah and ultimately and literally to the final restoration of the now dispersed Israelites.

CHAPTER FORTY-NINE

In this chapter is found the self-attestation of the Holy One, Israel's Redeemer, the Messiah, as to His person and work, the latter half of the chapter showing how desolated Israel is to be built anew from the Gentiles.

6 Yea, he saith, It is too light a thing that thou shouldst be my servant to raise up the tribes of Jacob, and to restore the preserved of Israel: I will also give thee for a light to the Gentiles, ¹that thou mayest be my salvation unto the end of the earth.

¹Or, *that my salvation may be*

Ver. 6. THE RESTORATION OF ISRAEL AND THE CALLING OF THE GENTILES.

Nagelsbach says, "The expression, 'raise up the tribes of Jacob' says more than one at first sight supposes. For it implies that the nation shall be restored according to its original distribution into twelve tribes."

"*the preserved of Israel*",—This, says Fausset, refers to "the elect remnant according to grace preserved for mercy."

8 Thus saith Jehovah, In an acceptable time have I answered thee, and in a day of salvation have I helped thee; and I will preserve thee, and give thee for a covenant of the people, to ¹raise up the land, to make them inherit the desolate heritages; 9 saying to them that are bound, Go forth; to them that are in darkness, Show yourselves. They shall feed in the ways, and on all bare heights shall be their pasture. 10 They shall not hunger nor thirst; neither shall the ²heat nor sun smite them: for he that hath mercy on them will lead them, even by springs of water will he guide them. 11 And I will make all my mountains a way, and my highways shall be exalted. 12 Lo, these shall come from far; and, lo, these from the north and from the west; and these from the land of Sinim.

¹Or, *establish the earth*

²Or, *mirage*

Vers. 8-12. THE PRESERVATION AND RESTORATION OF ISRAEL.

Ver. 8. In this verse and the first half of the next the address is made by Jehovah to His Chosen One, the Messiah.

"in an acceptable time . . . in a day of salvation",—Christ Himself by taking Isa. 61.1 as a text explains the time of His appearing as *"the acceptable year"*, which must be identical with the *"acceptable time"* of our text. But, says Nagelsbach, "The prophetic gaze, however, 'in the year of salvation' sees comprehensively all those points of time that belong, by way of preparation and development, to this central point of the redemption of Israel. It begins with the deliverance from Babylonian captivity and only ends in the completion of salvation in the world beyond."

"to raise up the land",—The country which has fallen into decay rises again and thus the promised land is restored to Israel.

"inherit the desolate heritages",—"The waste heritages", says Delitzsch, "become anew the property of their former owners."

Says Fausset, "Spiritually, the Gentile world, a moral waste, shall become a garden of the Lord; and literally, Judea, lying waste during Babylonian captivity, shall be possessed again by the Israelites, and Jesus, the anti-type of and bearing the same name as Joshua, will divide the land among its true heirs.

Ver. 9. In the second half of this verse the prophecy depicts the return of the redeemed. Says Rosenmuller, "Israel on its way back to the Holy Land shall not have to turn aside to devious paths in search of necessaries, but shall find them in all places wherever their route lies."

Vers. 10,11. Jehovah will abundantly supply all the wants of Israel on their way to the Holy Land, as He will those of spiritual Israel on their way to heaven, making all the mountains a way for the returning ones, and raising the paths of the desert, as it were, into artificially formed highways.

By Sinim in verse 12 is no doubt meant China.

17 Thy children make haste; thy destroyers and they that made thee waste shall go forth from thee. 18 Lift up thine eyes round about, and behold: all these gather themselves together, and come to thee. As I live, saith Jehovah, thou shalt surely clothe thee with them all as with an ornament, and gird thyself with them, like a bride. 19 For, as for thy waste and thy desolate places, and thy land that hath been destroyed, surely now shalt thou be too strait for the inhabitants, and they that swallowed thee up shall be far away. 20 The children of thy bereavement shall yet say in thine ears, The place is too strait for me; give place to me that I may dwell. 21 Then shalt thou say in thy heart, Who hath [1]begotten me these, seeing I have been bereaved of my children, and am [2]solitary, an exile, and wandering to and fro? and who hath brought up these? Behold, I was left alone; these, where were they? 22 Thus saith the Lord Jehovah, Behold, I will lift up my hand to the nations, and set up my ensign to the peoples; and they shall bring thy sons in their bosom, and thy daughters shall be carried upon their shoulders. 23 And kings shall be thy nursing fathers, and their queens thy nursing mothers: they shall bow down to thee with their faces to the earth, and lick the dust of thy feet; and thou shalt know that I am Jehovah; and they that wait for me shall not be put to shame. 24 Shall the prey be taken from the mighty, or [3]the lawful captives be delivered? 25 But thus saith Jehovah, Even the captives of the mighty shall be taken away, and the prey of the terrible

[1]Or, *borne*
[2]Or, *barren*

[3]Heb. *the captives of the just*

shall be delivered; for I will contend with him that contendeth with thee, and I will save thy children. 26 And I will feed them that oppress thee with their own flesh; and they shall be drunken with their own blood, as with sweet wine: and all flesh shall know that I, Jehovah, am thy God.

Vers. 17-26. DESOLATE ISRAEL BUILT AFRESH FROM THE GENTILES.

Ver. 17. Zion's children come again to build her fallen walls and those who made a desolate ruin of the holy city and land must depart from her midst.

"Thy children make haste",—The reference here, says Fausset, is to "Zion's literal children, who come on in haste to build up again the ruins and the waste places; to this the context refers especially, and only second-arily to her spiritual children by conversion to Christ."

Ver. 20. *"The children of thy bereavement"*,—Here again Fausset says that the context shows that her literal children are literally meant. Morgan thinks that by this expression the lost ten tribes are meant, as do also many other writers. "Only secondarily", says Fausset, "is the accession of spiritual Israel from the Gentiles meant."

Nagelsbach thinks these countless children are those converted to Jehovah from the Gentiles and that the reference is not to the returning Israelites. He contends that if they had been her own children or her children's children she would have recognized them as the children of her own body, and that they are therefore spiritual children of Israel. Delitzsch and most interpreters agree with Fausset in seeing in this the secondary reference of the passage only.

Ver. 22. *"Thy sons"*, says Fausset, "must be distinct from the Gentiles who carry them. The Gentiles shall aid in restoring Israel to her own land (Chap. 60.4 and 66.20), and this verse cannot therefore refer primarily to securing converts from among the Gentiles, but must the rather refer to the literal restoration of Israel."

Campbell Morgan, who contends for the literal restoration of Israel, believes this fact set forth in the verses before us, and he says, "While I am not able positively to deny that we, as a nation, are identical with the lost ten tribes, I am by no means satisfied of it; but I have no quarrel with those who hold that view. At all events God knows where they are; and back to the old land for which He has declared His love, shall come the scattered earthly people—not the two tribes, not Judah alone, but all the Israel of God."

Ver. 23. Instead of the nations, as in the previous verse, we now have their kings and queens who became her protectors and further her growth, which thing became true down through the ages, attended sometimes with good consequences and sometimes with evil.

Ver. 24. *"Shall the prey be taken from the mighty"*,—Israel has long been a prey to mighty Gentile nations, "whose oppression of her", says Fausset, "shall reach its highest point under Antichrist."

"the lawful captives be delivered",—The rendering of our text seems to refer to the Jews as justly consigned because of their sins as captives to the foe. (F.) The word is literally "just" or "righteous."

Hendewerk thinks the reference is to the Jews carried off as captives by the righteous Chaldeans, but this cannot be said of the Chaldeans even as accomplishing the judgment of Jehovah upon the wayward nation. This thought might be gathered from the marginal reading, *"the captives of the just"*, but it certainly cannot be the thought of the passage. The idea of *"just"* and *"righteous"* must be applied to the Israelites. Israel, ready to return home, is said to be righteous however sinful may have been those who were led away into captivity.

The best translation we believe is, *"the captive righteous ones be delivered"*. The rendering of our text gives a very proper idea, as Fausset says, but it is hardly in keeping with the original.

In a secondary sense Satan may be said to be the mighty one, the conqueror of man, upon whom his own sin gives to Satan a lawful claim, which claim is answered by Christ, by reason of which the guilty man goes free.

In verses 25 and 26 is found the answer of Jehovah to the question just propounded.

CHAPTER FIFTY

This chapter shows that the judgment upon Israel was provoked by her own iniquity, but that she was not to be altogether and finally cast off by God. In the first part is shown that their not receiving the Lord when He came to His possession was the cause of their temporary rejection; then in the second is set forth the suffering of the Messiah which He declares Himself willing to undertake; while in the last part of the chapter is shown the possibility of Israel's acceptance once again.

CHAPTER FIFTY-ONE

This chapter is taken up with the promised redemption of Israel, the argument being that the God who has so blessed one individual (verse 2) as to make him a mighty nation, can also increase and bless the small remnant of Israel, both that, as Fausset says, "left in the Babylonian captivity and that left in the present and latter days, the residue. (Chap. 13.8,9.)" In such verses as 11 and 14 many interpreters see the usual two-fold reference of a literal release from the then existing Babylon and anti-typically from the mystical Babylon, the last enemy of Israel and the Church, while of course still others, in keeping with their school of interpretation, spiritualize the meaning into the gathering of the Gentiles, the heathen of the present dispensation, into the Church, the spiritual Israel.

As to verses 17 and 18, Fausset says these cannot apply to the Babylonish captivity, because in that they had some one "to guide her"; they had Ezekiel and Daniel and Ezra and Nehemiah, and they soon awoke out of that sleep. The words apply, he says, to the Jews *now*, and will be still more applicable to them in their coming oppression by the Antichrist. But the premise of this writer's statement hardly warrants his conclusion, though his conclusion in itself may be a sound one. The thought of the passage is that Jerusalem was utterly devoid of any help on the part of her children; the suffering weighed so heavily on all the members of the exiled people, that, as Delitzsch says, "no one felt the joy and strength needful to rise up for her and to lay hold of her hand to guide her or to stay her up." Even the prophet is constrained, humanly speaking, to confess, "How shall I comfort thee?"

CHAPTER FIFTY-TWO

This chapter treats of the restoration of Jerusalem to glory. The first states that Jehovah must do this for the sake of the honor of His name, while the second part describes the accomplishment of the restoration.

CHAPTER FIFTY-THREE

This chapter portrays the humiliation and suffering of the Man of Sorrows, the prophecy regarding whose future no man believed. The first part, with which the last three verses of the preceding chapter should be connected, as presenting the theme of the prophecy, sets forth the lowliness of this Man as the Lamb that bears the sin of the people, while the last part of the chapter treats of His exaltation to glory.

CHAPTER FIFTY-FOUR

In this chapter are set forth the fruit of the Messiah's sufferings in the joyful salvation of Jehovah's people. In the first ten verses is portrayed the wondrous enlargement of Zion by the incorporation of the Gentile world, while in the remaining part the prophet describes the security and blessing of the restored nation.

CHAPTER FIFTY-FIVE

In this chapter the universal invitation to the Gentiles is given. The first part of the chapter designates believing acceptance of the word as the way of appropriating this new salvation, while the latter part speaks of the obstacles and scruples that must be set aside that the rich blessing offered may not be frustrated.

CHAPTER FIFTY-SIX

This chapter devotes itself to describing the preparation needed on the part of those who wish to partake of this new salvation. It consists both of a series of ethical instructions and of consolatory words for the eunuchs and the converts from the heathen to Israel and to Israel's God. Verses 6 and 7 says Campbell Morgan await complete and very literal fulfillment in the age to come, the Millennium age.

CHAPTER FIFTY-SEVEN

The prophet here returns to the time previous to the beginning of redemption, that is, to the time previous to the end of the exile. In the last verses of the preceding chapter he describes the mournful situation obtaining among the leaders of Israel, the watchmen and the shepherds, as well as among the people who lived during the exile, but in this chapter beginning with verse 15 he concludes that the believing remnant will be graciously cared for in spite of the conditions of the unpromising present which his eyes were forced to behold.

In verse 13 Fausset sees another promise of the literal restoration of Israel in coming days to the holy land.

CHAPTER FIFTY-EIGHT

The prophet now shows them how by a sincere repentance they must raise themselves out of the sphere of the flesh into that of the spirit, and contrasts the false worship with the true, setting forth the promises connected with the latter.

CHAPTER FIFTY-NINE

In this chapter the sins which hinder the accomplishment of redemption are still more directly laid bare. The people make their penitential confession by reason of which comes the consequent promise of the Messiah.

15 And Jehovah saw it, and it displeased him that there was no justice. 16 And he saw that there was no man, and wondered that there was [1]no intercessor; therefore his own arm brought salvation unto him; and his righteousness, it upheld him. 17 And he put on righteousness as a [2]breastplate, and [3]a helmet of salvation upon his head; and he put on garments of vengeance for clothing, and was clad with zeal as a mantle. 18 According to their [4]deeds, accordingly he will repay, wrath to his adversaries, recompense to his enemies; to the [5]islands he will repay recompense.

19 So shall they fear the name of Jehovah from the west, and his glory from the rising of the sun; [6]for he will come as [7]a rushing stream, which the breath of Jehovah driveth. 20 And a Redeemer will come to Zion, and unto them that turn from transgression in Jacob, saith Jehovah. 21 And as for me, this is my covenant with them, saith Jehovah: my Spirit that is upon thee, and my words which I have put in thy mouth, shall not depart out of thy mouth, nor out of the mouth of thy seed, nor out of the mouth of thy seed's seed, saith Jehovah, from henceforth and for ever.

[1]Or, *none to interpose.*
[2]Or, *coat of mail*
[3]Or, *salvation for a helmet*
[4]Heb. *recompenses*
[5]Or, *coast-lands*

[6]Or, *when the adversary shall come in like a flood, the Spirit of Jehovah will lift up a standard against him*
[7]Heb. *a stream pent in*

Vers. 15-21. The Promise of Jehovah's Intervention and the Redeemer Out of Zion.

Ver. 15. The prophet has now reached the point where he has to describe the judgment at hand. Jehovah investigates the situation and owns with displeasure that justice and equity has disappeared from the life of His people.

Ver. 16. *"And he saw that there was no man"*,—i. e., no one able to restrain, to remedy this corrupt condition; no man, says Fausset, "to atone by his righteousness for the unrighteousness of the people; no representative man able to retrieve the cause of fallen men."

"no intercessor",—i. e., no one to intervene, as intercessor, between God and the people, this expression corresponding largely in parallel to the one just before it, the former having a meaning analogous to and preparatory for the latter.

Understanding clearly then what was needed Jehovah proceeds to actual intervention, *"his arm"*, a symbol of His omnipotence, affording Him help, and *"His righteousness"* and the righteousness of His cause sustaining Him in His purpose.

Ver. 17.   The armour put on by the avenging Jehovah is now described under figures borrowed from the usages of war.   It is useless to conjecture as to the exact application of each particular part of the uniform. Righteousness, says Clericus, might just as well have been a sword, salvation a shield, vengeance a javelin or spear and zeal a torch with which to fire the hostile camp.   The first piece of armour is better understood as the habergeon or coat-of-mail from which all darts of the enemy rebound, while the helmet of salvation stands as a guarantee of the ultimate object for which He enters into the conflict, i. e., the deliverance and redemption of His people.   His vengeance is compared to the bright-colored military coat worn over the coat-of-mail, and His zeal to the fiery red military mantle.

Ver. 18.   *"to the islands"*,—i. e., representatives of the heathen world.   In this sentence, says Delitzsch, the prophet seems to conceal the special judgment upon Israel under the universal judgment upon all nations.

"This verse", says Fausset, "predicts the judgments at the Lord's second coming which shall precede the final redemption of His people (Chap. 66.13,15,16)."

Ver. 19.   As a result of this judgment, from all quarters of the earth, fear of Jehovah's name and of His glory becomes natural to the world of nations.   The last clause of this verse has been the subject of great controversy, commentators differing more or less as to the meaning of every word, as well as to the meaning of the clause as a whole.   There are two, among the many interpretations, that deserve especial attention:

(1) *"for he* (Jehovah) *shall come as a rushing river, which a strong wind* (Jehovah's own breath or Spirit) *driveth along."* (Lo. Na. Ew. Lut. Ges. Del.)   This is now the almost prevailing view, but in addition to a number of grammatical questions which it raises, it seems incongruous to liken Jehovah to a river which His own breath drives along, and the image of a stream rendered rapid by the wind is most unnatural.

(2) *"when he* (the enemy) *will come as a rushing stream the Spirit of Jehovah shall lift up a standard against him."*   This is the version of the English and the Dutch Bibles.   (V. F. He.)   This rendering is entirely defensible and it is difficult to see where that of our text has made any improvement over it.   It does have this objection to it, namely, that the context does not lead us to expect an allusion to the enemy coming against God but just the reverse; however, this is not a serious objection.   Cocceius has given us a somewhat ingenious interpretation, which Alexander has adopted, in the rendering, *"when He* (Jehovah) *approaches as their enemy, it will be like an overflowing stream, in which his spirit* (Jehovah's) *lifts up the banner of victory"*.

111

Ver. 20. There is of course no logical distinction between *"Zion"* and *"them that turn from transgression in Jacob"*, the apparent distinction being merely a rhetorical one.

Says Delitzsch, who reads *"for* Zion", "In Rom. 11.26 this utterance of God is cited by the apostle as a Scripture proof for the future restoration of all Israel."

Fausset says, "Paul applies this verse to the coming restoration of Israel spiritually."

"will come to Zion",—This is the reading of both the English and the Revised versions, but the particle can hardly be said to denote motion or direction, although it is sometimes used in this sense. It properly denotes, as Alexander says, relation in the widest sense and is commonly equivalent to *"as to"* or *"with respect to"* and the expression therefore seems to indicate that the Redeemer's coming has respect to Zion. The Septuagint version renders it *"for the sake of Zion"*.

Paul in quoting this verse makes it say *"out of Zion"*, supplementing the sense by inspiration from Psa. 14.7. He was and is come to Zion first with redemption, being sprung as a man out of Zion.

Alexander says, "Even Paul's translation, 'out of Zion', although it seems to completely reverse the sense, is not so wholly inconsistent with it as some have maintained; for though the Hebrew word does not mean 'from', it does mean that which may include 'from Zion' in its scope, because it might be by going out of Israel that He was to act as her deliverer, and the apostle might intend by his translation to suggest the idea that Zion's Redeemer was to be also the Redeemer of the Gentiles."

Scofield says, "The time when the Redeemer shall come to Zion is fixed relatively by Rom. 11.23-29 as following the completion of the Gentile Church. That is also the order of the great dispensational passage. (Acts 15.14-17.) In both, the return of the Lord to Zion follows the outcalling of the Church."

CHAPTER SIXTY

The following quotations set forth the method of approach to a passage of this kind by the two prevailing schools of interpretation.

Alexander says, "The chapter refers to spiritual Israel, the Church; though Israel's national pre-eminence was to be discontinued because of her sins the true spiritual Israel was to be ushered into a new and far more glorious experience which the prophet describes as a light rising upon her."

Fausset says, "This chapter is an ode to Zion upon her restoration at the second coming to her true position as mother of the Church from which the Gospel is to be diffused to the whole Gentile world. The first promulgation of the Gospel to the Gentiles beginning at Jerusalem was but an earnest of this."

1 Arise, shine; for thy light is come, and the glory of Jehovah is risen upon thee. 2 For, behold, darkness shall cover the earth, and gross darkness the peoples; but Jehovah will arise upon thee, and his glory shall be seen upon thee. 3 And nations shall come to thy light, and kings to the brightness of thy rising.
4 Lift up thine eyes round about, and

see: they all gather themselves together, they come to thee; thy sons shall come from far, and thy daughters shall be [1]carried in the arms. 5 Then thou shalt see and be radiant, and thy heart shall thrill and be enlarged; because the abundance of the sea shall be turned unto thee, the wealth of the nations shall come unto thee. 6 The multitude of camels shall cover thee, the [2]dromedaries of Midian and Ephah; all they from Sheba shall come; they shall bring gold and frankincense, and shall [3]proclaim the praises of Jehovah. 7 All the flocks of Kedar shall be gathered together unto thee, the rams of Nebaioth shall minister unto thee; they shall come up with acceptance on mine altar; and I will [4]glorify [5]the house of my glory. 8 Who are these that fly as a cloud, and as the doves to their windows? 9 Surely the isles shall wait for me, and the ships of Tarshish first, to bring thy sons from far, their silver and their gold with them, for the name of Jehovah thy God, and for the Holy One of Israel, because he hath [6]glorified thee.

[1]Heb. *nursed upon the side.*
[2]Or, *young camels*
[3]Heb. *bring good tidings of the praises*
[4]Or, *beautify*
[5]Or, *my beautiful house*
[6]Or, *beautified*

Vers. 1-9. THE GATHERING OF THE NATIONS TO JERUSALEM.

Ver. 1. *"Arise"*,—i. e., from the dust where thou hast been sitting as a mourning female captive.

"shine",—Gesenius translates with the margin, *"be enlightened"*, but our text is better, the literal of which is *"be light"*. She is to shine and so give spiritual light to others, but she is not to shine in her own light, but to let herself be enlightened, as the next clause shows.

"the glory of Jehovah",—This is a description of the kind of light that has come. It is the glory of the Lord in person, although there is doubtless an allusion to the Shekinah and the cloudy pillar such as rested above the Ark.

The words of this verse are not those of a prophetic chorus (V.), but of Isaiah speaking in the name of Jehovah.

Ver. 2. It is not that Zion shall be glorious because of the exclusive light she enjoys while other nations are sitting in gross darkness, but because the light which has shone upon her shall be "seen" (seen conspicuously, as the Hebrew word expresses it) by these nations and draw them to her.

Ver. 3. *"thy rising"*,—Literally *"thy sun rising"*, meaning the brightness that has arisen upon her.

Ver. 4. *"they . . . they"*,—Delitzsch makes these pronouns refer to the *"sons"* and *"daughters"* who bring the Gentiles with them, but it seems almost necessary to refer these pronouns to the *"nations"* of the previous verse, while the sons and the daughters are doubtless the Jews brought back or attended by the Gentiles who come to worship Jehovah.

"carried in the arms",—The Hebrew is *"nursed upon the side"*, i. e., carried, with an allusion to the oriental custom of carrying the child on the side astride the hip.

Alexander of course says this has reference only to the enlargement of the Church and has nothing to do with a return to Palestine after captivity or a future restoration of Israel. Others maintain that all three thoughts are contained in the expression. (F. Na. He. Lo. Del.)

Ver. 5. *"see"*,—About sixty manuscripts read *"fear"* (V. Um. Lo. Do. Jus. Ges. Mic.), meaning the painful sensation which often attends joy, and which is expressed in the next clause. Vitringa says "see" is a vain repetition of the preceding verse, while Knobel says to express "fear" twice in this verse is inexcusable tautology. The words in Hebrew are very alike, just a slight difference in the pointing. On the whole, *"see"* is to be preferred. (F. Na. Ew. He. Kn. Ma. Hit. Cle. Ros. Lut. Kim. Jer. Tar. Syr. Sept.) The idea then is the seeing of the bringing back of her sons and daughters.

"be radiant",—The word means "to brighten up" (for joy) as in Psa. 34.6.

"thy heart shall thrill",—i. e., tremble, because of the overpowering impression made by this complete change. (F. Al. Na. Ho. Del.) Henderson thinks it was because she had apprehension that she would not have room enough for all who were coming.

"and be enlarged",—i. e., dilate, swell, throb with joy.

"abundance of the sea",—i. e., the wealth, the costly things belonging to the islands and coast-lands. The Gentiles are to devote themselves and their possessions to the service of Jehovah.

Ver. 6. So many of the merchandise-bearing animals, the ships of the desert, shall come that they will *"cover"* her, i. e. the country will swarm with them.

Ver. 7. By a bold figure the rams are represented as offering themselves acceptably. The word rendered *"with acceptance"* signifies rather "with pleasure, delight" or "good-will" (V. F. He. Hit. Del.), "it being a general notion", says Lowth, "that prevailed with sacrificers among the heathen that the victims being brought without reluctance to the altar was a good omen; and the contrary a bad one."

"the house of my glory",—The temple was built for His glory, and now He will make its internal glory like its external glory by adorning it with the gifts brought in homage by the world of converted Gentiles.

Fausset says of the house of Jehovah's glory, "See the temple of Ezek. 41." Delitzsch says, "None of the prophets of the Old Testament is able to think of the worship of Jehovah by the Israel of the latter days without the offering of sacrifices; but it would be a return to the limited conceptions of the Old Testament if one were to conclude that animal sacrifice will ever be restored. The dividing-wall of national particularism and ceremonial observances forming shadows of things to come will never be re-established; and with the cessation of sacrificial worship since the fiery judgment fell upon the second temple, there has forever passed away the restriction of worship to any one central spot on earth (John 4.21)."

Says Donald Moore, "The picture drawn in this section perplexes those who understand it of the literal restoration of the Jews and of the future glory of the earthly Jerusalem. Hess, Baumgarten and others argue from verse 7 for the restoration of animal sacrifices. But Delitzsch justly rejects this notion as being utterly inconsistent with and contrary to the Christian system. But if the victims and the altar here spoken of are not to be taken literally, why should we look for a material temple or construe literally the other traits of the picture? The whole description represents not the material Jerusalem, but the Church of God under images, which, to be consistently interpreted, cannot be taken in a gross, literal sense."

Says Alexander, "Grotius supposes this prediction to have been literally verified in Herod's temple. Gesenius and other Germans easily dispose of it as a fanatical anticipation. It is much more embarrassing to those who make the passage a prediction of the future restoration of the Jews and the future splendor of the literal Jerusalem. Some of the most intrepid writers of this class consistently apply their fundamental principle of literal interpretation and believe that the Mosaic ritual or something like it is to be restored. But such interpreters as J. D. Michaelis and Henderson, who cannot go this length, are obliged to own that spiritual services are here represented under forms and titles borrowed from the old dispensation."

Ver. 8. Said perhaps, says Vitringa, with reference to the ships sailing in from the sea in cloud-like form with spread sails.

Ver. 9. *"the isles shall wait for me"*,—This is meant to be understood in the same way as in Chap. 51.5, and like the "expectant waiting" of the isles in Chap. 42.4, the word containing a firm expectation of something to be experienced.

"their",—This is by some referred to *"isles"* (F. Del.), but we prefer with our text, to connect it with *"sons"* as the nearer and more natural antecedent. (Al. Na.)

"the ships of Tarshish first",—The ships that trade to the most distant region shall be among the very foremost to bring back the sons of Israel.

10 And foreigners shall build up thy walls, and their kings shall minister unto thee: for in my wrath I smote thee, but in my favor have I had mercy on thee. 11 Thy gates also shall be open continually; they shall not be shut day nor night; that men may bring unto thee the wealth of the nations, and their kings led captive. 12 For that nation and kingdom that will not serve thee shall perish; yea, those nations shall be utterly wasted. 13 The glory of Lebanon shall come unto thee, the fir-tree, the pine, and the box-tree together, to beautify the place of my sanctuary; and I will make the place of my feet glorious. 14 And the sons of them that afflicted thee shall come bending unto thee; and all they that despised thee shall bow themselves down at the soles of thy feet; and they shall call thee The city of Jehovah, The Zion of the Holy One of Israel. 15 Whereas thou hast been forsaken and hated, so that no man passed through thee, I will make thee an eternal excellency, a joy of many generations. 16 Thou shalt also suck the milk of the nations, and shalt suck the breast of kings; and thou shalt know that I, Jehovah, am thy Saviour, and thy Redeemer, the Mighty One of Jacob.

Vers. 10-16. THE RESTORATION OF JERUSALEM TO GLORY.

Ver. 10. Delitzsch says on the first half of this verse, "The walls of Zion rise out of their ruins—foreigners, quite overcome through the interposition of Jehovah, rendering personal service in the work, while foreign kings are ready to help Zion; of this assistance the arrangements made through the decrees of Cyrus, Darius, and Artaxerxes Longimanus were but a prelude to what continued pointing to the latter days, though, *in the view of the prophet, the time after the exile is itself the time of the end.*"

Ver. 11. *"kings led captive"*,—Not so much "pompously attended" (Lo.), nor "escorted" (V. Ros. Kim. Ges.), but the word means *"conducted"*, i. e., *"led as captive"*, not, however, in the sense that their own people disgusted with their rule deliver them up (Hit.), but as Delitzsch says, "led by the Church which irresistibly enchains them, i. e., conquers their hearts so that they let themselves be brought as God's captives in triumphal procession to the Holy City."

Ver. 12.   A reason primarily for the promise of increase to Jehovah's people and secondarily for the Gentile kings submitting themselves to them in service.

Donald Moore says, "They who consider the literal Jerusalem to be the subject of this prophecy, and not the Church of God, may well ask themselves if literal destruction will really be the punishment of every nation and kingdom that will not serve the Jews.   But it is not they that are born of the flesh who are the heirs of this promise, but they who are Christ's, and so the true seed of Abraham, the Israel of God.   The Gentile Christians are not doomed to bondage."

Ver. 13.   *"The glory of Lebanon"*,—i. e., of her trees, her cedars and her luxuriant vegetation.

"to beautify the place of my sanctuary",—Many think the adornment is that of the buildings by the choicest kinds of timber, but others take it quite properly as the adornment of the grounds by living trees, this being more in keeping with the poetical tone of the context and more pleasing in itself.   (Na. Al. Kn. Ew. Hit. Del.)   The place of His sanctuary is of course Jerusalem.

"I will make the place of my feet glorious",—i. e., the place where I habitually stand and walk (Ma.), the place where He dwells in the midst of His people forever.

Says Nagelsbach, "Though He has no temple of stone there, He has still the place of His glorious presence, the place where His feet rest."   But, says Donald Moore, "If notwithstanding the words of Isaiah about the temple and the sacrifices (Chap. 2.2,3 and verse 7 of this chapter), we are justified in holding, as Nagelsbach does, that there will be in the Holy City of God no external temple and no animal sacrifices, may we not go further and seek a spiritual sense for the description of the future outward glory of Jerusalem contained in this chapter?"

Ver. 16.   This is not enrichment by plunder (Hit.), as of a vampire sucking a child, but a statement that Zion shall draw unto herself and enjoy all that is valuable of the possessions of the Gentiles.

17 For brass I will bring gold, and for iron I will bring silver, and for wood brass, and for stones iron.   I will also make thy officers peace, and [1]thine exactors righteousness.   18 Violence shall no more be heard in thy land, desolation nor destruction within thy borders; but thou shalt call thy walls Salvation, and thy gates Praise.   19 The sun shall be no more thy light by day; neither for brightness shall the moon give light unto thee: but Jehovah will be unto thee an everlasting light, and thy God thy [2]glory.   20 Thy sun shall no more go down. neither shall thy moon withdraw itself; for Jehovah will be thine everlasting light, and the days of thy mourning shall be ended.   21 Thy people also shall be all righteous; they shall inherit the land for ever, the branch of my planting, the work of my hands, that I may be glorified.   22 The little one shall become a thousand, and the small one a strong nation: I, Jehovah will hasten it in its time.

[1]Or, *thy taskmasters*

[2]Or, *beauty*

Vers. 17-22. THE NEW LIFE OF JERUSALEM TO BE ENJOYED BY THE
RESTORED.

Ver. 17. Some take the words *"peace"* and *"righteousness"* as predicates (F.), meaning that all her rulers shall be, as it were, peace and righteousness itself, but the majority (S. Na. Um. Del. Ges.) take it in the
sense that peace and righteousness shall rule. This is preferable. The
rulers may be peaceful and righteous but the city may be still disturbed
by unrighteousness, but when the government itself is peace and righteousness then all will be well. The word *"exactors"*, i. e., of tribute, is not
to be taken in an evil sense.

Ver. 18. *"thou shalt call thy walls Salvation and thy gates Praise"*,
—Delitzsch has put it well, "She has walls but in reality 'Salvation', the
salvation of her God is to her an impregnable fortification: she has gates,
but in reality all gates are rendered needless by her praise, the fame that
brings fear and reverence, with which Jehovah has invested her."

Ver. 19. Among the various comments on the meaning of this
verse the following are worthy of notice;

Alexander,—"All natural sources of illumination shall be swallowed
up in the clear manifestation of the presence, power and will of God."

Henderson,—"The superlative degree of happiness which shall be
enjoyed by the new and holy Jerusalem church, expressed in language of
the most sublime imagery."

Others make it a figurative promise of prosperity of which light is
the natural and common emblem, while still others make it God's residence
among His people clothed in such transcendent brightness as to make the
light of the sun and the moon useless.

Ver. 20. *"the days of thy mourning shall be ended"*,—There shall
be no national spiritual obscuration as in other days.

Ver. 21. *"the land"*,—Although the majority so translate (F. Na.
Del.) as a more literal and exact rendering, it must not be overlooked that
Scripture has attached to this prophetic formula a much higher meaning,
namely, the earth, the possession of the land being just such a type or
symbol of the broader, higher meaning.

Ver. 22. This verse on its face is simply a description of increase.
Vitringa and Alexander apply it to Israel itself. Gesenius and Delitzsch
say it means one without a family or a small family. Nagelsbach refers
it to the physically most insignificant, while Kimchi and Rosenmuller apply
it to number and not to size.

"it",—The reference is to this particular prophecy from verse 1 on
(Del.), and not to the whole preceding series of prophecies. (Kn. Al.)

"in its time",—i. e., the time which Jehovah hath appointed. The
word is not *"his"*, as in the Authorized version, but *"its"*, and so does not
refer to Jehovah, but modifies grammatically *"time"*, although the meaning
is as already shown one and the same thing.

CHAPTER SIXTY-ONE

1 The Spirit of the Lord Jehovah is upon me; because Jehovah hath anointed me to preach good tidings unto the ¹meek; he hath sent me to bind up the broken-hearted, to proclaim liberty to the captives, and ²the opening *of the prison* to them that are bound; 2 to proclaim the year of Jehovah's favor, and the day of vengeance of our God; to comfort all that mourn; 3 to appoint unto them that mourn in Zion to give unto them a garland for ashes, the oil of joy for mourning, the garment of praise for the spirit of heaviness; that they may be called trees of righteousness, the planting of Jehovah, that he may be glorified.

4 And they shall build the old wastes, they shall raise up the former desolations, and they shall repair the waste cities, the desolations of many generations. 5 And strangers shall stand and feed your flocks, and foreigners shall be your plowmen and your vinedressers. 6 But ye shall be named the priests of Jehovah; men shall call you ministers of our God; ye shall eat the wealth of the nations, and ³in their glory shall ye

¹Or, *poor*
²Or, *opening* of the eyes
³Or, *to their glory shall ye succeed*

boast yourselves. 7 Instead of your shame *ye shall have* double; and instead of dishonor they shall rejoice in their portion: therefore in their land they shall possess double; everlasting joy shall be unto them. 8 For I, Jehovah, love justice, I hate robbery ⁴with iniquity; and I will give them their recompense in truth, and I will make an everlasting covenant with them. 9 And their seed shall be known among the nations, and their offspring among the peoples; all that see them shall acknowledge them, that they are the seed which Jehovah hath blessed.

10 I will greatly rejoice in Jehovah, my soul shall be joyful in my God; for he hath clothed me with the garments of salvation, he hath covered me with the robe of righteousness, as a bridegroom ⁵decketh himself with a garland, and as a bride adorneth herself with her jewels.

11 For as the earth bringeth forth its bud, and as the garden causeth the things that are sown in it to spring forth; so the Lord Jehovah will cause righteousness and praise to spring forth before all the nations.

⁴Or, *for* (or, *with*) *a burnt-offering*
⁵Heb. *decketh himself as a priest*

Vers. 1-11.   THE GLORY OF THE OFFICE OF MESSIAH, THE SERVANT OF JEHOVAH.

The speaker in this chapter is the Messiah, the Servant of Jehovah. (F. V. Na. Or. Al. Dri. Del. Che.)

The Lord's use of this passage in His own time does not necessarily prove Him to be the speaker here (V.). There are, however, two parallel passages (Chap. 42.1-7 and 49.1-9) and all agree that the same speaker is here brought forward, and if therefore it is conceded that in these two passages just mentioned the speaker is the Messiah it is difficult to avoid the same conclusion in the passage before us. Gesenius, Umbreit and most modern expositors make the speaker to be the prophet himself, but this cannot only be allowed in a subordinate sense.

Ver. 1.   *"to proclaim liberty to the captives"*,—Said with manifest reference to the year of Jubilee (Lev. 25.10; Jer. 34.8,9), a year of general release from debts and obligations of all bondmen and bondwomen. The language may also be drawn from the deliverance of the Babylonish captivity. It is a figurative description, of course, of the deliverance from sin and death.

"opening of the prison",—The Hebrew is rather *"the most complete opening"*. The word is nowhere used of the opening of a room, but always of the opening of the eyes and because of the rest of the sentence we are here led to think of the eyes being opened as in contrast to the

gloomy darkness of the prison. It is a figurative expression, of course, prison being represented poetically as a state of darkness and deliverance from it as a restoration to light, just as proclaiming liberty refers to the deliverance from the bondage of sin.

Ver. 2. *"the year of Jehovah's favor"*,—The word *"year"* is used as a poetical equivalent to "day" and was suggested perhaps by the previous reference to the year of Jubilee. A year is assigned to grace but a day to vengeance. "Wrath is short, but grace is long."

Scofield says, "Observe that Jesus suspended the reading of this passage in the synagogue at the comma in the middle of the verse. The first advent, therefore, opened the day of *grace*, 'the acceptable year of Jehovah', but does not fulfill the day of *vengeance*. That will be taken up when Messiah returns. The vengeance precedes the regathering of Israel, and synchronizes with the day of the Lord."

"them that mourn",—The main reference is to Zion's mourners who are deeply affected by the desolations that have come to their city.

Ver. 3. *"a garland for ashes"*,—i. e., a crown, a tiara, worn in times of joy instead of a head-dress of ashes cast on the head in mourning.

"oil of joy",—Perfumed oil was poured on the heads of guests at joyous occasions.

"garment of praise",—i. e., bright-colored garments indicative of thankfulness.

"trees of righteousness",—Terebinth trees, symbolic of men strong in righteousness instead of being bowed down as a reed with sin and calamity.

Ver. 4. *"build the old wastes"*,—Delitzsch says these are not to be confined merely to what was lying waste during the exile, but that now the country is to be so densely populated that the former dwelling places will not be sufficient; hence what is meant are localities lying waste and situated beyond the limits of the Holy Land until now.

Henderson says, "This verse admits of no consistent interpretation except on the principle that the Jews are to be returned again to the land of their fathers; the desolations are those of cities that had once been inhabited and cannot without the utmost violence be applied to the heathen world."

Ver. 5. *"And strangers shall stand"*,—They shall stand, i. e., at their post, ready to offer their service.

Ver. 6. Your exclusive business will be the service of God, while others attend to your flocks and fields. (F. Na. Aba.)

"The Jews appear here as the priestly nobility and the Gentiles as those having to perform the hard work. But says the translator of Nagelsbach, "The conversion of Israel, instead of reducing the Gentiles to the position of menials, will conduce exceedingly to their riches, Rom. 11.12. The prophet is speaking here not of Israel after the flesh, but of the Israel of God, and does not here contradict what he elsewhere says about the equal privileges of converted Gentiles. (Chap. 19.24,25; 66.21.) Even in connection with the new heavens and the new earth our prophet speaks of the people, the inhabitants of Jerusalem *themselves* planting vineyards and eating their fruit (Chap. 65.17-23) and so not confining themselves to the exercise of priestly functions. Literally understood, these places are mutually exclusive and contradictory. They must be taken figuratively."

"and in their glory shall ye boast yourselves",—Some have thought that the idea is that of the dispossession of the Gentiles by the Jews of their wealth. But this does not necessarily inhere in the language even though the reading of our text be approved. The word rendered *"boast"* really means *"to push upward"*, to raise one's self up proudly (Del. Tar. Sep.), and may be taken as meaning that they shall become sharers in the glory and wealth of the Gentiles who have turned unto Jehovah.

Others again make the literal translation of the word to mean, "ye shall substitute yourselves," i. e., in their place. Alexander has said that all the latest writers, not excepting Gesenius, have gone back to Jarchi's explanation of the words as denoting "mutual exchange or substitution", thus making this verse and the previous one describe not exaltation on the part of the Jews and subjection on the part of the Gentile converts, but mutual exchange and intimate association. He says that context, etymology, and usage all favor this view, and consequently the true idea is that while the Jews shall be priests the Gentiles shall be their purveyors, the Jews supplying the spiritual wants of the Gentiles and the latter supplying the temporal wants of the Jews. (See Rom. 15.27.)

Ver. 7. *"Instead of your shame ye shall have double"*,—Double as much reward as your past share. (F. Al. Tar. Gès. Jar.) Twice as much reward as before they had shame. (He. Na.) Double possession in the land, which has been enlarged beyond the bounds of former occupation, as seen by the last half of the verse. (Del.)

The first explanation is much to be preferred.

"in their land they shall possess double",—Nagelsbach thinks the reference is not to an enlarged land and an enlarged inheritance of the individual in it, but that there is added to their own honor and their own possessions the wealth and possessions of the Gentiles.

Fausset says the expression marks the reference as being to literal Israel and not to the Church at large.

Ver. 8. *"I, Jehovah, love justice"*,—i. e., the justice which requires of me that I should restore my people and give them double in compensation for their former shame and suffering.

"I hate robbery with iniquity",—There seems to be a little redundancy here, as Jerome says, all robbery being iniquitous; but there are a multitude of places where such redundancy of expression occurs. The reference is to such robbery as was perpetrated on Israel. Delitzsch thinks it refers to the injustice formerly rampant in Israel, but his reasons are hardly sufficient.

Ver. 9. *"known"*,—i. e., known honorably.

Alexander here maintains that the Jews are represented as scattered among the Gentile nations instead of being gatherd out of them into their own land, because otherwise how could they be thus known.

Ver. 10. Zion gives thanks for God's returning favor.

Some (Al. Na. Del.) say the speaker here is still the Messiah, the Servant of Jehovah.

"decketh himself with a garland",—"Maketh himself a priestly head-dress (F.); "weareth the turban like a priest" (Del.), i. e., winds it around his head after the manner of a priest, the reference being to the tall mitre of the ordinary priest, and appropriate to the "kingdom of priests" dedicated to the offering of spiritual sacrifices to God continually.

Ver. 11. By *"bud"* is meant the tender shoot, by *"righteousness"*, moral excellence in particular, and by *"praise,"* the manifestation of excellence in general.

CHAPTER SIXTY-TWO

1 For Zion's sake will I not hold my peace, and for Jerusalem's sake I will not rest, until her righteousness go forth as brightness, and her salvation as a lamp that burneth. 2 And the nations shall see thy righteousness, and all kings thy glory; and thou shalt be called by a new name, which the mouth of Jehovah shall name. 3 Thou shalt also be a crown of beauty in the hand of Jehovah, and a royal diadem in the hand of thy God. 4 Thou shalt no more be termed Forsaken; neither shall thy land any more be termed Desolate: but thou shalt be called ¹Hephzi-bah, and thy land ²Beulah: for Jehovah delighteth in thee, and thy land shall be married. 5 For as a young man marrieth a virgin, so shall thy sons marry thee; and ³as the bridegroom rejoiceth over the bride, so shall thy God rejoice over thee.

6 I have set watchmen upon thy walls, O Jerusalem: they shall never hold their peace day nor night: ye that are Jehovah's remembrancers, ⁴take ye no rest, 7 and give him no ⁵rest, till he establish, and till he·make Jerusalem a praise in the earth. 8 Jehovah hath sworn by his right hand, and by the arm of his strength, Surely I will no more give thy grain to be food for thine enemies; and foreigners shall not drink thy new wine for which thou hast labored: 9 but they that have garnered it shall eat it, and praise Jehovah; and they that have gathered it shall drink it in the courts of my sanctuary.

10 Go through, go through the gates; prepare ye the way of the people; cast up, cast up the highway; gather out the stones; lift up an ensign ⁶for the peoples. 11 Behold, Jehovah hath proclaimed unto the end of the earth, Say ye to the daughter of Zion, Behold, thy salvation cometh; behold, his reward is with him, and his ⁷recompense before him. 12 And they shall call them The holy people, The redeemed of Jehovah; and thou shalt be called Sought out, A city not forsaken.

¹That is, *My delight is in her*
²That is, *Married*
³Heb. *with the joy of the bridegroom*
⁴Or, *keep not silence*
⁵Or, *silence*
⁶Or, *over*
⁷Or, *work*

Vers. 1-12. THE FURTHER DEVELOPMENT OF THE GLORY OF JERUSALEM.

Bredenkamp and most later interpreters think it is the prophet himself who is here speaking. Many others (S. Na. He. Al. Coc.) make the Messiah still the speaker. Delitzsch thinks it is Jehovah Himself, as shown by the first part of verse 6 and also by the expression employed. We see no reason for any change of speaker from the one who is represented as uttering the words of the former chapter, and if an exclusive subject must be chosen it is without doubt the Messiah.

Ver. 1. *"I will not rest"*,—This with the previous expression, *"I will not hold my peace"*, refers then not to the further predicting of Zion's glory, but to prayer on Zion's behalf, as most take it. Messiah is represented as unfainting in His efforts on behalf of His people.

"her righteousness—her salvation",—The same as in Chap. 61.10 and elsewhere.

Ver. 2.   *"thou shalt be called by a new name",*—i. e., as expressive of her new condition and character.

Ver. 3.   *"in the hand of Jehovah",*—i. e., that He might hold it fast and keep it safe (V.), that He might admire it (Ew. Bre.), that He might exhibit it (Coc.), that He might crown Himself with it (Pis.), that it might be at His disposal for bestowment (Mic.).   Gesenius says the hand of Jehovah is figurative for His power or protection, and this is perhaps the best solution to the problem, and therefore the first explanation made is to be preferred.

Ver. 4.   It would be better to retain all four words in the Hebrew, Azubah, Shemamah, Hephzibah and Beulah, or to put in the text their meaning in all four cases.
"thy land shall be married",—i. e., to Jehovah, implying His protection as well as His ownership.

Ver. 5.   *"so shall thy sons marry thee",*—There is here a seeming incongruity of sons marrying their mother.
Alexander says the word rendered *"marry"* means as well *"to inhabit"* and that it is used in this sense here and so the difficulty is avoided. Fausset following Lowth changes the points, which are of no authority in Hebrew and reads *"thy builder"* and refers the expression to Jehovah, in keeping with what has gone before and with the close of this verse.

Gesenius objects to this by calling attention to the fact that the word is plural and cannot therefore refer to God.   But this is not an objection, as seen by a comparison of Gen. 20.13; 35.7; II Sam. 7.23 whereas the plural form *"builders"* may ·be used here of Jehovah in reference, as husbands.   The real objection to the change is that it is not necessary.   The word, which in itself expresses only *"taking possession of"* may be used here as Alexander would have us believe, or we may think, as Delitzsch does of Israel and the homeland being blended and intertwined in the personification here employed.   Viewed in her relation to Jehovah she has Him for her Lord and Husband; viewed in her relation to her homeland she is the totality of those who are its possessors, and who call the land their own, as it were by the right of marriage.

Ver. 6.   *"watchmen",*—The reference is not to ''intercessory angels'' (Ew. Hah. Che.), nor to pious Israelites, who among the ruins of the walls await the return of the exiles (Ges.), because the appointment of such watchmen presupposes the existence of such walls and the restoration of the city, and if the watchers are upon the walls formerly destroyed but now rebuilt, then it must be a post-exilic picture to which our attention is being called.

Fausset says it is an image of the watchers set upon a city wall to look out for the approach of a messenger of good tidings, the good tidings in this case being the return of the exiles from Babylon, prefiguring the return of the Jews from their present time dispersion throughout the world.

The watchers are not necessarily there to give notice of the approach of enemies, as Nagelsbach says, thus showing that even then there will be enemies of Jerusalem, even though it be such a time as has been described; but the rather, as Delitzsch says, to lift up their entreating cry to Jehovah for the holy city entrusted to their care, the watchmen being the same as the *"remembrancers"* mentioned in the latter part of the verse. The post-exilian Jerusalem, says Delitzsch, is one with the Jerusalem of the last days in the eyes of the prophet.

The speaker is still here to be considered as Messiah (Na.) although Delitzsch insists that Jehovah is still speaking, while in the latter part of the verse this writer thinks the prophet is introduced in an address to "Jehovah's remembrancers". Others (F. Ges.) think the speaker is the prophet, even in the beginning of the verse, speaking in the name of the Messiah.

Ver. 8. These words come not so much as an answer to the prayer of the remembrancers (Na.) as an assurance to inspire them with confidence in prayer.

Ver. 9. *"In the courts of my sanctuary"*,—This is not to be construed that the harvest produce will be consumed only in this place, but that its enjoyment will be consecrated through a festal meal of a religious character.

Ver. 10. What has been solemnly promised in the two preceding verses is now to be fulfilled. Here at least we may concede that the speaker is the prophet speaking in the name of Jehovah.

Alexander thinks that the analogy of Chap. 57.14, together with the context here makes it probable that what is here described is "the entrance of the Gentiles into Zion, an event so frequently and so fully set forth in the preceding chapters."

Gesenius, followed by Delitzsch, thinks the address is to the exiled Jews in Babylon and other cities to go through the gates of these cities, to march out of Babylon upon their return from exile.

Henderson, Fausset, Rosenmuller and others think the address is to the Gentile nations to go through the gates of their own cities, in order to remove all obstacles out of the way of the returning Israelites.

The second explanation is perhaps more nearly correct, although there is little ground on which to rest the decision one way or the other. We are rather inclined to the idea of Nagelsbach, who thinks the address, while primarily to the Jews, includes the Gentiles also. They are all to pass through the gates and to prepare the way by the removal of obstacles and to assist in making the return home practicable, easy and glorious. The expressions that follow are rhetorical and not to be literally understood of course.

"lift up an ensign for the peoples",—Since the people are scattered much, not all being in one city, the command goes forth to lift up a standard *"high over"* (Al. Lut. Del.), not *"to"* (Vul. Sep.), or hardly *"for"* (our text, Mic.), the people so that the scattered ones in all places may see and come and join the outgoing procession back to the holy land.

Ver. 11. *"unto the end of the earth"*,—This shows that reference is not being made merely to a proclamation published in the realm of Cyrus, but to the very ends of the earth, wherever the scattered ones of

Israel are to be found—there it is to be told to the daughter of Zion that her salvation is coming.

"Say ye", etc.,—Those who are commanded to say this are not merely the prophets in Israel, but all the mourners in Zion wherever they may be. According to analogy of Chap. 40.10 the reference in the pronoun *"his"* in both cases is to Jehovah.

Ver. 12. *"And they shall call", etc.,*—The verb is indefinite and the expression means *"men shall call", etc.*

"Sought out",—The city will be sought after and loved by all and especially by Jehovah. The expression answers to *"not forsaken"* in the parallel clause. Jerusalem shall be no longer abandoned but highly prized and loved.

CHAPTER SIXTY-THREE

1 Who is this that cometh from Edom, with [1]dyed garments from Bozrah? this that is glorious in his apparel, marching in the greatness of his strength? I that speak in righteousness, mighty to save.

2 Wherefore art thou red in thine apparel, and thy garments like him that treadeth in the winevat?

3 I have trodden the winepress alone; and of the peoples there was no man with me; yea, I [2]trod them in mine anger, and trampled them in my wrath; and their [3]life-blood [4]is sprinkled upon my garments, and I [5]have stained all my raiment.

4 For the day of veangeance [6]was in my heart, and [7]the year of my redeemed is come.

5 And I looked, and there was none to help; and I wondered that there was none to uphold; therefore mine own arm brought salvation unto me; and my wrath, it upheld me.

6 And I [8]trod down the peoples in mine anger, and [9]made them drunk in my wrath, and I [10]poured out their lifeblood on the earth.

[1]Or, *crimsoned*
[2]Or, *will tread . . and trample*
[3]Or, *strength*
[4]Or, *shall be*
[5]Or, *will stain*
[6]Or, *is*
[7]Or, *my year of redemption*
[8]Or, *I will tread . . . and make . . . and will pour out*
[9]Another reading is, *brake them in pieces.*
[10]Or, *brought down their strength to the earth.*

Vers. 1-6. THE DAY OF VENGEANCE.

Ver. 1. The question here is to be put in the mouth of the prophet himself. The question is rhetorical, as the prophet well knows who it is, but the question is put to awaken our attention and direct it to the One whom the prophet sees coming. Messiah is pictured as approaching Jerusalem after having taken vengeance on the enemies of His people and Himself, and He is represented under imagery taken from the destruction of Edom, the last and most bitter foe of the people of Israel. He comes from Bozrah, the chief city of Edom, with garments *"dyed"* (crimsoned) with the blood of the Edomites.

"marching",—The literal is *"throwing back his head"*, in proud self-consciousness.

The last clause of this verse is Messiah's answer to the question.

"speak in righteousness",—Righteousness is here used adverbially, as frequently, and means to speak strictly according to the standard of truth, and the expression is not therefore with Fausset and others (Ma. Kn. Hit.)

to be rendered *"speak of righteousness,"* i. e., of salvation as the result of His righteousness.

Interpreters are much divided as to the meaning of the passage.

Rosenmuller thinks the restored Jews might be apprehensive of the enmity of certain neighboring nations, who had rejoiced in their calamity, and that the prophecy before us was intended to allay their apprehension.

Henderson thinks the prophet is deducing an argument from Jehovah's past dealings with His ancient people in favor of His graciously regarding them in their then distantly future dispersion, and that therefore no reference is made to any future judgments to be inflicted on the country formerly occupied by the Edomites.

Calvin disputes any reference to the Messiah whatsoever and finds here simply the announcement of a future judgment on Edom. This is practically also the view of Hitzig, Umbreit, Gesenius, Beck and a number of other modern scholars.

The Fathers applied the passage directly to the sufferings and ascension of Christ, and many of them put the question, *"Who is this that cometh,"* etc., in the mouth of angels who guard the gates of heaven.

Vitringa understands by Bozrah the city of Rome and Edom as the countries captured by Rome, and he applies the passage to the overthrow of the Antichrist (Rome) by the warrior who rides on the white horse in Rev. 19.11.

Stier is of the opinion that the one who is seen coming is Christ coming from the fulfillment of what is related in Rev. 14.20 and 19.18,21.

Delitzsch finds the historical fulfillment of the prophecy in what befell Edom at the hands of the Maccabean princes, while its final fulfillment, he thinks, is the destruction of the Antichrist and his hosts, which is the New Testament counterpart to this piece.

There is no doubt whatever but that the prophecy must be taken as a threatening against Edom and that Rosenmuller has the right idea as to the connection with what goes before it. As Delitzch says, "The discourse anticipates the question as to how Israel can rejoice in renewed possession of the land of its inheritance, if, as before, it is still to be surrounded by such malevolent neighbors as the Edomites." As to its typical reference it must be that of the judgment of the end-time upon the Antichrist.

Ver. 2. *"wine-vat"*,—The wine-press wherein grapes were trodden by the feet by reason of which the garments become stained with the juice.

Ver. 3. The reply of the Messiah. He treads the wine-press not as a sufferer, but as an inflicter. Many writers think that John had these words in mind when he wrote Rev. 19.13-15. (F. Na.) The verbs, as usual in animated discourse, are in the past tense.

"and of the peoples there was no man with me",—This indicates the universal antichristian spirit of the nations. The reason of this is that it was the nations themselves that were cut off like grapes and put into the wine-press.

Fausset says, "This final blow inflicted by the Messiah and His armies (Rev. 19.13-15) shall decide His claim to the Kingdom usurped by Satan and by the Beast to whom Satan delegates his power. It will be a day of judgment to the hostile Gentiles just as His first coming was a day of judgment to the unbelieving Jews."

Ver. 4. Since the verbs in verse 3 were rendered in the past tense it would seem best to so render them both here, "*was* in my heart", i. e., in my mind, in my thought, and "*had come*".

As in Chap. 34.8 and Chap. 61.2 the time of vengeance is described as a "*day*" and that of grace and reward to the redeemed as a "*year*."

Ver. 5. These are the same words as found in Chap. 59.16, except there the word "*righteousness*" is found instead of "*wrath*", the latter being an equivalent for the former, His wrath being but the executioner and agent of His righteousness and justice.

Says Nagelsbach, "It will happen again as it did in the days of Edom; the Lord will see none of the peoples of the world on His side."

7 I will make mention of the loving-kindnesses of Jehovah, *and* the praises of Jehovah, according to all that Jehov. h hath bestowed on us, and the great goodness toward the house of Israel, which he hath bestowed on them according to his mercies, and according to the multitude of his lovingkindnesses. 8 For he said, Surely they are my people, children that will not deal falsely: so he was their Saviour. 9 [1]In all their affliction he was afflicted, and the angel of his presence saved them: in his love and in his pity he redeemed them; and he bare them, and carried them all the days of old.

10 But they rebelled and grieved his holy Spirit: therefore he was turned to be their enemy, *and himself* fought against them. 11 [2]Then he remembered the days of old, Moses *and* his people, *saying,* Where is he that brought them up out of the sea with the [3]shepherds of his flock? where is he that put his holy Spirit in the midst of them? 12 that caused his glorious arm to go at the right hand of Moses? that divided the waters before them, to make himself an everlasting name? 13 that led them through the depths, as a horse in the wilderness, so that they stumbled not? 14 As the cattle that go down into the valley, the •Spirit of Jehovah caused them to rest: so didst thou lead thy people, to make thyself a glorious name.

15 Look down from heaven, and behold from the habitation of thy holiness and of thy glory: where are thy zeal and thy mighty acts, the yearning of thy heart and thy compassions are restrained toward me. 16 For thou art our Father, though Abraham knoweth us not, and Israel doth not acknowledge us: thou, O Jehovah, art our Father; our Redeemer from everlasting is thy name. 17 O Jehovah, why dost thou make us to err from thy ways, and hardenest our heart from thy fear? Return for thy servants' sake, the tribes of thine inheritance. 18 Thy holy people possessed *it* but a little while: our adversaries have trodden down thy sanctuary. 19 We are become as they over whom thou never barest rule, as they that were not called by thy name.

[1]Another reading is, *In all their adversity he was no adversary*
[2]Or, *Then his people remembered the ancient days of Moses &c.*
[3]Another reading is, *shepherd*.

Vers. 7-19. THANKSGIVING, CONFESSION AND SUPPLICATION OF JEHOVAH'S PEOPLE.

Ver. 7. The speaker here is the prophet speaking in the name of Jehovah's people. Favor in the past becomes the foundation of supplication for the future. The plurals, says Fausset, and the repetitions imply that language is inadequate to express all the goodness of God.

"The passage must be understood", says Alexander, "as relating to the favors experienced and the sins committed by the chosen people throughout the period of the old dispensation."

The prevailing opinion is that we have here a prophecy relating to the future restoration of Israel. (V. F.)

Fausset says, *"us"* refers to the Jews in the time just preceding their final restoration, while *"house of Israel"* points to Israel of all ages to whom God had always been good.

Ver. 8.   The prophet makes Jehovah the author of the saying here quoted, but nowhere has the Lord said or did He say that Israel would not lie and prove false; indeed He knew they would do so and would not keep faith with Him.

Fausset, and with him are the majority, explains the word *"said"* as a saying in His heart, i. e., He thought, as in Psa. 95.10.   Thus God is here said, according to human modes of thought, to say within Himself what He might naturally have expected as a result of His goodness to Israel, and thus the enormity of their *unnatural* perversity is the more vividly set forth.   The verb may therefore be taken as a future of hope.   Says Delitzsch, "Jehovah looked for their gracious requital of His covenant-grace by covenant-fidelity."

Ver. 9.   The first clause of this verse is famous for the diversity of explanation connected with it.

According to the rendering of our text the meaning is, as Delitzsch says, "Just as a man may feel pain while in his person he is raised above it, so God feels pain without His blessedness being hurt, and God felt His people's suffering; it moved Him inwardly."   (V. Ew. Um. Kn. Del. Lut. Hit. Cle. Hend.)

The rendering of our text, however, can hardly be sustained for the reason that in all the ancient manuscripts there is a *"not"* in the text, and critical presumption is much in its favor.   For this reason the marginal rendering must be substituted for that of the text.

Some of the other readings, which retain the "not" are as follows:

"In all their enmity He was not an enemy."   (D. Al.)

"In all their affliction there was no affliction", i. e., such as their sins merited.   (Jar.)

"In all their affliction He did not afflict them."   (Jer.)   But this can hardly be said to be true, unless some modifying clause is included in the explanation.

"In all their affliction He was not an adversary", i. e., though He afflicted them He did it not in hate.   (He.)   But this gives two different meanings to the same word.

"In all their distress there was no distress", i. e., of a real serious nature.   (Ges.)

"In all their straits there was no straitness in His goodness to them." (F.)

"In all their affliction there was no extreme, fatal affliction."   (Aurivillius.)

Those who adopt the rendering of our text think the *"not"* is in the text by mistake for *"to him"*, i. e., "In all their affliction there was affliction to Him."   But this contention can hardly be sustained.

"the angel of His presence",—This is the angel whom Jehovah sent

with Israel and who is identified with the presence of Jehovah (Ex. 33. 14,15), and in a certain sense with Jehovah Himself. It denotes the angel whose presence was the presence of Jehovah, or in whom Jehovah was personally present; therefore not an angel who stands always in the presence of Jehovah (Cle.), and so always beholds the countenance of Jehovah, but an angel who is Jehovah's countenance, or in whom Jehovah's countenance is to be seen. That this angel of Jehovah's presence was none other than that divine person who is represented in the New Testament as the brightness of the Father's glory and the express image of His person, in whose face the glory of God shines and in whom dwelleth all the fullness of the Godhead bodily, even Christ, the Messiah, there can be little if any doubt.

Ver. 10. *"he . . . himself"*,—i. e., Jehovah. He is changed into an adversary to those who resist His Holy Spirit.

Ver. 11. Here again are various interpretations.

The Dutch Bible makes Jehovah the subject of the first clause, but makes it all the language of the people, i. e., *"Once・He remembered the days of old, but now where is"*, etc. But the words *"but now"* are thus supplied without authority.

The Targum supplied *"lest they say"* before the second clause, which then becomes the language of Israel's enemies exulting in the failure of Jehovah's promises. But this idea is arbitrarily supplied and not expressed in the text.

All are agreed that the language from the second clause on is that of the people.

Fausset, following Jerome and Cyril, makes the first clause the language of Jehovah and the second with what follows, the language of the people. This is a possible construction and is that of our text. Notwithstanding their perversity Jehovah forgot not His covenant of old and therefore did not wholly forsake them. The transition, however, is somewhat abrupt, and not to be assumed without necessity.

The marginal reading is much to be preferred, Most modern writers since Vitringa are agreed that the first clause describes the penitent language of the people, while what follows gives their very language. (Del.)

However, instead of taking *"His people"* of the text as the subject, as is done by the marginal reading, it is better, Stier thinks, because of its remoteness, to leave it where it is and read *"they"* for *"He"*. Either construction, however, is acceptable.

The *"sea"* is the Red Sea, and the *"shepherds"* are Moses and Aaron and other leaders. If *"shepherd"* be read, then the reference is to Moses alone.

Ver. 12. *"caused his glorious arm to go at the right hand of Moses"*,—i. e., caused His almighty power, of which His arm is the established symbol, to be near or present with Moses when he needed its help.

Ver. 13. *"as a horse in the wilderness"*,—By *"wilderness"* is here meant the desert, free from inequalities over which a horse can run without stumbling. So He led them through the Red Sea.

Ver. 14. *"As the cattle that go down in the valley"*,—i. e., as the droves descending from the bare hills to the grassy tracts of the lowlands.

Ver. 15.   Here begins a fervent appeal to God to pity Israel now on the ground of His former mercies to them, an appeal which continues to the end of the chapter and throughout the following one.

Jehovah is called upon to look down from His dwelling place in heaven on their present distress and not restrain His love and might.   He is still their Father, and with great boldness He is besought as to why He permitted His people to become hardened and go astray, and He is called upon to return in His favor to His inheritance.   The complaint is made that His people had possessed only for a short time the promised land, while their enemies had trodden down the Sanctuary, and they had become as though they were not the chosen people of their God.

Ver. 16.   *"though Abraham . . . and Israel"*,—By some this is explained as meaning that these human progenitors were dead and so unable to render help.   (V. Na. Del.)   Others, who read *"when"* for *"though"* (Moore), and still others, who retain *"though"* (F.), make the meaning that natural affection and regard would cease rather than that God's paternal love should fail, or His covenant of adoption be annulled. "Even though Abraham, our earthly father, on whom we have prided ourselves, disown us, Thou wilt not."   (F.)

Ver. 17.   The question with which this verse opens must be taken in a permissive sense.   (F. Na. Del. Lut.)

Ver. 19.   The rendering of our text is approved by Nagelsbach, Delitzsch, Lowth and the majority, while Fausset, Alexander, Barnes and others prefer that of the Authorized Version, arguing from the analogy of verse 18 that while the first clause points to the Jews, the second one points to their foes.   Our text, however, is much the smoother, and the grounds for the change are far from sufficient.

CHAPTER SIXTY-FOUR

This chapter, the first verse of which in the Hebrew Bible belongs to the preceding one, contains Israel's further prayer that Jehovah would visibly intervene and show Himself to be the God and Father of His people as of old.   In violent agitation the prayer goes up that God would rend the heavens, bursting forth, as it were, to execute vengeance on His people's foe and put an end to Israel's distress (verses 1 and 2), a thing which only a God like Himself can do as proven by His acts of old (verses 3 and 4), in spite of which Israel had sunk deeper in corruption and sin (verses 5, 6 and 7).   But Jehovah is their Father and they the work of His hands; therefore let it please Him to be gracious (verses 8 and 9). All the cities, Zion and Jerusalem, have been made desolate (verses 10 and 11), and surely Jehovah cannot refrain from taking vengeance and delivering His people.

CHAPTER SIXTY-FIVE

JEHOVAH'S ANSWER TO THE PRAYER OF THE PEOPLE.

.1 I [1]am inquired of by them that asked not *for me*; I [2]am found of them that sought me not: I said, Behold me, behold me, unto a nation [3]that was not

[1]Or, *was inquired of*
[2]Or, *was found*
[3]Or, as otherwise read, *that hath not called upon*

called by my name. 2 I have spread out my hands all the day unto a rebellious people, that walk in a way that is not good, after their own thoughts; 3 a people that provoke me to my face continually, sacrificing in gardens, and burning incense upon bricks; 4 that ⁴sit among the graves, and lodge in the ⁵secret places; that eat swine's flesh, and broth of abominable things is in their vessels; 5 that say, Stand by thyself, come not near to me, for I am holier than thou. These are a smoke in my nose, a fire that burneth all the day. 6 Behold, it is written before me: I will not keep silence, but will recompense, yea, I will recompense into their bosom, 7 your own iniquities, and the iniquities of your fathers together, saith Jehovah, that have burned incense upon the mountains, and ⁶blasphemed me upon the hills: therefore will I ⁷first measure their work into their bosom.

⁴Or, *dwell*
⁵Or, *vaults*

⁶Or, *defied*
⁷Or, *measure their former work*

Vers. 1-7. NOT ALL ISRAEL SHALL BE SAVED.

Ver 1. Before promise comes first a rebuke and a menace. The penitent portion of Israel had in her prayer identified herself with the whole nation, but Jehovah answers that destruction and not salvation awaits a portion of the nation, and that the larger portion.

Many writers, and among them most of the modern scholars, think both this verse and the one following refers to unbelieving Jews. (Del.)

But there are serious objections to thus taking the words. Paul in Rom. 10.20 refers verse 7 to the Gentiles and this Delitzsch admits has very great weight. The difference between the Hebrew words as used for *"nation"* in verse 1 and *"people"* in verse 2 favors the reference of the word in verse 1, as Delitzsch also admits, to the heathen. The context seems also to favor the thought that Jehovah is here contrasting His success among the heathen with His want of the same among Israel. But most of all the expression, *"a nation that was not called by my name"* can hardly describe Israel even in her worst state of degradation.

This last objection Delitzsch relieves by using the marginal reading of our text, *"that hath not called upon my name"*, which is a possible and somewhat plausible rendering of the Hebrew. This author has also somewhat to say concerning Paul's application of the passage, but we are inclined to think he deals too lightly with this important testimony. The balance of argument certainly favors the reference to the Gentiles and to this opinion, for the reasons given, we incline. (F. S. Al. Na. Hof. Hend.)

Ver. 3. *"burning incense upon bricks"*,—

(1) Bricks come under the description of "hewn stones" and God's altars according to Mosaic law must be of unhewn stones and of earth. The heathen used hewn stones. Chiseling was also forbidden and therefore they could not inscribe superstitious symbols on them as the heathen did, and bricks were more easily inscribed than stone. (F. Na.)

(2) The flat brick-paved roofs of the houses upon which sacrifice to the sun was made. (Bo.)

(3) An allusion to some practice now unknown, but possibly connected with the curiously inscribed bricks found in modern times near the site of ancient Babylon. (Ros.)

(4) Altars hastily constructed and naturally out of brick as the superficial covering. (Al. Ges.) The first view, which is but little different from this last, is the preferable one.

Ver. 4. *"sit among the graves"*,—i. e., for the purpose of necromancy or communing with the dead (F. Na. Del.), or sacrificing to the dead, i. e., purificatory offering presented to the dead (V.), the former being the better explanation.

"lodge in the secret places",—i. e., consecrated precincts, the idol's inmost shrine (Ho.), where they used to sleep to have divine communications in dreams (Jer.), or perhaps, in keeping with the former clause, sepulchral caves. (Ma.)

The whole verse, with the one before it, is, as Alexander says, "a highly wrought description of idolatrous abominations."

Ver. 5. *"I am holier than thou"*,—The reference here is doubtless to the fact of their having gained initiation into the mysteries, or attained a high degree of sanctity by taking part in specially sacred heathen rites of purification which were not sanctioned by law. Such He says are the prey of a continual fire whose smoke goes up perpetually before Him. The fire of God's wrath was kindled at the sight and exhibited itself in smoking pantings from His nostrils. In Hebrew the nose is the seat of anger.

Ver. 6. *"it is written before me"*,—What is written before Him? The punishment, the divine sentence of judgment which follows (V. Al. Na. Ma.), or the eternal law of retribution (Um.), or their idolatrous practices, their sin, in scornful contempt of Jehovah's law (Del.)? Perhaps the former explanation is the better. The meaning may be that the fact that he will recompense is written in a document, as in Job. 13.26 and Jer. 22.30 (V. He. Na. Lo. Noy.), although nothing further than a decree in His own mind, an eternal purpose, is needed to give good meaning to the words.

"into their bosom",—Either a reference to the folds of the oriental dress where articles were carried and the thought of recompensing to them more than they can carry in their hand, i. e., a full, large measure of retribution; or, I will repay it *to the very person* from whom it emanated. The clause seems to be parenthetical, and is properly repeated at the close of the next verse.

Ver. 7. *"first measure their work"*,—The marginal reading cannot be right. For why should Jehovah punish only this? The word *"first"* is rightly taken as an adverb by our text. (Na. Ew. Or. Del. Bred.)

8 Thus saith Jehovah, As the new wine is found in the cluster, and one saith, Destroy it not, for a blessing is in it: so will I do for my servants' sake, that I may not destroy them all. 9 And I will bring forth a seed out of Jacob, and out of Judah an inheritor of my mountains; and my chosen shall inherit it, and my servants shall dwell there. 10 And Sharon shall be a [1]fold of flocks, and the valley of Achor a place for herds to lie down in, for my people that have sought me. 11 But ye that forsake Jehovah, that forget my holy mountain, that prepare a table for [2]Fortune, and that fill up mingled wine unto [3]Destiny; 12 I will destine you to the sword, and ye shall all bow down to the slaughter; because when I called, ye did not answer; when I spake, ye did not hear; but ye did that which was evil in mine eyes, and chose that wherein I delighted not.

13 Therefore thus saith the Lord Jehovah, Behold, my servants shall eat, but ye shall be hungry; behold, my servants shall drink, but ye shall be thirsty; behold, my servants shall rejoice, but ye shall be put to shame; 14 behold, my servants shall sing for joy of heart, but

[1]Or, *pasture*
[2]Heb. *Gad.* See Gen. 30.11
[3]Heb. *Meni*

ye shall cry for sorrow of heart, and shall wail for [4]vexation of spirit. 15 And ye shall leave your name for [5]a curse unto my chosen; and the Lord Jehovah will slay thee; and he will call his servants by another name: 16 so that

[4]Heb. *breaking*
[5]Heb. *an oath*

he who blesseth himself in the earth shall bless himself in the God of [6]truth; and he that sweareth in the earth shall swear by the God of [6]truth; because the former troubles are forgotten, and because they are hid from mine eyes.

[6]Heb. *Amen* See II Cor. 1.20; Rev. 3.14.

Vers. 8-16. NOT ALL ISRAEL SHALL BE CAST OFF. THE REMNANT TO BE SAVED.

Even as in a cluster of grapes, consisting of good and bad berries, there is a blessing, i. e., the wine-producing juice of the good berries, and therefore the whole cluster will not be thrown away; so God will spare the godly remnant while the ungodly mass of the nation shall be destroyed. The meaning is not therefore, as Knobel says, "He will not destroy the grapes along with the stem and husks", nor is the contrast between the good clusters and other bad clusters (Al.), but it is as J. D. Michaelis and others (F. Na. Del.) say, "He will not destroy the grapes that have good sap in them along with the preponderant bad ones."

"my servants",—The remnant according to the election of grace. (Rom. 11.28.)

Ver. 9. *"my mountains"*,—Not Mount Zion and Mount Moriah only (V.), but the whole of Palestine. (F. Al. Na. Del.)

Nearly all *modern* German commentators say this verse predicts the restoration of the Jews from Babylon.

Here again the two schools of interpretation are at widest divergence. Henderson says the future happy occupation of Palestine by a regenerated remnant of Jews is here clearly predicted; while Alexander says it predicts the perpetuation of the Jewish Church in the remnant which believed on Christ, and which, enlarged by the accession of the Gentiles, is heir to all the promises of the Church of the old dispensation.

Ver. 10. *"the valley of Achor a place for herds"*,—Achor means *trouble*. It is a valley near Jericho so called because of the trouble caused to Israel by Achan's sin. This valley, proverbial for whatever caused calamity, shall become proverbial for joy and prosperity.

As Sharon was noted for its verdure, so also, some think, was Achor, this last being made more probable from the fact that Hosea says it shall be a "door of hope".

Some think that because Sharon was on the Mediterranean and Achan was by the Jordan these two are chosen as showing the whole breadth of the land from west to east.

Ver. 11. The words *"Fortune"* and *"Destiny"* refer to two heathen deities and the last half of this verse refers to meals of the gods held in their honor. The Hebrew for the word is "Gad" and "Meni".

Gad, as the name of a divinity, means doubtless the star of fortune, of which the Babylonians had two, Jupiter, whom the Arabs named "Great Fortune", and Venus, whom they named "Little Fortune", and which in our text is represented by Meni, which Goddess was supposed to number the fates or the destiny of men.

Vitringa and Knobel think Gad refers to the sun and Meni to the moon.

The Authorized Version, and with it many interpreters, understands the word Gad as meaning "troop", as in Gen. 30.11, and Meni as meaning "number", the first pointing to the troops of planets and the multitude of stars as objects of worship, while the second refers to convivial assemblies connected with idolatrous worship.

The passage is descriptive of idolatrous worship which after all is the only point of importance.

Ver. 12. *"destine you to the sword"*,—Alexander has well remarked that it is better here to retain the word "number" as in the Authorized Version, instead of *"destine"*, as in our text, because the writer's idea is that they shall be cut off one by one, or rather one with another—all without exception. The same word is used elsewhere for the numbering of sheep. (Jer. 33.13.) The word thus translated would seem to have some bearing on the meaning of the word in the preceding verse.

Ver. 13. *"ye shall be hungry"*,—Fausset thinks this may refer to the destruction of Jerusalem wherein the Jews were so hungry that 1,000,-000 perished by famine, and that it may refer to a further fulfillment to take place just before the creation of the new heavens and the new earth, as the context in verse 17 implies.

Ver. 15. *"And ye shall leave your name for a curse"*,—This means more than to leave the name to be cursed; it means to leave it as a formula for cursing, so that men will say, "Jehovah slay thee as He slew them". The name of the Jew, as Fausset reminds us, has long been a formula of execration; if one wishes to curse another, he can utter nothing worse than this: "God make thee what the Jew is."

"my chosen . . . his servants",—The believing remnant.

"another name",—Nagelsbach says, "One name originally united the wicked and the godly, for they were all called 'Israelites'. Can the elect of the Lord still continue to bear the name which, after the judgment of God, has become cursed? No. The Lord will therefore give to His servants *'another name'*, and thus is the new covenant, that should come in the place of the old, intimated."

Some think the meaning is that as your name is to be a name by which men shall curse, so my servants shall have a name by which men shall bless. Others merely give it a more general sense as meaning that their condition shall be altogether different, while still others think that it relates to the name "Christian" as distinguished from the Jew. Alexander thinks that the correct explanation is to be found in a combination of all three views. In Chap. 62.2 of Jehovah's people it is said that they shall be given a *"new name"*, and according to Old Testament usage the promise of *"another name"* or a *"new name"* implies a different character and state.

Ver. 16. *"so that"*,—Whether the particle be so translated with Luther and others (Na. Del.), or translated "which" (with respect to which, i. e., by which), as Alexander renders it, it must in either case relate to the previously expressed antecedent *"name"*, by which the meaning would seem to be that the servants of Jehovah shall be called or named after the God of truth, so that His name and theirs shall be identical, and whoever blesses and swears by the one does so by the other also.   (Al.)

Blessing himself means praying for God's blessing, and swearing means the solemn invocation of God's presence as a witness.

"the God of truth",—i. e., the God of Amen; of what is true and firm; the God to whom that quality of covenant-keeping truth essentially belongs; the God who translates what He promises into Yea and Amen.

17 For, behold, I create new heavens and a new earth; and the former things shall not be remembered, nor come into mind.   18 But be ye glad and rejoice for ever in that which I create; for, behold, I create Jerusalem a rejoicing, and her people a joy.   19 And I will rejoice in Jerusalem, and joy in my people; and there shall be heard in her no more the voice of weeping and the voice of crying.   20 There shall be no more thence an infant of days, nor an old man that hath not filled his days; for the child shall die a hundred years old, and the sinner being a hundred years old shall be accursed.   21 And they shall build houses, and inhabit them; and they shall plant vineyards, and eat the fruit of them.   22 They shall not build, and another inhabit; they shall not plant, and another eat: for as the days of a tree shall be the days of my people, and my chosen shall [1]long enjoy the work of their hands.   23 They shall not labor in vain, nor bring forth for [2]calamity; for they are the seed of the blessed of Jehovah, and their offspring [3]with them.   24 And it shall come to pass that, before they call, I will answer; and while they are yet speaking, I will hear.   25 The wolf and the lamb shall feed together, and the lion shall eat straw like the ox; and dust shall be the serpent's food. They shall not hurt nor destroy in all my holy mountain, saith Jehovah.

[1]Heb. *wear out*
[2]Or, *sudden terror*
[3]Or, shall be *with them*

Vers. 17-25.   The Eternal Blessing of the Remnant in the New Earth and the New Heavens.

Ver. 17.   *"the former things shall not be remembered"*,—Most interpreters refer *"former things"* to the former troubles of verse 16; others simply construe it indefinitely as all former troubles.   The more natural explanation, however, is to refer it to the former heaven and earth, as the simple, more immediate and more exact parallel.   (Al. Del.) (See Jer. 3.16.)   The former heavens and earth, with all their sorrows under the fall, shall be so far from recurring that their very remembrance shall be obliterated by the many mercies which Jehovah will bestow upon the new heavens and the new earth.

Many expositors understand the reference to be to the renovation of the present earth with its skies after the destruction which shall occur at the end-time.   (F. Sco. Burnet.)

Scofield says that verse 17 looks beyond the kingdom age to the new heavens and the new earth, but verses 18 to 25 describe the kingdom age itself.

Alexander says, of course, that it is merely a prediction of entire change in the existing state of things, the precise nature of the change and the means by which it is to be brought about forming no part of the revelation here.

Ver. 18.   *"that which I create"*,—i. e., the new heavens and the new earth mentioned in the previous verse, Jerusalem being added for emphasis.   Jerusalem is to be created a rejoicing and her people a joy by

134

making these things the characteristics of her inner and outward life, her uniform, constant state.

Ver. 19.— (See Rev. 7.17 and 2.14.) (F. N.)

Ver. 20. *"no more thence"*,—i. e., from that time forward. Longevity of life is here promised as of old.

The particle translated "thence", and properly so, is however never used in regard to time, but always in regard to place. It refers to the place where the conditions prophesied are to exist. It does not therefore mean "from then", or "from that time forward", as Fausset translates it, although such thought is in keeping with the real meaning of the prediction. It simply means, "There, in that place, shall be no more an infant of days", or as Donald Moore puts it, "There shall no suckling thence arise or come into being who shall live only some days, whose age shall be counted by days".

"an infant of days",—i. e., an infant who shall live but a few days.

"an old man that hath not filled his days",—i. e., attained unto the regular measure of human life. None shall die, says Fausset, without attaining a full old age.

"the child shall die a hundred years old",—i. e., he who in other days had died as a youth, and whose death was considered premature, shall not die before his hundredth year. He that dies a hundred years old shall die a mere child.

"the sinner being a hundred years old shall be accursed",—This seems to mean that if a sinner shall die when he is a hundred years old, an age regarded in those days as mere childhood, it shall be deemed as the effect of a special visitation of God's wrath.

While the time predicted will be far superior to those of the present, it will not be perfect, because sin and death will still exist. (Rev. 20.7,8.) "Longevity is restored, but death, the last enemy", says Scofield, "is not destroyed till after Satan's rebellion at the end of the thousand years."

"It would be wrong", says Delitzsch, "to think that all this means less than what is said in Chap. 25.8 only in appearance. There the final annulling of death is spoken of; here only the limiting of its power." Nagelsbach thinks the last half of the verse contradicts the first half, for, says he, "if no one, not even an old man, falls short of the normal measure, then no one can die as a boy." To this his interpreter, Donald Moore, replies, "The prophet does not say that no one, not even an old man, falls short of the normal measure, in the former part of this verse. When one who dies at the age of a hundred years is counted a boy, and when a sinner who dies a hundred years old is regarded as prematurely cut off by the judgment of God, this is no contradiction of the declaration that the suckling's age will not be reckoned by days, and that old men will fill up the measure of their days. For the hundred years old sinner will not be included in the category of old men. If a sinner dies at a hundred he would be regarded as cursed by God. And if one of a hundred years should die a *natural* death (supposing such a case, which from what has been said cannot really occur), he would be only a boy at his death."

Ver. 22. *"as the days of a tree"*,—They shall live as long as trees, oaks, terebinths, palms, cedar, which live for centuries.

"shall long enjoy",—The word means "enjoy to the full". The Hebrew is really "to use up", "to consume", "to wear out", seeming to imply, as it were, that they shall live to enjoy the last of it.

Ver. 23. *"nor bring forth for calamity"*,—i. e., that which falls unexpectedly and carries their offspring, their children away (Del.), not bring forth children for a sudden death (F.). But Alexander says these are mere conjectures and that the Hebrew word means "extreme agitation and alarm" and that the meaning is that they shall not bring forth children merely to be the subjects of distressing solicitude.

"and their offspring with them",—Our text makes their offspring as well as themselves to be the seed of the blessed of Jehovah, which is of course true; but the marginal reading is to be preferred, "and their offspring shall be with them", i. e., not brought forth only to be cut off by sudden destruction or calamity.

Ver. 25. The curse seems to remain on the serpent. It will still creep in the dust, but without injuring man. (See Chap. 11.7.)

CHAPTER SIXTY-SIX

1 Thus saith Jehovah, Heaven is my throne, and the earth is my footstool: what manner of house will ye build unto me? and what place shall be my rest? 2 For all these things hath my hand made, and so all these things came to be, saith Jehovah: but to this man will I look, even to him that is poor and of a contrite spirit, and that trembleth at my word. 3 He that killeth an ox is as he that slayeth a man; he that sacrificeth a lamb, as he that breaketh a dog's neck; he that offereth ¹an oblation, *as he that offereth* swine's blood; he that ²burneth frankincense, as he that blesseth an idol. Yea, they have chosen their own ways, and their soul delighteth in their abominations: 4 I also will choose their ³delusions, and will bring their fears upon them; because when I called, none did answer; when I spake, they did not hear: but they did that which was evil in mine eyes, and chose that wherein I delighted not.

5 Hear the word of Jehovah, ye that tremble at his word: Your brethren that hate you, that cast you out for my name's sake, have said, Let Jehovah be glorified, that we may see your joy; but it is they that shall be put to shame. 6 A voice of tumult from the city, a voice from the temple, a voice of Jehovah that rendereth recompense to his enemies.

7 Before she travailed, she brought forth; before her pain came, she was delivered of a man-child. 8 Who hath heard such a thing? who hath seen such things? Shall a land be ⁴born in one day? shall a nation be brought forth at once? for as soon as Zion travailed, she brought forth her children. 9 Shall I bring to the birth, and not cause to bring forth? saith Jehovah: shall I that cause to bring forth shut *the womb?* saith thy God.

10 Rejoice ye with Jerusalem, and be glad for her, all ye that love her: rejoice for joy with her, all ye that mourn over her; 11 that ye may suck and be satisfied with the breasts of her consolations; that ye may milk out, and be delighted with the abundance of her glory. 12 For thus saith Jehovah, Behold, I will extend peace to her like a river, and the glory of the nations like an overflowing stream: ⁵and ye shall suck *thereof*; ye shall be borne upon the side, and shall be dandled upon the knees. 13 As one whom his mother comforteth, so will I comfort you; and ye shall be comforted in Jerusalem. 14 And ye shall see *it*, and your heart shall rejoice, and your bones shall flourish like the tender grass: and the hand of Jehovah shall be known toward his servants; and he will have indignation against his enemies.

¹Or, *a meal-offering*
²Heb. *maketh a memorial of*
³Or, *mockings*

⁴Or, *travailed with for but one day*
⁵Or, *then shall ye suck, ye &c.*

Vers. 1-14. EXCLUSION OF THE WICKED FROM END-TIME BLESSINGS.

Ver. 1. *"what manner of house will ye build unto me?"*,—Hendewerk, Knobel and Hitzig think that God here forbids the Jews, who meditated remaining behind in Chaldea, or in Babylon, to build a temple there, as the Jews did in Egypt at a later time at Leontopolis. But there is no support whatever in the text for this. The prophet is still describing the condition of things to be expected in the time of the end when there will be a new heaven and a new earth. He is addressing those about to return from exile, and the *"house"* of our text refers doubtless to the temple which is to take the place of the one destroyed (Chap. 64.9). He does not interdict them from building this temple (Chap. 44.28; 56.7; 60.7; Ezra 1.2-4; Haggai 1 and 2), but the thought is that the external temple is at all times a thing of minor importance; that, as Klostermann says, God does not need a temple at all, nor does He want men to forget His majesty in petty architecture, even though He promised the prospect of a rebuilt temple.

Umbreit thinks the reference is to the New Jerusalem in which there is no temple, as Nagelsbach also remarks, and where God forbids one being built. But Delitzsch reminds us that according to Chaps. 56 and 60 there is a temple in the New Jerusalem.

Barnes and Alexander both think it refers to the time when the temple of Herod was being finished.

"what manner",—This is much to be preferred to *"where"* of the Authorized text, since the query seems to have reference in both places to the nature or the quality rather than the mere locality of the edifice in question. (F. V. Al. Na. Del.)

Ver. 2. *"all these things"*,—i. e., heaven and earth, the world of visible surroundings.

In view of His creative dignity a temple is a small thing to Him, but His merciful look is directed to the mourners and the broken-hearted and those who have reverential fear toward His word.

Ver. 3. With each form of sacrifice is coupled an offering which was inadmissible and revolting. The first sacrifice mentioned counts as the slaying of a man, the offering of a human victim. The dog in the east has ever been regarded as unclean and in that light is coupled with the swine. To offer a dog would be an abomination, and the prophet here does not even honor this abomination by the use of the word sacrifice, but uses the degrading term, *"breaketh a dog's neck"*, the peculiar mode of killing a dog. To offer *"an oblation"*, a meal-offering, counts as the offering of swine's blood, and to burn frankincense counts as blessing an idol.

"blesseth an idol",—We see no good reason for not retaining the word *"idol"*, as does our text (Na. Hit), for certainly this particular meaning corresponds better to the context than does the general one of wickedness, or vanity (Al. Lut. Del.), and as all other secondary phrases refer to worship, it is better to understand it so here.

Delitzsch says the chapter starts with an address to the entire body ready to return from exile, and while not prohibiting the building of a temple upon their return says that as Creator of heaven and earth Jehovah needs no house made with men's hands, and then in verse 3, latter part, and verse 4 the address distinguishes between the penitent (the godly remnant) and those alienated from God (the majority) and rejects all worship and offering at the hand of the latter and threatens them with just retribution. Nagelsbach, on the other hand, asks, "Where is it by a single syllable intimated that verse 3, latter clause, and verse 4 is addressed solely to those estranged from God? If in Chaps. 56 and 60, as Delitzsch maintains, and in our chapter, verses 6 and 20, a temple and sacrificial worship is still spoken of, are we to suppose that the old temple of stone, with its material, bloody offerings, is intended? Even Jeremiah speaks of a time when the ark of the covenant will be no more thought of (Jer. 3.16). The prophet surveys the whole time of salvation from the time of the close of the exile to the age to come in one view, and while he sees a temple and sacrificial worship in this space of time, he declares them both to be insufficient, and he declares most unambiguously that this temple must disappear and give place to a better one. And when this shall have happened, then the prophet sees quite clearly that any animal sacrifice will be an abomination. He who in the Christian Church would present any such sacrifice would thus despise the blood of the Lamb of God. I cannot therefore agree with those who think the passage refers to the man who *with a disposition unholy and estranged from God* offers an ox, etc. In the time present to the mind of the prophet not only the sacrifice of the ungodly will be a crime, but *every* sacrifice will be as the offering of a man, dog or sow to God, a heinous crime."

The fact remains that if the address pertained to those of Old Testament times, even after the return from exile, it must have been made to or about the ungodly, whose sacrifices God abhors under any circumstances; but if the address pertains to those of the newer dispensation which the prophet saw coming the address is applicable to every sacrifice regardless of the disposition or character of the man who makes it, and in as much as the prophet seemingly conceives of all of this in one period there is truth in both of the above views, although the more important aspect of it rests with Nagelsbach.

Vitringa, and with him agree Alexander and Henderson, applies them to those who still adhered to the old sacrifices *after the great sacrifice* for sin was come and had been offered once for all, i. e., in the new dispensation.

Gesenius, somewhat after the manner of Delitzsch, thinks they refer to the practice of iniquity in general, which renders any sacrifice hateful to Jehovah.

Ver. 4. *"I will also choose"*,—i. e., in harmony with the law of retribution.

"their delusions",—This word answers to *"their own ways"* of verse 3. God chose these delusions by allowing them in His providence and causing the people to eat the fruit of them.

"will bring their fears upon them",—i. e., the things they fear. (F. Al. Na.)

Ver. 5. *"ye that tremble at His word"*,—The reference here is the same as in verse 2, to the believing portion of Israel.

"Your brethren that hate you",—Their own brethren, and what

aggravated the sin still more was that Jehovah's name was the ground on which they are hated by them.

Barnes and others (V. Al. Ka.) refer the expression to the Jews who hated and taunted the Christians during the early part of the Christian dispensation.

"that cast you out for my name's sake",—*"that cast you out"* of course belongs with what goes before, but Vitringa, Nagelsbach and others connect *"for my name's sake"* with what follows, but the majority rightly connect it with what goes before, as in our text, because the Jews would never admit that an Israelite was ever put out of the community for the sake of Jehovah's name. (Al. Del.)

"Let Jehovah be glorified",—The mocking words of the persecutors, as if their violence toward you was from zeal for the Lord, i. e., Let Him be glorified by manifesting Himself in your behalf. They regard the hope of the believers as a delusion and the words of the prophet as imagination.

Ver. 6. Fausset says that as verse 5 refers to the destruction of the unbelieving Jews, so it is said here that God from Jerusalem and the temple shall take vengeance on the hostile Gentiles, the abrupt language of the verse marking the suddenness with which these foes outside of Jerusalem shall be put to destruction.

Delitzsch and others (Ab. Na. Al. Bar.), on the other hand, rightly say that according to the context the enemies here meant are still primarily the God-estranged and yet arrogant mass of the Israelitish nation. Even Aben Ezra admits this.

"A voice of tumult from the city",—

The rejoicing of the Maccabees and their followers when Antiochus Epiphanes evacuated the temple. (Gro.)

The preaching of the Gospel by the Apostles beginning at Jerusalem. (Ju.)

A voice calling for vengeance on the Romans. (Jar.)

The blasphemies of the heathen. (Aba.)

The wail of such wicked Jews who may have gone up to Jerusalem from the exile in hope of worldly advantage and are smitten with divine judgments while there. (Ges.)

The voice is a joyful noise and not to be associated with the voice of Jehovah bringing vengeance (Na.)

All these explanations are opposed by the fact that the Hebrew word here used is never applied to a joyful cry or a cry of lamentation, but always to the tumult of war, and the rushing noise of battle.

Kimchi says it is the noise of tumult as applied to the destruction of Gog and Magog.

Hitzig says it is a description of the general judgment foretold by Joel (Joel 4.2), when all the nations should be judged at Jerusalem.

Knobel refers it to the confusion of punishment falling upon the antitheocratic Jews who remained in Babylon and especially upon the Babylonians themselves.

Vitringa, Henderson and Alexander apply it to the scenes connected with the destruction of the temple in the days of Herod, the noise being not only that of the Romans in taking Jerusalem (V.), but rather the whole confusion of the siege and conquest. (Al.)

Delitzsch says, "The thunder of judgment goes forth from the temple which has risen again, Jehovah's earthly dwelling place, of which He is again taking possession, followed by the faithful remnant of His people, and thence He renders recompense to His enemies, the God-estranged and yet arrogant mass of the exiles." This is by far the most satisfactory explanation, whatever the passage may further represent by way of typical significance.

Ver. 7. While the mass falls a prey to judgment, yet Zion is not left without children.

"*delivered of a man-child*",—i. e., a whole land full of people—a nation. Some take "*man-child*" merely in the sense of strength and numbers, Nagelsbach saying that the male-child is used because male-children are as a rule born harder, being larger, but here it is with apparent ease.

"Contrast this ease of the future Jewish Church", says Fausset, "with the travail of the Christian Church in bringing forth a man-child (Rev. 12.2,5)."

Vitringa and Alexander say the reference is to the call of the Gentiles.

Henderson says the language expresses the sudden and unexpected reproduction of the Jewish nation in their own land in the latter days.

Ver. 9. The meaning is, Shall I who have begun, not finish my work of restoring Israel?

Ver. 11. Jerusalem is thought of as a mother, and the rich, real comfort which she enjoys as the milk filling her breast, and with which she now richly nourishes her children.

Ver. 12. "*the glory of the nations*",—This comprehends all ˌthe desirable things in the way of outward blessings which the Gentiles may bring to her.

Since "*ye*" refers in each case to the faithful Jews, Delitzsch thinks the "*sides*" and the "*knees*" refer to the Gentiles, who vie with each other in showing them delicate attention, and that therefore the pronoun "*their*" should be used in each case instead of the article "*the*".

Ver. 14. "*shall be known toward*",—i. e., manifested in behalf of.

15 For, behold, Jehovah will come [1]with fire, and his chariots shall be like the whirlwind; to render his anger with fierceness, and his rebuke with flames of fire. 16 For by fire will Jehovah execute judgment, and by his sword, upon all flesh; and the slain of Jehovah shall be many. 17 They that sanctify themselves and purify themselves [2]to go unto the gardens, behind [3]one in the midst, eating swine's flesh, and the abomination, and the mouse, they shall come to an end together, saith Jehovah.

18 For I *know* their works and their thoughts: *the time* cometh, that I will gather all nations and tongues; and they shall come, and shall see my glory. 19 And I will set a sign among them, and I will send such as escape of them unto the nations, to Tarshish, Pul, and Lud, that draw the bow, to Tubal and Javan, to the isles afar off, that have not heard my fame, neither have seen my glory; and they shall declare my glory among the nations. 20 And they shall bring all your brethren out of all the nations

[1]Or, *in*
[2]Or, *in the*
[3]Or, *one* tree (or, Asherah; see Dt. 16.21)

for an oblation unto Jehovah, upon horses, and in chariots, and in litters, and upon mules, and upon dromedaries, to my holy mountain Jerusalem, saith Jehovah, as the children of Israel bring their oblation in a clean vessel into the house of Jehovah. 21 And of them also will I take for priests *and* for Levites, saith Jehovah.

22 For as the new heavens and the new earth, which I will make, shall remain before me, saith Jehovah, so shall your seed and your name remain. 23 And it shall come to pass, that from one new moon to another, and from one sabbath to another, shall all flesh come to worship before me, saith Jehovah. 24 And they shall go forth, and look upon the dead bodies of the men that have transgressed against me: for their worm shall not die, neither shall their fire be quenched; and they shall be an abhorring unto all flesh.

Vers. 15-24. A GENERAL PICTURE OF THE TIME OF THE END.

Ver. 15. *"with fire"*,—Some (Al. Del.) render with the margin, "in fire"; Lowth reads "as fire", but our text is quite appropriate, the meaning being the same according to any of the proposed renderings.

"to render his anger with fierceness",—i. e., to deal out His wrath with burning (Del.), or to apply His wrath with burning heat (Kn. Ges.)

Ver. 16. *"upon all flesh"*,—i. e., upon all who are the objects of His wrath. The judgment here predicted, says Delitzsch, is a general one and falls not only upon the heathen but upon the mass of unbelieving Jews as well. During this judgment the godly will be hidden away, says Fausset, referring to I Thess. 4.16,17.

Henderson applies the text also to the battle of Armageddon in Rev. 16 and 19, and Vitringa admits a reference to this also.

Alexander of course applies the judgment here mentioned to the destruction of Jerusalem under the Romans, and says the Apocalyptic prophecies borrow their images from the Old Testament prophecies, but are not exegetical of them.

Ver. 17. This verse refers to idolators whoever they may be and are the same persons doubtless as those in Chap. 65.3,5.

"to go unto the garden",—The idea is not that they purified themselves in the gardens, but on their way to the gardens, or in preparation for the gardens where idolatrous services were to be held.

"behind one in the midst",—The literal is *"one one in the midst"*. Gesenius reads, "following one in the midst",—i. e., a priest who led the rest in performing the sacred rites, and led the idolatrous procession through the garden.

Maurer reads, "following one in the midst", i. e., some idol or other, which out of contempt he does not mention. Vitringa says the word, twice mentioned in the text, is the name of a Syrian idol called Adad, the literal meaning of which is "one", and with him agree Bochart and other learned men of early date.

On the ground that the word "priest" is to be supplied, then the word which means *"in the midst"* means in the midst of the crowd—the priest who prescribes the rites stands in their midst and they follow him.

On the ground either that the word means "idol", or that the word "idol" is to be supplied, the identity of which idol no one can know, the word which means *"in the midst"* must refer to the garden—the idol in the midst of the garden.

Of the two explanations the former is by far the better. (Kn. Um. Na. Ro. Hit. Del. Ges. Baud. Hend. Beck, Pfeifer, Seinecke.) .

Some supply the word "tree" (Bo.) and think of one of the trees behind which they perform their lustrations; while others supply the word "pool" (Kim.) in which the lustrations are made.

All the things mentioned in the following words were forbidden to the Jew.

Ver. 18. *"and they shall come"*,—They will be impelled with enmity against Jerusalem and they shall come, but not without Jehovah's superintendence who makes even evil subservient to His plan.

"shall see my glory",—Not His glory as manifested in grace (S. Um. Ew. Hahn), but in judgment. (F. Al. Del.)

"I will gather all nations",—This includes the apostates of Israel, but it is evident from what follows in the next verse that the nations assembled against Jerusalem and perishing themselves in the enterprise are not to be taken as all nations without exception, because in the following verse many nations are mentioned by name who are situated outside the range of these great events.

Fausset says these nations shall gather together against Jerusalem, where the ungodly Jews shall perish, the apostate Jews, and then the Lord at last shall fight against those nations for Jerusalem's sake. He then says the survivors shall see Jehovah's glory. But why confine this to the survivors? Why is it not true of all present?

Alexander thinks this is a prediction of the calling of the Gentiles, both to witness the destruction of the apostate Jews and to supply their place in His Church or chosen people. He bases this much upon the fact, as he thinks, that the crimes described in the foregoing verses are those of the apostate Jews and not those of the heathen. But surely this learned expositor is wrong as to this latter proposition.

Ver. 19. The tidings of Jehovah are to be carried to the far-off heathen world. Fausset says, Tarshish is Tartessus in Spain in the west; Pul is East Africa and North Africa; Lud is the Lybians of Africa, famous as bowmen; Tubal refers to the Tibarennians in Asia Minor south of the Caucasus, and Java is the Greeks. The reference seems to be to the entire heathen world, and the prophet mentions only the farthest removed to intimate that to all—to the most remote—the joyful message should come."

"And I will set a sign among them",—The judgment is that which falls primarily upon the heathen, those mentioned in verse 17, to whom the *"them"* of this phrase refers, and they are primarily the ones mentioned also in verse 18 as being gathered, together with the apostate Jews.

Now most writers are agreed with Gesenius that the "sign" is to be taken in the same sense as that in Ex. 10.1,2, where God is said twice to have placed his signs *among* the Egyptians, and as these signs were the miraculous plagues, so here the reference must be to some miracle God will work in the midst of those gathered to judgment.

Calvin explains, "I make a sign on them", i. e., on the elect for their deliverance. But the sign is given to those who are judged and not to those who are saved.

Alexander says the sign is the whole display of miraculous power in the beginning of the new dispensation which the Apostles had bestowed upon them. But if there were no other objection to this interpretation it is exposed to the one just mentioned.

Fausset says it is "A banner on a high place to indicate the place of meeting for the dispersed Jewish exiles preparatory to their return to their own land"; while Gesenius thinks it is the extraordinary confluence itself of the Jews from all parts of the world. But these, too, are open to the objection just mentioned, and besides they commit themselves to the rather unfortunate arrangement of the verses proposed by Alexander whereby in point of time verse 19 is prior to verse 18, inasmuch as it is by the sign that the nations mentioned in verse 18 are gathered together at Jerusalem. Hitzig and Knobel consider the sign to be the dreadful miracle of the battle in which Jehovah fights against His enemies with fire and sword and inflicts His judgment upon them in their terrific slaughter. Delitzsch, however, says that if they were to witness the judicial glory of Jehovah, as verse 18 distinctly declares they shall, then if they were to have a sign set on them in that retributive sense it would be more appropriate for the words, *"I will set a sign on them"* to precede than to follow the words, *"they shall see my glory"*. The sign, therefore, he thinks, consists in the sparing of the remnant—the unexpected, surprising circumstance, considering the great slaughter, that a remnant is spared. (Del. Um. Ew. Seinecke.) But Nagelsbach asks, "Is it something so extraordinary and wonderful that individuals should escape from a slaughter, be it every so bloody?"

Stier refers the sign to the judgment upon apostate Israel. Nagelsbach says, however, that it seems strange to speak of the sign *after* the judgment has occurred and they have seen the glory of Jehovah. If, however, we place verse 19 after verse 18 in point of time, as do Alexander and the translator of Nagelsbach, and make verse 19, sign and all, the method by which the nations of verse 18 are gathered, the difficulty in Nagelsbach's mind must disappear.

It would be manifestly absurd to think of the nations in verse 18 being called to their own judgment in which they were to see the glory of God and then at the same time think of *"those that escape"* from this judgment going out to gather or call these same nations in. The only way therefore to consistently bring verse 19 in before verse 18 as to time is to think of those in verse 17 being apostate Jews who are to be judged, and after the judgment upon them had fallen, those that escape of them are to go out to the Gentiles of verse 18 and gather them in, not for judgment, but for mercy, to take the place of the apostate Jews, and this going out to them, as Alexander says, is the sign—the Gospel being preached to them.

Alexander in his exegesis of verse 18 says the Gentiles were brought in to witness the vengeance of God upon the Jews as well as to take their place. But this, of course, according to his own explanation could not be, because there would then as yet have been no remnant, none of *"those that escape"* to go out and gather the Gentiles in, as Alexander says they do, because there is no remnant until after the judgment on the apostate Jews has taken place, for the remnant is what is left out of that judgment. Our author must therefore eliminate the idea of the Gentiles being gathered in to witness the judgment in order to be consistent with himself.

However, this disarrangement of the flow of thought does not appeal to us, and there are reasons other than contextual why those mentioned in verse 17 can hardly refer to the apostate Jews, in as much as they were never guilty after the exile of the abominations mentioned in the verse.

It is impossible to tell what the sign is; the best is but conjecture. The translator of Nagelsbach thinks it refers to the Messiah, and Nagelsbach himself comes to pretty much the same conclusion.

We are now prepared to say that even though the sign is apparently placed among those upon whom the judgment falls, it does not at all follow that the sign is *upon* them in the sense that that retribution is to fall upon them. Any sign that could be given could be said with propriety to be *"among them"*, whether by *"them"* is meant those upon whom the judgment falls, or those who escape, or both, which is perhaps the better idea, although the close connection would seem to refer the first *"them"* of verse 19 to those mentioned in verse 18.

Of all the explanations given that of Delitzsch seems to be less open to serious objection.

"such as escape of them",—i. e., from the judgment previously mentioned. Alexander says these are the survivors of the Jewish nation upon the destruction of Jerusalem under Titus, the elect for whose sake the days were shortened when all besides them perished. These were the first preachers of the Gospel.

Nagelsbach agrees with Alexander and says the destruction of Jerusalem by the Romans was the first act in the judgment to which reference is made in the verses before us; because it could not, he says, be the general judgment to which reference is made, because after that there will be no nations to go to.

Henderson, on the other hand, says that any reference to the Jews here is "violent", and that those intended are the Gentiles who shall have been present at, but have not perished in the judgment of the great overthrow in Palestine, and who go as missionaries to all parts of the world.

Fausset also says they are the Gentile survivors spared by God. He maintains that other Old Testament passages (Isa. 2.2,3; Micah 5.7; Zech. 14.16-19) represent, not the Jews going as missionaries to the Gentiles, but that the Gentiles come up to Jerusalem to learn the ways of the Lord there.

Ver. 20. *"they"*,—Not the messengers of verse 19, who bring back converts to the true religion. These come by faith and not by litters and mules and dromedaries, and besides *"such as escape"* from the judgment could hardly have furnished all the expense attached to the process mentioned in this verse. Furthermore the *"they"* mentioned here is evidently regarded as different from the Israelites who are mentioned in the last part of the verse.

The reference is doubtless to the Gentiles mentioned in verse 19 (F. Na. Del.).

"your brethren",—This doubtless refers not to Gentiles (V. Al. Um. Ew. Ges.), but to the Jews (F. He. Ma. Kn. Na. and his translator, Hit. Hend.)

Ver. 21. *"And of them also will I take"*,—i. e., of the Gentiles.

(F. Um. Ew. Ma. Ges. Del. Ros.)   It refers to an abrogation of the ancient national distinction.   (Compare these same authorities under Chap. 61.5,6.)

Kimchi resolves the sentence or its meaning into, "I will take of them, i. e., of the Gentiles, for the priests and Levites, as drawers of water and hewers of wood, etc."

Hitzig, Knobel and Cheyne refer it to the scattered Jews, who will be brought home.   But why should being scattered deprive one of being a priest if he was of the tribe of Levi?

The reference is of course to the enjoyment of direct access to God which was formerly enjoyed by the ministers of the temple alone.   Vitringa refers it to the Christian ministry, to which Gentiles as well as Jews were admitted.   He says the words, *"I will take of them"*, implies selection of some kind from among the mass and so it is not to be allowed to all believers.   His criticism is not, however, well sustained.   Since all the priests were Levites, the two may have been mentioned here merely with a view to identify the two classes, both names being given lest either should appear to be excluded.

"bring their oblation",—This bringing of the Jews by the Gentiles will be regarded by God as a•precious, unbloody offering which the Gentiles offer unto Him.

Ver. 22.   This refers to the entire preceding promise including verse 21.   The name and seed of Israel, that is, Israel as a nation with the same ancestors and an independent name, is to remain forever.

Delitzsch says, "The prophet thus represents to himself the Church of the future on a new earth and under a new heavens, but he is unable to represent the eternal in the form of eternity; he represents it to himself as an unending continuation of temporal history.

Ver. 23.   *"from one Sabbath to another"*,—The Sabbath is therefore to be perpetually obligatory on earth.

"before me",—i. e., at Jerusalem, as the next verse certainly shows. The Jewish writers all say that the scene is laid in Jerusalem and the Septuagint actually has the name of Jerusalem inserted in this verse.

Henderson remarks that, "it is absolutely impossible that all should assemble at Jerusalem", but as the scene of the next verse is laid in the environs of Jerusalem, he seems to think the two verses are tantamount to saying that everywhere, all over the world, people will assemble for worship and go out to the environs of Jerusalem and see, etc.

Why may it not be that the nations could be there through their representatives?

Nagelsbach says, "It would have been impossible for the inhabitants of the circumscribed Palestine to have come up to Jerusalem once a month, but in the new conditions in that far off future of the new heavens and the new earth this will be possible for all flesh."

Alexander says the verse is merely a prediction of the general diffusion of the true religion with its stated observances and religious forms, and that the prophet, in accordance with his constant practice, speaks of the emancipated Church in language borrowed from the state of bondage.

Ver. 24. *"they"*,—i. e., all flesh.

"go forth",—i. e., to the environs of Jerusalem. South of Jerusalem is the valley of Hinnon where a perpetual fire was kept to burn the refuse thrown there.

"look upon the dead bodies", etc.,—The word denotes a qualified seeing, i. e., with pleasure, or interest, or satisfaction, or horror, as the case may be. Here it is with horror, says the translator of Nagelsbach. Fausset says it is with satisfaction, and this he says is not inconsistent with true love for them to thus look with satisfaction upon what God has done to the wicked.

"the dead bodies", i. e., of these slain by the Lord in that time of great judgment.

The neighborhood of Jerusalem becomes the scene of God's retributive judgment as predicted in verse 18.

Says Delitzsch, "Whereas we are forced to transfer what is set forth in verse 23, in accordance with Zech. 14.16, to the yet unglorified earth of those days; the last part of verse 24, on the other hand, looks like eternal punishment raised above the conditions of temporality. The prophet blends temporal and eternal. This world and the next coalesce to his view; the new creating of the heavens and the earth does not in his view go beyond the horizon of the present life; for the separation of what lies on this side of the gulf of the 'regeneration' and what lies beyond it we must look to the New Testament. The latter knows of a new setting up of the present Jerusalem after "the times of the Gentiles" have run their course, and of a glorious temporal restoration of Israel; but it knows also of a worm that dies not and of a fire that is never quenched beyond the history of time."

THE BOOK OF

JEREMIAH

(B. C. 629—B. C. 588)

CHAPTER THREE

14 Return, O backsliding children. saith Jehovah; for I am a husband unto you: and I will take you one of a city, and two of a family, and I will bring you to Zion. 15 And I will give you shepherds according to my heart, who shall feed you with knowledge and understanding. 16 And it shall come to pass, when ye are multiplied and increased in the land, in those days, saith Jehovah, they shall say no more, The ark of the covenant of Jehovah; neither shall it come to mind; neither shall they remember it; neither shall they [1]miss it; neither [2]shall it be made any more. 17 At that time they shall call Jerusalem the throne of Jehovah; and all the nations shall be gathered unto it, to the name of Jehovah, to Jerusalem: neither shall they walk any more after the stubbornness of their evil heart. 18 In those days the house of Judah shall walk [3]with the house of Israel, and they shall come together out of the land of the north to the land that I gave for an inheritance unto your fathers.

[1]Or, *visit*
[2]Or, *shall* that *be done*
[3]Or, *to*

Vers. 14-18. Promise of Final Restoration and Blessing to the Jews.

Ver. 14. There is no doubt that this verse as well as the whole passage contains an allusion to the final period.

"one of a city and two of a family",—Though there be but one or two Israelites in a foreign city they shall not be forgotten. All shall be restored. (F. Na. He. Noy. Kim. Ros.) There is another view which explains, "and even if so few fulfill the conditions of true reform". (Ei. Ew. Graf.) But this would seem to be a definite statement that only a few would return, and the other explanation is much to be preferred.

The expressions *"city"* and *"tribe"* intimate quite plainly that the cities and tribes of the heathen are in view.

Ver. 15. *"pastors"*,—Older commentators understand by these pastors, Zerubbabel, Joshua, Ezra and later the Apostles and their successors, and this is of course the case unless we see in the return under Zerubbabel, and in the Christian Church only the beginnings of the fulfillment of this promise, all of which will depend upon the view to be taken of the prophecy as a whole.

Ver. 16. *"when ye be multiplied"*,—The Israel of the future is first to become numerous in order to become fitted for the concluding and perfected revelation of the kingdom.

"The ark of the covenant",—This will be no more mentioned because the thing itself and every thought of it will have disappeared.

Ver. 17. *"Jerusalem the throne of the Lord"*,—What the ark had been to Jerusalem, Jerusalem is now to be in relation to all the nations. All Jerusalem is then to be the throne of the Lord. On the one hand this reminds us of Micah 4 but on the other of Rev. 21.

"all the nations",—So also is it in Revelation 21.

Ver. 18. Two distinct apostacies, that of Judah and that of Israel, were foretold (verses 8 and 10). There has been of course a developing fulfillment of this prophecy of reunion of the two tribes of Israel in spiritual Israel as God gathers one convert here and another there into His Church, but so far as the nation is concerned the two sections of it have never been united since the Babylonish captivity. The ten tribes are unknown to the present day and the prophet, gaze into the inconceivably distant future as he will, can see no restoration of these tribes. Nagelsbach reminds us that this prophecy was not fulfilled by the return under Zerubbabel and Ezra, because (a) not even the whole of Judah, to say nothing of the whole of Israel, then returned, and (b) not even Judah, to say nothing of the heathen, had then returned to the Lord. He also reminds us that it was not fulfilled by the founding of the Christian Church, because (a) the reunion of Judah and Israel has not yet taken place, the latter being unknown as to their whereabouts, (b) Israel in general has rejected the Lord and refused to enter the Christian Church, and (c) the heathen have not begun to come to the Lord and to the Jerusalem that is above in any such measure as prophesied. It would seem therefore that we must still wait for the complete fulfillment of this prophecy, and that it must be reserved for the final period to bring back the lost tribes of

Israel to the light of salvation, and to effect their restoration together with the tribes of Judah, if a literal as well as a spiritual fulfillment of this prophecy is to be looked for.   (Isa. 11.12,13; Ezek. 37.16-22; Hos. 1.11.)

The prophesied coming together in verse 18 of Judah and Israel seems to be the performance of the command given to them in verse 14.

CHAPTER TWELVE

14 Thus saith Jehovah against all mine evil neighbors, that touch the inheritance which I have caused my people Israel to inherit: Behold, I will pluck them up from off their land, and will pluck up the house of Judah from among them. 15 And it shall come to pass, after that I have plucked them up, I will return and have compassion on them; and I will bring them again, every man to his heritage, and every man to his land. 16 And it shall come to pass, if they will diligently learn the ways of my people, to swear by my name, As Jehovah liveth; even as they taught my people to swear by Baal; then shall they be built up in the midst of my people. 17 But if they will not hear, then will I pluck up that nation, plucking up and destroying it, saith Jehovah.

Vers. 14-17.   OBEDIENCE REWARDED BY FINAL UNION IN JEHOVAH.

Ver. 14.   *"evil neighbors",*—This expression refers to the Gentile nations, the Edomites, Moabites, Ammonites, Philistines and Assyrians, nations that were always endeavoring to assault Israel.   These nations, as well as Israel, were carried away into exile by Nebuchadnezzar.

"I will pluck them up from off their land",—The pronoun in this sentence points of course to these heathen nations and the expression is prophetic of their being carried away into exile.

"pluck up the house of Judah from among them",—Keil and Nagelsbach, with most commentators, take this in an evil sense also as referring to the carrying away of Judah into captivity, contending, as they do, that the same word *"pluck"* cannot occur in the two corresponding clauses in two different senses.   Judah and her neighboring nations, they say, will share the same fate, Judah directly and her neighbors indirectly, because what they did against Judah was done against Judah's God.   The carrying away of Judah, they say, involves her liberation from the attacks of her neighbors.   Calvin, Fausset and others, however, take the word *"pluck"* in a favorable sense and say it refers to the Jews who had fled to these nations and were being oppressed by them, the forcible word *"pluck"* being used because the heathen would never willingly give them up.   This latter is perhaps the better explanation, there being little force in the objection raised by the other authorities quoted.

Fausset would have us believe that God is here speaking consolation to the elect remnant among the Jews.

The *"them"* of verse 15 refers to the evil neighbors of verse 14.

CHAPTER SIXTEEN

14 Therefore, behold, the days come, saith Jehovah, that it shall no more be said, As Jehovah liveth, that brought up the children of Israel out of the land of Egypt; 15 but, As Jehovah liveth, that brought up the children of Israel from the land of the north, and from all the countries whither he had driven them. And I will bring them again into their land that I gave unto their fathers.

Vers. 14,15.   CONSOLATORY PROMISE OF FUTURE RESTORATION

"*from the land of the north*",—It was from the north that the Chaldeans came, and the primary reference is of course here to the restoration from captivity in Babylon. ·

"*from all the countries*",—Israel was not, save in a very limited sense, gathered from all the countries at the time of the return from Babylon, and while this return is doubtless the one primarily meant, it is perhaps true, as Fausset would have us believe, that "the return hereafter is the full and final accomplishment contemplated."

Campbell Morgan makes here the following interesting remarks, "The restoration is now compared with the deliverance out of Egypt and the assertion is made that marvelous as that exodus was, this final work of God for Israel will so transcend it in majestic power that 'it shall no more be said, The Lord liveth that brought up the children of Israel out of the land of Egypt'.   Here again I must ask you to note that the restoration is from a world-wide dispersion and that the 'land' is identified beyond peradventure as 'their land that I gave unto their fathers'—not the United States, not England, nor any land where the Jews may have temporary peace and prosperity, but Palestine.   It is impossible to seriously pretend that this prediction has been fulfilled in any sense.   Who, for example, ever referred to the return to Palestine under sufferance of a heathen king of less than fifty thousand men of Judah as an event so supremely wonderful as to efface by its greater splendor the amazing events of the exodus. The same comparison is repeated in Chap. 23.7,8."

CHAPTER TWENTY-THREE

1 Woe unto the shepherds that destroy and scatter the sheep of my pasture! saith Jehovah.   2 Therefore thus saith Jehovah, the God of Israel, against the shepherds that feed my people: Ye have scattered my flock, and driven them away, and have not visited them; behold, I will visit upon you the evil of your doings, saith Jehovah.   3 And I will gather the remnant of my flock out of all the countries whither I have driven them, and will bring them again to their folds; and they shall be fruitful and multiply. 4 And I will set up shepherds over them, who shall feed them; and they shall fear no more, nor be dismayed, neither shall any be lacking, saith Jehovah.

5 Behold, the days come, saith Jehovah, that I will raise unto David a righteous ¹Branch, and he shall reign as king and ²deal wisely, and shall execute justice and righteousness in the land. 6 In his days Judah shall be saved, and Israel shall dwell safely; and this is his name whereby he shall be called: ³Jehovah our righteousness. 7 Therefore, behold, the days come, saith Jehovah, that they shall no more say, As Jehovah liveth, who brought up the children of Israel out of the land of Egypt; 8 but, As Jehovah liveth, who brought up and who led the seed of the house of Israel out of the north country, and from all the countries whither I had driven them. And they shall dwell in their own land.

¹Or, *Shoot* Or, *Bud*
²Or, *prosper*
³Or, *Jehovah is our righteousness*

Vers. 1-8.   THE FUTURE RESTORATION AND CONVERSION OF ISRAEL.

Israel, or the Ten Lost Tribes, were carried away captive into Assyria in B. C. 725.   Their captivity was complete in number and time and to this day they have not returned. Judah was carried away captive into Babylon in B. C. 588. It was partial in number and time. They returned and remained until finally scattered about A. D. 70.

The shepherds mentioned in verses 1 and 2 are the ungodly monarchs on the throne of David who brought ruin to the kingdom and scattered Israel.

Ver. 3. In this and the following verses the restoration from Babylon is foretold in language which, Fausset and many others say, in its fullness can only apply to the final restoration of both Judah and Israel as set forth in verse 6.

"out of all countries",—As remarked in Chap. 16.15 Israel was not, save in a very limited sense, gathered out of *all* countries when they were brought back from Babylon (see also verse 8).

Ver. 4. *"neither shall any be lacking"*,—i. e., none shall be missing or detached from the rest. Neither these words nor those immediately preceding them, *"they shall fear no more"*, have ever yet been fully fulfilled.

Scofield says, "The restoration here foretold is not to be confounded with the return of the feeble remnant of Judah under Ezra, Nehemiah and Zerubbabel at the end of the seventy years (Jer. 29.10). At His first advent Christ, David's righteous Branch, did not 'execute justice and judgment in the earth', but was crowned with thorns and crucified. Neither was Israel the nation restored, nor did the Jewish people say, 'The Lord our Righteousness'. The prophecy is yet to be fulfilled."

Ver. 5. *"Behold the days come"*,—The phrase does not indicate any progress in time as compared with what precedes.

"righteous",—He would be righteous in distinction from the unrighteous rulers before Him who were brought into view in the previous chapter. Fausset calls attention to the fact that in the New Testament He is set forth not only as righteous Himself, but as righteousness to us, so that we become the righteousness of God in Him. (Romans 10.3,4; II. Cor. 5.19-21.) This, however, has nothing to do with our passage.

"unto David",—In fulfillment of the promise made to him. (I Chron. 17.12; II Sam. 7.12.)

"Branch",—Not precisely a limb of the tree but a shoot or sprout, which springing up from the root becomes itself the tree. This word, as a rule, has the collective sense, but not necessarily so. It has this sense when used of a plant of the field but this sense does not necessarily obtain when used in its spiritual signification.

Graf tries to show that the word is to be taken in its collective sense here but against this are the following facts:

1. Zech. 3.8 calls this same branch a man whose name is Branch.

2. Ezek. 34.23 says, "And I will set ONE Shepherd over them."

3. The Jews expected ONE great King.

4. Our verse says he shall reign as *"king"* and verse 6 says he shall be called *"our righteousness"*, and these things cannot be said of a series of kings.

Chap. 33.17 does not prove that the branch of David is a collective grouping together of all David's future posterity, but only that this one Branch of David shall possess the throne forever.

Some think that *"branch"* contradicts *"shepherds"*, the one being singular and the other plural, and they explain by rendering, "I will raise up shepherds, *then* the Messiah; or better shepherds, the chief of whom will be the Messiah." But the two promises are not to be joined. First we have the raising up of good shepherds in contrast to the evil shepherds that have destroyed the flock, the people; then the promise, says Keil, is further explained to the effect that these good shepherds shall be raised up to David in the *"righteous branch"*, that is, in the promised seed of his sons. The good shepherds are summed up in the person of the Messiah, as being comprised therein. In the one Branch of David the people shall have given unto them all the good shepherds needed for their deliverance.

Hengstenberg takes shepherds in a generic sense, a generic plural, which does not exclude the possibility of one shepherd being intended. But this will not do in as much as Jeremiah elsewhere presents the prospect of a multiplicity of rulers of the seed of David for the time of the great restoration. (See Chap. 33.17,18,22,26.)

Ver. 6. Says Fausset, "So far are the Jews as yet from having enjoyed the temporal blessings here foretold as the result of the Messiah's reign, that their lot has been for eighteen centuries worse than ever before. The accomplishment must therefore still be future."

"he shall be called Jehovah our righteousness",—Nagelsbach says this refers not to the Branch but to the people Israel, and he appeals to Chap. 33.16 for proof of his opinion. But this passage does not prove his case by any means, although of course grammatically he can support his decision. It is, however, much better with others to take it as referring to *"Branch"*, the Messiah. (K. F. Hit. Cow.)

It is hardly sound exegesis to take this expression as a proof of the divinity of Christ, or in the sense that His righteousness becomes ours by substitution or that we are justified in Him through the forgiveness of sins, as did the old commentators. Chap. 33.16, where the same expression is used of Jerusalem, the people, ought to make this plain. The expression is here, as elsewhere, the abbreviation of a sentence and means, "He by whom Jehovah deals righteousness", i. e., makes the people righteous in contrast to what other shepherds had done, and with this Chap. 33.16 corresponds well.

Vers. 7,8. (See Chap. 16.14,15.)

Of course there are those also who give a figurative or spiritual interpretation to the whole passage, maintaining that the reference in verse 3 is to the great ingathering of the Christian period and to the pastoral work of the Messiah as set forth in verses 5 to 8. The whole is, says Cowles, a magnificent picture of the Messiah's reign, and the reference in verse 6 is to the kingdom of the Messiah as enlarged by the accession of the Gentiles through the work of the Holy Spirit, the true Israel according to Gal. 6.16. There is no question as to the spiritual interpretation being possible; the question is as to whether these prophecies can be taken in a literal sense. If they can, they ought so to be taken.

20 The anger of Jehovah shall not return, until he have executed, and till he have performed the intents of his heart; in the latter days ye shall understand it perfectly.

Ver. 20. JEHOVAH'S UNALTERABLE PURPOSE AS TO ISRAEL AND HER ENEMIES.

"in the latter days",—This expression refers of course primarily to the days of their Babylonish captivity, but if there is an ultimate scope to the prophecy, as many would have us believe, it is that which points to the Jews in their final dispersion, who shall at last consider their sin and turn to the Messiah. (Hos. 3.5.)

CHAPTER TWENTY-FOUR

4 And the word of Jehovah came unto me, saying, 5 Thus saith Jehovah, the God of Israel: Like these good figs, so will I regard the captives of Judah, whom I have sent out of this place into the land of the Chaldeans, for good. 6 For I will set mine eyes upon them for good, and I will bring them again to this land: and I will build them, and not pull them down; and I will plant them, and not pluck them up. 7 And I will give them a heart to know me, that I am Jehovah: and they shall be my people, and I will be their God; for they shall return unto me with their whole heart.

Vers. 4-7. THE PROMISE OF RESTORATION AND CONVERSION OF ISRAEL.

The good figs represent the better classes taken away to Babylon. God sifted the nation and saved the more precious grain for replanting in the land after captivity. When Cyrus told them they could go back, the best men, the men of faith, would more quickly respond. While the primary reference is to the chastening effect of the Babylonish captivity, the language in its fullness, Fausset and others would have us believe, applies to the more complete conversion hereafter of the Jews *"with their whole heart"* (verse 7) through the painful discipline of the present dispersion.

CHAPTER TWENTY-FIVE

This chapter is devoted to the prophecy of the Seventy Years Captivity. In verse 5 the prophet reminds the people that the land had been promised to them and to their fathers for ever and ever, but because of their disobedience (verse 7) they were to be carried into the land of the north and there serve the king of Babylon for seventy years. This is one of the clearest and most definite of Jeremiah's predictions; but his prediction of the deliverance which Jehovah was to work out for His people is just as clear and just as definite. At the end of the seventy years redemption was to come to the holy nation along with judgment upon Babylon (verse 12) and all the kingdoms of the then known world (verses 19-26), including Jerusalem and the cities of Judah (verse 18).

The seventy years of captivity may be reckoned to begin with the first deportation of Judah to Babylon (B. C. 606), or with the final deportation (B. C. 588).

29 For, lo, I begin to work evil at the city which is called by my name; and should ye be utterly unpunished? Ye shall not be unpunished: for I will call for a sword upon all the inhabitants of the earth.

Ver. 29. If Jehovah does not spare His own city (verse 18) should the Gentile nations imagine that there is no judgment for them?

"all the inhabitants of the earth",—"The scope of this great prophecy", says Scofield, "cannot be limited to the invasion of Nebuchadnezzar. The prophecy leaps to the very end of this age. (See 'Day of the Lord', Isa. 2.10-22; Rev. 19.11-21; 'Armageddon', Rev. 16.14; 19.11-21.)"

While in what follows verse 25 no nation is mentioned by name the limits of the territory to be reached by the judgment are strictly defined by the words, *"all the inhabitants of the earth"* (verses 29,30), *"all flesh"* (verse 31), and *"from one end of the earth even unto the other end of the earth"*, and from this it would seem to follow that the prophet here beholds the judicial act of God in its last and highest stage.

"He now describes", says Nagelsbach, "the world-judgment, i. e., the judgment of all nations of the earth absolutely without regard to their greater or lesser importance. The storm rolls from nation to nation until the whole surface of the earth is covered with the slain. There is no possibility of escaping the day of slaughter though they howl and wallow as it breaks upon them (verses 34,35)."

CHAPTER TWENTY-NINE

12 And ye shall call upon me, and ye shall go and pray unto me, and I will hearken unto you.
13 And ye shall seek me, and find me, when ye shall search for me with all your heart.
14 And I will be found of you, saith Jehovah, and I will ¹turn again your captivity, and I will gather you from all the nations, and from all the places whither I have driven you, saith Jehovah; and I will bring you again unto the place whence I caused you to be carried away captive.

¹Or, *return to*

Vers. 12-14. ISRAEL TO BE REGATHERED TO HER ORIGINAL INHERITANCE.

There are those who would have us believe that there is here in verses 12 and 13 a brief renewal of the promise of Deut. 4.29,30, and in verse 14 a brief summary of the promise in Deut. 30.3-5. Notice the similarity of language. There can be no doubt, however, that the promise here looks primarily and specially, as seen by verse 10, to the times of Cyrus and Zerubbabel.

CHAPTER THIRTY

1 The word that came to Jeremiah from Jehovah, saying, 2 Thus speaketh Jehovah, the God of Israel, saying, Write thee all the words that I have spoken unto thee in a book. 3 For, lo, the days come, saith Jehovah, that I will ¹turn again the captivity of my people Israel and Judah, saith Jehovah; and I will cause them to return to the land that I gave to their fathers, and they shall possess it.
4 And these are the words that Jehovah spake concerning Israel and concerning Judah. 5 For thus saith Jehovah: We have heard a voice of trembling, ²of fear, and not of peace.

¹Or, *return to*
²Or, there is *fear, and no peace*

6 Ask ye now, and see whether a man doth travail with child: wherefore do I see every man with his hands on his loins, as a woman in travail, and all faces are turned into paleness? 7 Alas! for that day is great, so that none is like it: it is even the time of Jacob's trouble; but he shall be saved out of it. 8 And it shall come to pass in that day, saith Jehovah of hosts, that I will break his yoke from off thy neck, and will burst thy bonds; and strangers shall no more make him their bondman; 9 but they shall serve Jehovah their God, and David their king, whom I will raise up unto them. 10 Therefore fear thou not, O Jacob my servant, saith Jehovah; neither be dismayed, O Israel: for, lo. I will save thee from afar, and thy seed from the land of their captivity; and Jacob shall return, and shall be quiet and at ease, and none shall make him afraid. 11 For I am with thee, saith Jehovah, to save thee: for I will make a full end of all the nations whither I have scattered thee, but I will not make a full end of thee; but I will correct thee in ³measure, and will in no wise ⁴leave thee unpunished.

12 For thus saith Jehovah, Thy hurt is incurable, and thy wound grievous. 13 There is none to plead ⁵thy cause, ⁶that thou mayest be bound up: thou hast no healing medicines. 14 All thy lovers have forgotten thee; they seek thee not: for I have wounded thee with the wound of an enemy, with the chastisement of a cruel one, for the ⁷greatness of thine iniquity, because thy sins were increased. 15 Why criest thou ⁸for thy hurt? thy pain is incurable: for the ⁷greatness of thine iniquity, because thy

sins were increased, I have done these things unto thee. 16 Therefore all they that devour thee shall be devoured; and all thine adversaries, every one of them, shall go into captivity; and they, that despoil thee shall be a spoil, and all that prey upon thee will I give for a prey. 17 For I will restore health unto thee, and I will heal thee of thy wounds, saith Jehovah; because they have called thee an outcast, *saying*, It is Zion, whom no man ⁹seeketh after.

18 Thus saith Jehovah: Behold, I will ¹⁰turn again the captivity of Jacob's tents, and have compassion on his dwelling-places; and the city shall be builded upon its own ¹¹hill, and the palace shall ¹²be inhabited after its own manner. 19 And out of them shall proceed thanksgiving and the voice of them that make merry: and I will multiply them, and they shall not be few; I will also glorify them, and they shall not be small. 20 Their children also shall be as aforetime, and their congregation shall be established before me; and I will punish all that oppress them. 21 And their prince shall be of themselves, and their ruler shall proceed from the midst of them; and I will cause him to draw near, and he shall approach unto me: for who is he that ¹³hath had boldness to approach unto me? saith Jehovah. 22 And ye shall be my people, and I will be your God.

23 Behold, the tempest of Jehovah, *even his* wrath, is gone forth, a ¹⁴sweeping tempest: it shall burst upon the head of the wicked. 24 The fierce anger of Jehovah shall not return, until he have executed, and till he have performed the intents of his heart: in the latter days ye shall understand it.

³Heb. *judgment*
⁴Or, *hold thee guiltless*
⁵Or, *thy cause; for* thy *wound thou hast no medicines* nor *plaster*
⁶Heb. *for closing up,* or *pressing.*
⁷Or, *multitude*
⁸Or, *for thy hurt, because thy pain is incurable?*

⁹Or, *careth for*
¹⁰Or, *return to*
¹¹Or, *mound* Heb. *tel.*
¹²Or, *remain*
¹³Heb. *hath been surety for his heart.*
¹⁴Or, *gathering*

Vers. 1-24. ISRAEL IN TRIBULATION AND THE PROMISED DELIV-
            ERANCE.

There are some of course who think this chapter looks primarily to the restoration of the Jews from Babylon and the raising up of the Messiah, and while this is doubtless true there can, however, be scarcely any doubt but that it looks on further into the future, as the language plainly indicates, and that whatever restoration was made after the capture of Babylon was but a pledge of the fuller restoration which is yet to take place.

Ver. 3. The ten tribes (Israel) are mentioned first because their captivity had been longer. A few of them only returned with Judah, and this promise having never been fulfilled must await for its complete fulfillment for the days which are still to come.

Ver. 5. Jehovah here introduces the Jews as speaking for themselves. The dark background set forth in this and the following verses only sets off in stronger light the blessings that are to be revealed.

This verse and the two following do not refer to the political convulsion and calamities of the heathen nations that resulted in the capture of Babylon and the releasing of the Jews, as some think, but to the troubles of the Jews themselves.

With regard to verses 5 to 8 Campbell Morgan says, "Exposition is scarcely needed here. There cannot be two periods of unexampled tribulation, and Jeremiah and Jesus, in Matthew, therefore speak of the same period. The passages cannot refer to the destruction of Jerusalem for while that was a time of Jewish tribulation the Jews were not saved out of it, but were slain by the thousands and the remnant were carried away into slavery. Neither was the Davidic monarchy restored at that time. Jesus says it is the elect who are in tribulation, and Jeremiah tells us of whom Jesus speaks, namely the elect Jews. It is the time of Jacob's trouble. The period then is yet future."

Ver. 6. Nagelsbach says, "The prophet portrays with drastic vividness the effects of the terror by saying that he saw men behaving like women in the pangs of childbirth."

"Ask ye now",—i. e., ask anywhere, consult all the authorities; you will not find an instance.

Ver. 7. Here the cause of this terror is described.

"for that day is great",—The day is the same as that spoken of in verses 5 and 6, and by being "great" is meant that it is marked by great calamities. (Joel 2.11,31; Amos 5.18; Zeph. 1.14.)

Keil has quite properly said, "That day is for Jacob also, that is, for all Israel, a time of distress; for the judgment falls not merely on the heathen nations, but also on the godless members of the covenant people that they may be destroyed from among the congregation of the Lord, but the Israel of God will be delivered." The heathen nations are therefore included in the judgment, which is for both them and Israel, but Israel shall be saved out of it. It is clear therefore that the reference cannot be to the destruction of Jerusalem by the Chaldeans because this cannot be represented at the same time as a day of deliverance for the Jews.

Ver. 8. "in that day",—The day when Jacob shall be saved out of his trouble.

"his yoke",—The pronoun "his" as well as "thy" (thy neck) refers to Jacob, such a change from the third to the second person being quite frequent. God is both speaking about Jacob and addressing him. Foreigners shall no more make him their servant. After the deliverance from Babylon by Cyrus, Judah did become the servant of Persia, Alexandria, Antiochus Epiphanes and Rome, and therefore the full deliverance, it would seem, must be future.

Ver. 9. "David, their king",—The reference is no doubt here to the Messiah. The conception of a second David is analogous to that of the second Adam. The Messiah, it appears, is here called *"David"* not merely as a descendent of David, but as a real David in the highest sense and degree. (See Hos. 3.5.)

"whom I will raise up unto them",—This refers of course to the days of the Messiah which were to come, and is of course an incontrovertible argument that *"the time of Jacob's trouble"* looks *primarily* to a period prior to the appearance of the Messiah.

Ver. 10. *"thy seed"*,—Though you yourselves, by reason of the many years of captivity, may not see the restoration, the promise shall be fulfilled to your seed, "primarily", says Fausset, "at the return from Babylon and fully at the final restoration."

Ver. 11. *"I will not make a full end of thee"*,—Assyria and Chaldea were utterly destroyed, but Israel, after chastisement, was delivered.

Ver. 12. *"Thy hurt is incurable"*,—Her wounds were beyond her own power or that of any human helpers, but not, of course, beyond the power of God.

Ver. 14. *"All thy lovers"*,—i. e., the people formerly allied to thee, Egypt, Assyria and other nations with whom she had formerly made forbidden alliances.

Ver. 15. *"Why criest thou for thy hurt?"*—She had no right to complain and cry because she had brought on this suffering through her own sins.

Ver. 16. I prefer with Nagelsbach to connect this verse with verse 11, although it may quite as logically be connected with verse 13. (F. K. Cow.)

Ver. 18. *"tents"*,—This intimates their present dwelling in Chaldea as temporary only.

"have compassion on his dwelling places",—This means doubtless that the dwellings that have been destroyed will be restored.

"builded upon its own hill",—This rendering is much to be preferred, a hill being the usual site for a city. (F. K. Cow.) It also the better answers the parallel clause, *"after its own manner"*, i. e., in the same becoming way as formerly, than does the rendering of Nagelsbach, "upon its own heap of ruins."

"after its own manner",—This doubtless means *"according to its right"* (Deut. 17.11), that is, in accordance with what a palace requires, after its own fashion.

Cowles says, "When we cannot find an adequate fulfillment for a prophecy like this in its external and literal application, we are certainly justified in assuming its outlook onward to the better, brighter days of King Messiah." This is certainly true, and ought it not to be held as further true that, if in the days of the Messiah its complete fulfillment did not take place, we are justified in looking for a further fulfillment in the days that are yet to come. The restored city and temple under Zerubbabel never did reach the magnificence of the days of Solomon, and neither was this true of Herod's temple.

Ver. 20. *"Their children also shall be as aforetime"*,—Their children shall come into settled and precious relations to the Lord their God, enjoying the full blessings of the covenant even as in the days of old. They shall flourish as in the days of David.

"their congregation shall be established",—They shall no more be shaken or moved from their position.

Ver. 21. *"shall be of themselves"*,—i. e., be a Jew, and not a foreigner. That the words *"prince"* and *"ruler"* refer to the Messiah there can be no doubt, and they can be applicable to Zerubbabel only as a type of Christ, the Messiah.

"cause him to draw near and he shall approach unto me",—God will cause the *"prince"* and the *"ruler"* (the Messiah) to draw near as the great high priest through whom believers also have access to God. He is called *"king"* in verse 9, and here he is called *"prince"* and *"ruler"*. His priestly and kingly characters are similarly combined in Ps. 110.4 and Zech. 6.13. He may approach unto Jehovah and in this the mediatorial position of the king is announced.

"For",—This states the reason why the Lord leads the prince to Himself, i. e., because there is no other who would be capable of entering into this relation of nearness and communion with God.

In this last clause some introduce the word "otherwise", i. e., Who would otherwise, that is, without my special permission, dare commit his heart to approach unto me,—Who would dare such near approach if I had not invited and drawn him? But there is nothing in the Hebrew to represent this word "otherwise", and this alone is fatal to its use.

"who is he",—By some this is taken in the sense of surprise, astonishment, that any sinful mortal should dare such approach; by some as a question of rebuke and repulsion, as if to bid him begone; by some as if the question were one of offended dignity or at least of invaded dignity, inquiring the rank of the intruder who thus presumes to draw near to God. But all this is foreign to the course of the thought and the flow of feeling throughout the chapter. We must, as Cowles says, regard the question as implying on the part of God a joyous welcome to him who thus pledges his heart to draw near unto Him. The question is an emotional one and not a categorical one demanding an answer. Just as the question in Chap. 31.20 does not demand an answer but implies an outburst of parental emotion and gladly welcoming the prodigal home, so here whoever is conceived of as drawing near to God it is evident that God is pleased and gladly welcomes him. The question, Fausset says, implies admiration at one being found competent by reason of his twofold nature, as God and man, for the task.

"hath had boldness",—The literal Hebrew is, "hath been surety for his heart". Fausset gives to this a derived meaning such as "stake", "risk", "venture", and takes the word *"heart"* in the sense of "life", heart being used only as expressive of the courage it takes to undertake such a tremendous thing. Nagelsbach thinks this harsh and renders, "who stands bail for his heart", as if the prophet wishes to say, "Who can stand for his heart that it approach me?" Cowles says the action of the verb terminates upon one's own heart with reference to making approach unto God, hence it would seem that the sense must be "to pledge one's own heart, to

covenant with oneself, solemnly committing and earnestly purposing and endeavoring to approach unto God. Perhaps no better explanation can be found than that given us by Fausset, the answer implied being evidently, no one but the extraordinary person of the Mediator, the Christ, He alone having made His life responsible as the surety in order to gain access not only for Himself but for us."

Vers. 23,24. The reference here is as in Chap. 23.19,20, and refers perhaps *primarily* to the judgment brought on the land and the cities of Judah for their sins through the agency of the Chaldeans, although it must be understood of a judgment extending to Babylon and other heathen nations, the enemies of Israel, as well. It refers of course to all "wicked ones" and in such a way as that the godless members of the covenant people will be excluded from salvation.

"a sweeping tempest",—The idea is that of the rushing sound of the storm as it carries everything along with it. The Authorized Version, "continuing", gives hardly an appropriate meaning.

Hengstenberg connects the verses with what precedes, while Keil connects them with the judgment of verse 5 as a resumption, and Ewald connects them with the first verse of the following chapter, either of the latter two connections being preferable to that of Hengstenberg, as affording smoother transition.

CHAPTER THIRTY-ONE

1 At that time, saith Jehovah, will I be the God of all the families of Israel, and they shall be my people. 2 Thus saith Jehovah, The people that were left of the sword [1]found favor in the wilderness; even Israel, [2]when I went to cause him to rest. 3 Jehovah appeared [3]of old unto me, *saying*, Yea, I have loved thee with an everlasting love: therefore [4]with lovingkindness have I drawn thee. 4 Again will I build thee, and thou shalt be built, O virgin of Israel: again shalt thou be adorned with thy tabrets, and shalt go forth in the dances of them that make merry. 5 Again shalt thou plant vineyards upon the mountains of Samaria; the planters shall plant, and shall [5]enjoy *the fruit thereof*. 6 For there shall be a day, that the watchmen upon the hills of Ephraim shall cry, Arise ye, and let us go up to Zion unto Jehovah our God.

7 For thus saith Jehovah, Sing with gladness for Jacob, and shout [6]for the chief of the nations: publish ye, praise ye, and say, O Jehovah, save they people, the remnant of Israel. 8 Behold, I will bring them from the north country, and gather them from the uttermost parts of the earth, *and* with them the blind and the lame, the woman with child and her that travaileth with child together: a great company shall they return hither. 9 They shall come with weeping; and with supplications will I lead them: I will [7]cause them to walk by rivers of waters, in a straight way wherein they shall not stumble; for I am a father to Israel, and Ephraim is my first-born.

10 Hear the word of Jehovah, O ye nations, and declare it in the isles afar off; and say, he that scattered Israel will gather him, and keep him, as a shepherd doth his flock. 11 For Jehovah hath ransomed Jacob, and redeemed him from the hand of him that was stronger than he. 12 And they shall come and sing in the height of Zion, and shall flow unto the goodness of Jehovah, to the grain, and to the new wine, and to the oil, and to the young of the flock and

[1]Or, *have found . . . when I go*
[2]Or, *when he went to find him rest*
[3]Or, *from afar*
[4]Or, *have I continued lovingkindness unto thee*
[5]Heb. *profane*, or, *make common*. See Lev. 19.23-25; Dt. 20.6; 28.30.
[6]Or, *at the head*

[7]Or, *bring them unto*

of the herd: and their soul shall be as a watered garden; and they shall not sorrow any more at all. 13 Then shall the virgin rejoice in the dance, and the young men and the old together; for I will turn their mourning into joy, and will comfort them, and make them rejoice from their sorrow. 14 And I will satiate the soul of the priests with fatness, and my people shall be satisfied with my goodness, saith Jehovah.

15 Thus saith Jehovah: A voice is heard in Ramah, lamentation, and bitter weeping, Rachel weeping for her children; she refuseth to be comforted for her children, because they are not. 16 Thus saith Jehovah: Refrain thy voice from weeping, and thine eyes from tears; for thy work shall be rewarded, saith Jehovah; and they shall come again from the land of the enemy. 17 And there is hope for thy latter end, saith Jehovah; and *thy* children shall come again to their own border. 18 I have surely heard Ephraim, bemoaning himself *thus*, Thou hast chastised me, and I was chastised, as a calf unaccustomed *to the yoke*: turn thou me, and I shall be turned; for thou art Jehovah my God. 19 Surely after that I was turned, I repented; and after that I was instructed, I smote upon my thigh: I was ashamed, yea, even confounded, because I did bear the reproach of my youth. 20 Is Ephraim my dear son? is he a darling child? for as often as I speak against him, I do earnestly remember him still: therefore my heart [8]yearneth for him; I will surely have mercy upon him, saith Jehovah.

21 Set thee up waymarks, make thee guide-posts; set thy heart toward the highway, even the way by which thou wentest: turn again, O virgin of Israel, turn again to these thy cities. 22 How long wilt thou go hither and thither, O thou backsliding daughter? for Jehovah hath created a new thing in the earth: A woman shall encompass a man. 23 Thus saith Jehovah of hosts, the God of Israel, Yet again shall they use this speech in the land of Judah and in the cities thereof, when I shall [9]bring again their captivity: Jehovah bless thee, O habitation of righteousness, O mountain of holiness. 24 And Judah and all the cities thereof shall dwell therein together, the husbandmen, and they that go about with flocks. 25 For I have satiated the weary soul, and every sorrowful soul have I replenished. 26

[8]Heb. *soundeth*
[9]Or, *return to*

Upon this I awaked, and beheld; and my sleep was sweet unto me.

27 Behold, the days come, saith Jehovah, that I will sow the house of Israel and the house of Judah with the seed of man, and with the seed of beast. 28 And it shall come to pass that, like as I have watched over them to pluck up and to break down and to overthrow and to destroy and to afflict, so will I watch over them to build and to plant, saith Jehovah. 29 In those days they shall say no more, The fathers have eaten sour grapes, and the children's teeth are set on edge. 30 But every one shall die for his own iniquity: every man that eateth the sour grapes, his teeth shall be set on edge.

31 Behold, the days come, saith Jehovah, that I will make a new covenant with the house of Israel, and with the house of Judah: 32 not according to the covenant that I made with their fathers in the day that I took them by the hand to bring them out of the land of Egypt; [10]which my covenant they brake, although I was [11]a husband unto them, saith Jehovah. 33 But this is the covenant that I will make with the house of Israel after those days, saith Jehovah: I will put my law in their inward parts, and in their heart will I write it; and I will be their God, and they shall be my people. 34 And they shall teach no more every man his neighbor, and every man his brother, saying, Know Jehovah; for they shall all know me, from the least of them unto the greatest of them, saith Jehovah: for I will forgive their iniquity, and their sin will I remember no more.

35 Thus saith Jehovah, who giveth the sun for a light by day, and the ordinances of the moon and of the stars for a light by night, who [12]stirreth up the sea, so that the waves thereof roar; Jehovah of hosts is his name: 36 If these ordinances depart from before me, saith Jehovah, then the seed of Israel also shall cease from being a nation before me for ever. 37 Thus saith Jehovah: If heaven above can be measured, and the foundations of the earth searched out beneath, then will I also cast off all the seed of Israel for all that they have done, saith Jehovah.

38 Behold, the days come, saith Jehovah, that the city shall be built to Jehovah from the tower of Hananel unto the gate of the corner. 39 And the measuring line shall go out further straight onward unto the hill Gareb, and shall

[10]Or, *forasmuch as they brake my covenant*
[11]Or, *lord over them*
[12]Or, *stilleth the sea, when, etc.*

turn about unto Goah. 40 And the whole valley of the dead bodies and of the ashes, and all the fields unto the brook Kidron, unto the corner of the horse gate toward the east, shall be holy unto Jehovah; it shall not be plucked up, nor thrown down any more for ever.

Vers. 1-40. THE DECREE OF RESTORATION AND THE NEW COVENANT.

Ver. 1. *"At the same time"*,—i. e., in the time of the latter days. Cowles, who refers the fulfillment of the prophecy to the present dispensation, says that it indicates a great enlargement and increase of the visible Church and kingdom of the Messiah. Fausset, of course, calls attention to the fact that the prophecy has never yet been fulfilled.

Ver. 2. The prophet devotes more attention to the ten tribes, Israel, evidently because judging from all appearances they seem irrevocably lost forever, rejected of the Lord.

"left of the sword",—i. e., escaped from the sword of the Chaldeans and were carried captive into the wilderness.

By Ewald and others this verse is made to refer to those who were delivered from the captivity of Egypt. But this cannot be. The Ten Tribes did not then obtain a special deliverance; Pharaoh did not oppress them by the sword; Israel was then led through the desert as a whole and not as a remnant. The whole relates to the future as is proven by verses 4 to 6, which verses only particularize what was said in verses 2 and 3, the perfects in verses 2 and 3 being prophetical. The words *"escaped from the sword"* seem unconditionally to require us to refer the passage to the deliverance of Israel from exile. It is of course proper to conceive of the restoration of Israel from exile under the figure of their exodus out of Egypt into the promised land of their fathers, as in Hos. 2.15.

"when I went to cause him to rest",—This is perhaps better translated by Keil, "Let me go to cause him to rest". Nagelsbach renders it, "Up to bring him to rest", taking it as a command, as it were, from God to Himself. Both of these latter renderings take the words as an expression relating to the future.

Ver. 3. Israel gratefully acknowledges God's favor.

"of old",—Fausset says that this implies that God does not so appear to her now. We prefer the marginal reading, "from afar", implying that the Lord had kept Himself afar off, having almost, as it were, disappeared from their sight. (K. Na. Cow.) Keil says that so long as Israel was in exile the Lord had apparently withdrawn from them. "From afar" probably means from Zion where He was enthroned.

"with lovingkindness have I drawn thee",—This rendering is a proper one, but we prefer with Keil that of the margin as the better, i. e., "I have continued (drawn out) my loving kindness toward thee." (See Ps. 36.4.)

Ver. 5. *"Samaria"*,—i. e., the capital of the Ten Tribes.

"planters shall plant and shalt enjoy the fruit thereof",—The rendering of the Authorized Version is here much to be preferred since it not only gives a far more preferable meaning but adheres strictly to the original language. It shall no longer be that one shall plant and another shall eat the fruit. (See the law about this in Lev. 19.23-25, and see also Isa. 62.8.)

The idea contained in the marginal reading is that the fruits are to be applied to one's own use (Deut. 20.6), i. e., common (profane), no longer restricted to holy use as set forth in Lev. 19.

Ver. 6. *"the hills of Ephraim"*,—This stands for the whole mountainous region of the Ten Tribes.

"up to Zion",—i. e., up to the annual feasts as in the days of old.

Ver. 7. *"the chief of the nations"*,—The reference is to Israel. God estimates the greatness of nations not by man's standard of material resources, but by His electing favor. In this verse the people are urged with prayers and praises to supplicate for the restoration.

Ver. 8. *"and with them"*, etc.—So universal is the restoration to be that not even the most unfit will be left behind.

Ver. 9. *"weeping"*,—Tears of joy as well as penitential tears.

"Ephraim is my first-born",—(See Exodus 4.22). The designation of Israel as a whole in the Exodus passage is here transferred to Ephraim as the head and representative of the Ten Tribes. There is no trace in this prophecy of any preference given Israel over Judah. We have already seen why Ephraim is mentioned first and at greater length than Judah is mentioned a little later. The designation *"first-born"* here simply shows that Israel is not to be in any sense behind Judah; the love which God displayed toward whole Israel is to be shown toward this disobedient part of Israel, the Ten Tribes.

Ver. 10. Even heathen nations afar off will have their attention arrested by this wonderful happening to Israel, and even they must proclaim God's willingness to redeem graciously His people.

Ver. 12. *"to the goodness of the Lord"*,—i. e., to the Lord as the source of all good things.

Ver. 14. *"satiate with fatness"*,—The reference is to the fat pieces of the thank-offering, because numerous offerings will be made to the Lord in consequence of the blessings received from Him.

Ver. 15. Rachel, who so loved her children, is represented as lifting her maternal head from the tomb and looking around on the wild waste of ruin and sees none of her children in their native land.

Nagelsbach says the voice of Rachel is heard in Ramah because her tomb is there, but makes it the Ramah five miles north of Jerusalem. But Gen. 35.16 says Rachel was buried south of Jerusalem and near Bethlehem. Delitzsch says that Rachel's weeping is heard in Ramah, not because her tomb is in that neighborhood but because according to Jer. 40.1 the exiles were assembled there by Nebuchadnezzar before transportation into exile. But Keil rightly objects to this view because it was Jews who were assembled there and were from there to be carried away captive, whereas it was over Israelites or Ephraimites that *had* been carried away that Rachel weeps.

Samuel lived in Ramah, five miles north of Jerusalem, not far from Gibeah. (I Sam. 7.17.) All attempts to fix the tomb of Rachel at Ramah north of Jerusalem are groundless. If then she was buried near Bethlehem it was far away from Ramah, there being no Ramah near Bethlehem.

Keil says, and we feel rightly, that the weeping is heard at Ramah as the most northernly situated border town of the two kingdoms, whence the wailing that had arisen sounded far and near, and could be heard in Judah. She weeps as their common mother. As the people are often included under the notion of *"the daughter of Zion"* as their ideal representative, so here the great ancestress of Ephraim, Benjamin and Manasseh is named as the representative of the maternal love shown by Israel in the pain felt when the people are lost, the mother of the ruling tribe, Ephraim, appearing thus as the personification of the kingdom ruled by it.

This verse is quoted by Matthew after relating the story of the massacre of the children at Bethlehem. From this we can hardly conclude, as did the older theologians, that Jeremiah directly prophesied that event, because it will not fit in with the context of the prophecy. The expression used by Matthew only shows that the prophecy of Jeremiah received a new fulfillment through the act of Herod.

Ver. 16. *"thy work shall be rewarded"*,—i. e., thy parental weeping for thy children; all the pain and grief which thou hast borne and all thy toiling in love for Zion shall not go unrewarded; thy grief shall not be perpetual because thy children, the exiles, shall return.

Ver. 17. *"there is hope for thy latter end"*,—i. e., all thy calamities shall have a prosperous issue.

Ver. 18. *"Thou hast chastised me and I was chastised"*,—The first refers to the chastisement itself and the second to the beneficial effects of this chastisement.

"as a calf unaccustomed to the yoke",—As one therefore needing the goad. Fausset says that when Israel is restored, which as yet she has not been, she will confess that the chastisement was for her good.

Ver. 19. *"smote upon thy thigh"*,—i. e., as a sign of mourning, of terror and horror, of grief and indignation against oneself. (Ezek. 21.17.)

Ver. 20. To the question Fausset says a negative reply was to be expected, i. e., No, to judge from the way he has acted and lived. And yet God so regards him, and on Ephraim's being turned to God he is so welcomed. The question does not really call for an answer. It is, as Cowles says, the outburst and overflow of strong emotion. It seems almost like an expression of God's surprise at Himself for so considering Ephraim after all his sin. (Na. Ma. Ros. Cow.)

"speak against him",—i. e., threaten him on account of his idolatry.

Ver. 21. Waymarks and guide posts and heaps of stones to guide their way through the desert on their return.

"to these thy cities",—The words *"these"* shows that the author has his point of view in Palestine and not in the land of captivity,—the summons issues from the homeland.

Ver. 22. *"go hither and thither"*,—i. e., after human help.

"A woman shall encompass a man",—The Christian Fathers almost unanimously interpreted this of the Virgin Mary compassing Christ. A number of arguments are presented favoring this view but none of them

162

are very strong, while there are objections which are fatal to this interpretation. The new arrangement on earth, whatever it may be, is mentioned as a motive which should rouse Ephraim to return without delay to the Lord and to His cities. This should be borne in mind in trying to explain the meaning of this strange sentence. Therefore the following will not do:

1. Those who formerly behaved like women shall be men. (Lut.)
2. A woman shall change into a man. (Ew.)
3. The woman shall protect the man. (Ros. Ma. Ges.)
4. The woman shall turn the man to herself. (Na.)

None of these four interpretations furnish the motive mentioned and none of them can be lexically sustained because the word *"encompass"* does not bear the meanings thus given to it; nor can any of them with much propriety be called a new creative act or a new arrangement of things.

5. A fifth and very commendable interpretation is that of Keil, who thinks the word *"encompass"* is better rendered "embrace," and who translates as follows, "A woman shall embrace a man", the woman being the virgin Israel and the man being Jehovah. Hitzig renders, "make suit to a man", while Cowles retains the word *"encompass"*, but all three of these authorities rightly perceive that the general idea has been set forth with special reference to the relation between the woman, Israel, and the man, Jehovah, and their interpretations are practically one and the same thing. There is a change of relations between the Lord and Israel. The word means to compass with love and care, to lovingly embrace, the natural and fitting dealing on the part of the stronger to the weak and those who need assistance, and now the new thing that God creates consists in this, that the woman, the weaker nature, that needs help, will lovingly and solicitously surround the man, the stronger. God deals so condescendingly toward weak Israel that she can lovingly embrace Him. It is a new thing for a woman to woo a man. The word *"encompass"* means to go around about and the idea is that of soliciting the hand, wooing the heart, seeking the love of her rightful Lord.

Ver. 23. Here the prophecy turns to Judah and conceives of her as coming back from her captivity. Jerusalem was again to be the habitation of righteousness, and Zion will again be the seat of the Divine King.

Ver. 26. These words refer not to the people languishing in exile (Jer.), nor to God (Um. Ros. Mic.), such a thing as sleep being inappropriate as referred to God. They refer to the prophet. (K. F. Na. Hit. Cow. Hen. Kim.)

Ver. 29. Nagelsbach explains, "The fathers have begun to eat sour grapes, but not until the teeth of the children have become blunted by them", the meaning being that the punishment does not always come immediately upon the first who are guilty, but upon those of the second, third and fourth generations. But the change of tense in the verbs is against this, the first being perfect and the second imperfect, and this shows that the blunting of the children's teeth is set down as the result of the fathers' eating. The proverb means that the children atone for the misdeeds of their fathers.

Why shall they no more say this?

1. Because they will have no more occasion to say it. (K. Hit. Cow.) The children born in exile of their exiled parents complained doubtless that they were suffering for the sins of their fathers. It is true that during the season of exile the nation did suffer the retributions that had been accumulating for ages. The following verse would seem to favor this view of the matter.

2. Because they will no longer be disposed to thus reflect upon the government of God, as in that wicked proverb, but they will perceive that every one has to suffer for his own guilt. (Graf.) But the proverb is not a wicked one; it is true.

3. Because after the re-establishment of Israel, the Lord will make known to His people His grace in so glorious a manner that the favored ones will perceive the righteousness of His government and His judgments. (K.)

Ver. 30. This verse unquestionably contains the opposite of verse 29. It does not, however, says Keil, contain a judgment expressed by the prophet in opposition to that of his contemporaries, but it simply declares that the opinion contained in that current proverb shall no longer be accepted then, but the favored people will recognize in the death of the sinner the punishment due them for their own sins.

Ver. 31. *"a new covenant"*,—i. e., as compared with the old one made with their fathers at Sinai when the people were led out of Egypt.

"The remaining verses of this chapter", says Cowles, "have but one theme—the richer spiritual blessings of the Gospel age."

Ver. 33. *"after those days"*,—Keil thinks the inexact expression *"after"* owes its origin to the idea contained in the phrase, *"in the end of the days"*. The days meant are the coming days.

Fausset says, "With *'the remnant according to the election of grace'* in Israel the new covenant has already taken effect, but with regard to the whole nation its realization is reserved for the last days, to which Paul refers this prophecy in an abridged form in Romans 11.27."

Ver. 34. This verse does not contain a prohibition but a prediction. Why is this prediction to be true?

Is it because knowledge will be so universal that there is no longer occasion for teaching? The words, *"all shall know me"*, would seem so to imply. Yet the connection with the previous verse, which makes the teaching of the Spirit so prominent, would seem to indicate another reason, suggesting that far less teaching is left for man to do under the new covenant than under the old covenant. The words therefore do not mean that, "the office of the teacher must cease" (Hit.), but merely that the knowledge of God will, under the new covenant, be no longer dependent upon the communication and instruction of man. The Holy Spirit is a teacher so glorious as to eclipse all human agencies. The statement of the verse is comparative rather than absolute.

Ver. 36. *"these ordinances"*,—i. e., the established arrangements.

Though Israel's national polity has been broken up they are still reserved as a distinct people though scattered among the nations of the world for twenty centuries. Cowles insists that we must look beyond the outward Israel for the fulfillment of this prophecy to the spiritual Israel, the sanctified people of the living God, while others, conceding the view of Cowles as one proper form of interpretation, contend that there is yet to be an outward and literal fulfillment in the days that are yet to come.

Ver. 37. The measuring of the heavens and the searching out of the foundations of the earth are set forth as things impossible to be done and adduced to show that this casting off of Israel can never be.

Vers. 38-40. The measuring starts from the well-known *"tower of Hananel"* in the northwest quarter of the city, runs to the northwest corner gate, then includes Gareb, the hill of the leprous outside of the city on the northwest, then to the hill of Goah, the place of capital punishment; then finally the whole valley of the son of Hinnom, including Tophet defiled by the accumulated filth of the city with its worms and ever-burning fires. All these defiled places are to be embraced in the city and are to be made thoroughly clean and holy before the Lord.

By some the hill of Goah is supposed to be identical with Golgotha (V. Hen.), but by others (Hit. Fur.) it is taken as the projecting rock of the castle of Antonia on the southwest corner. It can hardly be identified as Golgotha because the latter was north or northwest of the city and the line was running down toward the southwest, while furthermore lexical considerations are against so taking it.

Says Keil, and with him agrees Cowles, "The prophecy does not refer to the building of Jerusalem after the exile, but to the erection of a more spiritual kingdom of God in the Messianic age—the prophecy reaches on to the time when the kingdom of God shall have been perfected—it contains under an Old Testament dress the outlines of the image of the heavenly Jerusalem which John saw on Patmos in its full glory."

CHAPTER THIRTY-TWO

36 And now therefore thus saith Jehovah, the God of Israel, concerning this city, whereof ye say, It is given into the hand of the king of Babylon by the sword, and by the famine, and by the pestilence: 37 Behold, I will gather them out of all the countries, whither I have driven them in mine anger, and in my wrath, and in great indignation; and I will bring them again unto this place, and I will cause them to dwell sately. 38 And they shall be my people, and I will be their God: 39 and I will give them one heart and one way, that they may fear me for ever, for the good of them, and of their children after them: 40 and I will make an everlasting covenant with them, that I will not turn away from following them, to do them good; and I will put my fear in their hearts, that they may not depart from me. 41 Yea, I will rejoice over them to do them good, and I will plant them in this land [1]assuredly with my whole heart and with my whole soul. 42 For thus saith Jehovah: Like as I have brought all this great evil upon this people, so will I bring upon them all the good that I have promised them. 43 And fields shall be bought in this land, whereof ye say, It is desolate, without man or beast; it is given into the hand of the Chaldeans. 44 Men shall buy fields for money, and subscribe the deeds, and seal them, and call witnesses, in the land of Benjamin, and in the places about Jerusalem, and in the cities of Judah, and in the cities of the hill-country, and in the cities of the lowland, and in the cities of the South: for I will cause their captivity to return, saith Jehovah.

[1]Heb. *in truth*

165

Vers. 36-44. FURTHER PROPHECY OF ISRAEL'S RETURN AND RESTORATION.

Ver. 36. *"Therefore thus saith the Lord"*,—These words correspond to the same words in verse 28. *"Therefore"*,—i. e., because nothing is too hard for the Lord. He is now drawing the second inference from the fact that nothing is too hard for Him to accomplish. Fausset would render, *"Now nevertheless"* without seeking connection with the *"therefore"* of verse 28. This is permissible, although the former construction appears to be the better one.

Ver. 37. This prophecy has never received as yet but meager fulfillment, and while some look solely to the Gospel age for their fulfillment, others believe the words look on to the last days, to the kingdom-age which is to follow, though accepting of course as a possible interpretation the view which finds their fulfillment in the Gospel age.

Ver. 40. *"they may not depart from me"*,—Fausset says this has never yet been fully realized as to the Israelites.

Ver. 41. *"assuredly with my whole heart"*,—The first planting was imperfect as was the first covenant because it was only hypothetical and because the Lord knew the condition would not be kept and He could not therefore be in it with His whole heart. Now He knows, for He Himself has promised (verse 40) that the condition will be fulfilled; therefore He can designate the planting as done *"assuredly"* (*"in truth"*— margin), without the reservation that it is only for a short time, and also as one which He performs with a whole and an undivided heart.

Ver. 42. The restoration from Babylon was only a slight foretaste, says Fausset, of the grace to be expected by Israel at last through Christ.

CHAPTER THIRTY-THREE

1 Moreover the word of Jehovah came unto Jeremiah the second time, while he was yet shut up in the court of the guard, saying, 2 Thus saith Jehovah that doeth it, Jehovah that formeth it to establish it; Jehovah is his name: 3 Call unto me, and I will answer thee, and will show thee great things, and [1]difficult, which thou knowest not. 4 For thus saith Jehovah, the God of Israel, concerning the houses of this city, and concerning the houses of the kings of Judah, which are broken down *to make a defence* against the mounds and against the swords; 5 while *men* come to fight with the Chaldeans, and to fill them with the dead bodies of men, whom I have slain in mine anger and in my wrath, and for all whose wickedness I have hid my face from this city: 6 Behold, I will bring

[1]Heb. *fortified*

it [2]health and cure, and I will cure them; and I will reveal unto them abundance of peace and truth. 7 And I will cause the captivity of Judah and the captivity of Israel to return, and will build them, as at the first. 8 And I will cleanse them from all their iniquity, whereby they have sinned against me; and I will pardon all their iniquities, whereby they have sinned against me, and whereby they have transgressed against me. 9 And *this city* shall be to me for a name of joy, for a praise and for a glory, before all the nations of the earth, which shall hear all the good that I do unto them, and shall fear and tremble for all the good and for all the peace that I procure unto it.

10 Thus saith Jehovah: Yet again there shall be heard in this place, whereof ye say, It is waste, without man

[2]Heb. *a bandage*

and without beast, even in the cities of Judah, and in the streets of Jerusalem, that are desolate, without man and without inhabitant and without beast, 11 the voice of joy and the voice of gladness, the voice of the bridegroom and the voice of the bride, the voice of them that say, Give thanks to Jehovah of hosts, for Jehovah is good, for his lovingkindness *endureth* for ever; *and of them* that bring *sacrifices* of thanksgiving into the house of Jehovah. For I will cause the captivity of the land to return as at the first, saith Jehovah.

12 Thus saith Jehovah of hosts: Yet again shall there be in this place, which is waste, without man and without beast, and in all the cities thereof, a habitation of shepherds causing their flocks to lie down. 13 In the cities of the hill-country, in the cities of the lowland, in the cities of the South, and in the land of Benjamin, and in the places about Jerusalem, and in the cities of Judah, shall the flocks again pass under the hands of him that numbereth them, saith Jehovah.

14 Behold, the days come, saith Jehovah, that I will perform that good word which I have spoken concerning the house of Israel and concerning the house of Judah. 15 In those days, and at that time, will I cause a Branch of righteousness to grow up unto David; and he shall execute justice and righteousness in the land. 16 In those days shall Judah be saved, and Jerusalem shall dwell safely; and this is *the name* whereby she shall be called: Jehovah our righteousness. 17 For thus saith Jehovah: [3]David shall never want a man to sit upon the throne of the house of Israel; 18 neither shall the priests the Levites want a man before me to offer burnt-offerings, and to burn meal-offerings, and to do sacrifice continually.

19 And the word of Jehovah came unto Jeremiah, saying, 20 Thus saith Jehovah: If ye can break my covenant of the day, and my covenant of the night, so that there shall not be day and night in their season; 21 then may also my covenant be broken with David my servant, that he shall not have a son to reign upon his throne; and with the Levites the priests, my ministers. 22 As the host of heaven cannot be numbered, neither the sand of the sea measured; so will I multiply the seed of David my servant, and the Levites that minister unto me.

23 And the word of Jehovah came to Jeremiah, saying, 24 Considerest thou not what this people have spoken, saying, The two families which Jehovah did choose, he hath cast them off? thus do they despise my people, that they should be no more a nation before them. 25 Thus saith Jehovah: If my covenant of day and night *stand not*, if I have not appointed the ordinances of heaven and earth; 26 then will I also cast away the seed of Jacob, and of David my servant, so that I will not take of his seed to be rulers over the seed of Abraham, Isaac, and Jacob: for I will [4]cause their captivity to return, and will have mercy on them.

[3]Heb. *There shall not be cut off from David.*
[4]Or, *return to their captivity*

Vers. 1-26. FURTHER PROMISE OF ISRAEL'S GLORIOUS FUTURE.

Ver. 2. *"Jehovah is His name"*,—In the name lies the guarantee of His action. The Lord not only has power to carry out His thoughts but He completes what He has spoken and determined on.

Ver. 3. This verse is probably addressed to Jeremiah though some think it addressed to Israel. It is a call to pray for that which the Lord has determined to grant, i. e., the restoration. (F. Na.)

"difficult",—The Hebrew means "inaccessible", incredible—hard to man's understanding, namely the restoration of the Jews, an event despaired of.

"which thou knowest not",—God had revealed this thing to Jeremiah, but the unbelief of the people in rejecting the grace of God had caused him to forget God's promise, as though the case of the people admitted of no remedy.

Ver. 4. *"against the mounds"*,—It is not that the houses are broken down by the missiles of destruction hurled from these mounds, as Fausset thinks; the houses are pulled down, according to Isa. 22.10, in order to fortify the walls of the city in defense against the attacks from these mounds of the besiegers. The houses of kings are mentioned along with others to show that no house is spared to defend the city.

Ver. 5. The Jewish soldiers go to fight with the Chaldeans but only to fill the houses with their own slain. (K. F. Cow.) The word *"them"* is a bit troublesome, inasmuch as the houses already thrown down cannot be filled and of other houses no mention has been made, unless the reference be to the houses before they have been thrown down. Changing the word *"Chaldeans"* to "Jerusalem" and making the mounds and the sword the subject of *"come"*, as Nagelsbach does, is hardly permissible.

Ver. 7. Fausset reminds us that the specification of both Judah and Israel can only apply fully to the future restoration.

"as at the first",—(Isa. 1.26. See also verse 11 of this chapter.)

Ver. 9. *"it"* refers to the city of Jerusalem, *"them"* to its inhabitants, and *"they"* to the Gentiles. (K. F. Na. Cow.)

"fear and tremble",—It is the idea of wholesome fear that is here most strongly set forth. The ungodly shall tremble for fear of God's judgment on them, and the penitent shall reverentially fear and turn to the Lord. That this latter thought is the predominating one is set forth in the fact that Jerusalem is to be a *"joy"* unto all the nations when they hear of what the Lord has done for it.

Ver. 13. *"pass under the hands of him that numbereth them",*— The usual mode of counting the flocks. The fact that they must be numbered speaks therefore of multitudes.

Ver. 14. The promise of verses 14 to 16 has already been given in Chap. 23.5,6, where see remarks.

"that good word",—(See Deut. 28.1-14).

This verse forms a transition from the promise of the restoration and blessings of Israel in the future to the special promise of the renewal and completion of the Davidic monarchy; the blessing promised to the people in the *"good word"* culminates in the promise (verse 15) that the Lord will cause a righteous spout to spring up for David.

Ver. 16. *"Jehovah our righteousness",*—The righteousness which the Messiah works in and on Jerusalem may, without changing the substance of the thought, be attributed to Jerusalem herself inasmuch as she reflects this righteousness bestowed upon her. This name in Chap. 23.5,6 is given to the sprout of David, and the transference of it to the city of Jerusalem is connected with the fact that the name only expresses what the Messiah is to the people.

Ver. 17. This prediction does not preclude a temporary interruption, and has been fulfilled in Christ, the Messiah.

Ver. 18. Hebrews say this priesthood is to give way to a higher one. Nagelsbach says, "Though lost in its outward, temporal and local form, it was really afterwards established in its ideal character." Fausset says, "Messiah's literal priesthood (Heb. 7.17,21,25-28) and His followers' spiritual priesthood and sacrifices (Rom. 12,1; 15.16; I Pet. 2.5,9; Rev. 1.6) shall never cease, according to the covenant with Levi, broken by the priests, but fulfilled in the Messiah (Num. 25.12,13; Mal. 24.5,8)."

Keil says, "The prophecy which follows shows clearly that the restoration spoken of will not be a reinstitution of the old form which was then perishing but a renovation of it, in its essential features, to a permanent existence."

Ver. 20. *"of the day"*,—Better rendered, "with the day", and so "with the night", answering to the covenant with David. The kingdom and the priesthood is to flourish in the Messiah, says Fausset, when the whole nation shall temporarily and spiritually prosper.

Ver. 22. *"as the hosts of heaven . . . the sands of the sea"*,—Jahn remarks that this would be a burden on the people if there is to be an unlimited increase of the royal and priestly posterity. But Exodus 19.6 says, "Israel shall be a kingdom of priests", and Isaiah 61.6 says, "ye shall be named the priests of Jehovah and men shall call you the ministers of our God." The priestly and royal character of the whole people is referred to, and this is only to be realized, says Nagelsbach, as the whole of regenerated humanity is included.

Vers. 24-26. The same promise is here repeated, especially to rebut the unbelieving cavils of some among the people. By saying what they did, they despised the Lord's people and insulted the Lord Himself by assuming that His promises were worthless. The *"two families"* are of course Judah and Israel, and it is hardly worth while to rebut the view of Hitzig that *"this people"* refers to foreign nations.

CHAPTER THIRTY-NINE

> 7 Moreover he put out Zedekiah's eyes and bound him with chains, to carry him to Babylon.

Ver. 7. THE BEGINNING OF THE TIMES OF THE GENTILES.

At this date began "the times of the Gentiles", from which time on Jerusalem has been "trodden down of the Gentiles", and this has been true from the time of Nebuchadnezzar even until this day. Jerusalem has been during all this time under Gentile rule and dominion.

CHAPTER FORTY-SIX

> 1 The word of Jehovah which came to Jeremiah the prophet concerning the nations.
>
> 27 But fear not thou, O Jacob my servant, neither be dismayed, O Israel: for, lo, I will save thee from afar, and thy seed from the land of their captivity; and Jacob shall return, and shall be quiet and at ease, and none shall make him afraid. 28 Fear not thou, O Jacob my servant, saith Jehovah; for I am with thee: for I will make a full end of all the nations whither I have driven thee; but I will not make a full end of thee, but I will correct thee in ¹measure, and will in no wise ²leave thee unpunished.
>
> ¹Heb. *judgment*
> ²Or, *hold thee guiltless*

Vers. 1,27,28. THE JUDGMENT OF THE GENTILES AND THE DE-
LIVERANCE OF ISRAEL.

Ver. 1. *"concerning the nations"*,—Scofield calls attention to the
fact that we are to distinguish between a near and a far fulfillment of
these prophecies against the Gentiles. The near vision, as seen in verse 2,
is of a Babylonish invasion of Egypt, but verses 27 and 28 look forward
to the judgment of the nations after Armageddon (Matt. 25.32), and the
deliverance of Israel.

On verses 27 and 28 see Chap. 30.10,11, from which place they
are here repeated.

CHAPTER FORTY-EIGHT

46 Woe unto thee, O Moab! the people of Chemosh is undone; for thy sons are taken away captive, and thy daughters into captivity.

47 Yet will I ¹bring back the captivity of Moab in the latter days, saith Jehovah. Thus far is the judgment of Moab.

¹Or, *return to*

Vers. 46,47. THE CONVERSION OF THE HEATHEN IN THE FINAL
PERIOD.

Ver. 46. This verse is copied from Numbers 21.29, and in the
verse which follows restoration is promised for the sake of righteous Lot,
their progenitor.

Ver. 47. In verse 42 it is said that Moab shall be destroyed. The
fact seems to be that under the Chaldean army, shortly after Jeremiah
wrote, Moab suffered severely, yet she rallied again and was prosperous
in the age of Josephus; but its nationality has long since ceased.

Gospel blessings, temporal and spiritual, to the Gentiles in the last
days are intended.

"in the latter days",—i. e., at the end of the days, in Messianic times
there is in store for them a turn in their fortunes. Similar promises are
made for Egypt (Chap. 46.26), and for Ammon and Elam, in Chap.
49.6 and 39.

CHAPTER FORTY-NINE

Vers. 6,39. (See remarks under Chap. 48.47.) There was but
partial fulfillment under Cyrus of these promises, but they were to have a
more complete fulfillment in Gospel times.

CHAPTER FIFTY

4 In those days, and in that time, saith Jehovah, the children of Israel shall come, they and the children of Judah together; they shall go on their way weeping, and shall seek Jehovah their God. 5 They shall inquire concerning Zion with their faces ¹thitherward, *saying,* Come ye, and ²join yourselves to Jehovah in an everlasting covenant that shall not be forgotten.

¹Or, *hitherward*
²Or, *they shall join themselves*

6 My people have been lost sheep: their shepherds have caused them to go astray; they have turned them away on the mountains; they have gone from mountain to hill; they have forgotten their resting-place. 7 All that found them have devoured them; and their adversaries said, We are not guilty, because they have sinned against Jehovah, the habitation of righteousness, even Jehovah, the hope of their fathers.

19 And I will bring Israel again to his ⁸pasture, and he shall feed on Carmel and Bashan, and his soul shall be satisfied upon the hills of Ephraim and in Gilead.

20 In those days, and in that time, saith Jehovah, the iniquity of Israel shall be sought for, and there shall be none; and the sins of Judah, and they shall not be found: for I will pardon them whom I leave as a remnant.

⁸Or, *fold*

33 Thus saith Jehovah of hosts; The children of Israel and the children of Judah are oppressed together; and all that took them captive hold them fast; they refuse to let them go.

34 Their Redeemer is strong; Jehovah of hosts is his name; he will thoroughly plead their cause, that he may give rest to the earth, and disquiet the inhabitants of Babylon.

Vers. 4-7,19,20,33,34. THE CHOSEN PEOPLE RESTORED AND UNITED IN ETERNAL COVENANT WITH THEIR GOD.

Ver. 4. *"In those days and in that time"*,—i. e., the time coincident with the fall of Babylon.

"they shall go on their way weeping",—Weeping doubtless with joy at their restoration and with sorrow at the remembrance of their sins and sufferings.

Fausset reminds us that this prophecy was fulfilled in part when some few of the Ten Tribes of Israel joined with Judah in a covenant with God at the restoration of Judah to its land, but that the full event is yet to come. (Chap. 31.9; Hos. 1.11; Zech. 12.10.)

Ver. 5. *"thitherward"*,—The Hebrew is "hitherward", Jeremiah's prophetic standpoint being at Zion.

Ver. 6. *"they have gone from mountain to hill"*,—These words have no meaning unless they are understood of the idolatrous dealings of Israel, the mountains and hills being those on which they sacrificed to idols.

"their resting place",—This is, according to verse 7, Jehovah the hope of their fathers.

Ver. 19. Carmel and Bashan were the most fertile tracts of the country and the mountains of Ephraim and Gilead furnished fodder in abundance for the sheep.

Ver. 20. Fausset says the mention of Israel as well as Judah shows that the full reference is to times yet to come.

"and there shall be none . . . and they shall not be found",—God's promise to grant pardon points to the time of the new covenant. God for Christ's sake will count them innocent. The reference is to Messianic times and the sin and iniquity refers not to idolatry but to the rejection of the Messiah, and of this it is predicted that they shall not be guilty in those days, though thus guilty now.

Ver. 33. He anticipates an objection in order to answer it, i. e., ye have been no doubt oppressed and therefore ye despair of deliverance; but remember your Redeemer is strong and therefore can and will deliver you.

Ver. 34. *"strong"*,—i. e., as opposed to the power of Israel's oppressor.

"thoroughly plead their cause",—God, as their advocate, delivers His people not by mere might but by righteousness.

THE BOOK OF

EZEKIEL

(B. C. 595—B. C. 574)

CHAPTER ELEVEN

17 Therefore say, Thus saith the Lord Jehovah: I will gather you from the peoples, and assemble you out of the countries where ye have been scattered, and I will give you the land of Israel. 18 And they shall come thither, and they shall take away all the detestable things thereof and all the abominations thereof from thence. 19 And I will give them one heart, and I will put a new spirit within you; and I will take the stony heart out of their flesh, and will give them a heart of flesh; 20 that they may walk in my statutes, and keep mine ordinances, and do them: and they shall be my people, and I will be their God. 21 But as for them whose heart walketh after the heart of their detestable things and their abominations, I will bring their way upon their own heads, saith the Lord Jehovah.

Vers. 17-21. ISRAEL PROMISED RESTORATION TO THEIR OWN LAND.

The literal fulfillment of this prophecy did actually take place in their restoration at the end of the Babylonian captivity. Yet it was only a partial fulfillment after all. Only a small portion, and these practically all from the house of Judah, returned.

Then further, while Israel did practically relinquish the practice of gross idolatry (verse 18), it did not then attain to that newness of heart predicted in verses 19 and 20. This only commenced with the preaching of John the Baptist and with the coming of Christ. The Shekinah glory had departed (Chap. 9.3; 10.18 and 11.23), the ark was not restored, nor was the second temple strictly inhabited by God until Christ came, who made it more glorious than the first temple (Hag. 2.9): Even then His stay was short, and ended in His being rejected. The full realization of the promise must then still be future, since the greater portion of Israel has still that hardness of the stony heart.

CHAPTER FOURTEEN

21 For thus saith the Lord Jehovah: How much more when I send my four sore judgments upon Jerusalem, the sword, and the famine, the evil beasts, and the pestilence, to cut off from it man and beast! 22 Yet, behold, therein shall be left [1]a remnant that shall be carried forth, both sons and daughters: behold, they shall come forth unto you, and ye shall see their way and their doings; and ye shall be comforted concerning the evil that I have brought upon Jerusalem, even concerning all that I have brought upon it. 23 And they shall comfort you, when ye see their way and their doings: and ye shall know that I have not done [2]without cause all that I have done in it, saith the Lord Jehovah.

[1]Heb. *they that escape*

[2]Or, *in vain*

Vers. 21-23. THE JUDGMENTS OF GOD JUSTIFIED BY THE DISOBEDIENCE OF THE PEOPLE.

This chapter from verse 12 to its close tells of the judgment of Jehovah upon Jerusalem.

The "*remnant*" in verse 21 are not those who save their lives or are spared by Jehovah because of their righteousness, but those who, after escaping, go to the captives in Babylon and by their wicked way and character cause the exiles there to acknowledge that Jehovah was justified in bringing severe judgment upon both Jerusalem and its inhabitants.

CHAPTER SIXTEEN

46 And thine elder sister is Samaria, that dwelleth at thy left hand, she and her daughters; and thy younger sister, that dwelleth at thy right hand, is *Sodom* and her daughters.

53 And I will ¹turn again their captivity, the captivity of Sodom and her daughters, and the captivity of Samaria and her daughters, and the captivity of thy captives in the midst of them; 55 And thy sisters, Sodom and her daughters, shall return to their former estate; and Samaria and her daughters shall return to their former estate; and thou and thy daughters shall return to your former estate.

¹Or, *return to*

60 Nevertheless I will remember my covenant with thee in the days of thy youth, and I will establish unto thee an everlasting covenant. 61 Then shalt thou remember thy ways, and be ashamed, when thou shalt receive thy sisters, thine elder *sisters* and thy younger; and I will give them unto thee for daughters, but not by thy covenant. 62 And I will establish my covenant with thee; and thou shalt know that I am Jehovah: 63 that thou mayest remember, and be confounded, and never open thy mouth any more, because of thy shame, when I have forgiven thee all that thou hast done, saith the Lord Jehovah.

Vers. 46,53,55,60-63.   THE HARLOTRY OF JERUSALEM FORGIVEN.

This portion of the chapter is exceedingly difficult to understand.

Ver. 46.   God says that in a sense Jerusalem is worse than her elder and younger sisters, Samaria and Sodom.   They were called her sisters because they both belonged to the same mother-land, Canaan, and perhaps more appropriately in a spiritual sense, because they were all animated by the same spirit of idolatry.   In what sense could Samaria be said to be older than Sodom?   None of the reasons given are at all satisfactory, and we are inclined to the explanation of Keil, who takes the words in the sense of "greater" and "smaller", i. e., with reference to the extent of the kingdoms.

That Samaria and Sodom stand for kingdoms is clearly proven by the expression "*daughters*", i. e., the cities adjacent and dependent upon the capital.

Ver. 53.   This verse announces the restoration of Sodom and Samaria as well as that of Jerusalem, so that all boasting on the part of Israel is precluded.   You shall be restored, but Sodom and Samaria shall be restored with you.

But we know nothing of an exile of Sodom.   Then, too, in what sense can Sodom be said to be restored since Sodom and all the cities of the plains together with their inhabitants were utterly destroyed and sunk into the depths of the Dead Sea?

Some think that Sodom stands for the Moabites and the Ammonites, Moab and Ammon being the offspring of Lot.   (F. Lap.)   But they were no more Sodomites than Lot was.

Some think Sodom stands for the heathen. (Ori. Jer. Hav.) But in what sense could Sodom stand for heathenism any more than Samaria could.

Some think they stand for the descendents of Sodom, who were carried captive to Elam in the expedition against Sodom mentioned in Genesis 14, and for those of Zoar, which city was spared at the petition of Lot. (Lap.) These descendents were destined to restoration just as it was also merely the descendents of Samaria and Jerusalem that could be restored. (Coc. Neteler.) The prophecy in this sense might be said to have commenced its fulfillment on the day of Pentecost when it is expressly stated the Elamites were present.

The only other explanation is that of Keil, who contends that the literal Sodom was meant, and yet he says, "We certainly cannot think for a moment of any earthly restoration of Sodom", for even if the cities could be found, how could the inhabitants, who perished in them, be restored, and, says Keil, "in this connection it is chiefly to them that the words refer." "Therefore", says Keil, "the realization of the prophecy must be sought for beyond the present order of things, in one that extends into the life everlasting, and can only take place on the great day of the resurrection of the dead in the persons of the former inhabitants of Sodom and her neighboring cities. Not only will the Gospel be preached to all nations before the end comes, but even to the dead." He thinks that all heathen nations that died before Christ or departed from this earthly life without having heard the Gospel preached will still have a chance to hear it and an opportunity to believe it.

It is difficult to decide with so little data before us, but perhaps that view which takes Sodom as representing the heathen in general is the more acceptable.

Ver. 55. *"return to their former estate"*,—If by Sodom the Moabites and the Amonites are represented there was a partial fulfillment in the return under Cyrus (Jer. 48.47), and if by Sodom is represented the heathen the full realization is yet future, says Fausset.

But what is their *"former estate"*?

It cannot be their wicked state before their punishment to which they are to be returned in order that they may thereafter be converted.

Keil thinks it is to their first estate in the sense of the restoration of all moral relations to their original moral constitution, which will begin by the reception of the heathen world, represented by Sodom, into the kingdom of Christ and will attain its perfection in the general restoration of the world to its original glory, the palingenesia. (II Pet. 3.13; Rom. 8.18; Matt. 19.28.) The forgiveness of the inhabitants of Sodom, he insists, can only take place on the great day of the resurrection of the dead.

If, however, Sodom be taken as representing the heathen in general (to which view it would seem that even Keil has committed himself), why may not the *"return to their former estate"* be a symbolical way of expressing the idea of bestowing pardoning grace, as simply relating to the pardon of Jerusalem and Samaria, the covenant nation, and of Sodom representing the heathen? If Sodom does not represent the heathen then of course her pardon must be delayed, if it is to come at all, until the resurrection day.

This much is certain under any explanation, namely, that the beginning of the fulfillment of this prophecy commenced with the establishment of the covenant made through Christ and with the reception of the believing portion of Israel in Judea, Samaria and Galilee (Acts 8.5; 9.31), and with the spread of the Gospel among the heathen and their entrance into the kingdom of Christ.

Calvin, and Fausset following him, says we do not have any promise at all until we reach verse 60, and that verses 53 and 55 mean, When Sodom and Samaria shall be restored, then Jerusalem also will be restored, i. e., *never!* This is sustained neither by the letter nor by the connection.

Ver. 60. The unfaithfulness of man can never alter the faithfulness of God. The reference is not to a new covenant, but to the renewing or perfecting of the old one, the fulfillment of the promise given to David in II Samuel.

Ver. 61. *"thou shalt receive thy sisters"*,—This of course means in this place not only Sodom and Samaria and their daughters, but heathen nations generally, great and small.

The prophecy goes even beyond Rom. 11.25 presenting, as it does, not only to the covenant nation but to all heathen nations the prospect of being eventually received into the kingdom of Christ.

"but not by thy covenant",—By what grammatical law Keil connects these words with *"daughters"* we fail to see. It must mean either the letter of the Old Testament, the covenant of works, upon which the Jews rested even while they broke it, or what is still better, the expression must be taken, as do the majority, as meaning, Not that thou on thy part hast stood to the covenant, but that I am the Lord; I change not.

CHAPTER SEVENTEEN

22 Thus saith the Lord Jehovah: I will also take of the lofty top of the cedar, and will set it; I will crop off from the topmost of its young twigs a tender one, and I will plant it upon a high and lofty mountain: 23 in the mountain of the height of Israel will I plant it; and it shall bring forth boughs, and bear fruit, and be a goodly cedar: and under it shall dwell all birds of every wing; in the shade of the branches thereof shall they dwell. 24 And all the trees of the field shall know that I, Jehovah, have brought down the high tree, have exalted the low tree, have dried up the green tree, and have made the dry tree to flourish: I, Jehovah, have spoken and have done it.

Vers. 22-24. PLANTING OF THE TRUE TWIG OF THE STEM OF DAVID.

Ver. 22. The Lord will fulfill the promise which He had given to the seed of David. As Nebuchadnezzar had broken off a twig from the top of the cedar and brought it to Babel (verse 13), but through it the kingdom of Judah had been brought to destruction, so will Jehovah Himself crop off a tender twig from the top of the high cedar and plant it upon a high mountain and it shall be a shelter to the whole world and shall be forever. This tender twig is none other than the Messiah, originally "a tender plant and root out of a dry ground". (Isa. 53.2.)

"the cedar",—i. e., the royal house of David.

"of its young twigs a tender one",—The idea of the tender "twig"

or "shoot" or "sprout" indicates not so much the youthful age of the Messiah (Hit.) as it does His lowly origin.

"a high and lofty mountain",—i. e., Zion, destined, says Fausset, "to be the moral center and eminence of grace and glory shining forth to the world, out-topping all mundane elevation. The kingdom, typically begun at the return from Babylon, and rebuilding of the temple, fully began with Christ's appearing and shall have its highest manifestation at His reappearing to reign on Zion, and thence over the whole earth."

Ver. 23. "and under it shall dwell all birds of every wing",—Says Keil, "All the inhabitants of the earth will not only find food from the fruit of this tree, but protection under its shadow." "The expression", says Schroeder, "points to Noah's ark of safety, and the meaning is, all the different nations and families of men upon earth." Says Fausset, "The Gospel 'mustard tree', small at first, but at length receiving all under its covert."

Ver. 24. "And all the trees of the field",—These are the collective ruling powers of the world, the kings and royal families of the earth, just as the cedar represents the royal house of David.

"high tree . . low tree . . green tree . . . dry tree",—The high tree, Schroeder thinks, points to Jehoiachin and the green tree to Zedekiah.

Keil says that the high and green tree naturally suggests the royal house of David and the dry tree Jehoiachin, and while these suggestions are not to be set aside, at the same time the words are not to be restricted to any particular persons, but are applicable to every high and green, or withered and lowly tree, i. e., not merely to kings alone, but to all men in common.

According to Hengstenberg the high tree is the worldly sovereignty, the green tree, Nebuchadnezzar's sovereignty of the world at the time; while the low tree and the dry tree represent the house of David with special reference here, of course, to the Messiah.

Thus Fausset says, "All the empires of the world, represented by Babylon, once flourishing (green tree), shall be brought low before the once depressed (dry), but then exalted kingdom of Messiah and His people, the head of whom shall be Israel."

CHAPTER TWENTY

33 As I live, saith the Lord Jehovah, surely with a mighty hand, and with an outstretched arm, and with wrath poured out, will I be king over you. 34 And I will bring you out from the peoples, and will gather you out of the countries wherein ye are scattered, with a mighty hand, and with an outstretched arm, and with wrath poured out; 35 and I will bring you into the wilderness of the peoples, and there will I enter into judgment with you face to face. 36 Like as I entered into judgment with your fathers in the wilderness of the land of Egypt, so will I enter into judgment with you, saith the Lord Jehovah. 37 And I will cause you to pass under the rod, and I will bring you into the bond of the covenant; 38 and I will purge out from among you the rebels, and them that transgress against me; I will bring them forth out of the land where they sojourn, but they shall not enter into the land of Israel: and ye shall know that I am Jehovah. 39 As for you, O house of Israel, thus saith the Lord Jehovah: Go ye, serve every one his idols, [1]and hereafter also, if ye will not hearken unto me; but my holy name

[1]Or *but hereafter surely ye shall hearken unto me and &c.*

shall ye no more profane with your gifts, and with your idols.

40 For in my holy mountain, in the mountain of the height of Israel, saith the Lord Jehovah, there shall all the house of Israel, all of them, serve me in the land: there will I accept them, and there will I require your offerings, and the [2]first-fruits of your [3]oblations, with all your holy things. 41 [4]As a sweet savor will I accept you, when I bring you out from the peoples, and gather you out of the countries wherein ye have been scattered; and I will be sanctified in you in the sight of the nations. 42 And ye shall know that I am Jehovah, when I shall bring you into the land of Israel, into the country which I [5]sware to give unto your fathers. 43 And there shall ye remember your ways, and all your doings, wherein ye have polluted your selves; and ye shall loathe yourselves in your own sight for all your evils that ye have committed.

44 And ye shall know that I am Jehovah, when I have dealt with you for my name's sake, not according to your evil ways, nor according to your corrupt doings, O ye house of Israel, saith the Lord Jehovah.

[2]Or, *chief*
[3]Or, *tribute*
[4]Or. *with*
[5]Heb. *lifted up my hand*

Vers. 33-44.   The Judgment Upon and the Future Restoration of Israel.

"The passage", says Scofield, "is a prophecy of the future judgment upon Israel, regathered from all nations into the old wilderness of the wanderings.   The issue of this judgment determines who of Israel in that day shall enter the land for kingdom blessing."

Fausset says, "Lest the covenant people should abandon their distinctive hopes, and amalgamate with the surrounding heathen, he tells them that as the wilderness journey from Egypt was made subservient to discipline, and also to the taking out from among them of the rebellious, just so a severe discipline should be administered to them during the next exodus for the same purpose, and so to prepare them for the restored possession of their land.   This was only partially fulfilled before and at the return from Babylon, and its full and final accomplishment is yet future.   The Jews now for long have been actually undergoing such discipline."

Ver. 33. *"and with wrath poured out"*,—These words, says Schroeder, strictly exclude any reference to a future leading into Canaan, because that is a thing of blessing and not of wrath.   He appeals to the later expression, *"into the wilderness of the peoples"*, maintaining that this means the conducting of Israel into another exile, an intensifying of their exile where Jehovah will contend with them.   With this Keil agrees; but this argument is not sufficiently sustained.   The wrath may be poured out on the nations from whom Jehovah's people are delivered, or it may refer to the judgment upon Israel herself through which she is to pass into the blessings which await her.

Ver. 34. *"out from the peoples . : . out from the countries wherein ye are scattered"*,—Keil says that this excludes any reference to the then existing exile, because Israel was then dispersed in one land only and among one people. (Kl.)   But this is not well maintained in view of the extensive empire of the king of Babylon. (Jer. 27.5.)   That there was a partial fulfillment of this prophecy in the return from Babylon cannot upon this ground be disputed.

Ver. 35. *"and I will bring you into the wilderness of the peoples"*, —Says Scofield here, "The passage is a prophecy of the future judgment upon Israel, regathered from all nations into the old wilderness of the wanderings. The issue of this judgment determines who of Israel in that day shall enter the land for kingdom blessing." It is, however, not only a question as to whether the expression should be so literally construed, but in case it is thus construed the wilderness ought the rather to be referred to the desert land lying between them and the land of Palestine, whether we think of the return as from Babylon alone, or from other nations as well whither they may have been scattered. (Hit. Ros.) The future guidance of Israel is depicted as a repetition of their earlier guidance from Egypt to Canaan, and as their Arabian desert experience was an experience of discipline preparatory to their entrance into Canaan (for which very reason the Arabian desert is called the "wilderness of Egypt", whereas it might, so far as geographical reasons are concerned, be called the "wilderness of Canaan", because it touched Canaan as well as Egypt), so is the wilderness experience into which they are now to be led to be one of discipline.

Keil thinks the expression is a figurative one applied to the world of nations, from whom the Israelites were spiritually distinct, whilst outwardly they were in the very midst of them and had to suffer from their oppression. "Consequently", he says, "the leading of Israel out of the nations is not a local and corporeal deliverance out of the heathen lands at all, but a spiritual severance from the heathen world in order that they might not be absorbed in it and so become inseparably blended with the heathen."

Keil's conclusion is, however, by no means a necessary or unavoidable one. The *"peoples"* are without doubt those referred to in verse 34 and *out from whom God says He will bring Israel*, and all this passage teaches, in case it is to be figuratively construed, is that in contrast to the literal *"wilderness of Egypt"* the *"wilderness of the peoples"* refers to Israel's spiritual state or period of trial, discipline and purification while exiles among these *"peoples"*.

Fausset says, "The full and final fulfillment is future. The wilderness state will comprise not only the transition period of their restoration, but the beginning of their occupancy of Palestine, a time in which they shall endure the sorest of all their chastisements, to *'purge out the rebels'* (verse 38), and then the remnant shall *'all serve God in the land'*. Thus the wilderness period does not denote locality, but their state intervening between their rejection and their future restoration."

Schroeder says that the expression, *"wilderness of the peoples"*, and the *"bringing out from the peoples"* as well must be taken spiritually as an aggravation of their exile condition, a spiritual experience of it, so that they should know and feel that they as the people of God were once more in the wilderness, but not at all in the same sense as before in the old wilderness wanderings on their way back from Egypt." This is in substantial agreement with Fausset.

The difficulty arising from the fact that the disciplinary experience in the *"wilderness of the peoples"* is *after* the *"bringing out from the peoples"* is relieved by some who adopt the figurative interpretation by referring the wilderness state to the transition period of discipline from the time Cyrus first decreed their restoration to the time of their complete settlement once more in their own land. Either this explanation must be adopted or that which takes the language literally and refers the *"wilderness of the peoples"* to the desert land lying between Babylon and Palestine. All things considered, the literal construction is the simpler and by far the less objectionable.

Ver. 36.   Though God saved them out of Egypt, says Fausset, He afterwards destroyed in the wilderness them that believed not; so, though He brings the exiles out of Babylon, yet their wilderness state of chastening and discipline continues, even after they were again in Palestine.

Ver. 37.   *"And I will cause you to pass under the rod"*,—The underlying figure is that of a shepherd causing his sheep to pass under his rod for the purpose of inspection and numbering (F. K. Hit.).   We think, however, its application here is that of the royal sceptre of Jehovah, agreeably to the expression *"rule over"* in verse 33.   The prominent idea in the figure being not so much subjection to government (Hen.), nor Jehovah's special care and guardianship (K.), but rather that of the closest inspection, with a view to purification and separation, as is distinctly expressed in verse 38.   (Schr.)

"the bond of the covenant",—This is no doubt said with an allusion to the giving of the covenant-law at Sinai after the passage of the Red Sea. Both the threats of the covenant and the promises are bonds by which God trains His people, and Israel is to be constrained to glad submission to it.

Ver. 38.   As applied to the future restoration the words, *"they shall not enter into the land of Israel"*, must be taken symbolically.   "Even though they enter Palestine", says Fausset, "it shall be to them an exile state; they shall not enter into the spiritual state of the restored favor of God to His covenant people, which shall be given only to the remnant to be saved."

Ver. 39.   This is not a command, but is really a powerful appeal to repent.   It is as if He said, If ye will not serve me, then go and serve your idols knowing now, as you do, the full consequence.

"and hereafter also",—This is hardly to be connected with *"serve"*, as if God anticipated the same apostacy afterwards (F. D.), nor can it be closely connected with what follows, as if it meant "and hereafter also, if ye will hearken to me, profane ye my name no more" (Ma. Ros.).   It is much better to allow it to stand by itself and take the following particle in the sense of an oath, i. e., verily, and translate "but afterwards (i. e., in the future) . . . verily, ye will hearken unto me, and my holy name ye shall no more profane", etc.   This is in virtual agreement with the marginal rendering, and thus it is taken by the majority.

Schroeder allows the expression to stand with a dash—joining it neither with what goes before or with what follows, and reads as follows, "if ye will not hearken unto me (in the present), then ye shall no more profane", etc.   The meaning, however, in any case is the same: Jehovah will have no hypocrisy; if they will not give up their idols, they cannot serve Him, and if they will not serve Jehovah alone, they may serve their idols, but He will not permit His holy name to be thus profaned by hypocritical worship.

Ver. 40.   *"all the house of Israel, all of them"*,—This wording seems to point to the healing of the breach between the house of Judah and that of Israel. Fausset says, "not merely individuals such as constitute the elect Church now; but the whole *nation*, to be followed by the conversion of the Gentile *nations*."

Ver. 41. The people purified by judgment shall be acceptable to Jehovah as a sweet savour, and in them, as a holy people, the holiness of their God shall be exhibited to the heathen.

CHAPTER TWENTY-EIGHT

25 Thus saith the Lord Jehovah: When I shall have gathered the house of Israel from the peoples among whom they are scattered, and shall be sanctified in them in the sight of the nations, then shall they dwell in their own land which I gave to my servant Jacob. 26 And they shall dwell securely therein; yea, they shall build houses, and plant vineyards, and shall dwell securely, when I have executed judgments upon all those that do them despite round about them; and they shall know that I am Jehovah their God.

Vers. 25, 26. RESTORATION TO THEIR OWN LAND PROMISED TO ISRAEL.

This, as Fausset would have us believe, was fulfilled in part only at the restoration from Babylon. The full accomplishment is yet future when Israel under Christ shall be the center of Christendom; of which an earnest was given in the woman from the coasts of Tyre and Sidon who sought the Saviour. (Matt. 15.21,24.)

CHAPTER TWENTY-NINE

21 In that day will I cause a horn to bud forth unto the house of Israel, and I will give thee the opening of the mouth in the midst of them; and they shall know that I am Jehovah.

Ver. 21. ISRAEL'S ANCIENT GLORY TO BE REVIVED.

"In that day",—i. e., primarily in the day when the judgment upon Egypt is executed by Nebuchadnezzar.

"I will cause a horn to bud forth",—The horn is the symbol of might and power. The very downfall of Egypt will be the signal for the rise of Israel because of God's covenant with her. Her ancient glory will begin to revive, which, says Fausset, is an earnest of Israel's full glory under the Messiah.

The horn which the Lord will then cause to bud forth unto the house of Israel is not the Messiah, but is the Messianic salvation, and the reason for thus connecting this salvation with the overthrow of Egypt is that Egypt, as Havernick says, presents itself to the prophet as the power in which the idea of heathenism was embodied and circumscribed; or as Keil says, "In the might of Egypt the world-power is shattered, and the overthrow of the world-power is the dawn of the unfolding of the might of the kingdom of God."

Schmieder has aptly observed that the annihilation of every earthly power that set itself against the Lord is to the prophet a type of the world's judgment. Thus *"in that day"* looks as well to the future, to what Hengstenberg calls "an ideal day", to the time of the Messiah, as Ewald has properly recognized, to the *"day of the Lord"* of Chap. 30.3, as Schroeder puts it.

"I will give thee the open mouth in the midst of them (Israel)*"*,— Fausset thinks this means, "When thy (the prophet's) predictions shall have come to pass, thy words henceforth shall be more heeded."

CHAPTER THIRTY

> Alas for the day! 3 For the day is near, even the day of Jehovah is near; it shall be a day of clouds, a time of the nations.

Ver. 3.   THE DAY OF JEHOVAH DRAWING NIGH.

The prophet here announces that the day of the Lord's judgment upon the nations is near at hand, and that it is about to burst upon Egypt. To the prophet the judgment upon Egypt was the beginning of a world-wide judgment upon all the heathen enemies of God.

"it shall be a day of clouds",—The day of the Lord was always a day of judgment and of taking vengeance.   When the clear light of day comes to be veiled it is because of a threatening storm, and the wrath of God is thus accordingly conceived as about to break forth.

"a time of the nations",—i. e., for taking vengeance upon them. (F. K. Schr.)

CHAPTER THIRTY-FOUR

11 For thus saith the Lord Jehovah: Behold, I myself, even I, will search for my sheep, and will seek them out.   12 As a shepherd seeketh out his flock in the day that he is among his sheep that are scattered abroad, so will I seek out my sheep; and I will deliver them out of all places whither they have been scattered in [1]the cloudy and dark day. 13 And I will bring them out from the peoples, and gather them from the countries, and will bring them into their own land; and I will feed them upon the mountains of Israel, by the watercourses, and in all the inhabited places of the country.   14 I will feed them with good pasture; and upon the mountains of the height of Israel shall their fold be: there shall they lie down in a good fold; and on fat pasture shall they feed upon the mountains of Israel. 15 I myself will be the shepherd of my sheep, and I will cause them to lie down, saith the Lord Jehovah.   16 I will seek that which was lost, and will bring back that which was driven away, and will bind up that which was broken,

and will strengthen that which was sick: but the fat and the strong I will destroy: I will feed them in justice.

17 And as for you, O my flock, thus saith the Lord Jehovah: Behold, I judge between sheep and sheep, the rams and the he-goats.   18 Seemeth it a small thing unto you to have fed upon the good pasture, but ye must tread down with your feet the residue of your pasture? and to have drunk of the clear waters, but ye must foul the residue with your feet?   19 And as for my sheep, they eat that which ye have trodden with your feet; and they drink that which ye have fouled with your feet.

20 Therefore thus saith the Lord Jehovah unto *them*: Behold, I, even I, will judge between the fat sheep and the lean sheep.   21 Because ye thrust with side and with shoulder, and push all the diseased with your horns, till ye have scattered them abroad; 22 therefore will I save my flock, and *they shall no more be a prey;* and I will judge between sheep and sheep.   23 And I will set up one shepherd over them, and

[1]Heb. *the day of clouds and thick darkness.*

he shall feed them, even my servant David; he shall feed them, and he shall be their shepherd. 24 And I, Jehovah, will be their God, and my servant David prince among them; I, Jehovah, have spoken it.

25 And I will make with them a covenant of peace, and will cause evil beasts to cease out of the land; and they shall dwell securely in the wilderness, and sleep in the woods. 26 And I will make them and the places round about my hill a blessing; and I will cause the shower to come down in its season; there shall be showers of blessing. 27 And the tree of the field shall yield its fruit, and the earth shall yield its increase, and they shall be secure in their land; and they shall know that I am Jehovah, when I have broken the bars of their yoke, and have delivered them out of the hand of those that made bondmen of them. 28 And they shall no more be a prey to the nations, neither shall the beasts of the earth devour them; but they shall dwell securely, and none shall make them afraid. 29 And I will raise up unto them a [2]plantation for renown, and they shall be no more [3]consumed with famine in the land, neither bear the shame of the nations any more. 30 And they shall know that I, Jehovah their God, am with them, and that they, the house of Israel, are my people, saith the Lord Jehovah. 31 And ye my sheep, the sheep of my pasture, are men, and I am your God, saith the Lord Jehovah.

[2]Or, *plant*
[3]Heb. *taken away*

Vers. 11-31.   ISRAEL RESTORED AND THE DAVIDIC KINGDOM SET UP.

Ver. 12.   *"in the cloudy and dark day"*,—Because these words are apparently taken from Joel 2.2, Hitzig, Klieforth, Fausset and others connect them with the principal clause and read, "I will deliver them in the dark and cloudy day out of all the places whither they have been scattered". But the reason given is entirely insufficient and it is much better with our text to connect them with the word *"scattered"*. This is not then the day of God's judgment upon all nations, the great day of the Lord, but it is, as Schroeder and Keil observe, the day of dispersion of the people of Israel, the punishment which befell them through the instrumentality of the heathen.

Ver. 16.   *"the fat and the strong I will destroy"*,—Another side of the pastoral fidelity of Jehovah.   The image is from fat cattle that wax refractory.   The fat and strong sheep are characterized in verses 18 and 19 and they refer to those rendered wanton by prosperity, the rich and strong, presumably the rulers and those occupying superior positions of the nation who oppress the humble and poor and treat them with severity.

Ver. 17.   The sheep are now themselves directly addressed.   Jeho-. vah judges between *"sheep and sheep"*, i. e., between one class of citizens and another, and will put an end to the oppressive conduct of the fat and strong ones.   He then, by what Schroeder calls an "enlarging apposition", designates the class about to be punitively judged, *"the rams and the he-goats"*, the idea being not that of a separation of the sheep from the goats, but that the sheep will be separated from the sheep in such a manner that the "fat and strong" among the sheep will be placed with the *"rams and the he-goats"* and kept apart from the others.   In the next verse Jehovah proceeds to address the rams and the he-goats.

Ver. 21.   *"scattered them abroad"*,—Grotius thinks, and perhaps rightly, that there is an allusion here to the carrying away to Babylon.

Ver. 22.   *"they shall no more be a prey"*,—Says Fausset, "After the restoration from Babylon the Jews were delivered in some degree from the oppression, not only of foreigners but from their own great people (Neh. 5.1-19). The full and final fulfillment of this prophecy is future."

Ver. 23. *"And I will set up one shepherd"*,—The Messianic hope closes each prophetic vision of the future. Compare John 10.14, where Jesus, doubtless thinking of this prophecy, says, "I am the good shepherd".

That the verse points to the Messiah, who is called David in Isa. 55.4, there can be no doubt. In Chap. 37.24 (compare Jer. 23.6) it is expressly said that the David to be raised up is to feed Israel and Judah, the two peoples that had before been divided.

"my servant David",—He is called *"servant"* not alone with reference to the obedience rendered (Hav.), but to the fact of His election as well. (Hen.) Says Klieforth, "This shoot of David comprehends in His one person the whole shepherd-offices of Israel, and fulfills them; they are to be done away with Him, but no other king over the people of God shall relieve Him."

Ver. 25. *"And I will make with them a covenant of peace"*,—i. e., such as is the natural consequence of the covenant relationship of God. It is not to be restricted to a covenant which God will make with the beasts in favor of His people, but the thought is a more comprehensive one and accords with Lev. 26.4-6, which is to be realized for the first time only under the Messiah.

Some think the evil beasts are the hostile human potencies and that the driving of the heathen world from its hitherto domineering position must be meant (Hav. Hen.) ; but this is not at all necessary nor a likely explanation.

Klieforth thinks of a literal return to the paradisical state is the final fulfillment of this picture.

Ver. 26. *"the places round about my hill"*,—This is by no means to be interpreted with Hengstenberg as referring to the heathen nations, but means just what it says, i. e., the land of Palestine round about Jerusalem. The thought is that God will make both the people and the land a blessing. (K. Kl. Hav.)

"showers of blessing",—i. e., the blessing brought by the fertilizing showers of their season.

Ver. 28. *"And they shall no more be a prey to the nations"*,—"The whole passage (11-31)", says Scofield, "speaks of a restoration yet future, for the remnant which returned after the seventy years and their posterity were continually under the Gentile yoke, until in A. D. 70 they were finally driven from the land into a dispersion which still continues."

Ver. 29. *"a plantation for renown"*,—What they planted should grow and prosper so as to be a glory for them, and the nations instead of scoffing at the heretofore fallen and ruined condition of the people would be convinced from the blessing upon them that they were indeed the people of God. The reading of our text is much to be preferred to that of the margin, which Fausset adopts and accepts as pointing to the Messiah. (K. Wh. Kl. Hit. Schr.)

Hengstenberg thinks the reference is to "a renewal of the paradisical plantation", but not only is there nothing in the connection for this, but

Chap. 36.99 shows that under these conditions there is to be "the rich distribution of *harvest* blessings".

CHAPTER THIRTY-SIX

In the first fifteen verses of this chapter a message is given to the mountains of Israel. The address is really to the land, the mountains being mentioned doubtless in antithesis to the mountains of Seir in the previous chapter. Because the heathen rejoice that the Holy Land has been laid waste and fallen to them for a possession, therefore the devastated land shall be sown again and become fruitful and be given once more to Jehovah's own people.

> 8 But ye, O mountains of Israel, ye
> shall shoot forth your branches, and
> yield your fruit to my people Israel;
> for they are at hand to come.

Ver. 8. RESTORATION FORETOLD.

"for they are at hand to come",—Some explain this in that the Israelites are about to return to their land, the primary reference being to the return from Babylon which was *"at hand"* or comparatively near. This, however, only in part fulfilled the prediction, the full and final blessing being yet future, the restoration from Babylon being but an earnest of the greater restoration yet to come. (F. Wh. Kl. Hen. Schr.)

However, most commentators say the Israelites are not the subject to be supplied and that the reference is to the blessings just promised, the branches and the fruits which the mountains are to bear.

In the next section of this chapter (verses 16-23) the reason is given why the Lord had scattered His people among the heathen. It was because of their incorrigible wickedness and the defiling of their land by sin, and the necessity, as Fairbairn says, "of God's vindicating the cause of His holiness by exercising upon them the severity of His displeasure".

In the last section of the chapter (verses 24-38) the purpose of the Lord for their future good is unfolded. There comes a promise first of restoration to their land, then of renewing their hearts to holiness and then of restoring them once more to a flourishing condition, after which is noticed the impression which the whole was to produce upon the minds of others.

24 For I will take you from among the nations, and gather you out of all the countries, and will bring you into your own land. 25 And I will sprinkle clean water upon you, and ye shall be clean: from all your filthiness, and from all your idols, will I cleanse you. 26 A new heart also will I give you, and a new spirit will I put within you; and I will take away the stony heart out of your flesh, and I will give you a heart of flesh. 27 And I will put my Spirit within you, and cause you to walk in my statutes, and ye shall keep mine ordinances, and do them. 28 And ye shall dwell in the land that I gave to your fathers; and ye shall be my people, and I will be your God. 29 And I will save you from all your uncleannesses: and I will call for the grain, and will multiply it, and lay no famine upon you. 30 And I will multiply the fruit of the tree, and the increase of the field, that ye may receive no more the reproach of famine among the nations. 31 Then shall ye remember your evil ways, and your doings that were not good; and ye shall loathe yourselves in your own sight for your iniquities and for your abominations.

32 Not for your sake, [1]do I *this*, saith the Lord Jehovah, be it known unto you: be ashamed and confounded for your ways, O house of Israel. 33 Thus saith the Lord Jehovah: In the day that I cleanse you from all your iniquities, I will cause the cities to be inhabited, and the waste places shall be builded. 34 And the land that was desolate shall be tilled, whereas it was a desolation in the sight of all that passed by. 35 And they shall say, This land that was desolate is become like the garden of Eden; and the waste and desolate and ruined

[1]Or, *do I work*

cities are fortified and inhabited. 36 Then the nations that are left round about you shall know that I, Jehovah, have builded the ruined places, and planted that which was desolate; I, Jehovah, have spoken it, and I will do it. 37 Thus saith the Lord Jehovah: For this, moreover, will I be inquired of by the house of Israel, to do it for them: I will increase them with men like a flock. 38 As the [2]flock for sacrifice, as the flock of Jerusalem in her appointed feasts, so shall the waste cities be filled with flocks of men: and they shall know that I am Jehovah.

[2]Heb. *flock of holy things*

Vers. 24-38. ISRAEL'S RESTORATION AND CONVERSION.

Ver. 24. This prediction was primarily fulfilled in the restoration from Babylon. It is, says Fausset, "ultimately to be fulfilled in the restoration from all countries whither the Jews are now dispersed".

Vers. 25-38. (See comments under Chap. 11.17-19.)

CHAPTER THIRTY-SEVEN

This chapter contains two revelations from God. In the first the prophet is given a vision of the resurrection of Israel to new life (verses 1-14), the latter verses of which (verses 11-14) being the explanation of the vision contained in the former.

11 Then he said unto me, Son of man, these bones are the whole house of Israel: behold, they say, Our bones are dried up, and our hope is lost; we are clean cut off. 12 Therefore prophesy, and say unto them, Thus saith the Lord Jehovah: Behold, I will open your graves, and cause you to come up out of your graves, O my people: and

I will bring you into the land of Israel. 13 And ye shall know that I am Jehovah, when I have opened your graves, and caused you to come up out of your graves, O my people. 14 And I will put my [1]Spirit in you, and ye shall live, and I will place you in your own land: and ye shall know that I, Jehovah, have spoken it and performed it, saith Jehovah.

[1]Or, *breath*

Vers. 11-14. THE VISION OF THE VALLEY OF DRY BONES EXPLAINED.

Ver. 11. *"the whole house of Israel"*,—i. e., both tribes, Judah and Israel united.

Ver. 12. The vision of the preceding verses is in these verses (11-14) explained as setting forth the raising up of the nation of Israel that has been given up to death, although many (Ca. Kl. Jer.) think the vision was intended to symbolize the raising of all the dead in general, the resurrection. To the people, speaking as they did in verse 11 the prophet is told to announce that the Lord will open their graves and bring them out, put His breath of life in them and lead them back into their own land.

"I will open your graves",—i. e., the abodes of their exile, since the people in exile considered themselves like dead men.

The passage from verses 1 to 10 has been used by the Fathers and many orthodox commentators as a basis for the doctrine of the resurrection from the dead. This may be quite appropriate, but what we are concerned about is whether it is to be taken as a direct and immediate prophecy of that great event which is still in the future, or merely as a type or figure of the waking up to new life of the Israel then dead in captivity. That it is the latter is seen not only from the fact that in the vision itself there are certain features to be found that do not apply to the literal resurrection of the dead, but as well from the fact that no other explanation can exhaust the meaning of the words in the first clause of verse 11.

Of course everybody acknowledges that verses 11-14 predict the raising to life of the nation of Israel, and the question arises how this is to be brought into harmony with the explanation which takes the first ten verses as a direct prophecy of the resurrection of the dead at the last day.

Jerome thought to resolve the matter by making the words, *"these bones are the whole house of Israel"* refer to the first resurrection, the resurrection of the saints. But this, as Keil has noted for us, "cannot be reconciled either with the words or with the context and has evidently originated in perplexity".

Klieforth would have us believe that verses 11-14 do not furnish an explanation of the vision at all, but simply make one application of it to the resusitating of the Israelitish nation. But certainly this does not do justice to the words, *"these bones are the whole house of Israel"*. The bones in the valley therefore must represent the whole house of Israel alone and not the resurrection of all men in general.

15 The word of Jehovah came again unto me, saying, 16 And thou, son of man, take thee one stick, and write upon it, For Judah, and for the children of Israel his companions: then take another stick, and write upon it, For Joseph, the stick of Ephraim, and ¹for all the house of Israel his companions: 17 and join them for thee one to another into one stick, that they may become one in thy hand. 18 And when the children of thy people shall speak unto thee, saying, Wilt thou not show us what thou meanest by these? 19 say unto them, Thus saith the Lord Jehovah: Behold, I will take the stick of Joseph, which is in the hand of Ephraim, and the tribes of Israel his companions; and I will put them ²with it, *even* with the stick of Judah, and make them one stick, and they shall be one in my hand. 20 And the sticks whereon thou writest shall be in thy hand before their eyes. 21 And say unto them, Thus saith the Lord Jehovah: Behold, I will take the children of Israel from among the nations, whither they are gone, and will gather them on every side, and bring them into their own land: 22 and I will make them one nation in the land, upon the mountains of Israel; and one king shall be king to them all; and they shall be no more two nations, neither shall they be divided into two kingdoms any more at all; 23 neither shall they defile themselves any more with their idols, nor with their detestable things, nor with any of their transgressions; but I will save them ³out of all their dwelling-places, wherein they have sinned, and will cleanse them: so shall they be my people, and I will be their God. 24 And my servant David shall be king over them; and they all shall have one shepherd: they shall also walk in mine ordinances, and observe my statutes, and do them. 25 And they shall dwell in the land that I have given unto Jacob my servant, wherein your fathers dwelt; and they shall dwell therein, they, and their children, and their children's children, for ever: and David my servant shall be their prince for ever. 26 Moreover I will make a covenant of peace with them; it shall be an everlasting covenant with them; and I will ⁴place them, and multiply them, and will

¹Or, of
²Or, *together with him unto* (or, *to be*) *the stick of Judah*

³Or, with a slight change of text, *from all their backslidings*
⁴Or, *give it them*

set my sanctuary in the midst of them for evermore. 27 My tabernacle also shall be ⁵with them; and I will be their God, and they shall be my people. 28

⁵Or, *over*

And the nations shall know that ⁶I am Jehovah that sanctifieth Israel, when my sanctuary shall be in the midst of them for evermore.

⁶Or, *I, Jehovah, do sanctify Israel*

Vers. 15-28. THE REUNITED TRIBES RESTORED TO THEIR LAND.

In this section of the chapter we have a prophecy of the reuniting of the two and the ten tribes and the bringing of them again into their own land.

"It is impossible," says Scofield, "seriously to pretend that this prophecy has ever been fulfilled in any sense. We have here a promise that the ten and two tribes shall no longer be divided into two kingdoms, and that the earthly center of the worship of God shall be in Jerusalem."

Ver. 22. *"and one king shall be king to them all"*,—The one king is the Shepherd David, whose reign is to be forever (verse 25). In this verse the promise first made in Chap. 11.17, and repeated many times, is made once more.

Ver. 23. *"but I will save them out of all their dwelling places"*,— This has been variously explained.

Hitzig, Hengstenberg and others think the *"dwelling places"* refer to their settlements in foreign lands, and that the meaning is that they will be removed from the scene of their idolatries during the exile in these lands. Most writers, however, think the *"dwelling places"* must be those of Canaan.

Hengstenberg takes the words in a spiritual rather than a local sense. Jehovah will first purify their hearts and then through their influence the land round about will be purified and made holy. But the "cleansing" in the clause before us takes place before the removal.

Klieforth, following the usual application of the words to Canaan, says the idea is "a leading out of these dwelling places", and therefore denotes the leading over of Israel from the present Canaan, or the Canaan of this life, to the glorified, new and eternal Canaan. But Keil has very properly said that such an interpretation is irreconcilable with the words themselves and the context, while verse 25 shows that it is not the glorified Canaan in which they are to dwell, but in the earthly Canaan in which their fathers dwelt.

Redpath prefers the marginal rendering of our text, "I will save them from all their backslidings". But this calls for a change in the text, which is not only unnecessary but hardly justifiable.

Keil, Whitby and others maintain that it means that God will remove from their dwelling places in Canaan everything that could offer them an inducement to sin. Jehovah will preserve them from the sinful influences of their dwelling places, which in other days had offered them such inducements to sin through the idolatry and moral corruption of the Canaanites who were left in the land. This we are inclined to think is the simple explanation.

Ver. 25. The David, who is Christ, will so rule over the reunited people that they will not be divided any more into two peoples and two kingdoms, and both the dwelling of Israel in Canaan and the government of David will be an everlasting one, as this verse together with verses 26 and 28 declare.

Ver. 26. *"I will make a covenant of peace with them"*,—The unchangeable covenant of grace so far superior to the old covenant of the law. This covenant, already expressed in Chap. 34.25, comprehends all the saving good which the Lord will bestow upon His people.

"will set my sanctuary in the midst of them",—Whatever further future reference may be contained in these words, and in the words of this entire section, it is certain that they find the commencement of their fulfillment in the days of Christ and during this present dispensation.

Hengstenberg says, "This promise has at all events come to be gloriously fulfilled in the election which forms the stem of the Christian Church."

Jerome says the sanctuary cannot be the temple built by Zerubbabel because this temple did not stand *forever*, and all these things are to be taken as referring to the Church in the time of the Saviour, when His tabernacle was placed in the Church.

Keil says, "The sanctuary which God will place forever among His people is the sanctuary seen by Ezekiel in Chap. 40, and this is merely a figurative representation of the dwelling of God in the midst of His people through His Son and the Holy Spirit, which began to be realized at the first coming of Christ, who 'became flesh and tabernacled among men' (John 1.14) and is continued in the spiritual dwelling of God in the hearts of believers (I Cor. 3.16)."

As to any further fulfillment, Keil continues in the quotation by saying this dwelling of God with His people "will be completed at the second coming of our Lord in 'the tabernacle of God with men' of the new Jerusalem, of which the Lord God Almighty and the Lamb are the temple, since Israel will then first have become in truth the people of God (Rev. 21.22)."

"The prophecy", says Whitby, "can never be fulfilled except by the ingathering of God's spiritual Israel into their permanent inheritance, the Christian Church and the heavenly Canaan."

"The territory of the blessing", says Fairbairn, "is no longer Canaan, but the region of which Christ is King and Lord."

"The prophecy is one of the future Church of salvation, the realized kingdom of priests", says Schroeder, who, with Vitringa, agrees with Keil, and refers to John 1.14; I Cor. 3.16, and Rev. 21.3; 7.15.

Ver. 27. *"My tabernacle also shall be with them"*,—*"My tabernacle"* really means *"my dwelling"* and should perhaps be so read in the text. The change in form from the saying concerning His *"sanctuary"* is not unintentional, and the word used is in reality not *"with them"*, as in our text, but *"over them"*, as in the margin. (K. Hit. Hen. Schr.)

Hitzig and Schroeder think the reference is to God's dwelling place in heaven over the temple of Jerusalem. But this is rather gratuitous and takes from the text much of its richness of thought.

Both Keil and Hengstenberg think the reference is to God's "protecting power", afforded, as Hengstenberg thinks, in the sanctuary of God, or perhaps better, as Keil takes it, who says that the expression is drawn from the site of the temple, towering above the city, and transferred to the dwelling of God in the midst of His people, to give prominence to the protecting power and saving grace of the God who rules in Israel.

"All this is the prelude", says Redpath, "to the erection of the sanctuary and tabernacle in the *ideal* Holy Land in Chap. 43.7, the same idea being in Rev. 21.3."

Fairbairn says these prophecies are descriptions of the future under the form and image of the past—not as if the past were actually to return again, but that its general spirit and character were to revive.

Hengstenberg says, "The New Testament knows nothing of a future possession of the land of Canaan."

Perhaps this section of Old Testament Scriptures, as much as any, is important in helping to decide the question as to how we are to understand the promises which tell of the restoration of all Israel to Canaan, to the land given to their fathers and where they are to dwell forever; whether, in a literal manner, by restoring the Jews to Palestine, or in a spiritual way, by the gathering together of the Israelites converted to God and introduced into the kingdom founded by Christ, in which latter case, Canaan, as the site of the Old Testament kingdom of God, would be a typical or symbolical designation of the earth wherever the sway and rule of Christ extends.

The exponents of the literal interpretation expect the Messiah to restore the Jewish nation to Palestine, re-establish the kingdom of David, rebuild the temple and once more institute the sacrificial worship of the Levitical law. Many of the deepest students of Scripture today believe that this, with more or less variation, is the only consistent explanation of the prophecies under consideration. Others, perhaps the majority, give to these Scriptures the spiritualistic interpretation noted above. (See remarks under the last section of Ezekiel's prophecy, page 196.)

CHAPTERS THIRTY-EIGHT AND THIRTY-NINE

"Gog, in the land of Magog, prince of Rosh, Meshech, and Tubal, will invade the restored land of Israel from the far distant northern land by the appointment of God in the last times, and with a powerful army of numerous nations (Chap. 38.1-9), with the intention of plundering Israel, now dwelling in security, that the Lord may sanctify Himself upon him before all the world (verses 10-16). But when Gog, of whom earlier prophets have already prophesied, shall fall upon Israel, he is to be destroyed by a wrathful judgment from the Lord, that the nations may know that the Lord is God (verses 17-23). On the mountains of Israel will Gog with all his hosts and nations succumb to the judgment of God (Chap. 39.1-8). The inhabitants of the cities of Israel will spend seven years in burning the weapons of the fallen foe, and seven months in burying the corpses in a valley, which will receive its name from this, so as to purify the land (verses 9-16); whilst in the meantime all the birds and wild beasts will satiate themselves with the flesh and blood of the fallen (verses 17-20). By this judgment will all the nations as well as Israel know that it was on account of its sins that the Lord formerly gave up

Israel into the power of the heathen, but that now He will no more forsake His redeemed people, because He has poured out His Spirit upon it." (Keil.)

The objections to a literal interpretation of the passage, as given by Fairbairn, are as follows:

1. The ideal nature of the name God; 2. The selection of the nations most remote from Israel and therefore most unlikely to act in concert; 3. The whole spoil of Israel could not have maintained the myriads of invaders a single day or given a handful to a tithe of their number; 4. The wood of the invaders' weapons was to serve for fuel to Israel for seven years; 5. *All* Israel were to take seven months to the burying of the dead. If a million Israelites were to bury each two corpses a day, the aggregate buried in the 180 working days of the seven months would be 300,000,000 corpses; 6. The smell from the unburied corpses, before they could be buried, would make it impossible to live in the pestilential stench; 7. The scene of the Lord's controversy here is different from that in Isa. 34.6 where it is Edom, thus creating a discrepancy; 8. God's dealings with His enemies is too grossly carnal for Messianic times. All of which, Fairbairn thinks, demands a non-literal interpretation, the final triumph of Messiah's truth over the most distant and barbarous nations being represented as a literal conflict on a gigantic scale.

Fausset, however, says that though the details are not literal, the distinctiveness in the picture gives probability to a more definite and *generally* literal interpretation, and that what Ezekial stated more generally, Rev. 20.7-9 states more definitely as to the antichristian confederacy which is to assail the beloved city.

CHAPTER THIRTY-EIGHT

1 And the word of Jehovah came unto me, saying, 2 Son of man, set thy face toward Gog, of the land of Magog, the ¹prince of Rosh, Meshech, and Tubal, and prophesy against him, 3 and say, Thus saith the Lord Jehovah: Behold, I am against thee, O Gog, ¹prince of Rosh, Meshech, and Tubal: 4 and I will turn thee about, and put hooks into thy jaws, and I will bring thee forth, and all thine army, horses and horsemen, all of them clothed in full armor, a great company with buckler and shield, all of them handling swords: 5 Persia, Cush, and Put with them, all of them with shield and helmet; 6 Gomer, and all his hordes; the house of Togarmah in the uttermost parts of the north, and all his hordes; even many peoples with thee. 7 Be thou prepared, yea, prepare thyself, thou, and all thy companies that are assembled unto thee, and be thou a ²guard unto them. 8 After many days thou shalt be visited: in the latter years thou shalt come into the land that is ³brought back from the sword, that is gathered out of many peoples, upon the mountains of Israel, which have been a continual waste; but it is brought forth out of the peoples, and they shall dwell securely, all of them. 9 And thou shalt ascend, thou shalt come like a storm, thou shalt be like a cloud to cover the land, thou, and all thy hordes, and many peoples with thee.

10 Thus saith the Lord Jehovah: It shall come to pass in that day, that things shall come into thy mind, and thou shalt devise an evil device; 11 and thou shalt say, I will go up to the ⁴land of unwalled villages; I will go to them that are at rest, that dwell securely, all of them dwelling without walls, and having neither bars nor gates; 12 to take the spoil and to take the prey; to turn thy hand against the waste places that are *now* inhabited, and against the people that are gathered out of the nations, that have gotten cattle

¹Or, *chief prince of Meshech*
²Or, *commander*
³Or, *restored*
⁴Or, *an open country*

and goods, that dwell in the ⁵middle of the earth. 13 Sheba, and Dedan, and the merchants of Tarshish, with all the young lions thereof, shall say unto thee, Art thou come to take the spoil? hast thou assembled thy company to take the prey? to carry away silver and gold, to take away cattle and goods, to take great spoil?

14 Therefore, son of man, prophesy, and say unto Gog, Thus saith the Lord Jehovah: In that day when my people Israel dwelleth securely, shalt thou not know it? 15 And thou shalt come from thy place out of the uttermost parts of the north, thou, and many peoples with thee, all of them riding upon horses, a great company and a mighty army; 16 and thou shalt come up against my people Israel, as a cloud to cover the land: it shall come to pass in the latter days, that I will bring thee against my land, that the nations may know me, when I shall be sanctified in thee, O Gog, before their eyes.

17 Thus saith the Lord Jehovah: Art thou he of whom I spake in old time by my servants the prophets of Israel, that prophesied in those days for *many* years that I would bring thee

⁵Heb. *navel.* See Judg. 9.37

against them? 18 And it shall come to pass in that day, when God shall come against the land of Israel, saith the Lord Jehovah, that my wrath shall come up into my nostrils. 19 For in my jealousy and in the fire of my wrath have I spoken, Surely in that day there shall be a great shaking in the land of Israel; 20 so that the fishes of the sea, and the birds of the heavens, and the beasts of the field, and all creeping things that creep upon the earth, and all the men that are upon the face of the earth, shall shake at my presence, and the mountains shall be thrown down, and the steep places shall fall, and every wall shall fall to the ground. 21 And I will call for a sword against him unto all my mountains, saith the Lord Jehovah: every man's sword shall be against his brother. 22 And with pestilence and with blood will I enter into judgment with him; and I will rain upon him and upon his hordes, and upon the many peoples that are with him, an overflowing shower, and great hailstones, fire, and brimstone. 23 And I will magnify myself, and sanctify myself, and I will make myself known in the eyes of many nations; and they shall know that I am Jehovah.

Vers. 1-23. THE DESTRUCTION OF GOG AND HIS GREAT ARMY OF NATIONS.

Ver. 2. Gog is perhaps a name arbitrarily extracted from the country, Magog, the latter being the name of a people mentioned in Gen. 10.2 as descended from Japheth, being according to tradition the great Scythian people. The word is used with the definite article, *"the"*, here and thus seems to designate the well known people from the time of Genesis. The title *"Gog"* may have been a common one for the kings of that country as the title "Pharaoh" was for the rulers of Egypt.

"Rosh, Meshech, and Tubal",—These were all peoples dwelling doubtless in the country of Taurus, and reckoned among the Scythian tribes, thus belonging to the neighborhood of Magog. These names might have been adopted by Ezekiel from the historical fact familiar to the men of his time, as ideal titles for the foes of the last great and ungodly confederacy against the people of Jehovah.

Ver. 5. *"Cush"* and *"Put"* refer to the Ethiopians and the Libyans, while Gomer of verse 6 refers to the Celtic Cimmerians, and Togarmah to the Armenians of the Caucasus south of Iberia.

Thus peoples living at the extreme north and east and south, on the borders of the then known world, make up the army of Gog. Where are their former foes, Ammon, Moab, Edom, and Syrians, and the old imperial powers of Egypt and Assyria and Babylon? These will all have passed from the stage of history, and the people of God will have spread so widely over the earth that its foes will, as Keil says, be found only on the borders of the civilized world.

Ver. 7. *"and be thou a guard unto them"*,—Spoken perhaps half ironically, i. e., if thou canst; for it will be seen immediately how the matter turns out.

Ver. 8. *"After many days thou shalt be visited"*,—These words remind one so vividly of Isa. 24.22 that it is impossible not to see here a play on the words of that passage. The words are used here as there in the sense of visited in wrath (K. F. Del. Schr.), *"visited"* being, as Keil says, a more general idea than punishment.

Havernick renders the word "missed", or "wanting", in the sense of their having perished as a result of the battle about to take place. But the word never has this meaning, and such meaning does not suit the context either here or in Isaiah.

Redpath, Hitzig, Klieforth and others translate, "thou shalt receive the command". But neither is this in accord with the context nor substantiated by the language. Gog has already, in verse 7, been appointed commander of the army and is not therefore to be placed in command *"after many days"*.

Hitzig says it is not time to speak of the punishment yet; but Schroeder replies that the expression means that punishment will begin to be prepared.

Both Keil and Schroeder explain the visitation as consisting in the fact of Gog's being moved by Jehovah to invade the land, which was the initial step in the judgment that was coming upon him.

"After many days",—These words are defined by *"in the latter years"*, and are the same as *"the end of the days"*, the last time—not the future generally, but the final future, the Messianic time for the coming of the kingdom of God. Says Whitby, "The time referred to is the 'terrible day of the end' of which the prophets so often speak."

Fausset gives the words a double reference by way of fulfillment, the times being those of *"the latter years"* just before the coming of Christ— fulfilled under Antiochus Epiphanes before His first coming, and to be fulfilled under the Antichrist before His second coming.

"the land that is brought back from the sword, that is gathered out of many peoples",—The predicates in these clauses show that in the word *"land"* the idea of its inhabitants predominates, for these only could be *"brought back"* and *"gathered out"*.

"gathered out of many peoples",—The word *"many"* Keil thinks points beyond the Babylonian captivity to the dispersion of Israel in all the world, which did not take place until the second destruction of Jerusalem, and which also shows that the "continual waste" spoken of denotes a much longer devastation of the land than the Chaldean devastation was.

"a continual waste",—Says Fausset, "Waste during the long period of the captivity, the earnest of the much longer period of Judah's present desolation, to which the words more fully apply."

Ver. 10. *"and thou shalt devise an evil device"*,—What this *"evil device"* is is seen in verses 11 and 12; the attacking God's people in their defenseless state.

Ver. 12. *"that dwell in the middle of the earth"*,—This is a figurative expression to be explained by Chap. 5.5, "Jerusalem in the midst of the nations". Palestine really was the center of the ancient civilized world. But the expression is hardly to be taken physically; it is rather to be taken morally, the land most glorious and richly blessed, so that its inhabitants occupy the most exalted position among the nations, and thus a central position for being a blessing to the world.

Ver. 13. *"the young lions thereof"*,—i. e., the daring princes and leaders.

Ver. 14. *"shalt thou know it"*,—i. e., that Israel dwells securely, not expecting any hostile invasion (K.), to thy cost through the punishment inflicted upon thee (F.). The former explanation is the better, as the words which follow show. Schroeder thinks the knowing refers to what the questioners of the previous verse had said, i. e., thou shalt know that just that very thing is true; while Ewald and Hitzig, by a slight altering of the text, read, "thou shalt set thyself in motion".

Ver. 17. *"Art thou he of whom I spake in old time"*, etc.,—Gog and his hosts are here identified with the enemies spoken of in other prophecies. (F. Wh. K. Schr.) It means of course, Thou art really he, the affirmative reply to the question being contained in the last words of the verse, *"I would bring thee against them"*.

Ver. 19. *"there shall be a great shaking in the land of Israel"*,—The reference is doubtless to physical agitations with accompanying social and moral revolutions, according to the customary figurative way of referring to such things. (Compare verse 22 with Rev. 8.7,16,21.)

CHAPTER THIRTY-NINE

1 And thou, son of man, prophesy against Gog, and say, Thus saith the Lord Jehovah: Behold, I am against thee, O Gog, [1]prince of Rosh, Meshech, and Tubal; 2 and I will turn thee about, and will lead thee on, and will cause thee to come up from the uttermost parts of the north; and I will bring thee upon the mountains of Israel; 3 and I will smite thy bow out of thy left hand, and will cause thine arrows to fall out of thy right hand. 4 Thou shalt fall upon the mountains of Israel, thou, and all thy hordes, and the peoples that are with thee: I will give thee unto the ravenous birds of every sort, and to the beasts of the field to be devoured. 5 Thou shalt fall upon the open field; for I have spoken it, saith the Lord Jehovah. 6 And I will send a fire on Magog, and on them that dwell securely in the [2]isles; and they shall know that I am Jehovah. 7 And my holy name will I make known in the midst of my people Israel; neither will I suffer my holy name to be profaned any more: and the nations shall know that I am Jehovah, the Holy One in Israel. 8 Behold, it cometh, and it shall be done, saith the Lord Jehovah: this is the day whereof I have spoken. 9 And they that dwell in the cities of Israel shall go forth, and shall make fires of the weapons and burn them, both the shields and the bucklers, the bows and the arrows, and the handstaves, and the spears, and they shall make fires of them seven years; 10 so that they shall take no wood out of the field, neither cut down any out of the forests; for they shall make fires of the weapons; and they shall plunder those that plundered them, and rob those that robbed them, saith the Lord Jehovah.

11 And it shall come to pass in that day, that I will give unto Gog, a place for burial in Israel, the valley of them that pass through [3]on the east of the

[1]Or, *chief prince of Meshech*
[2]Or, *coast-lands*
[3]Or, *in front of*

sea; and it shall stop them that pass through: and there shall they bury Gog and all his multitude; and they shall call it The valley of *Hamon-gog. 12 And seven months shall the house of Israel be burying them, that they may cleanse the land. 13 Yea, all the people of the land shall bury them; and it shall be to them a renown in the day that I shall be glorified, saith the Lord Jehovah. 14 And they shall set apart men of continual employment, that shall pass through the land, and, with them that pass through, those that bury them that remain upon the face of the land, to cleanse it: after the end of seven months shall they search. 15 And they that pass through the land shall pass through; and when any seeth a man's bone, then shall he ⁵set up a sign by it, till the buriers have buried it in the valley of Hamon-gog. 16 And ⁶Hamonah shall also be the name of a city. Thus shall they cleanse the land.

17 And thou, son of man, thus saith the Lord Jehovah: Speak unto the birds of every sort, and to every beast of the field, Assemble yourselves, and come; gather yourselves on every side to my sacrifice that I do sacrifice for you, even a great sacrifice upon the mountains of Israel, that ye may eat flesh and drink blood. 18 Ye shall eat the flesh of the mighty, and drink the blood of the princes of the earth, of rams, of lambs, and of goats, of bullocks, all of them fatlings of Bashan. 19 And ye shall eat fat till ye be full, and drink blood till ye be drunken, of my sacrifice which I have sacrificed for you. 20 And ye shall be filled at my

⁴That is, *the multitude of Gog*
⁵Heb. *build*
⁶That is, *multitude*

table with horses and chariots, with mighty men, and with all men of war, saith the Lord Jehovah.

21 And I will set my glory among the nations; and all the nations shall see my judgment that I have executed, and my hand that I have laid upon them. 22 So the house of Israel shall know that I am Jehovah their God, from that day and forward. 23 And the nations shall know that the house of Israel went into captivity for their iniquity; because they trespassed against me, and I hid my face from them: so I gave them into the hand of their adversaries, and they fell all of them by the sword. 24 According to their uncleanness and according to their transgressions did I unto them; and I hid my face from them.

25 Therefore thus saith the Lord Jehovah: Now will I bring back the captivity of Jacob, and have mercy upon the whole house of Israel; and I will be jealous for my holy name. 26 And they shall bear their shame, and all their trespasses whereby they have trespassed against me, when they shall dwell securely in their land, and none shall make them afraid; 27 when I have brought them back from the peoples, and gathered them out of their enemies' lands, and am sanctified in them in the sight of many nations. 28 And they shall know that I am Jehovah their God, in that I caused them to go into captivity among the nations, and have gathered them unto their own land; and I will leave none of them any more there; 29 neither will I hide my face any more from them; for I have poured out my Spirit upon the house of Israel, saith the Lord Jehovah.

Vers. 1-29.   THE JUDGMENT UPON GOG AND HIS HOSTS CONTINUED.

Ver. 2.   *"and I will turn thee about"*,—i. e., doubtless in the sense of misleading him.

Ver. 6.   *"them that dwell securely in the isles"*,—The judgment extends to all the heathen nations that are dwelling securely, carelessly and confidently in their distant homes, extending even to the land of Gog himself.

Ver. 9.   *"they shall make fires of them seven years"*,—Whitby says *"seven years"* is symbolical of completeness. Thus also Redpath, Fausset (nothing must be left to pollute the land), Keil, Schroeder and practically all.

Says Keil, "The number seven in the seven years as well as in the seven months of burying is symbolical, stamping the overthrow as a punishment inflicted by God, the completion of a divine judgment." Thus nearly all.

The reason is not as Havernick says, that weapons of war are irreconcilable with the character of the Messianic times of peace, but it is the complete annihilation of the enemy, the removal of every trace of him.

Ver. 11.   *"the valley of them that pass through on the east of the sea"*,—In place of this Cornill, Whitby, Redpath and others read, "The valley of Abarim", which leads to the frontier mountains of Israel, over against Moab, with the great, horrible sulphurous valley of the Dead Sea at its foot, through which ran the ancient road most traveled by invaders from the east.   But there is no satisfying reason for this interpretation; nor does it signify "the valley of the haughty ones" (Ew.), nor is there in it an allusion to the valley of Zech. 14.4 (Hit.), nor the valley of Jehosaphat, as Klieforth says.   It is doubtless the valley of the Jordan above the Dead Sea.

We think Keil is right in reading with the margin of our text, "on the front of" instead of with the text, *"on the east of"*, for the word scarcely, if ever, carries with it the meaning of *"east"*.   The burial place, therefore, as looked at from Jerusalem, the central point of the land, is probably the valley of the Jordan where is the principal crossing place from Gilead into Canaan proper, and which is the broadest part of the valley and therefore well adapted to be the burial place of the slaughtered multitude.

"And it shall stop them that pass through",—The burial ground is to be so large that it will block the way for passengers, the number of graves, or the impurity and uncleanness of the place causing traffic through the valley to cease.

Ver. 13.   *"and it shall be to them a renown"*,—Not that it is a source of honor to assist in such work, nor that they possess the grave of Gog (Hit.), but because they thereby cleanse the land and manifest their zeal to show themselves a holy people by sweeping away uncleanness. (K.)

Ver. 14.   *"with them that pass through"*,—The men employed in the burying were to be assisted by the passers through, by whom is doubtless meant the ordinary Israelitish travelers.   These do not belong to the official burial party.

Ver. 16.   Hamonah, the literal of which is "multitude", is the name of a city presumably built near the burial place, commemorating by its name the overthrow of the multitude of Israel's foes.

Ver. 18.   *"all of them fatlings of Bashan"*,—i. e., ungodly men of might, Bashan being famed for its fat cattle.   Grotius has correctly remarked that the names of all these animals, which were generally employed in the sacrifices, are to be understood as signifying different orders of men, chiefs, generals, soldiers, etc. (Compare these verses with Rev. 19.17,18.)

Ver. 20.   *"at my table"*,—i. e., the field of battle on the mountains of Israel.

Whitby and others think by *"chariots"* are meant riding beasts.

Ver. 25.   *"the whole house of Israel"*,—(See Rom. 11.26.)   "The restoration of Israel heretofore has been partial. There must yet be one that shall be universal." (F.)

Ver. 26. *"And they shall bear their shame"*,—This is not to be altered into "they shall forget their shame" (Hit. Dat.), but they will be ashamed of their past sins, and of their unworthiness of God's so great mercy.

Says Keil, "In order to determine with greater precision what is the heathen power thus rising up in Gog against the kingdom of God, we must take into consideration the passage in the Apocalypse (Rev. 20.8 and 9), where our prophecy is resumed."

Plumptre asks, "Will this prophecy ever be realized on this earth, or must we only look for it in the heavenly city whose builder and maker is God?"

Whitby says, "the conflict is to be on this earth, and the victory and peace which follows must be looked for here. It is not, however, a literal conflict between men armed with bows and arrows who shall be killed with bolts of lightning, but a spiritual battle between God's people and the powers of evil".

Scofield says, "That the primary reference is to the northern European powers, headed up by Russia, all agree. The whole passage should be read in connection with Zech. 12.1-4; 14.1-9; Matt. 24.14-30; Rev. 14.14-20; 19.17-21. The reference to Meshech and Tubal (Moscow and Tobolsk) is a clear mark of identification. Russia and the northern powers have been the latest persecutors of the dispersed Israel, and it is congruous both with divine justice and with the covenants that justice should fall at the climax of the last mad attempt to exterminate the remnant of Israel in Jerusalem. The whole prophecy belongs to the yet future 'day of Jehovah', and to the battle of Armageddon, but includes also the final revolt of the nations at the close of the kingdom age."

The time of this invasion is clearly set forth as *"in the latter years"* (verse 8), *"in the latter days"* (verse 16), and it is against the land *"that is brought back from the sword, that is gathered out of many peoples"*. "This," says Gaebelein, "shows us that the invasion takes place at the time when the Lord has brought back His people and resumed His relationship with the remnant of Israel. It must not be identified with the final revolt at the close of the Millenium, when Satan is loosed for a little season (Rev. 20.7-9). The invasion which Ezekiel describes takes place at the beginning of the Millennium, whereas the invasion of Gog and Magog in Revelation is postmillennial. The judgment upon Gog and Magog as here described completes and ends the judgment of the living nations at the beginning of the Millennial period."

CHAPTERS FORTY TO FORTY-EIGHT

Here in vision the prophet is carried back to the land of Israel and shown the new temple, the new order of service and the new division of the land among the tribes when they shall have returned. Jehovah had promised in the latter part of Chap. 37 that He would place His sanctuary, His temple, in the midst of them and dwell over them as their God forever.

The chapters before us now are the realization of that promise. The magnificent picture begins with the measurement of the new sanctuary, into which the glory of the Lord enters; it closes with directions for the re-division of the land among the tribes and the building of the new Jerusalem; while between these two portions the form of the ceremonial services of the temple are set forth, in the keeping of which Israel is to show itself to be the holy people of Jehovah.

As to whether the vision in these chapters is to be considered as one to be fulfilled literally, or in a figurative or symbolical way, commentators differ very widely from one another.

The figurative interpretation has been the predominate one even from the earliest period of Church history, having been supported by Ephraem Syrus, Theodoret, Jerome and many others. So generally did it prevail that L. Cappellus said, "That this is a setting forth of spiritual worship in types and figures, as portrayed in the picture and all the rites of this temple, which differ greatly from those of Moses, there is not a Christian who denies; nor any Jew, unless prejudiced and very obdurate, who ventures to deny, seeing that there are so many things in this description of Ezekiel's which not even the most shameless Jew has dared to argue that we are to interpret according to the letter."

In more recent times, however, many of our most learned critical scholars have not hesitated to champion the literal explanation of this prophecy, and have not only seen in many of the other prophecies, predictions of the literal restoration of Israel to the land of Palestine, but in this one the directions for the rebuilding of a new temple of the future in Jerusalem and the renewal of the Levitical worship in the Millennial age. (Ba. Au. Vo. Wh. Gab. Hof. Mor. Bro.) A curious combination of spirits in the flesh! most of whom make the community of God at the Lord's Second Coming to be an Israelitish one. Scofield would have us believe that the sacrificial offerings during the Millennium will doubtless be memorial, looking back to the cross, as the offerings of the Old Covenant were anticipatory, looking forward to the cross.

The Jews were not permitted to read these chapters in public because of the sharp discrepancies between these directions of worship and those of Moses, and because of the difficulty in understanding them.

That difficulties loom large when literal interpretation is attempted no serious minded student will deny.

1. The description is imperfectly worked out. There is no mention of a high priest and there is no mention of the second of the great yearly Jewish feasts. No satisfactory explanation for these omissions can be presented.

2. Every attempt to build a temple in the time of Zerubbabel or Herod utterly ignored these directions, and this, Farrar thinks, shows clearly that the Jews of those days did not take them literally. Some say the temple would have been thus literally made if the Jews had fulfilled literally the conditions set forth in Chap. 43.10,11. But Whitby reminds us that not one of Ezekiel's successors ever seems to have supposed that it was Israel's sin that caused the later temple to look more like Solomon's than Ezekiel's.

3. It would seem impossible to build such a temple upon the summit

of a mountain. This *"very high mountain"* unquestionably refers to the old site of the temple, and this little hill could, it would seem, be only thus designated in a moral or ideal sense.

4. The stream that issued from the east threshold of the temple and flowed into the Dead Sea, in the rapidity of its increase and the quality of its waters is, as Fairbairn says, unlike anything ever known in Judea or elsewhere in the world. To reach the Dead Sea it would furthermore have to run up hill, and how could it sweeten the waters of this Sea when this Sea has no outlet?

5. The distribution of the land is strangely supposed to be in equal portion among the twelve tribes without respect to their relative numbers, but the land cannot be equally divided by drawing lines east and west equi-distant between the Jordan river and the Mediterranean Sea, for while these sections would be of the same dimensions north and south they would differ greatly as to their width east and west. Fairbairn thinks there is difficulty also in supposing the separate existence of the twelve tribes, such separate tribeship no longer existing, and it being hard to imagine how they could be restored as distinct tribes, mingled as they now are.

6. The square of the temple (Chap. 42.20) is six times as large as was the circumference of the wall enclosing the old temple, and larger than the whole of the earthly Jerusalem, the boundary of Ezekiel's temple square being over three and a half miles, while the boundaries of the whole ancient city were only about two and a half miles.

7. The city of Ezekiel's vision has an area of between three and four thousand square miles, including the holy ground set apart for the prince, the priests and the Levites. This dimension would thus reach beyond the Jordan river, although this river, in Chap. 47.17, is made the border line of the same. This is nearly as large as the whole of Judea. Now as Zion lay in the center of the ideal city, the one half of the sacred portion extended to nearly thirty miles south of Jerusalem, that is, practically all of the southern territory. Yet five tribes were to have their inheritance on the south side of Jerusalem *beyond* the sacred portion. Where was the land to be found for them? "It would have required miracle after miracle", says Whitby, "to have made the land ready for such a temple. God could have done it, but such has never been the divine method."

8. But altogether apart from these natural impossibilities is it not true that the assumption of a literal temple and the restoration of the bloody sacrifices of Levitical worship is contrary to the spirit and teaching of the New Testament as set forth by Christ and His Apostles? And are we not justified by this spirit and this teaching in saying, with Douglass, "a temple with sacrifices now or in the future would be the most daring denial of the all-sufficiency of the sacrifice of Christ, and of the efficacy of the blood of His atonement. He who sacrificed before, confessed the Messiah; he who should sacrifice now, would most solemnly and sacriligiously deny Him."

"The catholicity of the Christian dispensation", says Fairbairn, "and the spirituality of its worship seems incompatible with a return to the local narrowness and 'beggarly elements' of the Jewish ritual and carnal ordinances, disannuled 'because of the unprofitableness thereof'."

It is in consequence of arguments like the foregoing that from the Fathers down the prevailing view of the Christian Church has been that of an ideal, a symbolical, a spiritual understanding of the vision and that it presents in grand outline the good in store for God's people during the times of the Gospel; in other words that it is a vision of spiritual realities pictorically presented, the historical presentation in temple-form merely supplying the mould into which it is cast, thus expressing under well-known symbols certain fundamental and eternal ideas with regard to the true worship of God.

Even Fausset, a literalist of the pre-millennial school, says, "There are things in the vision so improbable physically as to preclude a *purely* literal interpretation. The very fact that the whole is a vision, and not an oral, face-to-face communication such as that granted to Moses, implies that the directions are not to be understood so precisely literal as those given to the Jewish law-giver. Perhaps, as some think, the beau-ideal of a sacred commonwealth is given according to the then existing pattern of temple-service which would be the imagery most familiar to the prophet and his hearers at that time. The old temple *embodied* in visible forms and rites *spiritual truths* affecting the people when absent from it. So this *ideal* temple is made, in the absence of the outward temple, to serve by description the same purpose of symbolical instruction as the old literal temple did by forms and acts. In Revelation no temple is seen, as in the perfection of the new dispensation the accidents of place and form are no longer needed to realize to Christians what Ezekiel imparts to Jewish minds by the imagery familiar to them. The ideal temple exhibits, under Old Testament forms, not the precise literal outline, but the essential character of the worship of the Messiah as it shall be when He shall exercise sway in Jerusalem among His own people, the Jews, and thence to the ends of the earth."

Fausset certainly states the matter in a most finely discriminating way, especially from the standpoint of a believer in Jewish restoration to the land of their fathers. Yet in adopting a spiritual understanding of the temple-vision one quite naturally questions whether other Old Testament prophecies, especially those concerned with the restoration of the Jews to Palestine, ought not also to be understood in a similar way. This of course does not necessarily follow, as may be seen from the last paragraph of the quotation from Fausset just made.

Volck thinks, "it is impossible, without introducing unbounded caprice into our exposition, to resist the conclusion that, in all such passages as Joel 4.16-21, Micah 7.9-13, Isa. 24.1-23 as compared with Isa. 13.9 and Zech. 14.8-11, together with many other similar references, a time is depicted, when, after the judgment of God upon the power of the world, Israel will dwell in the enjoyment of blissful peace within its own land, now transfigured into paradisiacal glory, and will rule over the nations round about."

Keil, on the other hand, insists that Joel 4.16-21 does not mean that Edom will become literally a desert, nor that Egypt will, nor that the mountains will literally trickle with honey. Edom, he says, is a type of the world in its hostility to God, and so Judea is a type of the kingdom of God, and all that is taught is that the might and glory of the kingdoms of this world at enmity with God will be destroyed, and the glory of the kingdom of God established.

Neither do the other passages prove his point, says Keil, and even if they did, they do not, he maintains, prove such glorification of Palestine as taking place before the final judgment; while in Isa. 24.21 it is plainly said first that the earth will *fall and rise no more,* after which it is said that Jehovah will visit it, etc., placing therefore this visiting and reigning in heaven after the end of all things.

The vision of Ezekiel he understands not as depicting the rise and development of the new kingdom of God, the church of Christ, but as Ezekiel sees the temple as a *finished* building, so the vision sets forth the kingdom of God established by Christ in its perfect form. It is the Old Testament outline of the New Testament picture of the heavenly Jerusalem of the new earth as set forth in Rev. 21 and 22, namely the Father's house of many mansions, heaven itself, the city of God coming down from heaven upon the new earth, built of gold, precious stones and pearls and illumined with the light of the glory of the Lord, all of which takes place after the final judgment has been consummated. The tribes of Israel, therefore, which receive Canaan for a perpetual possession are not the Jews after their conversion to Christ, but the Israel of God, the people of Christ, gathered from among both Jews and Gentiles; and that Canaan is not the earthly Canaan between the Jordan and the Mediterranean Sea, but the New Testament Canaan, the kingdom of Christ whose boundaries reach from sea to sea and from the river to the ends of the earth. And the temple upon a *"very high mountain"* in the midst of this Canaan, in which the Lord is enthroned and causes the river of the water of life to flow down from His throne over His kingdom, so that the earth produces the tree of life with leaves as medicine for men, and the Dead Sea is filled with fishes and living creatures, is a figurative representation and type of the gracious presence of the Lord in His Church, which is realized in this present period of the earthly development of the kingdom of heaven in the form of the Christian church in a spiritual and invisible manner in the indwelling of the Father and the Son through the Holy Spirit in the hearts of believers, and in a spiritual and invisible operation in the church, but which will eventually manifest itself when our Lord shall appear in the glory of the Father, to translate His church into the kingdom of glory, in such a manner that we shall see the Almighty God and the Lamb with the eyes of our glorified body, and worship before His throne, and it is this worship which is described ideally, and quite naturally so, in our vision (Chaps. 43.13 and 46.24) as the offering of sacrifice according to the Israelitish form of divine worship under the Old Testament.

The question is indeed a most perplexing one. For ourselves it is difficult to get away from the conviction that a literal restoration to the land of their fathers is promised to the Jews in the Old Testament Scriptures, although we find it equally difficult to accept the literal interpretation of the temple vision.

THE BOOK OF
DANIEL
(B. C. 607—B. C. 534)

CHAPTER TWO

31 Thou. O king, sawest, and, behold, a great image. This image, which was mighty, and whose brightness was excellent, stood before thee; and the aspect thereof was terrible. 32 As for this image, its head was of fine gold, its breast and its arms of silver, its belly and its thighs of brass, 33 its legs of iron, its feet part of iron, and part of clay. 34 Thou sawest till that a stone was cut out without hands, which smote the image upon its feet that were of iron and clay, and brake them in pieces. 35 Then was the iron, the clay, the brass, the silver, and the gold, broken in pieces together, and became like the chaff of the summer threshing-floors; and the wind carried them away, so that no place was found for them: and the stone that smote the image became a great [1]mountain, and filled the whole earth.

36 This is the dream; and we will tell the interpretation thereof before the king. 37 Thou, O king, art king of kings, unto whom the God of heaven hath given the kingdom, the power, and the strength, and the glory; 38 and wheresoever the children of men dwell, the beasts of the field and the birds of the heavens hath he given into thy hand, and hath made thee to rule over them all: thou art the head of gold. 39 And after thee shall arise another kingdom inferior to thee; and another third

[1]Or, *rock*

kingdom of brass, which shall bear rule over all the earth. 40 And the fourth kingdom shall be strong as iron, forasmuch as iron breaketh in pieces and subdueth all things; and as iron that crusheth all these, shall it break in pieces and crush. 41 And whereas thou sawest the feet and toes, part of potters' clay, and part of iron, it shall be a divided kingdom; but there shall be in it of the strength of the iron, forasmuch as thou sawest the iron mixed with [2]miry clay. 42 And as the toes of the feet were part of iron, and part of clay, so the kingdom shall be partly strong, and partly [3]broken. 43 And whereas thou sawest the iron mixed with [2]miry clay, they shall mingle themselves [4]with the seed of men; but they shall not cleave one to another, even as iron doth not mingle with clay. 44 And in the days of those kings shall the God of heaven set up a kingdom which shall never be destroyed, nor shall the sovereignty thereof be left to another people; but it shall break in pieces and consume all these kingdoms, and it shall stand for ever. 45 Forasmuch as thou sawest that a stone was cut out of the mountain without hands, and that it brake in pieces the iron, the brass, the clay, the silver, and the gold; the great God hath made known to the king what shall come to pass hereafter: and the dream is certain, and the interpretation thereof sure.

[2]Or, *earthenware*
[3]Or, *brittle*
[4]Or, *by*

Vers. 31-45.   THE DREAM OF NEBUCHADNEZZAR AND ITS INTERPRETATION.

The head of gold was the Babylonian Empire (verse 38). A "king" and his "kingdom" are used interchangeably, as a rule, throughout the Scriptures. The dates of this Babylonian Empire were B. C. 606 to B. C. 538.

It is quite universally acknowledged that the breast and arms of the image represent the Medo-Persian Empire (B. C. 538 to B. C. 371), and the belly and thighs the Grecian Empire (B. C. 371 to B. C. 167).

What is the other kingdom, that represented by the legs of iron with feet and toes of mixed composition?

Of some five or six different views of this matter there are but two which call for any really serious consideration:

1. The Seleucid Empire, one of the four divisions of the Grecian Empire after the death of Alexander. (Zo. Ei. Po. St. Ju. Ma. Ber. Zel. Gro. Del. Wil. Len.)

2. The Roman Empire. (A. E. F. C. N. K. L. Pu. Zu. Kl. Fu. Bu. Au. Vo. Ze. Rob. Jer. Hen. Gab. Bla. Aug. Hav. Hof. Cas. Sta. Joa. The. Jos. Vel. Men. Gau. Gar. Prag., the majority of the Church Fathers, all the expositors of the Middle-age Church, Jewish expositors both before and after Christ's time, the whole Christian Church for four hundred years without any contradiction, and, says Zoeckler, a majority of the moderns, although he himself holds the other view.)

Personally we are convinced that the Roman Empire is the correct answer to the question before us; and for the following reasons:

1. The arguments used in favor of the Seleucid Empire are far from convincing;

   (a) The ten toes of the image (and the ten horns of the beast in Chap. 7) represent the ten kings of the Seleucid Empire, three of whom Antiochus Epiphanes is said to have uprooted. But neither the ten nor the three can be found. (See Chap. 7.7.)

   (b) The distinction between the unadulterated metal of the legs and the crumbling mixture of the feet and toes have their exact counterpart in the Seleucid Empire, but not in the Roman. This may, however, with propriety be held of the one empire as well as of the other.

   (c) Chap. 11 is an acknowledged account of the Seleucid Empire and the *"little horn"* of Chap. 8 is acknowledged to be Antiochus Epiphanes, and it is therefore hard to resist the conclusion that the *"little horn"* of Chap. 7 refers to the same person, and the fourth division of the image in Chap. 2 to the same dynasty.
   This sounds plausible at first thought, but it is not necessarily the case since quite sufficient reasons for interpreting otherwise will be found as we proceed.

2. One would expect *the four big world-powers* to be taken in order, and Rome would thus follow after Greece. The realm of the Seleucid Empire (the one of the four divisions of the Grecian Empire in which it is claimed the Antichrist, the *"little horn"*, Antiochus Epiphanes appeared) was territorially insignificant.

3. The description of the fourth kingdom (verse 40) seems to indicate a stronger kingdom than any of its predecessors, and this is especially true if, as all admit, this fourth kingdom corresponds to the fourth beast of Chap. 7, which with its great iron teeth was said to be "dreadful and terrible and strong exceedingly". In comparison with Rome this could hardly apply to the Seleucid Empire even under Antiochus Epiphanes.

4. The description of what the fourth kingdom and the fourth beast are said to do (Chap. 2.40,—"break—subdue—crush", and Chap. 7.23,—"devour *the whole earth,* tread it down and break it

into pieces") apply most aptly to the Roman Empire, but in no sense to the Seleucid Empire even during the time of Antiochus Epiphanes.

5. The division of the Roman Empire into the Eastern and Western kingdoms, as represented by the two legs of the image, favors this interpretation.

6. The periods of time assigned in Daniel for the fulfillment of the various prophecies favor their application to Rome, but there is absolutely no satisfactory adjustment of them to the Seleucid Empire. (See especially the exposition of the "seventy weeks" in Chap. 9.)

7. The vision of John in Revelation is markedly similar to these of Daniel, the same emblems and even the same phraseology being employed, and, if they do refer to the same thing, this points to a time at least far later than the Seleucid Empire. (See exposition under Chap. 7.)

8. The objections to the view that Rome is intended are not formidable:

   (a) The range of vision is too great because the greatness and the world-historical position of Rome was not known until 400 years after the captivity.
   But this applies as well to Greece, and besides it takes no account of the prophetic character of the vision.

   (b) The "stone cut out of the mountain" did not destroy the Roman Empire, but was rather assimilated with it for more than one thousand years.
   The principal part of this objection is just as true of the Seleucid Empire. The Seleucid Empire was not destroyed in B. C. 167 when Antiochus Epiphanes was ruling, and when it was destroyed in B. C. 65, it was destroyed not by the "stone", but by the Roman Empire itself. So the argument is even at this point. But if the smiting of the "stone" may be thought of as still future, the objection would then lose its force entirely.

9. In addition to these reasons the reader is referred to those with regard to the "fourth beast" in Chap. 7.7.
   Keil says, "The opinion that Rome is the fourth kingdom alone accords without any force or arbitrariness with the representation of these kingdoms in the visions both of Chap. 2 and Chap. 7, with each separately as well as with both together".

Ver. 31. "the aspect thereof was terrible",—i. e., terrible on account of its size and its brightness.

Ver. 33. "legs of iron",—These represent no doubt the two divisions of the Roman Empire into the Eastern and Western kingdoms. This Roman Empire conquered the four divisions of the Grecian Empire as follows: Elyricum and Epirus, B. C. 167; Pergamus, B. C. 132; the Seleucid Empire (Syria), B. C. 65, and Egypt, B. C. 29. Its beginning may therefore be said to have been in B. C. 167, and its end, as we know it, in A. D. 476. Some would date its beginning in B. C. 29, when it overthrew the kingdom of Ptolmey in Egypt.

Ver. 39. *"another kingdom inferior to thee"*,—This refers to an ethical rather than to a physical or political inferiority. This gradation runs throughout—gold, silver, brass, iron and clay.

Ver. 40. *"all these"*,—i. e., the materials already mentioned—gold, silver, etc.; the reference is not to the former kingdoms as such, but to the materials of which they were composed wherever found. Of course the ultimate reference is to the kingdoms themselves.

Ver. 41. *"part of potters' clay and part of iron"*,—Showing that it contains within itself the principle of an increasing disruption.

Ver. 43. *"they shall not cleave one to another"*,—The word *"they"* in each case refers to the people as well as to the kings, and the reference is, as Keil says, to the vain efforts of the hetrogeneous elements of the fourth kingdom to coalesce by juxtaposition or even by intermarriage among themselves.

Ver. 44. *"in the days of those kings"*,—This cannot refer to the kings of the four big successional monarchies because they are no longer in existence. Zoeckler, of course, refers it to the contemporaneous kings of the four divisions of the Grecian Empire. But if the *"legs of iron"*, the fourth kingdom of the image, be the Roman Empire, as we have seen reasons for believing it to be, then these kings must in some way be related to Rome. Some think it can hardly refer to Rome as a single kingdom because, as they contend, the plural, *"those kings"*, would then have been written in the singular. Many think therefore that the most consistent interpretation is that which refers these kings to the *"ten toes"* of the image, representing as they do ten kingdoms with their kings, which must consequently arise some time in the future when the Roman Empire shall in a sense have been revived. (F. Au. Gab. Sco.)

"nor shall the sovereignty thereof be left to another people",—There are to be no successors; it is to be an everlasting kingdom.

"consume all these kingdoms",—Not only the fourth, but the preceding three as having in a sense been incorporated in it, the whole image being, as it were, destroyed at once.

Ver. 45. *"stone cut out of the mountain"*,—This stone is the kingdom of Christ. In Matt. 21.44 and Luke 20.18 Christ clearly refers this Messianic prophecy to Himself and His kingdom.

"without hands",—i. e., not by human, but by supernatural and divine means. In answer to the question as to why the *"stone"* might not have been the kingdom of Christ as ushered in at His first coming, and the kingdom it smote the Roman Empire of Christ's time, Scofield remarks, "The smiting Stone destroys the Gentile world-system (in its final form) by a sudden and irremediable blow, not by the gradual process of conversion and assimilation; and then, and not before, does the Stone become a mountain which fills 'the whole earth'. Such a destruction of the Gentile monarchy-system did not occur at the first advent of Christ. On the contrary, He was put to death by the sentence of an officer of the fourth empire, which was then at the zenith of its power. Since the crucifixion the Roman Empire has followed the course marked out in the vision, but the Gentile world-dominion still continues, and the crushing blow is still suspended."

"It is important to note", says Scofield, "that the Gentile world-power is immediately followed by the kingdom of heaven, and that the God of the heavens does not set up His kingdom till after the destruction of the Gentile world-system." This same writer further remarks that *"the days of those kings"* (verse 44), i. e., the ten kings symbolized by the ten toes of the image, could not have been the days of the first advent of the Messiah, because that condition did not then exist, nor was it even possible until the dissolution of the Roman Empire, and the rise of the present national world-system.

CHAPTER SEVEN

1 In the first year of Belshazzar king of Babylon Daniel [1]had a dream and visions of his head upon his bed: then he wrote the dream and told the sum of the matters. 2 Daniel spake and said, I saw in my vision by night, and, behold, the four winds of heaven brake forth upon the great sea. 3 And four great beasts came up from the sea, diverse one from another. 4 The first was like a lion, and had eagle's wings: I beheld till the wings thereof were plucked, and it was lifted up from the earth, and made to stand upon two feet as a man; and a man's heart was given to it. 5 And, behold, another beast, a second, like to a bear; and [2]it was raised up on one side, and three ribs were in its mouth between its teeth: and they said thus unto it, Arise, devour much flesh. 6 After this I beheld, and, lo, another, like a leopard, which had upon its back four wings of a bird; the beast had also four heads; and dominion was given to it. 7 After this I saw in the night-visions, and, behold, a fourth beast, terrible and [3]powerful, and strong exceedingly; and it had great iron teeth; it devoured and brake in pieces, and stamped the residue with its feet: and it was diverse from all the beasts that were before it; and it had ten horns. 8 I considered the horns, and, behold, there came up among them another horn, a little one, before which three of the horns were plucked up by the roots: and, behold, in this horn were eyes like the eyes of a man, and a mouth speaking great things. 9 I beheld till thrones were [4]placed, and one that was ancient of days did sit: his raiment was white as snow, and the hair of his head like pure wool; his throne was fiery flames, *and* the wheels

thereof burning fire. 10 A fiery stream issued and came forth from before him: thousands of thousands ministered unto him, and ten thousand times ten thousand stood before him: the judgment was set, and the books were opened. 11 I beheld at that time because of the voice of the great words which the horn spake; I beheld even till the beast was slain, and its body destroyed, and it was given [5]to be burned with fire. 12 And as for the rest of the beasts, their dominion was taken away: yet their lives were prolonged for a season and a time.

13 I saw in the night-visions, and, behold, there came with the clouds of heaven one like unto a son of man, and he came even to the ancient of days, and they brought him near before him. 14 And there was given him dominion, and glory, and a kingdom, that all the peoples, nations, and languages should serve him: his dominion is an everlasting dominion, which shall not pass away, and his kingdom that which shall not be destroyed.

15 As for me, Daniel, my spirit was grieved in the midst of [6]my body, and the visions of my head troubled me. 16 I came near unto one of them that stood by, and asked him the truth concerning all this. So he told me, and made me know the interpretation of the things. 17 These great beasts, which were four, are four kings, that shall arise out of the earth. 18 But the saints of the Most High shall receive the kingdom, and possess the kingdom for ever, even for ever and ever. 19 Then I desired to know the truth concerning the fourth beast, which was diverse from all of them, exceeding terrible, whose teeth were of iron, and its nails of brass;

[1]Aram. *saw*
[2]Or, as otherwise read, *it raised up one dominion*
[3]Or, *dreadul*
[4]Or, *cast down*

[5]Aram. *to the burning of fire*
[6]Aram. *the sheath*

which devoured, brake in pieces, and stamped the residue with its feet; 20 and concerning the ten horns that were on its head, and the other *horn* which came up, and before which three fell, even that horn that had eyes, and a mouth that spake great things, whose look was more stout than its fellows. 21 I beheld, and the same horn made war with the saints, and prevailed against them, 22 until the ancient of days came, and judgment was given [7]to the saints of the Most High, and the time came that the saints possessed the kingdom.

·23 Thus he said, The fourth beast shall be a fourth kingdom upon earth, which shall be diverse from all the kingdoms, and shall devour the whole earth, and shall [8]tread it down, and break it in pieces. 24 And as for the ten horns, out of this kingdom shall ten kings

[7]Or, *for*
[8]Or, *thresh it*

arise: and another shall arise after them; and he shall be diverse from the former, and he shall put down three kings. 25 And he shall speak words against the Most High, and shall wear out the saints of the Most High; and he shall think to change the times and the law; and they shall be given into his hand until a time and times and half a time. 26 But the judgment shall be set, and they shall take away his dominion, to consume and to destroy it unto the end. 27 And the kingdom and the dominion, and the greatness of the kingdoms under the whole heaven, shall be given to the people of the saints of the Most High: his kingdom is an everlasting kingdom, and all dominions shall serve and obey him. 28 [9]Here is the end of the matter. As for me, Daniel, my thoughts much troubled me, and my [10]countenance was changed in me: but I kept the matter in my heart.

[9]Aram. *Hitherto*
[10]Aram. *brightness*

Vers. 1-28. THE VISION OF THE FOUR BEASTS AND ITS INTERPRETATION.

This vision of Daniel's without doubt refers to the same thing as Nebuchadnezzar's vision in Chap 2. (See Hos. 13.7,8.)

Ver. 2. *"the great sea"*,—The Mediterranean, as typifying the sea of heathen nations, the mere unorganized mass of mankind, the political sea.

"the four winds",—Used in keeping with the four beasts and referring to actual winds as representing the heavenly powers and forces by which God sets the nations of the world in motion.

Ver. 3. *"four great beasts"*,—These great beasts are four kings (verse 17) used interchangeably with the four kingdoms represented by their reign.

"came up from the sea",—Verses 6 and 7 show that they came up successively and were not therefore simultaneous kingdoms.

Ver. 4. *"The first was like a lion"*,—This refers to the Babylonian Empire with Nebuchadnezzar as king. Elsewhere Nebuchadnezzar is likened to a lion in strength (Jer. 4.7; 5.6; 49.19; 50.17) and to an eagle for swiftness (Jer. 48.40; 49.22; Lam. 4.19; Hab. 1.8; Ezk. 17.3, 12; 27.2).

"the wings thereof were plucked",—Its power of unrestrained motion was taken from it.

"lifted up from the earth",—To which it had been confined after having been stripped of its power.

"made to stand upon two feet as a man .... and a man's heart was given to it",—This is a reference no doubt to Nebuchadnezzar's derangement and restoration from the same, and emphasizing the greater

206

moderation and humanity of the Babylonian Empire after the king's restoration. (K. F. Zo. Rob.)

Ver. 5. *"a second like to a bear"*,—This is to be taken by common consent as referring to the Medo-Persian Empire.

"it was raised up on one side",—i. e., ready to spring, the reference being doubtless to its rapacious and warlike attitude, as Zoeckler says. It may also be taken as meaning that the brute was leaning sideways, with a reference to its weak and tottering condition (Kr. Ew. Hit.), or it may be taken, with Keil and Delitzsch, as meaning that the feet and shoulders of one side were raised as if going forward, representing the double sidedness of the empire, the weak and resting Median and the strong and aggressive Persian.

"three ribs were in its mouth",—These refer no doubt to Babylon, Egypt and Lydia, which kingdoms were conquered by the Medo-Persian power. (N. K. Zo. Eb. Hof.)

"and they said",—Doubtless the angel powers.

"devour much flesh",—i. e., subdue many nations.

Ver. 6. *"another like a leopard"*,—This likewise by common consent is to be taken as referring to the Grecian (Macedonian) Empire.

"four wings of a bird",—Pointing to the rapidity of the Grecian conquests.

"the beast had also four heads",—Referring to the four divisions which were embraced in the Grecian kingdom and into which it was divided upon the death of its king, Alexander. (Chap. 8.21,22.)

Ver. 7. *"a fourth beast"*,—This beast is acknowleged by all to refer to the same kingdom as that represented by the *"legs of iron"* in the vision of Chap. 2.40.

"stamped with its feet",—i. e., with its legs of iron.

"the residue",—i. e., what it could not devour and break.

"and it had ten horns",—These horns and the ten toes of the image of Chap. 2 refer to the same thing.

This *"fourth beast"* is said to be either the Seleucid Empire or the Roman Empire, according to the interpretation given to *"the legs of iron"* of the image in Chap. 2. (See authorities quoted there.)

The following arguments in favor of the Roman Empire seem rather conclusive:

1. One would naturally expect the four big world-powers to be taken in order and Rome would follow after Greece.

2. This beast was the most terrible of all and subdued the whole earth, and no one king of the Seleucid Empire or of any of the four divisions of the Grecian Empire answers either of these descriptions.

3. Greece did not have ten horns. In Chap. 8 it had four horns and in this chapter it has four heads, and to make the fourth beast the Seleucid Empire means to make it the tenth horn of the fourth head, which head this beast is not represented as having. This beast with its *one* head had itself ten horns.

4. Those who make Antiochus Epiphanes the *"little horn"* and the

eleventh king, cannot find the first ten. You can find seven, and then the three he is said to have unrooted would have to be Demetrius, the twelve-year-old heir who never was on the throne; Heliodorus, the usurper, who was on the throne but the briefest while, and Philometer, who also never was on the throne.

5. It is simply impossible to refer verses 9-14 and 22-28 to anything that occurred in the time of Antiochus Epiphanes (B. C. 164), or even at the close of the Seleucid Empire in B. C. 68.

6. If the vision refers to the same thing as the image of Chap. 2, then, as pointed out there, the *"legs of iron"* representing the eastern and western divisions favor the interpretation that points to the Roman Empire.

7. Pusey, who favors the Roman Empire, says, "The ten horns are ten kingdoms which shall issue *out of it* and must therefore be kingdoms which should arise at some later stage of its existence and not those first kings without which it could not be a kingdom at all".

8. The beast in Revelation 13 *is generally believed* to be identical with this one, and if it is, we must note the fact that Rev. 17.12 says the kings *"have as yet received no kingdom"*, and therefore the reference here cannot be to any kingdom prior to the Revelation date.

9. The ten horns or kingdoms are to be contemporaneous and are to continue on together until the eleventh, or *"little horn"* shall have risen up among them.

10. See also the arguments under *"the legs of iron"* of Chap. 2.

"ten horns",—Ten kings, as interpreted in verse 24.

1. To those who say the ten kings of the Seleucid Empire are here meant it is enough to refer the fourth of the preceding arguments.

2. To those who contend that ten is a round, symbolic number indicating a multiplicity of kings and that it is useless to attempt a specific interpretation, it is enough to reply that if the other figures are to be taken literally, this one, ten, ought also to be so taken.

3. Hengstenberg and many others (Lut. Ger.) say they are the ten kingdoms that resulted from the invasion of the Roman Empire from the north, namely, Syria, Asia, Egypt, Africa, Greece, Italy, Germany, France, Spain and England.

4. It seems, however, best to consider them as ten kingdoms yet to come—the Roman Empire in a sense still existing and to be revived. (F. K. Jer. Ira. Rob. Treg. Sco. Gab. Bla. Tor.)

Ver. 8. *"Another horn, a little one"*,—Literally *"the horn of little-ness"*—little in its beginning but becoming greater than them all (verse 20).

By some this *"little horn"* is referred historically to Antiochus Epiphanes and typically to the Antichrist of the New Testament (Zo. Po. Ju. Wil.). But if the *"fourth beast"* refers to Rome, as we are inclined to think it does, then the *"little horn"* must refer *directly* to the eschatological Antichrist of the New Testament (II Thess. 2.3,4). (E. K. Eb. Pu. Au. Zu. Ew. Hav. Hen. Rob. Jer. Sco. Bla. Tor. and nearly all the Church Fathers as well as nearly all Roman Catholic writers.)

By those who refer the *"little horn"* to Antiochus Epiphanes the *"fourth beast"* is said to be the Seleucid Empire with its ten kings, the last three of which were uprooted by Antiochus Epiphanes. Then Daniel sees God on His throne preparing judgment and sending it down upon Antiochus Epiphanes because of his great and blasphemous words (verse 11). Then in verse 13 the Son of man comes to God, the Ancient of days, and gets an everlasting kingdom, the reference being to the kingdom received by Christ at His first coming which is the same as the *"saints possessing the kingdom"* (verses 18 and 23). Then Daniel asks for more information about the *fourth beast* and was given a vision of this beast making war against the saints until Messiah came (His first coming) and gave justice to the saints, who then came into possession of the kingdom, as above stated. The angel then reveals to Daniel how the *"little horn"* *"shall subdue three kings"*, speak blasphemous words against God, wear out the saints, change times and laws and persecute the saints three and a half years until judgment is meted out to him, as it was in his death.

We have already mentioned reasons which seem sufficiently strong to invalidate this scheme of interpretation.

"three of the first horns plucked up by the roots",—Those accepting Antiochus Epiphanes as the historical fulfillment of the prophecy concerning the *"little horn"* must of course refer the horns *"plucked up"* to Demetrius, Heliodorus and Philometer, but we have already seen why this reference is scarcely to be admitted.

Calvin and some few others think that *"three"* should be taken as an indefinite number meaning many, but there is no sufficient reason for this, and it is best therefore to take it as a definite number meaning precisely three. (Bi. Me. Os. Pf. Jer. Mel. Bul. Rule.)

"eyes like the eyes of a man",—Showing that he was not some celestial being.

"a mouth speaking great things",—i. e., magnifying himself and *"speaking words against the most high"* (verse 25).

Ver. 9. *"ancient of days"*,—This expression is by many referred to Christ. (Oe. Gab. Cum. Rob. and others.) But the great majority rightly refer it to God, the everlasting Father. (K. F. Zo. Kr.) It thus harmonizes with the same expression in verse 13 where it refers without doubt to God.

Fausset says, "The Son would not judge in His own case, this cause being the one at issue with the Antichrist", while Irving says, "It is God judging the arch-enemy of His Son and preparing the way for the coming of His Son in the clouds of heaven."

"thrones were placed",—i. e., set up. Note the plural. Inasmuch as *"the ancient of days"* seems here the rather to indicate God than Christ, these thrones, it would appear, were not for the glorified saints, as Lightfoot and others take them, but for the angels of God, as Keil and Zoeckler would have us believe. (See Ps. 89.8.)

"His throne was fiery flames",—God's judgments are swift like rapid flames.

"the wheels thereof",—Oriental thrones moved on wheels.

Ver. 10. The thousands mentioned are His angels who stood before him to serve.

Ver. 11. The execution on earth of the judgment pronounced in the heavenly court.

"because of the voice of the great words",—Thus it is seen that it is the insolent rebellion of the little horn which is the cause and the occasion of the judgment.

"till the beast was slain",—Jerome and expositors in general, both Catholic and Protestant, interpret this as the destruction of the Antichrist at the second coming of Christ. Calvin indeed says, "All Christian expositors agree in treating the prophecy as relating to the final day of Christ's advent".

Others, of course, consistent with their former interpretations, explain this reference as pointing on typically to the Antichrist of the end of the age and to his kingdom, and see in its main reference that which points to Antiochus Epiphanes and the Seleucid Empire.

Ver. 12. This verse does not mean that *"the rest of the beasts"* continued to exist after the destruction of the fourth one, but that although deprived of their dominion they had continued to exist in certain fragmentary form along side of the fourth and were involved in a common ruin by the Messianic judgment just as the image of Chap. 2 was all destroyed at once. (K. N. Zo. Kr.)

Ver. 13. *"one like unto a son of man"*,—Jesus persistently called Himself the Son of man. Fausset calls attention to the fact that it is a title always associated with the second coming of Christ.

"with the clouds of heaven",—This is referred by most commentators to the second coming of Jesus to judgment.

Ver. 18. *"the saints of the most High"*,—These are not the angels of verses 10 and 16, but the people of God. But what people of God?

1. The glorified saints. (Oe. Rob.) But this cannot be, for verses 21 and 25 say that the *"little horn"* makes war on them and wears them out. They must therefore be God's people on earth. Verse 27 says the kingdom is *"under the whole heaven"*.

2. The people of Christ, the Church, the members of the house of Israel in its ideal, spiritual significance. (C. F. Zo. Ew. Lee, Bush.) If it is found that the Church is to pass through the Great Tribulation this explanation is quite plausible and probably the correct one.

3. Daniel's own people, the converted and God-fearing portion of them who are supposed to be on the earth after the Church has been caught away. (Au. Gab. Hof. Hit. Ber. Len.) If the Church does not go through the Great Tribulation, this explanation is without doubt the true one.

Ver. 21. *"made war with the saints"*,—A special feature connected with the devouring, breaking, stamping.

"prevailed against them",—Not ultimately, but only until the ancient of days came, which expression in the next verse refers without question to Christ Himself.

Ver. 22. *"judgment was given to the saints of the Most High"*,—The word *"judgment"* here includes the idea not only of justice but of rule as well.

210

Ver. 23. It is exceedingly difficult to refer the latter clauses of this verse to Antiochus Epiphanes because it cannot very appropriately be said to have been true of him.

Ver. 24. *"out of this kingdom shall ten kings arise"*,—Scofield says, "In the beast vision of Daniel 7 the fourth beast is declared to be 'the fourth kingdom', i. e., the Roman Empire, the 'iron' kingdom of Daniel 2. The 'ten horns' upon the fourth beast (Roman Empire), verse 7, are declared to be 'ten kings that shall arise' (verse 24) answering to the ten toes of the image vision of Daniel 2. The ten kingdoms, covering the regions formerly ruled by Rome, will constitute, therefore, the form in which the fourth or Roman Empire will exist when the whole fabric of Gentile world-dominion is smitten by the 'stone cut out without hands', i. e., Christ."

"put down three kings",—(See the remarks on verse 8.)

Ver. 25. *"change the times and the law"*,—The prerogative of God alone, blasphemously assumed by this individual. The *"times and the law"* refer to the legally appointed religious celebrations or ordinances in general, as determined by God; the great annual feasts, the monthly and also the weekly, Sabbaths, new-moons, etc. The ultimate realization of this must be looked for in the last times according to II Thess. 2.4; Rev. 18.8,11, even though its immediate historical fulfillment be found in Antiochus Epiphanes, to which latter, however, as we have seen, the prophecy can hardly with consistency be made to refer.

"they shall be given into his hand",—i. e., the saints of the Most High given into his hand to be persecuted.

"until a time and times and half a time",—According to frequent Chaldee usage the plural is put for the dual, and *"times"* means "two times", and the whole is equivalent to three and one-half.

Zoeckler says, "It must remain an open question whether ordinary calendar years are intended, or, what is scarcely less probable in itself, whether mystical periods are referred to, which are measured by a standard not known to men, but only to God." Zoeckler explains the symbolical reference of this time period by saying it is half of seven, seven standing for the whole. And just as the seven years passed in lycanthropy by Nebuchadnezzar were to be taken symbolically as representing an extended period, so this expression means a period of suffering shortened by one-half, and carries in it the same idea as that expressed by the Saviour when He said the season of tribulation would be shortened for the elect's sake. But we can hardly be satisfied with the inadequate explanation by this puzzled expositor of these sharply defined and often reiterated statements of time with reference to the events which are here predicted.

Keil likewise has contended against a literal interpretation of these chronological data, but he has of course been driven to this by his theory that this whole prophecy applies to the duration of the Roman Empire. The only satisfactory explanation of the expression is to take it in a literal sense, as meaning three years and a half, whether it be applied to Antiochus Epiphanes, as Zoeckler applies it (and even here the difficulty of reconciling the statement with events connected with the suffering of Israel under this Syrian despot are not so formidable as Zoeckler supposes), or whether it be applied, as we think it should be, to the suffering under the

Antichrist of the end-time. The reference is to be explained in harmony with the same expression in the twelfth chapter. The modern interpreters who hold to the "year-for-a-day" theory refer this *"little horn"* of this chapter, some to the papacy and others to Mohammedanism. There is, however, no really good and convincing evidence anywhere in Daniel of such a symbolical use of the word "day".

Zoeckler says, "This prophecy of the affliction of Israel during three and one-half years prior to its deliverance had a typical fulfillment in the history of Antiochus Epiphanes, but its final realization is reserved for the eschatological future."

Ver. 26. *"unto the end"*,—i. e., unto the end of the God-opposed world-power, which is to mark the end of the heathen world-power as a whole, and coincides with the erection of the kingdom of God.

Ver. 27. *"the kingdom and the dominion and the greatness of the kingdoms"*,—The dominion, power and greatness possessed by all the heathen kingdoms is intended, and these are to be conferred on Messiah's kingdom.

"under the whole heaven",—This, says Fausset, shows it to be a kingdom on earth, and not in heaven.

"his kingdom is an everlasting kingdom",—Says Fausset, "If everlasting, how can the kingdom here refer to the Millennial one? Answer. Daniel saw the whole time of *future blessedness* as *one period*, the Millennium and the time of the new heavens and new earth. Christ's kingdom is everlasting. Not even the last judgment shall end it, but only give it a more glorious appearance, the new Jerusalem coming down from God out of heaven, with the throne of God and the Lamb in it."

Ver. 28. *"Here is the end of the matter"*,—i. e., here is the end of the remarks of the interpreter, the conclusion of which coincides with the end of the dream.

"my thought troubled me",—i. e., after waking from his dream-vision. It shows perhaps that the Holy Spirit intended much more to be understood by Daniel's words than Daniel himself perhaps understood. "We are not", says Fausset, "to limit the significance of prophecies to what the prophets themselves understood." Many a seer has spoken wiser than he knew.

CHAPTER EIGHT

1 In the third year of the reign of king Belshazzar a vision appeared unto me, even unto me, Daniel, after that which appeared unto me at the first. 2 And I saw in the vision; now it was so, that when I saw, I was in Shushan the ¹palace, which is in the province of Elam; and I saw in the vision, and I was by the river Ulai. 3 Then I lifted up mine eyes, and saw, and, behold, there stood before the river a ram which had two horns: and the two horns were high; but one was higher than the other, and the higher came up last. 4 I saw the ram pushing westward, and northward, and southward; and no beasts could stand before him, neither was there any that could deliver out of his hand; but he did according to his will, and magnified himself.

5 And as I was considering, behold, a he-goat came from the west over the face of the whole earth, and ²touched not the ground: and the goat had a

¹Or, *castle*

²Heb. *none touched the ground*

212

notable horn between his eyes. 6 And he came to the ram that had the two horns, which I saw standing before the river, and ran upon him in the fury of his power. 7 And I saw him come close unto the ram, and he was moved with anger against him, and smote the ram, and brake his two horns; and there was no power in the ram to stand before him; but he cast him down to the ground, and trampled upon him, and there was none that could deliver the ram out of his hand. 8 And the he-goat magnified himself exceedingly: and when he was strong, the great horn was broken; and instead of it there came up four notable *horns* toward the four winds of heaven.

9 And out of one of them came forth a little horn, which waxed exceeding great, toward the south, and toward the east, and toward the glorious *land*. 10 And it waxed great, even to the host of heaven; and some of the host and of the stars it cast down to the ground, and trampled upon them. 11 Yea, it magnified itself, even to the prince of the host; and [3]it took away from him the continual *burnt-offering*, and the place of his sanctuary was cast down. 12 And [4]the host was given over *to it* together with the continual *burnt-offering* through transgression; and it cast down truth to the ground, and it did *its pleasure* and prospered. 13 Then I heard a holy one speaking; and another holy one said unto that certain one who spake, How long shall be the vision *concerning* the continual *burnt-offering*, and the transgression that maketh desolate, to give both the sanctuary and the host to be trodden under foot? 14 And he said unto me, Unto two thousand and three hundred evenings *and* mornings; then shall the sanctuary be [5]cleansed.

15 And it came to pass, when I, even Daniel, had seen the vision, that I sought [6]to understand it; and, behold, there stood before me as the appearance of a man. 16 And I heard a man's voice between *the banks of* the Ulai, which called, and said, Gabriel, make this man to understand the vision. 17 So he came near where I stood; and when he came, I was affrighted, and fell upon my face: but he said unto me, Understand, O son of man; for the vision belongeth to the time of the end. 18 Now as he was speaking with me, I fell into a deep sleep with my face toward the ground; but he touched me, and set me [7]upright. 19 And he said, Behold, I will make thee know what shall be in the latter time of the indignation; for it belongeth to the appointed time of the end. 20 The ram which thou sawest, that had the two horns, they are the kings of Media and Persia. 21 And the rough he-goat is the king of Greece: and the great horn that is between his eyes is the first king. 22 And as for that which was broken, in the place whereof four stood up, four kingdoms shall stand up out of the nation, but not with his power. 23 And in the latter time of their kingdom, when the transgressors are come to the full, a king of fierce countenance, and understanding dark sentences, shall stand up. 24 And his power shall be mighty, but not [8]by his own power; and he shall [9]destroy wonderfully, and shall prosper and do *his pleasure*; and he shall [9]destroy the mighty ones and [10]the holy people. 25 And through his policy he shall cause craft to prosper in his hand; and he shall magnify himself in his heart, and in *their* security shall he [9]destroy many: he shall also stand up against the prince of princes; but he shall be broken without hand. 26 And the vision of the evenings and mornings which hath been told is true: but shut thou up the vision; for it belongeth to many days *to come.*

[3]Another reading is, *the continual* burnt-offering *was taken away from him*
[4]Or, *a host was given to it against the &c.,* Or, *a host was set over the &c.*
[5]Heb. *justified*

[6]Heb. *understanding*
[7]Or, *where I had stood*
[8]Or, *with his power.* See ver. 22.
[9]Or, *corrupt*
[10]Heb. *people of the saints*

Vers. 1-26. Vision of the Desecrating Horn and Its Interpretation.

Ver. 3. "*a ram which had two horns*",—The ram stands for the kingdom of Media-Persia, the short horn referring to Media and the long one to Persia. (See verse 20.)

Ver. 4. The ram did not push eastward, not because Media-Persia came from the east (F. Kr. Len.), nor because the east already belonged to Media-Persia (Zo.), nor because their conquests did not extend in that direction (Hav.), but perhaps because their conquests in the east being very subordinate ones it was not essential to mention them in the unfolding of this kingdom as a world-power.

Ver. 5. *"a he-goat came from the west"*,—The reference here is to the kingdom of Greece.

"the goat had a notable horn",—By this horn is meant without doubt Alexander the Great. (See verse 21.)

Ver. 8. *"there came up four notable horns"*,—These Daniel later says were the four kingdoms, the divisions into which the Grecian Empire fell upon the death of Alexander. (See verse 22.)

Ver. 9. *"out of one of them"*,—i. e., out of the Seleucid Empire (the Syrian kingdom) as is universally acknowledged.

"came forth a little horn",—This by common consent is taken as a reference to Antiochus Epiphanes.

"the glorious land",—i. e., Palestine.

The little horn of this chapter is not to be confounded with the little horn of Chap. 7. (F. Au. Zu. Eb. Hav. Hen. Sco. Gab.)

Says Scofield, "The little horn here is a prophecy fulfilled in Antiochus Epiphanes, B. C. 175, who profaned the temple and terribly persecuted the Jews. He is not to be confounded with the 'little horn' of Chap. 7 who is yet to come and who will dominate the earth during the Great Tribulation. But Antiochus Epiphanes is a remarkable type of the Beast, the terrible 'little horn' of the last days. That the 'little horn' of Chap. 7 cannot be the 'little horn' of this chapter is evident. The former comes up among the 'ten horns' into which the 'fourth' empire (Roman) is to be divided; the 'little horn' of this chapter comes out of one of the 'four kingdoms' into which the third empire (Grecian) was divided (verse 23), and in 'the latter times' of the four kingdoms (verses 22 and 23). This was historically true of Antiochus Epiphanes. They are alike in hatred of the Jews and of God, and in profaning the temple."

Ver. 10. "This passage", says Scofield, "(verses 10-14) is confessedly the most difficult in prophecy, a difficulty increased by the present state of the text. Historically this was fulfilled in and by Antiochus Epiphanes, but in a more intense and final sense Antiochus Epiphanes but adumbrates the awful blasphemy of the *'little horn'* of Chap. 7."

"the host of heaven" and *"the stars"*,—By these expressions are meant the people of Israel, especially those who held positions of responsibility as did the princes, priests and rabbis.

Ver. 11. *"the prince of the host"*,—i. e., God Himself. (F. Zo. Gab.)

"him",—i. e., the prince of the host.

"took away the continual burnt-offering",—i. e., stopped the daily sacrifice.

Ver. 12. *"the host was given over to it"*,—The *"host"* here refers to the host of the Jews, and the pronoun *"it"* throughout the verse refers to the *"little horn."*

"through transgression",—This refers without doubt to the apostacy

of Israel because of which the host, i. e., the Jewish nation, was given over to the persecutions of the *"little horn"*, Antiochus Epiphanes. (K. F. D. Kr. Hav.) The construction of the verse is exceedingly difficult. There are some who render it, "and war is raised against the daily sacrifice with wickedness". (St. Eb. Wi. Hit. Hof. Gro.) See the margin for other translations, but the rendering of our text adheres more nearly to the original than any of the various other renderings and is much to be preferred.

"it cast down truth",—He forbade the worship of the true God.

Ver. 13. *"a holy one speaking"*,—i. e., a saint; here, an angel.

"How long shall be the vision", etc.?—How long shall the sacrifice be suspended and the profanation of the temple and the trodding under foot of the host of the Jewish people be continued, i. e., how long shall it last?

Ver. 14. *"Unto two thousand and three hundred evenings and mornings"*,—By no kind of impartial exegesis can this expression be taken to indicate two thousand and three hundred years. It must refer to days —not to 1150 days (Ew. Zo. Ka. Hil. Hit.), but to 2300 days. (C. F. K. St. Ber. Len. Hav. Hof. Der.) Antiochus Epiphanes took Jerusalem in B. C. 170. Three years later, B. C. 167, in June he sent Appolonius against the city who at that time caused all sacrifices to cease. On December of this same year Appolonius set up the heathen altar in the temple and on December 25 the heathen sacrifices began. Three years later on this same date, December 25, B. C. 164, Judas Maccabeus restored the true sacrifice and this was just three and one-half years after Appolonius stopped the sacrifice. The three years and a half dating from June, B. C. 167, was a period of severe oppression and sacrilege against the temple. Stuart and some others fix the first date mentioned above in B. C. 171 and accordingly set all the following dates back a year earlier, i. e., B. C. 171, 168 and 165.

These three and one-half years had their typical fulfillment in Antiochus Epiphanes, but it is generally conceded that its final realization is reserved for the last times, according to the New Testament writings, in the eschatological Antichrist.

Ver. 17. *"the time of the end"*,—This is the prophetic phrase for the time of fulfillment seen always at the end of the prophetic horizon. (Gen. 49.1; Num. 24.14.)

This refers of course primarily to the time of Antiochus Epiphanes, his overthrow and the judgment of the world-kingdom with the ushering in of the Messianic kingdom at Christ's first coming, but antitypically the reference is to the final period of the world's history, the close of the Christian era at the second coming of Christ. (K. F. St.)

Ver. 19. *"the latter time of the indignation"*,—i. e., of God's indignation.

"the appointed time of the end",—Says Scofield, "Two 'ends' are in view here; (1) historically, the end of the third, or Grecian Empire of Alexander out of one of the divisions of which the 'little horn' of verse 9 (Antiochus Epiphanes) arose; (2) prophetically, the end of the times of the Gentiles, when the 'little horn' of Chap. 7, the Beast, will arise— Daniel's final time of the end."

Ver. 22. *"not with his power"*,—Neither singly nor all taken together did the power of the four divisions of the Grecian Empire equal that of his, i. e., of Alexander's.

Ver. 23. *"when the transgressors are come to the full"*,—The *"transgressors"* are the apostate Jews whose sins have ripened them for judgment. (K. F. St. Rob. Gab.) The typical reference is of course to the time of Antiochus Epiphanes and the antitypical to the close of the Christian era.

"understanding dark sentences",—Literally "verses in riddle", i. e., crafty, clever and cunning.

Ver. 24. *"not by his own power"*,—It is by divine permission that he accomplishes his destructive work.

"the mighty ones and the holy people",—The leaders among the Jews and the Jewish people in general, the people of God.

Ver. 25. *"the prince of princes"*,—i. e., God Himself.

"he shall be broken without hand",—His destruction was to be due to the intervention of God.

We can hardly see wherein Scofield is warranted in thinking that verses 24 and 25 go beyond Antiochus Epiphanes and refer, as he says, "evidently to the *'little horn'* of Chap. 7, in fact pre-eminently so", although he does not exclude a reference to Antiochus Epiphanes. Certainly the *"king of fierce countenance."* of verse 23 is the same individual as the one referred to by the pronouns of verses 24 and 25.

Ver. 26. *"shut thou up the vision"*,—Daniel was told not to be too anxious about spreading the vision abroad, but to guard it carefully for later times when it would be better understood.

CHAPTER NINE

20 And while I was speaking, and praying, and confessing my sin and the sin of my people Israel, and presenting my supplication before Jehovah my God for the holy mountain of my God; 21 yea, while I was speaking in prayer, the man Gabriel, whom I had seen in the vision at the beginning, [1]being caused to fly swiftly, [2]touched me about the time of the evening oblation. 22 And he [3]instructed me, and talked with me, and said, O Daniel, I am now come forth to give thee wisdom and understanding. 23 At the beginning of thy supplications the commandment went forth, and I am come to tell thee: for thou art [4]greatly beloved: therefore consider the matter, and understand the vision.

24 Seventy weeks are decreed upon thy people and upon thy holy city, [5]to finish [6]transgression, and [7]to make an end of sins, and to [8]make reconciliation for iniquity, and to bring in everlasting righteousness, and to seal up vision and [9]prophecy, and to anoint [10]the most holy. 25 Know therefore and discern, that from the going forth of the commandment to restore and to build Jerusalem unto [11]the anointed one, the prince shall be [12]seven weeks, and threescore and two weeks: it shall be built again, with street and moat, even in troublous times. 26 And after the threescore and two

[1]Or, *being sore wearied*
[2]Or, *came near unto me*
[3]Or, *made me to understand*
[4]Or, *very precious* Heb. *precious things*

[5]Or, *to restrain*
[6]Or, *the transgression*
[7]Another reading is, *to seal up*
[8]Or, *purge away*
[9]Heb. *prophet*
[10]Or, *a most holy place*
[11]Heb. *Messiah*
[12]Or, *seven weeks: and threescore and two weeks, it shall be &c.*

weeks shall the anointed one be cut off, and [13]shall have nothing: and the people of the prince that shall come shall destroy the city and the sanctuary; and the end thereof shall be with a flood, and even unto the end shall be war; desolations are determined. 27 And he

[13]Or, *there shall be none belonging to him*

shall make a firm covenant with many for one week: and in the midst of the week he shall cause the sacrifice and the [14]oblation to cease; and [15]upon the wing of abominations *shall come* one that maketh desolate; and even unto the full end, and that determined, shall *wrath* be poured out upon the desolate.

[14]Or, *meal offering*
[15]Or, *upon the pinnacle of abominations shall be &c.*

Vers. 20-27. The Vision of the Seventy Weeks of Years and Its Interpretation.

The *"books"* in verse 2 refer to a collection of prophetic writings which Daniel had at hand including the writings of Jeremiah.

Daniel reckons in verse 2 the captivity, *"even seventy years"* from the fourth year of Jehoiakim, B. C. 606, when he himself was taken away by Nebuchadnezzar. (Dan. 1.1.) The vision of this chapter occurs B. C. 538 when the period was almost at its close.

Ver. 21. *"the man Gabriel"*,—i. e., the angel Gabriel in human form.

"the time of evening oblation",—i. e., three o'clock in the afternoon.

Ver. 24. *"Seventy weeks are decreed upon thy people"*,—It is conceded by all that these are weeks of years; more accurately "sevens of years", i. e., seventy weeks of seven years each, or 490 years. If they were taken to mean literal weeks the passage would have no sense or meaning whatever. Four hundred and ninety years are to elapse before any perfect deliverance is to come, before the national chastisement is to be ended and the nation re-established in everlasting righteousness. This is an amplification of the seventy actual years of Jeremiah which had made only an initial and imperfect fulfillment.

"to finish transgression",—i. e., to complete transgression. "Restrain", as in the margin, seems better suited to the context, i. e., to hem in, to hinder it, so that it can no longer spread about. (K. F.)

"to make an end of sins",—The literal of this is "to seal up", i. e., to conceal. "Removing them out of God's sight" (Hen.); "so as never more to be declared against us" (Pol. Wil.); "so as no more to be active or increase" (K. Kl. Hof.).

"reconciliation for iniquity",—The expression means to atone for by sacrifice. There is no word in the Old Testament properly rendered *reconcile*; atonement is invariably the meaning, the doctrine of reconciliation belonging to the New Testament.

"everlasting righteousness",—This refers to both the normal state between God and man through the righteousness of Christ imputed to man and the moral aspect of it,—the righteousness practiced by the believer. (K. F.)

"to seal up",—i. e., to conceal (as elsewhere), in the sense of causing it to cease in consequence of its fulfillment.

"vision and prophecy",—Not so much Jeremiah's prophecy concerning the seventy years, but the prophetic institution as a whole and its visions.

"to anoint the most holy",—This expression is not *once* used of a person anywhere, unless it be in I Chron. 23.13, and even here the reference is doubtful. It can hardly be taken therefore as referring to Christ. (C. Hen. Hav.), nor to Christ as the sacrificial altar of the New Testament Church (Zo.). Gaebelein maintains that the reference is to the Holy of Holies in the temple to be built during the time of Tribulation, while others (K. Pu. Kl. Hof. Rob.) take it as the new spiritual temple, the New Testament Church, as the dwelling place of God.

Ver. 25. *"from the going forth of the commandment"*,—Four commandments or decrees were issued from one of which it seems the *"seventy weeks"* ought to be dated, and each is supported by a number of commentators. They are:

1. The decree of Cyrus in the first year of his reign, B. C. 536 (Ez. 6.14 and Isa. 44.28). (C. U. Oe. Heg. Coc.)
2. The decree of Darius Hystapis in the second year of his reign, continuing that of Cyrus, B. C. 519 (Ez. 6.12). (B. Dr. Lut.)
3. The decree of Artaxerxes Longimanus in the seventh year of his reign, B. C. 457 (Ez. 7.1; 8.11). (Do. Fra. Cal. Pri. Gei.)
4. The decree of Artaxerxes Longimanus in the twentieth year of his reign, his second edict, B. C. 445 (Neh. 2.1,7). (Of. Re. Af. Sta. Hav. Hen. Gab. Der.)

There were also two prophecies given for the restoration of the city by Jeremiah from which some date the *"seventy weeks"*:

1. The first prophecy given B. C. 605 (Jer. 25.11). (Bl. Zo.)
2. The second prophecy given B. C. 598. (Jer. 29.10.)

Besides the above six starting points there are five others, each one of which has some advocates:

1. The first year of the reign of Darius the Mede, B. C. 539, the time of Daniel's prophecy itself. (Koc. Mic.)
2. The second year of the reign of Darius Nothus, B. C. 423. (Sca.)
3. The second year of the reign of Artaxerxes Longimanus, B. C. 462. (Lut. Mel.)
4. The tenth year of the reign of Artaxerxes Longimanus, or the earlier date of his second edict on the ground of his co-regency with his father, Xerxes, B. C. 454. (V. Pet.)
5. The second year of the reign of Xerxes, B. C. 483. (Faber.)

Besides these eleven starting points others have been conceived, but are hardly to be taken seriously.

The expositors of this remarkable passage introduced by verse 25 fall, generally speaking, into three classes:

1. Those who refer the whole passage to the time of Antiochus Epiphanes. (Ei. Ma. Ew. Bl. Kr. Zu. Ber. Len. Hit. Ros. Wie. Luc. Hil. Hof. Del. and others of the rationalistic school, together with a majority of the moderns.) Many of these give the passage also a typical eschatological meaning. It will be later seen why this view is an exceedingly difficult one to accept.
2. Those who make the passage a direct prophecy of Christ and the

destruction of Jerusalem by the Romans. (Au. Pu. Rei. Hav. and the majority of the older orthodox school.)

3. Those who give it an eschatological meaning directly, the periods of time being taken symbolically,—seven weeks till Christ; sixty-two weeks till the apostacy of the times of the Antichrist, and one week (divided into two times three and one-half), the rise and fall of Antichrist. (K. Kl. Ley.)

"Seven weeks, and three-score and two weeks",—With very few exceptions expositors take these two periods together, making sixty-nine weeks or 483 years. If you separate them you leave the last clause without any governing preposition. The fact that the sixty-two weeks are repeated in the next verse with the article *"the"* does not make them any more of an independent period than they otherwise would be, coming after the seven weeks. The abrupt pause before *"it shall be built"*, etc., is just what you would expect, being a resumption of the former statement that Jerusalem should be rebuilt. Neither is there sufficient evidence, as Zoeckler claims, for believing that the writer wants to make the building commence at the beginning of the sixty-two weeks. But we would expect the building to begin at once, at the beginning of the seven weeks (forty-nine years) for this was the very *terminus a quo* of the entire prophecy. Then the forty-nine years were after all historically the building period.

The expositors are conveniently divided into Messianic and anti-Messianic.

I. THE ANTI-MESSIANIC.

1. The destructive rationalistic class:

   (a) Daniel made a prediction never fulfilled. (Eckermann.)

   (b) Verses 25-27 are a gloss of some later rabbi. (Lowenheim.)

   (c) The weeks are ordinary weeks (490 days) and extend from the time of the vision to the time of Cyrus.

2. The more considerate class, who as a rule refer the fulfillment of the prophecy to the time of Antiochus Epiphanes. Of a score of interpretations we give a few, all of which break down historically.

   (a) Zoeckler and Farrar start with Jeremiah's prophecy and make the *"anointed one"* to be Cyrus at the end of seven weeks. But Cyrus became king and issued his edict B. C. 536. They make the *"anointed one cut off"* in verse 26 to be Onias III. who was murdered B. C. 171. Count back from B. C. 171 and the Cyrus date is missed sixty-nine years and the Jeremiah prophecy date as many.
   It misses the dates of the four decrees on an average of 150 years.
   Keil, arguing against starting with the prophecy of Jeremiah, well says, "All such references to Jeremiah are excluded by the fact that the angel names the commandment for the restoration of Jerusalem as the *terminus a quo* (the starting point) for the seventy weeks and could thus only mean a word of God, the going forth of which was somewhere determined or could be determined just as the appearance of the

anointed prince is named as the termination of the seventy weeks."

(b) Bleek and Maurice start with the prophecy of Jeremiah but refer the *"anointed one cut off"* to Philopator (Seleucis IV). But heathen kings can scarcely be said to be anointed. However Philapator was murdered B. C. 176 and counting back 483 years (seven weeks plus sixty-two weeks), we have B. C. 659, missing the Jeremiah dates by sixty years.

(c) Bertholdt makes the *"anointed one cut off"* refer to Alexander the Great. But he died B. C. 323 and no count can even approximate the Cyrus date (B. C. 536) or the Destruction of Jerusalem date (B. C. 588) with which he begins.

(d) Ewald starts with destruction of Jerusalem (B. C. 588) and makes the *"anointed one cut off"* to be Philopator, B. C. 175. But there is a shortage here of seventy years. Ewald says it was formerly in the text but has been lost.

(e) Hitzig and Lengerke start with the B. C. 588 date for both the forty-nine years and the 434 years (seven weeks and sixty-two weeks), paralleling the periods. Hitzig makes the *"cutting off"* refer to Onias III, B. C. 171, but counting back 434 years brings us to B. C. 605. Lengerke makes the *"cutting off"* refer to Philopator, B. C. 175, but counting back 434 years we have B. C. 609, thus missing the B. C. 588 date in both cases. *It would seem that historically the reference of this vision to the time of Antiochus Epiphanes is hardly justifiable.*

II. THE MESSIANIC.

1. **Those who hold the vision to be only typically Messianic:**

   (a) Kranichfeld reckons the forty-nine years from the destruction of Jerusalem, B. C. 588, which brings him to Cyrus, the anointed prince, which he takes to be B. C. 539, and from here he reckons 434 years to Christ, missing it 100 years, which period he says was unnoticed by the prophet in harmony with the law of perspective vision.

   (b) Some make the *"anointed one cut off"* to be Onias III (typical of Christ) from whose death, B. C. 171, they count back 434 years (sixty-two weeks) to B. C. 605. They then add one week (seven years) to B. C. 171, bringing it to B. C. 164, and then they transpose the seven weeks (forty-nine years) and add them to B. C. 164, or rather leave a hiatus between B. C. 164 and the first preaching of the Gospel in the time of Christ and the Apostles, from which latter time the seven weeks, a mystical period, begins and lasts until the second coming and judgment of the world. (Fu. Del. Hof. and Wies.)

2. **Those who hold that the vision is directly Messianic:**

(1) Christian expositors of older times.

   (a) Africanus reckons from the twentieth year of Artaxerxes (B. C. 445) to the death of Christ. (He reckoned on

Jewish lunar years, making only 465 solar years.) (Jer. Chr. Aug. Isi. Bed. Theo.)

(b) Hippolytus reckons from the decree of Cyrus, B. C. 536, sixty-nine weeks (483 years) to the birth of Christ, making the periods mystical, and refers the last mystical week to the time of the Antichrist in the final end.

(2) Christian expositors of recent times.

(a) The majority reckon from the decree of Artaxerxes in the twentieth year of his reign, B. C. 445 (Neh. 1.1; 2.1) and count 483 years to Christ's baptism, A. D. 28. To get this latter date they make the twentieth year of Artaxerxes B. C. 455 instead of B. C. 445. (Hav. Hen. Der. Less. Scholl.)

(b) Klieforth reckons from the edict of Cyrus, B. C. 536, and counts sixty-nine mystical weeks to the birth of Christ.

(c) Some reckon from the decree given by Artaxerxes in the seventh year of his reign, B. C. 457 (Ez. 7.8) and count 483 years to Christ's baptism in A. D. 26. (Pu. Au. Bla.)

(d) Some take the reckoning of Africanus as above. B. C. 445 to A. D. 32 is 476 years, or 173,740 days. This plus 116 days for leap years makes 173,856 days. The exact date of the crucifixion was April 6 (A. D. 32), and the exact date of the edict was March 14 (B. C. 445), giving twenty-four days more, which added to 173,856 makes 173,880 days. This is exactly 483 times 360 days (a prophetic year). (Gab. *Sir Robert Anderson.*)

In harmony with the direct Messianic interpretation of the prophecy *"the anointed one"* of verses 25 and 26 are the same person, i. e., Christ. (K. Pu. Au. Kl. Hav. Hen. Hof. Del.)

Of those who make the baptism of Christ the *terminus ad quem* of the sixty-nine weeks, most of the older and many of the later expositors make the "one week" (the last week—seven years) follow immediately, the crucifixion (the "cutting off") taking place at the end of three and one-half years (in the midst of the week) which put an end to O. T. sacrifices. The rest of the last week they leave indefinitely with no precise chronological determination, referring it to the founding of Christianity through the preaching of the Apostles.

Of those who make the crucifixion the *terminus ad quem,* some add next a hiatus of 2000 years and make the last week the period of the final Antichrist. (Gab. Sco. Mor. Tor. Mack.)

Klieforth, who holds the mystical theory, reckons the seven weeks from the edict of Cyrus to the advent of Christ, the sixty-two weeks from the advent of Christ to the Antichrist week which is the last week, the "one week".

"built again even in troublous times"—This occurs under Nehemiah

221

and Ezra, the enemies of God's people causing them much trouble. Historically the reconstruction period cannot be extended throughout the entire sixty-nine weeks, as some (F. Zo.) have interpreted. The temple was built as early as B. C. 515. (See Neh. 6.15 and Ez. 6.15.)

"The seventy weeks are divided into seven (forty-nine years); sixty-two (434 years), and one (seven years). In the seven weeks (forty-nine years) Jerusalem was to be rebuilt 'in troublous times'. This was fulfilled as Ezra and Nehemiah record. Sixty-two weeks (434 years) thereafter Messiah was to come. This was fulfilled in the birth of Christ." (Scofield.)

Ver. 26. "and shall have nothing",—All Hebrew scholars agree with this reading. The meaning is that He shall then possess nothing; He shall not possess the kingdom or be the acknowledged King; He shall be deprived of everything. (C. Eb. Kr. Kl. Ju. Gab. Mor. Sco.)

The following are some of the numerous other renderings:
1. "not for himself", i. e., not for His own sake will Christ die, but for humanity. (V. Ros. Wil. Hav. Bul)
2. "shall have no adherents". (Au. Gro. Marginal reading.)
3. "there shall be none to help him". (Vat.)
4. "there shall be nothing to Him", i. e., the city, the sanctuary and the Jewish people shall be His no more. (Pu.)
5. "it shall not be to him", i. e., His place as Messiah—He has lost it. (K.)

Hengstenberg adopts the fourth reading but makes it mean that the earthly kingdom for which the Jews had hoped shall come to nought.

All of the above five renderings together with that of our text refer "the anointed one" to Christ. Those who refer "the anointed one" to Onias or Philopator or Alexander translate, "he shall have no successor".

"the prince that shall come",—To whom does this refer? (See explanation under verse 27.)

"and the end thereof", etc.,—According to our text this must be taken as the end of the city and the sanctuary (F. Au. Del. Hav. Hit. Gei. Len.), but it may quite as properly be rendered "and his end" and refer to the prince that shall come, the final Antichrist. (K. Kl. Kr. Zo. Hof. Wie. Gab. Sco. Mor. Tor. Treg.)

"and even unto the end shall be war",—Unto what end?
1. The end of the city and the sanctuary. (Au. Hav.)
2. The end of the prince, i. e., until he is destroyed. (Wie. as well as all who take the prince to be Antiochus Epiphanes.)
3. The end of all things. (Kl.)
4. The end generally, i. e., the end of the last week, whether it be viewed as then in progress or as a week yet to come in the future. (K. Hen. Len. Hit.) This last is without doubt correct.

Scofield says, "The crucifixion is the first event of verse 26. The second event is the destruction of the city, fulfilled A. D. 70. Then "unto the end", a period not fixed, but which has already lasted 2000 years. To Daniel was revealed only that wars and desolations should continue (Matt. 24.6-14). The New Testament reveals that which was hidden from the Old Testament prophets (Eph. 3.1-10) that during this period should be accomplished the mysteries of the kingdom of heaven (Matt. 13.1-50), and the outcalling of the Church (Rom. 11.25). When the Church age will end and the 'seventieth week' begin, is nowhere revealed. Its duration can be but seven years; to make it more violates the principle of interpretation already confirmed by fulfillment."

"desolations are determined",—According to our text these words are to be joined to the preceding clause with a semicolon and are to be taken as an explanatory clause. (Kl. Kr.)

Many prefer the reading of the Authorized Version, "and unto the end of the war desolations are determined". (So. Fu. Ew. Hof. Ros. Vul. Sept.)

Another reading and one which we prefer is, *"and even unto the end shall be war, the determined desolations"*. The "determined desolations" are by this rendering taken in apposition with the word "war". (Au. Hit. Wie. Mau. Len. Hav.)

"determined",—i. e., decreed by God.

Ver. 27. *"make a firm covenant"*,—Many authorities take the word *"week"* to be the subject of this sentence, and explain the expression as follows:

1. The one week shall make the Old Testament covenant (adherence to the faith in Jehovah and to the theocratic law) hard (grievous) for many. (Hit.)
2. The one week shall confirm many in the covenant through tribulation and the trial of their faith. (Hof. Ros.)
3. The one week shall confirm a covenant to many through the seductive arts of Antiochus Epiphanes. (Len.)
4. The one week (especially by the death of the Messiah) shall lead to the conclusion of a new, strong and firm covenant with many. (Au. Hen. Hav.)

We prefer with our text to make *"he"* the subject of the sentence.

It would seem that *"he"* here must refer to the same person as does *"the prince that shall come"* in verse 26, and the reference in verse 26 must therefore be determined by the content of this verse 27 as well as by its own content.

It would seem evident therefore that *"the prince that shall come"* and the *"he"* cannot refer to Antiochus Epiphanes (Zo. Fa.), because, as Strong remarks, "the language was not fulfilled in any sense by Antiochus who aimed at the suppression of Jehovah's worship and virtually left the city and the sanctuary untouched"; nor can it refer to Christ, the Messiah (F. C. Rob. Wil. Str.) because it was not His people (verse 26) that destroyed the city and the sanctuary, nor is it without extreme difficulty that we can think of Him making a covenant for a week (seven years). His was an *"everlasting covenant"*. Once more, it can hardly refer to Titus (F. Bl. Ew. Len. Jos. Str.), because while verse 26 might be true of him, verse 27 can in no sense be said to be so. It would seem therefore that the reference in both verses must be to the Antichrist who is yet to come. (K. Kl. Kr. Sco. Mor. Gab. Wie. Hof.)

"many",—In the original the article *"the"* is found. Zoeckler and his class of interpreters make these to be the apostatizing Jews in the time

of Antiochus Epiphanes, but Keil well remarks that the mass of the Jews did not apostatize in his time, which this expression, by the use of the definite article *"the"* seems to make clear was the case. The reference, of course, consistent with our former explanation must refer to the Jews of the times of the final Antichrist. As Keil says, "That ungodly prince shall impose upon the mass of the people a strong covenant that they should follow him and give themselves to him as their God."

It must be noticed that, if *"the prince that shall come"* be taken as the Antichrist, it is not the Antichrist who destroys *"the city and the sanctuary"*, but the people of the Antichrist; that is, as Morgan says, "the people who are guided by the same principle of government that eventually characterizes the rule of the Antichrist".

Now, according to our explanation thus far, two distinct periods of time are referred to in the passages immediately before us. If we translate with our text, *"the end thereof"* in verse 26, and refer this to the end of the city and the sanctuary, then the end time in which the final Antichrist appears begins with verse 27, but if with Morgan and others we translate *"his end"* in verse 26, and refer this to the Antichrist himself, then the prophecy passes immediately after the semicolon on to events at the close of this age, when the Prince himself, the final Antichrist, shall be manifested. Then, as Morgan says, "The semicolon of Daniel is the coma which follows Isaiah's 'acceptable year of the Lord'."

"and in the midst of the week he", etc.,—The subject is of course the same throughout the verse. Says Scofield, "He will covenant with the Jews to restore their temple sacrifices for one week (seven years), but in the middle of that time, after three and one-half years, he will break the covenant and fulfill Dan. 12.11; II Thess. 2.3,4. Between the sixty-ninth week, after which the Messiah was cut off, and the seventieth week, within which the 'little horn' of Dan. 7 will run his awful course, intervenes this entire Church-age. Verse 27 deals with the last three and one-half years of the seven, which are identical with the 'great Tribulation', 'the time of trouble'; the hour of temptation; Matt. 24.15-28; Dan. 12.1; Rev. 3.10."

Those who refer the subject of this verse to Christ, the Messiah, maintain that the reference is to His perfect expiatory sacrifice on the Cross whereby He did forever away with the Levitical sacrifices. (F. Au. Str. Hav. Hen.) These authorities maintain, therefore, that half of Daniel's missing week has already gone in the three and one-half years of our Lord's earthly ministry. But the clear and distinct division of "weeks" in verses 26 and 27 rather argue against this view and lead us to believe that the whole of the missing week is still in the future.

"upon the wing of abominations shall one come that maketh desolate",—*"abominations"* mean "horrible things" and from the religious standpoint, "abominable idolatries".

"wing" is a literal translation. The word is equivalent to "screen, protection, covering, roof". It carries in it the idea of extension and so may be applied to the wing of a building. Some render it "pinnacle", but Bleek and Keil argue rather conclusively that the idea of extension which inheres in the word is always extension horizontally and never vertically. The idea of "pinnacle" may be gotten from one of its primal meanings.

i. e., "roof", and so by the rule of Synecdoche (a part being taken for the whole) the *"wing"* (extension) or the "roof" (pinnacle) may be applied to the entire building and so read "temple". The ancient versions all agreed in this. The Maccabean book, the most ancient translation of the words, so renders, as do also the most ancient translations, the Septuagint and the Vulgate. The literal reading would then be, "Upon the temple shall come the abominations of the one that maketh desolate", or "Upon the temple shall come the abominations of desolation", according as we translate "desolator" or "desolation". If the rendering "desolation" be adopted, this word would be considered as an apposition to "abominations", it being really a genitive of description.

Others translate, "Under the pinnacle of abominations comes the one temple where abominable idols were placed." (D. Oe. Os. Bul. Ges.) The last of these authorities translates with the margin of the Authorized Version, "On the pinnacle (of the temple) are the abominations of the one that maketh desolate". Jesus said, "When you see the abomination of desolation spoken of by Daniel". He quoted from the Vulgate and He also knew Hebrew and this lends pretty good evidence that the Vulgate translation is a good one. It would appear, however, that the only grammatically possible translation is that of our text.

Others translate, "Upon the pinnacle of abominations comes the one that maketh desolate". (K. Kl. Kr. Mau. Rei. Hen. Len.) The first three of these authorities makes the desolator to be the future Antichrist coming on the wings of idolatry, the power that moves and carries him over the earth. Still others translate, "On account of the pinnacle, or frightful height of abominations there shall come one that maketh desolate", thus giving the moral ground why in God's providence the desolator came. (F. Pu. Au. Eu. Gab.) Gaebelein translates, "On account of the protection of abominations there shall come one who maketh desolate".

Hitzig renders it, "Upon the extreme point of the abominations desolation shall come". This translation is much like that of our text, but by the "extreme point" he means the idol altar put up by Antiochus Epiphanes.

These different translations practically come to the same thing in their meaning; it was because of the idolatrous abominations that the desolator, or desolation, was to come upon the city and the sanctuary.

"even unto the full end",—Zoeckler says the expression for *"full end"* is an exact reproduction of Isa. 10.23; 28.22, and means "consumption", utter extinction, and he translates the last word of the verse *"desolator"*, referring it to Antiochus Epiphanes. Fausset and Tregellius translate with Zoeckler but while Fausset refers the word to Titus as a type of the final Antichrist, Tregellius refers it to the final Antichrist directly. The word in question, however, is passive and so means "desolate", and means, we presume, the people who are made desolate.

CHAPTER TEN

14 Now I am come to make thee understand what shall befall thy people in the latter days; for the vision is yet for many days.

Ver. 14.   THE PROPHECY OF THE END-TIME ANNOUNCED.

"the vision is yet for many days",—The idea here may be either:

1. The vision to be imparted to thee shall extend to these days.   (Kr. Hav.)

2. Yet a vision of those days I am now to reveal.   (Zo.)   According to this latter explanation the word *"yet"* seems to have a backward reference to the other visions given to Daniel.   Either view gives good sense and one has about as much in its favor as the other.

"many days",—These days refer to the days just mentioned, i. e., the latter days.   No content of this vision is given unless we refer it to the following chapter.

CHAPTER ELEVEN

31 And forces shall stand on his part, and they shall profane the sanctuary, even the fortress, and shall take away the continual burnt-offering, and they shall set up the abomination that maketh desolate.

32 And such as do wickedly against the covenant shall he ¹pervert by flatteries; but the people that know their God shall be strong, and do exploits.

33 And ²they that are wise among the people shall instruct many; yet they shall fall by the sword and by flame, by captivity and by spoil many days.

34 Now when they shall fall, they shall be helped with a little help; but many shall join themselves unto them with flatteries.

35 And some of ³them that are wise shall fall, to refine them, and to purify, and to make them white, even to the time of the end; because it is yet for the time appointed.

¹Heb. *make profane*
²Or, *the teachers of the people*
³Or, *the teachers*

Vers. 31-35.   THE "LITTLE HORN" OF DANIEL 8, ANTIOCHUS EPIPHANES, IN THE "GLORIOUS LAND" (PALESTINE).

In Chap. 11 the prophet first traces through prophetic vision the history of the two parts of the Grecian empire which had to do with Palestine and the Jews, viz., Syria and Egypt.   He brings this down to the time of Antiochus Epiphanes (verse 21), after which the vision concerns itself with the two expeditions of this king into Egypt, from the second of which he returns in verse 30 and on his way back to his own land (Syria) he takes out his revenge on the Jews, while at the same time he makes an affiliation with the apostate Jews, *"such as do wickedly against the covenant".*

Ver. 31.   *"forces shall stand on his part",*—He shall maintain an armed host in the Holy Land.

"profane the sanctuary, even the fortress",—The sanctuary was a stronghold not only in a physical sense but especially in a spiritual sense. Jehovah is called a "strong tower".

"set up the abomination",—"Abomination" is the common name for an idol in the Old Testament.   Appolonius, by direction of Antiochus Epiphanes, had an altar to Jupiter *Olympius* built on the altar of God in the temple; he also sacrificed a sow and sprinkled its broth about the temple.

"that maketh desolate",—i. e., that pollutes the temple.

Ver. 32. *"such as do wickedly against the covenant"*,—i. e., the apostate Jews.

"the people who know God",—This is said perhaps with special reference to the Maccabees and their followers. (See also Hebrews 11.34.)

Ver. 33. *"they that are wise"*,—Not special teachers (Hit.), but the understanding ones who know and keep the truth of God; men like Mattathias and his five sons and Eleazar.

Ver. 34. *"they shall be helped with a little help"*,—i. e., perhaps by the efforts and partial victories of Mattathias and his five sons. They however soon fell under the Romans and the Herodians.

"many shall join themselves unto them with flatteries",—The reference here is to the hypocritical Jewish adherents who joined Mattathias and his sons while fortune favored them, but who before had been deserters.

Ver. 35. Here is set forth some of the divine purpose in permitting the sufferings, namely, to refine, to purify and to make them "white".

"the time of the end",—Here, says Scofield, Daniel "overleaps the centuries to the time when he of whom Antiochus Epiphanes was a type, the *'little horn'* of Dan. 7.8, the Antichrist of the final end time, shall appear". Others of course will have us think here of the end of Antiochus Epiphanes himself.

"a time appointed",—This expression wherever found in this book of Daniel refers to a time of divine appointment, whatever may be the particular period of time in question. (See verses 27,29 also of this chapter.)

Vers. 31-35 are referred by some (Bi. Os. Pf. Cox. Rob) to the Papal power, with explanations as follows:

Ver. 31. *"forces shall stand on his part"*,—By various ways the Roman arms stood up over the Grecian power.

"profane the sanctuary",—This took place first on the siege of Jerusalem by Pompey when, says Josephus, "no small enormities were committed". It was polluted under Crassus and again when Sosius took the city.

"take away the continual burnt-offering",—This was done during the siege of the city by Titus.

"they shall set up the abomination",—This took place first when the Romans under Cestius assailed the temple; again under Titus when ensigns were brought into the temple and sacrifice offered to them, and again when a temple to Jupiter Capitolinus was built on the very site of the sanctuary of God.

Ver. 32. *"pervert by flatteries"*,—This refers to the alluring promises of the Roman magistrates.

Ver. 33. *"shall instruct many"*,—The primitive Christians, as they were dispersed everywhere, truly did so.

"yet they shall fall", etc.,—This was all fulfilled in ten general persecutions.

Ver. 34. *"they shall be helped with a little help"*,—i. e., under Constantine.

"Many shall join themselves unto them with flatteries",—Many did so because Christianity was made the religion of the empire.

Ver. 35. *"to refine and to purify and to make them white"*,—Many of the followers of Jesus became victims of Papal intolerance; a trying, purifying process. But the God-appointed end shall come.

Apart, however, from the impression which forces itself upon one that such reference to the Papal power is quite too arbitrary as well as lacking in appropriateness, it is not at all clear by what law of exegesis the subject of verse 31 can be made to differ from that of the preceding verse with which it is intimately connected. Certainly such a change of subject must be in some degree at least grammatically possible.

36 And the king shall do according to his will; and he shall exalt himself, and magnify himself above every god, and shall speak marvelous things against the God of gods; and he shall prosper till the indignation be accomplished; for that which is determined shall be done. 37 Neither shall he regard the gods of his fathers, nor the desire of women, nor regard any god; for he shall magnify himself above all. 38 But in his [1]place shall he honor the god of fortresses; and a god whom his fathers knew not shall he honor with gold, and silver, and with precious stones and pleasant things. 39 And he shall deal with the strongest fortresses by the help of a foreign god: [2]whosoever acknowledgeth *him* [3]he will increase with glory; and he shall cause them to rule over many, and shall divide the land for a price.

[1]Or, *office*
[2]Or, *whom he shall acknowledge and increase with glory*
[3]Or, *shall increase glory*

Vers. 36-39. THE WILFUL KING DESCRIBED.

It is difficult to determine to whom this section refers. It is referred by some (Zo. Wil.) to Antiochus Epiphanes with explanation as follows:

Ver. 36. *"magnify himself above every god"*,—i. e., in his proud imagination.

"speak marvelous things against the God of gods",—He forbade by a decree the worship of Jehovah.

"till the indignation be accomplished",—The reference here is to God's anger against the Jews in the execution of which He employed Antiochus Epiphanes.

Ver. 37. *"Neither shall he regard the gods of his fathers"*,—His Grecian fathers had adopted the gods of Syria, but he established the worship of Jupiter Olympius (Grecian) at Jerusalem and of Xenias (Roman) at Samaria.

"nor the desire of women",—

1. No respect for his marriage vows. (Gei. Cal. Lut.)
2. No regard for the supplication of women and especially of his wives that he cease from his attacks on Jehovah's religion. (Pol.)
3. No love for women. (Gro.)
4. Not allow his wives to worship any god but Jupiter Olympius (Pis.)

5. No regard for woman's love, the type of human affection for which even the worst man has some regard. (K.)

6. No pity for the sex. (Mal.)

7. No regard for the desire of women to be the mother of the coming Messiah.

8. No respect for the worship of the goddess Venus whose temple he plundered at Elymais and which goddess the women worshipped as their favorite deity. (Zo. Mau. Der. Hav. Ges. Mic.) We rather prefer this last explanation, if the passage is to be referred to Antiochus Epiphanes, in as much as the reference placed between two expressions referring to gods leads to the thought that a deity may have been in the mind of the speaker. The choice lies between this and the third explanation. But all is vague and uncertain.

"nor regard any god",—i. e., have no reverence for God or things divine. (K. Kl.)

"he shall magnify himself above all",—i. e., above all that is divine or human.

Ver. 38. "But in his place",—i. e., on his pedestal, the pedestal of his statue. (F. Zo. Ber. Hit. Hav. Len. Mau.)

"the god of fortresses",—Jupiter Capitolinus to whom he began to erect a temple in Antioch and which god, it is claimed by the authorities just mentioned, was unknown to his fathers.

Keil renders, "In the place of every god he will make war to be his god, that is, the taking of fortresses." The former view, however, is preferable.

Ver. 39. "And he shall deal with the strongest fortresses," etc.,— Out of a dozen different interpretations that of Keil seems the best, "He will deal with (proceed against) the strong fortresses with the help of this foreign god".

"whosoever acknowledgeth him",—i. e., Antiochus Epiphanes.

"and he shall cause them",—i. e., those who like him worship the god of fortresses. The reference is of course to the apostatizing Jews.

"and shall divide the land",—i. e., give them land for a reward.

There are some objections to referring these verses (36-39) to Antiochus Epiphanes:

1. The expressions "magnify himself above every god" and "nor regard any god" hardly apply to a man who sought to establish the worship of Jupiter; although it is true that he did identify himself with Jupiter and so claimed divine honors.

2. History knows nothing of his not regarding the desire of women, nor of his speaking marvelous things against God.

3. The worship of Jupiter Olympius, the Grecian god, can hardly be said to be "unknown to his fathers".

Pusey observes that of the many specified characteristics of this willful king only one agrees with the character of Antiochus Epiphanes.

Those who find in verses 31-35 a reference to the Papal power find here in these verses 36-39 a reference of course to the Pope.

Ver. 36. *"do according to his will"*,—The Pope claimed absolute sway over earthly rulers.

"magnify himself above every god",—Civil rulers claimed divine honors and were sometimes called "gods", and the Pope claimed to be above them.

"speak marvelous things against the God of gods",—i. e., by claiming equality with God. He is called, "Our Lord God, the Pope". The words of the 95th Psalm are applied to him on the day of his consecration in St. Peter's.

Ver. 37. *"Neither shall he regard the gods of his fathers"*,—He puts the Church above the word of God, imports paganism into worship (holy water), and takes his title, Pontifex, from the high-priest of ancient Roman idolatry.

"not regard the desire of women",—The Pope doesn't marry and claims it to be unlawful for ministers to do so. (I Tim. 4.3.)

"nor regard any god",—This is true whether "god" denotes the civil ruler or Jehovah.

Ver. 38. *"he shall honor the god of fortresses"*,—The word, it is said, denotes "god-protectors", and as such they worship Mary and the saints. They impose trust in relics of the saints and claim they afford them divine protection.

"honor with gold and silver", etc.,—The shrines of the tutelary saints and the images of the Virgin are adorned with costly offerings.

"divide the land for a price",—The choicest lands have been appropriated for the Church and the priests and their ministers have been given glory and honor.

Inasmuch as verses 31-35 cannot very properly, as we have seen, be applied to the Papal power, it follows that these verses, 36-39, can with no more propriety be referred to the Pope. At any rate the impartial scholar cannot but feel that any explanation which endeavors to apply them to the Pope must be necessarily somewhat warped and exaggerated, and as between the Pope and Antiochus Epiphanes the words are far more applicable to the latter than to the former.

By others again (Gab. Sco. Mor.) the verses (36-39) are referred to the final Antichrist, with explanation as follows:

He is self-willed; he will exalt himself *"above every god"*, and *"speak marvelous things against the God of gods"*. (II Thess. 2.)

"Neither shall he regard the gods of his fathers",—This is the reading of our text and would seem to imply that his fathers were heathen and Gentile, which Scofield seems to think accords with Dan. 9.26 which prophecy was fulfilled by the Gentile armies of Rome.

According to the reading of the Authorized Version, *"God of his fathers"*, the reference would be to Jehovah the God of the Jews, the Antichrist being as many think a Jew.

He will not regard Jesus Christ who is the desire of every Jewish woman.

He will honor a *"foreign god"*. To whom this foreign god refers is unknown. Gaebelein thinks it refers to the first beast of Rev. 13.

"The Antichrist", says Scofield, "is an apostate from Christianity, not from Judaism. Verses 38-45 describe his career. He substitutes the *'god of forces'* (i. e., the forces of nature) for the true god, and soon presents himself as that god (II Thess. 2.3,4)."

40 And at the time of the end shall the king of the south [1]contend with him; and the king of the north shall come against him like a whirlwind, with chariots, and with horsemen, and with many ships; and he shall enter into the countries, and shall overflow and pass through. 41 He shall enter also into the glorious land, and many *countries* shall be overthrown; but these shall be delivered out of his hand: Edom, and Moab, and the chief of the children of Ammon. 42 He shall stretch forth his hand also upon the countries; and the land of Egypt shall not escape. 43 But he shall have power over the treasures of gold and of silver, and over all the precious things of Egypt; and the Libyans and the Ethiopians shall be at his steps. 44 But tidings out of the east and out of the north shall trouble him; and he shall go forth with great fury to destroy and [2]utterly to sweep away many. 45 And he shall plant the tents of his palace [3]between the sea and the glorious holy mountain; yet he shall come to his end, and none shall help him.

[1]Heb. *push at*
[2]Heb. *to devote many*
[3]Or, *between the seas at*

Vers. 40-45. THE MARTIAL CAREER OF THE WILFUL KING.

It is equally difficult and even more so to know to whom these verses apply.

1. **Some refer them to Antiochus Epiphanes and make them a resume of verses 22-30.** (F. Ew. Der. Len. Mau. Hit. Kam.)
   (a) Verse 40 a resume of the first expedition in verses 22-25.
   (b) Verse 41 a resume of the former invasion of Judea in verse 28.
   (c) Verses 42, 43 a resume of the second and third expeditions in verses 23, 24, 29 and 30.
   If only two expeditions into Egypt are admitted the reference would be to the first one in verses 22-25, and the second one in verses 29 and 30.
2. **Others refer them also to Antiochus Epiphanes but make them an account of another and separate expedition into Egypt.** (St. Zo. Ju. Wil.)

Ver. 40. *"the time of the end"*,—This, it would seem, must refer to the same time as that mentioned in verse 35.

"the king of the south",—If the third expedition into Egypt just mentioned be admitted the king here mentioned is Euergetes, called Physcon, but if we have here a resume of the first expedition the king in question is Philometor.

"contend with him",—The Hebrew is "push at him", the king of the south being the aggressor.

"the king of the north",—i. e., Antiochus Epiphanes.

"he shall enter into the countries",—i. e., the countries adjoining Egypt through which his march would lead him, Coele-Syria, Palestine.

Ver. 41. *"the glorious land"*,—i. e., Palestine.

"Edom and Moab and Ammon",—The allies of Antiochus Epiphanes against the Jews and the leading representatives of tribal hostility to the theocracy.

Ver. 43. *"the Libyans and the Ethiopians shall be at his steps"*,— i. e., as enforced auxiliaries.

Ver. 44. This verse refers to the insurrection probably of the Parthians in Persia and the Armenians against whom, returning, he directed an expedition shortly before he died.

Ver. 45. *"the tents of his palace"*,—i. e., his palatial tents.
"the sea",—i. e., the Mediterranean.
"the glorious, holy mountain",—i. e., Mount Zion.
"he shall come to his end",—He died in the Persian town of Tabae a year or so after his campaign against the Parthians and the Armenians.

Keil says these verses cannot refer to a resume because of the expression, "at the end of the time", and because some new features are introduced. Whether this last expedition (if made) was a fourth or a third depends on whether verses 22-25 compose two or one expedition. If a last expedition be admitted it is preferably a third. Wiessler in Schaff-Hertzog says he made four expeditions, in the last of which he was stopped by the Romans, and on returning from which he stopped the worship of Jehovah and built the idol altar in the temple. Then came the victories of Mattathias and the Maccabees and his death in Tabae.

History, neither Livy, Polybius, Appian, Justyn, Maccabean books, nor Josephus, knows nothing about such a last expedition. Porphry alone mentions it and on the strength of his statement alone it is accepted by a goodly number of commentators. (K. St. Au. Fu. Jer. Wie.)

Stuart says that all histories of Antiochus Epiphanes are mere scraps (and this is true) and that since Daniel's accuracy is admitted elsewhere, why not accept him here and take this as a true account of another expedition. With Stuart we are inclined to agree, *if* the passage is to be referred to Antiochus Epiphanes.

Those who refer verses 31-39 to the Papal power and the Pope refer these verses 40-45 to the Saracens and the Turks in their crusade against the Roman empire. (Me. Br. Bul. Rob.)

Ver. 40. *"the time of the end"*,—i. e., the last times of the Roman empire.

The *"king of the south"* refers to the Saracens, and the *"king of the north"* refers to the Turks, both of whom "pushed against" the Romans, the first in A. D. 630 and the second in A. D. 1300, the *"him"* in both cases being the Roman empire.

After Rome had conquered Egypt and Syria, the Saracens took Egypt and the Turks took Syria.

Ver. 41. *"He shall enter into the glorious land"*,—*"He"* refers to the king of the north, mentioned in the preceding verse, i. e., the Turks, who entered Palestine in 1517.

Ver. 42. *"the land of Egypt shall not escape"*,—Sultan Selim took Egypt and established the government of the Turks.

Ver. 44. *"tidings out of the east and out of the north shall trouble him"*,—The uprisings of subdued nations or invasions from other quarters draw him from Egypt to Palestine. Robinson thinks that this part of the prophecy is not yet fulfilled.

Ver. 45. *"he shall come to his end"*,—The end of the hostile power *under its last form* is to come with the destruction of all the world powers that have set themselves in opposition to God's people and is still future.

Those who refer verses 36-39 to the final Antichrist refer of course these verses 40-45 likewise to this Antichrist, and by way of explanation say that the two kings push at him. First, the king of the south and with little success. No one knows who this king is to be. Then the king of the north will come against him, who also pushes down into Egypt, when tidings reach him out of the north and east and he returns in fury to encamp against the Holy City. Then Christ comes and this king of the north shall come to his end together with the overthrow of the Antichrist.

Gaebelein says the wilful king is the personal Antichrist, the *little horn* of Chap. 7 is the head of the revived Roman Empire, the first Beast of Rev. 13, and the *little horn* of Chap. 8 is the king of the north spoken of in this Chap. 11, verse 40. The personal Antichrist, he says, is the second Beast of Rev. 13.

CHAPTER TWELVE

1 And at that time shall Michael stand up, the great prince who standeth for the children of thy people; and there shall be a time of trouble, such as never was since there was a nation even to that same time: and at that time thy people shall be delivered, every one that shall be found written in the book. 2 And many of them that sleep in the dust of the earth shall awake, some to everlasting life, and some to shame and everlasting ¹contempt. 3 And ²they that are wise shall shine as the brightness of the firmament; and they that turn many to righteousness as the stars for ever and ever. 4 But thou, O Daniel, shut up the words, and seal the book, even to the time of the end: many shall run to and fro, and knowledge shall be increased.

5 Then I, Daniel, looked, and, behold, there stood other two, the one on the brink of the river on this side, and the other on the brink of the river on that side. 6 And one said to the man clothed in linen, who was above the waters of the river, How long shall it be to the end of these wonders? 7 And I heard the man clothed in linen, who

¹Or, *abhorrence*
²Or, *the teachers*

was above the waters of the river, when he held up his right hand and his left hand unto heaven, and sware by him that liveth for ever that it shall be for a time, times, and a half; and when they have made an end of breaking in pieces the power of the holy people, all these things shall be finished. 8 And I heard, but I understood not: then said I, O my Lord, what shall be the ³issue of these things? 9 And he said, Go thy way, Daniel: for the words are shut up and sealed till the time of the end. 10 Many shall purify themselves and make themselves white, and be refined; but the wicked shall do wickedly; and none of the wicked shall understand; but ²they that are wise shall understand.

11 And from the time that the continual *burnt-offering* shall be taken away, and the abomination that maketh desolate set up, there shall be a thousand two hundred and ninety days. 12 Blessed is he that waiteth, and cometh to the thousand three hundred and five and thirty days. 13 But go thou thy way till the end be: for thou shalt rest, and shalt stand in thy lot, at the end of the days.

³Or, *latter end*

Vers. 1-13. TRIBULATION AND RESURRECTION.

Ver. 1. *"And at that time"*,—If somewhere in the preceding chapter the transition has been made to the times of the final Antichrist, whether it be at verse 35 (Gab.) or at verse 40 (K.), then the reference in our expression here refers to the time just indicated in the preceding verse, i. e., in Chap. 11.45.

Zoeckler, who refers all of Chap. 11.21-45 to Antiochus Epiphanes, makes of course the same connection, referring it to the time (Chap. 11.45) when judgment shall overtake the impious oppressor, Antiochus Epiphanes, and when he shall come to his end *"without a helper"*. He says that nearly all recent expositors have so contended, and for three reasons:

(1) The conjunction *"and"* connects this new designation of time intimately with the preceding.

(2) It is impossible to regard the words *"at that time"* otherwise than as a reference to the time indicated in the context immediately preceding.

(3) The time referred to is immediately afterwards characterized as a time of trouble, which shows with sufficient clearness that the reference is to the period of persecution under Antiochus Epiphanes as heretofore described.

But while Zoeckler is right as to the connection, he must be wrong as to the content and reference of one or the other of these sections. While the words of that section may with propriety be referred to Antiochus Epiphanes, those of this chapter surely cannot be so referred. (K. Hav.) The statement regarding the time of trouble is far too strong for such a period, while the promised deliverance of Daniel's people does not accord with the facts of the Syrian oppression.

Now there is no doubt whatever that the first three verses of Chap. 12 refer to *"the time of the end"* in the sense of the *final* end-time. This being so, the transition from the narrative concerning Antiochus Epiphanes must be made somewhere, because there is likewise no doubt that verse 21 of Chap. 11 the narrative takes up the history of this king of Syria.

Gaebelein says the transition is at Chap. 11.35. He says verse 35 calls our attention to *"the time of the end"* and verse 36 transports us into it, and between them is the long unreckoned period of time.

Keil admits that the close connection made by the conjunction *"and"* will not admit of any break between the chapters, and he makes the transition at Chap. 11.40, which he says introduces *"the time of the end"* when the final hostile power, the final Antichrist, rises up to subdue the whole world, sets up his camp in the Holy Land, to destroy many in great anger and to utterly uproot them.

Most expositors maintain that from Chap. 11.21 on to the end of the chapter the reference is primarily to Antiochus Epiphanes, but that the final Antichrist is the antitypical reference, while of course, in a sense, it points to whatever other antichrists there may have been along the way, inasmuch as John says there are many antichrists. This is doubtless true, if the entire section (verses 21-45) be referred to this Syrian ruler, and it would be accordingly true of whatever portion of this section precedes the point of transition (if one is to be made) to the direct and primary reference to the final Antichrist.

Zoeckler escapes, as he thinks, the difficulty suggested above, by his close connection of the two chapters, by making the transition between the chapters. This might be allowable if he did not find in the first verses of Chap. 12 a direct reference to the troubles under Antiochus Epiphanes. What we contend is that these verses can in no way refer to the time of this king, and Fausset must likewise be wrong when he explains the words, *"at that time"* as "typically, towards the close of the reign of Antiochus Epiphanes; antitypically, the time when Antichrist is to be destroyed at Christ's second coming".

We are inclined to think there is little difference as to where the transition is made, although perhaps the one at Chap. 11.35 is to be preferred. But wherever it is put it must be something analogous to that found in the eschatological discourse of Christ in Matt. 24.29 and Mk. 13.24, and the transition here, as there, seems to stand as a connecting link between the near and the far distant application of the prediction.

"shall Michael stand up",—Michael is the prince of the angels, Israel's protector. The reference here is not to Christ, as Calvin and later Havernick, in accord with some of the older commentators suppose; the latter insisting that the reference is to the first appearance of Christ. He is, however, an archangel, and not the Lord Jesus, from whom he is distinguished in Jude 9.

In what particular way Michael executes the judgment committed to him on this particular occasion is not for us to inquire. An angel smote in one night 185,000 Assyrians that lay encamped about Jerusalem.

"a time of trouble",—Zoeckler, as we have seen, with Grotius, Chrysostom and others understand these troubles of the persecutions of Antiochus Epiphanes.

Calvin, Junius and others apply them to the troubles of the Church in the times of the Gospel.

Havernick understands them of the afflictions which the people of Israel endured at the destruction of Jerusalem under Titus, and which will be more fully realized at the second coming of Christ.

Most expositors rightly find in them the final time of the great tribulation at the termination of the present course of the world. (K. F. Ca. Hof. Gab. Sco. Tor. Mor.)

"at that time thy people shall be delivered",—This certainly has not been true of any period of persecution which the Jewish people (Daniel's people) thus far have gone through.

Says Fausset, "the same deliverance of Israel as in Zech. 13.8,9, 'the third part . . . brought through fire . . . refined as silver'. The remnant in Israel spared as not having joined in the antichristian blasphemy. This is not to be confounded with those who shall have confessed Christ before His second coming, 'the remnant according to the election of grace' composed of both Jews and Gentiles and being part of the Church of the firstborn, who will share Christ's Millennial reign in their glorified bodies. The delivered remnant will only know the Lord Jesus when they see Him, and when the Spirit of grace and supplication is poured out upon them."

"every one that shall be found written in the book of life",—This is by most expositors thought to have reference to the holy remnant of Daniel's people. (F. Au. Lee.)

Says Gaebelein, "These are the godly Jews, the believing remnant of the time of the end. For their sakes the days shall be shortened".

Keil and Hitzig say the reference is to the "book of life" (Phil. 4.3), containing the list of the citizens of the Messianic kingdom, and that in Isa. 4.3 it contains the names of those who reach it while living, but here in Daniel it contains the names also of those who must first be raised from the dead.

Zoeckler says, "The book is the same as that mentioned in the similar passage, Isa. 4.3, and hence the book of life. It is of course not to be regarded as containing a list of *living* Israelites; nor, probably as a 'record of those who shall be delivered in the decisive hour and be permitted to live'. It is rather a record of those who shall inherit eternal life, a 'list of the subjects of Messiah's kingdom', of *those who shall stand approved in the judgment*, whether they live until it transpires, or are raised from the dead to meet it, according to verse 2." With this view Zoeckler says Hofman substantially agrees, when he says, "A divine register of Israel, upon which are entered all who *truly* belong to Israel".

Ver. 2. *"And many of them that sleep in the dust of the earth shall awake"*,—Gaebelein says physical resurrection is not taught in this verse, because if it were it would teach a general resurrection and this would clash with the New Testament teaching concerning the resurrection. He says, "The passage has nothing to do with physical resurrection. Physical resurrection is here used merely as a type or figure of the national revival of Israel in the last day at the end of this age. They have been sleeping nationally in the dust of the earth, buried among the Gentiles. But at that time there will take place a national restoration, a bringing back from dispersion and a bringing together of the house of Judah and of Israel. It is the same figure as used in the vision of the dry bones in Ezekiel 37, and it concerns not the Gentiles but the Jewish people and is a national restoration and revival of these."

However, it is practicaly unanimous that the reference is to physical resurrection. Robinson says, "If a resurrection of the body is not here declared, it will be difficult to find where it is, or to imagine words in which it can be." But even so, Gaebelein's fears are none too well grounded, as may be seen in quotations, from many commentators, somewhat like the following from W. J. Erdman: "These words do not teach a general resurrection. The more literal translation, following Tregelles, would read, 'And many of them that sleep in the dust of the earth shall awake; these to everlasting life, and those to shame and everlasting contempt'. In the light of the context it is clear that the angel is speaking of Daniel's own people only. He is bringing together events of 'the time of the end', 'the great tribulation' and 'deliverance of every one that shall be found written in the book', 'even the remnant in Mount Zion and Jerusalem'; and the other event, the resurrection of the 'many' from out of the totality of the dead of Israel, the resurrection of the unraised belonging to some distant and undefined day."

Now if the reference is to a resurrection of the physically dead, then, if the last part of the preceding chapter and these words as well are to be referred to the time of Antiochus Epiphanes, Daniel either,

(1) thought it was going to take place right after the trouble under Antiochus Epiphanes, and *missed it*, as Hitzig, Bertholdt and other rationalistic interpreters say he did; or,

(2) he projected his vision onward to the period of resurrection which is still future. This latter view is of course the only acceptable one and the transition is to be found after the manner already noted.

Now if the resurrection is a physical future one, to what resurrection does it refer?

I. To the general resurrection at the end of all things. (C. Zo. Au. Kl. Zu. St. Hav. Hof. Aug.)

But the connection between the two verses is so close that it would seem they must go together, and then, according to the view now under scrutiny, the time of trouble, at the end of which all whose names are in the book are to be delivered, would be at the same time with this general resurrection, i. e., just before the end of all time. But this will hardly do. It would mean that Daniel's people were to continue in bad straits as long as the world lasts and that the last years were to be the worst, and that they would only be delivered at the last moment of all time. This objection is met by some by putting a hiatus between the two verses, thus making the deliverance of verse 1 something entirely different from the rising to everlasting life in verse 2.

An objection is registered against this hiatus, but to us it does not seem formidable.

The objection is that it takes away from the deliverance of verse 1 its real significance. But may that deliverance not consist in the deliverance of the believing *living* remnant from the oppression of their furious foes and from the severe judgments which are to come down on unbelieving Gentiles and apostate Jews as well, in which case the *"book"* would be a register of the living and not of the dead. To those who say the deliverance of verse 1 is the being raised to everlasting life of verse 2, it is sufficient to reply that this is not, as we have seen, necessarily so. At least this deliverance must not be limited to the dead. As between the living and the dead, it would more naturally refer to the former.

II. To a partial resurrection immediately after the tribulation, and prior to the last and general resurrection, and one confined to Israel, Daniel's own nation. (Fu. Kr. Ko. Hit. Bertholdt and the majority of writers since him.) There would then be a hiatus, unnoticed by the angel, between the rising of the good and the bad; or the content of the passage may be construed according to the translation of Tregelles, "And many of them that sleep in the dust of the earth shall arise; these (who arise) shall be unto everlasting life; but those (who do not arise at this time) to shame and everlasting contempt."

Zoeckler argues for the first explanation and against the second as follows:

(1) The expression, *"many of them that sleep in the dust of the earth"* is far too general in its character to admit of its being limited to the deceased of Israel.

(2) The mention of the eternal punishment of the wicked in the closing words of the verse would be incomprehensible, and serve no purpose, if they refer only to Israelites who are to be punished eternally.

(3) The *"many"*, which primarily implies the immeasurable extent

of the multitude of the resurrected dead (Hofmann translates "in multitudes") may as well designate the *entire world* of the dead arising from their graves as a large *fraction* of it, in the same way as *"many"* in the New Testament is frequently employed as synonymous with "all". (Matt. 20.28; 26.28; I John 2.2; I Cor. 15.22; Rom. 5.12,15,16.)

(4) Even if the earlier prophetic parallels (Isa. 26.19; 66.24; Ezek. 37.1-15), actually do foretell a partial resurrection which is confined to Israel (which can by no means be proven), this will not involve that the passage before us has a similar meaning.

(5) If this passage refers exclusively to a particular resurrection of the Israelites, then there is no place in the Old Testament where any substantiation of the doctrine of a general resurrection may be found, and inasmuch as the expectation of such a general resurrection of the dead is abundantly confirmed in the Apocryphal books (II Mac. 7.14), and in the New Testament (see especially John 5.28 and Acts 25.15) it ought also to be confirmed by some Scripture of the Old Testament.

(6) The intimate connection between these verses and the closing ones of the preceding chapter where the troubles under Antiochus Epiphanes are set forth does not militate against the universal character of the resurrection in question. It is evident that in the mind of the prophet that period of trial was the immediate precursor of the end of the world (!?). As he viewed it, the end of the persecution by Antiochus Epiphanes and the advent of the Messiah to introduce a new and eternal period of blessing were substantially coincident. He saw nothing at all of the long series of years that were to intervene between these Old Testament 'woes of the Messiah' and His actual birth and incarnation, nor did he observe the many centuries between His first and second advent, between the beginning of the end and the ultimate end of all things, because it was inconsistent with the nature of prophetic vision.

This last statement not only has little if any strength in it, but it certainly places the prophet in a false light. Daniel does not explicitly say that these events are simultaneous. He may not have clearly apprehended the length of the interval, but this is no evidence that he did not know there was any.

Zoeckler says that in the prophet's mind the universal judgment upon all flesh at the end time and the judgment that came upon Antiochus Epiphanes (the first antitypical and the second typical) were identical and it is therefore arbitrary to refer the judgment here under consideration to a special judgment over the good and bad of Israel alone, and thus deprive it of its universal character.

Zoeckler also says it is quite as arbitrary to refer verse 1 to the troubles under Antiochus Epiphanes and then refer verse 2 to the final time resurrection with an immense chasm between them, of which there is no indication in the text. This, however, is not unusual, after the manner of both Old and New Testament writers or speakers. Besides, Zoeckler must remember that not every one agrees with him in referring verse 1 to the times under Antiochus Epiphanes.

Keil remarks that "the angel has it not in view to give a general statement regarding the general resurrection of the dead, but only discloses on this point that the final salvation of the people shall not be limited to those still living at the end of the great tribulation, but shall include also those who have lost their lives during the period of this tribulation."

Fuller remarks that "the resurrection to shame is merely a passing observation, which might be omitted from the passage without damaging its meaning."

Certainly if the first class raised refers to the godly Israelites who were killed during the great tribulation, the second class can just as readily refer to the wicked of Daniel's nation whenever raised. The only objection of much force among those advanced by Zoeckler is the seemingly unnecessary limitation of the word "many". Keil, however, says that the word does not mean "all" and that the partitive interpretation "of" or "from among" is the only simple and natural one, and therefore, with most interpreters, he prefers it. Keil, however, does not limit the resurrection in question to the Jews, but thinks that the Israel here referred to consists not merely of Jews or of Jewish Christians, but embraces all the peoples who belong to God's kingdom of the New Covenant.

III. To a resurrection of the righteous just before Christ's second coming, and of the wicked at the end of all time, no notice being taken by the angel of the hiatus between them. (F.)

This places the resurrection of the righteous before the great tribulation. This is possible, of course, in as much as chronological sequence is not always necessarily observed in relating the details of an event. However, it is best not to make such transpositions unless absolutely demanded, and the resurrection in question here certainly is placed by the text after the time of great trouble.

Then, too, this interpretation takes the reference pretty largely away from Daniel's own people, inasmuch as many of them will have believed by that time. The Jews do not seem to be converted until after the time of trouble or during it and their experience with the Antichrist.

IV. To a resurrection of all that sleep in the dust after the time of great tribulation; the good, at that very time (immediately after) and the wicked later at the end of all time, with no notice taken by the angel of the hiatus or intervening time. (Au. Rob. New. Chal.)

According to this view the righteous, the Church, goes through the tribulation. This seemingly has more in its favor, and less against it than any of the other views, so far as the context is concerned, unless it is the first one, and this has other Scriptures which in the minds of many militate against it.

Ver. 3. "they that are wise",—i. e., the understanding ones of Chap. 11.33,35.

"shall shine", etc.,—i. e., in the resurrection.

"they that turn many to righteousness",—i. e., convert many to justification through Christ.

Ver. 4. "shut up the words and seal the book",—i. e., the whole book (K. Au. Kl. Hit. Ber.), and not just the final vision of Chap. 11.2 to Chap. 12.3 (Zo. Kr. Fu. Hav. Len.).

"shut . . . seal",—The reference here is to guarding it carefully; not that any one may not read it, but that it will be better studied and understood later.

"many shall run to and fro",—The word means to run about in order to search out and investigate. It cannot therefore mean mere increase of travel. It might mean travel for a purpose, the result of which is the increase of knowledge, but we prefer rather the meaning of to and fro in the sense of searching, scrutinizing the prophecy as a result of which knowledge of it will be increased.

Ver. 5. *"other two"*,—This refers to two angels and it is useless to conjecture who they were.

Ver. 6. *"the man clothed in linen"*,—The mighty angelic prince, who thus far had been the speaker addressing Daniel; perhaps Christ Himself, as Keil, Willet, Gaebelein and others think.

"How long shall it be to the end of these wonders?"—i. e., how long shall the time of great trouble last?

Ver. 7. *"a time, times and a half"*,—i. e., after a time and two times and a half time, or briefly, after three and one-half years. (Chap. 7.25; 8.14; 9.27.)

"when they have made an end of breaking in pieces the power of the holy people",—This is a second answer to the question, which substantially coincides with it as to the time involved.

The literal of *"breaking in pieces the power"* is "shattering the hand", the hand being the emblem of active power. The reading of our text is supported by many strong authorities. (K. Au. Ma. Kr. Kl. Fu. Ew. Hen. Hof.) It is to be preferred to that of Zoeckler, "and when the *scattering* of a *part* of the holy people shall have *ceased"*, which rendering is, however, supported by a number of strong authorities. (Zu. Len. Der. Ber. Ges. Hav. Lut. Vul. Theo.) It is true the word rendered "shatter" by our text is often in prophetic usage rendered "scatter", but the former is its more literal meaning; while the metaphorical significance of "hand", i. e., power, seems preferable as far more natural and usual than "part". The sense is not, however, materially different in either case; the reference being to the pouring out of the last dregs of the curse on the desolated, holy people, Israel's lowest humiliation being the precursor of her exaltation. The *"they"* of the text refers to Antichrist and his powers.

Ver. 8. *"what shall be the issue of these things"*,—i. e., by what event will it be possible to know that the last end has been reached? Daniel understood the main features of the vision, but not as to the times, and perhaps especially the reference with which the preceding verse closed.

Ver. 9. The desire of Daniel for knowing more is thus deferred to *"the time of the end"*. Zoeckler thinks this was to encourage and to lead to humble submission to the Divine guidance, whose purposes cannot at first be understood. Fausset says that John's Revelation in part reveals what here is veiled.

Ver. 10. *"many shall purify themselves . . . white . . refined"*,—i. e., by persecution and sufferings.

"they that are wise shall understand",—Says Fausset, "There is no need for fuller explanation of the *time*, for when the predictions so far given shall have come to pass, the godly shall be purified by the foretold

trials, and shall understand that the end is at hand; but the wicked shall not understand and so shall rush on to their own ruin."

Vers. 11,12. The first two clauses refer to one and the same point of time, the three and one-half years beginning with the taking away of the continual burnt offering and the setting up of the abomination that maketh desolate.

The difference in the figures has been variously explained. One thousand two hundred and sixty plus 30 equals 1290 plus 45 equals 1335.

1. If the figures are applied to the persecution under Antiochus Epiphanes, the best explanation is that of Stuart. He says the 1290 days are an exact account of the period of time stated in round numbers as three and one half years during which the abomination continued. Antiochus Epiphanes, he says, ordered the sacrifice removed June 1, B. C. 168, and Maccabaeus restored it Dec. 25, B. C. 165, 1290 days, or approximately three and one half years, and the 1335 days, that is forty-five days more, marks the death of Antiochus Epiphanes as reckoned by Klieforth and others (F. Ju. Ma. Ber. Hav. Len. Wie.) Zoeckler says the tribulation shall end in 1290, but not completely until 1335 days.

Bleek and Delitzsch say that some fact not now known in history marks the 1335 days.

Zoeckler, who has contended all along that the whole prophecy should be applied to Antiochus Epiphanes, says, "We are accordingly compelled to abandon every attempt to demonstrate an exact correspondence between the time indicated in the text and the period of Maccabean persecution." He therefore falls back with Keil upon a symbolical interpretation of the time element. But if the time element is symbolical only, then why the changes in the figures and why the exact figures that are given? Since the exact date of the death of Antiochus Epiphanes is not known, it is difficult to be certain about this matter if the contents be referred to him.

If the dates be referred to the Antichrist, as they doubtless must be, if not directly and primarily as we believe, then at least typically, the true explanation may perhaps be seen in some of the following:

(a) 1260 days marks the fall of the Antichrist; 1290 days, the restoration of the Jews, and 1335 days, the beginning of the Millennium. (New.)

(b) 1260 days marks the fall of the Antichrist and the deliverance of the Jews; 1920 days makes thirty days more during which the consciences of these Jews are awakened to faith in Christ, and 1335 days gives forty-five more for the gathering in of the outcast Jews and the full blessing. (Tre.)

(c) 1260 days marks the fall of the Antichrist; 1290 days gives an extra month for certain judgment events as mentioned in Matt. 25, and forty-five days later (1335) the Millennium begins. (Gab.)

Ver. 13. "thou shalt rest",—i. e., in the grave.

"at the end of the days",—i. e., at the end of the days just under discussion. Daniel was to go on to the end of his life, was to rest in his grave and was to rise again, to stand in his own lot, i. e., to enjoy his share of the promised inheritance.

THE BOOK OF

HOSEA
(B. C. 785—B. C. 725)

CHAPTER ONE

10 Yet the number of the children of Israel shall be as the sand of the sea, which - cannot be measured nor numbered; and it shall come to pass that, [1]in the place where it was said unto them, Ye are not my people, it shall be said unto them, Ye are the sons of the living God.

[1]Or, *instead of that which was said*

11 And the children of Judah and the children of Israel shall be gathered together, and they shall appoint themselves one head, and shall go up from the land; for great shall be the day of Jezreel.

Vers. 10, 11. The Future Blessing and Restoration of Israel.

The prophecy of these two verses may be considered, as to its fulfillment, in any one or all of the following three ways:

1. A literal fulfillment, though in a very small degree, at the return from Babylonish captivity when some of Israel joined with Judah.

2. A spiritual fulfillment through God's people, Jews and Gentiles, in Christ, as it is still being fulfilled today. (Romans 9.26.)

3. A complete literal fulfillment at the time of the restoration of the Jews which is still to come. (Romans 11.26.)

Ver. 10. *"children of Israel"*,—Keil refers this to the ten tribes (Israel) as distinct from the two tribes (Judah) as in verse 7; but it seems preferable with Schmoller to take the expression here as inclusive of both, separating them again as the passage does in verse 11.

"in the place",—In whatever place—no place in particular.

Ver. 11. *"one head"*,—Interpreting this and other expressions of this verse in harmony with the three views expressed above, the reference would be as follows: under (1) Zerubbabel; under (2) Christ, the Head of His Church; under (3) Christ, under Whom the *hereafter* united kingdoms of Judah and Israel will be realized at their restoration in Palestine.

"up from the land",—Under (1) from the land of exile, Babylon, back to Palestine; though Simcox and others make it mean up to Jerusalem from the Land of Palestine after they have come back; under (2) out of the sinful life into the Church of Christ marching on to Zion; under (3) out of the land of strangers, *where they are sojourners at this time*, back to Palestine, their own land.

"great shall be the day of Jezreel",—This is one of those obscure expressions where exact interpretation is impossible. It points back to verse 5 which has to do with a time of defeat for Israel.

Under views (1) and (3) as above the day of Jezreel is called great perhaps because in that place (the valley of Jezreel) where Israel's bow was broken, victory shall yet be achieved; and not, as Keil says, "because

242

that defeat formed the critical occasion by which the return of the recreant Israel and their reunion with Judah was made possible".

Under view (2), on this interpretation, the case is more difficult since there can be no local reference in the spiritual fulfillment of the words. The word *"Jezreel"* literally means, "God sows", and some prefer the appellative meaning, namely, that the valley of Jezreel where Israel's bow was broken is to become the place where God sows the seed of their renovation, the people being planted again in their own land. (F.) This would of course be true, though in a secondary sense, even though the other interpretation be accepted. Under (2) the appellative meaning would be found in the greatness of God's sowing as He through Christ is planting the kingdom of God today.

One thing is certain, the prophecy received very little, if any, fulfillment before the time of Christ, that is, according to (1), the first interpretation. The children of Israel did not go back with the children of Judah except the merest handful; they were not united under one head, the day of Jezreel, as explained, was not realized, and they did not become like the sands of the sea.

Another certain thing is that the prophecy was and is being spiritually realized in Christ. The fact, too, that Paul understood this prophecy as pointing to a spiritual fulfillment, as is clearly proven by Romans 9.26, is pretty good warrant for taking other and all similar predictions in the same way, although it will have to be admitted that many of the details of such prophecies, in many cases at least, utterly defy any reasonable interpretation when explanation is attempted in this way.

It remains yet to be said that we can see no prohibitive reason for not believing that the literal fulfillment of this prophecy may not yet take place as indicated under (3), the third explanation.

CHAPTER TWO

14 Therefore, behold, I will allure her, and bring her into the wilderness, and speak [1]comfortably unto her. 15 And I will give her her vineyards from thence, and the valley of [2]Achor for a door of hope; and she shall [3]make answer there, as in the days of her youth, and as in the day when she came up out of the land of Egypt. 16 And it shall be at that day, saith Jehovah, that thou shalt call me [4]Ishi, and shalt call me no more [5]Baali. 17 For I will take away the names of the Baalim out of her mouth, and they shall no more be [6]mentioned by their name. 18 And in that day will I make a covenant for them with the beasts of the field, and with the birds of the heavens, and with the creeping things of the ground: and I will break the bow and the sword and the battle out of the land, and will make them to lie down safely. 19 And I will betroth thee unto me for ever; yea, I will betroth thee unto me in righteousness, and in justice, and in lovingkindness, and in mercies. 20 I will even betroth thee unto me in faithfulness; and thou shalt know Jehovah.

21 And it shall come to pass in that day, I will answer, saith Jehovah, I will answer the heavens, and they shall answer the earth; 22 and the earth shall answer the grain, and the new wine, and the oil; and they shall answer [7]Jezreel. 23 And I will sow her unto me in the [8]earth; and I will have mercy upon [9]her that had not obtained mercy; and I will say to [10]them that were not my people, Thou art my people; and they shall say, *Thou art* my God.

[1]Heb. *to her heart*
[2]That is, *Troubling*
[3]Or, *sing*
[4]That is, *My husband*
[5]That is, *My master*
[6]Or, *remembered*

[7]Or, That is, *Whom God soweth*
[8]Or, *land*
[9]Heb. *Lo-ruhamah*. See Chap. 1.6
[10]Heb. *Lo-ammi*. See Chap. 1.9,10

Vers. 14-23. Israel's Conversion and the Renewal of the
        Covenant.

Ver. 14. *"Therefore"*,—A conclusion drawn from the whole preceding section, i. e., because the punishment of Israel for her sins has effected
its designed end and caused her to long for. God.

"lure",—i. e., in a friendly sense.

"into the wilderness",—The land of their captivity was to be to them
a wilderness for a disciplinary test (Deut. 8.2,3,15,16) where under
humbling providences they were made to be humble, where in poverty they
were made to be poor in spirit, etc.

Ver. 15. *"vineyards from thence"*,—i. e., as soon as they arrive
within the borders of Canaan, returning from the wilderness.

"valley of Achor",—It was in this valley on the edge of Canaan
returning from Egypt that Israel was deprived of the favor of God by the
sin of Achan, and where this favor was restored when the camp was purged,
and thus what seemed to be the valley of destruction became the door of
hope. And so the very trouble of Israel's wilderness state will be the door
of hope opening to better days.

"make answer there",—Israel will cry out in answer toward the place
where the Lord comes to meet her (verse 14), thankfully acknowledging
the tokens of His love and answering to them by suitable conduct.

Wolfendale and all English expositors interpret the word "sing" instead of *"make answer"*, with special allusion to the song of Miriam and
the Israelites after crossing the Red Sea. In this they interpret with the
Authorized Version, but we prefer with Hengstenberg and all German
expositors the rendering of the Revised Version, *"make answer"*, which
both adheres to the more literal meaning of the words and corresponds
better to the changed character of the people.

Ver. 16. *"Ishi"*,—meaning literally, "my husband". She will
recognize Jehovah as her true spouse.

"no more Baali",—meaning literally "my master". She will use
this expression no more because it had been perverted (verse 17) to express
the images of Baal whose name ought not to be taken upon their lips. It
would be possible thus to outwardly call upon Jehovah but at the same
time to have Baal in their minds.

Ver. 18. *"in that day"*,—In the day of their conversion when they
have done forever with their idols.

"for them",—i. e., for their benefit.

"covenant with the beasts",—Therefore the beasts are not to injure
them. Said perhaps by way of contrast with verse 12. It would seem
that this is a promise to be fully realized only in the Millennium.

"lie down safely",—i. e., cause them to be at rest, war having ceased.

Ver. 20. *"shall know Jehovah"*,—i. e., experimentally, and thus
be saved.

Ver. 21. We have here the grain, the new wine and the oil, the earth
and the heavens personified.

Ver. 22. The grain appeals to the earth, the earth (verse 21) appeals to the heavens and the heavens to God, and thus the grain, the new wine and the oil can answer Jezreel, i. e., Israel, "the sown of God", planted anew by divine grace. It is to be recalled here that the appellative meaning of the word *"Jezreel"* is "God soweth".

Of this prophecy we have to say like that of Chap. 1 (a) that it received only the smallest and feeblest fulfillment in the return of the Jews from exile, (b) that it was spiritually realized in fullness in Christ, the Messiah, and (c) that we see no insurmountable reason why its literal fulfillment may not yet be looked for in the promised land.

CHAPTER THREE

> 5 afterward shall the children of Israel return, and seek Jehovah their God, and David their king, and shall come with fear unto Jehovah and to His goodness in the latter days.

Ver. 5. THE FUTURE DAVIDIC KINGDOM.

"afterward",—i. e., after the *"many days"* of verse 4.

"David their king",—The Messiah of course is meant, a king of the family of David.

"the latter days",—The Messianic days.

This has not as yet taken place, save as we look upon Israel in a spiritual way as the children of God of this dispensation, but may it not be that the Jewish nation will yet return and seek Jehovah their God.

CHAPTER SIX

> 2 After two days will he revive us; on the third day he will raise us up, and we shall live before him.

Ver. 2. THE CERTAINTY OF ISRAEL'S RESTORATION.

The linking of days in this way is a method of expressing the certainty of an event within the period named, and it is used here only in the sense of a formula expressing what shall certainly take place at a future day.

"raise up",—This can appropriately be thought of as an expression of physical resurrection used to illustrate Israel's restoration, and it is not impossible therefore to find here a reference to the resurrection of Christ, the ideal Israel, Israel's restoration being taken as a type of our resurrection of which Christ is the firstfruits. (F. Ho. Wo. Pu.) This reference is, however, a very doubtful one and is opposed by Schmoller and the majority of the best students of this text.

CHAPTER ELEVEN

> 8 How shall I give thee up, Ephraim? *how* shall I cast thee off, Israel? how shall I make thee as Admah? *how* shall I set thee as Zeboiim? my heart is turned within me, my compassions are kindled together. 9 I will not execute

the fierceness of mine anger, I will not return to destroy Ephraim: for I am God, and not man; the Holy One in the midst of thee; and I will not ¹come in wrath. 10 They shall walk after Jehovah, who will roar like a lion; for

¹Or, *enter into the city*

he will roar, and the children shall come trembling from the west. 11 They shall come trembling as a bird out of Egypt, and as a dove out of the land of Assyria; and I will make them to dwell in their houses, saith Jehovah.

Vers. 8-11.   JEHOVAH'S PURPOSE TO RESTORE ISRAEL.

These verses refer to God's longing for Ephraim, the ten tribes, and His intention to bring them back from their dispersion.

He will *"not give them up"* (verse 8); He will *"not come in wrath"* (the best translation of the last clause of verse 9); He will *"roar like a lion"* against their enemies (verse 10), and He will *"make them to dwell in their houses"* (verse 11).

The same thing must be said as to the fulfillment of this prophecy as was said of those of the chapters which have gone before.

CHAPTER TWELVE

9 But I am Jehovah thy God from the land of Egypt; I will yet again make thee to dwell in tents, as in the days of the solemn feast.

Ver. 9.   FUTURE BLESSING AND RESTORATION AGAIN PROMISED.

When this promise is fulfilled it will be in remembrance (dwell in tents) of this their new deliverance out of bondage.

This prophecy had its primary, but only partial fulfillment, in the return from Babylon.   (Neh. 8.17.)   Those, however, who look beyond the spiritual fulfillment of this day, and see in all such passages a prophecy of literal fulfillment, refer the fulfillment of this prophecy to the time of final restoration from the present dispersion.   (Lev. 23.42,43; Zech. 14.6.)

CHAPTER THIRTEEN

14 I will ransom them from the ¹power of Sheol; I will redeem them from death: O death ²where are thy

¹Heb. *hand*

plagues?   O Sheol, ²where is thy destruction?   Repentance shall be hid from mine eyes.

²Or, *I will be*

Ver. 14.   THE BLESSING OF ISRAEL IN THE FUTURE KINGDOM.

These words are evidently to be taken in the sense of a promise, finding their fulfillment, as the other prophecies noted, partially in the restoration of Israel from Assyria; fully in a spiritual sense in Christ, Israel in this sense being the Israel of God, the New Testament Church of Christ; and finally, in keeping with other such passages, many see the literal fulfillment in the yet future restoration of Israel from their present dispersion and national death.

Because the verse before and after and all the chapter is a threat, Schmoller and others say that a promise is here unsuitable and accordingly make the clauses of the verse all questions implying a negative answer. But this inference is rather forced and the reading of our text is preferred by the majority.

The Septuagint translates after the manner of I Cor. 15.55, and from this Paul no doubt quoted. The verse is expressed in language alluding to the ideal Israel, and His victory over death and the grave, His own resurrection being the firstfruits of the full harvest to come in the resurrection at the end.

CHAPTER FOURTEEN

5 I will be as the dew unto Israel; he shall blossom as the lily, and cast forth his roots as Lebanon.

6 His branches shall spread and his beauty shall be as the olive-tree, and his smell as Lebanon.

7 They that dwell under his shadow shall return; they shall revive as the grain, and blossom as the vine, ¹the scent thereof shall be as the wine of Lebanon.

¹Or, *his memorial*

Vers. 5-7. THE EFFECTS OF THE LORD's LOVE RICH IN BLESSING ON ISRAEL.

Ver. 5. The dew falls copiously in the east; no plant is more productive than the lily, one root often producing fifty bulbs; while the trees of Lebanon cast down their roots as deeply as their height upwards, so that they are immovable.

Ver. 6. The olive never loses its verdure, while the fragrance of Lebanon with its cedars and aromatic shrubs is proverbial.

Ver. 7. The members of Israel (the first *"they"*) are here distinguished from Israel as a whole (the second *"they"*). The shadow mentioned here is Israel's and not God's, it being necessary that we hold to the same reference here as in verse 6. They that used to dwell under Israel's shadow, but who shall have been forced to leave it, shall return and be restored.

"the scent thereof",—i. e., of Israel's fame.

THE BOOK OF

JOEL

(B. C. 800)

The book of Joel falls easily into two divisions, Chap. 1.1 to Chap. 2.17, setting forth judgment upon the Gentiles, and Chap. 2.18 to Chap. 3.21 the promises of blessing for Israel.

CHAPTER ONE

4 That which ¹the palmer-worm hath left hath ¹the locust eaten; and that which the locust hath left hath ¹the canker-worm eaten; and that which the

¹Probably, different kinds of locusts, or locusts in different stages of growth.

canker-worm hath left hath [1]the caterpillar eaten.

6 For a nation is come up upon my
land, strong, and without number; his
teeth are the teeth of a lion, and he hath
the jaw-teeth of a lioness.

15 Alas for the day! for the day of
Jehovah is at hand, and as destruction
from the Almighty shall it come.

Vers. 4,6,15.   THE BEGINNING OF THE DAY OF JEHOVAH.

Is this description in the first chapter that of a plague of real locusts
in Joel's time or is it an allegorical prediction of a coming invasion by
some hostile human army?   A good case can be made out for either view.
In either case, however, it is an earnest or portent of a coming greater
calamity.

Arguments for the Allegorical View: (The Fathers, older expositors,
and more recently Po. Gr. Hav. Hen. Ber.)

1. Locusts are a natural figure for hostile invaders.   (See Rev. 9.3-12
   where they are allegorical.)

2. The scourge is called the "Northerner", while locusts come from
   the south.   (Chap. 2.20.)

3. The agent is described as a responsible one.   (Chap. 2.20.)

4. The imagery goes beyond the effects of locusts and threatens fire,
   drought, plague and assault upon cities.   (Chaps. 1.19,20 and
   2.6.)

5. Prayer is to be made for a removal of the scourge that the *heathen*
   may not rule over them.   (Chap. 2.17.)

6. The scourge was to be destroyed in a way physically inapplicable
   to locusts.   (Chap. 2.20.)

7. Ravages are to be remedied which locusts could not inflict, i. e.,
   Judah's captivity is to be turned and the land is to be recovered
   from the foreigners.   (Chap. 3.1,17.)

Arguments for the Literal View: (Sco.)

1. Joel addresses his own contemporaries and not a future generation.
   (Chap. 1.2.)

2. The plague had occurred *"before our own eyes"*.   (Chap. 1.16.)

3. He asks the old men if the like had ever occurred in their day.
   (Chap 1.2.)

4. The description is that of a physical and not a political plague,
   i. e., fields stripped, seeds shrivel, drought, etc.

5. He never hints at the invariable effects of human invasion, i. e.,
   plunder, massacre, bloodshed, etc.

6. The losses restored are the years which this army had *eaten*.
   (Chap. 2.25.)

7. He tells them to hand the story down to future generations.
   (Chap. 1.3.)

8. The locusts are compared to actual soldiers—run like horses, leap
   like men, climb, etc.; he never would have compared a real army
   to itself.

9. The name "Northerner" is typical of doom, a name employed
   always to express the instrument of God's wrath, and so Joel
   applies it to his fateful locusts.

10. *"that the heathen may not rule over them"* may, it is said, be translated with equal propriety, "that the heathen may not make satirical song about them", or "use a byword against them". (See margin.)

11. The assault on cities may be applied to locusts as well as to a human army; the expression, *"steal in at the windows"* being more applicable to the locusts than to a human army.

12. There is little if any force in what the Allegorists say about the responsible agent, as Chap. 2.20 may also be applied to locusts.

The balance of the argument we feel to be strongly in favor of the literal view, namely, that Joel was describing a plague of devouring locusts in his own day. This plague is shown, however, to have a spiritual significance, and is made the occasion for the prophecy of the day of the Lord in its two aspects of judgment on the Gentiles and blessing for Israel, this *"day of the Lord"* being more fully developed in the second chapter, where the literal locusts are left behind and the future "day of the Lord" fills the scene.

Ver. 4. Four successive swarms of locusts are described, literally, the "Shearer", the "Swarmer", the "Lapper" and the "Devourer", the same being four different poetic names for the locusts.

Ver. 6. *"nation"*,—The word used for nation here is one that has in it the idea of hostility, and is here used of locusts.

Ver. 15. *"Alas for the day"*,—i. e., the day then present in which the plague of the locusts was upon them. This day was so terrible that it might well be thought of as the beginning of the "Day of the Lord", which Joel describes as "at hand".

"the day of Jehovah",—This is always a day of judgment, a day of His anger. That the immediate reference is to the day then present is to be seen in the fact that in the next verse Joel returns at once to the devastation of the land then going on. However in this mention of the *"day of Jehovah"* may be seen a typical significance, a reference to the worse calamities about to come on them of which the locusts were but the prelude.

Verse 11 introduces an unusual drought, while verses 19 and 20 refer to the effect of the parching heat. Some refer the *"fire"* to forest fires.

CHAPTER TWO

Here it would seem the prophet passes into allegory and foretells a coming judgment through the invasion of a heathen army, and this he does under an imagery drawn from their then present experience of the locust plague.

1 Blow ye the trumpet in Zion, and sound an alarm in my holy mountain; let all the inhabitants of the land tremble: for the day of Jehovah cometh, for it is nigh at hand; 2 a day of darkness and gloominess, a day of clouds and thick darkness, as the dawn spread upon the mountains; a great people and a strong; there hath not been ever the like, neither shall be any more after them, even to the years of many generations. 3 A fire devoureth before them; and behind them a flame burneth: the land is as the garden of Eden before

them, and behind them a desolate wilderness: yea, and none hath escaped them.

4 The appearance of them is as the appearance of horses; and as [1]horsemen, so do they run. 5 Like the noise of chariots on the tops of the mountains do they leap, like the noise of a flame of fire that devoureth the stubble, as a strong people set in battle array.

6 At their presence the peoples are in anguish: all faces are waxed pale. 7 They run like mighty men; they climb the wall like men of war; and they march every one on his ways, and they break not their ranks. 8 neither doth

[1]Or, war-horses

one thrust another; they march every one in his path; and [2]they burst through the weapons, and [3]break not off *their course.* 9 They leap upon the city; they run upon the wall; they climb up into the houses; they enter in at the windows like a thief. 10 The earth quaketh before them; the heavens tremble; the sun and the moon are darkened, and the stars withdraw their shining. 11 And Jehovah uttereth his voice before his army; for his camp is very great; for he is strong that executeth his word; for the day of Jehovah is great and very terrible; and who can abide it?

[2]Or, *when they fall around the weapons, they &c*
[3]Or, *are not wounded*

Vers. 1-11. THE INVADING ARMY FROM THE NORTH.

Ver. 1. The priests were to sound the alarm horn to apprise the people of the coming judgment.

Ver. 2. *"A day of darkness"*,—This is a fit image of the coming day, suggested by the sun being obscured by swarms of locusts.

"as the dawn spread upon the mountains",—In the word *"spread"* is to be found the idea of beaten down, scattered, crushed by and with a mass of clouds as if in conspiracy to prolong the night. So shall come a great people and strong, bringing with them a day of darkness, etc. There may be a reference in the expression to the shining or the yellow light reflected by the rays of the sun from the wings of a swarm of locusts. (K. Ma.)

Some find the principal comparison in the rapidity with which and the wide extent over which the dawn spreads itself,—so shall a numerous people overspread the land. (Ma. Ba.)

Ver. 3. The word *"them"* throughout the verse refers to the army before the prophet's vision.

Ver. 4. *"The appearance of them"*,—i. e., of the figurative locusts, the army before the prophet's vision.

Ver. 7. This imagery is drawn from the well-known military order in the advance of swarms of locusts.

Ver. 8. They do not push each other out of their place.

Ver. 9. This verse completes the description, and together with verses 7 and 8 gives us a picture which is exactly true to nature. They rush through the weapons, the darts, and their ranks are not broken.

Ver. 11. *"his army"*,—Scofield takes verses 1 to 10 as descriptive of the invading army and verse 11 as referring to Jehovah's army which is to be marshaled against the invaders, the army, he says, being that which is described in Rev. 19.11-18, the battle foretold being that of Armageddon. But inasmuch as the reference is still to the day of Jehovah, even as in verse 1, there is no good reason why the antitypical human foes of Judea, of which the locusts are figures, should not be considered as the army of

Jehovah coming in judgment upon them. There can be, however, on the other hand no forcible objection to taking this army as Scofield does, if the chapter is to be referred to the still future day of Jehovah.

Vers. 12-17. A CALL TO REPENTANCE.

The reference to the *"meal offering"*, etc., in verse 14 finds its meaning in that God may give plentiful harvests so that these things could once more be offered.

Vers. 18-27. THE LORD'S PROMISE OF DELIVERANCE.

Ver. 20. *"the northern army"*,—Some take this as indicative of the Chaldeans and the Syrians, while others, thinking of the day of the Lord in the end time refer it to the Gentile world-powers headed up under the Beast and the false prophet. (Rev. 16.14.)

"eastern sea . . . western sea",—The Dead Sea and the Mediterranean.

"stench shall come up",—A metaphor from locusts which perish, when blown by a storm into the sea or the desert, and emit a stench from their putrefying bodies.

Ver. 23. *"the former rain"*,—The Autumn rain.

"in just measure",—i. e., as much as the land required. Literally it reads "according to right".

"the latter rain",—The Spring rain.

"in the first month",—i. e., in the month when first it is needed.

Some, who take Chap. 1 as allegorical prediction, see in the four kinds of locusts the four great world-powers, Babylon, Medo-Persia, Greece and Rome. (F. Hen., and the Jews in general.)

28 And it shall come to pass afterward, that I will pour out my Spirit upon all flesh; and your sons and your daughters shall prophesy, your old men shall dream dreams, your young men shall see visions: 29 and also upon the servants and upon the handmaids in those days will I pour out my Spirit. 30 And I will show wonders in the heavens and in the earth; blood, and fire, and pillars of smoke. 31 The sun shall be turned into darkness, and the moon into blood, before the great and terrible day of Jehovah cometh. 32 And it shall come to pass, that whosoever shall call on the name of Jehovah shall be delivered; for in mount Zion and in Jerusalem there shall be those that escape, as Jehovah hath said, and [1]among the remnant those whom Jehovah doth call.

[1]Or, *in the remnant whom, &c.*

Vers. 28-32. THE PROMISE OF SPIRITUAL GIFTS.

Ver. 28. Regardless of how the previous portion of this chapter is taken, it is certain that this verse and all that follows has a remote and ultimate reference.

"afterward",—This expression is a bit more indefinite but clearly identical with the formula used by the later prophets. It come from the Hebrew word meaning "latter", "last", and refers to the last days, the days under the Messiah after the deliverance of Israel from the northern army. The prophecy was fulfilled in Acts 2.17, but only in its beginning. Peter said the promise was also *"to all that are afar off"* (both in space and time), and thus while it has a partial and continuous fulfillment during

the *"last days"* which began with the first advent of Christ, its final and greater fulfillment awaits the *"last days"* as applied to the ultimate *"end time."*

"upon all flesh",—Not merely on a privileged few, as the prophets of the Old Testament, but upon mankind generally. (F. Pu. Sch.) Some think that the Jews only were in Joel's mind and that in his mind the heathen were to be destroyed. (George Adam Smith.)

"prophesy . . . dream . . . see visions",—The three modes whereby God revealed Himself under the Old Testament. Prophesying, here, does not relate so much to foretelling events but to preaching, speaking and witnessing under the inspiration of the Holy Spirit.

Ver. 30. Here begins a description of the cosmical signs preceding the day of the Lord.

This outpouring of the Spirit is viewed by the prophet as connected with the great day of the Lord and as *a sign of its coming.* It is described here only in a general way, its actual coming being set forth in Chap. 3. What the form of these phenomena shall be it is idle to conjecture. The allusion may be to the massacres and conflagrations attendant upon the destruction of Jerusalem as a type and earnest of the more terrible convulsions to occur before the final destruction of the ungodly world.

Ver. 32. *"shall be delivered"*,—As Christians were delivered from the destruction of Jerusalem by retiring to Pella, warned by the Saviour's utterance (Matt. 24.16), which was a type of the spiritual deliverance of all believers and of the last deliverance of the "elect remnant".

"in mount Zion and in Jerusalem",—Not to be taken in a local sense.

"as Jehovah hath said",—In Joel's own preceding words (F.), in Obadiah (K.), in an older writing of Joel (Ew.), in a lost prophecy (Mei.).

"among the remnant",—There shall be among them those whom the Lord shall call. The word literally means "the escaped".

"doth call",—i. e., according to the election of grace. (Rom. 11.5.) (F. Sch., and most older and later expositors.)

CHAPTER THREE

1 For, behold, in those days, and in that time, when I shall [1]bring back the captivity of Judah and Jerusalem, 2 I will gather all nations, and will bring them down into the valley of Jehosaphat; and I will execute judgment upon them there for my people and for my heritage Israel, whom they have scattered among the nations: and they have parted my land, 3 and have cast lots for my people, and have given a boy for a harlot, and sold a girl for wine, that they may drink. 4 Yea, and what are ye to me, O Tyre, and Sidon, and all the regions of Philistia? [2]will ye render me a recompense? and if ye recompense me, swiftly and speedily will I return your [3]recompense upon your own head. 5 Forasmuch as ye have taken my silver and my gold, and have carried into your temples my goodly precious things, 6 and have sold the children of Judah and the children of Jerusalem unto the sons of the Grecians, that ye may remove them far from their border; 7 behold, I will stir them up out of the place whither ye have sold them, and will return your [3]recompense

[1]Or, *return to*

[2]Or, *will ye repay a deed of mine, or will ye do aught unto me? swiftly &c.*
[3]Or, *deed*

upon your own head; 8 and I will sell your sons and your daughters into the hand of the children of Judah, and they shall sell them to the men of Sheba, to a nation far off: for Jehovah hath spoken it.

Vers. 1-8. THE RESTORATION OF ISRAEL AND THE JUDGMENT OF GENTILE NATIONS.

Ver. 1. *"For"*,—He is now to explain in detail what he had before mentioned in general.

"in those days",—i. e., the days to come, the "afterward" of the previous chapter.

"when I shall bring back the captivity",—This shows distinctly the object of the day of the Lord, namely, the bringing of deliverance to the people of God. To *"bring back"* means to reverse, to make an end of.

Ver. 2. *"all nations"*,—Primarily those that have offended against Israel but inclusive of the heathen world in general.

"valley of Jehosaphat",—This is the valley where Jehosaphat gained his victory over the Gentile army and is southwest of Jerusalem, and was called *"the valley of Berachah* (blessing) *unto this day"* (II Chron. 20). The valley between Jerusalem and the mount of Olives on the east was first called the valley of Jehosaphat in the fourth century and was therefore not so known in Joel's day. Jehosaphat means "Jehovah judges", and the expression used by Joel is no doubt a general term signifying the theatre of God's judgment on the nations, although undoubtedly the imagery was furnished to Joel by that great deliverance which God gave to Jehosaphat in II Chron. 20.

"execute judgment",—This is a much to be preferred rendering to "plead with" of the Authorized Version.

Ver. 3. A war custom of the heathen of that time in dealing with their captives.

Ver. 4. *"render me a recompense"*,—i. e., injure me (my people) for fancied wrongs. God here identifies Himself with His people.

"what are ye to me",—He counts them as aliens; they have no part in Him. The nations here mentioned had committed such crimes as those referred to.

Ver. 5. This alludes without doubt to II Chron. 21.16,17.

Vers. 7,8. Fulfilled by Alexander the Great. (Fa. Sch.)

"Sabeans",—These people occupied the remote extremity of Arabia Felix and were probably a partner with Tyre in slave selling.

"far off",—The remotest nation in the opposite direction from Greece.

9 Proclaim ye this among the nations; [1]prepare war; stir up the mighty men; let all the men of war draw near, let them come up. 10 Beat your plowshares into swords, and your pruning-hooks into spears: let the weak say, I am strong. 11 [2]Haste ye and come, all ye nations round about, and gather yourselves together; thither cause thy mighty ones to come down, O Jehovah. 12 Let the nations bestir themselves, and come up to the valley of

[1]Heb. *sanctify*

[2]Or, *Assemble yourselves*

253

³Jehosaphat; for there will I sit to judge all the nations round about. 13 Put ye in the sickle; for the ⁴harvest is ripe: come, ⁵tread ye; for the winepress is full, the vats overflow; for their wickedness is great.

14 Multitudes, multitudes in the valley of decision! for the day of Jehovah is near in the valley of decision. 15 The sun and the moon are darkened, and the stars withdraw their shining. 16 And Jehovah will roar from Zion, and utter his voice from Jerusalem; and the heavens and the earth shall shake: but Jehovah will be a refuge unto his people, and a stronghold to the children of Israel.

³That is, *Jehovah judgeth*
⁴Or, *vintage*
⁵Or, *get you down*

Vers. 9-16. THE DAY OF THE LORD IN RETROSPECT.

Ver. 9.   The nations are here summoned to come against Jerusalem not to destroy it but to be destroyed.

"Proclaim . . . prepare",—This is addressed not to the Jews but to the heathen nations, i. e., to their heralds who are to summon them to war. The word *"prepare"* is literally "sanctify" and Schmoller says it cannot therefore be referred to the heathen. But it is the same word exactly as used when Babylon was called upon to prepare war against Jerusalem (Jer. 6.4), and it is a well known fact that the heathen usually begin war with religious ceremonies.

Ver. 10.   *"let the weak say I am strong"*,—So mad shall be the fury of the world against God's people that even the feeble will not desire to be exempted from warring against them.

Ver. 11.   *"thither cause thy mighty ones to come down"*,—This is a prayer by Joel. The *"mighty ones"* are God's really mighty ones in contrast to the self-styled mighty ones of verse 9. Keil without warrant refers these to angels.

Ver. 12.   *"round about"*,—Not merely, as Henderson says, "round about Jerusalem", but all the nations from all parts who have maltreated the people of God. Thus also in verse 11.

Ver. 13.   God directs the ministers of His vengeance to execute His wrath. His command is to His mighty ones. His enemies are to be cut down like ripe grain and trodden (crushed) like grapes in the winepress.

Ver. 14.   *"valley of decision"*,—i. e., the valley of judgment, the place where the Judge renders His decision.

Ver. 16.   *"Jehovah will roar"*,—i. e., as a lion. It will be found that wherever this expression occurs it is in connection with the destruction of Gentile dominion (Jer. 25.30; Amos 1.2; 3.8; Isa. 42.13), and while it may have a near fulfillment it always looks forward to a vaster and more ultimate one.

17 So shall ye know that I am Jehovah your God, dwelling in Zion in my holy mountain: then shall Jerusalem be holy, and there shall no strangers pass through her any more.

18 And it shall come to pass in that day, that the mountains shall drop down sweet wine, and the hills shall flow with milk, and all the brooks of Judah shall flow with waters; and a fountain shall come forth from the house of Jehovah, and shall water ¹the valley of Shittim.

19 Egypt shall be a desolation, and

¹That is, *the valley of acacias*

Edom shall be a desolate wilderness, for the violence done to the children of Judah, because they have shed innocent blood in their land.

20 But Judah shall [2]abide forever, and Jerusalem from generation to generation.

21 And I will [3]cleanse their blood, that I have not cleansed; for Jehovah dwelleth in Zion.

[2]Or, be inhabited

[3]Or, hold as innocent

Vers. 17-21. THE BLESSINGS OF THE COMING KINGDOM.

Ver. 17. *"there shall no strangers pass through"*,—i. e., to attack or defile.

Ver. 18. *"mountains drop wine . . . hills flow with milk"*,—Figurative expressions for abundance of vines, and flocks yielding milk plentifully.

"a fountain shall come forth",—Here is a reference to the gushing and ever-flowing fountain of water under the temple. Thus blessings both temporal and spiritual shall issue from the house of God.

"valley of Shittim",—This is a valley on the border between Moab and Israel beyond the Jordan, an arid desert where the Acacia (sandalwood) grows.

Ver. 19. Egypt and Edom are mentioned because of their violence against the children of Judah and are taken as representatives of the enemies of Israel in general. (Amos 1.11; Oba. 10; Jer. 49.17.)

When Joel made this prophecy there were no symptoms whatsoever of decay on the part of the countries mentioned and yet how wonderfully has the prophecy been fulfilled.

Ver. 21. *"I will cleanse their blood"*,—It means to pronounce innocent, to free from guilt. Thus Judah was to be purged from her guilt (the shedding of blood), the climax of her sin which for long had been visited with judgments.

Nowack and Schmoller render, "I will avenge Israel's blood", i. e., I will not leave unpunished the shedders of it. The first explanation, however, adheres more closely to the original meaning of the word.

That Joel's prophecy is to find its final and completest fulfillment in *"the last day"*, in times yet to come, is the usually accepted view. As Schmoller says, "The final and complete fulfillment will come only with the consummation of the kingdom at the Parousia, or Second Advent of our Lord."

This explanation of the prophecy is favored by:

1. The usual two-fold application of this and similar prophecies.
2. Peter's statement that the promise is "unto them that are afar off".
3. The as yet unfulfilled verses 17 (of which the very opposite is as yet the case), 18 and 20.

Says Farrar, "By the expression 'a great people' in Chap. 2.2, the host of Assyria may be primarily meant (Isa. 37.36), but ultimately the last antichristian confederacy destroyed by special divine interposition is meant, and while Chap. 2.28 was fulfilled in earnest at Pentecost, it will be hereafter more fully fulfilled at the restoration of Israel (Isa. 53.13; Jer. 31.9,34; Ezk. 39.29; Zech. 12.10) and the consequent conversion of the whole world, (Isa. 11.9; 66.18-23; Mic. 5.7; Rom. 11.12,15), and while the reference of verse 16 of this last chapter may be to the victories of the Jews over their cruel foe Antiochus Epiphanes, under the Maccabees, the ultimate reference is to the last Antichrist of whom Antiochus Epiphanes was but the type."

Scofield says, "The whole picture is of the end-time of this present age, of the 'times of the Gentiles'; of the battle of Armageddon; of the re-gathering of Israel and of kingdom blessing. The order of events is: (1) The invasion of Palestine from the north by Gentile world-powers headed up under the Beast and the false prophet (Joel 2.1-10. See Rev. 16.14); (2) the Lord's army and the destruction of the invaders (Joel 2.11; Rev. 19.11-21; (3) the repentance of Judah in the land (Joel 2.12-17; Deut. 30.1-9); (4) the answer of Jehovah (Joel 2.18-27); (5) the effusion of the Spirit in the (Jewish) 'last days' (Joel 2.28,29; (6) the return of the Lord in glory and the setting up of the kingdom (Joel. 2.30-32; Acts 15.15-17) by the regathering of the nation and the judgment of the nations (Joel 3.1-16); (7) the full and permanent blessing (Joel 3.17-21; Zech. 14.1-21; Matt. 25.32)."

THE BOOK OF

AMOS

(B. C. 787—B. C. 763)

Amos prophesied in the northern kingdom (Israel). Within fifty years his warnings were fulfilled, the kingdom being utterly destroyed. The vision of Amos, however, did not stop with the northern kingdom, but included in certain respects the whole "house of Jacob".

The judgment on Judah was fulfilled in the seventy years' captivity, and that on Israel, the northern kingdom, in the world-wide dispersion which continues to the present day.

CHAPTER FIVE

16 Therefore thus saith Jehovah, the God of hosts, the Lord: Wailing shall be in all the broad ways; and they shall say in all the streets, Alas! alas! and they shall call the husbandman to mourning, [1]and such as are skillful in lamentation to wailing. 17 And in all vineyards shall be wailing; for I will pass through the midst of thee, saith Jehovah.

[1]Heb. *and* proclaim *wailing to such as are skillful in lamentation*

18 Woe unto you that desire the day of Jehovah! Wherefore would ye have the day of Jehovah? It is darkness, and not light. 19 As if a man did flee from a lion, and a bear met him; [2]or went into the house and leaned his hand on the wall, and a serpent bit him. 20 Shall not the day of Jehovah be darkness, and not light? even very dark, and no brightness in it?

[2]Or, *and*

Vers. 16-20. THE DAY OF JEHOVAH, A DAY OF RIGHTEOUS RETRIBUTION.

Ver. 16. *"Therefore"*,—God foresees that they will not obey the exhortation. The sense of the verse is that on every side there will be dead to mourn for.

"such as are skillful in lamentation to wailing",—The professional mourners who were employed at funerals. Not only these, but the husbandmen were called to mourn, inasmuch as there will not be enough of the former because of the universal mourning which will prevail.

Ver. 17. *"in all the vineyards shall be wailing"*,—As in the cities, so in the land among the vineyards where usually songs of joy were heard, there will be the death-wail.

"for I will pass through the midst of thee",—Said perhaps with an allusion to Exodus 12.12, as if what happened in Egypt at the smiting of the first born would be repeated.

Ver. 18. *"Woe unto you that desire the day of the Lord"*,—Because they fancied that they, the carnal Israel, and the true people of God were identical, and that this day must of course bring to them as well as to the rest of Israel deliverance from distress, as well as great joy and glory. Therefore they did not scruple to say in irony, as if in ridicule of the threatening of Amos, that they desired the day of the Lord to come. Would not that be a day of victory to Israel? But the prophet tells them that for them it would be a calamity and a day of righteous retribution.

Ver. 19. Therefore should they escape one danger they would the more certainly fall into another. The figures are taken from everyday life and are quite clear as to their meaning.

"leaned his hand on the wall",—i. e., to support himself from falling. Serpents often hide themselves in a fissure in the wall.

CHAPTER EIGHT

In this chapter, under the symbol of a basket of summer fruit, Israel is shown to be a people ripened by sin for the severe judgment of destruction pronounced upon them. So many shall be the dead that in every place they shall cast them forth in silence, meaning perhaps that the terror of God and the dread of the enemy would make them afraid to speak (verse 3). *"In that day"*, i. e., the day of judgment mentioned by the prophet, the sun will go down at noon and the earth will tremble. The primary reference of these severe pronouncements is, of course, to the calamity that came upon Israel fifty years later, but the bold and startling language with which the predictions are clothed shows that *they look forward to a vaster fulfillment in time still future*, and that the whole is a type of the judgments upon the ungodly people in the great day of accounts.

CHAPTER NINE

1 I saw the Lord standing ¹beside the altar; and he said, Smite the capitals, that the thresholds may shake; and break them in pieces on the head of all of them; and I will slay the last of them with the sword; ²there shall not one of them flee away, and there shall not one of them escape.

8 Behold, the eyes of the Lord Jehovah are upon the sinful kingdom, and I will destroy it from off the face of the earth; save that I will not utterly de-

¹Or, *upon*
²Or, *he that fleeth of them shall not flee away, and he that escapeth of them shall not be delivered.*

stroy the house of Jacob, saith Jehovah.
9 For, lo, I will command, and I will
*sift the house of Israel among all the
nations, like as grain is sifted in a sieve,

³Heb. *cause to move to and fro.*

yet shall not the least kernel fall upon
the earth. 10 All the sinners of my
people shall die by the sword, who say,
The evil shall not overtake nor meet us.

Vers. 1, 8-10. A Vision of Jehovah Executing Judgment.

Ver. 1. It is difficult to know whether this judgment is to be taken
as upon Israel alone, or upon both Israel and Judah. If upon the former
then the *"altar"* is in the idolatrous temple at Bethel (F. He. Sm. Gr. Sch.),
but if upon both Israel and Judah, the *"altar"* is at Jerusalem (K. C. Fai.
Fal. Hen.). The latter view makes the exegesis a bit smoother; but inasmuch as Amos was a prophet especially for Israel, and the book has been
largely devoted to Israel, and because of the connection (Chap. 8.14) the
altar at Bethel, which is denounced in other parts of the book (Chap.
3.14; 4.4), seems to be the one in the vision, and it would therefore seem
best to apply the chapter with its judgment to Israel, although there is to
be sure a reference to Judah in verse 11.

Ver. 8. *"the eyes of the Lord Jehovah are upon the sinful kingdom"*,—Here the difficulty begins. The *"house of Jacob"* would seem
to belong to the kingdom of Judah, and if we make *"the sinful kingdom"*
to be Israel only, then the exception, the house of Jacob, would lie outside
of the subject treated. Keil removes the difficulty by taking *"the sinful
kingdom"* as embracing both Israel and Judah in one; and there are no
insuperable objections to this interpretation.

Schmoller relieves the situation by saying that *"the house of Jacob"*
is literally "the stock of Israel" and is here to be referred to the ten tribes,
i. e., to Israel, and *"the sinful kingdom"* thus refers without difficulty to
the kingdom of Israel alone.

Perhaps the best explanation is to think of the house of Jacob before
there was any division, and the prophet here then conceives of the Jewish
nation as *one* and says that *this* part of the house of Jacob, this part of the
nation, the ten tribes (Israel) shall not be utterly destroyed. A remnant
was to be spared for Jacob's sake to fulfill the covenant whereby *"the seed
of Israel"* is hereafter to be "a nation forever". (Jer. 30.11; 31.36)

Ver. 9. *"yet shall not the least kernel fall upon the earth"*,—The
Godly elect, the solid grains, are preserved while the chaff, the dust, falls
through to the ground. (Rom. 11.26.)

11 In that day will I raise up the
tabernacle of David that is fallen, and
close up the breaches thereof; and I
will raise up its ruins, and I will build
it as in the days of old; 12 that they
may possess the remnant of Edom, and
all the nations that ¹are called by my
name, saith Jehovah that doeth this.
13 Behold, the days come, saith Jehovah, that the plowman shall overtake
the reaper, and the treader of grapes
him that soweth seed; and the mountans

¹Or, *were*

shall drop sweet wine, and all the hills
shall melt. 14 And I will ²bring back
the captivity of my people Israel, and
they shall build the waste cities, and
inhabit them; and they shall plant vineyards, and drink the wine thereof; they
shall also make gardens, and eat the fruit
of them. 15 And I will plant them
upon their land, and they shall no more
be plucked up out of their land which
I have given them, saith Jehovah thy
God.

²Or, *return to*

Vers. 11-15. THE BLESSINGS OF THE FUTURE KINGDOM.

Ver. 11. *"In that day"*,—i. e., in the dispensation of the Messiah.

"the tabernacle of David that is fallen",—The fallen condition of this kingdom, which occurred more especially in the time of the Babylonian captivity, is presupposed. (K. Gr.) The literal meaning of the word used is "hut", showing its low condition during the days of Amos and subsequently during the Babylonian captivity before the restoration, as well also as before the restoration under the Messiah.

This tabernacle of David Jehovah promises to *"raise up"*. This promise was but partially and temporarily fulfilled under Zerubbabel, because this restoration did not include Israel, the main subject of this prophecy, while furthermore the kingdom of Zerubbabel was not an independent and settled one and of its subjects it could not be said, *"they shall no more be plucked up out of their land"* (verse 15).

The prophecy in this verse 11 certainly does turn to Judah, yet, as Schmoller says, "not so much as a separate kingdom, but only insofar as it furnishes the divinely appointed basis and point of departure for the restoration of the entire people".

Ver. 12. *"the remnant of Edom"*,—Edom, as the representative of all heathen nations, is mentioned because of these nations they were the most hostile to Israel, and by *"the remnant"* is expressed that part of Edom which had not already been subjugated.

"called by my name",—This expression, wherever used, is applied only to the covenant people of God, in conformity with which the meaning here must be that the recreated kingdom shall bear sway over Edom and other heathen nations which shall in consequence become a part of the covenant people. This seems therefore to be a prophecy of the calling of the Gentiles, and as such is quoted by James in Acts 15.17. Concerning this expression Fausset says, "who belong to me, whom I claim as mine (Psa. 2.8); in the purposes of electing grace, God terms them already called by his name". The possession then spoken of here is to be spiritually realized. (F. Gr.) (Isa. 49.8; 54.8; Rom. 4.13.)

Amos shows that nothing was to be hoped for by the ten tribes apart from connection with Judah.

Ver. 13. *"Behold the days come"*,—i. e., when Israel is "planted upon their land" (verse 15) when the Jews shall have been restored to their own land.

"the ploughman . . . . . and the treader",—Such shall be the abundance of the harvest and the vintage that they can hardly be gathered before the time shall come for the preparing for the next crop.

Ver. 15. *"they shall no more be plucked up out of their land"*,— (See Jer. 32.41.) This is most certainly a distinct expression of the final abolition of an exile; never again shall the restored exiles be carried away by enemies. The promise in verses 11 to 15 is to the nation as a whole.

Schmoller says, "An unprejudiced comparison shows that the prophecy transcends the experience. This fact does not show that the threatening is unfounded, but that it has an eschatological character. The prophet, indeed, sees the last decisive judgment arise, but still the judgment which came historically upon the ten tribes was not this last decisive one. The prophecy was further fulfilled when Jerusalem was destroyed by the Romans, but it still awaits its complete fulfillment in the last judgment at the *Parousia* upon the entire body of the apostate members of the people of God of whom Israel was a type." This same expositor further says that because the judgment was fulfilled in literal Israel is no sign that the promise must likewise be so fulfilled in Israel after the flesh. He with many others think of this promise as being fulfilled now in the New Testament Israel. James says in Acts 15.17 that verse 12 was fulfilled in Christ, and if this be so, then in a very certain sense the fulfillment of the raising up of the tabernacle of David ought also to be found in Christ.

If this, and other prophecies like it, are to be taken literally, then we must look for a literal restoration of the Jews to the land of Palestine sometime in the future, inasmuch as it did not occur in times now past. (See "Doctrinal and Moral" in Lange's Commentary under this chapter.)

THE BOOK OF

OBADIAH

(B. C. 586)

Vers. 1-16. The condemnation and coming destruction of Edom together with the rest of the foes of Israel.

15 For the day of Jehovah is near upon all the nations; as thou hast done, it shall be done unto thee; thy ¹dealing shall return upon thine own head. 16 For as ye have drunk upon my holy mountain, so shall all the nations drink continually; yea, they shall drink, and ²swallow down, and shall be as though they had not been.

¹Or, *recompense*

²Or, *talk foolishly*

Vers. 15,16. THE DAY OF JEHOVAH AND THE PUNISHMENT OF THE UNGODLY.

Ver. 15. *"the day of Jehovah"*,—The day in which the Lord will manifest Himself as the righteous punisher of the ungodly people. It is the day introduced in verse 8.

"upon all the nations",—"The range", says Klieforth, "extends to a universal judgment." "It shows", says Fausset, "that the fulfillment is not exhausted in the punishment inflicted upon the surrounding nations by the instrumentality of Nebuchadnezzar, but as in Joel 3.14 and in Zech. 12.3, the last judgment to come on the nations confederate against Jerusalem is referred to."

Ver. 16. *"ye"*,—Some explain, "ye Jews", the prophet suddenly shifting his address for a moment. (F. Sm. Ma.) Others explain, "ye Edomites". (C. Kle.) By the first explanation *"drunk"* refers to the cup of affliction, being dispossessed of their goods and lands by Edom and all the nations: so shall all the heathen nations drink the same cup. By the second explanation *"drunk"* refers to the cup of exultation, i. e., taking part in the wild revelry of the destroyers and so shall they drink the cup of wrath from God's hand.   The latter seems preferable.

17 But in mount Zion there shall be those that escape, and it shall be holy; and the house of Jacob shall possess their possessions.   18 And the house of Jacob shall be a fire, and the house of Joseph a flame, and the house of Esau for stubble, and they shall burn among them, and devour them; and there shall not be any remaining to the house of Esau; for Jehovah hath spoken it.   19 And they of the South shall possess the mount of Esau, and they of the low-land the Philistines; and they shall possess the field of Ephraim, and the field of Samaria; and Benjamin *shall possess* Gilead.   20 And the captives of this [1]host of the children of Israel, [2]that are *among* the Canaanites, *shall possess* even unto Zarephath; and the captives of Jerusalem, that are in Sepharad, shall possess the cities of the South.   21 And saviours shall come up on mount Zion to judge the mount of Esau; and the kingdom shall be Jehovah's.

[1]Or, *fortress*
[2]Or, shall possess *that which* belongeth to *the Canaanites, even &c.*   Or, *that are* among *the Canaanites, even unto Zarephath, and &c.*

Vers. 17-21.   THE RE-ESTABLISHMENT OF THE JEWS IN THEIR OWN POSSESSIONS.

Ver. 17.   *"those that escape"*,—Unlike Judah's heathen foes of whom no remnant shall escape, a remnant of the Jews shall escape when the rest of the nation has perished.

"it shall be holy",—It shall be inviolable, no longer profaned by strangers.

Ver. 18.   The *"house of Jacob"* is the kingdom of Judah, and the *"house of Joseph"* is the kingdom of Israel, and through the burning zeal of God in them, the one shall become a *"fire"* and the other a *"flame"*, the two forming one kingdom, their former feuds being laid aside.

"This was but an earnest", says Fausset, "of the future union of Judah and Israel in the possession of the enlarged land as one kingdom. (Ezek. 37.16.)"

Ver. 19.   *"And they of the South"*,—The men of Judah, who in the coming time are to occupy the south of Judea, shall also possess in addition to their own territory the adjoining mountainous region of Edom.

"and they of the lowland",—This refers also to Judah, who in the coming time is to occupy the lowland in the west of Judea, but shall also possess the land of the Philistines, the people being here put for the land.

"and they",—The reference is still to the men of Judah.

Ephraim and Samaria formerly belonged to the Ten tribes.

"and Benjamin",—The other tribe composing Judah shall possess Gilead, east of the Jordan, and so the dominion returns to Judah (Gen. 49.10) and the whole land is brought back to the House of David by the two tribes who had remained true to it.   (Jer. 32.44.)

The *"they"* of this verse is by some referred to the Ten tribes.   This makes an abrupt and an unnatural passage from the previous subject, but it makes them possess the land that was originally theirs (Ephraim and Samaria).   These same authorities then refer *"the children of Israel"* of verse 20 to the Ten tribes also, and this seems natural because Jerusalem of verse 20 refers to Judah, the Two tribes, and thus the parallelism is the better carried.   But all things considered, the explanation we have already given is the preferable one.

Ver. 20.   *"captives"*,—Those who were "carried away".

"host of the children of Israel",—The twelve tribes united under Judah.

"among the Canaanites",—In Phoenicia and western Palestine.

"even unto Zarephath",—Near Zidon.   Mentioned in Luke 4.26.

"in Sepharad",—A district of western Asia about Lydia and near the Bosphorus.   (F. Vul. Jer. Say. Che. Kle.)

There are four interpretations of the first clause of this verse:

1. "And the captives of this host of the children of Israel that are among the Canaanites even unto Zarephath, and the captives that are in Jerusalem, that are in Sepharad shall possess the cities of the South."   (He. Ma. Um. Pu. Cas.)

2. "And the captives of this host of the children of Israel shall become the Canaanites which there are even unto Zarephath", etc. This is the view of Kleinert, but it will hardly do to arbitrarily supply, as he does, the words "shall become" and "there are".

3. "And the captivity of this host of the children of Israel shall possess that of the Canaanites, even unto Zarephath, and the captivity of Jerusalem, which is in Sepharad, shall possess the cities of the South."   (A. V. F. Sm. Hit. Sep.)

4. The rendering of the Revised Version as set forth in our text.

Both the third and fourth views supply "shall possess" before the words, *"even unto Zarephath"*.   This is quite allowable, but between the two the rendering of the Revised Version is preferable.   In fact, it is far more natural than either of the other views, the word *"among"*, which it supplies, corresponding with the word *"in"* in the latter part of the verse.

Inasmuch as the distribution of the land as set forth in these verses has never taken place, it would seem as though it ought to take place in the future.   The general conception of the true Israel, the people of God in a spiritual sense, inheriting the earth may be set forth as a spiritual fulfilling of the Old Testament prophecies in general, but how such minute details as the very portions of land which the different tribes shall possess can be spiritualized is difficult to see.

Ver. 21.   *"saviours"*,—This does not refer to kings, but the rather to heroes like the Maccabees.

Edom is, of course, a type of Israel's foes and of God's last foes.   Keil calls attention to the fact that the destruction of Edom and the occupation of Seir by Israel must, according to Numbers 24.18, proceed from the Ruler that shall arise out of Jacob, the Messiah.   According to Amos 9.11, however, not until the setting up of the tabernacles of Judah that have fallen down, and not until, according to Obadiah, on the day of Jehovah, at and after the judgment of all the peoples, will it follow.   The fulfillment of verses 17 to 21 can therefore only belong to the Messianic period, so that it began in a spiritual sense with the establishment of the kingdom of Christ on earth and proceeds with its extension among the peoples of the earth, and will in this sense be fully accomplished with its final completion at the second coming of the Lord. But in the literal sense it would seem, as we have shown, to call for a fulfillment which is yet altogether in the future.

THE BOOK OF

MICAH

(B. C. 750—B. C. 710)

CHAPTER TWO

12 I will surely assemble, O Jacob, all of thee; I will surely gather the remnant of Israel; I will put them together as the sheep of Bozrah, as a flock in the midst of their pasture; they shall make great noise by reason of the multitude of men.

13 The breaker is gone up before them: they have broken forth and passed on to the gate, and are gone out thereat; and their king is passed on before them, and Jehovah at the head of them.

Vers. 12,13.   THE PROMISE TO THE REMNANT.

Some authorities put verses 12 and 13 in the mouth of the false prophets. (Ew. Kle. Hof. Hart.) But there is hardly sufficient ground for this view, although the words do seem a bit abrupt when put in the mouth of Micah. However, the reference to the *"remnant"* is hardly appropriate to the false prophets, and so we prefer with the majority to refer the words to Micah. (F. K. Pu. Ma. Hen. Hit. Cas.) For a similar transition see Hos. 1.9,10.

Ver. 12.   *"all of thee"*,—The restoration from Babylon was but partial, and this is of course therefore Messianic and finds its spiritual fulfillment in the people of God of this dispensation, and its literal fulfillment, as Fausset says, in the still future restoration of Israel as mentioned in Romans 11.26.

"remnant",—The elect remnant which is to survive all previous calamities.

"Bozrah",—A region famed for its rich pastures.

"multitude of men",—God can make a remnant into a multitude.

Ver. 13.   *"the breaker"*,—The Messiah.

"they",—The returning Israelites.

"through the gate",—i. e., the gate of the foe's city where they had been held captive.

"their king",—The king out of the House of David, the Messiah, the "Breaker".

"Jehovah at the head of them",—As in the marches in the desert. (Num. 10.35; Ex. 13.21.)

263

CHAPTER FOUR

1 But in the latter days it shall come to pass, that the mountain of Jehovah's house shall be established [1]on the top of the mountains, and it shall be exalted above the hills; and peoples shall flow unto it. 2 And many nations shall go and say, Come ye, and let us go up to the mountain of Jehovah, and to the house of the God of Jacob; and he will teach us of his ways, and we will walk in his paths. For out of Zion shall go forth [2]the law, and the word of Jehovah from Jerusalem; 3 and he will judge [3]between [4]many peoples, and will decide concerning strong nations afar off: and they shall beat their swords into plowshares, and their spears into pruninghooks; nation shall not lift up sword against nation, neither shall they learn war any more. 4 But they shall sit every man under his vine and under his fig-tree; and none shall make them afraid: for the mouth of Jehovah of hosts hath spoken it. 5 For all the peoples walk every one in the name of his god; and we will walk in the name of Jehovah our God for ever and ever. 6 In that day, saith Jehovah, will I assemble that which is lame, and I will gather that which is driven away, and that which I have afflicted; 7 and I will make that which was lame a remnant, and that which was cast far off a strong nation: and Jehovah will reign over them in mount Zion from henceforth even for ever. 8 And thou, O tower of [5]the flock, [6]the hill of the daughter of Zion, unto thee shall it come, yea, the former dominion shall come, the kingdom of the daughter of Jerusalem.

9 Now why dost thou cry out aloud? Is there no king in thee, is thy counsellor perished, that pangs have taken hold of thee as of a woman in travail? 10 Be in pain, and labor to bring forth, O daughter of Zion, like a woman in travail; for now shalt thou go forth out of the city, and shalt dwell in the field, and shalt come even unto Babylon: there shalt thou be rescued; there will Jehovah redeem thee from the hand of thine enemies. 11 And now many nations are assembled against thee, that say, Let her be defiled, and let our eye [7]see our desire upon Zion. 12 But they know not the thoughts of Jehovah, neither understand they his counsel; for he hath gathered them as the sheaves to the threshing-floor. 13 Arise and thresh, O daughter of Zion: for I will make thy horn iron, and I will make thy hoofs brass; and thou shalt beat in pieces many peoples: and I will devote their gain unto Jehovah, and their substance unto the Lord of the whole

[1]Or, at the head
[2]Or, instruction
[3]Or, among
[4]Or, great

[5]Or, Eder. See Gen. 35.21.
[6]Heb. Ophel
[7]Or, gaze upon

Vers. 1-13. THE FUTURE KINGDOM AND THE REGATHERING OF ISRAEL.

Ver. 1. The first three verses of this chapter are almost word for word like Isa. 2.2-4. The majority seem to think that Isaiah quoted from Micah.

"In the latter days",—The word "latter" literally means the "hindmost", the "farthest", whether of space or time—the last of the days, and is translated by Alexander and others, "in the end of the days". The phrase according to Jewish interpreters always means the days of the Messiah.

"the mountain of Jehovah's house",—Mount Zion in the widest sense including Mount Moriah where the Temple stood.

"on the top of the mountains",—It is better to retain the literal reading of the margin, "at the head of the mountains". Alexander translates, "high among". It means raised and fixed above the other mountains so as to be visible in all directions.

"exalted",—The reference is to a moral exultation and dignity and not to physical elevation.

Kleinert insists that we have here a figurative reference to the Christian

Church and that the ideal significance of both sentences is proven by the parallel third member, the *"flowing"* being a spiritual one (verse 3) and compatible with the nations *"afar off"* staying at home.

Fausset, on the other hand, declares that the restoration from Babylon is but a type of the restoration of Israel hereafter and that Israel, and not merely the Christian Church, is the ultimate subject of the prophecy, one of the encouragements for this contention being the unsearchable wisdom of God's thoughts as set forth in Isa. 55.8 as the ground for this restoration, which matter he says is again in mind in verse 12 of this chapter. The truth is, of course, to be found in both of these views taken together.

Ver. 2. *"mountain of Jehovah"*,—Mount Zion.

"the law",—The word means literally, "instruction", and the reference is not merely to the Jewish law as such but to a rule of life from God.

Ver. 3. *"judge between"*,—This does not mean to "rebuke" (A-V.), nor to "convince" (C. V. Coc.), but to "decide concerning". It means to arbitrate, to decide their differences.

"beat their swords into plowshares",—The more particular reference here is to the swords still drawn against God's kingdom. (Joel 4.10.)

Ver. 5. *"all the peoples"*,—All the heathen peoples walk in the name of their several gods, but as for the Jews in dispersion they will walk in the name of Jehovah forever.

Their Babylonian captivity cured them of their idolatry, and so it seems their present dispersion must cure them of their unbelief.

Ver. 6. *"lame . . . driven away . . . afflicted"*,—The suffering children of Israel will then after hard blows and rejection, be graciously gathered together again.

Ver. 7. *"remnant"*,—They were to be treated as the remnant to whom the promise applies and were to be made into a strong nation.

"Jehovah",—The Messiah, of course, is meant although Micah speaks of Him as Jehovah.

"from henceforth",—i. e., from the time of the fulfillment on.

Ver. 8. *"tower of the flock"*,—That Jerusalem is meant is proven by the next clause, *"the hill of the daughter of Zion"*, which hill was an impregnable height on Mount Zion. The reference is probably to the tower of David. In large pastures it was customary to erect wooden towers so as to overlook the flocks, and therefore it is a shepherd relation between Jehovah and His people that is here mentioned. (F. K. Hen.)

"the former dominion . . . . the kingdom",—The kingdom in its former glory.

Ver. 9. *"Is there no king in thee?"*—This is asked tauntingly,—there is a king in Zion but he is powerless to help against the advancing foe.

"counsellor",—This is an explanatory synonym for "king".

The first question of this verse is addressed to Zion as she sees the Assyrian army approaching.

Ver 10. *"now shalt thou go forth out of the city"*,—i. e., upon its capture.

"dwell in the field",—Defenseless instead of being in a fortified city.

"unto Babylon",—Micah looks beyond the threatening Assyrian power to the captivity under Babylon.

"there will Jehovah redeem thee",—Through Cyrus, the type of the coming Messiah.

Ver. 11. *"many nations"*,—Many see here a reference to the oppression under Antiochus Epiphanes. This, however, seems to be opposed by *"now"* and by the term *"nations"*, which can hardly refer to the mercenary collections of this king, but may very properly designate the subject peoples composing Babylon's army, together perhaps with Edom, Amon, etc., who exulted in Judah's downfall.

Ver. 13. *"Arise and thresh"*,—i. e., destroy the foes gathered by Jehovah as sheaves.

CHAPTER FIVE

1 Now shalt thou gather thyself in troops, O daughter of troops: he hath laid siege against us; they shall smite the judge of Israel with a rod upon the cheek.

2 But thou, Beth-lehem Ephrathah, which art little to be among the ¹thousands of Judah, out of thee shall one come forth unto me that is to be ruler in Israel; whose goings forth are from of old, ²from everlasting. 3 Therefore will he give them up, until the time that she who travaileth hath brought forth: then the residue of his brethren shall return ³unto the children of Israel. 4 And he shall stand, and shall feed *his flock in* the strength of Jehovah, in the majesty of the name of Jehovah his God: and they shall abide; for now shall he be great unto the ends of the earth. 5 And this *man* shall be *our* peace. When the Assyrian shall come into our land, and when he shall tread in our palaces, then shall we raise against him seven shepherds, and eight ⁴principal men. 6 And they shall waste the land of Assyria with the sword, and the land of Nimrod in the entrances thereof: and he shall deliver us from the Assyrian, when he cometh into our land, and when he treadeth within our border. 7 And the remnant of Jacob shall be in the midst of many peoples as dew from Jehovah, as showers upon the grass, that tarry not for man, nor wait for the sons of men. 8 And the remnant of Jacob shall be among the nations, in the midst of many peoples, as a lion among the beasts of the forest, as a young lion among the flocks of sheep; who, if he go through, treadeth down and teareth in pieces, and there is none to deliver.

9 Let thy hand be lifted up above thine adversaries, and let all thine enemies be cut off.

10 And it shall come to pass in that day, saith Jehovah, that I will cut off thy horses out of the midst of thee, and will destroy thy chariots: 11 and I will cut off the cities of thy land, and will throw down all thy strongholds. 12 And I will cut off witchcrafts out of thy hand; and thou shalt have no more soothsayers: 13 and I will cut off thy graven images and thy ⁵pillars out of the midst of thee; and thou shalt no more worship the work of thy hands; 14 and I will pluck up thine Asherim out of the midst of thee; and I will destroy thy ⁶cities. 15 And I will execute vengeance in anger and wrath upon the nations ⁷which hearkenth not.

¹Or, *families.* See Judg. 6.15
²Or, *from ancient days*
³Or, *with*
⁴Or, *princes among men*
⁵Or, *obelisks*
⁶Or, *enemies*
⁷Or, *such as they have not heard*

Vers. 1-15. THE BIRTH OF THE KING, THE DISPERSION OF ISRAEL, AND THE KINGDOM AGE.

Lest they fall into carnal security he reminds them of the calamities which are to precede the prosperity.

Ver. 1. *"daughter of troops"*,—She is so-called because of her numerous troops.

"he",—i. e., the enemy, Assyria-Babylon.

"smite upon the cheek",—The greatest of insults.

"the judge"—The one who stands at the head. If the king is meant he was perhaps not so called because that dignity was reserved for the Messiah just to be announced. Hengstenberg says the expression marks a time when there was no king.

Ver. 2. *"the thousands of Judah"*,—Each tribe was divided into "thousands", each thousand containing a thousand families.

Ver. 3. *"them"*,—i. e., Israel, given into the hands of her enemies.

"she who travaileth",—"This", says Fausset, "cannot be restricted wholly to the Virgin Mary (Hen.), for Israel is still given up, though the Messiah has been brought forth eighteen and a half centuries ago. But the Church's throes are to be included, which are only to be ended when Christ shall at last appear as the Deliverer of Jacob, and when the times of the Gentiles shall have been fulfilled, and Israel, as a nation, shall be born in a day." (Isa. 66.7-11; Lu. 21.24.) Kleinert thinks the people of Judah are meant. (See Chap. 4.8.)

"then the residue of his brethren shall return",—The remainder of the Israelites dispersed in foreign lands both of Judah and the ten tribes. (F. K. Kle. Hof. Cas.)

Scofield's remarks are of interest at this point; he says, "Micah 5.1,2 forms a parenthesis in which the 'word of the Lord' goes back from the time of the great battle of Armageddon (closing part of preceding chapter), yet future, to the birth and rejection of the King, Messiah-Christ. This is followed by the statement that He will 'give them up until the time that she which travaileth hath brought forth'. There is a twofold travail of Israel: (1) that which brings forth the 'man-child' (Christ) (Rev. 12. 1-3); and (2) that which, in the last days brings forth a believing 'remnant' out of the still dispersed and unbelieving nation (ver. 3; Jer. 30. 6-14; Mic. 4.10). In verse 7 we have the 'man-child', the Christ of Rev. 12.1-3; in verses 8-24 the remnant established in kingdom blessing. The meaning of verse 3 is that from the rejection of Christ at His first coming Jehovah will give Israel up till the believing remnant appears; then He stands and feeds in His proper strength as Jehovah; He is the defense of His people, and afterward the remnant go as missionaries to Israel and to all the world."

Ver. 4. *"he"*,—The Messiah.

"they",—Both the returning remnant and the Israelites previously delivered.

"great unto the ends of the earth",—His kingdom becomes a universal kingdom of great power.

Ver. 5. *"this man"*,—i. e., the one just mentioned.

"the Assyrian",—Whatever Assyrian it may be, i. e., Assyria as the representative of all the foes of Israel in all ages.

"seven shepherds and eight principal men",—An idiom for a full and sufficient number.

Ver. 6. *"land of Nimrod"*,—i. e., Babylon.

"he",—This in both instances in this verse means the Messiah.

Ver. 7. *"as dew"*,—i. e., quickening them by a blessed influence as dew does the grass.

Ver. 8. *"as a lion"*,—i. e., striking terror by her power into all opponents.

Ver. 9. *"Let thy hand be lifted up"*,—i.e., that through it and by it God may smite.

Vers. 10,11. *"horses . . . . strongholds"*,—Israel will no longer depend upon these because war will be no longer.

"I will cut off witchcrafts",—i. e., the witchcraft which thou now useth.

Ver. 13. The reference here is to stone and molten images and statues for idolatry.

Ver. 14. *"Asherim"*,—i. e., *"groves"*,—the idolatrous symbol of Astarte.

"thy cities",—The cities where were the seats of false worship or near which the "groves" existed.

CHAPTER SEVEN

1 Woe is me! for I am as when they have gathered the summer fruits, as the grape gleanings of the vintage: there is no cluster to eat; [1]my soul desireth the first-ripe fig.
2 The godly man is perished out of the earth, and there is none upright among men: they all lie in wait for blood; they hunt every man his brother with a net.
3 [2]Their hands are upon that which is evil to do it diligently; the prince asketh, and the judge is ready for a reward; and the great man, he uttereth the evil desire of his soul; thus they weave it together. 4 The best of them is as a brier; [3]the most upright is *worse* than a thorn hedge: the day of thy watchmen, even thy visitation, is come; now shall be their perplexity. 5 Trust ye not in a neighbor; put ye not confidence in a [4]friend; keep the doors of thy mouth from her that lieth in thy bosom. 6 For the son dishonoreth the father, the daughter riseth up against her mother, the daughter-in-law against her mother-in-law; a man's enemies are the men of his own house.

7 But as for me, [5]I will look unto Jehovah; I will wait for the God of my salvation: my God will hear me. 8 Rejoice not against me, O mine enemy: when I fall, I shall arise; when I sit in darkness, Jehovah will be a light unto me. 9 I will bear the indignation of Jehovah, because I have sinned against him, until he plead my cause, and execute judgment for me: he will bring me forth to the light, *and* I shall behold his righteousness. 10 Then mine enemy shall see it, and shame shall cover her who said unto me, Where is Jehovah thy God? Mine eyes shall see *my desire* upon her; now shall she be trodden down as the mire of the streets. 11 [6]A day for building thy walls! in that day shall the [7]decree be far removed. 12 In that day shall they come unto thee from Assyria and the cities of [8]Egypt, and from Egypt even to the River, and from sea to sea, and *from* mountain to mountain. 13 Yet shall the land be desolate because of them that dwell therein, for the fruit of their doings.
14 [9]Feed thy people with thy rod, the flock of thy heritage, which dwell

[1]Or, *nor first-ripe fig which my soul desired*
[2]Or, *Both hands are put forth for evil to do it, &c.*
[3]Or, *the straightest is* as it were taken *from &c.*
[4]Or, *confidant*

[5]Or, *in Jehovah will I keep watch*
[6]Or, *In the day that thy walls are to be built*
[7]Or, *boundary*
[8]Heb. *Mazor*
[9]Or, *Rule*

solitarily, in the forest in the midst of Carmel: let them feed in Bashan and Gilead, as in the days of old. 15 As in the days of thy coming forth out of the land of Egypt will I show unto them marvellous things. 16 The nations shall see and be ashamed of all their might; they shall lay their hand upon their mouth; their ears shall be deaf. 17 They shall lick the dust like a serpent; like crawling things of the earth they shall come trembling out of their close places; they shall come with fear unto Jehovah our God, and shall be afraid because of thee.

18 Who is a God like unto thee, that pardoneth iniquity, and passeth over the transgression of the remnant of his heritage? he retaineth not his anger for ever, because he delighteth in lovingkindness. 19 He will again have compassion upon us; he will [10]tread our iniquities under foot; and thou wilt cast all their sins into the depths of the sea. 20 [11]Thou wilt [12]perform the truth to Jacob, *and* the lovingkindness to Abraham, which thou hast sworn unto our fathers from the days of old.

[10]Or, *subdue our iniquities*
[11]Or, *Thou wilt show* thy *faithfulness &c.*
[12]Heb. *give*

Vers. 1-20. THE VOICE OF THE REMNANT IN THE LAST DAYS.

Personified Israel is here speaking through the prophet. In other words Micah speaks as the organ of the true Israel.

Ver. 4. *"the day of thy watchman"*,—i. e., the day foretold by thy true prophets, the day of their visitation, the day of the Lord.

"their",—i. e., those to whom reference has just been made.

"now",—i. e., in the day of their perplexity.

Ver. 7. *"I will look unto Jehovah"*,—"She did so under Babylonian captivity", says Alford, "and she shall do so again hereafter when the Spirit of grace shall be poured upon her." (Zech. 12.6.)

Ver. 8. *"rejoice not against me"*,—Israel addresses her triumphant foe. This foe is a type of her last and worst enemy. (Ps. 137.7,8.)

Ver. 9. *"execute judgment for me"*,—i. e., against my enemies.

"bring me forth to the light",—i. e., out of the darkness of captivity.

"his righteousness",—His gracious faithfulness to His promises.

Ver. 11. The anticipation of the exile goes forward and from the certainty of the threatenings the prophet expects the restoration of Jerusalem.

"a day for building thy walls",—i. e., by Cyrus. Fausset says, "And again hereafter when the Jews shall be restored". (Amos 9.11; Zech. 12.6.)

"in that day shall the decree be far removed",—It is impossible to discover the exact meaning of this phrase. The word *"decree"* may also mean "law" or "boundary". Among the explanations are the following:

1. The tyrannical decree or rule of Babylon. (F. Hen.)
2. The decree of God for her captivity. (Henry.)
3. The law in its widest and most general sense and the reference is to its abolition in New Testament times. (Kle.)
4. The boundary of the city shall be extended, i. e., so as to contain the people flocking into it from all nations. (Ma.)
5. The boundary of the land shall be far extended, her territory increased. (Cas.)

6. The boundary between Israel and the nations shall be removed, and so shall Israel's exclusiveness be removed. (K.)

Views 1 and 2 taken together furnish perhaps the best explanation.

Ver. 12. *"unto thee"*,—i. e., the restored Zion.

"they",—i. e., the heathen peoples.

"from Assyria",—i. e., first of all from the nation that had been her scourge.

"the River",—i. e., Euphrates.

"from sea . . . from mountain",—Perhaps from the Mediterranean on the west to the Persian sea on the east, and from Mount Zion on the south to Mount Lebanon on the north.

Ver. 13. They must not forget the visitation of calamity upon their land which must intervene.

Ver. 14. Here personified Israel speaks again.

"dwell solitarily",—i. e., in the midst of captivity.

Ver. 15. Jehovah answers the prayer.

"them",—i. e., Israel.

Ver. 16. Here Micah speaks.

"lay their hand upon their mouth",—Their speech shall be taken away by reason of astonishment.

"Their ears shall be deaf",—They shall close their ears, "so as not to be compelled to hear of Israel's successes", (F.), "before the thunder of Jehovah's mighty deeds". (Hit. Kle.)

Ver. 17. *"close places"*,—i. e., hiding places.

"thee",—Maurer refers this to Jehovah, but it is better with Fausset and others to refer it to Israel.

Ver. 18. Personified Israel speaks again.

"remnant",—The elect remnant of grace.

Ver. 19. The *"us"* and the *"our"* refer to Israel in the first person, and the *"their"* refers to the same in the third person.

THE BOOK OF

ZEPHANIAH

(B. C. 630—B. C. 611)

CHAPTER ONE

7 Hold thy peace at the presence of the Lord Jehovah; for the day of Jehovah is at hand; for Jehovah hath prepared a sacrifice, he hath consecrated his guests.

14 The great day of Jehovah is near, it is near and hasteth greatly, even the voice of the day of Jehovah; the mighty man crieth there bitterly.

15 That day is a day of wrath, a day

of trouble and distress, a day of wasteness and desolation, a day of darkness and gloominess, a day of clouds and thick darkness, 16 a day of the trumpet and alarm, against the fortified cities, and against the high ¹battlements.

¹Or, *corner towers*

Vers. 7,14-16. JEHOVAH'S DAY OF WRATH COMING UPON JUDAH.

Ver. 7. *"Jehovah hath prepared a sacrifice"*,—The reference is to a slaughter of the guilty Jews, the Chaldeans being the guests.

The day of Jehovah is called, in verse 8, *"the day of Jehovah's sacrifice"*, and in verse 14 this day is described.

Ver. 14. *"The great day of Jehovah is near"*,—The day is always looked upon as near at hand. The reference is here of course to the judgment upon Judah through the Chaldeans.

"even the voice of the day of Jehovah",—As if Jehovah ushered in that day with a roar of vengeance. The word *"voice"* may as properly be taken as an interjection, "Hark, the day of Jehovah".

"the mighty man crieth bitterly",—Because he cannot save himself from the power of the foe.

Ver. 15. Of this verse Keil says, "All the words supplied by the language are crowded together to describe the terrors of the judgment". This Day of Jehovah is to be accompanied by terrible signs of destruction on earth and by troublous agitation of the elements.

Ver. 16. *"trumpet"*,—The war-signal of the besieging army.

"the high battlements",—The corner towers or embattlements behind which the wicked people vainly imagine themselves to be secure.

CHAPTER TWO

1 Gather yourselves together, yea, gather together, O nation that hath no ¹shame; 2 before the decree bring forth, ²*before* the day pass as the chaff, before the fierce anger of Jehovah come upon you, before the day of Jehovah's anger come upon you. 3 Seek ye Jehovah, all ye meek of the earth, that have kept his ordinances; seek righteousness, seek meekness: it may be ye will be hid in the day of Jehovah's anger.

6 And the sea-coast shall be pastures, with ³cottages for shepherds and folds for flocks.

7 And the coast shall be for the remnant of the house of Judah; they shall feed their flocks thereupon; in the houses of Ashkelon shall they lie down in the evening; for Jehovah, their God, will visit them and ⁴bring back their captivity.

11 Jehovah will be terrible unto them; for he will famish all the gods of the earth; and men shall worship him, everyone from his place, even all the ⁵isles of the nations.

¹Or, *longing*
²Or, (*the day passeth as the chaff*)
³Or, *caves*
⁴Or, *return to*
⁵Or, *coast-lands*

Vers. 1-3,6,7,11. REPENTANCE COMMANDED AND RESTORATION PROMISED.

Ver. 1. *"hath no shame"*,—i. e., the insolent and audacious nation. It is literally, "doth not grow pale". The word may be translated "longing", and thus mean there is no longing on the part of the nation to return to God. The address is to Judah.

Ver. 3. *"it may be you will be hid in the day of Jehovah's anger"*,

—This does not express doubt as to the fact of their deliverance, but the difficulty of it.

Ver. 6.   Philistia, instead of a land of thick population, shall become a pasture land.

"cottages",—The reference is doubtless to caves or dug-outs to protect the shepherds from the sun.

Ver. 7.   *"for the remnant of the house of Judah"*,—Judah after her judgment, upon her return from exile, is to inherit this pasture land for her flocks.

"Jehovah will visit them",—i. e., in mercy.

Ver. 11.   *"worship him everyone from his own place"*,—Some read into the word *"from"* the sense of *"going up to Jerusalem"*, and so make this the same idea as that in Micah 4.1 and Zech. 14.6, where the idea of going on pilgrimage to Jerusalem for worship is set forth.   (K. Kle. Hit.) But we see no reason for taking this other than it reads, and so we refer it to worshipping God everywhere, each one in his own home land.   (F. Ma. Wo.)

CHAPTER THREE

8 Therefore wait ye for me, saith Jehovah, until the day that I rise up to the prey; for my [1]determination is to gather the nations, that I may assemble the kingdoms, to pour upon them mine indignation, even all my fierce anger; for all the earth shall be devoured with the fire of my jealousy.

9 For then will I turn to the peoples a pure [2]language, that they may all call upon the name of Jehovah, to serve him with one [3]consent. 10 From beyond the rivers of Ethiopia [4]my suppliants, even the daughter of my dispersed, shall bring mine offering.   11 In that day shalt thou not be put to shame for all thy doings, wherein thou hast transgressed against me; for then I will take away out of the midst of thee [5]thy proudly exulting ones, and thou shalt no more be haughty in my holy mountain.   12 But I will leave in the midst of thee an afflicted and poor temple, and they shall take refuge in the name of Jehovah. 13 The remnant of Israel shall not do iniquity, nor speak lies; neither shall a deceitful tongue be found in their mouth; for they shall feed and lie down, and none shall make them afraid.

[1]Heb. *judgment*
[2]Heb. *lip*
[3]Heb. *shoulder*
[4]Or, *shall they bring my suppliants, even the daughter of my dispersed, for an offering unto me*
[5]Or, *them that exult in thy majesty*

14 Sing, O daughter of Zion; shout, O Israel; be glad and rejoice with all the heart, O daughter of Jerusalem.   15 Jehovah hath taken away thy judgments, he hath cast out thine enemy: the King of Israel, even Jehovah, is in the midst of thee; thou shalt not [6]fear evil any more.   16 In that day it shall be said to Jerusalem, Fear thou not; [7]O Zion, let not thy hands be slack.   17 Jehovah thy God is in the midst of thee, a mighty one who will save; he will rejoice over thee with joy; he will [8]rest in his love; he will joy over thee with singing.   18 [9]I will gather them that sorrow for the solemn assembly, who were of thee; *to whom* the burden upon [10]her was a reproach.   19 Behold, at that time I will deal with all them that afflict thee; and I will save that which is lame, and gather that which was driven away; and I will make them a praise and a name, whose shame hath been in all the earth.   20 At that time will I bring you in, and at that time will I gather you; for I will make you a name and a praise among all the peoples of the earth, when I [11]bring back your captivity before your eyes, saith Jehovah.

[6]Another reading is *see*
[7]Or, and to *Zion*
[8]Heb. *be silent*
[9]Or, *They have been sorrowful for the solemn assembly which I took away from thee*, for the *lifting up of reproach against her*
[10]According to another reading, *thee*
[11]Or, *return to*

Vers. 8-20.　Jerusalem Denounced But Her Joyful Re-estab-
　　　　　lishment Promised.

Ver. 8.　This verse is addressed not to the ungodly (C. Ma.), but
to the pious Jews.

"*rise up to the prey*",—i. e., like a savage beast rising from his lair
greedy for his prey.　(Matt. 24.28.)

"*gather the nations*",—i. e., against Jerusalem, to pour out his indignation upon them there (F. Kle.), and not in the sense that those among
them desirous of salvation shall fall a prey to Jehovah.　(See Joel 3.2:
Zech. 12.2 and 14.2.)

It is, says Kleinert, "the last act of the judgment, as it is a fixed
element of the prophetic eschatology, the final gathering of the heathen
nations before Jerusalem in order to be destroyed in the decisive struggle".
(Micah 4.12.)

Ver. 9.　"*For then*",—i. e., after the punishment and as a result of it.

"*peoples*",—The peoples which have hitherto with unclean lips
called upon their idols.

"*a pure language*",—Literally "a pure lip".

Ver. 10.　"*Ethiopia*",—The southern extremity of the then known
world, and here made the representatives of all Israel which shall be restored.

"*my suppliants, even the daughter of my dispersed*",—The reference
is of course to Israel.　This rendering, which makes the words nominative
and which is preferable, is supported by the context and also by Isa. 18.7.
(Lut. Hit. Mar. Kle. Vul.)

Others prefer the marginal reading.　(K. F. D. Wo. Hen. Stra.)
This puts the words "*suppliants*" and "*daughter*" in the objective case,
and thus represents the heathen as converting the Israelites dispersed among
them and as bringing them to God as an offering; but this is no doubt introduced from the reference in Isa. 66.20.

Ver. 11.　"*thou*",—i. e., Israel.

"*shalt not be put to shame*",—Because their transgressions will have
been removed.

"*proudly exulting ones*",—It is pride that brings shame, and there
had been those who boasted of their temple and their election as God's
people, etc.

"*no more be haughty*",—The converted remnant shall be of humble
spirit.

Ver. 12.　The blessed effect of sanctified affliction on the Jewish
remnant.

Ver. 14.　The prophet in mental vision sees the joyful day of Zion
and bids her rejoice at it.

Ver. 15.　"*thy judgments*",—When sin is renounced (verse 13)
judgments are removed.　The judgments are those threatened in verses
5 and 7.

Ver. 17. *"rest in his love"*,—The Hebrew word for *"rest"* is "be silent" and the reference is no doubt to the calm, quiet joy which He has in the possession of the object of His love.

Ver. 18. *"will gather"*,—i. e., from the dispersion.

"them that sorrow for the solemn assembly",—i. e., the solemn assembly which they could not celebrate in captivity.

"were of thee",—i. e., of Israel, of thy origin and thy descent.

"to whom",—i. e., to Israel. The meaning of the text as rendered is, "To whom (Israel) the burden (of Israel's captivity) upon her (Israel) was a reproach". This rendering follows the Hebrew more closely than does that of the Authorized Version, although either is allowable and makes practically the same sense, the reference in either case being to Israel in dispersion and longing for the solemn assembly.

Ver. 20. *"bring you in"*,—In the sense of Deut. 33.3,5.

"captivity",—This word is plural in the Hebrew and is so used to express perhaps all their captivities and the different places from which they will be caused to return.

"before your eyes",—Your own eyes shall see it, incredible as it may seem.

THE BOOK OF

HAGGAI

(B. C. 520)

CHAPTER TWO

6 For thus saith Jehovah of hosts: Yet once, it is a little while, and I will shake the heavens, and the earth, and the sea, and the dry land; 7 and I will shake all nations; and ¹the precious things of all nations shall come; and I will fill this house with glory, saith Jehovah of hosts. 8 The silver is mine, and the gold is mine, saith Jehovah of hosts. 9 The latter glory of this house shall be greater than the former, saith Jehovah of hosts; and in this place will I give peace, saith Jehovah of hosts.

¹Or, *the things desired* (Heb. *desire*) *of all nations shall come*

Vers. 6-9. THE GLORY OF THE FUTURE TEMPLE.

Ver. 6. The prophet calls upon the old men to witness to the insignificance of the present temple in comparison with the magnificence of the temple in the days of Solomon, and then he utters a prophecy concerning a temple which shall be built the glory of which shall be greater even than that of Solomon's.

"Yet once, it is a little while",—There are several translations of this phrase, all of which amount to practically the same thing, namely, that it would be only a little while until, etc.

    1. *"One period more, a brief one it is"*,—There will be one period more, and a brief one, between the then present and the predicted

great change of the world. (Hit. Hof. Del.) This is perhaps overworking the passage a bit.

2. "It is yet a little while",—The Hebrew for "once" is by this view considered an indefinite article or numeral adjective. (F. C. Ew. Um. Ru. Hen. Moo. Gro. Lut. Tar.) This view is quite acceptable, as the one or two grammatical objections which have been urged against it are not at all weighty.

3. "Once more (i. e., yet once), it is a little while",—This is perhaps the least objectionable grammatically and is therefore to be preferred. (K. Kle. Coc. Mar. Koe. Pre. Sep.)

"and I will shake the heavens", etc.,—The principal reference here is perhaps a figurative one. God's judgments are often represented under images drawn from the phenomena of nature. (Psa. 62; Psa. 18.7-15; Isa. 13.13; 64.1-3.) The thought then of this expression is that of violent political convulsions and judgments on His foes. Physical prodigies are not necessarily to be excluded. (Matt. 24.7,29.)

Ver. 7. "I will shake all nations",—i. e., I will judge among the nations (Psa. 110.6), shake them down until they shall lose hostility to Him. Fausset calls attention to the fact that Paul condenses together the two verses of Haggai, both 6 and 7 as well as 21 and 22, implying thereby that it was one and the same shaking of which the former verses of Haggai denote the beginning and the latter the end; and Fausset says, "The shaking began introductory to the first advent; it will be finished at the second. Concerning the former compare Matt. 3.17; 27.51; 28.2; Acts 2.2 and 4.31; concerning the latter compare Matt. 24.7; Rev. 16.20; 18.20 and 20.11."

Sir Isaac Newton says here, "There is scarcely a prophecy of the Messiah in the Old Testament which does not to some extent at least refer to His second coming."

"the precious things of all nations shall come",—The Authorized Version reads, "The Desire of all nations shall come", and the usual idea is that this refers to the Messiah.

This rendering has always been a favorite one. It is the rendering of the Vulgate, of all the Reformers excepting Calvin, of the older orthodox commentators, quite generally of the English expositors, and has more recently been adopted by Fausset. So confidently has this opinion been held that Ribera suspected the later Jews of having changed the verb to the plural so that it could not refer to the Messiah, after they had found that He had not, as they maintain, come to the temple and that it had been destroyed by Titus in A. D. 70. Of course this is not to be taken seriously. It is quite natural, as McCurdy says, that the Christian Church, in whose hymns and prayers this interpretation is still daily heard, should be loathe to give up a prediction which seemed to embody such a great and inspiring truth. But such an interpretation cannot as we will now see, stand the test of correct criticism.

The rendering of our text, "the precious things", or "the desirable things", is favored by the following considerations:

1. The Hebrew word means the quality of a thing rather than the thing itself, i. e., desirableness, beauty, etc.

2. The Messiah can hardly be said to be the desire of *all* nations. He was "a root out of a dry ground", having "no beauty that we should desire Him". (Isa. 53.2.)

3. If my *"all nations"* the Gentiles only are meant, what encouragement would it have been to the Jews to build the temple, which is the matter in mind, to tell them that One was coming who was the desire of all the Gentiles, i. e., *"all nations"?*

4. The *person* of the Messiah does not well connect with the expression, *"silver and gold"* of verse 8, which is introduced as confirmatory of this verse 7.

5. The verb *"shall come"* is plural and cannot therefore have a singular subject. This is the strongest objection to the Authorized rendering and it is impossible to evade the force of it.

Fausset prefers the old rendering, and answers the above objections to it after the following manner:

1. To the first objection he says the abstract is often put for the concrete. A "man of desires" is one desired or one who is desirable. (Dan. 9.23; 10.3,11.)

2. To the second objection he replies that if the Messiah was not desired, and it is not implied that the nations definitely desired Him, yet He was the only one to satisfy the yearning desires which all unconsciously felt for a Saviour, shown in their painful rites and bloody sacrifices. Moreover, while the Jews as a nation desired Him not (to which people Isa. 53.2 refers), the Gentiles, who are plainly pointed out by *"all nations"*, accepted Him; and so to them He was peculiarly desirable.

4. As to the fourth objection, he thinks that verse 8 harmonizes quite as well with the Authorized Version of verse 7; in the former of which verses Jehovah says that the silver and gold are His and consequently He could so adorn this temple if He chose, but He says He will adorn it with a glory far more precious, i. e., with the presence of His divine Son, in His veiled glory first, and at His second coming with His revealed glory. Then shall the nations bring offerings of those precious metals which ye now miss so much. (Isa. 2.3; 60.3,6,7; Ezek. 43.2,4,5; 44.4.)

5. To the fifth objection he replies that when a plural noun depends upon and follows a singular one, the verb in Hebrew may agree with the plural noun, being nearest to it. But this can be true only when the predicate may naturally be referred to the governed word as containing the controlling idea of the sentence. But this is not the case here; it is not the *nations* who are to come, but *the desire*, or as we prefer to translate, *the desirable things*, in which latter case there is no difficulty in explaining the plural verb.

It is quite evident from the above discussion that the rendering of our text is by far to be preferred, the more especially so since it is grammatically unassailable. The *"desirable things"* therefore refer to the precious things, i. e., gold, gifts, etc. Most of the later commentators have adopted this view. (K. C. Gr. Ma. Co. Ew. No. Ne. Cl. It. Hen. Hof. Koe. Sep. Syr. Ros. Moo. Kle. McC. Kim. Mor. Sco. Dru.)

It will not, however, do to think, with Henderson, of the things desired by the nations, realized in the blessings of the Messiah's reign. This explanation is not only irrelevant to the discourse as a whole, but it must be discarded as well because of the want of connection with the context. Some few authorities (Um. Ru. Hit. Fue.) take the word collectively and make the passage mean, "the most desirable among the Gentiles shall come". This is allowable so far as the Hebrew is concerned, but here also the connection with verse 8 fails us.

Cocceius resolves the difficulty presented to the rendering of the Authorized Version by the plural verb by translating as follows: "I will shake all nations, that they may come to the desire of all nations." This is more admissible grammatically than Fausset's explanation of the plural verb, but the third consideration in favor of our text, as given above, is decisive also against this rendering.

"and I will fill this house with glory",—

According to the Authorized Version this would mean the glory of Christ, who Himself was to enter into this house. The outward adornment of the temple is by this view lost sight of entirely. As Fausset says, "The first temple was filled with the cloud of glory, the symbol of God; this temple was to be filled with the glory of God *veiled* in the flesh (John 1.14) at Christ's first coming when He entered into it, i. e., into Herod's temple, performed miracles there and taught in it. (Christ 'sat daily teaching in the temple'); but that glory is to be *revealed* at His second coming, as this prophecy in its ulterior reference foretells (Mal. 3.1)."

According, however, to our rendering the primary reference must be to the outward and inward glory of the silver and gold adornments, in keeping with the clause just preceding.

Ver. 8. *"The silver is mine, and the gold is mine",*—

According to our text this merely means that there will be plenty of it to outshine the glory of the first temple:

According to the Authorized rendering the thought of this and the following verse would be, "Fear not; the Messiah is coming and I will fill this latter house with His glory. The silver and the gold are mine and I could make this house outshine the first with the glory of such things, but I will see to it that the glory of this latter house shall be greater than that of the first one because it will be filled with the glory of Christ."

Ver. 9. *"The latter glory of this house shall be greater than the former",*—The view of the old rendering has just been given, but in keeping with our text, if we regard the immediate context the interpretation becomes self-evident. The display of gold and silver in the first temple was mournfully remembered by the people in their poverty, but the outward adornments of those other days would be more than surpassed, as Calvin says, "when the nations would come, bringing with them all their riches, that they might offer themselves and all their possessions a sacrifice to God."

What now as to the fulfillment of this remarkable prediction? According to the older view, that of the Authorized Version, this question has already been answered by the remarks of Fausset, whether we think of the typical fulfillment of Herod's time or of the ultimate reference of the prophecy to the time of Christ's second coming.

Scofield adopts this view but refers the entire passage to the end-time and says, with certain other commentators, following the interpretation of Abarbanel and other Jewish expositors, that *"this latter house"* can only refer to the temple *yet to be built* as predicted in Ezek. 43. The expression, *"I will shake all nations"*, he says refers to the great tribulation and is followed by the coming of Christ in glory. There is no great force in McCurdy's objection to this on the ground of the prophet's announcement of a speedy fulfillment. The student must of course make his decision here consistent with his interpretation of the remarkable passage in Ezekiel just referred to.

According to the rendering of our text it is quite certain that there has as yet been no literal fulfillment of this prediction. The gifts to be brought are most certainly those which are to be prompted by the spirit of reverence and piety and godly fear. This was not the case with the adornments of the temple of Herod's time. Herod, it is true, was a foreigner, but his labors for the temple were prompted by worldly policy and were utterly out of harmony with the spirit of this prediction. Even so the adornments of this temple did not outshine those of Solomon's. It is doubtful therefore whether this temple has any right to consideration at all in connection with this prophecy (C. Hen. McC.), for thus in either case the prophecy will have been a failure. Of course there were some few proselytes from heathenism to Judaism in the days of the temple of Herod, and the offering of themselves with their gifts may be taken as but the merest fraction of a literal fulfillment of the promise in these verses when, according to representation elsewhere the nations of the world with their possessions shall flow unto Jerusalem. We must therefore either, (1) look for the literal fulfillment in times still future according to the premillennarian teaching of the kingdom which is to follow the second coming of Christ, or (2) seek a spiritual interpretation of the prophecy, because the prediction is given as a revelation from God and its fulfillment is certain, and the decision must rest of course with one's view of the entire teaching of prophetic Scripture along these lines.

According to the spiritual interpretation the temple must be merged into the Church of Christ or the kingdom of the present dispensation, and the coming of the early converted Gentiles, offering themselves and their gifts, was but a pledge of the higher and more glorious fulfillment which is still to come as more and more the world is gathered into the fold of the kingdom of Christ, the inward glory of the New Testament dispensation far exceeding the outward glory of the dispensation of the Old.

"in this place will I give peace",—

Says McCurdy, following the school of spiritual interpretation, "It is the presence of Jehovah that sheds glory upon the Church, His temple and dwelling place, that imparts inward peace and joy and outward peace and prosperity to its members in ever increasing measure."

Fausset, of the older school, says, " *'in this place will I give peace'*, viz., at Jerusalem, the metropolis of the kingdom of God, whose seat was the temple; where Messiah made peace through the blood of the cross. Thus the glory consists in this peace, inward peace and outward, between man and God and between man and man."

20 And the word of Jehovah came the second time unto Haggai in the four and twentieth *day* of the month, saying, 21 Speak to Zerubbabel, governor of Judah, saying, I will shake the heavens and the earth; 22 And I will overthrow the throne of kingdoms; and I will destroy the strength of the kingdoms of the nations; and I will overthrow the chariots, and those that ride in them; and the horses and their riders shall come down, every one by the sword of his brother. 23 In that day, saith Jehovah of hosts, will I take thee, O Zerubbabel, my servant, the son of Shealtiel, saith Jehovah, and will make thee as a signet; for I have chosen thee, saith Jehovah of hosts.

Vers. 20-23. THE FUTURE DESTRUCTION OF GENTILE POWER.

Ver. 21. *"I will shake the heavens and the earth",*—(See verses 6,7.) Zerubbabel may have asked concerning these convulsions, the Jews possibly believing they would lead to the overthrow of their own national existence.

Ver. 22. *"the throne of the kingdoms",*—i. e., their governments. All other kingdoms, says Fausset, are to be overthrown to make way for Christ's universal kingdom. (Dan. 2.44.)

"by the sword of his brother",—The heathen nations are doubtless to be stirred up against each other and thus the wars will be mutually destructive.

Ver. 23. *"In that day",*—i. e., the period, however long, during which the political convulsions and overthrow of the nations are commenced and completed.

"I will make thee as a signet",—i. e., a ring with a seal on it, thus making Zerubbabel, as the representative of his people, the signet ring of Jehovah. The signet being worn on the finger it was the object of constant regard, in all which points of view, says Fausset, "the theocratic people, and their representative Zerubbabel the type, and Messiah his descendent the Antitype, are regarded by God."

During the commotions God would take care of Zerubbabel. He would be building the temple and convulsions would be taking place all around him, but God promises to preserve him. Of course Zerubbabel fitly represents all the rulers of the Jews during the period within the range of the prophecy and the promise extends to all the faithful rulers who were to follow him, and thus the prophecy becomes indirectly and typically Messianic, the Messiah and His kingdom being prefigured in Zerubbabel and his kingdom. (F. He. Kle. McC. Moo.) Thus Fausset says, "Messiah is the antitypical Zerubbabel. He is the signet ring on God's finger and with Him God makes the covenant in which the Israelites are included. He is the Representative and King. In Him, in Whom God hath chosen the people as His own, they are assured of safety."

Others say the prophecy is directly Messianic and that by Zerubbabel the Messiah is meant. We are inclined to the indirect or typically Messianic interpretation. There is, of course, no doubt that the prophecy of verses 6 and 7 are directly Messianic. Those who spiritualize the prophecy of verses 6 and 7 take the shakings mentioned in two entirely different ways. Says McCurdy, "The shaking of the heaven and the earth illustrates in both cases the violent commotions among the Gentiles through the divine power, but the result in the former was to be their ultimate conversion, in the other their destruction. The allusion in the former must be to all movements in the history of humanity either before or since the coming of Christ which have disposed men to own Christ as their Lord and Saviour, those which changed the aspect of the civilized world and adjusted the nations for the ready reception and rapid spread of the Gospel, the conquests of Alexander and the wars of his successors, then the progress of Roman supremacy, and all subsequent events in the world's history, political, social or moral, which have subserved the growth and glory of the Church of Christ. The view, therefore, of Keil and Hengstenberg is beside the mark, who suppose that the shaking of the nations is intended to set forth the punitive judgments of God upon the heathen, as leading them to submit themselves to His rule. As a matter of fact it was not to any great extent the judgments of God that led the heathen to accept the Gospel."

THE BOOK OF

ZECHARIAH

(B. C. 520—B. C. 487)

The Book of Zechariah is designed to console and encourage God's people still in a condition of weakness and suffering.

CHAPTER ONE

7 Upon the four and twentieth day of the eleventh month, which is the month of Shebat, in the second year of Darius, came the word of Jehovah unto Zechariah, the son of Berechiah, the son of Iddo, the prophet, saying,

8 I saw in the night, and, behold, a man riding upon a red horse, and he stood among the myrtle-trees that were in the ¹bottom; and behind him there were horses, red, sorrel and white.

9 Then said I, O Lord, what are these? And the angel that talked with me said unto me, I will show thee what these are.

10 And the man that stood among the myrtle-trees answered and said, These are they whom Jehovah hath sent to walk to and fro through the earth.

11 And they answered the angel of Jehovah that stood among the myrtle-trees, and said, We have walked to and fro through the earth, and, behold, all the earth sitteth still, and is at rest.

12 Then the angel of Jehovah answered and said, O Jehovah of hosts, how long wilt thou not have mercy on Jerusalem and on the cities of Judah, against which thou hast had indignation these three score and ten years?

13 And Jehovah answered the angel that talked with me with good words, even comfortable words.

14 So the angel that talked with me said unto me, Cry thou, saying, Thus saith Jehovah of hosts; I am jealous for Jerusalem and for Zion with a great jealousy.

15 And I am very sore displeased with the nations that are at ease; for I was but a little displeased, and they ²helped forward the affliction.

16 Therefore thus saith Jehovah: I am returned to Jerusalem with mercies; my house shall be built in it, saith Jehovah of hosts, and a line shall be stretched forth over Jerusalem.

17 Cry yet again, saying, Thus saith Jehovah of hosts: my cities shall yet overflow with prosperity; and Jehovah shall yet comfort Zion, and shall yet choose Jerusalem.

¹Or, shady place

²Or, helped for evil

Vers. 7-17. THE RIDER ON THE RED HORSE. THE FIRST OF TEN VISIONS IN ONE NIGHT.

Ver. 8. *"man",*—The angel of the Lord, i. e., Christ. (See verse 11.)

"red horse",—Representing blood-shed and implying vengeance on the foes of Israel.

The horses next mentioned are red in color, dark red (Ges. Zur.), brown (Hen.) bay (Ch. Koe. Moo.), the idea being that of flame colored referring to burning and destroying. Next are mentioned "sorrel" horses or "speckled" (K. Um. Ma. Pe. A-V.), and then "white" horses, the last being perhaps a symbol of victory, although the significance of the color is not to be pressed.

"in the bottom",—The word means deep places, or shady places, and is a symbolical designation of the abyss-like power of the world in which the Jewish Church stands like a feeble and lowly shrub.

Ver. 9. *"my Lord",*—Whether this is addressed to the man on the red horse of verse 8 or to the angel of interpretation (the angel that talked with me) of this verse is a difficult question to decide. Some think the *"man"* of verse 8, *"my Lord"* and *"the angel that talked with me"* of this verse, and the *"man"* of verse 10 and the *"angel of the Lord"* of verse 11 are all one and the same, the prophet having addressed the man on the red horse as *"My Lord",* but having perceived, when the reply came, that it was but an angel. (Sco.)

Others because of the expression *"the angel of Jehovah"* think the man on the red horse to be Christ. The language of verse 9 seems to imply a distinction between the party addressed and the one making the reply, in case we consider the question put to the man on the red horse. The context does not furnish sufficient ground for a positive decision one way or the other; neither is it a matter of great importance which view is taken, but on the whole we prefer that which takes the *"angel of Jehovah"* as Christ.

Vers. 10,11. The man on the red horse answers, and then in verse 11 the attendant angels answer the angel of Jehovah.

"all the earth sitteth still and is at rest",—The nations at large were dwelling in calm and severe repose undisturbed by any foe, a vivid contrast to their own prostrate and suffering condition. This gives occasion for the following intercession.

Ver. 12. *"seventy years",*—The angel of Jehovah intercedes for the land against a world at ease. It is not implied here that the seventy years were just drawing to a close, but it seemed as if the exile condition would never end although they were back in their own land.

Ver. 16. *"a line shall be stretched forth over Jerusalem",*—A measuring line for extending the city. The contents of this and the following verse were all practically fulfilled under Ezra and Nehemiah. But this was only a beginning. Says Chambers, "Zechariah looks down the whole vista of the future and utters predictions which do not exhaust themselves in any one period."

281

18 And I lifted up mine eyes, and saw, and behold four horns.

19 And I said unto the angel that talked with me, What are these? And he answered me, These are the horns which have scattered Judah, Israel and Jerusalem.

Vers. 18,19. THE VISION OF THE FOUR HORNS.

Ver. 18. *"four horns"*,—A horn is the symbol of power and here stands for a Gentile foe. The expression *"four horns"* doubtless refers to the four cardinal points of the compass. Which ever way Israel had looked she had found threatening foes on every side. (C. F. Um. Ma. Ch. Hit. The. Koe.)

Ver. 19. Jerusalem is mentioned here merely for emphasis, while in verse 21 Judah alone is mentioned as including both the two and the ten tribes.

By many the four horns are referred to the four great world-empires of Daniel (K. Ba. Wor. Hen. Kim. Jer.) The only objection to this view is not that two of the powers were still in the future, because God's Spirit in the prophets regards the future as present, but that the Medo-Persian power did not persecute Israel, and also each succeeding world-power destroyed its successor while here the four powers are destroyed by four other powers. These objections are not necessarily fatal to the view, nor need this view be taken to show that the exhaustive fulfillment is yet future.

20 And Jehovah showed me four smiths.

21 Then said I, What 'come these to do? And he spake, saying, These are the horns which have scattered Judah, so that no man did lift up his head; but these are come to terrify them, to cast down the horns of the nations, which lifted up their horn against the land of Judah to scatter it.

Vers. 20, 21. THE VISION OF THE FOUR CARPENTERS.

Ver. 20. *"carpenters"*,—The various powers which God raised up and employed to overthrow Israel's foes.

Ver. 21. *"no man lifted up his head"*,—All were in a prostrate condition.

CHAPTER TWO

1 And I lifted up mine eyes, and saw, and, behold, a man with a measuring line in his hand. 2 Then said I, Whither goest thou? And he said unto me, To measure Jerusalem, to see what is the breadth thereof, and what is the length thereof. 3 And, behold, the angel that talked with me went forth, and another angel went out to meet him, 4 and said unto him, Run, speak to this young man, saying, Jerusalem shall ¹be inhabited as villages without walls, by reason of the multitude of men and cattle therein. 5 For I, saith Jehovah, will be unto her a wall of fire round about, and I will be the glory in the midst of her.

6 Ho, ho, flee from the land of the north, saith Jehovah; for I have spread you abroad as the four winds of the heavens, saith Jehovah. 7 Ho, Zion, escape, thou that dwellest with the daughter of Babylon. 8 For thus saith Jehovah of hosts: ²After glory hath he sent me unto the nations which plundered you: for he that toucheth you toucheth the apple of his eye. 9 For, behold, I will shake my hand over them,

¹Or, *dwell*

²Or, *After the glory, he hath &c.*

and they shall be a spoil to those that served them; and ye shall know that Jehovah of hosts hath sent me.

10 Sing and rejoice, O daughter of Zion; for, lo, I come, and I will dwell in the midst of thee, saith Jehovah. 11 And many nations shall join themselves to Jehovah in that day, and shall be my people; and I will dwell in the midst of thee, and thou shalt know that Jehovah of hosts hath sent me unto thee. 12 And Jehovah shall inherit Judah as his portion in the holy land, and shall yet choose Jerusalem. 13 Be silent, all flesh, before Jehovah; for he is waked up out of his holy habitation.

Vers. 1-13. The Vision of the Man with the Measuring Line.

This chapter is a prophecy of the enlargement and security of the Covenant people.

Ver. 1. *"man"*,—There is no data for positive opinion as to these characters, but there is no reason why this man should not be thought of as the same with the one in Chapter 1, i. e., Christ, here the author of Jerusalem's coming restoration.

"a measuring line",—"The measuring line", says Scofield, "is used by Ezekiel (Ezk. 40.3,5) as a symbol of preparation for rebuilding the city and temple in the kingdom-age. Here also it has that meaning, as the context (verses 4-14) shows. The subject of the vision is the restoration of the nation and the city. In no sense has this prophecy been fulfilled."

Ver. 2. *"to measure Jerusalem"*, i. e., its present dimensions with a view to its future indefinite enlargement.

Ver. 3. *"went forth"*,—i. e., from me, Zechariah.
"another angel",—i. e., one sent by the Measuring Angel.

Ver. 4. *"young man"*,—Zechariah, so-called because of his age.

"without walls",—So many shall be its inhabitants that all cannot be contained within the walls.

Ver. 6. Addressed to the Jews still remaining in the *"land of the north"*, i. e., Babylon, a type of the various Gentile lands where the Jews had been scattered.

"as the four winds",—To be thus scattered is a symbol of violence. The verse assigns a reason why the return was a possible one, i. e., I who scattered you can gather you.

Ver. 7. *"Zion"*,—Zion is here put for the inhabitants of Zion.
"daughter of Babylon",—i. e., the people of Babylon personified.

Ver. 8. *"after glory hath he sent me"*,—The meaning is, after restoring the glory of God's presence in Jerusalem, he (God) hath sent me (Christ) to execute judgment on the nations.

"apple",—This refers to the pupil of the eye, the most precious and most easily injured which has therefore a double claim to protection.

Vers. 10-13. These are of course purely Messianic and are by some referred to the people of God in this dispensation, while *Scofield and others of his school refer them to the "full blessing of the earth in the kingdom-age."*

Ver. 11. *"many nations"*,—This was true to some extent upon their return from exile, but in Messianic times, whether now or in the future, the kingdom of God will not be confined to the Jews but will be enlarged by the reception of many heathen peoples.

Ver. 12. (See Deuteronomy 32.9.)

Ver. 13. *"his holy habitation"*,—i. e., heaven.

CHAPTER THREE

Divine forgiveness the sure foundation for the promises made.

1 And he showed me Joshua the high priest standing before the angel of Jehovah, and [1]Satan standing at his right hand to be his adversary. 2 And Jehovah said unto Satan, Jehovah rebuke thee, O Satan; yea, Jehovah that hath chosen Jerusalem rebuke thee: is not this a brand plucked out of the fire? 3 Now Joshua was clothed with filthy garments, and was standing before the angel. 4 And he answered and spake unto those that stood before him, saying, Take the filthy garments from off him. And unto him he said, Behold,

[1]That is, *the Adversary*

I have caused thine iniquity to pass from thee, and I will clothe thee with rich apparel. 5 And I said, Let them set a clean mitre upon his head. So they set a clean [2]mitre upon his head, and clothed him with garments; and the angel of Jehovah was standing by.

6 And the angel of Jehovah protested unto Joshua, saying, 7 Thus saith Jehovah of hosts: If thou wilt walk in my ways, and if thou wilt keep my charge, then thou also shalt judge my house, and shalt also keep my courts, and I will give thee [3]a place of access among these that stand by.

[2]Or, *turban*
[3]Or, *places to walk*

Vers. 1-7. THE VISION OF JOSHUA THE HIGH PRIEST.

Ver. 1. *"he"*,—i. e., the interpreting angel.

"Joshua, the high priest",—He represents here the Jewish people.

"standing before the angel of Jehovah",—i. e., in his official function as a high priest performing his duties.

"Satan",—This refers to the chief of evil spirits, Satan himself, and not to a human adversary such as Sanballat (Ew. Kim.).

"at his right hand",—The usual place of the accuser.

Ver. 2. *"Jehovah"*,—This is generally acknowledged to mean the angel of Jehovah, it being not unusual in prophecy to have these terms used interchangeably.

"a brand plucked out of the fire",—The reference is to the Babylonish exile from which Joshua, in the sense that he represents the people, had been pulled out as a brand.

Ver. 3. *"clothed with filthy garments"*,—These represent the sins of the people.

Ver. 4. *"those that stood before him"*,—i. e., the Lord's ministering angels.

Ver. 5. *"I"*,—i. e., Zechariah. He wants the assurance that the priesthood with its official purity would be fully restored.

Ver. 6. *"protested"*,—i. e., solemnly declared,—a forensic term.

Ver. 7. *"keep my charge"*,—i. e., keep the ordinances, ritual and moral.

"keep my courts",—i. e., preside over the temple ceremony as high priest.

"a place of access",—This relates to a promise of some kind of association or influence with Jehovah's ministering angels. It really means "places to walk" and pertains doubtless to ingress and egress, free access to God among his ministering servants in the discharge of his priestly functions. (C. Ch. Ma. Ew. Hit. Fur. Koe.)

Some translate *"walkers"*,—i. e., angels, who as messengers, go between the high priest and god (Pe. Ba. Gro.), while others translate "guides", i. e., from among the angels. But these last two require somewhat of an alteration of the text.

> 8 Hear now, O Joshua the high priest, thou and thy fellows that sit before thee; for they are men that are a ¹sign: for, behold, I will bring forth my servant the ²Branch. 9 For, behold, the stone that I have set before Joshua: upon one stone are seven eyes: behold, I will engrave the graving thereof, saith Jehovah of hosts, and I will remove the iniquity of that land in one day. 10 In that day, saith Jehovah of hosts, shall ye invite every man his neighbor under the vine and under the fig-tree.
>
> ¹Or, *wonder*
> ²Or, *Shoot* Or, *Sprout*

Vers. 8-10. THE VISION OF JEHOVAH'S SERVANT, THE BRANCH.

Ver. 8. *"thy fellows that sit before thee"*,—His associates in the priestly office; not that they were then actually sitting before him, but that this was their usual posture when in consultation about the duties of the priesthood.

"men that are a sign",—The literal rendering is "men of wonder". They are a sign of what is to come. They are typical and as such are pledges to the desponding Jews that the priesthood should be preserved until the great antitype should come. The address seems suddenly to have been shifted to the ministering ones and the talk is of Joshua and his colleagues in the third person.

"my servant, the Branch",—The Messiah. This seems to show His original obscurity and the gradual development of his character.

Ver. 9. *"the stone that I have set before Joshua"*,—There are two views as to the meaning of this stone:

1. The foundation stone of the temple which had been set up (laid) before Joshua by the hand of Zerubbabel by God as the chief builder, and therefore your labor in building shall not be in vain. (F. He. Hit. Ros. Neu.)

   Antitypically then the stone is Christ, the chief corner stone of the foundation of the Church, "and", says Fausset, "the stone that shall crush all the world kingdoms".

   The "eye" is a symbol of Providence and seven is the symbol of perfection; so the watchful eyes of God are fixed upon it. And upon Christ are the eyes of the angels (I Tim. 3.16) and of the saints (John 3.14,15; 12.32) and of the patriarchs and the prophets (John 3.56; I Peter 1.10) and, above all, the eyes of the Father.

2. The Jewish Church, with the same interpretation of the seven eyes as that just given. (Ch. Moo.)
There is little data for definite decision but we unhesitatingly prefer the first view.
The "seven eyes" may also be conceived as the seven-fold radiation of the Spirit of God preserving and fitting for the glorious purpose involved.

Both of these views of the "seven eyes" consider them not as engraved on the stone but as directed toward it. Calvin perhaps better considers the eyes to be carved on the stone, which would then refer to Christ's own sevenfold or perfect fullness of grace and of the gifts of the Spirit, and His watchful care for the Jews in building the temple, and always for the Church, His spiritual temple.

"I will engrave the graving",—i. e., make it a beautiful and precious stone.

"I will remove the iniquity",—Not alone the iniquity but its consequences as well.

"that land",—i. e., this land, the land of Israel, the inhabitants of which of course stand for the whole Church.

"in one day",—Primarily the reference is to the "great day of atonement" (tenth day of the seventh month); typically the reference is to the atonement of the Messiah on the cross "once for all".

Ver. 10. "under the vine and under the fig-tree",—This is to be taken perhaps both spiritually and literally. "It is", says Fausset, "a type of peace with God through Christ and of Millennial blessedness." Scofield says that verse 10 marks the time of fulfillment as in the future kingdom. He says, "It speaks of a security which Israel has never known since the captivity, nor will know until the kingdom comes."

CHAPTER FOUR

1 And the angel that talked with me came again, and waked me, as a man that is wakened out of his sleep. 2 And he said unto me, What seest thou? And I said, I have seen, and, behold, a candlestick all of gold, with its bowl upon the top of it, and its seven lamps thereon; [1]there are seven pipes to each of the lamps, which are upon the top thereof; 3 and two olive-trees by it, one upon the right side of the bowl, and the other upon the left side thereof. 4 And I answered and spake to the angel that talked with me, saying, What are these, my lord? 5 Then the angel that talked with me answered and said unto me, Knowest

[1]Some MSS have, and seven pipes to the lamps, &c.

thou not what these are? And I said, No, my lord.
6 Then he answered and spake unto me, saying, This is the word of Jehovah unto Zerubbabel, saying, Not by [2]might, nor by power, but by my Spirit, saith Jehovah of hosts.
7 Who art thou, O great mountain? before Zerubbabel thou shalt become a plain; and he shall bring forth the top stone with shoutings of Grace, Grace, unto it.
8 Moreover the word of Jehovah came unto me, saying,
9 The hands of Zerubbabel have laid the foundations of this house; his hands shall also finish it; and thou shalt know that Jehovah of hosts hath sent me unto you.

[2]Or, an army

10 For who hath despised the day of small things? for these seven shall rejoice, and shall see the plummet in the hand of Zerubbabel; these are the eyes of Jehovah, which run to and fro through the whole earth.

11 Then answered I, and said unto him, What are these two olive-trees upon the right side of the candlestick and upon the left side thereof?

12 And I answered the second time, and said unto him, What are these two olive-branches, ³which are beside the two golden spouts, that empty ⁴the golden oil out of themselves?

13 And he answered me and said, Knowest thou not what these are? And I said, No, my lord.

14 Then said he, These are the two anointed ones, that stand by the Lord of the whole earth.

³Or, *which by means of the two golden spouts empty*
⁴Heb. *the gold*

Vers. 1-14. THE VISION OF THE GOLDEN CANDLESTICK AND THE TWO OLIVE TREES.

"This is, as we know from Rev. 11.3-12", says Scofield, *"a prophecy to be fulfilled in the last days of the present age."*

Ver. 1. *"out of his sleep"*,—This was perhaps an ecstatic slumber of astonishment at the former vision.

Ver. 2. *"seven pipes to each of the lamps"*,—The literal is "seven sevens" (forty-nine in all), and our text is doubtless right in taking the expression distributively. For an exact parallel see II Sam. 21.20 and compare I Chron. 20.6.

"bowl",—This is the oil vessel.

"its seven lamps",—The candlestick symbolizes the Jewish theocracy and ultimately the Church. The seven lamps indicate the fullness of the light that was shed, and the forty-nine pipes the number and variety of the channels by which grace is imparted to the luminary.

The seven lamps are united in one stem: so in Ex. 25.32, but in Rev. 1.12 the seven candlesticks are separate. Says Fausset, "The Gentile Churches will not realize their unity until the Jewish Church as the stem unites all the lamps in one candlestick (Rom. 11.16-24)."

Ver. 3. *"two olive trees by it"*,—(See verses 12-14.)

Ver. 6. *"Not by might"*, etc.,—As the candlestick gave light because it was supplied with oil, so the work on the temple and the establishing of his people could only be accomplished by the same agency, oil being a symbol of the Holy Spirit.

Ver. 7. *"O great mountain"*,—Some take this as a reference to the Persian kingdom (K. Hen. Hit. Kim. Jer. Cha.), but it is better to take it with others as a figure of any and all mountain-like difficulties. (F. Kl. Ch. Neu.)

"he",—Zerubbabel, as the next verse plainly shows.

"grace, grace unto it",—May God grant His grace to the stone, the grace that completed it preserve it forever.

Ver. 8. *"me"*,—i. e., the divine angel, as also in verse 9.

Ver. 10. *"who hath despised the day of small things"*,—An admonition to the people and their rulers not to despise small beginnings such as they had experienced. Who hath, i. e., with any reason? A negative answer is implied. (K. Ch. Wor,)

"these. seven",—i. e., the seven eyes of the Lord.

"shall see the plummet",—An indication that the work is going forward to completion.

Ver. 12. Without waiting for an answer he renews his question with slight alteration.

"branches",—i. e., the channels through which the oil flowed into the bowl of the lamps.

"spouts",—We are inclined to think that the marginal reading which is that of the Authorized Version, gives the same sense with a somewhat clearer way of expression.

Ver. 14. *"the two anointed ones"*,—Literally "the two sons of oil", i. e., Joshua and Zerubbabel (F. He. Pre.). Not the believing members of the Jews and the Gentiles (Kl.), for this would confound the olive trees with the candlestick; nor Haggai and Zechariah (Ba. Hof.).

Joshua and Zerubbabel typify the royal and priestly office of Christ. Fausset says that the *"great mountain"* of verse 7, representing mountainlike obstacles, antitypically refers to the antichristian last foe of Israel, the obstacle preventing her establishment in Palestine, about to be crushed before Messiah. (Jer. 51.25; Dan. 2.34,44; Matt. 21.44.) He says also the bringing forth of the "top stone" antitypically refers to the time when the full number of the spiritual Church shall be completed, and also when "all Israel shall be saved". (Rom. 11.26; Heb. 11.40; 12.22,23; Rev. 7.4-9.)

Scofield says, "The whole scene forms a precursive fulfillment of the ministry of the two witnesses of Rev. 11, and of the coming of the true 'headstone', Prince Messiah, of whom Prince Zerubbabel is a type. Joshua and Zerubbabel were the two olive trees for that day, as the two witnesses of Rev. 11 may, in turn, but point to Christ as Priest-King in the kingdom-age."

CHAPTER FIVE

Vers. 1-4. THE VISION OF THE FLYING ROLL.

The curse of God upon the thief and the profane man.

Vers. 5-11. THE VISION OF THE WOMAN IN THE EPHAH.

We have here as some think a prophecy of the present dispersion of the Jewish people. Scofield thinks that prophetically the application to the Babylon (land of Shinar, verse 11) of Revelation is obvious, the Gentile Church in which time full of iniquity falls under the severe judgment of God. (Rev. 18.)

CHAPTER SIX

1 And again I lifted up mine eyes, and saw, and, behold, there came four chariots out from between two mountains; and ¹the mountains were mountains of brass.

2 In the first chariot were red horses;

¹Or, *the two*

and in the second chariot black horses; 3 and in the third chariot white horses; and in the fourth chariot grizzled strong horses.

4 Then I answered and said unto the angel that talked with me, What are these, my lord?

5 And the angel answered and said unto me. These are the four ²winds of heaven, which go forth from ³standing before the Lord of all the earth. 6 The chariot wherein are the black horses

²Or, spirits
³Or, presenting themselves

goeth forth toward the north country; and the white went forth after them; and the grizzled went forth toward the south country. 7 And the ⁴strong went forth, and sought to go that they might walk to and fro through the earth: and he said, Get you hence, walk to and fro through the earth. So they walked to and fro through the earth. 8 Then cried he to me, and spake unto me saying, Behold, they that go toward the north country have quieted my spirit in the north country.

⁴Some MSS have, red

Vers. 1-8. THE VISION OF THE FOUR CHARIOTS.

Ver. 1. "chariots",—i. e., chariots to execute God's judgments on the wicked Gentile nations.

"brass",—A symbol of impregnable strength and permanency.

"two mountains",—A valley guarded by two brazen mountains is a fit symbol of the resistless might of Him who sends forth the executioners of His will. There has been considerable speculation as to which mountains are intended, Mt. Zion and Mt. Moriah (Ma. Um.), Mt. Zion and Mt. Olives (K. Moo.), the two horns of Medo-Persia (He.). But there is no need for seeking such explanations.

"four",—i. e., indicating like the four points of the compass, universality, a judgment going in every direction.

Can there be an allusion in the number "four" to the four world-kingdoms of Daniel? It is thought by some that this is true insofar at least as their existence lay in the future. God's judgment on Babylon had already been executed unless the reference be to the punishment by Darius on Babylon two years later for her rebellion against the Medo-Persian conqueror.

Vers. 2,3. "Red" denotes war and bloodshed; "black" denotes sorrow and death; "white" denotes victory, and the "grizzled" (piebald, speckled, dapple) denotes a mixed dispensation or judgment of perhaps "famine and pestilence" (K. Ch.), or of "adversity and prosperity" (F. Wo. He.), or a combination of all (Moo.).

"strong",—This is the usual sense of the word and is so taken by the majority but it is strange to find an epithet of quality immediately connected with one of color. Some therefore derive the word from an Arabic root meaning "to shine", hence, shining red. (C. Ch. Ew. Or. Coc. Koe. Kim. Fur. Cha. Sep. Syr. Aq. A-V.) One cannot be sure, but it is best perhaps to adhere to the usual sense of the world and translate "strong" as in our text.

Ver. 5. "winds",—Some translate "spirits" (F. A-V. He. Neu.), but it is nowhere else in the Bible so translated (certainly not in Ps. 104.4), and it is better to adhere to the word "winds". God makes the winds His angels, His ministers of judgment.

Ver. 6. "north country",—i. e., Babylon, the territory washed by the Tigris and the Euphrates.

"the white went forth after them",—The white horses, following perhaps to victoriously subdue Medo-Persia who had before the days of this vision been used of God to subdue Babylon. In this case of course the white horses would represent the Grecian (Alexander's) kingdom, i. e., in case we adopt the four world-power explanation.

"the south country",—i. e., Egypt "being a part of Alexander's kingdom and standing for the whole of it", says Fausset, and in this case the grizzled horses would represent Rome.

Ver. 7. *"strong"*,—He seems until now to have omitted the destination of the first chariot with the red horses. All are agreed that verse 7 refers to what the red horses of the first chariot were to do, and it will not therefore be worth while to busy ourselves with the practically insoluable difficulty as to why the word *"strong"* is used here. These first horses seem not content with going forth to a single territory but asked permission to go through the whole earth and it was given.

If the reference to the world kingdoms be retained the work of these horses is to be completed hereafter when the final form of the Roman empire has been assumed and Israel's last great foe, the antichristian confederacy, is overthrown. (Kl. Hof. Wor. F.)

But the contemporaneousness of their going forth, their destinations, the fact that Babylon had been overthrown before the vision and that Egypt was only one of the divisions of the Grecian empire somewhat invalidate the four world-empire explanation. (K. Sco. Coc. Koe.)

Scofield says, "That which is symbolized by the four chariots with their horses is not the four world-empires of Daniel, but the 'four spirits of heaven which go forth from standing before the Lord of all the earth', as is plainly shown in verse 5. These spirits are angels (Lu. 1.19; Heb. 1.14), and are most naturally interpreted of the four angels of Rev. 7.1-3; 9.14,15. These have also a ministry earthward and of judgment, even as these spirits of Zechariah. The vision, then, speaks of the Lord's judgments upon the Gentile nations north and south in the day of the Lord. (Isa. 2.10-22; Rev. 19.11-21.)"

Ver. 8. *"quieted my spirit"*,—i. e., have caused my spirit to rest, have appeased my anger. (F. Wo. A-V.)

Babylon alone in the days of the prophet was punished. God's wrath had been satisfied in that direction.

9 And the word of Jehovah came unto me, saying, 10 Take of them of the captivity, even of Heldai, of Tobijah, and of Jedaiah; and come thou the same day, and go into the house of Josiah the son of Zephaniah, whither they are come from Babylon; 11 yea, take of *them* silver and gold, and make [1]crowns, and set them upon the head of Joshua the son of Jehozadak, the high priest; 12 and speak unto him, saying,

[1]Or, *a crown, and set it*

Thus speaketh Jehovah of hosts, saying, Behold, the man [2]whose name is the [3]Branch: and he shall [4]grow up out of his place; and he shall build the temple of Jehovah; 13 even he shall build the temple of Jehovah; and he shall bear the glory, and shall sit and rule upon his throne; and [5]he shall be a priest upon his throne; and the counsel of peace shall be between them both. 14 And the [6]crowns shall be to Helem, and to

[2]Or, *whose name is the Bud; and it* (or, *they*) *shall bud forth under him*
[3]Or, *Shoot* Or, *Sprout*
[4]Or, *shoot*
[5]Or, *there shall be*
[6]Or, *crown*

Tobijah, and to Jedaiah, and [7]to Hen the son of Zephaniah, for a memorial in the temple of Jehovah. 15 And they that are far off shall come and build in the temple of Jehovah; and ye shall

[7]Or, *for the kindness of the son &c.*

know that Jehovah of hosts hath sent me unto you. And *this* shall come to pass, if ye will diligently obey the voice of Jehovah your God.

Vers. 9-15. The Crown upon Joshua's Head.

This communication although given at the same time as the visions and closely connected with them, does not itself take the form of a vision. Zechariah is told to go to the house of Joshua where three men had carried silver and gold sent as gifts, through them, by the exiles in Babylon to help in building the temple in Jerusalem. He was to go on that very day and take the silver and the gold and make crowns, etc.

Ver. 11. *"crowns"*,—The word is plural and is to be taken in the sense of circlets of which the crown was woven, or better perhaps, in keeping with the connection which treats of two distinct offices in one person, priest and king.

Ver. 12. *"Behold the man"*,—This may be referred to Joshua as typical of the Messiah (K.), but is better referred directly to the Messiah as if He were present.

"Branch",—(See Chap. 3.8 and Isa. 4.2.)

"shall grow up out of his place",—

1. Grow up from His own land and nation as a genuine root-shoot from the stock to which the promise had been made. (K. Ba. Ch. Coc. Hen.)
2. Under Him "it", the Church, shall grow forth. (Ma. Margin.)
3. Grow up of Himself, without man's aid, of His own power, in His miraculous conception. (He.)
4. Grow up out of His place of obscurity. (Moo.)

The first explanation is by far the more preferable.

"temple",—The spiritual temple of which Solomon's and the one they were then building were only types. (F. Wo. Ch. Hen. Tho. Coc. Koe.)

Fausset says, "It raises their thought beyond the material temple they were then building to the spiritual temple and also to the future glorious temple to be reared in Israel under Messiah's superintendency." (Ezk., Chaps. 40,41,42,43.)

Ver. 13. *"a priest upon his throne"*,—He is to be both king and high-priest on one and the same throne.

"peace between them both",—Not between the Branch and Jehovah (Vit. Coc.), nor between the Branch and an ideal priest (Ew. Bu.), nor between the royal and priestly offices (Hen. Ros.), but between the king and the priest who sit on the throne united in one person, the Branch. (F. Ch. Um. Koe.) This is typified by Joshua and Zerubbabel working harmoniously together.

"counsel of peace",—The glorious scheme of reconciliation between God and man effected by the joint exercise of the regal and sacerdotal offices of the Lord Jesus Christ.

Ver. 14. The crowns are not to be Joshua's personal property but are to be preserved in the temple as a memorial of the three men who brought them and to Joshua for his gracious hospitality. They were to be left there also to extend the typical significance of the whole proceeding. These men sending from afar their gifts for the house of God were types of many who would one day come from heathen lands and help to build the temple of God.

"Chelem" is a copyist's error for Cheldai and *"Hen"* is doubtless another name for Joshua.

Ver. 15. *"they that are afar off"*,—The reference is primarily to the distant stranger, including of course the Jews of the dispersion, the return of the latter and the conversion of the former.

"ye shall know",—i. e., when the events correspond to the prediction.

"if",—This does not mean that their unbelief could set aside God's gracious purpose as to the coming of the Messiah, but that His glory should not be manifest to the disobedient Jews unless they turn to Him with manifest repentance.

Says Scofield, "The invariable order is followed, first the judgments and then the kingdom, and we have here a symbolical representation of Christ in His kingdom glory. The fulfillment of the Branch will infinitely transcend the symbol. He shall 'bear the glory' as the Priest-King on His own throne. Christ is now a Priest, but still in the holiest within the veil and seated on the Father's throne. He has not yet come out to take His own throne. The crowns were laid up in the temple to keep alive this larger hope of Israel."

CHAPTER SEVEN

PAST RESULTS OF DISOBEDIENCE.

CHAPTER EIGHT

1 And the word of Jehovah of hosts came *to me,* saying, 2 Thus saith Jehovah of hosts: I am jealous for Zion with great jealousy, and I am jealous for her with great wrath. 3 Thus saith Jehovah: I am returned unto Zion, and will dwell in the midst of Jerusalem: and Jerusalem shall be called The city of truth; and the mountain of Jehovah of hosts, The holy mountain. 4 Thus saith Jehovah of hosts: There shall yet old men and old women [1]dwell in the streets of Jerusalem, every man with his staff in his hand [2]for very age. 5 And the streets of the city shall be full of boys and girls playing in the streets thereof. 6 Thus saith Jehovah of hosts: If it be marvellous in the eyes of the remnant of this people in those days, should it also be marvellous in mine eyes? saith Jehovah of hosts. 7 Thus saith Jehovah of hosts: Behold, I will save my people from the east country, and from the west country: 8 and I will bring them, and they shall dwell in the midst of Jerusalem; and they shall be my people, and I will be their God, in truth and in righteousness.

[1]Or, *sit*
[2]Heb. *for multitude of days*

Vers. 1-8. PROMISE OF FUTURE BLESSINGS FOR OBEDIENCE

Ver. 3. *"I am returned"*,—i. e., determined to return.

"The city of truth",—i. e., the city where truth is found

292

Ver. 4. A beautiful picture of long life, security and happiness. The strict fulfillment is to be referred to Messianic times and in complete fulfillment to the Millennium times.

Ver. 6. *"the remnant"*,—This refers, as also in verses 11 and 12, to the remnant of Judah which returned from Babylon, and among whom Zechariah was prophesying. If the thing predicted seemed impossible to them, i. e., in their eyes, it was not so in His, Jehovah's.

Ver. 7. He will save His people from all lands as far as the sun shines. They are now found in countries especially west of Jerusalem. The dispersion under Nebuchadnezzar was only to the east. It would appear therefore that the restoration is as yet future. In a spiritual sense Jerusalem stands for the Messianic kingdom, while the literal interpretation (F. He. Sco. Pre. Koe.) calls for an actual restoration to their own land.

Campbell Morgan says here, "This is a prophecy never yet fulfilled; and I believe one of the very first things after the Apocalypse of Jesus with His saints, and when the man of sin has been destroyed, will be the gathering of God's ancient people to their own city."

9 Thus saith Jehovah of hosts: Let your hands be strong, ye that hear in these days these words from the mouth of the prophets that were in the day that the foundation of the house of Jehovah of hosts was laid, even the temple, that it might be built. 10 For before those days there was no hire for man, nor any hire for beast; neither was there any peace to him that went out or came in, because of the adversary: for I set all men every one against his neighbor. 11 But now I will not be unto the remnant of this people as in the former days, saith Jehovah of hosts. 12 For *there shall be* the seed of peace; the vine shall give its fruit, and the ground shall give its increase, and the heavens shall give their dew; and I will cause the remnant of this people to inherit all these things.

13 And it shall come to pass that, as ye were a curse among the nations, O house of Judah and house of Israel, so will I save you, and ye shall be a blessing. Fear not, but let your hands be strong.

14 For thus saith Jehovah of hosts: As I thought to do evil unto you, when your fathers provoked me to wrath, saith Jehovah of hosts, and I repented not; 15 so again have I thought in these days to do good unto Jerusalem and to the house of Judah: fear ye not. 16 These are the things that ye shall do: Speak ye every man the truth with his neighbor; [1]execute the judgment of truth and peace in your gates; 17 and let none of you devise evil in your hearts against his neighbor; and love no false oath: for all these are things that I hate, saith Jehovah.

18 And the word of Jehovah of hosts came unto me, saying, 19 Thus saith Jehovah of hosts: the fast of the fourth month, and the fast of the fifth, and the fast of the seventh, and the fast of the tenth, shall be to the house of Judah joy and gladness, and cheerful feasts; therefore love truth and peace.

[1]Heb. *judge truth and the judgment of peace*

Vers. 9-19. THE RESTORATION PROPHETS ARE TO BE HEEDED.

Ver. 9. *"prophets"*,—Haggai and Zechariah himself.

"before those days",—i. e., in which work on the temple was resumed.

"went out or came in",—i. e., engaged in their ordinary occupations.

By *"adversary"* is doubtless meant the foe without and by *"every one against his neighbor"* is meant intestine discord.

Ver. 11. *"But now"*,—i. e., now and from now on.

Ver. 12. *"the seed of peace",*—There is no doubt but that the meaning is the seed shall be prosperous. (F. Ch. Wo. He. Pre. A-V.)

Keil and others render, "The seed of peace, namely, the vine shall", etc.; but the vine is no more a vegetation that grows in peaceful times than other kinds of vegetation.

Ver. 13. *"ye shall be a blessing",*—They were to be an example of blessedness as they were before an example of an accursed people, i. e., a people upon whom the curse of God had rested.

Fausset says, *"The distinct mention of Judah and Israel proves that the prophecy has not yet had its full accomplishment, since Israel (the ten tribes) has never yet been restored, although individuals of Israel did return with Judah."*

Ver. 16. *"gates",*—The place where justice was usually administered.

Ver. 19. The fast of the fourth month was on account of the taking of Jerusalem (Jer. 39.2); that of the fifth month was on account of the burning of the city and temple by Nebuchadnezzar; that of the seventh month on account of the murder of Gedaliah and his friends (Jer. 41.1), and that of the tenth month was on account of the commencement of the siege against Jerusalem (Jer. 52.4). These were all to be turned into festivals of joy.

20 Thus saith Jehovah of hosts: It shall yet come to pass, that there shall come peoples, and the inhabitants of ¹many cities; 21 and the inhabitants of one city shall go to another, saying, Let us go speedily to entreat the favor of Jehovah, and to seek Jehovah of hosts: I will go also.

22 Yea, many peoples and strong nations shall come to seek Jehovah of hosts in Jerusalem, and to entreat the favor of Jehovah.

23 Thus saith Jehovah of hosts: In those days it shall come to pass, that ten men shall take hold, out of all the languages of the nations, they shall take hold of the skirt of him that is a Jew, saying, We will go with you, for we have heard that God is with you.

¹Or, *great*

Vers. 20-23. JERUSALEM YET TO BE THE RELIGIOUS CENTER OF THE EARTH.

Ver. 20. *"peoples",*—i. e., entire nations. The connection is dropped at the end of the verse and resumed in verse 22.

Ver. 21. *"I will go also",*—The prompt response of each of the parties addressed.

Ver. 22. *"many peoples and strong nations",*—This is of course Messianic, but it is entirely consistent as well with the literal interpretation that reserves the full accomplishment till Jerusalem becomes the center of Christianized Jewry. (Rom. 11.12,15.)

Ver. 23. *"ten",*—A definite number put for an indefinite. (Gen. 31.7.)

The heathen will not only go in streams to Jerusalem but will seek intimate connection with the Jewish nation.

"of all the languages of the nations",—i. e., of the nations of all languages.

"take hold of the skirts",—A gesture of entreaty.

"go with you",—i. e., not only to the house of God (Hit.), but in other ways as well. (Ruth 1.16.)

"in those days",—The days when Jerusalem has been made the center of the earth's worship. Says Scofield, "The Jew will then be the missionary, and to the very 'nations' now called 'Christian'."

CHAPTER NINE

Chapters 9 to 14 were written thirty years later.

Vers. 1-8. A graphic account of Alexander's conquests in Syria in the language of prophecy and also a prophecy of Philistia's incorporation with Judah.

"The greater meaning of these verses", says Scofield, *"converges on the yet future last days, as the last clause of verse 8 shows, for many oppressors have passed through Jerusalem since the days of Alexander."*

9 Rejoice greatly, O daughter of Zion; shout, O daughter of Jerusalem: behold, thy king cometh unto thee; he is just, and ¹having ²salvation; lowly, and riding upon an ass, even upon a colt the foal of an ass. 10 And I will cut off the chariot from Ephraim, and the horse from Jerusalem; and the battle bow shall be cut off; and he shall speak peace unto the nations; and his dominion shall be from sea to sea, and from the River to the ends of the earth.

11 As for thee also, because of the blood of thy covenant I have set free thy prisoners from the pit wherein is no water. 12 ³Turn you to the stronghold, ye prisoners of hope: even today do I declare that I will render double unto thee.

13 For I have bent Judah for me, I have filled the bow with Ephraim; and

I will stir up thy sons, O Zion, against thy sons, O Greece, and will make thee as the sword of a mighty man. 14 And Jehovah shall be seen over them; and his arrow shall go forth as the lightning; and the Lord Jehovah will blow the trumpet, and will go with whirlwinds of the south. 15 Jehovah of hosts will defend them; and they shall devour, and shall tread down the slingstones; and they shall drink, and make a noise as through wine; and they shall be filled like bowls, like the corners of the altar. 16 And Jehovah their God will save them in that day as the flock of his people; for *they shall be as* the stones of a crown, ⁴lifted on high over his land. 17 For how great is ⁵his ⁶goodness, and how great is ⁵his beauty! grain shall make the young men flourish, and new wine the virgins.

¹Heb. *saved*
²Or, *victory*
³Or, *return*

⁴Or, *glittering upon, &c.*
⁵Or, *their*
⁶Or, *prosperity*

Vers. 9-17. SAFETY AND PEACE BECAUSE OF THE COMING MESSIAH WHOSE DOMINION IS TO BE UNIVERSAL.

Ver. 10. "This and the verses which follow", say some, "look forward to the end-time and the kingdom." Its immediate reference is perhaps to the deliverance under the Maccabees from the tyranny of Antiochus Epiphanes.

"from Ephraim . . . from Jerusalem",—Both the ten and the two tribes, "which", says Fausset, "are to be restored hereafter".

"sea to sea",—Primarily the Red Sea and the Mediterranean.

"the River",—The Euphrates. These boundaries fulfill Gen. 15.18; Ex. 23.31 and Ps. 72.8. "This", says Fausset, "is to be the center of the Messiah's future kingdom and from thence extended to all the earth."

Ver. 11. *"thee"*,—i. e., the whole nation, the ten and two tribes.

"blood of thy covenant",—i. e., the covenant between them ratified by the blood of sacrifices.

"the pit wherein is no water",—An image of the misery of the Jews in exile.

"set free",—i. e., delivered them from the oppression of Antiochus Epiphanes, this deliverance being a type of the future deliverance from their last great persecutor hereafter. (Isa. 51.14; 60.1.)

"prisoners",—This is not necessarily to be restricted to the Jews in exile but is to be taken rather of the entire people.

Ver. 12. *"the stronghold"*,—An emblem of the security they are to find in the Messiah.

"prisoners of hope",—i. e., the hope just expressed, hope in a covenant-keeping God.

"render double",—i. e., double the prosperity you formerly had (Ch.), or perhaps better, doubly greater than your adversity. (F. Wo.)

"even today",—i. e., in spite of all threatening circumstances.

Vers. 13-15. The Maccabean deliverance.

Ver. 16. *"lifted on high"*,—Many prefer the marginal reading, "glittering on high". (K. Ew. Ch. Ma. Koe. Fur.) The reference is to the gems of a crown flashing from the brow of a conqueror as he stalks over the land.

Ver. 17. *"his"*,—i. e., Jehovah's. (F. He. Ch. Ew. Hen. Pre.)

"goodness . . . beauty",—i. e., which He bestows upon His people.

"corn" and *"wine"*,—i. e., indicating peace and prosperity.

CHAPTER TEN

1 Ask ye of Jehovah rain in the time of the latter rain, *even of* Jehovah that maketh lightnings; and he will give them showers of rain, to every one grass in the field. 2 For the teraphim have spoken vanity, and the diviners have seen a lie; and [1]they have told false dreams, they comfort in vain: therefore they go their way like sheep, they are afflicted, because there is no shepherd. 3 Mine anger is kindled against the shepherds, and I will punish the he-goats; for Jehovah of hosts hath visited his flock, the house of Judah, and will make them as his goodly horse in the battle. 4 From him shall come forth the corner-stone, from him the nail, from him the battle-bow, from him every [2]ruler together. 5 And they shall be as mighty men, treading down *their enemies* in the mire of the streets in the battle; and they shall fight, because Jehovah is with them; and the riders on horses shall be confounded. 6 And I will strengthen the house of Judah, and I will save the house of Joseph, and I will bring them back; for I have mercy upon them; and they shall be as though I had not cast them off; for I am Jehovah their God, and I will hear them.

7 And they of Ephraim shall be like a mighty man, and their heart shall rejoice as through wine; yea, their children shall see it, and rejoice; their heart shall be glad in Jehovah.

8 I will hiss for them, and gather them; for I have redeemed them; and they shall increase as they have increased.

[1]Or, *the dreamers speak falsely*
[2]Or, *exactor*

Vers. 1-8. FORMER MERCIES RESTORED TO JUDAH AND ISRAEL.

Ver. 1. The promise of rain and the fruitful season. Scofield says that there is here both a physical and a spiritual meaning; rain as of old will be restored to Palestine, but also, there will be a mighty effusion of the Spirit upon restored Israel.

Ver. 2.   Idolatry, the cause of their affliction, to cease.

Vers. 3-5.   Deliverance through God's blessing upon her own native rulers. "The whole scene", says Scofield, "is of the events which group about the deliverance of the Jews in Palestine in the time of the northern invasion under the 'beast' (Dan. 7.8; Rev. 19.20), and 'Armageddon' (Rev. 16.14; 19.17). The final deliverance is wholly effected by the Return of the Lord. That there may have been a precursive fulfillment in the Maccabean victories can neither be affirmed nor denied from Scripture."

Ver. 6.   Fausset here claims that the distinct mention of Israel, the ten tribes, shows that there is yet a more complete restoration than that from Babylon when Judah alone with a very few Israelites returned.

"bring them back",—He promises to bring them back and cause them to dwell as in olden time in their own land.

Ver. 8.   *"hiss for them"*,—This refers to calling them together as do the keepers of bees by a hissing sound or whistle.

"So Jehovah, by the mere word of His mouth, shall gather back to Palestine His scattered people. The multitudes mentioned by Josephus, as peopling Galilee two hundred years after this time were but a pledge of the future more perfect fulfillment of the prophecy."   (Fausset.)

9 ¹And I will sow them among the peoples; and they shall remember me in far countries; and they shall live with their children and shall return.

10 I will bring them again also out of the land of Egypt, and gather them out of Assyria; and I will bring them into the land of Gilead and Lebanon; and place shall not be found for them.

¹Or, *And though I sow them . . . . they shall remember, &c.*

11 And he will pass through the sea of affliction, and will smite the ²waves in the sea, and all the depths of the Nile shall dry up; and the pride of Assyria shall be brought down, and the sceptre of Egypt shall depart.

12 And I will strengthen them in Jehovah; and they shall walk up and down in his name, saith Jehovah.

²Or, *the sea of waves*

Vers. 9-12.   THE DISPERSION AND THE REGATHERING OF ISRAEL.

Ver. 9.   *"I will sow them"*,—Never does this word, when applied to men, have the sense of scattering, abandoning, destroying (He. Hit. Fur.), but always the idea of increase. It therefore means here to cause to increase. The dispersion was with a special design. It is a Hebrew future and is said of that which has been done, is being done, and may be done afterwards.

Ver. 10.   *"Egypt and Assyria"*,—These are types of the present universal dispersion.

"Gilead and Lebanon",—Their old dwellings east and west of Jordan, with special reference perhaps to northern Palestine, the former home of the ten tribes.

Ver. 11.   *"he will pass through the sea with affliction"*,—i. e., He will afflict the sea. "As before at the Red Sea, so now He marches through

the deep at the head of His chosen and smites down the roaring waves."
(Chambers.) He will cause such things to cease to be an obstacle to their
restoration.

CHAPTER ELEVEN

Israel's rejection caused by her persistent and deliberate wickedness.

Vers. 1-6. THE WRATH AGAINST THE LAND.

This, says Scofield, was fulfilled in the destruction of Jerusalem after
the rejection of the Messiah.

7 So I fed the flock of slaughter, verily ¹the poor of the flock. And I took unto me two staves; the one I called ²Beauty, and the other I called ³Bands; and I fed the flock.

¹Or, *the most miserable of sheep*

²Or, *Graciousness*
³Or, *Binders* Or, *Union*

Vers. 7-14. JEHOVAH'S WRATH CAUSED BY THE SALE AND REJECTION
OF THE MESSIAH.

Ver. 7. *"Beauty . . . . Bands"*,—Literally, "graciousness" and
"union", the first signifying God's attitude toward His people Israel in
sending His Son, and the second, His purpose to reunite Judah and
Ephraim.

"poor of the flock",—"This is", says Scofield, " 'the remnant according to the election of grace' (Rom. 11.5); those Jews who did not wait
for the manifestation of Christ in glory, but believe on Him at His first
coming, and since. Of them it is said that 'they waited upon me', and
'knew' (verse 11). Neither the Gentiles nor the Gentile Church cor-
porately are in view; only the believers out of Israel during this age."

15 And Jehovah said unto me, Take unto thee yet again the instruments of a foolish shepherd.

16 For, lo, I will raise up a shepherd in the land, who will not ¹visit those that are ²cut off, neither will seek ³those that are scattered, nor heal that which

¹Or, *miss*
²Or, *lost*
³Or, *the young*

is broken, nor feed that which ⁴is sound; but he will eat the flesh of the fat sheep, and will tear their hoofs in pieces.

17 Woe to the worthless shepherd that leaveth the flock! the sword shall be upon his arm, and upon his right eye: his arm shall be clean dried up, and his right eye shall be utterly darkened.

⁴Heb. *standeth*

Vers. 15-17. THE JUDGMENT OF THE WICKED SHEPHERD.

Ver. 15. *"implements"*,—The crook, bag, pipe, knife, etc.
"foolish",—Literally, "wicked".

Ver. 16. *"tear their hoofs in pieces"*,—This may refer either to
cruelty, even as the flock is driven over rough and rocky places (F. Ew.
Hit.), or to the ferocious greed of the shepherds who will even rend these
extremities rather than lose a shred of the flesh. (Ch.)

Ver. 17. *"arm . . . eye"*,—The judgment is upon the arm that
ought to have defended and the eye that ought to have watched.

Who is meant by the *"wicked shepherd"*?

1. Herod. (He.)
2. The Roman rulers. (K. F. Hof. Koe.)
3. The whole body of native rulers. (Hen.)
4. The Beast of Dan. 7.8 and Rev. 19.20. (Sco.)

The primary reference is doubtless to the Roman rulers, although they stand no doubt as a type of the later antichristian power which is to rise in the last times.

Scofield says, "The reference to the Beast is obvious; no other personage of prophecy in any sense meets the description. He who came in His Father's name was rejected; the alternative is one who comes in his own name."

Fausset says, "They were given up to Rome and shall be again given up to the Antichrist, the instrument of judgment by Christ's permission. Antichrist will first make a covenant with them as their ruler, will break it, and they shall feel the iron yoke of his tyranny as the false Messiah because they rejected the light yoke of the true Messiah. But at last he is to perish utterly (verse 17) and the elect remnant of Judah is to be saved gloriously."

CHAPTER TWELVE

Scofield contends that Chaps. 12-14 form one prophecy, the general theme of which is the Return of the Lord and the establishment of the kingdom.

1 The ¹burden of the word of Jehovah concerning Israel.
Thus saith Jehovah, who stretcheth forth the heavens, and layeth the foundation of the earth, and formeth the spirit of man within him: 2 Behold, I will make Jerusalem a cup of reeling unto all the peoples round about, and ²upon Judah also ³shall it be in the siege against Jerusalem. 3 And it shall come to pass in that day, that I will make Jerusalem a burdensome stone for all the peoples; all that burden themselves with it shall be sore wounded; and all the nations of the earth shall be gathered together against it.

¹Or, oracle
²Or, against
³Or, shall it fall to be

Vers. 1-3. JERUSALEM WHEN BESIEGED TO BECOME THE INSTRUMENT OF JUDGMENT ON HER FOES.

Ver. 2. "a cup of reeling",—i. e., a cup containing God's wrath, the drinking of which will cause them to reel and fall in hopeless weakness, etc.

"upon Judah also shall it be",—i. e., she shall be involved in the same trial and be also a cup of trembling to her foes.

Ver. 3. "a burdensome stone",—This is taken from one of the sports of the young men who test their strength by lifting great stones by which they are sometimes crushed.

Fausset says, "The Jews fell on the stone of offense, Messiah, and were broken; but the stone shall fall on Antichrist who 'burdens himself with it' and grind him to powder."

"all the nations of the earth",—Here again those who interpret literally mention the fact that the antichristian confederacy against the Jews shall be almost universal.

4 In that day, saith Jehovah, I will smite every horse with terror, and his rider with madness; and I will open mine eyes upon the house of Judah, and will smite every horse of the peoples with blindness. 5 And the chieftains of Judah shall say in their heart, The inhabitants of Jerusalem are my strength in Jehovah of hosts their God. 6 In that day will I make the chieftains of Judah like a pan of fire among wood, and like a flaming torch among sheaves; and they shall devour all the peoples round about, on the right hand and on the left; and *they of* Jerusalem shall yet again dwell in ¹their own place, even in Jerusalem. 7 Jehovah also shall save the tents of Judah first, that the glory of the house of David and the glory of the inhabitants of Jerusalem be not magnified above Judah. 8 In that day shall Jehovah defend the inhabitants of Jerusalem; and he ²that is feeble among them at that day shall be as David; and the house of David shall be as God, as the angel of Jehovah before them. 9 And it shall come to pass in that day, that I will seek to destroy all the nations that come against Jerusalem.

10 And I will pour upon the house of David, and upon the inhabitants of Jerusalem, the spirit of grace and of supplication; and they shall look unto ³me whom they have pierced; and they shall mourn for him, as one mourneth for his only son, and shall be in bitterness for him, as one that is in bitterness for his first-born.

¹Heb. *her*

²Or, *that stumbleth*

³According to some MSS., *him*

Vers. 4-10. THE SIEGE ITSELF.

Many scholars would have us believe that the reference is to the battle of Armageddon.

Ver. 4. *"I will open mine eyes upon the house of Judah"*,—i. e., to guard over her, Judah standing here for the whole nation.

Ver. 6. *"all the peoples round about"*,—Many persist in finding an ultimate reference here to the final antichristian foes of Israel. Fausset says that Daniel represents the Antichrist more as a king with his conquests, St. John dwells more on his spiritual tyranny, while here in Zechariah his army is more fully described.

Ver. 7. *"save the tents of Judah first"*,—The unprotected open land as against the fortified city, the latter of which must know that in either case the victory was from God.

Ver. 8. *"shall be as David"*,—David was to the Jew the highest type of strength and glory.

"the house of David shall be as God, as the angel of Jehovah",—It shall exceed even its highest fame of old.

Many commentators refer this prophecy, as we have seen, to the dealings of God with the national Israel in the last days, in the last great struggle of ungodliness. (V. F. K. Mi. Dat. Sco.)

Chambers objects to this interpretation, but says, however, "It is manifestly easier to interpret the passage in its details upon this literal view of its application." (See Lange's Commentary in loco.)

Ver. 10. *"the Spirit of grace and supplication"*,—i. e., the Spirit which brings grace, producing in the minds of men the experience of the grace of God and so leading to supplication.

"whom they have pierced",—The reference is here plainly to the Messiah.

"me . . . him",—This change of person is not uncommon in Hebrew.

"The conversion and restoration of the Jews", says Seiss, "the Saviour Himself connects with His promised return, as also does the Apostle Paul, thus leaving no room for a Millennium of universal peace and righteousness before His second coming. Thus here the Lord says, 'I will pour upon the house of David, and upon the inhabitants of Jerusalem the Spirit of grace and supplication; and they shall *look upon me* whom they have pierced'."

11 In that day shall there be a great mourning in Jerusalem, as the mourning of Hadadrimmon in the valley of Megiddon. 12 And the land shall mourn, every family apart; the family of the house of David apart, and their wives apart; the family of the house of Nathan apart, and their wives apart; 13 the family of the house of Levi apart, and their wives apart; the family of the Shimeites apart, and their wives apart; 14 all the families that remain, every family apart, and their wives apart.

Vers. 11-14. THE REPENTANCE OF THE REMNANT.

Ver. 11. The mourning shall be as the mourning of the city of Hadadrimmon for King Josiah who fell in the valley of Megiddon.

Ver. 12. *"every family apart"*,—Retirement is natural and needful for deep religious mourning and personal religion.

Four families are enumerated, two from the royal line under the names of David and of his son Nathan, and two from the priestly line, Levi and his grandson Shimei, after which he embraces all together. (F. K. Ch. He. Lut. Hen. Koe.) Thus one leading family and one subordinate family of both the royal and priestly order is mentioned to show that the grief pervades all from the highest to the lowest.

Ver. 14. *"all the families that remain"*,—Perhaps it is best to think with Chambers of the remainder after those just specified, although Newman refers it to those who are left after the judgment. Thus also Fausset, who says it refers to those who are left "after the fiery ordeal in which two thirds fall. (Chap. 13.8,9.)"

CHAPTER THIRTEEN

1 In that day there shall be a fountain opened to the house of David and to the inhabitants of Jerusalem, for sin and for uncleanness. 2 And it shall come to pass in that day, saith Jehovah of hosts, that I will cut off the names of the idols out of the land, and they shall no more be remembered; and also I will cause the prophets and the unclean spirit to pass out of the land. 3 And it shall come to pass that, when any shall yet prophesy, then his father and his mother that begat him shall say unto him, Thou shalt not live; for thou speakest lies in the name of Jehovah; and his father and his mother that begat him shall thrust him through when he prophesieth. 4 And it shall come to pass in that day, that the prophets shall be ashamed every one of his vision, when he prophesieth; neither shall they wear a hairy mantle to deceive: 5 but he shall say, I am no prophet, I am a tiller of the ground; for I have been made a bondman from my youth. 6 And one shall say unto him, What are these wounds between thine [1]arms? Then he shall answer, Those with which I was wounded in the house of my [2]friends.

[1]Heb. *hands*
[2]Or, *lovers*

Vers. 1-6. IDOLATRY AND FALSE PROPHESYING TO CEASE.

Ver. 1. *"a fountain opened"*,—It had long been opened but then only will their eyes be opened to see it.

"for sin and for uncleanness",—i. e., for judicial guilt and for impurity. The reference is to the two-fold ritual of Moses. It is the blood which cleanses from all sin.

Ver. 2. *"cut off the names of the idols"*,—The reference is to the total extinction of idolatry, idolatry here representing all forms of ungodliness and immorality.

"prophets",—i. e., false prophets.

"the unclean spirit",—The spirit of uncleanness in opposition to the spirit of holiness. The reference is to those who profess to be divinely inspired but are in league with Satan, an active agency in direct contrast to the Spirit of grace. (Chap. 12.10.)

Ver. 3. If such a false prophet prophesies his very parents would not let parental affection keep them from punishing him.

Ver. 4. The revolution is to be so great that the false pretender will be ashamed of his claims and will strip off his *"hairy mantle"*, the badge of a prophet and a symbol of grief for the sins he is supposed to reprove, by means of which in this case he was deceiving the people.

Ver. 5. Charged with his crime he denies it.

Ver. 6. He is asked about the tell-tale wounds between his arms, i. e., on his breast, which to the questioners is palpable evidence that he was wounded in connection with idolatrous worship. (See I Kings 18.28.)

"wounded in the house of his friends",—Fausset takes this as an implied admission that he had pretended to prophesy and his friends in their zeal for God had wounded him.

Hengstenberg says the word *"friends"* should be translated "lovers" and made to refer to idols, which is also tantamount to admitting the charge.

Chambers takes it as an evasion; they are simply chastisements he had received from his friends or relatives.

7 Awake, O sword, against my shepherd, and against the man that is my fellow, saith Jehovah of hosts: smite the shepherd, and the sheep shall be scattered; and I will turn my hand upon the little ones. 8 And it shall come to pass, that in all the land, saith Jehovah, two parts therein shall be cut off and die; but the third shall be left therein.

9 And I will bring the third part into the fire, and will refine them as silver is refined, and will try them as gold is tried. They shall call on my name, and I will hear them: I will say, It is my people; and they shall say, Jehovah is my God.

Vers. 7-9. THE SHEPHERD SMITTEN, THE FLOCK SCATTERED AND THE REMNANT REFINED AND SAVED.

"Awake",—This is addressed to the sword personified. The sword is here used representatively for any means of taking life. (See Jer. 47.6.)

"smite",—In Matt. 26.31, where this is quoted, it is said, "I will smite", thus showing that it is God's act.

"my fellow",—Used only here and a number of times in Leviticus. It denotes a close and intimate connection. Who is this and who is the "fellow"? It is the Messiah Himself, as the Fathers, Reformers and most moderns take it. Other interpretations are "the foolish shepherd" of Chap. 11.15 (Ma. Ew. Hit.), but this it cannot be, for God's "fellow" could not in any appropriate sense be applied to an unworthy person. Judas Maccabaeus (Gro.), Pekah (Bun.), Jehoiakim (Ma.), Josiah (Pre.), the whole body of rulers including Christ (C.).

"the sheep",—The covenant nation. The scattering of the Disciples on His arrest was an initial fulfillment, a pledge of the dispersion of the whole Jewish nation. Says Fausset, "The Jews are still His sheep waiting to be gathered by Him. (Isa. 49.9,11.)"

"my hand upon the little ones",—These are doubtless to be taken as the humble followers of Christ from the Jewish Church, the "little flock", the "wretched of the flock" in Chap. 11.7,11, mercifully revisited.

Ver. 8. Keil says, "The dispersion of the flock will deliver two thirds of the nation in the whole land to death, so that only one third will remain alive." (See Ezek. 5.2-12.)

"cut off and die",—This seems to show that literal death is meant. Fausset says, "Since this has never been fulfilled it must await fulfillment in the future under the Antichrist."

Ver. 9. "shall call on my name",—Hence, says Fausset, "it appears that the Jews' conversion is not to precede but to follow their external deliverance by the special interposition of Jehovah."

"in all the land",—Chambers, consistent with his method of spiritual interpretation, says, "This is not to be taken in a literal sense, but as representing the domain covered by the kingdom of God", while others (K. F. Hen. Sco. Koe.) refer it to the holy land, Palestine.

Some say the third part is the entire race of Jews during the present dispensation (Mi. Koe.), but as Hengstenberg justly argues in that case unbelieving Judaism would be regarded as the whole and legitimate continuation of Israel, and this is simply impossible. Chambers says the third part is the entire kingdom of God on earth whether composed of Jews or Gentiles."

Scofield contends that in these last two verses Zechariah is returning to the subject of Chap. 12.10, and that they refer to the sufferings of the remnant preceding the great battle of Armageddon.

CHAPTER FOURTEEN

1 Behold, a day of Jehovah cometh, when thy spoil shall be divided in the midst of thee.

2 For I will gather all nations against Jerusalem to battle; and the city shall be taken, and the houses rifled, and the women ravished; and half of the city shall go forth into captivity, and the residue of the people shall not be cut off from the city.

3 Then shall Jehovah go forth and fight against those nations, as when he fought in the day of battle.

Vers. 1-3. THE GREAT BATTLE IN THE DAY OF JEHOVAH.

The final conflict and triumph of God's kingdom.

Ver. 1. *"a day of Jehovah"*,—A day appointed for the manifestation of His glory and power.

"thy spoil",—i. e., that which the enemy takes from her.

Ver. 2. *"half the city"*,—Fausset to reconcile this with the two-thirds of Chap. 13.8,9 says that there it was two-thirds of the entire land, while here it is one half of the city.

To what does the event refer?

1. The time of the Maccabees. (C. Gro.)
2. The siege of Jerusalem by Titus. (Lo. Cl. He. Cy. The. Marc.) But Titus did not have all nations under his banner, nor did he leave one-half of the people in the city. For the same reason it cannot apply to the Chaldean conquest.
3. The period just before the Babylonian exile. (Ma. Kn. Ew. Hit. Bert.) But this is not at all consistent with facts.
4. All conflicts of the Church of God with her foes from the commencement of the Messianic era to its close. (K. Ch. Hen.)
5. A period yet future. (F. Ne. Co. Sco. Wor. Moo. Blay.) It would seem that only according to this last view is it at all possible to interpret the passage without meeting insurmountable difficulties.

"This", says Campbell Morgan, "is an Old Testament prophecy of the Apocalypse of the Lord with His holy ones, being that stage of His coming elsewhere called His manifestation."

Ver. 3. The Deliverance of His People.

"as when He fought",—Perhaps at the Red Sea (Hen.), although the more general reference may seem better, that is, as shown on many former occasions. (K. Ch. Koe.)

4 And his feet shall stand in that day upon the mount of Olives, which is before Jerusalem on the east; and the mount of Olives shall be cleft in the midst thereof toward the sea and toward the west, and there shall be a very great valley; and half of the mountain shall remove toward the north, and half of it toward the south. 5 And [1]ye shall flee [2]by the valley of [3]my mountains; for the valley of the mountains shall reach unto Azel; yea, ye shall flee, like as ye fled from before the earthquake in the days of Uzziah, king of Judah; and Jehovah my God shall come, and all the holy ones with thee.

6 And it shall come to pass in that day, that [4]there shall not be light; the bright ones shall withdraw themselves: 7 but it shall be one day which is known unto Jehovah; not day, and not night; but it shall come to pass, that at eventime there shall be light.

8 And it shall come to pass in that day, that living waters shall go out from Jerusalem; half of them towards the eastern sea, and half of them toward the western sea: in summer and in winter shall it be.

[1]Or, as otherwise read, *the valley of my mountains shall be stopped*
[2]Or, *to*
[3]Or, *the*

[4]Or, *the light shall not be bright nor dark*

Vers. 4-8. THE RETURN OF THE MESSIAH TO THE MOUNT OF OLIVES, AND THE PHYSICAL CHANGES IN THE LAND.

Ver. 4. The valley is to run east and west.

The prediction that His feet shall stand on the mount of Olives, Erdman says, is a proof that the Lord is to return to this earth.

Ver. 5. *"by the valley"*,—i. e., through it.

"my mountains",—i. e., those made by the cleavage.

"reach unto Azel",—This refers to a place near Jerusalem of which no trace exists today.

One derivation of the word makes it mean "adjoining". (F. He. Koe. Jer.) Fausset says, "The valley reaches up to the city gates so as to enable the fleeing citizens to betake themselves to it immediately on leaving the city".

Another derivation makes it mean "ceasing" (Hen.), the valley reaching to Azel where they will find cessation from danger. This puts the place east of the mount of Olives.

"earthquake",—This is referred to in Amos 1.1 but of it we have no further information.

"with thee",—The narrative here passes from indirect to direct address suddenly because of the rapture of the moment,—a thing not uncommon in Hebrew.

"all the holy ones with thee",—All agree that angels are meant, and to these are added by premillennarians redeemed men, glorified saints.

Ver. 6. This is a very difficult verse.

1. A very great preponderance of manuscript authority (Tar. It. Pe.) as well as many commentators (He. Lut.) translate, "It will not be light, but cold and ice".

2. Exegetical necessity almost compels one to accept the translation of either the A-R-V or the A-V., and the preponderance of authority is greatly on the side of the former. (K. Kl. Ch. Hen. Hof. Pre. Fur. Van. Koe.) The whole verse then indicates a day of darkness.

Ver. 7. *"one day"*,—i. e., an unique day.

"known to Jehovah",—And by implication to no one else.

"not day and not night",—These words are easier explained in harmony with the Authorized Version reading of verse 6. Both verse 6 and verse 7 would then refer to an admixture like a dark day in which it is hard to distinguish between the darkness and the light. If the reading of our text, which we have preferred, in verse 6 be retained it is still possible to find reference to the kind of a day just mentioned. Chambers, however, explains. *"not day and not night"* in the sense of not being able to determine what is day and what is night because the lights of heaven have been put out, and this is in harmony with what is said elsewhere of the Day of the Lord, i. e., a day of darkness.

"at eventime there shall be light",—When darkness would be expected it suddenly becomes light.

Cowles says, "There is a gradation through three distinct stages, first, utter darkness; then, a dim twilight like that of an eclipse; then at the close when you might expect darkness to cover the earth, lo! the effulgence of the full and glorious day."

Ver. 8. An ever-flowing stream toward the Dead Sea and toward the Mediterranean, a lively image of abundance.

9 And Jehovah shall be King over all the earth: in that day shall Jehovah be one, and his name one.

10 All the land shall be made like the Arabah, from Geba to Rimmon south of Jerusalem; and she shall be lifted up, and shall dwell in her place, from Benjamin's gate unto the place of the first gate, unto the corner gate, and from the tower of Hananel unto the king's winepresses.

11 And men shall dwell therein, and there shall be no more [1]curse; but Jerusalem shall dwell safely.

12 And this shall be the plague wherewith Jehovah will smite all the peoples that have warred against Jerusalem: their flesh shall consume away while they stand upon their feet, and their eyes shall consume away in their sockets, and their tongue shall consume away in their mouth.

13 And it shall come to pass in that day, that a great [2]tumult from Jehovah shall be among them; and they shall lay hold everyone on the hand of his neighbor, and his hand shall rise up against the hand of his neighbor.

14 And Judah also shall fight at Jerusalem; and the wealth of all the nations round about shall be gathered together, gold, and silver, and apparel, in great abundance.

15 And so shall be the plague of the horse, of the mule, of the camel, and of the ass, and of all the beasts that shall be in those camps, as that plague.

[1]Or, *ban* Or, *devoting to destruction*   [2]Or, *discomfiture*

Vers. 9-15. THE KINGDOM ESTABLISHED UPON THE EARTH.

Ver. 9. *"be one and His name one"*,—i. e., be so recognized. He alone will be worshipped and the worship of idols and other gods will disappear.

Ver. 10. *"Arabah"*,—The largest of the Judean plains running from Lebanon to the further side of the Dead Sea.

"Geba and Rimmon",—Cities on the northern and southern borders of Judea.

"she",—i. e., Jerusalem.

"from Benjamin's gate (on the north) *to"*, etc.,—It is a question whether *"the first gate"* (the old gate, Neh. 3.6) was on the east or on the west. Some make the line run east to the *"first gate"* and west to the *"corner gate"* (F. K. Hen.), while others, with less probability, make the *"first gate"* and the *"corner gate"* the same and place it on the northwest corner.

The idea is that the city is to have its former limits. Some put the tower of Hananel at the northeast corner and the wine presses at the south; others put the former at the south and the latter in the center of the city.

Ver. 11. This verse is used in Rev. 22.3 to describe the New Jerusalem.

"The last day will end everything." (Au.)

"Temporal blessings and spiritual prosperity go hand in hand in the Millennium." (F.)

"In the nature of the case", says Seiss, "what is here foretold in verses 9 to 11 can only be realized as the result of the great consummation. It is, moreover, prefaced with the description of judicial administrations, in which 'the Lord shall go forth, . . . and His feet shall stand in that day upon the mount of Olives, which is before Jerusalem on the east'."

Ver. 12. The foe that is here punished, says Fausset, is the last antichristian confederacy.

Ver. 13. *"lay hold"*,—Not for help, as some maintain, but to assail him. (F. Ch.)

Ver. 14. *"fight at Jerusalem"*,—Not against Jerusalem (C. Ma. Jer. Lut. Coc. Kim.), but fight at Jerusalem against her foes. (F. K. Ch. Kl. Hen. Koe.)

Ver. 15. Even the beasts of the foes shall be overtaken by the divine curse.

16 And it shall come to pass, that every one that is left of all the nations that came against Jerusalem shall go up from year to year to worship the King, Jehovah of hosts, and to keep the feast of tabernacles.

17 And it shall be, that whoso of all the families of the earth goeth not up unto Jerusalem to worship the King, Jehovah of hosts, upon them there shall be no rain.

18 And if the family of Egypt go not up, and come not, neither shall it be upon them; there shall be the plague wherewith Jehovah shall smite the nations that go not up to keep the feast of tabernacles.

19 This shall be the [1]punishment of Egypt, and the [1]punishment of all the nations that go not up to keep the feast of tabernacles.

20 In that day shall there be upon the bells of the horses, HOLY UNTO JEHOVAH; and the pots in Jehovah's house shall be like the bowls before the altar.

21 Yea, every pot in Jerusalem and in Judah shall be holy unto Jehovah of hosts; and all they that sacrifice shall come and take of them, and boil therein: and in that day there shall be no more a Canaanite in the house of Jehovah of hosts.

[1]Or, *sin*

Vers. 16-21. THE WORSHIP AND SPIRITUALITY OF THE NEW ORDER.

Ver. 16. *"all the nations shall go up"*,—This of course could not be literally so, but they might go up by representatives. (F. He.) Those who allow only a spiritual interpretation·to the prophecy see here a striking method of depicting the entrance of the heathen into the kingdom of God.

There is a bright side to our Lord's coming, even to the nations. It is clearly taught that every one that is left of the nations and kings and princes shall worship and serve Jesus. (See Isa. 49.7; Psa. 2.8; 72.8-11.)

Says W. J. Erdman, "The return of Christ is followed by the conversion of the world, as is plainly shown by Paul in Rom. 11.25-27. A fullness of Gentile believers is now coming in while Israel as a nation remains in hardness of heart. When the number of the elect Church is complete, the Redeemer comes out of Zion and turns away ungodliness from Jacob and takes away their sins, and so 'all Israel shall be saved', and when Israel is converted, the whole Gentile world will also be converted. The same order of events was recognized by the apostolic Council at Jerusalem. (See Rom. 11.12-15 and Acts 15.13-18.)"

"to keep the feast of tabernacles",—Why is this feast designated?

1. Because it was held during the best season for travel. (The. Gro. Ros.)

2. Because it was the holiest and most joyful feast. (Pre. Ort. Kos.)

3. Because of its relation to the ingathering of the harvest. (Koe.)

4. Because it could be held without any compromise of New Testament principles. (He.)

5. Because the reference being to Messianic times the other two great feasts (Passover and Pentecost) have had their antitypes fulfilled and are gone. (F.)

6. Because of its interesting historical relation. (Ch. Mi. Hen. Dac.)

The last is perhaps the best reason. It was a feast of thanksgiving after their pilgrimage through the desert. It was so kept on their return from Babylonish captivity, and so after their long dispersion it will be appropriate again for the same reason. To the Gentiles also it will be significant after their long wandering in their moral wilderness.

Ver. 17. *"no rain"*,—Rain is one of the greatest blessings of God because of the fruitfulness that follows it.

It is true, as Chambers says, that this does not compel us to believe that at this period there will still be godless people. It may be taken as a rhetorical enforcement of the thought that there will be none. It may however be used with some propriety as authority for the view that there will be.

Fausset, referring the fulfillment of the prophecy to Millennium times, says, "That there shall be unconverted men during and under the Millennium appears from the outbreak of Gog and Magog at the end of it (Rev. 20.7-9), but they, like Satan their master, will be restrained during the Millennium."

Ver. 18. *"Egypt"*,—Even Egypt, who is not dependent on the rain for her fertility, but on the Nile, is mentioned to show that not even she shall escape. However, the Nile depends at its source on rain, and so the better reason for this special mention of Egypt might seem to be the fact that she was Israel's old hereditary foe. Not even she shall escape.

Vers. 20,21. Every thing holy. Even the pots of the temple (used for boiling the sacrificial flesh) shall be as holy as the *"bowls before the altar"* (which receive the blood of the victim), yea, and *"every pot"*, (pots even for ordinary use) shall be as holy as them.

"no more a Canaanite in the house of Jehovah",—The word does not mean "merchant", as in Prov. 31.24 (Aq. Tar. Jer. Gro. Hit. Bun.), nor literal Canaanite by birth (Kl. Hof. Dru.), but as Chambers and others say, it is an emblematic designation of godless members of the covenant nation. Canaan was cursed among Noah's children. It means here no unclean or ungodly person.

"holiness, etc., on the bells",—This does not mean that these bells should be used for religious purposes or worship or used to make sacred vessels (Cy. Gro.), nor that horses and other means of warfare should be consecrated to the Lord (Mi. Ma. Ew. Hit.), but that the distinction between holy and profane should cease and all things should be sacred.

THE BOOK OF

MALACHI

(B. C. 397)

CHAPTER THREE

1 Behold, I send my messenger, and he shall prepare the way before me: and the Lord, whom ye seek, will suddenly come to his temple; [1]and the [2]messenger of the covenant, whom ye desire, behold, he cometh, saith Jehovah of hosts. 2 But who can abide the day of his coming? and who shall stand when he appeareth? for he is like a refiner's fire, and like fuller's soap: 3 and he will sit as a refiner and purifier of silver, and he will purify the sons of Levi, and refine them as gold and silver; and they shall offer unto Jehovah offerings in righteousness. 4 Then shall the offering of Judah and Jerusalem be pleasant unto Jehovah, as in the days of old, and as in ancient years. 5 And I will come near to you to judgment; and I will be a swift witness against the sorcerers, and against the adulterers, and against the false swearers, and against those that oppress the hireling in his wages, the widow, and the fatherless, and that turn aside the sojourner *from his right*, and fear not me, saith Jehovah of hosts. 6 For I, Jehovah, change not; therefore ye, O sons of Jacob, are not consumed.

[1]Or, *even*
[2]Or, *angel*

Vers. 1-6. THE MISSION OF JOHN THE BAPTIST AND THE COMING OF THE LORD.

Ver. 1. The answer to the last question of the last verse of the preceding chapter.

"*my messenger*",—i. e., the one familiar to them from Isaiah's prophecy. (Isa. 40.3.) The reference is of course to John the Baptist.

"*the Lord*",—The word here used is applied only to God, but this same person is called in this same verse "*the messenger* (angel) *of the covenant*", and therefore by "*the Lord*" it is evident that here the Christ is meant, thus setting forth the deity of the Son of God.

"*whom ye seek*",—i. e., whom ye desire—spoken perhaps ironically with reference to "*where is the God of justice*" of the preceding verse.

"*suddenly*",—i. e., unexpectedly. (F. Wo. Poc.)

"*covenant*",—This is understood by Keil and others of the Old Covenant, but by most commentators it is taken as a reference to the New Covenant. Perhaps the chief thought is that of the New Covenant, but we see no reason for restricting it either to the one or the other exclusively. The first clause of this verse is quoted of John the Baptist (Matt. 11.10; Mk. 1.2; Lu. 7.27), but the second clause, "*the Lord whom ye seek*", etc., is nowhere quoted in the New Testament. With reference to this Scofield says, "The reason is obvious: in everything, save the fact of Christ's first advent, the latter clause awaits fulfillment (Hab. 2.20). Verses 2-5 speak of judgment—not of grace. Malachi, in common with the other Old Testament prophets, saw both advents of the Messiah blended in one horizon, but did not see the separating interval described in Matt. 13, consequent upon the rejection of the king (Matt. 13.16,17). Still less was the Church-age in his vision. The "*messenger of the Covenant*" is Christ in both of His advents, but with special reference to the events which are to follow His return."

Ver. 2. *"who can abide"*,—The day of the Lord is *"great and very terrible"*, (Joel 2.11). It is a day of judgment. That the two comings of Christ seem to be blended in one is quite the universal opinion of scholars both ancient and modern.

Augustine says, "The first and second advents of Christ are here brought together".

Fausset says, "His mission is here regarded as a whole from the first to the second advent". He further says, "The process of refining and separating the godly from the ungodly beginning during Christ's stay on earth, and going on ever since, is to continue until the final separation (Matt. 25.31-46). The refining process whereby a third of the Jews is refined, as silver of its dross, and a whole two thirds perish is described. (Zech. 13.8,9)."

Ver. 3. *"he will purify the sons of Levi"*,—These are the priests and judgment begins at the house of God.

"in righteousness",—i. e., in a proper state of heart.

Ver. 4. *"offering of Judah"*,—The Hebrew word used here for *"offering"* is not that of expiation, but of prayer, thanksgiving and self-dedication.

"as in the days of old",—i. e., in the days of David.

Ver. 5. *"near to you to judgment"*,—Not only will the priests be judged, but all the people also. The sins mentioned are those of which the Jews were then and later guilty.

16 Then they that feared Jehovah spake one with another; and Jehovah hearkened, and heard, and a book of remembrance was written before him, for them that feared Jehovah, and that thought upon his name. 17 And they shall be mine, saith Jehovah of hosts, even mine own possession, in the day that I [1]make; and I will spare them, as a man that spareth his own son that serveth him. 18 Then shall ye return and discern between the righteous and the wicked, between him that serveth God and him that serveth him not.

[1]Or, *do this*

Vers. 16-18. THE REWARD OF THE FAITHFUL REMNANT.

Verses 7 to 15 are taken up with the complainings of the ungodly which was the occasion for *"they that feared the Lord"* to talk to one another in defense of God.

Ver. 16. *"a book of remembrance was written"*,—A book written for their advantage against the day of judgment when those found faithful are rewarded.

Ver. 17. *"mine own possession"*,—Literally, "mine own peculiar treasure".

"in the day that I make",—With the reading of our text agree most of the authorities (Pa. Ma. Jer. Tar. Sep.), except that they differ somewhat as to the word *"make"*. Literally this word means "do", as in Chap. 4.3.

Calvin translates, "in the day in which I will do it", i. e., fulfill the promises made.

If the word *"make"* is retained the meaning is doubtless, as Grotius says, "in the day that I make those things come to pass foretold in verse 5".

Ver. 18, *"ye"*,—i. e., the wicked murmerers.

"return",—i. e., to a better state of mind. The word may be taken as an adverb and rendered "again", and the "and" omitted, i. e., "Then shall ye again discern", etc. (K. Pa. He. Ges. Koe.)

CHAPTER FOUR

1 For, behold, the day cometh, it burneth as a furnace; and all the proud, and all that work wickedness, shall be stubble; and the day that cometh shall burn them up, saith Jehovah of hosts, that it shall leave them neither root nor branch. 2 But unto you that fear my name shall the sun of righteousness arise with healing in its ¹wings; and ye shall go forth, and gambol as calves of the stall. 3 And ye shall tread down the wicked; for they shall be ashes under the soles of your feet in the day that I ²make, saith Jehovah of hosts.

4 Remember ye the law of Moses my servant, which I commanded unto him in Horeb for all Israel, even statutes and ordinances.

¹Or, *beams*

²Or, *do* this

Vers. 1-4. THE DAY OF THE LORD AND THE SECOND COMING OF CHRIST.

Ver. 1. *"the day cometh"*,—This is the *"great and terrible day"* mentioned in Joel 2.31. There are those who refer this to the destruction of Jerusalem while others of course refer it to the last great day. That there may be a reference here to the destruction of Jerusalem cannot be denied but certainly this does not exhaust the meaning of the verse unless we confess to a gross exaggeration. It would seem that we have here again the principle of successive fulfillment, the destruction of Jerusalem being but an earnest of the later coming day of judgment.

"leave neither root nor branch",—Not one shall escape, the expression being one of utter destruction.

Ver. 2. *"the sun of righteousness"*,—Jewish commentators and many others (K. Hen. Koe. Rei. Moo.) agree with the text of the American Revised Version and make the idea that of "righteousness as a sun", i. e., the consummation of salvation. But from parallel passages such as Isa. 9.1; 49.6, etc., from exegetical tradition and from internal evidence, it is, as Packard says, better to understand it personally of Christ. (Pa. He. Eu. Cy. The., the Fathers, the early and a majority of the modern commentators.)

"healing",—i. e., salvation. The beams of the sun are here compared to the outstretched wings of a bird.

Ver. 3. *"the wicked"*,—i. e., those who have troubled them.

"they shall be ashes",—i. e., after having been burnt with the fire of judgment.

Fausset thinks the reference is to the righteous who shall be the army attending Christ in His final destruction of the ungodly. (Mic. 7.10; Zech. 10.5; I Cor. 6.2; Rev. 2.26,27.)

Ver. 4. *"Remember ye the law"*,—The way in which the coming judgment is to be averted. They would be apt to forget it in the absence of living prophets of whom Malachi was the last for four hundred years.

5 Behold, I will send you Elijah the prophet before the great and terrible day of Jehovah come. 6 And he shall turn the heart of the fathers [1]to the children, and the heart of the children [1]to their fathers: lest I come and smite the [2]earth with a [3]curse.

[1]Or, *with*

[2]Or, *land*
[3]Or, *ban* Or, *devoting to destruction*

Vers. 5,6. ELIJAH TO COME BEFORE THE DAY OF THE LORD.

Ver. 5. This seems to be a repetition of the promise of Chap. 3.1 in more specific form.

Christ said that John the Baptist fulfilled both of these prophecies in Malachi and that he was the fore-runner meant in each of them.

"This is he of whom it is written 'Behold I send my messenger before thy face and he shall prepare the way before thee'."

"And if ye will receive it, this is the Elijah who was to come."

"Elijah is come already and they knew him not." "Then understood they that He spoke to them of John the Baptist."

The angel said to John the Baptist's father before the birth of his son, *"And he shall go before him* (Christ) *in the spirit and power of Elijah."*

This is enough to prove that John the Baptist was meant by the *"messenger"* in Malachi 3.1, and by *"Elijah"* in Malachi 4.5, so far as the first coming of Christ is concerned.

When John the Baptist in John 1.21 denied that he was Elijah he meant only in the sense to which the Jews had reference, because he knew they were naturally thinking of a literal, personal Elijah, according to their interpretation of Malachi's prophecy. But John in fact said that he was the Elijah of Malachi, in this other sense, when he affirmed, *"I am the voice of one crying in the wilderness, 'Make straight the way of the Lord'."*

The Jews hold that a literal, personal Elijah was meant by Malachi in Chap. 4.5 and that it referred to Christ's first coming, and therefore they say that Christ has not yet come because the literal, personal Elijah has not yet come.

Most of the Fathers, Cy. Or. Chr. The. Jer. Ter. Aug. Theo., the Romish interpreters and many modern Protestant commentators hold also that a literal, personal Elijah is meant in Chap. 4.5, but these teach that the prophecy has a double fulfillment; that John came in the spirit and power of Elijah before Christ's first coming, but that the real, literal, personal Elijah will come before the second coming of Christ. (S. A. O. F. Ma. Ry. Ew. Hit. Sco.)

Alford says, "John the Baptist only partially fulfilled the great prophecy which announced the real Elijah (the words of Malachi will hardly bear any other than a literal, personal meaning) who is to fore-run the second and greater coming."

Now Christ said in Matt. 17.10, *"Truly Elijah shall first come and restore all things"*. Some commentators explain this by saying that Christ put Himself back in Malachi's time and uses these words with a future reference from there, but it is far more in keeping with careful exegesis to refer them to a future and second coming after the time when the words were uttered by Christ, as do all the expositors mentioned above, except of course the Jewish commentators.

Therefore that Elijah will come before the second coming of Christ seems quite certain, although it is not determined with absolute certainty whether he will be the personal Elijah (against which, however, no strong objection can be urged) or another John, as it were, in the spirit and power of Elijah. The natural inference is that he will be the real, personal Elijah.

Ver. 6. Some refer this to a restoration of family harmony. (He. Ma. Ew.) It is better, however, to refer it to the reconciliation to be effected between the unbelieving, disobedient children and their godly, believing ancestors. They had been estranged from the piety of their ancestors and the bond of union which had been broken will be restored. If this reconciliation is not thus effected Messiah's coming would prove a curse and not a blessing.

MATTHEW

(A. D. 37)

CHAPTER TEN

> 23 for verily, I say unto you, Ye
> shall not have gone through the cities
> of Israel, till the Son of man be come.

Ver. 23. THE COMING OF THE LORD IN THE DESTRUCTION OF JERU-
SALEM.

"gone through",—This means literally "to make an end of", i. e.,
you shall not have finished your mission to the cities of Israel.

"till the Son of man be come",—This expression here is most certainly a direct reference to the destruction of Jerusalem which historically
put an end to the old dispensation and which is of course a type of the final
coming of the Lord. It is what Alford calls "an immediate literal and
distant foreshadowing fulfillment". This interpretation has more in its
favor and less against it than any other. (A. R. Eb. Mi. Glo. Moe. Ges.
Schot.) Indeed every other view is either entirely gratuitous and far-
fetched or if it has any due regard at all for the accepted meaning of the
phraseology it becomes the subject of insurmountable difficulty.

Meyer says the personal second coming of Christ is meant. He says
the phrase, *"the Son of man cometh"*, always has a definite doctrinal signification, and always refers to Christ's personal coming, and that Jesus
here speaks of this coming as being thus near, even as He does in Chap.
16.28. But this is hardly in keeping with Christ's own statement that
He Himself did not know the day of His coming, inasmuch as a prophecy
that it was so near at hand would imply that He did know somewhat as
to the time, while furthermore it is difficult to conceive of Christ being the
author of any such misconception as to the time of His personal second
coming at the end of the age.

It will be interesting to note the various expedients to which commentators have committed themselves in attempting to resolve the difficulty
of the passage before us. One of the most curious is that of Blackstone,
who, with Meyer, says the reference is to the personal second coming of
Christ, but who escapes the embarrassment this view involves by declaring
that not even yet in this twentieth century have the followers of Christ
gone through the cities of Israel. The work, begun in the day of the
Disciples, has been interrupted, but will be resumed in the last days and
then Christ will come. But this cannot appeal with any great force to
the impartial exegete, being, as it seems, rather something of a convenient
makeshift which avoids the real issue of the text.

The expression is explained by some as a vague "coming of the Son
of man to their help". (Chr. Bez. Kui. The. Eut. Zig. Theo.) This view
is advanced from the feeling that the connection demands reference to
something that was to happen *very* soon. But such explanation does not

suit the earnest *"verily"*, nor the fact that in reality it was *they* who came back to Jesus. (Lu. 9.10.)

Others make *"gone through"* mean "finish" in the sense of bringing to Christian perfection, and thus in this way remove the time for Christ's coming far into the future. (Hi. Hof. Mal. Jan. Zeg.) This Meyer rightly calls "an erroneous makeshift".

Neither must the expression be explained as a coming through the Holy Spirit (C. Ca. Bl. Gro.); nor allegorically, i. e., until the victory of Christ's cause comes (B-C); nor yet, *"until the Son of man overtake you"*, seeing that the Disciples in their mission only preceded Christ. (L. Heub.)

Olshausen says the Resurrection, the coming through the Holy Spirit at Pentecost and even the destruction of Jerusalem were *all* too remote from the Disciples during the first period of their ministry, and he says the words involve by way of anticipation a wider range of vision and blend the early mission of the Disciples with their subsequent one. But is such liberty of extension of the thought of Christ on the part of Matthew altogether warranted with reference to any teaching?

Says Campbell Morgan, "This was the first reference that Christ ever made to His coming in any other sense than that of His presence with them in the world at the time. It was an incidental word, and I personally feel that there can be no escape from the conviction that upon that occasion His reference was not to the coming with which He dealt at a later period, but to His visitation of Jerusalem in judgment at her destruction a generation after His Cross."

CHAPTER TWELVE

18 Behold, my servant whom I have chosen;

My beloved in whom my soul is well pleased:

I will put my Spirit upon him,

And he shall declare judgment to the Gentiles.

19 He shall not strive, nor cry aloud;
Neither shall any one hear his voice in the streets.

20 A bruised reed shall he not break,
And smoking flax shall he not quench,
Till he send forth judgment unto victory.

Vers. 18-20. THE END-TIME JUDGMENT UPON THE GENTILES.

Practically all scholars are agreed that by *"declaring judgment to the Gentiles"* reference is made to Christ as Judge announcing final judicial sentence to the Gentiles at the day of judgment. All are equally agreed that by *"until he send forth judgment unto victory"* is meant "until He cause His judgment to end in victory in the day of final decision, so that no further conflict will remain", i. e., "until He shall have led forth unto victory at the last day the judgment announced by Him". The holding of the final assize is the victory of the judgment.

Alford has rightly said of the last clause of verse 18 that "it contrasts the majesty of His future glory with the meekness about to be spoken of".

Verses 19 and 20 then refer to the disposition of the lowly Christ in His day and ours. "In the present day", as Morgan says, "He does not strive nor cause His voice to be heard in the streets: neither will He break the bruised reed, nor quench the smoking flax, *till*—there is an emphasis on that word which we must regard if we are to understand the passage—

till He send forth judgment unto victory." Verse 20, in fact, has nothing to do with the dispensation in which we live, and the *"bruised reed"* and *"smoking flax"* do not refer, as is usually supposed, to "men and women whose aspirations after Him are weak but will not be despised", because there is a time coming when He will break the bruised reed and quench the smoking flax. These expressions, therefore, refer to His enemies, as will be seen by referring to the original of the quotation in Isa. 42.1-4. In His day of grace and mercy He is longsuffering with those who stand out against Him, but in the time yet to come beyond this day of grace and mercy, "He will break and quench His enemies, and He will sweep before the majesty of His coming, as chaff of the threshing floor, the evil things which so affright us by their tremendous hold upon our age. In that day He will send forth judgment unto victory."

CHAPTER THIRTEEN

Vers. 24-30.   (See explanation under verses 38-43.)

31 Another parable set he forth before them, saying, The kingdom of heaven is like unto a grain of mustard seed, which a man took and sowed in his field: 32 which indeed is less than all seeds; but when it is grown, it is greater than the herbs, and becometh a tree, so that the birds of heaven come and lodge in the branches thereof.

Vers. 31,32.   THE KINGDOM OF HEAVEN LIKE UNTO A MUSTARD SEED.

Ver. 32.   *"less than all seeds"*,—This is not to be pressed in its literal sense, the mustard seed being a well-known Jewish type for anything exceedingly small.

It is quite natural to interpret this parable in harmony with the mingling of good and evil as set forth by the previous ones. Thus Morgan says, "A tree, in Scripture, is always the figure of power. Our Lord simply teaches that Christendom shall become a great power and force—nothing more. I suggest for your consideration that the fowls of the air are emblems of evil and not of good; and that their lodging in the branches of the tree teaches the corruption of even Christendom itself."

Most pre-millennial scholars agree in general with this interpretation, and we are not prepared to say that such an explanation is not in accord with the general teaching of Christ concerning the kingdom.

Assuredly, however, there is an aspect of the kingdom which portrays the growth of Christianity from small beginnings, and it would seem to be far more natural for any mind not warped by doctrinal prejudice to think of this parable as representing the insignificant beginning of the kingdom and then its increase and growth and progress while the nations of the earth are drawn into it, whether we think of these nations as mere external adherents, mere nominal Christian nations, or as representing those who are sincerely coming into the kingdom. The fact is it would be better not to press either of these views concerning the *"birds of heaven"* too far. The idea of growth as represented by a tree is the central teaching of the parable, and the birds lodging in the branches quite naturally belong to the picture, without attaching to themselves any particular significance as a part of the parable. Any picture, as a whole, may stand for a truth, without calling for a definite significance of every detail. The parable represents, says Erdman, Alford, and other ardent pre-millennarians, "the small beginnings and wide extension of the message of the kingdom and of its effects".

33 Another parable spake He unto them; the kingdom of heaven is like unto leaven, which a woman took, and hid in ¹three measures of meal, till it was all leavened.

¹*A little more than a bushel*

Ver. 33. THE KINGDOM OF HEAVEN LIKE UNTO LEAVEN.

"like unto leaven",—Because leaven, in the Scriptures, usually represents an evil influence (Ex. 12.15; I Cor. 5.6,7; Matt. 16.6; Gal. 5.9), many take it thus here and explain it of the progress of the corruption and deterioration in the outward visible Church. (Gab. Mor. Sco. Bla. and most pre-millennial scholars.)

But there are strong arguments, as set forth by Lange, against so taking it.

1. It is contrary to the rules of hermenutics to treat an allegorical figure like a dogmatic statement. Thus a lion is used as a figure of Satan but also as a figure of Christ.
2. All the other parables in this section, and especially the preceding one, bear upon the development of the kingdom of heaven, and so this parable would be quite out of place if taken otherwise.
3. It is impossible to conceive of the kingdom of heaven as leavened by evil and thus hopelessly destroyed.
   (We might also remark that the passage does not say that the kingdom is like unto three measures of meal with which the leaven becomes mixed up, but it says the kingdom is *like* unto *leaven*, and says Alford, a pre-millennarian, "How are we to explain that it is said that the kingdom of heaven is *like* this leaven, and if it is like it in the sense of corruption, then there is an end of all the blessings and healing influence of the Gospel?"
4. Leaven may indeed be employed as a figure of sin and evil in the sense of being stronger than the individual Christian when left in his own strength to combat with error, but not in that of being more powerful than the kingdom of heaven itself.
5. Leaven *as such* is nowhere in the Bible a figure of evil, but a neutral figure of an all-pervading, contagious power. (See Leviticus 23.17, where it says, *"They shall be baken with leaven; they are the first fruits unto the Lord."*)

We find therefore on the other hand that many take the leaven here not as an evil principle but as a gracious influence. Thus Alford, Lange, Trench, Stier, Meyer, Olshausen and Godet among pre-millennialists, as well as all post-millennialists.

Trench says that because leaven was as a rule used in an evil sense, Christ was not therefore the less free to use it in a good sense, while Stier says that the growth of the kingdom like a mustard seed doubtless brought to the mind of Jesus the thought of the corrupting influences that would creep into the Church like an evil leaven, and having this in mind, He purposely placed in opposition to it His good leaven, the kingdom of heaven. The kingdom of heaven is thus seen to be the good leaven pene-trating by degrees the whole mass of humanity, as seen in the general world improvement.

Trench, followed by Meyer, limits the parable to an individual refer-ence as indicating the regenerating and transforming of the soul. Meyer is worth quoting here, although the limitation mentioned is hardly a per-missible one. He says, "The parable of the mustard seed is designed to show that the great community, consisting of those who are to participate in the Messianic kingdom, i. e., the true people of God as constituting the body politic of the future kingdom, is destined to develop from a small beginning. The parable of the leaven on the other hand is intended to show how the specific influence of the Messiah's kingdom gradually pene-trates the whole of its future subjects until by this means the entire man is brought intensively into that spiritual condition which qualifies it for being admitted into the kingdom."

"until the whole be leavened",—This of course is never true of the entire dough of humanity, for what then would be made of the tares and the separation at the end? Just to what degree it is true individually and personally of the elect is also a question, even though one limit the parable to its individual reference.

No allegorical explanation of the *"three measures"* is to be sought, and those advanced are far-fetched and unwarranted. It was the amount usually taken for a batch.

Vers. 37-43.   (See Vers. 24-30.)

37 And he answered and said, He that soweth the good seed is the Son of man; 38 and the field is the world; and the good seed, these are the sons of the kingdom; and the tares are the sons of the evil one; 39 and the enemy that sowed them is the devil: and the har-vest is [1]the end of the world; and the reapers are angels. 40 As therefore the tares are gathered up and burned with fire; so shall it be in [1]the end of the world. 41 The Son of man shall send forth his angels, and they shall gather out of his kingdom all things that cause stumbling, and them that do iniquity, 42 and shall cast them into the furnace of fire: there shall be weeping and gnashing of teeth. 43 Then shall the righteous shine forth as the sun in the kingdom of their Father. He that hath ears, let him hear.

[1]Or, *the consummation of the age*

Vers. 37-43. THE KINGDOM AND THE TARES.

Ver. 38. *"sons of the kingdom"*,—Not by the old covenant as in Chap. 8.12, but ·by the effectual grace of adoption.

"sons of the evil one",—Their ethical nature being derived from the Devil.

"the field is the world",—Stier says, and rightly, that Christ could not have possibly said anything else here than *"world"*, and that all who without reason substitute "Church" lose thereby a highly important ground feature of the parable.

Others think of the world here as the Church, i. e., the visible Church, nominal Christendom seeking to pervade and occupy the whole world. (R. A. M. O. Tr.) The sense, however, in the ultimate is practically the same. The kingdom of heaven began with Christ's incarnation, the good seed being sowed by the Gospel.

Ver. 39. *"the end of the age"*,—The reference is to the end of the dispensation or period of time in which we are now living. This expression is not found in any other Gospel. The Jews said in substance, "When the Messiah comes, this age will end." Christ and His Disciples took this phrase of the Jews and referred it to the second coming of the Messiah which is to introduce the Messianic judgment. (M. L. O. R. A.)

"the reapers are angels",—This is not a figure of speech any more than the Devil is a figure of speech. (See Chap. 24.31.)

On the words, *"let both grow together"*, in verse 30, Trench says, "Pregnant words, which tell us that evil is not, as so many dream, gradually to wane and disappear before good; the world is to find itself in the Church, but each is to unfold itself more fully out of its own root, after its own kind." There is to be the intermixture of good and evil until the end of time.

Ver. 41. *"gather out of His kingdom"*,—Meyer says this judgment is to take place as soon as the earth has undergone that process of regeneration which is to transform it into the scene of the Messiah's kingdom. The words *"gather out"*, says Lange, "clearly show that the end of the age must be regarded as a period of time, an interval of time, and hence indicates that there is a period intervening between the Second Coming of Christ and the first resurrection connected with it, and the last resurrection."

"things that cause stumbling",—Men who by their unbelief and sin put temptation in the way of others.

"furnace of fire",—Gehenna, hell. (Chap. 25.41; Rev. 20.15.)

Ver. 43. *"shine forth"*,—This conveys the idea of a sublime display of majestic splendor like the glory of Christ at the transfiguration. They shall shine forth *"like the sun"* when the clouds have rolled away. (Dan. 13.3.)

"who hath ears",—The conclusion is in keeping with the importance of the parable. It behooves men to heed a prophecy respecting the destiny of all men.

> 44 The kingdom of heaven is like unto a treasure hidden in the field; which a man found and hid; and [1]in his joy he goeth and selleth all that he hath, and buyeth the field.
>
> [1]Or, *for joy thereof*

Ver. 44. THE KINGDOM LIKE A TREASURE HID IN A FIELD.

The kingdom of heaven can become ours only on condition that we are prepared joyfully to surrender for its sake every other earthly treasure. The field is the outward visible Church, and this man, says Alford, without any earnest seeking unexpectedly finds in some part of it the treasure of true faith and hope.

> 45 Again the kingdom of heaven is like unto a man that is a merchant seeking goodly pearls; 46 and having found one pearl of great price, he went and sold all that he had, and bought it.

Vers. 45,46. THE KINGDOM LIKE A MAN SEEKING PEARLS.

This is a parable not merely of a finder but of a seeker, a seeker after truth. The Pearl of Great Price is Christ Himself.

"one",—There is only *one* such pearl.

47 Again, the kingdom of heaven is like unto a [1]net, that was cast into the sea, and gathered of every kind: 48 which, when it was filled, they drew up on the beach; and they sat down, and gathered the good into vessels, but the bad they cast away. 49 So shall it be in [2]the end of the world: the angels shall come forth, and sever the wicked from among the righteous, 50 and shall cast them into the furnace of fire: there shall be weeping and the gnashing of teeth.

[1]Gr. *drag-net*

[2]Or, *the consummation of the age*

Vers. 47-50. THE KINGDOM LIKE A DRAG-NET.

The ultimate separation of the holy and the unholy in the Church.

The net is the Church, the outward visible Church, gathering from the sea of nations. The parable teaches the development side by side of good and evil in this Church and the world.

"they sat down",—Intimating perhaps that some time is to be taken in the work of separation.

CHAPTER SIXTEEN

27 For the Son of man shall come in the glory of his Father with his angels; and then shall he render unto every man according to his [1]deeds. 28 Verily, I say unto you, There are some of them that stand here, who shall in no wise taste of death, till they see the Son of man coming in his kingdom.

[1]Gr. *doing*

Vers. 27,28. THE COMING OF THE LORD IN THE DESTRUCTION OF JERUSALEM.

Ver. 27. Christ at His Second Coming is to appear as Judge and His attendants shall be His angels.

"shall come",—This is not a simple future, and Lange is inclined to see in it the meaning that the event is impending, i. e., He shall come—is about to come.

"in the glory of his Father",—The same glory as that which belongs to God and which He now shares with God.

"deeds",—The total outward manifestation of his inner life as a believer or an unbeliever.

Ver. 28. Olshausen says, "This saying, which the first three evangelists have with such unanimity preserved in the same connection, was one of the strongest supports of the Apostolic age that there would be a speedy and visible return of Christ."

"some of them that stand here",—The Disciples and the people standing about Him. (Mark 8.34.) This much we must accept as certain, namely that it presupposes that the majority of them will have died previous to the event in question.

"coming in his kingdom",—

1. Many commentators refer this to the following transfiguration. (Be. Va. Fa. Chr. Ken.)

   But,

   (a) *"some not tasting death"* implies a distant event, at least one more distant than six days.

(b) The evangelist could not have applied this expression to such an exceptional and transitory incident.

(c) The transfiguration could not, save in the sense of a foretaste, be called a coming in His kingdom.

2. Lange refers it to His resurrection, to the coming in the glory of His kingdom within the circle of the Disciples, which took place when He arose from the dead and revealed Himself in their midst; the moment being close at hand when their hearts were to be set at rest by such manifestation of His glory.

But the first objection (a) to the view above applies equally here.

3. Godet refers the expression to a spiritual coming of Christ, to an inner experience of the soul in accordance with the inward nature of the kingdom itself (the kingdom of God is within you); in order to enjoy this sight a new sense, a new birth, is needed, which some of them standing there should receive with the coming of the Holy Spirit at Pentecost, when they were to behold with their inward eye those wonderful works of God which Jesus calls His kingdom, or the kingdom of God.

But the objection just recorded obtains here. It is furthermore an altogether too easy method of resolving a difficulty.

4. Many other authorities refer the expression to the progress and conquests of the Gospel, especially between Pentecost and the Destruction of Jerusalem. (Al. Fa. Whe. Dor. Era. Klo. Schen.)

But there is the same fatal objection to this view, as without doubt practically all of them saw at least the beginning of such a fulfillment.

5. Barnes interprets the passage spiritually and refers it to the day of Pentecost and the founding of the Church. But,

(a) The same common objection applies equally to this view.

(b) Jesus and the Holy Spirit are two distinct persons. Jesus said, "I will send you *another* Comforter", and if the Holy Spirit be *"another"* Comforter, He cannot then be Christ Himself, and it is therefore inconsistent to confound this event with the coming of the Son of man.

(c) Furthermore, it will not do to identify the Church with the Kingdom. The Church is to suffer and to reign with Christ in His Kingdom. (Rom. 8.17.)

6. Wordsworth substitutes, "shall not taste of the bitterness of death", i. e., shall not taste of the death of the soul until, etc., much less shall they after He comes!

But this is an interpretation altogether too fanciful. Blackstone says the words may have this significance, as in the sense of John 8.51 and Hebrews 2.9, but he merely suggests this explanation, and is quite convinced that the word *"till"* more than intimates that some of them standing there should taste death, and that therefore natural death or the separation of soul and body was meant.

7. Meyer and Olshausen refer it to His ultimate glorious Parousia.

They say the kingdom cannot come without the King, and that the coming of this verse and the one just before it are one and the same, the former verse emphasizing the certainty of the Second Coming and the latter one the nearness of it.

But—

(a) This coming can hardly be the same as that mentioned in the preceding verse because there He comes in the glory of His Father, while here He comes in His kingdom.

(b) How could Christ, not knowing the time of His Parousia Himself (Mark 13.32) utter such a determinate prophecy of it?

(c) Christ could not have labored under such a misapprehension. Olshausen says Christ thought His personal return was really so near at hand. But this is equivalent to saying the Lord was mistaken.

(d) Stier says, *"not tasting death until He comes"* implies that they will taste it after He comes, and that therefore this cannot refer to His final Parousia.

8. Blackstone maintains that it is at Christ's coming in His kingdom that He is to be manifested in His glory, and that the expression here means His coming in the Parousia at the end of this age, even as do Meyer and Olshausen, but, in a manner hardly consistent with sound interpretation, he refers the prophecy of this passage to the visions given to the three Disciples on the Mount of Transfiguration, to Paul when caught up into the third heaven, and to John when in Patmos, as set forth in the Book of Revelation. But apart from the fact that the nearness of the Transfiguration is, as we have already so often stated, fatal to this part of the explanation, it will not do to deprive in this way the thing prophesied of its actuality and to fill up its meaning with a vision. Whatever they were to see must have been in some sense a real coming of Christ in His kingdom, and not merely a vision of it.

9. Still others refer the expression to the Destruction of Jerusalem (Chap. 10.23) as a type and an earnest of the final Second Coming of Christ. (A. E. R. S. Ow. Oo. Eb. Bl. Gro. Wet. Cap. Kui. Glo. Schot.) With this view we are inclined to agree. It has against it none of the objections enumerated and Chap. 25 seems to support it.

CHAPTER NINETEEN

27 Then answered Peter and said unto him, Lo, we have left all, and followed thee; what then shall we have? 28 And Jesus said unto them, Verily I say unto you, that ye who have followed me, in the regeneration when the Son of man shall sit on the throne of his glory, ye also shall sit upon twelve thrones, judging the twelve tribes of Israel.

Vers. 27, 28. THE DISCIPLES TO JUDGE ISRAEL AT THE LORD'S RETURN.

Ver. 27. A question doubtless prompted by the words, *"shalt have treasure in heaven"* spoken to the rich young man.

"what shall we have therefore?"—This is a question of reward. Not "What therefore will there be for us still to do?" (Pau.); nor "What is waiting for us? Are we, too, to be called upon to undergo such a test as the young man has just been subjected to?" (O.)

Ver. 28. *"in the regeneration",*—Some (Aug. Eut. Fri. Theo.) interpret this expression of the Resurrection; but this sense is too restricted and is besides contrary to regular New Testament usage.

Hilary, Hammond and others apply the expression to the first regeneration, and, connecting it with *"followed me"*, render, "Ye who have followed me in the regeneration, or as regenerated persons". Similar to this is the view which takes the words as referring to the state of things on earth after Christ's resurrection, when He had sat down, after His ascension, upon His throne. (C. Bl. Li. Gro. Whe.) But the Disciples could only have conceived of the renovation of the world as something taking place contemporaneously with the actual setting up of the kingdom at the return of the Lord. Others accordingly and rightly take them as signifying the change by which the whole world is to be restored to that original state of perfection in which it existed before the fall and which is to be brought about by the coming of the Messiah, at which time it seems, in the minds of the Disciples, there would take place the setting up of His kingdom. (M. D.) Lange combines the last two views.

"judging the twelve tribes of Israel",—There are two views of this passage:

1. The symbolical view, i. e., that the expression applies to the spiritual administration and rule of the Disciples in subordination to the will of the Master. Lange says that it is a figurative representation of Christ's presence and power in the infant Church, laying down rules and sitting in judgment through His vice-regents, the Disciples. The Disciples appear here therefore in the ideal rather than in their individual capacity, and that therefore the twelve tribes of Israel must be taken in a symbolical sense as applying to the whole body of believers. (L. D. C. Bl. Gro. Whe.)

   But against the symbolical view the following good reasons obtain:

   (a) The period after Christ's resurrection was not the time of their reward but of trial and persecution.

   (b) It does not furnish a pertinent reply to Peter's question.

   (c) Godet says that in the parallel passage in Luke 22.30, the expression, *"eat and drink at my table"*, almost compels one to go further than the spiritual or symbolical interpretation, and interpret *"in my kingdom"* as in Luke 22.16,18, and so it would seem that the reference is to a kingdom He was to establish in the future.

   (d) Meyer says that the Disciples could only conceive of the renovation of the world contemporary with the setting up of the Messianic kingdom.

2. The literal view, which attaches to the word *"judging"* its usual literal significance. It must at least have so appeared to the minds of the Disciples. (M. O. G. Pl. Ow. Carr.)

Ellicott well says, "Whatever approximations to a literal fulfillment there may be in the far-off future lies behind the veil." That is, we do not know exactly what is the nature of this function, but the arguments all seem to strongly favor the literal view of the same. Judging, it would seem in the minds of the Disciples, would refer not alone to judging every man according to his works, as assessors of the divine King; but judging in the old sense of the word as well, i. e., redressing wrongs, ruling, governing.

Owen would have us think of a mere "concurring" in the sentence of the Judge.

Ellicott says, "The words receive at least an adequate fulfillment if we see in them the promise that in the last triumphant stage of the redeeming work the Apostles should still be recognized and held in honor as guiding the faith and conduct of their countrymen. So I Cor. 6.2 refers in like manner not solely nor chiefly to any share which the Disciples shall have in the actual work of the final judgment, but to the assured triumph of the faith, the laws, the principles of action of which they were then the persecuted witnesses."

Meyer, advocating the literal view, says, "Believers generally are to share in the future glory and reign of Christ (Rom. 8.17; II Tim. 2.12) and to have part in judging the non-Christian world (I Cor. 6.2), but to the Disciples the special prerogative is here accorded of having part in the judgment of the Jewish people, it being evident from I Cor. 6.2 that the Jewish people will then still form part of the unconverted world."

CHAPTER TWENTY

21 She saith unto him, Command that these my two sons may sit, one on thy right hand, and one on thy left hand, in thy kingdom.

Ver. 21. THE KINGDOM MISINTERPRETED.

This request seems to have arisen from the promise given in Chap. 19.28, and this mother was doubtless one of those who thought that the kingdom was immediately to appear. (Matt. 27.56; Mark 15.40; Luke 19.11.)

CHAPTER TWENTY-ONE

43 Therefore say I unto you, the kingdom of God shall be taken away from you, and shall be given to a nation bringing forth the fruits thereof.

44 And he that falleth on this stone shall be broken to pieces; but on whom soever it shall fall, it will scatter him as dust.

Vers. 43,44. THE REJECTION OF THE JEWISH NATION.

Ver. 43. Returning to the parable, our Lord announces more plainly than ever to them their rejection by God.

"a nation bringing forth the fruits thereof",—The reference is no doubt, as Alford says, to the holy nation, the peculiar people of God, the Church of the truly faithful. (1 Pet. 2.9 and Acts 15.14.) It is quite true, as Whedon says, that our Lord here predicts again the fall of the Jews and the call of the Gentiles, but as Meyer, Olshausen and Fausset say, the community of believers referred to consists not of the Gentiles in particular (Eu. Vol. Keim.), but of the whole of the future subjects of the kingdom, conceived of as one people, consisting chiefly of Gentiles of course until *"all Israel should be saved"*.

Gaebelein objects to the view just stated by saying that the Church is called *"the body of Christ"*, *"the Bride of Christ"*, *"the habitation of God by the Spirit"*, *"the Lamb's wife"*, but never a nation. He therefore refers the expression to the believing remnant of the Jews, but there is hardly sufficient argument in support of his objections and of his view.

Ver. 44. There is no doubt here a reference to the second chapter of Daniel. The idea is, Whoever falls on Christ, i. e., stumbles over Him as a *"rock of offense"* (I Pet. 2.8; Isa. 8.14,15) in the days of His humiliation shall be broken, i. e., shall have great sorrow; but to incur His wrath, to have Him fall on them at His Second Coming to judgment means utter destruction.

"scatter him as dust",—Literally, "shall winnow him", suggested by Dan. 2.35 where the image broken to pieces became as the chaff of the threshing floor. The idea is that of being thrown off like chaff from the winnowing fan.

Ellicott, Whedon and others, who refer both parts of the expression to the present dispensation which began with the first coming of Christ, say the second part of the verse refers to Christ, or the Church with which He identifies Himself, coming into collision with the powers that oppose Him, when it shall grind them to pieces and scatter them like dust.

While the reference is a general one, Gaebelein says with propriety that the first part of the verse refers to the Jews and the second part to the Gentiles. The first part has been fulfilled and the second part will be when at His coming He falls on the world-powers, the Gentile governments, and grinds them to powder.

Godet, who seems to agree with Gaebelein, says, "It is dangerous to encounter this stone whether by dashing against it while yet it is laid on the ground, as Israel is doing, or whether when it shall be raised to the top of the building, men provoke it to fall on their own heads as other nations shall one day do."

CHAPTER TWENTY-THREE

> 39 For I say unto you, Ye shall not see me henceforth, till ye shall say, Blessed is he that cometh in the name of the Lord.

Ver. 39. THE GLAD WELCOME OF OUR LORD AT HIS SECOND COMING.

You shall not see me henceforth until that day, the subject of all prophecy, when the repentant Jewish nation shall turn with true and loyal Hosannahs and blessing to greet Him whom they have pierced. (Deut. 4.30,31; Isa. 66.20; Hos. 3.4,5; Zech. 12.10; 14.8-11.)

"he that cometh",—Not in the destruction of Jerusalem (Wet.), because Christ was not then hailed as here predicted; but that Second

Coming when He shall appear in the glory of the Messiah. (M. E. A. G. S. B. L. Au. Oo. Ew. Hof. Whe. Theo. Sche.) It is a mistake therefore to take the verse as the conversion of Israel in her development down *to* the Second Coming.

Ellicott says, "There can be little doubt that our Lord points to the Second Advent and to the welcome that will then be given Him by all the true Israel of God. For the generation of His day and for the outward Israel as such the abandonment was final."

Owen, who will not think of a visible, bodily return of Christ, says, "Prophecy discloses to us the fact that the Jewish nation as such will eventually acknowledge Jesus as Messiah. He will then come, not in bodily form, but in the Spirit to sit upon the throne of His father, David, and then shall be uttered this *'blessed'*."

CHAPTER TWENTY-FOUR

1 And Jesus went out from the temple, and was going on His way; and his disciples came to him to show him the buildings of the temple. 2 But he answered and said unto them, See ye not all these things? verily I say unto you, There shall not be left here one stone upon another, that shall not be thrown down. 3 And as he sat on the mount of Olives, the disciples came unto him privately, saying, Tell us, when shall these things be? and what shall be the sign of thy [1]coming, and of [2]the end of the world? 4 And Jesus answered, and said unto them, Take heed that no man lead you astray. 5 For many shall come in my name, saying, I am the Christ; and shall lead many astray. 6 And ye shall hear of wars and rumors of wars; see that ye be not troubled: for these things must needs come to pass, but the end is not yet. 7 For nation shall arise against nation, and kingdom against kingdom; and there shall be famines and earthquakes in divers places. 8 But all these things are the beginning of travail. 9 Then shall they deliver you up unto tribulation, and shall kill you: and ye shall be hated of all the nations for my name's sake. 10 And then shall many stumble, and shall [3]deliver up one another, and shall hate one another. 11 And many false prophets shall arise, and shall lead many astray. 12 And because iniquity shall be multiplied, the love of the many shall wax cold. 13 But he that endureth to the end, the same shall be saved. 14 And [4]this gospel of the kingdom shall be preached in the whole [5]world for a testimony unto all the nations; and then shall the end come.

[1]Gr. *presence*
[2]Or, *the consummation of the age*
[3]See ch. 10.4.
[4]Or, *these good tidings*
[5]Gr. *inhabited earth*

Vers. 1-14. THE COURSE OF THIS PRESENT AGE.

It is difficult to exegete this twenty-fourth chapter of Matthew and the parallel chapters in Mark and Luke intelligently without knowing whether the various parts refer to the Destruction of Jerusalem or to the Parousia. Some say that this chapter refers exclusively to the invisible return of Christ at the Destruction of Jerusalem; but verses 29-31 contradict this.

Godet says, "Matthew combines in the answer of Jesus the two subjects indicated in the question as Matthew has expressed it, and he unites them in so intimate a way that all attempts to separate them in the text from Chrysostom to Ebrard and Meyer have broken down."

It must be remembered that we have here only a partial report of the discourse of Jesus, and even when taken with the account in Mark and

Luke, it is quite probable that only a fraction of all that Jesus said has been preserved for us.

Prof. Erdman, too, thinks with Godet that the Lord is describing not one event, but two, "prophesying", as Erdman says, "the literal overthrow of the holy city by the armies of Rome, but using the colors of this tragic scene to paint the picture of His own coming in glory."

The question of the Disciples in Mark and Luke refers presumably only to the Destruction of Jerusalem, and so, presumably, the answer of Jesus as well.

Alford says the events in this chapter run parallel;

Verses 4 to 28 describe the Destruction of Jerusalem primarily and the Parousia secondarily.

Verses 29 to 44 describe the Parousia primarily and the Destruction of Jerusalem secondarily.

Verses 45 to 51 describe the Parousia alone.

Ebrard gives us much the same division except that he ascribes verses 4 to 14 to the Parousia.

Owen refers verses 4 to 44 to the Destruction of Jerusalem and with Alford and Ebrard refers verses 44 to 51 to the Parousia.

Others again refer the first 14 verses to the Destruction of Jerusalem and verses 15 on to the Parousia.

Gaebelein and his school, on the other hand, refer the entire chapter to the Parousia and contend that no reference is to be had to the Destruction of Jerusalem in this part of the Lord's discourse, this being set forth wholly by Luke in his Gospel.

The first section of the discourse, the one with which we are now concerned, ends with verse 44, and we have accordingly four different ways of viewing the content of this remarkable passage:

(a) Those who think it was all fulfilled in the past at the time of the Destruction of Jerusalem.

(b) Those who think it is all to be yet fulfilled during the time of the great tribulation just before the coming of the Lord in glory and in judgment on the antichristian forces of the world after the Church has been caught up according to the fourth chapter of I Thessalonians.

(c) Those who think it is being fulfilled in this present dispensation and is to find its final and more awful fulfillment in the great tribulation through which the Church herself will pass in the time of the end.

(d) Those who see part fulfillment in the Destruction of Jerusalem and the other part in the Parousia which is still in the future.

We shall endeavor to deal fairly with all these views, carrying them along side by side, that the student may the more easily resolve the situation, if indeed it can be done with unquestioning satisfaction.

Some say that Jesus thought of the Destruction of Jerusalem and His Second Coming as at the same time, but,

1. This denies His infallibility.

2. It is a contradiction of His own words in Mark 13.32.

3. Luke 21.24 proves conclusively that He did not so think, nor think of His Second Coming as so near at hand.

Ver. 1. In pointing out the magnificence of the temple they doubtless had in mind the reference made to it by Christ in Chap. 23.38.

"his disciples",—Luke says "some", while Mark says, "one of his disciples", probably Peter.

Ver. 2. "See ye not", etc.,—This sentence in Luke is an affirmation, but whether it be taken as an affirmation or a question the sense is the same, serving to call attention to the prophetic doom awaiting the city.

Ver. 3. "the disciples",—From Mark we learn that it was Peter, James, John and Andrew.

There are only two questions here; they wanted to know when the destruction foretold would take place, and then they wanted to know the sign of two things, namely, His coming and the end of the world, which two things in their minds were to occur at the same time. (Gab.)

"the sign of thy coming",—The word here is "Parousia" (presence) and is the ordinary expression for the Coming of the Lord.

Whedon says, "the word 'Parousia' never in the whole New Testament signifies anything else than a bodily presence, and the Destruction of Jerusalem is never implied by this term."

Olshausen says this Parousia is synonomous with "appearing" (I Tim. 4.14) and "his revelation" (I Cor. 1.7).

Olshausen further maintains that as the Old Testament prophets made no distinction between Christ's coming in humiliation and His coming in glory, i. e., His first and second coming; so the Gospel makes no distinction between His coming in glory at the end of the age and the end of the world, supposing as they did that both would take place at the same time. So also Meyer says, "In the Gospels we find no trace of the Millennium idea of the Apocalypse."

"the end of the world",—Literally, "the end of the age", which in their minds were the same. It means, as Alexander says, "When will this existing state of things, this system of dispensation be completed, wound up or brought to a conclusion."

Alford says, "Christ gave them enough to guide them from error in supposing the Second Coming to be near at hand and at the same time from carelessness in not expecting it as near."

Meyer says, this age is to have a stormy and a wicked end during the time called in I Peter 1.5, "the last time", and in Acts 2.17 and II Tim. 3.1, "the last days". He warns us, however, against confounding these designations with the expression, "the last day" of John 6.39 and 11.24, at which time, he says, the advent, the resurrection and the judgment are to take place.

Ver. 4. According to a large number of authorities verses 4 to 14 record the answer of Jesus as it relates, primarily at least, to the Destruction of Jerusalem. (A. O. E. B. G. Ow. Ca. Hof. Whe. Ros. Gro. Krebs.)

This is quite the natural view inasmuch as the first question of the Disciples relates to this event, and besides in Luke the only question asked concerned the Destruction of Jerusalem and in answering it Jesus made use practically of the very same language as that found here in Matthew.

Gaebelein, on the other hand, says this part of the discourse is a prediction of how the Jewish age will end, the age following the Rapture of the Church, the age which therefore has not ended but which has been "interrupted" by this present dispensation, *"until the times of the Gentiles be fulfilled"*, the end of the age referring to the seventieth week of Daniel, and verses 4 to 14 referring to the first three and one-half years of that period.   This author calls attention to the fact that there is not a word in this discourse about Jerusalem or the Destruction of the temple: that this is reserved for Luke; that Luke says that after the siege the Jews were led away captive and Jerusalem was trodden down, whereas in Matthew, instead of a scattering of the elect people, we have a gathering of them (verse 31), the word *"elect"* referring to literal Israel.   But this is hardly fair, because this passage about the elect may be and is referred to the Parousia even by the majority of those who take the former portion of the chapter as referring to the Destruction of Jerusalem.

There is, however, no strong reason why the passage may not be taken here, as it may also in Luke, as a brief summary of the course of this present age (L. Er. Sco.), and there are some statements in the passage that can be thus resolved with less difficulty than otherwise.   We shall therefore so explain it here, carrying along with the explanation, however, such reference as incline others to apply the passage to the Destruction of Jerusalem, or even yet to the time after the Rapture of the Church, as some contend.

Ver. 5.   *"in my name"*,—Not in the name or authority of Jesus, but claiming the title of Jesus, claiming to be the Messiah, the Christ Himself.

"I am Christ",—History records no such pretenders before the Destruction of Jerusalem, although doubtless there may have been.   Barcochba did not appear until after the Destruction of Jerusalem, and Simon Magus, Theudas, Meander and Dositheus, who have been referred to as cases in point by those referring the passage to that event, did not pretend to be the Christ.

Olshausen admits that the fact no such false Messiahs are recorded prior to the Destruction of Jerusalem indicates that the whole prophecy was not fulfilled at that time, but points further on to the coming of the Lord at the end of the age.

Gaebelein says that the false Christs of other days and of today are but faint shadows of what will take place in the end time soon to come.

Ver. 6.   *"wars and rumors of wars"*,—Not perhaps as Meyer says, "Wars in the neighborhood and wars in the distance of which only the rumors are heard", but rather the rumors of wars are the conflicting, exaggerated and frightful rumors which precede the approach of war and which cause so much panic.

Lange says that all wars are meant down to the Parousia, while De Wette, Meyer, and others say that history records no such wars prior to the Destruction of Jerusalem.   Alford, on the other hand, makes mention of these wars as well as divers earthquakes and famines.

"these things must come to pass",—In pursuance of the divine purpose.   The words are calculated to inspire a calm and reasonable frame of mind.

"but the end is not yet",—The *"end"* referred to is doubtless *"the end of the age"* mentioned in verse 3 (L. D. Ow. Bl. Eb. Au. Cre. Hoe. Chr. Ges.), although others refer it to the end of the tribulation before the Destruction of Jerusalem.

Ver. 7.   De Wette says that no particular instances can be enumerated, but Lange on the other hand, who contends that the passage combines in one view the whole period down to the end, says, "These insurrections, famines, earthquakes and other plagues which are here adduced were before the Destruction of Jerusalem by no means so insignificant as for instance De Wette asserts."

Godet says, "The time which preceded the Destruction of Jerusalem was signalized in the east by many calamities, a dreadful famine which took place under Claudius, and by the earthquake which destroyed Laodicea and other cities in A. D. 68.   At Cæsarea 20,000 Jews were massacred in a fight with the Gentiles, and 30,000 died in Rome of a pestilence." Tacitus gives us a narrative full of earthquakes, wars and crimes, and describes the period as one "rich in calamities, horrible with battles, rent with seditions, and even savage in peace itself."

This passage could therefore be made to refer to the Destruction of Jerusalem as well as to this present age or the times at the end of this age.

Gaebelein says the *"pestilences and earthquakes"* of our times are but harbingers of the far greater ones during the actual *"end of the age"* still to come.

Ver. 8.   *"the beginnings of travail"*,—They stand in relation to what is to follow as the beginnings of the birth-pangs do to the much severer pains which follow.

Ver. 9.   *"Then"*,—Not *after* the things of verses 6 and 7 have taken place, but during that time.   (L. A. M.)

In Luke it says, *"before all these things"*,—This seems to present a contradiction which Godet escapes by taking the word *"before"* not in the sense of time but in the sense of importance, i. e., above all things else. Meyer, however, says the word *"before"* can only be taken in the sense of "previous to", and certainly this is its more natural meaning.   There is no contradiction between the account of Luke and that of Matthew and Mark, and in order to see this we need not take the preposition in any other than its natural sense, "before—previous to".   Matthew says *"then"*, and this seems to imply, as does the narrative in Mark, that the persecutions would follow the signs, but in verse 6 of Matthew we are told what shall take place before the end comes and this verse corresponds to verses 8 and 9 in Luke.   Then verses 7 and 8 in Matthew correspond to verses 10 and 11 in Luke, and these verses both in Matthew and Luke, which tell of certain things which are *"the beginnings of sorrow"*, are in each case a parenthetical warning of what shall happen before the end. Then having stated that *"these things are the beginnings of sorrow"*, the chronology is resumed in all three accounts, the *"then"* in Matthew going back to verse 6 while in Luke the word *"before"* refers back to the same time, the word itself meaning "before the things mentioned in the parenthetical statement".   The whole difficulty arises from not rightly appreciating the force of the expression, *"the beginnings of sorrow"*.

"hated of all nations",—They were slandered by Jewish enemies and considered as atheists and devourers of children. Tacitus charged them with being the enemies of the human race.

This verse may apply with equal fitness to either of the three times under consideration. Gaebelein of course refers those *"delivered up and killed"* to the martyrs of the Jewish remnant during the great tribulation after the rapture of the Church as mentioned in Rev. 6.9-11.

"Certainly", says Lange, "this must refer to religious persecutions of modern times as well as to those of earlier times, the Disciples being in this the representatives of all Christians."

Ver. 10. *"Then"*,—As in verse 9.

"many",—Christians.

"stumble",—Renounce Christ and become apostate because of persecution, or, especially if the verse be applied to this age, because of new phases of truth presented, or because of the delayed coming of the Lord, the first reason being, however, the chief one.

"deliver up one another",—The apostates shall deliver up the Christians, says Meyer, while Lange thinks of the persecutions inflicted by one Christian sect upon another.

Ver. 11. *"false prophets"*,—False teachers. They should not be more precisely defined as to the nature of their prophecy or their particular teaching.

Ver. 12. *"the love of many shall wax cold"*,—Doubtless of the majority.

Ver. 13. *"he that endureth to the end"*,—The *"end"* here is not death (Eb. Ow. El. Kui.), which the context forbids; but the end of the period of which the Lord was speaking.

If the passage be referred to the Destruction of Jerusalem, then the being *"saved"* will doubtless refer to escape through flight to Pella from the doom of those involved in the destruction of the city. (E. Hof. Ros. Kre.)

If, on the other hand, it be referred to the end of the age, then the deliverance is that which comes to the faithful who go through the Great Tribulation before the coming of the Lord. (M. L. Whe.)

Ver. 14. *"this Gospel of the kingdom"*,—The Gospel which Christ was then preaching, i. e., the Gospel of the Messianic, universal kingdom.

"in all the world",—Mark reads, "among all nations"; Alford and Ellicott limit this to the Roman Empire, but it refers rather to the then inhabited earth.

Olshausen says that this preaching is now going on and this verse opposes the view that refers this part of the discourse to the Destruction of Jerusalem alone, because such a proclamation of the Gospel he declares did not take place before that event. Owen and others, on the other hand, maintain the very opposite.

The fact is it is impossible for any one to say when this witness is complete. (Er. Bla.) When the Gospel was preached at Pentecost there were present *"devout men out of every nation under heaven"*. The Disciples *"went forth and preached everywhere"* (Acts 8.4 and Mark 16.20).

In Romans it says, *"their words went unto the ends of the world"* (same word as in our text). Paul says in Col. 1.23 that the Gospel had already been *"preached to every creature which is under heaven"*.

Again there are those who make a distinction between the Gospel of grace to which we have just been referring, and the *"Gospel of the kingdom"* mentioned in our text, declaring that this latter is to be preached not for the purpose of gathering the Church, but *"for a witness to all nations"*, and that it is the Gospel mentioned in Rev. 14.6 as preached by the Jewish remnant during the time of the great tribulation. (Sco. Gab. Mack.)

But there is scarcely sufficient warrant for this limitation, nor is it a necessary part of the general view of the Lord's coming which the authorities just quoted maintain.

"for a testimony",—

1. Owen says it was that the whole world might be acquainted with the fact of the Jewish rejection of Christ by reason of which Jerusalem was to be destroyed. But this is quite too limited.

2. Ancient expositors largely agree with Meyer in making it mean for the conviction and condemnation of the Gentile nations. It does not, however, say "against" the nations but *"unto"* them.

3. Whedon says it was in order that all might believe and be converted, but Dorner says, and we think rightly, that it was in order that all might accept or reject the Gospel thus preached, resulting accordingly in either life or death.

"then shall the end come",—The *"end"* is unquestionably *"the end of the age"* about which the Disciples asked in verse 3, and seemingly the end of the troubles that are to precede the Messianic advent. Owen and others of course apply it to the overthrow of Jerusalem. Others (L. Bl. Eb. Whe. Dor. Hof. Cre.) say the reference here, as in verse 13, is to the end of the world proper. It is not said in this verse that all shall be converted.

15 When therefore ye see the abomination of desolation, which was [1]spoken of through Daniel the prophet, standing in [2]the holy place (let him that readeth understand), 16 then let them that are in Judea flee unto the mountains: 17 let him that is on the housetop not go down to take out the things that are in his house; 18 and let him that is in the field not return back to take his cloak. 19 But woe unto them that are with child and to them that give suck in those days! 20 And pray ye that your flight be not in the winter, neither on a sabbath: 21 for then shall be great tribulation, such as hath not been from the beginning of the world until now, no, nor ever shall be. 22 And except those days had been shortened, no flesh would have been saved: but for the elect's sake those days shall be shortened.

[1]Dan. 9.27; 11.31; 12.11.
[2]Or, *a holy place*

Vers. 15-22. THE GREAT TRIBULATION.

This section is made to refer to the Destruction of Jerusalem by perhaps the great majority of commentators. (L. M. B. D. S. E. A. O. Bl. El. Wi. Eb. Ev. Ow. Chr. Eut. Hug. Whe. Gro. Wet. Wie. Kui. Pau. Fri. Jer. Wor. Theo. Nast, and most Fathers.) There are three principal reasons why it is so taken by the authorities just mentioned:

1. The same instruction about fleeing to the mountains are given in Luke where the reference is without doubt to the Destruction of Jerusalem and it is only natural to think of these words being used in the same sense in the passage in Matthew. The destruction of Jerusalem would then be a type of the final catastrophe, and, says Olshausen, "whatever the abomination of desolation was, it is a type of what is recorded in II Thess. 2.4, to which this prophecy properly and finally refers". There is considerable force in this argument.

2. It was to this, they say, that the question of the Disciples chiefly referred and it is but natural to think that Christ is answering the question proposed to Him. But it is by no means clear that this was the principal question of the Disciples. It was this of course that led to the questioning, but the latter question about the end of the age was fully as prominent and important and a matter about which the Disciples were far more concerned than they could possibly be about the Destruction of Jerusalem. The reason would have more force in it if it were true, as so many maintain, that the three events mentioned in the third verse of this chapter lay in the minds of the Disciples as occurring at one and the same time.

   But Luke 21.24 shows conclusively that Luke at least did not so think of these events. We must so conclude or concede that the last part of the verse is an interpolation, or that Luke wrote after the Destruction of Jerusalem, neither of which opinions we are inclined to think of as tenable. If then Luke did not conceive of the three events as being simultaneous what right have we for concluding that the other writers did?

There are, on the other hand, some arguments of considerable worth against so taking the passage and in favor of referring it to the great tribulation period just before the coming of the Lord:

1. The quotation from Daniel 12 says, *"At that time thy people shall be delivered"*, and most assuredly they were not delivered in the days of Titus when Jerusalem was destroyed—they were massacred by the millions and dispersed in every direction. It must be true therefore that Daniel speaks of an end far later than that of the Destruction of Jerusalem.

2. The difficult connection with the words of verse 29, *"Immediately after the tribulation of those days"*, is altogether resolved by this explanation.

Alford, who parallels the two events in his explanation, says, "This citation from Daniel has in the Destruction of Jerusalem its immediate fulfillment, but its final fulfillment is yet future; for Daniel is speaking of the end of all things."

Ver. 15. *"Therefore"*,—This is not to be taken, as Wiesler says, as "resuming the thread broken by verse 3", but rather signifying a transition to the announcement which follows, and so to be taken, with De Wette and Meyer, as meaning "therefore", i. e., in consequence of these sorrows which are but the beginning of the greater calamity now about to be announced. It seems to connect what follows with that which went before as something following in natural sequence, and it would seem therefore that if this section be referred to the Destruction of Jerusalem, so ought the former one; and so too if this section be referred to the great tribulation, then ought the former one be referred to the course of this present age down to its close, or to the earlier part of the Great Tribulation itself, as Gaebelein takes it.

"abomination of desolation",—

Among the views of those referring the passage to the Destruction of Jerusalem are the following:

1. The statue of Titus or Hadrian erected on the sight of the desolated temple. (Chr. Eut. Theo., and most Fathers.) But this was after the destruction of the temple; and furthermore it was not in the temple.

2. The Roman army with its standards planted on the sacred soil which surrounds the city (G.), an abomination because pagan and a desolation because conquering and devastating (Whe.).

3. The internal desecration of the temple by the Jewish Zealots under pretense of defending it. (A. E. S. Bl. El. Hug. Wer. Nast.)

Alford says that the first two evangelists were writing as Jews to the Jews, and therefore give the inner or domestic sign of the approaching calamity which was to be seen in the temple and which was to be the abomination which was to cause the desolatiɔn; but that Luke, writing for the Gentiles, gives the outward state of things corresponding to this inward sign, the inward sign being the profanation of the temple by the Zealots and the outward sign being the approach of the army under Cestius.

Olshausen says that neither the work of the Zealots nor the Roman army can be the thing in mind for three reasons:

(a) Neither has a religious character, which character is indicated by the term *"abomination"* as used in connection with the Holy Place.

(b) The term *"holy place"* must relate only to the temple and cannot relate to the holy land nor to the land around the temple.

(c) The word *"standing"* is incompatible with either of the two explanations mentioned.

There is little if any force in the first objection of Olshausen, while the second certainly has no bearing on the inward sign, and the third puts a construction on the word *"standing"* which ought not to be unduly pressed.

4. Meyer says the expression refers to the "vile and loathesome abominations practiced by the conquering Romans on the place where the temple stood," while others (B. D. L. Gro.) refer it to the "Roman eagles, as military ensigns, rising over the site of the temple".

There are those who oppose this view because the expression refers to something that took place before the destruction of the temple; nor will they permit it to refer to the besieging legions of Cestius because it is said to be *"standing"* in the holy place. But Luke's account, where the reference to the Destruction of Jerusalem is unmistakable, says, *"when ye see Jerusalem encompassed with armies"*

The words simply say, *"the abominable desolation in the holy place"*, and the safest interpretation is that which sees reference to the doings of the heathen conquerors during and after the siege of the temple (B. D. L. Eb. Gro. Wet. Wie.), although the reference to the Zealots in the temple may reasonably be included.

"the holy place",—This refers to the temple or the place of the temple, and not to Palestine nor the neighborhood about Jerusalem (B. Wie. Schot.), nor to the mount of Olives (Gro.), these interpretations having been adopted on the ground that it would be too late to flee after the temple was taken.

Those who refer the passage to the time of the Parousia, with which is connected the great tribulation, refer the expression to the Antichrist of II Thess. 2.4. (Ew. Sco. Gab. Ori. Lud. Klo. Mack.) It is under his rule that the great tribulation is to take place.

"let him that readeth understand",—These are the words of Matthew himself, intimating the near approach of the signs and warning his readers to note the admonition to escape. (M. B. L. Ow. Whe.) This is by far the most preferable explanation and is favored by Mark 13.14. It is not therefore to be considered as a marginal note by the copyist (A.), nor as the words of Jesus Himself, pointing to the reading in Daniel, *"Know therefore and understand"*. (E. S. Ba. Chr. Wor. Hen. Eut. Pau. Nast.) If they were the words of Jesus would He not have used "heareth" instead of *"readeth"*?

Ver. 16. *"In Judea"*,—Not perhaps Judea in distinction from Jerusalem (M. Whe.), but both Jerusalem and the contiguous places (Ow.) as is plainly indicated in Luke. Those in the city were to get out and those out of the city in Judea round about were not to enter the city but to flee also.

Those who refer the passage to the Destruction of Jerusalem find the fulfillment of this and the following verses in the flight of the Christians to Pella, while Gaebelein and his school refer it to admonition given to the Jewish Christians who will be in Judea at the time of the appearing of the Antichrist. It could hardly with appropriate sense be applied to the Church in general which some are inclined to think is to pass through the great tribulation. The fact also that the admonition is to those *"in Judea"* points strongly to one or the other of the other views. It is quite certain also that if the Church is not to pass through the great tribulation there could then be no propriety whatever in advising Christians to flee at the coming of their Lord or to pray that their flight be not in winter when the days were short and severe or on the Sabbath day when the gates of the towns were closed and food could not be procured or that a woman might not be giving suck to a child.

Ver. 17. A man could run on the top of the flat-roofed houses to the walls of the city and so escape (E. Mi. Fri. Win. Pau. Kui.); the primary thought, however, being as others say (L. B. Ow. Gro. Wet.), that they should not come down to go into the house for any household goods but should escape at once.

Ver. 19. The tone is of pity rather than denunciation. Christian mothers would find escape harder. Jewish mothers, it developed, during the siege of Jerusalem ate their own children in their awful extremity.

Ver. 20. In the winter the days were short, the roads were bad and it was cold. On the Sabbath day the gates of the towns would be closed and the securing of provisions would be difficult. Should the same conditions prevail concerning the Sabbath during the time of the great tribulation as prevailed during the time before the Destruction of Jerusalem their flight might be hindered in either case by the Jews if they in any way disregarded the Jewish law about travel on the Sabbath, which was to be only five furlongs.

Ver. 21. If the verse be referred to the Destruction of Jerusalem it is a fact that over one million Jews perished. Josephus says nothing like it was ever known before, and Bloomfield says, "Never to this day has it been paralleled."

Ver. 22. *"those days"*,—To be taken either as the days of the destruction of Jerusalem (L. M. E. A. Ow. Whe.) or of the great tribulation at the end of the age yet to come.

"had been",—i. e., by the decree of God. Their length had been fixed in the eternal counsels of God.

"shortened",—It is not that the length of the days themselves were shortened (Li. Fri.), but that the number of the days were shortened. (L. M. A. D.)

"no flesh",—i. e., no man. This verse may be explained appropriately according to either view. How the siege of Jerusalem was providentially shortened is a matter of history, else the whole nation would have perished.

"for the elect's sake",—If the great tribulation be thought of as before the rapture, the elect here mentioned must refer to all of Christ's followers then living; if it be thought of as after the rapture, with the Church having been caught away, the elect must refer to the elect remnant of the Jews, whereas if it be thought of in connection with the Destruction of the Jews the elect will refer to the Christians then among the Jews (M. E. Whe.), although some (A. L. Eb. Ow.) include those who were in the future to be converted and gathered in from among the Jews and Gentiles.

Gaebelein declares that the term *"elect"* in the Epistles always refers to the Church, but that in this chapter, as well as throughout the Gospels, always means His earthly people, the Jews.

23 Then if any man shall say unto you, Lo, here is the Christ, or, Here; believe [1]it not. 24 For there shall arise false Christs, and false prophets, and shall show great signs and wonders; so as to lead astray, if possible, even the elect. 25 Behold, I have told you beforehand. 26 If therefore they shall say unto you, Behold, he is in the wilderness; go not forth: Behold, he is in the inner chambers; believe [2]it not.

[1]Or, *him*

[2]Or, *them*

27 For as the lightning cometh forth from the east, and is seen even unto the west; so shall be the [3]coming of the

[3]Gr. *presence*

Son of man. 28 Wheresoever the carcase is, there will the eagles be gathered together.

Vers. 23-26.   PREDICTION CONCERNING THE FALSE CHRISTS.

It is at this point that such expositors as Alford and Olshausen, who find the twofold reference in the prophecy, think that the narrative begins to point more to the future Second Coming and less to the Destruction of Jerusalem, while Lange says the transition is here marked without doubt to the Parousia at the end time.   It will under no circumstances do to say with Calovius that Christ here passes to His spiritual advent through the Gospel.

Ver. 23.   "*Then*",—i. e., when the desolation and flight shall take place.   Christ is still speaking of the time of that period of distress in verse 21.   It will hardly do therefore with Lange to say that the word "*then*" refers to the New Testament interval between the Destruction of Jerusalem and the Parousia.

"*believe it not*",—He shows them in verse 27 that His Second Coming was to be from the sky, while these false Christs appear on earth.   The fact that history knows little if anything of such false Christs prior to the Destruction of Jerusalem and the fact that these words could have no possible application to Christians of this age who are instructed to "*wait for the Son of God from heaven*" lends some support to the view that the time in question is that after the rapture of the Church and that the warning is intended for the Jewish believing remnant, although it may have a possible reference to the time of the overthrow of the holy city.

Ver. 24.   "*false Christs*",—i. e., Antichrists,—pretenders.

"*false prophets*",—Not perhaps false Christian teachers (L.), nor apostles of the false Christs (Gro.), nor giving themselves out as prophets raised from the dead, Elias, and others (Kui.), but rather false prophets among the Jews pretending to be sent from God and trying to impose upon their fellow countrymen as had been done during national misfortunes of other days.

"*great signs and wonders*",—The reference here is to miracles performed by Satanic agencies as in II Thess. 2.9.   Meyer, Lange, Owen and others think here of "lying wonders", pretended miracles, but not real.

"*the elect*"—To be taken either as the Christians in Judea and Jerusalem who had been converted from among the Jews, or as the believing remnant of the Jews during the times of the Great Tribulation, in keeping with one or the other of the two views under consideration.

Ver. 26.   Olshausen and Alford say this verse and the following can have no sense whatever except as applied to the coming of Christ in the clouds of heaven, the reference to the Destruction of Jerusalem being but a very faint one indeed.

It is in the openness of Christ's coming to universal observation as contrasted with the secrecy and deception that the words of this verse and the next find their real force.

Ver. 27. The coming of the false Christs shall be more or less concealed in the wilderness or in the secret chamber, the quiet of the desert and the secrecy of the chamber being convenient places for the fomenting of new movements or of rebellion, but the Coming of Christ shall be open and discernible like an all-illuminating flash of light which no one can mistake, its presence to be announced everywhere from east to west over the whole world.

Whedon suggests the splendor of the Coming Son of man suspended in the heavens while the earth makes one complete revolution.

If this verse were to be interpreted allegorically it could afford no protection whatever against the wiles of the false Christs, because if the coming of Christ was to be invisible and figurative and could be fulfilled in the coming of the Roman armies or of Titus, how then could the warning of verse 26 have any force? No, it is the contrast between the personal coming of a false Christ and the personal coming of the true Christ; the first earthly and lurking, the second heavenly and lightning-like.

Owen, of course, insists that the primary reference here is still to the Destruction of the Holy City while its secondary, though higher sense, he says, is to the final Coming of Christ.

Ver. 28. *"eagles"*,—The reference is to carrion-kites, a species of vulture.

Some would have us believe there is an allusion here to the eagles of the legions of Cestius. It is better perhaps to think of Christ adopting the term to designate the enemy falling upon its prey, thus founding His expression upon the same symbol that led the armies to adopt the eagles for their standard.

"Wheresoever", etc.,—That is, says Meyer, "Wheresoever there is a carcase there will Christ come in vengeance."

It is quite generally accepted that this explanation of the eagles is the proper one, i. e., Christ coming to judgment, but to what must we refer the *"carcase"*? Among the different views the following may be noted:

1. The carcase is Christ crucified and the eagles are His saints hastening to meet Him at His Second Coming. (C. Ca. Ze. Jan. Cla. Fri. Fle. Chr. Jer. Eut. Lut. Mue. Era. Bez. Theo.)

2. The carcase refers to the Christian Jews, the elect of Israel, and the eagles to the Messiah. (Witt.) But this overlooks the universal character of the Advent, and besides the carcase can hardly be conceived of as something Christian.

3. The carcase is Jerusalem and the eagles are the Roman army. (Li. Ow. Wol. Cle. Wet. Ham.) There is some merit in this view if in the Roman army we recognize the judgment of God and consider the same as a figurative coming of Christ in judgment upon the Jewish nation at that time.

4. The carcase is Jerusalem and the eagles Christ and His angel host at the Parousia, at His coming in glory and judgment at the end of the great tribulation. This is quite similar to the view of Gaebelein, who takes the carcase as the unbelieving portion of the Jewish people living at that time.

5. The carcase is by some referred to corruption in general and the eagles to the false Christs who always gather wherever this is found. But the conjunction *"for"* connects the expression directly with the Coming of Christ. Others think of the eagles as the Church, or a certain class of "advanced believers". But this is weak and fanciful and deserving of little if any attention.

6. There are others who think that whether we make the primary reference of the carcase to Jerusalem at the Parousia and the secondary one to Jerusalem at its destruction by Titus, or vice versa, such interpretation is too narrow and localized for such a far-reaching comparison, and that what the Disciples saw fulfilled in the Destruction of Jerusalem is to repeat itself scores of times in the world's history and to be fulfilled on the largest scale at the Second Coming of Christ. This is all the more true, they seem to think, since it is this advent which seems to be here in question, and furthermore verses 23 to 27 would seem to be against referring this primarily to any definite locality. This, they say, is a confirmation of the truth of verse 27 that the Advent will announce its presence everywhere, and that from the point of view of the retributive punishment which the Coming One will be called upon to execute. The carcase, therefore, while having doubtless a specific reference to Jerusalem, seems to be a metaphorical expression denoting that which is spiritually dead and doomed to Messianic destruction. (M. G.)

29 But immediately after the tribulation of those days the sun shall be darkened, and the moon shall not give her light, and the stars shall fall from heaven, and the powers of the heavens shall be shaken: 30 and then shall appear the sign of the Son of man in heaven: and then shall all the tribes of the earth mourn, and they shall see the Son of man coming on the clouds of heaven with power and great glory. 31 And he shall send forth his angels [1]with [2]a great sound of a trumpet, and they shall gather together his *elect* from the four winds, from one end of heaven to the other.

[1]Many ancient authorities read *with a great trumpet, and they shall gather &c.*
[2]Or, *a trumpet of great sound*

Vers. 29-31. THE RETURN OF THE KING IN GLORY.

Ver. 29. *"immediately after the tribulation of those days"*,—We are now to deal with the difficulty anticipated when we took the section beginning with verse 15 as a reference to the Destruction of Jerusalem. Nearly every expositor takes the words now before us as a reference to the Parousia of Christ at the end-time. Perhaps no portion of Scripture has been the subject of more widely divergent opinions as to the time element included in it than this one. It would seem that we have in each of the three Gospels but a partial report of this great discourse of the Master, and we must therefore compare the accounts one with the other, and we must also bear in mind that even then we may not have before us the prophecy in its entirety.

Charles R. Erdman has said, "It is evident that our Lord is describing not one event, but two; He is prophesying the literal overthrow of the Holy City by the armies of Rome, but He is using the colors of this tragic scene to paint the picture of His own coming in glory. So interwoven are these two series of predictions that it is extremely difficult at times to be certain whether the reference is to the nearer or to the more remote of these great events."

Among the various explanations of the words under consideration are the following:

1. Weber says that the word *"immediately"* belongs to the preceding verse. But all manuscript authority is against such connection.

2. Nast refers verse 29 to the Destruction of Jerusalem, and, to avoid the difficulty, proposes a figurative interpretation of verses 29-36, and sees here a picture of "a judicial visitation on nominal Christendom by Christ in order to destroy all ungodly institutions and principles in Church and State, of which visitation the overthrow of the Jewish polity was but a type and which is itself in turn the full type of the final and total overthrow of all powers of darkness on the great day of judgment." This makes the Lord's coming in verses 29 to 36 a providential one and without reference to His final personal coming. The language, however, throughout the entire context is too plain to admit of a toning down of this kind which pulls out of it the very heart of its meaning.

3. Hammond and Schott say that the translators have made a mistake and that instead of *"immediately"* it should have been "suddenly", or, "unexpectedly", the nature of the Advent being described as swift and surprisingly sudden. But the word used can hardly be made to bear this meaning. Olshausen calls this interpretation a "makeshift".

4. Owen refers the preceding verses to the Destruction of Jerusalem, and says that the word *"immediately"* may be taken in the sense of "very soon after", and refers to the comparative brevity of the intervening centuries between the Destruction of Jerusalem and the final Parousia as compared with eternity. But this is not at all satisfying, and something of the objection just made to the explanation preceding this one applies to this one.

5. Wetstein and others do not allow any reference here whatever to the final Parousia but refer the entire context to the Destruction of Jerusalem. They think that verses 32 to 34 refer undoubtedly to the Destruction of Jerusalem and ask, therefore, why verses 29 to 31 should be interposed if they refer to a different and more distant and more august event. They contend also that a reference here to the Parousia would make Christ reply to the simple question of the Disciples in a very confused and perplexing way. They explain the language used as that of prophetic imagery. But the marvelous signs and the details as here presented hardly seem suited to the Destruction of Jerusalem.

   Then, again, if verses 29 to 31 be referred to the Destruction of Jerusalem, how can the tribulation of verse 21 be represented as *past*, since the Destruction of Jerusalem, in this case, is the very culmination of that tribulation?

6. Ellicott and many others (M. D. Cl. Rob. Erd.) say the Parousia is here represented as following immediately upon the Destruction of Jerusalem. Meyer says that all fanciful interpretations of the

word *"immediately"* come from the supposition that Jesus could not have possibly so spoken; but this, he says, is contrary to all exegetical rule, considering that Jesus repeatedly makes reference elsewhere to His Second Coming as an event that is near at hand. Ellicott, in defense of his explanation, explains the word *"immediately"* in three ways:

(a) By II Pet. 3.8, where a thousand years are said to be as one day with God. Olshausen says this is not permissible here because the representation is evidently adopted to human conception.

(b) God often postpones or hastens His plans, even as man's purposes are oftentimes modified.

(c) Christ, as He has assured us, in His human nature did not know the time of His coming, and so here He spoke in the telescopic sense with the vision of two mountain peaks before him, one beyond the other, but with no intimation of the time intervening between them. This last explanation is the one preferred by Ellicott.

7. Alford, Lange, Gordon and others (Au. Cre. Whe. Kel.) get rid of the difficulty by transporting Luke's account into Matthew's and so making *"those days"* cover all the time mentioned in Luke's passage, namely, the times of the Gentiles during which Jerusalem is downtrodden, immediately after which, etc.

Alford then says, in agreement with Ellicott, as above, "All the difficulty arising from the word *'immediately'* comes from confounding the partial fulfillment (the destruction of Jerusalem) with the ultimate one (the Parousia), of which latter He now speaks directly and mainly."

A. J. Gordon says, "After using language that can only apply to that appalling event (the Destruction of Jerusalem) (verses 19 and 20), He adds, *'For there shall be great tribulation, such as was not since the beginning of the world to this time,—no, nor ever shall be'*. How long shall this tribulation continue? Until Christ's Second Coming. For our Lord declares that *'immediately after the tribulation of those days'* the signs of the advent shall be witnessed, when *'they shall see the Son of man coming in the clouds of heaven with power and great glory'*. So closely are these two events connected in the prediction that some have argued that Christ's advent must have actually occurred at the Destruction of Jerusalem in a spiritual or providential sense. But a careful examination of the language used proves beyond question that it is a literal coming that is here described, and that a literal immediateness after the great tribulation is affirmed by the word, *'immediately'*. If we turn to Luke's Gospel, however, and read his parallel report of our Lord's words, all becomes plain (Luke 21.23-27). For he makes the tribulation to include the dispersion of the Jews among all nations, and the treading down of their Holy City by the Gentiles, until the times of the Gentiles be fulfilled. In other words, the Great Tribulation covers the entire age from Zion's captivity to Messiah's coming."

8. Gaebelein, Scofield and others find no reference at all in this entire chapter to the Destruction of Jerusalem, but refer it all to the final Parousia at the Second Coming. "It is important", says Gaebelein, "to see that the record of the discourse, as given by the Holy Spirit, passes over the answer to the first question, *'When shall these things be?'* This is evident by the fact that the Lord says not a word in the discourse about Jerusalem or the destruction of the temple; while in Luke we hear that Jerusalem is to be besieged by armies, and the inhabitants are seen falling by the edge of the sword and *led away captive into all the nations,* and Jerusalem trodden down by the Gentiles—in Matthew we do not find a word of this at all; instead of a scattering of the elect people at the close of the Great Tribulation, we have a gathering of the elect."

We frankly confess that none of the above explanations, to our mind, fully meet the situation; and we just as frankly confess that we have no better explanation of our own. Our choice lies between the last three. The difficulty with the last explanation is not only that it leaves the main question of the Disciples unanswered, but the similarity of language, as used in both Matthew and Luke, certainly must have some reference to one and the same thing. Compare the statements and the words of Matt. 24.4 to 9 with those of Luke 21.8 to 12 and also the words of verses 16 to 20 of the former with those of verses 21 to 23 of the latter, and it certainly must appear that it looks like an utter wresting of language to make these accounts refer to two entirely separate and distinct occurrences. If this last explanation be set aside the choice must then rest between that of Ellicott (view number 6) and that of Gordon (view number 7). Yet it becomes apparent that if either one of these views be accepted, the other must also be taken as a supplement to it, and consequently these two views become in reality one, and perhaps are to be taken as the best solution of the problem we have been endeavoring to solve.

"the sun shall be darkened",—

1. Dorner says this is a prophetical, figurative delineation of the fall of heathenism, the sun, moon and the stars signifying the nature worship of the heathen.

2. Hengstenberg says the language is figurative and merely illustrative of sad and troublous times.

3. Meyer, Olshausen and others (B. Ow. B-C. Pau. Schot.) contend that the language must be taken literally in the sense of obscuration. This is much to be preferred, the obscurations finding their explanation in II Pet. 3.10-12.
   Owen explains the expression as a total eclipse of the sun as the result of a smoky, lowering atmosphere such as usually precedes earthquakes and similar convulsions of nature, the description being a frequent one in Scripture.

"the moon shall not give her light",—To be explained similarly with the expression concerning the sun.

"the stars shall fall from heaven",—

1. Allegorically:
   (a) The downfall of the Jewish commonwealth. (Wet.)

342

(b) The downfall of heathen star-worship. (Dor.)

(c) The downfall of those who shone brightly in the Church. (Wor.) Wordsworth also refers the darkening of the sun to the solar light of Christ's truth being dimmed, and the moon not giving its light he refers to the lunar orb of the Church being obscured by heresy. Augustine also refers the expression to the obscuration of the Church.

2. Stars literally falling, according to the notion that they were fixed in the heavens. Meyer says, "The falling of the stars, i. e., the whole of the stars, as the expression must be taken, is impossible; but it need not surprise us to see such an idea introduced into a prophetic picture so grandly poetical as this. But this seems to ascribe an error to Christ or at least His acquiescence in one; and furthermore we must surely see something more than mere poetry in this description.

3. Phenomenal appearances, shooting stars and meteors popularly mistaken for real stars. (C. Ow. Fri. Kui.)

4. Literal obscuration finding explanation in II Pet. 3.10-12, as above. (B. O. L. Pau.) Lange says the reference is to the planets becoming disassociated from the solar system and taking their places in heavenly constellation according to II Pet. 3.10-12. But there is too much surmise about this phase of this last explanation.

The fourth view is perhaps the more acceptable.

"the powers of heaven shall be shaken",—

1. The host of stars. This is a very common view (Isa. 34.4), but it is a bit tautological after the words, *"the stars shall fall"*.

2. The angel world. (O. Jer. Chr. Eut.) But this is somewhat inconsistent with the word *"shaken"*, and besides the whole reference is to the physical domain.

3. The laws and forces by which the sun, moon and stars are kept in the courses, i. e., the powers which uphold the heavens, which stretch them out and produce the phenomena. (E. A. L. M.) This is by far the better view.

"shaken",—The word refers to a literal tossing to and fro as a ship on the waves.

Ver. 30. Says Ewald, "While the whole world is being convulsed the heaven-sent Messiah appears in glory."

"then shall appear",—Not merely to the elect (Cre.), but universally, to be in keeping with what follows. (M.)

"the sign",—i. e., the sign inquired about in verse 3.

Perhaps this sign cannot be imagined until it comes, but among the various views the following will be of interest:

1. The star of the Messiah. (O. Bl. Fle.)

2. The rending of heaven and the appearing of angels. (Heb.)

3. A Cross. (Hi. Cy. Wor. Chr. Jer. Aug. and Alford with some reserve.)

4. A lightning flash.

5. The signs of verse 29. (Hui. Schot.) But the definite article *"the"* requires a definite sign. The word *"then"* is also apparently against this view.

6. The Son of man Himself. (Dan. 7.13.) (E. B. Ew. Hen. Hof. Fri.) But this is seemingly inconsistent with the following, *"They shall see the Son of man"*, and it is inconsistent also with the question of the Disciples who asked for *a sign of His coming*.

7. The dawning of the Messianic glory, growing brighter and brighter until Christ appears in the midst of it. (M. D. L. Whe.) This is the better explanation.

"all the tribes of the earth",—In Zech. 12.10 this seems to be confined to the tribes of Israel, but here it seems the rather to be universal.

"mourn",—The words, it would seem, apply to the inhabitants of the whole earth. The reference is primarily to those who have done evil, who pierced Him then and in every age since. (E. L. M. Ew. Dor.) Ewald rightly says that penitence is not to be excluded from the mourning.

It may be interesting just here to note the words of Owen, who insists that these verses together with all that has gone before refer to the Destruction of Jerusalem. He says the appearance is not a literal one, but virtually so; Christ's vengeance was to be so real that they would recognize His hand in it just as though they had really seen Him with their own eyes.

"coming on the clouds of heaven",—The clouds are doubtless literal clouds lighted by His glory. It seems to indicate with evident clearness that this coming of Christ is to be a visible one.

Alford says that the coming of this verse is the same as that in I Thess. 4.16-17, and that it is a coming for judgment which occurs at the commencement of the Millennium when Christ first establishes His Millennial Kingdom. Alford furthermore says the reference is not to the judgment in Matt. 25.31, which judgment he refers to the end of the Millennial Kingdom.

"with power and great glory",—The power and glory of the kingdom which is displayed in the accompanying angel hosts of verse 31.

Ver. 31. *"he shall send forth"*,—i. e., from the clouds of heaven.

"with a great sound of a trumpet",—It is not that the individual angels blow each one a trumpet, but what is meant is the trumpet of God, which is sounded while Christ is sending forth His angels especially employed in His service.

When is this trumpet sounded?

According to Scofield, Torrey, Morgan, Gaebelein, Pettingill and others of this school it is the trumpet sounded at the close of the supposed seven years and at the beginning of the Millennium, when Christ comes *with* His saints (the raptured and resurrected Church), and the elect, who are gathered out, refer especially to the believing Jews who have been converted during the seven years of tribulation, the resurrection of other believers and the transformation of living believers having taken place at, or just before, the beginning of the seven year period.

Most pre-millennial expositors do not seem to make any place for the seven year period just mentioned, but say that this passage refers to the time of the resurrection of believers, commonly called the First Resurrection, and they refer the trumpet to the one blown in I Thess. 4.16. (M. A. G. L. E.) Meyer and Lange identify this trumpet also with that of I Cor. 15.52, but Alford refers this latter to the great trumpet of what he calls the general resurrection at the end of the Millennium.

"*his elect*",—These elect are, of course, according to the authorities just quoted, the chosen of God of all ages who are caught up at the coming of the Lord, but according to Scofield, and those of his school, they must refer to certain elect ones, the Jews, who have believed during the time of the tribulation, the supposed seven year period.

"*they shall gather together*",—This is to be interpreted according to the reference to be found in the word "*elect*", as just discussed. The "*gathering together*" is toward the place where He is in the act of appearing on earth. (M. L.)

Those who will hear nothing of a Millennium on earth refer these verses to the final end of the world, and say that while these angels gather the Christians to the right hand of the judgment seat, the evil angels will bring the wicked to the left hand. (Whe.)

Owen, of course, refers this passage primarily to the Destruction of Jerusalem, and in a higher sense to the final end of the world. He says the "*angels*" refer to the guardian angels who in the Destruction of Jerusalem protected and guided the Christians to a place of safety; and with Kuionel, he says the "*four winds*" and the "*from one end of heaven to the other*" means from all parts of Judea and from one horizon to the other in Judea.

Lange says that as between Christ, the first-fruits and the first resurrection there is a long period, so probably between the first resurrection of the Christians and the end there is another period, as intimated in John 5.28,29. In this second period Lange places the judgment on the clerical office (verse 45); then upon the collective Church (Chap. 25.1); then upon its individual members (Chap. 25.14), and finally upon all nations (Chap. 25.31). This, says Lange, points to the judgment of Christ upon earth during the 1000 years of Revelation 20, and the sending of the angels is to collect around Christ on earth His elect, although the greeting and reception is to be regarded as conducted in the air.

Olshausen says the passage cannot refer to Palestine alone because of the expressions, "*from the four winds*" and "*from one end of heaven to the other*", both of which phrases metaphorically denote the widest extent of the earth. He says that since the Disciples only asked for the time and the signs of His coming, the passage before us must refer to something prior to that coming itself and prior to the resurrection of the Christians and the transformation of the living saints. Therefore, he says, it does not apply to the general union of all the saints in the kingdom of God after Christ's coming, or at His coming; but it applies to the dispersed of Israel who are to be gathered together just before the resurrection of the just, in order that they may be separated from the mass of unbelievers and be united so they can all see the coming of the Son of man. Only thus, he says, do the exhortations to watchfulness and fidelity have any true significance; for this implies the possibility of escaping the dreadful events at the Parousia and being taken to a place of safety. The angels, he says, are human messengers of the Lord, the sound of the trumpet being the power of the Holy Spirit. (Tho.)

32 Now from the fig tree learn her parable: when her branch is now become tender, and putteth forth its leaves, ye know that the summer is nigh; 33 even so ye also, when ye see all these things, know ye that [1]he is nigh, *even* at the doors. 34 Verily I say unto you, This generation shall not pass away, till all these things be accomplished. 35 Heaven and earth shall pass away, but my words shall not pass away. 36 But of that day and hour knoweth no one, not even the angels of heaven, [2]neither the Son, but the Father only. 37 And as *were* the days of Noah, so shall be the [3]coming of the Son of man. 38 For as in those days which were before the flood they were eating and drinking, marrying and giving in marriage, until the day that Noah entered into the ark, 39 and they knew not until the flood came, and took them all away; so shall be the [3]coming of the Son of man. 40 Then shall two men be in the field; one is taken, and one is left; 41 two women *shall be* grinding at the mill; one is taken, and one is left. 42 Watch therefore: for ye know not on what day your Lord cometh. 43 [4]But know this, that if the master of the house had known in what watch the thief was coming, he would have watched and would not have suffered his house to be [5]broken through. 44 Therefore be ye also ready; for in an hour that ye think not the Son of man cometh.

[1]Or, *it*
[2]Many authorities, some ancient, omit *neither the Son.*
[3]Gr. *presence*
[4]Or, *But this ye know*
[5]Gr. *digged through*

Vers. 32-44. THE SECOND COMING TO BE SUDDEN AND UNEXPECTED.

Ver. 32. *"putteth forth its leaves"*,—i. e., about Passover season, about the last of March. The fruit of the fig tree accompanies the mature leaf.

"the summer is nigh",—i. e., the harvest time of fruit in general. As surely as the leaves of the fig tree are the sign of summer so shall the signs of which He speaks portend most certainly the coming of the Son of man. Alford says that as the withered fig tree, which the Lord cursed, represented the Jewish race in their unfruitfulness, so this fig tree represents the reviviscence of that race.

Ver. 33. *"all these things"*,—(1) the signs in verse 30 (L.); (2) the signs in verses 29 to 31 (M.); (3) all that Christ said in answer to the question of the Disciples (O. Ow.). The second reference is the more preferable.

"he is nigh",—Meyer says the subject is *"the summer"* of verse 32, i. e., the summer time, the harvest reward in the Messianic kingdom. This extending of the subject *"summer"* from verse 32 is permissible, but it seems more direct to supply the subject *"he"* as in our text; or it is quite as proper to supply the subject *"it"* as in the margin of our text and in the Authorized Version, and make it refer to the Parousia, the end of the age, inasmuch as that is what the Disciples were inquiring about.

In Luke it reads, *"the kingdom of God"*, and if this idea be read into the narrative here, with Olshausen, Auberlen and others, then the word *"it"* as in the margin must be supplied.

Olshausen says, "The kingdom of God is a state of things commencing at the second coming of Christ, i. e., the kingdom of the saints upon the renovated earth as in Revelation 20."

346

Ver. 34. *"This generation"*,—Here again opinions are widely divergent:

1. The people then living. (E. O. D. M. F. G. Ow. Al.)
2. The Jewish race. (L. A. S. Ca. Au. Dor. Rig. Jan. Sto. Heu. Heb. Sco. Gab. Pet. Mor. Wor. Tor. Bla. Mack. Nast.)
3. Creation. (Mal.)
4. The human race. (Jer.)
5. There is a sudden shift here to the Destruction of Jerusalem. (Schot.)
6. The generation of believers, i. e., *"the body of my disciples"*. (L. Cl. Pau. Cla. Eut. Chr. Ori. Theo.)
7. *"All will begin to take place now in this time while you live"*,— i. e., you will survive the beginning of these things. (Lut. Ger. Sta.)
8. The rationalizing interpreters say the prophecy has failed.

There does not seem to be any foundation whatever for views 3 and 4. View 7 is a mere expedient, and view 8 is of course not to be thought of. Such a sudden change as is suggested in view 5 cannot be supposed, as there is nothing whatever to support the supposition. View number 6, like view number 7, seems to be an evasion of the issue, and the choice must therefore rest as between views number 1 and number 2.

In regard to the second view it must be said that there is much objection to it on the part of commentators.

Ellicott says there is not the shadow of authority for this interpretation. Olshausen says the word here employed (genea) is not once used in the sense of "race", either in the New Testament, nor in profane writers, and only once in the Septuagint.

Godet says the interpretation is a forced one; Whedon says it has met with little favor among scholars; while most German critics treat the explanation as a sheer invention without the shadow of authority either in classical or Hellenistic usage; they say that some lexicons do not mention it, even to condemn it.

On the other hand those who accept view number 1 must refer the passage to the Destruction of Jerusalem. But then we will have difficulty with the expression, *"all these things"*. These words look back to the preceding verses, and however far back it might seem necessary to carry their reference, the words of verses 29 to 31 must be included in it. But when we ask the question as to whether *"all these things"* really did take place at the time of the overthrow of Jerusalem by Titus in A. D. 70; whether the Gospel of the kingdom had been preached in all the world, whether the Son of man had come in the clouds in visible glory, and whether the elect had been gathered from the four winds, history answers that nothing of the kind ever occurred at that time.

Whedon and Owen refer *"all these things"* to the *"these things"* of verse 3; but this is hardly fair in view of all that has come between that verse and the one before us.

Now, if the reference here be to the Parousia at the end-time, then the word must be taken in the sense of "race". The fact remains that many of the lexicons do give as the primary meaning of the word, *Race, Kind, Family, Stock, Breed.*

Says Alford, "Meyer, who strongly contends for the meaning 'generation', states in a note that the word (genea) never *absolutely means* 'nation', but that it may by the context acquire this *sense accidentally* from its meaning as 'race'. This is exactly what is here wanted. Never was a nation so completely one genea (race) in all accuracy of meaning as the Jewish people."

Dorner, with especial truth and force, notices that verses 34 and 36 would contradict each other if Christ announced everything still for the same generation—as well as that the first Christians, nay, the Apostles, could not possibly have continued to *wait for* Him, when Israel was not converted and Christ did *not* come, therefore that they cannot have so understood the words in the sense merely of the generation then living.

Alford in his commentary, and Stier in his "Words of the Lord Jesus", set forth practically incontrovertible arguments for the use of the word genea here in the sense of "*race*", and to these writings the student will do well to refer.

Ver. 35. He claims for His words the eternity which belongs to the word "*Jehovah*". (Psa. 102.26.)

"*my words*",—i. e., generally, but with special reference here to the prophetic utterances preceding.

"*shall not pass away*",—i. e., in any way whatever fail of their accomplishment.

Meyer rightly observes that the first clause of this verse cannot be regarded as a leading idea of it, but only as a subsidiary one by way of background for what is immediately after said of "*my words*".

Ver. 36. "*of that day and hour*",—i. e., the exact time; as we would say, "the hour and the minute".

"*neither the Son*",—

1. This is referred to Christ's human nature as consistent with the statement that He increased in wisdom. (Lu. 2.52). (A. M. E. C. D. S. Al. Ow. Gro. Fri.)

2. He knew personally, but not officially, i. e., Christ was using hyperbolical language as showing the great event was to be kept a profound secret, the knowledge not having been given Him *as regards to us*, i. e., for the purpose of being communicated to us. (B. L. W-W. Wor. Lut., and many of the Fathers.) But this seems something of an attempt to evade the plain meaning of the expression, the ignorance referred to being the same as that of man and angels with which it is connected.

3. Schaff, who does not like this dualistic separation between Christ's two natures, assumes a voluntary self-limitation of knowledge on the part of Christ, i. e., a sacred unwillingness to know.

Of the three views the first is by far the most satisfactory.

Meyer does not hesitate to say that Christ taught that His second coming was to take place in the lifetime of the generation then living but that no one knew upon what day or hour. But this makes Christ to be the author of erroneous prediction.

Ver. 37. The comparison here is not alone with the ignorance of the exact time, but also with the sudden and unexpected manner in which the two events took place.

Ver. 38.   They were living in thoughtless security and gross sensuality.   That the reference in the section before us is not to the Destruction of Jerusalem, but to the end time, is seen from the fact that no such day of surprises came upon Jerusalem; she died by inches.

Vers. 40,41.   *"one is taken"*,—The verb is the same as that translated *"receive"* in John 14.3.

1. The reference is to the Destruction of Jerusalem, and while one is seized and put to death or led away captive, the other providentially escapes.   (Wet. Kui.)   This, however, is ungrammatical inasmuch as the verb *"taken"* cannot be the equivalent of "capture in war"; while furthermore the reference to the Destruction of Jerusalem is, at this point, as we have already seen, hardly warranted.

2. Alford refers this to the Millennial dispensation and to the gathering of the elect at that time, as set forth in I Thess. 4.16-17.

3. Ellicott and others (M. Whe.) refer it to the last day, to the final judgment when the holy angels will come and snatching one will bear him to the right hand of Christ, while the other is left to be borne by evil angels to his doom at the left hand of Christ.

   Meyer refers it to verse 31 and says if it pointed to I Thess. 4.16-17 the preposition *"up"* would have been used in the make-up of the verb instead of *"along side of"*, as is the case.   But there is little if any force in this, and the view of Alford seems much the simpler.

Ver. 42.   If the second coming of the Lord were not possible in our day; if it is still distant by the lapse of a thousand years of Millennial glory, or must wait until a good part of the world has been converted, this injunction, it would seem, could hardly have any significance for us of this day, as it could not have had for them to whom it was directly spoken.

Ver. 43.   If the master of the house had been warned, as you have been, he would have been watching, the exact time of the thief's coming not having been included in the warning.

Owen, who applies the preceding verses to the Destruction of Jerusalem, says the prediction here passes to the day of final judgment.

Ver. 44.   The same remarks are to be made under this verse as those made under verse 42.

45 Who then is the faithful and wise [1]servant, whom his lord hath set over his household, to give them their food in due season?   46 Blessed is that [1]servant, whom his lord when he cometh shall find so doing.   47 Verily I say unto you, that he will set him over all that he hath.   48 But if that evil [1]servant shall say in his heart, My lord tarrieth; 49 and shall begin to beat his fellow-servants, and shall eat and drink with the drunken; 50 the lord of that [1]servant shall come in a day when he expecteth not, and in an hour when he knoweth not, 51 and shall [2]cut him asunder, and appoint his portion with the hypocrites: there shall be the weeping and the gnashing of teeth.

[1]Gr. *bondservant*

[2]Or, *severely scourge him*

Vers. 45-51. The Watchful and the Careless Servants.

Ver. 45. The image changes from a householder watching for a thief to a servant watching for his master.

"*Who then*",—i. e., considering the necessity for watchfulness.

"*set over his household*",—To dispense and apportion food.

"*food in due season*",—i. e., suitable food and at the proper time.

The verse applies especially to the ministers of the Gospel, but it has a wider reference to all of God's ministering servants.

Ver. 46. Here is the answer to the question of verse 45. Instead of saying, "*It is he who*," etc., prominence is given to the blessedness of such a servant.

"*find so doing*",—i. e., in accordance with the duty assigned to him in verse 45. It is our duty, not to be idly looking at the clouds in radiant expectation of His appearance, but to be found "*so doing*", i. e., busy at our appointed task, even though we knew the hour of His coming.

Ver. 47. This statement is not to be pressed too strongly in its spiritual application and so give the sense of one saint being placed over another. It gives completion to the story, but in the diffusion of love, the more each one has the more there is for all.

Ver. 48. The conduct of the evil servant springs from unbelief with regard to the coming of his Lord.

"*that evil servant*",—i. e., on the supposition that he is evil. He also was set over the household, but proved unfaithful.

"*My Lord tarrieth*",—Lange says the expression marks an internal mocking frivolity. It describes a temper identical with that portrayed in II Pet. 3.3-4—he is a long time in coming.

Ver. 49. "*his fellow servants*",—i. e., such as are faithful servants of their absent master.

"*eat and drink with the drunken*",—i. e., with his drunken companions, guests and outsiders and such fellow servants, who like him may have been evil.

Ver. 51. "*shall cut him asunder*",—Owen says the reference is to "severe flagilation", pointing out that he survived the punishment.

On the other hand, Meyer, Whedon and others adopt the literal interpretation, i. e., actually cut him to pieces, in two parts.

There is little force in the objection of Owen to the literal interpretation, because what follows, "*portion with the hypocrites*", is only a statement of the thing itself which the likeness of that terrible punishment is intended to illustrate, and we, therefore, see no reason to depart from the literal sense of the expression, this sense of course, as applied to the parable, not being intended to be carried over into the thing it illustrates, i. e., the future judgment.

Ellicott gives the expression a figurative sense, i. e., his lord with the sharp sword of judgment smites through the false apparent unity of his life and reveals its duplicity.

Among other interpretations are the following: "scourge" (D. O. Pau. Schot.), "mutilate" (Mi.), "exclude from service" (Bez. Gro. Mal.), "withdraw from him his spiritual gifts" (Theo.), "extreme punishment" (Chr.).

"with the hypocrites",—i. e., such as he had proved himself to be, being in reality in the service of the world but professedly in that of Christ.

"there",—i. e., in hell.

CHAPTER TWENTY-FIVE

1 Then shall the kingdom of heaven be likened unto ten virgins, who took their ¹lamps, and went forth to meet the bridegroom. 2 And five of them were foolish, and five were wise. 3 For the foolish, when they took their ¹lamps, took no oil with them: 4 but the wise took oil in their vessels with their ¹lamps. 5 Now while the bridegroom tarried, they all slumbered and slept. 6 But at midnight there is a cry, Behold, the bridegroom! Come ye forth to meet him. 7 Then all those virgins arose, and trimmed their ¹lamps. 8 And the foolish said unto the wise, Give us of your oil; for our ¹lamps are going out. 9 But the wise answered, saying, Peradventure there will not be enough for us and you: go ye rather to them that sell, and buy for yourselves. 10 And while they went away to buy, the bridegroom came; and they that were ready went in with him to the marriage feast: and the door was shut. 11 Afterward came also the other virgins, saying, Lord, Lord, open to us. 12 But he answered and said, Verily I say unto you, I know you not. 13 Watch therefore, for ye know not the day nor the hour.

¹Or, *torches*

Vers. 1-13. THE FIVE WISE AND THE FIVE FOOLISH VIRGINS.

Some authorities say that the affair took place according to the Jewish custom that the bridesmaids should wait at the bridegroom's house while he brought his bride from her father's house, usually after sunset. (E. Whe.) Others say the ordinary custom is reversed and that the wedding took place in the home of the bride, because the thing signified is the coming of the Lord to the bride, the Church. (M. L. D.)

Still others say the bridesmaids were with the bride at her father's house waiting for the bridegroom to come for her from whence they would all go to his house for the marriage supper.

It is better perhaps to adhere to this last explanation, the ordinary custom, and interpret accordingly where we can.

Ver. 1. *"Then"*,—i. e., at the period spoken of at the end of the preceding chapter, the coming of the Lord.

All pre-millennialists, of course, refer this to Christ's personal coming to establish His reign on earth, while all post-millennialists refer it to His final coming in judgment at the end of the world.

"Then shall the kingdom of heaven be likened",—i. e., in respect to the principle of admission and exclusion that will be followed when that kingdom shall be set up.

"ten",—This represents perhaps only a definite number. It was the usual number of bridesmaids, although sometimes, in case of rich marriages, as many as seventy were used.

351

"virgins",—i. e., unmarried females, but not necessarily representing, as Whedon would have us believe, holy character. They refer to all believers, faithful souls bearing their lamps. (A. Scha.)

"went forth",—Not perhaps from the bride's house (M.), but from their own homes to go to the bride's house, from whence they were to go out to meet the coming bridegroom and escort him and the bride to his house.

Alford says that the bride here is, in strict interpretation, the Jewish Church and the ten virgins are the Gentile congregations accompanying her.

Ver. 2. There is no contrast here between chastity and its opposite, as Cremer suggests; nor does it represent the foolish as having a dead faith (lamps without light). All this is quite beside the parable. The lamps were all burning at first and for a certain length of time.

Vers. 3,4. The foolish seem vain and thoughtless, going forth through excited feeling.

Ver. 5. *"tarried"*,—This is the same word as that in Chap. 24.48, *"My Lord tarrieth"*, where the Lord seems to hint that the real time of His coming might be more distant than the words predicting its nearness literally expressed.

"they all slumbered and slept",—The first word implies the nodding and the second the continual sleeping.

Some apply this to sleeping in death. But this will not fit the machinery of the parable (verse 8), and it also assumes that none of the faithful (*"they all"*) would be living on the earth when the Lord comes.

Ver. 6. The approach of the bridegroom was made known by the light of the torches they carried. The hour was later than the virgins expected.

"a cry",—i. e., by the porter (A.), by the waiting spectators (M.), or possibly by the bridegroom's party (E. L. Ow. Whe.).

Owen says the bride is the Church of which the virgins are the members, the representatives, and that the cry is identical with the blast of the last trumpet at the final day of judgment. This is of course consistent with his exegesis of the whole of this section of Scripture.

Ver. 7. All now seem alike; all wanted their lamps trimmed.

Ver. 9. *"Peradventure there will not be enough"*,—No man can have more of this provision than will supply his own wants.

"go ye rather",—Spoken not in mockery, but in earnest.

Vers. 10,11. Alford says this feast is the marriage supper of Rev. 19.7-9, *after which* the foolish will be judged in common with the rest of the dead.

Ver. 13. Olshausen, Alford and others suppose the foolish virgins to be excluded only from the Millennial kingdom, but not from the ultimate kingdom of heaven. Schaff, a post-millennialist, says that *"I know you not"* and *"the door was shut"* argues against this, and he says Alford tries to evade the difficulty by making a distinction between *"I never knew you"* of Chap. 7.23 and *"I know you not"* of this passage. (See comment on Chap. 24.42.)

14 For *it is as when* a man, going into another country, called his own [1]servants, and delivered unto them his goods. 15 And unto one he gave five talents, to another two, to another one; to each according to his several ability; and he went on his journey. 16 Straightway he that received the five talents went and traded with them, and made other five talents. 17 In like manner he also that *received* the two gained other two. 18 But he that received the one went away and digged in the earth, and hid his lord's money. 19 Now after a long time the lord of those [1]servants cometh, and maketh a reckoning with them. 20 And he that receiveth the five talents came and brought other five talents, saying, Lord, thou deliveredst unto me five talents: lo, I have gained other five talents. 21 His lord said unto him, Well done, good and faithful [2]servant: thou hast been faithful over a few things, I will set thee over many things: enter thou into the joy of thy lord. 22 And he also that *received* the two talents came and said, Lord, thou deliveredst unto me two talents: lo, I have gained other two talents.

[1]Gr. *bondservants*
[2]Gr. *bondservant*

23 His lord said unto him, Well done, good and faithful [2]servant; thou hast been faithful over a few things, I will set thee over many things; enter thou into the joy of thy lord. 24 And he also that had received the one talent came and said, Lord, I knew thee that thou art a hard man, reaping where thou didst not sow, and gathering where thou didst not scatter; 25 and I was afraid, and went away and hid thy talent in the earth; lo, thou hast thine own. 26 But his lord answered and said unto him, Thou wicked and slothful [2]servant, thou knewest that I reap where I sowed not, and gather where I did not scatter; 27 thou oughtest therefore to have put my money to the bankers, and at my coming I should have received back mine own with interest. 28 Take ye away therefore the talent from him, and give it unto him that hath the ten talents. 29 For unto every one that hath shall be given, and he shall have abundance: but from him that hath not, even that which he hath shall be taken away. 30 And cast ye out the unprofitable [2]servant into the outer darkness: there shall be the weeping and the gnashing of teeth.

Vers. 14-30. THE PARABLE OF THE TALENTS.

In the parable of the ten virgins the simple idea is that of waiting, watching, in constant readiness for the coming bridegroom. In this parable of the talents it is *active* watchfulness that is enjoined. The first sets forth the contemplative side of the Christian life, while the second sets forth the active side of it. The foolish virgins thought their part too easy, while the wicked servant thought his part too hard.

Ver. 14. *"it is"*,—i. e., the kingdom of heaven is.

"going into another country",—i. e., as our Lord ascended into heaven.

"his own servants",—The reference is to Christians and not to the world at large.

"delivered unto them his goods",—i. e., for investment; an oriental custom. So Christ entrusts to Christians in this world the treasure of His spiritual life.

Ver. 15. Spiritual gifts are regulated by personal capacity.

Vers. 16, 17. The first two made an increase equal to the amount of their trust, endowment. Of each one will be required as much as he has been given.

Ver. 18. This servant is not to be confounced with the wicked servant of Chap. 24.48. This is not actively an evil doer, but a do-nothing, a hider of talents.

Ver. 19. *"after a long time"*,—Here, as in the previous parable, is a faint suggestion, as it were, of a longer delay than men looked for in the coming of Christ, which is the counterpart of this.

"the .lord of those servants cometh",—Says Alford, "This is the judgment of the Millennial advent, which for the servants of Christ is their final judgment, but not that of the rest of the world."

Ver. 21. *"good and faithful"*,—The genus and species of an upright character.

"enter thou into the joy of thy lord",—i. e., participate in the happ - ness which thy master is enjoying.

In the application of this parable this joy, according to post-millennialists, refers to the heavenly rewards in eternal glory; but according to pre-millennialists it refers to the millennial joys, just as *"set thee over many things"* is by them referred to the same period.

The joy of the Lord, Alford refers to that arising from the completion of His work and labor of love, of which the first Sabbatical rest was typical and of which His faithful servants shall in the end partake.

Ver. 24. *"reaping where thou didst not sow"*,—This is a man's lie.

"scatter",—This means to winnow, by casting grain to the wind which carries the chaff away.

Ver. 25. *"and I was afraid"*,—i. e., of the consequences in case he lost the money. The fear is a pretended one. It would have been more commendable if he had lost it by investing it as the others had done.

"thou hast thine own",—Another lie. He did not account for his time and his labor which belonged to his lord, and so he did *not* give to the lord *what was his*.

Ver. 26. *"thou knewest that I reap where I sowed not"*,—i. e., according to his own statement. These words are not, however, concessive, but hypothetical and not admitting himself to be such a hard master. It is as if he had said, "If thou hadst really thought me such a hard master thou oughtest, etc., in order to avoid utter ruin."

Ver. 28. *"Take ye away the talent therefore from him"*,—This shows the talent to refer to external opportunity, inasmuch as a man's ability cannot be taken from him.

Ver. 29. The words of this verse justify the preceding judgment by appealing to a principle founded on universal experience.

31 But when the Son of man shall come in his glory, and all the angels with him, then shall he sit on the throne of his glory: 32 and before him shall be gathered all the nations: and he shall separate them one from another, as the shepherd separateth the sheep from the goats; 33 and he shall set the sheep on his right hand, but the goats on the left. 34 Then shall the King say unto them on his right hand, Come, ye blessed of my Father, inherit the kingdom prepared for you from the foundation of the world: 35 for I was hungry, and ye gave me to eat; I was thirsty, and ye gave me drink; I was a stranger, and ye took me in; 36 naked, and ye clothed me; I was sick, and ye visited me; I was in prison, and ye came unto me. 37 Then shall the righteous answer him, saying, Lord, when saw we thee hungry, and fed thee? or athirst, and gave thee drink? 38 And when saw we thee a stranger, and took thee in? or naked, and clothed thee? 39 And when saw we thee sick, or in

prison, and came unto thee? 40 And the King shall answer and say unto them, Verily I say unto you, Inasmuch as ye did it unto one of these my brethren, *even* these least, ye did it unto me. 41 Then shall he say also unto them on the left hand, [1]Depart from me, ye cursed, into the eternal fire which is prepared for the devil and his angels: 42 for I was hungry, and ye did not give me to eat; I was thirsty, and ye gave me no drink; 43 I was a stranger, and ye took me not in; naked, and ye clothed me not; sick, and in prison, and ye visited me not. 44 Then shall they also answer, saying, Lord, when saw we thee hungry, or athirst, or a stranger, or naked, or sick, or in prison, and did not minister unto thee? 45 Then shall he answer them, saying, Verily I say unto you, Inasmuch as ye did it not unto one of these least, ye did it not unto me. 46 And these shall go away into eternal punishment: but the righteous into eternal life.

[1]Or, *Depart from me under a curse*

Vers. 31-46. THE JUDGMENT BASED UPON WORKS.

There are four views of this passage which present themselves for consideration, and they are as follows:

I. It refers to a final judgment of unbelievers at the end of the Millennium. (K. R. O. A. S. B-C.) In favor of this view is adduced:

    1. Those only are judged who are distinguished from Christ's brethren, but nothing is said of a judgment upon these brethren themselves. The strength of this argument depends largely upon who are meant by the brethren.

        (a) If these brethren constitute a third audience, either Jews according to the flesh, as many think, or the elect saints in general, the Church, as others think, then both the sheep and the goats would represent naturally two different classes of unbelievers.

        (b) If, however, the brethren be conceived of as consisting of the sheep on His right hand, which many maintain is quite as natural, then the right hand group would consist of Christians who had been kind to one another as the brethren of Christ, while the goats, of course, as not having been so disposed, would consist of unbelievers upon whom an adverse judgment falls.

    2. The verdict turns upon works and not upon faith, and therefore it does not relate to believers.

        (a) However, Christians are judged also according to their works; not works as such, but rather as the outgrowth of the faith and love which prompted them.

    3. No one but an unbeliever, such a one as never had the consciousness of a personal relation to Christ, could say what is contained in verses 37 to 39, because Christians do these things distinctly with reference to Christ and for His sake. This is the strongest argument for the view we are now discussing.

        (a) But may not the answer have been the language of humility? Still it is hard to think, even as Olshausen says, of Christian humility devoid of consciousness in respect to a matter of this kind. In this case the language of the goats would be the language of self-justification.

Certain things, however, militate very strongly against this view:

(1) It is contrary to Scripture usage to call any other than Christians *"sheep"*, or *"righteous"*, or *"blessed of my Father"*, or to say that *"the kingdom was prepared for them from the foundation of the world"*, in which last expression Alford strongly maintains that the elect in general seem to be exclusively involved.

(2) It would seem that Christians only would be given to doing the things mentioned in verses 35, 36 and 40, which Christ represents as done unto Him.

(3) If they were unbelievers and heathen, to save them because of their behaviour toward Christ's brethren would manifest not only what Keim calls "a remarkable toleration", but it would seem to be utterly inconsistent with the whole tenor of New Testament teaching.

(4) This judgment it seems is one of works only, and if so, it is consistent that Christians should appear in it, as we have already seen; and in this case there would at least be included people who were converted during the Millennium, granted that all other Christians were translated and judged before the Millennium; otherwise it leaves only the heathen to be judged from among whom some are saved and that because of their works.

II. It refers to a final judgment upon professing believers only at the end of the Millennium. (Gro. Eut. Lact.)

This is the oldest view, and in favor of it the following is adduced:

1. Verse 34 shows the sheep to have been real Christians, while their actions as set forth in verses 35 and 36 show the same thing; the goats by the same test proving themselves to have been unfaithful or false professors of the faith.

2. Of no one but Christians would the things mentioned have been expected, and only Christians do such things as those recited in verses 35 and 36.

3. From any other standpoint it would establish the doctrine of salvation by works and show that some out of the heathen will be saved because of their works.

4. Meyer says the expression *"all nations"* proves it. He says the word *"nations"* does not necessarily exclude the Jews, and calls attention to Matt. 28.19; 24.9; John 11.50; II Cor. 5.10; Rom. 14.10. He maintains that the judgment of unbelievers forms a distinct and separate scene.

(a) But the expression *"all nations"* proves Meyer's contention only on the ground that the universality of Christianity is presupposed, everybody practically having at least professed faith in Christ.

But against this second view is to be urged the fact that verse 37 could not be the language of real Christians (A. O. E.). These authorities just quoted declare that the words could, however, be used by the merciful among the heathen. The argument used, however, seems weak and dangerous. For instance, Alford, much to our surprise, says, "These who are judged know not that all their deeds of love have been done to and for Christ. They are overwhelmed at the sight of the grace which has been working in them and for them and the glory which is now their blessed portion. It is not works as such but the love which prompted them—that love which was their faith—which felt its way, though in darkness, to Him who is love—which is commended. Any good that they did was the fruit of Christ's Spirit, and this Spirit is purchased for man by Christ, and thus they are blessed of His Father and the kingdom is prepared for them. The Scriptures assure us of the Second Resurrection; the First, of the dead in Christ to meet Him and to reign with Him and to hold judgment over the world (I Cor. 6.2); the Second, of all the dead, to be judged according to their works. And to what purpose would a judgment be if all were to be condemned?"

III. It refers to a final judgment upon both unbelievers and believers at the end of the Millennium. (R. Scha.)

In favor of this is adduced the following:

1. The expression *"all nations"* seems to favor this interpretation.
    (a) Olshausen objects to this on the ground that *"my brethren"* is distinguished from both the sheep and the goats. It could, however, in this case refer to those on the right hand, the righteous themselves, or to some special class of believers. (See notes under verse 32.)

    With regard to the expression *"all nations"*, Whedon calls attention to the fact that it is not a judgment of the nations as such any more than the twelve are commended in Chap. 28.19 to teach *"all nations"* as such; but the reference, he says, is to the individuals who compose the nations.

2. As verse 34 would seem to refer to Christians whose answer is to be construed as one of humility, or of surprise as having been done to Christ personally; so verse 46 would seem to refer to the wicked and unbelieving.

    The objections to be urged against this view are:
    (1) Christians could not use the language of verses 37 to 39. Olshausen says it could not be the language of humility because Christian humility cannot be thought of as devoid of consciousness.
    (2) The New Testament teaches that Christians shall not be brought into the judgment. Some, however, as we have seen, conceive of this as a judgment for works in which it is proper for Christians to have part.

IV. It refers to a judgment of the living nations at the beginning of the Millennium. (Sco. Bla. Gab. Mor. Tor. Pet. Mack.)

Says Scofield, "This judgment is to be distinguished from the judgment of the great white throne. Here there is no resurrection; the persons judged are living nations; no books are opened; three classes are present, sheep, goats, and brethren; the time is at the return of Christ (verse 31); and the scene is on the earth. All these particulars are in contrast with Rev. 20.11-14, the scene of the final judgment at the end of the Millennium. The test in this judgment is the treatment accorded by the nations to those whom Christ here calls *'my brethren'*. These *'brethren'* are the Jewish remnant who will have preached the Gospel of the kingdom to all nations during the great tribulation. The test in Rev. 20.11-17 is the possession of eternal life." This same author says those who are found upon the right hand form the Gentile nucleus of the population of the Millennial earth, while those upon the left go away into eternal punishment.

Ver. 31. *"the Son of man"*,—The Lord here identifies Himself as the Son of man described in the vision of Daniel. The passage which follows is a proof text of His divinity inasmuch as all judgment is committed into His hands by the Father.

"in his glory",—i. e., the glory which belongs to Him as the Messiah. Both Alford and Olshausen say that Chap. 24.30 has to do with an *earlier* period in the revelation of His glory, which glory in Chap. 24.30 is that also of His saints with whom He is there to be accompanied. They are right, though only, of course, on the ground of their theory that the coming of the Son of man in our verse is to take place at the *end* of the Millennium, while that of Chap. 24.30 takes place, according to these same authorities, at the beginning of the Millennium.

"all the angels with him",—i. e., as witnesses and executors of His will.

Olshausen thinks that as verse 40 seems to imply that the saints are present also, the expression *"angels"* is here taken in a comprehensive sense so as to include the saints, the just made perfect (Heb. 12.33). If by the expression *"my brethren"* is meant the saints in general, Olshausen's idea may be conceded.

Owen says that according to I Thess. 4.16,17 the Christian dead are raised first and then the Christian living are caught up together with them, and then the wicked are raised, and so to the wicked the saints seem to come to judgment with the Lord.

"then shall he sit",—An expression of finished victory.

"the throne of his glory",—The literal is "his glorious throne", i. e., the throne which He shares with the Father, says Ellicott.

Ver. 32. *"and before him shall be gathered all nations"*,—(See introductory discussion as to the subjects of this judgment.)
1. All nations, then universally Christianized, i. e., Christendom, then co-extensive with all nations, all having professed the Christian faith. (M. L.)
   This makes the judgment refer exclusively to professing Christians.
   "my brethren", they say, refers either
   (a) to the poor, obscured and despised who were always with Him on earth, and with whom He represents Himself as now surrounded. (M. Au.)
   (b) to Christians generally, and pre-eminently the least of them. (K. L. O. Ke. Hil. Geo. Cre.)
2. All unbelievers as distinguished from the elect. (A. O. E. S.)
   "my brethren", then refers, they say, either
   (a) to any of the great family of men. (A.)
   (b) to believers in Christ who are with Him in glory by the side of the throne. (O. Cre.)

3. All believers and all unbelievers of all ages and all continents—all stand before Him. (Ow. Whe. Ken.)

"*my brethren*", these authorities say refers either
  (a) to the Apostles and by inference to all messengers of Christ in all ages. (Whe. Ken.)
  (b) to one of the least of your own number, believers in Christ like yourselves. (Ow.)

4. All living Gentile unbelievers to be judged at the beginning of the Millennium. (Mor. Sco. Gab. Tor. Pet. Bla. Mack.)

"*my brethren*" then refers to the believing Jews then present, the judgment taking place on earth.

"*he shall separate them*",—The two classes are probably mingled together up to this time; pastured together, as Meyer says. The separating involves the idea of judging. The work is done probably by the ministry of the angels.

"*as a shepherd*",—As the Shepherd of all mankind He knows how to distinguish them perfectly.

Ver. 33.   The right hand and the left are understood, says Ellicott, according to the laws of what we might call a natural symbolism, as indicating respectfully good and evil, acceptance and rejection.

The wicked are conceived under the figure of goats, doubtless, as Meyer and De Wette say, because goats were considered worthless, and not perhaps on account of the stench and wantonness of goats (Gro.), or their stubbornness (L. The. Mal.), or both combined (Nast).

Ver. 34.   "*the King*",—Here for the first and only time Christ gives Himself this name. He comes forward in all His kingly dignity since He has now appeared in His kingdom.   (Chap. 16.28.)

"*Come*",—Not to be taken in a local sense but as an expression of encouragement and incitement.

"*ye blessed of my Father*",—The idea is one of possession, *belonging to* the Father rather than of being *blessed* by Him.

This, say Meyer, Lange and others, means blessed as the regenerate, renewed by the Holy Spirit, the elect of God, who by their works have proven their faith and profession.

"*inherit the kingdom*",—This kingdom all post-millennialists, of course, refer to heaven.

Some pre-millennialists make it to be the kingdom of Christ here on earth during the Millennium (Sco. Mor. Gab. Pet. Tor.), while Alford, Lange and all other pre-millennialists who place this judgment scene at the end of the Millennium, refer the kingdom to the time of the new heavens and the new earth after the Millennium.

Ver. 35.   "*ye took me in*",—i. e., numbered me among your own circle (A. Ow.), introduced me to your family (M.).

Vers. 37-39.   This is taken by some as a modest exhibition of humility on the part of the believers in Christ.   (M. D. Ow. Whe. Ori.)   Meyer says it is a declining with humility as not having rendered the service to *Christ Himself*.

On the other hand others maintain that believers in Christ could not be so surprised and that this proves they were not believers, not Christians (E. O. A.), or as Auberlen says, "they have not as yet been leading consciously the New Testament life".

Olshausen remarks here, "To those who have been actuated by a humble child-like love there will then be a disclosure of a living faith, the living connection that subsists between the Redeemer and His people."

Ver. 40. *"these my brethren"*,—See exposition under verse 32 and the discussion introductory to this section of Scripture, to which add also the view of Ludhardt, "the Christian Church in distress".

Ver. 41. *"Depart from me, ye cursed"*,—The omission of *"of my Father"* is significant. He is not the author of the curse. (E. A. O. L. S.)

The words, *"prepared from the foundation of the earth"*, are not repeated here, but are to be understood as known to the hearer as a matter of course.

"eternal fire which is prepared",—This is not followed by *"for you"*, but by *"for the devil and his angels"*, because the fall of the angels (II Pet. 2.4) took place, as Scripture tells us, before the introduction of sin among men and so the fire was prepared for the devil and his angels, but as men became partakers of the guilt of the devil they are of course condemned to share in his punishment.

Ver. 44. The ignorance here expressed is of another kind and closely connected with self-righteousness. As if they would have been glad to serve Him (!), and thus trying to excuse themselves.

Ver. 46. *"eternal punishment"*,—The punishment is as eternal as the reward, the death as everlasting as the life.

Regarding the entire passage Owen says that according to the pre-millennial view the righteous should be acquitted before the wicked are even raised, whereas here the wicked are raised, tried and condemned before the righteous enter at all upon their reward. They escape, he says, somewhat the difficulty they confront in this judgment scene by making the scene 1000 years long, beginning at the beginning of the Millennium, but he declares that there is no support in the passage for this.

Alford says he cannot see how the features of this whole description can agree with the idea of this judgment being previous to the Millennium.

CHAPTER TWENTY-SIX

> 29 But I say unto you, I shall not drink henceforth of this fruit of the vine, until that day when I drink it new with you in my Father's kingdom.

Ver. 29. (See exposition on Luke 22.16-18.)

> 64 Jesus saith unto him, Thou hast said: nevertheless I say unto you, Henceforth ye shall see the Son of man sitting at the right hand of Power, and coming on the clouds of heaven.

Ver. 64. THE SECOND COMING IN A FIGURATIVE AND EVER PRESENT SENSE.

"Thou hast said",—i. e., he was what the words they had uttered

had implied. It was a solemn affirmation of the truth involved in the question. In other words, He said, "I am." Alford thinks a reference is made to a previous conviction and admission by Caiaphas himself (John 11.49,50), but this is not likely.

"*nevertheless*",—i. e., however apart from what I have just affirmed ye shall henceforward have reason to be satisfied from actual observation that I am the Messiah who was seen by Daniel in his vision.

"*henceforth*",—i. e., from now on, from the accomplishment of this trial, i. e., after my death. (M. A. Ow.)

Says David Brown "The word rendered '*hereafter*' (Authorized Version) means not 'at some future time', as now the word 'hereafter' commonly does, but what the English word originally signified, 'after here', 'after now', or 'from this time'. Accordingly in Luke 22.69 the words used mean 'from now', or 'from this time'. So that though the reference we have given it to the day of His glorious Second Appearing is too obvious to admit of doubt, He would, by using the expression, 'from this time', convey the important thought which He had before expressed, immediately after the traitor left the supper table to do his dark work, '*Now is the Son of man glorified*'."

The glorification of Christ is by Himself said to begin with His betrayal. (John 13.31.)

"*ye shall see*",—i. e., in the course of experience.

The expression, says Lange, must not be limited to the final appearing of Christ, but refers to His whole state of exaltation, i. e., to the personal exaltation which reveals itself in the almighty power and universal influence exercised by Him throughout the whole course of history.

"*on the right hand of Power*",—The power here is that of the eternal One, and the expression is equivalent to the right hand of God. The reference is to His omnipotence. (Psa. 110.1.) It is "*the*" power, the abstract for the concrete, the Mighty One being conceived of as power and the reference is to His share in the governing of the world in which His glory is manifested.

"*coming on the clouds*",—The expression looks on, as Alford says, to the awful time of the end when every eye shall see Him, but the reference is not specifically to this, as De Wett says, but rather, as Lange puts it, "to the whole judicial administration of Christ, which commences immediately after His resurrection, but more especially at the destruction of Jerusalem, and shall be completed in the end of the world." The reference is therefore mainly to a figurative coming in the shape of those mighty influences which from His place in heaven He will shed upon the earth,—His sovereign sway. (M. L. Bez. Nea. Holt. Weis. Ges. Schen.)

Meyer seems rightly to say that, " '*henceforth ye shall see*' can only be said of something that beginning now is continued henceforth". The sitting cannot therefore be regarded as an object of actual sight. The "*henceforth*" here, says Meyer, requires for what follows the *figurative* sense. He also thinks that the expression in Mark (Chap. 14.64), "*sitting at the right hand of Power*", requires the figurative meaning as well, while Luke alone, he maintains, gives the literal meaning.

THE GOSPEL ACCORDING TO

MARK

(A. D. 57—A. D. 63)

CHAPTER FOUR

26 And he said, So is the kingdom of God, as if a man should cast seed upon the earth; 27 and should sleep and rise night and day, and the seed should spring up and grow, he knoweth not now. 28 The earth [1]beareth fruit of herself; first the blade, then the ear, then the full grain in the ear. 29 But when the fruit [2]is ripe straightway he [3]putteth forth the sickle, because the harvest is come.

[1]Or, *yieldeth*

[2]Or, *alloweth*
[3]Or, *sendeth forth*

Vers. 26-30. THE KINGDOM OF GOD FROM SEED-TIME TO HARVEST.

This beautiful parable is not merely an appendix to the preceding one, as Braune says; it is rather, as Stier says, an independent link in the chain or cycle of parables in Matthew 13. It is found here only. Weizsacker finds in this parable a proof that the Gospel of Mark was not written until after the Destruction of Jerusalem, when the delaying of the Parousia had become evident. But the establishment of the kingdom is not at all depicted here under the specific form of the Parousia, and nothing is said at all about the delaying of it.

Stier has rightly said, "The self-inherent growth-power of the kingdom of God (as a whole, as well as in individuals) in its independence of human care and labor,—this and nothing else is the theme."

Ver. 26. *"And he said"*,—Notice the omission of "to them", the address probably being now to the people.

"The kingdom of God",—This, says Meyer, is the Messianic kingdom conceived of as preparing for its proximate appearance and then (verse 29) appearing at its time.

"as if a man",—This does not refer to Christ, as Gerlach maintains; because the sleeping during the night is not applicable to Him, as is not the expression *"he knoweth not how"*. Nor does it refer exactly to Christ's ministers, as the putting forth the sickle seems inapplicable to them. The main point, however, is the seed with its self-inherent power, the agent being quite in the background. The *"man"* therefore is anybody, that is, just the farmer, the sower, the idea being only that of human agency.

Ver. 27. *"and should sleep and rise night and day"*,—i. e., live as usual without further care as to the seed sown.

"he knoweth not how",—The growth of the seed depends upon a mysterious power implanted by God within it, the working of which is hidden from the human eye.

Ver. 28. *"The earth beareth fruit of herself"*,—i. e., without man's assistance. Says Alford, "No trouble of ours can accelerate the growth, or shorten the stages through which each seed must pass." As a seed grows according to a certain inherent law, so also does growth take place in the

362

kingdom of grace, i. e., in the kingdom of God in general and in the individual.

"first the blade", etc.,—A beautiful allusion to the succession of the stages of growth. The maturity of the kingdom or of the individual does not come at once. The lesson is one of patience. We must not lose heart because of small beginnings.

Ver. 29. "when the fruit is ripe",—The Greek may be rendered, "when the fruit shall have yielded itself", or, according to the more usual sense, "when the fruit alloweth", i. e., when it is ripe. The thought of the independency of human agency is kept up.

"he putteth forth the sickle",—The sower reaps the benefit, though God alone giveth the increase. Alford says there is a reference in this verse to Joel 3.13.

Riddle says, "The parable possibly has a historical application; the sowing referring to the institution of the Church by Christ; the intervening period to His absence, during which the growth continues according to the laws of the Spirit's influence; and the harvest to His return."

Meyer says, "The teaching of the parable is: Just as a man, after performing the sowing, leaves the germination and growth, without further intervention, to the earth's own power, but at the time of ripening reaps the harvest, so the Messiah leaves the ethical results and the new development of life, which His word is fitted to produce in the minds of men, to the moral self-activity of the human heart, through which these results are worked out in accordance with their destination, but will, when the time for the establishment of His kingdom comes, cause the righteous to be gathered into it (by the angels, Matt. 24.31; these are the reapers, Matt. 13.39)."

Vers. 30-32. THE PARABLE OF THE MUSTARD SEED.
(See Matt. 13.31 and Luke 13.18.)

CHAPTER EIGHT

38 For whosoever shall be ashamed of me and of my words in this adulterous and sinful generation, the Son of man also shall be ashamed of him, when he cometh in the glory of his Father with the holy angels.

Ver. 38. THE DISOWNER OF CHRIST DISOWNED AT HIS COMING.

The reference, says Meyer, is to the Parousia. "And as to this mighty decision, how soon shall it emerge! (Chap. 9.1.)"

Here the reference to his own glory is omitted. In Luke 9.26 the glory is threefold, His own, His Father's, and His holy angels'.

"It can scarcely be doubted", says Oosterzee, "that the Saviour directs His eye toward His last Parousia, at the end of the age. But before the thought of its possibly great distance could weaken the impression of the warning, He concludes with a nearer revelation of His kingly glory in the first verse of the next chapter."

Says Godet, "All the several glories of the royal advent of Jesus will be mingled together in the incomparable splendor of that great day (II Thess. 1.7-10)." (See exposition on Luke 9.26.)

CHAPTER NINE

> 1 And he said unto them, Verily I say unto you, There are some here of them that stand by, who shall in no wise taste of death, till they see the kingdom of God come with power.

Ver. 1. THE COMING OF THE LORD IN THE DESTRUCTION OF JERU-SALEM.

(See exposition on Matt. 16.28 and Luke 9.27.)

Riddle says, "The coming referred to was probably at the day of Pentecost, or the destruction of Jerusalem, and the consequent triumph of Christianity."

Says Meyer, "When in this place the coming of the kingdom is spoken of, it is the same nearness of the Parousia that is meant as in Matt. 16.28; not the constituting of the Church (Bl.), nor the emergence of the *idea* of the kingdom into historical realization (Wei.), nor the triumph of the Gospel (Schen.), and the like. With interpretations of this nature the specification of time, pointing, as it does, to the term of the then existing generation, is not at all in keeping."

We are inclined to agree with Oosterzee when he says, "It cannot be difficult to decide which coming of the Saviour He wished to be immediately understood by this saying. He has here in mind, as in Matt. 26.64, the revelation of His Messianic dignity at the desolation of the Jewish state, which was to take place within a human generation." But see our exposition on Matt. 16.28 and Luke 9.27.

CHAPTER ELEVEN

> 10 Blessed is the kingdom that cometh, the kingdom of our father David: Hosanna in the highest.

Ver. 10. THE KINGDOM MISINTERPRETED.

"the kingdom of our father David",—Whatever may be said as to what this kingdom is, it is certain that here the thing in mind was the outwardly glorious kingdom toward which their carnal hopes were outwardly directed.

Alford says, "The words clearly set forth the idea of the people that the Messianic kingdom, the restoration of the throne of David, was come."

The Lord was here recognized as the royal Messiah, who, as Riddle says, was to restore the throne of David.

Lange says it refers to the kingdom of the Messiah as the *spiritual* restoration of the kingdom of David, which kingdom of David was for them a type of the Messianic one. The exact meaning of the word "spiritual" at this place is difficult of appreciation. (See notes on *"the kingdom"* under Matt. 3.2.)

CHAPTER THIRTEEN

(For the exegesis of this entire Chapter see exposition under Matthew 24 and Luke 21.)

> 10 And the Gospel must first be preached to all the nations.

Ver. 10. A CONDITION OF HIS COMING.

Riddle says the sense is the same as in Matt. 24.14, as does also Meyer. Says Riddle, "Their martyrdom would spread the Gospel, and this spread should precede the end of the woes. A twofold fulfillment of this verse is most probable." Riddle, Lange and Meyer are agreed in their explanation.

Says Olshausen, "In Matthew the expression is *'the Gospel of the kingdom'*, which is the object of the glad tidings to be proclaimed by the preachers; that message, however, is to be viewed as combining both the external and the internal; only that here the connection naturally leads to this, viz., that the proclamation would invite to receive the spirit of the new living community, so that at the Parousia, when it shall appear in between 9:00 P. M. and 6:00 A. M.

> 13 And ye shall be hated of all men for my name's sake: but he that endureth to the end, the same shall be saved.

Ver. 13. REDEMPTION THROUGH ENDURANCE.

"he that endureth to the end, the same shall be saved",—The endurance, says Lange, refers to the entire state of trial which they should pass through faithfully, confessing His name, as the context implies. (R. M. L.)

> 33 Take ye heed, watch [1]and pray: for ye know not when the time is. 34 *It is* as *when* a man, sojourning in another country, having left his house, and given authority to his [2]servants, to each one his work, commanded also the porter to watch. 35 Watch therefore: for ye know not when the lord of the house cometh, whether at even, or at midnight, or at cockcrowing, or in the morning; 36 lest coming suddenly he find you sleeping. 37 And what I say unto you I say unto all, Watch.
>
> [1]Some ancient authorities omit *and pray*
> [2]Gr. *bondservants*

Vers. 33-37. WATCHFULNESS IN VIEW OF THE RETURN OF THE LORD.

This passage is peculiar to Mark, and contains in somewhat condensed form the substance of Matt. 24.43-47.

Ver. 34. *"commanded also the porter to watch"*,—It would be the office of the door-porter to look out for approaching travelers. The idea here is that the injunction was given to him at the door just as the master of the house was going away, i. e., the last thing he said. Does not this point to the official duty of the ministers of religion?

Ver. 35. By *"even"* is meant 9:00 P. M.; by *"midnight"*, 12:00; by *"cockcrowing"*, 3:00 A. M., and by *"morning"*, 6:00 A. M. "These periods", says Lange, "may denote the same unexpectedness:—the evening, the evening of the old world (Matt. 20.8); the midnight, the frame of mind of the slumbering Church (Matt. 25.6) ; the cockcrow, the voice of the watchers (Isa. 21.11) ; the morning, the dawn of Christ's appearing, the breaking into day of the new world (Mal. 4.2)." (See Matt. 14.24.) The night-season Meyer thinks belong to the pictorial effect of the parable, and is in keeping with the figurative *"watch"*, without exactly expressing "a dark and sad time", as Lange thinks. The coming, which is to be unexpected and sudden, is pictured as taking place in the night between 9:00 P. M. and 6:00 A. M.

Ver. 37. *"I say unto all, Watch"*,—All believers, as well as the Apostles and ministers of the Gospel, are to be incessantly watchful.

CHAPTER FOURTEEN

> 25 Verily I say unto you, I shall no more drink of the fruit of the vine, until that day when I drink it new in the kingdom of God.

Ver. 25. (See exposition on Luke 22.16-18.)

> 62 And Jesus said, I am: and ye shall see the Son of man sitting at the right hand of Power, and coming with the clouds of heaven.

Ver. 62. (See exposition on Matt. 26.64 and Luke 22.69.)

THE GOSPEL ACCORDING TO

LUKE

(A. D. 63—A. D. 68)

CHAPTER ONE

> 32 He shall be great, and shall be called the Son of Most High: and the Lord God shall give unto him the throne of his father David: 33 and he shall reign over the house of Jacob [1]for ever; and of his kingdom there shall be no end.
>
> [1]Gr. *unto the ages.*

Vers. 32,33. CHRIST TO BE KING FOREVER ON DAVID'S THRONE.

Says Campbell Morgan, "Jesus will be King, in as direct and positive a sense as any ruler the world has ever known, but with larger empire and more autocratic sway. He will be Judge as well as King, and the final Arbitrator in any disputes that may arise among men. The announcement made to Mary in these two verses concerning Jesus has never yet been fulfilled, but will be when the time comes for His personal reign. He will be the King of God's ancient people gathered in Jerusalem; and through them, the Governor of the whole earth."

These words are but an echo of the sublime prediction of Isa. 9.6,7.

"he shall be called",—This expression signifies here that He shall be universally recognized as such, and that because He is such in fact.

"He shall be great",—What follows is an explanation to Mary of this greatness, although a full explanation was scarcely possible.

"the Son of the Most High",—Meyer rightly says this is a description of His recognition as the Messiah, and as such the angel still more definitely designates Him as the One to whom the throne of David is to be given. The expression is not used in a metaphysical sense, but only in a theocratic one. Of course the expression denotes a personal and mysterious relation between this child and the Divine Being, but had the notion of the pre-existence of Christ as the eternal Son of God been emphasized Mary could not have comprehended it, and Gerlach has very wisely remarked that had the proper divinity of her son been definitely revealed to Mary, neither she nor Joseph would have been in a position to bring the child up.

The expression points to the anointed King, so long foretold by the prophets, and to whom so fully apply the words of II Sam. 7.14; Psa. 2.7; 89.28.

"the Lord God shall give unto Him the throne of His father David", —Says Alford, "This announcement makes it almost certain that *Mary also* was of the house of David. No astonishment is expressed by her at this part of the statement, and yet, from the nature of her question, it is clear that she did not explain it by supposing Joseph to be the destined father of her child."

In these words His Messiahship is distinctly made known. Mary, who was intimately acquainted with the Old Testament, would so understand them, especially in the light of such promises as II Sam. 7; Isa. 9; Micah 5, etc.

Says Godet, "These expressions in the mouth of the angel keep their natural and literal sense. It is, indeed, the theocratic royalty and the Israelitish people, neither more nor less, that are in question here; Mary could have understood these expressions in no other way. The unbelief of Israel foiled the plan, and subverted the regular course of history; so that at the present day the fulfillment of these promises is still postponed to the future."

Ver. 33. *"over the house of Jacob"*,—Mary no doubt understood these words literally according to the national expectation of the Jews.

"The house of Jacob", says Meyer, is not, with Olshausen, Bleek and others, to be idealized into the "spiritual Israel". "The conception of the kingdom in our passage", says this same expositor, "is Jewish-national, which, however, does not exclude the dominion over the Gentiles according to prophetic prediction."

Says Oosterzee, "The announcement of His universal spiritual reign would have been, at this time, even more incomprehensible to Mary; it lies hidden, however, in the promise, 'Of His kingdom there shall be no end'. We must not therefore regard these words of the angel as an accommodation merely to the exclusively Jewish expectations then prevailing concerning the kingdom of the Messiah."

"of His kingdom there shall be no end",—Riddle says, "This hints at the universal spiritual reign of the Messiah. But the literal sense is also correct. Salvation is really of the Jews and will one day return to Israel."

CHAPTER FOUR

16 And he came to Nazareth where he had been brought up: and he entered, as his custom was, into the synagogue on the sabbath day, and stood up to read. 17 And there was delivered unto him [1]the book of the prophet Isaiah. And he opened the [2]book, and found the place where it was written, 18 [3]The Spirit of the Lord is upon me, [4]Because he anointed me to preach [5]good tidings to the poor:

He hath sent me to proclaim release to the captives,
And recovering of sight to the blind,
To set at liberty them that are bruised,
19 To proclaim the acceptable year of the Lord.
20 And he closed the [2]book, and gave it back to the attendant, and sat down: and the eyes of all in the synagogue were fastened on him.

[1]Or, *a roll*
[2]Or, *roll*
[3]Is. 61,1 f.
[4]Or, *Wherefore*
[5]Or, *the gospel*

Vers. 16-20.   THE SECOND COMING SET FORTH BY IMPLICATION.

The fact that Christ will yet one day come in judgment glory is as clearly set forth by His actions on this occasion as if it had been expressly here declared.   Turn to the place from which the quotation comes and it will be seen that in reading the passage from Isaiah 61.1,2 He omitted the words, *"And the day of vengeance of our God"*.   There was no stop after the words, *"the acceptable year of the Lord"*, in the roll from which Jesus read, but, although He had come as well to procliam *"the day of vengeance of our God"*, at the point indicated He ceased reading and closed the book.   Says Morgan, "In publicly reading the words of a Hebrew prophet who hundreds of years before had foretold the coming of Christ, no one else would have ended there, for Messiah's work included the proclamation of God's day of vengeance.   Christ's immediate purpose, however, was to indicate the first aspect of His mission, *'the acceptable year of the Lord'*, as then beginning in Himself.   With equal certainty shall the Messiah once more take up that old-time prophecy, and fulfill it to the letter as regards *'the day of vengeance of our God'.''*

CHAPTER NINE

26 For whosoever shall be ashamed of me and of my words, of him shall the Son of man be ashamed, when he cometh in his own glory, and the glory of the Father, and of the holy angels.

Ver. 26.   THE DISOWNER OF CHRIST DISOWNED AT HIS COMING.

Ver. 26.   *"when he cometh"*,—The reference is to His second coming, and the glory, says Meyer, is threefold, "His own, which He has of and for Himself as the exalted Messiah; the glory of God which accompanies him as coming down from God's throne, and the glory of the angels who surround Him with their brightness."   (See Mk. 8.38.)

27 But I tell you of a truth, There are some of them that stand here, who shall in no wise taste of death, till they see the kingdom of God.

Ver. 27.   THE COMING OF THE LORD IN THE DESTRUCTION OF JERU-SALEM.

"the kingdom of God",—This is not a less definite expression but is

a more simple one than that of Matthew and Mark, the reference being the same, i. e., the kingdom of the Messiah—the Son of man coming in His kingdom. (See Matt. 18.28.)

CHAPTER TEN

8 And into whatsoever city ye enter, and they receive you, eat such things as are set before you: 9 and heal the sick that are therein, and say unto them, The kingdom of God is come nigh unto you. 10 But into whatsoever city ye shall enter, and they receive you not, go out into the streets thereof and say, 11 Even the dust from your city, that cleaveth to our feet, we wipe off against you: nevertheless know this, that the kingdom of God is come nigh. 12 I say unto you, It shall be mode tolerable in that day for Sodom, than for that city.

Vers. 8-12. PARTICIPATION IN THE COMING KINGDOM THE REWARD OF CHRISTIAN HOSPITALITY.

Ver. 9. *"the kingdom of God is come nigh unto you"*,—A promise of participation in the coming kingdom of the Messiah, which they conceived as being near at hand.

Ver. 11. *"the kingdom of God is come nigh"*,—This seems to be a threatening reference to their penal exclusion from that kingdom.

Ver. 12. *"in that day"*,—This may denote either the destruction of Jerusalem or the last judgment. The two punishments are blended together in this threatening of the Lord, as doubtless in that of John the Baptist in Chap. 3.9, yet the idea of the last judgment seems to be the prevailing one from what follows in verse 14.

CHAPTER TWELVE

35 Let your loins be girded about, and your lamps burning; 36 and be ye yourselves like unto men looking for their lord, when he shall return from the marriage feast; that, when he cometh and knocketh, they may straightway open unto him. 37 Blessed are those [1]servants, whom the Lord when he cometh shall find watching: verily I say unto you, that he shall gird himself, and make them sit down to meat, and shall come and serve them. 38 And if he shall come in the second watch, and if in the third, and find *them* so, blessed are those *servants*. 39 [2]But know this, that if the master of the house had known in what hour the thief was coming, he would have watched, and not have left his house to be [3]broken through. 40 Be ye also ready: for in an hour that ye think not the Son of man cometh.

[1]Gr. *bondservants*

[2]Or, *But this ye know*
[3]Gr. *digged through*

Vers. 35-40. CONSTANT EXPECTATION OF AND PREPARATION FOR THE LORD'S COMING.

Ver. 35. The connection is with verse 32, *"It is your Father's good pleasure to give you the kingdom"*; let that free you from anxiety, but let it also be the motive to labor and to watch for the King.

"Let your loins be girded about",—That there may be no delay in opening the door, the faithful servant must have his loins girt about, without which by reason of the long, loose garments of the Orientals, activity and service were impossible.

"your lamps burning",—He must be in readiness for His master's return in case he came at night. Both activity and watchfulness are enjoined.

Ver. 36. *"the marriage feast"*,—The main thought here is only that he is away at a feast and will return. The marriage in question is not that of the master himself, but of a friend. (G. S. M.) The Master's own marriage is *after* the Parousia.

Olshausen says the feast in question here is the *heavenly* marriage feast, i. e., His union with the Church in heaven, *from* which He comes *to* the marriage feast with His saints in the air. If this distinction is warranted, it is then after all the Master's own marriage feast to which reference is made.

Ver. 37. *"come and serve them"*,—John 13.1 was a foreshadowing of this last great act of self-abasing love. The Lord Himself in the great day of His glory—the marriage supper of the Lamb—will reverse the order of human requirements and in the fullness of His grace and love will serve His brethren.

Ver. 38. The four watches were: (1) 6:00 P. M. to 9:00 P. M., (2) 9:00 P. M. to Midnight, (3) Midnight to 3:00 A. M., (4) 3:00 A. M. to 6:00 A. M.

Jesus does not mention the first watch because in this the marriage feast took place; nor the fourth watch because so late a return would have been unusual, and in this place contrary to the decorum of the events that were represented. (M. A.) He does name the first watch because it would weaken the whole representation of the watchful servants; nor does He name the fourth watch simply for the reason that the Disciples from that should understand that His return was by no means to be expected as late as possible. "The Parousia does not come so quickly as impatience, nor yet so late as carelessness supposes."

Farrar says, "It is very important to observe that often as our Lord bade His Disciples to be ready for His return, He as often indicates that His return might be long delayed. He always implied that He should come suddenly, but not necessarily soon."

Godet says the parable teaches that the coming of Christ, the Parousia, may be long delayed—much longer than the Disciples imagined—and that this delay will be the means of testing their fidelity. The same thought, he says, is found in Matt. 25.5, *"tarried"*, and in Matt. 25.19, *"after a long time"*.

CHAPTER THIRTEEN

> 35 Behold your house is left unto you desolate; and I say unto you, Ye shall not see me, until ye shall say, Blessed is he that cometh in the name of the Lord.

Ver. 35. THE GLAD WELCOME OF OUR LORD AT HIS SECOND COMING. (See Matt. 23.39.)

Some writers have said that the time pointed to here is Palm Sunday on which Jesus received the homage of the people. (Wie. Pau. Era. Schm. Stein.) But surely this is what Fausset calls a "frivolous interpretation", and is unnaturalness itself.

CHAPTER FOURTEEN

> 15 And when one of them that [1]sat at meat with him heard these things, he said unto him, Blessed is he that shall eat bread in the kingdom of God.
>
> [1]Gr. *recline*

Ver. 15. THE KINGDOM MISUNDERSTOOD.

"*the kingdom of God*",—The Messianic kingdom which was about to be set up. The Jews connected the advent of the Messianic kingdom with banquets of food more delicious than manna, and as Riddle says, "It is probable that the man hearing of the resurrection of the just, at once thought of the great feast which the Jews expected would follow, and thus spoke with the common Jewish idea that his admission to that feast was a certainty."

CHAPTER SEVENTEEN

> 20 And being asked by the Pharisees, when the kingdom of God cometh, he answered them and said, The kingdom of God cometh not with observation: 21 neither shall they say, Lo, here! or, There! for lo, the kingdom of God is [1]within you.
>
> [1]Or, *in the midst of you*

Vers. 20, 21. THE KINGDOM IN THE SENSE OF A PRESENT REALITY.

Ver. 20. "*being asked by the Pharisees*",—Some say the question was a mocking one. (C. Pau. Kui. Eut. Theo.) But the more preferable view is that they asked the question with a view to entangle Him. (A. M. G. R.)

"*when the kingdom of God cometh*",—They refer, of course, to the actual, external kingdom of the Messiah.

"*not with observation*",—There is no indication here of any reference to Jewish astrology, nor is the translation, "pomp" (Gro. Bez. Wet.) a good one, as it conveys more than the text warrants.

Riddle says, "It will not be of such a character that men can see outward tokens of preparation for it, and determine when it is to come."

Oosterzee says, "Of this unnoticed coming of the kingdom of God the Saviour could not well give any more striking proof than this, that the kingdom of heaven had already in its incipiency appeared among them, without their having even yet in their earthly-mindedness observed it."

Ver. 21. "*the kingdom of God is within you*",—Godet says, "Their question rested on a purely external view of this divine kingdom. His advent appeared to their minds as a sudden and great dramatic act. In the Gospel point of view this expectation is certainly not altogether false; but humanity must be prepared for the new external and divine state of things by a spiritual work wrought *in the depths* of the heart, and it is this internal advent which Jesus thinks good to put first in relief before such questioners. Now that the kingdom is not established in a visible way, it might happen that it should be present without men suspecting it. And that .this is exactly the case, Jesus is here represented as saying."

Olshausen says that the two aspects of the kingdom mutually complete each other; it shows itself spiritual in the beginning, but external in its perfection; it appeared in its spiritual form within men's hearts while Jesus was here in humiliation; in its external manifestation it will reveal itself at its final Parousia.   (C. Ko. Vat. Chr. Era. Lut. Fri. Hil. Theo. Gloe. Sche. Heub. Schau.)

Other commentators, indeed, Godet says, "almost all modern commentators", explain the words in the sense of "in the midst of you", "among you", "in your neighborhood".   (M. A. B. S. D. Ew. Bl. Fa. Oo. Ca. Pau. Kui. Bez. Gro. Wol. Hof. Fle. Bor. Kae. Schlei.), and this reading is defended by Oosterzee as follows:

1. In this way the antithesis between the external coming and the being already present is kept more sharply defined.

2. The kingdom of God was most certainly not within the hearts of those Pharisees to whom Jesus was talking.

3. This same thought is expressed in another way in John 1.26; 12.35; Luke 7.16; 11.20, while on the other hand for the apparently profound, but really not very intelligible statement that the kingdom of God is found within man no other proofs are to be found in the words of our Lord.

4. This view is favored by the context and especially by the connection.   The kingdom was already in their midst, it having come potentially into their neighborhood.

Alford stands strongly for "among you", although he says that this meaning includes of course the deeper and personal one, "within each of you" but the two are not controvertible.

Philologically either view is correct, although the rendering "among you" is much to be preferred.   In either case Jesus implied that His kingdom had already come while they were straining their eyes forward in curious expectation.

22 And he said unto the disciples, The days will come, when ye shall desire to see one of the days of the Son of man, and ye shall not see it.   23 And they shall say to you, Lo, there! Lo, here! go not away, nor follow after *them*; 24 for as the lightning, when it lighteneth out of the one part under the heaven, shineth unto the other part under heaven; so shall the Son of man be [1]in his day.   25 But first must he suffer many things and be rejected of this generation.   26 And as it came to pass in the days of Noah, even so shall it be also in the days of the Son of man. 27 They ate, they drank, they married, they were given in marriage, until the day that Noah entered into the ark, and the flood came, and destroyed them all. 28 Likewise even as it came to pass in the days of Lot; they ate, they drank, they bought, they sold, they planted, they builded; 29 but in the day that Lot went out from Sodom it rained fire and brimstone from heaven, and destroyed them all: 30 after the same manner shall it be in the day that the Son of man is revealed.   31 In that day, he that shall be on the housetop, and his goods in the house, let him not go down to take them away: and let him that is in the field likewise not return back.   32 Remember Lot's wife. 33 Whosoever shall seek to gain his life shall lose it; but whosoever shall lose his life shall [2]preserve it.   34 I say unto

[1]Some ancient authorities omit *in his day*.

[2]Gr. *save it alive.*

you, In that night there shall be two men in one bed; the one shall be taken, and the other shall be left. 35 There shall be two women grinding together; the one shall be taken, and the other shall be left. 36 There shall be two men in the field; the one shall be taken, and the other shall be left.[3] 37 And they answering, say unto him, Where, Lord? And he said unto them, Where the body is, thither will the [4]eagles also be gathered together.

[3]Some ancient authorities add ver. 36, *There shall be two men in the field; the one shall be taken, and the other shall be left.* Mt. 24, 40.
[4]Or, *vultures.*

Vers. 22-37. THE SECOND COMING TO BE SUDDEN AND UNEXPECTED.

He now begins to speak of His kingdom in the sense that it will come with observation, and He now addresses only His Disciples, the Pharisees having probably withdrawn. He answers for the Disciples the question of the Pharisees but carries them to the actual solemn appearing of the Messiah in the Parousia.

Ver. 22. *"one of the days of the Son of man",*—Many give the interpretation that the time was to come when they would long for another day such as they were then enjoying when they had Christ with them. (A. B. Kui.)

Others say it means that the time will come when they will long for a day of the Messianic period, the period when Christ has returned, the age to come, in order to refresh themselves by its blessedness. (M. O. D. L. G. Bl. Oo. Gro.)

Oosterzee says that having said that the kingdom was already among them, He feared perhaps that some of the Disciples might think that He was therefore forever to remain with them, and *"restore at that time the kingdom of Israel"*, and He is led to tell them that He is going away and that the days would come when they would long for His return and for a single day of the blessedness which that return was to bring with it. This latter is perhaps the better view of the matter, although there is really not much difference after all between them; if the days referred to were after He had left them, their longing would of course look forward to His return, and yet it might be and doubtless would be for just such a day as they were then enjoying that they would be looking forward to. This is what they would long after, although the day when realized would be far more glorious than any they had ever yet enjoyed.

"shall not see it",—Beause the day would not be there, the point of time of the Parousia not yet having come.

There is a slight intimation here that in His mind the Parousia would not come in their day.

Ver. 23. (See Matt. 24.36.) A warning to those who cry *"Lo, here"* every time war breaks out.

Ver. 24. (See Matt. 24.27.)

The comparison seems to lie not in its unexpectedness but in its visibility, and it would seem to be an appearance that will manifest itself in a moment and universally.

Godet says, "The Lord's coming will be universal and instantaneous.

Men do not run here and there to see a flash of lightning. It shines simultaneously on all points of the horizon. So the Lord will appear at the same moment to the view of all living."

"in his day",—The day of His Parousia.

Ver. 25. *"of this generation"*,—The reference is to the Jewish contemporaries of Christ.

Vers. 26-30. (See Matt. 24.37.) The point of comparison is surprise in the bosom of security.

Vers. 28, 29 are peculiar to Luke.

Ver. 30. *"in the day that the Son of man is revealed"*,—The day of His Parousia.

Ver. 31. *"In that day"*,—It is difficult because of the connection here to refer this to anything other than the day of His Parousia just mentioned in the preceding verse. (G. R. M. Oo.) See Matt. 24.16-18, where the same words are by nearly all writers applied to the destruction of Jerusalem, although even there some (Gab.) have applied them to the Parousia, as here. It will hardly do with Stier and De Wette to refer the words here in Luke to the Destruction of Jerusalem and think of them as unsuitably occurring in this place.

The reference is doubtless here to the catastrophe which immediately precedes the Parousia, and which is described in Matt. 24.29-31.

"let him not go down", etc.,—This indicates undelayed flight, but not, says Meyer, "as in the flight at the Destruction of Jerusalem, but flight for deliverance to the returning Messiah at the catastrophe which immediately precedes His Parousia, when nothing temporal should fetter their interest". This is seemingly favored by the example of Lot's wife. Oosterzee says, on the other hand, that the main thought is merely that no temporal possessions ought to engage the interest when eternal good must be won at any price.

Luke has been condemned for applying to the Parousia the counsel to flee, but no such counsel is given according to either of the above two views.

Ver. 33. (See Chap. 9.24 and John 12.25.)
There are two views of the meaning of this verse:

1. The man who throughout his preceding life seeks to save his life shall in the catastrophe just prior to the Parousia lose it.
2. The man who seeks to save his life during the catastrophe just prior to the Parousia will at the moment of the Parousia lose it.

The first view is preferable and is favored by Matt. 10.39.

Godet very appropriately explains as follows: "To save one's life by riveting it to some object with which it becomes identified is the means of losing it, of being left behind in this perishing world at the time of the Parousia; to give one's life by quitting everything at once is the only means of saving it, by laying hold of the Lord who is passing." Thus the saving or the losing is fixed at the Parousia.

Ver. 34. *"In that night"*,—There is no reason for thinking of the night as an image of misery and taking the expression in a figurative sense as meaning "in that time of calamity". (Bl. Gro. Kui.)

On the other hand it is not with De Wette to be pressed to the conclusion that the Parousia is definitely ordained to take place in the night. The grinding at the mill is an occupation for the daytime. It matters little anyway, because for one hemisphere it will be night; for the other it will be day.

Vers. 35, 36. (See Matt. 24.40 and 41.)

The best authorities omit verse 36.

Ver. 37. *"Where, Lord"*,—The Pharisees had asked about the time; now the Disciples ask about the place. They were doubtless entangled somewhat in the Jewish mistake that all descendants of Abraham would, by virtue of the same, participate in the kingdom of the Messiah; but now that Jesus had spoken so plainly of separation, they doubtless think He is referring to the heathen world and certainly not to Jerusalem. They utter surprise; "Where? Surely, Lord, this cannot be true of Judea, of Jerusalem!" They did not understand the universality of the matter.

The Parousia is still the subject of the discourse, although in Matt. 24.28, we find precisely the same words and thought applied by nearly all writers to the Destruction of Jerusalem.

In the Lord's answer the universality of this judgment is shown. He simply says that where the corruption of death is, there will the Carrion-Kites come. Jesus assigns moral and religious decay as the ground for destruction, and in so far as this corruption had seized the people of Israel they too were the subjects of destruction.

Godet says, "The carcass is humanity entirely secular and entirely destitute of the life of God and the eagles represent punishment alighting on such society."

Alford says that here in Luke the Parousia is the only subject, and that this discourse is an entirely distinct one from that in Matthew where the reference is to the Destruction of Jerusalem. He says it is entirely distinct also from the discourse in Luke 21.

CHAPTER EIGHTEEN

1 And he spake a parable unto them to the end that they ought always to pray, and not to faint; 2 saying, There was in a city a judge, who feared not God, and regarded not man: 3 and there was a widow in that city; and she came oft unto him, saying, [1]Avenge me of mine adversary. 4 And he would not for a while: but afterwards he said within himself, Though I fear not God, nor regard man; 5 yet because this widow troubleth me, I will avenge her, [2]lest she [3]wear me out by her continual coming. 6 And the Lord said, Hear what [4]the unrighteous judge saith. 7 And shall not God avenge his elect, that cry to him day and night, [5]and yet he is longsuffering over them? 8 I say unto you, that he will avenge them speedily. Nevertheless, when the Son of man cometh, shall he find [6]faith on the earth?

[1]Or, *Do me justice of*: and so in ver. 5, 7, 8

[2]Or, *lest at last by her coming she wear me out*
[3]Gr. *bruise*
[4]Gr. *the judge of unrighteousness*
[5]Or, *and is he slow to punish on their behalf?*
[6]Or, *the faith*

Vers. 1-8. THE LOSS OF FAITH THROUGH THE DELAY OF THE LORD'S COMING.

This parable is not an addition inserted without a motive. (Ko.

Holt.), nor are there any intervening dialogues omitted (O. Schlei.), but it follows naturally after the thought of what precedes about the Parousia.

Ver. 1. The parable was spoken to His Disciples.

"always to pray",—Compare II Thess. 5.17, which refers to the believer's prevailing frame of mind (Prayer as the breath of the inner man. O.), which kind of prayer Olshausen and Alford think is referred to here, but it is much better to refer it to the unwearied petition for the same object believed to be in accordance with the will of God.   (R. F. M.)

"not to faint",—We are not to become discouraged and give up through the weight of overpowering evil.

Ver. 2. The expressions describing the judge are those indicating an unprincipled and depraved and reckless person.   The thought is, "Were God like this judge He could not resist the prayers of the Church; how much less, being what He is?"

Ver. 3. *"there was a widow"*,—The widow represents the Church, although there is an individual application to be found in the parable as well.   (A. M. G. R. O. Oo.)

The Old Testament always demanded protection for the widow. The condition of the Church after the Lord's departure is like that of a widow, and of a widow deprived of her rights.

"Avenge me of mine adversary",—The justice of her cause is implied throughout.   She wants a sentence from the judge to stop the practices of her adversary.   The word *"avenge"* does not include so much the notion of vengeance, as of justice rendered to the oppressed.   The margin of the Revised Version really catches more of the spirit of the entreaty.

Ver. 4. *"for a while"*,—Not necessarily for a long time, and yet it is an indefinite indication of the comparatively long time during which all entreaty might appear in vain in the day of the tribulation, days which must be spent in prayer and which will reach an end as surely as the widow's trial. (Matt. 24.32,33.)

Ver. 5. *"lest she wear me out by her continual coming"*,—"lest at last by her coming she wear me out" is the better reading.   (A-R-V. M. G. O. S.)   This gives the more actual meaning of the word translated *"continual"* by both the Authorized and Revised Versions.   Bleek and some others take the verb *"wear out"* in its literal sense and render, "Lest at last she come and beat my face black and blue".   The Dutch translation is, "come and break my head".   Very few, however, adhere to the literal sense.

Vers. 6,7. While there is in a sense an individual application, the main application is to the elect as a collective body, with reference to the final release from the days of sorrow at the return of the Lord.   The poor widow is the Church, contending with her adversary, the Devil, and in this case she has the additional claim in that she is the elect of God.

"yet he is longsuffering over them",—That the word *"them"* refers to the elect there can be no doubt, but it is not absolutely necessary to refer the *"longsuffering"* to them as well.

1. The verb really means "to be slow to punish", and would therefore seem to have for its object, not the elect, but their oppressors. (A. M. G. R. B. Ew.)

   But why this longsuffering toward their enemies?

   (a) For the sake of allowing His elect time for more perfect sanctification. (B. Ew.)

   (b) For the sake of the oppressors themselves. (Romans 2.4.) (G.)

Alford renders, "And yet in their case He is longsuffering", i. e., over their enemies.

Riddle renders, "Though He delays His vengeance on their account." Meyer renders it as a qustion, "And in their case does He tarry", i. e., delay to take vengeance on their enemies? The negative answer is implied.

2. On the other hand the *"longsuffering"* is referred to the elect. (S. O. Oo. Fa.)

The first two authorities, just quoted, give the verb the exceedingly refined meaning of "delay", which, says Olshausen, is implied in the meaning of *"longsuffering"*, the object of which delay is the purification of the elect.

Oosterzee renders, "And is it His way with reference to the elect to delay His help?" He says the idea is not forbearance toward the elect, which is here not at all in place; nor is it that He for their sakes postpones His punishment of their oppressors, which though a truth, is not taught here; but He is simply saying that God cannot to the last withhold a help for which His elect so earnestly prayed.

The fact of the matter is that the Lord does delay His coming, at which time He will take vengeance on the enemies of the elect, and the purpose of this delay is both that the enemies may have time to repent (Rom. 2.4), and the elect time for sanctification; and yet we are hardly justified in reading all this into the one word *"longsuffering"* used in this case.

If, however, the root meaning of the words *"slow to punish"* be emphasized here and the word be referred accordingly to the enemies of the elect, the purpose of this delay or longsuffering may best, in view of the construction, the context and the preposition used, be referred to the purification of the elect.

Yet it is not wise to unduly press the root-meaning of the verb, in as much as a modified meaning in a Greek verb is quite as much the rule as otherwise, and in view of the evident thought of the passage and the simple construction of the words, it seems altogether best to take the word in that refined sense of delay given to it by Olshausen and Stier, and this with a view to the spiritual betterment of the elect themselves.

Ver. 8. *"avenge them speedily"*,—This doubtless refers to the shortness of time before the deliverance is to take place (M. R. A. Oo. Fa.), rather than to the suddenness with which the deliverance takes place when it does come. (O. S. G.)

Meyer says it declares the speedy advent of the Parousia and·that it is vain to weary oneself and twist about in the vain attempt to explain away this simple meaning of the words.

Riddle says this avenging is still future after eighteen centuries, but however long delayed in man's estimation, the Day of the Lord will quickly come as God regarded it.

"when the Son of man cometh",—There is not the least reason for understanding any other here than the last coming of the Son of man. (M. O. R. G. Oo.)

"shall he find faith on the earth",—It is literally, "the faith". Not some faith in general; not faith that Jesus is the Messiah (M.); nor does it refer, as DeWette says, to the faithfulness of His Disciples in general, as in Chap. 12.35-48, but it is such a faith as the widow had, faith in God as a righteous Judge, which on account of the delay of the Parousia and of the hearing of their prayer, will sustain a severe conflict. (A. R. P. S. G. O. Oo. Fa.)

The special form of faith therefore which will be lacking is faith in the return of the Lord as evidenced by the lack of importunate prayer for the hastening of that event.

There is a certain intimation of doubt on the Saviour's part that He will find this faith at His Parousia. (M. G. R. Oo.)

CHAPTER NINETEEN

11 And as they heard these things, he added and spake a parable, because he was nigh to Jerusalem, and *because* they supposed that the kingdom of God was immediately to appear. 12 He said therefore, A certain nobleman went into a far country, to receive for himself a kingdom, and to return. 13 And he called ten ¹servants of his, and gave them ten ²pounds, and said unto them, Trade ye *herewith* till I come. 14 But his citizens hated him, and sent an ambassage after him, saying, We will not that this man reign over us. 15 And it came to pass, when he was come back again, having received the kingdom, that he commanded these ¹servants, unto whom he had given the money, to be called to him, that he might know what they had gained by trading. 16 And the first came before him, saying, Lord, thy pound hath made ten pounds more. 17 And he said unto him, Well done, thou good ³servant: because thou wast found faithful in a very little, have thou authority over ten cities. 18 And the second came, saying, Thy pound, Lord, hath made five pounds. 19 And he said

unto him also, Be thou also over five cities. 20 And ⁴another came, saying, Lord, behold, *here is* thy pound, which I kept laid up in a napkin: 21 for I feared thee, because thou art an austere man: thou takest up that which thou layedst not down, and reapest that which thou didst not sow. 22 He said unto him, Out of thine own mouth will I judge thee, thou wicked ³servant. Thou knewest that I am an austere man, taking up that which I laid not down, and reaping that which I did not sow; 23 then wherefore gavest thou not my money into the bank, and ⁵I at my coming should have required it with interest? 24 And he said unto them that stood by, Take away from him the pound, and give it unto him that hath ten pounds. 25 And they said unto him, Lord he hath ten pounds. 26 I say unto you, that unto every one that hath shall be given; but from him that hath not, even that which he hath shall be taken away from him. 27 But these mine enemies, that would not that I should reign over them, bring them hither, and slay them before me.

¹Gr. *bondservants*
²*Mina* here translated a pound is equal to one hundred drachmas. See Chap. 15.8.
³Gr. *bondservant*

⁴Gr. *the other*
⁵Or, *I should have gone and required*

Vers. 11-27.   THE PARABLE OF THE POUNDS AND THE POSTPONED
        KINGDOM.

Calvin, Meyer and Olshausen say this is the same parable as the one found in Matt. 25.   But if this be true, then we must give up the idea of the historical accuracy of the Gospels and all idea that they furnish us with an accurate account of the words of our Lord.   They are different parables altogether.   That of Matthew is more complete and was addressed to the Disciples alone.   The parable in Luke was the earlier of the two and probably furnished to the Lord's mind the ground-work for the later one in Matthew.

There is a close relation between the preceding conversation and this parable, the parable being given, as Riddle says, to controvert the idea that the kingdom would be set up at once without a previous separation of the Master from His servants to whom He would return as King.

Chap. 17.34 shows that the Disciples were as yet by no means cured of their earthly Messianic hopes.   They imagined that the present journey to Jerusalem, undertaken as it had been with such publicity and accompanied with such wonderful miracles, was for the purpose of revealing and setting up the Messianic kingdom.

Ver. 11.   "they",—Not the Disciples exclusively, but more especially the murmurers of verse 7, although the Disciples may have been included and doubtless were.

"these things",—The reference is to the things heard in verses 8, 9 and 10.

"kingdom of God was immediately to appear",—The same excited anticipation which the Disciples had after the resurrection of Jesus. (Acts 1.6 and 7.)

"appear",—Literally, "come to light".   The people think of the glorious setting up of the Messianic kingdom in which they had always believed, the palpable, sensuous kingdom that was now to be set up inasmuch as the Son of man was come.

Ver. 12.   "nobleman",—This represents the Lord Jesus and a certain intimation of His kingly descent and dignity.

"went into a far country",—Archaleus, one of the governors, had just made such a journey to Rome to receive appointment by the Emperor, and perhaps from this Jesus drew His illustration.   Jesus was of course going to heaven.

"far country",—Godet and Olshausen say the words suggest the long absence that would intervene between the departure of the Lord and His return at the Parousia, and that Christ was trying to show that His Parousia was not so near at hand.

Baur and Zeller say these words remove the Parousia beyond the lifetime of that generation, but Meyer objects to this because the return has to do with the same servants.   There is not a great deal of force in the objection of Meyer because the setting of the parable could have taken no other form.   That there is a certain intimation of long absence it would seem necessary to grant.

"to receive a kingdom",—The installation of Jesus into His kingly power. The going to receive a kingdom was not going to receive a kingdom which was in heaven, but a going there to receive His crown and to return to his kingdom here. Jesus is coming back.

Ver. 13. *"ten pounds"*,—One pound to each servant, about $15.00.

In Matthew He committed His whole property to His servants, but here only a slight gift. The giving of so small an amount corresponds to what is so carefully emphasized in the parable, i. e., the relation of faithfulness in the least to the largeness of reward for the same. It was given as a test of fidelity.

The best reading gives the idea of "while I am on my journey" instead of *"till I come"*, and yet this does not fully bring out the sense of the word, which means "come". It really means "while I am coming", and pictures His coming as a constant one, somewhat in keeping with the idea in Matt. 26.64, according to which passage His ascension was the first step in His return and He has always been returning ever since.

Ver. 14. The kingdom referred to in verse 12 is that over His own citizens, the Jews. Here in this verse *"him"* in each case, and *"this man"* refers to Jesus, and the verse describes the resistance of the Jews to the Messianic sovereignty which still continues to this day. The citizens of this verse must not be confounded with the servants of verse 13.

Ver. 15. Before He deals with the citizens, His enemies, He will first take an accounting with His servants.

"what they had gained by trading",—The idea is rather, "what business they had carried on". It was not so much the amount gained but the thought of fidelity to their trust that was in the mind of the Lord.

Ver. 16. *"thy pound"*,—In deep humility the servants acknowledge that the gain was not their own but the Lord's; therefore they say, *"thy pound"*. In Matthew's parable the trust was according to ability, but here it is the same in every case. In Matthew the gain was in proportion to the trust (five talents gained other five), but here the proportion was on a larger scale, the one pound gaining ten others, etc.

Ver. 17. *"have thou authority over ten cities"*,—The reward is proportioned to the gain and corresponds with the kingly dignity of the returned Lord. At the coming of the Lord, at the Parousia, each servant will share in the power of his Master, now become a King, in proportion to his activity during the time of his probation. Faithfulness in the smallest way becomes the source of inexhaustible blessing.

Ver. 20. This servant doubtless argued that if he lost the pound he would be punished for it, and if he gained anything by investing it his lord would come and pluck the fruit, and thus strengthened in his natural slothfulness he remained idle and met his lord with the answer of this and the next verse.

Ver. 21. (See Matt. 25.24,25 for the same excuse.) A typical description of injustice forbidden alike by the Jewish and the Greek law.

Ver. 22. *"out of thine own mouth"*,—The Lord does not concede that he is a hard man, but only refutes the idle servant on the position he himself had so arbitrarily taken.

Ver. 23. *"into the bank"*,—Literally this means "on a banker's table". It is not "the" bank, and this, says Riddle, opposes the view that the bank represents the Church and the putting of the pound there as a resignation of his office. Godet says the reference is to prayer, i. e., why did you not avail yourself of divine omnipotence by prayer? But this is mere surmise. It means just what it says.

Ver. 24. *"them that stood by"*,—Not the other servants (Kui.), but the attending officers who surround Him when He appears in majesty.

"the ten pounds",—The pounds mentioned in verse 16. The pound was given to the servant who had shown himself the most active.

Ver. 25. This by many is considered parenthetical. (A. M. Oo. Ew. Fa. Lach.) It gives the king occasion to more particularly give the reason for his severe determination.

Ver. 26. (See Matt. 25.29.)

Ver. 27. *"enemies"*,—The citizens of verse 14.

This strong expression sets forth the hopelessness and the severity of the judgment that shall fall upon the enemies of Christ. It was spoken as in verse 24 to his attending officers. His enemies, although absent, are spoken of as present in the idea of the speaker and the hearers.

It doubtless has its primary reference to the Jewish nation, and then a wider one to the opposing world; being a figure first of the punishment which fell upon Jerusalem, and secondly of that which is to follow at the judgment when He comes again. (R. A. G.)

CHAPTER TWENTY-ONE

5 And as some spake of the temple, how it was adorned with goodly stones and offerings, he said, 6 As for these things which ye behold, the days will come, in which there shall not be left here one stone upon another, that shall not be thrown down. 7 And they asked him, saying, Teacher, when therefore shall these things be? and what *shall be* the sign when these things are about to come to pass? 8 And he said, Take heed that ye be not led astray: for many shall come in my name, saying, I am *he*; and, The time is at hand: go ye not after them. 9 And when ye shall hear of wars and tumults, be not terrified: for these things must needs come to pass first; but the end is not immediately. 10 Then said he unto them, Nation shall rise against nation, and kingdom against kingdom; 11 and there shall be great earthquakes, and in divers places famines and pestilences; and there shall be terrors and great signs from heaven. 12 But before all these things, they shall lay their hands on you, and shall persecute you, delivering you up to the synagogues and prisons, [1]bringing you before kings and governors for my name's sake. 13 It shall turn out unto you for a testimony. 14 Settle it therefore in your hearts, not to meditate beforehand how to answer: 15 for I will give you a mouth and wisdom, which all your adversaries shall not be able to withstand or to gainsay. 16 But ye shall be [2]delivered up even by parents, and brethren, and kinsfolk, and friends; and *some* of you [3]shall they cause to be put to death. 17 And ye shall be hated of all men for my name's sake. 18 And not a hair of your head shall perish.

[1]Gr. you *being brought*
[2]Or, *betrayed*
[3]Or, *shall they put to death*

19 In your [4]patience ye shall win your [5]souls. 20 But when ye see Jerusalem compassed with armies, then know that her desolation is at hand. 21 Then let them that are in Judæa flee unto the mountains; and let them that are in the midst of her depart out; and let not them that are in the country enter therein. 22 For these are days of vengeance, that all things which are written may be fulfilled. 23 Woe unto them that are with child and to them that give suck in those days! for there shall be great distress upon the [6]land, and wrath unto this people. 24 And they shall fall by the edge of the sword, and shall be led captive into all the nations: and Jerusalem shall be trodden down of the Gentiles, until the times of the Gentiles be fulfilled. 25 And there shall be signs in sun and moon and stars; and upon the earth distress of nations, in perplexity for the roaring of the sea and the billows; 26 men [7]fainting for fear, and for expectation of the things which are coming on [8]the world: for the powers of the heavens shall be shaken. 27 And then shall they see the Son of man coming in a cloud with power and great glory. 28 But when these things begin to come to pass, look up, and lift up your heads; because your redemption draweth nigh. 29 And he spake to them a parable: Behold the fig tree, and all the trees: 30 when they now shoot forth, ye see it and know of your own selves that the summer is now nigh. 31 Even so ye also, when ye see these things coming to pass know ye that the kingdom of God is nigh. 32 Verily I say unto you, This generation shall not pass away, till all things be accomplished. 33 Heaven and earth shall pass away: but my words shall not pass away. 34 But take heed to yourselves lest haply your hearts be overcharged with surfeiting, and drunkenness, and cares of this life, and that day come on you suddenly as a snare: 35 for so shall it come upon all them that dwell on the face of the earth. 36 But watch ye at every season, making supplication, that ye may prevail to escape all these things that shall come to pass, and to stand before the Son of man.

[4]Or, *stedfastness*
[5]Or, *lives*
[6]Or, *earth*
[7]Or, *expiring*
[8]Gr. *the inhabited earth*

Vers. 5-36. THE DESTRUCTION OF JERUSALEM FORETOLD.

In this discourse Luke seemingly contemplates exclusively the Destruction of Jerusalem.

Ver. 8. (See Matt. 24.5.)

"the time is at hand",—The time meant is the time of the establishment of the Messianic kingdom. These are not the words of Jesus, but of the many false prophets. (M. A. R.)

Ver. 9. (See Matt. 24.6 and 7.) (See also Meyer on II Cor. 6.5.)

"be not terrified",—This refers perhaps to the temptation of premature flight.

Ver. 10. Jesus could here have easily passed to verse 20, but after these preliminary warnings He preferred to enter a bit more upon the further description of the impending judgment.

Ver. 11. *"terrors and great signs from heaven"*,—The *"terrors"* as well as the *"great signs"* belong to *"from heaven"*. Godet thinks of meteors, eclipses, etc., to which was readily attached a prophetic significance. For seven and a half years it is said that Jesus, the son of Hanan, cried, *"Woe, woe, woe"*. Strange rumors were afloat, of monstrous births, of the vast brazen temple gates suddenly opening, of a sword shaped comet appearing in the heavens, and of fierce, fiery warriors fighting upon the clouds, all of which things the blind multitude would interpret in their own favor.

Ver. 12.   The best comment on this verse is found in Acts 4.3; 5.17-41 and other such passages.

Ver. 13.   *"for a testimony"*,—It would give them an opportunity to testify for their Lord.   (R. A. M. G. L.)   This in itself is regarded as something great and honorable.   (Phil. 1.28.)

Ver. 18.   *"And not a hair of your head shall perish"*,—This verse, which seems to contradict the last part of verse 16, means, according to Lange, that they were not to perish as long as they were needed on the earth in the service of the Lord.   Godet explains it, that while some individuals were to perish, the community as a whole was to escape the extermination which was to overtake the Jewish people.

It is far better to explain it in a spiritual sense rather than in a literal sense.   (R. A. M. O. Fa.)

Ver. 19.   *"in your patience"*,—Your patient endurance of these things.

"win your souls",—By embracing the means which seems the way to lose everything they shall save themselves.   Jeremiah says, *"I will give thee thy life for a prey."*

Ver. 20.   *"When ye see Jerusalem compassed with armies"*,—This verse gives the direct answer of Jesus to the question of the Disciples.   Up to now Jesus has been warning believers not to give way to hasty measures; now He guards them against the fanatical delusions of the Jews who to the end will cherish the belief that God will not fail to save Jerusalem; but, No, says Jesus, Jerusalem is doomed; *"When ye see"*, etc.

Luke is writing for the Gentiles, and therefore he does not mention the prophecy of Daniel, as do Matthew and Mark, but speaks merely of its fulfillment.

Godet says that he sees nothing to hinder us from regarding this sign as identical in sense with that announced by Matthew and Mark in the words of Daniel, *"the abomination of desolation standing in the holy place"*.

Olshausen says that the most consistent hypothesis is that reference is made to some form of idolatrous worship; but the difficulty is to fix upon anything definite because the historical accounts respecting the attempts made to introduce it afford us so very little real satisfactory information about it.

Ver. 21.   *"them that are in Judea"*,—The Christians.

"her",—Jerusalem.

"them that are in the country",—Christians who are in the fields round about.   (M. O. L. A. Fa.)   The reference is hardly to the Provinces.   (D. Bret.)

Ver. 22.   *"days of vengeance"*,—Days in which the Lord accomplishes His judgments upon His enemies.

"that all things which are written may be fulfilled",—The prophecy of Daniel is meant along with the rest.

Ver. 23. *"Woe unto them that are with child"*, etc.,—(See Matt. 24.19.)

"upon the land",—This is referred by Meyer, Alford and others to the land in general, while *"wrath upon this people"* is referred by the same authorities to the Jews of Judea in particular. If the first is general, then the particular reference is of course to be found in the second expression. Riddle and Godet more accurately refer both phrases to Judea and the Jews.

Ver. 24. *"led captive into all the nations"*,—The whole world was open to them, but henceforth the Holy City was closed against them. A million perished, while ninety-seven thousand were taken prisoners and dragged into Egypt and her provinces.

"trodden down",—This refers to the oppression and contempt which always follows conquest. This has been true during all the ages since.

"until the times of the Gentiles be fulfilled",—This shows that after the fall of Jerusalem there is still a period of indefinite duration to be waited.

In the use of the plural *"times"* Lange sees a *long* interval of time intimated. But from this alone the idea of long duration is not to be concluded, there being no particular significance in the use of the plural form, it having doubtless been used because the Gentiles are in the plural, i. e., nations.

There are two views of the meaning of this passage:

1. Some say it refers to the appointed time of Gentile dominion over Jerusalem, i. e., until the Gentiles shall have finished this judgment of wrath. (M. O. L. S. Bl.)

But with regard to this view it may be said:

(a) The words contain no express information respecting the relation of Israel to the Gentiles at the termination of their power over her.

(b) It would be tautology to say, "Jerusalem shall be trodden down by the Gentiles until the time of Gentile dominion comes to an end."

(c) If there is any significance at all in the use of the plural *"times"*, this view does not account for it.

(d) It does not account for the choice of the Greek word for *"times"* (kairos), which means opportunity, instead of the word "kronos" which means merely a space of time.

2. The second explanation, which for the reason just noted it seems best to accept, is that it refers to the period of grace during which the Gospel is offered to the Gentiles. (G. B. R. A. Eb. Fa.)

Olshausen says, "The time of the conversion of the Gentiles is not the period referred to. The Lord here does not speak of the Gentiles in so far as they are the object of Divine favor, but so far as they are used as instruments in the divine government of the world." The proof, however, which Olshausen attempts to produce is, we feel, quite too scanty. The inference, of course, may be a legitimate one, but it would seem best not to read anything into the passage.

Riddle says that opinions differ as to whether this dispensation of the Gentiles implies their conversion to Christ or their rejection of Him. He says, "All analogy points to the former and subsequent prophesies confirm this view."

But after all the question raised by Riddle does not enter into the discussion here; other Scriptures must settle this.

Alford is doubtless nearer the truth when he says that it refers to the fulfillment of the Gentile dispensation just as the time of Jerusalem was the end, the fulfillment of the Jewish dispensation, and that it more likely refers to the rejection of Christ by the Gentile world which answers to His rejection by the Jews.

Ver. 25. It is purely arbitrary to assert, as Meyer and De Wette do, that Luke, writing after the Destruction of Jerusalem, omits for this reason the *"immediately"* of Matthew, as he necessarily must do. For this reason, says Meyer, Luke could not link the Parousia onto the Destruction of Jerusalem, as Matthew and Mark did, by means of the word *"immediately"*. Jesus is simply stating what shall take place after the times of the Gentiles shall be fulfilled, i. e., what shall take place before His Parousia. (R. A. M. G. Oo.) This is plainly enough indicated by the consecutive *"and"*.

The signs are to be taken literally in keeping with the Old Testament representations and descriptions elsewhere, and allegorically or metaphorically; the eclipse of nations and the downfall of potentates (Fa.); the sun meaning Antichrist (Starke), the moon meaning antichristian teachers (Besser), and the roaring sea, the tumult of nations (Fa.).

Ver. 26. *"fainting for fear"*,—The margin has "expiring", and Meyer renders, "giving up the ghost" as corresponding more to the progressive coloring of the description. *"Fainting"*, however, is a permissible rendering.

Ver. 27. (See Matt. 24.30.)

Godet says, "It is not said that the Lord shall return to the earth to remain there. This coming can only be a momentary appearance destined to effect the resurrection of the faithful and the ascension of the entire Church (I Cor. 15.23; Luke 17.31-35; I Thess. 4.16,17)." Godet, like most pre-millennial expositors, makes no provision for any period between the Lord's coming for His saints and His coming with them, and consequently refers the redemption of verse 28 and the elect of Matt. 24.31 to the saints in general, and not to the elect of Israel, as do Scofield, Petingill, Gaebelein and others.

Ver. 28. *"these things"*,—The appearances of verse 25 and the facts mentioned in verse 26.

"look up, and lift up your heads",—Their heads until then are to be bowed down under affliction.

"your redemption draweth nigh",—It is brought to them by the appearing, the Second Coming of their Lord. (M. A. G. R. O. Oo.)

A few have thought that Jesus here returns to the principal subject of the Chapter, the Destruction of Jerusalem. The deliverance would then be the emancipation of the Jewish-Christian Church from the persecuting Jewish power, the coming of the kingdom of God (verse 31) would refer to the propagation of the Gospel among the Gentiles, and *"this generation shall not pass away"* would indicate quite naturally the date of the Destruction of Jerusalem. Yet there is no evidence whatever for this departure from the subject of the Parousia at this point, and this subject is quite too solemn when once mentioned to be treated as a purely accessory idea.

Vers. 29,30. The reviving of the Jewish nation is to be taken as a sign of the near approach of the Parousia of Christ. (See Matt. 24.32.)

Ver. 31. *"the kingdom of God is nigh"*,—The Messianic kingdom to be established at the time of Christ's Parousia.

Vers. 32,33. (See Matt. 24.34 and 35.)

Ver. 34. *"overcharged with surfeiting"*,—This is referred by Oosterzee to heaviness such as drunkenness of yesterday gives. *"Drunkenness"* makes them unfit for today, and *"cares of life"* plague them for tomorrow.

Ver. 35. It is to be a universal judgment, a universal surprise. The idea of "sitting securely" is implied in the word *"dwell"*.

Ver. 36. *"at every season"*,—Some join this expression to *"watch"*, some to *"making supplication"*, and some to both.
"escape all these things",—The reference is to the calamities connected with the coming of the Lord; the Parousia itself no one can escape.
"stand before the Son of man",—This does not exactly mean to stand before Him acquitted in the judgment (Kui. Bez. Gro. Era.), but the rather gathered there by the angels in the presence of the glorified Son of man where they are to stand erect. In fact it does not refer to a coming into judgment but standing fearlessly and composed before His throne to view Him, to serve and glorify Him, which is both the beginning and the substance of the highest happiness.

CHAPTER TWENTY-TWO

> 16 for I say unto you, I shall not eat it, until it be fulfilled in the kingdom of God.
> 18 for I say unto you, I shall not drink from henceforth of the fruit of the vine, until the kingdom of God shall come.

Vers. 16,18. THE LORD'S KINGDOM, AT HIS RETURN, UNDER THE IMAGE OF A FEAST.

Ver. 16. *"I shall not eat of it"*,—Most authorities very properly read into the words the meaning, "I shall not eat of it any more", because all admit that Jesus did eat of that Passover. What He means is that He would eat of it now, but never again until, etc. The strong desire of the Lord to eat of this Passover may be explained from Chap. 12.50.
"until it (the Passover) *be fulfilled in the kingdom of God"*,—The Lord sees in the paschal celebration a symbolic setting forth of the perfect

joy in the Messianic feast of the future alluded to in verse 30 and in Matt. 27.29, and taking place at the Parousia.

Oosterzee says very properly, "To wish to conclude now from this that the Lord expects a literal Passover at the revelation of His divine kingdom is purely arbitrary, since it is plain enough that He here, as often, describes the joy of the perfected Messianic kingdom under the image of a feast.   The Passover is only fulfilled when the outer form, the Passover celebration, is entirely broken down and the eternal idea, the perfect feast of deliverance, is realized."

The impersonal view which makes it mean "until the establishment of the kingdom is brought about" (Pau. B-C), is purely an evasion opposed by the context; while the rationalistic interpretation, "you shall hereafter enjoy with me in heaven more intimate and supreme joy" (Kui.), is purely arbitrary.

Ver. 18.   "until the kingdom of God shall come",—This points to the same event as in verse 16.

Alford says the words of these two verses carry on the meaning and continuance of this eucharistic ordinance even into the new heavens and the new earth.   He quotes Thiersch as most excellently saying, "The Lord's supper points not only to the past but to the future also.   It has not only a commemorative, but a prophetic meaning.   In it we have not only to shew forth the Lord's death, *until He come*, but we have also *to think of the time when He shall come* to celebrate His holy supper with His own, new, in His Kingdom of Glory.   Every celebration of the Lord's Supper is a foretaste and a prophetic anticipation of the *great Marriage Supper* which is prepared for the Church at the second appearing of Christ."

Says Riddle, "He is done with earthly rites, and at this sad moment points them to a future reunion at the Marriage Supper of the Lamb." (Scha.)

In both Matthew and Mark it reads, *"when I drink it new"*, and Meyer thinks the reference is to a newness different in respect of quality, as Bengel says, "it indicates evidently a peculiar newness".

"This conception of the new Passover wine", says Meyer, "which is to be the product of the coming aeon and of the glorified creation, is connected with the idea of the renewal of the world in view of the Messianic kingdom."

Riddle gives the word *"new"* something of an adverbial sense, i. e., "on some peculiar and exalted festal occasion".

"until the kingdom of God shall come",—Matthew reads, *"until that day when I drink it new with you in my Father's kingdom"*, while Mark reads, *"until that day when I drink it new in the kingdom of God"*. (See also the 16th verse in Luke's rendering, *"until it be fulfilled in the kingdom of God"*.

The expression, says Meyer, can only be intended to designate the kingdom of the Messiah.   Riddle says it points to the time of the Church triumphant, and our continued celebration of it is an expression of assured victory on the part of His militant Church.

"He consecrates this sad moment", says Lange, "as the anticipatory festival of a common enjoyment in the world of glory."

Kuionel says, "The new wine of the glorified world is a symbol of the future festal blessedness of the heavenly world."

28 But ye are they that have continued with me in my temptations; 29 and ¹I appoint unto you a kingdom, even as my Father appointed unto me, 30 that ye may eat and drink at my table in my kingdom; and ye shall sit on thrones judging the twelve tribes of Israel.

69 But from henceforth shall the Son of man be seated at the right hand of the power of God.

¹Or, *I appoint unto you, even as my Father appointed unto me a kingdom, that ye may eat and drink &c.*

Vers. 28-30, 69. THE DISCIPLES TO JUDGE ISRAEL AT THE LORD'S RETURN.

Ver. 28.   The Lord does not reproach them but praises them for their steadfastness.   He speaks of His whole life as one of trial and temptation. The reference is to the many injuries, persecutions, snares, perils of life. etc., and the expression *"temptation"* is none too strong.

Ver. 29.   *"and I"*,—i. e., I, in my turn, as a reward for their fidelity to Him.   The meaning is, "I ordain for you a dominion in my kingdom as my Father, etc."

The word appoint has in it the idea of a disposition such as a dying man forms when he makes his will for those who are left behind.   Meyer objects to this idea in the word because it could not be retained in the second clause where it is said that the Father hath appointed unto Christ a kingdom.   It is nevertheless true that the verb used is applied to testamentary disposition.   (G. A. Oo.)

Ver. 30.   *"that ye may eat and drink at my table"*,—This is without doubt to be taken in the same sense as in verses 16 and 18.

"sit on thrones",—Does He refrain from saying *"twelve thrones"* as in Matthew because of Judas?

Godet says, "The kingdom mentioned here is the power exercised by man on man by means of divine life and divine truth.   As Christ Himself reigns over Christians, so Christians by the life and the truth which they possess through Him shall reign over all.   Are not Peter, James and Paul at the present day the rulers of the world?"   He says in substance that this is only another form of the thought expressed in John 13.20, *"He that receiveth whomsoever I send receiveth me; and he that receiveth me, receiveth Him that sent me."*   But this is an altogether uncalled-for weakening of the meaning of these profound and solemn words.

Ver. 69.   (See exposition under Matt. 26.64.)   The words at once recall Dan. 7.13,14.   Meyer thinks that Luke alone gives the literal meaning, while in the accounts of both Matthew and Mark the figurative sense must be maintained; in Matthew by the expression *"Henceforth"*, i. e., from now on, and in Mark by the words, *"sitting at the right hand of power"*.

CHAPTER TWENTY-FOUR

> 21 But we hoped that it was he who should redeem Israel. Yea and besides all this, it is now the third day since these things came to pass.

Ver. 21. THE KINGDOM AGAIN MISINTERPRETED.

"But we",—That is, on our part, as over against what the rulers had done.

"hoped that it was he",—It does not say they were still hoping, but that they had once hoped until their hopes had been checked by the events they mentioned.

"who should redeem Israel",—This is, doubtless, to be taken in the sense of Acts 1.6, which redemption in their minds doubtless included both political and religious deliverance.

"the third day",—This was spoken with reference to His promise to rise on the third day. Their faint hope had grown fainter.

The subject, of course, is Jesus, and the more literal rendering is, "He passes this present day as the third", but the rendering of our text sets forth the meaning sufficiently clear.

THE GOSPEL ACCORDING TO

JOHN

(A. D. 85—A. D. 90)

CHAPTER FIVE

> 21 For as the Father raiseth the dead and giveth them life, even so the Son also giveth life to whom he will. 22 For neither doth the Father judge any man, but he hath given all judgment unto the Son; 23 that all may honor the Son even as they honor the Father. He that honoreth not the Son honoreth not the Father that sent him. 24 Verily, verily, I say unto you, He that heareth my word, and believeth him that sent me, hath eternal life, and cometh not into judgment, but hath passed out of death into life. 25 Verily, verily, I say unto you, The hour cometh, and now is, when the dead shall hear the voice of the Son of God; and they that [1]hear shall live. 26 For as the Father hath life in himself, even so gave he to the Son also to have life in himself: 27 and he gave him authority to execute judgment, because he is a son of man. 28 Marvel not at this: for the hour cometh, in which all that are in the tombs shall hear his voice, 29 and shall come forth; they that have done good, unto the resurrection of life; and they that have [2]done evil, unto the resurrection of judgment.

[1]Or, *hearken*
[2]Or, *practised*

Vers. 21-29. CHRIST, THE AUTHOR OF RESURRECTION BOTH FOR THE RIGHTEOUS AND THE WICKED.

1. Some refer this whole passage to the bodily resurrection and the final judgment. (B. Ew. Ow. We. Bez. Ter. Era. Gro. Kui. Sto. Kae. Chr. Baum, Schot. Buser.)

But against this Meyer rightly urges the following:

(a) *"that ye marvel not"* (verse 20) refers to a continuous marveling.

(b) *"whom he will"* is in keeping only with a spiritual reference.

(c) *"that ye may honor"* expresses a result taking place in the present and continuing.

(d) *"out of death"* (verse 24) cannot be referred to physical death.

(e) *"and now is"* can refer only to a present spiritual awakening.

(f) The literal resurrection is distinctly marked out by Christ in verses 28 and 29 as distinct and as something greater than the awakening He had just been referring to.

2. Others refer the whole passage to a spiritual awakening. (Ei. Ec. B-C. Amm. Schw.) This is manifestly without proper support.

3. Still others refer verses 21 to 27 to the ever continuing spiritual quickening and judging, and verses 28 and 29 to the final bodily resurrection and judgment. (M. C. D. Le. Ca. Mai. Wor. Nea. Hun. Hen. Hil. Lam. Lu. and the majority.) This is the prevailing view.

4. There are those, however, who slightly modify the last mentioned view by seeing in the passage not only a progression from the spiritual to the bodily, but from a general to a particular; that is, they take verses 21 to 23 as collecting in a unity the total quickening work of Christ spiritual and bodily, and then progressing from this general thought to the particular, first to the spiritual quickening and judgment in verses 24 to 27 and then to the bodily quickening in verses 28 and 29. (L. A. G. K. Lud. Tho. Wei.)

These last two views are alike as to 'the main portion of the passage, and either view as to verses 21 to 23 may be taken without violence to the distinction to be maintained in the main portion, but on the whole the third view is to be preferred, especially since *"whom he will"* seems more naturally to refer to spiritual quickening than to the final bodily resurrection.

Ver. 21. Jesus now specifies the greater works of verse 20.

"the Son also giveth life",—The tense is present, for He was doing it then and is doing it now.

"whom he will",—No one can doubt that these words lie implicitly in the first part of the verse also, but the thought is expressed only with reference to the Son.

There is no suggestion here of an absolute decree: He wills to quicken those who will to believe, as seen in verse 24.

Lunneman refers the expression to the Jews who imagined that as descendents of Abraham they had a necessitating right to eternal life, while Lange finds in it a reference to the Jews who were trying to stop Jesus in His work of quickening and giving life, as evidenced by verse 18. But these are both rather far-fetched findings. It simply means that in every case where He wills the results invariably follow.

Those who take the verse literally refer the expression to the raising of Lazarus and other similar cases. But for these few cases this expression is neither appropriate nor adequate.

Ver. 22. *"For neither"*,—This seems to mean that as the Father does not Himself, by His own proper act, give life to any, but commits all such quickening to the Son, so it is with the judging also. Indeed Christ's giving life to whom He will is an exercise of judgment (D. M. Lu. Tho.), and this verse is a justification of Christ's giving life to whomsoever He wills to give it. As Godet says, "To make alive is to absolve; to refuse to make alive is to condemn."

"judge",—Meyer, Lange, Riddle and others refer this to the judgment of condemnation, the sentence of spiritual death. Godet, however, we think rightly prefers to take it in its general sense. It refers not only to the last day, but to the progress of judgment in time whereby the *"whom He will"* is decided.

Ver. 24. *"cometh not into judgment"*,—Says Mackintosh, "The idea of Christians being arraigned at the bar of judgment to try the question of their title and fitness for heaven, is as absurd as it is unscriptural. How can we think of Paul standing to be judged as to his title to heaven, after having been there for two thousand years? If the question of our title to heaven has to be settled at the day of judgment, then clearly it was not settled on the Cross. If it be maintained that Christians shall only stand in the judgment in order to make it manifest that they are clear through the death of Christ, then would the day of judgment be turned into a mere formality, the bare thought of which is most revolting to every pious and well-regulated mind."

Ver. 25. This is quite generally referred to the spiritual awakening from the dead.

"the hour cometh and now is",—The first part of this expression doubtless refers to Pentecost (A. G.), and the whole is an expression of that which is to characterize the spiritual kingdom of Christ which was even now begun among men, but was yet to come in its fullness.

"hear the voice",—His call to awake in the widest and deepest sense, which call was to be heard in His own preaching and that of his Apostles and ministers. The meaning is the same as that of verse 24, the word *"voice"* being used instead of *"word"* because the hearers are spoken of as dead. This *"hour"* has already lasted 2000 years. (Mack.)

Olshausen would have us refer verse 24 to the spiritual resurrection and this verse to the first bodily resurrection—that of believers, he says, at the Parousia; and then verses 28 and 29 he would have designate the final, universal resurrection.

Those who agree with Olshausen must refer the expression, *"and now is"* to the resurrection of a few believers who appeared after the resurrection of Christ or, as some do, to the few miraculous resurrections wrought by Jesus in the course of His ministry. But these are rather narrow limitations of the words. Indeed Olshausen's explanation of this expression is not open to discussion, as nothing in the text authorizes us to see here the indication of any resurrection different from that of verse 24.

Godet says, "Undoubtedly Jesus admits a distinction between the first resurrection, the resurrection of the just, and the final, universal resurrection", but Olshausen's explanation he considers entirely out of the question.

Ver. 28. *"Marvel not at this"*,—Because something far more marvelous you are about to hear.

"shall hear his voice",—i. e., the voice of the Son of God as in verse 25.

Ver. 29. *"done good"*,—The Greek verb for the word *"done"* as here used refers more to the permanent good, the good which remains, while in the expression *"done evil"* the verb used refers more to the habit of action, i. e., practicing evil, as though one were, as Stier puts it, the servant of evil.

"the resurrection of judgment",—This, says Godet, "is a resurrection leading to judgment in a condemnatory sense, to eternal death in Gehenna." (Thus Tholuck, Lange, Alford, Riddle, Schaff and most all authorities.) "It is," says Lange, "a resurrection from death temporal to death eternal."

Tholuck says, "If *'life'* had simply the idea of duration in it, then *'judgment'* here, its antithesis, would mean annihilation. The New Testament idea of life, however, includes happiness, and judgment here must be that of misery." The one comes forth to a continuing life and the other to a continuing judgment.

Olshausen makes verse 24 refer to spiritual resurrection and verse 25 to the first bodily resurrection, while verses 28 and 29 he refers to the last, final and general resurrection in which both good and bad are involved (Rev. 20.12), *"judgment"* referring to absolute condemnation. But this contention can hardly be supported.

Mackintosh argues from verse 29 that, "We have indicated in the most unmistakable terms the two resurrections. True, they are not distinguished as to time in this passage; but they are as to character. We have a *life* resurrection, and a *judgment* resurrection, and nothing can be more distinct than these. There is no possible ground here upon which to build the theory of a promiscuous resurrection."

Hodge, on the other hand, argues from the use of the word *"hour"* in verse 28 that the resurrection of the righteous must take place at the same time with that of the wicked, and it would not therefore be premillennial. But if the *"hour"* in verse 25 has lasted now for 2000 years, and the *"hour"* mentioned in Chap. 4.21,23 has lasted quite as long, why may not the hour which is to be signalized by the resurrection of all the dead from their graves, for all these words teach, also denote a period of centuries, asks Dr. Kellogg.

In these verses "it is as little said that *'all'* shall be raised at the same time as in verse 25 it is said that all the spiritually dead shall be quickened at the same time. The *'orders'* which Paul in First Corinthians distinguishes at the resurrection and which are in harmony with the teachings of Judaism and of Christ Himself regarding a twofold resurrection finds room also in the word *'hour'* which is capable of prophetic extension." (Meyer.)

Alford refers the judgment here to Matt. 25.31-46.

CHAPTER SIX

39 And this is the will of him that sent me, that of all that which he hath given me I should lose nothing, but should raise it up at the last day. 40 For this is the will of my Father, that every one that beholdeth the Son, and believeth on him, should have eternal life; and I [1]will raise him up at the last day.

44 No man can come to me, except the Father that sent me draw him: and I will raise him up in the last day.
54 He that eateth my flesh and drinketh my blood hath eternal life; and I will raise him up at the last day.

[1]Or, *that I should raise him up*

Vers. 39,40,44,54. THE BELIEVER'S RESURRECTION AT THE LAST DAY.

That the bodily resurrection of the believer is here set forth is beyond all dispute, and it is presented here as the necessary crowning of the spiritual work accomplished by Christ in the believer.

Meyer says, "It is the first resurrection that is meant, that to the everlasting life of the Messianic kingdom, and, as a matter of course, it includes the transformation of those still living." This is in keeping with his explanation of Chap. 5.29.

Lange says, "It is the period of resurrection and judgment from the second coming of Christ to the general resurrection, Rev. 20."

Alford says, "It refers to the only resurrection which is the completion of the man in his glorified state."

Riddle says, "It is the one great period of resurrection for the whole Church of God, the glorious consummation, the final resurrection."

Blackstone says, "This is the great Millennial day ushered in and ending with resurrection and judgment, and during which Christ shall rule the nations and judge the world in righteousness, as Paul says in Acts 17.31. Some argue that if this is the *'last day'* there cannot follow a thousand years before the unbelievers are raised; but Peter says, *'One day is with the Lord as a thousand years and a thousand years as one day'*."

CHAPTER ELEVEN

23 Jesus saith unto her, Thy brother shall rise again. 24 Martha saith unto him, I know that he shall rise again in the resurrection at the last day. 25 Jesus said unto her, I am the resurrec-tion, and the life: he that believeth on me, though he die, yet shall he live; 26 and whosoever liveth and believeth on me shall never die. Believest thou this?

Vers. 23-26. THE LAST-DAY RESURRECTION AND THE ETERNAL LIFE OF BELIEVERS.

Ver. 23. *"Thy brother shall rise again"*,—Some think Jesus refers to the immediate resurrection of Lazarus (G. S. M.), while others refer the words to the resurrection at the last day (A. L. Hen.). The words might easily denote either, but in keeping with what He came to do (verse 11) and the meaning of the answer in the next verse the former and more common interpretation appeals to us as the more preferable one. The words were designedly ambiguous, so put for the trial and development of her faith.

Ver. 24. Martha, it seems, failed to grasp the true meaning of the Master's words. The great unqualified *"rise again"* was, as Godet says, "too strong for her thoughts to connect it with the present". Her answer expresses not merely "the resignation of disappointed expectation" (M.). There is a tone of inquiry in it (D. C.) ; she seems to be feeling her way, as Lange says. We must not therefore, with Riddle, think of Martha as "having lost the hope which the sight of Jesus had awakened" (verse 22). She is implying the rather in her answer that she was expecting something more, and so she gently repels, as Alford says, the insufficient comfort of her brother's ultimate resurrection. She is giving Jesus a chance to explain Himself, as Godet says, "and to declare expressly what she scarcely dares to hope for in the present case." But Martha's faith is not as spiritual as it is strong, and it is to the development of that faith in a more spiritual sense that Jesus in the next verse gives Himself.

"In the resurrection at the last day",—This *"last day"* in the mind of the Jew was the closing day of the age that then was, and the resurrection of the pious Jews was by them thought to be the opening act of the Messianic kingdom, as had already been announced in Dan. 12.2 and II Macc. 7.9,14. This belief, says Godet, "was generally spread abroad in Israel, and that especially in the circles in which Pharisaic teaching prevailed".

Ver. 25. *"I am the resurrection and the life"*,—i. e., I am the personal power of both, the One who raises and who makes alive.

Some contend that *"life"* here is the positive result of the resurrection (M. Luc.). This it assuredly is, but it is more: it is the ground, the condition, the cause and true principle of the resurrection (S. O. G. L. Ew. Lud. Hun.). Christ is the Life in the highest and most absolute sense of the word and therefore He is the Resurrection.

Jesus then goes on to say, He that believeth on Me, even if he shall have died physically, will live eternally, and every one who is still alive physically and believes on Me shall not die forever, i. e., *"shall never unto eternity die"*, as the Greek has it.

In the first clause death is physical and life is spiritual, while in the second clause life is physical and death is spiritual.

Ver. 26. There is no reference here, as some maintain, to the Second Coming and those who are to be alive at that time, as in I Cor. 15.51. Such an interpretation would set aside all reference to Lazarus, or to present circumstances. In First Corinthians Paul is speaking of believers primarily, but that saying is to be equally true of unbelievers, on those bodies the change from corruption to incorruption must sometime also take place, in the case of those who are living when the time for that change arrives, whereas the saying here is one setting forth the exclusive privilege of the believer.

CHAPTER FOURTEEN

3 And if I go and prepare a place for you, I will come again, and will receive you unto myself; that where I am, there ye may be also.

18 I will not leave you ¹desolate; I come unto you.

¹Or, *orphans*

21 and I will love Him and manifest myself unto him.

23 Jesus answered and said unto him, If a man love me, he will keep my word; and my Father will love him, and we will come unto him, and make our abode with him.

28 Ye heard how I said to you, I go away, and I come unto you.

29 And now I have told you before it come to pass, that, when it come to pass, ye may believe.

Vers. 3,18,21,23,28,29. HOW THE LORD IS TO COME AGAIN.

Ver. 3. *"I will come again"*,—Just what Jesus had in mind is by no means certain.

1. Ebrard finds in the words a reference to His resurrection. But the true reunion (*where I am, there ye may be also*) with His own did not take place then.

2. Others refer it to death. (L. B-C. Ni. Tho. Gro. Reu. Hen. Kna.) But this would be their going to Christ rather than Christ's coming to them. Nowhere does the New Testament speak of Christ coming to receive believers at death. Neither Luke 16.22, Acts 7.58 nor John 21.22, as argued by Lange, is to the point.

3. Still others refer it to His Second Coming, the Parousia, and say that the disciples would be at once reminded of His words in Matt. 24. (M. C. K. Ew. Lud. Wei. Ori. Hof. Lam. Bru. Tor. Mack.) Certain objections register themselves against this view, namely:

   (a) The present *"I come"* denotes a right speedy return as calculated to console the sorrowing Disciples.

   (b) By this interpretation He would have consoled them by an event which not one of them ever saw and which is still future after 2000 years.

   (c) It presupposes that Christ and the Disciples conceived of the Parousia as so imminent in a chronological sense. Meyer in accepting this view indeed does so attribute this belief to them. It may have been true of the Disciples and the Church, but can it with confidence be maintained of Jesus? Did He not on several occasions at least intimate rather the opposite? (See Matt. 25.5; Luke 12.28, and Mark 13.35.)

   (d) The reunion mentioned here is to be in heaven, whereas at the Parousia the reunion is to be rather on earth with its future destiny of glorification.

4. Again there are those who see in the words a reference to the return of Jesus through the Holy Spirit at Pentecost and thereafter abiding with them. It is claimed that this view is favored by the fact that the whole chapter deals with the coming of the Comforter. (G. O. R. Lu. Nea.)

   The chief objection to this view is that Christ is speaking of coming to fetch them to a prepared place whose locality is determined, and as Torrey says, "Jesus at the coming of the Holy Spirit does not receive us unto Himself to be with Him, but the rather He comes to be with us."

   Both Godet and Riddle relieve this embarrassment by affirming that the two promises contained in the words must not necessarily refer to the same time. The *"I come"* is put in the present tense, while the *"I will receive"* is future, the first referring to something soon to take place, while the second refers to the introduction of the believer into the Father's house either at death or at the Parousia if he be then still living.

5. Alford and Stier take a comprehensive view. They would have us bear in mind what Stier calls the "perspective" of prophecy and refer this coming not to any single act, but to the great complex of them all.

   Alford says, "The coming is begun in His Resurrection (verse 18), carried on in the spiritual life (verse 23), further advanced when each by death is fetched away to be with Him, and fully completed at His coming in glory when they shall be with Him forever."

This last view is rather an amplification of the one just preceding it, and it would seem that between these two views and the third the decision must lie. All things considered the objections to the third view appear to us as the less formidable. Manifestly the words mean that having gone to prepare a place for them, His coming was to take them away to that place where they were henceforth to be with Him.

Ver. 18. *"I come unto you"*,—This expression plainly applies to the coming by the Spirit, who is one with Christ. (A. S. M. C. O. R. G. Lu. Tho. Baum.), although some (Be. Lud. Aug. Hof.) refer it to the Parousia, and others (Ew. Chr. Ori. Eut. Era. Gro. Rup. Theo.) to the manifestations subsequent to His resurrection, while still others (L. D. Bez. Lut. Lam.) claim that Christ had in view both His corporeal and His spiritual return, upon the former of which (His corporeal return at His Resurrection) the latter (His spiritual return) depended.

Ver. 21. *"I will manifest myself unto him"*,—The reference is to the manifestation of Christ through the Holy Spirit (L. A. S. G. M.), and not to His manifestation at the Parousia (Lud.), nor to His appearings after His Resurrection (Gro. Hil.).

Ver. 23. *"and we will come unto him and make our abode with him"*,—This is to be taken in the same sense as in verse 18, i. e., a coming and an indwelling of the Holy Spirit.

Ver. 28. *"I come unto you"*,—These words are of course to be interpreted in harmony with those of verse 3.

Ver. 29. *"come to pass"*,—This refers not to His coming again, but to His going to His Father, His exaltation by means of His death, His Resurrection and His Ascension.

CHAPTER SIXTEEN

> 13 Howbeit when he, the Spirit of truth, is come, he shall guide you *into all truth*; for he shall not speak from himself; but what things soever he shall hear, these shall he speak; and he shall declare unto you the things that are to come.

Ver. 13. THE REVEALER OF THINGS TO COME.

"things to come",—This is said no doubt with a reference to verse

12, being especially the eschatological references scattered through the Acts and the Epistles and most fully in the Apocalypse where the *"things to come"* are distinctly the subject of the Spirit's revelation.

These *"things to come"*, properly interpreted, are not, as Milligan says; so much revelations wholly new, as new applications of what had already been revealed. That Christ had the Disciples alone in mind Tholuck thinks is clearly proven by Chap. 14.26 and Chap. 15.26,27, and therefore it will not do to think with the Quakers and the Mystics that this special revelation of the Spirit goes on now in the illuminated in general, that is, in all spiritually-minded followers of Jesus. Godet, too, thinks the reference is to special revelation granted to the Apostles, distinct from that which every Christian receives by means of theirs. The expression *"all the truth"* contains the thought, says Godet, "that during the present economy no new teaching respecting Christ will come to be added to that of the Apostles".

16 A little while, and ye behold me no more; and again a little while, and ye shall see me.
20 Verily, verily, I say unto you, that ye shall weep and lament, but the world shall rejoice: ye shall be sorrowful, but your sorrow shall be turned into joy.
22 And ye therefore now have sorrow: but I will see you again, and your heart shall rejoice, and your joy no one taketh away from you.

Vers. 16,20,22. THE COMING OF CHRIST THROUGH THE HOLY SPIRIT.

"a little while",—The first *"little while"* refers of course to His death, and the *"not seeing"* refers of course to physical sight. But to what does the second *"little while"* refer and what kind of sight is involved in *"ye shall see"*? There are three views:

1. That which refers the second *"little while"* to the Resurrection. (L. Eb. Ew. Hen. Wei. Lut. Aug. Tho.) But this not only seems inconsistent with verse 23, because in that day they did ask Him questions (Acts 1.5,6), but the sequel, as seen in verses 25 and 26, seems to prove the impossibility of this explanation.

2. That which refers the second *"little while"* to the Parousia. (Hof. Lud. Brow.) But this hardly seems consistent with the expression *"a little while"*. The first *"little while"* was only one day, and the second one would then be at this present time 2000 years long. Luthardt thinks that because of the expression, *"yet a little while"*, the Disciples were to see in the transitory return of the Risen One a pledge of the future Parousia. But of this Jesus certainly says nothing, either here or in what follows.

3. That which refers the second *"little while"* to the coming of Christ through the Holy Spirit at Pentecost, and makes the *"seeing"* a spiritual vision. (M. G. O. R. Tho. Mil. Scha.) That this is its main reference, even as in Chap. 14.18, there can be little doubt.

Alford and Stier concede that the expression receives its *main* fulfillment at the day of Pentecost, but in all these prophecies assumes a perspective of continual unfolding fulfillments beginning at the Resurrection (at which time their spiritual vision might be said to have really begun) and going on through Pentecost to its final completion in the great return of the Lord.

The Disciples were perplexed; they could not reconcile this *"little while"* with what the Master had said in verse 10 about going to His Father. Jesus therefore proceeds in verses 20 and 22 to describe the *not seeing* and the *yet seeing again* by their effects.

Ver. 20. *"ye shall weep and lament"*,—They would mourn for Him as dead.

"the world shall rejoice",—This rejoicing was first seen in its derision at the Cross.

"turned to joy",—i. e., when the *"ye shall see me"* takes place. Says Godet, "The appearance of the Risen One only half healed the wound; the perfect and enduring joy was given only on the day of Pentecost."

Alford, in keeping with his method of interpretation, says with refined insight that *"ye shall be sorrowful"* goes deeper than the *"weeping and lamenting"* just mentioned, and shows that the whole refers not only to the grief while Christ was in the tomb, but to the grief continually manifesting itself in the course and conflict of the Christian, which grief is turned into joy by the advancing work of the Spirit of Christ and into the perfect consummation of joy at the Second Coming of the Lord.

It is here that David Brown says, "The transport of joy of the widowed Church at the personal return of her Lord is certainly here expressed."

Ver. 22. *"but I will see you again"*,—This is only a correlate designation of the same fact expressed in verses 16 and 19, and the reference is mainly no doubt, as in the previous verses, to the communion with them through the Holy Spirit. (M. G. Mil.)

Lange, with others of like view, refers it to the Resurrection exclusively, as seen in their exegesis above, while Alford, consistent with his view throughout, says, "at My Resurrection—by My Spirit—at My second coming".

CHAPTER EIGHTEEN

> 36 Jesus answered, My kingdom is not of this world; if my kingdom were of this world, then would my [1]servants fight, that I should not be delivered to the Jews: but now is my kingdom not from hence.
> [1]Or, *officers*: as in verses 3,12,18,22

Ver. 36. CHRIST'S KINGDOM NOT A WORLDLY ONE.

"not of this world",—i. e., not belonging to, not springing from, not arising out of the world and therefore not to be supported by this world's weapons.

Blackstone says, "True, it is not of the spirit of this world, just as believers are not of this world (John 15.19). The correct rendering of the passage is, 'My kingdom is not (ek) *out* of this world.' That is, it does not emanate from the world. He is not (ek) out of this world. (John 8.23.) Both He and His kingdom are from above (Col. 3.1). But His kingdom will be set upon this earth, in accordance with the prayer which He taught us, '*Thy kingdom come; Thy will be done, as in heaven, so in earth'.*"

"*my servants*",—The reference here is not to angels (S.), nor to His Disciples (Lam.), but to such officers and soldiers as He would have had if His kingdom had been of this world. (A. Lu. Hen.)

"*but now*",—This is not a temporal particle; it means, "as the case now stands".

CHAPTER TWENTY-ONE

21 Peter therefore seeing him saith to Jesus, Lord, ¹and what shall this man do? 22 Jesus saith unto him, If I will that he tarry till I come, what *is that* to thee? follow thou me. 23 This saying therefore went forth among the ¹Gr. *and this man, what?*

brethren, that that disciple should not die: yet Jesus said not unto him, that he should not die; but, If I will that he tarry till I come, what *is that* to thee?

Vers. 21-23. THE SECOND COMING AND THE DEATH OF JOHN.

Ver. 21. "*what shall this man do?*"—What did Peter mean?

1. Some take the question as a disapprobation of John's unauthorized following after Christ and Peter. (Pau.)
2. Some take it as mere curiosity. (Tho.)
3. Some take it as an expression of petty jealousy. (M.)
4. Some say Peter doubtless understood Christ's words about his (Peter's) coming martyrdom, and prompted by an affectionate feeling, he gave expression to the longing he naturally felt for his friend, as he asks, "And what shall befall him?" (A. G. L. Lud. Era. Chr.)

Ver. 22. "*what is that to thee?*"—The reply of Jesus seems to contain a gentle rebuke, and so there must have been something at least indiscreet in Peter's question. The rebuke is, however, hardly so severe as some would have us think. It is as if Christ had said, "Do thou think of what I command *thee*, and leave to God His own secrets." We are inclined to think it was affection mingled with curiosity that prompted the question of Peter.

"*tarry*",—i. e., live, be preserved in life in opposition to Peter's martyrdom.

"*till I come*",—In what sense is this coming to be taken?

1. It is not His coming in the Holy Spirit at Pentecost, since Peter as well as John was present at that event.
2. It is not His coming to John in death, for this would be equivalent to saying, "If he live until he die", which would be nonsense. Or if it be taken that John shall have a gentle and natural death at the end of a long life (O. L. Ew. Ze. We. Gro. Lam. Rup. Wor. Cla.), it is equivalent to saying that Jesus only comes in death to such, which is not only absurd, but is disproved by the case of Stephen.
3. It is not His coming to the place where John is to wait. (Pau.)

4. It is not His coming to lead him out of Gallilee, where John was to remain, to the scene of Apostolic activity.

5. It is practically agreed by all able exegetes that the Parousia is the time to which Christ referred.   But the Parousia in what sense?

I. The final Second Coming (M. D. Tor. Wei. Reu. Lus. Bla. Mil. Sco.), the passage teaching that John would be among those caught up without dying (I Cor. 15.51). Thus the Jews understood it until John died, and even then they had a legend that he was alive in the grave and that the tomb moved when he breathed.   There is no doubt that there was at that time a belief in the nearness of the Parousia.

One of two things must be true if this view be accepted:

1. That Jesus shared the error of His contemporaries in relation to the nearness of His return, as Weiss maintains, which is, of course, in itself inadmissible as well as contrary to His testimony elsewhere.

2. That Jesus was speaking hypothetically, i. e., "*even should I will*", etc. (M. Tho. Tr.), which is also inadmissible, because Jesus could not have presented as possible (on the condition of His good pleasure) a thing which was impossible, as Godet says.   Alford furthermore says that "such a mere hypothetical saying would be strangely incongruous in the mouth of our Lord, especially in these last solemn days of His presence on earth".

II. There is but one other possible interpretation of this Second Coming of Christ, namely, that which seems so often to be alluded to in the three other Gospels, i. e., the establishment in full of the dispensation of the kingdom by the destruction of the nation, the temple and the city of the Jews at Jerusalem as the beginning of the Parousia of Christ. (B. A. S. G. Lud.) Alford says, "At the Destruction of Jerusalem *began that mighty series of events* of which the Apocalypse is the prophetic record and which is in the complex known as the 'coming of the Lord', ending, as it shall, with His glorious and personal advent."

This the beloved Apostle alone lived to see.   The fact that John far outlived this event does not, as Weiss maintains, militate against the view, since the *"until"*, as Godet says, has nothing exclusive in it.

Ver. 23.   *"he should not die"*,—John does not explain the meaning of Christ's words, which perhaps he did not know; he only corrects the misapprehension that he was not to die.

THE ACTS

(A. D. 65)

CHAPTER ONE

6 They therefore, when they were come together, asked him, saying, Lord, dost thou at this time restore the kingdom to Israel? 7 And· he said unto them, It is not for you to know times or seasons, which the Father hath ¹set

¹Or, *appointed by*

within his own authority. 8 But ye shall receive power, when the Holy Spirit is come upon you: and ye shall be my witnesses both in Jerusalem, and in all Judæa and Samaria, and unto the uttermost part of the earth.

Vers. 6-8. THE KINGDOM CONFUSED.

Ver. 6. *"come together"*,—Luke 24.49,50 makes it plain that this coming together was not at the same time as in verse 4 (A. D.), but on a subsequent occasion, though perhaps on the same day. (G. O. M. Ha.)

"asked Him",—This is not an expression of astonishment, "Lord, wilt Thou restore the kingdom to those who have so treacherously dealt with Thee as to crucify Thee?" (Li.), or, "Lord, wilt Thou at this time, when the hatred of the rulers is so strong and our power is so weak, try to erect your banners?" (Bark.); for thus, in either case, the Lord's answer would be irrelevant.

"at this time",—Having promised them that not many days hence the Baptism of the Spirit would take place, and having always connected this with the coming of the kingdom, they were led thus to ask the question. All the more did they think they might assume this from verse 4. (M. Le.)

"kingdom to Israel",—Still entangled in the Jewish hopes, thinking the Messiah to be destined for Israel as such; still looking for a temporal, visible kingdom, although after so long an association with Jesus their views could hardly have been altogether carnal; and they must have had some more advanced ideas as to the spirituality of the kingdom than the rest of the Jews.

Ver. 7. Jesus answered them only as to time. He does not correct their erroneous notions, knowing that the Holy Spirit, so soon to be given, and the course of events would do that. He did not, however, give such an answer as would take away all prospect of a future manifestation of His kingdom, which He knew would yet one day display itself in a visible, external dominion.

Olshausen well remarks that the Apostles were to be less prophets of the future and more witnesses of the past. As it was not for them to know, neither is it for us.

"times",—The reference is to time absolutely without regard to circumstances.

"seasons",—In this word the reference is to definite, determined periods and epochs, seasons of greater and less duration respectively.

"set within His own authority",—The word *"set"* is by Alford and Gloag rendered "kept", but our reading keeps closer to the original. Meyer renders it "established", which has quite the same meaning as the text. It involves in it of course the idea of "appoint" (marginal reading), the period referred to being that of the arrangement of the divine counsels of redemption.

"within His own authority",—i. e., in the sovereign exercise of it.

Ver. 8. A reproof, by implication, of their carnal anticipation of the kingdom for the Jews only at Jerusalem. Still they did not seem to understand. (See Chap. 11.9.)

"witnesses",—i. e., of My teachings, life, death, resurrection and ascension.

"ends of the earth",—There is no warrant here for the untenable position that the Apostles themselves went to the ends of the earth, nor does the expression mean the ends only of the land of Palestine, but of the whole world.

9 And when he had said these things, as they were looking, he was taken up; and a cloud received him out of their sight. 10 And while they were looking stedfastly into heaven as he went, behold two men stood by them in white apparel; 11 who also said, Ye men of Galilee. why stand ye looking into heaven? this Jesus, who was received up from you into heaven, shall so come in like manner as ye beheld him going into heaven.

Vers. 9-11. THE ASCENSION AND THE PROMISED RETURN.

Ver. 9. *"cloud"*,—A bright cloud. (Matt. 17.5.)

"The visible manifestation of the presence of God who takes to Himself His Son into the glory of heaven." (Meyer.)

"The bright cloud so often appearing to the Israelites and which rested on the mercy seat, the visible symbol of the presence of God, the Shekinah of the Jews." (Gloag.)

Alford says, "There was a manifest propriety in the last withdrawal of the Lord while ascending; not consisting in a *disappearance* of His body as on former occasions since the Resurrection; for thus might His abiding humanity have been called into question. As it was He went up in human form, and so we think and pray to Him."

Baumgarten beautifully says, "While the ascension of Elijah may be compared to the flight of a bird which none can follow, the ascension of Christ is as it were a bridge between heaven and earth laid down for all who are drawn to Him by His earthly existence."

Ver. 10. *"two men"*,—i. e., angels.

Ver. 11. *"why stand ye looking into heaven?"*—

Calvin thinks perhaps they thought He might return, that He had not really gone away into heaven but only up into the clouds.

Some think it was a rebuke to their astonishment because He had told them that He must ascend to His Father, and they should not have been so astonished when He did so.

It is more probable that the words were spoken in a comforting manner, i. e., "Why stand ye gazing as if you were never more to see Jesus; He will come back again?"

"so come",—This refers of course to the *manner* of His coming, in a cloud, bodily, visibly and, of course, in His glorified humanity. (O. M. B. D. A. E. Gl. Ha.)

Hackett has well said that the assertion that the words refer only to the *certainty* of Christ's return, namely, that as He had departed, so He would certainly come back, is contradicted by every passage in which the phrase occurs. (Chap. 7.8; Matt. 23.27; Lu. 13.34; II Tim. 3.8.) The phrase always indicates manner, and the literal translation here is, "thus shall come in the manner which".

Dr. Torrey has well said, "If the Bible teaches anything definitely and distinctly, it teaches that the Lord Jesus who was taken up visibly and bodily from Mount Olivet into heaven so that the Disciples saw Him as He went, is coming again visibly and bodily so that people shall see Him as He comes."

17 [1]And it shall be in the last days, saith God,
I will pour forth of my Spirit upon all flesh:
And your sons and your daughters shall prophesy,
And your young men shall see visions,
And your old men shall dream dreams:
18 Yea and on my [2]servants and on my [3]handmaidens in those days
Will I pour forth of my Spirit; and they shall prophesy.
19 And I will show wonders in the heaven above,
And signs on the earth beneath;
Blood and fire, and vapor of smoke:
20 The sun shall be turned into darkness,
And the moon into blood,
Before the day of the Lord come,
That great and notable day:
21 And it shall be, that whosoever shall call on the name of the Lord shall be saved.

[1]Joel 2.22 ff.
[2]Gr. *bondmen*
[3]Gr. *bondmaidens*

CHAPTER TWO

Vers. 17-21. THE EFFUSION OF THE HOLY SPIRIT IN THE LAST DAYS.

A reproduction almost verbatim of Joel 2.28-32, following the Septuagint. (See Joel for further and fuller explanation.)

Ver. 17. *"in the last days"*,—In the Hebrew of Joel it is *"afterwards"*, and in the Septuagint it is *"after these things"*. The expression was used in the Old Testament to signify the age of the Messiah. It was used by the Rabbis for that period of time which extends from the coming of the Messiah to the end of the world, and therefore it signifies this age. or the period in which we now live. Of course the Jews believe the Messiah has not yet come.

The "Age of the Messiah" was called *"the last days"* because it was to be the last dispensation of religion. (Isa. 2.2; Micah 4.1; Heb. 1.1; II Tim. 3.1; I John 2.18.)

Meyer says, "This denotes the days immediately preceding the erection of the Messianic kingdom, which, according to the New Testament view, could only take place by means of the speedily expected Parousia."

"will pour",—The outpouring figuratively describes the copious communication.

"upon all flesh",—Joel doubtless had the Jews only in mind, and that as the people of God, the collective body of whom, and not merely as formerly individual priests, who were to receive the divine inspiration. But by this expression as used by Peter all believers without any distinction as to race were to receive the Spirit as thus specially outpoured. (B. A. Le. Gl. Ha. Lum.)

"prophesy",—Signifying not merely to foretell future events but more especially to communicate religious truth in general under divine inspiration. (See Chap. 19.6 and Chap. 21.9.)

"your sons and your daughters",—Male and female members of the people of God—all without exception.

"visions .... dreams",—Divine revelations by day and by night.

403

Ver. 18.   A solemn repetition of verse 17.

The reference is not to slaves, as might be the case in Joel, but by the addition of *"my"* the reference is plainly to God's servants and God's handmaids, all true Christians, male and female, inasmuch as they recognize that they belong to God.

Ver. 19.   *"blood and fire, and vapours of smoke"*,—

"The mode of speaking here", as Hackett has well said, "is founded on the popular idea that, when great events are about to occur, wonderful phenomena foretoken their appearance."

We are not therefore to understand, with Meyer, natural signs such as blood-shedding and conflagrations, as this is opposed to their grammatical relation to *"wonders"* and *"signs"*.   They are the portents themselves and not the calamities portended.   (A. D. Ha. Gl.)

Ver. 20.   A day is at hand which will be one of thick gloom, of sadness and woe.   The sun will become dark and the moon will appear as blood.   (Compare Matt. 24.29; Isa. 13.10; Ezek. 32.7.)

Ver. 21.   The covenant of the new and spiritual dispensation. "The gates of God's mercy are thrown open in Christ to all people."

How did Peter understand this prophecy?   And how are we to understand it?   There are many who refer *"the Day of the Lord"* with its *"signs"* and *"wonders"* to the destruction of Jerusalem.   Hackett thinks this the primary reference for four reasons:

1. Since Peter applied the first part of the prophecy to the early times of the Gospel, so also, by the law of correspondence, should the last part of the prophecy be applied to the same period.
2. The Day of the Lord, by common usage in the Hebrew prophets, denotes a day when God comes to make known His power in the punishment of His enemies, a day of vengeance for the rejection of His long-continued mercies and the commission of aggravated sins, and the destruction of Jerusalem appropriates fully every trait of just such a day.
3. The language coincides almost verbally with that of Matt. 24.29, and if the language there, as understood by most interpreters, describes the destruction of Jerusalem, we may justly infer that it does here.
4. The phraseology, according to the laws of prophetic language, is strikingly appropriate to represent the unsurpassed horrors and distress which attended the siege and destruction of Jerusalem, and to announce the extinction of Jewish power and the glory of the Jewish worship.

Hackett's reasons are hardly sufficient to warrant his conclusion although part of the truth lies in the position he has taken.   But even he says, "We are also to recognize the wider scope of the prophecy, and this fulfillment is but a type of another and fuller fulfillment in the days yet to come."   And Howson well says, "Neither Pentecost and the miraculous powers bestowed upon the early Church on the one hand, nor the siege of Jerusalem on the other has exhausted the great prophecy of Joel which

Peter took up and repeated; these are only partial fulfillments; the full accomplishment still tarries and will assuredly precede that awful day of the Lord, the time of which is known to the Father only." In harmony with this we find Gloag saying, "The wonders and signs predicted were as yet future, but they were regarded by Peter as unavoidable and imminent. In the destruction of Jerusalem as well as in Pentecost there *was* a striking fulfillment of the prophecy, but this was only typical of what was to take place before the second coming of the Lord."

It must be borne in mind that in prophetic language the day of the Lord was regarded as following close upon the outpouring of the Spirit, because, as Alford says, "it was to be the next great event in the divine arrangement." The prophetic forecast did not take cognizance of the long period between what we know as the first advent of the Messiah and His coming again. In fact the Disciples were not expecting so long a season of waiting, and it may be that they associated the destruction of Jerusalem, which their Master had foretold, with His coming again according to His promise. At any rate the day of the Lord was to be in the program of the Lord's return, and Peter was right in taking Pentecost with its accompanying miracles as the fulfillment of Joel's prophecy. It was the beginning of its fulfillment, the beginning of the signs of the end, and then, as Alford says, "follows the period, *known only to the Father*, the period of waiting—the Church for her Lord's return—and then the signs shall be renewed and the day of the Lord shall come."

29 Brethren, I may say unto you freely of the patriarch David, that he both died and was buried, and his tomb is with us unto this day. 30 Being therefore a prophet, and knowing that God had sworn with an oath to him, that of the fruit of his loins [1]he would set *one* upon his throne; 31 he foreseeing *this* spake of the resurrection of the Christ, that neither was he left unto Hades, nor did his flesh see corruption. 32 This Jesus did God raise up, [2]whereof we all are witnesses. 33 Being therefore [3]by the right hand of God exalted, and having received of the Father the promise of the Holy Spirit, he hath poured forth this, which ye see and hear. 34 For David ascended not into the heavens: but he saith himself,

[4]The Lord said unto my Lord, Sit
　　thou on my right hand,
35 Till I make thine enemies the footstool of thy feet.

36 Let [5]all the house of Israel therefore know assuredly, that God hath made him both Lord and Christ, this Jesus whom ye crucified.

[1]Or, one *should sit*
[2]Or, *of whom*
[3]Or, *at*

[4]Ps. 110.1
[5]Or, *every house*

Vers. 29-36. THE HEIR TO DAVID'S THRONE.

Ver. 29. The object of these words is to show that the remarks just made could not have referred to David.

"*freely*",—He was not deficient in any respect to his memory, but was to state a matter of fact which could not be denied.

"*patriarch*",—As being the founder of the royal family.

"*with us*",—Here in this city.

Ver. 30. In this and the next verse we have the application of the prophecy to Christ. Unless David meant himself, he must have meant the Messiah.

"*knowing*",—Through knowledge received from the prophet Nathan as related in II Sam. 7.12,16; see also Ps. 132.11.

"he would set one upon his throne",—Namely, the Messiah of whom David was speaking and who was to be the theocratic consummator of David's kingdom.

Ver. 31. *"foreseeing"*,—Prophetically looking into the future.

"was left",—This and the following verb are in the aorist because the speaker thinks of the prediction as now accomplished.

Ver. 32. *"whereof"*,—This is better than *"of whom"*, as the verb naturally suggests as antecedent the resurrection itself, and of this the Apostles considered themselves to be especially the witnesses. (M. Ha. Gl.)

Ver. 33. *"by the right hand of God exalted"*,—That this rendering is the correct one there can be little doubt. (A. M. C. E. Gl. Le. Kui. Win.) Others, however, render it "to the right hand of God exalted". (O. D. Ha. Ba. Wor. Rob. Nea.)

This latter rendering agrees best perhaps with what follows in verse 34 but it is hardly in harmony with the structure of the Greek language, and we must not set aside one suitable sense for another when a violation of syntax is involved. It is not true, as De Wette claims, that the former rendering is inappropriate and meaningless; for on the contrary it shows that God's mighty power is seen in the exaltation of Christ as well as in His resurrection.

"the promise of the Holy Spirit",—This refers to the promise above cited from Joel, and not of course to the promises made by Himself to the same effect, although this latter may also have been in Peter's mind. The phrase refers to the fulfillment in the bestowal of the Holy Spirit, and is therefore equivalent to *"having received the promised Holy Spirit"*.

"this",—To be taken not as referring to the Holy Spirit (Bez. Era. Kui.), but as *just* this,—*this* merely, this thing which ye see and hear, leaving it to the hearers themselves to infer that what was poured out was none other than the effusion of the promised Holy Spirit.

Ver. 34. *"For David ascended not into heaven"*,—Therefore the prediction could not be applied to him.

"my Lord",—i. e., David's Lord, the Christ.

"on my right hand",—i. e., as the partner of the throne having participation in the supreme dominion.

Ver. 35. The dominion here received belongs to Christ as Mediator and is to cease when the objects of His kingdom as Mediator are accomplished.

Ver. 36. The conclusion from all that has been said.

"Lord",—The supreme King, ruler generally.

"Christ",—In the full and glorious sense in which, as Alford says, that term was prophetically known.

It is not possible to decide from this passage alone whether or not Jesus is now sitting on the throne of David. It is quite certain that the passage has no reference to the original dominion which Christ as God possesses. It is also just as certain that it is the mediatorial throne, as the result and reward of His sufferings, which is here primarily intended and to which He, as Lord and Christ, is exalted.   But is this the throne of David?

It is true that at first thought the passage does seem to imply this, as seen in verse 30 and the following references to Christ's resurrection. Dr. Brown, in his famous work, "The Second Coming", says, "That Christ is now on the throne of David is as clearly affirmed by Peter in this sermon as words could do it."   He argues that He has been sitting there from the time that God raised Him from the dead.

But an impartial exegesis does not necessarily make the passage teach anything of the kind.

1. Dr. Brown follows the Authorized Version and makes the words *"raise up"* in verse 30 refer to the resurrection of Christ.   But:

(a) The words *"raise up"* must, according to preponderating manuscript authority, be omitted as spurious. (See Revised Versions.)

(b) Even if we accept the words, they do not, when standing by themselves, denote a raising from the dead, but according to usage they mean "to raise up in history", as when God is said to have raised up for His own purpose Moses, Cyrus or some other historical personage.

(c) If we accept the word and give to it the meaning Dr. Brown maintains, it does not necessarily follow that the assumption of David's throne took place *immediately* upon or after the resurrection.

It was necessary for Christ to be raised to sit upon David's throne and all the passage can be said to unquestionably teach is that this session followed the rising from the dead, but as to how soon after the resurrection it began no hint is given.   There is all the more force in this argument when we remember that, as Dr. Kellogg has said, "the prophets almost invariably speak of related events, without indicating any interval of time, whether great or small, which may elapse between them."

CHAPTER THREE

19 Repent ye therefore, and turn again, that your sins may be blotted out, that so there may come seasons of refreshing from the presence of the Lord; 20 and that he may send the Christ who hath been appointed for you, *even* Jesus: 21 whom the heaven must receive until the times of restoration of all things, whereof God spake by the mouth of his holy prophets that have been from of old.

Vers. 19-21.   THE SEASONS OF REFRESHING AND THE RESTORATION OF ALL THINGS.

Ver. 19.   *"blotted out"*,—As the blotting out or the erasure of a handwriting. (Col. 2.4.)

"that so",—In order that.   (M. O. D. A. Ha. Gl. Er. Kel. Wor. Win. Chr.)   The meaning of the particle absolutely forbids the old rendering of the Authorized Version.

"from the presence of the Lord",—God is the author of these seasons of refreshing.

"seasons of refreshing",—The following explanations have been made of this expression:

1. That which connects it with the second coming of Christ, as Alford says, ushering in the seasons of refreshing. (A. M. O. Er. Ha. Gl. Le. Kel. Lum.)
2. The spiritual refreshing which comes from believing in Christ. (S. Al. Kui.)
3. The deliverance of Christians at the destruction of Jerusalem. (Li. Ham. Gro.)
4. The period of rest after death. (Schu.)

Only the first two of these views are worthy of any extended attention. The second of these views would certainly present us with the most natural meaning if it were not for the following things:

1. The grammatical connection with the next verse seems to demand, as Olshausen declares, that it be connected with the second coming of Christ. Hackett correctly says that the order of the clauses decides nothing against this opinion, it being quite as natural to think first of the effect and then to assign the cause, as the reverse.
2. It is in favor of the first view that it refers the verbs *"may come"* and *"may send"* to the same period and event, as the close connection of the verbs would lead us to expect.
3. The fact that the verb *"come"* is in the aorist tense and used in a conditional sentence seems to refer to a definite arrival. If it had been for repeated occurrence of refreshings the present tense would have been used.
4. The fact that the seasons of refreshing are said to come from the presence of the Lord is more favorable to the first than to the second view.

We believe therefore that Gloag very properly says, "All those interpretations which refer the *'seasons of refreshing'* to anything unconnected with the second coming of Christ are to be rejected. No other meaning it seems to me will suit the words."

Does not this passage therefore represent the second coming of the Lord as immediately conditioned in the divine plan by the repentance of the Jewish nation? Does not Peter seem to directly teach that whenever Israel repents Christ will come? Is it not true, as Alford says, that by the expression under consideration, "is clearly meant some future refreshment which the conversion of the Jews was to bring about"? Most authorities are quite agreed in answering these queries in the affirmative. (A. M. O. Ha. Gl. Kel. Lum. How.)

Alford contends that this was not only the plain inference from prophecy but that doubtless Peter was so taught by his risen Lord, and that this holds true *even now*.

If it therefore be objected that the Jews by their nonconversion are holding back the Parousia, Alford replies that however true this may be in fact, the truth above is fully borne out by the manner of speaking throughout the Scriptures.

Says Olshausen, "The conversion of men therefore and the diffusion of faith in Christ are the conditions of the speedy approach of that blessed time, a thought which occurs again in II Pet. 3.9."

Ver. 20. *"may send"*,—Contemporaneous with the *"may come"* of the preceding verse.

"appointed",—i. e., from all eternity.

"for you",—i. e., as your Messiah.

Ver. 21. *"whom the heaven must receive"*,—This is the much more natural and usual rendering of the verb. (A. D. M. Le. B-C, Ha. Gl. Lum. Kui. Bez. Ern.) The other rendering which is made doubtless in the interests of Christ's ubiquity, "who must occupy heaven", is likewise supported by good scholars. (O. B. L. S. Hei. Ca. Lut. Wei.) But this rendering is not only a forced one but a very unusual one, there being only two or three instances of it and then it takes the meaning of "possessing as property". The emphatic position of *"heaven"* with the particle attached to it is quite decisive against this rendering, because, as Alford has said, "this particle in a sentence of the present form is always attached to the subject and never to the object".

"until the times of the restoration of all things",—We are inclined to think that the reference here is to the same epoch as the times of refreshing of verse 19. (A. D. O. Ha. Gl.)

Some render, "until the times of the *fulfillment* of all things *of which* God spake", etc. (S. Gro. Theo. Whitby.) But this is against all precedent. Some render *"during* the times of the restoration", etc., and explain the passage in the sense of the present spiritual restoration which is going on through the work of the Holy Spirit in the hearts of men today. But this is also without precedent altogether.

What then shall be restored? The following quotations from eminent scholars will furnish satisfactory answer to this question.

1. "All that God has spoken by the mouth of His holy prophets shall be restored and placed in its original order, and in that condition which God designed and promised." (Lechler.)

2. "It is a restoration to a state of primeval order, purity, holiness and happiness such as will exist for those who have part in the kingdom of Christ at His second coming." (Hackett.)

3. "I understand it of the glorious restoration of all things, the pallingenesia', which as Peter says here, is the theme of all the prophets from the beginning. The key to the construction and the meaning is to be found in our Lord's own words, *'Elijah shall come and restore all things'*. (Matt. 17.11)." (Alford.)

4. "There will be a moral restoration; the present disorders of this world will be removed; the good will finally triumph over evil; holiness and happiness will prevail throughout the world. The idea of the Apostle seems to be that so long as the unbelief of Israel continues, Christ will remain in heaven, but that their repentance and conversion will bring about the times of refreshing and the restoration of all things, which will either precede or coincide with the second coming." (Gloag.)

Meyer contends that this *"restoration of all things"* cannot be the same as *"the times of refreshing"*. He says the second coming of Christ does *not* take place before the *"restoration of all things"*, and that the *"age to come"*, which is the time after the second coming, is the same as *"the times of refreshing"*, and is therefore a different period of time than that of *"the restoration of all things"*.   The *"restoration of all things"*, he says, refers to only such time as shall precede the second coming of Christ.   Therefore it cannot refer to such restorations as are mentioned in the four views noted above, in as much as the restoration to which they refer coincides with or immediately follows the second coming of the Lord. "The correct explanation", says Meyer, "must start from Mal. 4.6 as the historical seat of the expression, and from Matt. 17.11 where Christ made it His own.   Christ stays in heaven until the moral corruption of the people of God is removed, and the thorough moral renovation of all their relations shall have ensued.   Then and then only is the exalted Christ sent from heaven to the people and then only does there come for them the times of refreshing from the presence of the Lord.   What an excitement neither to neglect nor to defer repentance and conversion as the means to this restoration of all things . . ."

"whereof",—This belongs to *"times"* and not to *"all things"*.

"from the beginning",—This is to be taken relatively; from the earliest times of prophetic revelation.

CHAPTER TEN

> 42 And he charged us to preach unto the people, and to testify that this is he who is ordained of God *to be* the Judge of the living and the dead.

Ver. 42.   CHRIST AS JUDGE OF THE QUICK AND THE DEAD.

"he",—i. e., the risen Christ.

"the people",—It was the Jewish people that Peter doubtless had in mind when he spoke, seeing that the context speaks of no other (verse 41).   (A. M. Ha. Gl.)   (See also verse 2.)

The reference must be to some unknown expression of the risen Christ other than that referred to in Matt. 28.29, seeing that their contents are so different.   Acts 1.8 may have been in the writer's mind, but even there the Disciples thought of the charge as referring to the Jews only.

"he",—The Greek has the intensive form, *"he, himself"*, i. e., he himself and no other.

"the living and the dead",—The reference here is of course to those physically alive and physically dead.   Olshausen has no ground for understanding here the righteous and the wicked, that is, those spiritually alive and those spiritually dead.   *There is a law of interpretation which should always be borne in mind, and that is that a figurative sense of words is never admissible except when required by the context.*

When is this judgment to take place?   At the time, of course, when He comes to judgment, at His second coming, His Parousia (M. A. Ha. Le. Gl.), whatever may be the view one holds with regard to the succession of events during that period.

There is nothing in this verse whatever to intimate a twofold resurrection and judgment of the dead, one of the righteous dead and a later one of the wicked dead, although it can be interpreted as quite in harmony with such teaching if it can be shown that the same is elsewhere taught in the Scriptures.

CHAPTER FOURTEEN

22 confirming the souls of the disciples, exhorting them to continue in the
faith, and that through many tribulations we must enter into the kingdom
of God.

Ver. 22. THE KINGDOM OF GOD ENTERED THROUGH TRIBULATION.

Blackstone quotes this verse as proof that the kingdom of God, the Messianic kingdom, the Millennium was still future in the day when Paul so exhorted the brethren.

Meyer says, "We Christians must, through many afflictions, enter into the Messianic kingdom, the kingdom of God, to be established at the Parousia."

Gloag likewise says that here the kingdom of God is the Messianic kingdom, but refers it to the state of the redeemed in heaven. He says, "As these converts had already entered the Church of Christ, and so were members of Christ's visible kingdom, 'the kingdom of God' here must refer to the state of the redeemed in heaven."

"The kingdom of God is here", says Hackett, "the state of happiness which awaits the redeemed in heaven." This expositor does not, however, identify the expression with the Messianic kingdom, as does Gloag. Thus also Howson, Lechler and others.

CHAPTER FIFTEEN

14 Symeon hath rehearsed how first God visited the Gentiles, to take out of them a people for his name. 15 And to this *agree* the words of the prophets; as it is written,
16 [1]After these things I will return,
And I will build again the tabernacle of David, which is fallen;
[1]Am. 9.11,12

And I will build again the ruins thereof,
And I will set it up:
17 That the residue of men may seek after the Lord,
And all the Gentiles, upon whom my name is called,
18 Saith the Lord, [2]who maketh these things known from of old.
[2]Or, *who doeth these things* which were *known &c.*

Vers. 14-18. THE RESTORATION OF THE KINGDOM OF DAVID AND THE CALLING OF THE GENTILES.

(See the exegesis on Amos 9.11,12.)

The royal house of David, which is here represented as a tabernacle fallen into ruin, had been weakened by the revolt of the Ten Tribes and reduced by repeated disasters. God promises to restore it and to make it flourish as in olden times and to make the Gentiles a part of the theocracy.

Whatever fulfillments of this prophecy may have taken place, they most certainly have been only very partial and its full accomplishment is to be received only in the Messiah.

This great passage has been most aptly called "the divine program of this age and the next", says Scofield. He says, "I must again call attention to the words 'take out', in verse 14. It is exactly what we see. Not the conversion of *all*, but the taking out of *some*. After this taking out, Christ 'will return', and then follows the conversion of the world."

THE EPISTLE OF PAUL TO THE

ROMANS

(A. D. 60)

CHAPTER EIGHT

16 The Spirit himself beareth witness with our spirit, that we are children of God: 17 and if children, then heirs; heirs of God, and joint-heirs with Christ; if so be that we suffer with *him*, that we may be also glorified with *him*.

18 For I reckon that the sufferings of this present time are not worthy to be compared with the glory which shall be revealed to us-ward. 19 For the earnest expectation of the creation waiteth for the revealing of the sons of God. 20 For the creation was subjected to vanity, not of its own will, but by reason of him who subjected it, [1]in hope

[1]Or, *in hope; because the creation &c.*

21 that the creation itself also shall be delivered from the bondage of corruption into the liberty of the glory of the children of God. 22 For we know that the whole creation groaneth and travaileth in pain [2]together until now. 23 And not only so, but ourselves also, who have the first-fruits of the Spirit, even we ourselves groan within ourselves, waiting for *our* adoption, *to wit*, the redemption of our body. 24 For [3]in hope were we saved: but hope that is seen is not hope: [4]for who [5]hopeth for that which he seeth? 25 But if we hope for that which we see not, *then* do we with [6]patience wait for it.

[2]Or, *with us*
[3]Or, *by*
[4]Many ancient authorities read *for what a man seeth,·why doth he yet hope for?*
[5]Some ancient authorities read *awaiteth.*
[6]Or, *stedfastness*

Vers. 16-25. THE WHOLE CREATION AWAITS THE COMING OF CHRIST.

Ver. 17. *"heirs of God"*,—The inheritance which God transfers to His children is the salvation and glory of the Messianic kingdom (M.), the kingdom of glory (R. L.). Says Lange, "As He Himself will be all in all, so shall His children receive with Him, in His Son, everything for an inheritance." After all, His heritage is Himself, and the best He can give His children is to dwell in them. ·

"joint heirs with Christ",—It is quite natural that Paul should have in mind here the Roman law which made all children, even adopted ones, equal heritors (R. A. M. Tho. Fri.), rather than the Hebrew law which gave the firstborn a double portion (L. Ph.), although the controversy, as Schmoller says, appears somewhat pedantic. It is not so much that Christ is the rightful heir, who shares His inheritance with the other children, but it is as adoptive children that we get the inheritance, Christ being the means of it, however, as it is He who gives us power to become the sons of God.

"if so be",—There is a latent admonition in this conditional form. It is the order, rather than the reason, for obtaining the inheritance that is here set forth. (C. R.) We enter into possession of the common inheritance of glory only by accepting our part of the common inheritance of suffering. If we suffer with Him we shall also reign with Him. (II Tim. 2.11,12.)

"that we may be",—This is God's purpose, not ours; in our case it is the result.

"also glorified with him",—i. e., when He comes in His glory our own glory shall then only become fully manifest, as we participate with Him in His own glory. Hodge says this refers to the blessedness of the future state.

Ver. 18. *"For"*,—This is not to be connected alone with *"glorified with Him"* (St.), but the rather with the whole of the preceding thought which culminates in verse 17. (R. L.) It introduces a reason why the present sufferings should not lead to discouragement.

"I reckon",—i. e., I judge after calculation. The thought is, I, myself, as one having embraced this course, am convinced, etc.

"not worthy",—The literal is "not of weight". The idea of our worthiness or of any merit of our own because of the sufferings we endure is foreign to the context, and perhaps the phrase may be better translated, "insignificant in comparison with".

"the glory which shall be revealed to us-ward",—i. e., at the apocalypsis of Christ (A.); at the end of the present time, when full redemption comes with the coming of the Lord (R.); at the Parousia, when the glory which is now hidden in heaven shall be revealed.

"This glory is to be revealed," says Godet, "and is therefore already in existence; it exists not only in the plan of God decreeing it to us, but also in the person of Christ glorified, with whose appearing it will be visibly displayed."

"this present time",—Meyer says this expression marks off from the whole of *"this age" the period then current*, which was to end with the approaching Parousia, assumed as near throughout the entire New Testament, and was thus the time of the crisis. The expression, however, does not necessarily indicate that the Parousia was, to the Apostle's mind, near at hand. It may imply this, but the evidence for or against the view must be sought elsewhere.

"to us-ward",—The preposition is not "en" (A-V.), but "eis", and the idea expressed is a very pregnant one. It does not mean merely "to us" as spectators, but "on us" and "for us" and "in us". We are, as Riddle says, "its subjects, its possessors and its center, for even creation shares in it".

"The glory", says Godet, "will not consist only in our own transformation, but also in the coming of the Lord Himself, and the transformation of the universe. Thus it will be displayed at once *for* us and *in* us."

Lange says, "If it is imparted through the inward life of believers and through nature, it nevertheless comes from the future and from above."

Ver. 19. *"For"*,—This particle here introduces not a proof of the certainty of the manifestation of this glory, though this secondary thought is perhaps in the background, but it presents the proof of the transcendent greatness of the glory mentioned.

"the earnest expectation",—This translation comes from one of those admirable words with which the Greek language so fully abounds and which it so easily forms. It is composed of three elements; *"the head"*, *"to wait for"* and the preposition *"from afar"*, and hence it means "to wait with uplifted head looking toward the horizon from which the

expected object is to come". "An artist", says Godet, "might make a statue of hope out of this Greek term."

"creation",—Here Campbell Morgan says, "For His coming, not only the Church, but the whole creation, waits. Today the sons of God, as such, are unknown, or despised and persecuted; but when the Master comes, they will be revealed with Him—and it is for this consummation that the earth is waiting."

There is an astonishing variety of answers given to the question as to what the word *"creation"* refers to. The word in itself means the totality of created things, but it very often takes a more restricted meaning according to the context. Among the various interpretations are the following:

1. All inanimate creation. (C. Ar. Fri. Chr. Bez. Lut. Theo. Schm.) But there is no sufficient reason why animal creation should be excluded; and furthermore, the expressions *"not of its own will"* (verse 20), and *"groaneth and travaileth"* (verse 22) imply life.

2. The entire universe without any limitation. But believers ought here to be excluded from the expression because in verse 23 they are mentioned as forming a class by themselves.

3. The entire universe excluding believers. (R.) But unbelievers ought also to be excluded, for (1) either they will be converted before the expected time, and will in that case be found among the children of God, or (2) if they are not then converted, they will not participate, even indirectly, in the glory in question.

4. The totality of created things except humanity. This is, in view of all the statements of the context, without doubt the correct interpretation. (A. M. G. D. H. B. Ru. Ca. Ew. Um. Ph. Es. Us. Le. Nea. Tho. Wol. Gro. Ire. Mel. Lap. Coc. Mai. Bis. Del. Nie. Hof. Zah. Reic. Gloe.)

"waiteth",—Here is another splendid combination of words, being formed from the verb "to receive", and two prepositions, "ek" (out of, i. e., here, out of the hands of), and "απο" (from afar), the whole meaning "to receive something from the hands of one who extends it to you from afar".

"the revealing of the sons of God",—Says Hodge, "The time when they shall be manifested in their true character and glory as His sons. *'Beloved, now are we the sons of God; and it doth not yet appear what we shall be: but we know that when He shall appear we shall be like Him'* (I John 3.2)."

Says Riddle, "The final revelation of Christ's glory is here spoken of as that *'of the sons of God'*, and in this glory creation shall share."

The expression is explained, says Godet, by Col. 3.4, *"When Christ, our life, shall be manifested, then ye also shall be manifested with Him in glory"*.

This is what our Lord calls the coming of the Son of man, and it is only the deep-seated consciousness of fellowship with Him that leads the Apostle to use the expression *"sons of God"*. With the coming of Christ the glory of creation will find its full expression; then it will be manifested in its full glory.

Ver. 20.   It was God who, in consequence of the fall of man, subjected creation to vanity, i. e., it became empty, as the word signifies; lost its original significance, and became a prey to corruption.

"in hope",—The subjection of creation, however, was not final and hopeless.   Some consider the previous part of this verse as parenthetical and join *"in hope"* with verse 19.   This is permissible and has much to commend it, but it cannot be insisted upon, and it is better to make the connection, as in our text, with *"was subjected"*, rather than with "who subjected it", though the sense in either case would be the same.

Of course God was not the moral cause of the curse on nature.   This belongs either to man or to Satan.   This has led some (Tho. Chr. Schn.) to refer the *"him who subjected it"* to Adam, while Hammond has referred it to Satan himself.   Godet, who rejects the idea of God as the author here, inclines to the view of Hammond, though not pronouncedly so.   He says the expression, *"by reason of him"*, with "dia" as the preposition makes the agent, whoever he may be, the moral cause of the curse, and this he says of course is not true of God, who is but the efficient cause of the curse. He thinks that if the Apostle had meant Adam, or man, he could have avoided the strange mysteriousness of the passage by simply saying, "by reason of the man".   Then too he thinks *"he who subjected"* applies hardly as well to man, who, in this event, so far as nature is concerned, played a purely passive part.

"in hope" could, of course, only be referred to *"who subjected it"* in case the subject of this clause is God.   Godet therefore refers the expression to *"was subjected"*, and says it signifies that from the first, when this chastisement was inflicted, it was only with a future restoration in view.

Alford says this view hardly needs refutation, as it is entirely unsubstantial.   He says *"in hope"* must not be connected with *"who subjected it"* (C. O. Es. Ori. Vul. Lut. Pis. Schm. Cast.), because then the hope becomes the hope of the one who subjected nature to its curse; but with *"was subjected"* (R. G. L.), the hope belonging to that which was subjected.

The sense, however, in the ultimate, as Hodge says, amounts to the same thing.

Ver. 21.   *"the bondage of corruption"*,—i. e., its subjection to the law of decay; the state of frailty and degradation mentioned above.

Meyer, Riddle, Tholuck and others take the word *"corruption"* as in apposition to *"bondage"*.   Lange and Godet object to this, but without good reason, as this sense preserves the proper distinctions.   As Riddle says, "The *corruption* is the consequence of the *vanity*; the unwilling subjection to a condition which is *under vanity*, and results in *corruption*, is well termed *bondage*."

"into the liberty of the glory",—Not to be rendered "glorious liberty", by which the "glorious" is merely an epithet whereby the liberty is characterized; but, as in our text, the freedom is described, as Alford says, as consisting in, belonging to, being one component part of, the glorified state of the children of God; and thus the thought is carried up to the state in which the freedom belongs.

The creation itself shall in a glorious sense be delivered into that freedom from debility and decay in which the children of God, when raised up in glory, shall expatiate. (C. B. D. O. H. A. M. Ph. Tho. Bez.)

The glory, says Riddle, is that which is spoken of in verse 18; it will appear at the revelation of the sons of God.

Ver. 22.   This verse introduces the proof, not of *"the bondage of corruption"* (Zah.), nor of *"the earnest expectation of creation"* (Ph.), which is much too distant, but of the existence of the hope, "For", as Meyer says, "if that hope had not been left to it, all nature would *not* have united its groaning and travailing *until now."* He further says, "This phenomenon, so universal and so unbroken, cannot be conducted without an aim; on the contrary it presupposes as the motive of the painful travail that very hope toward the final fulfillment of which it is directed." (M. R.)   The connection thus goes back to either *"in hope"* of verse 20 or to the hope as expressed in verse 21. (G).

"we know",—This is an appeal to the Christian consciousness.

"together",—The marginal rendering, "with us", (C. Ew. Um. Kop. Oec.) can hardly be allowed.   The word comes from the preposition *"with"* used in connection with each of the verbs, and verse 23 seems decisive against the marginal rendering.   It denotes rather the common sighing of all the elements, comprised in the collective expression *"the whole creation"*.   (M. A. R. L. G. H.)   "All its parts uniting and sympathizing."   (H.)

"travaileth in pain",—"All nature groans and suffers anguish, as if in travail, over against the moment of its deliverance."   As the poet says, *"She feels in her womb the leaping of a new universe."*

"until now",—i. e., from the beginning until now, no reference being made to the future, because *"we know"* expresses the results of experience.   (A. R. M. H.)   The sighing and travail commenced when creation was subjected to vanity (verse 20.)

Says Campbell Morgan, "Creation is to be freed from its groaning and travailing in pain; the blight upon nature will be removed, and a perfect manifestation of its beauty will take the place of all it now suffers in company with fallen humanity."

Ver. 23.   *"And not only so"*,—Not only is it true that the whole creation groaneth, etc.

"the first fruits of the Spirit",—

(1) The first outpourings of the Spirit in point of time, the early Christians being the recipients; the full harvest of which will be the impartation of the Spirit to all believers. (M. D. O. Era. Wet. Kos. Kol. Reic.)

Some among those who take this view restrict these firstfruits to the Apostles alone.   (Ori. Gro. Oec. Mel.)

But Godet asks what importance this difference can have for the spiritual life, and where is a trace of such distinction to be found in the New Testament.

(2) What all Christians now possess is but the first fruits; the harvest will be the full outpouring of the future, i. e., what we shall receive hereafter.   (R. H. A. C. St. Es. Ca. Ph. Fl. Sem. Tho. Bez. Bis. Chr.)

Says Alford, "The reference is to the indwelling and influences of the Holy Spirit *here,* as an earnest of the full harvest of His complete possession of us, body, soul and spirit, hereafter. That this is the meaning seems evident from the analogy of St. Paul's imagery regarding the Holy Spirit: He treats Him as an earnest and a pledge given to us, and of His full work in us as the efficient means of our full glorification hereafter."

Godet says, however, that the Apostle is not here contrasting an imperfect with a more perfect spiritual state; he is contrasting an *inward* state already relatively perfect with an *outward* state which has not yet participated in the spiritual renewal.

The reference, however, to the full glorification at the close of the verse strongly favors this second view.

(3) Others again, including Godet, say that the firstfruits of our redemption consists in the possession of the Holy Spirit Himself. (G. B. K. L. B-C. Ru. Hof. Mai. Zah.) This places the word *"Spirit"* in apposition to *"firstfruits".* Although usage is against this, Lange and Godet argue strongly in its favor. Either view (2) or (3) is to be preferred, and as between them the balance is in favor of (2).

"groan within ourselves",—We, although we have the firstfruits, are far from being complete.

"waiting for our adoption",—We are already adopted children, but the outward condition corresponding to this new relation is not yet complete. This, says Meyer, must wait upon the Parousia, whereupon the *"revelation of the sons of God"* and their *"glory"* ensues.

"the redemption of our body",—Redemption *from* the body (Ew. Era. Fri. Cle. Reic.), although linguistically admissible, is altogether incorrect, for the whole thought of this chapter pertains not to freedom from the body but to the glorification of the body at the coming of Christ.

At the moment of this redemption, says Meyer, the body shall be freed from all the defects of its earthly condition; through which redemption it shall be glorified into the incorruptible body similar to the glorified body of Christ, or shall be raised up as such, in case of our not surviving the Parousia.

Says Hodge, "The time of the resurrection of the body, or the manifestation of the sons of God, is the time of the second advent of Jesus Christ. (See I Cor. 15.23; I Thess. 4.16.) This is the period toward which all eyes and all hearts have been directed, among those who have had the firstfruits of the Spirit, since the fall of Adam; and for which the whole creation groaneth and is in travail even until now."

Ver. 24. *"For in hope we were saved",*—We must not with some authorities identify hope and faith and find here the idea of salvation by faith, as is implied in the marginal reading of our text. Paul always distinguishes faith and hope (I Cor. 13.13), and he always bases salvation on faith, from which hope thereupon proceeds. The fact of salvation places us in a condition of which hope is a characteristic. Luther finely says, "We are indeed saved, yet in hope." *"In hope"* does not express the means by which the thing is done, but the condition or circumstance in which it is, or the way and manner in which it occurs.

"hope that is seen is not hope",—Says Riddle, "By these self-evident statements about hope, the Apostle leads his readers up to the thought of

verse 25, which is both an encouragement and an exhortation. In the words, *"hope that is seen"*, the term *hope* is taken for the object hoped for, while in the words following, *hope* resumes its subjective meaning. Hence the meaning of the last two propositions of the verse is quite clear and self-evident.

"for who hopeth for that which he seeth?"—The thought here is, "Who hopeth *at all* for that which he seeth?", while that of the margin is, "Why doth a man still hope for that which he seeth?" The marginal rendering seems the better established by manuscript authority and is preferable only for that reason, the meaning being quite the same, "Why doth he still (yet) hope, when there is no more ground or reason for it?" (M. L. R. G. H.)

Ver. 25. *"then do we with patience wait for it"*,—The idea is that of steadfastness, which includes patience as its consequence. The hope which the Christian has furnishes one strong motive for his patient endurance of the sufferings of this present time. Because he hopes for a glory yet to be revealed at the coming of the Lord, he perseveringly waits for it.

CHAPTER NINE

27 And Isaiah crieth concerning Israel, [1]If the number of the children of Israel be as the sand of the sea, it is the remnant that shall be saved: 28 for the Lord will execute *his* word upon the earth, finishing it and cutting it short.

[1]Is. 10.22 f.

29 And, as Isaiah hath said before, [2]Except the Lord of Sabaoth had left us a seed, We had become as Sodom, and had been made like unto Gomorrah.

[2]Is. 1.9

Vers. 27-29. THE ELECT REMNANT OF ISRAEL.

Ver. 27. The words spoken by Isaiah of the return from captivity of a remnant of Israel. Hosea in verse 25 speaks of the Gentile unbelievers, but Isaiah is speaking of the rejection of Israel except the believing remnant.

"crieth",—The word represents the impassioned manner of Isaiah, and sets forth the bold declaration of a truth very offensive to the people.

"the remnant",—The article *"the"* before the word *"remnant"* shows that it is a thing known. Indeed one of the most frequent notions of Isaiah is that of the holy remnant which survives all chastisements of Israel and which, coming forth from the crucible, becomes each time the germ of a better future.

"shall be saved",—The Hebrew word is "shall return", that is, from captivity; but Paul applies the phrase in its fullest sense, taking the Septuagint translation which, of course, was used in a more restricted sense. The thought of the verse is that however numerous the people of Israel might be, only a remnant of them are to be saved. (O. H. G. L. M. A. R.) These authorities all reject the view of Hofmann and others who insist that the meaning is that this remnant will certainly *subsist;* but this, as Godet well remarks, is not the question at all.

Hofmann makes the passage mean that the whole of the people of Israel which return, be they ever so numerous even like the sands of the sea, is called a remnant, because they have come out of a severe time of distress, and that Paul rightly understood that the remnant which obtains salvation is one with the people which is as numerous as the sands of the sea.

But this is utterly inconsistent with both the original Hebrew and the idea which the Septuagint plainly had in mind when they made their translation; and the fact that Paul follows the Septuagint is likewise against this view of Hofmann's.

Ver. 28.   This verse explains the idea of the saved remnant.   The judgment, says Isaiah, will be a sudden and a summary execution which will fall not upon this or that individual but upon the whole nation.

The literal Hebrew of Isaiah is, "Extirpation is decided, overfloweth with righteousness; for extirpation and decree shall the Lord of Hosts make in all the land."

The Septuagint translation runs, "The Lord fulfills the sentence; He cuts short righteously (in righteousness), because He makes a rapidly accomplished word (utterance) upon all the earth."

"word",—This is a good translation, although "utterance" (M. A. R.) is better still.

Godet renders it "reckoning", but this in connection with the Greek word used would be contrary to idiom.

Others render "matter of fact".   (Bez. Mel. Kop. Cast.)   But this it never denotes with Paul.

Calvin, with the Authorized Version, translates, "work", but this also is a signification which it never has.

Olshausen, and perhaps the majority, take it in the sense of decree. But the Greek word never means this, although this idea doubtless underlies the passage and is found in the Hebrew.

"cut short",—Referring to the rapid accomplishment of what the Lord had said.

"in righteousness",—This refers to the judicial justice of God which punishes in order to save the remnant.   The former thought is the prominent one, as is to be inferred both from the context and from the original. The sense of the whole verse then is, "He (the Lord) is finishing and cutting short the utterance (making it a fact by rapid accomplishment) in righteousness; for a cut-short utterance (one rapidly accomplished) will the Lord make (execute, render actual) upon the earth."

The Septuagint, we feel, has preserved most fully the thought of the original Hebrew, in fact conveying it to the mind of a reader familiar with the Greek more clearly than could have been done by a literal rendering of the Hebrew.   It is a fact, however, that the Septuagint is a faulty translation of the Hebrew, and because Paul quoted from the Septuagint, Meyer and others say he endorsed an incorrect rendering of the word of God. But the only fair way to handle such a proposition is to think that Paul quoted wittingly, because he felt that the Septuagint conveyed his own meaning in simple and more emphatic form, the meaning in either case being the same.

Some interpret the whole of God's mercy, of His cutting short judgment.   But this gives to righteousness the sense of mercy, and it is foreign to the Hebrew and inappropriate here where Paul is emphasizing the fact that only a remnant will be saved.

"The main purport of the verse", says Moule, "is clear: the prophet foretells severe and summary judgments upon Israel such as to leave ere long only a remnant able and willing to return."

419

Ver. 29. *"left us a seed"*,—The rescued Israelites are in Isaiah called *"a holy seed"* (Isa. 6.13), because out of them, as a small beginning, the nation shall rejuvenate itself and the true spiritual Israel shall proceed. The Hebrew has "remnant", but Paul follows the Septuagint, the sense being precisely the same. The Hebrew word means "that which remains", and the word *"seed"* as used in this passage means the seed reserved for sowing. The meaning of this saying is that without quite a peculiar exercise of grace on the part of the Lord, the destruction as announced in verses 27 and 28 would have been more radical still, as radical as that which overtook the cities of the plain.

"before",—Some explain this word by the circumstance that in the book of Isaiah this passage occurs before that which has just been quoted in verses 27 and 28.

Others (A. C. Gro. Bez. Era.) refer the *"before"* to a preceding part of the book of Isaiah; but this is opposed by others (M. R. D. G. Mi. B-C. Tho.) as quite puerile. The word is used merely in the sense of a prediction and refers to the time of Isaiah as prior to that of the Apostle who is here recording what Isaiah had before (in other days) prophesied.

CHAPTER ELEVEN

5 Even so at this present time also there is a remnant according to the election of grace.

11 I say then, Did they stumble that they might fall? God forbid: but by their ¹fall salvation is come unto the Gentiles, to provoke them to jealousy. 12 Now if their fall is the riches of the world, and their loss the riches of the Gentiles; how much more their ful-

¹Or, *trespass* Comp. Chap. 5.15 ff.

ness? 13 But I speak to you that are Gentiles. Inasmuch then as I am an apostle of Gentiles, I glorify my ministry; 14 if by any means I may provoke to jealousy *them that are* my flesh, and may save some of them. 15 For if the casting away of them *is* the reconciling of the world, what *shall* the receiving *of them be*, but life from the dead?

Vers. 5,11-15. THE ELECT REMNANT OF ISRAEL ACCORDING TO GRACE.

Ver. 5. *"a remnant according to the election of grace"*,—This refers to the apparently insignificant number of believing Jews whom God's grace has chosen out of the totality of the people. As God reserved to Himself in the days of Elijah a number, larger than the prophet believed it to be, even so now He hath graciously chosen a number, a remnant according to the election of grace. May it not be that this number is larger than is generally supposed? The Apostle James speaks of myriads of believing Jews. (Acts 21.20.)

Still, it is small comparatively, and it became more and more so as the distinctive character of the New Testament teaching came out and the nearer the last crisis of the old order approached. The election refers not so much to such and such individuals but to the remnant in its entirety.

"at this present time",—The time of Israel's national rejection.

Ver. 11. *"I say then"*,—This introduces a possible but a false conclusion from verse 7 and implies a negative answer.

"Did they stumble that they might fall?"—The first verb expresses

420

a shock against an obstacle while the second expresses the fall which follows it, the first being a figure for the taking offense at Christ and the second for being involved in everlasting destruction.

The only possible correct view of the meaning of these words is, Did they stumble in order that they might lie prostrate, plunged into perdition? Was their stumbling permitted by God with a view to the fall? Was their stumbling designed to be a permanent casting them out of the kingdom of Christ? No, says Paul.

This view is substantiated by the whole subsequent discussion in which it shows that the Jews as a nation are to be saved. The stumbling of the Jews was not attended with the result of their utter and final ruin but was the occasion of the bringing of the Gospel to the Gentiles. It was therefore not designed to lead to the former but to the latter result. God had a double purpose—to open the gateway of salvation to the Gentiles and to provoke the Jewish nation to jealousy and thus to finally save them. (G. R. A. M. L. H.) The primary purpose, however, if one must distinguish, was not the final salvation of the Jews, but the rather the gathering in of the Gentiles, which was occasioned by the stumbling of the Jews.

"they",—The hardened ones of verse 7 gives us the nearest subject for this word, and the fact that the verbs are plural is in favor of so taking it, but we quite agree with Alford and Meyer that the fact that the nation as a whole is the general subject throughout the chapter ought to incline us to so taking it here, and the more especially since the pronoun of the following verse favors this interpretation.

"by their fall",—While the word "fall" suggests a reference to the previous word "fall", its reference here is more properly to the idea contained in the word "stumble" previously used, it being intended to mark a temporary and not a final false step or falling. (R. A. M. H. Vul.)

Riddle aptly remarks, "The word 'fall' here must be taken as a less strong expression than the verb which precedes it if the view be adopted which denies the fact of a final fall. We must then hold that the national fall into utter ruin is denied throughout, while the stumbling and the moral fall of the individuals is admitted."

"salvation is come",—This was the historical fact and this fact had as its purpose the provoking of the Jews to jealousy.

"jealousy",—"emulation" is a better word.

Ver. 12. "Now if",—The "if" is logical, not conditional.

"riches of the world",—Enriched through the Gospel preached unto it: so also with the Gentiles.

"loss",—The fundamental meaning of this word is, to be in a state of inferiority, to fall below a normal state, and it may be applied qualitatively or numerically.

In the qualitative sense the meaning would be, "The moral degradation of Israel has become the cause of enriching the Gentiles." This, however, is not only repugnant, but it would require the word "fulness" to be taken also in a qualitative sense, i. e., their perfect spiritual state, but this in view of verse 25 is impossible because there the idea is that of the totality of the Gentile nations.

We must therefore accept the numerical meaning and the better translation is "diminishing", i. e., their diminishing to a small number of believers. (G. M. R. L. Mo. Tho.)

"fulness",—This word must accordingly be conceived of as meaning the restoration of the Jewish nation to the complete state of a people, the totality of the living members of the people of Israel at the time the Apostle holds in his mind.

This word is here used in the sense of that with which a thing is filled and in its application here we must regard the abstract notion of a people as the empty frame to be filled, and the totality of the individuals in whom this notion is realized as that which fills the frame.

Riddle says aptly, "If the diminution of Israel through unbelief has had such a blessed result, how much more their full number when they as a nation become believers; in other words, if the rejection of the Jews has been the occasion of so much good to the world, how much more may be expected from their restoration."

There are some who apply the word "loss" or "diminution" to the believing Jews, by which reference the meaning would be, "If so small a number of believing Jews has done so much good to the world, how much more will the conversion of the entire nation do?" (D. B. O. B-C. Es. Chr. Era. Bez. Wet. Reic. Theo. Bucer.) But it was the loss of the unbelieving Jews that brought this good to the world about. Paul does not say that the conversion of a few Jews has been the occasion of good to the Gentiles, but the rejection of the nation had. Besides the pronoun *"their"* excludes this view, because in the three propositions it can only apply to the same subject, the Jewish people in general.

Meyer well remarks, "Through the fact that a part of the Jews was unbelieving the people suffered an overthrow, like a vanquished army, being weakened in numbers, inasmuch, namely, as the unbelieving portion by its unbelief practically seceded from the people of God." Their diminution came because of their sin, and the argument in a nutshell is, "If their sin had done so much, how much more their conversion?"

Ver. 13. *"Gentiles"*,—i. e., Gentile Christians who no doubt preponderated in the congregation at Rome.

"glorify my ministry",—This does not mean to praise his office (Gro. Lut. Reic.), but, "I strive to honor my office by its faithful discharge in striving for the conversion and edification at all times of the Gentiles." (D. M. R. L. A.)

Alford says that this verse gives answer to the question, "Why make it appear as if the treatment of God's chosen people was regulated, not by a consideration of them, but of the less favored Gentiles?" But it is quite unlikely that the Gentiles would raise such a question.

Godet finds in this verse a proof that the Apostle was laboring for the ultimate benefit of the Gentiles by seeking the conversion of the Jews, since the latter would result in life from the dead, etc.

Riddle thinks the verse is meant to meet a thought that might arise in the minds of the Gentiles, namely, that his ministry as the Apostle to the Gentiles had no reference to the Jews, and consequently he shows that the blessed results to the Jews formed a part of the purpose of his labors. To us the view of Riddle seems by far the more preferable. With it agree both Meyer and Lange.

Ver. 14. The reason why Paul desired the conversion of the Gentiles, but of course only one of the many reasons. Since the salvation of both classes was intimately related there was no occasion for ill feeling on the part of either.

"As, however, Paul says, *'may save some of them'*, it is clearly a mistake to suppose that the Apostle continued, at the date of the Epistle to the Romans, to imagine our Lord's second coming to be as near as he had thought when he wrote to the Thessalonians. For, as appears from verse 25, he expected the conversion of all Israel at the advent; consequently, if he had still regarded this as so near, he would have chosen some more comprehensive expression instead of *'some'*. It might indeed be said that Paul left the conversion of the mass of the Jews to the Twelve, and Himself only hoped to convert some Jews incidentally to his proper work. And if so, no conclusion could be drawn from this passage as to Paul's views respecting the nearness of Christ's coming. Still, the Epistle to the Romans gives the impression that Paul no longer considered the second coming so near." (Olshausen.)

Ver. 15. *"For"*,—This introduces the reason for verses 13 and 14.

"the casting away of them",—Analogous to but not quite identical with the *"loss"* or *"diminishing"* of verse 12. The Jewish nation was, as Paul here asserts, by reason of its rejection of Christ, under temporary exclusion.

"the receiving of them",—Referring to their reception to and participation in salvation by their conversion.

"life from the dead",—There is no doubt that Paul had here in mind something beyond "the reconciliation of the world", some greater blessing than the gradual conversion of the Gentiles through the Gospel, and this, whatever it was, he terms, *"life from the dead"*.

There are two views as to the meaning.

1. The literal resurrection which, it is said, is to follow the conversion of the Jews. (M. D. Ru. To. Hof. Era. Ori. The. Chr. Sem. Fri. Bey, Nie. Theo. Gloe. Reic.) Meyer says, "It is the blessed resurrection life which will set in with the Parousia. (I Thess. 4.14-17.)

But there are serious objections to this view, as follows:

   (a) The lack of evidence in the Bible that the literal resurrection will immediately follow the conversion of the Jews.

   (b) *"Life"* has often a wider signification than *"resurrection"*, and why did Paul not use the word *"resurrection"* if he had a literal resurrection in mind?

   (c) Why did he not use the article "the" before the word *"life"*, which he doubtless would have done if he had meant to refer to an event to which he so often refers elsewhere.

   (d) Paul has in view a blessing to the Gentiles through the Jews and a literal resurrection or even the resurrection life would be in no way peculiar to the Gentiles.

(e) There is a causative connection just as in the previous clause, but how could this be if *"life"* meant literal resurrection?

(f) Paul does not say the second event will follow closely upon the first, but he goes the length of identifying the two facts of which he speaks,—*"What shall the reception be but a life"*, etc.

2. It is evident therefore from the above reasons that the expression must be applied to a powerful spiritual revival which will be wrought in the heart of Gentile Christendom by the fact of the conversion of the Jews. (R. B. C. G. Mo. Le. B-C. Ca. Ph. Aug. Mel. Bez. Cra. Boe. Mai. Car. Theo. Bucer.) Philippi says it is "at once the extensive diffusion of the kingdom of God and a subjective revivification of Christendom which had become largely dead".

There are far less objections to the spiritual view than to the literal one.

To combine the two views seems improper (A. L. O. Um. Ew.), viz., "the final completion of all history down to and including the literal resurrection" (Ew.), "a spiritual resurrection which is succeeded by the bodily resurrection" (L), or which takes place in the bodily resurrection (O.). Some take the expression metaphorically, "the highest joy" (H. Kol. Kop. Ham. Oec. Gro.); "a joy like that of the resurrection" (St.). But this is a toning down of the words hardly warranted.

Some apply the phrase to the blessedness of Gentile Christendom in consequence of the conversion of the Jews (G.), while others limit it to the Jews themselves (Fl. Tho. Bez. Theo. Hengle), but we prefer the wider reference to the entire body of believers, although there is much to be said in favor of the first application.

Auberlen says, "A new life in the higher charismatic fullness of the Spirit shall extend from God's people to the nations of the world, compared with which the previous life of the nations must be considered dead."

Godet says, "We are little affected by the objection of Meyer, who says that according to Saint Paul the last times will be times of tribulation, those of the Antichrist, and not a time of spiritual prosperity. We do not know how the Apostle conceived the events. It seems to us, however, that according to the Apocalypse, the conversion of the Jews must precede the coming of the Antichrist and consequently also precede the coming of Christ."

> 25 For I would not, brethren, have you ignorant of this mystery, lest ye be wise in your own conceits, that a hardening in part hath befallen Israel, until the fulness of the Gentiles be come in; 26 and so all Israel shall be saved.

Vers. 25, 26. ALL ISRAEL YET TO BE SAVED.

Ver. 25. *"For"*,—Paul is saying in the use of this particle that he does not rest this announcement that the Jews shall be grafted in again on mere hope or probability, but that he has a direct revelation from the Holy Spirit as to the matter, which decisive proof is to be found in the prophetic announcement not to be made.

"mystery",—A thing undiscovered by men themselves and which

is made known to them by revelation from God. Paul seems to be assuming that the contents of this mystery were as yet unknown to his readers. (R. A. M. H. Mo.)

"lest ye be wise in your own conceits",—They should not hold for truth their own views on the expulsion of the Israelitish people, taking credit for wisdom superior to the Jews in having acknowledged and accepted Christ, and therefore dismissing the subject, careless whether there were or were not any future mercy for Israel in the divine plan.

"that a hardening in part hath befallen Israel",—The word *"hardening"* is used instead of *"hardness"* because it is a process rather than a state that is indicated. The word *"that"* introduces the content of the mystery which extends to the word *"saved"* in verse 26.

"in part",—This may be taken extensively (M.), or it may be taken intensively, as our text seems to take it. Meyer would join the word to the verb, *"hath befallen"*, whereas if taken intensively it should be joined preferably to *"hardening"*, but in neither case to *"Israel"* (Es. Sem. Kop. Fri.). It seems better to take the expression intensively, inasmuch as the *whole* nation became unbelieving, and not a part of it. It is intended to soften the severity of the notion which Paul graciously calls to their attention.

"until the fulness",—Most commentators agree in referring this phrase to the totality of the Gentiles, to the nation as a whole, although some refer it to the complement from the Gentiles which is to take the place of the rejected Jews (O. Mi. Ph. Wol.); but this seems unnatural.

The expression is to be taken numerically, not that every individual shall be saved but that the nation as a whole shall be.

Meyer says this is before the Parousia and not by means of it.

Ver. 26. *"all Israel"*,—This does not mean the great majority (Ru. Tho. Fri. Wet. Oec.), nor does it mean all the true people of God. (C. Gro. Lut. Aug. The.), nor yet "all the elect Jews"; all that part of the nation which constitutes the remnant according to the election of grace (O. B. Ca.), but it refers to the nation as a whole. (H. A. M.)

Says W. J. Erdman, "This *'all Israel'* or sum total of the believing nation is called in a previous message *'their fulness'* and the argument is that when Israel is converted the whole Gentile world also will be converted."

CHAPTER THIRTEEN

11 And this, knowing the season, that already it is time for you to awake out of sleep: for now is [1]salvation nearer to us than when we *first* believeth. 12

[1]Or, *our salvation nearer than when &c.*

The night is far spent, and the day is at hand: let us therefore cast off the works of darkness, and let us put on the armor of light.

Vers. 11,12. THE COMING OF THE LORD DRAWING NEAR.

Ver. 11. *"And this"*,—i. e., "let us do this", namely, live in no debt but that of love (verse 8), and that for other reasons, but especially for the following one. (H. A. M. R. B. Ph. Tho.)

Because of the remoteness of verse 8 and the fact that there is no special connection between it (the duty of justice) and what follows in this verse before us, Godet and Moule make the expression refer to all the foregoing precepts enumerated in Chapters 12 and 13. The former explanation, however, is to be preferred.

"knowing the season",—The word is "kairos", which does not mean time in general, but a portion of time considered as an appropriate period of time; the reference being therefore to the general character of the time.

"sleep",—The state of worldly carelessness and indifference to sin.

"for now is salvation nearer to us",—The reference is to the Messianic salvation in its completion as introduced by the Parousia. (M. A. G. R. L. O. D. Mo. Ph. Tho., and nearly all German commentators.) It does not therefore refer to deliverance by death (Pho.), nor to the Destruction of Jerusalem, a fortunate event for Christianity (Mi.), nor to the preaching among the Gentiles (Mel.), nor to "the inner spiritual salvation of Christianity (Ca. Fl. Mor. Schr.).

Riddle says, *"It is difficult for an unlettered believer to read the New Testament and not find this expectation of the second coming, while even the most learned now find it."*

Stuart, Hodge and others, on the other hand, understand the verse as the consummation of salvation in eternity—deliverance from this present evil world. They object to the reference to the second coming of Christ, and Stuart is shocked at it as being inconsistent with the inspiration of Paul's writings.

"But," says Alford, "because Paul in II Thess. 2 corrects the mistake of imagining it to be just at hand or even already actually come is no sign that he did not expect it soon." Alford says that to argue this is quite beside the purpose. On the certainty of the event, he says, our faith is grounded; by the uncertainty of the time our hope is stimulated and our watchfulness is aroused.

"than when we believed",—When we were brought into the faith.

Ver. 12. *"the night"*,—The time before the Parousia, which ceases when the Parousia ushers in the day. Night and day are therefore figures for *"this age"* and *"the age to come"*.

Most all of the more recent commentators now, in keeping with all the most ancient commentators, admit that the reference is not to the approach of the end of the earthly life, but that it without doubt refers to the Parousia.

CHAPTER SIXTEEN

20 And the God of peace shall bruise
Satan under your feet shortly.

Ver. 20. GOD'S SUMMARY DEALING WITH THE EVIL ONE.

This is a similitude from Genesis 3.15. There is not here the expression of a wish, but it is a prophetic assurance and encouragement in bearing up against all adversities, that the great Adversary himself would shortly be bruised under their feet.

"God of peace",—This is said with a reference to the division and strife caused by those mentioned in verse 17.

"bruise under your feet",—This refers to the triumph over error, sin and death and final deliverance from all trial of each of His followers, and

is to be interpreted in keeping with that interpretation of the word *"shortly"* which sees in it not necessarily any reference to the time of the Parousia.

"shortly",—It is maintained, and rightly, by most authorities that there is here not necessarily implied any reference to the return of Christ. The expression for *"shortly"* is usually translated by "soon", which would signify "at a time near when I write you". It is because of this that Schultz and many others find here the idea of Christ's near return. But the word here is "tachus" (shortly) and this word and its derivatives do not denote imminence, nearness of the event. They denote rather the swiftness with which the event is accomplished. The Greek word "euthus" denotes imminence. "We think also that it is wrong to translate Rev. 22.20, *'I come soon* (my arrival is near)'; the meaning is rather, 'I come quickly', that is to say, 'I move rapidly even though my arrival may be yet a great way off'. Paul means therefore that the victory will be speedily gained when once the conflict is begun, and not that the victory itself is near". (Godet.)

Meyer explains, "When the authors of division appear among you".

Shedd refers it to the preservation from the fatal errors that soon assailed Christianity.

Riddle says the word for *"shortly"* is usually taken in the sense of "soon", no matter to what the reference of the passage is applied.

Moule says, "In the eternal day so near at hand (Chap. 13.11,12) when all enemies shall be made the footstool of the Messiah and of His saints through Him".

THE FIRST EPISTLE OF PAUL TO THE

CORINTHIANS

(A. D. 59)

CHAPTER ONE

> 7 so that ye come behind in no gift, waiting for the revelation of our Lord Jesus Christ; 8 who shall also confirm you unto the end, that ye be unreprovable in the day of our Lord Jesus Christ.

Vers. 7,8. WAITING THE COMING OF CHRIST AN EVIDENCE OF CHRISTIAN MATURITY.

Ver. 7. *"waiting for the revelation of our Lord Jesus Christ"*,— This waiting was one of the results of their not being behind (*"come behind"*), and is a proof of the maturity and richness of their spiritual life. This is by far the simplest and most satisfactory explanation and it is thus taken as a parallel clause with the one that precedes it.

Paul is not therefore trying to alarm them by the thought of approaching judgment (Chr.), as this would not be very appropriate for a thanksgiving; nor is it a reproof to those who deny the resurrection (Ru. Gro.), since he is not here talking of the resurrection but of the Second Coming; nor yet is it an ironical reference to the fancied perfection of the Corinthians (Mos.), for this is inconsistent with the friendly, winning style of the introduction. A commendation is intended. Some take it as an encouragement to them, i. e., as those who are waiting the Lord's advent with confidence, for ye possess all the graces that suffice for that time. But this goes farther than the contents of the Epistle warrant.

"*revelation*",—The Greek is "apocalypsis" and it means to uncover, unveil, disclose. It is used seven times of Christ's return and is used of both the blessed aspect and the punitive side of that event.

Ver. 8. "*who*",—Many refer this to "God" of verse 4. (A. O. D. Ew. Fl. Os. Hof. Bil. Pot. Schr.) We must, however, decide for the more immediate connection with "Christ" of verse 7. The word "God" at the beginning of verse 9 favors the reference to "Christ" in verse 8. The other view makes the whole passage from verses 5 to 7 a mere parenthesis. The repetition of the expression, "*the day of the Lord Jesus Christ*", in verse 8 is not at all an insurmountable barrier to the view we have taken, inasmuch as it was a customary and solemn formula.

"*also*",—This word implies a continuation of that which had already been wrought in them.

"*unto the end*",—The reference is not to the end of one's life, but to the end of the present dispensation, to the Second Coming of Christ.

"*that ye may be unreprovable*",—i. e., liable to no accusation. This is not only because of a reputed righteousness, but since he is speaking of their condition at the appearing of Christ it is to be taken likewise in the sense of an actual or perfected holiness.

"*the day of our Lord Jesus Christ*",—The decisive day of His Second Coming. This day as related to the Parousia is not quite the same as the day of the Lord. The former relates always to saints and their reward while the latter relates to sinners and their punishment. Erdman says, "The transactions associated with '*the day of Christ*' or '*the day of our Lord Jesus Christ*', in *every* Scripture where it is found, pertain exclusively to the risen and transfigured Church and are radiant with holy joy and triumphant blessedness; but the events associated with '*the day of the Lord*', both in the Old Testament and in the New, concern especially the Jews and the nations of an apostate Christendom, and are dark with the wrath of God upon the wicked."

CHAPTER THREE

13 each man's work shall be made manifest; for the day shall declare it, because it is revealed in fire; [1]and the fire itself shall prove each man's work of what sort it is.

[1]Or, *and each man's work, of what sort it is, the fire shall prove it.*

Ver. 13. EVERY MAN'S MINISTRY MADE MANIFEST AT THE COMING OF THE LORD.

"*shall be made manifest*",—It shall not remain hidden.

"the day shall declare it",—This does not refer to time in general (Fl. Gro. Wol. Vor.), nor to the time of clear knowledge of the Gospel (C. Era. Bez. Vor.), nor the day of tribulation (Ca. Aug.), nor least of all that never ending refuge of poor critics, the day of Jerusalem's destruction (Li. Ham. Scho.), for what had those Corinthians to do with that? But it refers, as nearly all commentators of our time maintain, to the day of the Parousia of the Lord, the Second Advent. (M. A. G. O. D. B. Ew. Os. Ru. Hof. Hey. Kli. Bil. Pot. The. Chr. Ter. Schr. Schot.)

"it is revealed in fire",—What is revealed in fire? We prefer to think of the *"day"* as the subject, the thought, if not the words, being in keeping with II Thess. 1.8; II Pet. 3.10-12. (H. O. D. M. A. Es. Ru. Ew. Wor. Pot. Bil. Hof.)

Others, and in fact the majority, make *"work"* the subject, saying that the day is never spoken of as being revealed. This view, however, make an intolerable tautology with the following proposition.

"in fire",—The element in which the day will be revealed. The reference, in keeping with the passages above quoted, seems to be to literal fire, but this fire, the bursting forth of which will perhaps be the visible herald of Christ's coming, is but as the symbol of that *"fiery"* judgment which shall search to the bottom every case, as immediately expressed. This is not the fire of *"hell"* into which the costly stones will never enter, but the fire of judgment in which Christ will appear and by which all works will be tried.

"and the fire itself shall prove",—Godet rightly says, "It must not be forgotten that the building to be proved exists only figuratively, and consequently the fire which is to put it to the proof can only be figurative fire. The term can therefore only here denote the incorruptible judgment pronounced by the omniscient and consuming holiness of the Judge who appears. His Spirit will thoroughly explore the fruit due to the ministry of every man."

CHAPTER FOUR

> 5 Wherefore judge nothing before the time, until the Lord come, who will both bring to light the hidden things of darkness, and make manifest the counsels of the heart; and then shall each man have his praise from God.

Ver. 5. JUDGMENT OF CHRIST'S SERVANTS TO AWAIT HIS COMING.

"judge nothing",—i. e., with respect to me. Refrain from all premature decisions concerning me, says Paul.

"before the time",—Explained by the following, *"until the Lord come"*.

"until the Lord come",—The verb is subjunctive, and in the expression *"until"* there is a particle which designates the coming as problematic, not as to the fact of His coming but as to the time of it, i. e., until the Lord come, whenever that may be.

"both",—Many translate this "also", i. e., among other things He will also. (M. A. Ru. Os. Kli.) Godet renders it "even". Either of

these translations is permissible, but *"both"* is preferable. The strengthening force of "even" is uncalled for, and as to the calling attention to other things, we are tempted to ask what they are, and can see no reason for bringing them into the passage.

"the hidden things of darkness",—All things in general, the good as well as the bad things which are hidden in darkness. (M. O. H. G.) (Rom. 2.16.)

"the counsels of the heart",—The motives and purposes by which men are governed.

"his praise",—The praise which is his due,—commendation.

Alford says Paul has in mind the boastings among themselves, the various parties giving exaggerated praise to certain teachers; let them wait until the day when fitting praise will be given, be it what it may.

Meyer thinks that Paul speaks of praise only because he has in mind only Apollos and himself, and therefore leaves out of sight the undeserving. The view of Alford is good, but perhaps that of Meyer is a little safer.

CHAPTER FIVE

> 5 to deliver such an one unto Satan
> for the destruction of the flesh, that the
> spirit may be saved in the day of the
> Lord Jesus.

Ver. 5. REDEMPTION OF THE SPIRIT IN THE DAY OF THE LORD'S COMING.

"deliver to Satan for the destruction of the flesh",—(See I Tim. 1.20 for the only similar expression.)

1. Excommunication pure and simple. (C. O. Ow. Bez. Hei. Bon. Tur. Poo.)
2. A handing over to Satan for corporeal infliction, as in the case of Job, without excommunication. (Li. Hof. Hols.) Godet finds it a sentence of death.
3. Excommunication with bodily punishment added through the disciplinary power of Satan let loose upon the offender by the Apostle, i. e., through the Apostle's apostolic authority and power. (H. A. M. Os. Ru. Bar. The. Chr.) This view is by far the more preferable. It is clearly revealed in Scripture that bodily afflictions are often brought about by the agency of Satan, and it is also clear that the Apostles were invested with the power of miraculously inflicting such evils. (Acts 5.1,11; 13.9-11; I Cor. 10.8; 13.10.)

"for the destruction of the flesh",—This is taken by many in the moral sense of the word, that is to say, of the sinful tendencies in consequence of the pain and repentance produced in him by his expulsion. (Es. Gro. Bez. Ger. Bon. Brow.)

But,—

(a) *"destruction"* is never used in a beneficent sense, but always in a threatening one involving real loss.
(b) Such a delivering over to Satan might have an effect opposite to that of repentance.

(c) The connection points to an operation of Satan.

(d) It is opposed by the antithesis between *"flesh"* and *"spirit"*.

These objections incline Alford, Meyer and others to the view of Chrysostom, that the sinful, fleshly nature is intended, the working-place of his desires and lusts, which was to be emptied of its enemy of sinful life by the pains of bodily sickness. This is without doubt the correct interpretation.

Godet argues that since *"spirit"* refers not to spiritual life but to the spirit itself, so *"flesh"* does not mean the fleshy life, but the flesh itself and that therefore the destruction of the man's earthly existence (death) is what is involved. This is possible, both from the meaning of the word and from example (Ananias and Saphira), but this presses the case seemingly too far and hardly accords with the ethical relations of it. To meet this objection Godet says the reference is to a wasting disease, giving the man time to repent.

"that the spirit may be saved",—The discipline was for a wholesome effect, the punishment being in reality a merciful one.

"in the day of the Lord Jesus",—The day of the approaching Parousia, the time, says Godet, "when Jesus will appear again on the earth to take to Him His own". Some authorities omit the word *"Jesus"*, but the evidence is weightier in favor of its retention.

CHAPTER SIX

2 Or know ye not that the saints shall judge the world? and if the world is judged by you, are ye unworthy [1]to judge the smallest matters? 3 Know ye not that we shall judge angels? how much more things that pertain to this life?

[1]Gr. *of the smallest tribunals*

Vers. 2,3.   THE SAINTS TO SIT IN JUDGMENT ON THE WORLD.

Ver. 2.   *"Or know ye not"*,—A formula used ten times in this Epistle and alluding no doubt to doctrines he had taught them at the time of the founding of their church.

"the saints shall judge the world",—This means as assessors of Christ at His coming. (A. C. O. D. M. G. Es. Ru. Bez. Gro. Wol. Bil. Kli. Stan. Brow.)   All attempts to elude this plain meaning of the words are futile.   Some of them are the following:

1. An indirect judgment as in Matt. 12.21, *"The men of Ninevah shall rise up in judgment against this generation"*.   (Wor. Chr. Era. Theo.)

2. The saints will merely assent to the judgment pronounced by Christ. (Es. Bar. Mai.)

3. The saints' particular ability to estimate here and now the value of the world's opinions and doings, in the sense of Chap. 2.15,16.

4. It refers to the general notion of the Kingdom and glory of believers yet to come.   (Fl.)

5. The saints are to possess as the princes and rulers of the world judicial functions in the future; that is, the Gospel will some day become supreme and the courts of law will be composed of Christians.

The objections to these several views are at once apparent. This is the only direct enunciation of this truth, but it is in perfect harmony with the conclusions elsewhere furnished.

What was said in Matt. 19.28 of the Apostles is here extended to the saints in general, and Paul is speaking of such judicial work of the saints as is ascribed to them in Daniel 7.22. (O. A. G. M. Kli.)

"if the world is judged by you",—Those for whom the idea of the saints judging the world, in the sense we have taken the passage, is intolerable, try to escape this conclusion by putting such stress upon the present tense of the verb *"judge"* in this clause and upon the meaning of the preposition translated *"by"*.

But the previous word *"judge"* is future as well as the word *"judge"* in the next verse, and these control the word *"judge"* in the intervening clause, which here expresses, as Godet says, "not an actual fact, but a principle", and consequently, as Olshausen says, "there can be no reference to a present function of believers", but, as Meyer and Alford maintain, that the saints are to be the judges sitting in judgment.

They would further have us believe that the preposition means *"in"*, i. e., in your example. The preposition is indeed "en", but its real meaning is "among", in your midst, and therefore "before you". It is the expression meaning to be "judged before", as found in all classic Greek, and means here not "through" (Gro. Bil.), nor "in" (Chr.), but *"before you"*, although *"by you,"* as in the text, gives the meaning quite appropriately.

"to judge the smallest matters",—Since the original Greek, as in the margin ("of the smallest tribunals") makes fine sense we see no reason for the change in the text. The idea is then, "Are ye unworthy of holding or passing judgment in such inferior courts?" The word translated *"matters"* can hardly be said to mean this. It means first, "tribunal" or place of trial, and then the trial itself, but it never means the matter of dispute.

Meyer takes the word in its second sense and translates, "Are ye unworthy to hold judgment in very trivial trials?" Either this, or the rendering of the margin is proper, but that of the Revised Version, while it expresses the idea all right, is contrary to all usage. The world to be judged by the saints can only designate those who have rejected the Gospel appeal.

As to the saints judging the world, Klieforth says, "Whatever these functions may be, the language which describes them plainly implies the exercise of an active supremacy in the affairs of the world."

Hodge, Barnes and other post-millennialists, of course, refer this to the last judgment, the future and final judgment at the end of all time, but by others, and the very great majority, it is referred to judging with Christ during His kingdom of millennial reign.

Ver. 3. *"we shall judge angels"*,—Many authorities think that good angels are here meant and that they are to be judged for their service, their ministry (Heb. 1.14) for which they are to render account. (M. A. H. G. Kli. Brow.) They say that the word *"angels"* always means good angels. But this is not true, since in II Peter the word is used and means without any doubt bad angels.

Others, and the majority, say that bad angels are meant. (B. C. Ca. Bez. Poo. Era. Oec. The. Theo.)

It is maintained by some that both good and bad angels are meant. (O. Lap. Hof. Bes.)

There is nothing of a more detailed nature on the subject in Scripture, but the interpretation of "bad angels" best accords with the word *"world"*, and besides nowhere is it taught in Scripture that the elect angels are to be judged for their ministry. This, together with the fact that good angels are represented as furnishing a part of Christ's retinue in judgment, and as acting the part of organs and witnesses of His judicial work, induces us to the opinion that bad angels are intended here.

Godet says it is worthy of note that in the parables of the tares and the drag-net it is the angels who effect the division between the good and the bad, while here the saints are said to judge the angels, and apparently therefore bad angels.

Lightfoot says the only thing that is meant is that the influence of the kingdom of Satan is to be destroyed by Christianity. But with such exegesis the Apostle may be made to say anything.

Some make the first clause a question and the second one an exclamation; others make the whole one question with a comma after *"angels"*, while still others take the two clauses as two questions. Either method of punctuation is admissible, but we prefer that first mentioned.

CHAPTER SEVEN

29 But this I say, brethren, the time [1]is shortened, that henceforth both those that have wives may be as though they had none; 30 and those that weep, as though they wept not; and those that rejoice, as though they rejoiced not; and those that buy, as though they possessed not; 31 and those that use the world, as not using it to the full: for the fashion of this world passeth away.

[1] Or, *is shortened henceforth, that both those &c.*

Vers. 29-31. Sundry Exhortations Based on the Near Approach of the Lord's Return.

Ver. 29. *"the time is shortened"*,—The word *"shortened"* means contracted, compressed, brought within narrow limits. (M. A. G. D. Os. Ew. Wei. Hof. Mai.) Some take it as meaning "calamitous". (O. Ru. Fl. Pot. Ros. Hey. Nea. Schu.) But it never has this signification. In the passages they refer to, it means humbled, cast down, but this is as applied to persons, and this definition cannot be applied to time.

"the time",—This does not refer to the space of a man's life on earth (C. Es. Vor.), for however true this thought and however legitimate this application, it certainly is not the thought in the mind of Paul, nor does it agree with his usage elsewhere of the word (Rom. 13.11; Eph. 5.16), nor with that of the great prophecy of the Lord which is the key to this chapter (Luke 21.8; Mark 13.33). It is the time between the moment he was speaking to the coming of the Lord that was compressed into a small space according to the literal meaning of *"shortened"*.

"henceforth",—The connection here is disputed. Some make it belong to what follows. (H. C. M. Ti. Ru. Es. Ter. Jer. Vul. Era. Lut. Hey. Blo. Hof. Lach. and both the Revised and Authorized Versions.)

Others refer it to what precedes. (A. G. O. D. Pe. Os. Ew. Chr. The. Gro. Bez. Bil. Mai. Nea. Theo.) The first view is preferable inasmuch as the second view hardly gives to the word its full and legitimate meaning.

The punctuation of the Revised Version is much to be preferred as that of the Authorized Version breaks the continuity of the passage, leaves the word *"henceforth"* to stand alone and does not give to it its full and true sense.

"that",—This introduces the design of the shortened time on God's part. (M. A. H. Kli.) It depends therefore upon *"shortened"* and not upon *"this I say"* (Bez. Hof. Bil.), as it is not the end of his assertion he has in view, but the rather of the thing asserted.

The idea in what follows is that each one should keep himself inwardly independent of the relations of his earthly life. They must not rob us of our moral freedom nor of our standing as a Christian in heart and life. He is not laying down rules, that the married ought to be as though unmarried. Meyer well says it is, "In order that those who wait for the coming kingdom may keep themselves loose in heart from worldly relationships and employments; that the married may not fetter his interests to his wedlock, nor the mourner to his misfortunes, nor the joyous to his prosperity, nor the man of commerce to his gain, nor the user of the world to his use of the world."

"for the fashion of this world passeth away",—This, says Alford, shows again that in the Apostle's mind the time was short, while Godet says, "It is connected by *'for'* with the preceding *'the time is shortened'*, and we are obliged to apply it to the near coming of the Lord."

Klieforth remarks, "This does not refer to the transitoriness of earthly things in general, but to the mighty revolution attendant upon the advent of Christ—the entire vanishing or destruction of the form of this world, its outward appearance and mode of existence. This great change presents itself as one close at hand and he therefore speaks of it as present."

Meyer says, "It refers to the world-embracing catastrophe of the Parousia, the transformation of the form of this world, and therewith of its whole temporal constitution into the new heavens and the new earth."

The word *"fashion"* does not therefore mean, as some say, worldly affairs in general, but it refers to the present external form or state of things, and this expression seems to prove that this world itself will not disappear, but that it will take on a new mode of existence and development.

It is hard to read this whole passage and understand how anyone can but feel that Paul thought the Parousia not very far away. Calvin says, "Without doubt Paul wrote these words in expectation of a near and approaching transformation of the fashion of this world, and the introduction of the age to come with the kingdom of God."

It must not, however, be overlooked that in the selection of the particular word here used for time, Paul did not perhaps have in mind so much the idea of duration as of favorable, opportune time, the time in which one can yet prepare himself for the great change which is one day to take place.

CHAPTER TEN

> 11 Now these things happened unto them [1]by way of example; and they were written for our admonition, upon whom the ends of the ages are come.
>
> [1]Gr. *by way of figure*

Ver. 11. THE ENDS OF THE AGES COINCIDENT WITH THE PRESENT DISPENSATION.

"by way of example",—The literal is "typically", but our text expresses the correct thought, and the idea of type is not to be taken in a theological sense.

"upon whom the ends of the ages are come",—"ages" is plural, indicating the great epochs in which all history is unfolded. "ends" is also plural, indicating the successive terminations of the several epochs. (See such references as Heb. 1.1; 9.26; Matt. 13.39; 25.3; I Cor. 1.8; 15.24; I Peter 4.7; 1.20 and I John 2.18.)

Meyer says, "Upon the supposition of the Parousia being close at hand the last times of the world were now come; the ages were running out their final course; with the Parousia, the ages to come begin to run."

"are come",—The ages are represented as coming to meet the living (G.), into whose lifetime they are entered (Kli.); they have reached unto us, have fallen upon our lifetime and are now here (M.).

Neander says, "Paul had always good reason for considering the final catastrophe as near at hand, although he held the last time to be shorter than it really was."

Paul, however, did not himself know or pretend to know the duration of this final period in the culmination of the ages, this present dispensation of which he was speaking, and which in his mind coincided with the development of the Church; but the phrase, *"the ends of the ages"*, shows that he did not regard it as short as is commonly alleged that he did. (See also Chap. 7.29.)

CHAPTER ELEVEN

> 26 For as often as ye eat this bread, and drink the cup, ye proclaim the Lord's death till he come.

Ver. 26. THE LORD'S SUPPER A PLEDGE OF HIS COMING AGAIN.

Paul here proceeds in his own words.

"ye proclaim the Lord's death",—You do solemnly declare in connection with this ordinance that Christ has died for you. The word *"proclaim"* is by no means to be taken as imperative (Ew. Ru. Gro. Lut. Hols.), but as indicative. (M. A. G.)

"until he come",—The Holy Supper is the link between the two comings of Christ; the monument of the first and the pledge of the second. It is the compensation of the Church for the absence of her Lord. When He comes it will be discontinued. It is connected with remembrance, and remembrance ceases when the Lord appears.

CHAPTER FIFTEEN

20 But now hath Christ been raised from the dead, the firstfruits of them that are asleep. 21 For since by man *came* death, by man *came* also the resurrection of the dead. 22 For as in Adam all die, so also in [1]Christ shall all be made alive. 23 But each in his own order: Christ the firstfruits; then they that are Christ's, at his [2]coming. 24 Then *cometh* the end, when he shall deliver up the kingdom to [3]God, even the Father; when he shall have abolished all rule and all authority and power. 25 For he must reign, till he hath put all enemies under his feet. 26 The last enemy that shall be abolished is death.

[1]Gr. *the Christ*

[2]Or, *If in this life only we have hoped in Christ &c.*

[3]Gr. *presence*

Vers. 20-26. THE ORDER OF THE RESURRECTION.

Ver. 20. *"But now"*,—i. e., as the matter stands the case is far otherwise.

"the first fruits of them that are asleep",—"The allusion", says Brown, "is as obvious as it is beautiful." On the morrow after the first Sabbath of the Passover (Easter Sabbath) a sheaf of the first fruits of the barley harvest was reaped and waved before the Lord as a joyful pledge of the full harvest to come. Even so on the morrow after the first Sabbath of the Passover when our Lord was crucified, did He rise, the first fruits of His sleeping people.

It is probable, from many considerations, that such a reference was in Paul's mind, but since he indicates nothing more minutely the matter must be left undecided.

The resurrections from the dead recorded in the Old Testament and the translations of Enoch and Elijah do not contradict what is here said of Christ as the first fruits, because in the case of the former there was no arising to an immortal life, and in the case of the latter there was no dying, and so a resurrection could not occur. (Rev. 1.5 and Col. 1.16.) In the first fruits is contained not only the idea of the earliest, but of the most costly and the pledge of a full resurrection harvest, and as such dedicated to God.

"them that are asleep",—Who are meant? Inasmuch as the expression is that used in the New Testament of the death of saints always, and the idea of fellowship with Christ as the first fruits, and as the totality of believers seems to be the thing conceived of, we think here only of departed saints. However, the word *"dead"* in the next verse might seem to refer the expression to the dead in general. The matter must be decided by an exposition of what follows where the explanation of this verse is made, first in a divine rule that what has been taken away from us by man shall by man also be restored to us. Note, however, that if the expression be restricted to the departed saints, it is not thereby said that Christ is not the raiser also of the unbelieving dead. He is not, however, their first fruits.

Ver. 21. *"death"*,—As death here is physical so also by the *"resurrection of the dead"* is meant the resurrection of the body. Hodge, while making this the primary reference, declares that the expression involves also the moral death and the moral life. But of this Paul says nothing here, although it is of course true.

436

Says Meyer, "The evil which arose through a human author is by divine arrangement removed also through a human author."

Ver. 22. As verse 21 was the ground and explanation of verse 20, so verse 22 gives the reason for verse 21.

"in Adam all die",—That this includes the whole human race all expositors agree.

"in Christ shall all be made alive",—There are two explanations of this clause, either of which is acceptable though each is attended with difficulties.

1. That which adheres to the idea of physical resurrection and makes the *"all"* refer to everybody. (A. C. M. D. O. Am. Blo. Kli. Bar. Bez. The. Chr. Theo. Brow.)

2. That which reads into the second clause the idea also of eternal bliss and limits the *"all"* to believers. (H. G. B. Fl. Ew. Es. Ru. Ed. Le. Os. Mc. Dod. Aug. Bil. Mai. Gro. Hof. Mul. Hein. Stan. Beet. Lutt. Hols.)

In favor of the second view it may be said that: (a) As a rule *"made alive"* is never referred to unbelievers, but always when used of the work of Christ as imparting spiritual life; (b) If Paul had meant only bodily resurrection he would have retained the word used in verse 21; (c) Paul is speaking throughout of the resurrection only of believers; (d) *"They that are Christ's"* of the next verse favors this view; (e) The other view would seem to imply that Christ is the first fruits of the wicked; (f) The analogy between Adam and Christ includes more than physical death.

Hodge says there is a limit in each *"all"*, i. e., all who are in Adam die and all who are in Christ shall be made alive. The order of the Greek words, however, will hardly allow this, although this thought may have been in Paul's mind. The great objection to this view is the change of parallelism and the possibility of reading into it the doctrine of the final restoration of all mankind, as indeed done by some. This, however, is inconsistent with the last part of verse 25, and is opposed by such Scriptures as II Thess. 1.9; Acts 25.15.

The principle arguments in favor of the second view are:

1. It retains unimpaired the parallel between the two *"alls"*.

2. Paul is speaking of physical resurrection throughout the whole chapter.

3. The *"each"* of the next verse seems to imply that the wicked are included in the number.

The principal objection to this view is in the use of *"in Christ"*, which it is declared cannot be said of the unbeliever's resurrection.

But Klieforth has well said, "Inasmuch as it is universally recognized that Christ is the head of humanity, the reference may well be to an organic union of the race in Christ as it is in Adam, and the *"in"* shows that each process of development has its ground or source in its peculiar head." The being in Christ then would refer not to the incorporation into Christ's mystical body of believers by faith, but to their being taken in under Christ's headship of the race, as they were previously in under the headship of Adam by descent.

It is, of course, Christ's power that awakens both good and bad, and it is, as Godet says, "the relation of both the good and the bad to Christ that determines their return to life either to glory or to condemnation."

We are inclined to think the force of the argument is in favor of the first view.

Ver. 23. *"each in his own order"*,—As forming part of it and involved in it.

"order",—This means not so much priority, but rank, troop, division of an army. The believers are conceived of as rising together and of course the same will be true of the unbelievers.

"Christ the first fruits",—The first fruits are as the lump, a community of nature being involved.

"they that are Christ's",—Not Christ's followers in the days of His flesh (Vul. Scho.), nor professing Christians, good and bad (M.), but true believers. (H. G. Ed.)

"at his coming",—At His Parousia, His Second Coming.

This is another of the proof texts used by Dr. Brown against the premillennarians as showing that no one can be saved after the coming of Christ. He insists that as the foregoing words, *"in Adam all die"*, include *"the whole federal offspring of Adam"*, so the words *"they that are Christ's"* must include the whole federal affspring of Christ, i. e., the total number of the saved. To Dr. Brown at this point Kellog replies, "But it so happens that the meaning which Dr. Brown insists that the phrase, 'they that are Christ's' *must* have, is just the one meaning that it *cannot* have. It is absolutely certain that the words, 'they that are Christ's'—as denoting those who shall rise from the dead at His coming—do *not* include 'the whole federal offspring of Christ'. First, it is certain that, in the nature of the case, Enoch and Elijah must be excluded. In the second place, it is no less certain that we must exclude all those many saints of the old dispensation of whom we read in Matt. 27.52,53, that they came out of their graves after Christ's resurrection and appeared to many. In the third place, it is equally clear that we must exclude all those of 'Christ's federal offspring' who shall be found alive at His coming, of whom Paul himself says that they shall not sleep—but shall be changed. As they shall never die, they cannot be raised. These three exceptions are enough to settle the question that what Dr. Brown declares the words *must* mean, they *cannot* mean. If, then, the phrase 'they that are Christ's at His coming', does not denote all the saved, but only a certain portion of them, then it is evident that if it be elsewhere taught, as we have abundant reason to believe, that the subjection of all nations to Christ must follow His second coming, then these words teach nothing which is inconsistent with this."

Ver. 24. *"then"*,—The first preposition *"then"* in verse 23 is "epeita", and the second *"then"* in this verse is the same word with the preposition (epi) left off. They are adverbs of time and mark a sequence of course, sometimes depending on temporal succession and sometimes on the nature of the things enumerated. There is absolutely nothing in the words to designate a shorter or longer period of time. If the idea of *immediate* succession was found in either word it would more aptly inhere in the first one where the preposition is added, and yet we know that more than 2000 years have intervened between the two points of time mentioned. If the first *"then"* looks down the ages for 2000 years it is possible for the second one to do the same so far as the two words themselves are concerned.

Principal Edwards says, "eita" does not mean "at that time", but "after that", as in Matt. 24.6,14; Mark 13.7; Luke 21.9.

The second "eita" is the same word as that used in Mark 4.28, *"First the blade, then the ear, then the full corn in the ear"*, and here of course an intervening period of time must be figured in between each preposition.

Then, too, if Paul had wanted to say that the end came there and then immediately after the resurrection of *"they that are Christ's"* he could easily have done so by using the word "tote".

Blackstone reminds us that in this same chapter (verses 5-7) "eita" is used interchangeably with "epeita"; that it here signifies *next in order,* but not necessarily *immediately,* and that when the Holy Spirit means *immediately* He uses τότε, ἐξαμτῆς, εὐθέως, or Μαραχρῆμα.

Godet says with seeming propriety, "The 'eita' does not allow us to identify the time of the end with that of the advent; it implies in the mind of the Apostle a longer or shorter interval between the advent of Christ and what he calls the *'end'."*

Alford says, "It ought to be needless to remind the student of the distinction between this Parousia and the final judgment; it is here peculiarly important to bear this in mind."

"the end",—Not the end of the resurrection (M. B. Os. The. Oec. Kil. Hey. Grimm), nor yet the end of the Gospel dispensation (Bil. Gro. Whe.), but the end of the world, the end of all things absolutely. (A. H. G. O. Ed.)

"he shall deliver up the kingdom",—The royal power itself, the dominion exercised, the reign of Christ (G. M. A.), and not the subjects of His kingly rule nor the citizens of the kingdom as raised from the dead (Bez. Hey.).

"shall have abolished",—There is a very fine distinction in the use of the subjunctive aorist here. Above we had the future, *"shall deliver"* (equivalent to the certain present), but here the tense shows that he is looking backward and referring to what is to take place before the end. The meaning is "after having abolished", and it would seem to prove an epoch of judgment before the end.

"he",—Not God (B. Bez. Gro. Hen. Hey.), but Christ (A. M. G. H.).

"all rule, and all authority and power",—The powers intended are hostile powers no doubt, and not earthly, political powers legitimate and even ordained of God, as Calvin thinks, nor all rule, good and evil, even that of the Son of God, as Olshausen would have us believe.

Godet makes them invisible hostile powers, while others make them invisible hostile powers and earthly powers. (H. M. Us. Ca. Lut. Nea. Bil. Hey. Chr. Kil.) However the primary reference here is to spiritual powers as is evident from the words used. The words signify different orders of angels, the highest, a lower and a still lower in the order of the words. In Eph. 6.12 the first two words are used of the *"spiritual hosts of wickedness"*.

Alford maintains that all powers are meant, invisible hostile powers and earthly powers good and bad, but the view of Hodge and others as just expressed is perhaps the better, especially in view of verse 25, although what Alford says may be thought of as being true. All legitimate authorities are to come under His kingdom; kings shall submit to Him and the kingdoms of this world shall become the kingdoms of Christ.

Ver. 25. The subject throughout the verse is not God (B. Es. Bil. Gro. Hof. Bez.), but Christ .(A. D. H. Os. Ru. Ew. Ed. Kil. Nea. Mai. Brow.).

"must";—A necessity in accordance with divine counsel and decree as well as the eternal fitness of things. It is as if he had said that Psalm 110 must be fulfilled. Paul appropriates, not quotes, this Psalm.

Godet remarks, "The essential object of Christ's reign is the carrying out of this judgment on the opposing powers which still remain after the advent", while Edwards says, "The reign of Christ is not a millennium of peace, but a perpetual conflict ending in final triumph."

Ver. 26. This is accomplished by and through the resurrection, by taking his victims from him and seeing that he gets no more, because all dying will be over.

Impartial searchers after truth will appreciate a quotation like the following from Principal Edwards. He says, "Death has not, it appears from this, been destroyed at the second coming and at the resurrection of those who are Christ's. The Apostle seems, it must be acknowledged, to teach that there will be two resurrections, the former of believers only, the latter of all others when at last death itself will die. I may add that my interpretation of the Apostle's words is not the result of having adopted any theory on the general question. I know next to nothing of Millennial literature, but after reading Bishop Waldegrave's 'New Testament Millennarianism', and Dr. David Brown's 'Second Advent', *I am not convinced that the Apostle does not teach the doctrine of two resurrections.* Neither of these writers so far as I have observed touches upon the argument that death is not destroyed at the advent."

50 Now this I say, brethren, that flesh and blood cannot inherit the kingdom of God; neither doth corruption inherit incorruption. 51 Behold, I tell you a mystery: [1]We all shall not sleep, but we shall all be changed, 52 in a moment, in the twinkling of an eye, at the last trump: for the trumpet shall sound, and the dead shall be raised incorruptible, and we shall be changed. 53 For this corruptible must put on incorruption, and this mortal must put on immortality. 54 But when [2]this corruptible shall have put on incorruption, and this mortal shall have put on immortality, then shall come to pass the saying that is written, [3]Death is swallowed up [4]in victory. 55 [5]O death, where is thy victory? O death, where is thy sting? 56 The sting of death is sin: and the power of sin is the law: 57 but thanks be to God, who giveth us the victory through our Lord Jesus Christ. 58 Wherefore, my beloved brethren, be ye stedfast, unmovable, always abounding in the work of the Lord, forasmuch as ye know that your labor is not [6]vain in the Lord.

[1]Or, *We shall not all &c.*
[2]Many ancient authorities omit *this corruptible shall have put on incorruption, and.*
[3]Is. 25.8
[4]Or, *victoriously*
[5]Hos. 13.14
[6]Or, *void*

Vers. 50-58. SOME BELIEVERS NEVER TO TASTE DEATH.

Ver. 50. *"this I say"*,—This refers to what follows and not to what goes before. He is impressing upon them something that might be overlooked.

"flesh and blood",—Our present physical organism; human nature in its present, material, mortal, corruptible state. It is not to be taken in an ethical sense, as *"flesh"* in Romans 8.12,15, because *"flesh and blood"* never have this meaning.

Some of the Jews believed in a flesh and blood resurrection, and others in a spiritualistic, ethereal one, and some (O. Us. Bil.) think Paul meant to combat the first and to make concessions to the latter. But this is purely an importation into the Apostle's thought. He is simply confirming what he had already said, by affirming that not only is the change already mentioned possible, but it is necessary because the inheriting of the kingdom of God by flesh and blood is impossible by the very nature of the thing.

"neither doth corruption", etc.,—The same idea expressed in abstract terms. They are mutually exclusive and antagonistic.

Godet would have us refer *"flesh and blood"* to Christians alive at the coming of Christ and *"corruption"* to Christians dead and already in a state of dissolution, each of whom must be transformed, one by change and the other by resurrection. This is perhaps carrying the application a bit too far (although it is true), as corruption is not to be thought of so much as distinct from flesh and blood, as the dead are distinguished from the living, but it exhibits to us a prominent characteristic of our present state, flesh and blood being corruptible.

"kingdom of God",—Olshausen remarks, "We are here to understand the kingdom of God on earth, which the Scriptures inform us will be set up immediately upon the coming of our Lord."

Hodge of course, in keeping with his general view, refers it to the kingdom of Christ after the general and final resurrection.

"This verse is quoted", says Blackstone, "to support the assertion that the kingdom of God is only spiritual and that there is nothing literal or material in it. But Paul says nothing of the kind and his whole argument is entirely to the contrary. He asserts that our bodies which are sown in corruption, dishonor and weakness will be raised in incorruption, glory and power, or if living, will be changed in the twinkling of an eye. In these glorified bodies we shall *'inherit the kingdom prepared for us from the foundation of the world'*. Christ, the rightful heir of all things, will be there and we shall be there to reign with Him."

Ver. 51. *"mystery"*,—A thing unknown except through revelation.
All are agreed as to what Paul means by the following clause, namely, that at the coming of Christ some would be alive and that these without dying would be changed. Yet each class of expositors accuses the other of making Paul say something other than that. Many renderings have been given of the clause in question.

    1. The text of the Revised Version, *"We all shall not sleep but we shall all be changed."* (M. Kli. Win.)

2. We shall all die but we shall not all be changed. But this is contradicted by the next verse.

3. All of us shall rise but all of us shall not be changed. There is insufficient manuscript authority for this. Both these two last views are inconsistent with the fact that the entire discussion refers to believers only.

4. Some transfer the word *"not"* and read, "Not all of us shall sleep but all of us shall be changed". (Fl. Os. Hey. Chr. Hen. Reic. and most all older commentators.) But this makes the *"change"* refer to all—both the living and the dead, the former being transformed alive and the latter resurrected. The strongest objection to this is not that the transposition of *"not"* is not grammatically allowable, because its position is not so rigorously observed, and the Septuagint seems to have instances of the same thing. The strongest objections are, however: (a) the stricter meaning of the word *"change"*, and (b) the fact that verse 52 says apparently that only the living are changed while the dead are to arise.

5. Some place the emphasis on the word *"all"* and render "All of us shall not sleep but we all shall be changed". (A. H. Ed. Stan.) But the same objections registered against the view just considered are pertinent in this case.

Godet and Alford say that the reading of our text teaches that not one Christian shall die before the Parousia, which, of course, they declare is an absurdity. Meyer admits this absurdity only if the subject is made to be all Christians living when Paul was speaking, but he affirms that the subject in Paul's mind was all Christians (himself included, as he doubtless hoped) who were to be alive at the Parousia. These are to be changed, he says, and only these, while the dead are to be raised according to verse 52. Meyer contends that Paul transfers himself in thought to the moment of the Parousia, i. e., "We all who are alive at the Parousia shall not die but we all who are alive at that time shall be changed." But how easy for Paul to have said, "Not one of us who are alive at the Parousia shall die, but we all who are then alive shall be changed."

The rendering of our text seems a bit forced to avoid applying the word *"changed"* to the dead. This word *"changed"* in verse 52 does apparently refer to the living, and inasmuch as it is the same word in both cases, it does present something of a difficulty when made to cover in verse 51 both the dead and the living. There is, however, not much choice between the two.

6. There is, however, still another translation which relieves the difficulty altogether, namely, "We shall not all sleep, but we all (who do not sleep—who are alive at the Parousia) shall be changed."

This thought could easily have been in the Apostle's mind, and yet have been expressed just as he has expressed himself so far as the wording of the sentence is concerned, and this we prefer because it makes Paul say what all agree he had in his mind, and at the same time confines the word *"changed"* to those living at the time of the Parousia.

Ver. 52. *"moment"*,—Literally, an "atom", a little indivisible point of time.

"at the last trump",—The reference is to the divine signal by which the *"moment"* will be proclaimed, manifesting the divine will to the beings of the invisible world. It does not therefore mean the last among any particular number (D. The.), nor the last of the seven trumpets which the Jews thought would sound the seven successive stages of the resurrection. This conception was foreign to Paul, seeing that he represents the resurrection as instantaneous. (H. A. M. G. Ed.)

This trump no doubt corresponds to the last trump mentioned in Revelation, but this does not mean that Paul had this in mind, not necessarily so at least, as Olshausen thinks.

Brown thinks the sound will be audible. But what it is and how it is to sound is not to be searched out, but is to be left with God.

The connection gives us no right to assume a non-literal, imaginative representation. Most expositors, however, agree with Godet that the reference is not to a literal trumpet, but that the expression is a figurative one, the symbol for expressing the idea of a gathering multitude (H.), a stupenduous spiritual influence arousing mankind for some mighty purpose (O.), an all-agitating command or nod of God. (Us. Nea. Bil. Hof. Theo.)

"last trump",—While Hodge says this is the last trumpet that is ever to sound and refers to the last day of the world's economy, others, however, rightly say that the idea of *"last"* is not to be pressed too hard or too far; it is the last in a wide and popular sense, and not necessarily the last that is ever to sound. Olshausen says it is the last of the seven trumpets in Revelation 8, and cannot therefore mean the trumpet sounding in the last day, but the last sounding trumpet, i. e., the last of the trumpets but not necessarily the trumpet of the last day. It is without doubt the trump of God mentioned in I Thess. 4.16, and is the last trumpet of this age or dispensation.

"the dead",—The Christians who have already died up to that time. He is speaking of Christians throughout.

"we shall be changed",—This is consistent with his hope that he might be alive when his Lord returned. (M. A. O. G. Kli.)

It is possible of course to think of him speaking, as Hodge says, of believers as a whole and meaning, "Those of us who are dead will arise and those of us who are alive will be changed", although in view of other Scriptures it is better to take it the other way.

"we shall be changed",—This refers without doubt to the living Christians. Godet well says, "There is no difficulty in taking it in a more restricted sense here than in verse 51, because here it is contrasted with rising and not with being dead."

Ver. 53. This is the idea of verse 50 reproduced in positive form, showing in the necessity here mentioned, the reason why we must be changed.

It is safer, as Klieforth says, to refer *"corruptible"* and *"mortal"* both to the living, rather than with Bengle and Godet to refer the first to the resurrected bodies and the second to those living.

"this",—It is better to think of him, as Brown says, referring to the mortality of the saints in general, as in II Cor. 5.1, *"our earthly house"*,

rather than to think of Paul pointing to his own body (A. M. Theo.) and making, as Edwards says, a personal application of the doctrine to himself.

"put on",—This points to the continuance of personal identity; the perishable, mortal body not to be destroyed, but to be clothed upon, changed to an incorruptible condition of existence. (O. M. A. G. H.)

Ver. 54. Paul here quotes from Isa. 25.8 and intentionally changes the last word from *"forever"* to *"in victory"*, as the Septuagint frequently does.

"in victory",—So as to result in victory. Death is to be completely conquered, its prey rescued from it and none thereafter to be given to it through dying.

It ought to be borne in mind that Paul is still speaking of believers. Edwards, referring to II Cor. 5.4, says the reference here is only to the living; but we have seen no other commentator take any notice of such a distinction, and the most natural reference, it would seem, is to both the resurrection and the transformation, as Hodge maintains.

Ver. 55. Hodge says, "The Apostle places himself and his readers in the presence of the Saviour and the risen dead and the transformed living arrayed in immortality, and in view of that majestic scene he breaks out in these words of triumph.

Paul quotes from the Septuagint of Hosea 13.14 with free alteration.

"victory",—Death had conquered us, but Christ conquers death and takes his victory away from him.

"sting",—Not of a goad driving us to death (Fl. Bil. Hein.), but of a venomous serpent. (H. A. M. G. Ed. Kil.)

Ver. 56. *"The sting of sin is death"*,—This is so because in a subjective way it is sin that arms death with all its terrors, but more especially in an objective way it is sin that imparts to death its fatal power. Death is by sin. (Rom. 5.12.)

"The power of sin is the law",—

1. Because without law there would be no sin. (Rom. 4.15.)

2. Because if there be no law there can be no condemnation. (Rom. 5.13.)

Klieforth prefers the subjective meaning, namely, that the law awakens sin in man, excites, exasperates and thus strengthens it, in the sense of Rom. 7.7. But the subjective aspect in both clauses of the verse seems foreign to the connection.

This is a discussion of the Resurrection, and as Godet says, it would seem that we have here nothing to do with the trouble experienced by the dying man or the peace enjoyed by the believer.

"the law",—Not the Mosaic law, which would make the declaration amount to nothing, but the law of God in its widest sense.

Ver. 57. *"giveth"*,—The present tense, representing this future victory as sure and certain.

"the victory",—The victory over death.

"through our Lord Jesus Christ",—Because:

1. He has satisfied the demands of the law and it has no power to condemn those who are clothed in His righteousness. (Rom. 8.1.)
2. He new creates the soul after the image of God and repairs all the evils which death had inflicted.

Ver. 58. *"Wherefore"*,—Seeing that this victory is sure. (A. O. M. G. Kil. Brow.)

"steadfast, unmovable",—In reference to the doubt which some attempt to raise among you on this matter. (A. M. G. Ed.)

"the work of the Lord",—The Christian life with its duties, especially that of bringing others to the knowledge of the Lord. (M. A. Ed. Kil.)

"knowing",—Being convinced by what has been said.

"not in vain",—This it would be if there were no resurrection. In the resurrection you will get your reward. This is the thought rather than that their work will not be in vain in its results, i. e., in converting many, etc.

"in the Lord",—This does not belong to *"your labor"*, nor yet altogether to *"in vain"* (M.), but the rather to the whole sentence, your labor, etc.

THE SECOND EPISTLE OF PAUL TO THE

CORINTHIANS

(A. D. 60)

CHAPTER FOUR

> 14 knowing that he that raised up the Lord Jesus shall raise up us also with Jesus, and shall present us with you.

Ver. 14. THE JOYFUL PRESENTATION OF BELIEVERS BEFORE THE THRONE OF CHRIST.

"knowing",—This gives the ground of the speaking (M. A.) and not the matter or content of it.

"shall raise up us also with Jesus",—Because of the preposition *"with"*, this is taken by some as a figurative resurrection, viz., of the overcoming of the constant perils of death (verses 10-12), which it is held is a resurrection *"with"* Jesus, insofar as through it there arises a fellowship of destiny with the risen Christ. (Ru. Nea. Schu.)

These authors claim that the Apostle could not thus speak of his physical resurrection because he expected to be alive at the coming of the Lord. But this objection is best refuted by this very passage; he speaks here exactly in the same sense that he did in I Thess. 4.15.

Then, too, it is possible to conceive under the general idea of being *"raised up"* the more special one of a simple change, the raising up here having respect rather to the contrast of the future glory with the present suffering, and not therefore necessarily implying one or the other side of the alternative of being quick or dead at the Lord's coming, but embracing all, quick and dead, in one blessed resurrection state.

The figurative interpretation is not demanded by the words *"with Jesus"*, which, by the way, is no doubt the correct reading. This reading is supported by overwhelming authority, and the *"by"* of the Authorized Version was introduced no doubt because of the supposed impropriety of *"with"* in reference to a future resurrection, Christ having already been raised. It is true that the resurrection of the dead takes place *"by"* (dia) Jesus, but as Meyer says, "Christians may be conceived and designated as one day becoming raised *'with'* Jesus, since they are members of Christ and Christ is the first fruits of those who rise from the dead. The believer, in virtue of his connection with the Lord, knows himself already in his temporal life as risen with Christ, and what he thus knows in faith emerges at the last day into objective completion and outward reality."

The possibility of dying was always before Paul's mind, and that too before the Lord came. (I Cor. 15.31; II Cor. 1.8; 5.18; Phil. 1.20; Acts 20.25,38.)

"present us with you",—viz.,

"Before the judgment seat of Christ as perfected men of God." (O.)

"Before the judgment seat of Christ for the reception of the great prize, i. e., as companions of Christ in His kingdom." (Kli.)

"Before the judgment seat of Christ to receive the eternal glory." (M.)

The idea of judgment is of course foreign to the passage except in the sense of reward as noted by the authorities just quoted, and certainly there is here no allusion whatsoever to the awful scenes of the last judgment. The reference is rather to the joyful, blessed presentation referred to so often elsewhere by the Apostle. (Chap. 11.2; Eph. 5.27; Col. 1.22; Jude 24.)

CHAPTER FIVE

1 For we know that if the earthly house of our [1]tabernacle be dissolved, we have a building from God, a house not made with hands, eternal, in the heavens. 2 For verily in this we groan, longing to be clothed upon with our habitation which is from heaven: 3 if so be that being clothed we shall not be found naked. 4 For indeed we that are in this [1]tabernacle do groan, [2]being burdened; not for that we would be unclothed, but that we would be clothed upon, that what is mortal may be swallowed up of life. 5 Now he that wrought us for this very thing is God, who gave unto us the earnest of the Spirit. 6 Being therefore always of good courage, and knowing that, whilst we are at home in the body, we are absent from the Lord 7 (for we walk by faith, not by [3]sight); 8 we are of good courage, I say, and are willing rather to be absent from the body, and to be at home with the Lord. 9 Wherefore also we [4]make it our aim, whether at home or absent, to be well-pleasing unto him. 10 For we must all be made manifest before the judgment-seat of Christ; that each one may receive the things done [5]in the body, according to what he hath done, whether it be good or bad.

[1]Or, *bodily frame* Comp. Wisd. 9, 15.
[2]Or, *being burdened, in that we would not be unclothed, but would be clothed upon*
[3]Gr. *appearance*
[4]Gr. *are ambitious.* See Rom. 15.20 marg.
[5]Gr. *through*

Vers. 1-10. WHY DEATH HAS NO TERROR FOR THE BELIEVER.

Ver. 1. This verse gives the reason for Chap. 4.17. 'Paul, whom we are inclined to believe felt strongly the possibility of his living to the time of the Parousia, is here supposing the possibility of his death before that time.

"*we know*",—This is not the general "it is known", but Paul is here speaking (with the inclusion of Timothy) of himself, as in the whole context.

"*earthly house of our tabernacle*",—His then present physical body.

"*tabernacle*",—This is a genitive of apposition; the tabernacle and the house are one and the same. The literal of "*tabernacle*" is "tent", the well-known expression among the Greeks for the earthly habitation or covering for the soul.

"*if*",—This is hypothetical, involving the possibility that he might not die. This is disputed by some, but both the context and the meaning of the particle favors this view.

"*dissolved*",—Undergo the process of dissolution.

"*we have*",—Present tense as referring to the time of the dissolution.

"*a building from God*",—A building originating with God and furnished by Him; not as contrasted with our earthly body, for that too is from God, but a building prepared in a special manner for us by God.

"*a house not made with hands*",—This is not to be contrasted with our earthly body, for that too is not made with hands; but with the other houses and buildings which are hand-made.

What is this house not made with hands?

1. Heaven itself. (H. Ca. Ros. Wol. Hof.)

Hodge argues for this view as follows:

(a) Heaven is so often called in Scripture a habitation, a house of many mansions, a city in which are many houses.

(b) The appropriateness of the metaphor.

(c) The agreement of the description here given with other descriptions of heaven. (Heb. 9.11; 11.10.)

(d) A body after death or in the resurrection could not be spoken of as present in the heavens, or as to be received from heaven, whereas Christ expressly authorizes such language respecting the mansions He is preparing.

(e) The building here spoken of is evidently to be entered upon at death. When Paul dies this was to save him from being found naked and this could not be at the final resurrection.

(f) Believers are said to pass immediately into glory at death. (Matt. 22.32; Phil. 1.22; Heb. 12.23; Luke 16.22.)

But on the other hand it is to be said:

(a) This view destroys the parallelism. If the earthly house is a body the heavenly house must be a body also.

(b) It does not say that the house was to *be* heaven, but that it was then *in* heaven.

(c) The change of the preposition from "*in*" of verse 1 to "*out of*" or "*from*" in verse 2 is against the view of Hodge. If

Paul meant the same thing this is certainly a very loose use of prepositions.

(d) The special form of the verb *"clothed upon"*, "to put on over", in contrast with the same verb without the preposition is not at all favorable to this view.

(e) The simple idea of heaven, if found in verse 1, does not consist with the idea of a house *"out of"* or *"from"* heaven in verse 2.

2. The resurrection body received at the Parousia. (M. A. Kli. Nea. Brow.)

This is the opinion of almost all recent expositors, with the exception of Hodge, who alone adopts the view that the house mentioned is heaven, and he argues for it very ably, as we have seen, and yet not with success, for a body which is said to be now in heaven and afterwards to come from heaven can hardly be identified with heaven itself. In spite of the apparent difficulty of Paul's representation that he receives the investiture at death, the arguments favor strongly the second view, namely that Paul has in view here the body to be received at the time of the resurrection.

Meyer explains very appropriately the use of the present tense, *"have"*, by saying that he who dies has from that moment a glorified body, not yet indeed as a real possession, but as an ideal possession (he has it *"in the heavens"*) to be realized at the Parousia.

Olshausen thinks the reference is solely to the transformation of the living. But in the case of transformation, there is no such thing as dissolution, which Paul mentions here as taking place before the house from heaven belongs to him.

Some say the reference is to an immediate pneumatic bodily organ in heaven, which is to clothe the soul only until the time for the resurrection body. (Au. Fl. Us. Nea.) But the word *"eternal"* is against this. Webster and Wilkinson argue for a permanent spiritual corporeity capable of coexisting with the body of the resurrection. But of all this, Scripture knows absolutely nothing.

The reason why Paul did not refer to the intermediate state between death and the Parousia or the resurrection is perhaps because he had as yet received no revelation on the point whether he and his fellow Christians of that age would live until the Parousia, and so whether there should be any such state to those of whom he was speaking. That it was in Paul's mind is perhaps evident from the distinction between the prepositions *"in"* and *"from"* in verses 1 and 2 respectively. It is not necessary therefore to say with De Wette that he over-leaped it, or with Osiander that he omitted its mention because of what he believed would be its shortness, viz., the time between his death (in case he died) and the resurrection.

"in the heavens",—This properly modifies the verb *"have"*, although the same sense will be preserved if it is taken as an adverbial phrase limiting building.

Ver. 2. The certainty of verse 1 confirmed by the longing, etc.

"in this",—i. e., in this body, Paul's then present body.

"longing",—The reason for the groaning.

"clothed upon",—The figure is here changed to a garment—to have superimposed upon, to put on over.

"with our habitation which is from heaven",—The reference is here the same as in verse 1, where this habitation was said to be *in* heaven, but now considered as brought at the resurrection time with the Lord from (out of) heaven at His coming.

The expression, *"clothed upon"*, seems to indicate that he is thinking of the same thing he said in I Cor. 15.51 and the following, namely, his being transformed alive. The additional preposition, *"epi"*, seems to lend strength to this supposition. (M. O. A. W-W. Kli.)

Olshausen says, "Paul regards it as an especial happiness not to taste death at all, not to be obliged to put off this body, but to be glorified living, drawing the heavenly body over this present mortal body like a garment, but of course in such a manner that the mortal body is absorbed in the nature of the spiritual body." The authorities quoted are very strong indeed in their advocacy of this view, and we see no good reason for not accepting it.

Ver. 3. This verse is a substantiation and explanation of the preceding one.

"if so be that",—This particle carries in it, in Classic Greek as well as here, the idea of full certainty, and this thought is here confirmed by the context. However, since to the English mind there is always a shade of doubt attached to the word *"if"*, we prefer to read "seeing that".

Paul is no doubt speaking with the deniers of the resurrection in mind. The passage is somewhat difficult, but we can see no other reasonable interpretation than that the Apostle says, in confirmation of what had preceded, that when Christ comes we shall be found clothed (having the resurrection body) and consequently shall not be found naked (in a disembodied state), i. e., we will not be disembodied spirits in that day. This, of course, would be true of Paul whether he were dead or alive at the Parousia.

"naked",—This is the very word used by the Greeks to express the disembodied spirit or condition. Anselm makes *"naked"* refer to naked of Christ; Hunsius to being without faith; Olshausen to naked of the robe of righteousness. But if by *"naked"* Paul had meant any other kind of nakedness than that which the similitude obviously implies, he most certainly would have indicated it.

The most current exposition on the part of others is that which refers the *"being clothed"* to being still clothed in the earthly body when the Parousia takes place, and the word *"naked"* to being not dead (not disembodied). Alive when the Lord comes he would of course then be changed. The rendering is:

1. If so be we shall be found clothed (in the earthly body) and not naked (not in the disembodied state of the dead), or as Grotius puts it,
2. If so be we shall be found among the changed and not among the naked (the disembodied). (B. Em. Ca. Es. Gro. Con. Ter. Wol. Mos. Schr.), or as Bilroth renders it,

3. If we, having been once clothed (with the earthly body) shall not be found naked (without the earthly body).

There are three objections to these views, or rather to these renderings, because the views really come to the same thing in the end:

(a) The clause would have to begin with a different particle, for which there is considerable but still insufficient authority.

(b) It fails to translate the particle "kai", which by the way is also overlooked by the Revised Version.

(c) "*clothed*" should according to this view be in the perfect tense, instead of in the past.

De Wette renders, "Seeing that when we are also clothed (in the heavenly dwelling, which is also a body) we shall not be found naked." But this makes "*clothed*" and "*naked*" to coexist, whereas they are by the text made to be the very opposite one of the other.

There is another reading, "*unclothed*", not quite so well substantiated, by which the rendering would be, "If we, provided that we shall be unclothed (shall have died before the Parousia) shall be found not naked."

Klieforth prefers the reading "unclothed" and translates, "Although we, even if an unclothing has ensued (if we have died before the Parousia), will not be found naked." The particle however, never means "although". Yet the sense of this rendering is good. But the reading "unclothed" is not sufficiently substantiated.

The literal rendering is, "If so be that being clothed, not naked we shall be found", and the rendering given by the discussion at the start is the only one that suits both the text and the context.

Ver. 4.   This verse expresses again the wish of verse 2 and confirms and explains it.

"*this tabernacle*",—As before, Paul's then present body.

"*being burdened*",—The reason for the groaning and for the being burdened is seen in what follows. The being burdened is not therefore because of troubles, etc. (Em. Pis. Fri. Schu.)

"*unclothed*",—That is, to suffer the process of physical death.

"*not for that we would*",—This can be a little better expressed for the English mind by, "because we do not wish", or "because that we do not wish". He is expressing the natural disinclination as to death; not that he feared to die, but perhaps regarding the Parousia as near, he would naturally prefer to be transformed.

"*that what is mortal*",—By speaking of what is mortal as existing in that day when Christ comes, he shows he is referring to the change or transformation of the living, for if he were referring to himself as being dead at that time there would have been no mortal part left, as he himself at that time under those conditions would be a disembodied spirit.

"*life*",—The new, immortal power of life which is imparted to us in the moment of the change at the Parousia when we are clothed upon.

Ver. 5.   This verse expresses the ground of his wish.

"*wrought us for*",—Made us ready for, and this He did through redemption, justification and sanctification.

Others refer this to the creation. (The. Bez. Chr. Theo. Schn.) But this has no place here, not even as the beginning of the preparation indicated.

"this very thing",—This does not have its reference in the groaning of the previous verse (B. Hof.), but to what he has just said about being *"clothed upon"* in order that that which is mortal may be swallowed up of life.

"the earnest of the Spirit",—i. e., the Holy Spirit as an earnest.

Meyer says, "The Holy Spirit given him as an earnest of the fact that he shall not fail to be clothed upon with the body waiting for him at the Parousia, which Paul was convinced he would live to see."

Alford, however, is nearer the truth when he says, "Paul in this verse seems to be treating no longer exclusively of his own wish to be transformed alive, but is showing that *the end itself* (which it seems he in common with others then living wished accomplished by transformation without death) is, under whatever form brought about, that for which all the preparation by grace of Christians is carried on and to which the earnest of the Spirit points forward."

Ver. 6. This verse shows the effect of verse 5 on Paul's mind.

"always of good courage",—No matter what the troubles, or as Alford prefers, "whether hoping to be clothed upon by transformation, or shrinking from being unclothed by physical dissolution."

Paul in verses 6 to 8 is saying that whether his particular wish as to the method of receiving the new body be realized or not, he is prepared to accept the alternative of being denuded of the body, seeing that it will bring with it a translation into the presence of the Lord.

"and knowing",—This is the ground for the *"willing"* of verse 8. It is an additional thought and correlative with *"being of good courage"*, and not a ground for the latter (Ca.), nor an exception to it (O. Es. Fl. Em. Ros.) as if it were to be taken in the sense of "although".

"at home in the body",—That is, residing here in our physical body.

"absent from the Lord",—Literally, away from home from the Lord, sojourning in a foreign country. (For the same thought see Phil. 1.3; I Thess. 4.17; Heb. 11.13.)

Ver. 7. We do not believe this verse ought to be taken as a parenthesis. Paul started to write, "Being therefore always of good courage and knowing that whilst we are at home in the body we are absent from the Lord, we are willing rather," etc., as in verse 8. But he was carried away from this by the intervening thought of verse 7, and accordingly took up the thought again in verse 8 with a change of construction. (A. M. Kil.) Others want to make a parenthesis out of both verse 7 and verse 8; but this most certainly interferes with the true trend of the thought.

"sight",—This cannot refer to a subjective process. It means that we are not surrounded by the actual appearance of heaven itself; we are not seeing the objective realities. It is the Lord in His glory concerning whom we now walk by faith, but one day will walk with His actual glory shining around and before us.

Ver. 8.   If verse 7 be taken as a parenthesis (and there is no strong objection to this construction), the particle translated *"I say"* must be so translated.   It is a picking up again of the thought interrupted by the parenthesis.

We, however, prefer, in keeping with our thought that no parenthesis ought to be allowed, to read the particle *"But"*, the adversative, and to start the sentence thus, "But we are", i. e., even though we do now have to walk by faith.

"at home with the Lord",—Though having expressed a preference to live until the Parousia, he says now, since being in his present body means absence from the Lord, he is willing, i. e., prefers to suffer even physical dissolution inasmuch as he knows this will bring him into the presence of the Lord.   The reference is not then in this place to the putting on of the immortal body at the Parousia.

Ver. 9.   *"Wherefore"*,—i. e., this being so, namely, our confidence being such, in event whether of death or of life until the coming of the Lord.

"whether at home or absent",—This phrase must be connected with *"to be well-pleasing unto him"*.   (B. Ca. Es. Em. Fl. Hof. Gro. Bez. Chr.) By many it is taken with *"make it our aim"*.   (C. D. Os. Ew. Ru. Bil.) But how can we, when we are absent from our body and present with the Lord, make it our aim *then* to please Him?   This connection brings commentators into all sorts of difficulty.   The thought of the passage may be expressed as follows: "Wherefore also we make it our aim now while we are in the body to be well-pleasing unto Him at His coming whether we are at that time in the body or out of it."

Ver. 10.   This verse gives the reason and the motive for the aim of verse 9.

"all",—All Christians, myself among the number, with special reference to those to whom they have preached.

Alford well says, "No more definite inference must be drawn from this verse as to the place which the saints of God shall hold in the judgment than it warrants, viz., that they as well as others shall be manifested and judged by Him.   When or in company with whom is not here even so much as hinted."

"be made manifest",—Made to appear in our true light (A. M. B. Bez.), and not merely to stand before.   (Gro.)   It is the same word used concerning the manifestation of Christ.

"before the judgment seat of Christ",—This does not refer to a mere judicial inquiry with respect to each man immediately after death (Fl.), for of this the Scriptures know nothing.

"the things done in the body",—Literally, "the things through the body", i. e., the body as the medium or organ of action, the things being done of course while in the body.

"in the body",—This was taken by some earlier writers (Ter. The. Chr. Oec.) and later by Osiander as indicating the resurrection body in which each receives back according to that which he did while in the physical body.   But this agrees neither with the context, nor with the

sense in which the body is used throughout the passage, nor with the actual words as used in this place.

"receive",—This really means to carry away.   Moral actions are here conceived as something deposited, laid up, and which at the judgment are received back, carried away in equivalent reward and retribution.

"whether it be good or bad",—That is, the things he hath done.

THE EPISTLE OF PAUL TO THE

EPHESIANS

(A. D. 64)

CHAPTER ONE

10 unto a dispensation of the fulness of the [1]times, to sum up all things in Christ, the things [2]in the heavens, and the things upon the earth;
[1]Gr. *seasons*
[2]Gr. *upon*

Ver. 10. The Present Age the Dispensation of the Fullness of the Times.

"unto",—i. e., with a design; with a view to. It belongs to the preceding "purposed in him".   (M. E. R. A. H. Ea. Bra.)

"dispensation of the fulness of the times",—The primary meaning of the word "dispensation" is house management, stewardship; but transferred to the spiritual sphere it means arrangement, economy, the ordering of events.   Practically all are agreed that the reference is to the first coming of Christ and that the dispensation referred to is the Gospel dispensation inaugurated by that coming; though Scofield quite arbitrarily makes it "the seventh and last of the ordered ages which condition human life on earth", and says it is "identical with the kingdom covenanted to David, and gathers into itself under Christ all past 'times'."

"fulness of the times",—The word "fulness" may mean (1) that which fills; or (2) that which is filled, and hence the state of fullness; or (3) the act of filling.   The last sense is out of the question; a fair interpretation could be gotten out of the first meaning, but all agree that the second meaning is the best one for the context in this place.

Eadie says, "The pleroma (fulness) is regarded as a vast receptacle into which centuries and millenniums have been flowing, but now it was filled."   In Gal. 4.4 where the word is "time", a fixed point of time is the thought in Paul's mind, that point of time being the birth of Christ, the time before Christ being conceived of as a unit; but in our passage, where the word is "times", the expression refers to a series of periods, to sections or seasons of time strung out through one complete whole which constitutes the fullness.

Alford complains that most expositors go astray in making the expression refer to a point of time rather than to a series of seasons.   As, for instance, Vincent says, "It is the moment when the successive ages of the Gospel dispensation are completed", and Ellicott says, "The reference is to that moment which completes the ordained seasons of the Gospel dispensation." Most expositors have had difficulty in making themselves clear on this point.

Riddle, on the other hand, says, "The main question is whether the phrase, *'the fulness of the times'*, as a whole, refers to the entire Gospel dispensation or to the period of the first advent alone. As the explanatory clause which follows points to what is still future, we accept the wider reference." With Riddle most authorities are agreed. (A. H. S. Mo. Ca. Ru. Ea. Mat. Bra.)

But there is still a question as to what periods of time the expression is meant to designate. We believe the majority of commentators have missed the exact meaning here. The *"times"* are pre-Messianic. There is no difference whatever between this statement and that in Gal. 4.4 except that this latter text conceives of the pre-Messianic ages as a unit, while our passage conceives of them as a series of periods. But as much as the word *"dispensation"* carries with it in itself the idea, not of a point but of a period of time, we must conceive of the time after Christ's first advent as included also in the *"fulness"* to which reference is made. This is substantially the view of Meyer, save that he closes the *"fulness"* with the last of the pre-Messianic periods.

All times, past, present, and future, come to their fullness at the beginning, in the course of, and at the completion of the dispensation of the Gospel.

CHAPTER TWO

7 that in the ages to come he might
show the exceeding riches of his grace
in kindness toward us in Christ Jesus:

Ver. 7.   POST-PAROUSIA BLESSEDNESS FOR THE BELIEVER.

"ages to come",—There are two views as to what is the time meant:

1. The ages which are successively arriving until Christ's Second Coming. (A. E. R. H. Ea. Bra. Wol.) These authorities conceive of Paul as speaking of the period between the resurrection of Christ and His Second Coming as the *"ages to come"* according to the technical, Jewish way of speaking and thinking.
2. The time after the Parousia. (M. O. Mo. Gro. Har.) Certainly the ordinary reader would take it in this sense, and Olshausen says that New Testament usage in the singular, its derivative meaning and the context favor this interpretation.

The arguments against this view by Alford are not at all formidable:

(a) The plural *"ages"*. (But see Chap. 3.21 and Jude 25 and the expression, *"unto the ages of ages"*.)
(b) The passage in Col. 1.26,27. But there is no mention there of *"the ages to come"*, and we cannot see how that passage bears very strongly on this one.
(c) The Second Coming is hardly ever alluded to in Ephesians. But there is no argument in this.

(d) The present tense of *"coming"*. But this as in other places may be a present of certainty with a future meaning. The very same word is used in the singular in the present tense in Luke 18.30 and Mark 10.30, in both of which places it is used with *"age"* and refers without doubt to the time after the Parousia. Certainly if usage counts for anything the balance is in favor of this second view.

This verse is used by many who favor the first view, in showing that Paul did not believe the Parousia to be near, but that he expected *"coming ages"* to intervene before that time.

But this is not at all a necessary, nor is it hardly a legitimate conclusion from the viewpoint under discussion, for if Paul used the phrase in its technical sense, that is from the standpoint of Jewish teaching as they looked forward to the ages of glory that were to follow close upon the appearance of the Messiah, it is at once evident that by the expression, *"ages to come"* no such time of waiting for the glory of the Messiah to come such as this present dispensation has brought to us was ever associated with the use of the words in question, as used by the teachers of Jewish doctrine.

CHAPTER FOUR

> 30 And grieve not the Holy Spirit
> of God, in whom ye were sealed unto
> the day of redemption.

Ver. 30. REDEMPTION FULLY REALIZED IN THE DAY OF CHRIST'S COMING.

"the day of redemption",—The reference here is to the day "when at the Parousia the certainty of the deliverance unto salvation becomes a reality" (M.); "when the body is glorified with the Spirit" (Mo.); "when the redemption shall be fully realized" (E. A.).

CHAPTER FIVE

> 5 For this ye know of a surety, that
> no fornicator, nor unclean person, nor
> covetous man, who is an idolater, hath
> any inheritance in the kingdom of Christ
> and God.

Ver. 5. THE KINGDOM OF CHRIST THE INHERITANCE OF THE PURE IN HEART.

"the kingdom of Christ and God",—"The kingdom", says Meyer, "which Christ opens at His Parousia and rules under the supreme dominion of God (I Cor. 15.27) until the final consummation whereupon He yields it up to God as the sole ruler (I Cor. 15.24,27)."

Riddle perhaps more appropriately says, "This kingdom is not merely the future kingdom of glory but the present kingdom of grace (Matt. 13)."

27 that he might present the church
to himself a glorious *church*, not having spot or wrinkle or any such thing;
but that it should be holy and without
blemish.

Ver. 27. THE JOYFUL PRESENTATION OF THE SAINTS BEFORE CHRIST'S THRONE AT HIS COMING.

That this presentation is to take place at the Second Coming is generally admitted, the more so since that event is so frequently referred to as a marriage. (R. A. E. O. Ea. Bra.) This is the purpose both of the sanctification, in verse 24, and of the giving up of Himself, in verse 25. The Church is to be presented as a bride, not as an offering.

"a glorious church",—This is somewhat inexact; the Church is to be presented as glorious, this word being emphatic by reason of its position, and explained by what follows.

"that he might present",—We prefer the rendering, "that He might Himself present to Himself", as supported not only by preponderant manuscript evidence, but as more appropriate to the actual circumstance. What takes place is not as in the case of the bringing home of actual brides by others, but Christ Himself presents the Church to Himself as a Bride at the Parousia. (A. R. O. M. E. Ea. Bra.)

Riddle remarks that, "Clearly enough the Church is not yet ready to be thus presented; but the Bridegroom is preparing her for it." This certainly is true so far as the Church visible is concerned, but as to how far it is true of the actual Bride one cannot be so certain.

Dr. David Brown adduces this verse, together with Col. 1.22, I Thess. 3.13 and Jude 24, in proof that the Church will be absolutely complete at His coming, and that therefore there can be no conversion of the nations after that event, and that therefore the universal turning of the nations to God, and the consequent Millennium, must take place before the second advent of the Lord.

Whatever the teaching of Scripture elsewhere on this point, in order that this verse shall be valid evidence of Dr. Brown's contention, it will be necessary to show first that the word *"church"*, as here used, denotes the total number of those who shall be saved; and even if it should thus comprise the totality of the redeemed, it must be equally shown that there never shall be in the future more than one manifestation of Christ in connection with this earth; and even so, inasmuch as the word Parousia (translated *"coming"*) really means "presence" and therefore a period of time rather than a point of time, many of the opponents of Dr. Brown's teaching contend that it is nowhere declared in Scripture that this presentation of the Church to Himself takes place immediately upon His glorious appearing.

CHAPTER SIX

13 Wherefore take up the whole
armor of God, that ye may be able to
withstand in the evil day. and, having
done all, to stand.

Ver. 13. THE CHRISTIAN'S ARMOR FOR THE EVIL DAY.

"the evil day",—Not the day of death (Era. Schm.), nor the day of

judgment (Jer.), nor the present life, hinting also at the idea of its brevity (Chr. Oec. Theo.), in which case "age" would have been used instead of "day."

Two other views remain, both of which agree that the definite article indicates some special time.

1. Any felt crisis in the soul's resistance whenever it may be. (E. O. A. R. B. D. Ru. Ba. Bl. Bra. Mel. Mat. The. Har. Winz.)
   The day of violent temptation.
   Moule says, "The definite article in such a phrase does not isolate a solitary occasion, but denotes distinct occasions of the one class in question."

2. "The day in which the Satanic power puts forth its last and greatest outbreak, which last outbreak of the anti-christian kingdom Paul expected shortly before the Parousia." (M. Us.)

This second view is possible but we feel that the first view is safer exegesis, i. e., the more conservative method of exegesis. The whole passage seems to be concerned with a present wrestling with or against present enemies.

The Epistle is quite silent on the subject of the Second Coming of Christ as compared with the other of Paul's writings.

THE EPISTLE OF PAUL TO THE

PHILIPPIANS

(A. D. 64)

CHAPTER ONE

6 being confident of this very thing, that he who began a good work in you will perfect it until the day of Jesus Christ.

10 so that ye may [1]approve the things that are excellent; that ye may be sincere and void of offence unto the day of Christ;

[1]Or, *distinguish the things that differ*

Vers. 6,10. THE CHURCH PRESENTED IN PERFECT HOLINESS AT THE DAY OF CHRIST.

Ver. 6. *"the day of Jesus Christ"*,—i. e., the day of His Second Coming. Thus practically every commentator. While the day of the Lord and the day of Christ refer to the same period of time, on examination it will be found that while the day of the Lord relates more to the sinner and his punishment, the day of Christ relates the rather to the saint and his reward. Erdman has said, "The transactions associated with the day of Christ in *every* Scripture where it is found, pertain exclusively to the risen and transfigured Church, and though presenting solemn judicial aspects to His saints, they are nevertheless radiant with holy joy and triumphant blessedness."

"will perfect it until",—Alford and Meyer say this expression assumes the nearness of the Coming of Christ. There is, of course. nothing in the

expression itself to warrant this deduction, but they say that unless this is assumed there exists a difficulty of some considerable seriousness. If Christ were to come in their time, then at His coming the good work begun in them would be completed and there is no difficulty in the expression. But if His coming was to be delayed, then what about those who die in the meantime?

This has caused Estius to refer the expression to each one's death, and Hackett to assume "that the reason Paul did not say 'death' is because the day of one's death and the final advent of the Lord coincide so essentially in their moral consequences that this advent was habitually near to the feelings and consciousness of the first Christians." But this is both gratuitous and unnecessary.

The fact is that some Christians were already dead and Paul knew it (I Thess. 4.14), so if there is any difficulty in this direction, thinking that Paul believed the Second Coming near at hand does not relieve it.

Calvin says the dead are still in process of being perfected, because they have not yet reached the goal. But this is a makeshift. It is difficult to see how the difficulty referred to presents itself, but so far as the nearness of the advent is concerned, the facts are now before us, and if Paul did so believe, we will need proof stronger than this passage affords to substantiate it.

Ver. 10. *"the day of Christ"*,—The day is the same as that in verse 6. The expression here is introduced by *"unto"*, which is a different preposition from that introducing it in verse 6. It means "for". Our word "against" expresses it well, i. e., so that when that day comes ye may be found, etc. It marks the destination.

CHAPTER TWO

16 holding forth the word of life;
that I may have whereof to glory in the
day of Christ, that I did not run in
vain neither labor in vain.

Ver. 16. *"day of Christ"*,—The same day as that of verses 6 and 10.

CHAPTER THREE

9 and be found in him, [1]not having a righteousness of mine own, even that which is of the law, but that which is through faith in Christ, the righteousness which is from God [2]by faith. 10 that I may know him, and the power of his resurrection, and the fellowship of his sufferings, becoming conformed unto his death; 11 if by any means I may attain unto the resurrection from the dead.

[1]Or, *not having as my righteousness that which is of the law*
[2]Gr. *upon*

Vers. 9,10,11. THE RESURRECTION OUT FROM AMONG THE DEAD.

Ver. 9. *"be found in him"*,—i. e., now and especially at His Coming. (M. A. R.)

Ver. 10. *"know him"*,—i. e., in the fullness of experimental knowledge.

"power of his resurrection",—The reference here is not to the power by which He was raised (Gro.), but the power which His resurrection exercises on believers, in assuring them of their justification (Rom. 4.25), and of their being raised with Him (Rom. 6.4; Col. 2.12).

Ver. 11. *"if by any means I might attain unto the resurrection from the dead"*,—

The two particles translated *"if by any means"* are used when an end is proposed but the possibility of failure to reach it is presumed. This at once shows that Paul had something else in his mind other than any general resurrection, because Paul knew quite well that he would be resurrected. It was the Christian's resurrection to which Paul was of course referring. Now certainly there is a difference between a Christian's resurrection and that of an unbeliever. There is this difference whenever the resurrection takes place, whether the dead are all raised at once or a thousand years apart.

But does the time element enter into this verse? Does this verse give support to the distinction between a first and a second resurrection? The literal for the word *"resurrection"* is "rise up", but here Paul has added another preposition, and the literal of the word *"resurrection"* as here used by Paul is "rise up out of", the verb thus having two prepositions connected with it, and it is the only instance where it is so used.

Next we come to the words, *"from the dead"*, and here is the preposition *"from"* used with *"the dead"* in addition to the two prepositions used in the word *"resurrection"*. The whole expression is then literally "rise up out of from among the dead", the two prepositions *"out of"* and *"from"* being one and the same word, *"ek"*.

It is this expression, as thus literally translated, that causes many here to find the reference to what is known as the first resurrection. Meyer has sought to eliminate this preposition *"ek"* (from among) standing before *"the dead"* from the text, but it is entrenched entirely too strongly by manuscript authority to be thus set aside.

Meyer says the word *"resurrection"*, as used here by Paul, is to be distinguished neither in substance nor style from the more simple word which Paul ordinarily uses, but is to be explained solely from the more vividly imaginative view which the Apostle has in mind. But a contention of this sort seems rather groundless in face of the most unusual, and otherwise uncalled for, form which the Apostle has given to the expression.

Meyer together with Alford, Ellicott, Braune and many other scholarly commentators say the expression refers to *"up out of"* the *earth*. This may be true, but we are still confronted with the other expression, *"from among the dead"*. There are those expositors who claim that the word *"resurrection"* alone, in the form here used by Paul, means "up out of the dead", but whether this be so or not, certainly taken with the rest of the expression, it must refer to some sort of an eclectic resurrection.

Olshausen declares that "the phrase would be inexplicable if it were not derived from the idea that out of the mass of the dead some would rise first". If this is not true we are simply at a loss to know why Paul piled up these expressive prepositions the way he did, and why he was not here content to use the simple word he used in other places, where he spoke of the resurrection of the dead, as for instance in Acts 24.15, where he was speaking to those who were utterly incapable of entering into the Christian's proper hope.

Of course it is not out of the range of possibility that Paul was here speaking of his own hoped for Christian resurrection, which of course would be a resurrection out of the place where the dead are, a resurrection to such blessed glory as might well be the hope and inspiration of every child of God, and that the rest of the dead and their destiny did not necessarily enter into the Apostle's concept.

We cannot, however, force ourselves from the inclination toward the other explanation, and to this it must be added that if the teaching of a first and second resurrection is found in Scripture anywhere, and if such was accordingly the belief of the Apostle, it is only natural to think that he must have had this distinction in mind when he made use of the particular prepositions in this passage.

However, altogether apart from the above discussion, the resurrection to which Paul made reference, is, as all admit, *"The blessed resurrection of the dead in Christ in which those who are Christ's shall rise at His Parousia. (I Cor. 15.23 and I Thess. 4.16)."* (A. M. E. Bra.)

It is, of course, the plain teaching of the Scriptures that the Christian shall rise first,—*"each in his own order; Christ, the firstfruits; then they that are Christ's at His coming"*; then, of course, the wicked, but just how long after most certainly does not enter into the content of this verse in Paul's letter to the Philippians.

CHAPTER FOUR

> 5 Let your ¹forbearance be known
> unto all men.   The Lord is at hand.
> ¹Or, *gentleness.*   Comp. 2 Cor. 10.1.

Ver. 5.   THE SECOND COMING OF THE LORD NOT TO BE LONG DELAYED.

"The Lord is at hand",—The words may apply either to the foregoing or to the following, or better still be taken with reference to both. Of course the reference is to the Second Coming of Christ, concerning the immediateness of which, Riddle says, there was wide-spread expectation.

Meyer says, "The expression points to the nearness of Christ's Parousia."

Ellicott says, "The inspired Apostle regards the Second Coming of Christ as nigh, yet not necessarily as immediate, nor as necessarily happening in his own life-time."

Hackett, while admitting that the reference is more probably to Christ's nearness in point of time, says, "There is no necessary, certainly no exclusive reference here to a definite expectation of the near advent of Christ."   Some *simply will not* have it so.

THE EPISTLE OF PAUL TO THE

COLOSSIANS

(A. D. 64)

CHAPTER ONE

> 13 who delivered us out of the power
> of darkness, and translated us into the
> kingdom of the Son of His love.

Ver. 13. THE KINGDOM HERE AND NOW.

"translated us into the kingdom of the Son of His love",—This is a historical fact realized at our conversion, and the kingdom is that which is now present. With this agrees almost everyone but Meyer, who pertinaciously maintains all such references exclusively refer to the future kingdom which is to set in at the Parousia. He, of course, must here take *"translated"* proleptically, as something already consummated.

CHAPTER THREE

> 4 When Christ, who is ¹our life, shall
> be manifested, then shall ye also with
> him be manifested in glory.
> ¹Many authorities read *your*

Ver. 4. CHRIST'S MANIFESTATION THE TIME OF HOLY PERFECTION.

"our life",—Alford has well remarked that Christ is personally Himself that life, and that we possess it only by union with Him and His resurrection.

"shall be manifested",—i. e., shall come forth from His present concealment at the Parousia, be personally revealed. This word is never used of the coming of Christ to judge the wicked or to punish them. All of its transactions pertain only to the blessed phase of the Advent.

"with him be manifested in glory",—This manifestation in glory of believers who are still living takes place through their being changed in the moment of rapture, as the readers were aware, and, of course, of the departed through their resurrection.

Braune and Meyer and many other splendid authorities say that the believers too shall be manifested visibly, their bodies having been glorified.

Alford has said, "It includes in itself both spiritual, ethical and corporeal; and the realization so far as possible here is the sum of the Christian's most earnest endeavors; but the life itself in its full manifestation is that perfection of body, soul and spirit, in which we shall be manifested with Him at His appearing."

CHAPTER FOUR

> 5 Walk in wisdom toward them that
> are without, ¹redeeming the time.
> ¹Gr. *buying up the opportunity*

Ver. 5.   *"redeeming the time",*—Many see in this expression a reference to the shortness of the time before the coming again of the Lord. (Ca. Bah. Oec. Chr.)   But even Meyer says this is gratuitously imported, and surely when Meyer doesn't catch this idea in a passage, it is not to be found.

THE FIRST EPISTLE OF PAUL TO THE

THESSALONIANS
(A. D. 54)

CHAPTER ONE

> 10 and to wait for his Son from heaven, whom he raised from the dead, even Jesus, who delivereth us from the wrath to come.

Ver. 10.   WAITING FOR THE SECOND COMING A COMMENDABLE CHARACTERISTIC OF THE CHRISTIAN'S LIFE.

To wait for Christ's return (this verse) and to serve the living and true God (verse 9) are here set forth as the aim of conversion and the characteristic of the Christian life.   It comes like a surprise that hope of the Second Coming is raised here to such explicit and emphatic emphasis. We would rather have expected faith in Christ to have been set forth as the other characteristic mark of the Christian life alongside of the service of God.   But this hope presupposes faith, while Christ's deliverance of us from the wrath to come points to faith as its necessary condition.

"to wait",—So far as the word itself is concerned we are warranted to assign to it nothing more than the notion of patience and confidence. But in view of what seems to have been their understanding concerning the matter, it is quite conceivable that they would read into the word the idea of nearness, i. e., nearness of the Second Coming.   (A. Dw. Lu.) This verse cannot, however, be taken as a proof text for this opinion on the part of the Apostles and early Christians.

"whom he raised from the dead",—The resurrection of Jesus from the dead is the great fact by which He is shown to be the Son of God (Rom. 1.4), and by which at the same time His return is rendered possible and certain. (I Pet. 1.3-5.)

"wrath to come",—i. e., at the judgment which Christ will hold at His advent.

CHAPTER TWO

> 12 to the end that ye should walk worthily of God, who [1]calleth you into His own kingdom and glory.
> 19 For what is our hope, or joy, or crown of glorying?   Are not even ye before our Lord Jesus at His [2]coming? 20 For ye are our glory and our joy.
>
> [1]Some ancient authorities read *called*
> [2]Gr. *presence.*   Comp. 2 Cor. 10.10.

Vers. 12,19,20.   THE LORD'S COMING THE TIME OF REWARD FOR THE FAITHFUL SERVANT.

Ver. 12.   *"to the end",*—This belongs to all three of the preceding particles as expressing their purpose (A. D. Rig. Coc.) rather than their object, as introducing the thing they were exhorted and encouraged and testified unto to do, as Lunneman says.

"who calleth",—We have here the present because the action is extended on into the future.

"his own kingdom and glory",—Both words have the same rank and the same emphasis. It is not therefore the *"kingdom of His glory"* nor the *"glory of his kingdom"* (O. Ben. Kop. Bol. Tur.). The glory is not the glory of the kingdom, but the glory of God.

It is not implied that the Thessalonians are already in that kingdom, but that they are only called to be citizens of it at some future time. The kingdom is that which is to be established at His coming. Lillie has put it well, "God calls you to a participation in His own kingdom which will appear at Christ's second advent, and to a participation in His own divine glory, into which believers then enter through the change of the living (I Cor. 15.21) and the resurrection of the dead (I Thess. 4.17)." The glory is that which God Himself has and which our Lord Jesus had with Him before the world began.

Ver. 19. A reason for the twice formed resolution (verse 18) of the Apostle to return to the Thessalonians.

The second clause of the verse is a confirmatory and explanatory question set forth as an answer to the one just propounded in the first clause. The rendering of the Authorized Version forms a very acceptable translation. The Revised Version differs only in punctuation, placing a comma after *"ye"*.

The punctuation of the Revised Version makes *"before our Lord Jesus at His coming"* modify all three of the preceding predicates. It seems as though Paul had written, *"For what is our hope or joy or crown of glorying? Are not even ye?"*, and then as a closer definition of what he meant he added, *"before our Lord Jesus at His coming"*.

With this view we feel that a dash after *"ye"* instead of a comma would be preferable. Westcott and Hort put a dash there and also one after *"glorying"* instead of the question mark there, and satisfy the passage with a question mark at the close after *"coming"*.

This rendering of the Revised Version, which is perhaps preferable, designates the presence of the Lord at His coming as the place of the hope and joy and glorying, and at the same time states or emphatically implies that the Thessalonians are to be present and accepted of the Lord at the time of His coming. The Authorized Version emphasizes this last point and implies the former.

Some critics seem by their exposition to refer the hope and the joy to the then present life of Paul and the glorying to the time of the presence of the Lord at His coming.

Lunneman, for instance, says that the hope consists in this, that Paul is confident that the Thessalonians will not be put to shame but will be found blameless in that day, and the joy consists in the fact that by the conversion of the Thessalonians and their Christian conduct the kingdom of God has been promoted. But even though Lunneman's idea of the hope and the joy be accepted, there is no reason why it should not be thought of as operating at the same time and place with the glorying.

However, most expositors take *"hope"* as the anticipation of reward on account of the conversion of the Thessalonians as effected by Paul. (L. Au. Es. Hof. From. Roos.) This is perhaps the most natural explanation, and the thought of the whole passage has been aptly expressed, and no doubt correctly, by Roos, "We hope on your account to have rich experience at the Coming of Christ, when we shall be able to joy over you, and to parade with you as one parades with a crown won in a contest of games." This reference to the crown as won in the game is the ground thought in the expression, *"crown of glorying"*, as admitted by all.

Ver. 20. An impassioned answer to the question in verse 19.

Some refer verse 19 to the Parousia and verse 20 to the then present. (A. Fl. Hof.) But had Paul intended this distinction of time he would have marked it, and the change is vigorously opposed by Ellicott, Lunneman and most other scholars of note.

CHAPTER THREE

12 and the Lord make you to increase and abound in love one toward another, and toward all men, even as we also do toward you; 13 to the end he may establish your hearts unblamable in holiness before [1]our God and Father, at the [2]coming of our Lord Jesus with all his saints.

[1]Or, *God and our Father*
[2]Gr. *presence*

Vers. 12,13. THE BELIEVER UNREPROACHABLE AT THE COMING OF THE LORD.

Ver. 12. *"the Lord"*,—The reference is here preferably to Christ (E. O. Lu. Rig.), although it may with propriety be referred to God (A.).

"increase",—Not in numbers (The.), but in grace, in faith and knowledge and richness of gifts, etc.

"even as we do",—It is possible to connect this phrase with both *"increase"* and *"abound"*, although by most it is connected only with the latter.

Ver. 13. *"to the end"*,—Expressing the aim of the contents of verse 12.

"in holiness",—This belongs to *"unblamable"* and not to *"establish"*. It specifies the sphere in which the blessedness is to be known.

"before our God and Father",—This belongs grammatically to the whole *"unblamable in holiness"*, the genuineness of which is assured by its being not before the eyes of men but before the eyes of God.

"at the coming",—Parousia; presence.

"with all His saints",—This means either angels (D. Lu.), glorified believers (Fl. Hus. Hof. Ger.), or both (A. E. Pl. Ba. Rig.)

Some of these writers, thinking that the word must refer to glorified believers because the word is never used in the New Testament of angels, throw the expression back and join it to *"unblamable in holiness"*. But this is awkward and it is not necessary even from the standpoint of these writers, because it is a fact that angels do come with Christ at His advent

(Matt. 16.27), and the word is used in the Hebrew of the Old Testament and in the Septuagint exclusively of angels, unless Zech. 15.5 be excepted. The word is "agioi". It is used, as we have said, in the Old Testament of angels, but in the New Testament it is never used of angels, but always of believers—and how often!

But do holy men, glorified believers, come with the Lord at His advent? The added *"his"* makes one think of believers because angels are never elsewhere called His.

The collective mass, *"with all"*, makes one think of believers because it is hardly conceivable that *all* the heavenly hosts should accompany Christ when He comes, but it might be that *all* believers should.

Now if it can be shown from any other passages of Scripture that glorified believers do accompany Christ when He comes, then it would seem preferable to take the expression here as referring to both angels and glorified saints, if not to the latter alone, in keeping with New Testament usage. That this can be shown there is no doubt and is quite generally acknowledged.

Alford says, "We need not enter into any discussion whether these are angels or saints properly so-called. The expression is an Old Testament one and was probably meant by Paul to include both. Certainly He will be accompanied by the angels, but also with the spirits of the just. (Matt. 25.31; II Thess. 1.7; I Thess. 4.14.)."

Riggenbach says, "Saints are with Christ immediately after death, and He will bring them with Himself, raising them before the rapture of the living, and thus they may be described as coming with Him."

CHAPTER FOUR

13 But we would not have you ignorant, brethren, concerning them that fall asleep; that ye sorrow not, even as the rest, who have no hope. 14 For if we believe that Jesus died and rose again, even so them also that are fallen asleep [1]in Jesus will God bring with him. 15 For this we say unto you by the word of the Lord, that we that are alive, that are left unto the [2]coming of the Lord, shall in no wise precede them that are fallen asleep. 16 For the Lord himself shall descend from heaven, with a shout, with the voice of the archangel, and with the trump of God: and the dead in Christ shall rise first; 17 then we that are alive, that are left, shall together with them be caught up in the clouds, to meet the Lord in the air: and so shall we ever be with the Lord. 18 Wherefore [3]comfort one another with these words.

[1]Gr. *through.* Or, *will God through Jesus*
[2]Gr. *presence*
[3]Or, *exhort.* Chap. 5.11.

Vers. 13-18. The Rapture at His Coming, the Believer's Blessed Hope.

Ver. 13. *"But .... brethren"*,—A common formula of transition to the imparting of weighty information by the Apostle.

"fall asleep",—i. e., from time to time among you. It was, as Alford says, "an expression conveying definite meaning to the Thessalonians as importing the dead in Christ."

It seems as though Paul had gotten notice in some way of a misunderstanding on the part of the Thessalonians, and he in this verse rectifies it. What were these Thessalonian Christians worrying about?

We quote for what they are worth in the estimation of the reader the following words from Olshausen. He says, "They seem not to have been duly informed as to the first resurrection and its relation to the universal one. The dead they thought would not return to life till at the general resurrection of the dead after the coming kingdom of Christ on earth, and would therefore be debarred from the bliss of this kingdom."

We have thought much over this passage and if Olshausen is not right as to the reason for their sorrow it is a seriously difficult matter to understand just why they seem to have been so troubled. Olshausen goes on to say, "To their misunderstanding Paul now opposes the information that those dead in the faith would rise before the general resurrection and accordingly those living at Christ's coming could not possibly anticipate the former." Let us bring the matter home to ourselves. It is exceedingly hard to get away from this explanation. They were disturbed about their departed loved ones. If there is to be but one general resurrection, as many believe, and this resurrection is to be at some future time when the Christian people now living, and who have departed loved ones, are likewise to be in the grave awaiting that resurrection, what advantage shall we who are now living have at that time over those who are now dead, if they died in the faith? Now this same thing would have applied to the Thessalonian Christians had they had this same belief about the resurrection.

They must have felt therefore that they who were living were in some way advantaged as to their own believing dead, and in what way this could have been, other than that mentioned above, it is not easy to see. It would seem therefore from this passage, as thus explained, that these Thessalonian believers were rather expecting to be living at the time of the return of the Lord.

"that ye sorrow not",—Many find in this the thought that the Thessalonians should not mourn in the same degree, not so excessively, because the Apostle could not possibly forbid every mourning for the dead. (C. Ca. Fl. Hem. Pis. Lap. Ben. Pel. Bis. Coc. Hof. Rig. Blo.) But if Paul had meant this he would have stated it differently; and besides the particle *"even as"* is only a particle of comparison and not of degree. It is absolute. The Apostle forbids sorrowing altogether. (A. Lu. Pl.)

But we must remember what sort of sorrow it was—not that we are forbidden to mourn our loss, but that we must not be sorrowful for theirs. That is, we are not to sorrow at all as those who look upon death as annihilation and have no hope of the resurrection. Death has no sting for the Christian.

"the rest",—The heathen and unbelievers in general, including especially such Jews as did not believe in the resurrection at all.

Ver. 14. Now comes the reason why they were not to sorrow.

"if we believe",—Lunneman says, and rightly, "It is clear that he supposes the fact of the death and resurrection of Christ as an absolute recognized truth, as indeed, among the early Christians generally no doubt was raised concerning the reality of this fact."

"even so",—This expression is designed to bring forth the agreement of the fate of Christians with that of Christ, i. e., even so, as Christ died and rose again, them also, etc.

The expression has been taken, but hardly with sufficient ground, in two other ways: (1) "even so, if they are asleep with this belief, them also", (Hof. Coc.); (2) "even so, if this our belief is true, them also" (Rig.).

"asleep in Jesus",—The literal is "asleep through Jesus". The preposition is *dia*, through.

This has caused some to say that it refers to those who were brought to death through Jesus, i. e., on account of Him., i. e., the Christian martyrs. (Me. Ar. Ham. Thi. Mus. Til. Salm.) But—

1. This is entirely foreign to the Apostle's design, to limit this participation in the glory of the returning Christ to so small a portion of Christians.
2. The indications in both Epistles have nothing to do with persecutions that ended in bloody death.
3. The expression is entirely too weak to express death through martyrdom.
4. What, in any case, would this have to do with the question in hand?

Many others follow the rendering of our Version and connect the preposition with *"fallen asleep"*, and translate, "fallen asleep in Jesus". (C. Es. Ca. Wh. Jo. Hil. Rig. Vor. Hem. Zan. Chr. Lap. Bez. Gro. Wol. Ben. Mac. Kop. Cali.) This is all right so far as the general trend of the Apostle's thought goes, for he is manifestly throughout this section speaking of the Christian dead. This is confirmed especially in verse 16.

But this rendering hardly gives the proper sense to the preposition (dia), *"through"*. Then again, the very fact that in verse 16 Paul uses the preposition (ἐν) *"in"* leads one to believe that if he had meant "in" here, he would have used that preposition, namely (ἐν) *"in"*, and not (ζιά) *"through"*. If the Apostle meant the same thing in each place why did he so quickly bring into use a different preposition?

This has caused some to join (dia) *"through"* to the word *"bring"*, as in the margin of the Revised Version. (O. D. Lu. Hof.; and Riggenbach says "almost all moderns".) This gives to *dia* its exact sense and harmonizes with the fact that elsewhere Christ is the instrument through which God brings to pass the resurrection. (I Cor. 15.21 and John 5.28.)

The meaning by this interpretation would then be that these sleeping ones God through Jesus would bring with Jesus.

The objection that *"bring"* already has a modifying clause in *"with him"* is no valid objection to this rendering, but Alford's objection that it gives us a "flat and dragging expression which I am persuaded the Apostle could never have written", is not without some weight.

Since, however, either of the two views above mentioned are consistent with the general thought, it matters little how we choose between them. The rendering of the Revised Version runs a bit more smoothly, but since it lays the Apostle open to the charge of a loose use of the prepositions, we are inclined to decide for the last view mentioned and accordingly read with the margin, which connects *"through Jesus"* with the verb *"bring"*.

Alford indeed has another view but it is arbitrary and insufficient. He retains the sense of *"through"* and still connects the words with *"fallen asleep"*. He unduly presses the distinction between being asleep and being dead. "Why", he asks, "are the departed Christians asleep, and not dead?" "By whom", he asks, "have they been thus privileged? Certainly through Jesus." He inappropriately regards such constructions as Rom. 1.8; 5.1; II Cor. 1.5, etc., as analogous expressions. His interpretation, with which certain other writers agree (E. Mi. Bar. Wor. Vau.), is entirely too strained.

"bring with him",—This is a pregnant expression which gives, instead of the act of resurrection, that which follows the act in time. Their resurrection is implied in their being brought.

"with him",—i. e., with Jesus.

Ver. 15. *"this"*,—i. e., what follows.

"by the word of the Lord",—It was not by Paul's subjective opinion, but by the very word of the Lord, i. e., there can be no mistake in what is about to follow.

Where did the Lord say this?

The expression no doubt refers to a direct revelation by the Lord to Paul. That Paul had many such revelations we know from various other passages. (O. E. A. D. Ar. Tur. Ben. Kop. Rig. Mold. Ges.)

Some (Bol. Pel. Mus.) suppose him to refer to the words of Jesus in Matt. 24.31, to which Ewald adds Lu. 14.14 and Hofmann adds Matt. 26.27 and Zwingli adds Matt. 25.1, but all these expressions, as Lunneman says, "are too general to be identified with the special thought of our passage", nor do they correspond to the expression, *"by the word of the Lord"*, which points to positive information on the definite subject in question.

Calvin appeals to a lost expression of Christ's, but this is quite arbitrary, and furthermore we have no evidence of, nor can we think of any inducement to Christ to set forth such special instruction in His day.

"we that are alive",—Paul does not say, "they that are alive"; he says *"we"*, thus presumably including himself.

It will not do with Calvin, much to our surprise, to charge the Apostle with little pious fraud; supposing that he, although he was convinced of the distance of the event, nevertheless represented himself as surviving in order in this way to stimulate believers to be in a state of spiritual readiness at every instant.

It will be well to note first that the revelation of the Lord refers only to the chief idea of the relation of the living to the dead at the Lord's coming—that those who are alive will not go before those who are dead; but that it does not refer to the question of who shall or who shall not be among the different classes in that day. If Paul had said, "I know by a revelation from the Lord that we shall witness the advent of Christ", the case would be different.

It is, however, unreasonable to contend that the possibility of their being alive at the Parousia cannot attach itself to the Apostle's thought. It does look as if Paul should have said, had he thought that the coming was to be long delayed, "Don't worry about your dead, for long before the Lord comes you will be in the same condition as they are now." In fact it would seem that the whole doctrine could not have the slightest practical significance for them unless the coming of the Lord was deemed possible before their death.

1. That Paul did mean for them to infer the possibility of his own and their being alive at that time is accordingly the view of many.

Lunneman says, "Every unprejudiced person must, even from these dogmatic suppositions, recognize that Paul here includes himself along with the Thessalonians, among those who will be alive at the second advent of Christ."

Alford says, "Beyond doubt he himself expected to be alive, together with a majority of those to whom he was writing, at the Lord's coming. That this was Paul's expectation we know from other passages, especially from II Cor. 5.1-10. It does not seem to be so strong toward the end of his course. (Phil. 1.20-26.)"

Olshausen says, "It is unmistakably clear from this that Paul deemed it possible that he and his contemporaries might live to see the coming again of Christ."

Dods says, "That the words of Paul are susceptible of a meaning which would imply that he expected to live until the Lord came again is evident from the circumstances that some of the Thessalonians, with whom the Greek was the mother tongue, did so understand the words."

On the supposition that this view is correct, Alford, who strongly espouses it, says, "It need not surprise any Christian that the Apostles should in this matter of detail have found their personal expectations liable to disappointment, respecting a day of which it is so solemnly said that no man knoweth its appointed time, not the angels in heaven, nor the Son, but the Father only."

What the above quoted authorities have to say about Paul's conviction in regard to this matter may be looked upon with favor, but the conclusion must not be made to rest too largely upon the inference that may legitimately be drawn from this verse. The fact is that the word "we" has little if anything to do with the question at issue. Paul doubtless hoped that he might be alive when Christ returned, but he has nowhere told us that he believed that he would be of the number living at that time; for how, then, could he have spoken so doubtfully about it in Phil. 1.21; 2.17; II Cor. 5.9, and in a still different tone in II Tim. 4.6?

Again, in I Thess. 5.1 he says that we do not know the time; consequently he could not have had any fixed belief about the matter one way or the other.

Again, if by "we" he meant to say that he would be alive at the Parousia, then the same thing would have to be true of every one of the Thessalonians, which thing is manifestly absurd.

But still again, and this is rather conclusive, if Paul had believed that he would be of the number living at the Parousia, and manifested the same by the use of the word "we", then by the very same argument it is conclusive that he believed that he would be dead and in his grave at that time, because he said in I Cor. 6.14, "God will raise us up". Note also that this last is used in the same Epistle in which he said, "We shall all be changed". (See also II Cor. 4.14 and compare I Thess. 5.10 and Acts 20.29.)

2. Consequently, there have been those who have maintained that Paul here speaks neither of himself nor yet of his contemporaries, but of a later period of Christianity. Lunneman says this view has been almost universally maintained, and it is indeed the view of a very great number of interpreters. (C. B. Fl. Wh. Ca. Era. Chr. The. Oec. Mus. Bul. Zan. Hun. Vor. Bal. Lap. Lau. Ben. Cali. Theo.)

These expositors take the plural only conversationally as not intending the idea that Paul and his readers might be alive at the second coming of Christ.

We are inclined to believe that Paul did use the plural "only conversationally", but this by no means excludes the possibility of the probability that Paul did have in mind the thought that he as well as the Thessalonians might be alive when his Lord returned, although it would hardly be legitimate to draw this conclusion, either from the use of the word *"we"* or from this one verse as a whole.

Paul seems simply to have opposed the two classes one to another—those who were dead with those who were living—and of course classed himself with the latter and spoke in a representative way, in the sense that one could just as appropriately say the same thing today, without believing in anything more than the possibility or perhaps the probability of the Parousia occurring in our day. Paul certainly had just as much reason for believing in the imminency of the Parousia as has anyone today.

There are other renderings, some of which express possible explanations of the matter in hand, but which cannot be substituted for the rendering of the text for grammatical reasons:

(a) "We, provided we are then alive, etc." (Tur. Pel. Hof.)

(b) "We, so many of us as are alive, etc." (L.)

It is certain that it was concerning them that had fallen asleep (verse 13) the Thessalonians were worried and anxious. It is also evident that they expected the Lord to come before they themselves died (wherever they got their information), else their worry would have been about their own selves after they had died, and their question would have been, "What about us?" Lunneman strangely thinks that the Thessalonians did not believe in a resurrection at all. But there is nothing in the passage before us to indicate this. Again, Paul did not reprove them for any such belief, or unbelief rather, as he did in the case of the Corinthians. Nor do the words of verse 13 prove in any sense that they did not believe in the resurrection at all. Olshausen rightly says, "Had the Thessalonians believed in no resurrection at all, then there could have been no talk of the living preceding the dead."

Lunneman draws his inference from the last clause of the verse, *"sorrow not even as the others who have no hope"*. But this does not say that the Thessalonians had no hope, any more than when in Chap. 5.5 he says, *"Indulge not in lust, even as the Gentiles who know not God"*, it proves that the Thessalonians know not God. It is the rather, Because you do know Him, be not like those who know Him not. And so in verse 13 it is, "Sorrow not as those who have no hope, because you do have hope", that Paul says.

But what kind of a hope did they have?   It was the hope of the last resurrection, what is known as the general resurrection, which hope of course the unbeliever did not have.

It is supposed by some (O. D. Hof.) that they had no doubt about the resurrection at the final consummation, but that they knew nothing about a first resurrection prior to that time.   If there is a resurrection of this kind, then this solution is doubtless the correct one, and the idea would be that in the kingdom just at hand, as they supposed, their beloved dead have no part.

It would seem that if the Thessalonians had believed that all the dead would rise at the coming of the Lord they would have had none of the anxiety that led Paul to say what he did to them, for if all the dead were then to arise, most assuredly their own dead would be among the number.

Olshausen contends that it is only on the ground that they believed in the general resurrection at the end of the kingdom, and that Christ was soon to come and establish that kingdom in which they, being alive when He came, hoped to have a part, that the anxiety could have arisen, because in this case their dead would have no part in the kingdom reign and glory.

"*shall in no wise precede*",—i. e., get before, so that the dead be left behind and fail of the prize.

Ver. 16.   "*the Lord Himself*",—In contrast to any other kind of a revelation of Himself through angels or other operations.   (O. Es. Ham. Bis.)

It seems to be as Alford says, that this is "said for solemnity's sake and too that it will not be a mere *gathering* to Him, but He Himself will descend and we shall all be called to meet Him."

"*with a shout*",—This refers to a signal shout of any kind given by the voice and is usually used as a word of command.

To whom is the shout to be referred?   It seems as though Paul set forth first and primarily the shout, and then defines it by the two following expressions, "*the voice of the archangel*" and "*the trump of God*".   If this is so, then it would seem best to refer the shout to the archangel, who for the publication of it uses partly his voice and partly a trumpet.   The content of the shout is the imperative call or command which reaches the sleeping Christians to summon them from their graves, consequently the resurrection-call.   (A. E. Jo. Lu. The. Hof. Dod. Cali. Stea.)

Others have referred the shout to God—to His imperative call to bring about the advent.   (Hun. Bis.)   But this would make it refer to an act preceding the descending, and would call for another preposition than the one used.

Still others have referred the shout to Christ.   (O. Gro. Oec. Rig.) But this comes into collision with the expression, "*the voice of the archangel*".   Riggenbach says it is the shout of Christ, as that of a victorious Captain, whose order summons to battle, for the destruction of His enemies and the extermination of the anti-Christian powers.   He says, "We have three particulars following each other in rapid succession: the Commander's call of the King Himself; the voice of the archangel summoning the other angels; and the trumpet of God which awakes the dead and summons believers.   The sounds will be heard and the signs will be seen."   To inquire which archangel is futile.

The trumpet, as used by the archangel, is called the trumpet of God, either because it excels all earthly trumpets in the power of its sound (B. Ba. Ca. Lap. Wol. Ben. Bol.), or because it will be blown at the command of God (O. Bal. Lau. Pelt. Schot.), or because it belongs to God and will be blown in His service (D. A. E. Koc. Stae.).

"The dead in Christ shall rise first",—Schott arbitrarily attaches *"in Christ"* to *"shall rise"*, on the ground that if we conceive of Paul as here speaking of the dead in Christ being raised that the doctrine of two resurrections is thereby taught. This is a bold but unwarranted exegetical stroke to avoid a disagreeable conclusion.

The expression does not denote, as some maintain (Oec. Theo.), the first resurrection in contrast to the resurrection of all men at a later period, which distinction is left entirely unnoticed in this passage, the contrast being only between what will take place in case of the righteous dead and the righteous living. (O. A. Lu. Jo. Rig.)

Ver. 17. *"then"*,—i. e., immediately after the dead in Christ have arisen.

"with them",—i. e., with the resurrected dead in Christ.

"caught up",—This is after the change indicated in I Cor. 15.51,52 and II Cor. 5.2-4. The word means "snatched away", and is an expression depicting swiftness and irresistible force.

"in the clouds",—i. e., enveloped in the clouds, or perhaps *on* the clouds. The same idea is to be found in Psa. 104.3; Dan. 7.13; Acts 1.9,11; Matt. 24.30. Alford and Lunneman connect these words with *"caught up"*, but the meaning is the same whether thus connected or connected with *"meet"*. The latter connection appeals to us the better, however, from the fact that the words are nearer each other, and *"caught up"* already has one modifying clause.

"and so shall we ever be with the Lord",—Some have taken this to mean that we are to have our permanent abode with Him in the air. (We. Us. Pelt. Stae.) But II Cor. 5.1 says our permanent abode is in heaven.

Paul goes no further here because his purpose was accomplished, it being wholly and entirely to satisfy the doubt raised by the Thessalonians concerning the advent of Christ. It was for this same reason doubtless that he remained quiet about the change of believers who may be alive at the time of the advent.

Some have taken the words to indicate that we shall remain with Him in the air and in the heavens and that He does not therefore come down to earth for the establishment of an earthly kingdom. The fact is Paul says nothing about this here one way or the other. However, from the fact that the narrative stops with the meeting of the saints in the air with the Lord, lends strength to the intimation that what is here said is more favorable to an abiding of His people with the Lord elsewhere than on the earth in a personal reign. And yet from the words alone one is not warranted in drawing any positive conclusion one way or the other.

Lillie calls attention to the fact that the word used for *"meet"* is used in only three other places in the New Testament, and in all of them (Matt. 25.1,6; Acts 28.15) the party met continues after the meeting to advance still in the direction in which he was moving previously. This in interesting, but of course it proves nothing with any degree of certainty in this case.

Olshausen says that after Christ meets the saints He returns with them to heaven, into His heavenly abode at the right hand of God, and that we nowhere read that Christ and the glorified believers will reign on the earth during the Millennium, and that to *"reign upon the earth"* in Rev. 5.10 is really to "reign over the earth", and that this they can do from heaven and that both Christ and the saints may perhaps even now and then appear to individuals as Christ did during the forty days after the resurrection.

Ver. 18. *"with these words"*,—i. e., the words Paul had just spoken to them, and not the doctrines of the faith in general. (O. Ar. Fl. Pelt.)

CHAPTER FIVE

1 But concerning the times and the seasons, brethren, ye have no need that aught be written unto you. 2 For yourselves know perfectly that the day of the Lord cometh as a thief in the night. 3 When they are saying, Peace and safety, then sudden destruction cometh upon them, as travail upon a woman with child; and they shall in no wise escape. 4 But ye, brethren, are not in darkness, that that day should overtake you ¹as a thief: 5 for ye are all sons of light, and sons of the day: we are not of the night, nor of darkness; 6 so then let us not sleep, as do the rest, but let us watch and be sober.

¹Or, *as thieves*

Vers. 1-6. THE SUDDEN AND UNEXPECTED COMING OF THE DAY OF THE LORD.

Ver. 1. *"times and seasons"*,—The same expression is used by Christ in Acts 1.

Times denotes times in general, while seasons denotes the definite points or periods of time in the former.

It is probable the expression had become a common one for giving a greater completeness than either word alone would give and that the distinctive meaning of each word had been somewhat lost sight of. There can be, of course, no way to be certain of this, but if the two terms are to be distinguished, the above distinction is the correct one. The expression, as Campbell Morgan says, is no haphazard one, but refers to the whole providential arrangement marked out by God, and is here used with special bearing upon the time of the end when the Lord was to come again.

Riggenbach thinks that the idea of longer duration lurks in the use of the plural of these words as here used by Paul.

"have no need",—It was not because such instruction would not be useful to them (Oec. Theo.), nor because no instruction could be given unto them (Zw. Es. Fl. Ba. Hun. Koc. From. Pelt.), but because Paul had already by word of mouth taught them as much as could be known, which was that the time was unknown and could not be known. (A. Lu. Rig. Dod.)

This had doubtless formed the topic of frequent discussions among the Thessalonians and perhaps they had sent the question to Paul through Timothy.

Ver. 2. *"the day of the Lord",*—This is not a day of twenty-four hours. It refers to a period of time commencing at His coming but stretching out beyond that through the time of the judgment. It is the day mentioned by Joel and other prophets as the day of judgment, and must not be thought of in any sense as the day of the destruction of Jerusalem (Ham. Har. Scho.), nor the day of each man's death (Chr. Blo.). It relates itself perhaps more nearly than any other time-end expression to what is in reality the Parousia, which last word literally means "presence". (A. O. Lu. Rig.)

Riggenbach says, "The reference is, indeed, partly to particular, preliminary judgments, but more and more to the conclusive, final judgment."

"The day of the Lord" in the Old Testament denotes a time when God will manifest His punitive justice and also His goodness and power. It is the day of His wrath on His enemies and of the deliverance of His people. (Joel 1.15; 2.11; Ezek. 13.5; Isa. 2.12.)

"thief in the night",—The idea of suddenness and unexpectedness is the prominent one in this expression. (O. E. A. Lu.)

The image is conceived from a secure state of worldly complacency on which the advent of Christ comes like the unexpected thief into the well-guarded house, plundering the members of the house of their possessions and of that to which their hearts cling.

"cometh",—This is not used instead of a future (Fl. Vor. Kop. Pelt.), but it is the present expressing, as is so often the case, the absolute certainty and truth of that which is predicated.

Ver. 3. *"they",*—i. e., men in general,—the people of the world as opposed to the people of God.

"peace and safety",—The one word refers to inward repose and the other to a secureness not interfered with by outward opposition.

"as travail upon a woman",—The point of comparison is the sudden and inevitable occurrence of the rending pain.

Alford is right when he says that De Wette, followed by Lunneman, presses the comparison too closely when he says that it "assumes the day to be near—for that such a woman, though she does not know the day or the hour, yet has a definite knowledge of the period." It is not the woman nor her condition that is the subject of comparison, but the suddenness and unexpectedness of the pang that comes upon her.

Ver. 4. *"not in darkness",*—This expression refers to the ruined condition of the unbelieving world that knows not God and is expressive of its ignorance and moral slumber.

"that",—It seems as though this must be taken in the sense of "in order that" as referring to the purpose or design of God. (A. E. Lu. Fri.)

Lunneman perhaps best interprets the thought for us, "Ye are not in darkness, and thus the design which God has in view in reference to those who are in darkness, namely, to surprise them by the day of the Lord, can have no application to you."

Olshausen says that this interpretation, "in order that", as expressing design, does great violence to the sentence. Accordingly many join

Olshausen in translating "so that" as expressive of result.   (D. Ba. W-W. Fl. Rig. Hof. Bis. Jow. Pelt.)

The idea of result does better suit the thought, but it is hard to get that meaning out of the particle used.   This is, however, given in Thayer's Lexicon as a third meaning of the particle,—"with the issue that".   But Winer seems to have rather conclusively shown that this meaning cannot attach to any New Testament use of the particle, and Thayer says that wherever the interpretation "in order that" can be taken, it ought by all means to be so taken.

"*that day*",—Here, of course, is meant the day of the Lord, but it is called merely "*the day*" as the time of light breaking in on darkness.

Ver. 5.   "*sons of light and sons of day*",—The "*day*" is a strengthening synonym for "*light*" and is that in which we have our origin and our specific nature.

Ver. 6.   "*the rest*",—i. e., the unbelievers.

> 23 And the God of peace himself sanctify you wholly; and may your spirit and soul and body be preserved entire, without blame at the ¹coming of our Lord Jesus Christ.
>
> ¹Gr. *presence*

Ver. 23.   THE BELIEVER PRESENTED IN PERFECT HOLINESS BEFORE THE LORD AT HIS COMING.

"*sanctify you wholly*",—In view of what follows it is best to take this in a quantitative sense, as referring to the whole personality, viz., in your entire extent, through and through.   (A. E. O. D. W-W. Lu.)

There are those who take it in an ethical sense, "*so that ye be pure and blameless*".   (Jer. Lut. Kop. Pelt.)   But this qualitative sense is fully enough expressed in the words "*without blame*".

"*may your spirit and soul and body be preserved entire*",—The Revised Version we feel has interfered somewhat with the real thought of the passage by transferring the word "*entire*" to the place it now occupies in the text.   The word is an adjective and modifies all three of the words, spirit, soul and body, although being placed in the Greek just before the word "*spirit*" it takes its gender from that noun.   The word "*entire*" means consisting of all its parts.   The words "*wholly*" and "*entire*" seem to be one the synonymy of the other and refer to that which is perfect, not in the ethical sense so much, but spoken of things to which nothing belonging to their nature is wanting, i. e., quantitatively.

"*spirit and soul and body*",—The Apostle seems here to teach the three-fold division of human nature, the spirit being the highest and distinctive part of man, the immortal and responsible part, while the soul is the lower or animal part containing the passions and desires.

"*without blame*",—In a word Paul prays that the whole personality, each part in its entirety, may be preserved so that it will be found blameless in the day of His coming.

"*coming*",—The word is as usual, Parousia, meaning, literally, presence, and the verse as a whole sets forth the blessed truth that this is the time when the believer is to be presented in perfect holiness before his Lord and Saviour.

THE SECOND EPISTLE OF PAUL TO THE

THESSALONIANS

(A. D. 54)

CHAPTER ONE

4 so that we ourselves glory in you in the churches of God for your [1]patience and faith in all your persecutions and in the afflictions which ye endure; 5 *which is* a manifest token of the righteous judgment of God; to the end that ye may be counted worthy of the kingdom of God, for which ye also suffer: 6 if so be that it is a righteous thing with God to recompense affliction to them that afflict you, 7 and to you that are afflicted rest with us, at the revelation of the Lord Jesus from heaven with the angels of his power in flaming fire, 8 rendering vengeance to them that know not God, and to them that obey not the [2]gospel of our Lord Jesus: 9 who shall suffer punishment, *even* eternal destruction from the face of the Lord and from the glory of his might, 10 when he shall come to be glorified in his saints, and to be marvelled at in all them that believed (because our testimony unto you was believed) in that day.

[1]Or, *stedfastness*

[2]Gr. *good tidings*: and so elsewhere. See marginal note on Mt. 4.23.

Vers. 4-10. THE PERSECUTED BELIEVER'S REST AT THE REVELATION OF CHRIST.

Ver. 5. *"which is a manifest token"*,—The word denotes a sign, a guarantee, a proof. It is to be taken as referring to all of verse 4 beginning with *"for your patience"*, etc. (A. D. E. Lu. Fri. Lil.), and not to the subject of *"endure"*, i. e., the Thessalonians (Es. Era.), nor to *"all your persecutions and tribulations"*. (C. Zw. Ew. Bul. Are. Wol. Kop. Bis. Pelt.)

"the righteous judgment",—Alford says, "The judgment which will be completed at the Lord's coming, but is even *now* preparing, this being an earnest and token of it."

The majority of expositors agree with Alford in this, referring the judgment especially to that which will take place at the coming of Christ. (C. D. E. Lu. Lut. Hof. Dod. Pelt.) The use of the definite article *"the"* and more especially the following verse seem to favor this interpretation. The unjust sufferings of the righteous show that justice is not meted out sometimes as it should be here and that therefore there comes the demand for a future judgment.

Riggenbach and Olshausen strongly contend against this view and maintain that the righteous judgments of God were those which the Thessalonians were then suffering on earth, the end of which or the purpose of which is that they might be counted worthy, etc. Olshausen asks, "How can the *present* patiently endured suffering for the sake of the kingdom of God be a sign or an evidence of the *future* righteous judgment of God?" This view of course represents their present afflictions and persecutions as the righteous judgment of God upon them, merited because of their sin, but endured for their perfection and being made worthy of God's kingdom.

If it were not for the following context Olshausen's view would be the preferable one. But in view of what follows, their present sufferings may be taken as a proof of the coming judgment upon their adversaries

476

and the adversaries of God, because it made it obvious that in this world men do not receive their just deserts and therefore a future judgment is demanded for the sake of justice.

Ellicott says, "To refer *'righteous judgment'* solely to present sufferings, as perfecting and preparing the Thessalonians for future glory (O.) is to miss the whole point of the sentence. The Apostle's argument is that their endurance of suffering in faith is a token of God's righteous judgment and of a future reward, which will display itself in rewarding the patient sufferers, as surely as it will inflict punishment on their persecutors."

There is no good reason why both views should not be combined after the manner of Alford and Fausset.

"to the end that",—This depends on *"righteous judgment"* (A. D. E. Lu. Ew. Rig.), and not on *"endure"* (B. Es. Za. Bis. Hof.). It means "the result of which judgment will be" (E. Lu.), rather than "the purpose of which judgment shall be" (A. D. Ew. Rig.). God's righteous judgment, the proof and demand for which is seen in their patient endurance of affliction, will result in their being esteemed worthy of the kingdom in the day of the Lord's coming.

"the kingdom of God",—This, says Olshausen, is the kingdom to be established at Christ's coming, expected then as quite near at hand. (Lu. Bla.) Riggenbach says, "The kingdom of God here mentioned is the holy dominion, which shall one day be revealed by the return of the King in victorious glory." He says, however, that this is a kingdom which flesh and blood cannot inherit.

"for which ye also suffer",—Not as purchasing the kingdom by suffering as meritorious, but they suffer for the kingdom's sake.

Ver. 6. *"if so be that"*,—This does not express doubt, but is put hypothetically for the very purpose of strengthening its import, and to indicate that it is altogether incontestable, the writer appealing to the reader's own judgment.

"it is a righteous thing",—This points back to the righteous judgment of verse 5.

Ver. 7. *"rest"*,—Liberation from earthly affliction is one of the glories of the kingdom.

"with us",—i. e., with Paul and his companions who were in like manner being persecuted; and not with Christians generally (D. Tur.), for all Christians were not being persecuted, which is the case as implied in our verse; nor with us, the saints of Israel (B. Ew. Mac.), seeing that the Thessalonians were Gentiles.

"at the revelation"—Riggenbach says, "The same thing as Parousia, only it conveys more than His presence; He will be unveiled in His glory." The word is "apocalypsis".

"angels of His power",—Not "mighty angels" (Fl. Pis. Oec. Ben. Theo.) The power is Christ's; His angels are His servants and the instrumentality through which He manifests His power. They are the executors of His power.

Some translate "with His angelic host" (Mi. Hof. Dru. Kop.). But the Greek word for *"power"* is never translated in the sense of "host" or "army"; besides this translation would require the words *"angels"* and *"power"* to exchange places.

"in flaming fire",—The natural symbol of perfect purity and unapproachable majesty. This is to be taken as a further specification of the mode of His revelation. (A. E. Lu. Rig.) In the Old Testament God is described as appearing in flames of fire and especially is His coming to judgment described as a coming in fire. Here the description is referred to Christ. The words are not therefore to be connected with what follows as the instruments of His taking vengeance. (Es. Lap. Har. Mac. Hil. Hof. Schm. Mold.)

Ver. 8. *"rendering vengeance"*,—i. e., distributing it as their portion.

The rest of this verse is taken by Olshausen and others as referring to unbelievers in general who were criminally ignorant of God and who obeyed not His Gospel that was preached unto them. (O. C. D. Rig. Tur. Hem. Pelt. Schot.) But the repetition of *"to them"* usually compels to the distinction of two different classes and so many others take the first as referring to the Gentiles and the second to unbelieving Jews. (B. E. A. Ba. Ew. Bis. Kop. Ben. Gro.)

The fact that the Gentiles are in a number of places elsewhere called by Paul, *"those who know not God"*, and that disobedience was the characteristic of the theocratic nation of the Jews, together with the repetition of the *"to them"* inclines us to the latter view.

Ver. 9. *"eternal destruction"*,—"A testimony this", says Ellicott, "to the eternity of future punishment that is not easy to be explained away."

"from" and *"from"*,—Three explanations:

1. To be taken in a local sense, i. e., separation from. This is by far the best explanation and is approved by the majority of scholars. (A. E. Lu. Rig. Bis. Kop. Blo. Pic. Bez. Cali. Schot.)
2. To be taken in the sense of time,—immediately upon the appearance of His face and His glory, describing thereby the swiftness and facility of the punishment; Christ has but to appear. (Va. Es. Oec. Chr. Era. From. Theo.) But this is a very artificial interpretation.
3. To be taken in the sense of cause. (Ca. Kop. Bol. Pelt.) ; some taking *"from the face of the Lord"* arbitrarily as "from the Lord"; and others with equal arbitrariness understanding the word *"face"* as of a wrathful countenance. But this would make the verse a mere repetition of verses 7 and 8.

De Wette objects to the first view on account of the word *"might"*. This word at first glance might seem to favor the second view; but it may be taken as a genitive of origin.

The meaning is "from the glory which is a creation (visible—localized result,—A.) of his might." (Lu.)

Alford and Lunneman understand this glory as that imparted to believers, and not as Christ's own glory. But this is a bit far-fetched; the parallelism leads us rather to think of something belonging to the

Lord, although it may extend in reference here to the believers as well who are at that time to be glorified.

Ver. 10.   *"saints"*,—Not angels (Mac. Schr.), but Christians, glorified believers.

"in",—Not "through", as many render; nor "among", but *"in"*, the element in which, so that the glorification of His saints becomes a glorification of Christ Himself—as the sun in reflected in a mirror—as a teacher is glorified in her scholars.   Dods says, "The saints are the risen and glorified companies of believers."

Olshausen says, "It is not stated here that Christ comes *with* His saints, as it was said in verse 7 that He comes *with* the angels, but according to I Thess. 4.17 (their gathering together with Him), this must here to be necessarily assumed."

"to be marveled at in all them that believed",—This may mean that in the hearts of His believers there is an admiring adoration, but in view of the apparent parallelism between the two members, it is better to take it that Christ will be admired or wondered at *because of those* who have believed on Him.   Lunneman says, "The blessedness of believers being admired, Christ also is therein admired as the Author of that blessedness."

If Christ is the object of this admiration, who is the subject?   Some think it is those who are now stiff-necked.   But it is best, however, to take it in a universal sense of all creation, even of the angels as well as of men believing and unbelieving, the wonder and admiration of the glorified increasing, while the unbelievers are at least amazed at such a person.

"because . . . believed",—A parenthetical statement designed to bring forward the certainty that also the Thessalonians belonged to the believers.

"in that day",—To be connected with *"glorified"* and *"marveled at"* (A. Lu. Rig.); not with *"believed"* (Gro. Syr.), taking this last word in the future sense.   The verb is an aorist and the aorist can never be taken in the sense of a future.   Nor is it to be connected with *"testimony"* (Es. Fl. Ba. Ros. Kop.), nor with the too remote *"shall come"* (B. O. Zeg. Pelt.).

There is another of Dr. Brown's proof texts against pre-millennialism.   He says the expression *"all that believed"* must include all that ever have believed or ever shall believe on Christ to all eternity, and that hence at His coming, when all such admire Him, it is plain that the number of the elect must be complete, and that therefore no more can be saved after the Parousia takes place.   But, however the case may be presented elsewhere, Dr. Brown's position can hardly be said to be clearly established by the passage before us.   Kellogg replies as follows:

1. When Moses delivered Israel from Egypt he saved all that believed on him.   Does that prove that none could have believed on Moses after that?   Will any say that Christ could not be said to be admired by all believers at His coming, if any believed on Him after His coming?

2. What proof is there that in this place the word *"all"* must thus include all that could possibly be put into it?   That this word is not thus used in every case is so certain as not to be denied by anyone.   The same principle which Dr. Brown assumes here,

carried elsewhere would prove from Rom. 5.18 the universal salvation of all men, and from Col. 1.20 even the salvation of the Devil and all his angels. The mere use of the word *"all"* proves very little. That in any particular case it has the broadest sense possible always needs to be proved. That it has such a sense here no evidence is offered.

3. But when we look at the Greek text of the passage we find that the evidence is on the other side; for the particle which is rendered in the Authorized Version, *"them that believe"*, is in the past tense, so that the word *"all"* is thereby strictly limited to all those who have believed before the Advent. The New Testament revisers have accordingly rendered the participle in the past, *"them that believed"*. The sense of the words, then, is simply that all who up to the time of the Advent shall have believed on Jesus will then admire Him. As to whether, after the Advent, others shall be saved or not, the words teach absolutely nothing. They are equally consistent with either supposition.

CHAPTER TWO

1 Now we beseech you, brethren, [1]touching the [2]coming of our Lord Jesus Christ, and our gathering together unto him; 2 to the end that ye be not quickly shaken from your mind, nor yet be troubled, either by spirit, or by word, or by epistle as from us, as that the day of the Lord is just at hand; 3 let no man beguile you in any wise: for *it will not be*, except the falling away come first, and the man of [3]sin be revealed, the son of perdition, 4 he that opposeth and exalteth himself against all that is called God or [4]that is worshipped; so that he sitteth in the [5]temple of God, setting himself forth as God. 5 Remember ye not, that, when I was yet with you, I told you these things? 6 And now ye know that which restraineth, to the end that he may be revealed in his own season. 7 for the mystery of lawlessness doth already work: [6]only *there is* one that restraineth now, until he be taken out of the way. 8 And then shall be revealed the lawless one, whom the Lord [7]Jesus shall [8]slay with the breath of his mouth, and bring to nought by the manifestation of his [2]coming; 9 *even he*, whose [2]coming is according to the working of Satan with all [9]power and signs and lying wonders, 10 and with all deceit of unrighteousness for them that [10]perish; because they received not the love of the truth, that they might be saved. 11 And for this cause God sendeth them a working of error, that they should believe a lie: 12 that they all might be judged who believed not the truth, but had pleasure in unrighteousness.

13 But we are bound to give thanks to God always for you, brethren beloved of the Lord, for that God chose you [11]from the beginning unto salvation in sanctification of the Spirit and [12]belief.

[1]Gr. *in behalf of*
[2]Gr. *presence*
[3]Many ancient authorities read *lawlessness*
[4]Gr. *an object of worship.* Acts 17.23.
[5]Or, *sanctuary*
[6]Or, *only until he that now restraineth be taken &c.*

[7]Some ancient authorities omit *Jesus*
[8]Some ancient authorities read *consume*
[9]Gr. *power and signs and wonders of falsehood*
[10]Or, *are perishing*
[11]Many ancient authorities read *as firstfruits*
[12]Or, *faith*

Vers. 1-13. THE DAY OF THE LORD AND THE MAN OF SIN.

Ver. 1. *"touching"*,—This translation hardly expresses what the preposition contains. Many take it as a form of adjuration, "by", but this meaning the preposition never has in the New Testament.

It is more correctly taken in the sense of "in respect to". (D. Fl. Ba. Ew. Zeg. Vor. Gro. Ham. Wol. Noe. Kop. Hey. Win. Wie. Blo. Rig. Pelt. Schot.)

However this is not quite the thought. There seems to be a touch of concern about the event as though he would guard it from misrepresentation, and perhaps it is best to translate with the margin of the text, "on behalf of". (A. E. Lu. Er.)

"coming",—Parousia, presence.

"our gathering unto him",— (See I Thess. 4.17).

Ver. 2. *"to the end that"*,—The aim and object of *"beseech"*.

"shaken from your mind",—*"mind"* is to be taken quite generally, your mental apprehension of the subject (A. E. Lu.), and not as "your former more correct sentiment on the subject as received through personal instruction by the Apostle". (Fl. Os. Es. Hem. Bul. Pis. Lap. Gro. Hey. From. Mold.)

"shaken",—Used especially of a sea agitated by a storm.

"quickly",—i. e., soon and without due consideration. This meaning, doubless, soon after the instruction received by them from the Apostle (O. Ca. Pis.), though some take it, soon after my departure (Lan.), soon as ever the matter is spoken of at any time. (A. Lu. Dod.)

"either by spirit",—i. e., prophetical discourses by members of the Church and falsely given out as divine revelation. (A. O. Lu. Rig. Dod.) (See I Thess. 5.20.) Not a dream (Schr.), nor deceitful revelations by spiritual appearances (Schm.), nor falsely understood prophecies of the Old Testament (Krause).

"as from us",—i. e., pretending to be from us when in reality it is spurious.

Since all three words are governed by the same word, *"by"*, some say *"as from us"* must modify all three of them, or the last one only. (C. Ew. Zw. Rig. Hof. Chr. Theo.) Grammatically this appears to be true. But since it cannot modify the first word, *"spirit"*, inasmuch as a prophetic discourse of the Apostle could not be invented, it being necessary for the Apostle's presence for such an utterance, the above authorities have confined *"as from us"* to the last word only, *"letter"*, and they take *"word"*, not as some sayings of Paul hawked around, but as a *teaching* that reasoned perhaps from the Scriptures and not from prophetic rapture as was the case in connection with the first word, *"spirit"*. Others, however, refer *"as from us"* to the last two words as closely connected, showing that someone carried around a pretended oral utterance, while others did even the same with a spurious letter. (E. A. D. Lu. Gro. Wet. Theo.)

"word" therefore means either "teaching" in accordance with the first view noted, or it means an oral statement attributed to Paul if the second view is followed. We incline hesitatingly to this second view.

By *"word"* is not meant therefore a traditional falsified word of Jesus (Ba.), nor the prophecy of Jesus in Matt. 24, Mk. 13, Lu. 21 (Noe.), nor *"reckoning"*, with reference to Daniel's week of years. (Mi. Ty.)

"epistle",—It is a bit difficult to know whether Paul was simply referring to the possibility of such a letter being circulated (Jow.), or whether he means to say that such a letter was actually in circulation (A. Lu.), or whether he refers to his first epistle. (Bl. Hil. Bez. Ham. Reu.)

1. The phrase *"as from us"* may intelligibly be made to mean, "Be not troubled by letter as if I had said," i. e., do not understand my former letter to have taught, etc.

2. It seems natural that in this his second epistle, which might seem to contradict what he had said in his first one, that he would draw attention (Chap. 3.15) to his signature as evidence that both epistles were from him.

3. If a forged letter had existed it is probable that he would have dealt more severely with it.

4. It is a bit improbable that while Paul was within so easy reach, so daring a forgery would have taken place, and a forgery so profitless.

5. Dods says that if Paul had meant a forged letter he would have doubtless used another preposition more distinctly expressing the source from which the thing eminates.

However, all this does not establish the case for a reference to a first epistle, and as between the possibility of such a fraud and the actuality of it, it is safer to decide for the latter, as more in keeping with the expression as used by the Apostle.

"day of the Lord",—Preponderating authority is against the reading of the Authorized Version, "day of Christ".

"just at hand",—The word means "just on the point of commencing" (A-R-V); "immediately imminent" (Dod.), or "already present" (R-V); "is now present" (A. Er. Tor. Bla. Rig.), "has really come" (Lil.), "is now come" (E.).

Alford says, and rightly, "Paul could not have written as in the Authorized Version, 'at hand', because he and all other New Testament writers had been writing all along that the day of the Lord was at hand, but they had never said it was *just on the point of coming* or was *even then present*."

Dr. Brown makes strong use of this passage to prove that the Millennium was still in Paul's mind many centuries removed. But the Parousia of Christ (which others believe is to usher in the Millennium) could still be *"at hand"* and yet be a year or many years away; in other words, *"at hand"* is not indicative of nearness as the verb here used implies. The Thessalonians apparently either thought He had already come and that their rapture (I Thess. 4.17) had not taken place, or that He was just on the point of coming any minute, hour or day.

Riggenbach says, "The emphatic position of the verb at the front shows that the Apostle does not intend generally to put far away the expectation of the last day; they were merely not to let themselves be surprised by the cry, 'Here it is now!' The verb denotes a standing at the door, immediate presence."

The verb occurs in six other places in the New Testament and Alford says always in the sense of "being present". (Rom. 8.38; I Cor. 3.22, 7.26; Gal. 1.4; II Tim. 3.1; Heb. 9.9.)

Says Alford, "They imagined the day to be already come, and accordingly were deserting their pursuits of life, and falling into other irregularities, as if the day of grace were closed."

Blackstone says, "The persecuted Thessalonians thought that they were *in* the Tribulation period, and that the Day of the Lord had set in. But Paul corrects them, first by reminding them that the Lord had not come for *them as yet,* as He had said that He would (I Thess. 4.15-17), and then by adding certain other things which must occur before the Day of the Lord should come."

Morgan says, "The people of Thessalonica misinterpreted Paul's first epistle, thinking that the day of Christ had come because they were in tribulation. Paul therefore wrote a second letter wherein he corrected this error, showing how that day must be preceded by certain signs, and the Church waiting for her Lord, will not pass through the tribulation, but will be taken from the earth before it comes. In the opening verse of Chap. 2 there is a wonderfully clear and concise distinction between the *'coming'* and the *'day'* of Christ. Before *'that day'* dawns, *the* final apostacy (the definite article is very distinct) is to be inaugurated by the revealing of the man of sin—not a system, but an individual."

Torrey says, "The Thessalonians were troubled by the teaching that had arisen among them that the day of the Lord was already present and that they were in the midst of the judgment, *'the day of the Lord'*. They were greatly excited and perturbed by the fact. Paul shows them that this could not be because the *'man of sin'*, who was to be especially dealt with in *'the day of the Lord'*, had not yet been revealed. The *'day of the Lord'* is not the coming of Christ to receive His Church, but that which follows upon it. It is the time of the Lord's coming to the earth."

C. H. Mackintosh says, "The Christians at Thessalonica were passing through intense persecution and tribulation, and it is evident that false teachers had been disturbing their minds by leading them to think that they were even then surrounded by the terrors of the day of the Lord, that it was already present. He beseeches them, first, on the ground of the coming of the Lord Jesus Christ and the rapture (verse 1) not to so think, thus drawing a clear distinction between the coming at the time of the rapture of the saints and the *'day of the Lord'*. And then further he reminds them that *'that day'*, i. e., the day of the Lord, shall not come except there be first a falling away from the faith and the revelation of the man of sin."

Kellogg says, "What troubled the Thessalonians was not the possible imminence of the Advent, which could only have filled them with gladness, but what had been suggested by some false teachers, who taught—like some in our own time—that the *'day of the Lord'* was *'now present'*, and had brought with it no personal return of the Lord, and no resurrection of those whom they had laid to sleep in Jesus."

Dods says, "The expression, *'shaken out of your mind'*, implies that wild spiritual excitement prevailed among the Thessalonians; that they were really acting as people who had lost their senses, giving up perhaps their ordinary occupations and scandalizing sober-minded people."

But no wonder, if they thought that the "*day of the Lord*" had really come, and that the events of I Thess. 4.15-17 had not taken place.

But let us examine the matter a bit more carefully. It is not so easy to think that the Thessalonians believed the day of the Lord had already come; because they knew that no rapture had taken place, no gathering together unto the Lord in the air (not even of Paul himself), no resurrection of *"the dead in Christ"*, no appearance of their Lord, as they had been taught in the first epistle of Paul, to them would take place (I Thess. 4.15-17). Then again if they had so thought, would not Paul have reminded them most clearly and emphatically that they were mistaken, by the very fact that these things had not taken place, and then have added, as another reason why their actions were unwarranted, the fact that there must first come the apostasy and the revelation of the man of sin? But instead of this Paul emphasized only the latter reason, telling them that the apostasy and the revelation of the man of sin had first to take place prior to the time to which reference is had in the passage.

Now we are not so sure that the Thessalonians or other Christians of their day knew of the distinction, much emphasized in our day by certain teachers concerning the end-occurrences, between the *"coming of Christ"* and *"the day of the Lord"* or His revelation, at least in the sense that the latter occurred some time after the former, a period, as some believe, of seven years intervening.

Campbell Morgan says this distinction was made "very distinct" as between the last verses of the fourth chapter and the first verse of the fifth chapter of First Thessalonians. But certainly this noted expositor's vision must be exceedingly keen to gather with such emphatic assurance this knowledge from the passages in question.

Even C. H. Mackintosh, one of the staunchest champions of this school of interpretation, says, "They knew that Jesus was to return; but as for any distinction between His coming *for* His people and His coming *with* them at a later time, between His coming and the day of the Lord, they were, at the first, (i. e., until Paul made it plain in the verses to which Morgan refers) they were wholly ignorant."

At any event the distinction is not well drawn. Does not the *"day of the Lord"* begin at the same moment with the coming of Christ for His people (if not before)?

Even Morgan says, "The day of the Lord is, in one sense, begun by His coming; but it is a whole period which stretches out beyond that coming, the Millennium itself being included in that phrase."

So also W. J. Erdman, a strong pre-millennarian, who says, "The rapture is the opening event of the day of the Lord."

And most certainly the Thessalonians thought of the day of the Lord in this sense, and not as something to take place a number of years later by a single event, when Christ was to come back with His risen and glorified saints, because it was doubtless the persecution and suffering through which they were going that led them to believe that the day of the Lord was either present or just breaking upon them.

If therefore this time distinction is to be conceded it should be made, not between the *"coming of Christ"* and the *"day of the Lord"*, but between the *"coming of Christ"* and *"the revelation of Christ"* with the *"day of the Lord"* between the two and stretching on out past the *"day of Christ's revelation"*, including, if you wish, the Millennium, even as Morgan maintains.

Now it would seem that it was in the sense just set forth that Paul thought of *"the day of the Lord"*, viz., as beginning immediately after the coming of Christ, if not before, but at least not as beginning seven years or any number of years after that coming. This seems apparent because it was the matter of the persecution and suffering of the Thessalonians that became the moving cause of his admonitions to them.

Now we have further to state that so far as the expression, "*shaken from your mind*", is concerned, it denotes, as Olshausen has rightly said, "all violent passions of joy, grief or fear". Lunneman has likewise said, "This effect might be produced both on those who regarded the advent with longing desire and on those who regarded it with fear."

Now, for the reasons already given, we repeat it is difficult to think of the Thessalonians as imagining that the time had passed for the rapture and the resurrection, and that they were in the "*day of the Lord*" which was to follow immediately thereafter. If this be the case, then their state of mind was indeed one of fear and overwhelming despondency. But if, on the other hand, because of the persecution and trial that was beginning to gather so hard about them, they thought the coming of Christ was just about to take place, then their state of mind would naturally be one of great joy and extravagant excitement due, as Ellicott says, "to wild spiritual anticipations", in which they may well be pictured as forsaking their daily vocations and dissipating their property because of the happy prospect of the coming rapture and departure from the earth to meet the coming Lord. It is to this latter view we find ourselves inclined, and for this reason prefer the reading of our text, "*as that the day of the Lord is just at hand*".

W. J. Erdman even identifies the expression, "*the day of the Lord*", with the "*coming of our Lord Jesus Christ, and our gathering together unto Him*" of verse 1. He says, "The Apostle beseeches the saints touching (Gr., in behalf of) this very coming (Parousia) of the Lord to gather them together into His presence, not to be troubled or shaken from the teaching they had received from him; and he beseeches them concerning this coming and gathering together as something that has not taken place and cannot take place before the '*man of sin*' has been revealed."

Now it would seem from this that in either case the Apostle puts the "*apostacy*" and the "*revealing of the man of sin*" before the coming of Christ for His saints, and if this be true, just because this revelation of the man of sin must be thought of as during the day of the Lord, the supposed period of time between "*the coming of Christ*" and "*the revelation of Christ*" vanishes altogether, or shrinks, as it were, into a mere point of time, thus bringing the two events together and throwing the period, "*the day of the Lord*", before them both, and this again would mean that the Church will go through the "*day of the Lord*", which is the same with the "*time of great tribulation*".

Thus W. J. Erdman, "The Church throughout the world will be contemporary with the '*man of sin*' and in the '*great tribulation*'. The man of sin is the author of the great tribulation; the Day of the Lord (he means what we have designated as the revelation of Christ) in which he meets his doom, comes after the great tribulation; the Church is delivered at the opening of that day from the wrath which overtakes him; therefore the Church must have been contemporary with him and *in the great tribulation*."

We therefore see no reason thus far in the Apostle's teaching to consider the day, the coming, the appearing, the manifestation and the revelation of Christ other than one so far as the time element enters into their conception.

And thus Dwight, with many others, "The question whether the Apostle thought of the Parousia as probably to take place within twenty or thirty years or not, must be determined so far as this passage is concerned, by the length of time which must be allowed for the occurrence of what he declares is to take place before the day of the Lord."

Ver. 3. *"beguile"*,—This is better than *"deceive"* of the Authorized Version because the word does not precisely carry the idea of deceit from an evil intention. "Befool" is a good rendering.

"in any wise",—Neither by any of the three ways mentioned, nor by any other way.

"for . . . . ",—There is an elipsis here, but it is not necessary to think of the Apostle intending to fill it out but forgetting it after the lengthy description which follows (Lu.), but the elipsis supplies itself readily in the reader's mind, as in either the rendering of our text or that of the Authorized Version.

Two things must precede that day, the apostacy and the revelation of the man of sin.

"falling away",—Apostacy. This is preceded by the definite article *"the"*, and therefore refers to the apostacy as well known to the Thessalonians, either through the oral instruction of the Apostle (verse 5), or through the Old Testament prophecies, or the prophecy of Jesus in Matt. 24.10-12.

It must be taken in the sense of a religious apostacy and not in a political or semi-political sense. This is made certain by the relation of Antichrist to it, by the description of it in verse 7 and by the constant Biblical usage.

"man of sin",—Not the cause of the apostacy (D. Pelt., appealing to verses 9 and 10), but the historical completion and climax of it. (A. Lu.)

"revealed",—As Christ in His time, so Antichrist in his time is to be revealed.

"the son of perdition",—The primary meaning is that perdition is his inheritance (A.); he falls a prey to perdition (Lu. Rig.), and not that he is the cause of perdition to others (Pelt); although we see no good reason for not including the latter in the former, as do many (O. H₂y. Oec. The. Schot.). Olshausen aptly says, "He not merely has sin and falls into destruction, but that sin and destruction proceeds from him as their source and he drags every one else into sin and destruction after him."

The article *"the"* before *"man of sin"* only admits of the reference to a definite, known personality.

Olshausen says, "The name 'man' characterizes him at the same time as a real man with body and soul, whom Satan, the principle of evil, thus makes his dwelling, as the Son of God united Himself with the man Jesus."

Zwingli and a few others take the word collectively as denoting every bad man altogether fallen under the power of sin, but the article forbids this and the following description shows plainly that a single personality is in Paul's mind.

Ellicott says, "Even as Christ is now spiritually present in His Church, to be personally revealed more gloriously hereafter, even so the power of Antichrist is now secretly at work, but will hereafter be made manifest in a definite and distinctive bodily personality."

The man of sin means the one who wholly belongs to sin (Rig.), in whom sin predominates, the genitive of predominating quality (E.), in whom sin is the principle matter (Lu.), in whom sin is personified as righteousness is in Christ (A.).

That by *"the man of sin"*, the Apostle means the Antichrist is shown;

(a) By the connection with apostacy.
(b) By the genitive "anomias", verse 7.
(c) By the words, *"son of perdition"*.
(d) By the words, *"he that opposeth"*, etc.
(e) By his sitting in the temple of God.
(f) By the connection of his coming with the working of Satan.
(g) By the application to him of the words *"Parousia"* and other words which are used of Christ's coming.
(h) By the contrast of the deceit of unrighteousness with the truth.

The Antichrist is not the Devil himself because he is distinguished from the Devil in verse 9. He is, according to verse 9, the instrument of the Devil.

Ver. 4. *"he that opposeth"*,—Whom does he oppose. Not the human race (Mi. Ba.), but God (see immediately following) and more especially Christ, as the entire context shows. (A. Lu. Hey. Schot.) He is the Antichrist (I John 2.18), the antagonist, the adversary and caricature of Christ.

"against all that is called God",—Not only against the true God but against heathen gods as well. He treads all religion under his feet. He does not promote idolatry, but seduces men from the true God and from all idols as well, and sets himself up as the only object of adoration. He wants to be the only god and suffers none else beside himself.

"Compare", says Alford, "the close parallel in Dan. 11.36,37."

Says Ellicott, "This characteristic of impious exaltation is in such striking parallelism with that ascribed by Daniel to 'the king that shall do according to his will' (Dan. 11.36), that we can scarcely doubt that the ancient interpreters were right in referring both to the same person—Antichrist. The former portion of the prophecy in Daniel is apparently correctly referred to Antiochus Epiphanes, but the concluding verses (verse 36, etc.) seem only applicable to him of whom Antiochus Epiphanes was merely a type and a shadow."

Riggenbach says, "The Apostle's brief picture reminds us of Dan. 7.8,11,20, etc. The modern interpreters see in this for the most part Antiochus Epiphanes; more correctly we shall recognize in this little horn of the 7th Chap. the yet future adversary of whom Antiochus Epiphanes, described in similar terms, was but a type."

"that is worshipped",—A generalization of the idea God—whatever else is an object of divine adoration.

"he sitteth in the temple of God",—Because of the word *"sitteth"*, and the repetition of the article *"the"*, many say the one definite temple

of the one definite God is meant, i. e., the temple at Jerusalem. (D. E. Lu. Wh. Gro. Cle. Wie. and Scho.—with reserve). But the article is no formidable reason for this view because the very same expression is used elsewhere in a metaphorical sense, as all acknowledge. There is some strength in the argument from the word "*sitteth*". It seems as though it means a literal setting of one's self down. And the fact that the temple no longer exists is not sufficient argument against it because some are ready with an argument, not without some strength, that the temple is to be rebuilt. For this reason Ellicott leans strongly to an ultimate fulfillment in a future temple (Ezek. 37.26) at Jerusalem. However, the figurative sense of holding a place of power, sitting as a ruler, is very frequently found in connection with the same word, as for instance where our Lord is said to "*sit on the right hand of God*".

Inasmuch as this is true and Paul used the expression,"*the temple of God*" metaphorically in I Cor. 3.17 (See also I Cor. 6.16 and Eph. 2.21), others have taken the expression in a metaphorical sense. We see no reason why it should be interpreted with such rigid literality as that of Lunneman and others. The passage will be satisfied if the homage due to God is drawn aside to something human. The reference is said by Olshausen and others to mean the Christian Church as such in all lands; and indeed the Church is called the temple of God.

But what Paul does is, as Riggenbach says, "to depict an act, which as a symbol of permanent spiritual significance, is confined to no locality, and means to say: He places himself in God's room and forces himself on mankind as a Divine ruler. He portrays, indeed, an outward act that connects itself with the temple; but this act is the expression of an abiding disposition and purpose that is not confined to the one house of stone. Who will see beforehand where or in what form of outward action it will come to pass that the Man of Sin shall force himself on all the world as God? The language of a prophet must be understood according to the analogy of the prophets."

This interpretation does not necessarily conflict with the literal one and yet it both satisfies the prediction and relieves it of whatever embarrassment the literal interpretation might attach to it. If, however, it can be shown that the temple is to be literally rebuilt in Jerusalem there can then be no embarrassment in accepting the literal interpretation of our passage, and it would seem that it ought under such circumstances to be so accepted.

"*setting himself forth as God*",—Publicly predicating of himself divine dignity and worthiness of adoration, and this perhaps not only in word (D. O. Rig. Bis. Hey. Oec. Chr. Theo. Schot.), but by deceitful miracles (verse 9).

Ver. 5. Inserted with a slight accent of surprise mingled with a tone of reproach that they should have made so little of this previous oral instruction. He was telling them nothing new apparently. Notice the force of the "elegon", "*I was telling, I used to tell*". It appears somewhat as though he had repeatedly talked to them of the advent and the things about which he was now writing.

Ver. 6. "*now*",—There are four explanations of the connection:
1. A particle of transition to a new communication, i. e., "And now —to pass to another point—ye know", etc. They knew this

from Paul's oral instruction and needed only to be reminded of it. This is by far the most commendable view. (D. A. E. Lu. Ew.)

Other views are:

2. A temporal adverb in opposition to *"yet"* of verse 5, the present time in contrast to the time Paul was with them, i. e., "I told you orally that the Antichrist must come before the advent of Christ, but now after my written declaration (verse 3) ye know that the apostacy must come before the Antichrist." (B. Fl. Hil. Storr.) But this is not what the verse says. It says, *"ye know what restraineth"*, and of this Paul had written nothing in verse 3, for surely the apostacy is not the same as that which restraineth. Even so, to have expressed this contrast would have taken a different construction.

3. A temporal adverb modifying restraineth, i. e., "And ye know that which now restraineth". (O. Wh. Ba. Hey. Wie. Bis. Mac. Schr.) But with this we would have expected the word *"now"* to have been placed immediately before *"restraineth"*.

4. A particle of time, i. e., "And now, when ye recall my oral instruction, ye know", etc. (Rig.) Riggenbach says the oral instruction would then have extended to an explanation also of that which restraineth, and that this may account for the brevity with which Paul mentions it here, having referred to it more fully in his oral instruction.

"that which restraineth",—i. e., hinders. Not what hinders me from expressing myself freely about the Antichrist (Heinsius), nor the coming of Christ (No.), but that which hinders the appearance of the Antichrist. The expression is a neuter one and so denotes a power or a principle, while the *"one that restraineth"* in verse 7 is a masculine and denotes a person. At least, says Riggenbach, "this is apriore the most natural suggestion."

"his own season",—i. e., the time appointed him by God.

Ver. 7. *"mystery"*,—Made very emphatic by being placed first and by being separated from its further definition "of lawlessness" by the verb and the adverb.

"lawlessness",—i. e., ungodliness, wickedness in general. It corresponds to the apostasy of verse 3. There are three views as to its grammatical relation, each of which amount to the same thing. It is either:

1. A genitive of apposition—the mystery which consists in lawlessness. (A. D. Lu.); or

2. A genitive of possession—the mystery which belongs to lawlessness; or

3. A genitive of characterizing quality—the mystery which is characterized by lawlessness. (E.)

It refers to a concealed, mysterious wickedness—to lawlessness insofar as it is still a mystery.

Olshausen goes beyond Scripture when he makes the expression equivalent to the Antichrist himself as an incarnation of Satan.

"doth already work',—i. e., in a yet hidden, mysterious way, which perhaps many as yet did not recognize, but in it all, Paul sees the beginning of the final rebellion against final grace.

"*only*",—This word must be connected with what follows. It cannot. be connected with what precedes, either with "*mystery*"—only as a hidden mystery (Wor.), or with "*work*" (Ky.), because this word is defined by "*already*".

The rendering of our text is certainly very awkward. It is better to supply the verb, "will restrain", as is done in the Authorized Version, which certainly gives the proper sense to the verse. (B. Es. Wh. Zw. Os. Vul. Syr. Era. Bez. Zeg. Bal. Lap. Cap. Lan. Sto. Cali. Pelt., et al.) The Authorized Version, however, has an unhappy rendering of the verb supplied. It is, however, perhaps better, especially from a grammatical standpoint, to supply nothing, to conceive of "*one that now restraineth*" being placed before "*until*" for the sake of emphasis, and to transfer in thought "*until*" to its proper place immediately after "*only*", and read, "Only until he who now restraineth is taken out of the way", i. e., "The mystery of lawlessness doth already work, but only will it work in this hidden, mysterious way until he who now restraineth is taken out of the way." (A. Rig. Lil. Ros. Hey. Noe. Schot.)

Some supply "*there is*", as in our text, (W-W. Ba.), but this does not get rid of the troublesome "*until*" except in what is rather an awkward way, although the sense is the same. All in all we prefer the marginal reading of our text.

"*be taken out of the way*",—The phrase is used of any person or thing which is taken out of the way whether by violence or death or any other way.

What the restraining power is and who the restraining one is (if this distinction is allowed to stand) is the darkest point in the whole passage. It will be discussed a little later.

Ver. 8. "*the lawless one*",—The same as the Man of Sin—the Antichrist.

"*revealed*",—He will then throw off every veil, bringing himself forth into the light. The same word (apocalypsis) is used of Christ.

"*slay*",—i. e., destroy; consume.

"*with the breath of his mouth*",—This is an expression denoting the ease with which omnipotence accomplishes its object. It is not to be taken in a sensuous way, as of a fiery wind; nor to be idealized so as to mean a "word" or "shout of command". It is a figure of speech. As Lunneman says, "It describes the power and irresistible might of the reappearing Christ, the breath of whose mouth is sufficient to destroy his opponents." (Compare Rev. 19.15,21, "*a sharp sword out of His mouth*".) (Compare also Isa. 11.4, "*with the breath of His lips shall He slay the wicked*".)

"*bring to nought*",—i. e., overthrow; not as Olshausen says, "deprive of influence" merely. (See Rev. 19.20.)

"*manifestation of His coming*",—Coming is Parousia,—Greek, "*presence*". The Authorized Version rendering is rather thoroughly backed up, since it is approved by many strong authorities. (Os. Wh. Mus. Bul. Hem. Lap. Era. Cle. Tur. Ben. Mac. Kop. Bol. Hey. Wie. Schm. Cali. Scho. Pelt. Schot., et al.)

It is better, however, to adhere to the original meaning of the words and take them in the sense they are used elsewhere by Paul, and so even preferable to our text is the rendering, "appearance of His coming". The mere advent of His presence (Lu.), the mere outburst of His presence (A.), the first gleam of the advent (B.), is enough to bring the adversary to nought.

Lillie remarks, "That there is an interval of time between our Lord's descent from the right hand of the Father into the region of the air, where His gathered saints are admitted into His presence, and His coming *with them* to the judgment of the nations, is not only in itself a perfectly reasonable and scriptural idea, but one of use in harmonizing the various and at first sight apparently discrepant descriptions of the manner of the advent, and the condition of the world in that day." This is the first remark of this kind we have found among the expositors.

Ver. 9. *"whose coming"*,—Antichrist too has a Parousia (Gk. presence).

"is",—The present as describing the certainty of the coming in the future.

"according to the working of Satan",—i. e., in conformity with it, the Devil working in and through him. Satan gives him power even as God gives power to Christ.

"with all power", etc.,—It is better to read as in the margin, "with all power and signs and wonders of falsehood". Both *"all"* and *"falsehood"* belong to all three nouns. They all have falsehood as their base, essence and aim. (A. E. D. Lu. Ar.)

Is the reference to a deception of the senses by sham miracles, or real miracles misleading to a false belief in them as if performd by divine power. Riggenbach says that Augustine prefers the second explanation as most others do. Roos says, "They are miracles of falsehood because men who regard them as proofs of the divinity of the Antichrist are thereby miserably deceived." Riggenbach says, "Performed by dark, gloomy powers, they are at bottom nothing but assumptions, imitations, manifestations of a sham strength which at last is a wretched impotence—monstrosities without any saving object, but not therefore mere juggleries."

Ver. 10. *"deceit of unrighteousness"*,—i. e., deceit which leads to, belongs to and consists in unrighteousness. (D. A. Lu. Es. Ar. Gro. Rig.) It is the agency of the Man of Sin.

"for them that perish",—Here is a limitation of his power and influence. Only those who are perishing succumb under it. It is a present participle and thus characterizes this future fate as already decided. Some restrict the connection of this phrase to *"with all deceit of unrighteousness"* (Fl. Lil. Hey. Hof.), but it is better with Riggenbach and Lunneman to conceive of it as belonging to the whole sentence from verse 9 onward.

"because they received not the love of the truth",—They loved falsehood and darkness more than truth and light. The natural man has no love for truth and the awakening of a love for truth must precede the reception of the truth itself. When every advance of grace to stir up the love of truth is repulsed, there neither can truth itself be subsequntly received. The high degree of guilt is thus represented. Truth is here

not necessarily the Christian truth but truth generally as opposed to falsehood which characterizes the workings of the Man of Sin.

Ver. 11. *"and for this cause"*,—i. e., because they received not the love of truth.

"God sendeth",—Not merely permits to come, but sends. To be compelled to believe the lie they chose to believe is their punishment—sin punished by sin. "It is", says Lunneman, "a holy ordinance of God that the wicked by their wickedness shall lose themselves always the more in wickedness."

"a working of error",—i. e., the active power of seduction.

"that they should believe a lie",—Not a definite lie, but rather the element of falsehood in opposition to the truth. Alford and Ellicott take it, because it has the article *"the"* as referring to the definite falsehood which the mystery of sin is working among them.

Ver. 12. *"that"*,—The ultimate purpose of God. It depends on *"believe"* of the preceding verse.

"be judged",—i. e., condemned (A. Lu.), as the context shows.

"the truth",—Here the Christian truth is meant as seen by its contrast to unrighteousness.

THE TEACHING CONCERNING ANTICHRIST

The teaching concerning the Antichrist may perhaps be conveniently classified under a fourfold division.

I. The teaching is not prophecy at all.
1. Paul was speaking of his own subjective anticipations of the future of Christianity. (D. Jow.)
   (a) But this involves the question of Inspiration or No Inspiration. It is enough to assert again that we believe, as Alford says, "that Paul was giving utterance not to his own subjective human opinions, but to truths which the Spirit of God had revealed to him."
2. Paul was simply quoting opinions from a letter received from the Thessalonians, and step by step refuting these opinions. As if he were saying, "You certainly wrote to me saying that the day of the Lord will not come except there be first a, etc., but don't you remember I told you about this when I was with you, etc." (Tychsen.)
   (a) This view only deserves attention on account of its strangeness and hardly deserves any refutation.

II. The teaching is prophecy already fulfilled; the coming of the Lord took place in the destruction of Jerusalem.
   Under this view (1) The Antichrist, (2) The Apostacy, (3) That which restraineth, and (4) The one who restraineth, were according to the different authorities as follows:
   (1) Simon Magus, (2) the falling off of Christians to Gnosticism, (3) the union between the Christians and the Jews, (4) the civil law. (Ham.)

(1) The rebel Jews and their leader Simon, (2) the rebellion of the Jewish people against the yoke of Rome, (3) whatever hindered the open breaking out of that rebellion, (4) King Agrippa and the Roman Pontifices. (Cle.)

(1) The Jewish people, (2) the falling away of Jewish converts to Judaism, (3) the Roman government, (4) the Emperor Claudius. (Wh.)

(1) Pharisees, Rabbis and Doctors of the law, (2) the rebellion against Rome, (3) and (4) the Christians in prayer. (Scho.)

Other authorities found the Antichrist in Caligula, Titus, the High Priest Ananias, the Jewish Zealots, etc.

But all these interpretations which conceive of the prophecy as fulfilled already, and that, in the coming of Christ at the destruction of Jerusalem have against them the one fatal objection, viz., that it is utterly impossible to conceive of the destruction of Jerusalem as in any sense corresponding to the Parousia as the term is used by the Apostle Paul.

III. The teaching is prophecy yet unfulfilled.

1. The Church Fathers, for whose opinion profound respect must of course be held.

These all agree in referring the prophecy to the personal coming again of Christ yet to take place, and in conceiving of the Antichrist as an individual. Most of them took *"that which restraineth"* as the Roman Empire, and *"the one that restraineth"* as the Roman Emperor.

Some of these authorities, however, took *"that which restraineth"* as the purpose of God. This view would naturally make *"the one that restraineth"* to be God Himself. But how then can it be said that God must be taken out of the way? It is contended by some that the expression can be made equally applicable to a voluntary withdrawal. It was the usual expression among the Greeks for declining battle.

2. The Reformers who stood out in opposition to the Church as she rose to the head of secular power with an imposing hierarchy at her own head. They looked upon the Pope as the Antichrist. The Pope in turn said the Antichrist was Luther. They explained *"that which restraineth"* and held back the destruction of the Papacy to be the Roman Empire, i. e., the imperial power which they held to be a revival of the old Roman Empire.

The Apostasy, they taught, was the fall from pure evangelical doctrine to the traditions of men, and the *"one that restraineth"* they said was the Roman Emperor. The temple of God they held to be the Christian Church and the *"sitting in it"* to be the tyrannical power which the Pope usurps over it. (C. N. B. Zw. Os. Ar. Ca. Za. Mi. Bez. Wol. Lan. Tur. Ben. Mac. Lut. Schm. Cali.) Some of the Reformers referred to Mohammed as the Antichrist, and said the apostasy was the falling off of many oriental and Greek churches to Mohammedanism. Some held that there was an eastern and a western Antichrist, Mohammed and the Pope. (Mel. Bul. Pic. Bucer.)

3. Moderns.

(1) Those who made the Antichrist to be Napoleon; the Apostacy the enormities of the French Revolution; the power that restraineth, the German Empire. This Empire, however, ended in 1806 and this alone convicts this view of error.

(2) Those who give the description a general, ideal or symbolical sense.

(a) Paul was following the general import of Jewish expectations that there was to be a season of ungodliness before the end, the full eruption he expected only after his own death, he himself being the one that restraineth. (Kop.)

(b) The Man of Sin is Atheism, with its open authority and contempt for religion. (Ni.)

(c) Many of the interpretations of the past are right but do not exhaust the import of the prophecy. The various untoward events and ungodly persons which have hitherto been mentioned, including the godlessness of the present time, are all prefigurations of Antichrist, but contain only some of his characteristics, but not all. It is the union of all in some one personal appearance that shall make the full Antichrist. That which restraineth is the moral and conservative influence of political states, restraining this great final outbreak. (O. E. A. Ba. Bis. Hof. Lud. Ger. Thi. Heub., these authorities all agreeing in the main.)

So far as the Fathers are concerned, their idea of interpreting *"that which restraineth"* and *"he who restraineth"* as respectively the temporal political power and he who wields it, may be considered appropriate. They then of necessity referred to the Roman Empire and the Roman Emperor. But these have passed away and the Antichrist has not yet come, and so in the particularization they were of course wrong.

So far as the Reformers are concerned the Pope does not and never did fulfill the prophecy, and furthermore if Papacy be the Antichrist, then has the Antichrist been revealed and endured now for more than 1500 years, and yet the Day of the Lord has not come, which, as Alford says, "by the very terms of our prophecy such manifestation is to immediately precede."

We still look for the Man of Sin, as the final and central embodiment of lawlessness and resistance to God. The Apostacy is still going on, Papacy, Mohammedanism, Mormonism, Christian Science, etc. Of *"that which restraineth"* and *"the one who restraineth"*, the one, the general hindrance and the other, the person in whom that hindrance is summed up, Alford says, "As the Fathers took them of the Roman Empire and the Roman Emperor, standing and ruling in their time, repressing the outbreaking sin and enormity,—so have we been taught by history to widen this view and understand them of the fabric of human polity and those who rule that polity, by which the great upbursting of godliness is kept down."

Ellicott says, "The restraining power of well-ordered human rule, the principles of legality as opposed to those of lawlessness, of which the Roman Empire was the then embodiment."

Riggenbach says, "The falling away is the general rush of violent departure from the faith that precedes the final disclosure of the Antichristian despot."

Heubner says, "However the delicate and tender-hearted may shudder at the idea of such a degenerate, atheistical, as it were devilish generation, yet according to the course of things it is probably what we have to expect." (For other quotations see Lange Commentary on II Thess., page 138.)

Others think that since the restrainer is a person—"he", and since a "mystery" always implies a supernatural element, this Person can be none other than the Holy Spirit in the Church. (Sco.)

Torrey says, "It is only natural to think that this restraining power has something to do with the Church; and the inevitable implication seems to be that the Church must be removed from the earth before 'the lawless one' can be revealed on the earth."

Says Scofield, "The order of events is: (1) The working of the mystery of lawlessness under divine restraint which had already begun in the Apostle's time (verse 7); (2) the apostacy of the professing Church (verse 3); (3) the removal of that which restrains the mystery of lawlessness (verses 6, 7); (4) the manifestation to the lawless one (verses 8-10); (5) the day of Jehovah (verses 9-12); (6.) the coming of Christ in glory and the destruction of the lawless one (verse 5)."

THE FIRST EPISTLE OF PAUL TO

TIMOTHY

(A. D. 65)

CHAPTER FOUR

> 1 But the Spirit saith expressly, that in later times some shall fall away from the faith, giving heed to seducing spirits and doctrines of demons.

Ver. 1. THE APOSTACY OF THE LATTER TIMES.

"*but*",—Connects this verse, and by way of contrast, with the beginning of verse 16 of Chap. 3.

"*expressly*",—Distinctly, in express words. This is the only place in the Bible where the Holy Spirit is said to have spoken "*expressly*". We are inclined to think this was a direct prophecy by the Spirit to Paul himself, although it may have been through the words of others spoken by the Spirit. Paul may have been familiar with the word spoken by our Lord in Matt. 24, and the predictions of other Apostles and of the prophets then present in the church. These suggestions may be looked upon with favor, but the suggestion of Wiesinger that Paul had before him prophecies of this kind in which allusion was had to the prophecies of the Old Testament is at least doubtful, since in that case he would doubtless have said, "The Scriptures saith", or "The Lord saith".

"in later times",—There is an interesting distinction here to be noted. Expositors all seem pretty much agreed that this expression is not quite equivalent to the one in II Tim. 3.1. Our verse, they say, points simply to the future, while that of II Tim. 3.1 (II Pet. 3.3; James 5.3) points to the last time of the future immediately preceding the second coming of Christ. (A. E. Hu. Oo. Hof.)

"some",—i. e., those who are led away from the faith by the heretics. (Hu. Oo. Pli.)

"seducing spirits",—The reference here is to the evil spirits which inspire the heretics, and which are the tools of the Devil himself. (A. E. Wi. Oo. Hu. Pl.) (See Eph. 2.2.; 6.12.) Mack and Coray, on grounds quite insufficient, think they refer to the heretics themselves.

"doctrines of demons",—i. e., doctrines of which demons are the source. (E. A. B. O. D. Wi. Oo. Hu. Con. The. and the Fathers generally.) It is not doctrines regarding demons (Hey.), nor are these demons to be referred to the heretics. (C. Mos. Mack.)

We wonder if there is not a bit of evidence here to show that the spirits which are around in the Spiritualistic seances and sittings of the present time are not the spirits of our departed loved ones at all, but spirits whose distinguishing characteristics are a cloven hoof, a forked tail and a lying tongue.

CHAPTER SIX

14 that thou keep the commandment, without spot, without reproach, until the appearing of our Lord Jesus Christ; 15 which in [1]its own times he shall show, who is the blessed and only Potentate, the King of [2]kings and Lord of [3]lords;

[1]Or, *his*

[2]Gr. *them that reign as kings*
[3]Gr. *them that rule as lords*

Vers. 14,15. The Appearance of Jesus in God's Own Time.

Ver. 14. *"commandment",*—i. e., all that Christ has commanded, the rule of the Gospel, the Gospel viewed as the rule of life. (O. A. E. Hu. Wi. Hof. Leo.) Not merely the exhortation to fight the good fight (Oo.), nor the commandment to flee avarice (verse 11), nor even yet all the doctrine that had been enjoined upon Timothy. (C. D. Bez.)

"without spot, without reproach",—Timothy is charged to keep the commandment that it may not be stained and open to reproach. (A. E. D. Hu. Oo. Pli. Hof. and nearly all ancient interpreters.)

These epithets are in the New Testament as a rule, if not always, referred to persons and for this reason some refer them to Timothy. (Wi. Es. Leo. Mat. Hey. Bez.) Estius says they can only refer to persons, but De Wett has shown with examples from classical Greek that this is not the case, and the construction here and the general good sense thus secured seem to make it preferable to refer them to the commandment.

"appearing",—This does not refer to Christ's coming to Timothy in death (Chr. Theo.), but to the visible appearing of our Lord at His

second coming.   It is the time mentioned in I Thess. 4.16,17 and is the
day of reward for the saints. (II Tim. 4.8.) It is the word, as Huther says,
that "brings into prominence the element of visibility in the Parousia".
"From such passages as this", says Alford, "we see that the apostolic age
maintained that which ought to be the attitude of all ages, constant expectation of the Lord's return."

This verse has been used by many as a proof that Paul believed the
second coming of Christ to be near at hand.   (D. Hu. Pl. Oo. Reu.)

Ellicott says, "It may perhaps be admitted that the sacred writers
have used language with reference to their Lord's return which seems to
show that the longings of hope had almost become the convictions of
belief, yet it must be observed that (as in the present case—'its own
times') this language is often qualified by expressions which show that
they also felt and knew that the hour was not immediately to be looked
for (II Thess. 2.2), but that the counsels of God, yea, and the machina-
tions of Satan must require time for their development."

Alford calls this a mistake and says that the word "epiphany"
(appearing) and the very words "in its times" should have kept Ellicott
from making it.   We cannot see how the expression "in its own times"
lends any weight one way or the other in regard to the nearness or remoteness of that coming, and whatever argument Ellicott gets for his view of
this matter from II Thess. 2.2 depends entirely upon his interpretation of
that much disputed passage.

Our verse is by no means a strong proof passage for the belief for
which Paul has been given credit by the authorities mentioned above, but
whatever ground they feel they have for the view taken doubtless comes
from the fact that Paul told Timothy to thus *keep* the commandment
until the *appearing*.   The Greek for this last word is "epiphany".   It is
found in five other passages (II Tim. 4.8; II Tim. 4.1; Titus 2.13; Acts
2.20; II Thess. 2.8) and is rendered *"appearing"* in every passage except
II Thess. 2.8, where it is *"brightness"*.

Ver. 15.   *"its own times"*,—This is better translated "his own
times".   (A. E. Hu. Oo. Pl.)

These words at least show that even if Paul did entertain a hope of
the near return of Christ, it did not lead him to fix arbitrarily the day
when that return would take place.

"he",—God.

"shall show",—i. e., cause to appear, make visible, display.

This passage shows that it is God who will bring to pass the epiphany
of Jesus Christ, and He will do this in His own times. (See Titus 1.3;
Gal. 4.4; I Tim. 2.6; Acts 1.7.)

The following ascription beginning with *"who is the blessed"*, etc.,
refers to God.

THE SECOND EPISTLE OF PAUL TO
TIMOTHY

CHAPTER ONE

10 but hath now been manifested by the appearing of our Saviour Christ Jesus, who abolished death and brought life and [1]immortality to light through the [2]Gospel.

12 For which cause I suffer also these things; yet I am not ashamed; for I

[1]Gr. *incorruption.* See Rom. 2.7.
[2]Gr. *good tidings*

know Him whom I have believed, and I am persuaded that He is able to guard [3]that which I have committed unto Him against that day.

18 The Lord grant unto him to find mercy in that day.

[3]Or, *that which he hath committed unto me.* Gr. *my deposit*

Vers. 10,12,18. PAUL'S CONFIDENCE AS TO HIS SECURITY IN THE DAY OF HIS LORD'S COMING.

Ver. 10. *"the appearing of our Saviour Christ Jesus"*,—The word is "epiphany" and it is the only place in the New Testament where this word is applied to the first coming, the incarnation, of our Lord.

Ver. 12. *"For which cause"*,—i. e., because he was appointed as a preacher of the Gospel, and yet it was not because of the appointment considered in itself alone but to the fact that to this appointment was related Paul's activity in proclaiming the Gospel. It refers to the immediately preceding verse. (A. E. Oo. Hu. Wi.)

"suffer also these things",—Paul was in prison.

"not ashamed",—Prison for Paul was not a disgrace but a matter for glorying. Said with reference to verse 8 and as an encouragement to Timothy.

"him",—i. e., God.

"know Him",—I have the most unquestionable proof of His power and His love—I *know* Him.

"whom I have believed",—The literal of this is "to whom I have given my faith". The figure is that of a deposit made and the depositor trusting the depositary, and it is this which has induced the Revised Version rendering ("guard"), although there is really no better translation than that of the Authorized Version.

"that which I have committed unto Him",—The literal Greek is "my deposit", and this may mean what I have deposited with God or what God has deposited with me, as in the margin.

The former is without doubt the correct view, but what, according to this view, did Paul deposit with God?

1. His eternal reward, the crown laid up for him. (Wi. Oo. Pli. Ca. Tho. Bez. Wol.) But Alford rightly remarks that "This represents this reward not as a matter of God's free grace but as Paul's own delivered to God for safe keeping."

2. His salvation. (C. Am. Hu.) This is quite similar to the view just noted and is open to the same objection.

3. The believers who had been converted by his means; his converts. But this is unsupported by the context and hardly needs refutation.

4. His soul, himself, as in I Pet. 4.19. (A. B. Gro. Pau. Con. Hof.)

What did God commit to Paul according to the second view? The meanings assigned to *"my deposit"* are very numerous and it must be confessed that not one of them is free from difficulty.

1. The Holy Spirit. (The.)
2. The Gospel and its proclamation to the world. (E. Fl.)
3. The apostolic office as a stewardship. (D. Hei.)
4. His own soul as entrusted to him by God. (Bret.)
5. His converts as committed to him by God.

In verse 14 and in I Tim. 6.20 we have the same word, *"deposit"*, and used with the same verb, and because of this De Wette and others argue that the sense and meaning must be the same. But this is a lax and careless way of reasoning. As a rule this is possible and true but it is by no means necessary. Wiesinger gives three good reasons why in this case it proves just the reverse:

1. In these other references Timothy is the guardian and in our verse the guardian is plainly God and the guardian is usually the one to whom the deposit is committed.
2. In these other references the deposit seems to refer to the doctrines committed to Timothy, while in our verse it is a personal possession which belongs to Paul.
3. In these other references it is a question of right action on Timothy's part, while in our verse it is a question of confidence and consolation in the right action of another, namely, God.

I am inclined to think, therefore, with Alford that when we inquire what this deposit was, the answer is to be found in the previous words, *"in whom I have believed"*; and that Paul had entrusted himself, body, soul and spirit, to the keeping of his heavenly Father, and lay safe in His hands, confident of His abiding and effectual care.

"against that day",—The day meant here is the day of Christ's second coming, the Parousia, "The day of the coming of Christ", says Oosterzee, "when the crown of life will be given to all who love His appearing." It is the day referred to in I Thess. 4.16,17.

Another strong reason in our mind against taking the *"deposit"* as something committed to Paul is that Paul would then have to render up his trust, whatever it be, at the end of his life, and *"that day"* here referred to would then mean the day of his death; and this is entirely contrary to usage on the part of Paul.

Ver. 18. *"in that day"*,—The same day as that mentioned in verse 12, the day of the Parousia, of the second coming of Christ.

"the Lord grant unto him to find mercy of the Lord",—The repetition of the word *"Lord"* seems at first glance a bit confusing. Some refer both words to God while others again refer both to Christ. Some refer the first word to God and the second to Christ, while others just reverse

this order, and each with a reason of course sufficient for himself. Inasmuch as all judgment is said to be committed to the Son (John 5.22), it would seem best to refer the second word to Christ regardless as to whom the first word is referred. But why not refer them both to Christ. Paul had used the well-known formula, *"The Lord grant"*, and might simply have finished by saying, *"to find mercy in that day"*, but in his mental vision of the judgment, seeing Christ as Judge, he writes down, *"from the Lord"*, just as it occurs to him, without recalling that he had begun with *"The Lord grant unto him"*.

CHAPTER TWO

12 If we endure we shall also reign with Him; if we deny him, he also shall deny us.

Ver. 12. THE BELIEVER SHALL REIGN WITH HIS COMING KING.

"we shall also reign with Him",—All are agreed as to the reference of this reigning to the time after the Parousia, when the Messianic kingdom shall be revealed in its full glory. (A. E. Oo. Pl. Hu. Wi.)

(See Rom. 5.17; 8.17; I Cor. 4.8; Matt. 19.28.)

Not only shall we live with Him but we shall be kings with Him and share in His glory and dominion.

CHAPTER THREE

1 But know this, that in the last days grievous times shall come.

9 But they shall proceed no further; for their folly shall be evident unto all men, as theirs also came to be.

13 But evil men and impostors shall wax worse and worse, deceiving and being deceived.

Vers. 1,9,13. THE LAST DAYS ARE TO BE TIMES OF DISTRESS.

Ver. 1. *"in the last days"*,—That the reference here is to a time still in the future ought to be sufficiently evidenced to an unbiased mind by the use of the future verb, *"shall come"*, and with this practically all unbiased scholars agree and refer the time to that immediately preceding the second coming of Christ, the Parousia. (A. E. Oo. Eb. Wi. Hu. Pl.) It is the *"last hour"* of I John 2.18, and Alford again calls attention to the fact that they of that time wrote and spoke of that hour and that day as if it were to appear in the not very far away future.

The time referred to is not, therefore, the time between the first and second coming of Christ, as Heydenreich maintains, nor as Mack says, the time in which the errors spoken of shall come to an end. Such renderings are purely arbitrary.

As another evidence that Paul thought the end not far away is noted the fact that by verse 5 it would seem as though the times mentioned had, at least in their beginnings, already set in, inasmuch as he tells Timothy to turn away from these evil men who are to come in the last days.

"grievous times",—The idea is of distress rather than of danger as conveyed by the word *"perilous"* of the Authorized Version. By De Wette it is translated "critical times" and by Wiesinger, "severe times", "evil times".

The following verses describe in what sense the *"last days"* are to be grievous.

Ver. 9. *"but they shall proceed no further"*,—There seems to be a contradiction between these words and those of verse 13 and of Chap. 2.16. Paul certainly does not mean to contradict himself, nor is it likely, if it could be possible at all, that he would do it in statements so close together. The apparent difficulty must be relieved in one or the other of two ways: either conceive of Paul as not speaking of the same people or as having in mind a different kind of progress to be made by the same people, and of the two the latter is without doubt the better explanation.

What the Apostle says is that there shall be no real and ultimate advance. In Chap. 2.16 the Apostle seems to be speaking of an immediate spread of error, while here he is looking to its ultimate defeat and distinction. Wiesinger says verse 13 treats of an intensive progress and the more rapid their advance to the worse the more speedily will their folly expose itself. The advance is not denied, but what is denied is the successful advance without detection and exposure. The authorities are quite agreed as to this explanation. (A. E. Oo. Hu. Wi. Pl. Chr.)

"as theirs also came to be",—i. e., as the folly of Jannes and Jambres of verse 8. (See Ex. 8.18 and 9.11.)

Ver. 13. The chasm is to grow wider and wider until the final issue.

"But",—The contrast is rather with verse 12, to the godly in their persecutions (A. E. Oo. Wi. Mat. Chr. Hey.), than with verse 10, Paul's godly life (D. Hu.). Either reference is permissible but on the whole that with the immediately preceding verse 12 is preferable.

"evil men",—i. e., evil men in general, and then particularized by the next word, *"impostors"*, the impostors being included in the general term.

"impostors",—This comes from a word meaning *incantations by howling*, and from this it passes to the practice of magic arts in general, and then by a very natural transition to deception and imposture. The word really means "magicians" and Paul doubtless uses it with express reference to verse 8.

Ellicott aptly says, "We cannot indeed definitely infer from this term that magic arts were actually used by these impostors, but there is certainly nothing in such a supposition inconsistent either with the context, the primary meaning of the word, or the description of similar opponents mentioned elsewhere in the New Testament."

"wax worse and worse",—The language here not only can, as De Wette says, but must be taken intensively, as practically all are agreed. It is the same word as used in verse 9, but it denotes a greater degree of wickedness while verse 9 refers the rather to increase in extent.

"deceiving and being deceived",—Here the mode of progress is indicated. "He who leads others astray", says Huther, "is himself led astray."

CHAPTER FOUR

1 ¹I charge thee in the sight of God, and of Christ Jesus, who shall judge the living and the dead, and by his appearing and his kingdom;

¹Or, *I testify, in the sight . . . dead, both of his appearing &c.*

3 For the time will come when they will not endure the ²sound ³doctrine; but having itching ears, will heap to themselves teachers after their own lusts,

²Gr. *healthful*
³Or, *teaching*

Vers. 1,3. THE APPEARING OF CHRIST AN INCENTIVE TO MINISTERIAL FIDELITY.

Ver. 1. *"in the sight of"*, etc.,—As though both God and Christ, as visible witnesses, were considered personally present.

"the living and the dead",—It is altogether wrong to suppose with Peile that the spiritually living and dead are meant, but all expositors are agreed that it is the physically alive and the physically dead who are to be judged at the time in question.

I have found no distinction in the minds of any of the expositors as to any difference in the time of the judgment upon the living and the dead respectively. If there is such a distinction, this verse assuredly must not be taken as one of the proof references, although a fair exegesis does not prohibit its interpretation in harmony with such distinction.

Of course the judgment in question is related in some temporal way with the appearing, the coming of Christ. It is doubtful, however, whether this verse says so in so many words. According to the Authorized Version it does. This version reads, *"at his appearing and his kingdom"*, and very many expositors adopt this reading and interpret *"at"* as a preposition of time modifying the word *"judge"*. But Tischendorf, Tregelles, Lachmann, and by far the best manuscript authority favor the conjunction *"and"* of the Revised Version and make it modify the word *"charge"*.

In considering the question of time it might be well also first to note the distinction between the words *"appearing"* and *"kingdom"*. These words do not refer to one and the same thing, but the first refers to Christ's epiphany, His coming as mentioned in I Thess. 4.16,17, and the second refers to His kingdom then to reveal itself in glory. Notice the repetition of *"his"*. This is not without significance; each point is conceived independently and in its own full significance; His coming at which we shall stand before Him and His kingdom in which we hope to reign with Him. It is without doubt the kingdom which begins with the return of our Lord.

Still the question as to the time of the judgment is before us. Those who place the time of Christ's coming after the Millennium refer this verse to the general judgment of all the living and all the dead at that time, and they of course quote I Thess. 4.16,17 and I Cor. 15.51,52 as being in harmony with this interpretation.

Those who place the time of Christ's coming before the Millennium place the judgment of the living at the beginning of the Millennium and the judgment of the dead at its close (Mack). As we have already said, the verse may be made exegetically to conform to either view, but it can scarcely be said to lend evidence one way or the other, and the matter must be settled by one's thought in regard to the matter as shaped by the teaching of other portions of the Word.

There is an interesting turn in the expression, *"shall judge"*, which we have noticed nowhere else; it really means "about to judge". There is no doubt but that grammatically this rendering is correct. The word "mellontos" does carry, according to all lexicons consulted, the idea of "to be about to do anything", and this is all the more true when used with a present infinitive. Thus Thayer in his lexicon defines the word, with the infinitive present, "to be on the point of doing something". It cannot therefore be thought over-refined or arbitrary to see in the expression, as used by Paul, an added evidence of his feeling that the coming again of his Lord was not to be conceived of as in the far distant future.

Ver. 3. *"the time will come"*,—The same time is here meant as that in Chap. 3.1, the time he has been talking about.

"not endure",—They will find it intolerable because it is not con sistent with their desires.

"itching ears",—The word means to scratch or tickle. Their desire is to hear something tickling to the ear.

"heap to themselves",—The idea here is' to procure in multitudes, and the word involves the idea of contempt.

"after their own lusts",—i. e., their own willful, selfish desires instead of obedience under the divine will.

> 8 henceforth there is laid up for me the crown of righteousness, which the Lord, the righteous Judge, shall give to me at that day, and not to me only, but also to all them that have loved his appearing.

Ver. 8. THE HOPE OF HIS COMING IS INCONSISTENT WITH UNRIGHTEOUS LIVING.

"henceforth",—i. e., as to what remains for me. At the end of his life-course nothing remains but to receive the crown.

"laid up",—The prize is already prepared and laid up for him and cannot possibly escape him.

"the crown of righteousness",—This is to be explained as the crown which is bestowed as a recognition of righteousness—that which rewards the righteous course of life. (A. E. D. Wi. Pl. Pli. The. Chr.)

There is another explanation which takes the word righteousness as an apposition to crown, that in which the crown consists. (Hu. Oo. Dw. Leo. Holt, Grimm.) Reference is made to Jam. 1.12; I Pet. 5.4; Rev. 2.10, where this kind of construction doubtless prevails.

This view is of course possible, but if it is accepted, *"righteousness"* must be vested only with its ordinary meaning, and not with the forensic sense as though it were the righteousness of Christ imputed, as Calovius and Mosheim take it. Analogy with the other passages mentioned seems to favor this view, but since the word *"righteousness"* in all cases in these epistles appears to have not a dogmatical but a practical reference, it seems better to take the first view. Wiesinger well remarks that righteousness could hardly be taken as the reward of righteousness, and that the reward is always elsewhere represented as *life* or *glory*, and that the first view is in harmony with the figure being used, which is not true of the second view.

"the Lord",—i. e., Jesus Christ.

"shall give",—Alford reads "shall award". The word itself does not necessarily convey any sense of due, requittal, reward, although, as Ellicott says, "such a meaning can be grammatically sustained and confirmed by examples", and in keeping with our explanation above it is better for us to so take the word here.

"at that day",—i. e., the day of His appearing; the day of Christ's Parousia, which Paul now of course no longer expected to see on earth. (I Thess. 4.16,17.)

"have loved",—i. e., those who at that day shall be found to have loved, and still to be loving—those who have looked forward with longing and earnest joy.

"his appearing",—His Parousia, the epiphany at the second coming.

> 18 The Lord will deliver me from every evil work, and will save me unto his heavenly kingdom; to whom be the glory ¹forever and ever. Amen.
> ¹Gr. *unto the ages of the ages*

Ver. 18. THE KINGDOM AWAITING THE BELIEVER IMMEDIATELY UPON DEATH.

"The Lord",—i. e., Christ.

"every evil work",—This does not mean from the evil one (Mos. Pel.), nor from every evil circumstance (Lut. Mat.), which would be out of harmony with verse 6 and would be against the essential meaning of the word *"evil"*, which in the New Testament always refers to moral evil and not to external affliction.

There are two other views, each of which has many strong advocates:

1. The evil works which he himself might do, i. e., yield to temptation and apostatize through faint-heartedness. (A. D. Pl. Gro. Hey. Bez. Chr.)

   Oosterzee well remarks, "But at this high state of his spiritual development, and with death immediately before him, as he well knew, it is not probable that the aged Apostle could have felt and expressed fear in this respect."

2. The evil acts and designs of his enemies toward him. (E. Oo. Wi. Hu. Hof.) It was not that Paul expected to be delivered from prison (verse 6), but that he knew that through the Lord he would be delivered from the attacks of the evil One and his agents so that they could do him no harm. In other words, "Stone walls do not a prison make; nor iron bars a cage." Of course so far as outward circumstances went, his enemies had the best of him, and could do with him as they pleased and this Paul knew. The Lord in His providence had not seen fit to deliver him from them in this respect, and this does not seem to enter into Paul's concern. If any harm then came to him or was at all likely to come to him through their treatment of him, and from which he might well hope to be rescued, it would be that of faint-heartedness and apostasy, but the possibility of this being so far removed for the reasons above stated, it would seem on the whole best to adhere to the second view as above.

"his heavenly kingdom",—This is the only place in the New Testament where this exact expression occurs, and some have declared that the term and the idea are alike foreign to the Apostle, who knows only of a kingdom of God which Christ will introduce at His coming. But surely this is an ill-considered conception. There is a three-fold aspect of the kingdom and Paul is familiar with them all. A glance back at verse 1 shows his familiarity with the idea of the kingdom to be established at Christ's coming. In Col. 1.13 he says that we as Christians are already

translated into the kingdom of His dear Son; and in Phil. 1.23 the Apostle anticipates for believers immediately after death an entrance into a heavenly kingdom in which there is a fuller fellowship with Christ than that which any earthly existence can afford. The kingdom referred to in this verse is the same as that in Phil. 1.3.

"Why then", says Wiesinger, "even though the precise expression does not occur elsewhere, regard the idea as un-Pauline, when the Apostle recognizes elsewhere a being with Christ after death, regards Christ as reigning in the heavens, and the establishment of His kingdom on earth, to which he naturally adverts when he would mention the closing period, as but the manifestation of the sovereign authority with which He is already invested?"

THE EPISTLE OF PAUL TO

TITUS

(A. D. 65)

CHAPTER TWO

> 13 looking for the blessed hope and appearing of the glory [1]of the great God and our Saviour Jesus Christ.
>
> [1]Or, of our great God and Saviour

Ver. 13. THE BELIEVER'S BLESSED HOPE.

"looking for",—And of course expecting. (Lu. 2.25; Mk. 15.43.)

"the blessed hope",—Looking for a hope sounds strange, but this strangeness is relieved when we remember that hope here does not so much designate subjectively the form or the act of hoping, as rather objectively the contents and the object of the hope, the thing hoped for. And yet it will not do to take "hope" too objectively. It is rather hope contemplated under objective aspects, our hope being thought of as something definite and substantial.

Alford aptly says, "Nearly objective,—the hope as embodying the thing hoped for; but keep the vigour and propriety both of language and thought, and do not tame down the one or violate the other."

"blessed",—This hope is thus described because it brings the expected blessedness, and the expectation of it blesses the believer.

"appearing",—The Greek is epiphany. There are two great epiphanies, the Epiphany of Grace (verse 11), when Christ first appeared in humility, and the Epiphany of Glory (this verse), when Christ is to appear again in power, which last Epiphany beyond doubt denotes the Second Coming of Christ.

Epiphany, it seems, differs only from Parousia in that it emphasizes the visibility of the Second Coming.

"glory",—It is better to join this word with both "hope" and "appearing" rather than with the latter word alone.

The rendering of the Authorized Version, "the glorious appearing", is incorrect and unfortunate.

"of our great God and Saviour Jesus Christ",—This is the rendering of the Revised Version and it makes the *"Saviour Jesus Christ"* to be the great God, while the rendering of the Authorized separates the two. The authorities for these two renderings are about evenly divided.

The settlement of this question does not lie within the scope of the purpose of this study. It may be said, however, in passing that even Winer admits that the question cannot be settled on purely grammatical grounds.

Ellicott says, "It does indeed seem difficult to resist the conviction that our blessed Lord is here said to be our great God, and that this text is a direct, definite and even studied declaration of the divinity of the eternal Son."

We are inclined, for reasons not in place here to enumerate, to feel about the passage rather much as Wiesinger says, "Whoever will simply read and translate the words without doctrinal prejudice will have as little hesitation in referring them to one and the same subject, as in understanding, for instance, in II Pet. 1.11, the words, *'kingdom of our Lord and Saviour Jesus Christ'*, as relating to the same subject."

THE EPISTLE TO THE

HEBREWS

(A. D. 64)

CHAPTER ONE

2 God hath at the end of these days spoken unto us in [1]*his* Son, whom he appointed heir of all things, through whom also he made the [2]worlds;
8 but of the Son *he saith,*

[1]Gr. *a Son*
[2]Gr. *ages.* Comp. 1 Tim. 1.17

[3] *'Thy throne, O God, is for ever and ever;
And the sceptre of uprightness is the sceptre of thy [5]kingdom.*

[3]Ps. 14.6 f.
[4]Or, *Thy throne is God for &c.*
[5]The two oldest Greek manuscripts read *his*

Vers. 2,8. THE END OF THESE DAYS AND THE EVERLASTING KING-DOM OF CHRIST.

Ver. 2. *"at the end of these days"*,—It is very plain that the end of any time may be thought of as a point of time, the terminus itself, or as a portion of time. In this latter sense we speak of a week-end visit, meaning the end of the week in the sense of one or more days. It is in this sense the word *"end"* is used both by the prophets of the Old and New Testament writers.

What days are to be understood? Of course the particular time to which the writer referred is the same as that meant in Chap. 9.26, *"at the end of the ages"*, the time between the coming and the crucifixion of Christ, the time when the fulfillment of Messianic prophecy commenced.

But how is *"the end of these days"* to be interpreted in harmony with this statement of the case? Just what did the writer mean by *"these days"* and *"the end"*?

Lunneman says he means the very days in which he and his readers were actually living, and he says the writer uses *"the end"* because he was thinking of the near approach of the Second Coming, i. e., the closing days of *"these days"*, the last part of them, their culmination.

But the period between the coming and the crucifixion of Christ was at the beginning and not at the end of those days. If Lunneman were right it would be quite as appropriate for us to say the same thing in these days of ours, and certainly the time when God spoke through His Son is not A. D. 1923!

The reference cannot be to the days of the prophets because those days did not extend down to the time of Christ, and furthermore the antithesis between *"days of old"* and *"these days"* would then be lost.

With good reason therefore we must refer the phrase to the technical Old Testament expression, "be-acharith-ha-yamim" (Num. 24.14), which in the Septuagint is rendered so many times, *"in the last days"* or *"at the end of the days"*. These expressions which in themselves denote simply the end of certain days, became to the ancient Jews an expression for "the times of the Messiah". Thus what Peter meant at Pentecost was, "We are now in what Joel called *'the last days'*." (Acts 2.17.)

The Jews divided the religious history of the world into two periods. One period they called Olam Hazzeh, the time before the Messiah whom they were expecting, the time which preceded the fulfillment of prophecy concerning the Messiah. The other period they called Olam Haba, the time after the Messiah had come, which coming, in their minds, was to be accompanied by the resurrection. They knew nothing of a second coming and a delayed resurrection.

The Jews called the former of these periods "this age" (Greek, aion outos), and the latter period they called "the age to come" (Greek, aion mellon).

Now the actual days of the Messiah seem to have been regarded as a transition between these two ages, sometimes being included in the former and sometimes in the latter. They could therefore very properly be said to be the end of the pre-Messianic age (which the Jews called "this age"), and they could quite as properly be called the beginning of the post-Messianic age (which the Jews called "the age to come"). In fact this Messianic period was by the Rabbis sometimes reckoned with the one and sometimes with the other.

The Jews of course did not and could not foresee that it would be necessary for the Apostles and for us to again divide the portion of time known as the end. But they rejected the Messiah and He went away, promising that He would come back again, and consequently to all who believe in this promise there is still another "age to come", another "future age", which is to begin at the time of our Lord's return, and the days that now are and which were in the writer's time are in a sense, chronologically distinct from Jewish conception, "the present age", "this age" (aion outos).

507

The following diagram will help in distinguishing these various divisions of time, the expressions above the line being the Jewish expressions of the times as related to the Messiah, while those below the line are made from the Apostolic and Christian standpoint, the star standing for the actual days of the Messiah and the arrow for His return.

Olam hazzeh	Olam haba
aion outos	aion mellon
this age	age to come
	the last days
	the latter days
	be-acharith-ha-yamim

this age	age to come
aion outos	aion mellon
the last days	
the latter days	

As the Christians believed that the Messiah had come, the former period, as conceived by the Jews, had, in their mind, already ended, and they themselves were living in the Olam haba, in what was in reality the "age to come" of the Jews.

Now Moll says, "The 'these days' are not the days in which the readers and the author lives, but they correspond to what the Jew knew as 'this age' (aion outos), and the 'end' is to be taken as indicating the close of the pre-Messianic time." This will be found consistent with what we have already said if the actual Messianic days be counted with the former of the two Jewish divisions of time as the ending days of that period.

But why did the writer say "these days"? All agree as to the time which was actually in the writer's mind, and the only difficulty is to harmonize the word "these" with it.

There can be only one answer to this question and that is that the writer would have them know that the days in which they were living belonged to "the end of the days", not the end in the sense that the Second Coming of Christ was near (against Lunneman), but the end in the Old Testament technical sense.

Says Lindsay, "The word 'these' was added plainly to indicate that the days referred to had already begun. They were styled 'the end of the days', 'the last days' from the most ancient times; but now, says Paul, they are 'these last days' because the long expected Messiah has appeared."

The explanation of Moll is indeed most simple and there is much to say in its favor, but between it and this other we are inclined to the latter. In the former, "these" points to time before the arrival of the Messiah and in the latter to time after His arrival, and we cannot get away from the conviction that the writer used the word with the latter thought in his mind.

Ver. 8. "Thy throne, O God, is forever and ever",—That the word "God" is here in the vocative case and applies to Christ there can be no doubt. Other explanations are absurd and sometimes preposterous. The marginal reading of the Revised Version will not do; it puts Christ above

God, as he who sits upon a throne is always superior in dignity and importance to the throne itself.

"forever and forever",—Greek, "unto eternity of eternity". The phrase is unique in the New Testament and means that the dominion of Christ is to endure forever.

Lindsay says it is His mediatorial throne to which reference is here to be seen.

CHAPTER THREE

7 Wherefore, even as the Holy Spirit saith, ¹*Today,* if ye shall hear his voice, 8 Harden not your hearts, as in the provocation, like as in *the day* of the trial in the wilderness.

13 But exhort one another day by

day, so long as it is called *Today,* lest any one of you be hardened by the deceitfulness of sin.

15 While it is said, ¹*Today* if ye shall hear His voice, harden not your hearts as in the provocation.

¹Ps. 95.7 ff.

CHAPTER FOUR

7 He again defineth a certain day, *Today,* saying in David so long a time afterward (even as hath been said before), ¹*Today* if ye shall hear His voice,

¹Ps. 95.7 f.

Harden not your hearts. 8 For if ²Joshua had given them rest, he would not have spoken afterwards of *another day.*

²Gr. *Jesus.* Comp. Acts 7.45

Here are a number of instances in which the word *"day"* is used to express a greater period of time than twenty-four hours. In verses 7,13,15 of Chap. 3 and verses 7 and 8 of Chap. 4, the word will have, as Westcott says, "various interpretations in accordance with its connections. For the Church it is the whole time until Christ's Second Coming. For the believer it is the period of his life."

Specifically *"today"* refers to the day when this word of God is read, whether in private or when the Psalm from which it is taken was read in public as it was accustomed to be read, "whenever", as Alford says, "that might be".

The *"certain day"* of Chap. 4.7 is the *"today"* mentioned in the various other verses.

"The day of temptation" in Chap. 3.8 refers specifically to the second murmuring against Moses and Aaron for want of water at the close of the fourth year's wilderness experience, while *"the provocation"* refers to the first murmuring of the same kind at the beginning of the wilderness experience; hence the whole forty years are covered by the two expressions. (See Num. 20.1-13 and Ex. 17.1-7.)

CHAPTER EIGHT

7 For if that first covenant had been faultless, then would no place have been sought for a second. 8 For ¹finding fault with them he saith, ²Behold the days come, saith the Lord, that I will ³make a new covenant with the house of Israel

¹Some ancient authorities read *finding fault* with it, *he saith unto them &c.*
²Jer. 31.31 ff.
³Gr. *accomplish*

and with the house of Judah; 9 Not according to the covenant that I made with their fathers, in the day that I took them by the hand to lead them forth out of the land of Egypt; for they continued not in my covenant, and I regarded them not, saith the Lord. 10 For this is the covenant that *I will make with the house of Israel after those days, saith the Lord; I will put my laws in their mind, and on their hearts also will I write them; and I will be to them a God, and they shall be to me a people;

*Gr. *I will covenant*

11 And they shall not teach every man his fellow-citizen, and every man his brother, saying, Know the Lord. For all shall know me, from the least to the greatest of them. 12 For I will be merciful to their iniquities, and their sins will I remember no more.

Vers. 7-12. THE NEW COVENANT IN CHRIST.

Ver. 7. *"if that first covenant had been faultless"*,—i. e., if it had fulfilled perfectly the purpose to which it pointed. The law is not blamed; the fault lay with those who received it.

"no place . . . for a second",—i. e., no place in the development of the divine purpose and consequently no place in the history of the world.

Ver. 8. *"them"*,—i. e., the Israelites. Grammatically this word can be taken either with *"finding fault"* or *"saith"*. The authorities are about equally divided, but all things considered it seems best to retain the reading of our text, thus making it the people who are blamed and not the covenant. If it is taken with the word *"saith"* then some word must be supplied as the object of *"finding fault"*, and the sentence would read, "finding fault with (it, i. e., the covenant) He saith to them."

"the days come",—The words are from Jeremiah 31.31-34, and the days to come are the days to be introduced by the Messiah.

"make",—This is not the same word as that used in verses 9 and 10. This word really means "to accomplish" and seems to be used intentionally to set forth the completeness of the new covenant (A. Lu.) and to emphasize the efficacy of it. (W. Del. Aug.)

"Israel and Judah",—Both went into captivity after the prophecy here quoted was made by Jeremiah, and both are specified in God's promise of grace and restoration. The once divided and exiled people are again to be brought together, says Jeremiah; the schism is to have no existence under the new covenant.

That Jeremiah, when he made the prophecy here quoted, had in mind a broader conception than merely that of national Israel seems rather certain because the writer of Hebrews quotes him and uses his words, *"Israel and Judah"*, with a reference wide enough to take in all the people of God. The new covenant, the New Testament Covenant, takes in all of us who are God's people and the writer speaks of it as a covenant with the house of Israel and the house of Judah. Therefore it would seem that this expression means something more than Jews, at least so far as this passage goes.

Ver. 9. *"with"*,—The preposition here used really means "to", and it therefore excludes the notion of reciprocity in the covenant making, the people of Israel being only recipients and not co-agents in the making of it.

"regarded them not",—i. e., did not concern Himself about them as formerly. Yet their unfaithfulness did not annul the faithfulness of God, for this He proved by establishing a new covenant when the old one failed to accomplish His gracious purpose.

Ver. 10. *"house of Israel"*,—This refers to the whole nation; the division having ceased the people of God is again called by its own name. The reference here also as understood by the writer of Hebrews is to the people of God in general and not to Israel after the flesh.

"after those days",—This may be taken either with Delitzsch as meaning *"after the days that are coming"* as mentioned in verse 8, which is the same from the viewpoint of time as *"after the end of these days"* in Chap. 1.2 as advocated by Westcott; or it may be taken with Alford as meaning *"after those days of disregard"* as mentioned in verse 9, which is the same thing from the viewpoint of time as "after the days which precede the coming days of verse 8", as advocated by Lunneman. The latter explanation seems to be favored more by the context and the more precise meaning of the preposition *"after"*.

"mind . . . hearts",—Says Lindsay, "They are not only to be known and remembered but loved, cherished and obeyed."

Ver. 11. This does not mean that there shall be no religious instruction but that the knowledge of the Lord would be widely spread in the Church. There needs to be no privileged class interposed between the mass of men and God, but the people being brought by the Holy Spirit into true fellowship with God are themselves to be privileged by an immediate knowledge of Him. (Read Joel 2.28,29; Isa. 54.13; Matt. 11.11; Lu. 7.28; John 6.45; I John 2.20,27.)

"from the least to the greatest",—There is to be no distinction of age, station or endowments.

Ver. 12. The New Covenant rests upon forgiveness on the part of God and not on performance on the part of man. It is this fact that insures us against any repetition of failure such as the Old Covenant had produced. As yet this prophecy has received only partial fulfillment, and we look patiently forward to its more ample and complete fulfillment in the days when *"The knowledge of the Lord shall cover the earth as the waters cover the sea."*

CHAPTER NINE

25 Nor yet that he should offer himself often, as the high priest entereth into the holy place year by year with blood not his own; 26 else must he often have suffered since the foundation of the world; but now once at the [1]end of the ages hath he been manifested to put away [2]sin by the sacrifice of himself.

[1]Or, *consummation*
[2]Or, *by his sacrifice*

27 And in as much as it is [3]appointed unto men once to die, and after this cometh judgment; 28 so Christ also, having been once offered to bear the sins of many, shall appear a second time, apart from sin, to them that wait for him, unto salvation.

[3]Gr. *laid up for.* Col. 1.5; 2 Tim. 4.8

Vers. 25-28. CHRIST'S APPEARING THE SECOND TIME UNTO THEM THAT LOOK FOR HIM.

Ver. 25. *"nor yet* (hath he entered into heaven) *that he should offer himself often"*,—By many authorities *"offer Himself"* is referred to His sacrificial death upon the cross. (W. D. Lu. Ow. Lin. Tho.)

By as many others it is made the offering of Himself before God, His self-presentation in the heavenly holiest place. (A. An. Dw. Bl. Del. Hof. Mol. Kur. Boe. Schli.)

The argument in favor of the first view rests upon the general usage by the writer of the word *"offer"*. This argument has considerable weight for the word used is the usual one for the taking of the victim to the altar and not for the carrying of its blood within the veil.

This single argument, however, weighty as it may be, is hardly weighty enough to outbalance what is to be said in favor of the other view. Dwight has well said, "The high-priest's ministry in the presence of God is the thing or the subject constantly kept before the reader's mind throughout, and the sacrifice here, as everywhere in this section, is subordinate to the offering of the blood in the sanctuary."

This fact, together with the use of the word *"suffered"* in verse 26, which refers to His death on the cross, the *"entered in"* and *"to appear"* of verse 24, the *"entereth"* of verse 25, the contrast with *"suffered"* of verse 26, all seem to show that the word *"offer"* denotes Christ's presentation of Himself with His blood before God in the heavenly Holy of Holies.

Ver. 26. *"else"*,—Here must be supplied, "if that were the case".

"often have suffered since",—But how could Christ have suffered often? How could He have offered Himself in sacrificial death more than once? We might well say the thing is impossible, and yet explanations have been given.

Lunneman says by a series of incarnations and crucifixions and entrances into heaven, while Delitzsch says He would have had to sacrifice Himself just as many times on earth as He expected to present Himself in the heavenly sanctuary, i. e., accumulate, as it were, a stock of sacrificial deaths on earth.

Moll, who with Hofman, Alford and others supports this last explanation, says it is far more probable than the more common view of Lunneman. I see very little to choose between the two, but the view of Delitzsch it seems to me is much the harsher and the more unnatural and improbable of the two.

But the speculation is a useless one, for this very verse (verse 26) shows the unreasonableness of them both and relieves us of making any choice between them, and for this purpose it would seem the first clause of this verse was introduced.

Christ entered into the heavenly Holy of Holies free from the necessity of returning for further sacrifice of Himself and without any necessity for having suffered more than once before He went.

"now",—i. e., as things actually are. The word does not express any temporal idea.

"once",—i. e., once for all, without need of renewal.

"at the end of the ages",—Ages is here plural to imply that the course of history is regarded as a succession of various periods, of which the appearance of Christ forms the conclusion.

The word for *"end"* in the original is one which expresses rather a consummation, an end involving more than one part or phase.

The end of the ages marks a point of termination of a series of preparatory ages, the ages being pre-Messianic and covering the whole period indicated by *"since the foundation of the world"*.

By many the expression is taken as denoting the end of the world and there is much to be said in favor of this interpretation.

Wherever *"ages"* occurs in the plural in the Epistle to the Hebrews it means the world. (Chaps. 1.2; 11.3.) In the Gospels the word here used for *"end"* repeatedly occurs with the singular or the plural of the word *"age"*, and always means the end of the world. The contrast between this expression and the *"foundation of the world"* seems also to call for this meaning.

Then, too, there is a sense in which this rendering is perfectly proper. Two thousand years have now passed since the first coming of Christ, but certainly this is not what the primitive Church was expecting. "The first Christians", says Alford, "universally spoke of the second coming of the Lord as close at hand, and indeed it ever was and is." In comparison with the long ages gone the writer might well conceive of the end of the world as near, even though he allowed it to be several hundred years away, although evidence does not seem to be wanting that he thought of it as nearer than that. Paul contended that he was living in *"the last times"* and he might have thought of those times as the end of the world, which in a very certain sense they were and are.

There is, however, one fact that inclines us to the view we have already taken, that the ages refer to pre-Messianic times, the end of the Jewish economy. It is this: In the expression, *"foundation of the world"*, the writer had just used another word for *"world"* (kosmos), and had he meant *"world"* in our passage we most certainly would have expected him to use the same word. (W. A. C. St. An. Fa. Lu. Del. Mol. Mac. Tho. Ham.)

"hath he been manifested",—i. e., in the flesh at His incarnation.

"put away sin",—The word really means "annulment". Sin is vanquished, set at naught in its guilt and in its power.

"by the sacrifice of himself",—This belongs to *"put away sin"* and not to *"manifested"*.

Ver. 27. *"And in as much"*,—This introduces a reason for what has been said. As in the case of man it is appointed unto him to die but the once, so is this true of Christ who is a partaker of our human nature.

"judgment",—Since judgment follows death, Christ upon His return will not again have to offer Himself for the cancelling of sin as He has already once done, and nothing remains for Him but to return as Judge in glory. The judgment is therefore not passed upon the soul at death (Fa. Kur.), but at the last day. (W. B. A. Bl. Lin. Bis. Del. Mai. Tho.)

Ver. 28. *"having been once offered"*,—The verb is passive, the offering being on one side voluntary but on the other the result of some outward compulsion. For the agent some supply "by Himself" (Chr.), some "by God" (Kur. Hof.), and some "by men" (Del., "the demoniac violence of the act of betrayal and crucifixion"). If an agent must be supplied, Alford has given perhaps the best answer to the query, i. e., "through the Eternal Spirit, as in verse 14—the divine submission of our Lord subjecting Himself to the external force which was exerted against Him—that force being in some part the agent, but not without His own will cooperating."

"to bear the sins of many",—The reference here is plainly to Isa. 53.12, where the same word is used in the Septuagint, the original Hebrew of which combines the meaning of *"bear"* and *"take away"*. The former meaning *"bear"*, i. e., "to take upon one's self", is the only one properly represented by the word in our text. The thought therefore is that of the vicarious sacrifice, to bear the penalty of, make atonement for, the vicarious endurance of punishment for the sins of others. (D. A. Eb. Ew. Es. Del. Aug. Boe. Bis. Mai. Mol. Kur. Hof. Con. Rie. Schm.)

"many",—i. e., mankind in general. The notion is simply that of multitude without any regard to the question whether this plurality constitutes the totality of mankind or not. (A. C. W. Lu. Del. Lin.)

"appear a second time",—This is the same verb as the one usually used of the appearances of Christ after His resurrection. It refers here of course to His second appearance before the eyes of men at His Parousia.

"apart from sin",—These words form a contrast, not to Christ's character during His first visit to this world, but to His work in reference to sin. It does not mean, therefore, as Edward Irving contended, that Christ had not been altogether without sin when first in this world. The sense is manifestly, "without any further sin laid upon Him". He is to come, when He returns, not as a sin bearer, but as a Judge.

"to them that wait for him",—The believers who cease not to desire the return of their Lord and wait for Him even as the people of Israel waited for the return of the high-priest from the Holy of Holies after the atonement had been made.

"unto salvation",—These words belong to *"appear"* and not to *"them that wait"*. He comes to accomplish or rather to consummate salvation. It was worked out by vicarious atonement during His first appearance, but its complete realization awaits His second coming.

CHAPTER TEN

13 henceforth expecting till his enemies be made the footstool of his feet.

Ver. 13. PATIENT WAITING FOR THE LORD'S RETURN.

"henceforth",—i. e., from the time of His sitting down at the right hand of God.

"expecting",—i. e., looking for Him, awaiting with expectancy, in fulfillment of the divine promise that He is one day to come again.

"till",—i. e., until the time of His Parousia, waiting until the time of His second coming, which waiting period was expressed in *"henceforth"*.

"enemies",—All opposing powers.

The order of the subduing of His enemies Paul describes in I Cor. 15.23-26, between which passage and this one in Hebrews there is no discrepancy, as some maintain there is. It is said that here all enemies are represented as subdued before Christ leaves the right hand of God and returns to earth, while in Corinthians Christ first comes to earth and then subdues His enemies.

But the fact is that in Hebrews the second coming of Christ is not taken into account, i. e., it is not the thing stressed. It is rather the contrast between the suffering and triumphant Christ that is stressed in

Hebrews, whereas in Corinthians the Apostle concerns himself especially with the order of events.

Then, too, as Lindsay says, "We must not attach a too local conception to 'the right hand of God'. That simply means participation in the rule of the universe, and Christ's return to this world, so far from being an abdication of His authority, is an exercise of it. When a prince leaves his palace and capital for a distant part of his dominions, he does not thereby give up his right and title. The real thing that is meant by the figure of Christ sitting at the right hand of God, really continues after Christ's return to this world." How splendidly Paul brings this out in Corinthians; first, He comes (verse 23), then He subdues His enemies (verse 24), and then what? "For He must reign until He hath put all enemies under His feet." (verse 25.)

> 25 not forsaking our own assembling together, as the custom of some is, but exhorting one another; and so much the more, as ye see the day drawing nigh.

Ver. 25.   THE LORD'S RETURN AN INCENTIVE TO FIDELITY.

"not forsaking the assembling of ourselves together",—The right interpretation is that the writer means to admonish them against neglecting the practice of coming together at stated periods for worship. (A. D. Lu. Eb. An. Fa. Lin. Chr. Del. Tho. Hof. Mol.)

The expression, "assembling ourselves together", must not be taken as meaning the Church and the whole phrase as embodying an admonition against apostasy. (C. Bl. Kui. Cap. Sey. Bret.) The Church is always styled "ecclesia" and the word used for "gathering" is never applied to the Church or the religious community. Furthermore the following phrase, "as is the custom", shows that apostasy is not meant, inasmuch as apostasy is not a custom or a habit.

In the neglect of public worship the writer no doubt saw the dangerous germ of apostasy, as seems evident from the following admonition, "exhorting one another", and by the awful caution which is found in the next verse.

"exhorting one another",—In the place of public worship and in private to fidelity, love and good works.

"the day",—The day of Christ's second coming, the day of His reappearing, the Parousia. It is the day of days, "the breaking up", as someone has said, "for the Church of the redeemed the night of the present." Of all the various designations of Christ's second coming this one is the briefest.

Lunneman says, "It is the day of the coming in of the Parousia of Christ, which the author thinks of as quite near at hand (verse 37), and which the readers themselves already saw drawing nigh in the agitations and commotions which preceded the Jewish war, such as had already begun to appear."

Lindsay thinks the writer here refers to the destruction of Jerusalem because they could "see" the signs of this day approaching, but not of the other far away day of the second coming. But as to this the signs may as easily have been those referred to by Christ Himself in Matt. 24, as the signs of His coming.   And then, too, verse 37 clearly refers to the second coming of Christ.

That the New Testament writers thought the Parousia of Christ to be not far away is too clearly revealed to be denied, and who knows but that they may have thought the forthcoming destruction of Jerusalem would be the time of that coming.   It was at least one of the great types and foretastes of it, "the bloody and fiery dawn", as Delitzsch finely calls it, "of the Great Day."   He further says, "The approaching judgment on Jerusalem of which so many signs filled the sky, brought home the thought of His coming in a peculiarly vivid manner."

> 37 ¹For yet a very little while. He
> that cometh shall come, and shall not
> tarry.
> ¹Hab. 2.3 f.

Ver. 37. THE SECOND COMING OF JESUS NOT TO BE LONG DELAYED.

"*a very little while*",—The original is "a very, very little while", or "a little, little while", or more literally still, "for yet how, how little".

"*He that cometh*",—Literally, "the Coming One", so-called because since His ascension *He has always been coming,* His return being a matter of constant expectation.

It is by nearly all commentators rightly referred to Christ's personal second coming, although by some (Me. Eb. Din. Ern. Hei. Blo. Carp.) referred to the Destruction of Jerusalem.

The words, "*a very little while*", are not a part of the quotation, but proceed from the author himself.   It is perhaps a reminiscence of and may be an allusion to Isa. 26.20, where they are found.   That which follows is a quotation from the Septuagint rendering of Hab. 2.3,4.

In Habakkuk it runs, "*If it delays, wait for it; it comes, it comes; it will not tarry.*"   By "*it*" is meant the vision, and the vision concerns the overthrow of the Chaldeans by the judgment of God.   Now the word "*vision*" in Hebrew is feminine, and the Septuagint in making their translation used the masculine form in the verb "*comes*", thus evidently referring to some one indicated by the vision.   The writer of Hebrews uses the quotation as found in the Septuagint, not necessarily adducing it as a proof, but evidently as expressing his own ideas in regard to the coming of the Messiah a second time; and he makes it clear that he refers to this coming person because he attached the article "*the*" to the word "*coming one*", which article is not found in the Septuagint.

"*shall not tarry*",—There is to be no delay beyond the final term fixed by the divine wisdom, long-suffering and mercy.

Blackstone says, "There is no prophesied event which has to be fulfilled before His coming in the air to receive His Church."   To those who complain that it has been more than "*a little while*", he says, "Wait until you have realized a few of the mighty cycles of eternity, and then these eighteen centuries will indeed appear to be '*a very, very little while*'.   God speaks to you as an immortal soul.   The '*little while*' of Hag. 2.6-7, we believe has not ended yet, and it certainly covered the 500 years up to Christ's first coming."

CHAPTER ELEVEN

35 Women received their dead by a resurrection: and others were tortured, not accepting their deliverance; that they might obtain a better resurrection.

Ver. 35. TORTURE NOT WORTHY TO BE COMPARED WITH THE RESURRECTION OF THE JUST.

"by a resurrection",—These examples here are without doubt taken from the life of the woman of Sarepta and of the Shunamite who received their children back in the way of resurrection. As the women are mentioned by the writer, rather than the prophets Elijah and Elisha, who, respectively, by the power of God, raised the dead in question, it is doubtless the faith of the women rather than that of the prophets that he had in mind.

"others were tortured",—From the term used it is probable that the reference is to a mode of torture in which the victim was stretched on a wheel and then beaten to death with a club.

"that they might obtain a better resurrection",—While this refers, of course, to the resurrection of the just *"at the last day"*, it can hardly be urged, with Blackstone, as an argument for a first resurrection as distinguished from a later one at the end of the Millennium.

It is possible that the future resurrection is here called *"better"* in comparison with the temporal *"deliverance"* previously mentioned (Lu. Tho. Mol. Win. Hei. Ham. Schm. Gerh.), but it is far more natural to refer it to the resurrection already spoken of. These blood-witnesses gave up their lives to obtain a resurrection to eternal life which was far better than a mere restoration from death back again into this life. (O. A. B. D. Eb. Bl. St. Chr. Lin. Del. Boe. Schu.) Others, again, understand the expression as contrasted with the resurrection of the ungodly to judgment, using Dan. 12.2 as a reference verse. (Oec. Theo.) But there is nothing in what goes before to suggest this idea; and besides there is nothing good at all in the resurrection to judgment, and the word *"better"* therefore, according to this interpretation loses entirely its force.

CHAPTER TWELVE

26 Whose voice then shook the earth; but now he hath promised, saying, [1]Yet once more will I make to tremble not the earth only, but also the heaven. 27 And this word, Yet once more, signifieth the removing of those things that are shaken, as of things that have been made, that those things which are not shaken may remain.

[1]Hag. 2.6

Vers. 26,27. THE OLD EARTH AND HEAVENS GIVING WAY TO THE NEW.

Ver. 26. *"then"*,—At the promulgation of the Mosaic law.

"shook the earth",—This refers to a literal shaking (A. An. Ed. Lu. Lin. Mol. Del.), and not to a figurative one, the emotions produced among the Israelites. (Es.)

"now",—i. e., under the New Testament dispensation hath he (God) whose voice it was that spoke at Sinai, promised, etc.

Without a doubt the promise referred to is the prediction in Haggai 2.6, and the *"now"* points to the period to which the prediction referred, i. e., with regard to the present Christian dispensation hath He promised, etc.

"yet once more",—This expression implies that the shaking is to be such as makes any repetition of a similar shaking superfluous. It means "once more and then not again". "All that admits of being shaken will then forever have been removed", says Westcott.

What the writer in verse 26 appears to say is that the God whose voice shook the earth in the old dispensation at the giving of the law on Mount Sinai, hath *"now"*, with reference to this dispensation, promised to shake not only the earth but the heaven and that with a shaking which was to be final; and in verse 27 he says this *"yet once more"*, this final shaking signified that all things shakable were by the shaking to be removed and the unshakable things were then forever to remain.

There are two views as to the reference contained in these verses:

1. It is the opinion of Lindsay and others (Coc. Lap. Boe. Klee) that *"mount Zion"* and *"the city of the living God"* and *"the heavenly Jerusalem"* of verse 22 are figures of the new order of things, in short of the Gospel Church, and they accordingly understand the shaking of heaven and earth here mentioned as figurative descriptions of the great political and social changes which accompanied the introduction of the Gospel.

2. On the other hand there are those, and these are the great majority, who take the expressions of our passage as descriptive of the great physical convulsions by which a new heaven and a new earth are to emerge out of the ruin of the old. (A. O. D. W. S. An. Ed. Lu. Bl. The. Era. Bez. Tho. Mol. Del. Theo.)

Lindsay says these authorities refer the expressions of verse 22 to "the glorious condition that awaits the saints after the resurrection" and upon this build their explanation of the passage now under consideration.

We are inclined to think, however, that Dr. Lindsay allows the expressions found in verses 22-25 too large a part in the explanation of the passage before us. Not one of the authorities, who take the second view, says anything one way or the other, as he deals with the three expressions in verses 22-25, as to the time element being either after or before the resurrection of the saints.

But altogether apart from what the three expressions in verses 22-25 mean, there are other expressions in the verses noted, some of which evidently refer to the saints now on earth and some to such saints as are now in their glorified condition, and that too before their resurrection, as practically every one of the authorities supporting the second view above mentioned admits.

For instance, *"the Church of the firstborn who are enrolled in heaven"* (verse 23) without doubt refers to the saints living on earth, the Church below (A. An. Bl. Eb. Mol. Gro. Mos. Boe. Kui. Lin. Tho. Del. Hof. Prim. Schu. Schli. Knapp, Riehm), although some (C. B. S. Lu.) insist that saints already glorified are meant, and others still would include both (O.).

It is equally certain that *"the spirits of just men made perfect"*, whether we include in the expression Old Testament saints only (D. Bl.

Eb. Lap. Wol. Schu. Schli.), or New Testament saints only (B. Ba. Lu. Gro. Mos. Schm.), or both (A. An. Fa. Lin. Del. Tho. Bis. Boe. Kui. Mol. Knapp, Riehm), (and of this we are convinced) refers to the saints who are *now* in glory.

Those who take the second view above mentioned are quite ardent in its support. Thus Alford says, "It is clearly wrong to understand this shaking of the mere breaking down of Judaism before the Gospel, or of anything which shall be fulfilled *during* the Christian economy, short of its glorious end and accomplishment." Thus the prophecy of Haggai seems to point to the same great final bringing of all the earth under the kingdom of God, which is spoken of in Zech. 14, when the Lord shall come with all His saints. The heaven that is to be shaken here is the material heaven stretched above the earth.

Few points have been more contested than this. On hardly any portion of the Epistle have commentators left us so much in the dark. Interpreters, who otherwise are rich in exegetical pearls, have seemingly hurried over this passage as an undesirable place to tarry.

It is true, as Lindsay says, that the primary object of this Epistle is to show that under the New Covenant we have advantages and privileges that were not enjoyed under the Old, and that contrast all along has been between the heavenly, spiritual elements of the New Dispensation and the worldly, material, perishable elements of the Old. But what the writer of the Epistle is doing here is to base upon that contrast, so finely and fully brought out in verses 22-24, certain much needed warnings and instructions. He therefore says, "See that ye refuse not Him that speaketh, whose voice then (at Mount Sinai) shook the earth, but who now (as regards this Dispensation) hath promised to shake not the earth only, but also heaven." We repeat therefore that we must not look back to verses 22-24 for the key to the interpretation of the passage under consideration.

Furthermore to confine the fulfillment of the promise of Haggai to that which took place at the introduction of the Gospel by the first coming of Christ, as does Lindsay in the first of the two views noted above, is to put upon the prophecy the stamp of at least partial failure, for most assuredly that prophecy does not seem as yet to have met with its full and complete accomplishment.

Again, this Epistle does not anywhere describe the passing away of the Old Covenant as a violent catastrophe, but rather as that of something which has grown old and decayed, whereas the coming death of the Lord is elsewhere and often spoken of as accompanied with great convulsions of nature.

The fact is that the prophets of the Old Testament made no distinction between the beginning and the consummation of the age to be inaugurated by the appearance of the Messiah they foretold. They expected the consummation to come speedily upon His arrival. To them it was not given to see the two thousand years which God in His longsuffering has allowed to intervene while He is gathering out a people for Himself. The two advents of the Messiah are therefore regarded as one, even as two peaks in a mountain range seen from a distance seem to be one close upon the other or practically together but which are in reality many miles apart, and the shaking which was promised began at the first advent of the Messiah and will be completed at the second; the convulsions connected with the overthrow of Jerusalem foreshadowing those which shall take place upon the return of the Lord, the announcement of which is to the ungodly a terror but to believers a promise to the fulfillment of which they can look forward with joy. This is practically the view of Alford and the majority to which attention has already been called.

Ver. 27. The last clause of this verse, beginning with *"that"*, is most properly joined to the word *"removing"* as indicating some inferiority in the things that were shakable and hence removed. (A. W. D. S. Lu. Bl. An. Lin. The. Oec.)

It has by others been joined to the preceding word *"made"* and two explanations of the thought are set forth:

1. *"made to the end that the unshakable things might remain"*, i. e., remain by the passing away of the unshakable things. (B. Gro. Tho. Del.). This thought is beautiful enough indeed but this connection not only destroys the logic and the rythm of the sentence, but it is forced and unnatural. Of course if the things are unshakable they must of necessity remain.

2. *"made in order that they may await the unshakable things"*, i. e., that they may remain until the unshakable things arrive. (Sto. Boe. Kui. Klee, Bauldry.) But this would rather call for the present tense than the aorist, and besides it gives to the Greek word a sense (wait) hardly suitable to the scope of the passage.

Eternal reality abides only in the ideal. The material world is unreal and evanescent. When it has served its purpose, it will be removed and the new heavens and the new earth, God's heavenly city and eternal kingdom, the things unshakable, will abide forever.

THE EPISTLE OF

JAMES

(A. D. 60)

CHAPTER FIVE

3 Ye have laid up your treasure in the last days.

7 Be patient therefore, brethren, until the [1]coming of the Lord. Behold, the husbandman waiteth for the precious fruit of the earth, being patient over it, until [2]it receive the early and latter rain.

[1]Gr. *presence*
[2]Or, *he*

8 Be ye also patient; establish your hearts; for the [1]coming of the Lord is at hand. 9 Murmur not, brethren, one against another, that ye be not judged: behold, the judge standeth before the doors.

Vers. 3,7,8,9. Exhortations in View of the Coming of the Lord.

These are the only four verses in the whole of the Epistle of James which are devoted to the subject of the Second Coming of Jesus Christ. It is evident, however, from these four verses that he shared in the prevalent hope of the near approach of *"the Parousia of the Lord"*. To him it was both a day of blessing for the Christian and a day of judgment for the ungodly.

Ver. 3. *"in"*,—Not "against" nor "for" as in the Authorized Version; neither is the word "wrath" to be supplied to the word *"treasures"*, as in Rom. 2.5 (C. Es. Lau.). The treasures are amply described in the foregoing verse as treasures of riches.

"the last days",—In harmony with the rest of the Epistle these words are to be taken as the last days before the Second Coming of Christ (A. G. Hu. Pl. Gl.), and are not to be referred to the last days of their lives (Wol. Mor.), nor to the last days just before the coming national judgment on the Jews in the destruction of Jerusalem (L.).

Ver. 7. *"patient"*,—The literal is "longsuffering" and it is an exhortation to forbearance toward their oppressors and to a trustful waiting on God for deliverance.

"coming of the Lord",—James uses the usual expression, Parousia— presence. By *"Lord"* is meant Christ (A. L. Fr. Hu. Wi. Bru. Bou.) according to constant Christian usage, and not God (D. Aug. Thie.).

The whole context shows that James is thinking of Christ's Second Coming as the judge of the wicked ones, and of course at the same time as a rewarder of the righteous.

Some, of course, relate the matter to the destruction of Jerusalem, and Fronmuller says that the Apostles thought that the coming of Christ at the end of the age was to take place at the same time with the destruction of Jerusalem, and so combine the two views.

"early and latter rain",—The rain of Autumn and Spring. James is illustrating by example.

Ver. 8. *"establish"*,—This means to confirm and strengthen, which things are required for patience to which he had been exhorting them.

"is at hand",—The literal here is "hath drawn near". The verb is in the perfect tense; if the coming of the Lord had drawn near, it was then most assuredly *"at hand"*. The reference is of course to the Second Coming at the end of the age.

How could James say this? It was certainly the general expectation of the day, but James would not base his statement upon this unless he had reason for believing it. Was he, as some say, looking through the eye of faith and seeing as God sees, that one day with the Lord is as a thousand years? No, hardly. He was saying what he did as a comfort to the Christians to whom he was writing as something which might take place in the near future, not necessarily before they died, yet there is little if any doubt but that believers in that day were taught to live in constant expectation of the coming again of their Lord.

Ver. 9. *"murmur not one against another"*,—The reference here is to a sinful irritability towards each other because of impatience, and not to an imprecation of divine vengeance on one another (C. L. Hot. Mor. Geb.).

"that ye be not judged",—i. e., when the day of judgment comes. Murmuring thus involves judging one another, and this violates our Lord's injunction in Matt. 7.1.

"the judge standeth before the doors",—This of course can be taken in no other sense than that it is used to indicate the nearness of Christ's coming to judgment, and is evidently quite equivalent to the expression used in the preceding verse. It gives all the more reason why the Christian should be patient and leave all judgment to the Lord.

The sneering ones at Jerusalem used to ask Saint James, "Which is the *door* of Jesus?", "By which *door* will He come?"

THE FIRST EPISTLE OF
PETER
(A. D. 60)

CHAPTER ONE

5 who by the power of God are guarded through faith unto a salvation ready to be revealed in the last time.

7 that the proof of your faith, being more precious than gold that perisheth though it is proved by fire, may be found unto praise and glory and honor at the revelation of Jesus Christ.

13 Wherefore girding up the loins of your mind, be sober and set your hope perfectly on the grace that [1]is to be brought unto you at the revelation of Jesus Christ.

20 who was foreknown indeed before the foundation of the world, but was manifested at the end of the times for your sake.

[1]Gr. *is being brought*

Vers. 5,7,13,20. THE REVELATION OF CHRIST THE TIME OF FULL SALVATION.

Ver. 5. *"by the power of God"*,—This expression is related to the omnipotence of God, and is not to be understood of the Holy Spirit, as some do. The Holy Spirit is never so designated in Scripture; not even in Lu. 1.35. God's power is the efficient cause of the guarding, while *"through faith"* is the effective means by which the power of God effects the preservation.

"ready to be revealed",—This refers, of course, to the salvation.

Says Fausset, "When Christ shall be revealed, it shall be revealed."

There are those who are ever insistent that Paul shall be made to say the coming of the Lord is near if the language used permits of the least possible turn in this direction. Here this turn is found in the word *"ready"*. Fronmuller, for instance, remarks, "Paul thinks of the salvation as not far distant but as close at hand, and he says in Chap. 4-5, *'Who shall give an account to Him that is ready to judge the quick and the dead.'* Sharing the opinion of the other Apostles concerning the nearness of Christ's advent to judgment, he describes the salvation as *ready* to be revealed. (See Jam. 5.7,8; Rev. 1.3; 22.10,20; Heb. 10.25,37; Jude 18; I John 2.18; Rom. 13.11,12; I Cor. 15.51; II Cor. 5.2,3; Phil. 4.5; I Thess. 4.17)."

And Huther says, "When this time will be the Apostle does not say, but his whole manner of expression indicates that in hope it floated before his vision as one near at hand."

We might say that it is in no wise certain that the reference in Chap. 4.5 refers to the nearness of the judgment, and furthermore that the stress of being *"ready"* here is not on the nearness of the *"revelation"*, but on the fact of the salvation being ready, prepared, completed for the revelation when it comes.

The tense of the infinitive after *"ready"* gives the idea of the rapid completion of the act of the revelation as contrasted with the guarding mentioned.

"in the last time",—This is elsewhere called *"the end of the age"* (Matt. 13.39,40). It is absolutely the last time, beginning with the Parousia, and is not to be thought of in the Jewish technical sense as *"the last times"* beginning at the first advent of Christ.

"The last time", says Fausset, "is the last day, closing the day of grace; the day of judgment, of redemption, of the restitution of all things, and of perdition of the ungodly." "It is", says Salmond, "the time closing the present order of things, and heralding Christ's return. Pre-Messianic times began to fade to their extinction with Christ's First Advent; post-Messianic times entered conclusively with Christ's Second Advent. The former was known as *'this age'*, to which, although Christ had appeared, the Apostle's own time was spoken of as belonging. The latter was called *'the age to come'*, the final reality of which was as near as was the Messiah's glorious return. This Second Advent, therefore, was the crisis once for all separating the two, and the time which marked the end of the one period and ushered in the other was *'the last day'* ,*'the last time'*. Christ's return will announce the close of the *'last time'* of the old order, and in a moment uncover what God has prepared in secret."

"The hope of the Church", says Morgan, "is, in this aspect, a salvation to be revealed in all its fullness when Jesus Christ Himself shall come." This salvation, or *"inheritance incorruptible, and undefiled, and that fadeth not away"*, for which the Christian is guarded, and which is said to be *"ready to be revealed in the last time"*, is in verse 4 said to be reserved in heaven. This means, of course, that the inheritance, which has been prepared for us from the beginning, has been laid up in reserve for us in the heavens where God Himself is. It is thus made doubly safe in that it is laid up for us, as Lillie says, "among God's own treasures, under His own eye, and within the shelter of His omnipotence", and we are guarded and kept by the power of God through faith against the day of its revealing. The expression, however, *"reserved in heaven"*, was much used by the Fathers and Greek interpreters as an argument against the Millennarian doctrine.

Fausset says, "It does not follow that because it is *now* laid up *in heaven*, it shall not *hereafter* be *on earth* also."

Ver. 7. *"at the revelation of Jesus Christ"*,—The reference is to the Parousia, when Christ, who is now withdrawn from our sight, will appear again, and with His revelation shall come also the revelation of the saints of God. (Rom. 8.9; I John 3.2.)

Ver. 13. *"at the revelation of Jesus Christ"*,—This is to be taken in the same sense as in verse 7. (A. D. C. Hu. Fr. Es. Wi. Oec. Gro. Car. Sta. Bez. Sem. Hof. Theo. Pott.)

However, there are those who take it as the revelation of grace made by the Gospel in which Jesus Christ is revealed. (B. Zo. Ca. Wei. Era. Gerh. Steig.) But in no passage is the revelation of the Gospel called "the revelation of Jesus Christ", and this view is not only contrary to the New Testament usage of this expression, but it is contrary to the immediately previous usage by John in verse 7, and contrary as well to the general significance of the present participle, *"is being brought"*, which is the literal rendering and which cannot be taken in the sense of a past tense, but must be looked upon as a realization of the future.

Ver. 20. *"manifested"*,—This same word occurs in Chap. 4.4 of the Second Coming of Christ, but here it refers to His first coming, which is represented as an emerging, as it were, from obscurity through the manifestation of the incarnation.

"at the end of the times",—This expression in Chap. 1.5 and in II Pet. 3.3, where it is *"the end of the days"*, refers to time yet future, immediately preceding the Second Coming of Christ, but the expression is here conceived of in the technical sense as *"the last times"*, the entire period beginning with the first coming of Christ.

Alford has put it, "This manifestation of Christ marks this time, this present dispensation, as *'the end of the times'* and it will endure only so long as the *'manifestation'* requires."

CHAPTER FOUR

5 who shall give account to him that is ready to judge the living and the dead.
7 But the end of all things is at hand; be ye therefore of sound mind and be ye sober unto prayer.

13 but insomuch as ye are partakers of Christ's sufferings, rejoice; that at the revelation of His Glory also ye may rejoice with exceeding joy.

Vers. 5,7,13. THE RETURN OF CHRIST AN INSPIRATION TO SOBER MINDEDNESS AND PATIENT ENDURANCE.

Ver. 5. *"ready to judge"*,—Here again many expositors read into the word *"ready"* the idea that the judgment is pointed out as near at hand. But this is far-fetched. It simply states that God is fully prepared; all the means and necessary conditions are in His hand.

"the living and the dead",—Whether living or dead at the appearing of the Judge, none can escape. (See remarks under II Tim. 4.1.)

It is strange that by anyone this should be understood of Christians only (Wic. Schot.), or that others should refer it alone to those who speak evil. It refers, of course, to all who are living or dead at the time when the judgment mentioned is to take place. There can be no doubt, however, that there is a special reference here to the blasphemers and the natural inference is that Peter was saying that they should not remain unpunished whether they die before the day of judgment or not. There is to be found here consequently just another touch of that thought of the nearness of the end which seemed to hold the minds of the Apostles and early Christians.

Ver. 7. *"But the end of all things is at hand"*,—It is hard to see how any one can find anything in this expression other than just what its surface meaning indicates, namely, that Peter thought that the end of all things was about to transpire, and that with the coming of the Lord there was to arrive a time of joy and reward for the believer and a time of wrath and destruction upon the ungodly. Consistent with this we call attention to the following quotations, hundreds of which of similar import might be added:

Alford,—"This was the constant expectation of the Apostolic age."

Huther,—"That the Apostle, without fixing the time or the hour of it, looked upon the advent of Christ and the end of the age therewith connected, as near at hand *must be simply admitted.*"

Salmon,—"The vivid realization of the nearness of the end, which appears in all the Apostolic writings, is especially characteristic of Peter; to him the close of the present dispensation was so near that nothing seemed to stand between him and it."

Fronmuller,—"Peter in common with the other Disciples expected that the second advent of Christ and the end of the whole present dispensation were nearly impending."

Says John Calvin, "It ought to be the chief concern of the believer to fix his mind constantly on Christ's second advent."

Ver. 13. *"at the revelation of his glory"*,—The expression is found only here and it refers to the time of His Parousia. Whoever is a partaker of Christ's sufferings and rejoices therein will one day have the glad privilege of rejoicing everlastingly in His glory. Otherwise the day of the revelation of Christ and His glory would be to them a day of terror.

CHAPTER FIVE

1 The elders therefore among you I exhort, who am a fellow elder, and a witness of the sufferings of Christ, who am also a partaker of the glory that shall be revealed.

4 And when the chief Shepherd shall be manifested, ye shall receive the crown of glory that fadeth not away.

Vers. 1,4. THE BELIEVER'S GLORY AT THE MANIFESTATION OF THE LORD.

Ver. 1. *"the glory that shall be revealed"*,—The reference is to the day of the revelation of Jesus Christ. Peter may have had in mind the words of his Master in John 13.36, but it is safer exegesis to think he was glancing back to the *"revelation of glory"* in Chap. 4.13.

The present participle is used here and Alford, as is his invariable custom, reads into it the idea of nearness and translates "about to be", but the rendering of the Revised Version, *"shall be"*, is better. The participle with the passive infinitive, which is used here, expresses something that is determined and certain rather than something that is near, although the verb from which the participle comes (mello) does mean "about to be".

Ver. 4. *"shall be manifested"*,—This word like the word *"revelation"* relates to the visible return of the Lord. While the reference is clearly here to the Second Coming, Peter uses the same word, as seen in Chap. 1.20, to express the first coming of Christ.

Says Alford, "It would not be clear from this passage alone whether Peter regarded the coming of the Lord as likely to occur in the life of his readers, or not; but as interpreted by the analogy of his other expressions on the same subject, it would appear that he did."

THE SECOND EPISTLE OF
PETER

CHAPTER ONE

11 for thus shall be richly supplied unto you the entrance into the eternal kingdom of our Lord and Saviour Jesus Christ.

16 For we did not follow cunningly devised fables, when we made known unto you the power and the [1]coming of our-Lord Jesus Christ, but we were eye-witnesses of his majesty.

19 And we have the word of prophecy made more sure; whereunto ye do well that ye take heed, as unto a lamp shining in a [2]dark place, until the day dawn and the day-star arise in your hearts.

[1]Gr. *presence*

[2]Gr. *squalid*

Vers. 11,16,19. THE RETURN OF THE LORD, THE DAY-DAWN OF THE HEART.

Ver. 11. *"the eternal kingdom of our Lord and Saviour Jesus Christ"*,—Whether you take this to be the kingdom into which the believer enters at the moment of his death or that which the Lord established at His Coming will depend upon your conclusion from the study of the entire subject of the *"kingdom"* as presented throughout the Scriptures, and whether you consider the Second Coming of Christ to take place before or after the Millennial period.

Notice it is *"the"* entrance, the well understood entrance which formed the object of every Christian's hope.

Ver. 16. *"the power and coming of our Lord Jesus Christ"*,—

"power",—The whole treasure of divine power is centered in Him. (Matt. 28.18.) The Apostle is thinking of the Transfiguration (verses 17,18), and *"power"* denotes, as Salmon says, "the fullness of might of the glorified Lord as it will be more especially revealed in His Coming."

"coming",—The word here is the usual Greek word, "Parousia", and in harmony both with New Testament usage, and the connection of the thought here (verses 4,17; Chap. 3.4), relates to the Lord's Second Coming. (A. D. Hu. Es. Sem. Die. Hof. Kna. Bru.)

It must not, therefore, be taken as referring to His human birth, His first coming (Va. Hor. Jac.), nor to His presence during the time He appeared on earth (Schm.), nor to "his appearing with miraculous powers in the flesh along with His expected appearance in glory" (Fr. Han.)

Ver. 19. *"in your hearts"*,—These words make the interpretation of the whole verse somewhat difficult.

They do not belong to *"take heed"* (Schot.), nor to the following *"knowing this first"* (Hof.), to which is opposed the position of the words. They belong to the clause immediately preceding, *"until the day dawn and the day-star arise"* (D. Hu. Fri. Wi. Bru.), which clause itself is to be connected not with *"shining"* (B. Hof. Schot.), but with *"take heed"* (A. Hu.). Because of the words *"in your hearts"* some think, as Salmon says, that a subjective application must be given to the whole verse and the following explanations are made of the various terms:

"dark place",—

Fronmuller refers this to the condition of the readers before they were Christians, and the *"day dawn"*, etc., to the idea of a man's conversion. But the context makes clear the fact that Peter's words were to those who were Christians.

By others the words are made to refer to a low state of spiritual knowledge and experience which is to give way to a higher state of illumination and assurance in the case of Christians.

The time when the day dawns in the hearts of the Christians and the morning star arises, and when consequently they can do without the light, has been variously interpreted. The expression is taken by Grotius to mean their attainment of the gift of prophecy; by De Wette, "the arrival at the full conviction of the certainty of the coming of Christ"; and by Alford, "that degree of Christian experience where faith rests not on external evidence, but upon the inward revelation of the Holy Spirit."

The *"day-star"* means, of course, the morning star which always accompanies the dawning of the day and is added here to complete the picture.

On the other hand there are those who take the objective interpretation of the words to be the proper one and think of the *"dark place"* as a figure of the world itself.

The time spoken of, as is seen by the very wording of the verse, must be the time present with the readers, and therefore any reference to Old Testament times is out of place. It is the world in its present condition to which reference must be had. (Hu. Wi. Bru. Sal. Die.) The place where the Christians are and where the light shines are one and the same, and if they did not take heed unto this light they would be in darkness.

The analogy of similar figures (Rom. 13.11) favors the objective view. The majority of those who take this objective view refer it to the Parousia, the Second Coming of Christ.

"The reference therefore", says Salmon, "seems to be to the day of Christ's Second Coming, in comparison with which the present state of the world is the time of night and darkness."

According to this view the particular point of time in view is that immediately heralding the Second Advent itself, *"the time when the sign of the Son of man appears"* (Matt. 24.30), when believers are to lift up their heads because their redemption draweth nigh (Lu. 21.28) when accordingly the morning star which ushers in the day shall arise in their hearts, i. e., in their hearts shall arise a light and an assurance like the dawn of day with its morning star.

There is no doubt that the evidence warrants the application of the expression to the Second Coming of Christ, although it is possible, as Alford says, that "the Apostle may have mingled both ideas together as he wrote the words; seeing that even in our hearts the fullness of the spiritual will not have arisen until that time when we see face to face and know even as God knew us."

CHAPTER TWO

4 For if God spared not the angels when they sinned, but [1]cast them down to [2]hell, and committed them to [3]pits of darkness, to be reserved unto judgment;

[1]Or, *cast them into dungeons*
[2]Gr. *Tartarus*
[3]Some ancient authorities read *chains*. Comp. Wisd. 17.17

9 the Lord knoweth how to deliver the godly out of temptation, and to keep the unrighteous under punishment unto the day of judgment;

Vers. 4,9. THE INTERMEDIATE STATE OF JUDGMENT.

Ver. 4. *"when they sinned"*,—The reference is to the revolt. of Satan and his associates. (See Jude 6.)

"cast them down to hell",—The word is "Tartarus" and is found nowhere else in the New Testament nor in the Septuagint. It is not "hades", and it is not synonomous with "Gehenna", which is the place of final punishment; but it is the intermediate scene or state of punishment, the preliminary place of confinement and state for the spirits similar to what sheol is for men.

"judgment",—The final judgment. Jude reads, *"unto the judgment of the great day"*.

"reserved",—The word has in it the idea of being held in custody.

Ver. 9. *"temptation"*,—Including, as in I Pet. 1.6, not only temptation in the limited sense, but all species of trials, persecutions and the like.

"under punishment",—Not "to be punished", as in the Authorized Version, but held in reserve *"for the final judgment of the great day"* (A. Hu. Fr. Wi. Sal. Bru. Schot.)

CHAPTER THREE

3 knowing this first, that [1]in the last days mockers shall come with mockery, walking after their own lusts. 4 and saying, Where is the promise of his [2]coming? for, from the day that the fathers fell asleep, all things continue as they were from the beginning of the creation. 5 For this they wilfully forget, that there were heavens from of old, and an earth compacted out of water and [3]amidst water, by the word of God; 6 by which means the world that then was, being overflowed with water, perished; 7 but the heavens that now are, and the earth, by the same word have been [4]stored up for fire, being reserved against the day of judgment and destruction of ungodly men. 8 But forget not this one thing, beloved, that one day is with the Lord as a thousand years, and a thousand years as one day. 9 The Lord is not slack concerning his promise, as some count slackness; but is longsuffering to you-ward, not wishing that any should perish, but that all should come to repentance. 10 But the day of the Lord will come as a thief; in the which the heavens shall pass away with a great noise, and the [5]elements shall be dissolved with fervent heat, and the earth and the works that are therein shall be [6]burned up.

[1]Gr. *in the last of the days*
[2]Gr. *presence*
[3]Or, *through*
[4]Or, *stored with fire*

[5]Or, *heavenly bodies*
[6]The most ancient manuscripts read *discovered*

Vers. 3-10. MOCKERS OF HIS COMING AND THEIR DESTINY.

Ver. 3. *"knowing this first"*,—They are to consider it as a principal point of the prophetical words they are now to read.

"in the last days",—Literally, "in the last of the days". The times referred to are those immediately preceding the Second Coming of Christ,

and, says Salmon, "immediately introducing the age described as *'the age to come'* "

"mockers shall come with mockery",—The form of the expression gives sharp emphasis to their conduct, and the Authorized Version by omitting *"with mockery"* strips the statement of its most graphic stroke.

"walking after their own lusts",—Says Salmon, "The lustful life and the scoffing voice are not associated here without a purpose."

"own lusts",—This brings out the self will and the opposition of these men to the will of God—no longer wolves in sheep's clothing, but walking openly in their wolfish natures.

Ver. 4. *"Where is"*,—Implying that it is nowhere; it has passed away and disappeared.

"promise",—That made by Jesus in the Gospels and especially the promise in Acts 1.11.

"his",—They did not use the name of Christ because of their disdain for His name, say some. (Fr. Wi. Hof. Gerh.)

The question shows how familiar the subject was among everybody in that day.

"fathers",—The first generation of Christian believers received the promise and lived in the hope of its sure and speedy fulfillment. They died without witnessing it, and this would be used as an argument with their children for discrediting the promise itself. (D. Fr. Hu. Sal. Hof. Thi. Hes.)

Wiesinger refers the word to the Old Testament patriarchs, but the fact that they died before the fulfillment of the promise of the Lord's return would be a strange argument for these mockers to urge against the Christian hope.

Wiesinger argues that the time element will not permit our interpretation; but this was written in A. D. 67, and then it must be remembered that Peter is speaking from the standpoint of the last times, some little time at least in the future.

"as they were",—Better, "as they are". The meaning is well expressed as follows, "Ever since the death of our fathers to whom the promise was given, things have continued as we now see them and as they always have continued even from the beginning of the creation." (A. Fr. Sal.) The fact that the scoffers would ask such a question shows that the people of that time expected by reason of some great manifestation or world disturbance to know when Christ came. This is a strong argument against the Millennial Dawn teaching of His unobserved coming, and that only gradually will it dawn upon the world that He is here when once He does come.

Ver. 5. *"For"*,—Introducing the reason for their making such a statement as that in verse 4.

"wilfully forget",—Shut their own eyes. Some authorities refer the word *"this"* to the assertion of the preceding verse and give to *"wilfully"* the meaning of "asserting", and read, "For, asserting this, they forget", etc. But this gives a most unusual sense to the word *"wilfully"*, and nearly all commentators hold to the rendering of the Revised Version.

"from of old",—From the first origin of all things.

"compacted",—i. e., brought together, made solid, "consisting of", as in the Authorized Version of Col. 1.7.

"by the word of God",—Not of its own will, not by a fortuitous concurrence of atoms, but as in the record of the Word of God.

Our rendering, *"compacted"*, looks to the water as the *material "out of"* which the earth was made, and the meaning of the word is strongly in favor of this, the Revised Version reading. (A. Hu. Sal.)

The Authorized Version reads "standing" for *"compacted"*, and so makes the earth rise up *"out of"* the water in which it lay buried. (B. Wi. Win. Hof. Schot.)

Ver. 6. Peter shows that the world was once destroyed and that therefore the assertion that it had continued as it was from the beginning of creation was not true.

"perished",—This means, not that it was annihilated, but that it lost its form and substance as a world; reduced to another form and state.

"by which means",—These words are to be explained in one or the other of three different ways:

1. They may refer to the *"heavens"* and the *"earth"*, the heavens opened and the fountains of the earth broken up to cause the destruction. (Fr. Hof. Bez. Oec. Wol. Horn, Steinf.)
   Some of these authorities take *"the world that then was"* as the world of living creatures and some take it as the material system which perished by means of the very things by which it consisted, while still others combine the two, which last is certainly, if the view under consideration is accepted, the proper way to take the expression.

2. They may refer to *"water"* and *"the word of God"*, i. e., the seemingly constant order of things perished through the agents that first formed it. (Wi. Bes. Bru. Sal. Gerh.) With this view it is also best to take *"the world that then was"* as the whole order of things, the earth with men and other living creatures occupying it.

3. They may refer to *"water"* alone, out of which and through which the heavens opened and the fountains of the deep broke up. *"The world that then was"* is, under this view, to be taken in the same way as that preferred above. (A. C. Hu. Lum. Pott. and the majority.)

These views are all equally substantial. The third view makes the flow of thought a bit easier than the others, while the reference in the next verse to the word of God again, *"by the same word"*, seems to favor the second view.

Ver. 7. *"for fire"*,—Some would have this modify *"reserved"* (A. Hu. Fr. Bru.), but with others we prefer the arrangement of our text. (Wi. Sal. Hof. Schot.) Why should anyone think that Peter got this idea of the destruction of heaven and earth by fire from Greek or Stoic philosophy or Oriental mythology when the Old Testament is full of it, and the more especially since it was promised that the world would not again be destroyed by water, and the destruction of Sodom and Gomorrah would naturally be taken by him as a type of the future judgment of the world.

Ver. 8. This is not a second refutation of the scoffers but a removal of an obstacle which believers might find in the delay of Christ's coming.

As he quotes from Psalm 90, the *"Lord"* here is not to be referred to Christ, but to the Lord of the Psalms, Jehovah, God.

Says Stier, "He who created the heavens and the earth in six days because He thus willed it, may also suddenly accomplish in one day that which under other circumstances would require a thousand years; in like manner He may ordain thousands of years to be to the world week-days and work-days before His great Sabbath begins to dawn."

Ver. 9. God's purpose in the delay concerning the promise of the coming again of Christ is a gracious one.

"some",—The reference here, we feel, is primarily to believers of weak faith (Fr. Hu. Sal.), and not to the scoffers (A.), although of course these are still in his mind.

"as some consider slackness",—i. e., as some consider it to be, namely, His delay.

Ver. 10. *"shall come"*,—This is placed at the head of the sentence for emphasis. He will come in spite of the delay and of the assertion of the scoffers.

"as a thief",—The idea is that of unexpected suddenness rather than that of dread.

"day of the Lord",—The Lord here, as throughout the passage, is evidently not Christ but God as in verse 12.

"a great noise",—The better translation is "a rushing sound". The word has in it the idea of whirring, whizzing motion as well as of sound. De Wette refers it to the crash with which the heavens shall fall, and Oecumenius to the actual noise of the flames. The writer probably thinks of both.

"elements",—The reference here is doubtless to the heavenly bodies, the constituent elements making up the heavens. The word means the component parts which make up a thing, and while it is true that wherever else used in Scripture it has an ethical sense, it has in Peter clearly a physical sense, and it seems best to take it here in a broad sense as applying to the parts of which the heavens in particular, or the system of things generally, are made up, and it doubtless denotes much the same as *"the powers of the heavens"* in Matt. 24.29, the idea being that these heavens shall pass away by having their constituent parts dissolved.

It will not do to think of the four elements, earth, air, fire and water (Be.), nor just *"earth, air and water"*, because fire would not be represented as being consumed by fire (Horn), nor yet as "air and water" (Es.).

"with fervent heat",—The word is a participle which means "being scorched up" and properly belongs with *"elements"*, but the Revised Version rendering gives the right thought exactly and may be allowed to remain.

"works",—The works of God and man, nature and art. (B. Wi. Fr. Die. Bru. Schot.) It is not merely man's works (Ros. Hof. Steinf.), nor yet merely God's work, the earth and the fullness thereof (Hu.), nor is it to be taken only as the wicked works of man after I Cor. 3.15.

"burned up",—It is true that *"burned up"* is difficult to account for, the best manuscript authority being in favor of the marginal reading, "discovered", and this reading is supposed by the latest scholarship to have arisen from a corruption of another, which would mean "shall flow (or melt) away". The wide variety of readings is a witness to the early uncertainty of the text. One manuscript reads, "shall disappear"; one version inserts a "not", and reads "shall not be found".

If the word "discovered" be retained, the sense would likely be, "found out judicially" or "made to appear as they are". Some turn it into a question, "Shall the earth and the works therein be found then?", i. e., shall they continue? There is, however, no uncertainty whatever as to the sense that is meant to be conveyed.

11 Seeing that these things are thus all to be dissolved, what manner of persons ought ye to be in *all* holy living and godliness, 12 looking for and [1]earnestly desiring the [2]coming of the day of God, by reason of which the heavens being on fire shall be dissolved, and the [3]elements shall melt with fervent heat? 13 But, according to his promise, we look for new heavens and a new earth, wherein dwelleth righteousness.

14 Wherefore, beloved, seeing that ye look for these things, give diligence that ye may be found in peace, without spot and blameless in his sight. 15 And account that the longsuffering of our Lord is salvation; even as our beloved brother Paul also, according to the wisdom given to him, wrote unto you; 16 as also in all *his* epistles, speaking in them of these things; wherein are some things hard to be understood, which the ignorant and unstedfast wrest, as *they do* also the other scriptures, unto their own destruction. 17 Ye therefore, beloved, knowing *these things* beforehand, beware lest, being carried away with the error of the wicked, ye fall from your own stedfastness. 18 But grow in the grace and knowledge of our Lord and Saviour Jesus Christ. To him *be* the glory both now and [4]for ever. Amen.

[1]Or, *hastening*
[2]Gr. *presence*
[3]Or, *heavenly bodies*
[4]Gr. *unto the day of eternity*

Vers. 11-18. HASTENING THE COMING OF THE DAY OF THE LORD.

Ver. 11. *"these things"*,—Not merely the works, but all the things before mentioned.

"to be dissolved",—This is the present of certainty (A. Hu. Fr.), and not "are dissolving", are now in process of dissolution, as Salmon puts it.

"what manner", etc.,—Beginning with these words the Revised Version takes all the words to the end of verse 12 as a question. The arrangement of the words in the Revised Version cannot be improved upon, but it is more in accord with usage to take the whole expression as a solemn declaration in an exclamatory sense. (Hu. Sal. Hof.)

Ver. 12. *"earnestly desiring"*,—The passages quoted in support of this rendering by the Revised Version really do not support it at all. They all mean to prosecute with zeal something that is present. We are inclined most strongly to the marginal reading of the Revised Version and to the text of the Authorized, "hastening", i. e., hurry on. (A. B. D. Wi. Hu. Fr. Era. Hof. Sal.) The idea is that of accelerating the advent of that day by our holy lives and our labors for the advancement of the Gospel.

"the coming (presence—Parousia) of the day of God",—This expression is found only here and this is the only place where we read of the Parousia of a day, it being commonly used of a person, and usually of the presence or advent of the Lord Himself.

Lachmann says that Peter had given up the hope of Christ's return, and mixed it up with God's future day of judgment. This is sheer nonsense. Peter treats of the coming of Christ in other places in his writings. The term, *"day of God"*, ought not to surprise us if we have due respect to teaching of the Old Testament.

"by reason of which",—i. e., by reason of the day of God.

"fervent heat",—As in verse 10.

"melt",—There is no gainsaying the fact that the word means "melt" in the most literal sense, although De Wette says the meaning is not to be literally pressed. Alford on the other hand says, "Why not?" and refers to the liquefaction that has actually taken place in the crust of the earth wherever the central fires have acted upon it. He asks, "Why should not that day, in its purifying process, produce a similar effect on the earth again?"

In spite of the strong expressions used by the writer, it is not decidedly stated that the world is to be dissolved into nothing, and the passage cannot be said to finally settle the dispute as to whether annihilation or transformation is in the writer's mind, whether the dissolution refers to substance or to quality. Salmon has said very aptly that the use to be made of the passage must be a very guarded one, so far as theorizing about the nature of the end is concerned. He says that Peter is speaking in terms of the lofty imagery of the Old Testament. The idea is not annihilation, says Alford, but change. (Wor. Sal.)

Ver. 13. *"his promise"*,—God's promise in the Old Testament. (Isa. 65.17; 66.22.)

Ver. 14. *"found"*,—i. e., at His coming.

"in peace",—With God and man and one's self.

Ver. 15. The delay is not slackness but longsuffering, which is to be valued as *"salvation"*, that is in the sense of the suspension of judgment with a view to a prolonged offer of grace.

"wrote unto you",—Doubtless in the First Epistle to the Thessalonians, although there is a great diversity of opinion as to what writing Peter actually refers to.

Ver. 16. *"these things"*,—i. e., the things of the Second Coming of the Lord about which Peter had been talking, the things of the end. Of course those who contend that the *"even as"* of verse 15 does not refer to the things of which Peter had just been discoursing, the Day of the Lord, must refer *"these things"* to something else, i. e., doctrines of justification and so forth.

"wherein",—If it were not for the form of the pronoun this would naturally refer to *"these sayings"*, thus affirming the truth that in the teaching concerning the Second Coming of Christ there are some things hard to be understood, but the form of the pronoun as used compels the connection of *"wherein"* with *"epistles"*.

"other scriptures",—referring doubtless to other New Testament writings.

Ver. 17. *"before hand"*,—The announcement of which things had occupied practically the whole of the chapter he had just written.

Ver..18. *"forever"*,—The literal of the expression is "to the day of eternity,—the day which shall dawn at the end of time and itself know no end". The word *"eternity"* is literally "aeon", and the expression literally translated means, "unto the day of the aeon", and is found only here.

THE FIRST EPISTLE OF

JOHN

(A. D. 90)

CHAPTER TWO

18 Little children, it is the last hour; and as ye heard that antichrist cometh, even now have there arisen many antichrists.

22 Who is the liar but he that denieth that Jesus is the Christ? This is the antichrist, even he that denieth the Father and Son.

28 And now, my little children, abide in him; that, if he shall be manifested, we may have boldness, and not be ashamed [1]before him at his [2]coming.

[1]Gr. *from him*
[2]Gr. *presence*

Vers. 18,22,28. THE SPIRIT OF THE ANTICHRIST DEFINED.

Ver. 18. *"it is the last hour"*,—The expression plainly refers in some sense to the last period of the world.

Yet it is not "the last dispensation", i. e., from Christ's first coming in grace to His Second Coming in judgment (C. D. Be. Sa. Aug. Bez. Luc. Wol. Nea.), because:

1. This idea is unsuited to the context.

2. Verses 8 and 17 and especially verse 28 show that it is the Second Coming of Christ that he has in mind.

3. The sign *"whereby we know"* proves the reference to be to the last part of the dispensation in which John was living.

4. The fact of many antichrists being already in existence corresponds well with the prophecy given by the Lord which plainly referred to the last days of the present dispensation and to which John here no doubt has reference.

With these reasons and with the view that John referred to the last days of the dispensation in which he was living many of the best expositors agree. (A. Ba. My. Er. Eb. Hu. Nea. Luc. Ger.) (See A. and Hu. *in loco*.)

The reference is not therefore to the last hour of John's life (B.), nor of the Apostolic age (Ste.), nor of the Judean nation, the time immediately preceding the destruction of Jerusalem. (Li. So. Me. Ham. Gro.) Dusterdieck refers *"the last hour"* to the destruction of Jerusalem as opening the period of judgment which shall precede the end and the length of which is nowhere laid down.   But this leaves uncertain that of which the Apostle speaks of with certainty.

These different explanations arise from the desire to acquit John of making a mistake as to the nearness of the time of the Parousia.   But John speaks as did the other Apostles and as we might well speak today.

"as ye heard",—i. e., from the preaching of the Apostles, from John and especially from Paul.

"cometh",—This is a present tense used in the sense of a fixed certainty.

"antichrist",—The word may mean either "against Christ" or "instead of Christ", i. e., a false Christ.   The decision cannot rest on philology alone, but the context shows plainly that John used the word in a sense antagonistic to Christ, and this is now commonly recognized.

A false Christ is not necessarily a willful enemy of Christ.   The man himself may be deceived.   John was acquainted with the Greek for "false Christ", but he chose not to use it.   He used *"antichrist"*, showing plainly that he meant the idea of enmity to be read in the word.   Furthermore, in the Greek Fathers we do not find a trace of the idea of "false Christ" in Antichrist, but it is always the thought of antagonism that is emphasized.

"many antichrists",—Grotius says there are the false Christs prophesied by Christ Himself in Matthew, and refers them to the false Christs prior to the destruction of Jerusalem, the chief of whom was Barchochebas, whom Grotius declares to have been the Antichrist.   But the false Christs of our verse went out from the Christian Church (*"out from us"*—verse 19), which those to whom Grotius refers, being Jews, most assuredly did not do; and furthermore, what would the nearness of the destruction of Jerusalem, viewed as a Jewish event, have to do with the subject of this Epistle of John?

These antichrists in John's time were the heretical teachers who had gone out from the Church, who were clothed with the attributes, had the spirit of and were the forerunners of the coming personal Antichrist.   Does John in this verse mean to say that the Antichrist is already here, i. e., in a collective sense, being in fact the aggregate of these many antichrists? In other words, is the Antichrist collective or is he personal?

1. Since the antichrists are personal so must the Antichrist be.
2. Christ and Antichrist stand over against each other and if one is personal the law of analogy requires that the other should be personal also.
3. Chap. 4.3 does not say that the *spirit* then prevalent was Antichrist, but it says that it is the spirit *of* Antichrist, and in this place the article *"the"* is used before Antichrist.
4. The present of fixed certainty (cometh), as referred to Antichrist is set over against *"have arisen"* and *"is"*, as referred to the antichrists, showing that there is a distinction between the Antichrist who is to come and the many antichrists who have already come.

The word *"antichrist"* is found only in the Epistles of John.   "Almost all commentators", says Huther, "have correctly supposed that John understands by this enemy the same as Paul speaks of in II Thess. 2.3, the features which appear in the description of the Apostle Paul and in the statements of John corresponding too closely to admit of this being denied."

Ver. 22. *"who is the liar?"*,—The *"the"* should not be omitted as in the Authorized Version. It refers to the preceding lie of verse 21 as embodied in concrete form in the Antichrist. John certainly has the particular lie of the antichrists of his time in view, and the *"liar"* and the *"antichrist"* are identical.

"this",—i. e., the liar just described.

"denieth the Father and the Son",—This is a clause of more particular definition, stating the full, unhappy consequence of that antichristian lie. Therefore the denial that Jesus is the Christ is in its very essence a denial of the Father and the Son.

Antichrist is obviously here not used as predicating the one person in whom the character shall be finally and centrally realized, but as setting forth the identity of character with him and participation in the same development of the antichristian principle.

Ver. 28. *"that, if he shall be manifested"*,—There is no intimation in this clause of the time or the nearness of His coming. The particle *"if"* marks reality rather than time, and has been correctly substituted for the "when" of the Authorized Version. Of course in view of John's thought concerning the nearness of the expected return of the Lord, it is doubtless true that this was in his mind as he wrote the words of our verse, although it will not do to draw this information out of this verse taken in itself.

"shall be manifested",—This manifestation of Christ is His Parousia which is to take place at the end of the *"last hour"*. It is the same word as that used of His manifestation in the flesh at His first coming. (Chap. 3.5,8.)

"his coming",—Parousia,—presence; it is only this once that the word is found in John.

"The *'if'* in this verse", says Morgan, "casts no doubt upon His appearing, but is indicative of His coming at any time. In the words, *'boldness'* and *'ashamed'*, an alternative possibility is suggested as to the attitude of Christians at that coming. They may have *'boldness'* or they may *'be ashamed'*. *'Boldness'* suggests the freedom of speech that comes of the perfect familiarity of friendship; there will be no embarrassment and awkwardness of speech arising from the constraint of being strangers to Him. The root meaning of the word *'ashamed'* is 'disgraced', so that it is allowable to read, 'and not be disgraced from (the preposition is 'apo') Him at His coming'. This is not addressed to the outside world, but to believers in Christ. In that verse there is a very clear division which, to my mind, answers the question as to whether believers may not pass through the great tribulation. Some will be ready to enjoy freedom of access to Christ and familiarity with Him; but the *'little children'* of God who have been living only in the elements of the world will be disgraced at His appearing."

CHAPTER THREE

2 Beloved, now are we children of God, and it is not yet made manifest what we shall be. We know that if [1]he shall be manifested, we shall be like

[1]Or, *it*

him; for we shall see him even as he is. 3 And every one that hath this hope set on him purifieth himself, even as he is pure.

Vers. 2,3. PRACTICAL EFFECTS OF THE BELIEVER'S BLESSED HOPE.

Ver. 2. *"is not yet"*,—We have here a past tense and the more forceful reading is "has not yet".

"made manifest",—It is not the *knowledge* of what we shall be that is to be manifested (Eb.), but the future condition itself that is meant, i. e., shown forth in reality. (A. Hu. Dus. Bra.)

"if he shall be manifested",—The majority read "it" for *"he"*, and consequently make *"like him"* and *"see him"* and *"he is"* (all of this verse) and *"on him"* and *"he is"* of verse 3 refer to God. (A. B. D. Hu. So. Ep. Sp. Lu. Sa. Ba. Bra. Oec. Lut. Ben. Ros. Nea. Dus. Schli.)

Grammatically this seems the better view and the translation would then call for the following, *"What we shall be has not yet been made manifest, but we know that if it* (what we shall be) *is made manifest, we shall be like him"*, i. e., like God.

But in spite of all arguments this does not agree with the context, and inasmuch as it is just as grammatical to supply *"he"*, and inasmuch as the thing John is talking about is not primarily that we are the children of God, but the significance of the coming of Christ (Chap. 2.28), we are led with others to read *"he"* and refer the same to Christ, and so throughout. (C. Be. Ar. Es. Ca. Wh. Sy. Bez. Hor. Mor. Sem., the Tyndall and Cranmer versions, the Authorized Version and all Revised versions.)

"for",—The meaning may be made somewhat clearer by translating "because". It may mean either (1) that we are quite sure we shall be like Him, from the very fact that we are to see Him (C. Ri. My. So. Hu. Mor. Schm. Pope), or (2) that seeing Him will cause us to be like Him (D. A. B-C. Sp. Eb. Nea. Dus. Kos. Bra. Wei.)

Pope says, "The final glorification into the image of Christ is never said to be the result of seeing that image; but conversely, likeness to Him is the preparation for seeing Him." Therefore because we shall see Him we know that we must and will be like Him. (See II Cor. 3.18.)

On the other hand, Alford says the *"for"* or the "because" contains the real cause and ground of that which follows, and that therefore the seeing Him as He is is not merely a proof that we shall be like Him, but we shall be like Him *because* we shall see Him face to face.

Campbell Morgan says, "It seems to me that this transformation must first take place; and the fact that I am to see Him is the proof that I shall be like Him. If my vision of Christ on the resurrection morning is to be the cause of my transformation, the presupposition is that I shall not be changed until I look at Him, and that therefore my first view of Him will be in my unchanged condition. This is, in some respects, a beautiful thought, but incorrect, as I think. I believe we shall be changed in a moment, in the twinkling of an eye; and that when changed by the power of God, we shall look at Christ. Almost all who have any right to deal

with the original tongue lean to this exposition rather than to the other."
To this explanation we incline.

Ver. 3. "*this hope*",—i. e., the hope of being like Him.

"*purifieth himself*",—This self-purification does not spring out of
the nature of man; the will to do it lies in this hope, and therefore it is
the expression of his spiritual state as worked out in him through the Holy
Spirit of God.

CHAPTER FOUR

2 Hereby know ye the Spirit of God: every spirit that confesseth that Jesus Christ is come in the flesh is of God; 3 and every spirit that [1]confesseth not Jesus is not of God; and this is the spirit of the antichrist, whereof ye have heard that it cometh; and now it is in the world already.

[1]Some ancient authorities read *annulleth Jesus*

Vers. 2,3.   THE SPIRIT OF THE ANTICHRIST ALREADY IN THE WORLD.

Ver. 2.   "*the Spirit of God*",—The Holy Spirit, as is evident from
the expression itself and from its antithesis to the Antichrist.

"*confesseth*",—Oral confession with the mouth is meant.   That the
life may agree with the profession is not implied in the expression, although
as Braune says, "Only a confession with the mouth emanating from the
faith of the heart under the influence of the indwelling Spirit of God can
be meant."

"*in the flesh*",—If this does not directly assert the Incarnation it
certainly implies it.   (A. D. Lu. Hu. Dus. Bra.)

Ver. 3.   "*Jesus*",—The reference here is to the historical Christ in
the complex of all that He is and has become, involved as it is in His having
come in the flesh.

The particular negative particle used is one that denotes not only
denial, but contradiction as well.

"*this*",—i. e., this spirit.

Practically all commentators agree with our text in supplying "*spirit*"
and thus the meaning is, "and this spirit is the spirit of the Antichrist."

Very strangely some refer "*this*" to the previous denial, the refusal to
confess, and so supply "matter" or "nature" instead of "*spirit*" and make
it the "antichristian nature" that is referred to.   (Hu. Ep. Val. May.)
But this is decidedly uncalled for and subverts the real sense of the passage.

"*have heard*",—This refers doubtless to the previous instructions
they had received, and not to Chap. 2.18.

"*it is in the world already*",—By "*it*" is meant the spirit of the Antichrist.   It is in the world in the person of these false prophets.   John does
not say that the Antichrist is already in the world but only that the spirit
of the Antichrist is already in the world.

The word "*already*" is added doubtless not alone to intensify the
"*now*" but to point to the future time when the personal Antichrist is to
appear, for which appearing the world is already being made ready.

SECOND EPISTLE OF
JOHN

7 For many deceivers are gone forth
into the world; even they that confess
not that Jesus Christ cometh in the flesh.
This is the deceiver and the antichrist.

Ver. 7. THE FIRST COMING OF CHRIST DENIED.

"deceivers",—i. e., false teachers.

"are gone forth",—The expression in itself does not denote separation from the Church, but inasmuch as the verb is in the past tense, the *"from us"* of John's First Epistle 2.19, is doubtless in his mind.

"confess not",—The same negative is used and with the same meaning as in I John 4.3, on which passage see remark.

"cometh in the flesh",—Oecumenius wrongly interprets, "is to come", taking it as a future participle and referring it to the Second Coming of Christ, but it is to be taken exactly as in John's First Epistle in Chap. 4.2, except that here the present participle is used which expresses the idea in itself altogether apart from the idea of time. (A. D. Lu. Sa. Hu. Dus. Bra.)

"this",—i. e., the one who denies and does not confess. It points to a class, making each one of these in its place a representative and precursor of the one coming Antichrist.

Braune says, "The Antichrist is personally behind the many who are his forerunners. From '*deceivers*' to '*deceiver*' is plurality expressed in unity; it is a transition from the plural to the distributive singular."

The word *"antichrist"* with which the verse closes gives prominence to a further characteristic of the deceiver.

THE EPISTLE OF
JUDE
(A. D. 66)

6 And angels that kept not their own
principality, but left their proper habitation, he hath kept in everlasting bonds
under darkness unto the judgment of
the great day.

Ver. 6. THE FALLEN ANGELS RESERVED UNTO THE DAY OF FINAL JUDGMENT.

Ver. 6. *"their own principality"*,—i. e., the one originally assigned to them. Most of the best expositors rightly translate with our text (A. B. D. Hu. Wi. Pl. An. Hof. Bra. Schot.), although many (C. Lut. Gro.

Bez. Hor. Era.) approve the rendering of the Authorized Version, "first estate", i. e., original condition.

"*their proper habitation*",—i. e., heaven, or whatever habitation of light may have been assigned to them.

"*under darkness*",—i. e., in the depths of the underworld, in the abyss, covered over with darkness.

"*unto the judgment of the great day*",—This is the last and final judgment day for which they are kept, taking place at the end of the world, doubtless at the same time with the judgment upon Satan just prior to that upon the wicked in general.

Scofield says, "The '*great day*' is the day of the Lord (Isa. 2.9-22)", The day of the Lord, then, according to Scofield extends from the Second Coming of Christ on through the Millennium period, as Morgan and others also maintain.

Just to what sin reference is here to be had is not known.

We are inclined to think it is to that to which vague reference is made in Gen. 6.2, and that Jude got his more particular information from the Book of Enoch. (A. K. Hu. Pl. Die. Del. Hof. Kur. Jus. Cyp.)

Others say that Gen. 6.2 refers to the marriage of the Sethites to the descendants of Cain, and that the sin referred to in Jude is that of the first fall in the realm of the spirits, namely, the revolt of Satan and his angels. (F. C. An. Es. Fr. Ph. Af. Bra. Mel. Lut. Hor. Eph. Hen. and writers of the Middle ages in general.) (I John 3.8,10.)

The second view is adopted on the ground that it is doubtful whether Jude quotes from the Book of Enoch, that the first view is inconsistent with what we are elsewhere in Scripture taught of the angelic nature. But when this view is taken there seems to be a conflict with the other teachings of the New Testament where we are told that Satan and his angels have their residence in the air, exercising power over unbelievers and laying snares for believers. This is reconciled by the supporters of this view by saying that Satan's continued activity is by special permission from God, or by saying, as others do, that although they do inhabit the air near this earth of ours they may well be said to be chained or kept in everlasting bonds because they are restrained from recovering the glory and happiness they have lost.

The arguments in favor of the first view are the difficulty just mentioned, the fact that the references in the Book of Enoch are too many and too extended and too plain not to be reckoned with, the similarity of language as seen especially in the expression, "*the judgment of the great day*", all pointing to a reference of Jude to Enoch or of both to some common source, and finally the expression, "*in like manner with these*", in verse 7 without doubt refers to these angels and therefore distinctly puts the sins mentioned in both verses in practically the same class. If this view is adopted the passage is at once relieved of all difficulty because only a special class of angels are then included in Jude's passage.

14 And to these also Enoch, the seventh from Adam, prophesied, saying, Behold, the Lord came with ¹ten thousands of his holy ones, 15 to execute judgment upon all, and to convict all the ungodly of all their works of ungodliness which they have ungodly wrought, and of all the hard things

¹Gr. *his holy myriads*

which ungodly sinners have spoken against him. 16 These are murmurers, complainers, walking after their lusts (and their mouth speaketh great swelling *words*), showing respect of persons for the sake of advantage.

17 But ye, beloved, remember ye the words which have been spoken before by the apostles of our Lord Jesus Christ; 18 that they said to you, In

the last time there shall be mockers, walking after ²their own ungodly lusts. 19 These are they who make separations ³sensual, having not the Spirit. 20 But ye, beloved, building up yourselves on your most holy faith, praying in the Holy Spirit, 21 keep yourselves in the love of God, looking for the mercy of our Lord Jesus Christ unto eternal life.

²Gr. *their own lusts of ungodlinesses*
³Or, *natural* Or, *animal*

Vers. 14-21. JUDGMENT UPON APOSTATE TEACHERS AT THE COMING OF THE LORD.

Ver. 14. *"And to these"*,—This rendering of our text is better than that of the Authorized Version, *"of these"*, or *"with reference to these"*, as many take it. These latter renderings spoken in Jude's day could give the prophecy's fulfillment a restrospective character, while the rendering of our text spoken to them of Enoch's time could throw it ages into the future.

"Enoch, the seventh from Adam",—i. e., counting Adam the first and Enoch the seventh. He is so designated several times in the Book of Enoch.

To Adam was given the promise of the first advent of our Lord as Saviour; to Enoch was given the first promise of His second advent as Judge. Stier says that Enoch is a personal type of the sanctified of the seventh age of the world, the great earth Sabbath, the seventh millennium.

"the Lord came",—The tense is past because Enoch speaks in a vision in which the future appears to him as present. It is what scholars call "the historic sense of prophecy", or "the prophetic past".

"ten thousands of His holy ones",—The Greek is "his holy myriads". The terms include, as Riddle says, "not only angels but redeemed men."

The prophecy here quoted is found almost verbally in the Book of Enoch. Jude must at all events have known of the tradition of Enoch's prophecy and considered it true as to its kernel, even if he did not have the Book of Enoch before him.

Ver. 15. *"to execute judgment"*,—i. e., to pronounce the doom and to see that it is carried out. Thus the coming of the Lord with His angels and His saints is here clearly shown to be a coming for judgment.

Ver. 17. The reference in this verse is to that of simple priority. The idea of the prophetical does not lie in the words. Jude here doubtless refers to such passages as II Tim. 3.1; Acts 20.29,30; I Tim. 4.1; II Pet. 3.3.

Ver. 18. *"In the last time"*,—Meyer says the time in view here is that just prior to the second coming of Christ, and similar to this is Alford's comment, "the last age of the Church". (See II Pet. 3.3 and our exegesis there.) There is here a glance backward to what was said in verse 15 as to the characteristic quality of the works there brought into view.

Ver. 21. *"looking for the mercy of our Lord Jesus Christ"*,— *"looking for"* here points to the future, and the *"mercy"* therefore is that by which Christ will glorify Himself in His saints in His great day, the mercy which He will show at His second coming.   (A. M. Hu.)

"*unto eternal life*",—This phrase may be connected with "*mercy*" (D.), or with "*keep yourselves*" (Hu.), or with "*looking for*" (B.), while Alford connects it with both of the last two.

> 24 Now unto him that is able to guard you from stumbling, and to set you before the presence of his glory without blemish in exceeding joy,

Ver. 24.   THE JOYFUL PRESENTATION OF THE BELIEVER BEFORE THE THRONE OF CHRIST AT HIS COMING.

"*before the presence of his glory*",—The reference is to the special manifestation which will take place in connection with His Parousia.

"The glory", says Alford, "being that which shall be revealed when the Son of man shall come."

This verse taken in connection with Eph. 5.25-27; Col. 1.22; I Thess. 3.13, is taken by David Brown as proof that when Christ comes the Church will be complete and that therefore after His coming there can be no salvation for any others who at that time may be as yet unsaved. Whether this be true or not, the fact of its being so can hardly, on the basis of sound exegesis, be drawn from these passages, unless several other things can be shown to be true in connection with it, namely:

1. That the word "*Church*" as used in Eph. 5.25-27 can be shown to denote the total number of those who are to be saved;

2. That the Scriptures clearly prove that there can never be in the future more than òne manifestation of Christ as it relates to this earth; and

3. That this presentation is to take place immediately upon Christ's return.   And even if this latter point could be established, unless the other two can be equally established, the presentation of the saints in question could be associated with the first manifestation quite as properly as with any later ones.   The arguments produced by Dr. Brown at this point are not at all convincing.

THE REVELATION OF JOHN
(A. D. 96)

CHAPTER ONE

1 The Revelation of Jesus Christ, which God [1]gave him to show unto his [2]servants, even the things which must shortly come to pass: and he sent and signified [3]*it* by his angel unto his servant John; 2 who bare witness of the word of God, and of the testimony of Jesus Christ, *even* of all things that he saw. 3 Blessed is he that readeth, and they that hear the words of the prophecy,

[1]Or, *gave unto him, to show unto his servants the things &c.*
[2]Gr. *bondservants*
[3]Or, *them*

and keep the things that are written therein: for the time is at hand.

4 John to the seven churches that are in Asia: Grace to you and peace, from him who is and who was and [4]who is to come; and from the seven Spirits that are before his throne; 5 and from Jesus Christ, *who is* the faithful witness, the firstborn of the dead, and the ruler of the kings of the earth. Unto him that loveth us, and [5]loosed us from our sins [6]by his blood; 6 and he made us *to be* a kingdom, *to be* priests unto [7]his God and Father; to him *be* the glory and the dominion [8]for ever and ever. Amen. 7 Behold, he cometh with the clouds;

[4]Or, *who cometh*
[5]Many authorities, some ancient, read *washed.* Heb. 9.14; comp. Chap. 7.14
[6]Gr. *in*
[7]Or, *God and his Father*
[8]Gr. *unto the ages of the ages.* Many ancient authorities omit *of the ages*

and every eye shall see him, and they that pierced him; and all the tribes of the earth shall mourn over him. Even so. Amen.

8 I am the Alpha and the Omega, saith the Lord God, [9]who is and who was and [4]who is to come, the Almighty.

9 I John, your brother and partaker with you in the tribulation and kingdom and [10]patience *which are* in Jesus, was in the isle that is called Patmos, for the word of God and the testimony of Jesus. 10 I was in the Spirit on the Lord's day, and I heard behind me a great voice, as of a trimpet.

[9]Or, *he who*
[10]Or, *stedfastness*

Vers. 1-10. THE COMING OF THE LORD THE THEME OF THE REVELATION.

Ver. 1. *"The revelation of Jesus Christ"*,—This is not a revelation of which Jesus is the object, as Seiss maintains, but one of which He is the subject or author. (A. L. F. Eb.) It is not a revelation about Jesus Christ by someone else, but a revelation which Jesus Christ Himself gives. It is not John's revelation, but Christ's. It is made to us all, to all of Christ's *"servants"* through John, either from Christ Himself or an angel on His behalf.

"must",—i. e., by necessity of divine decree.

"shortly come to pass",—There are three views of this phrase:

1. It refers to the swiftness with which the things prophesied will take place when they do occur, without any reference to their nearness or remoteness, i. e., in swift succession. (L. Eb.)

2. It refers to the speedy coming of what is to happen. (Dus. Hen.)

3. It means "before long", according to the method of computation of Him with whom 1000 years are as one day, and does not therefore necessarily mean near at hand as we compute nearness. (A. F. D. V. Wol.)

The first view is hardly consistent with the past tense of the verb *"come to pass"*, nor with the context, nor with the closing clause of verse 3, nor especially with Chap. 22.7 where Christ Himself, speaking through His angel and using the same Greek words, says, *"I come quickly"*.

The second view cannot be accepted, as it attributes not alone to John but also to Christ, who uses the same word in Chap. 22.7, the teaching that His second coming was quite near according to our conception of nearness.

The third view is therefore the one to which we are necessarily driven. It is after all but a modification of view 2. It is God's speedy time in the same sense as in Luke 18.7,8 where delay is evidently implied.

Among the things which *"must shortly come to pass"* are events after a millennium period of a thousand years more or less and events beyond that are mentioned in the book, and consequently it must have embraced considerable time in its whole content. The expression is therefore most appropriately taken as a prophetic formula to teach us how short our time and the time of the world really is in comparison with time as it stretches out in the vision of God.

Though the time is near, we are told to *wait* patiently for it, both explicitly (Chaps. 1; 13.10; 14.12) and by the very organism and content of the book, as well as by the succession of the seals which shows that many intermediate events must first elapse, says Fausset. This reference to the seals, however, has weight only if we think of them as *succeeding* each other and occurring in the history of the world from the time John had his vision on down through the centuries, the so-called Historical view.

"his angel",—Lange's explanation of the angelic appearance throughout the book, of "Christ appearing in the quality of an angel", will not do, as Chap. 22.9 clearly proves. If the angel of our verse refers to one definite angel, some see here a difficulty in that he does not appear as revelator until Chap. 17.1, and that other personages performed this office in the meantime. It would seem, however, that the expositors are creating a difficulty for themselves. The angel voice of verse 10 is followed in verse 11 by the voice of Christ who opens the revelation. In Chap. 4.1 the angel of verse 10 speaks again; in Chap. 6.1 it is the four living creatures who speak; in Chap. 7.13 it is one of the twenty-four elders; in Chap. 10.8,9 it is the Lord and another angel; in Chaps. 17.1; 21.9 and 22.1,6 it is one of the seven angels who speaks, which angel it would seem, according to Chap. 22.6, is the same as the angel of our verse, and with whom we see no objection whatever to identifying the angel of Chap. 1.10.

Ver. 3. *"the time is at hand"*,—The word for *"time"* as used here is "kairos", which always expresses a fixed or expected point of time, a season or certain period of time. "Kronos" means time in general.

"at hand",—To be explained in the same sense as *"shortly come to pass"* of verse 1.

Ver. 4. *"which is and which was and which is to come"*,—This reference to God the Father is a paraphrase of the name Jehovah implying His unchangeableness, His immutability. It is the Father as distinguished from Christ who is here meant.

Instead of *"which is to come"* we would have expected "which shall be" as more in keeping with the other two verbs, but inasmuch as the Father and the Son are one, there is a sense in which it may be said of the Father that He too is to come, and for this reason perhaps the phrase *"which is to come"* was used. The idea, however, of a future coming of God Himself as contained in the last part of the clause is not to be pressed. To God the present, the past and the future are one and the same eternal now.

"seven spirits",—The Holy Spirit in His own complete fullness and diverse activities (Isa. 11.21); sevenfold in His operations, the author and the giver not only of seven but of all spiritual gifts, seven being the number of perfection and denoting multiplicity.

Ver. 5. *"faithful witness"*,— (John 18.37). He faithfully made known all that He had heard of the Father and testified always to the truth concerning Himself even before Pilate and in the hour of death. The reference is to His general mission, although there is no good reason for not extending it to the attestation of the apocalyptic truth about to be revealed.

"the first begotten of the dead",—Lazarus rose to die again; Christ rose to die no more. The resurrection is a birth.

"the ruler of the kings of the earth",—This He is in a sense now, but He will especially prove Himself to be so in the judgment at His advent.

Lange says, "Now dynamically ruling over the kings of the earth, and destined in the end to prevail over the antichristian powers also, He works on and on until His appearance as the King proper."

Ver. 6. *"made us to be a kingdom"*,—All that can be legitimately maintained here is that the redeemed are the kingdom of God in the sense that they are the subjects of it and the blessed sharers in it. (E. D. Eb. Dus.) The royal sovereignty of believers is hardly taught in this verse, according to the best attested reading. This truth is brought out in Chap. 5.10 where we have the fact clearly set forth that in this kingdom the saints reign. Hengstenberg and some others insist that the word *"kingdom"* even here carries with it in conjunction with the word *"us"* the idea of "a people invested with kingly power", i. e., kings. But grammatically this is scarcely tenable. The reading *"for us"* would give this meaning, but it is not well enough attested.

"priests",—The distinction of priests and people, nearer and more remote from God, has ceased and all people have nearest access to God, come immediately to God, offer their prayers and give themselves to Him in holy service. A similar idea appears in Chap. 21.22 where the new Jerusalem appears without a temple.

"unto Him",—i. e., unto Jesus Christ.

Ver. 7. The theme of the Apocalypse.

"he",—i. e., Jesus Christ.

"cometh with the clouds",—(See Acts 1.9,11). Whether on them or in them is not expressed. It is a coming to judgment. While the clouds are symbolic (a symbol of wrath) they are nevertheless real, the clouds of heaven. Among the later Jews the Messiah is actually called the "Cloud Man". It is the coming *"with His saints"*, after the Great Tribulation, that is here meant.

"every eye shall see him",—If the coming of Christ *with* His saints is to occur after the Millennium, this expression is best understood of the whole human race, all the risen, both good and bad, as well as those then living.

In this case *"they that pierced him"*,—which is a singling out from the more general group of a special class, may refer either

1. to all who pierced Him in all ages by their rejection of Him, the then living rejectors being present at His coming and the rejectors then dead being raised to appear with them in judgment; or
2. to the Jews who actually did pierce Him, being then risen to meet Him in judgment (Dus.) ; or, preferably,
3. to the persons referred to by Christ in Matt. 26.64, i. e., those who were His murderers whether the Jews who delivered Him

to be crucified or the Romans who actually inflicted His death. (A.)

If this coming of Christ is to take place before the Millennium, this expression, *"every eye shall see him"*, must refer to all save the wicked dead. This will be true whether the Church goes through the Great Tribulation or not, although in the latter case the righteous dead, having been raised, will have been *"caught up"* with the living but transformed Church, and so will come with the Lord when He returns at the time when *"every eye shall see him"*. In this case *"they that pierced him"* must refer either to the living wicked in general, or preferably to the Jewish nation in particular then living, and perhaps as well to the Romans, as the representatives of those who actually did the work of delivery and crucifixion. The post-millennial view affords the simpler explanation of the verse, although it may be explained quite as consistently from the viewpoint of the pre-millennialist.

"all the tribes of the earth shall mourn",—Practically all are agreed that this is the fulfillment of Zech. 12.10, and the prophecy is without doubt an allusion to Matt. 24.30 in which place the mourning is distinctly stated to be *"immediately after the tribulation days"*.

It has been said with certain propriety, "The mourning is both hostile and penitential; the hostile by the unrepentant wicked in fear of impending consequences; the penitential especially by the then penitent Jews, and even by the holiest saint because of his sins which had once pierced his Lord." (B. A. F.) The reference, however, in this quotation to the mourning of the *"holiest saint"* can be approved only on the supposition that the Church is on earth at this coming and has not been *previously "caught up"*.

Dusterdieck limits the mourning to the unrepentant wicked, the unconverted for whom the day of repentance was then past, while Fausset says that the antichristian confederacy will mourn in discomfiture at His pre-millennial advent, and all the unconverted at the general judgment.

Ver. 8. Here the eternal Father speaks. Seiss claims it is Christ Himself who is here speaking, and who here formally proclaims Himself to be the very God, the Almighty. It is, however, by no means necessary to take this position, though Christ is indeed all this and virtually so asserts in verses 17 and 18, and perhaps in Chap. 22.13. The reference of the words of our verse to God Himself seems the more natural one. (A. L. Dus.)

"is to come",—(See verse 1).

Ver. 10. *"on the Lord's day"*,—It was on the Lord's day when John got his instructions to write. Seiss says this was the *"day of the Lord"* at the end of the age, the so-called *"seven years"* or *"last week"* of Daniel's *"seventy weeks"*. The evidence, however, for this view we hold is hardly sufficient, and the *"Lord's day"* is rightly taken by nearly all as the first day of the week and is to be referred to the time in which John was living and writing.

> 19 Write therefore the things which thou sawest, and the things which are, and the things which shall come to pass hereafter;

Ver. 19. THE THREEFOLD NATURAL DIVISION OF THE BOOK OF
REVELATION.

"the things which thou sawest",—i. e., the vision just vouchsafed
to him.

"the things which are",—By many this expression is rendered, "what
they (the things thou sawest) signify". (A. D. Ew. Bl. Kl. Ar. Hei. Her.
Alc. Eic.)

Alford calls attention to the fact that the verb of the last clause is
singular while that of this clause is plural.   But this is hardly of sufficient
weight to decide the case for this rendering although grammatically it is a
possible one.   Neither is the antithesis of the next clause favorable to
this view.

Adhering to the text of our version we still have two explanations of
the words:

1. That which refers to *the state of things in the churches when John
   was writing,* as seen in the contents of Chaps. 2 and 3. (B. L.
   F. V. Zu. Eb. Ly. Ca. Lap. Are. Luc. Dus. Hen. Wol. Gro.)
2. That which takes them in the prophetic sense as portraying *the
   course of the Church from the time of John on down to the end
   of this age,* the time of our Lord's return.   (Gab. Sco. Mor.)

Morgan says, "The words reveal progress, good or bad, in Church
life and movement.   We find both Laodicean and Philadelphian churches
now. 'The things which are' exist in the present dispensation."   It would
seem, however, from the simplest reading of the words that the view which
refers them more especially to the conditions existing in the time of John's
vision is the more preferable one.

Scofield has some interesting remarks just here, and remarks that are
worthy of consideration.   He says, "The messages to the seven churches
have a fourfold application: (1) Local, to the churches actually addressed;
(2) admonitory, to all churches in all time as tests by which they may
discern their true spiritual state in the sight of God; (3) personal, in the
exhortations to him *'that hath an ear'*, and in the promises *'to him that
overcometh'*; (4) prophetic, as disclosing seven phases of the *spiritual*
history of the Church from, say, A. D. 96 to the end.   It is incredible
that in a prophecy covering the church period there should be no such
foreview.   These messages must contain that foreview if it is in the book
at all, for no church is mentioned after Chap. 3.22.   Again, these messages by their very terms go beyond the local assemblies mentioned. Most
conclusively of all, these messages *do* present an exact foreview of the
spiritual history of the Church, and in this precise order."

"the things which shall be hereafter",—These words refer without
doubt to the things symbolically represented in Chaps. 4 to 22.   The
time referred to is either (1) the period after the time in which John wrote
extending on into the future from that time to the general judgment at
the end (A. E.), which view is known as the Historical View; or (2) it is,
according to the prophetic view of Morgan and others, the so-called seven
year period, which they place immediately after the rapture of the saints
and just before the Millennium, together with the time which extends on
to the general judgment at the end, which view is known as the Futurist
View.

The literal of the words is, *"the things which shall be after these things"*, *"these things"* referring to *"the things which are"* in the previous clause. It is somewhat to be regretted that our text did not retain the more literal translation, "after these things", instead of *"hereafter"*. It must be admitted that the most natural inference from the words is that which refers their content to what transpired immediately afterwards and on down through the ages, while many of our best Greek scholars would have us believe that the words, *"after these things"* (μετα ταῦτα), carry with them always the idea of "immediately"; but this must not be pressed too vigorously and must be determined somewhat by the contents of the vision.

Says Elliott, "The subject matter I assume to be *the continuous fortunes of the Church and of the world* (that is *of the Roman world and the Christian Church* settled therein) *from the time of the revelation being given,* or the time of St. John's banishment, to the end of all things. If the words, 'these things' mean the state at that time of the apocalyptic churches, as described in the seven epistles—a point which, I suppose, few will doubt—then must Christ's declaration distinctly and all but necessarily imply that the foreshadowing of the future should begin *from the time of John's banishment,* or soon thereafter. This is indeed admitted by the most competent judges. I believe the words must have positive violence done them in order to extract therefrom any other meaning than that which I have given to them."

CHAPTER TWO

The reference in verses 5 and 15 are not to Christ's second coming but to His coming in special judgment to the church of Ephesus and of Pergamum. The expression, *"the second death"* in verse 11, is a description of damnation; it is the Gehenna of Matt. 5.29; Mk. 9.43-49 and Lu. 12.15. It is defined in Chap. 20.14 as *"the lake of fire"*.

25 Nevertheless that which ye have, hold fast till I come. 26 And he that overcometh, and he that keepeth my works unto the end, to him will I give authority over the [1]nations: 27 and he shall rule them with a rod of [2]iron, as the vessels of the potter are broken to shivers; as I also have received of my Father: 28 and I will give him the morning star.

[1]Or, *Gentiles*

[2]Or, *iron; as vessels of the potter, are they broken*

Vers. 25-28. THE SAINTS TO REIGN AND RULE WITH CHRIST.

Ver. 25. *"that which ye have",*—This is not to be restricted to their steadfastness against Jezebel and her teaching, but it refers to Christian doctrine, hope and privilege in general. (Jude 3.1.c.)

"hold fast till I come",—The expression in Greek by the use of the particle "ἄν" gives an uncertainty to the time of the Second Coming which our language cannot express.

Ver. 26. *"my works",*—i. e., in contrast with *"her works"* (verse 22); the works which Christ commands.

"to him will I give authority over the nations",—It is rightly said that this refers to the authority to be conferred on the saints when they shall inherit the earth and reign with Christ in His kingdom. (M. F. Dus. Crav.) Says Fausset, "At Christ's Second Coming the saints shall possess

548

the kingdom under the whole heaven and therefore over this earth", and, says Dusterdieck, "The victor is to share in the work of establishing the kingdom at the coming of the Lord."

Some would have us believe that this authority is being gradually realized but shall only at the Second Coming find its full realization. (A. L.) The natural reference of the words, however, hardly seems to favor this modification; and besides the power of the Christian over the world now is hardly that of the *"iron sceptre"*, the power of government.

Ver. 27. *"he shall rule them"*,—Literally, "shepherd them".

"a rod of iron",—i. e., "a sceptre of severity", as Lyra says. The sense is then, "He shall shepherd them with a rod of iron" instead of "He shall break them to pieces with a rod of iron" as in the Hebrew of Psalm 2.9. The Septuagint translation made the change by slightly altering the Hebrew word, and John quotes the Septuagint perhaps with the thought of mingling mercy with judgment; "severity first, that grace may come afterward", says Fausset. That, however, severity is the chief idea is seen both in the expression, *"rod of iron"* and the parallel expression, *"broken to shivers"*.

"broken to shivers",—This is because they fail to answer the design of the maker, the act being of course a spiritual one.

"as I also",—(See Psalm 2.9). The power there conferred on Christ He will share with His victorious servant. (Lu. 22.29.)

Ver. 28. *"And I will give him the morning star"*,—This does not refer to "the glorified body of Christ" (Ly.), nor to "the Devil" (Are. And.) (Isa. 14.12), nor to "a share in my kingdom at its first appearance" (Tait). It refers either to Christ Himself (V. Eb. Be. Kl. Ca. Lap. Wol. Plu. Prim. Stern.), or to the heavenly glory with which the victor is to be endowed (Dan. 12.3; Matt. 13.42; I Cor. 15.40). (A. D. Ar. Gro. Hen. Dus.) While neither of these quite satisfy the words *"give to him"*, yet of the two the latter is to be preferred as referring by way of poetic imagery to him as clad in the glory of that star, putting it on, as it were, as a jewel or as a glittering robe.

CHAPTER THREE

"I will come as a thief", in verse 3, is not a reference to His Second Coming yet it is expressed in language which in its fullest sense describes His Second Coming. (A. F. L. Dus.) It is a reference to a coming in special judgment, as in Chap. 2.5 and 16.

10 Because thou didst keep the word of my [1]patience, I also will keep thee from the hour of [2]trial, that hour which is to come upon the whole [3]world, [4]to try them that dwell upon the earth.

11 I come quickly: hold fast that which thou hast, that no one take thy crown. 12 He that overcometh, I will make him a pillar in the [5]temple of my God, and he shall go out thence no more; and I will write upon him the name of my God, and the name of the city of my God, the new Jerusalem, which cometh down out of heaven from my God, and mine own new name.

[1]Or, *stedfastness*
[2]Or, *temptation*
[3]Gr. *inhabited earth*
[4]Or, *tempt*

[5]Or, *sanctuary*.

Vers. 10-12. THE FAITHFUL TO BE KEPT FROM THE HOUR OF TRIAL.

Ver. 10. *"I will also keep thee from the hour of trial"*,—Some authorities restrict this promise to this church of Philadelphia alone as a special exception (B. Eb. Ei.) ; but this is an altogether arbitrary assumption exhibiting an exegetical helplessness at all times to be discouraged.

"keep thee from",—The precise meaning of the preposition *"from"* is not altogether clear. In the Greek it is "ek" and means primarily "out of". Thus Paul speaks of attaining unto the *"ek-resurrection of the dead"*, i. e., the resurrection "out of" or "out from among" the dead. *"the hour of trial"*,—

1. This expression may refer to the period known as the Great Tribulation, mentioned by our Lord in Matt. 24.21 and by Peter in his first epistle, Chap. 4.12. (F. A. L. Dus. Hen. Mor. Sco. Gab. Crav.)

    The definite article *"the"* used in the Greek in connection with it seems to favor this view, i. e., *the* hour, the well-known hour.

    (a) Now if the Church is caught up before the Great Tribulation occurs this fact furnishes an answer as to how they were to be *"kept from"* this time of trial. (Mor. Gab. Tor. Sco. Pet. Bla., and most pre-millennarians of the present time.) "There is no way to escape from it", says Blackstone, "but to be taken out of the world by the Rapture, in as much as the Great Tribulation covers the whole habitable earth." This view, however, if accepted, must rest for its vindication upon other evidence than that furnished by the verse before us.

    Dusterdieck contends that if this were the idea, the preposition "apo" would have been used as in James 1.27. But this distinction between the two prepositions is somewhat exaggerated by our author and cannot be pressed, inasmuch as the idea of exemption, or being taken away from, may, so far as the preposition is concerned, be with propriety attached to our passage as well as to the one in James. Dusterdieck appeals to Rev. 7.14, but there the matter is decided by the meaning of the verb itself.

    (b) If the Church is not caught up until after the Great Tribulation and consequently is to go through this period of trial, then the meaning here is "to deliver out of" in the sense of bringing safely through the trials they will be called upon to endure, just as in John 17.15, where the same preposition is used and the meaning is without doubt "to pass unscathed through the evil." (F. V. L. D. Zu. Ew. Ly. Hen. Dus.) We have in the Old Testament an historical example which furnishes us at least a reasonable surmise of what might be true here, namely, that just as the Israelites were kept from the plagues in whose midst they lived, so may the believer during the days of the Great Tribulation be safeguarded therein and thus kept from the trials that shall come upon them that dwell upon the earth.

2. The expression is taken by some, who conceive of the Church being caught up before the Great Tribulation, as referring to a period of severe conflicts of faith through which the Church must pass just before the Great Tribulation. (Moorehead.)

Such authorities take the second view just noted, namely that of being safeguarded during the time of these trials, and in defense of which Moorehead presents four arguments:

(a) The word *"trial"* seems deliberately chosen to distinguish the period from the Great Tribulation.

(b) The natural and obvious meaning, as well as the use of the preposition "ek" favors the idea of safeguarding in the midst of the trial.

(c) The use of the same preposition in and the evident meaning of John 17.15 seems almost decisive in the matter.

(d) The explanation is confirmed by the words that follow, *"Behold I come quickly; hold fast that which thou hast, that no one take thy crown"*. "Christ lays upon them the responsibility of vigilance, of continual effort. Philadelphia, no less than the others, is to be in the trial, but kept safely in it, not raptured away before the trial begins."

"to try them that dwell upon the earth",—This expression, as a rule, refers to the mass of men in contradistinction to believers, as in Chaps. 8.13 and 13.8, and this agrees nicely with the view just expressed above. If, however, the expression be taken to include all men (and this, of course, must be considered as allowable), then the words *"keep thee from"* are better explained in harmony with the thought of Dusterdieck, the trial bringing out the fidelity of those who are Christ's and are kept by Him (Chap. 7.3), and hardening the unbelieving reprobates. (Chaps. 9.20,21 and 16.11,12.)

Ver. 11. *"I come quickly"*,—"A constantly recurring announcement designed for the awakening and terrifying of the foes and for the consolation and elevation of the pious", says Lange.

"hold fast that which thou hast",—The reference here is not only to the grace especially mentioned in verse 10, but in general to whatever of grace and truth and piety they possessed.

"that no man take thy crown",—Not that another could secure it for himself, but that in the time of trial you might by inconstancy lose it.

Ver. 12. *"the new Jerusalem which cometh down out of heaven"*,—(See Chap. 21.2,3).

Ver. 21. *"to sit down with me in my throne"*,—This grandest and crowning blessing is not made especially to correspond to the special greatness of the victory to be gained by the Laodiceans (Eb.), but rather because coming at the end of the letters it is natural that such a promise should be expressed as would gather all the promises into one.

This promise is not to be regarded as partially fulfilled in this life. The aorist tense of the verb points to a final and complete act. Then too the example of Christ, *"as I overcame and sat down"* forbids such a conception. It means to have a share with Christ in His kingly glory and power (Chaps. 2.27 and 20.6), and must refer to something still in the future.

It is impossible to tell from this verse alone whether a distinction is here to be made between the throne of God and the throne of Christ. As the words stand here it would seem that such a distinction is tenable, and to this view of the matter we are inclined. Some say that the thrones are different and that Christ's peculiar throne is to be set up over the whole earth at His Second Coming, and that in this the victorious saints shall share. (F. Ca. Sco. Gab. Mor.) This seems to be in keeping with Matt. 19.28; Lu. 1.32,33; Acts 2.30,34,35; 15.14,15,16. Chap. 21.1, however, seems to identify these thrones, and so it is taken by some. (L. A. Dus.)

CHAPTER FOUR

At Chapter Four begins the revelation proper, the third division of the book, *"the things which shall come to pass hereafter"*. John is caught up by the Spirit into heaven, which means that he is now in a trance or in a heavenly ecstacy and is given a vision of the judgments which are to come upon the earth. Before these judgments are related we have in Chaps. 4 and 5 the heavenly scenery described which furnished the local grounds for the visions.

1 After these things I saw, and behold, a door opened in heaven, and the first voice that I heard, *a voice* as of a trumpet speaking with me, one saying, Come up hither, and I will show thee the things which must ¹come to pass hereafter. 2 Straightway I was in the Spirit: and behold, there was a throne set in heaven, and one sitting upon the throne; 3 and he that sat *was* to look upon like a jasper stone and a sardius: and *there was* a rainbow round about the throne, like an emerald to look upon. 4 And round about the throne *were* four and twenty thrones: and upon the thrones *I saw* four and twenty elders sitting, arrayed in white garments; and on their heads crowns of gold. 5 And out of the throne proceed lightnings and voices and thunders. And *there were* seven lamps of fire burning before the throne, which are the seven Spirits of God; 6 and before the throne, as it were a ²sea of glass like unto crystal; and in the midst ³of the throne, and round about the throne, four living creatures full of eyes before and behind.

¹Or, *come to pass. After these things straightway &c.*
²Or, *glassy sea*
³Or, *before.* See Chap. 7.17, Comp. 5.6

7 And the first creature *was* like a lion, and the second creature like a calf, and the third creature had a face as of a man, and the fourth creature *was* like a flying eagle. 8 And the four living creatures, having each one of them six wings, are full of eyes round about and within: and they have no rest day and night, saying,

Holy, holy, holy, *is* the Lord God, the Almighty, who was and who is and ⁴who is to come.

9 And when the living creatures shall give glory and honor and thanks to him that sitteth on the throne, to him that liveth ⁵for ever and ever, 10 the four and twenty elders shall fall down before him that sitteth on the throne, and shall worship him that liveth ⁶for ever and ever, and shall cast their crowns before the throne, saying,

11 Worthy art thou, our Lord and our God, to receive the glory and the honor and the power: for thou didst create all things, and because of thy will they were, and were created.

⁴Or, *who cometh*
⁵Gr. *unto the ages of the ages*

Vers. 1-11. THE VISION OF THE THRONE.

Ver. 1. *"after these things"*,—i. e., after Christ had gotten through dictating to John the letters to the seven churches, or, after John had gotten through writing these letters. The second view would indicate a break in the vision. Some prefer this because of the fact that he *"was in the Spirit"* in Chap. 1.10 and the fact that here again in verse 2 it says he was *"immediately in the Spirit"* inclines them to believe that he had come out of the Spirit and had written the letters to the churches and then went into another trance. (G. Ar. Cr. Ca. Gro. Hen.) We think it, however, better with the majority not to see any break in the vision at this point, but to conceive of the whole as imparted in one vision, one continuous revelation composed of many parts.

The phrase therefore, *"after these things"*, denotes merely the transition from one part of the vision to another—it marks the succession of the visions and not of time.

"I saw",—i. e., with the eye of ecstatic vision.

" a door opened in heaven",—It is not that heaven is to be regarded as the house of God where He is enthroned (Dus.), nor as a temple (V. Zu.), nor as a firm arch (Hei.), but the *"door"* is that through which John is caught up by the Spirit into heaven. (A. L. F. D. Gro.)

Nor does it mean that John saw the door open. It is a perfect participle; the door was "standing open".

"the first voice that I heard",—i. e., the voice of Chap. 1.10. The voice is not to be thought of as God's (Lap.), nor hardly as the voice of Christ (L. S. Ew. Hen.), inasmuch as the voice in Chap. 1.10 was followed by Christ's voice, not as a trumpet but as the sound of many waters. It is doubtless the voice of an angel. (A. F. Eb. Dus.) If, however, we take it to be the voice of an angel it is not to be thought of as an angel speaking in the person of Christ (Ly.), nor as the voice of an unknown angel (A. F. Dus.), but rather as that of the angel of Chap. 1.1. Against this identification we can see no valid objection whatever.

"Come up hither",—i. e., through the opened door.

Scofield says, "This call seems clearly to indicate the fulfillment of I Thess. 4.14-17. The word 'church' does not occur again in the Revelation."

"The whole book of Revelation", says Torrey, "after Chap. 4.1 has to do with the time after the rapture of the Church." Thus practically all who belong to the Futurist School of interpretation.

Alford, on the other hand, says, "I cannot regard the futurist scheme with approval. The seven seals, trumpets and vials run on to the time close upon the end. Any scheme of interpretation which does not recognize this common ending of the three seems to me to be thereby convicted of error." (See under Chap. 6 a discussion of the various methods of interpretation.)

"hereafter",—Literally, "after these", i. e., after *"the things that are"* (Chap. 1.19), and to be interpreted accordingly as we take the expression, *"the things that are"*. (See Chap. 1.19.)

Ver. 2. *"I was in the Spirit"*,—i. e., in a trance or ecstacy. (See Chap. 1.10.)

"a throne set in heaven",—It does not mean that the setting or placing of it there formed part of the vision. The word *"set"* is literally "lay". We best express it by the English word "stood".

"one sitting",—The eternal Father. (F. A. L. B. V. Al. Gro. Wet. Hen. Dus. Stern.) He is not named because John simply describes what he saw and as he saw it. For the same reason he did not expressly name Christ in Chap. 1.13.

Ver. 3. *"a jasper stone and a sardius"*,—A description symbolic of the glory of God.

"a rainbow round about the throne",—"The brightness of His glory and the fire of His judgment is ever girded by and found within the refreshment and surety of His mercy and goodness", says Alford.

Ver. 4. *"four and twenty elders"*,—If these are redeemed human beings, they are not to be taken as representative of the entire assembly of the ministers of the Word, pastors of the New Testament Church (V. Ca.), nor are they to be taken as representing the Christian martyrs (Eic.); they are rather, if redeemed human beings, the representatives of the entire people of God, the Church generally. (A. Sw. Dus. Sei. Mil. Vau. Moor.) This is the usually accepted view. Their designation, their robes, their crowns and their employment, and especially their redemption (especially if *"us"* is the right word to be supplied in Chap. 5.9) seem to favor this view.

Ludhardt says the true reading of Chap. 5.10 is *"them"* and that this distinguishes these elders from redeemed men, and so he objects to the view just given. He says it is the heavenly council of unfallen spirits representing the hosts of God in heaven. (See Craven in Lange.) There is much to be said in favor of Ludhardt's view, although it is impossible to be absolutely certain one way or the other, in as much as the weight of evidence on each side is about equal. Happily the decision one way or the other does not affect the interpretation of the general content of the book. Craven thinks the view of Ludhardt gives a unity to the heavenly scene not found in any other view, especially if the four living creatures are to be taken as unfallen heavenly spirits, personal non-human beings who are executors of the will of God.

However, even if the reading *"them"* be accepted (as it evidently must be) the inference of Ludhardt does not necessarily follow. They could include themselves even though they used the pronoun "them", the use of this pronoun being a mark of modesty, just as is often seen in the use of language today. Inasmuch as the proper reading and determination of the writer's thought in Chap. 5.9,10 has much to do with the true explanation of the twenty-four elders, it is fitting to discuss the same at this point.

The Authorized Version has *"redeemed us"* in verse 9 and *"made us"* in verse 10. It would seem that the same persons must be referred to in each instance.

But the *"us"* in verse 10 must be replaced it seems by "them" according to the manuscripts K. A. B., and it is so taken by practically all. (B. R-V. W-H. Ti. Gri. Syr. Vul. Lach. Copt.) This would seem to call for the deletion of *"us"* in verse 9, for which in fact there is no word in the original text, and it is accordingly omitted by the majority (A. L. R-V. Ti. Wor. Lach.), and in its place is supplied the word "men", inasmuch as some word harmonizing with *"them"* of verse 10 must seemingly at least be supplied.

The Authorized Version follows אB'P, all of which have the word *"us"* in the original of verse 9, and this reading is followed by some authorities. (Tre. Vul. Sei.) Seiss is insistent that the *"us"* be retained, setting forth the fact that Tregellius argued for it even before א was discovered, and that certainly with this added evidence in its favor there can be no doubt as to its place in the text. But even with ℵ in its favor, the "us" is hardly sufficiently well attested to claim for itself a place in the original, and with the "them" of verse 10, for which the weight of manuscript authority so preponderates, it does not appear how "us" could be used consistently in verse 9.

Although we would expect "us" in both places, if the elders are representatives of human beings, let it be noted once more that by the use of "men" in verse 9 and "them" in verse 10, they do not necessarily exclude themselves from the redemption, but, as Fausset says, it may be taken as a Hebrew construction of the third person for the first and as giving a more modest sound than "us". There is really no need for any word to be expressed in verse 9. For similar construction see Matt. 25.8; I John 4.13.

While Craven accepts the view which is held well nigh universally by commentators, namely, that the elders are representatives of the glorified Church, redeemed human beings, he suggests that inasmuch as the omission of "us" in verse 9 and the rendering "them" in verse 10 releases us from the necessity of including the elders among the redeemed, it might be better to take them as the princes of the heavenly host, unfallen spirits, as Ludhardt does. He says:

1. The doxology was raised in view of the general fact of redemption and not of the personal redemption of those who united in it, and it furnishes no evidence that any who united in it were themselves the subjects of it.

2. Apart from this doxology there is no evidence that the elders were in any way connected with the Church, while everything else in Revelation seems to point to the contrary. Although they are mentioned several times it is never as representing the redeemed or being among them or joining in their hallelujahs.

   (a) If there are any specially favored among the redeemed and glorified saints they ought to be found among the martyrs, but while the elders are on the thrones the martyrs are beneath the altar.

   (b) When the great multitude in Chap. 7.9 stood before the throne and raised their hallelujahs, the elders were not with them but were with the living beings and the angels, offering a separate worship and uniting in a separate hymn of praise. In speaking to the Seer about that glorified throng one of the elders spoke of "them" and not of "us", spoke not as one of their number but as a mere spectator of their glory.

   (c) In Chap. 11.15-18 when the elders and four living beings burst forth in a doxology because the Kingdom of the Messiah was fully established on the earth, they made no allusion to any personal participation in the rewards that were to be bestowed on the saints.

   (d) When the Lamb stood with the 144,000 on Mt. Zion, the elders and the four living beings stood apart from the throne, and the song of the redeemed was sung *before*, not *by* them. As representatives of glorified humanity they should have been among the 144,000.

In reply to Craven it may be said that inasmuch as the 144,000 and other groups in question may quite as properly refer to special classes of the glorified it does not at all become necessary that the elders be included among them. This fact together with the fact that the use of *"men"* and the pronoun *"them"* in Chap. 5.9 and 10 does not necessarily exclude the elders from those redeemed, and the significance of their designation, their robes, their crowns, the number and finally their employment will incline one perhaps to abide by the old and preponderant view which takes these elders as representatives of the glorified Church. Thus L. A. V. R. Sw. Hen. Dus. Sei. Gab. Sco. Eic. Mil. Vau. Bos. Cal. Dean, Gebh. Moor.

These elders, however, cannot be the totality of the redeemed already raised up and glorified, because the souls of the martyrs, certainly the noblest part of the redeemed, are seen beneath the altar as disembodied spirits having had as yet no resurrection nor reward, and other martyrs are to follow these. (Chap. 6.11.) Perhaps the most discriminating explanation is that given by Swete, who says, "The twenty-four elders are the Church in its totality, but the Church idealized and therefore seen as already clad in white, crowned, and enthroned in the divine presence—a state yet future, but already potentially realized in the resurrection and ascension of the Head."

While retaining the old and accepted view, we repeat that no serious objection can be registered against the view of Ludhardt, which Craven suggests for consideration, namely that we have in these twenty-four elders representatives not of the glorified Church, but the heavenly council, composed of the representatives of the hosts of God in heaven—of unfallen spirits.

From the wording of Chap. 5.9,10 according to the Authorized Version, it would seem that the four living beings as well as the elders joined in the song about their redemption. But this is rendered dubious by the fact that the anthem is sung to the music of the harps and the harps are the property only of the elders.

As to why there are twenty-four elders it is useless to speculate. Of the many surmises only two are worthy of any consideration:
1. It is derived from the order of the priests. As the twenty-four priests are but one course out of 24,000 (I Chron. 23.3,4), so these twenty-four crowned priests wearing white robes are the representatives of many thousands upon thousands. (F. V. Al. Ca. Ze. Ew. Hil. Eic. Sei.)
   Some object to this because these elders are not priests as seen in Chap. 5.8, their occupation being simply connected with their representative character. (A. Dus.)
2. The other and usually accepted explanation is that they represent the Old Testament and the New Testament Church—the twelve patriarchs and the twelve apostles, not in their personal but in their representative character; and so in Chap. 15.3 the conquerors sing the song of Moses and the Lamb, and in Chap. 21.12 the names of the twelve tribes and of the twelve Apostles are inscribed on the gates and on the foundation respectively of the New Jerusalem. (Mil.)

The white robes signify purity and the crowns kingly authority. They imply conflict and endurance and strongly argue for the twenty-four elders being redeemed human beings, though not conclusively by any means.

Ver. 5. *"lightnings and voices and thunders"*,—Showing forth God's omnipotence particularly as exercised in judgment and wrath which is about to proceed from the throne. (A. Sei. Dus. Bar. Hen.)

"seven lamps of fire burning before the throne",—The Holy Spirit in His seven-fold operation as the light and life giver and fiery purifier of the Godly and the consumer of the ungodly. (A. F.)

Ver. 6. *"as it were a sea of glass like unto crystal"*,—It is of course impossible to be absolutely sure of the interpretation of this as well as of many other symbols of this book. Many explanations are mere guesses. Calovius thinks the glassy sea is a symbol of baptism; Joachim, of the Holy Scriptures; Alexander, of repentance; Bullinger, of the present transitory world; Hengstenberg, of the judgments of God. Dusterdieck and Ludhardt say it is identical with the river of life in Chap. 22; but this is untenable inasmuch as the vision in Chap. 22 is quite distinct from this and each has its own propriety in detail.

Others say it is symbolic of the glorified Church, calm and peaceful in contrast to the turbulent sea representing the mass of nations in their ungodly state (L. Eb. Ar. Kl. Wor. Gro.), while Vitringa says it represents the basis of righteousness and grace whereon the throne of God is founded.

Others say it is the clear ether in which the throne of God is upborne, in front of the throne to separate it from John and all else, and signifying the purity and calmness and majesty of God's rule. (A. F. D.)

Dusterdieck objects to this view as well as to that of Vitringa because the sea is not beneath the throne but before it; but this objection is by no means a formidable one inasmuch as it could be beneath it and before it at the same time. Our decision is perhaps best found among the last three views and of these the view of Alford, Fausset and De Wette is not only the simplest but it is the least open to objection and is more in keeping with the earlier usage in the Old Testament. (See Ezek. 1.22 and Ex. 24.10,11.)

It is almost universally admitted that John did not look upon the real heaven but that the scenes he beheld were symbolical. But were they?

A symbol is an image; either—

1. Material,—as for instance the bread and the wine, symbolic of the body and blood of Christ.
2. Visional,—an appearance, as beheld in ecstatic vision or trance.

In respect to their relation to the object symbolized they may be divided as follows:

1. Immediate,—representing without further medium the object contemplated, as a visional image of heaven, angels, etc.
2. Mediate,—representing the object through the medium of some other object, as when Christ is represented through the visional image of a lamb.

The four living creatures are generally admitted to be Mediate symbols. They are identical with the Cherubim of the Old Testament (Ezekiel

1.5-10 and 10.20), although certain differences are traceable. If they are symbols there is not the slightest intimation given in the Word of God as to what they symbolize. All we have is the pure imagination of the commentators. Someone has aptly said, "They are the sphinx of the Bible."

The following are some of the explanations:

1. The four Gospels. (Vic.)
2. The four elements. (Al.)
3. The four principal angels. (Lap.)
4. The four cardinal virtues. (Ar.)
5. The four faculties of the soul.
6. The four principal attributes of God. (St.)
7. The four greatest fathers of the Church.
8. The four fundamental forms of divine government. (L.)
9. The four patriarchal churches, Jerusalem, Antioch, Alexandria and Constantinople. (Ly.)
10. The four great Apostles, Peter, James, Matthew and Paul. (Gro.) Others mention other Apostles.
11. The four great events in redemption, Incarnation, Passion, Resurrection and Ascension. (Ar.)
12. The four representatives of the New Testament Church, as were the four standards of the four chief tribes of the Old Testament Church. (Me.)
13. Glorified saints who have been raised to special eminence. (Lord.)
14. The ministers of the Church on earth. (Dau.)
15. All the ministers and teachers of the Church in every age. (V.)
16. Saints who are to attend Jehovah as assessors in the judgment. (Ham.)
17. The Church militant. (E.)
18. The Church triumphant. (Bush.)
19. The creative power of God. (Eb.)
20. Animated creation. (A. D. B. Dus. Hen. Rei. Vau.) "We have thus", says Alford, "the throne of God surrounded by His Church and by His animated world, the former represented by the elders and the latter by the four living beings."
21. They are not symbols at all, but personal non-human ministers of the throne. (Crav.)

View number 1 is the oldest and was at one time almost universally accepted and for this reason some moderns are again taking it up. It is really not the Gospels that are symbolized but the evangelists, and that not as expressing *their* personal character, but the personal character of Christ,—in Matthew, the lion as representing his royalty; in Mark, the ox, as representing his patience; in Luke, the man, as representing his brotherly sympathy; in John, the eagle, as representing his soaring majesty, etc. But not one of the Gospels, with perhaps the exception of the last one, has any substantial accord with the character thus assigned. This is seen in the fact that each one of the living beings has been assigned by different scholars to each of the four Gospels.

Now if the four living beings in the doxology of Chap. 5.9,10 spoke of themselves as redeemed by the blood of Christ, then they *must* be human beings, and so must be symbolic of redeemed individuals. But the reading *"us"* of the Authorized Version is *far* from being certain. Indeed it is quite certain that the reading *"them"* of the Revised Version is the correct one (see discussion *en loco*), and therefore it is not *necessary* to think of them as human beings at all. In either case, however, it is not clear that they joined in the doxology with the twenty-four elders. There are reasons for believing they did not.

On the ground that they were not human beings the views of Alford and of Lange are perhaps the most worthy of serious attention; but of the two, that of Alford suits better the setting and the context, i. e., that they are representatives of animated nature,—the animal life of the world.

But even if they are not human *they may still be personal*. The best way to clarify the subject is to see what the same *"living beings"* (the cherubim) of the Old Testament stood for. They stood no doubt as executors of the will of the One on the throne. (See Ezekiel 1.) And so here too the simplest and most consistent explanation is to see in the living beings personal ministers of the divine government. As such they are not symbols at all. Therefore:

I. Taken as *non-personal beings* they may best be considered as symbols or representatives of animated nature. (A. B. Dus.) There is much to be said in favor of this view. (See Craven in Lange.)

II. Taken as *personal beings* they are either:

1. Personal *human beings,* and as such they are symbols either of,

   (a) The redeemed in general, the redeemed, glorified Church. (F.) But this seems quite too indefinite to meet the requirements of the vision, and would confuse them with the twenty-four elders in case these latter are taken to represent the redeemed Church.

   (b) A certain pre-eminent class of the eclectic resurrection and translation saints who serve as executors while the elders serve more as counselors. (Sei. Mor.)
   Says Morgan, "The living creatures mark the inner circle of the Church, which God has selected, elected, chosen, and which Jesus is coming to gather unto Himself."
   But this is rather far-fetched and a bit too fanciful.

2. Personal *non-human beings,* i. e., unfallen heavenly spirits who are the personal ministers of the throne of God; and so not symbols at all. To this view we strongly incline.

Of course the forms they assume are symbolic,—the lion for courage, boldness and victorious strength; the ox for patience, industry, endurance and sacrifice; the man for human sympathy, and the eagle for soaring aspiration, contemplation and striving after the ideal.

Milligan and others, however, say that the qualities represented are those that strike terror, i. e., the ferocity of the lion, the power and rage of the ox (*"bull-calf"*), and the eagle hastening vulture-like to his prey.   They are vice-generals of God; the assessors of the throne.

"in the midst round about",—Not that they moved round about in the midst of a transparent throne (Eb.), nor "under as supporting it" (Ew. Hen. Eic.), but one on each side and at the middle of the side in each case. (D. A. F. Zu. Dus.)

Ver. 7.   *"calf"*,—While *"calf"* is the primary meaning, "ox" is the preferable translation according to usage in the Septuagint and as determined by the context.

Ver. 8.   *"full of eyes round about and within"*,—The *"round about"* of this verse really comprises the *"before and behind"* of verse 6, while the *"within"* refers to the inner part of the half-opened wings and that part of the body otherwise covered by the wings.

The six wings are here to be understood as in Isaiah 6 and are a figurative representation of the ministerial relation in which the creature stands to its God.

The eyes are signs of intense intelligence (omniscience) as well as of constant wakefulness, day and night, ceaselessly declaring the glory of God.   (A. Dus.)

Ver. 9.   *"when"*,—Better taken in the sense of "whensoever".   (A. F. L. Bar. Wor.)

"give",—Not to be pressed as an absolute future, but more as a frequentative signification (V. B. Eb. Dus. Han.) and as implying eternal repetition of the act.   (A.)

Ver. 10.   *"fall down . . . cast crowns"*,—An expression of reverence and humility and recognition of the fact that to Him belongs all honor, etc.

Ver. 11.   *"because of thy will"*,—Because Thou didst will it.

"they were",—i. e., they existed, as in contrast to their previous non-existence.

CHAPTER FIVE

1 And I saw [1]in the right hand of him that sat on the throne a book written within and on the back, close sealed with seven seals.   2 And I saw a strong angel proclaiming with a great voice, Who is worthy to open the book, and to loose the seals thereof?   3 And no one in the heaven, or on the earth, or under the earth, was able to open the book, or to look thereon.   4 And I wept much, because no one was found worthy to open the book, or to look thereon: 5 and one of the elders saith unto me, Weep not; behold, the Lion that is of the tribe of Judah, the Root of David, hath overcome to open the book and the seven seals thereof.   6 And I saw [2]in the midst of the throne and of the four living creatures, and in the midst of the elders, a Lamb standing, as though it had been slain, having seven horns, and seven eyes, which are [3]the seven Spirits of God, sent forth into all the earth.   7 And he came, and he [4]taketh *it* out of the right hand of him that sat on the throne.   8 And when he had taken the book, the four living creatures and the four and twenty elders fell down before the Lamb, having each one a harp, and golden bowls full of incense, which are the prayers of the saints.   9 And they sing a new song, saying,

Worthy art thou to take the book,
and to open the seals thereof: for
thou wast slain, and didst purchase

[1]Gr. *on*
[2]Or, *between the throne with the four living creatures, and the elders*
[3]Some ancient authorities omit *seven*
[4]Gr. *hath taken*

unto God with thy blood *men* of every tribe, and tongue, and people, and nation, 10 and madest them *to be* unto our God a kingdom and priests; and they reign upon the earth.

11 And I saw, and I heard a voice of many angels round about the throne and the living creatures and the elders; and the number of them was ten thousand times ten thousand, and thousands of thousands; 12 saying with a great voice, Worthy is the Lamb that hath been slain to receive the power, and riches,

and wisdom, and might, and honor, and glory, and blessing.

13 And every created thing which is in the heaven, and on the earth, and under the earth, and on the sea, and all things that are in them, heard I saying,

Unto him that sitteth on the throne, and unto the Lamb, *be* the blessing, and the honor, and the glory, and the dominion, [5]for ever and ever.

14 And the four living creatures said, Amen. And the elders fell down and [6]worshipped.

[5]Gr. *unto the ages of the ages*
[6]See marginal note on Chap. 3.9

Vers. 1-14. THE SEVEN-SEALED BOOK WHICH CHRIST ALONE IS WORTHY TO OPEN.

Ver. 1. *"a book"*,—i. e., "a book-roll", according to contemporary practice, in which stands written what must come to pass.

"in the right hand",—It is really "on"; not "on the right side of Him who sat on the throne" (Eb.), but on His open right hand (A. F. L. Dus.) as if on God's part there was no withholding of His future purposes as contained in the book. (See verse 7 and Chap. 20.1.)

"written within and on the back",—It was written on the side next to the staff and on the side turned outwards in unrolling and so betokening the completeness of the contents as containing the divine counsels.

"closed sealed with seven seals",—Expressing the idea of both mystery and security.

Many think there were seven successive leaves rolled on the staff, each with its own seal, and so only the seal to the outer one was visible to the Seer. (L. V. D. Ew. Gro. Wet.) It is better, however, to think of all the seals on the end, each one holding together a number of turns on the staff and so all of them visible at the same time. (A. F. D. Eb. Dus.)

WHAT IS REPRESENTED BY THE BOOK?

1. The Old Testament. (V.)
2. The Old Testament and the New Testament. (Be. Ew. Jer. Aug.)
3. Divorce from God written against the Jews. (Wet.)
4. Christ Himself. (Heterius.)
5. The sentence designed against the enemies of the Church. (Scho.)
   All of these are more or less surmise.
6. The true explanation is that which refers it to that part of the Apocalypse which deals with what is to follow. But as to how much of what is to follow scholars are again at widest variance. Does it refer to Chap. 6 only (L.), or to Chaps. 6 to 8 (Hen.), or to Chaps. 6 to 11 (Al.), or to Chap. 6 on to the end (A. V. D. F. Me. Dus. Lap.)? This last is by far the most acceptable view.

The fact that the seals were broken by the Lamb would lead one to suppose that the roll was unfolded and read, but there is no record that anything was read out of the book. The book seemingly was never actually opened nor any part of it read. The revelations given to the Seer, as seal after seal is broken, is in images which represent the contents of the book. (A. F. Eb. Sei. Dus. Hen.)

"There is no hint", says Moorehead, "that the book was read, that its contents were disclosed. We are told of the events which succeed the opening of the seals, but of the contents written within it nothing is said. Did the book contain the events? Doubtful. It would be unwarranted to affirm so much."

What is in the book will be made known, says Fausset, at the visible setting up of the kingdom of Christ at His return and the opening of the seals are the successive steps by which God in Christ prepares or clears the way for this.

Moorehead says it is Christ's "title deed" to the kingdoms of this world, the inheritance which He had purchased by His obedience unto death, that Dan. 7.9-14 points to the same great transaction, and that this majestic scene has not yet taken place.

Ver. 3. *"under the earth",*—This does not mean "in the sea" (Gro.), but the reference is to hades, the place of departed spirits. (A. F. Dus.)

"no one was found worthy to open the book or to look thereon",— Not perhaps, as Lange says, "not even so much as to look upon it", i. e., before it was opened; but rather to look upon it with a view to reading it after it was opened. (A. F. D. Ew. Dus.)

Ver. 4. *"And I wept",*—It is difficult to know just why John wept. Lange says it was because he already knew the contents of the book and the dreadful things which were about to take place. It was perhaps because the promise of Chap. 4.1 seemed about to be frustrated.

Ver. 5. *"one of the elders",*—Some say the reference is to Matthew; others to Peter and others to Jacob. But all this is mere guesswork.

"the root of David",—Some refer the expression to Christ's divine nature alone as the source, the divine root which brought forth David. (Ca. Coc.) Others refer it to His human nature alone. (A. D. Ew. Eb. Ei. Ly. Lap. Hen.), the reference being to His descent from the tribe of Judah (being the Lion who has victoriously fought) and from the family of David, the branch or sucker come up from the ancient root, i. e., the descendant of David.

Others say the reference is to both His divine and human nature. (L. A.) There is a possibility of reading the first explanation (Ca. Coc.) into the expression, although by no means must the other be overlooked. But the explanation which refers it to his human nature is better, as the evident design is to set forth Christ as springing from the tribe of Judah and the lineage of David and His victory as His exaltation through suffering.

"hath overcome to open the book",—The idea is not that He "prevailed to open the book" (A-V. B. Ew.), but it refers the rather to His absolute victory. It is best read, "hath overcome, so as to open the book". His right and power to open the book is the result of His victory over the power of darkness and sin and death. (R-V. A. F. L. D. Eb. Dus.)

Ver. 6. *"in the midst"*,—Not *"on"* the throne (Eb.), but at the middle point between the throne and the twenty-four elders. (A. D. L. F. Dus. Hen.) De Wette further says, *"on the glassy sea"*; but nothing is said as to this, whereas Chaps. 7.17 and 22.1 lend no strength to the idea.

"a Lamb",—The form is diminutive, a little lamb, as expressing, not His short life as against the long life of the elders (B. Heñ.), but perhaps it is meant as De Wette says, "to put forward more prominently His innocence and meekness".

"standing",—This is chosen no doubt with reference to the words, *"as though it had been slain"*, to show that it is still living and strong. By falling He stood.

"as though it had been slain",—i. e., retaining the appearance of death wounds on his body, looking as if it had been slain.

"having seven horns",—Representing perfect might. (A. F.) (Matt. 28.18.)

"and seven eyes",—Representing watchful, active operation.

"the seven Spirits of God",—i. e., the Holy Spirit in His sevenfold perfection belonging to and profluent from the incarnate Redeemer, just as the seven lamps represent this Spirit immanent in the Godhead.

"which are",—This does not refer to the horns but to the eyes alone.

"sent forth into all the earth",—Referring to His world-wide energy. The word *"apostle"* is derived from the word here used for *"sent"*.

Ver. 8. *"each one"*,—This applies only to the elders, as seen:

First, by the masculine form, the four living beings being feminine in form, while the twenty-four elders are masculine in form;

Second, by the unnaturalness of ascribing harps and vials to beings as fashioned in Chap. 4.7;

Third, by the incongruence of such beings as the four living beings, whether non-human personal unfallen spirits or representatives of animate creation, having the office of offering the prayers of the saints.

"golden bowls full of incense",—i. e., one in the hand of each elder. It is said by some that the bowls (vials) represent the prayers of the saints just as the harps represent their praise. (A. L. Dus. Wor.) Grammatically this is possible, yet it is not only grammatically just as possible to refer the prayers to the incense, but it is far more natural and appropriate. (V. Bar. Crav.) (See Psalm 141.2 and the temple ceremony.)

"the prayers of the saints",—Seiss says the reference is to the saints of all ages whose prayers, *"Thy kingdom come"*, are now about to be answered. He says, "The picture is not that of saints in heaven officiating for saints on earth; but of saints in heaven holding up to Christ their own prayers, that now they may be answered in the ushering in of the kingdom for which they have through all ages prayed." This seems a bit too fanciful and far-fetched.

Hengstenberg says, "By the saints are primarily to be understood the saints on earth. Still there is no reason for excluding the saints in glory (compare Chaps. 11.18 and 18.20). These look down upon the sufferings and conflicts of their brethren, who are still in the flesh, and entreat

God to accomplish their redemption and to perfect His Church." But is this not somewhat productive of confusion?

It is better, we feel, with others to refer it to Christians on earth exclusively. (A. D. F. Ew. Gab. Dus. Crav.) The prayers of the saints on earth are, as it were, inclosed in the golden vials, and by the ideal Church divested of their earthly, unbounded and immoderate affections and thus presented to Christ.

Though the elders and the angel be employed by God in some way unknown to us to present the prayers of the saints, nothing is here said of their praying for the saints, and even though it be admitted, as many would have us think (B. St. Hen. Lap. Lut.), that the glorified saints in heaven pray for the saints on earth, it does not involve the utterly un-scriptural idea that prayer may be offered to the glorified saints.

Ver. 9. *"And they sing"*,—It is their blessed occupation con-tinually.

"a new song",—In Chap. 4 it was the song of creation; here it is the song of redemption and its immediate reference is to the worthiness of the Lamb to open the book, acquired through His work of redemption. The theme is the Incarnation, the Passion and the Redemption of Christ.

"didst purchase unto God with thy blood men of every tribe",—(See explanation under Chap. 4.4.)

Ver. 10. *"and madest them"*,—(See explanation under Chap. 4.4).

"a kingdom",—(See explanation under Chap. 1.6).

"and they reign upon the earth",—Many commentators following weighty manuscript authority read here in the present tense (R-V. A. L. Vau. Lac. Tre. Wor Dus.), while others argue for the future (A-V. F. Crav.) The weight of authority, both of manuscript and scholarship, is about equally divided. We must not forget, however, that elsewhere of the saints it is said that they *shall* reign over the earth (Dan. 7.22,27; Lu. 22.29,30). It is this fact which inclines us to agree with the view that gives to the verb here the future sense, as well as the fact that they who utter the song are in heaven.

Fausset thinks the weightiest authority favors the future and that even if the present tense be acceptd it is a prophetical present denoting the certain future (See Chap. 11.15,18), and that the saints shall share Christ's King-Priest throne in the Millennial Kingdom.

Others, on the other hand, say the whole aspect and reference of this heavenly vision is not future but present and that even now the Church in Christ, her Head, is reigning over the earth. (A. L. Dus. Vau.)

"upon the earth",—The preposition is "epi" and the Greek justifies the translation "over", according to which the saints themselves do not necessarily need to remain or be upon the earth. The translation in our text is, however, justified by the use of this preposition as is elsewhere made plain.

The natural inference is that the four living beings join in the song. If they represent a special class of glorified saints for some reason more highly privileged than others, as some believe, they of course did join in the song. Even as non-human beings they could have joined in it with the elders providing we do not think of the elders as including themselves among the redeemed, but having already conceded that the elders probably did include themselves, it will not do to think of the four living beings as included in the song inasmuch as we have taken them to be non-human personal unfallen spirits.

Since "*having each one*" in verse 8 refers only to the elders it is quite proper to refer the "*they*" of verse 9 to the elders as those to whom the words immediately preceding refer, all the more especially since the song of the four living beings is given at verse 14. Lange, followed by Milligan and Hengstenberg, calls attention to the fact that the song is sung to the music of the harps held by the elders and so by the elders only is the song sung. Says Hengstenberg, "Harps, human instruments, are found elsewhere in the Apocalypse only in the hands of the members of the Church (Chap. 14.2,3; 15.2), and a celebration of the deeds of Christ is nowhere else found in the mouths of the cherubims and indeed does not appear to suit them."

Dusterdieck, who takes the four living beings as representatives of the entire living creation and elders as representatives of redeemed humanity, makes the four living beings unite in the song; but this he can do only by making the song refer to the general fact of redemption rather than to any personal participation in it. It is, however, best not to think of these living beings as uniting in the song unless they are made likewise, with the twenty-four elders, representatives of redeemed human beings.

Ver. 11. "*And I saw and I heard*",—This is not to be generalized into meaning, "I saw, that is to say, I heard"; but John most certainly saw the host of angels whose voices he heard.

"*round about*",—i. e., surrounding on all sides the smaller circle hitherto described.

Ver. 12. The items in the ascription here given are seven, to express their holy completeness. The article is used only before the first one and thus makes all seven to be, as it were, a single word or expression.

"*riches*",—This is not to be confined to spiritual riches (D. Hen.), but is to be taken generally, all riches and fullness, earthly as well as spiritual.

Ver. 13. "*And every created thing*",— That the reference is primarily to animated creatures seems affirmed by the fact that heaven, earth and sea are mentioned as the abodes of these creatures or creations.

"*in the heaven*",—The living beings, including the angels and the glorified saints.

"*on the earth*",—i. e., collective humanity and all other creatures.

"*under the earth*",—Not demons (V. Hen.), but the departed spirits in hades. (A. Dus.) (Phil. 2.10.)

"*on the sea*",—Not ships, but the sea animals which are here conceived as being on the sea's surface, with perhaps special reference to seabirds, flying fish, whale, etc.

"*in them*",—i. e., in the several spheres just mentioned.

Ver. 14. "*worshipped*",—i. e., in silent adoration of God and of the Lamb.

CHAPTER SIX

There are four Systems of Interpretation of the Book of Revelation which must be borne in mind in entering upon the study of the time reference and the meaning of the various Seals now to be set before us, as well as of the Trumpets and Vials which are to follow.

I. THE SPIRITUAL SYSTEM.

The Book of Revelation deals only with great principles, and is a poetic and prophetic depiction of the struggle that has always been going on between righteousness and sin, between Christ and Satan, the struggle which began with the fall of man and which will end only with the end of time. Among the advocates of this view are some able and devout scholars such as Prof. Milligan, Prof. Randell, Archdeacon Lee, and the author's own revered instructor, George Tybout Purves.

The Book of Revelation, however, claims to be genuine prophecy, while furthermore this novel theory deliberately ignores the distinct and definite chronological data furnished by the writer. There is of course truth in the deductions of this method of explaining the Book, but as a System of interpretation it is altogether inadequate, and has never been acceptable to the Church either of Ancient, Medieval or Modern times.

II. THE PRETERIST SYSTEM.

This School of Interpretation holds that the Revelation has largely been fulfilled, and that it has special and immediate reference to conditions and events in John's own time, having to do with the Roman State, the Jews, the Destruction of Jerusalem and the Christians of the first century and the Apostolic age. The School was launched by the Jesuit Alcazar in 1614. (D. St. Sw. Ew. Ei. Sim. Ham. Dus: Luc. Bos. Dav. Desprez, Le-Clerc, and Prof. Ramsey.) Most advocates of this System of Interpretation place the date of the Book at A. D. 68, accept Nero as the Beast of Chap.`13, believing John to have adopted the absurd fiction that Nero did not die by his own hand and that he was somewhere concealed till the hour should arrive for his reappearance at the head of a great army to overthrow Rome, annihilate Christianity, deliver Israel and become the Antichrist.

But—

(a) Historical facts and events have proven, as Moorehead has well said, that the Book is totally mistaken, false and untrustworthy if it be based upon the foundation just described, for Nero did not appear, the seventh head of the Beast did not become Antichrist, Rome did not fall, but Jerusalem did, and Israel instead of being delivered and exalted, went into an exile that still endures.

(b) Certainly the awful figures and celestial phenomena of the sixth Seal, as well as the events described in other portions of the Book are not satisfied with merely that which took place at the overthrow of Jerusalem.

(c) It is now generally conceded that Revelation was not written until A. D. 96, twenty-six years after the Destruction of Jerusalem.

(d) This view gives us essentially the rationalistic interpretation of the Book, the recognition of its inspiration being wholly inadequate. It has few supporters at the present time. Among recent scholars adopting it are Ramsey, Swete and Simcox, who, however, date the Book in A. D. 96 and make Domitian the Beast of Chap. 13 by whose ascension the deadly wound of Nero was healed, but their exposition utterly gives way when confronted with the historical facts in the case.

III. THE HISTORICAL SYSTEM.

The School of Interpretation holds that the prophecies of Revelation embrace the whole history of the Church and its foes from the time of its writing to the end of the world. This School originated about the eleventh century among those who began to protest against the growing corruptions of the Church of Rome.

This School must again be divided into two classes:

1. The Consecutive or Continuous Historical view which makes the different visions refer to successive historical events following one after the other along the way from the beginning of John's time to the final consummation of all things. (B. V. N. Me. El. Br. Bi. Lut. Bul. Cun. Dau. Gor. Gui. New. Bale, Foxe, Frere, Keith, Irving, Pareus, Faber, Whiston, Bicheno, Marlorat, Woodhouse, Habershon, Chytraeus, Bickersteth.)

For the best discussion of the views of this School read Elliott's "Horae Apocalypticae", and Guinness' "The Approaching End of the Age". The majority of these writers agree as to the following points, with some diversity of course as to detail:

(a) The First Seal refers to the temporary prosperity, and Seals two, three and four to the decline of the Pagan Roman Empire.

(b) The Fifth Seal to the martyrdom of Christians which commenced under Diocletian in A. D. 303.

(c) The Sixth Seal to the fall of the Pagan Roman Empire under Constantine.

(d) Trumpets one to four to the Gothic invasions, Trumpet five to the Saracen invasion and Trumpet six to that of the Turks.

(e) The little "opened book" to the Reformation.

(f) Chapter eleven to the Papal persecution of the saints as heretics.

(g) Chapter twelve to the depression and recession from view of the true Church during the Papal ages.

(h) The Beasts of Revelation to aspects of the Papacy.

(i) The Vials to the great French Revolution and its results.

(j) Chapter seventeen to Rome.

(k) Chapter eighteen to the Papacy.

(l) A day is the symbol of a year.

As set forth by Elliott this view may be stated in general as follows: "The Seals, Trumpets and Vials are to be interpreted as connected and consecutive series,—the Seventh Seal unfolding itself in the seven Trumpet-visions, and the Seventh Trumpet in those of the seven Vials; and this with no intermission or interruption, save only that of the *supplemental retrogressive Part* (which Ellicott supposes to have occupied the *outside* of the Scroll), their historic matter being respectively as follows:

I.   That of the coming temporary prosperity, and then the decline and fall of Pagan Rome, before the power of Christianity:—the subject of the first six Seals.

II.   The ravage and destruction of Rome Christians, after its apostacy, in its divisions both of east and west; of the western empire by the Goths, of the eastern by the Saracens and the Turks:—the subject of the first six Trumpets.

III.   The history of the Reformation, as introduced about the middle of the Sixth Trumpet.

IV.   The supplemental and explanatory history of the rise, character and actings of the Papacy and Papal Empire, which sprung out of the Gothic inundations of Western Europe.

V.   The preliminary judgments on, and then the final overthrow of the Papacy and Papal Empire under the outpourings of the vials of God's wrath; followed by the coming of Christ to judgment; consequent on which is depicted,

VI.   The glorious consummation, including the descent of the heavenly Jerusalem, and the reign of Christ and His saints on the renovated earth.

Of which parts the first four seem to me to have been accomplished already; and of the fifth part the prefigured events to be now far advanced in progress of fulfillment."

That this method of interpretation is a possible one can hardly be doubted by any one who has given close study to the profane and ecclesiastical history of the world since the time of Christ, but as a System of Interpretation many scholars think it quite too incomplete.

(a)   It leaves huge gaps in the history it is supposed to cover. The 500 years between A. D. 1000 and 1500 it leaves almost untouched.

(b)   The periods are not well defined; they run into and are embodied one with another.

(c)   The awful figures of the Sixth Seal are hardly satisfied by the sack of Rome, as Elliott interprets, or by the invasions of the Goths and Vandals from the north upon the Roman Empire, as Barnes explains.

(d)   The year-day theory, making a day stand for a year, does not commend itself to sober scholars as once it did, not a few believing that Tregelles has demonstrated it to be fallacious and unbiblical.

(e)   The utter lack of harmony among the interpreters of this School as to historical reference and especially as to the starting point of the 1260 days (years, as they interpret) so frequently mentioned in the Book does not commend the system any too highly, although this cannot be taken as an altogether sufficient reason for its condemnation.

It might be well just here to insert a quotation from Milligan, who strongly opposes this method of interpretation; he says, "All the greatest incidents, and, it must be added, some of the most trivial details, of the past or present (such as the red color of the stockings of the Romish cardinals) are to be seen in its prophetic page; and the pious mind derives its encouragement and comfort from the thought that these things were long ago foretold. But the whole school of historical interpreters has been irretrievably discredited, if not by the extravagance of paltriness of its explanations, at least by their hopeless divergence from, and contradiction of, one another. Besides this, it has to be observed that to make the Apocalypse deal almost exclusively with these historical incidents belonging to later history of the Church, is to make a book that must have been useless to those for whom it was written. How could the early Christians discover in it the establishment of Christianity under Constantine, the rise of Mohammedanism, the Lutheran Reformation, or the French Revolution? Of what possible use would it have been to foretell to them events in which they could have no interest? Would they be either wiser or better if they had known them? Would they not have substituted a vain prying into the future for the study of those divine principles which, belonging to every age, bring the weight of universal history to enforce the lessons of our own time? Nothing has tended more to destroy the feeling that there is value in the Apocalypse than this continuous historical interpretation of the book. The day, however, for such interpretations has passed, probably never to return."

2. The Contemporaneous or Synchronous Historical view which holds that the first five Seals, as well as Trumpets and Vials, are synchronous, beginning as to their development at the time John had the vision and continuing on down through history with reference to certain contemporaneous events, the Sixth Seal ushering in the Second Coming of Christ.

IV. THE FUTURIST SYSTEM.

This School of Interpretation throws the whole book, beginning with Chap. 4, forward to the times of the Second Coming of Christ. (Sco. Gab. Pet. Sei. Mor. Tor. Bla. Gra. Will. Todd, Tyso, Burgh, Maitland.)

These authorities refer all seven Seals, Trumpets and Vials to the seven years just prior to the Second Coming of Christ *with* His saints in judgment, and declares that all Christians will have been caught up in the Rapture when these judgments are enacted.

This school was launched in 1580 by the Jesuit Ribera, who, as Guinness says, "moved like Alcazar, to relieve the Papacy from the terrible stigma cast upon it by the Protestant interpretation (the Historical School), tried to do so by referring these prophecies to the distant *future*, instead of like Alcazar to the distant *past*."

This view gives to literal Israel a very large place in the book of Revelation, and refers the word *"saints"* very largely to Jewish believers during the time of the Great Tribulation, whereas the Historical view refers the prophecy very largely to the experiences of the Christian Church during the present dispensation.

The Spiritual and Preterist Systems of Interpretation, as we have seen, have very little to commend them, and we are left to a choice as between the Historical and the Futurist.

It has already been admitted in the discussion under Chap. 1.19 that the most natural inference at that place seems to favor some form of the historical method of interpretation; but there is so much in the book for which it seems hard to find a place in the history of the world, as we know it, that one is much tempted to look into the future for the *"things which must shortly come to pass"*; although some look upon this as an easy way to escape the difficulties of the text.

Should the Futurist view be taken, it must be borne in mind that there are also two aspects of this view; one which puts all the happenings *after* the Christians have been caught up and during the Great Tribulation; the other which puts all the happenings just *before* the Christians are caught up and during the Great Tribulation which precedes this Rapture.

The references to the Futurist interpretation throughout our study will be confined, unless otherwise noted, to the first division of this school, to which belong by far the greater number of Futurist commentators.

> 1 And I saw when the Lamb opened one of the seven seals, and I heard one of the four living creatures saying as with a voice of thunder. Come[1]. 2 And I saw, and behold, a white horse, and he that sat thereon had a bow; and there was given unto him a crown; and he came forth conquering, and to conquer.
>
> [1]Some ancient authorities add *and see*

Vers. 1,2.   THE FIRST SEAL.

Ver. 1.   *"voice of thunder"*,—A tone of terror, majesty and judgment, not belonging particularly to the first being as resembling a lion, nor has it anything to do with the contents of the First Seal (Hen.), but as belonging to all four alike and to be accounted for by their mysterious and supernatural nature.   It is accredited only to the first being because it is the first to speak.

"Come",—The *"and see"* of the Authorized Version is hardly well enough attested to be received and must therefore be omitted.

Some say the address is to John to draw close to see accurately what proceeds from the unsealed book.   (Dus. Gro.)   Lange says this idea is void of meaning since it is a visional appearance that is referred to.   Alford objects to it on the ground (1) that John was already there and that the *"come"* could not have been repeated as it was in verses 3, 5 and 7 unless we conceive of John drawing near each time and then retiring; (2) that he would have no need to be addressed in a voice of thunder; and (3) that the verb is never used in this sense without some particle which does not here appear.

Others say it is addressed to Christ and is the groaning of creation for the second coming of Christ (Rom. 8.9) (A. F. Mil.).   They remind us that at the Fifth Seal the martyrs make the same prayer and that at the Sixth Seal Christ's coming takes place.   They refer also to Chap. 22.17,20. This idea fits in beautifully with their interpretation of the four living creatures as representing animated creation, but (a) it is unexampled and unnatural as an address to Christ, and (b) Chap. 22.17,22 is a call to *"the* water of life", and (c) thunder is the voice of command and not of prayer; all of which reasons discourage us from accepting this view.

Still others say it is a command issuing from the ministers of God for the riders to come forth and is accordingly addressed to them. (Sei. Crav.) Any explanation here can be little more than a surmise, but this last view seems to have the least against it whether we translate by the word "Come" or the word "Go" as Seiss does.

Ver. 2. Roman victors always rode on white horses. We have here, it would seem, the image of the victorious warrior going forth to conquer.

Lange, though not identifying the horses necessarily with those of Zech. 1.8, thinks them no doubt related in a general way, as do many others, including Hengstenberg. But Dusterdieck well says that "neither the forms of the horses in Zechariah nor the attached significance agrees with the vision of our passage; even the color of the horses are not the same, much less their meaning." We are not inclined to attach any significance to the horse itself or its color or to the bow. Any attempt to go further is liable to land in the arbitrary and ofttimes frivolous and ridiculous, and is altogether uncalled for.

"he that sat thereon",—The Consecutive Historical view makes the rider of this horse to be the Roman emperor, the time under consideration being that during the reigns of the five good emperors, Nerva, Trajan, Hadrian and the two Antonines. Elliott maintains that the differences between the rider of the white horse in Chap. 19 and here are so many and so great that they must have been purposely set forth in order to set aside all idea of any identity btween the two riders. Gibbon represents this as the "Golden Age" of the Roman Empire.

According to the Synchronous Historical view this seal represents the triumphing image of Christ, the same as in Chap. 19.11. (F. L. Kl. Eb. Se. Be. Ca. Ly. Dus. Hen. Gro. Lap. And.)

"to conquer",—He goes forth not only as a conqueror but he is to gain a victory that shall be final and everlasting. The crown may find its parallel in Zech. 6.11 and the bow may be identified with the imagery of Hab. 3.9 where God goes forth for the salvation of His people. (See also Isa. 41.2; Zech. 9.13, and especially Psalm 45.4,5.)

Almost all scholars down to A. D. 150 took the image as a sympol of the preached Gospel and its success.

Inasmuch as the other three riders are personifications, this is taken by many (D. B. Ei. Ew. Her.) as a personification of victory, while Alford and Stern take it as a personification of Christianity breaking down earthly power and making the kingdoms of this world to become the Kingdom of our Lord and His Christ. However it is hard to perceive of a personification of Christianity except in the person of Christ, and if the Synchronous Historical view is taken it is better to see in the image the person of Christ as above noted.

Craven, however, who also belongs to this school, makes this image a symbol of a false Christ, i. e., Human Culture, Science. He thinks this in harmony with Matt. 24, as it is in harmony with the fact that the other riders are symbolical or personifications. There is not a little to be said in favor of the view of Craven but it is hardly to be preferred above the other.

The Futurists make the image a personification also of a false Christ, and see here a picture of the Antichrist during the last days proclaiming peace indeed but a false peace upon the earth.

Most Futurists place this as well as the other Seals after the Rapture, but Moorehead, who thinks we have here a picture of "triumphant militarism", places this Seal and the three following ones during *"the beginning of sorrows"* (Matt. 24.5-14) before the Rapture, "before", he says, "Daniel's Seventieth Week begins its course".

3 And when he opened the second seal, I heard the second living creature saying, Come[1]. 4 And another *horse* came forth, a red horse: and to him that sat thereon it was given to take [2]peace from the earth, and that they should slay one another: and there was given unto him a great sword.

[1]Some ancient authorities add *and see*

[2]Some ancient authorities read *the peace of the earth*

Vers. 3,4. THE SECOND SEAL; PEACE TAKEN FROM THE EARTH.

Ver. 4. *"a red horse"*,—i. e., war personified. Expositors are united concerning the essential significance of this vision. The color of the horse in each case has reference to the employment of the rider.

According to the Consecutive Historical view it is civil war that is here depicted, inasmuch as they were to *"kill one another"*, and it was therefore from the Roman *"earth"* that the peace left by the former Seal was to be taken away, the period referred to being that during the time of Emperor Commodus and his successors (A. D. 192 to A. D. 249). Says Sismondi, "During the ninety-two years from the death of Commodus on, thirty-two emperors and twenty-seven pretenders, alternately hurled each other from the throne by incessant civil warfare." "It was the period", says Elliott, "of civil wars and bloodshed in the Roman Empire."

According to the Synchronous Historical view it is, as Alford says, "one of the world-long and world-wide preparations for Christ's coming", the *"earth"* referring not to Judea, nor to the Roman Empire, nor to any special portion of the earth.

Dusterdieck thinks the reference is to the wars mentioned in Matt. 24.7,8, as the first presage of the coming of Christ.

Stern thinks the reference is to the persecution of Christians by the world-powers, the red horse being the Roman Empire and the rider being Nero. (Ly.) Calovius refers the horse to antichristianity and its rider to the Devil. With him agree many others, including Bede, who says, "against the victorious and conquering Church a red horse (an unfavorable populace) goes forth bloody from their rider the Devil." But they were to *"kill one another"* and therefore the persecution of Christians cannot be thought of, nor are we according to the view under discussion to think of the last three horsemen as occupying a hostile attitude toward the first one.

The figure is rightly apprehended as general by Alford and others. (L. F. Eb. Dus. Hen. Mil.) "The war thought of", says Milligan, "is not between the Church and the world but between different portions of the world itself. A world that will not accept the rule of the Prince of Peace brings upon itself the curse of war."

According to the Futurists war comes to take away the promise of peace made by the false rider of the first horse. (See II Kings 3.22, the horse blood-colored.)

5 And when he opened the third seal, I heard the third living creature saying, Come[1]. And I saw, and behold, a black horse; and he that sat thereon had a balance in his hand. 6 And I heard as it were a voice in the midst of the four living creatures saying, [2]A measure of wheat for a [3]shilling, and three measures of barley for a [3]shilling; and the oil and the wine hurt thou not.

[1]Some ancient authorities add and see

[2]Or, A choenix (i. e. about a quart) of wheat for a shilling—implying great scarcity. Comp. Ezek. 4.16 f.; 5.16
[3]See marginal note on Mt. 18.28

Vers. 5,6.   THE THIRD SEAL.

Ver. 6.   "as it were a voice",—The one from whom the voice proceeds remains unknown, though doubtless it was from one of the four living beings.

"measure",—Greek, "Choenix",—a man's daily nourishiment; a quart.

"shilling",—Greek, "Denarius",—a man's daily wage.

The Consecutive Historical School takes the symbol of that of the fiscal oppression and injustice on the part of the Roman Provincial Governors who are supposed to be represented by the rider on the horse, and who were intrusted in each province with the collection of the produce and the revenue.

According to the Synchronous Historical School the reference, of course, must be more or less general, although the specific reference may appropriately be to the time just before the Parousia of Christ, and to one of the four judgments by which the way of the Lord's coming will be opened.   (A. Dus.)

The figuration, according to this school of interpretation, is to be taken as that of Famine, the horse being black, the color of hunger (Lam. 4.8,9), and it is to be taken here not so much as denoting the grief of those afflicted by the plague (D. Hen.), but as indication of the mournful nature of the employment of the rider on the horse, i. e., famine.

The "balance" is taken by this school as the symbol of scarcity.   (A. L. E. Hen. Mil. Dus.)   (Ezek. 4.10,16.)

"the oil and wine hurt not",—This is to be taken under any circumstances as a command to the horseman limiting the plague.   It is taken by the school, whose view we are now considering, as an injunction to let them grow as ordinarily.   Fausset surmises that they were to be spared for the refreshment of the sufferers—mercy tempering judgment.

The arguments of the Consecutive School against taking the figuration in this Seal as that of famine are not without weight.

The measure of wheat (a quart) was a man's daily provision and this he got for a shilling, a day's wage, which Elliott declares though not a cheap price, was far from being a famine price.   But he got three days' provision of barley for one day's work, which certainly is not a famine price!   "Did ever man hear of such a famine as this?" asked Elliott. "The 'balance'," says Elliott, "in John's day was a symbol of justice, and is to be associated here not with the weighing, out of a scanty measure for

573

his own or his family's eating, but with the buying and selling of corn, and so may as well be taken as a symbol of plenty as of famine."

The oil and wine, when housed and secured by the owner in his casks and cellars, were not things to be *"hurt"*, nor can they be put here figurative for growing olives and vines, and the best translation, Elliott thinks, is "do not deal unjustly in"; though this rendering Alford will not allow.

According to the Futurist School the plague of famine begins after the Rapture of the Church and runs parallel with the other Seals on through the time of the Great Tribulation.

Purely arbitrary are all such allegorizings as "false brethren whose works are black" (Be.), "dearth of spiritual nourishment" (V.), "personified heresies" (Stern), and that of Lyra who says, "the horse means the Roman army, the rider, Titus, while wheat and barley mean the Jews, and the oil and the wine mean the Christians".

The reference is, of course, not specifically to the famine under Claudius (Gro. Wet. Hei. Boe.), nor so much to famine in general (B. Hu. Ca.).

> 7 And when he opened the fourth seal, I heard the voice of the fourth living creature saying, Come[1]. 8 And I saw, and behold, a pale horse: and he that sat upon him, his name was Death; and Hades followed with him. And there was given unto them authority over the fourth part of the earth, to kill with sword, and with famine, and with [2]death, and by the wild beasts of the earth.
>
> [1]Some ancient authorities add *and see*
>
> [2]Or, *pestilence.* Comp. Chap. 2.23 marg.

Vers. 7, 8. THE FOURTH SEAL.

Ver. 8. *"a pale horse"*,—The color here is that of a corpse, i. e., livid, the greenish pallor of death.

"Death; and Hades followed with him",—Both Death and Hades are here personified. By *"hades"* we are not to understand the inhabitants of Hades (Ei. Eb.), which idea would people the earth with ghosts. But *"Hades followed with him"*,—ready to engulf and detain his victims.

"the fourth part of the earth",—According to the Consecutive Historical school the horse here symbolizes the Roman empire and people, appearing deadly pale and livid under the influence of Death, who brings his curse upon the Roman earth with all the four sore judgments of God. Such an era of terrible mortality, Elliott assures us actually did take place in Roman imperial history immediately following the time of the preceding Seal and thereafter. During a part of this period (A. D. 248 to A. D. 296), says Gibbon, "five thousand persons died daily in Rome; and many towns that escaped the hands of the barbarians were entirely depopulated."

Elliott finds difficulty with the expression, *"the fourth part of the earth"* (i. e., according to him, the Roman earth), inasmuch as the plague extended over all of it, as he has set forth. This difficulty he escapes by adopting a rendering of Jerome's Latin Vulgate, "over the four parts of the earth", and by showing how the Roman empire was actually divided at that time into four parts, West, East, Illyricum, and Central Italy.

The Continuous Historical School gives the word *"earth"* its regular significance. Lange says that as four is the number of the world, the fourth part is the worldly part. But certainly, if these plagues take place before the Rapture of the Christians, as they must according to the Synchronous and Historical views, they are not confined to unbelievers, but they must, according to this view, as Dusterdieck says, refer as well to "believers who have patiently endured and hoped for the coming of the Lord as well as unbelievers."

Alford says *"the fourth part"* merely specifies his position as being one of the four riders and not that he divided the earth with the other three riders. But this is unsatisfactory and finds no analogy in Chap. 8, where a third part is spoken of.

By most expositors it is taken to mean merely a considerable portion. Milligan says that this judgment was limited because if it extended over the whole earth there would be no room for the extension of th judgments that are to follow and he thinks the Seer used the fourth part as the estimate simply because this number together with the number three was most often in his mind and that he chose it as being a smaller portion than a third.

We have seen no explanation altogether satisfactory of the expression under discussion, and can find none of our own unless it was necessary on account of the nature of this plague (death) to limit its ravages (as it was not in the case of the less severe ones) lest the whole earth perish, the *"one fourth"* being taken not geographically but quantitatively.

The four agents enumerated here are the same as those in Ezekiel 14.21, death being used in this instance in the sense of pestilence; the wild beasts multiplying in consequence of depopulation.

Alford says, "All four seals are judgments upon the earth; the beating down of earthly power, the breaking up of earthly peace, the exhausting of earthly wealth and the destruction of earthly life." He says, "The cry of the first beast is answered, not by Christ Himself, but by a symbol of His victorious power; Seals two, three and four hold a somewhat subordinate place to the first one, the destined concomitants of the growing and conquering power of Christ, methods by which He carries out His conquering career; the four seals being contemporaneous and each of them extending through the whole lifetime of the Church." Alford admits that "they may receive continually recurring, or even ultimate fulfillments, as the ages of the world go on, in distinct periods of time, and by distinctly assignable events."

The Futurists make these first four seals also synchronous but place them after the rapture of the Christians and during the tribulation which they believe immediately follows.

Entirely arbitrary are all the allegorizing interpretations such as "death-bringing heresies" (Be.), "spiritual death, complete falling away from Christ" (Stern), the "Saracens and the Turks" (V.), the "Romans under Dominitian" (Ly.), "migration of natives" (Hus.), "mortal sufferings of the Jewish war" (Gro. Wet. Her. Boe.).

9 And when he opened the fifth seal, I saw underneath the altar the souls of them that had been slain for the word of God, and for the testimony which they held: 10 and they cried with a great voice, O Master, the holy and true, dost thou not judge and avenge our blood on them that dwell on the earth?

11 And there was given them to each one a white robe; and it was said unto them, that they should rest yet for a little time, until their fellow-servants also and their brethren, who should be killed even as they were, should [1]have fulfilled *their course.*

[1]Some ancient authorities read *be fulfilled in number*

Vers. 9-11. THE FIFTH SEAL.

Ver. 9. The scene is now changed to an altar which is in heaven.

"underneath the altar",—The reference here is not to the altar of incense (D.), but to the altar of burnt offering, the altar of sacrifice. (A. E. F. L. V. B. Eb. Ew. Hen. Dus. Wor.)

"underneath the altar",—The blood of sacrifice was always poured out at the foot of the altar. (Lev. 4.7.) It is no doubt to be taken, as Alford says, symbolically, carrying out the likening of the martyrs to victims slain on the altar.

"the souls of them that had been slain",—There are three explanations:

1. Martyrs clothed with subtile bodies (Ei.). But for this meaning there is no use whatever except the unnecessary attempt to make the souls visible to John.
2. The disembodied spirits of the martyrs as in Chap. 20.4. (A. L. Dus. and the majority of commentators.)
3. Their animal life only as represented in their blood, crying for vengeance, as in Gen. 4.10. (F. Su. Hen. Mil. Crav.)

The last view is worthy of thoughtful consideration and we are rather inclined to accept it. The second view has this against it, that the spirits of the martyrs must be in bliss with Christ, and furthermore it makes Stephen say one minute, *"Lord, lay not this sin to their charge",* and the very next minute cry for vengeance on them. Hengstenberg says the passage in Chap. 20.4 makes this last view all the more necessary.

"the testimony which they held",—i. e., the testimony borne by them concerning Christ. (A. F. L. E. Bl. Ew.)

Ver. 10. *"O Master, the holy and true",*—It is God who is here addressed (L. A. V. Ew. Dus.), and not Christ (V. Gro.). The idea in the word *"true"* is that of a God who is faithful to His promises (V. A. B. D. Hen.), rather than to a God whose essence is truth (Dus.).

The Consecutive Historical School refers this Seal to the martyrdom of Christians which commenced under Diocletian in A. D. 303.

According to the Synchronous Historical School the reference here is, as Alford says, to "the cry of the martyrs' blood which has ever been going up to God since Stephen's fall; ever and anon at some great time of persecution it has waxed louder and so on through the ages it shall gather strength and accumulate until the great issue of the parable of Luke 17.1 is accomplished."

The Futurists refer it, of course, to the tribulation martyrs, those who are to give their lives during the years of the Great Tribulation. They hold these martyrs do not pertain to the Church because their cry for vengeance indicates that they were on other ground than Christian. But the language is precisely the same as that used by our Lord in Luke 18.7, and the argument therefore for the Rapture of the Church at the opening of Chap. 4 *on this ground* loses its force. Moorehead contends that they are Christians, belong to the Body of Christ, the time referred to being just before Christ's Advent and after the riding forth of the four horsemen by whose order the martyrs were doubtless slain, the first resurrection not yet having taken place, which resurrection "occurs when Christ returns to earth in visible majesty and overwhelming power and glory".

Milligan and some others think the reference is not to those who have been actually killed or martyred, but to all the saints of the Old Testament, and that by *"their fellow-servants also and their brethren who should be killed"* is meant the saints of the New Testament. The arguments, however, adduced by Milligan for this view are far from convincing.

Ver. 11. *"a white robe"*,—"The vestment of acknowledged and glorified righteousness, in which the saints walk and reign with Christ." (A.) The white robes are not to be thought of as having at that time been actually bestowed (as all receive these robes on entering glory), but as appearing to be bestowed in the vision of the Seer, because until this moment only one side of the martyr's intermediate state had in the vision been presented, i. e., their slaughter and their cry for vengeance.

"they should rest",—Not merely to quit crying for vengeance (B. D.), but to rest in blessedness. (A. Dus. Hen.)

"for a little time",—This is to be taken as corresponding with the entire view of the Apocalypse and is to be interpreted as everywhere else throughout the book. Dusterdieck says that John really thought the time was to be very short but that John was mistaken.

"who should be killed",—i. e., martyred.

"should have fulfilled their course",—i. e., as to their number (D. Eb. Dus. Wol.), although there is quite as much manuscript authority for the marginal reading preferred by many others. (A. Li. Tre. Hen.)

12 And I saw when he opened the sixth seal, and there was a great earthquake; and the sun became black as sackcloth of hair, and the whole moon became as blood; 13 and the stars of the heaven fell unto the earth, as a fig tree casteth her unripe figs when she is shaken of a great wind. 14 And the heaven was removed as a scroll when it is rolled up; and every mountain and island were moved out of their places. 15 And the kings of the earth, and the princes, and the [1]chief captains, and the rich and the strong, and every bondman and freeman, hid themselves in the caves and in the rocks of the mountains; 16 and they say to the mountains, and to the rocks, Fall on us, and hide us from the face of him that sitteth on the throne, and from the wrath of the Lamb: 17 for the great day of their wrath is come; and who is able to stand?

[1]Or, *military tribunes;* Gr. *chiliarchs*

Vers. 12-17. THE SIXTH SEAL.

(See Matt. 24.29 and Joel 2.31.)

Ver. 12. The Sixth Seal, says Elliott, of the Consecutive Historical School, surely betokened some sudden and extraordinary *revolution in the Roman empire* which would follow chronologically after the era of martyrdom depicted under the Seal preceding; a revolution arising from the triumph of the *Christian cause*. This he declares to have taken place under

Constantine, and calls it the dissolution of the Pagan firmament, the expressions concerning the earthquake and the heavenly firmament being all taken metaphorically as referring to political changes.

Alford, on the other hand, representing the Continuous Historical School, says, "We may unhesitatingly set down as wrong all interpretations which view as the fulfillment of this passage any period except that of the coming of the Lord."

Craven says, "That the Sixth Seal introduces the end of the age and the coming of the Lord for the establishment of the Kingdom there can be no doubt; that it in any proper sense can be said to usher in the final consummation and the final judgment is exceedingly questionable. If the earth quaked and the rocks rent and the sun was darkened when the God-man died, is it not rational to expect in view of these prophesies that similar portents will precede or accompany His second coming to Glory?"

Alford further says, "Thus we are brought to the very threshold of the great day of the Lord's coming, to the time described in Matt. 24.30. But before He comes His elect must be gathered out."

On the other hand Dusterdieck says, "It is the subject of a vision and not something objectively real and when it occurs no further life on this earth will be possible as the day of the Lord will have come and the final judgment have taken place", while Lange says, "It is the catastrophe of the final judgment, the finale of this world's history."

The only difference between the view of Alford and those of his school and the Futurist on this point is that Alford thinks of the saints as going through the period of Great Tribulation and being caught up at the close of this Tribulation just before the Lord descends, while the Futurist school thinks of the saints as having been caught up before the period of the Great Tribulation and the coming of the Lord here under discussion as occurring at the close of the tribulation period, some years, usually figured as seven, after the Rapture of the saints.

"the whole moon became as blood",—i. e., the full moon.

Ver. 13. "as a fig tree casteth her unripe figs",—It is perhaps winter figs that are here meant which always fall off unripe.

Ver. 14. "as a scroll when it is rolled up",—Since the heavens stretch out like a sheet they are said to vanish as a scroll. (Isa. 34.4.)

"every mountain and island were moved out of their places",—The earth's foundations to be overthrown.

Says Alford, "This total disruption shall be the precursor of the new earth just as the pre-adamic convulsions were preparative for its present occupants."

Ver. 15. "the strong",—The special reference here is to the physically strong.

Ver. 17. "who is able to stand",—i. e., to stand justified before the judge and not be condemned.

Entirely groundless are the allegorical interpretations which find here only figurative prophecies of events pertaining to the development of the Church; viz.:

    1. The earthquake means "revolutions in political or ecclesiastical spheres." (V. Boe.)

2. The sun darkened means "the blasphemed Christ" (Ly.), "prophecy" (Doc.), "worldly emperors and kings" (V.).

3. The blood red moon means "the Church reddened by the blood of martyrs" (Ly. Are.), "the law" (Boe.), "spiritual princes" (V.).

4. The fallen stars mean "the fallen exalted Church teachers" (Ly. V.), "the Jews who desert Christ for Judaism" (Boe.).

5. The mountains mean "prophets and philosophical pursuits" (Are.).

CHAPTER SEVEN

1 After this I saw four angels standing at the four corners of the earth, holding the four winds of the earth, that no wind should blow on the earth, or on the sea, or upon any tree. 2 And I saw another angel ascend from the sunrising, having the seal of the living God: and he cried with a great voice to the four angels to whom it was given to hurt the earth and the sea, 3 saying, Hurt not the earth, neither the sea, nor the trees, till we shall have sealed the [1]servants of our God on their foreheads. 4 And I heard the number of them that were sealed, a hundred and forty and four thousand, sealed out of every tribe of the children of Israel: 5 Of the tribe of Judah *were* sealed twelve thousand; Of the tribe of Reuben twelve thousand; Of the tribe of Gad twelve thousand; 6 Of the tribe of Asher twelve thousand; Of the tribe of Naphtali twelve thousand; Of the tribe of Manasseh twelve thousand; 7 Of the tribe of Simeon twelve thousand; Of the tribe of Levi twelve thousand; Of the tribe of Issachar twelve thousand; 8 Of the tribe of Zebulun twelve thousand; Of the tribe of Joseph twelve thousand; Of the tribe of Benjamin *were* sealed twelve thousand.

[1]Gr. *bondservants*

Vers. 1-8. THE SEALING OF THE ONE HUNDRED AND FORTY-FOUR THOUSAND.

Ver. 1. *"after this"*,—Showing that the Sixth Seal is complete and that Chap. 7 comes in as an episode and parenthetically (A. F. D. Ei. Ew. Eb. Hen. Dus.), although Elliott contends that the two visions of this chapter constitute the second half of the Sixth Seal.

"four angels",—Not bad angels (B. Ze. Ca. Are.), nor necessarily the *"angels of the winds"* (D. Zu. Lap.) Chap. 16.5, but *"at the four corners of the earth"*, i. e., the four cardinal points from which the winds blow.

Ver. 2. *"Another angel"*,—Not Christ (Be. Ze. Ca. Hen.) nor an archangel (Stern), nor the Holy Spirit (V. L.), but simply an angel. (A. B. D. Ew. Eb. Dus.)

"from the sun-rising",—The east designated not because of the Christian lands where the Gospel light first shone (Stern), nor because omens from the east were thought to be favorable (Blo.), nor because the Jews always turned first toward the east (D.), nor because the throne of God whence the angel proceeded is regarded as in the east (Ew.), nor because plagues have their origin in the east (B.), but because it is the side

from which life and light are brought by the sun (A. Eb. Dus. Hen. Lap. Vol. Weid.), and thus, as Alford further says, it agrees with the angel's salutary and victorious work.

"*seal*",—What is on it?

1. The stamp of the cross. (Be. Lap. Gro. Boe.)

2. The name of God and the Lamb. (D. A. Eb. Ew. Ei.) This is the more likely view but the text says nothing.

"*living God*",—Because it is He as the living God who gives life (B. Ew. Dus. Hen. Kli.) and also as giving to the seal solemnity and vital import. (A. D.)

"*great voice*",—Not used here as referring to the certainty of the command (Hen.), nor to his desire to restrain the angels anxious to begin (B.), but perhaps that the call might penetrate to the ends of the earth where the angels were. (Dus.) It is, however, peculiar to heavenly beings.

Ver. 3. "*hurt not the earth*", etc.,—The meaning is that they were not to hurt the earth by letting the winds loose which, as yet, they were holding in. (A. V. D. Ew. Eb. Dus. Hen. Lap.) It does not mean by restraining the winds and so allowing the earth to become parched and sultry. This last would make the cry a command to let the winds loose. (Her.)

"*we*",—i. e., the angel and his associates, who need not be further mentioned. Not necessarily the four angels assisting (Hen.), nor the Father and the Son (Ca.), although these explanations are possible.

"*the servants of our God*",—By some this is taken as Israel alone, i. e., Jewish Christians, while by others it is taken as the Israel of God, i. e., Christians in general. The expression because of the article could be taken in the latter sense. However, see explanation further on.

"*on their foreheads*",—The noblest as well as the most conspicuous part of the body.

Ver. 4. "*And I heard*",—i. e., probably from the other angel of verse 2.

"*a hundred and forty and four thousand*",—Twelve times twelve taken one thousand times, the symbol of fixedness and full completion, and perhaps not a literal number at all. Alford says, "No one that I am aware of has taken the 144,000 literally". He thinks it means a full, complete number known to the Lord and none of whom shall fail. In latter years, however, some have taken it literally, just 144,000, as Seiss for instance.

WHAT IS THE PURPOSE OF THIS SEALING?

1. Exemption from tribulation; that is, they are not to experience the impending visitations. (A. V. B. D. F. Eb. Ew. Ei. Bl. Hil. Hen. Hei. Lap. Stern.) They point to Exodus 12.7,13; Ezek. 9.4, and Rev. 9.4. Dusterdieck says in reply that in Exodus and Ezekiel it was not a sealing but a marking for the specific purpose of assuring those thus marked of the impending judgments, and that in Rev. 9.4 it is a special case of exemption from the plague from the abyss, but not because they as sealed were thus secure from all plagues. He further says the view under consideration

is against the teaching of the New Testament in general (Matt. 24.30) and against the Apocalypse in particular which admonishes to patient steadfastness to the end in the midst of trial and tribulation. Fausset says the saints are not to be thought of as exempt from all trial (see verse 14) but their trials are distinct from the destroying judgments that fall on the world, because from these they are exempt as were the Israelites from the destroying plagues of Egypt. With this Alford agrees and says Dusterdieck's trouble comes from failing to note this distinction. He says further that the four angels are commanded not to begin their work of destruction until the sealing has taken place and for what imaginable reason could such a prohibition be uttered, unless those who were to be sealed were to be marked out for some purpose connected with that work, and for what purpose could they thus be marked out if not for exemption?

2. Not *exemption from* tribulation but *preservation in* tribulation. (El. St. Dus. Sei. Gab. Sco. Pet. Weid. Moor.)

The preservation in question is a preservation from apostasy under tribulation, says Weidner. Dusterdieck remarks that, "The servants of God do not remain entirely untouched by all the sufferings whereby judgment comes upon the world, but their sealing designates the immutable firmness of their election which is not to be affected even by the trial of the last Great Tribulation." "The purpose of the seal", says Stuart, "was to make them secure against all harm."

The arguments for the first view do not seem sufficiently strong to guarantee it and we are at this juncture inclined to the second view, namely of preservation in tribulation.

WHO ARE THE SEALED?

1. **Jewish Christians only.** (F. B. G. Ei. Eb. St. Au. Zu. Dus. Gro. Bul. Ire. Hof. Blo. Hei. Gab. Sco. Pet. Sei. Tor. Mor. Bla. Weid. Moor. Burger, and all Futurists.) In proof of this it is affirmed:

(a) It does not say "Israel" nor the "children of Israel", but it does say the *"tribes"* of the children of Israel and then proceeds to mention them by name.

(b) If the elders be taken as representing the glorified Church, then they appear in Chap. 14.3 as a wholly distinct body from the 144,000.

(c) These same 144,000 in Chap. 14.4 are called the *"first-fruits unto God and the Lamb"*. But this they were anyhow if they are to be taken as the representatives of redeemed humanity, of the glorified Church, and therefore the 144,000 must be the first-fruits unto God of another order.

Weidner remarks that though Israel may elsewhere mean spiritual Israel, the Israel of God, it is not so written here.

Fausset says, "Out of the Tribes a believing remnant will be preserved from the judgments which shall destroy all the antichristian confederacy, which remnant shall faithfully resist the seductions of the Antichrist, while the rest of the nation restored to Palestine in unbelief are his dupes and at last his victims."

2. **The elect of the Lord, i. e., spiritual Israel,** the Israel of God, Christians in general. (A. D. L. V. Kl. Me. Ph. El. Hen. Wor. Kli. Gebh. Beck.)   In proof of this it is affirmed:

(a) That no good reason can be conceived why only Jewish and not Gentile Christians should be sealed.

(b) In Chap. 21.9 the Israel of God must be meant and it is an accepted rule always to interpret an ambiguous term by the use of the same term in the place or places where its meaning is clear and unmistakable.   Of course in Chaps. 2.9 and 3.9 real Jews are meant, but the circumstances there and here are different.

(c) John in the Apocalypse makes no distinction between Jewish and Gentile Christians and sometimes designates Christians as Israel and sometimes as the elect of all nations and tongues or as the elect of the earth.

(d) In verse 3 they are called absolutely the *"servant of our God"* and in Chap. 14.1 they appear as the redeemed.

(e) Those coming forth (verse 14) are not such as have been preserved in the calamities but such as were exempt from them.

(f) The 144,000 is a complete number and can hardly be Jewish believers alone but must be the Church of Christ in its final comprehensiveness.

(g) In Chap. 14 the vision of these same 144,000 follows the description of the enemies of Christ as they have reference to the whole Church and not to any one part of it; and at the same time the vision precedes the vintage of the earth which is to be as comprehensive as the whole Church of the redeemed the world over.

(h) In Chap. 14 we have the *"Father's name written on their foreheads"* and in Chap. 22 this is true of all the saints of God in the New Jerusalem.

(i) The changes made in the tribes as given argues against taking them as literal Israel.

(j) As the mark of the Beast is imprinted on all his followers so ought we expect that the seal of God should be likewise stamped on all His followers.

(k) As the plagues to come threatened all just alike, the Gentiles as well as the Jews, so should the seal in like manner protect all believers.

(l) If the Gentile Christians are not included in the 144,000 then they are nowhere spoken of as sealed at all.

(m) To the twelve reasons already enumerated for taking the 144,-000 as spiritual Israel, or Jewish and Gentile Christians combined, Hengstenberg adds yet another, namely, that it is to be argued from the fact that John takes just 12,000 out of the tribe, from the small tribes as well as from the large ones.   "It cannot be imagined", says Bossuet, "that there were precisely in each tribe twelve thousand elect, neither more nor less, to make up this total number of 144,000."

Dusterdieck replies in answer to

(a) that even though the sealing be referred only to Jewish believers, even so it shows that the Gentile Christians in the innumerable throng were not inferior in that which the sealing really meant;

(b) that Israel as used of the inhabitants of heaven is something different from when it is used of people who are still upon the earth, as is undoubtedly the case here, and though Israel may elsewhere mean the Israel of God, Christians in general, it is not so stated *here*;

(c) that this is not the case, and it can only be referred to Jewish Christians here because the individual tribes of Israel are mentioned by name directly afterwards;

(d) that the designation of *"the servants of our God"* and *"the redeemed"* suit Israel, Jewish Christians, pre-eminently;

(e) that this rests upon a false conception that exemption from instead of preservation in is meant, and upon the unjustifiable transformation of the present *"come"* into a past tense, and the confused conception of verse 14 in general.

It might further be said in reply to

(f) that the 144,000 as a complete number can apply to a complete and well rounded number of Jewish Christians as well as to the same idea with reference to Jewish and Gentile Christians;

(g) that while this is true it, by no means, furnishes any conclusive proof that the 144,000 thus mentioned in Chap. 14 cannot refer to Jewish Christians alone;

(h) that the Father's name as written on the 144,000 in Chap. 14 and on all the saints of God in Chap. 22 is the indication of their regeneration and has nothing to do with the seal mentioned in this seventh chapter. The Father's name on their forehead is merely the indication that they are children of God and is the foundation upon which the sealing takes place. The sealing came later and they could not have been sealed had they not prior to the sealing been born again and thus become the children of God bearing the Father's name;

(i) that this argument is not at all conclusive;

(j) that this is an inference which is in some considerable measure gratuitous;

(k) that while this would seem to be a natural conclusion it does not, however, dispose of the fact that in God's mind there may have been sufficient reason for applying the seal to Jewish Christians only as a part of His dispensational plan for His own peculiar people;

(l) that while this is true the Gentile Christians, who are at least included in the throng mentioned in verse 9 and who are before the throne, etc., received everything which the seal could have possibly meant to the Jewish Christians. The fact that they are before the throne, etc., proves this, it would seem.

While the arguments for taking the "sealed" as spiritual Israel are not altogether conclusive, and some of them are of little if any value at all, we find it very hard to get away from arguments such as those given under (a) and especially under (b), to the last of which the reply of Dusterdieck is not at all satisfactory, and we find ourselves inclined toward the view which takes them as spiritual Israel, i. e., both Jewish and Gentile Christians, although even in the moment of this decision we find ourselves wondering whether after all the reference may not be to Jewish believers only, as the naming of the tribes would seem to indicate.

It must not be overlooked that the tribes are also mentioned by name in Chap. 21.12, not indeed so written in this book of Revelation but so written upon the gates of the City of God.

It may also be said that the decision of this matter one way or the other does not bring us into conflict with any other part of the Revelation, and is therefore not a matter of vital importance.

WHEN DOES THIS SEALING TAKE PLACE?

1. The Consecutive Historical School refers the saints in question to the converts of the faith, Jewish and Gentile, succeeding the age of Constantine (El.); others refer them to the Albigenses and the Waldensians; others to the Reformation period, and some to the times after the fall of Bonaparte in 1815. Elliott says that the four destroying tempest-angels are the "threatening tempest of barbarians" destined ere while to desolate the Roman earth, while the sealing was represented as a preservative. He identifies the 144,000 with the innumerable throng of the second vision in verse 9, and says this second vision of their ultimate blessedness is given by way of encouragement. "The sealing," he says, "appertains chronologically to the times following on the politico-religious revolution under Constantine and his immediate successors in the fourth century, and the twelve tribes of Israel, and the 144,000 mentioned in them, designate respectively the visible professing Church in the Roman empire, and Christ's true Church, the election of grace, gathered out of it."

2. The Synchronous Historical School refers the saints in question to the elect of the Lord who shall be living upon the earth at the time of the Second Coming of the Lord and so place the time of this sealing before the Rapture of the Church, and thus cause the Church, the saints of the latter days to go through the Great Tribulation.

3. The Futurists, as a rule, place this sealing right after the Rapture of the Church and usually refer it to what is known as the Remnant, i. e., Jewish believers only.

    Placing the sealing after the Rapture does not, however, militate against the view which takes the sealed ones as spiritual Israel, inasmuch as there would be as many Gentiles as Jews who would believe at a time like that.

    Moorehead says, "The time of the sealing belongs almost certainly to a point before the Tribulation begins, for these believing Jews are no doubt the fruit of the testimony of the Two Witnesses, and if so, their sealing belongs to the time of the four riders." In this, however, our author seems confused, since he puts the four riders before the opening of the Seventieth Week, and the preaching of the Two Witnesses during the first half of it.

4. The Spiritual School of Interpretation refers the sealing to that which is going on among the redeemed all the time while the Church is on the earth. But this is a sealing of the Holy Spirit that comes immediately at regeneration in the forgiveness of sins (Eph. 1.13 and 4.30), while the sealing mentioned here is for the particular purpose of protection.

5. The Preterists refer the passage to the Jewish Christians who escaped to Pella at the time of the Destruction of Jerusalem, and the same reference is given to verses 15 and 17.

We think it better not to take this vision as belonging to the latter part of Seal Six, as Elliott does, but to take it rather as a parenthetical section, and refer the sealing in question to something still in the future, for whatever else one may be inclined to say in favor of Elliott's general scheme of interpretation, his treatment of the two visions of this chapter is not at all necessary to its consistency. But whether this sealing is to be placed before or after the Rapture of the Church must wait on further exegesis.

THE NAMING OF THE TRIBES.

1. It does not follow any assignable principle.

2. Each tribe is given the same number. In the divine gifts of grace all have like share.

3. The tribe of Dan is omitted. This is because:

   (a) The Antichrist is to come from this tribe, say nearly all ancient expositors (Gen. 49.17).

   (b) It was the first tribe to fall into idolatry. (V. Wet. Hen. Wor. and most expositors.) (Jud. 18.)

   (c) It had long before been as good as extinct. (D. A. Ew. Eb. Gro. Dus.) (I Chron. 4.)

4. Joseph is mentioned instead of Ephraim because of idolatrous recollections concerning Ephraim (L. Dus.), or perhaps because by Joseph, Ephraim is meant. (A.)

5. Levi is included. "Since the Levitical ceremonies have been abandoned Levi is found again on equal footing with his brethren. All are priests; all have access, not one through the other, but one with the other." (B. Dus. Mil.) But this is hardly a sufficient reason since in some of the Old Testament catalogues Levi was not omitted.

9 After these things I saw, and behold, a great multitude, which no man could number, out of every nation and of all tribes and peoples and tongues, standing before the throne and before the Lamb, arrayed in white robes, and palms in their hands; 10 and they cry with a great voice, saying,

Salvation unto our God who sitteth on the throne, and unto the Lamb.

11 And all the angels were standing round about the throne, and about the elders and the four living creatures; and they fell before the throne on their faces, and worshipped God, 12 saying,

Amen: [1]Blessing, and glory, and wisdom, and thanksgiving, and honor, and power, and might, be

[1]Gr. The blessing and the glory

585

unto our God [2]for ever and ever. Amen.
13 And one of the elders answered, saying unto me, These that are arrayed in the white robes, who are they, and whence came they? 14 And I [3]say unto him, My lord, thou knowest. And he said to me, These are they that come out of the great tribulation, and they washed their robes, and made them white in the blood of the Lamb. 15 Therefore are they before the throne

[2]Gr. *unto the ages of the ages*
[3]Gr. *have said*

of God; and they serve him day and night in his [4]temple: and he that sitteth on the throne shall spread his tabernacle over them. 16 They shall hunger no more, neither thirst any more; neither shall the sun strike upon them, nor any heat; 17 for the Lamb that is in the midst [5]of the throne shall be their shepherd, and shall guide them unto fountains of waters of life: and God shall wipe away every tear from their eyes.

[4]Or, *sanctuary*
[5]Or, *before.* See Chap. 4.6; comp 5.6

Vers. 9-17. The Saints of the Great Tribulation.

Ver. 9. *"After these things",*—This is doubtless another distinct vision. (A. Dus. Crav.)

"before the throne and before the Lamb",—They were in heaven itself as described in Chap. 4. Gaebelein says that this is an earth-scene at the beginning of the Millennium, a millennial scene. But this will not do. It is the same throne surrounded by the same elders, the same living creatures and the same angels as in Chap. 4 and it will not do to shift this scene from heaven to earth for the convenience of any preconceived plan as to how the arrangements of those times should seem to be.

"arrayed in white robes",—Significant of their victory and also emblematic of their righteousness. (Chap. 6.11.)

"palms in their hands",—The mark of festal joy.

Ver. 10. *"salvation unto our God",*—i. e., their salvation; the praise for it.

Ver. 13. *"one of the elders answered",*—i. e., to John's thoughts asking, as it were, the question which might have been expected to arise in John's mind. (F. B. Hen.) An elder from among the representatives of redeemed humanity is a fitting interpreter of the scene.

Ver. 14. *"My Lord",*—An address of deep reverence.

"thou knowest",—i. e., I do not know, but thou dost. (A. F. B. D. Ew. Hen. Dus.)

"They that come",—Not "came" (A. V.), nor "shall come" (Dus. Hen.), as though the multitude was still on the earth, nor "coming" (L.), as if the number was not yet completed, but *"come",* implying that they have just come. (A. B. D. Ew.)

"out of the great tribulation",—The literal rendering is, "the tribulation, the great one," and it must therefore refer to the Great Tribulation announced in Matthew 24.21, just before the coming of Christ in judgment and which, it seems, the Seventh Seal is to introduce. (D. Ew. Eb. Hen. Dus.)

"The Great Tribulation," says Scofield, "is the period of unexampled trouble predicted in the passages cited under that head from Psalm 2.5 to Rev. 7.14 and described in Rev. 11-18. Involving in a measure the whole earth (Rev. 3.10), it is yet distinctively 'the time of Jacob's trouble' (Jer. 33.7), and its vortex is Jerusalem and the Holy Land. It involves the people of God who will have returned to Palestine in unbelief. Its duration is three and one-half years, or the last half of the Seventieth Week of Daniel."

"washed their robes and made them white",—There is no reference here to the blood of martyrs as if there was a cleansing power in martyrdom. The robes are made white by the washing, and it is not that the washing refers to forgiveness, and the making white to sanctification, as Hengstenberg says. It was through their faith in Christ that their robes were washed and made white.

Ver. 15. *"and they serve him"*,—i. e., doing whatever high and blessed service He may delight to employ them in.

"day and night",—The meaning is "eternally" and the manner of speaking is after our custom.

"spread his tabernacle over them",—The literal is, "shall tabernacle upon them," an expression hard to represent in our language. No more as in an earthly covering by pillars of smoke and fire, but as Dusterdieck says, "in the heavenly immediateness". His dwelling among them is secondary to the thought of His being their covert. The glory of Shekinah or the over-shadowing presence of God is now to sink down from the throne upon the blessed and spread itself out protectingly over them.

Ver. 16. *"hunger no more neither thirst anymore"*,—i. e., as they did when here.

"neither shall the sun strike upon them",—The thought relates itself to the hot oriental sun in its overpowering effects.

"nor any heat",—Heat that is intense like that of the sirocco. (See Isa. 49.10 from which the whole sentence is taken.)

Ver. 17. *"in the midst of the throne"*,—i. e., in the middle point in front of the throne.

"It is not", says Dusterdieck, "without many tears that they come out of the Great Tribulation, but when they have overcome, God Himself shall dry their tears and change their weeping into joy."

OF WHOM IS THIS INNUMERABLE THRONG COMPOSED AND WHAT RELATION DO THEY BEAR TO THE 144,000?

They are not identical, as some would have us believe, because:

1. The first are numerable and the second are innumerable.
2. The first are sealed and of the second this is not said.
3. The first are on earth and the second are in heaven.

There are many views as to the relationship between these two groups of believers, but perhaps those deserving the most attention are the following:

1. The first are Jewish Christians immediately after the Rapture and the second are Gentile Christians on earth before the Millennial throne (Gab.), or in glory as most of the Futurists believe. (Mor. Tor. Sco. Pet. Bla. Sei. Moor.)

The remarks of G. Campbell Morgan, one of the prominent Futurists of our day, will be of interest just here. He says, "The passage refers to the great company of those who come, not through trials such as yours and mine, but, by God's grace, out of *the* Great Tribulation which follows the taking away of the Church and the revealing of the man of sin. How is this ingathering to be accomplished? I give you my answer with reserve, because many devout students of prophetic truth differ with me here. Personally, I am convinced that not all Christian people will be taken to be with Christ on His return, but only those who by the attitude of their lives are ready for His appearing. They who remain and pass through the Tribulation will be awakened by the stupendous events of their times to the privilege and responsibility of witnessing for the truth in that age. Even in the day of Jewish sorrow God will dwell with His ancient people, who will then become heralds of the Cross; and under stress of plague, famine and suffering beyond imagination, an innumerable multitude will 'wash their robes and make them white in the blood of the Lamb.' Those years will be such as the world has never seen—first, in regard to the manifestation of evil in forms more awful than we have ever known; and, secondly, in the marvelous crowding to Jesus Christ of a 'great multitude which no man can number.' What of the Church during that time of Tribulation? She is in the heavens with her Lord, all the retarding forces and probationary days of earth being ended."

Scofield, another of the Futurists, says, "The Great Tribulation will be, however, a period of salvation. An election out of Israel is seen as sealed for God (Rev. 7.4-8), and, with an innumerable multitude of Gentiles (Rev. 7.9), are said to have come *'out of the great tribulation'* (Rev. 7.14). They are not of the priesthood, the Church, to which they seem to stand somewhat in the relation of the Levites to the priests under the Mosaic Covenant. The Great Tribulation is immediately followed by the return of Christ in glory."

2. The first are Jewish Christians and the second are Jewish and Gentile Christians, the second being inclusive of the first. (B. F. St. Zu. Ei. Dus. Bul. Hof. Gro. Hei. Weid.)

3. The first are Jewish and Gentile Christians and the second are the same in larger numbers with Gentiles preponderating. (A.)

In keeping with former explanations we are inclined to this last view, although we cannot agree with Alford as to whom this second and innumerable group represents. He says it is the great final assembly of saints in heaven after the last resurrection and after the final judgment of the Great White Throne, which judgment, he says, is that mentioned in Matt. 25.31-46, the scene here being that of all the assembled believers in final gathering in heaven.

This cannot be, because it is said that they come out of the Tribulation, the great one, and this cannot be said of all the finally assembled believers in heaven. It cannot be said of those who are saved during the Millennium and it cannot be said of the millions who will have died before the Great Tribulation. This being the case, the throng, although innumerable, represents but a part, and a small part, of the sum total of glorified believers who are finally to be assembled in heavenly glory. This innumerable throng must therefore represent a scene in final glory of those who pass through the Great Tribulation, and no reference is made to the far greater number who are likewise to be assembled there with them. Fausset and Lange say the expression, *"the great tribulation,"* includes retrospectively all the tribulations of which the saints of all ages have had to pass through. With this Alford agrees, but how Alford can arrive at such a conclusion after having himself called attention to the original reading of the expression, *"the tribulation, the great one,"* is a difficult thing to see. We believe a fair exegesis will compel one to take the expression at its face value and to see in the innumerable throng, as already stated, those who come out of the Great Tribulation which our Lord foretold should come upon the earth *during the last days.*

CHAPTER EIGHT

1 And when he opened the seventh seal, there followed a silence in heaven about the space of half an hour. 2 And I saw the seven angels that stand before God; and there were given unto them seven trumpets.

3 And another angel came and stood [1]over the altar, having a golden censer; and there was given unto him much incense, that he should [2]add it unto the prayers of all the saints upon the golden altar which was before the throne.

[1]Or, *at*
[2]Gr. *give*

4 And the smoke of the incense, [3]with the prayers of the saints, went up before God out of the angel's hand. 5 And the angel [4]taketh the censer; and he filled it with the fire of the altar, and cast it [5]upon the earth: and there followed thunders, and voices, and lightnings, and an earthquake.

6 And the seven angels that had the seven trumpets prepared themselves to sound.

[3]Or, *for*
[4]Gr. *hath taken*
[5]Or, *into*

THE SEVENTH SEAL.

Ver. 1. *"he opened the seventh seal"*,—

Of what does the Seventh Seal consist?

1. Some make it to consist of the silence alone. (A. V. Hen.) But certainly this will not do. After what took place in connection with the other seals something in the way of a fullness of significant content is to be expected in the Seventh Seal.

2. Others refer it to the silence and to all that follows up to and through verse 5. (Gab. Braun.) But this will hardly do, because in verse 2 the trumpet angels have already entered, and verses 2 and 5 are a preparation for the following trumpets.

3. Others make it inclusive of all that follows, the silence, the offering of the incense and the casting of the coals upon the earth, the sounding of the seven trumpets and the emptying of the seven vials. This view, which is supported by many authorities (B. D. F. Eb. Ew. Ar. Ca. El. Dus. And. Are. Bul. Crav. Weid. Stern) more strongly appeals to us, and a careful reading of the text seems to confirm this conclusion.

"a silence in heaven",—

What does this silence mean?

It refers doubtless to the anxious expectation of the heavenly inhabitants awaiting the contents of the Seventh Seal. (B. D. F. Eb. Ew. Ar. Ca. St. Dus. Are. Hei. Crav. Weid. Stern.)

"Indicative of the solemn things which are now to come," (Gab.)

"The deep and fearful sympathy with the expected sequel." (St.)

"The heavenly company's silence of astonishment and fear at what was about to happen." (Hei.)

"Expressing the solemnity of the crisis which has now arrived." (Weid.)

"The earnest, adoring expectation with which the blessed spirits and angels await the succeeding unfolding of God's judgments." (F.)

Other explanations are:

1. Some, who think the Book consists of a triple series of visions chronologically parallel with each other and each reaching on to the consummation, explain the silence as the thousand years of rest before the final period of eternity. (V. L. Tichonius.)
Elliott contends that this had been depicted before in the palm-bearing vision of the Sixth Seal of Chap. 7, and furthermore that a Millennium of joyous, active rest could hardly be prefigured by a single half hour of silence in heaven.

2. Others, who likewise think of the visions as chronologically parallel, explain the silence simply as a pause in the heavenly representations indicative of a break of separation between the two parallel series of prophecies. Thus Bullinger and Aretius explain it as a mark of transition from the Seals to the Trumpets. Elliott thinks in this case the silence ought to have occurred *before* and not *after* the opening of the Seventh Seal, and that furthermore, in this case there ought to have been a similar pause between the second and third series.

3. Others who regard the contents of the visions as chronologically consecutive, think the silence prefigures the Church's silence in prayer before the First Trumpet's sounding during the incense offered by the angel priest, even as the Jews were wont to pray silently in the court without, while the priest went within the temple to offer incense (Luke 1.10). (Me. Dau. New.)
But the silence is here depicted as beginning *before* the action of the angel-priest.

4. The peace and Sabbath-rest of the Church in some brief interval between Antichrist's destruction and the second coming of Christ. (Be. Hof. Chri.)

5. The silencing of Christ's enemies. (Hen.) But how can we think of enemies of Christ *in heaven!*

6. Alford thinks the reference is to the beginning of the eternal rest in heaven and that it imports silence as to what the roll contains so far as John is concerned, i. e., the withholding of that which the Seventh Seal revealed. This author thus places the opening of this Seal in heaven after the Millennium and at the time eternity begins. He says, "The Day of the Lord's coming is gone by and this vision reaches far beyond it into the blissful eternity, because then, and not till then, shall the Seventh Seal, which looses the roll of God's eternal, be opened and the book read to the adoring Church in glory."

7. Elliott, in keeping with his scheme of interpretation representing the tempest-angels as the symbols of barbarian invading hosts, says the silence refers to stillness from storm in the firmamental heaven, the four winds being authoritatively restrained from blowing, and the expression is to be taken as indicative of the brief interval

between the opening of the Seventh Seal and the first outbreak of the tempest of barbarian invasion, the matter affecting John as the half hour's stillness before a storm might do in common life.

Ver. 2. *"I saw"*,—i. e., not at the end of the silence (A. Eb.), but during the silence (L. Dus.), which lasted doubtless until verse 5.

"the seven angels",—Not the archangels (D. Stern), nor the seven spirits of God, Chap. 4.4 (Eu. Are.), nor seven angels selected from a greater number on account of the seven trumpets (L. Eb. He.), but seven particular angels as the definite article shows.

Ver. 3. *"another angel"*,—Not Christ (V. Se. El. Ca. Be. Gab. Boe. Sco.), nor the Holy Spirit, both of which views are adopted in deference to theological propriety; but an angel, a real angel; and not an angel symbolical of Christ (A. Hen. Dus.), which latter view leads those who hold it to resort to all sorts of arbitrary expedients in the interpretation of what follows. No countenance is given by the above view to angelic intercession. He is merely offering incense to mix with the prayers of the saints and is serving only as a ministering spirit. Christ is the One through whom the prayers are offered. "The angel does not," says Fausset, "provide the incense; it is given to him by Christ, whose meritorious obedience and death are the incense, rendering the prayers of the saints well-pleasing to God."

"over the altar",—He so presents himself to John's view that he rises above the altar, the altar being between the angel and John.

"altar",—This is not the altar of incense (D. Eb. Gro. Hen.) but the altar of burnt-offering.

Ebrard says the first altar is the altar of burnt-offering and the second one is the altar of incense, but this is a precipitate inference and uncalled for inasmuch as a more definite description of this altar is given in the last part of the verse, because the employment at the altar is there spoken of. It is the same altar as in Chap. 6.9. There is nothing said in Leviticus 16 of an altar of incense and therefore appeal to that passage is not legitimate.

"add it unto the prayers",—So perfecting and making the prayers efficacious as a sweet-smelling savor to God. (A. L. V. F. Ca. Dus.)

"all the saints",—If the general scheme of interpretation presented by the Consecutive Historical school of interpretation is to be accepted, it is best to see with Elliott here a reference to the saints immediately after the time of Constantine who were on earth during the years immediately following A. D. 395, saints, by the way, whom Elliott conceives to be represented by the 144,000 sealed ones and later by those of the palm-bearing vision.

Alford and others, on the other hand, interpret these saints as those of the whole Church of God as well as those of Chap. 6.9. But this is hardly in keeping with the context, and besides the prayers of the martyrs of the Church were not for vengeance, but the rather as Stephen cried, "Lord, lay not this sin to their charge."

If, therefore, we are to interpret this Seventh Seal as occurring in connection with the second coming of the Lord, it seems better to find here a more special reference to the prayers of the saints who must pass through the Great Tribulation now about to be disclosed and which takes place either just before the coming of the Lord, or as others (Gab. Sco. Pet. Mor. Tor. Weid.) think, just after it, this view being confirmed by the fact that the answer to the prayers of these saints is seen to bring severe judgments upon the earth.

Ver. 4. Weidner aptly says, "The whole imagery suggests that the saints' prayers on earth and the angel's incensing in heaven are simultaneous and that God will graciously hear the prayers of His saints during the great trials which come upon the earth by means of the judgments disclosed by the trumpets about to be blown."

Ver. 5. *"take the censer"*,—i. e., after having shaken from it the incense, and laid it down perhaps.

"cast it upon the earth",—i. e., the fire, to signify that the answer to the prayers was about to descend in the fire of God's vengeance upon the ungodly of the earth (F. A. B. D. Ew. Lap. Dus. Hen.), and not, as Barnes says, "to show that notwithstanding the prayers that would be offered the judgments would come anyhow," nor, as Lange says, "the fire was the fire of saving grace by which the earth is rendered capable of bearing the judgments which follow".

"thunders, and voices, and lightnings and an earthquake",—Symbolic precursors of the divine judgments about to be inflicted.

7 And the first sounded, and there followed hail and fire, mingled with blood, and they were cast [1]upon the earth; and the third part of the earth was burnt up, and the third part of the trees was burnt up, and all green grass was burnt up.

[1]Or, *into*

Ver. 7. THE FIRST TRUMPET JUDGMENT.

Elliott of the Consecutive Historical School says the first four Trumpet judgments were poured out upon the Roman earth, and that they depict the destruction through a series of tempests (barbarian devastations) successively affecting the third part of the Roman earth, sea, rivers and luminaries or Roman rulers. The judgments of these Trumpets, he takes with most English expositors, as the ravages of the Goths in the fifth century which ended in the overthrow of the Western part of the Roman Empire. The sun and other heavenly luminaries, he says, are well-known symbols of earthly rulers.

Many of the Contemporaneous Historical School contend that the prophecy begins again with the First Trumpet and recapitulates, the First Trumpet running parallel with the First Seal, and so on. (V. L. Eb. Be.) "Now he recapitulates," says Bede, "from the beginning in order to say the same thing in another way."

Alford, however, of this same school, says that the vision of the Trumpets takes up the great world-wide vision of the Seals at the point where it was said to the vengeance-invoking martyrs that they should rest awhile, and that the judgments of the Trumpets vision occur during the time of that waiting.

Weidner of the Futurists says the Trumpet judgments are a recapitulation not so much of the six seals as of the Sixth Seal, disclosing more fully the terrors that are to come upon the earth in connection with the destruction of the Antichrist. Gaebelein of the same school says, "The first five seals would seem to constitute what Matt. 24.8 calls the *'beginning of sorrows'*, while the Trumpet judgments would seem the rather to introduce the Great Tribulation proper during the years immediately preceding the coming of the Christ to destroy the Antichrist." This author is evidently right as to the Trumpet judgments. (Moor.)

The Preterists refer all these Trumpet judgments, of course, to the Jewish-Roman war and events preceding the Destruction of Jerusalem.

Our attention is called by most exegetes to the fact that the first four trumpets affect natural objects chiefly, while the last three, the woe trumpets, are expressly said to be inflicted upon men. The language of these judgments seems to be largely reproduced from the description of the plagues of Egypt.

"hail and fire mingled with blood",—The *"blood"* here Elliott refers to the destruction of life in connection with the Gothic invasions, while the literalists, who look for the fulfillment as still in the future, think of the hail-stones and balls of fire falling in a shower of blood as in a shower of rain.

"the third part",—This Elliott refers to the Western division of the Roman empire, one of its three divisions according to the tripartition in A. D. 311. Mede thinks it refers to the whole Roman earth as constituting about one-third of the known world at the time of the Evangelist. Thus also Daubuz and Bishop Newton, while Alford, who shares here very largely the views of the literalists, remarks with some force that a comparison with Chaps. 6.8 and 11.15 shows the idea of amount and not fractional division in strictness as being uppermost in the thought. "The idea seems therefore," he says, "to be that though the judgment is to be fearful in extent, yet God spares more than He smites, two-thirds escaping in each case while only one-third is smitten."

Gaebelein refers *"the third part"*, repeatedly mentioned in these Trumpet judgments, to the revived Roman Empire, though he gives no good reason for this opinion.

The plague seems quite similar to that in Ex. 9.24. Weidner seems wisely to say, "Why attempt to explain away the plain significance of this trumpet judgment? If the ten plagues of Egypt were historical and were visited upon the enemies of God's people, why may we not expect a repetition of these judgments in the days of the Antichrist? And although we may not fully understand what special form these judgments may assume, their reality, the certainty of their coming and their terribleness are here clearly disclosed."

The Allegorists are quite as confused in their attempt at satisfactory explanation. By *"the third part"* they say that simply a large part is meant; by the *"trees"*, the great ones of the earth are meant, the eminent Jews; and by the *"green grass"* is meant the ordinary Jews. Stern refers this judgment to the persecution of the Church by false heathen doctrines. *"Hail and fire"* are referred to erroneous doctrines cast by Satan upon the earth, the *"trees"* being the teachers of godliness and the *"grass"* the ordinary Christians. (Ar. Ze.) Ebrard refers the whole to spiritual famine. Even Gaebelein passes, at this place, over into the Allegorical School and makes the green things symbols of agriculture and commercial prosperity; man's boasted prosperity ending in great calamity.

Dusterdieck quite aptly remarks here, "To explain allegorically is an undertaking, there being no ground for it in the text, that can lead to nothing but arbitrary guess-work."

Lange on the other hand says, "By sticking to the letter of the text we arrive at the conclusion that one-third of the earth and one-third of the trees and all the grass is burned up. All the abortive interpretations in the world cannot make us abandon our conviction that the Apocalypse has an allegorical meaning."

8 And the second angel sounded, and as it were a great mountain burning with fire was cast into the sea: and the third part of the sea became blood; 9 and there died the third part of the creatures which were in the sea, even they that had life; and the third part of the ships was destroyed.

Vers. 8,9. THE SECOND TRUMPET JUDGMENT.

Just as Elliott of the Consecutive Historical School interpreted the First Trumpet as the Gothic invasion under Alaric, embracing chiefly some dozen years from about A. D. 400 to A. D. 410, so he interprets the Second Trumpet as the second Gothic invasion under Genseric in A. D. 429 in which upper Africa and the western part of the Mediterranean were devastated, the creatures of the sea which had life, being the islands of Sicily and Sardinia, and the ships destroyed being those of the Romans in the harbors around Carthagena, the blood referring, as under the First Trumpet, to the loss of life.

Perhaps as good an allegorical explanation as can be conjectured is that of Gaebelein of the Futurist School, who says, "The sea here is typical of nations; some kingdom internally on fire, signifying probable revolution, will be precipitated into the restless sea of nations and the result will be a still greater destruction of life and of commerce which is represented by the ships."

Others after all think it better to accept the plain signification of the text as describing a great pestilence, the reference being to a burning mass so large as to look like a mountain (*"and as it were"*), or perhaps a meteor falling into the sea and causing putrescence and the destruction of many ships of commerce. (See Ex. 7.20,21.)

The judgments of these plagues are apparently those which in Chap. 7.3 were held back until the sealing took place, and must consequently, many think, be in very close conjunction with the coming of the Lord to destroy the Antichrist.

10 And the third angel sounded, and there fell from heaven a great star, burning as a torch, and it fell upon the third part of the rivers, and upon the fountains of the waters; 11 and the name of the star is called Wormwood: and the third part of the waters became wormwood; and many men died of the waters, because they were made bitter.

Vers. 10,11. THE THIRD TRUMPET JUDGMENT.

Ver. 10. *"there fell from heaven a great star"*,—This star in falling scattered its sparks and fell upon a third part of the fresh waters of the earth.

Ver. 11.   The star is called in Greek "absinthe," i. e., "*wormwood*," because it made the waters bitter and many who drank died from the effects of the poisonous bitterness.

This Third Trumpet is referred by most of the Consecutive Historical School to the third stage of the Gothic irruption, the "great star" being Atilla, "the scourge of God," who also ravaged the Western or third part of the Roman Empire during the years around A. D. 450.

Among the Futurists, Weidner says, "There shall come a time when as a divine punishment men will drink again of '*the waters of Marah*' (Ex. 15.23-25) for which there is no healing, and in many cases death shall result as in the days of Elisha (II Kings 2.19-21)", while Gaebelein, of the same school, joins with the Allegorists, and refers it to some apostate and thinks it may refer to the Antichrist himself.

By Lyra it is referred to Pelagius, by Luther to Origen, by Bengel and Vitringa to Arius and by Laurentius to Gregory the Great; all of which show how really arbitrary this method of interpretation really is and how hopeless is the task of ever trying to solve the problem from their standpoint.

Petingill says the star symbolizes Satan, whose fall from heaven is described in detail in Chap. 12.

12 And the fourth angel sounded, and the third part of the sun was smitten, and the third part of the moon, and the third part of the stars; that the third part of them should be darkened, and the day should not shine for the third part of it, and the night in like manner.

13 And I saw, and I heard [1]an eagle, flying in mid heaven, saying with a great voice, Woe, woe, woe, for them that dwell on the earth, by reason of the other voices of the trumpet of the three angels, who are yet to sound.

[1]Gr. *one eagle*

Vers. 12,13.   THE FOURTH TRUMPET JUDGMENT.

Ver. 12.   This plague is in many respects the same in character as that in Ex. 10.21. "The absence of any instrument in this fourth vision," says Alford, "teaches us not to place too much import upon the instruments by which the previous judgments are brought about."

Elliott of the Consecutive Historical School says that the reference of this Fourth Trumpet is to the overthrow of the Emperor and rulers in general of the Western division of the Roman Empire, the name and office being abolished by Odoacer, the leader of the fourth stage of the Gothic devastation about the year A. D. 476.

Others of the Contemporaneous or Synchronous Historical School think it quite evident that this judgment runs parallel with the Sixth Seal. while Gaebelein of the Futurist School says, "The sun is the symbol of the highest authority, the moon of derived authority and the stars of subordinate authority, and the symbolical meaning of this trumpet judgment is that all authority within the revived Roman Empire will be smitten by the hand from above and as a result the most awful moral darkness will ensue."

The Allegorical interpreters are guilty here, even as Lange admits, of the most aimless and arbitrary play of interpretation, i. e., the troubling of the Church by false brethren (Be.); heresy (Ly.); Islam (Stern): political disorders (Wet. Her.).

"the third part of it",—Alford and Dusterdieck think the limitation is manifestly to time, while Fausset and others (B. L. Kl. Zu.) think it is to brightness, while the reference to the *"night"* is to the night, Alford thinks, insofar as she is by virtue of the moon and the stars a time of light. We have already seen that Elliott refers all this to the rulers of the third part of the Roman Empire, the Western section of it.

Ver. 13. *"an eagle"*,—Not an eagle in the form of an angel (D. Ei. Ew. Bl. Stern), but an eagle; and that not in antithesis to the dove (Hen., referring to John 1.36), nor as a bird of omen (Ew.), but far more probably, "the symbol of judgment and vengeance rushing to its prey" (A.). Nor is it to be identified with the eagles of Matt. 24.28, which is a mere proverbial saying rather than a prophetic one.

"in mid heaven",—i. e., where the sun at noon-time reaches the meridian and where the eagle could be seen and heard of all to whom its message pertains.

"that dwell on the earth",—i. e., as in Chap. 6.10, the ungodly men of the world.

The Preterists, of course, see in the eagle the eagle of the Roman legions.

Allegorically the eagle is the voice of eminent teachers in the Church (Be.); some prophet to be expected at the end of the world (Lap.); Gregory the Great protesting against the title "Universal Bishop" (E. Jo.); a special messenger, probably Christ Himself (Wor.). Weidner remarks, "Is it any wonder that men regard the Apocalypse as an enigma with such interpretations as guides."

CHAPTER NINE

1 And the fifth angel sounded and I saw a star from heaven fallen unto the earth: and there was given unto him the key of the pit of the abyss. 2 And he opened the pit of the abyss; and there went up a smoke out of the pit, as the smoke of a great furnace; and the sun and the air were darkened by reason of the smoke of the pit. 3 And out of the smoke came forth locusts upon the earth; and power was given them, as the scorpions of the earth have power. 4 And it was said unto them that they should not hurt the grass of the earth, neither any green thing, neither any tree, but only such men as have not the seal of God on their foreheads. 5 And it was given them that they should not kill them, but that they should be tormented five months: and their torment was as the torment of a scorpion, when it striketh a man. 6 And in those days men shall seek death, and shall in no wise find it; and they shall desire to die, and death fleeth from them. 7 And the [1]shapes of the locusts were like unto horses prepared for war; and upon their heads as it were crowns like unto gold, and their faces were as men's faces. 8 And they had hair as the hair of women, and their teeth were as *the teeth* of lions. 9 And they had breastplates, as it were breastplates of iron; and the sound of their wings was as the sound of chariots, of many horses rushing to war. 10 And they have tails like unto scorpions, and stings; and in their tails is their power to hurt men five months. 11 They have over them as king the angel of the abyss: his name in Hebrew is Abaddon, and in the Greek *tongue* he hath the name [2]Apollyon.

12 The first Woe is past: behold, there come yet two Woes hereafter.

[1]Gr. *likenesses*
[2]That is, *Destroyer*

Vers. 1-12. THE FIFTH TRUMPET JUDGMENT AND THE FIRST WOE.

Ver. 1. *"a star from heaven"*,—Not a good angel (B. D. Bl.

And.), for his description and his work refute this, but an evil angel (V. Dus. Weid. Todd); doubtless Satan himself according to the analogy of Isa. 14.12; Luke 10.18. (A. El. Me. Vol. Gab. Pet. Dau. New.)

"fallen unto the earth",—It had already fallen when John saw it.

"the pit of the abyss",—The present abode of the Devil and his angels, as distinct from Gehenna, the lake of fire and brimstone (Rev. 20.10) which is to be their abode after the final judgment.

Ver. 2. *"And he opened the pit of the abyss"*,—To John in vision it appeared as if this abyss was under the earth, having a shaft after the manner of a well leading to it, says Weidner, and this well or pit was shut down by a cover and locked.

Ver. 3. *"And out of the smoke came forth locusts"*,—It was not an apparent mass of smoke which proved to be locusts (V. Ei. Zu. Eb.), but the locusts ascended under cover of the smoke. (Ew. Dus.)

These infernal locusts differed from earthly ones in that God gave them power to sting like scorpions, thus being able to hurt men, while this is not true of earthly locusts.

Ver. 4. *"grass...green thing...tree"*,—i. e., the usual objects on which locusts prey.

"such men as have not the seal of God",—This fixes the time of this Fifth Trumpet after the sealing of Chap. 7. Gaebelein and others who refer the sealed ones of Chap. 7 to Jewish believers only, the Remnant, maintain that these unsealed ones upon whom the judgment falls must be unbelieving Israel. But of this there is no hint in the text. The plague shall fall upon all alike, whether Jews or Gentiles, if they have not the seal of God on their forehead. Others say of this plague, that the saints are not partakers. (F. Weid.) But they must be unless we include them among those who are sealed, and think of the 144,000 as spiritual Israel, which interpretation neither of the authorities just quoted accept and we cannot see therefore how they can consistently maintain their position.

Ver. 5. *"not kill them"*,—i. e., the ungodly, the unsealed.

"five months",—The ordinary time during the year in which locusts continue their ravages. (A. F. D. Ew. Ei. Ca. Dus.)

"their torment",—i. e., the torment of the sufferers (A. F.), and not of the locusts (Dus.), it being the objective and not the subjective.

Ver. 6. *"seek death . . . desire to die"*,—i. e., because of the excruciating pain of these tormenting locusts. The word really means to "vehemently desire."

Ver. 7. *"like unto horses"*,—This resemblance has often been noted by travelers and is especially true when the horse is equipped for war.

"crowns like unto gold",—Dusterdieck refers this to the ragged elevation in the middle of the thorax, while Ewald refers it to the antennae; but perhaps the best explanation is that of Alford, who says it refers to "the crown-shaped fillet of the locust's head resembling gold in material

just as the wings of some of the beetle tribe might be said to blaze with gold and gems."

"as men's faces",—Hengstenberg says this refers actually to faces of men. This would be true if they were actually human soldiers; but the text says only *"as the faces of men"*. Attention has been called to the fact that the head of a locust has actually a faint resemblance to the human profile, which resemblance was even more noticeable in the case of these supernatural locusts. (A. D. Zu. Ew. Dus.)

Ver. 8. *"hair as the hair of women"*,—An Arabic proverb compares the antennae of locusts to the hair of girls. Ewald refers it to the hair on their legs or bodies. These might be acceptable explanations, but it belongs rather to the supernatural portion of our description.

"teeth of lions",—Illustrating their desolating voraciousness, the teeth being rather to terrify than to bite. It is, however, another purely graphic feature and does not apply to the plague to be inflicted. (A. Dus.) (See Joel 1.6.) The Allegorists (Ca.) say the teeth refer to the false doctrines with which heretics have lacerated the orthodox Church.

Ver. 9. *"as it were breastplates of iron"*,—The plate which forms the thorax, stronger than that of the natural locust, being as of iron. (A. L. F. Dus.)

"as the sound of the chariots of many horses",—The natural locusts in their flight make a most fearful noise, and the reference here is to the mingled sound of chariot wheels and the hoofs of the horses, the chariots being regarded as appendages to the horses.

Ver. 10. *"tails like unto scorpions"*,—Another difference between natural and demoniacal locusts. It is not that the tails themselves are like unto scorpions (B. Hen., with an appeal to verse 19), but that they have tails like unto scorpion tails. (A. L. Dus.)

Ver. 11. *"angel of the abyss"*,—Hardly Satan (F. Eb. Ca. Gro.) nor the Antichrist. (Pet.) Some think him the same as the star in verse 1. (Hen. Wei.) We rather think of him as one of the chiefs among Satan's angels and who has special charge over the abyss. (B. A. D. Ew. Dus. Weid.) His name is the Hebrew word for "destruction", namely *"Abaddon"*, the Greek equivalent for which is "Apollyon", which comes from the word meaning "to destroy", i. e., the Destroyer. His name is the place of destruction personified. With the Jew, Abaddon is the lowest place in hell. It designates in the Old Testament the kingdom of destruction or corruption in a local sense, and so the angel who is the personal representative of the place is given the name.

The Preterist School refers this plague of the locusts to the Roman wars in Judea (Gro. Wet. Her.), the "fallen star" being the demon Nero.

The Allegorists make the locusts heretics raging against the orthodox, of the Zealots of the Jewish war.

The Spiritualist system of interpretation says that the woe is obviously spiritual and cannot find its fulfillment in mere wars or calamities of any kind; that the woe falls upon the whole world but that it is not allowed to affect the redeemed Church.

Alford of the Contemporaneous Historical School says, "There is an endless babble of allegorical and historical interpretation of these locusts from the pit. The most that we can say of their import is that they belong to a series of judgments on the ungodly which will immediately precede the second advent of our Lord; that the various mysterious particulars of the vision will no doubt clear themselves up to the Church of God when the time of its fulfillment arrives; but that no such clearing up has yet taken place, a very few hours of research among histories of Apocalyptical interpretation will serve to convince any reader who is not himself the servant of a preconceived system."

The Consecutive Historical School in general refers it to the ravages of Mohammedanism, the Saracens or Arabs out of Arabia, that part of the earth which their devastations covered being the eastern part of the Roman empire. (N. Me. El. Wor. Bar. Will. Dodd. Dau. Scot. Keith. Faber. Frere.) The locust itself, Elliott contends, is peculiarly Arabic, while each part in the description of these strangely constructed locusts was peculiarly figurative of the Arabs, even to the beard which he supposes to belong to the faces which were *"as the faces of men"*. The abyss, he thinks, signifies the prison-place of evil spirits, and it is figurative of the false religion of Mohammedanism, and it was out of this, after embracing Islamism, that the Arabian (Saracen) hordes burst forth in fury on Roman Christendom.

Elliott declares it to have been a peculiarity of the Saracens that they did not destroy the trees or any green thing. They were only to torment and not to kill or annihilate politically Roman Christendom and this Elliott declares to have been true of them because of the many checks given them in their career of devastation and destruction. The five months, or 150 days he interprets as 150 years, according to the year-day theory, and finds this time as fixed between Mohammed's public opening of his mission A. D. 612 and the removal of the Caliphate to Bagdad in A. D. 762.

That there is a remarkable parallelism between this prediction and the rise and progress of the Mohammedan power the candid student must admit. Even Kelly, a staunch Futurist, admits the interpretation to be well founded. "The difficulty lies, however, in this," says Moorehead, "that the Woe Trumpets sound at the time of the end, in Daniel's Seventieth Week, and hence events which occurred a thousand years ago cannot possibly exhaust this mighty prophecy. They adumbrate it, but are not its complete fulfillment."

The fact that in these wars as waged by the Saracens many of the saints, the sealed ones, were made to suffer and were killed weighs heavily against this view, as it likewise does against the allegorical view.

Of the Futurists some think the locusts symbolize evil spirits, demons (Gab.), while others think that literal locusts are intended. (DeBurgh.) Moorehead takes the locusts as the symbol of an invading army, even as does Elliott, although the former places the event in the time of the end. This invading host he thinks identical with Ezekiel's Gog, prince of Rosh, and suggests that Russia will have the chief part in this invasion supported by swarms of other peoples, animated by a satanic spirit and filled with the fury of demons. Hebart looks for the fulfillment in the future appearance of just such locusts. He says, "The fact that such creatures have never yet been seen ought not make us conclude that they never can or never will come. In the last times many things until then unheard of shall come to pass—much hitherto unseen shall greet mortal eyes." Dusterdieck remarks, "He who like Hebart looks for the literal fulfillment of all these visions, expecting for instance the actual appearance of the locusts described, certainly does more justice to the text than does the allegorist."

If the Futurist explanation be adopted there is no good reason why the literal interpretation of Hebart and DeBurgh should not be accepted, although the view of Gaebelein and others, who see in the locusts only symbols of demon powers might appear to be attended with less difficulty.

13 And the sixth angel sounded, and I heard [1]a voice from the horns of the golden altar which is before God, 14 one saying to the sixth angel that had the trumpet, Loose the four angels that are bound at the great river Euphrates. 15 And the four angels were loosed, that had been prepared for the hour and day and month and year, that they should kill the third part of men. 16 And the number of the armies of the horsemen was twice ten thousand times ten thousand: I heard the number of them. 17 And thus I saw the horses in the vision, and them that sat on them, having breastplates as of fire and of hyacinth and of brimstone: and the heads of the horses are as the heads of lions; and out of their mouths proceedeth fire and smoke and brimstone. 18 By these three plagues was the third part of men killed, by the fire and the smoke and the brimstone, which proceeded out of their mouths. 19 For the power of the horses is in their mouth, and in their tails: for their tails are like unto serpents, and have heads; and with them they hurt. 20 And the rest of mankind, who were not killed with these plagues, repented not of the works of their hands, that they should not worship demons, and the idols of gold, and of silver, and of brass, and of stone, and of wood; which can neither see, nor hear, nor walk: 21 and they repented not of their murders, nor of their sorceries, nor of their fornication, nor of their thefts.

[1]Gr. *one voice*

Vers. 13-21.   THE SIXTH TRUMPET JUDGMENT.

Ver. 13.   *"golden altar"*,—The same as in Chaps. 6.9 and 8.3

"a voice",—The voice probably proceeded from the altar itself (Chap. 16.7) and the command to the angel to loose the four angels is the result of the prayers of the saints offered on this altar, and it is represented as uttering the cry of vengeance for the blood shed on it (Chap. 6.9), i. e., the answer to the prayers bringing down the fiery judgments. (A. D. F. Eb. Bl. Kli. Hof. Hen. Dus.)   Literally it is "one voice", but this is not to be interpreted as "the four horns giving forth simultaneously one and the same voice" (Hen.), because not only does the "four" not belong to the text, but the sense itself is forced and feeble.

Ver. 14.   Alford rightly says that this sixth angel is not necessarily by the text made the active agent in the loosing of the four angels.   It says *"they were loosed,"* and the sixth angel may have been addressed only as the herald and the representative of what was to take place.

"the four angels",—These four angels are hardly to be identified with the four angels of Chap. 7.1-3 (El. Wor. Hei.), because their mission and their locality are altogether different.   Hengstenberg and others (D. Dus.) would have us believe that the word *"four"* indicates perhaps that the army is to be led on all four sides of the earth.

Some say they are good angels (Hen. Wor.), but it is far better to think of them as evil angels, as seen from the fact of their being bound and their leading an infernal army, and also from their position, i. e., on the Euphrates. (B. Be. Ew. Eb. St. Dus. Will. Weid. Stern.) Moorehead thinks they may refer merely to the providential restraints of armed forces from the east.

"Euphrates",—Whence all the chastisements of Israel have always come. Todd calls our attention to the fact that "it was the almost universal opinion of the ancients that Antichrist was to arise from this region".

Dusterdieck maintains that the river cannot be taken literally because the rest of the vision, the army, etc., must be t ken mystically. But this is a mistake. In Psalms 88.8 the vine, boughs and branches are of course mystical, while Egypt, the sea and the river are literal: Just so here there is nothing to prevent the Euphrates being taken literally, as Alford says, even though the army and the angels be taken mystically.

The Preterists refer this of course to the army of Titus against Jerusalem. (Ei. Gro. Wet. Her. Hei.)

Elliott of the Consecutive Historical School, taking the Euphrates literally, of course, refers this Sixth Trumpet to the invasion of the Turkman power which dwelt beyond the Euphrates, the *"third part of men"* referring to the Grecian Empire as at that time (about A. D. 1055) constituting one of the third parts of the Roman world. (Thus also V. N. Me. Dau. Dodd. Faber, Forbes, Keith and others.)

The Futurists for the most part refer the army not to a human but to an infernal host constrained to work out God's will during the days of the Great Tribulation. (F. Dus. Weid.)

Moorehead, however, says, "This great army is human, and not a countless multitude of evil spirits, as some think. It may be the imperial army of the Antichrist and possibly consist mainly of Mohammedans. There is a parallelism between this prediction and the interpretation of Elliott, but if the invasion of western Asia by the Turks be conceded to be an accomplishment of the vision, it was but a partial and anticipatory one, because the vision belongs specifically to the time of the end."

Ver. 15. *"for the hour"*, etc.,—i. e., appointed by God. Only one article is used, and by many it is taken as referring to the fixed hour in the fixed day in the fixed month in the fixed year, this very hour being determined by God. (V. St. Dau. Hei.)

Elliott contends that these time terms must be aggregated together and so signify a continuous period, namely, the interval between the loosing of the angels and their accomplishment of the stated purpose of their loosing, viz., to slay the third part of men, the period from A. D. 1055 to the capture of Constantinople by the Turks and the fall of the Grecian Empire, namely A. D. 1453, this time period being worked out on the year-day system.

"kill the third part of men",—Elliott, as we have seen, refers this to the eastern part of the Roman Empire, the Grecian division. Others take it in what is seemingly its more natural sense that one-third of those who dwell upon the earth (Chap. 8.13), the ungodly, shall perish, as previously a third of the trees, ships and creatures were destroyed.

Ver. 16. *"twice ten thousand times ten thousand"*,—i. e., two hundred million. Hengstenberg sees here only an allegorical collective designation of all armies.

Dusterdieck has something to say here worthy of thoughtful consideration. He says that John uses the Euphrates in a schematical way, it being in the Old Testament the place from whence the plagues came upon Israel, and so John works this idea into his scheme, the local designation, as Hengstenberg says, "being only a seeming one". So here Dusterdieck thinks the number is schematical, the army appearing in a supernatural numerical quantity and denoting nothing definite.

Elliott thinks it expressive merely of large numbers and refers it of course to the soldiers and especially the horsemen of the Turks and Tartars, who he says, by the way, had the custom of using the term *myriads* in the numbering of their forces.

Beck and others interpret this immense army of a future literal army and explain it by a universal war involving all races of men.

Petingill of the Futurists says it refers to the nations of the world gathered against Israel to cut them off from national existence.

"*I heard*",—through the voice of prophecy.

Ver. 17. "*in the vision*",—Added not to show that the things were merely seen (Hen.) and that the present vision is merely allegorical (B. L. Hen.), but doubtless because what has thus far been made known in the Sixth Trumpet vision has been heard. (A. Dus.)

"*breastplates*",—Referred by some (L. B. D. Bl. Ew. Heb.) to the riders only; but rightly by others (A. Eb. Zu. Dus. Weid.) to both horses and riders, although the horses are the main objects of interest and not the riders.

"*fire*",—i. e., fiery red.

"*hyacinth*",—i. e., our dark blue iris.

"*brimstone*",—i. e., yellow, sulphur-colored.

These correspond to the fire, smoke and brimstone proceeding out of the mouths of the horses.

Elliott says these descriptions suit well the uniforms of the Turkish army.

"*as the heads of lions*",—The reference here is possibly to the size of the mouths and the length of the manes; a definite monstrous appearance rather than the idea of ferocity, though Elliott contends for the latter as characteristic of the Turkish armies.

Ver. 18. Elliott refers the fire, the smoke and the brimstone of this verse to the cannon as used by the Turks in their siege of Constantinople. Others of the Futurist School refer them to three plagues of the latter times. Weidner has remarked, and seemingly well, "that all this imagery describes a judgment of plagues coming upon the earth in connection with the days of the Antichrist is plainly evident, but to attempt to set forth the exact character of the plagues would be the height of presumption, because nobody knows."

Ver. 19. "*the power of the horses is in their mouths*", i. e., as seen in the previous verse.

"*and with them they hurt*",—i. e., by their fangs, their bite.

The fact that these horse-tails have "*heads*" Elliott thinks is suggestive of *rulers*, and in these tails he sees the horse-tails borne by the Turkish

Shahs as symbols of authority. But what then becomes of their serpent-like character? Alford says of this view of Elliott's, "I venture to say that a more self-condemnatory explanation was never broached than this of the horse-tails of the Shahs."

Among other allegorical and historical interpretations of these tails the following may be mentioned, though, like Elliott's, to one's amusement rather than to his edification.

1. Grotius, who as a Preterist connects the whole thing with the destruction of Jerusalem, sees in them the foot soldiers on the backs of the horses behind the horsemen.

2. Volkmar refers them merely to the "kicking back" of the horses.

3. Bengel sees in them the turning back of the Turkish cavalry to the sudden detriment of their pursuers.

4. Hengstenberg finds in the expression the malignity of war symbolized.

Many, both of the Contemporaneous Historical and of the Futurist Schools of interpretation, who contend for the parallelism of this Sixth Trumpet with the Sixth Seal, would have us believe that events are intended immediately preceding the Second Coming of Christ to destroy the Antichrist.

Ver. 20. *"repented not"*,—This and the following words show that ungodly men are meant.

"the work of their hands",—The reference is more particularly to the idols which their hands had made (A. F. B. Ew. Hen. Dus.) rather than to the entire course of their life (D. Eb.). (See Acts 7.41 and Deut. 4.28.)

Ver. 21. The chief sins of the heathen. "It is clear," says Alford, "that he is thinking of the heathen (A. Dus.), and even thus will the heathen world continue in the main until the second coming of Christ of which these judgments are the immediate precursors." (See Gal. 5.20.)

Ludhardt says, "Such moral corruption will occur at the end in spite of advanced culture; for culture of itself does not promote morality, but as history teaches, may be employed as well in the service of ungodliness and immorality."

Elliott, of course, refers verses 20 and 21 to the religious state during the time between the fall of Constantinople and the Reformation.

CHAPTER TEN

1 And I saw another strong angel coming down out of heaven, arrayed with a cloud; and the rainbow was upon his head, and his face was as the sun, and his feet as pillars of fire; 2 and he had in his hand a little book open: and he set his right foot upon the sea, and his left upon the erath; 3 and he cried with a great voice, as a lion roareth: and when he cried, the seven thunders uttered their voices. 4 And when the seven thunders uttered *their voices*, I was about to write: and I heard a voice from heaven saying, Seal up the things which the seven thunders uttered, and write them not. 5 And the angel that I saw standing upon the sea and upon the earth lifted up his right hand to heaven, 6 and sware by him that liveth [1]for ever and ever, who created the heaven and the things that are therein, and the earth and the things that are

[1]Gr. *unto the ages of the ages*

therein, and the sea and the things that are therein, that there shall be [2]delay no longer; 7 but in the days of the voice of the seventh angel, when he is about to sound, then is finished the mystery of God, according to the good tidings which he declared to his [3]servants the prophets.

8 And the voice which I heard from heaven, I heard it again speaking with me, and saying, Go, take the book which is open in the hand of the angel that standeth upon the sea and upon the earth.

[2]Or, *time*
[3]Gr. *bondservants*

9 And I went unto the angel, saying unto him that he should give me the little book. And he saith unto me, Take it, and eat it up; and it shall make thy belly bitter, but in thy mouth it shall be sweet as honey. 10 And I took the little book out of the angel's hand, and ate it up; and it was in my mouth sweet as honey: and when I had eaten it, my belly was made bitter. 11 And they say unto me, Thou must prophesy again [4]over many peoples and nations and tongues and kings.

[4]Or, *concerning*

Vers. 1-11. THE STRONG ANGEL AND THE LITTLE BOOK.

Ver. 1. As after the Sixth Seal, so after the Sixth Trumpet we seem to have a passage containing two episodes, a parenthetical passage containing the incidents of the little book and the two witnesses. (Chap. 10.1 to Chap. 11.14.)

"another strong angel",—Many refer this, and not without considerable propriety, to Christ Himself. (V. Be. Me. Ze. El. Ar. Al. Ca. Hen. Gab. Pet.) But not only is the very style of the oath seemingly inappropriate to Christ, but throughout the book when angels are mentioned it is to ministers of the divine purpose that reference is made, and when John means to indicate the Son of God he does so in plain and unmistakable language.

Others say the reference is to an angelic image of Christ (L. Wor.). But the text says *"angel"*, and further than this we need not go, and he is therefore to be thought of as an angelic minister of Christ. (A. F. B. D. Dus. Lap. Sad. And. Sim. Weid. Boyd. Carp. Stern.)

"another",—This is doubtless to distinguish him from the strong angel of Chap. 5.2, who also had a book (A. B. F. Eb. Dus.), and not from the foregoing angels of the trumpets (D. L. Hen.).

"arrayed with a cloud",—i. e., as a messenger of divine judgment. (A. F. Eb. Dus. Hen.)

"the rainbow was upon his head",—Notice the definite article *"the"*, i. e., the well-known rainbow, the emblem of covenant mercy to God's people.

"his face was as the sun",—i. e., indicating the divine glory with which he was invested.

"his feet as pillars of fire",—Another emblem of judgment, the whole of the symbols betokening perhaps judgment tempered with mercy.

Ver. 2. *"in his hand"*,—Doubtless the left hand. (See verse 5.)

"a little book",—i. e., a little scroll. It is called *"little"* perhaps in comparison with the larger book in Chap. 5 (A. F. Ew. Dus.), rather than with reference to John's eating it (Ei.), or in comparison to the size of the angel (B.).

"and he set his right foot", etc.,—The whole imagery would seem to represent the glory and majesty of Christ whose messenger the angel is.

"Sea and earth," says Alford, "are to be taken literally, and both are by this action claimed as belonging to Christ, and indicate that the tidings to be brought are for the whole earth, and that the power of God in judgment extends over the whole world." John was no doubt thinking of the Mediterranean and of Palestine.

Ver. 3. *"and he cried"*,—What, the text in no way indicates. Hardly, as Bengel says, what is described in verse 6.

"with a great voice as a lion roareth",—Representing perhaps the threatening character of the revelation.

"the seven thunders uttered their voices",—Wordsworth calls the use of the article *"the"* here the prophetic use of the article, i. e., the thunders, of which more hereafter. Ewald's idea that it means all the thunders of heaven, i. e., the whole heavens exclaimed with a thunderous voice, is without foundation. I think perhaps the better explanation is that by a part of the Apocalyptic symbolism they are marked by the article as well-known, even as the seven stars, the seven churches, the seven seals, the seven trumpets and the seven vials.

Ver. 4. *"I was about to write"*,—i. e., in obedience to the command of Chap. 1.19.

"and I heard a voice",—The voice of Christ, says Bengel, while others claim it to have been the voice of the angel of Chap. 1.1. At best it is but a conjecture.

"from heaven",—This does not compel us to think of John as being on the earth (D. L.) any more than does verse 1.

"seal up the things",—i. e., by not writing them.

The Preterists see in the entire episode a prelude to the destruction of Jerusalem.

Elliott of the Consecutive Historical School says that the divine intervention portrayed by the opening clause of this chapter refers to the Reformation of the sixteenth century as inaugurated by Martin Luther, that the *"strong angel"* of verse 1 is Christ, and that the *"little book"* is the open Bible through the knowledge of which the Reformation was brought about.

Others of the same school with Elliott (V. N. Me. New. Faber, Frere, Cuninghame) refer the little book, like that in the commencement of the prophecy in Chap. 5, to another prophetic roll, the same being called a *"little book"* because it contained but a small portion of God's purposes, and it was *"open"* because God was ready to disclose its contents.

What did the voices of the seven thunders utter? Whether the thunders spoke as one voice or whether each thunder spoke its own special voice an intelligible revelation was brought to John thereby because he understood them and was about to write them for others. That the utterances were of fearful import is implied by the thunder. Many think it is vain to inquire what the voices uttered because no intimation whatsoever is given in the text. There are, however, many conjectures:

(1) The praises of God. (B.)
(2) The seven Crusades. (V.)
(3) Emblems or warnings of the Seven Vials of the Seventh Trumpet. (Me. Cuninghame, Bickersteth.)

(4) Seven wars between the Reformation and the sounding of the Seventh Trumpet at the French Revolution. (Keith.)

(5) The echo of laws confirmatory of the Protestant doctrine of seven kingdoms that embraced the Reformation. (Dau.)

(6) The blessed mystery of the new world. (Hof.)

(7) What is announced later concerning the destruction of the enemies of God. (Hen.)

(8) Seven future acts of God to occur before the beginning of the Seventh Trumpet. (Eb.)

(9) The Papal Anathemas during the Reformation. (El.)

This last conjecture brings before us Elliott's explanation of the *"seven thunders"* themselves. These he thinks of as referring to the Papal Antichrist, which had arisen in the Church visible even before the days of the Reformation, especially in Pope Leo the Tenth, who had assumed for himself and had ascribed to him in various ways all the attributes of the mighty angel Christ as mentioned in the three previous verses, the vision before us being that of Christ coming down to fight against this Antichrist and to claim this world as His own. Alford remarks that "no interpretation could be more unfortunate—none more thoroughly condemnatory of the system which is compelled to have recourse to it. For, merely to insist upon one point—if it were so, then the Apostle sealed the utterances in vain, for we all know what those thunders (the papal anathemas) have uttered."

Why was John forbidden to write what the seven thunders uttered? It was not that they exceeded human comprehension (Ew.), because John understood them and was about to write them for others; not because thereby the mysteriousness was increased (D.). The fact is that God has given no account as to why. Of course we may readily surmise the effect (and this may have also been in the aim), viz., the Godly are kept from brooding over the evils to come, and the ungodly will know that all the terrors of the judgment are not yet exhausted.

Ver. 6. Elliott of the Consecutive Historical School thinks that as verses 1 and 2 gave to Luther and the Reformers a discovery of Christ and verse 3 gave to them a discovery of the Antichrist, so what now follows is a further revelation to them, in due chronological order of sequence, signifying further advance and progress in the Reformation. They are now shown, he says, that the ill-fated time of the Antichrist's final foredoomed destruction, and therewith also the coming of Christ's kingdom, and the ending of God's great prophetic mystery, is near at hand, though indeed not yet fully come.

"him that liveth forever and ever",—The Almighty God, as Creator, who is to consummate the mystery of God, as noted in verse 7.

"there shall be delay no longer",—Not as the Authorized Version implies, that time shall end and eternity begin (Be. Are. Oec. Will.), which view is refuted by the words of the first half of verse 7, and furthermore by the fact that the next Trumpet was to issue in the reign of Christ and His saints.

The words according to many authorities (A. F. V. D. Ca. Ew. Ei. Gro. Dus. Lap. Hen. Moor. et al.) express the immediate consummation of what in the next verse is called the fulfillment of the mystery of God.

And yet these authorities are by no means agreed as to the point of time involved. Hengstenberg says it means that no time is to intervene between the sound of the Seventh Trumpet and the fulfillment of the prophetic oracles. But verse 7 says that the fulfillment of the mystery of God, the fulfillment of all prophecy, is to occur just at the time of the Seventh Trumpet. The real meaning is doubtless that no more time is to intervene between the present point of time and the Seventh Trumpet which ushered in the finishing of the mystery of God. (A. Eb. Dus. Gab. Wor. Weid.) The appointed time of delay is at an end. The martyrs have no longer to wait for the answer to their prayers (Chap. 6.11); the hour for vengeance has struck.

Elliott translates, "there shall be time no longer extended," and of course means thereby that time shall no longer be extended to the mysterious dispensation of God which has so far permitted the reign of evil including the power of the Papal Antichrist's mock thunders, the Seventh Trumpet's era being its fixed determined limit.

Ver. 7. When the Seventh Trumpet sounds, the completed time of the fulfillment is, as Alford says, simultaneous with his blowing, so that it is properly said that the fulfillment comes in the "days when he is about to sound".

"in the days",—Bengel says that the angel is heard continuously throughout these days. But this conflicts with the analogy of the other trumpet voices. There seems to be in the expression an intermingling of the fulfillment with the prophecy, the standpoint of the vision not being strictly preserved.

As Weidner says, "The moment that the Seventh Trumpet shall sound the mystery shall be made clear, for the fulfillment comes in the days when it sounds."

"the mystery of God",—The meaning of this phrase is determined by the fact of its fulfillment being placed in the time of the Seventh Trumpet, and by the fact that it is a communication of a message of joy. Hence all of the following are correct: The mystery of God's scheme of redemption (F.); The eschatological mystery of the world's history (L.); The glorious completion of the divine kingdom (Dus.); The mystery of the kingdom as unfolded in the course of God's dispensation (A.). Weidner tersely and with correctness says, "This finishing of the mystery of God is the glorious consummation of God's kingdom when the kingdoms of this world shall have become the kingdoms of our Lord and of His Christ, when He shall reign forever and ever." The verse is anticipatory of Chap. 11.15-18.

Ver. 9. *"And I went unto the angel"*,—i. e., in idea, in vision, says Lange, who also conceives of John as now in the earth. Some think of him as leaving heaven and changing his standpoint of observation and so coming near to where the angel stood. (A. F. Dus.)

Verses 8 to 11, Elliott of the Consecutive Historical School conceives to be the special commissioning by Christ (the angel holding the little book) of the ministers of the Reformation to preach His Gospel in various countries and languages, the Apostle John standing in the vision as the representative of these ministers, and the word *"prophesy"* being taken in the sense of preaching, proclaiming the Gospel.

Alford of the Contemporaneous Historical School, as well as all the Futurists, think of the *"little book"* not as the Bible or the New Testament, but as another scroll of prophecy relating to the fulfillment of the mystery of God.

"eat it up",—i. e., as Bede says, "Take into your inward parts as contained within the space of the heart." (Jer. 15.16.)

"bitter and sweet",—Different sensations of the one book in different parts of John's body, says Alford. The reference is not therefore to different portions of the book, its sad and its joyous contents (Ew. Hei.); nor is it that the first bitterness leads afterwards to sweetness and joy (Her. Rink); nor that the bitterness indicates the persecution with which the preaching of John and the Church met; and the sweetness, his declaration of it to others (Be. Ar.). The right idea seems to be that the roll was sweet to the taste because he knew it to be the will of God, and the thought that God was to be glorified gave to him the sweetest pleasure, but as its contents were digested he was embittered with grief at the message of judgment to be announced. (F. V. D. A. Hen. Dus. Lap. Stern.)

Ver. 11. *"They say"*,—An indefinite expression for "it was said", the speaker or speakers being left unknown.

"Thou must prophesy again",—This necessity is laid upon him by the will of God and not because of an inner subjective necessity caused by eating the book.

"many peoples",—The inhabitants of the earth as before. (Chap. 6.9.)

"again",—Not after returning from exile (Be. Orim.); nor in contradistinction to the old prophets (B.); nor as referring to the composition of John's Gospel; nor as one of the two witnesses (Crav.); but perhaps, "as thou hast done before in writing the former part of the Apocalypse." (A. L. D. F. Eb. Al. Hen. Gro. Dus.) He is to prophecy what he finds in the little book, which book relates to the fulfillment of the mystery of God, and which prophecy is given in that part of the Apocalypse which begins at Chap. 11. (A. B. D. L. F. Be. Al. Ew. Eb. Lap. Hen.)

There can be but little, if any, doubt but that the little book contains the mystery of God spoken of above. Practically all are agreed here but they do not by any means agree either as to the relation of the little book to the book of Chap. 5, or as to how much from Chap. 11 on is included in the little book.

Weidner thinks the prophesying again of John begins with Chap. 12 and goes on to the end of the Apocalypse.

Alford seems rightly to say, "The contents of the little book cannot well be confined to Chap. 11.1-13, or we should not have had so solemn an inauguration of it, nor so wide-reaching an announcement of the duty of the Apostle consequent upon receipt of it."

There are four views as to the relation of this little book to the book of Chap. 5.

1. *The two books are identical.* (Ze. Ca. Lap.) But John thus far has been prophesying on the ground of the book of Chap. 5 and

now he is to begin anew, again, with the contents of the little book. This would seem to prove the books to be different.

2. *The two books have no relation at all.* (A.)
   (a) The little book contains only Chap. 11.1-3 and this refers to the fate of Jerusalem. (Ew. Ei. Gro. Wet.)
   (b) The little book contains only Chap. 11.1-13 and this refers to judgments on the degenerate Church. (Hen.) The fact that he is to prophesy concerning peoples and kings militates against (a) and (b).
   (c) The little book contains Chap. 11.1-13, including a reference to Antichrist, announcing the conversion of Israel. (G.)
   (d) The little book contains the testimony of the two witnesses. (De Burgh.)
   (e) The little book contains all from Chap. 11 to the end of the Apocalypse.

3. *The little book is the latter part of the book of Chap. 11 and contains:*
   (a) Chap. 11.1-13, which refers to the calamities of the Western Church. The objection to (a) and (b) above holds also here.
   (b) Chap. 11 on to the end of the Apocalypse. (Dus.)

4. *The little book is a repetition of the other book.* (Vol.)

Either (e) under 2 or (b) under 3 is the proper view. They agree as to the contents of the little book but not in its relation to the book of Chap. 5. Alford argues that the book of Chap. 5 was not to be opened at all until the end; while Dusterdieck argues that it is inconceivable that the book of fate in Chap. 5 should contain nothing as to the fate of Jerusalem (Chap. 11), the degenerate Church. We incline to the view of Alford, (e) under 2.

We are inclined to think the vision refers to that which is still future and that after the judgments announced by the first six trumpets have come to pass, the beginning of the final consummation, when Antichrist will be destroyed, will be ushered in, and the judgments which shall come upon the world in connection with this destruction and which are to mark the times of the Great Tribulation are accordingly to be conceived of as the contents of the little book.

CHAPTER ELEVEN

1 And there was given me a reed like unto a rod: [1]and one said, Rise, and measure the [2]temple of God, and the altar, and them that worship therein. 2 And the court which is without the [2]temple [3]leave without, and measure it not; for it hath been given unto the [4]nations: and the holy city shall they tread under foot forty and two months.

[1]Gr. *saying*
[2]Or, *sanctuary*
[3]Gr. *cast without*
[4]Or, *Gentiles*

Vers. 1,2. THE SAINTS SET APART FOR DELIVERANCE.

Many regard this chapter as a compendium summary of and introduction to the more detailed prophecies of the same events to come in Chaps. 13 to 20. (A. F. Weid.)

Alford remarks, "We cannot understand this prophecy at all except in the light of those that follow, for it introduces by anticipation their *dramatis personae.*"

Ver. 1. *"And there was given me a reed",*—Probably by the angel of Chap. 10 (B.), or perhaps by Christ, who seems to be the speaker in verse 3, but by whom is left undetermined by the text.

"and one said",—literally, "saying". The giver of the reed is of course meant.

"the temple of God",—The word is "naos" and it refers to that part of the temple which contains the sanctuary, namely the Holy Place and the Most Holy Place, i. e., the temple proper in distinction from the entire space of the outer courts. (Dus. Weid.)

"and the altar",—Not the altar of Burnt Offering which stood outside in front of the Holy Place (V. El. Bar. Gro. Hen.), but the altar of Incense which stood in the Holy Place not far from the entrance into the Most Holy Place. (F. A. L. Ei. Eb. Hei. Dus. Stern.)

"and them that worship therein",—i. e., in the "naos", the temple.

Dusterdieck rightly says, "That John beholds believers in the Most Holy Place, otherwise open to priests only, is due to his knowledge of the priestly character of believers."

Others, however, refer the preposition *"in"* to its nearest noun, *"altar,"* and render this word "altar court", and thus make *"them that worship therein"* emblematic of the Church on earth, while the Most Holy and its blessed company represent that part of the Church already gathered into Paradise, and by the *"court without"* is symbolized the apostate Roman Catholic Church.

"Rise and measure",—What is meant by this measuring?

The things are measured as a sign that they are not to be devoted to destruction, while the outer court, not being measured, is indicative of destruction. The action which John is commanded to perform is of course a symbolic one, the "naos" being symbolical of worshipping believers and the outer court symbolical of the unbelieving and the apostate.

Ver. 2. *"the court which is without",*—Not the court of the Gentiles only (V. El. Zu. Ew.), but all outside the temple (naos) as conceived in verse 1, i. e., both the court of the Gentiles and the court of Burnt Offering. (F. A. L. D. Eb. Dus. Hen.)

"leave without",—i. e., out of your measurements. The literal is "cast out", i. e., reckoned as unhallowed. (F. A. L. B. D. Ei. Eb. Ew. Hen.)

"it hath been given",—i. e., by divine appointment. (A. F. Dus.)

"unto the nations",—i. e., unto the Gentiles. Not that the Gentiles shall one day worship there (B.), nor that the altar of Burnt Offering standing in the outer court is thereby to be maintained (D.), but as the next clause indicates, that together with the Holy City it shall be trodden under foot.

"forty and two months",—This and the 1260 days and the three and one-half years seem equal enough and doubtless are periods of the same length, although Alford rightly remarks that we have no right to suppose

them in any two given cases to be identical unless so required by the context. While of equal length, no doubt they may refer to different periods of time. There are three main views as to the period of time here referred to:

1. That it is to be taken symbolically of "the times of the Gentiles", whether their beginning be dated from the Babylonish captivity or from the destruction of Jerusalem by Titus, and continuing down to the Second Coming of Christ.

2. That each day represents a year and we have therefore 1260 years. This is the view of nearly all the supporters of the Consecutive Historical School, each one, however, of whom has a different beginning time for the 1260 years, it being impossible for any two of them to agree, Joachin beginning with A. D. 1; Mede with A. D. 455; Cuninghame with A. D. 533; Bengel with A. D. 576; Fleming with A. D. 606; Elliott with A. D. 608; Melancthon with A. D. 660; Guinness with A. D. 672; Fysh with A. D. 727, etc.

3. That the period is to be interpreted literally and that it refers to the last half of the Seventieth Week, the days of the Antichrist.

It will be seen therefore that the answer to the question as to who are the believers and unbelievers, as typified by the temple and the outer court, must depend upon the school of interpretation one is inclined to follow in seeking an explanation of the entire passage.

The Consecutive Historical School, especially Elliott, refers the passage to the Reformation and the causes which led to it. The reed he makes a type of the authority given to Luther and the Reformers by Elector John. The measuring, he says, was the ecclesiastically constituting of what was called the Evangelic Church, the introduction of new forms of worship after the principles laid down by Luther, and the non-measuring was the removal from the Church and church worship of Roman images and superstitions and the exclusion, as heathen-like and apostate, of the Church of Rome herself.

The Contemporaneous Historical School, especially Alford, says the whole expression, "the temple, the altar and them that worship therein" is to be taken symbolically, and refers to "the Church of the elect servants of God (I Cor. 3.16,17), partakers of the first resurrection, the Church of the first born". "These," he says, "are they who, properly speaking, alone are measured, i. e., estimated again and again in this book by tale and by number." This measuring, he says, consists in the distinction which John so accurately draws in the subsequent chapters between God's servants and those who bear the mark of the Beast. Noticing that nothing further is said of the measuring, Alford remarks, "Either then it never took place (which is inconceivable), or it did take place and no result is communicated to us (which is hardly probable), or the result of it is found in the subsequent prophecies in the minute and careful distinctions between the servants of God and those who receive the mark of the Beast." The nations to whom the outer court is given, are, he says, "those outside of the elect Church of the first-born over whom the Millennial reign of Chap. 20 shall be exercised, the dwellers on the earth, the material upon which judgment and mercy are severally exercised in the rest of the book." As to the periods of time mentioned Alford says, "No solution at all

611

approaching to a satisfactory one has ever yet been given of any one of these periods. This being so, my principle is to regard them as still among the things unknown to the Church and awaiting their elucidation by the event. It is our duty to feel our way by all the indications which Scriptures furnish, and by the light which history, in its main and obvious salient events, has thrown on Scripture; and when those fail us, to be content to confess our ignorance. An Apocalyptic commentary which explains everything is self-convicted of error."

The Futurists take the time periods literally and refer the worshipping believers to the faithful remnant of the Jews, as symbolized by the temple, and the unbelievers to the apostate Jews and the Gentiles, the time in question being at the end during the days of the Seals, Trumpets and Vials, or more specifically during the last three and one-half years of the Seventieth Week of Daniel.

Todd, who is a Futurist, advocates the teaching that Jerusalem will be inhabited again, the temple rebuilt, then the city sacked by the Gentiles, the outer court of the temple seized and profaned while the sanctuary itself and a remnant of them that worship therein graciously preserved, says, "There is nothing impossible, nothing inconsistent with faith or reason, nothing which can furnish the smallest justification to us for departing from the natural meaning of the words."

Fausset, to whom the measuring stands parallel to the sealing of the elect of Israel, and who takes the measuring literally, says, "The fact that the temple is distinguished from them that worship therein favors the view that the spiritual temple (believers) is not exclusively meant, but that the literal temple must also be meant. It shall be rebuilt on the return of the Jews to their land. The measuring then at once implies the exactness of the proportions of the temple to be restored and the definite completeness of the numbers of the Israelitish and Gentile elections." He further says, "Literal Israel in Jerusalem and with the temple restored shall stand at the head of the elect Church. The sealed elect of Israel, the head of the elect Church, alone shall refuse Antichrist's claims. These constitute the true sanctuary which is here measured, i. e., accurately marked and kept by God."

Thus also Godet, who takes those who worship in the sanctuary to be the body of faithful Jews who refuse to worship Antichrist at the time of his reigning in Jerusalem.

We can ourselves see no good reason for departing from the literal interpretation of these periods of time.

3 And I will give unto my two witnesses, and they shall prophesy a thousand two hundred and threescore days, clothed in sackcloth. 4 These are the two olive trees and the two [1]candlesticks, standing before the Lord of the earth. 5 And if any man desireth to hurt them, fire proceedeth out of their mouth and devoureth their enemies; and if any man shall desire to hurt them, in this manner must he be killed. 6 These have the power to shut the heaven, that it rain not during the days of their prophecy: and they have power over the waters to turn them into blood, and to smite the earth with every plague, as often as they shall desire. 7 And when they shall have finished their testimony, the beast that cometh up out of the abyss shall make war with them, and overcome them, and kill them. 8 And their [2]dead bodies *lie* in the street of the great city, which spiritually is called Sodom and Egypt, where also their Lord was crucified. 9 And from among the peoples and tribes and tongues and

[1]Gr. *lampstands*

[2]Gr. *carcase*

nations do *men* look upon their [2]dead bodies three days and a half, and suffer not their dead bodies to be laid in a tomb. 10 And they that dwell on the earth rejoice over them, and make merry; and they shall send gifts one to another; because these two prophets tormented them that dwell on the earth. 11 And after the three days and a half the breath of life from God entered into them, and they stood upon their feet; and great fear fell upon them that beheld them. 12 And they heard a great voice from heaven saying unto them, Come up hither. And they went up into heaven in the cloud; and their enemies beheld them.

Vers. 3-12. THE TWO WITNESSES.

Ver. 3. *"And I will give"*,—What is given is declared by what follows, i. e., power and authority to prophesy. There is, therefore, no use to conjecture such objects as "consistency and wisdom" (Ly. Lap.), "the Holy Spirit" (Bez.), "direction and power" (D.).

"my two witnesses",—literally "the two witnesses of me." "The" implies well-known witnesses, at least to John; "me" has its reference in Christ, although Christ is not necessarily to be regarded as speaking (B. Eb. Hen.), but it is the same heavenly voice which has been speaking in the name of Christ (A. Dus.). That it cannot be Christ Himself who here speaks is made plain by verse 8, where it is said, "where also their Lord was crucified." The *"witnesses"* may be taken literally, i. e., two individual men, or symbolically as representing bodies of men who embody the principles and characteristics of the true witnesses here mentioned. The fact that they were said to be clothed in sackcloth strongly favors the literal interpretation, as Alford admits, and this fact also shows that they preached repentance and approaching judgment. If taken as individuals the reference to Moses and Elijah seems the best one (F. B. Be. Dus.), because of the character of miracles described and because they appeared with Christ at the transfiguration which fore-shadowed his coming Millennium kingdom. Enoch was substituted for Moses to avoid making Moses die twice, since both witnesses are killed.

The early Church almost universally believed in the literal fulfillment of this prophecy just as the words are written. They all accepted Elijah as one of the witnesses, and most thought the other to be Enoch, since it is said that these two alone of mankind had not tasted death. (Pet.)

But the deeds of these two witnesses seem to link them more closely with Moses and Elijah than with Enoch and Elijah, and it has been said that the passing away of Moses was also miraculous, as was that of the other two. Most modern commentators take the characters as Moses and Elijah or at least of two prophets with miraculous powers similar to Moses and Elijah, which interpretation is probably the right one.

The Allegorical interpretation says they are the Old and New Testaments, the fire coming out of their mouths is being fulfilled in the insults now being offered to the Two Testaments. (Tichonius, Frere, Irving.)

The Consecutive Historical School makes them a long line of witnesses for Christ during the 1260 years of the Papal Antichrist preceding the Reformation, beginning about A. D. 533, their death signifies the entire cessation of such witnessing during the few years just before the Reformation, and the three and one-half years indicates exactly the time between the ninth session of the Lateran Council, May 5, 1514, and the posting of the ninety-five Theses on the Wittenberg cathedral door, Oct.

31, 1517, their resurrection, the revival of the Gospel preaching by Luther and his associates, and their ascension the peace of Augsburg, 1555. Wiedner, a Futurist, remarks, "Is it a wonder that the book of Revelation has fallen largely into disrepute and been regarded as an enigma, when such interpretations are seriously set forth and considered as bringing out the meaning of God's word?"

Moorehead, however, just as ardent a Futurist, says, "We have no good reason to reject this application of the prophecy as at least a partial and proleptic fulfillment. But it does not meet all the facts. The witnesses beyond all question prosecute their ministry in Jerusalem (verse 8), and they appear just before the Seventh Trumpet sounds when the consummation is reached."

"*a thousand two hundred and threescore days*",—1260 days. This means no doubt they will prophesy daily during this period, which is here not to be identified with the forty-two months. The time of their prophesying is, according to the Futurist School, doubtless during the first half of the times of the Antichrist, while the forty-two months no doubt refer to the last half of this period.

Ver. 4. "*Two olive trees*",—Lange says John has seen in the olive trees of Zech. 4 perfectly admissible types of New Testament affairs. John has amplified the symbolism of Zechariah in the case of candlesticks, making two here instead of one there, "carrying it on," perhaps, as Alford says, "by the well known figure of light (two candlesticks), as representing God's testifying servants."

They are called "*olive trees*" because the energy and power of the Holy Spirit rests upon them. (Gab.)

Ver. 5. Elliott takes the statements of this and the following verse as figurative, the fire proceeding out of their mouths referring to the fiery judgments of God destroying the apostates nationally who might have persecuted them. Alford, on the other hand says, "Individuality could not be more strongly indicated. The literal sense seems to be stamped here by the double announcement. And the '*if any man*' and '*he must be killed*' can hardly take a national sense, as Elliott supposes."

2 Kings 1.10 is referred to by way of example. (D. L. F. Ew.) If the passage be taken literally it presents a most fearful reality. God causing fire to come down and consume their enemies can answer the demands of the passage. Allegorists are much puzzled here.

Ver. 6. The miracles performed by Moses and Elijah, thus pointing to them as the two witnesses. Apart from this there is no hint whatsoever that these two witnesses are sent to earth from the unseen world. Indeed the passage does not require such an interpretation; if two men shall appear in the last days bearing witness in the spirit and power of Elijah and Moses the terms of the prophecy will have been fully met.

Some take these plagues spiritually, i. e., closing the heavens spiritually and holding back the rain of the Gospel (V. L. Ly. El. Eb. Ca. Hen.), and causing bloodshed to come from the preaching of the Gospel (V.), "the bloodshed of wars inflicted in God's providence on the enemies of the witnesses" (El.); but there is no reason, as Dusterdieck says, why they should not be taken literally, just the same as in I Kings 17.1 and Ex. 7 sqq.

Ver. 7. *"when they shall have finished"*,—The verb as used shows that the whole period of their testimony shall have come to an end when that which is next said shall happen. Allegorists try to escape this, but in vain; as for instance, "when they shall be about finishing" (Me.), and Elliott, who says it does not necessarily mean when they shall have completed their whole testimony, but any one complete deliverance, and this he places in the opening of the sixteenth century just before the Reformation. The same verb is used of Paul's ending his life by violent death.

"the beast",—The first mention of this beast, and it is evidently the same as the one mentioned in Chaps. 13.1 and 17.8, and is doubtless that *"little horn"* spoken of by Daniel "which made war with the saints and prevailed against them" (Dan. 7.8-21). His infernal nature can be seen in that he comes up out of the abyss. When he makes war with the saints, it is then that the company of martyrs mentioned in Chap. 6.11 will be gathered. Weidner says, "This beast is evidently the Antichrist who now manifests himself in all of his diabolical power as the Man of Sin."

Ver. 8. *"dead bodies"*,—The Greek (which is singular) does not properly signify a dead body, but that which is fallen, be it of one or of many.

"the great city",—The arguments of Alford against taking this as Jerusalem are not conclusive. He makes it Babylon because it was the usual term for Babylon, and is used of Babylon eight times elsewhere in Revelation. But the connection, its spiritual designation, and the last clause of verse 8 decide the case in favor of Jerusalem. (L. F. D. Ew. Bl. Dus. Sei.) Sodom (Isa. 1.10) and Egypt are not to be thought of in their individual relations (first—immoral practices; second—religious corruption [Hen.]), but together as representing entire enmity to God and his servants. (D. Bl. Ew. Dus.) Alford, followed by Ebrard, Hengstenberg and Elliott, spiritualizes *"crucified"*, i. e., even as we crucify him today. But the past tense of the verb is against this view.

It is only possible to surmise why John here calls Jerusalem great. Perhaps because "Sodom and Egypt" and "holy" would not be proper in the same breath, while *"great"* emphasizes its greatness and power as the vain foundation of its godless security and enmity against the Lord and his witnesses calling it to repentance.

In the times of the Antichrist Jerusalem may well be called "Sodom and Egypt" because of her corruptions, and Fausset says, "she can be called great by reason of her becoming the world's capital of idolatrous apostasy, such as Babylon originally was, and as Rome has been". De Wette remarks that John couldn't call her "holy" any more after her desecration.

Elliott must, in keeping with his scheme of interpretation, explain this *"great city"* as the one wherein all martyrdom of the saints had originated or taken place, i. e., Rome, and he must accordingly interpret the word *"crucified"* in a spiritual sense as meaning crucified afresh, even as Alford does who thinks of the *"great city"* as Babylon.

Ver. 9. *"suffer not their dead bodies to be laid in a tomb"*,—Gaebelein says, and rightly, "The wicked are so elated over the silencing of the testimony that they refuse to permit their burial so that they may feast their eyes upon the sickening spectacle. Many from among the Gentiles and the Jews seem to have assembled in Jerusalem." Elliott having taken the witnesses and the slaying symbolically must of course take this expression also in the same way, although he remarks that here as elsewhere the figure may have been drawn 'from life inasmuch as the Lateran Council denied burial to the heretics, the faithful anti-papal witnessing body of Christ. Because of the *"among"* Fausset says the reference is to all save the elect.

Lange, with insufficient reason, says this verse refers to those who look upon them friendly; not allowing them to be buried, hoping they would revive (they looked on in sorrow), while verse 10 refers to the ungodly.

"three days and a half",—Not with reference to Christ lying in the grave (Lap. Hen.), nor merely designating a short time (Ze.), nor because it meant longer than was proper (Ew.), but only from the analogy of the three and one-half years, verse 2. (A. F. D. Dus.)

For the interpretation by the Consecutive Historical School of this expression see under verse 3.

Ver. 10. *"they that dwell upon the earth"*,—Because of this expression some say that Jerusalem is not meant as the city, but Papal Rome, or rather Romish Papacy, which extends over all the earth. (V. Ca.) But this effort to represent all dwellers on the earth miscarries. The ungodly in Jerusalem are to be taken as representing the entire mass of such dwellers on the earth. It is the generic idea (Dus.) and not the numerical mass here thought of.

"send gifts one to another",—i. e. as on a day of festival.

"tormented them",—i. e., by the plagues above mentioned.

Ver. 11. *"breath of life"*,—Not the Spirit of life (A. L. F. Hen.), but as in the text (Dus.).

"from God",—i. e., miraculously, immediately. It is not, however, unallowable to take "spirit of life" as one conception and "of God" as modifying it in the sense of Alford and others, as above. John doubtless had before him the imagery of Ezekiel 37.

Ver. 12. *"they heard"*,—i. e., the two witnesses.

"And they went up into heaven",—Alford says that little if any attempt has been made to explain this ascension by those who interpret the witnesses figuratively. He says that the modern Historical School which can interpret such a phrase, as Elliott does, as "calling up to political ascendancy and power" surely needs no refutation. From those highest for the time being in the heaven of political authority there was issued a Decree, says Elliott, a Decree issued by the Roman Emperor, celebrated as the Pacification of Nuremberg, by which full toleration was accorded to Protestantism so recently the object of such persecution on the part of the Beast, the Popes of Rome and the secular Roman power under them.

"in the cloud",—Because of the definite article *"the"* Fausset thinks the same cloud is meant which took Christ up. But this can hardly be vigorously maintained.

13 And in that hour there was a great earthquake, and the tenth part of the city fell; and there were killed in the earthquake [1]seven thousand persons: and

[1]Gr. *names of men, seven thousand.* Comp. Chap. 3.4.

the rest were affrighted, and gave glory to the God of heaven.

14 The second Woe is past: behold, the third Woe cometh quickly.

Vers. 13,14. THE SECOND WOE.

Ver. 13. *"earthquake"*,—Literal earthquake (Dus.) as in Chap. 6.12 (see Matt. 27.5 and 28.2), and not some dreadful event to be discerned only from the fulfillment of the prophecy. (Eb.) The numerical specifications favor the literal view.

"the tenth part of the city",—Ebrard refers to the tenth part of the fourth world-power, over which the Antichrist is to extend his dominion.

"seven thousand persons",—Literally, "the names of men seven thousand," showing that the number is carefully and precisely stated, as if the name of each one were recounted.

Fausset says, "According to the literal view, one-tenth of Jerusalem fell under the Antichrist and, according to the Consecutive Historical view, one of the ten Roman apostate world-kingdoms fell."

"the rest",—Not the remnant of the Israelites who were not slain (F. Weid.), but the rest of the inhabitants of the city. (A. Dus.)

"gave",—an attempt has been made to supply "the two witnesses" as the subject here, but this will not do. The subject is *"the rest."*

"gave glory to God",—

1. Were converted. (F. A. Dus. Weid.) (See Chap. 16.9 and Jer. 13.16.)
2. A giving of glory only inspired by fear. They do not turn in true repentance to God. (Gab.)

Ver. 14. Weidner remarks, "We are still under the Seventh Seal, for the entire series of trumpet visions is developed out of the Seventh Seal; the first Six Seals bringing in preliminary judgments, while .the coming Seventh Trumpet, under the Seventh Seal, introduces the final and partly anticipated judgment under the Sixth Seal."

15 And the seventh angel sounded; and there followed great voices in heaven, and they said,
The kingdom of the world is become *the kingdom* of our Lord, and of his Christ: and he shall reign [1]for ever and ever.
16 And the four and twenty elders, who sit before God on their thrones, fell upon their faces and worshipped God, 17 saying,
We give thee thanks, O Lord God, the Almighty, who art and who wast; because thou hast taken thy great power, and didst reign. 18

[1]Gr. *unto the ages of the ages*

And the nations were wroth, and thy wrath came, and the time of the dead to be judged, and *the time* to give their reward to thy [2]servants the prophets, and to the saints, and to them that fear thy name, the small and the great; and to destroy them that destroy the earth.

19 And there was opened the [3]temple of God that is in heaven; and there was seen in his [3]temple the ark of his covenant; and there followed lightnings, and voices, and thunders, and an earthquake, and great hail.

[2]Gr. *bondservants*
[3]Or, *sanctuary*

Vers. 15-19. THE SEVENTH TRUMPET JUDGMENT.

Ver. 15. Before introducing the third woe in detail there is ·given the thanksgiving song of the elders for the establishment of the kingdom and the hour of vengeance, etc.

"And the seventh angel sounded",—Alford calls attention to the fact that the seventh member in each series of visions, seals, trumpets and vials, are all differently accompanied from any of the preceding series in each case. (a) At each seventh member we hear what is done not on earth, but in heaven; (b) each seventh member is followed by the statement that there followed voices, thunders, lightnings and earthquake; (c) at each seventh member it is plainly indicated that the end is come or is close at hand. All this, he says, forms grounds for inference that the three series of visions are not continuous but resumptive; not, indeed, going over the same ground with one another, either of time or occurrence, but each evolving something that was not in the former and putting the course of God's Providence in a different light. They are not, therefore, to be thought of as in mere temporal succession.

The Seventh Trumpet is to be limited to verses 15 to 18, although some include verse 19. But verse 19 is to be taken as traditional, belonging to and forming a transition to what follows. (A. Eb. Gab. Weid.)

"great voices",—i. e., of the four beasts (Ew.), of the angels (D.), of the innumerable hosts of Chap. 7.9 (Hen.), of the armies of heaven (Weid.). The view of Weidner is perhaps the best, although it may be well to think of them as the armies of heaven and the four living beings as distinguished from the elders' voices in the next verse. The question, says Dusterdieck, is neither to be asked or answered. That these voices have a proleptical import is seen in the fact that they describe as something already done what really does not occur until Chap. 18. (Ew. Dus. Lap.)

"in heaven",—i. e., whither the look of John is directed, John at this time not being in heaven. (D. Dus.)

"the kingdom of the world",—i. e., the regal dominion over the world. (A. B. D. Hen. Dus.) (See Psalm 2.2.)

"shall reign",—(See Dan. 7.14.) Fausset says it is the setting up of heaven's sovereignty over the earth visibly and that here begins the Millennial reign, the consummation of the mystery of God.

"This Seventh Trumpet", says Seiss, "is the last trumpet, at the sound of which the dead are raised and the prophets and saints receive their rewards, and it is only then that the voice declares, *'The kingdom of this world is become the kingdom of our Lord and of His Christ'*. It is therefore directly against the record here given to think of this reign of universal peace and righteousness, the Millennium, as taking place before the resurrection of the saints and before the second coming of the Lord."

Weidner, with a reference to I Cor. 15.24-28, says this points to the final end and judgment and is no temporal rule on earth, but eternal in the heavens.

Ver. 17. *"We give thee thanks"*,—Not because they consider themselves partakers of the great power and government of God (Hen.), but because the answer to the prayers of the saints for vengeance on their oppressors has been furnished by the judgment of the trumpets. (A. F. L.)

"Who art and who wast",—"Who is to come" is naturally omitted, the consummation having already come, i. e., proleptically.

Ver. 18. *"And the nations were wroth",*—Antichrist and his armies shall rise up against Christ. (Psa. 2.1-3.)

"the time of the dead to be judged",—Stated proleptically and does not actually occur until Chap. 20.11. (Dus. Gab.)

"servants",—This is to be referred only to the *"prophets",* which latter word is in apposition with the former.

"them that fear thy name",—The entire mass of the godly.

"them that destroy the earth",—The antichristian secular power.

Ver. 19. God's response to the songs of adoration.

"the ark of his covenant",—i. e., in the holy of holies; the symbol of God's faithfulness in bestowing grace on His people and inflicting vengeance on His enemies. It is indicative of what nature the succeeding visions are to be, i. e., they relate especially to His own covenant people.

"lightnings and voices", etc.,—"The solemn salvos of the artillery of heaven with which each series of visions is concluded." (A.) "The threatening foretokens of that with which the actual execution of the judgment comes upon the antichristian world." (Dus. Kli.)

CHAPTER TWELVE

1 And a great sign was seen in heaven: a woman arrayed with the sun, and the moon under her feet and upon her head a crown of twelve stars; 2 and she was with child; and she crieth out, travailing in birth, and in pain to be delivered. 3 And there was seen another sign in heaven: and behold, a great red dragon, having seven heads and ten horns, and upon his heads seven diadems. 4 And his tail draweth the third part of the stars of heaven, and did cast them to the earth: and the dragon standeth before the woman that is about to be delivered, that when she is delivered he may devour her child. 5 And she was delivered of a son, a man child, who is to rule all the ¹nations with a rod of iron: and her child was caught up unto God, and unto his throne. 6 And the woman fled into the wilderness, where she hath a place prepared of God, that there they may nourish her a thousand two hundred and threescore days.

7 And there was war in heaven: Michael and his angels *going forth* to war with the dragon; and the dragon warred and his angels; 8 and they prevailed not, neither was their place

¹Or, *Gentiles*

found any more in heaven. 9 And the great dragon was cast down, the old serpent, he that is called the Devil and Satan, the deceiver of the whole ²world; he was cast down to the earth, and his angels were cast down with him. 10 And I heard a great voice in heaven, saying,

³Now is come the salvation, and the power, and the kingdom of our God, and the authority of his Christ: for the accuser of our brethren is cast down, who accuseth them before our God day and night. 11 And they overcame him because of the blood of the Lamb, and because of the word of their testimony; and they loved not their life even unto death. 12 Therefore ⁴rejoice, O heavens, and ye that dwell in them. Woe for the earth and for the sea: because the devil is gone down unto you, having great wrath, knowing that he hath but a short time.

13 And when the dragon saw that he was cast down to the earth, he persecuted the woman that brought forth the man *child.* 14 And there were given to the woman the two wings of

²Gr. *inhabited earth*
³Or, *now is the salvation, and the power and the kingdom, become our God's and the authority is become his Christ's*
⁴Gr. *tabernacle*

THE REVELATION OF JOHN

the great eagle, that she might fly into the wilderness unto her place, where she is nourished for a time, and times, and half a time, from the face of the serpent. 15 And the serpent cast out of his mouth after the woman water as a river, that he might cause her to be carried away by the stream. 16 And the earth helped the woman, and the earth opened her mouth and swallowed up the river which the dragon cast out of his mouth. 17 And the dragon waxed wroth with the woman, and went away to make war with the rest of her seed, that keep the commandments of God, and hold the testimony of Jesus.

Vers. 1-17. THE SUN-CLOTHED WOMAN AND THE MAN-CHILD.

Says Moorehead, "After the Seventh Trumpet has sounded and the consummation is at length come, the Seer goes back and starts once more with a fresh vision".

Elliott of the Consecutive Historical School says that this vision and the two subsequent ones are *supplemental and explanatory* of what has gone before and that they have therefore a *retrogressive* character.

Alford of the Contemporaneous Historical School remarks also that, "the principal details of this section are descriptive rather than prophetical, relating to things past and passing."

Ver. 1. *"a great sign"*,—i. e., important in its meaning as well as vast in its appearance. (F. A. Dus.)

"sign",—i. e., a symbol (A. Eb. Hen. Dus.); one of those appearances by which something is signified to the Seer (Chap. 1.1). (A. Dus.)

Dusterdieck well remarks that the context and the very word itself shows it must be taken symbolically since the woman must be taken to represent something.

The rest of this verse can be the better understood when a decision has been reached as to whom the woman represents.

1. Sadler, Bernard, and especially the Romanists say she represents the Virgin Mary. (Are. Lap.) But the ideal description of the woman and the events pertaining to her, as well as her relation to the rest of her seed, precludes this.

2. The New Testament or Christian Church. (V. B. El. Be. Ly. Ar. Ca. Ham. Wor. Bar. Ira. Lord.) Stuart thinks the reference is to this Church particularly at the time of Christ's birth, while others (Chri. Stern) refer it to the time of the Antichrist. If the man-child refers to Christ, as most authorities think, then this view, according to Lange, Moorehead and others, miscarries in verse 5, because most assuredly, say these authorities, the New Testament Church did *not* give birth to Christ.

   Elliott takes this view, referring the expression to *Christ's true visible Church on earth* inclusive only of those that are alive at any particular time on earth. The *"heaven"* meant is that of the political heaven, the sun and the moon representing the chief rulers of the state, while in the same way the stars signify the lesser rulers, the former to be referred to the ruling powers of the Roman world decorating and supporting the Church at the particular time of the vision, while the latter is to be referred to the ecclesiastical rulers or Bishops recognized at the time to which the vision points as dignified authorities before the world. The man-child he takes as representing the children of the Church united into a *body politic* and raised to *dominant power*.

3. The Old Testament and the New Testament Church in undivided unity. (D. H. L. Au. Vic. And. Chr. Hen. Geb. Sei. Beck.) But there seems to be no hint of this in the prophecy and it also raises the question as to who could be represented by her seed.

4. The Old Testament Church, the Old Testament congregation of God (A. F. Au. Ew. Eb. Zu. Vol. Hei. Hof. Lud. Her. Gab. Pet. Weid. Moor.), the woman's travail representing the Old Testament believers' ardent longing for the promised Redeemer. "Israel, of whom according to the flesh Christ came, who is over all, God blessed forever." (Rom. 9.5.)

Lange, Elliott and others seem to think this view is incompatible with the wilderness experience, but a careful exegesis will show, we are inclined to think, that this last interpretation is the only tenable one. (See Isa. 7.14; Micah 4.10; 5.2-4.)

"clothed with the sun",—There is endless conjecture as to what the sun and the moon and the stars represent. Many make the sun stand for Christ, who to Israel is the Sun of Righteousness (V. N. Ar. Me. Ca. Pet. Gab. And. Dau. New. Lap. Gro. Stern), while by many of these same authorities the moon is referred to the reflected light of the Old Testament typical system.

Alford refers the stars to the twelve Patriarchs, while others (V. Be. Ar. Lap. Stern) refer them to the twelve Apostles, and yet others (Dus. Pet. Gab. Weid.) to the twelve tribes of Israel.

Perhaps it is well enough to see with Fausset and Weidner the thought that the Old Testament Church, clothed with the sun, is the bearer of divine, supernatural light in the world, and that by the moon under her feet, she will, as Ludhardt says, "in spite of her trials, finally triumph over night which for her has passed away"; or it may be better still to see, as Dusterdieck does, in all these designations only poetic descriptions of brilliancy, glory, etc.

Ver. 3. *"a great red dragon"*,—Elliott says this is the fit representative of any heathen persecutor but here it symbolizes Imperial Rome as an antichristian persecuting power. By the great majority of commentators, however, the dragon is taken to mean the Devil. (V. D. Ar. Ly. Eb. Hen. Dus. Lap. Gab. Moor.)

Dr. Maitland says, "What meaning is there in language, if we can make the dragon anything but the great enemy of man; while we read, 'The great Dragon was cast out, that old Serpent called the Devil and Satan'?" (See verse 9.)

"great",—i. e., great in size, from which is inferred his dreadful power.

"red",—i. e., fiery red, symbolical of destruction and corruption (Eb.); perhaps also because he is a murderer from the beginning (Dus.) (John 8.14), and is intent upon the murder of the child to be delivered and of all believers. (Chap. 6.4.)

The assumption by the dragon of so many of the details of the Beast of Chap. 13.1 indicate that he lies in wait for the child in the form of that antichristian power which is afterwards represented by the Beast.

"seven heads",—Not seven deadly sins (Tirinus), nor a caricature of the Seven Spirits of God, i. e., seven evil spirits (Au.), nor the non-unitous power of Satan (Hof.), but perhaps the perfection of diabolical subtlety and wisdom (D. Pet.).

The seven heads, says Dusterdieck, refer to the antichristian secular power of the Roman empire, which is seen in Chap. 13 under another form, the number of heads, horns and diadems being based upon the historical relations of that empire, the seven crowned heads referring to the imperial successions, and the ten horns representing ten rulers, the number all to be taken in literal accuracy.

"ten horns",—A symbol of his earthly power. (D. Weid.)

"seven diadems",—Implying universality of earthly dominion as held by the Prince of this world. (A. F. Gab. Weid.)   Note that the dragon has *seven* diadems on his *heads,* while the Beast of Chap. 13.1, the Antichrist, has *ten* diadems on his *horns.*   In Chap. 17.9-13 John explains these heads and horns as so many kings.

Ver. 4.   *"And his tail draweth"*, etc.,—(See also Dan. 8.10).

Elliott of the Consecutive Historical School says the reference is to a time when the antichristian persecuting power was in supremacy in only one-third of the Roman political heaven, namely in the fourth century (about A. D. 313), the dragon symbolizing Maximim, who ruled in the Asiatic third of the Roman world and who severely persecuted the Church even while in the other two-thirds it enjoyed toleration and protection, the "drawing with his tail and casting down to earth of the stars" referring to his degrading and even killing the bishops and rulers in ecclesiastical affairs.

There are those (Ei. Ew. Dus.) who think the reference to the dragon's tail is a poetic trait and represents his eagerness for combat; while others still (A. Weid.) think it represents the magnitude and fury of the dragon, while the reference to the *"third part of the stars"* many of these authorities (Eb. Vic. Pet. Sad. Will. Weid.) are inclined to think refers to the angels which the Devil drew down with him to perdition at the time he was cast out of heaven. (Jude 6.)

"standeth before the woman",—Simcox says that this evidently "symbolizes the enmity of the serpent against the seed of woman, beginning with the intended treachery of Herod and the massacre of the innocents, but including also that malice which pursued Him through life, the temptation and at last the cross."

Ver. 5.   *"delivered of a son"*,—The words, *"rule all nations with a rod of iron"*, cited verbatim from Ps. 2.9, leave no possibility of doubt as to who is here intended. It is the Lord Jesus and none other, and the reference is to the historical birth of Jesus. (A. L. F. D. Eb. Dus. Pet. Gab. Sad. Hen. Lee. Sim. Weid. Boyd. Carp. Rinck, Currey, Moor.)

Some wrongfully regard the child as Christ formed mystically in believers and so of all regenerated children of God (Be.) ; others take the being "born" as the professing of the Nicene Creed and so becoming a child of God in the midst of the persecutions of the heathen secular powers (B. Ap. Ar. Ca. Stern) ; while others (Ei. Hei. Her.) say the child is the Christian Church proceeding from the Jewish Church, while still others

622

claim the reference is to the Roman Catholic Church. It is, however, impossible to dispose of the reference by any of these interpretations.

"caught up unto God and unto his throne",—Elliott of the Consecutive Historical School interprets this as the enthroning of Constantine over the Roman Empire in the character of a Christian emperor, inclusive of other orthodox Christian Roman emperors after him. It was, he says, Constantine, *the son of Christ's faithful Catholic united Church*, elevated to an avowedly Christian throne, that might well be called the throne of God, like Solomon's, and thus was Christianity caught up to the place of supremacy in the Roman Empire. Thus, as Gibbon says, "Christianity was seated on the throne of the Roman world." It was Constantine and other emperors, such as Theodosius, who ruled the heathen *"with a rod of iron"*, discountenancing them and finally putting an end to all toleration of Paganism.

The idea, however, is that of deliverance from danger, and the reference is doubtless to Christ's historical ascension (V. A. L. D. Eb. Hen. Dus. Gab. Tor. Mor. Sco. Gra. Weid. Moor.) after a conflict, as Alford says, with the prince of this world who came and tried Him and found nothing in Him. "Words can hardly be plainer than these," says Alford. "It surely is but needful," he continues, "to set against them, thus understood, the interpretation which would regard them as fulfilled by the 'mighty issue of the consummated birth of a son of the Church, a baptized emperor, to political supremacy in the Roman empire,' 'united with the solemn public profession of the divinity of the Son of man'."

All Futurists, however, contend that it was not with the history of the present-day Church that the vision was concerned. Christ, they say, ascended and took His place at the right hand of God. Then the present age began. It is not even mentioned or recorded in the vision at all. It is the whole history of the Old Testament Church, the Old Testament congregation of God, and of Israel, in God's covenant relation to His chosen people. down to the very end of time that John sees. In the thought of John and of all the Apostles no such period as twenty centuries was to intervene.

Weidner remarks, "The thought here that this man-child is to rule all the nations with a rod of iron brings by anticipation this very period of the final end before us," while Moorehead likewise remarks, "The chapter touches the first advent and then sketches the events that pertain to the time of the second advent."

Petingill, Mackintosh and a few others have a curious idea here. They think the "catching up" does not refer to the historical, bodily ascension of Christ from the mount of Olives, but to His spiritual body, believers who are to be caught up at the coming rapture, that the man-child therefore is still in progress of birth, the Church not being fully formed as yet, and that the dragon is still seeking to destroy the man-child, the true Church of Christ in the world today.

Ver. 6. This verse anticipates what is more minutely described in verses 13 to 15. (V. A. Dau. Ew. Dus. Hof. Hen. Weid.)

Ver. 7. *"war in heaven"*,—Elliott says the reference here is to Christianity contending against heathenism in the time of Julian, the Apostate, which ended in the final downfall of paganism on Julian's death in A. D. 363, whose death-cry was, "O Galilean, thou hast conquered", and the downfall of heathenism Elliott interprets as the Dragon and his angels being cast out of heaven.

Alford and others think that the war here mentioned occurred at the time of Christ's ascension into heaven. Their view of the matter is that the Dragon not being able to overcome Christ while on earth, pursued the Man-child at His ascension even to the throne of God, and this caused the war; "carried the war," as Weidner says, "into heaven itself, returning thither with his angels, with the vain hope of supplanting Christ on the throne of heaven—God permitting it, in His eternal counsels, for the sake of the glory of His Son."

Says Alford, "I would appeal in passing to the solemnity of the words here used, and the particularity of the designation, and ask whether it is possible to understand this of the mere casting down of paganism from the throne of the Roman empire?"

Alford, referring to Luke 10.18 and John 12.21, thinks this casting down of Satan from the office of accuser in heaven is evidently connected with the work of redemption. He accordingly says, "The day of acceptance in Christ has dawned and Satan's voice is to be heard before God no longer, and his angels, those rebel spirits, whom he led away, are cast down with him into the earth, where now the conflict is raging during the short time which shall elapse between the Ascension and the Second Advent when he shall be bound."

The casting down of Satan from heaven took place directly after the ascension of Christ, immediately upon the issue of the war.

The one rather formidable objection to this view is that in verse 12 it is said that the Devil knew he had but *"a short time"* before he was to be bound, and inasmuch as this is said from the standpoint both of the supernatural knowledge of the Devil and the elders in heaven it can hardly bear the same relation to the idea of duration as the same expression could, and indeed does, when used by the Apostles in their expressions of "short time", "shortly come to pass", etc., and doubtless therefore means just what we would mean by the same expression, namely, a very little while indeed, and not 2000 years and more from the ascension of Christ. And then, too, Ephesians 6.12 seems to imply that Satan is still in the heavenly places, even while he is the prince of this world. These objections are not, however, altogether unsurmountable. But because of the foregoing, and because of other reasons, the Futurists take the position that this war in heaven occurred after the Rapture of the saints, and that Satan will be then present, accusing the brethren before God day and night, whereupon (Zech. 3.2) Christ rebukes him and Michael leads the hosts of heaven against him with the result already known.

These authorities remind us that Satan and his angels were first cast out of heaven at some time previous to the fall of man (II Pet. 2.4 and Jude 6), yet he was still permitted at least in Old Testament times to enter into the presence of God in heaven as the accuser and adversary of man (Job 2.1-7 and 16.12; Zech. 3.1,2), and that there is no reason to believe, especially in view of Eph. 6.12, that this was not true in New Testament times and will be true *until the end of this war* when he will be cast down to enter heaven no more forever.

"Michael",—Not Christ (L. V. Hen.), inasmuch as Michael of this verse and the child of verse 5 cannot be the same person. He is Michael, the archangel, the adversary of Satan in their strife about the body of Moses, and in the Old Testament the guardian of the Jewish people in their conflict with heathenism, and the leader of the good angels in all their conflicts with the power of Satan. (See Dan. 10.13,21; 12.1 and Jude 9.) (B. D. A. Ew. Au. Eb. Hof. Dus. Gab. Weid.) The construction is irregular and is best explained by supplying *"going forth"* as in our text.

Ver. 8. *"neither was their place found any more in heaven"*,—He was no longer to maintain any place in heaven.

Ver. 9. The various designations describe his nature and activity as completely as possible. It shows what the saints on earth, whence he is cast, have to expect from him.

"serpent",— (See Gen. 3.1).

"Devil",—The Greek for "slanderer", "accuser".

"Satan",—The Hebrew for "adversary".

Ver. 10. *"a great voice in heaven"*,—Whose, is left unknown. Not of angels (Be.), for they would scarcely have called the saints *"our brethren"*, nor of the already perfected saints (B. V.), for they would have spoken in the first person rather than in the third, and said "our accuser", and "we overcame". It is probably that of the Elders representing the Church, inasmuch as the expression, *"our brethren"* suggests this.

Elliott, of course, thinks *"heaven"* to be symbolical of political elevation and power, and that this song prefigures some similar song of the Christians of the Roman world on the occasion of their triumph and exaltation over Heathenism under the reigns of Maximin and Licinius and Julian.

"Now is come",—i. e., is realized. In the ultimate the textual and marginal readings are practically the same. The song, it would seem, is introductory to the final events which are now about to occur.

"our brethren",—Elliott, of course, finds here a reference to the martyr-victors of the antichristian persecution days of the Roman empire, the *"kingdom of our God"* referred to in the former part of the verse being that of Constantine with Christianity dominant in it.

"The dispensation of the kingdom, *'the kingdom of our God,'* etc.," says Scofield, "begins with the return of Christ to the earth, runs through the 'thousand years' of His earthly rule, and ends when He has delivered up the kingdom to the Father (See II Sam. 7.8 and I Cor. 15.24.)."

"accuseth day and night",— (Derived from Zech. 3 and Job 1 and 2.)

Ver. 11. *"they overcame him"*,—*"They"* of course refers to *"our brethren"*.

"because of the blood of the Lamb",—"Their victory over Satan was grounded in and was the consequence of the Lamb having shed His blood; without that the charges of the Adversary against them would have been unanswerable." (A.)

"because of the word of their testimony",—It is because they give a faithful testimony unto death that they are victorious; this is their part and the shedding of the blood was the Lamb's part.

Ver. 12. *"rejoice"*,—Because of what is said in verses 10 and 11. Those who place the war at the time of the historical ascension of Christ (A. D. Dus. Weid. Crav.) give as the principal reason for rejoicing only the fact that Satan has been cast down, and are of course compelled to look upon what is said in verse 11 as proleptical, i. e., something recorded as past but which is still to take place in the future.

"knowing that he hath but a short time",—Depending upon the fact that "the time is at hand" and that the Lord will soon come to judge Satan together with all his instruments.

Elliott of the Consecutive Historical School insists that the *"woe"* here announced is to be regarded as a detached and solemn notification by the *dictating prophetic Spirit* of some woe soon to come upon the Roman empire, the reference being to heretical persecutors within the Church, and to the Gothic scourge which soon came. The first of these he finds in verse 13, which refers to persecution by bitter Arian emperors, and the second in the Dragon's attempt to drown the Church in the Gothic scourge as prefigured in verse 15. The fleeing into the wilderness he interprets as a serious decline in the piety and spiritual state of the Church soon after the establishment of Christianity in the Roman empire, and the two wings given unto it as the protection afforded the Church by the Eastern and Western divisions of the Roman empire under Theodosius the Great. Verse 16 he interprets as the overthrow and disappearance of Arianism by practically all of the Roman *earth*, and verse 17 as Satan's efforts against the doctrines of such men as Augustine and others of the seed that "kept the commandments of God and held the testimony of Jesus."

Ver. 13. *"he persecuted the woman"*,—Satan now turns his fury toward the mother of the child. If the woman is taken as the Old Testament Church, in keeping with the explanation already adopted, she must here, it would seem, be thought of either in one or the other of the two following ways:

(1) The remnant of Isreal (Moorehead says the 144,000) converted doubtless by the preaching of the Two Witnesses during the last days (Gab. Pet. Mor. Sco. Tor.) after the Rapture of the Church.

(2) The Old Testament Church must be supposed to have passed in the interim into the new form of the Christian Church, which is the view of Alford and others of his school, and in this case the further persecutions of Satan, as directed against the woman, will relate to the whole of the Church of this dispensation. If, however, the object of Satan's further hostility is to be considered as thus directed, an easier solution of the problem might present itself if the woman be taken in the first place as representing the Old Testament and the New Testament Church in undivided unity, or as representing the New Testament or Christian Church alone. (See under verse 1, page 620, views 3 and 2.)

Says Alford, "I own that considering the analogies and the language used, I am much more disposed to interpret the persecution of the woman by the Dragon of the various persecutions by the Jews which followed the Ascension, and *her flight into the wilderness* of the gradual withdrawal of the Church and her agency from Jerusalem, finally consummated by the flight to the mountains on the approaching siege, commanded by our Lord Himself."

Ver. 14. *"the two wings of the great eagle"*,—A figure of God's delivering Providence. The figure is taken from Ex. 19.4 and Deut. 32.11. The article must not be supposed to identify the eagle with that of Chap. 8.13 (Eb.), nor with the figures in Exodus and Deuteronomy. The article is simply generic. (A. D. Dus.)

"into the wilderness",—(For views of the Historical Schools see above.) According to the view of the Futurists the reference is here perhaps to the place of isolation among the nations of the earth during the last days. John has of course before his mind the picture of Israel fleeing out of Egypt.

"into her place",—i. e., prepared for her by God. (Verse 6.) (See Ex. 23.20.)

"she is nourished",—As God nourished Israel in the wilderness, so will He care for these saints (the Jewish remnant, according to the Futurists) against whom the Dragon is endeavoring to vent his rage.

Some because of this expression, interpret the woman as the *invisible* spiritual Church of Christ, the flight into the wilderness meaning that God's true servants are withdrawn from the eyes of the world. But this they have been just as much at all times and will continue so until the great manifestation of the Sons of God.

"from the face of the serpent",—Not to be connected with *"fly"* (V. Zu.), but with *"nourished"* (A. B. D. El. Ew. Dus. Hen.), importing *safe from, hidden from*.

"time and times and half a time",—In explaining this expression we must adopt one or the other of three different views:

(a) The year-day theory which reckons a day a year. According to this mode of reckoning, a day will be a year, a month will be thirty years and a year will be 360 years.

(b) The symbolic view which gives the expression but a mystical meaning without chronological force, involving no particular length of time.

(c) The literal view which makes the period designated to be just three years and a half, one time (year), two times (two years) and a half of a time (half year).

Elliott of the Consecutive Historical School adopts, as we have seen, the year-day theory, as do practically all interpreters of this school. It is however difficult to find the period. If we think of the flight into the wilderness as taking place any time between the Ascension and the Destruction of Jerusalem, 1260 years would bring us to no event which can with any propriety be pointed out as putting an end to the wilderness state of the Church. Elliott makes the flight to begin soon after the establishment of Christianity in the Roman empire (the flight consisting in a serious decline in the piety and spiritual state of the Church, thus "vanishing in its distinctive features from public view"), but then the 1260 years brings us to a period which is not, says Alford, altogether satisfying as meeting the requirements of the prophecy. It is also in order to ask here, if the decline in piety spoken of is the beginning of the wilderness state, was the open establishment of the Protestant churches the end of it, and this Elliott would hardly allow.

If we adopt the second view, "we seem," as Alford says, "to incur the danger of missing the prophetic sense, and leaving unfixed that which apparently the Spirit of God intended us to ascertain."

Futurists in general take the literal view and place this period after the Rapture of the Church. Petingill refers it to the first half of the time of Antichrist, while others (Gab. Weid, et al.) refer it to the last half of the same period. Of course the period is the same as the 1260 days of verse 6, but this need not necessarily refer to the same actual time as the 1260 days of Chap. 11.3 which we saw referred, according to the Futurist view, to the first half of the period under consideration. The most natural inference would be that of Petingill's, but then the question would arise as to the woman's place and protection during the last half of the time of Antichrist when she would be especially in need of God's nourishing care. This consideration inclines us, in case the Futurist interpretation be accepted, to the view of Gaebelein, and Weidner and others of this school of interpretation.

Alford says of all prophecies the literal view of this time period can be applied least satisfactorily to this one. "The conflict," he says, "is that between Satan and the Church, whose seed, as expressly interpreted to be, is God's Christian people, and is it likely that a few days or years will limit the duration of a prophecy confessedly of such wide import?"

Ver. 15. Satan's attempt to destroy the saints with a flood. Compare the passage of Israel through the Red Sea; although Dusterdieck seems to think that John is simply forming living images from the symbolical mode of speech of the Old Testament, and here gets his concept from passages such as Ps. 18.5-17; 32.6; 42.8, rather than from the passage of Israel through the Red Sea. The various intrepretations of this *"river"* are so numerous as to bewilder one.

The Allegorists, pointing to Chap. 17.1, where the "many waters" are expressly explained as a figure of many nations, make these expressions identical, and thus we have here a "river of people" which will roll against the Church. "The abundance of Godless men or various trials" (And.).

Among the Preterists and Historical interpretations are the following: "The flight of the Christians to Pella" (Ew.); "The armies of Vespasian" (Wet.); "Roman persecutions after Nero" (Ham.); "The flood of barbarous nations" (Wor. Stern); "The Saracens" (V.); "The wild Germanic masses flowing against Rome" (Au.); "The army of Antichrist" (Lap.); "The Arian heretics" (Ca.); "The force of persecutions" (Hen. Eb.). All of these interpretations take from the passage of course any and all reference to prophecy yet to be fulfilled. Alford, interpreting the flight into the wilderness as the flight of the Christians before the destruction of Jerusalem, says, "Then the river which the dragon sent out of his mouth after the woman might be variously understood,—of the Roman armies which threatened to sweep away Christianity in the wreck of the Jewish nation,—or of the persecutions which followed the Church into her retreats, but eventually became absorbed by the civil power turning Christian,—or of the Jewish nation itself, banded together against Christianity wherever it appeared, but eventually itself becoming powerless against it by its dispersion and ruin,—or again, of the influx of heretical opinions from pagan philosophers which tended to swamp the true faith; I confess that not one of these seems to me satisfactory to answer the conditions; nor do we gain anything by their combination. But anything within reasonable regard for the analogies and symbolism of the text seems better than the now too commonly received Consecutive Historical interpretation, with its wild fancies and arbitrary assignment of words and figures."

Weidner remarks, "Although we do not profess to understand or explain any of these prophecies concerning events still lying in the future, we deem it far better to accept the idea that God will in some way bring about all these events as here indicated, than to adopt the strange and arbitrary fancies with which the allegorists and historical interpreters seek to becloud us."

Perhaps one of the simplest explanations, whether we adopt the Historical or the Futurist view, is that of Gaebelein, who sees in the water cast out by Satan a symbol of the hatred which Satan stirs up against the faithful.

Ver. 16. Some are inclined with Weidner, to take the contents of this verse literally (see Num. 16.26-35); while others take it symbolically, as Gaebelein for instance, who says it refers to the help rendered the believing remnant of Jews by the Gentile nations among whom they are in isolation, and who have been converted by believing the final message of the Gospel of the Kingdom.

Ver. 17. *"the rest of her seed"*,—This verse presents another puzzling inquiry. Elliott, as we have seen, refers the verse to Satan's attempts to subvert the doctrines of such men as Augustine and Vigilantius. Others of the Historical School say the reference is to the Christians who survived the earlier persecutions. But in reality there was no "rest" in this sense, because the efforts of the Dragon as thus conceived were entirely unsuccessful.

Alford finds himself wondering if the woman after all may not symbolize *the true visible Church*, which continued as established by our Lord and His Apostles, in unbroken unity during the first centuries, but which as time went on was broken up by evil men and evil doctrines, and has remained, unseen, unrealized, her unity an article of faith, not of sight, but still multiplying her seed, those who keep the commandments of God and have the testimony of Jesus, in various sects and distant countries, waiting the day for her comely order and oneness again to be manifested, when the Lord's prayer for the unity of His people being accomplished, the world shall believe that the Father sent Him. "If," says Alford, "we are disposed to carry out this idea, we might see the great realization of the flight into the wilderness in the final severance of the Eastern and the Western churches in the seventh century, and the flood cast after the woman by the Dragon in the irruption of the Mahometan armies. But this, though not less satisfactory than the other interpretations, is as unsatisfactory."

Among the Futurists, who place the time of all this Satanic hostility after the Rapture of the Church, the following interpretations are found:

Weidner thinks the reference is to those believers among the Gentiles who in that day accept the Gospel.

Gaebelein refers it to the godly remnant in the land of Palestine in distinction from those in isolation among the nations into which the woman had fled. Similar to this is the view of Moorehead, who refers the fleeing woman to the 144,000 sealed among the Jews, and the *"rest of her seed"* to the Jewish martyrs of the last three and one-half years which constitute the time of the Great Tribulation, and in this expression he thinks perhaps the countless throng of Gentiles, as seen in Chap. 7.9-14, may be included.

The question I own is a puzzling one, but its answer must be sought in keeping with the school of interpretation to which the student finds himself inclining.

CHAPTER THIRTEEN

1 and [1]he stood upon the sand of the sea. And I saw a beast coming up out of the sea, having ten horns and seven heads, and on his horns ten diadems, and upon his heads names of blasphemy. 2 And the beast which I saw was like unto a leopard, and his feet were as *the feet* of a bear, and his mouth as the mouth of a lion: and the dragon gave him his power, and his throne, and great authority. 3 And *I* saw one of his heads as though it had been [2]smitten unto death; and his deathstroke was healed: and the whole earth wondered after the beast; 4 and they [3]worshipped the dragon, because he gave his authority unto the beast; and they [3]worshipped the beast, saying, Who is like unto the beast? and who is able to war with him? 5 and there was given to him a mouth speaking great things and blasphemies; and there was given to

him authority [4]to continued forty and two months. 6 And he opened his mouth for blasphemies against God, to blaspheme his name, and his tabernacle, *even* them that [5]dwell in the heaven. 7 And it was given unto him to make war with the saints, and to overcome them: and there was given to him authority over every tribe and people and tongue and nation. 8 And all that dwell on the earth shall [3]worship him, *every one* whose name hath not been [6]written from the foundation of the world in the book of life of the Lamb that hath been slain. 9 If any man hath an ear, let him hear. 10 [7]If any man [8]*is* for captivity, into captivity he goeth: if any man shall kill with the sword, with the sword must he be killed. Here is the [9]patience and the faith of the saints.

[1]Some ancient authorities read, *I stood &c.*, connecting the clause with what follows
[2]Gr. *slain*
[3]See marginal note on Verse 12
[4]Or, *to do* his works *during* See Dan. 11.28
[5]Gr. *tabernacle*
[6]Or, *written in the book . . . slain from the foundation of the world*
[7]The Greek text in this verse is somewhat uncertain
[8]Or, leadeth *into captivity*
[9]Or, *stedfastness*

Vers. 1-10. THE BEAST OUT OF THE SEA.

Ver. 1. *"and he* (the Dragon) *stood upon the sand of the sea"*,— In order to call forth the beast out of the sea, to whom he is to give all his power and authority.

"out of the sea",—By the vast majority of commentators the sea is taken, and rightly, as symbolic of the disordered and confused life of the Gentile nations of the world. (L. F. E. A. Be. Eb. Bar. Hen. Hof. Vic. And. Lap. Coc. Kli. Wor. Pet. Lee. Cow. Weid. Moor. Stern.)

"ten horns",—Mentioned first not because they are crowned (A. F.), but doubtless because appearing first as the beast rises from the sea. (B. Hen. Weid.)

"upon his heads names of blasphemy",—It is not, as Zundel says, one letter on each head; nor perhaps as others (D. Ew. Hen. Dus.) say, the same name on each head. The meaning is doubtless that each one of the heads appears to have a frontlet with an inscription on it that was blasphemous, in that it ascribed some attribute to this power that belonged to God alone. Alford seems to think the reference is to the divine titles given to kings.

The beast, which is the same as that in Chap. 17, has seven heads and ten horns, on each horn a crown, and on each head a name of blasphemy. In Chap. 17.9 we are told that the seven heads are seven mountains; in Chap. 17.10 we are told that the seven heads are seven kings; in Chap. 17.11 we are told that the beast himself is an eighth king, and in Chap. 17.12 we are told that the ten horns are ten kings. It would seem that this beast bears some relation to the fourth beast which Daniel saw rising out of the sea. Daniel saw four beasts coming up out of the sea. Daniel's fourth beast had ten horns and among them there was a *"little horn"* which came up and plucked up three of the other horns, and made war with the saints.

Ver. 2. Dusterdieck and Cowles say this description of the beast refers merely to its rapacity and power uniting in itself the most dreadful weapons of the strongest beasts.

The first of Daniel's beasts was like a lion, the second like a bear, the third like a leopard and the fourth was a strange nondescript with ten horns. The beast which John saw, as will be seen from its description, seems to be a compound of Daniel's first three beasts, the beast of John being himself identical with Daniel's fourth beast. (A. L. F. El. Pet. Gab. Sco. Will.)

Says Scofield, "The three animals, leopard, bear and lion, are found in Dan. 7.4-6 as symbols of the empires which preceded Rome, and whose characteristics all entered into the qualities of the Roman empire; Macedonian swiftness of conquest, Persian tenacity of purpose and Babylonish voracity. This first beast of John is the same as the fourth beast of Daniel (Dan. 7.24). The 'ten horns' are explained in Dan. 7.24 and Rev. 17.12 to be ten kings, and the whole vision is of the last form of Gentile world-power, a confederate ten-kingdom empire covering the sphere of authority of ancient Rome. The first three verses of this chapter refer to the ten-kingdom *empire*, while verses 4-10 refer to the ten-kingdom *emperor*, who is emphatically *the* beast. (See Rev. 19.20.)"

It would seem, as Williams says, that "he represents some great principle of evil found in all the heathen kingdoms."

"the dragon gave him his power", etc.,—In order to use him as the instrument of his diabolical wrath against the rest of the seed of the woman.

Ver. 3. *"and his deathstroke was healed"*,—The whole chapter is a difficult one to interpret and this and other perplexing expressions must be explained in keeping of course with the interpretation which is given to the beast introduced by the first verse of the chapter.

It is a much mooted question as to just what the beast refers. Some declare that it represents merely the aggregate or sum total of the God-opposed empires of the world and that it is not to be restricted to any particular manifestation. But David Brown has very properly said, "The beast is described with such precision as well as fullness of detail that it will not do to generalize it away by calling it simply the great world-power which in every age is antagonistic to the kingdom of God. It is contrary to all principles of strict interpretation to dispose of detail so specific, so varied and so peculiar in this way."

This beast and the one in verse 11 are doubtless, as Cowles says, co-ordinate and co-operative and therefore contemporaneous.

Interpreters of the Historical Schools here unite in referring the whole description to Rome, but they are all so divided among themselves that utter confusion really prevails.

Some of them refer the whole chapter to Papal Rome, exercising both political power, as represented by the first beast, and ecclesiastical power as represented by the second beast, the second beast representing the Papal Priesthood. (B. V. El. Ca. Coc. Lud.) As a fair example of this interpretation the following is gleaned from Elliott. He says in substance:

The *"sea"* is the flood of invading Goths; the image of the beast is the Papal Councils of Western Europe. The *"Antichrist"* of Saint John and the *"little horn"* of Daniel are one and the same.

When the angel in Chap. 17.9 said the seven heads of the first beast were seven hills he fastened the symbol at once to Rome, the seven hills of the city of Rome, which at once refutes any interpretation that refers the heads to the seven successive world powers, of which it is said in Chap. 17.10 that five had fallen before John's time (Egypt, Assyria, Babylon, Persia, Greece), while the sixth, which then was, referred to Rome during John's own time; the remaining one which is yet to come being variously understood.

When the angel further said that the seven heads were seven "kings" or "kingdoms" he makes it plain that he refers to seven heathen-like Governors or rather successive forms of government. The first six heads are (and this is the generally received Protestant interpretation) Kings, Consuls, Dictators, Decemvirs and Military Tribunes (the first five which are fallen) and the imperial form commencing with Augustus Caesar. The seventh head was the government under Diocletian and his three colleagues.

Under Julian the last heathen head of the Roman empire was struck down through an edict by Theodosius (which was the wound unto death), the pagan sacrifices and temples being suppressed, but in the rise of Papacy this deadly wound of the last pagan ruling head was healed. The ten horns sprouting from the beast's last or Papal head refer to ten kingdoms existing about A. D. 532, Anglo-Saxons, Franks of Central, Alleman-Franks of Eastern, Burgundic-Franks of South Eastern France, Visigoths, Suevi, Vandals, Ostrogoths, Bavarians, and the Lombards. The ten horns all sprout from ·the eighth head and this eighth head is the Popes. The Popes are the Antichrist and all that is said of the persecution and blasphemy of the beast is true of the Popes. The miracles are pretended miracles and 666 means *Lateinos*.

Others refer the first beast to Pagan Rome and the second beast to Papal Rome. (Bar. Faber, Bickersteth, Cuninghame.) As a fair example of this interpretation the following is gleaned from Barnes. He says in substance:

> The ten horns refer to Rome contemplated as made up of ten subordinate kingdoms just after the invasion of the Northern hordes and at the time the Papacy was about to rise. After the time of Constantine the Pagan Roman empire began its decline, and, as if wounded to death, would have become extinct had it not been revived in the days of Charlemagne under the influence of Papal Rome, which latter is the second beast of verse 11.

> The worship mentioned in verse 4 is not religious worship, but homage such as is shown to one whom we deem our superior and all such homage rendered under Papal Rome was really homage to Satan.

> Verses 6 and 7 refer to the Albigenses and the Waldensians. The miracles are only pretended miracles, i. e., "signs and lying wonders." Making an image of the beast and causing it to live means that John saw in a vision such a state of things existing *as if*, or similar to what would be the case if an image had been made of the beast, or Pagan Roman empire, and the people did homage to it. All this would have been fulfilled if Pagan Rome, the old Roman secular imperial power, should become to a large extent dead or cease to exert its influence over men (wounded, as it were, to death), and if then the Papal spiritual power should cause a form of domination to exist strongly resembling the former in its general character and extent; and this very thing was done in the empire that sprung up in the days of Charlemagne through the influence of the Papacy. In this we discern the image of the former Roman power. Causing the image to breath and speak, in verse 15, means giving signs of life and issuing authoritative commands, while *"worship"* again refers to homage shown to the empire or the emperors.

> The *"mark"* of verse 16 means that there would be some mark of distinction, some indelible sign, something that would designate with entire certainty those persons who belonged to the Papacy, and this is true inasmuch as one can usually tell the Roman Catholic. Verse 17 refers to the Papacy trying to control the markets and the wealth of the world. Often they have prohibited trade or traffic with the Protestants.

Others again refer the whole chapter to Pagan Rome, the second beast representing the Pagan Priesthood. (D. Al. Be. Ew. Ei. Bl. Lu. Cow. Vic. Gro. Ham. Bos. Wet. Her. Dus. Alc.)

Cowles says the second beast cannot be Papal Rome because Papal Rome did not exist in the age of the first seven emperors whose regime was 600 years before Papal Rome became a well-defined system and 1000 years before she became a persecuting power. He says it referred to the Pagan Priesthood which everywhere ministered to the idolatrous homage paid to the Roman emperors and everywhere inspired the animus of Paganism.

Others again refer the first beast to the secular persecuting power (Pagan or Papal) and the second beast to the sacerdotal (priestly) persecuting power. While this latter refers primarily to the Pagan Priesthood, inasmuch as it was this that made the image of the emperors, compelled the Christians to do homage to the same, and wrought the pretended miracles mentioned, it refers as well to the Papal or so-called Christian Priesthood. (A.) The wounded head, says Alford, represents the Roman empire, which, having long been a head of the beast, was crushed and to all appearances exterminated, but was healed in the establishment of the Christian Roman empire. The image of the Beast for the time being would be the image of the reigning emperor, the giving of life to the image referring doubtless to some lying wonders permitted to the Pagan priests to try the faith of God's people. The buying and selling refers to the commercial and spiritual interdicts laid on nonconformity, both of Pagan and Papal persecutors.

Craven, who wavers between the Historical and the Futurist views, says in substance:

The wounded head is the sixth or Roman world-power, the wound consisting not only in the fact of Rome's nominal conversion under Constantine but also to the fact that shortly after Constantine it ceased to be a Roman sovereignty. The empire under Charlemagne cannot be the seventh head since it never extended over the field of the Eastern Churches and not indeed over all the Western. If the seventh head is to be analogous with the other six we must look for it still in the future. He does not deny the possibility of the Futurist view and in fact commits himself to the view that the consummate fulfillment is still in the future.

The seven heads and ten horns are, as we have seen, variously interpreted. Among those who refer the beast to Pagan Rome many explain the seven heads as seven individual emperors of Rome. (D. Bl. Ei. Ew. Lu. Vic. Hil. Cor. Bau.) Hammond and Grotius refer the seven heads and the ten horns to the seven hills of Rome and the ten servant kings.

Dusterdieck, who applies the beast to Pagan Rome, says the seven heads are seven emperors and the ten horns are ten emperors, seven of whom were real emperors (one for each head) and the other three were usurpers growing up between the fifth and sixth heads, the tenth horn therefore corresponding to the seventh head being still in the future.

Of those who restrict the beast to Papal Rome, some refer the seven heads and ten horns to seven forms of Roman government and the ten kingdoms subservient to the Papacy from the French kingdom to the Polish.

Among those who decline to restrict the reference of the beast to Rome we have the seven heads referred to "the seven world-periods" (And.), "the seven kings before the appearance of the Antichrist" (Lap.), "the seven persecutions of Christians" (Al.), "the seven powers hostile to Christianity corresponding to the seven periods of the New Testament history" (Stern), and as we have before seen, Craven joins with others (A. K. Eb. Hen. And. Mil. Dau. Bur. Glas.) in referring the seven heads to the seven world-powers, which they interpret as Egypt, Assyria, Babylon, Medo-Persia, Greece, Rome and finally, as the seventh, the Roman empire with its ten horns which followed the downfall of Rome upon the Barbaric invasion and under which we now live; while others (Fu. Hof. Lud.) omit Egypt and starting with Assyria give us the following, Assyria, Babylonia, Persia, Macedonia, Syria under Antiochus Epiphanes, Rome, and finally, as seventh, the future Apocalyptic Kingdom.

Burgh says the generally received interpretation that the whole chapter refers to Papal Rome in its political and ecclesiastical character, i. e., the empire and the Hierarchy of the Papacy, is refuted by the following:

1. No one has ever found the ten-fold division of the empire. Twenty-eight different commentators have named sixty-five different kingdoms, reckoning only once the kingdoms common to the different lists. What would it be if all the commentators were consulted!

2. Study the meaning of "blasphemy" in the Bible and you will find that while the character of Rome is corruption and perversion of the truth, it is not that of daring and open-mouthed blasphemy.

3. Papal Rome never, either politically or ecclesiastically, had such power over all the world is here depicted.

4. Even if the 1260 days mean "years" none of them have been able to agree as to when they begin or when they end; whether they have already ended or whether the saints are yet in the power of the beast: and the saints themselves do not seem to know!

5. The word *"miracles"* is the same word as that used not of pretended or trick miracles, but of real miracles, and as such they have never yet been performed by the Papal Priesthood.

6. The Papacy does not kill those who do not worship as it dictates and it never has.

7. This class of interpreters has as many different interpretations of 666 as there are interpreters.

Burgh says that beasts uniformly represent "kingdoms" and horns, "kings". In Chap. 17 it is plainly said that the ten horns are ten kings who receive power for one hour (the same hour), and they have one mind, showing plainly that ten contemporaneous kings are meant, whose history embraces only a short time. Kingdoms may be extended through many centuries and that is why it was substituted here for "kings", because it suited better the historical system of the men who did the translating.

Among other Historical interpretations of the head that was wounded the following may be noted:

It was given to the Roman empire by the migration of nations but was healed by the rising of a new Roman empire whose chief strength lay in the Germanic nations. (L. Au. Eb. Ca.)

It was the Grecian part of the Roman empire wounded by Julian restoring the worship of the Gods and healed by the removal of Julian and the succession of Javian. (Coc.)

It was the Roman empire invaded by the Moors for 700 years and healed by their expulsion by King Ferdinand. (Nicolai.)

It was Papal Rome wounded by the humiliation of Pope Alexander III by Emperor Frederick and healed by the humiliation of Frederick by the Pope in 1177.

It was the influence of Christ's victory on the Cross that made the wound, and the healing was the later outward prosperous condition of the Roman empire, the new life which it displayed, the success that attended its persecutions, etc. (Hen.)

It refers to the death of Nero, who was actually put to death by a sword stroke. Thus most of those who refer the seven heads to seven individual kings. (D. Lu. Bl. Ei. Dus. Cor. Hil. Vol. Vic. Bau. Renan.)

Many of these last quoted commentators refer the healing to Nero's return from hell to be the final Antichrist. But Dusterdieck quite properly disposes of this assumption, while in turn he makes the healing refer to the restoration of the empire by Vespasian to its ancient strength and vitality. The only way you can get Nero out of 666 is by the use of the Hebrew alphabet and the value of the letters as understood in that day, but Brown protests and rightly against this in a book written entirely in Greek. The seven heads of the beast Dusterdieck refers to seven emperors, Augusta, Tiberius, Caligula, Claudius, Nero, Vespasian and Titus, while the ten horns he refers to the same emperors with Galba, Otho and Vitellius, the usurpers coming in between Nero and Vespasian, thus making Titus correspond to the seventh head. Together with the authorities quoted above, he makes the wounded head to be Nero, the fifth head. Others (Au. Eb. Hen.) who make the seven heads refer to seven world-powers, refer the wounded head to the sixth world-power, i. e., the Roman world-power of John's time. Chap. 17.8-11 says the future eighth king would be the personified beast himself.

Having given pretty largely the interpretation of the chapter from the standpoint of the Historical School, we will now follow quite largely the interpretation of the Futurists.

The Futurist School, of course, thinks of the beast as a symbol of that which is still future and refer the prophecy to the days of the Antichrist which are still to come.

Scofield says, "Fragments of the ancient Roman empire have never ceased to exist as separate kingdoms. It was the *imperial* form of government which ceased; the one head wounded to death. What we have practically in Rev. 13.3 is the restoration of the *imperial* form of government as such, though over a federated empire of ten kingdoms; the 'head' is 'healed', i. e., restored; there is an emperor again—the beast."

Most of the Futurists say the first beast is undoubtedly the Antichrist himself (Pet. Lee. Will. Weid. Moor.), although others of this school make the second beast, the beast out of the earth, to be the Antichrist. (Sco. Gab.) The Futurists expect that in the days of the Antichrist there will be a revived Roman empire and that the ten horns of the beast stand for the ten kingdoms into which this empire is to be divided.

Moorehead says the seven heads are seven successive empires, the first being Egypt, and the sixth the Rome that was, while the seventh is still future, the revived Roman empire which is the beast out of the sea, the emperor which is the same as "*little horn*" of Dan. 9.27 and the Antichrist.

Gaebelein says the first beast *is* this revived Roman empire. He says the seven heads refer to the seven forms of government which have characterized the empire in the past. The seventh head becomes the eighth and it is this eighth head which is wounded as unto death, denoting, as he claims, the imperial form of government which had died and is now revived in the person of the leader, the *"little horn"* of Daniel. He thinks the second beast is the Antichrist. He explains the identification of the first beast as a person and an empire by the famous statement of Louis XIV, who said, "I am France."

Petingill says this first beast, the Antichrist, comes up out of the sea of the Gentile world and is a Roman prince, though at the same time an apostate Jew.

Ver. 4. *"and they worshipped the dragon . . . the beast"*,—"Such is the final issue of modern civilization, of all this vaunted progress in thought, art, science and methods of education." (Weid.) "The very phraseology in which they express their worship," says Dusterdieck, "seems like a blasphemous parody of the praise with which the Old Testament Church celebrates the incomparable glory of the living God."

"who is able to make war with him",—Implying seemingly a desire to begin the conflict with the Christians who did not worship the beast, and referring perhaps to the great battles for which all things in the Apocalypse are preparing.

Ver. 5. *"given him"*,—i. e., by God (L. Bl. Dus. Weid.); permitted to use his mouth in such a way. Only in accordance with God's will can the dragon equip his beast—a consolation for believers.

"speaking great things and blasphemies",—i. e., words of outrageous arrogance and self-glorification.

"to continue",—better "to work during" (as in the margin). (See Dan. 8.24 and 11.28.) (A. V. F. D. Zu. Hen. Dus.)

"forty and two months",—The well-known period of the three and one-half years of the Antichrist. The last half of Daniel's "seventieth week," says Weidner. Lange says this expression is not to be chronologically calculated. (See other opinions in previous exegesis on page 633.)

Ver. 6. Describing together with verse 7 more fully what is said in verse 5.

"blaspheme His name",—Calumny against God Himself, especially fulfilled by the beast usurping divine names.

"his tabernacle",—Doubtless referring to heaven. (A. F. Dus.)

"them that dwell in heaven",—i. e., the angels and the departed souls of believers. Fausset also includes believers on earth who have their citizenship in heaven.

Ver. 7. *"over every tribe"*, etc.,—i. e., universal empire and dominion.

"and to overcome them",—Insofar perhaps as the saints must succumb to his power and suffer prison, affliction and death. Weidner remarks, "Though many shall fall away and worship the beast even among professing Christians (Matt. 24.9-12), the true believers shall be preserved through (or exempted from,—according to the exegesis adopted) the Great Tribulation." Gaebelein and those who teach the "any moment rapture" and that the Church will be caught up before the Great Tribulation takes place, make the saints here the Jewish saints, while those who

believe the Church will go through the Great Tribulation make them the saints who will be living on the earth just prior to the coming of Christ.

Ver. 8. *"all that dwell upon the earth"*,—A description usual for those who are in antithesis to those whose conversation is in heaven, i. e., unbelievers, the ungodly, worldlings.

"shall worship him",—Not the *"dragon"* (L. Dus.), but the beast. All this points to the great and final apostacy predicted by our Lord. (Matt. 25.11,12) and of which we read also in II Thess. 2.3.

"from the foundation of the world",—Taken by many with our text as modifying *"written"*. (L. A. R. V. B. D. Zu. Eb. Bl. Ew. Dus. Hen. Hei. Ham. Gro. Mil. Crav. Weid. Brown.) By others it is taken as modifying *"slain"*. (A. L. F. Be. Bl. Eb. Pl. Vul. Wor. Lee. Sad. Carp. Boyd, Blunt. Curry, Pearson.) I Peter 1.19,20 and John 17.24, and the position of the words here favor the latter view. Chap. 17.8 does not contradict this verse here because no other element than that of writing is introduced there. Yet it does have an influence in deciding this question. Furthermore, as Craven says, the foreordination of a thing and its occurance are two different things. The Lamb was not *slain* from the foundation of the world, though in the counsel of God it was so ordained. We think, therefore, the former view is to be preferred.

Ver. 9. Bespeaking solemn attention to what follows.

Ver. 10. The Greek text here is uncertain. The reading of our text is a prophetic declaration of how it shall fare with the saints in the day of persecution, their trials being severally appointed by God's fixed counsel. (See Jer. 43.11 and Zech. 11.9.) The verse is both a warning to believers to suffer with patience without having recourse to weapons of carnal welfare, because "they that take the sword shall perish by the sword" (Weid.), and a warning to the persecutors that they shall be punished with retribution in kind; while in this last fact, namely, that God will avenge his elect, some see an intended consolation to believers.

"here is",—i. e., in the patient endurance of these afflictions.

11 And I saw another beast coming up out of the earth; and he had two horns like unto a lamb, and he spake as a dragon. 12 And he exerciseth all the authority of the first beast in his sight. And he maketh the earth and them that dwell therein to [1]worship the first beast, whose deathstroke was healed. 13 And he doeth great signs, that he should even make fire to come down out of heaven upon the earth in the sight of men. 14 And he deceiveth them that dwell on the earth by reason of the signs which it was given him to do in the sight of the beast; saying to them that dwell on the earth, that they should make an image to the beast who hath the stroke of the sword and lived. 15 And it was given *unto him* to give breath to it, *even* to the image of the beast, [2]that the image of the beast should both speak, and cause that as many as should not [1]worship the image of the beast should be killed. 16 And he causeth all, the small and the great, and the rich and the poor, and the free and the bond, that there be given them a mark on their right hand, or upon their forehead; 17 and that no man should be able to buy or to sell, save he that hath the mark, *even* the name of the beast or the number of his name. 18 Here is wisdom. He that hath understanding, let him count the number of the beast: for it is the number of a man; and his number is [3]Six hundred and sixty and six.

[1]The Greek word denotes an act of reverence whether paid to a creature, or to the Creator.

[2]Some ancient authorities read *that even the image of the beast should speak; and he shall cause &c.*

[3]Some ancient authorities read *Six hundred and sixteen.*

Vers. 11-18. THE BEAST OUT OF THE EARTH.

Ver. 11. *"another beast coming up"*,—This second beast, an accomplice of the first, leading the people to worship him, seems to be a personification of false prophecy. (See Chaps. 16.13; 19.20; 20.10 and Matt. 24.11,24.)

"out of the earth",—Dusterdieck thinks this refers to the fact that this beast is to work upon the inhabitants of the earth. Others (Hen. Lee) see here a symbol of the earthly, sensual, worldly, demoniacal nature of the beast. Alford and Fausset say it means "out of human society and its progress, just as *'out of the sea'* was an empire rising up out of confusion into order and life." We are inclined to the view of Milligan and others, who, regarding the sea as the Gentile nations opposed to God, would refer the earth to the Jews as God's prophetic and priestly people, the beast thus having a religious and not a secular origin.

"two horns like unto a lamb",—We hardly think this is meant as a contrast with the lamb of seven horns (Chap. 5.6) as of less power, and as though the two-horned beast claimed to exercise all the power of Christ, even though this may be true. If there is any contrast it is with the first beast, but we are inclined to think that the number in itself has no special significance, but only expresses the resemblance of a lamb and designating the peculiarity of false prophetism, and as a lamb it must necessarily have two horns. (See Matt. 7.15 where is found the warning of Christ against false prophets.)

"spake as a dragon",—"Though the appearance and profession of this second beast are sacerdotal its words and acts are devilish," says Alford, who doubts not that the term dragon is chosen on account of the dragon before mentioned even though ·we did not hear the first dragon speaking (which Dusterdieck offers as an objection to the reference).

"He looks like Christ and is like Satan", (Sim.)

Scofield says, "This beast out of the earth is the same as the false prophet of Chaps. 16.13; 19.20; 20.10 and is the Antichrist. He is the last ecclesiastical head, as the beast of verses 1-8 is the last civil head. For purposes of persecution he is permitted to exercise the autocratic power of the emperor-beast." (Bla. Gab.)

Ver. 12. *"in his sight"*,—i. e., beneath the eyes of the first beast as a prime minister would serve his king.

"whose deathstroke was healed",—(See verse 3, the cause of the astonishing adoration.)

Ver. 13. *"doeth great signs"*,—Of course all those who refer this second beast to Papal Rome, as does the Historical School, say that these miracles are not real, but ostensible, illusive wonders. (L. A.)

Others claim them to be real from the fact that the same noun and verb are used as John used in his Gospel and the noun is the same as that generally used to designate the miracles of Christ. (Crav.) Still others say they are real but are miracles of demoniacal kind and by demon aid like those of the Egyptian magicians. (V. F. Weid.)

"that",—Whether we read "so that" (A. B. Hen.) or *"that"*, the sense is quite the same. In the latter case *"that"* explains the conception of *"great"*, i. e., miracles, great,—so great *"that"*,

"causeth fire to come down",—mimicing Pentecost, says Bede. But this is hardly to be thought of. We are more apt, as Dusterdieck says, to think of the miracles of Elijah (I Kings 18) and so regard this false prophet as the forerunner of the Antichrist even as Elijah went before the true Christ and shall again precede Him at his second coming.

Ver. 14. This power to perform miracles was given to Him by Satan subject to the will of God and by these diabolical miracles the worldly-minded are deceived.

"make an image of the beast",—Lange, though not a Futurist, is quite right we think in saying, "It is not an image of the first beast in the abstract but in his quality of having the deathstroke and reviving again that is commanded", or as Weidner, a Futurist, puts it, "Just as Paul maintained that Jesus Christ was declared to be the Son of God by His resurrection from the dead (Rom. 1.4), so in the times of the Antichrist stress will be laid on the fact that though this first beast had received his deathstroke, nevertheless he had lived again and that therefore he had established his right to claim divine majesty and worship."

Ver. 15. *"cause"*,—The subject of this verb is not the false prophet (D. Ew. Zu.) but the image now made alive (Bl.).

Dusterdieck says, "The description contains a suggestion of what has been reported concerning divine images actually speaking and John appears to presuppose the reality of such demoniacal miracles." But John could hardly be so superstitious as this explanation would involve. Dusterdieck of course refers the image to that of the deified emperors, such Christians being put to death as would not worship the same.

Gaebelein thinks the image will most likely be put up outside of the land of Palestine, perhaps in Rome, while Weidner suggests that it will be placed in the temple at Jerusalem and constitute the abomination of desolation that Christ refers to in Matthew and to which Daniel referred three times. (Pet.)

Gaebelein says the first beast is a political power, the second a religious leader; the first a Gentile power with a Gentile head, and the second, a Jew, else his claim of being Israel's true Messiah would not be accepted by the Jews. He says the second beast is the final, personal Antichrist, the man of sin, the son of perdition. His two horns are an imitation of the priestly and kingly power of Christ.

Ver. 16. *"He"*,—the second beast.

"a mark",—Even as masters brand their slaves, and kings their subjects. Dusterdieck says that they put the mark on themselves by the mere fact of their being deceived by the second beast to worship the first beast. But Chaps. 14.9; 16.2; 19.20; 20.4 to which he refers hardly support his view, and the stamping is more naturally understood of those whose office it is, the subject here being left uncertain.

"on their right hand and on their forehead",—the most conspicuous part of the body where it is most readily presentable to the eye. The purpose being visibility, whether it be attached to the one or the other place is a matter of indifference. Hengstenberg thinks, "on the forehead for confession and on the right hand as the instrument for action", while

Fausset says, "a prostration of bodily and mental powers to the beast's domination is implied". But these are, of course, mere surmises.

Ver. 17. The mark is the name of the beast, or the number of his name, i. e., the number which the letters of his name make when added together according to the practice of thus calculating the numerical value of letters in names which was widely prevalent. "Most commentators," says Weidner, "think that we dare not interpret here literally of an actual mark impressed,—that as in the case of the servants of God no actual visible mark is intended, so here the mark signifies, as Alford says, 'rather conformity and addiction to the behests of the beast'."

"to buy or to sell",—Those bearing the mark will hinder the intercourse even in business of the saints who do not have the mark. The Antichrist will control the labor market. In order to buy or sell one will have to join the organization of which the Antichrist is the head.

Dennett says, "Under the mask of the welfare of the empire all will be subjected to this awful tyranny under the pains and penalties of the deprivation of the commonest liberty of the individual." Petingill calls it, "The logical heading up of the boycott system."

Ver. 18. "Here is wisdom",—It takes wisdom to understand the mysterious mark.

"it is the number of a man",—The number can be found because it is expressed in a human way, i. e., counted as men generally count.

"six hundred and sixty-six",—These figures must not be taken as an expression of time. (Be.) Others think that we must not accept any interpretation of them that does not find in them the indication of some name.

It is well known that each letter of the alphabet in the Greek as well as the Hebrew had a value attached to it, as noted above. Among the Historical School of interpreters more than 100 attempted solutions or guesses, some of them very ingenious, have been tabulated. If the Hebrew alphabet is used, perhaps the name of Nero furnishes the best solution. This is at present a very popular interpretation and the modern school of rationalism boastingly claims it as the only possible solution. (Thus Ew. Fri. Hit. Hil. Vol. St. Da. Cow. Gebh. Baur. Renan, Benary, Reuss, Hausrath.) However, by far the larger number of scholars agree that it is entirely out of place to use the Hebrew alphabet for this name in a book that is written entirely in Greek.

The most plausible of the explanations in which the Greek alphabet is used is the word Lateinos, meaning Latin, and thus containing a reference to the Roman empire. The numerical value of the letters are as follows: 30-1-300-5-10-50-70-200, making in all 666. To this view are inclined A. D. F. Ei. Eb. Bl. Ca. Dus. Wor. Sad. Lee. Crav. Schaff. From the viewpoint of the Futurist School we see no reason at present why the solution of Lateinos may not be retained with a reference of course to the revived Roman empire, although we have nowhere seen this view advocated.

Some of the Futurists take the figures symbolically, it being, says Petingill, "the number of incompleteness thrice repeated. It is ever short of the perfect seven, showing that however the Antichrist may try to show himself forth as God, he will fail to deceive at least the very elect." Says Gaebelein, "Six is incomplete and is man's number. It is humanity fallen, filled with pride, defying God."

Of the two solutions, Lateinos and the symbolical interpretation we are inclined to the former, but until the Antichrist comes the mystery will not be solved, but when he comes believers will be able to recognize him by this number.

CHAPTER FOURTEEN

This chapter contains seven visions recording apparently the main events of the closing days of this age.

1 And I saw, and behold, the Lamb standing on the mount Zion, and with him a hundred and forty and four thousand, having his name, and the name of his Father, written on their foreheads. 2 And I heard a voice from heaven, as the voice of many waters, and as the voice of a great thunder: and the voice which I heard *was* as *the* voice of harpers harping with their harps: 3 and they sing as it were a new song before the throne, and before the four living creatures and the elders: and no man could learn the song save the hundred and forty and four thousand, even they that had been purchased out of the earth. 4 These are they that were not defiled with women; for they are virgins. These *are* they that follow the Lamb whithersoever he goeth. These were purchased from among men, *to be* the firstfruits unto God and unto the Lamb. 5 And in their mouth was found no lie: they are without blemish.

Vers. 1-5. THE LAMB AND THE 144,000 ON MOUNT ZION.

Says Dusterdieck concerning the purpose of this first vision, "The manifestation of *the blessed with the Lamb in eternal glory* is intented to give believers who are on earth, and exposed to persecution on the part of the Dragon, a pledge inspiring courage and patience, that if they remain faithful they too shall attain to that glory." (Bar.) Says Dennett, "In Chap. 13 the frightful oppression and persecution of the saints is seen; and in this vision they are displayed as having been tried and come forth as gold."

Ver. 1. *"I saw and behold"*,—Marking the unexpected, forcible contrast to the preceding vision and the lively introduction to that which follows.

"on the mount Zion",—Says Alford, "I would call attention of the reader to the fact, essential to the right understanding of the vision, that the harpers and the song are in heaven and the 144,000 on earth." (A. D. St. El. Gab. Pet. Den. Weid.) On the other hand many place the 144,000 in heaven as well. (V. B. Eb. Ei. Zu. Ew. Gro. Hen. Lap. Dus. Lord, Stern.)

Hengstenberg says, "As certainly as the voice from heaven in verse 2 is the voice of the 144,000, so certainly must the mount Zion where the Lamb stands with them be the heavenly one. According to verse 3 the throne of God is on Mount Zion, but this belongs to the heavenly Zion and not to the earthly."

The arguments as presented by either side are not at all strong or convincing. Hearing the voice *"from heaven"* immediately after seeing the 144,000 some claim implies by contrast that the 144,000 were on earth. But there is little, if any, strength in this argument. The statement, however, in verse 3 that the 144,000 were *"redeemed from the earth"* might seem to imply that they were in heaven, while the fact that they learn and join in the song lends added weight to this fact. We see no good reason at this time why they should not be thought of as being in heaven. They are redeemed believers. This is certain. The vision is for the comfort and encouragement of those believers who are to endure the persecutions of the beast. Terrible judgments are about to fall and the visions of this chapter and the next are given to prepare the people for them.

"having his name, and the name of his Father, written on their foreheads",—While the ungodly are marked with the name of the beast, these children of God are here shown as marked with the name of Christ and the Father.

"the hundred and forty and four thousand",—Dusterdieck objects to identifying these with the 144,000 of Chap. 7.4 because of the lack of the definite article. But this in itself is evidence quite insufficient. It would seem as if the two groups were to be considered identical from the fact, (1) that the number is the same, (2) that both are sealed and the seal of Chap. 7.4 may easily be the same as here, (3) that both are elect and firstfruits, though it is not distinctly so stated of the 144,000 in Chap. 7.4. Moorehead, referring to Chap. 3.10, suggests that there may be Gentiles among them. Many writers (Bl. Vo. Are. Lap. Nea.) agree with Dusterdieck but the vast majority of commentators identify the two groups. (A. L. F. V. B. D. St. Eb. Ew. Zu. Ei. Gro. Hil. Hei. Hen. Kli. Gab. Pet. Crav. Weid. Glas. Moor. Gebh. Lord, Renck.)

Ver. 2. *"a voice from heaven",*—

1. If the 144,000 are in heaven, this is doubtless their voice. (B. V. Hen.) Hengstenberg calls attention to the fact,

    (a) that in Chap. 15.2 it is those who have gotten the victory over the beast who have the harps of God;

    (b) that the *"new song"* is in Scripture always represented as being sung by those to whom it relates;

    (c) that harps belong to the Church according to Chap. 5.8, and the expression *"before the elders"* (verse 3) presents no difficulty, because it is perfectly proper to distinguish believers (he makes the 144,000 represent the whole redeemed Church) from their representatives. Of course the voice belongs to the harpers. They are harp-singers, accompanying the harps with their voices.

2. If the 144,000 are on earth, then the harp-singers must be found in another body. Weidner conceives them to be angels. Gaebelein says they are the martyrs seen in connection with the fifth seal and including those slain during the Great Tribulation.

"many waters and great thunder",—"Divinely sweet and yet divinely terrible." (See Chaps. 1.15 and 6.1.)

Ver. 3. *"they sing",*—i. e., the harp-singers, of course, as above.

"as it were",—i. e., what sounded like.

643

"a new song",—"New in that it has reference to the faithfulness of God and the Lamb whereby believers, on the ground of redemption through Christ, are preserved amid the enticements and persecutions of the antichristian power and brought to victory and eternal glory." (Dus.)

"no man could learn the song",—Not merely "understand" (D. Ew.), but appreciate and join in. (Dus.) The 144,000 could thus learn the song because they alone have the experience of that which is celebrated in the song, namely "matters of trial and triumph, of deep joy and heavenly purity of heart". (A.)

"purchased out of the earth",—Thus even angels could not learn the song.

Ver. 4. *"that were not defiled with women"*,—Alford says, "The past tense shows that their course is ended and looked back on as a thing of the past, and so serves to refute all interpretations which regard them as representing saints while in the midst of their earthly conflict and trial." So Dusterdieck says, "The subject pertains to the past earthly life of those who have died." So also the first clause of verse 5.

"they are virgins",—Three explanations of this epression have been given:

1. Kept themselves in entire abstinence from all sexual intercourse, i. e., celibacy. (A. Be. Aug. Dus. Jer. And. Nea. Sim. Weid. Rothe.) Matt. 19.12 and I Cor. 7 do prove, as Simcox says, on any fair interpretation that a devout celibacy gives special means for serving God. This interpretation, however, seems inconsistent with Heb. 13.4, and furthermore we can hardly conceive of John attributing this special blessedness to 144,000 unmarried gentlemen. Barnes calls attention to the fact that the word "defile" applies only to that which is unlawful and cannot therefore be applied to the marriage relation wherein intercourse is lawful and proper. Dusterdieck says that even in the Old Testament sexual union itself even in wedlock was defiling. (Deut. 15.18.) In a sense this is so, and yet a blessing indeed is attached in the Old Testament to marriage and the bearing of children.

2. Kept themselves from all fornication as we understand it, i. e., illegitimate intercourse. (D. B. Ei. Bar. Hen.) This meaning Barnes thinks is determined by the word *"defiled"*, especially as used with the words *"with women"*. Stuart says that to take it in this sense would be a singular eulogy because the context says nothing at all of impurity which is the opposite and therefore there is nothing here to make it emphatic.

3. Kept themselves pure in a religious sense, i. e., spiritually, free especially from idolatry. (L. F. V. St. Ze. Gab. Vic. Wol. Coc. Gro. Glas. Gebh.) Stuart thinks that a comparison with verse 8 makes this meaning certain. He says the expression is a symbol of purity and not of sex, and therefore in any case the reference need not apply exclusively to men.

We find ourselves inclining to this last and figurative view as involving less embarrassment than either of the others.

"*follow the Lamb*",—The tense is present; not therefore on earth *even unto death, etc.;* (V. D. B. Eb. Ew. St. L. Gro. Coc. Wol. Hen. Wor. Glas.), but in Millennial glory, having the privilege of a special nearness to Him. (A. F. Zu. And. Aug. Dus. Weid. Stern.)

"In the regeneration when the Son of man shall sit on the throne of His glory (Matt. 19.28), they shall be the constant retinue of the Lamb." (Weid.)

"*were purchased from among men to be the firstfruits*",—All the redeemed are so purchased and purchased as the firstfruits of creation (James 1.18), but these are evidently the firstfruits from among the purchased themselves. (A. B. F. L. Ew. Dus. Sim. Bar. Weid.) To those who say this 144,000 represents all of God's people (D. Hen. Gla. Crav.) Lange rightly replies that as Chap. 7 made a distinction between the 144,000 there and the innumerable throng, so here a special selection is likewise intended. There is a sense in which all true believers constituting the Church are first-fruits (Rom. 8.23; Jas. 1.18; I Cor. 15.20-22) and the consequent general ingathering of Israel and the nations is the harvest.

Ver. 5. "*no lie*",—i. e., no falsehood. There may be a certain contrast to the sphere of falsehood in which the false prophet and worshippers of the beast move, but it is better to take the word in its general sense (Dus.), and not to limit it to idolatry (B. Gro.), nor to the denial of Christ (Hen.). They lived their earthly life in utter truthfulness.

Alford and Lange rightly say that the vision of this chapter has not a backward reference to Chap. 13, but a forward reference to the mystic Babylon and to the consummation of punishment and reward.

Elliott, with strange persistence, contends that the primary emblem of the Lamb with the 144,000 on Mount Zion depicted generally Christ's policy or government of the faithful all through the reign of the beast, characterized as it proved to be with severe Papal persecutions. The singing of the "*new song*" by the harp-singers he conceives to prefigure some happy crisis in the earthly fortunes of Christ's saints and faithful ones, and this crisis he would have us believe was the glorious Reformation. The "*new song*" he refers to the blessed doctrine and central truth of the Reformation, viz., *Christ our righteousness,* and during the days of general decline in spirituality throughout the Church, following close on after the death of Luther and Melancthon, none but those illumined and quickened and sealed by the Spirit of the Lord Jesus, the faithful, who followed the Lamb whithersoever He went, even unto death, the spiritual virgins who were "*without blemish*", in short, the 144,000 could sing it. The angel with the eternal gospel prefigures the missionary era which directly followed.

6 And I saw another angel flying in mid heaven, having [1]eternal good tidings to proclaim unto them that [2]dwell on the earth, and unto every nation and tribe and tongue and people; 7 and he saith with a great voice, Fear God, and give him glory; for the hour of his judgment is come: and worship him that made the heaven and the earth and sea and fountains of waters.

[1]Or, *an eternal gospel*
[2]Gr. *sit*

Vers. 6,7. THE ANGEL WITH THE EVERLASTING GOSPEL.

Ver. 6. Fausset thinks that as the former portion of this chapter related to the Israelitish world, so here begins the portion relating to the Gentile world.

"*another angel*",—i. e., besides those already mentioned, with no particular reference to any other one angel or to the angels of the heavenly choir, as Stuart thinks. It may be interesting to note that the old Protestant expositors referred this angel to Luther and the other two to Wicliffe and Huss.

"*eternal good tidings*",—The article is wanting here just as in Rom. 1.1. It is preached not to the heathen merely (Eb.) but to all the dwellers on the earth.

The special content of this angel's message is shown by the next verse to be the second coming of Christ and the hour of His judgment (Ew. Zu. Dus. Gro. Hen.), but the Gospel here mentioned is, as all the older expositors have taken it, the Gospel in its universal sense, the Gospel of salvation in Christ (A. L. Eb. Lue. Gebh.) and is not to be confined, as Fausset confines it, to the Gospel of the kingdom about to be set up on this earth, the Millennial kingdom. It is eternal as declaring the eternal truth of God; eternal as to its contents, its origin and its effects.

The preaching of the Gospel as here mentioned is to have its fulfillment in the future, and has, as Gaebelein says, nothing to do with the preaching of the Gospel during this present time. Its reference lies in the latter times, during the days of the Great Tribulation, whether we think of the Tribulation as before or after the Rapture. Gaebelein says the preaching is done by the faithful remnant of the Jews.

Scofield comments upon the preaching of the Gospel as follows, namely:

(a) That the Gospel was seemingly first preached as the Gospel of the Kingdom; it was so proclaimed by John the Baptist and continued by Jesus and His Disciples until the Jewish rejection of the King. This Gospel will doubtless be emphasized again in the last days. It is the good news that God purposes to set up His kingdom on earth in fulfillment of the Davidic covenant.

(b) That upon the rejection of the King by the Jews came the preaching of the Gospel of Grace, as it is being preached today, the good news that Christ died on the cross for the sins of the world.

(c) That the Gospel mentioned here in verse 6, the "*eternal good tidings*", the "everlasting Gospel", is to be preached to the earth-dwellers at the very end of the Great Tribulation and immediately preceding the judgment of the nations, which he thinks is set forth in Matt. 25.31.

Ver. 7. "*the hour of His judgment is come*",—The time of the end is close at hand, the time for the destruction of the Antichrist. This is not perhaps the general judgment but that upon the beast and his followers.

"*worship Him*",—i. e., turn from idols and the worship of the beast to serve the true and living God.

8 And another, a second angel, followed, saying, Fallen, fallen is Babylon the great, that hath made all the nations to drink of the wine of the wrath of her fornication.

Ver. 8. THE JUDGMENT OF BABYLON ANNOUNCED.

"*Fallen, fallen is Babylon the great*",—The name of the Old Testament God-opposed, secular power, proud, haughty, insolent, oppressive. The Preterists understand this Babylon to be Pagan Rome; the Historical interpreters refer it chiefly to Papal Rome; the Futurists refer it of course to the chief city of the antichristian world-power of the last days,—the capital of Antichrist; some maintaining it to be the Rome of the future, while others refer it to Jerusalem as ruled over during that time by the Antichrist. At any rate Babylon is here the type of the world-power which persecutes the Church of God. (See Chaps. 17 and 18.)

"*wrath*",—i. e., God's wrath. There is, as Simcox says, a blending of two ideas; the wine of Babylon's fornication of which she made all nations to drink, and the wine of God's wrath of which she and her followers are made to drink. The latter is the retribution for the former. The whole is from Jer. 51.7,8. (A. D. F. Dus.)

"*fornication*",—i. e., idolatry.

9 And another angel, a third, followed them, saying with a great voice, If any man ¹worshippeth the beast and his image, and receiveth a mark on his forehead, or upon his hand, 10 he also shall drink of the wine of the wrath of God, which is ²prepared unmixed in the cup of his anger; and he shall be tormented with fire and brimstone in the presence of the holy angels, and in

¹See marginal note on Chap. 13.12
²Gr. *mingled*

the presence of the Lamb: 11 and the smoke of their torment goeth up ³for ever and ever; and they have no rest day and night, they that ¹worship the beast and his image, and whoso receiveth the mark of his name. 12 Here is the ⁴patience of the saints, they that keep the commandments of God, and the faith of Jesus.

³Gr. *unto ages of ages*
⁴Or, *stedfastiness*

Vers. 9-12. THE JUDGMENT OF THE BEAST-WORSHIPPERS ANNOUNCED.

"The most dreadful of all threatenings contained in the whole of Scripture," says Bengel.

Ver. 10. "*he also*",—i. e., as well as Babylon (Ew. Dus. Weid.), or, as well as having drunk the wine of Babylon's fornication (L. A. Hen.).

"*unmixed*",—The meaning is without doubt that this wine is not to be tempered with water. There is no element of grace or hope or compassion blended with the judgment. (L. F. A. D. Eb. St. Ew. Dus. Hen. Bar. Will. Weid.)

"*tormented*",—i. e., in hell proper, Gehenna.

"*with fire and brimstone*",—A figurative expression referring doubtless to the pangs of remorse and conscience. (V. St. Gro. Bar. Crav.)

"*in presence of the holy angels*",—Not "according to the judgment of" (D.), but as stated, "before the eyes of" (Luke 16.23). (A. Dus. Sim.) Dusterdieck notes that an aggravation of their punishment is signified by the fact that the holy angels and the despised and persecuted Lamb are spectators of it. The words indicate only that the angels and the Lamb acquiesce in the justice and necessity of God's awful judgments.

Ver. 11.   The eternity of the punishment is here explicitly set forth. (St. Den. Bar. Weid. Will.)

Ver. 12.   A digression of the Seer, as in Chap. 13.10.

"here",—i. e., "in the inference to be drawn from the certainty of this everlasting torment is the ground for the patient endurance of the saints." (A. Dus. Hen.)

13 And I heard a voice from heaven saying, Write, Blessed are the dead who die ¹in the Lord from henceforth: yea, saith the Spirit, that they may rest from their labors; for their works follow with them.

¹Or, *in the Lord.   From henceforth, yea, saith the Spirit.*

Ver. 13.   THE BLESSEDNESS OF THE HOLY WHO DIE HENCEFORTH.

"a voice from heaven",—It is not said whose voice and it is useless to speculate. Alford thinks, however, the word *"write"* points somewhat to the angel of Chap. 1.1. Hengstenberg says it is the voice of one of the elders or of a departed saint. Lange with some propriety says it is the Spirit mentioned in the next clause, and that two distinct voices are not to be thought of.

"from henceforth",—Some connect this word with *"blessed"*, while others connect it with *"die"*.

1. The reference is not to the *dying henceforth,* i. e., to those who die during the terrible persecutions which are soon to follow, but to the *blessedness henceforth* of all who die in the Lord, because full and complete blessedness of the holy dead is *just about to begin.* (A. F. D. Dus. Hen.)
2. Not that all who die in the Lord are not blessed, but that those who so die during the coming persecutions were to be peculiarly blessed. (Zu. Bar. Gab. Coc. Ham. Sim. Gla. Weid.)

The order of the words seems somewhat to favor the second view; although the supporters of the first view escape the force of this argument somewhat by declaring that the word *"blessed"* is thrown forward to the front of the sentence for emphasis sake. That in which the blessedness consists will be helpful in deciding the matter. At any rate *"die in the Lord"* must not be taken as referring to martyrs (Zu. Coc. Ham.), for to this alone it cannot assuredly refer. In what therefore does this blessedness consist? This seems to be explained by the rest of the verse.

"that",—Introducing the ground of the blessedness, i. e., "in that".

"their labors",—i. e., work, toil, persecution, etc.

"their works follow with them",—Not simply in blessed memory, as Alford says, but there is evidently here a reference to the reward which is theirs for their works. (D. L. Gro. Weid.)

The blessedness therefore seems to consist especially in their being relieved from the awful sufferings and persecutions of those last troublous times (Sim.), although their reward in glory whence their works follow them is not by any means to be overlooked in the estimate. This blessedness together with the position of the word *"henceforth"* and the fact that the present tense of the verb *"die"* points rather to death at the time under consideration than to those who have died in the Lord in past ages, would all seem to favor the explanation which attaches *"henceforth"* to the verb *"die"* All who die in the Lord are blessed in that they are delivered from the miseries of this wretched world, but this will be especially true of those who so die in the awful times which John says are about to come. One thing is certain, namely, that those who die in the Lord in those days, whether by martyrdom or otherwise, cannot be any more blessed in glory than those who have so died in the Lord during all ages. The blessedness must either consist in the fact mentioned above or the first view mentioned above must be accepted, namely, that which attached *"henceforth"* to *"blessed"*, and the blessedness made to consist in the fact that the interval is so short before "the perfect consummation and bliss" of all who have died in the Lord.

"Yea, saith the Spirit",—The Holy Spirit's ratification to what has been said.

Fausset says the voice mentioned first in the verse is the voice of God, while here it is the voice of the Holy Spirit speaking in the Word and in the saints. (Chap. 22.17; II Cor. 5.5; I Pet. 4.14.)

Lange maintains that the voice in each instance is the voice of the Holy Spirit Himself in the Church triumphant. Alford and Dusterdieck say it is the first voice still speaking, giving the Holy Spirit's ratification.

There can be no doubt, however, that the voice in the second instance is the voice of the Holy Spirit by whom John was inspired and by whose command John recorded what was written, the Holy Spirit who spake within John himself. (L. F. St. Hen. Bar. Dodd.)

14 And I saw, and behold, a white cloud; and on the cloud *I saw* one sitting like unto a son of man, having on his head a golden crown, and in his hand a sharp sickle. 15 And another angel came out from the [1]temple, crying with a great voice to him that sat on the cloud, Send forth thy sickle, and reap: for the hour to reap is come; for the harvest of the earth is [2]ripe. 16 And he that sat on the cloud cast his sickle upon the earth; and the earth was reaped. 17 And another angel came out from the [1]temple which is in heaven, he also having a sharp sickle. 18 And another angel came out from the altar, he that hath power over fire; and he called with a great voice to him that had the sharp sickle, saying, Send forth thy sharp sickle, and gather the clusters of the vine of the earth; for her grapes are fully ripe. 19 And the angel cast his sickle into the earth, and gathered the [3]vintage of the earth, and cast it into the winepress, the great *winepress*, of the wrath of God. 20 And the winepress was trodden without the city, and there came out blood from the winepress, even unto the bridles of the horses, as far as a thousand and six hundred furlongs.

[1]Or, *sanctuary*
[2]Gr. *become dry*
[3]Gr. *vine*

Vers. 14-20. CHRIST'S PAROUSIA AND THE VISION OF ARMAGEDDON.

Ver. 14. *"one like unto a son of man"*,—Not an angel in the likeness of Christ, or representing Christ (V. D. B. Zu. Gro.), which is a makeshift to avoid bringing Christ and his Parousia in at this juncture, and springing from a desire to interpret the whole series of visions continuously, as fulfilled in chronological order. But as Chap. 11.7 is anticipatory of the same events as Chap. 13, and Chap. 12 is retrospective, looking back to events earlier probably than any others indicated in the book, so this may be anticipatory of what is more fully described later, as for instance in Chap. 20. The reference is to Christ Himself. (A. F. L. Ew. Eb. Ei. St. Be. Ca. Vol. Hen. Dus. Pet. Gab. Bar. Weid. Moor.) The *"son of man"*, *"white cloud"*, *"crown"*, the parallelism of Dan. 7.13 and Matt. 26.64, the harmonious contrast between the three following angels and the three preceding ones, all argue this expression as referring to Christ.

"golden crown",—Implying that the time for His triumphant victory has come.

"a sharp sickle",—A symbol of beginning judgment and implying that the time for harvest has come, the earth being ripe for judgment.

Ver. 15. *"out of the temple"*,—i. e., as immediately sent from God with a message to His Son, and so not improper to present the following command to Christ, as Dusterdieck objects.

"send forth thy sickle",—A remembrance of Christ's own words (Mark 4.29). (See also Joel 4.13.)

Ver. 16. *"and the earth was reaped"*,—What reaping is this and what is the difference between this reaping and the one that follows, inasmuch as it would be pointless to have the two images worked successively out if they meant exactly the same thing?

There can be little if any doubt, as Simcox says, that this first reaping refers to the gathering of the elect. (A. F. B. L. Bar. Weid. Moor.)

Says Wordsworth, "It is the manifestation of God's love in the gathering of the good wheat into the heavenly barn." (Matt. 13.30,39.)

"Christ," says Weidner, "does not do this reaping directly, but indirectly, sending forth His angels to do it. (Matt. 24.31; Mk. 13.27.)"

Bengel says, "By means of the harvest a great multitude of the righteous, and by means of the vintage a great multitude of the ungodly are removed from the earth."

Says Moorehead, "I Thess. 4.13-18 is another account of this majestic scene, the gathering of God's people into His everlasting kingdom by resurrection and translation. This does not occur before the Great Tribulation, but it does occur before the wrath of God is poured out."

It is the true harvesting of earth's harvest fruit for God. (L.)

Fausset says, "By the harvest-reaping the elect righteous are gathered out; by the vintage the antichristion offenders are removed out of the earth, the scene of Christ's coming kingdom." The fact that there seems to be two reapings, and that the former seems to be over before the latter begins, favors the thought that the reapings refer to two different classes; and the fact that Christ appears in the first and only an angel in the second, and especially that there is a casting into the wine-press of God's wrath in the second case and not in the first favors the thought that the second reaping is of the wicked and the first is of the righteous, the elect. (A. F. Eb. Gla.) Still there are some who refer the whole of the two reapings to the harvest of the wicked. (St. Gab. Pet.)

Stuart says, "What is here begun is consummated in the sequel."

Petingill says that the whole passage refers to the gathering out of the tares and that Chap. 15 shows us the wheat garnered into the barn.

This is more in keeping with the reference in Matt. 13, "gather up first the tares and bind them in bundles to burn them; but gather the wheat into my barn. The harvest is the end of the age and the reapers are angels".

We are inclined to the view which sees in the reaping of this verse, the harvest of the righteous and in the following verses the harvest of the wicked.

Ver. 18. "out from the altar",—The same altar of incense beneath which the souls of the martyrs lie crying for vengeance. (Chaps. 6.9; 8.3; 16.7.)

"power over fire",—i. e., that on the altar, and so perhaps the same angel as in Chap. 8.3-5.

Ver. 19. What the winepress is for the common cluster, that is the wrath of God for these.

Ver. 20. This verse, as Weidner says, describes the terrific nature of the punishment that shall overtake the enemies of Christ at the time of His coming to destroy the Antichrist. (Chap. 19.11-21.) "The battle of Armageddon comes now into view for the first time." (Gab.)

"without the city",—i. e., in the country or field. What city? It is of course the city of the Beast, doubtless Jerusalem (A. F. Bar. Dus. Sim. Gab. Weid. Moor.), although not a few authorities prefer to think of Rome. It is the slaughter of the wicked that is here spoken of and not their eternal punishment. (B. F. Weid.)

"bridles of the horses",—Some think the reference is to the horses of the avenging armies of heaven (St. Hen.), but the expression is meant perhaps as a mere measure, as Simcox says,—that any horseman riding there would find his horse bridle-deep in blood. Some have conceived of the blood as having been merely splashed as high up as the bridles of the horses. The idea in any case is that an exceedingly great slaughter is predicted.

"a thousand and six hundred furlongs",—A square number merely denoting completeness and universality; four times four hundred, or four times four times one hundred, or forty times forty. With four, the world number, as the basis the 1600 is thus built up.

Four times four hundred, denoting the four quarters of the earth and the four regions of heaven, as a designation of great expanse. (Be. Vic.) A great distance, or a wide extent is all that can well be supposed to be meant. (A. St. Dus. Bar. Weid.)

Alford says it is either this or it is a riddle of the Apocalypse to which not even an approximate solution has ever yet been given. Some suggest that 1600 is derived from the square of four, the world number, multiplied by the square of ten, which is the sign of completeness, thus indicating that no created being can escape the judgment of God.

Other interpretations are:

1. Forty (the number of punishment) times forty as the symbol of terrible punishment. (Eb.)
2. The river in the valley of Jehosaphat to be discolored with blood for 1600 furlongs. (B.)

3. Symbolical of terrible punishment extending beyond the present age into future ages, a state of misery to which the eye can see no limit. (L.)

4. The length of the Holy Land (160 Roman miles,—140 English miles). (B. Ei. Ew. Zu. Pet.· Hei.)

5. The breadth of Italy, Rome being the city referred to. (St.)

Barnes rightly says it merely denotes that the slaughter would be great and that we cannot tell why 1600 is chosen, nor need we inquire.

Says Wordsworth, "The casting of grapes into a winepress and the act of treading them under the feet, so that the juice flows out of them in purple streams, is emblematic in Scripture of the destruction of enemies in battle with great carnage; so when the day of grace is passed, and the season of the world's vintage is come, will He tread all His enemies under His feet with the same ease as the treader of grapes in a winepress tramples the ripe, luscious fruit."

CHAPTER FIFTEEN

1 And I saw another sign in heaven, great and marvellous, seven angels having seven plagues, *which are* the last, for in them is finished the wrath of God.

2 And I saw as it were a ¹sea of glass mingled with fire; and them that come off victorious from the beast, and from his image, and from the number of his name, standing ²by the ¹sea of glass, having harps of God. 3 And they sing the song of Moses the ³servant of God, and the song of the Lamb, saying,

Great and marvellous are thy works, O Lord God, the Almighty; righteous and true are thy ways thou King of the ⁴ages.

4 Who shall not fear, O Lord, and glorify thy name? for Thou only art holy; for all the nations shall come and ⁵worship before thee; for thy righteous acts have been made manifest.

5 And after these things I saw, and the ⁶temple of the tabernacle of the testimony in heaven was opened: 6 and there came out from the ⁶temple the seven angels that had the seven plagues, arrayed ⁷with *precious* stone, pure *and* bright, and girt about their breasts with golden girdles. 7 And one of the four living creatures gave unto the seven angels seven golden bowls full of the wrath of God, who liveth ⁸for ever and ever. 8 And the ⁶temple was filled with smoke from the glory of God, and from his power; and none was able to enter into the ⁶temple, till the seven plagues of the seven angels should be finished.

¹Or, *glassy sea*
²Or, *upon*
³Gr. *bondservant*
⁴Many ancient authorities read *nations*. See Jer. 10.7
⁵See marginal note on Chap. 13.12
⁶Or, *sanctuary*
⁷Many ancient authorities read *linen*. See Chap. 19.8
⁸Gr. *unto the ages of the ages*

VERS. 1-8. THE SEVEN LAST PLAGUES AND THE BOWLS OF GOD'S WRATH.

A compendious description of the following vision extending to the end of the sixteenth chapter, and referring to events that shall take place on earth just before the coming of Christ to destroy the Antichrist.

Ver. 1. *"great and marvelous"*,—Not only in that the seven angels appear simultaneously, but also in their peculiar equipment, and perhaps also in the terrible nature of the events signified by them.

"having seven plagues . . . the last",—The last because they introduce the final and victorious coming of Christ, and because *"in them is finished the wrath of God"*. How they have and hold these plagues is not known; it belongs to the wonder of the vision.

"finished the wrath of God",—Not that this is the final judgment (Hen.), but only the consummation of His wrath in sending the plagues on the earth, at the close of which He will come (Chap. 19.11), the finishing of His wrath having reference to the beast, the consummation of whose punishment is now about to take place. (A. L. F. Dus.)

Ver. 2. *"as it were a sea of glass"*,—Not an actual sea, but something appearing like one. It is the same sea as that of Chap. 4.6, the personages being the same, the omission of the article not being a sufficient reason (Eb.) for differentiating this sea from that of Chap. 4.6. (A. Dus. Sim.)

"mingled with fire",—"Added here, and not in Chap. 4.6, because here it introduces an element belonging to this portion of the prophecy of which judgment is the prevailing complexion." (A. Bar. Weid.)

"harps of God",—Such as serve only for the praise of God. (B. A. L. Dus. Bar. Weid.) (See Chaps. 5.8 and 14.2.) Simcox calls attention to the fact that the harpers here are not the same as those in Chap. 5.8 and not (probably) the same as those in Chap. 14.2, although Gaebelein thinks those of Chap. 14.2 and here are identical.

"standing by the sea of glass",—"Upon" hardly harmonizes with the scenery of Chap. 4.6 and is in itself somewhat unnatural, although a sea of glass would be a solid support; or it might be they stand and walk upon the sea like their Lord, sustained by faith. But *"by the side of"* accords better with the children of Israel when they sang the song to which allusion is made; and furthermore it is justified by a similar use of the preposition in Chaps. 3.20 and 8.3. (L. A. Sim. Crav.)

This vision in Chap. 15 is given for the encouragement of those who will have to pass through the Great Tribulation.

"mingled with fire",—This expression has caused many curious interpretations, of which we are entitled to our choice or are privileged to surmise another.

1. The mass of Gentile Christians inflamed with love to God. (Gro.)
2. The peace of the world (sea) and the operation of the Holy Spirit in the world. (Coc.)
3. Grace will not be denied to penitents (the sea standing for baptism) in the midst of the flames of divine wrath. (Ca.)
4. The firm ground of truth (the sea upon which they stand) illumined by the fire of divine righteousness. (V.)
5. Dusterdieck says that the sea of glass refers to the eternal fullness of joy in God's presence with which the victors will be rewarded, and that the fire refers, as Alford says, to judgment, and that thereby is designated the unity of God's saving grace and righteous judgment.

Who are these that come victorious from the beast?
1. The martyred company worshipping in glory, the harpers of Chap. 14.2-3. (Gab.)
2. The great multitude which no man could number, of Chap. 7.9. (Pet.)
3. Both the martyrs of Chap. 14.2-3 and the great multitude of Chap. 7.9. (D. L. Weid. Moor.)

4. Barnes and others of the Historical School of course refer them to those who remain true in the midst of the papal persecutions of the past ages.

Ver. 3.   *"Moses, the servant of God"*,—(See Exodus 15 and also 14.31.)

"song of Moses and of the Lamb",—Not two songs, one of the saints of the Old Testament and the other of the New Testament saints (And.), nor is any allusion made to the connection between prophecy and the Gospel (Coc.). Nor is it the song of Moses applied to Christ and the things of Christ (V. D. Eb. Ca. Gro. Hen.); neither can we say it is a song composed at once by Moses and the Lamb (Ew. Dus.). It is one song doubly designated. It betokens the unity of the Old Testament and the New Testament Church, and is the celebration in one song of the typical redemption of Moses at the Red Sea and the real redemption by the Lamb. It is at the same time the song of Moses and of the Lamb, the song being one and the same. It is the whole redemption as mediated by Moses and the Lamb. (L. Ger. Sim. Weid.)

Fausset, "This is the new song mentioned in Chap. 14.3. The singing victors are the 144,000 of Israel, the first fruits, and the general harvest of the Gentiles."

Ver. 4.   *"all the nations"*, etc.,—Says Fausset, "The conversion of the nations shall therefore be when Christ comes and not till then, and the first moving cause will be Christ's manifested judgments preparing all hearts for receiving Christ's mercy."

Milligan suggests that the worship of the nations referred to is one of "awe, of trembling and of terror" (Phil. 2.10,11), but Weidner, agreeing with Fausset above. says it is better to refer it to the events occurring after the coming of Christ and during the time of the Millennium.

"thy righteous acts have been made manifest",—Both in the publication of the Gospel and in the destruction of His enemies. Fausset says, "The elect after their trials, especially those arising from the beast, shall be taken up before the vials of wrath are poured on the beast and his kingdom. The Lord coming with the clouds and in flaming fire, shall first catch up His elect people and then shall destroy the enemy."

Ver. 5.   *"thy temple of the tabernacle of the testimony"*,—The temple (naos) is the "Holy Place" of the tabernacle (Chap. 11.1) (A. L. Ew. Dus. Hen.), and not the "Holy of Holies" (Eb. St. Gro.), and it is here mentioned in its quality of being the place of testimony (Hen.), which, says Alford, "is peculiarly appropriate seeing that the witness and the covenant of God are about to receive their great fulfillment", reminding, as Weidner says, "of judgment and of God's faithfulness in avenging His people." The tabernacle was called the *"tabernacle of testimony"* because it was a testimony or witness of the presence of God among His people, i. e., it served to keep up the remembrance of Him.

Ver. 6.   *"arrayed with precious stone"*,—The reading of "linen" instead of *"stone"* is accepted by A. L. Tich. Weiss. The manuscript authority is about equally divided with perhaps a slight weight in favor of *"stone"*. The word "linen" seems to suit the sense a little better and better agrees with the two adjectives, which by some are taken as the emblem of holiness (the common representation in regard to the heavenly inhabitants,—Bar.) ; by some, as symbolical of the righteousness which demands the judgment wrath about to be poured out; and by others as a description of the angelic priestly attire.

If the word *"stone"* be retained, it cannot be referred to Christ Himself as the Corner Stone (I Peter 2.26), nor to "the various adornment of virtues" (Be. And.), but it means that each angel wears a garment set with a pure and brilliant gem or with many such gems. (Dus. Weid.)   Later expositors accept the reading "linen", but the considerations above noted, together with the fact that *"stone"* is the more difficult reading, and therefore the more likely to be the original, seem to favor the translation of our text.

"golden girdles",—Another emblem of divine righteousness (Gab.) Thus also was Christ girded (Chap. 1.13), and these angels were clothed with authority and divine righteousness to act for Christ.

Ver. 7.   *"bowls"*,—This is a better word than "vials", the Greek word designating that which is broad rather than deep, more like the vessels used in the temple below.

"full of the wrath of God",—Filled with that which represents his wrath, as it were with a poisonous mixture.

Ver. 8.   *"the temple was filled with smoke"*,—

1. A sign of His divine majesty. (B. Dus. Weid.)
2. A sign of His unapproachableness in the manifestation of His holiness. (L. Mil.)
3. A sign of the wrath of God. (B. Eb. Gro. And. Hen. Hei.)
4. A sign of the incomprehensibility of the divine judgments. (Lap.)

The first three views are each very proper and should perhaps be combined.

"God cannot be approached at the moment when He is revealing Himself in all the terrors of His indignation (Ex. 19.21)." (Mil.)

The whole description, says Weidner, "conveys an impression of the awful sacredness of God's presence."

"When God pours out His fury, it is fit that even those who stand well with Him should withdraw for a little, and should restrain their inquiring looks." (B.)

"from the glory," etc.,—i. e., from His presence in which His glory and His power were displayed.

"till the plagues should be finished",—When satisfaction has been rendered His holy wrath, then access to Him shall be possible.

CHAPTER SIXTEEN

1 And I heard a great voice out of the [1]temple saying to the seven angels, Go ye, and pour out the seven bowls of the wrath of God into the earth.

2 And the first went, and poured out his bowl into the earth; and [2]it became a noisome and grievous sore upon the men that had the mark of the beast, and that [3]worshipped his image.

3 And the second poured out his bowl into the sea; and [2]it became blood as of a dead man; and every [4]living soul died;

[1]Gr. *sanctuary*
[2]Or, *there came*
[3]See marginal note on Chap. 13.12
[4]Gr. *soul of life*

even the things that were in the sea.

4 And the third poured out his bowl into the rivers and the fountains of the waters; [5]and [2]it became blood. 5 And I heard the angel of the waters saying, Righteous art thou, who art and who wast, thou Holy One, because thou didst thus [6]judge; 6 for they poured out the blood of saints and prophets, and blood hast thou given them to drink: they are worthy. 7 And I heard the altar saying, Yea, O Lord God, the Almighty, true and righteous are thy judgments.

8 And the fourth poured out his bowl upon the sun; and it was given unto [7]it to scorch men with fire. 9 And men were scorched with great heat: and they blasphemed the name of God who hath the power over these plagues; and they repented not to give him glory.

10 And the fifth poured out his bowl upon the throne of the beast; and his kingdom was darkened; and they gnawed their tongues for pain, 11 and they blasphemed the God of heaven because of their pains and their sores; and they repented not of their works.

12 And the sixth poured out his bowl upon the great river, the *river* Euphrates; and the water thereof was dried up, that the way might be made ready for the kings that *come* from the sunrising. 13 And I saw *coming* out of the mouth of the dragon, and out of the mouth of the beast, and out of the

[5]Some ancient authorities read *and they became*
[6]Or. *judge. Because they . . . prophets, thou hast given them blood also to drink*
[7]Or, *him*

mouth of the false prophet, three unclean spirits, as it were frogs: 14 for they are spirits of demons, working signs; which go forth [8]unto the kings of the whole [9]world, to gather them together unto the war of the great day of God, the Almighty. 15 (Behold, I come as a thief. Blessed is he that watcheth, and keepeth his garments, lest he walk naked, and they see his shame.) 16 And they gathered them together into the place which is called in Hebrew [10]Har-Magedon.

17 And the seventh poured out his bowl upon the air; and there came forth a great voice out of the [11]temple, from the throne, saying, It is done: 18 and there were lightnings, and voices, and thunders; and there was a great earthquake, such as was not since [12]there were men upon the earth, so great an earthquake, so mighty. 19 And the great city was divided into three parts, and the cities of the [13]nations fell: and Babylon the great was remembered in the sight of God, to give unto her the cup of the wine of the fierceness of his wrath. 20 And every island fled away, and the mountains were not found. 21 And great hail, *every stone* about the weight of a talent, cometh down out of heaven upon men: and men blasphemed God because of the plague of the hail; for the plague thereof is exceeding great.

[8]Or, *upon*
[9]Gr. *inhabited earth*
[10]Or, *Ar-Magedon*
[11]Or, *sanctuary*
[12]Some ancient authorities read *there was a man*
[13]Or, *Gentiles*

Vers. 1-21. THE JUDGMENT OF THE SEVEN BOWLS OF GOD'S WRATH.

The pouring out of these bowls all occurs during the blowing of the Seventh Trumpet.

The Historical School of interpretation construes these bowls as prefiguring events which are of course already past; Elliott, for instance, referring them to the French Revolution.

Alford here joins with the Futurist School of interpretation and referring to the last words of Chap. 15.1, *"seven plagues which are the last, for in them is finished the wrath of God"*, he says, "There can then be no doubt here, not only that the series reaches on to the time of the end, but that the whole of it is to be placed very close to the same time. It belongs by its very conditions to the time of the end."

The Futurists, of course, place all these occurrences in the times of the Great Tribulation at the close of this dispensation.

Blunt says, "They appear to represent those human woes and convulsions of nature to which our Lord referred when in Matt. 24.29 and Luke 21.11. He speaks of the signs that will precede His Second Coming."

"God now begins," says Weidner, "in a direct way to bring to an end the Great Tribulation through which His faithful ones are passing by visiting judgment upon the followers of the Antichrist."

Ver. 1.   *"a great voice out of the temple"*,—According to Chap. 15.8, the voice of God. (A. B. L. F. Zu. Dus. Hen. Weid.)

THE FIRST BOWL.

Ver. 2.   *"went and poured"*,—Each angel as his turn comes leaves the heavenly scene and from the space between heaven and earth pours his bowl out upon the appointed object.   (See Exodus 9.9.)

"noisome and grievous",—A more general expression for "bad and evil". As usual the Allegorical and Historical interpretations of this plague have been of infinite variety. Elliott, with many other interpreters (Faber, Keith, Galloway, Cuninghame), explains it to prefigure "that tremendous outbreak of social and moral evil, of democratic fury, atheism and vice, which was speedily seen to characterize the French Revolution."

While some take the sores literally, others (Gab.) interpret symbolically of the breaking out of the internal corruption of the world in its vile and apostate condition.

THE SECOND BOWL.

Ver. 3.   *"as of a dead man"*,—Not the idea of a great pool of blood as of many slain (D. Ei. Hen.) but loathesome and corrupting blood clotted and putrefying as when a dead man lies in his own blood. (A. B. Zu. Dus.)

Elliott interprets this bowl as a judgment that would fall on and destroy the maritime power, commerce and colonies of the countries of Papal Christendom; that is, of France, Spain and Portugal, these being the only Papal kingdoms to which such maritime colonies and power attached. And the fulfillment of the prophecy, he says, stands conspicuous in the history of the wars that arose out of the French Revolution.

Perhaps most commentators interpret all these vial judgments symbolically, making the sea in this instance represent the nations in restless state and this vial as designating the moral and spiritual death among the nations. The future alone can decide the question, but the close resemblance to the Egyptian plagues suggests that the fulfillment may be a literal one.

THE THIRD BOWL.

Ver. 4.   *"and it became blood"*,—It does not say "they became", i. e., the waters, although some ancient authorities so read. The reading may be, however, as in the margin, "there came", which reading is also proper in connection with the first two vials. The singular, however, *"it became"*, can be retained and, in harmony with the analogy of Chap. 8.11 and the first two vials, it seems best to think of the rivers and the fountains becoming blood. The rivers and fountains may be taken together and be regarded as neuter, and so the singular *"it"* be used.

Ver. 5.   *"the angel of the waters"*,—Not the angel who emptied the bowl into the waters. (Eb. Gro. Weid.) A definite angel is meant who is placed over the streams as his special sphere.   (D. A. F. Ew. Zu. And. Lap. Hen.)

"who art and who wast",—The "who is to come" is absent here as in Chap. 11.17 because the coming is already in process of fulfillment.

"thus judge",—Literally, "judge such things"; the "such things" being the equivalent of *"thus"* and referring to verse 4, as seen by verse 6, where the blood of these rivers is referred to as their drinking water.

Ver. 6.   *"they are worthy"*,—i. e., have merited this judgment and they have to taste the vileness and the bitterness of their apostasy.

Ver. 7.   *"I heard the altar saying"*,—The simplest way of understanding these words is that they represent a personification of the altar. (A. F. D. Dus. Weid.)   The altar speaks just as the blood of Abel is said to cry, and the stones of Jerusalem are said to cry out. Many expedients are resorted to to avoid this explanation. Some supply a personality, "another angel of" (Zu. Lut.); "the angel who guards the spirits of the martyrs" (Gro.); "an inhabitant of heaven standing by the divine altar" (Ew.).   Others resort to allegory: "The inner affection of the saints, angels, or men who by teaching rule the people." (Be.)   "The angelic powers as bearers of our prayers." (And.)   None of these explanations are deserving of serious attention.

Elliott explains this bowl of a judgment of war and bloodshed that would begin to be poured out on the countries watered by the Rhine and the Danube and on the sub-Alpine provinces of Piedmont and Lombardy, all of which, he says, was fulfilled during the French Revolutionary wars.

THE FOURTH BOWL.

Ver. 8.   *"given unto it"*,—Not to the angel (B. El. Ew. Hen.), but to the sun (A. F. D. L. Dus.).   So far as the grammar goes it could be either *"unto it"* or "unto him", but the sense of the passage refers it to the sun, while the gender testifies as strongly for the one as for the other. While some take the sun literally, Gaebelein prefers the symbolical meaning, the government ruling them, i. e., the Roman empire.

"to scorch men with fire",—The fire of the sun and not some other fire, as it is taken by some (B. Hen.), who refer *"it was given unto it"* to the angel.

"men",—This is perhaps to be taken generically simply as referring to men, although because of the definite article *"the"* it is possible to find reference here, as does Fausset, to the particular men who had the mark of the Beast.

This bowl Elliott interprets of the darkening, partially or entirely, either of the power of the German emperor, who might be considered as most properly the sun in the symbolic firmament of Papal Christendom, or perhaps of the sovereigns of those Papal kingdoms, more in general, all of which was accomplished in the wars of the French Revolution.

THE FIFTH BOWL.

Ver. 10.   *"the throne of the beast"*,—The throne given to it by the Dragon (Chap. 13.2).   The throne of the beast refers here to the spot, the place where the power and presence of the beast had its proper residence.   The actual center of his entire kingdom is here meant.   The lands over which he ruled were covered with darkness as in the ninth Egyptian plague. (Exodus 10.21-23.) Says Moorehead, "Judicial blindness smites his kingdom; madness and defiance rule."

"*his kingdom*",—The kingdom of the beast considered according to its geographical extent (A. Dus.), those lands which owned his rule.

"*was darkened*",—Occasioned not by an injury to the sun but by a special miraculous act. (A. D. Dus.)

"*they*",—i. e., the inhabitants, the worshippers of the beast.

"*gnawed their tongues for pain*",—Not because of the darkness so much, as this is no cause for pain; but because, as verse 11 shows, of the plagues poured upon them by the preceding bowls, although the darkness makes them all the more unbearable.

Ver. 11. This verse shows that the first three plagues are still continuing: the sores are still in force. It shows that the bowls are cumulative and not successive.

Elliott interprets the throne of the beast as the Papal seat of Rome, the judgment consisting in the abolition of the Pope's temporal authority over the Roman state accompanied by insults and injuries heaped by the French on the Papal power from almost the very commencement of the French Revolution, the Pope himself being torn from his throne and carried a prisoner into France, where he died in exile in 1799.

THE SIXTH BOWL.

Ver. 12. "*for the kings that come from the sun-rising*",—The interpretation of these kings from the sun-rising is various indeed. The view of Ebrard, that they are the four angels of Chap. 9.4, and that of Ewald, that they are the Parthian allies federated with Nero going against Rome need merely to be mentioned to be set aside.

Wordsworth says that the prediction is not necessarily a literal one, but that what is signified is that the Roman empire must be attacked, divided and weakened by enemies, and that this is most significantly expressed here by adverting to the only enemies, *Parthia and her allies*, who, when this book was written, were able to make any impression upon that empire. But this view has no more in its favor than many other such which have been advanced in the interest of the Synchrono-Historical interpretation.

Elliott of the Consecutive Historical School explains the Euphrates as the Turkish power, the same as that prefigured under the Sixth Trumpet as "loosed from the Euphrates", which power, having overflown its Euphratean banks over Grecian Christendom, is here, as a symbolic river-flood, represented as being dried up, the process starting by internal revolt and insurrection in the Turkish empire in 1820, as the next great event after the out-pouring of the fifth bowl on the throne of the Beast. Elliott then calls attention to the fact that the Turkish power has been the greatest bulwark to the Mohammedan religion, and that Mohammedanism has been the most formidable obstruction to the Christianization of the *Eastern world*, and he therefore asserts, somewhat gratuitously it would seem, that what is here intended by the coming of the kings of the east is their conversion, the coming of eastern princes and peoples into the Christian faith.

But Alford rightly says that "to suppose the conversion of the Eastern nations or the gathering together of Christian princes to be meant, or to regard the words as referring to any auspicious event, is to introduce a totally incongruous feature into the series of bowls which confessedly represents *judgment*, the seven last plagues."

By others the expression has been taken of *the restoration of the Jews to their own land.* (Me. Br. New. Cun. Burgh.) But Alford's objection weighs equally strong against this. Besides the Jews are not represented in Scripture to be so concentrated in eastern countries at the close of their dispersion, and furthermore they are not represented at this time as "kings", but as "a nation scattered and peeled and trodden down".

The remarks of Alford, given above, bear equally against the view which makes these kings to be Jews adopting the Christian faith; or the Babylonian Jews going to the aid of the Palestinian Jews, and it weighs especially against the view of Fausset who, following the ancient interpretation of Primasius, says these kings are primarily the transfigured saints coming with the King of kings, at His Second Coming, these saints being kings and priests, as set forth in Chap. 1.6. Fausset of course, in harmony with his interpretation, takes the drying up of the Euphrates in a figurative or symbolic sense, it being the mystical river of the antichristian Babylon, and its drying up the diminution of that Babylon's power for opposition to the truth.

We are inclined to think that the only understanding of the words under consideration which will suit the context or the requirements of this series of prophecies is that the kings of the whole earth are to be gathered in battle against God and the Lamb, and the way is thus prepared for those coming from the east. (A. D. Bl. Ew. Dus. And. Gab. Pet. Sco. Weid.)

The circumstance has its basis no doubt in the dividing of the waters of the Red Sea for the passage of the children of Israel.

From the rising of the sun, the land beyond the Euphrates, conquering hordes were wont to come from the earliest times down upon lower Asia and especially upon Canaan. This affair must, in keeping with the other bowls, represent a judgment upon the ungodly. These kings of the east are doubtless a part of the *"kings of the whole earth"* (verse 14) and are instruments of the dragon and the beast who go up to war, not against Babylon (the apostate Church) but against believers. The plague of the sixth vial does not lie in the fact that these kings of the sun-rising come (L.), but that they assemble at Armageddon *for their own destruction.*

On account of the saying that the river Euphrates was dried up, some (D. Eb. Hof. Bru.) maintain that a battle of the eastern kings against the spiritual Babylon is intended. But Hengstenberg says well, "that the expedition is directed not against spiritual Babylon, that is, Rome, but against Canaan, that is, the Church, is rendered manifest by verse 16, and as well by verse 14, and by the fact that all the other vials bear an oecumenical character, and sweep over all the earth, the whole of the God-opposing wickedness, and not merely some particular phase of it." "The Euphrates", says Hengstenberg, "is mentioned here merely in respect to the hindrance it presented to the march of the ungodly power of the world into the Holy Land, against the Holy City; against the Church."

The drying up of the river Euphrates may be taken of course symbolically of any barriers whatsoever which may have held back the kings of the east, the removal of which is symbolized by the drying up of the river. On the other hand it may quite as well be taken in an altogether literal sense. (A. Sim. Pet. Gab. Dus. Weid.) Dusterdieck, whose interpretation in the main we believe to be correct, contends that these kings from the sun-rising refer proleptically to the ten kings of Chap. 17.12 who give their power to the beast, and that in Chap. 17 will be found the details of their defeat. This is, however, perhaps more than we are warranted in drawing from the text.

Vers. 13-16. These verses contain without doubt a parenthetical vision.

Ver. 13. *"the false prophet"*,—The second beast of Chap. 13.11.

"unclean",—Designating also the demoniacal nature of these spirits.

"as it were frogs",—The form in which the spirits appeared. The likeness is to be explained from the uncleanness, offensiveness and pertinacious noise of the frogs. The representation may rest upon I Kings 22.20-22.

Here again all sorts of interpretations too numerous to mention are given by the Allegorical and Historical Schools, such as, "three forms of divination in which Maxentius trusted" (Gro.); the sophists, Faber, Eck and Emser (Lut.); the Jesuits, Capuchins, and Calvinists (Ca.)

Elliott interprets these spirits as the spirit of infidelity proceeding from the mouth of the Dragon, the Devil; of popery proceeding from the mouth of the Beast, the Papal Antichrist; of priestcraft proceeding from the mouth of the False Prophet, the apostate Papal priesthood; all of which manifested themselves throughout France and England and other lands with great intensity beginning about the year 1830, and are still operating in the world today.

Ver. 14. Here we find the definition of these spirits, *"spirits of demons"*, and here it would seem the limits of interpretation are clearly set. Weidner says, "We must insist that these spirits are just as real as the dragon and his two beasts from whose mouths the spirits actually proceed."

"working signs",—Lange says these are "lying, apparent miracles". But it is the word always used for miracles in John's Gospel. As the false prophet used miracles to seduce men to the worship of the beast, so do these spirits in order to gather the kings together for the great battle.

"the kings of the whole earth",—The rulers of the inhabitants of the earth worshipping the beast.

"unto the war",—The final conflict for the kingship of the world. This gathering is the signal for Christ's coming as set forth in II Thess. 1.7,8.

"the great day of God, the Almighty",—Explained in detail in Chap. 19. It is evidently, as Craven says, the day of Christ's appearing to establish His Millennial kingdom, and not the future final-end judgment (B. D. L. Dus.); nor yet is it hardly to be taken with Hengstenberg in a comprehensive way, denoting all the phases of God's judgments.

"This great gathering of the beast and of the kings of the earth against God and the Lamb, is," says Alford, "the signal for the immediate and glorious appearing of the Lord. And therefore follows in the next verse an exhortation to be ready and clad in garments of righteousness when He comes."

Even this, some of the Historical interpreters refer to the devastation of Rome. (Ei. Ew.)

Ver. 15. *"I come as a thief"*,—The Lord Himself speaks. John apparently hears, and writes down as he hears, the words of Christ spoken in the midst of his vision. (F. L. Sim. Mil. Sei. Hen. Weid.) Others say it is the Seer speaking in the name of Christ. (A. D. Dus.)

"keepeth his garments",—The figure of a man keeping watch in his clothes in apprehension of the coming thief. In a spiritual sense the garments are the robes of righteousness put on by faith in Christ, the destitution of which will cause the shame spoken of in that day.

Ver. 16. *"And they gathered"*,—i. e., the three unclean spirits. (A. F. D. Bl. Dus. Sim. Weid.)

If the English version "he" is retained, the reference would be to God (L. Eb. Hen. Gab.), and not to the angel of the Sixth Bowl (B.), nor to the Dragon (Ew.).

"them",—i. e., the kings just mentioned and their armies.

"Har-Magedon",—"Har" means hill, mountain. "Magedo" means slaughter. Magedo is the name of the place where occurred the overthrow of the Canaanite kings by God's miraculous interposition under Deborah and Barak. (Judges 5.9.) Here also Josiah was defeated and slain. (II Kings 23.29.)

Gebhart uses this last reference, viz., that as once in Magedo the Theocracy was borne to its grave in the defeat of Joshua, so in Har-Magedon the Lord will avenge the crime of the heathen. The point of comparison, however, is rather with the first reference, namely, the defeat of God's enemies, the Canaanites. (A. B. Eb. Dus. Kli. Weid.)

Ar-Magedon means City of Magedon, or City of Slaughter; Har-Megedon means Hill of Magedon, or Hill of Slaughter. There is some reason for believing that, whether the one or the other word is used, it should not be regarded as the name of any one particular place, but that it rather gives the special characteristic of this final world-conflict. In fact we read in the Hebrew of "the waters of Megedo" (Jud. 5.19) and of "the valley of Megedo" (Zech. 12.11), but nowhere in the Hebrew Bible do we read of "the hill of Megedo" or of "the city of Megedo". The Megedo of Palestine is not a mountain, not even a hill, nor is it a city. In the neighborhood of Megedo (Megiddo), as Thompson, in his "The Land and the Book" tells us, there is "only a little hillock or heap of sand", while in the common parlance of the Arabs and Syrians today the Megedo of Palestine is the very antithesis to a hill. It is a plain, and the Palestinian might therefore the more likely be the great ancient plain of Esdraelon, the great world's battleground of all past ages.

In keeping with the interpretation which makes the word descriptive of a characteristic (great slaughter) rather than a definite place, there are those who think the last world war just closed was indeed the very battle of Har-Magedon, and that therefore, as John Robertson says, "The Second Advent of our Lord is now by Prophetical schedule due, and may at the next tick of the watch in your pocket be seen in the sky."

"It is evident," says Weidner, "that we must distinguish between the battle of Har-Magedon and the Day of Judgment; for in Zech. 14.4,5 the mount of Olives, and in Joel 3.12 the valley of Jehosaphat, is represented as the scene of that great event."

THE SEVENTH BOWL.

Ver. 17. "upon the air",—Perhaps as the abode of the powers of darkness, Satan being the prince of the powers of the air.

"a great voice",—i. e., of God. (A. Sim. Wor. Dus. Weid.)

"It is done",—That is, the end has come, the time for the overthrow of the Antichrist. The Lord has come!

Some (B. D. Dus. Hen.) say that was done which was commanded in verse 1. But it is better to explain as above and take the expression in a proleptical sense, importing that the outpouring of the seventh vial had done that which should accomplish all and bring in the end. "It is," says Alford, "as if one who had fired a train should so speak even though the explosion had not yet occurred." (L. F. Sim. Weid.)

Ver. 18. Here we have the same signs as in Chap. 11.9, though extremely heightened. Verse 21 shows that verses 18-21 do not conclude the effects of the Seventh Bowl, but rather begin them, which effects do not cease until the overthrow of Babylon and the destruction of the great antichristian forces.

Ver. 19. "And the great city",—

1. Papal Rome. (A. El. Bar.)

2. Heathen Rome, the great heathen metropolis. (D. Ew. Al. Bl. St. Vol. Dus.)

3. Jerusalem, which at that time will be antichristian and the seat of the Antichrist. (B. Eb. Zu. Mil. And. Lap. Sim. Her. Hof. Weid. Stern.) (See Chap. 11.8.)

4. An ideal city embracing all anti-christianity, of which at that time heathen Rome was the highest representative point. (E. L.)

Views 2 and 4 are quite the same in essence, Fausset declaring that the reference is to spiritual Babylon (heathen Rome), the capital and seat of the apostate Church.

It is, after all, a matter of conjecture as to which city is intended. In favor of view 3, is the fact that it would be pointless to suppose Babylon to be mentioned twice in this one verse, while taken the other way there is a climax. The identical expression, "the great city", is used of Jerusalem in Chap. 11.8. It must not be overlooked, however, that Babylon is even more often called "the great".

The objection to view 3 by Hengstenberg that the judgment of the vials is upon the heathen worldly power as opposed to God has no weight in view of the fact that if the interpretation of Jerusalem is here accepted, it must refer of course to Jerusalem as at that time under the power of the Antichrist. Dusterdieck argues in favor of view 2 that it follows from the connection of Chap. 13 as well as from the context here; but the strength of his argument is not apparent. One cannot afford in a case like this to be arbitrary in his choice of expositions, but to us the inference seems to favor taking *"the great city"* as Jerusalem.

"divided",—i. e., split by the earthquake.

"into three parts",—(See Zech. 14.4,5). The meaning is doubtless that the city was broken up and overthrown, sustaining a very large and severe damage. It seems that the number *"three"* is here taken in a symbolical sense, as Stuart says, and that the reference is to the fact that the city was reduced to a ruinous state. Stuart, however, admits that the meaning may be that chasms in the earth divided the city into three parts.

"cities of the nations fell",—Other great cities in league with the antichristian forces also fell from the violence of the earthquake.

"Babylon the great",—The reference here is doubtless to spiritual Babylon, that is, heathen Rome, whose fate is referred to by way of anticipation. (See Chap. 14.8.)

Some make *"Babylon the great"* and *"the great city"* one and the same, referring both to Jerusalem (Mil.) or both to heathen Rome, but as already noted it would seem best to distinguish them.

"remembered in the sight of God",—All the plagues were but preparatory, the divine intent being in the midst of them, to make Babylon drink the cup of His wrath in the judgment which is now to follow. (See Acts 10.31 on the expression, and Psa. 10.13 on the thing designated.)

"fierceness",—The boiling-over outburst.

Ver. 20. (See Chap. 6.14.) Islands and mountains disappear, but earth remains. The case is different in Chap. 20.11, says Burger. Hengstenberg says the islands and mountains are indicative of kingdoms, and this may be true, but there is no strong reason for not taking the expression literally, as the result of earthquakes frequently is an effect of this kind.

Ver. 21. *"the weight of a talent"*,—Fifty-seven pounds Attic, or ninety-six pounds Hebrew; sixty times heavier than ever known before.

Says Ebrard, "We are assuredly not to imagine that actual, natural hail is meant." Thus also Barnes and Stuart and many others who think it only a frightful image to denote the terrible and certain destruction that is to come upon Babylon, symbolizing the tremendous blows of suffering and sorrow which the antichristian world sustains in this time of revolution. There is, however, no incontrovertible reason for not taking the hailstones in a literal sense. (F. Pet. Gab. Sim. Weid.)

"and men blasphemed God",—i. e., those not being struck by the hail, the others being killed. A different issue than in Chap. 11.13.

The destruction of Babylon alluded to is described in the following chapters.

Elliott here joins, as it were, the Futurists and interprets this Seventh Bowl as symbolizing events yet future, although he gives to the entire passage a figurative meaning. The *"air"* he explains to be the European political and moral atmosphere just as he explains the Apocalyptic firmament elsewhere to mean the political firmament, and the result of the pouring out of the Seventh Bowl is to be a convulsion, vitiation, and darkening of the moral and political atmosphere of Western Europe. The thunders, lightnings and voices indicate, he says, the wars and tumults which are to follow, while the hailstorm, he seems to think, indicates that France, the most northerly of the Papal kingdoms, is to become at least one of the chief operators or instruments of the plague, inasmuch as he thinks a judgment from the North is indicated. Other expositors, comparing this prophecy with the one in Ezekiel 38 and 39, prefer to explain the hailstorm of Russia, inasmuch as the prophecy in Ezekiel seems to point to Russia's taking part in the pre-millennial conflict. This last view, Elliott says, "is also not improbable."

Vitringa explains the hailstorm simply to indicate a judgment immediately from heaven, and refers to the hail which fell in the seventh Egyptian plague, and also that which fell on the Canaanites, as described in Josh. 10.11.

Elliott also says, "It seems to me very possible that there may be here, too, that which shall literally answer to the prediction. Compare the as yet unfulfilled prophecy in Isa. 30.30. But the analogy of all the Apocalyptic prefigurations requires primarily a *symbolic* explanation."

The dividing of the great city into three parts Elliott explains as "the final breaking up of that decemregal form of the Papal empire, which has now characterized it for nearly thirteen centuries, into a new and tri-part form."

CHAPTER SEVENTEEN

1 And there came one of the seven angels that had the seven bowls, and spake with me, saying, Come hither, I will show thee the judgment of the great harlot that sitteth upon many waters; 2 with whom the kings of the earth committed fornication, and they that dwell in the earth were made drunken with the wine of her fornication. 3 And he carried me away in the Spirit into a wilderness: and I saw a woman sitting upon a scarlet-colored beast, [1]full of names of blasphemy, having seven heads and ten horns. 4 And the woman was arrayed in purple and scarlet, and [2]decked with gold and precious stone and pearls, having in her hand a golden cup full of abominations, [3]even the unclean things of her fornication, 5 and upon her forehead a name written, [4]MYSTERY, BABYLON THE GREAT, THE MOTHER OF THE HARLOTS AND OF THE ABOMINATIONS OF THE EARTH. 6 And I saw the woman drunken with the blood of the saints, and with the blood of the [5]martyrs of Jesus. And when I saw her, I wondered with a great wonder.

[1]Or, *names full of blasphemy*
[2]Gr. *gilded*
[3]Or, *and of the unclean things*
[4]Or, *a mystery, Babylon the Great*
[5]Or, *witnesses.* See Chap. 2.13.

Vers. 1-6.   THE MYSTERY OF THE SCARLET WOMAN AND THE BEAST. THE DIVINE VIEW OF "BABYLON".

THE JUDGMENT OF BABYLON.

Twice before has the fall of Babylon been introduced by way of anticipation (Chaps. 14.8 and 16.9), but in this and the succeeding chapter we are to have a detailed account of it. The time referred to is that immediately preceding the second coming of Christ.

Ver. 1.   *"one of the seven angels"*,—Probably the one who poured out the seventh vial, because it was during the outpouring of his vial that reference is made to the fact that God remembered Babylon in the fierceness of His wrath. We are not, however, told which angel it is and it is useless to conjecture. It is the same angel who showed John, according to Chap. 21.9, the Bride, the Lamb's wife.

"Come hither",—Barnes says, "The reference is not to local motion but to a certain direction of the contemplation."

"I will show thee the judgment",—A promise not immediately fulfilled in verse 3, nor indeed even in this chapter. The harlot is shown in her antichristian form, but not until Chap. 18.1 does the judgment occur.

"the great harlot",—This is explained in verse 18 as being a symbol of "the great city which reigneth over the kings of the earth". It is not uncommon in Scripture to represent a city under the image of a woman.

"sitteth upon many waters",—This was literally true of the old Babylon. Verse 15 shows that by *"waters"* is here meant "peoples, and multitudes, and nations and tongues" over which the city or government, symbolized by the woman, ruled.

WHO IS THE GREAT HARLOT?

1. Babylon to be rebuilt on the Euphrates.
2. A great world-city of the last days, either, one to be built as the seat of the antichristian government, or in an ideal sense, any and all great cities that have directed persecution against the people of God.
3. Jerusalem. (Zu. Her. Hartwig.)
4. Heathen Rome. (Dus. Hen. Sim.)
5. Papal Rome. (A. B. V. El. Ca. Gab. Bar. Coc. Glas.)
6. The apostate church of the future in general, Roman Catholic, Greek Catholic and unfaithful Protestantism. (F. Au. Mil. Pet. Hahn. Moor.)

The first three views are not to be seriously considered.

1. Literal Babylon on the banks of the Euphrates which is to be the seat of government during the end of this age. This cannot be, because:
   (a) That city was not built on seven hills, but on the plains of Shinar.
   (b) Literal Babylon was never a part of the Roman empire, and as the Babylon of the seventeenth and eighteenth chapters is seen in closest identification with this empire and for a time at least its center and capital, the Babylon in Asia is ruled out at once.

The objection of Petingill that Babylon had long before John's time ceased to "reign over the kings of the earth" is hardly relevant because Isa. 13.20-22 seems to imply that it is to be rebuilt. But even so, the two objections noted above outweigh any evidence that might be quoted in Babylon's favor.

2. A great world-city of the last days. There are no arguments of any strength adduced in favor of this view. Milligan gives four arguments against the view, but they are of little weight, expressing themselves as they do from the standpoint of the School of Spiritual Interpretation.

3. Jerusalem. This city is also built on seven hills, four large and three small. But the fact that Jerusalem as well as Babylon is called *"the great city"* (Chaps. 11.8 and 16.19) is not sufficient ground for applying the reference here to that city.

As to which one of the other three views should be accepted will perhaps be the easier decided after the exposition of this chapter.

Ver. 2. The fornication here mentioned committed by the kings of the earth as well as by all the nations is of course of a spiritual sort and suggests that the harlot will seduce men from the worship of the true God to worldliness and sin and to the worship of the beast.

Ver. 3. *"carried me away in the Spirit"*,—This expression is found only here and at Chap. 21.10 where the vision of the New Jerusalem is introduced. It denotes spiritual ecstacy and here refers to a change wrought in the ecstatic direction of the spirit of the Seer, and not bodily removal.

"into a wilderness",—Amidst all her pomp and luxury the place where she reigns is really desolate. Many think in keeping with verse 16 that the harlot is to be seen in the wilderness because of the complete desolation pending over her. (D. Ew. St. Dus. And. Lap. Hof. Hen. Ros. Bar.) Hengstenberg confirms this conclusion by reference to the fundamental passages of the Old Testament (Jer. 50 and 51 and Isa. 21.1). He further says we are led to this conclusion by the contrast of the great and high mountain in Chap. 21.10.

The desert place or wilderness Elliott explains as a reference to the Campagna of Rome which is even now in an actual desolate state, a state which began when first the ten-horned beast of western anti-Christendom having emerged into existence, the harlot Church of Rome rose on its back to supremacy, and has so continued ever since.

"a scarlet-colored beast",—The same beast as in Chap. 13.1. (F. A. L. St. Dus. Hen. Mil. Gab. Weid. Glas. Moor.), not only because of the features they have in common, and that he is always afterwards mentioned as the beast, but Chap. 19.19,20 clearly identifies them.

"scarlet colored",—Not the color of a covering (D. Zu.), but of the beast itself. It is a fiery red and is a sign of the blood shed by it. It implies blood-guiltiness and deep-dyed sin.

"full of names of blasphemy",—These were found before only on the head of the beast, but now as ridden and guided by the harlot, over all the beast tenfold more blasphemous in its titles and assumptions than ever.

"having seven heads and ten horns",—As did the beast in Chap. 13. (See verses 9 and 12 for the explanation of these heads and horns.)

Ver. 4. *"purple and scarlet"*,—Purple was the color of the imperial robe placed on Christ (John 19.2) and here indicates royal sovereignty, while the *"scarlet"* evidently refers to her being stained with the blood of the saints. (St. Dus. Weid.)

Many Protestant commentators see in this verse a description of the robes of the Roman popes and cardinals, and perhaps not altogether unjustly, especially if in any sense the harlot can refer to Papal Rome. (A. B. V. El. Gab.)

Alford refers the words *"scarlet"* and *"purple"* to the same thing, but while this is possible it is superfluous to designate by two emblems the same thing.

"a golden cup full of abominations", etc.,—The language is probably founded on Jer. 51.7. Not that the cup serves her to drink the blood of saints and martyrs (verse 6), but the cup with which she invites and entices to drunkenness and uncleanness, the cup with which she seduces and corrupts the nations.

Here the Allegorist has opportunity to give reign to his imagination, as for instance, "hypocrisy" (Be.), i. e., the enticement of feigned truth; "worldly happiness, the majesty of government" (Lap.); "Scripture distorted by wicked interpretation" (Coc.); "papal doctrine; the cup of the Mass" (Ca.).

Elliott finds in it a reference to the indulgences, the worship of relics and other sacrilegious impositions of the Romish Church, while in the purple and scarlet dress and precious stones he finds a prefigurement of the robes of the Romish dignitaries and the costly embellishment of their chapels and churches.

About all we are warranted in reading from the text is that just as she was arrayed in gold, etc., so is the cup golden but is full of abominations, holding as it does the wine of her fornication.

"full of",—This is first followed by a genitive (*"abominations"*) and then by an accusative (*"unclean things"*). Many (A. Bl. Ew. Hen.) make both depend upon *"full of"*. This gives a change of construction which is most remarkable, but Hengstenberg says it is allowable to avoid so many genitives inasmuch as another genitive follows; while Alford says it is to mark a difference between the more abstract designation of the contents of the cup as *"abominations"* and the specification of them in the concrete as *"unclean things"*

Others (L. Dus.) avoid all this by connecting the accusative *"unclean things"* with the verb *"holding"* and saying it is a later interpretation of the *"abominations"*. They regard it as parallel with *"cup"*. But this would seem to put the unclean things in her hand and not in the cup.

Stuart more appropriately regards it as in apposition with *"cup"* and as exegetical of its meaning.

Our text tries to adopt the idea of Dusterdieck and Lange by a pure apposition, but this is most crude. Of the four views that of Alford and the margin of our text appeal to us most strongly, although the difficulty has to us no satisfactory solution.

Ver. 5. *"a name written"*,—As was customary with harlots.

"MYSTERY",—It is difficult to decide whether this word is to be regarded as a part of the name, or as indicating the symbolical character of the city. Many (A. Hen. Wor. Lil.) think it belongs to the name. Lillie gives some five reasons for this view but they are hardly strong enough to be convincing, and it is better with other authorities (St. Dus. Bar. Sim. Mil. Weid.) to take it as indicating that what follows is to be symbolically, mystically, spiritually understood.

According to some, the words following *"Babylon the Great"* are not to be considered a part of the inscription, but an exclamation of the author, inasmuch as Babylon would not thus openly and shamelessly wear a frontlet proclaiming such a character. (St.)

"BABYLON THE GREAT",—(See Chaps. 14.8 and 16.9). The chief city as the concrete representation of the whole antichristian empire in the days of the Antichrist.

"MOTHER OF HARLOTS",—She is the chief of these and the cause of the rest being what they are. She made her own daughters, the cities of the Gentiles, to be harlots, and gave them to drink of her own cup of abominations, says Dusterdieck.

She was the mother of "that spiritual apostacy from God, which in the language of the prophets is called adultery, and the promoter of lewdness by her institutions." (Ba.)

Ver. 6. *"drunken with the blood"*,—A reeling, intoxicated harlot. "The phraseology," says Stuart, "is derived from the barbarous custom of drinking the blood of enemies slain in the way of revenge."

"saints and martyrs",—There is no distinction in kind here. It is by their testimony as saints that they become martyrs.

Here Elliott finds reference to the bloody persecutions which have characterized the Romish Church more especially during certain periods of her history.

"I wondered with great wonder",—There are many explanations advanced:

1. That such a woman could finally be the product of the historical development of the Church of faith then existent. He wondered at the degeneracy of the apostate Church. (L. Moor.)

2. Because of the change in the beast which he had seen in **Chap.** 13.1. (Eb.)

3. Because of the phenomenon of so powerful a beast being constrained to carry the woman. (B.)

4. Because he recognized in the harlot the woman he had seen in the wilderness in Chap. 12 and marveled at the contrast. (A. F. Au.)

5. Both the woman and the beast were each one a mystery, but it is the complex mystery of the beast bearing the woman that caused the wonder, and it was this that the angel explained in the following verses. (Dus. Crav.)

Dusterdieck calls the fourth explanation as just given an egregious mistake because there is nothing in the text to occasion it; the mystery must be the thing the angel explained, and of the relation of the harlot to the woman of Chap. 12 not a word does the angel say.

Moorehead objects to this view on the ground that the woman of Chap. 12 symbolizes Israel, the Messianic nation; and furthermore the woman, as protected in the wilderness in chapter 12, whoever she may symbolize, could hardly in so short a time become the vile and guilty harlot of Chap. 17. This latter objection, of course, is made on the ground that the wilderness experience of the first woman occurs but three and one-half years before the content of the present vision is to be realized, according to the Futurist view; but from the viewpoint of Alford and others who hold this fourth explanation this objection of Moorehead's loses its force, because they think of the woman of Chap. 12 as the Christian Church of Apostolic times.

The fifth view above is perhaps the right one.

7 And the angel said unto me, Wherefore didst thou wonder? I will tell thee the mystery of the woman, and of the beast that carrieth her, which hath the seven heads and the ten horns. 8 The beast that thou sawest was, and is not; and is about to come up out of the abyss, ¹and to go into perdition. And they that dwell on the earth shall wonder, *they* whose name hath not been written ²in the book of life from the foundation of the world, when they behold the beast, how that he was, and is not, and ³shall come. 9 Here is the ⁴mind that hath wisdom. The seven heads are seven mountains, on which the woman sitteth: 10 and ⁵they are seven kings; the five are fallen, the one is, the other is not yet come; and when he cometh, he must continue a little while. 11 And the beast that was, and is not, is himself also an eighth, and is of the seven; and he goeth into perdition. 12 And the ten horns that thou sawest are ten kings, who have received no kingdom as yet; but they receive authority as kings, with the beast, for one hour. 13 These have one mind, and they give their power and authority unto the beast. 14 These shall war against the Lamb, and the Lamb shall overcome them, for he is Lord of lords, and King of kings; and they *also shall overcome* that are with him, called and chosen and faithful. 15 And he saith unto me, The waters which thou sawest, where the harlot sitteth, are peoples, and multitudes, and nations, and tongues. 16 And the ten horns which thou sawest, and the beast, these shall hate the harlot, and shall make her desolate and naked, and shall eat her flesh, and shall burn her utterly with fire. 17 For God did put in their hearts to do his mind, and to come to one mind, and to give their kingdom unto the beast, until the words of God should be accomplished. 18 And the woman whom thou sawest is the great city, which ⁶reigneth over the kings of the earth.

¹Some ancient authorities read *and he goeth*
²Gr. *on*
³Gr. *shall be present*
⁴Or, *meaning*
⁵Or, *there are*
⁶Gr. *hath a kingdom*

Vers. 7-18. THE LAST FORM OF GENTILE WORLD-POWER.

Ver. 8. *"The beast . . . was, and is not; and is about to come"*, etc.,—This expression occurring twice in this verse and also in verse 11 with slight variation identifies the beast in each of these instances as one and the same. The explanation is found in verse 10.

"shall wonder",—i. e., in admiration, and shall worship him. (Chap. 13.3,4,8.) Fausset says, "They exult· with wonder in seeing that the beast which had seemed to have received its death-blow from Christianity, is on the eve of reviving with greater power than ever on the ruins of that religion which had tormented them."

Ver. 9. *"Here is the mind that hath wisdom"*,—See Chap. 13.18 and Dan. 12.10, where spiritual discernment is required in order to understand the symbolical prophecy. Hengstenberg translates, "Here belongs the understanding that hath wisdom," meaning that wisdom here has its right place, and intimating that a problem is presented here which it is the province of the more profound spiritual insight to handle. The words seem to indicate, says Simcox, that the mind which hath wisdom will recognize the meaning of the image, though it is obscurely expressed.

The reference is to wisdom enlightened from above. The words bespeak attention and challenge spiritual discernment. (El.)

"The seven heads are seven mountains",—In the next verse these same heads are said to be seven kings—seven mountains and seven kings—

and thus is presented a problem which it is utterly impossible to solve to general satisfaction. The usual interpretation is that by these words the city of Rome is pointed out. (A. D. El. St. Gab. Pet. Dus. Lee, Bar. Sim. Moor.)

Others say that while the specific reference is or may be to Rome, i has a wider reference to the various world empires which have arisen like great mountains in the world's history, the specific reference being doubtless to Egypt, Assyria, Babylon, Medo-Persia, Greece, Rome and the empire which is to come. (F. Mil. Hen. Sad. Crav. Will. Gebh.)

There are four arguments of considerable weight in favor of this last view:

1. It is unreasonable to literally interpret the seven heads first of *"mountains"* and then of *"kings"*.
2. We are told in Chap. 13.3 that one of the heads was wounded to death and such a description cannot apply to a literal mountain.
3. In the symbolic language of Scripture, Isa. 2.2; Dan. 2.35, and especially of the Revelation, mountains signify kingdoms.
4. The explanation of *"seven kings"*, or "kingdoms", the terms being interchangeable in Scripture, seems to confirm the interpretation adopted.

We would have then a double description of the same object, first *"mountains"* and then *"kings"*. The thought of Rome may have been present in the mind of John as one, perhaps even as the most important, phase of a much wider truth.

But the text says plainly that the seven heads *"are seven mountains on which the woman sitteth"*, and verse 18 says, *"the woman is the great city which reigneth over the kings of the earth"*. The seven heads of the beast, then, as related to the woman, must apparently find their reference in something that has primarily to do with the city of Rome. But these heads are also related to the beast and in this respect they are said in the next verse to be kings.

Ver. 10. *"and they are seven kings"*,—There are three general interpretations of this expression.

First. That which takes it as referring to actual kings.

Dusterdieck says that the entire force of the context demands this. This results especially, he says, from the description in this verse, and furthermore the entire sense of verse 11 depends upon this conception inasmuch as the future eight kings are contemplated as the human-personal manifestation of the whole beast.

There is considerable difference in the enumeration of these kings.

Of the schools of interpretation which place the fulfillment of the prophecy in the past, some start the five with Caesar, make the sixth (which is) Nero, and the seventh (which is to come) Galba (St. Wet.), while others claim that Caesar was a Dictator and not an Emperor, and start the five with Augustus, make the sixth (which is) Galba, and the seventh (which is to come) Otho.

Dusterdieck, Simcox and others claim that with these enumerations the rest of the prophecy receives nothing that can be considered even as a typical fulfillment, and holding that Galba, Otho, and Vitellius, his successor, were only usurpers reigning but a few weeks each, they begin their enumeration of the five with Augustus, make the sixth (which is) Vespasian, and the seventh (which is to come) Titus, who continued but a short while, reigning only two and one-half years.

Lange says it is no more necessary to take these *"kings"* as so many actual, literal kings than it is to take the beast as an actual, literal beast or animal, while Alford says it misses the propriety of the symbolism and introduces utter confusion.

Alford also calls attention to a fact in which there is considerable force, namely that the word *"fallen"* refers to a violent fall, an overthrow such as applies to the downfall of empires, and cannot refer to kings who die in their beds. It is also difficult to reconcile this view with the facts of the case, there being so much confusion introduced in the effort to name the kings. Nor is it hardly probable that John would enter into the minute details of the internal government of any heathen nation.

Second. That which takes the seven kings as so many forms of government which the Roman empire would be under from its early origin to its final destruction. (B. El. Ar. Os. Gab.)

The five which are fallen are Kings, Consuls, Dictators, Decemvirs, and Military Tribunes. The sixth, or the one which is, is the imperial form of government of John's day, commencing with Augustus Caesar.

As to this disposition of the first six forms of government, scholars adopting this method of interpretation are practically unanimous.

The seventh, or the one which is to come and continue a short while, is variously interpreted; the Dukedom of Rome (New.), the Christian emperors from Constantine to Augustulus (Cun.), the Western Government after the division of the Roman empire into East and West (Me.).

But all of these views make the seventh head a Christian headship. How then can the eighth head be *of* the seventh?

The seventh form of government Elliott conceives to be that ushered in under Diocletian, and which received its death wound under Julian through the Christian emperor Theodosius. The healing of the wound and the living again of the beast in its *eighth* head Elliott conceives to be the rising to prominence of the Papacy, as seen perhaps first in Pope Gregory, whereby the Popes of Rome began to be a new head to the empire, and this in the distinct character of Antichrist.

Among the Futurists we have the following from Gaebelein: "The seventh, the one which is to come, is the revived Roman empire of the future, the final form of Roman government. The eighth is the beast, as the text distinctly says, and is the emperor of this revived Roman empire, the *'little horn'* of Daniel's prophecy."

Simcox says of this method of interpretation in general, "Considering that the Dictatorship, the Decemvirate and even the Military Tribunes were but transitory episodes in the Roman government—the first avowedly exceptional, the second both exceptional and ephemeral, and all three, as well as the primitive monarchy, probably unknown to John's original readers—this view does not appear even plausible." Other objections have been registered against taking the expression as referring to forms of government, but neither they nor Simcox's are at all formidable.

Third. That which takes the beast as the embodiment of the God-opposed worldly imperial spirit, a general symbol of secular antichristian power, and takes the *"seven kings"* here mentioned as empires or kingdoms. (A. K. L. Au. Eb. Hen. Mil. Hof. Lud. Weid.) Here again is much division of opinion. The *majority* of commentators who follow this method of interpretation are agreed that the five fallen are Egypt, Assyria, Babylon, Medo-Persia, and Greece.

And *all* such commentators are agreed that the sixth, or the one that is, is the imperial Rome of John's day.

The seventh, or the one which is to come, presents the difficulty. Some think of the Christian Roman empire beginning with Constantine, during which time the beast (antichristian pagan imperial Rome) ceases to be. (A. Mil. Sad. Will. Au.) Others think of the kingdoms, or world-powers of modern Europe, which have taken the place of the Roman empire, i. e., the present system of European governments. (K. Lud. Hof. Hen. Lee. Weid.)

If the third method of interpretation be adopted (and to this we are inclined), then either explanation of the seventh king or kingdom may be appropriately taken.

Alford says, "As related to the beast these heads are kings; not kings over the woman or the city she symbolizes, but kings in relation to the beast of which they are the heads. Therefore to interpret these kings as emperors of Rome, or the successive forms of government over Rome (which, by the way, have never been made out) is to miss the propriety of the symbolism altogether and to introduce utter confusion."

The difficulty in Gaebelein's interpretation is that he begins with a form of government in which kings rule, then makes his seventh form of government also a kingdom (the revived Roman empire), and then in interpreting the beast himself as number eight (as the text does) he suddenly refers the beast, not to a form of government, but to the *"little horn"* of Daniel ruling over the revived Roman empire, the seventh form of government. It is to be noticed that while the third method of interpretation makes the heads to be world-kingdoms and the second method makes them different forms of government of the one Roman kingdom, they both unite in making the sixth head to be imperial Rome of John's day. At this point the difficulty begins. To make the revived Roman empire (the beast himself, as Gaebelein admits and in fact contends) to be the seventh head (which is to come) as Gaebelein does, is to find ourselves without an eighth, for the text plainly says the beast himself is the eighth. Then, too, most certainly this revived Roman empire must be the last form of antichristian imperial power, and to make the *"little horn"* of Daniel, who plainly is to be the ruler over the empire represented by the beast, to be the eighth head of a regime which must of necessity follow the seventh is certainly not the most discriminating sort of interpretation. In other words he seems to make the beast represent both the seventh and the eighth head. It is for this reason we accept the third explanation as given above.

"he must continue a little while",—Calls attention to the fact that this expression does not refer to a short continuance, but rather means "some little time", it being duration and not nonduration which is being stressed.

Others think that the idea of brevity is made prominent, i. e., his kingdom shall soon come to an end. (Dus.)

The decision here must be made to fit in with the view, or rather the result of the view, taken above of the *"seven kings"*.

Ver. 11. *"And the beast that was, and is not, is himself also an eighth"*,—This is the beast named in verse 8.

Among those who interpret the *"seven heads"* as seven actual kings is Simcox, who thinks that here the reference is to Nero, who is yet to return from the dead as Antichrist. Nero killed himself A. D. 68—*"was and is not"*, i. e., he had been and wás not at the time of this vision, but his reappearance was looked for by man.

This eighth beast, it would seem, is to be the eighth world-power concentrating in itself, as Weidner says, all the rage and God-opposed spirit of the seven preceding kingdoms, and is the last and worst manifestation of the ungodly power of the world. Its king, he says, will doubtless be the Antichrist, prefigured by the *"little horn"* of Daniel. (F. Sad. Weid.)

"and is not",—This refers to the time during which it was *"wounded to death"*, and has the *"deadly wound"* of Chap. 13.3.

Dusterdieck says, "This eighth king cannot be symbolized by a head on the beast, because he is not one of their series and has a different position from them." Thus the explanation of Hengstenberg and Klieforth who maintain that in the seventh head the eighth is also found, cannot be accepted; nor can that of Vitringa be accepted, who maintains that there is a true head of the beast distinct from the seven and that this is the eighth. No single head can fully represent it, says Milligan.

Elliott says the seventh head *visible* on the beast is in order of existence its eighth, this eighth head having evidently sprouted up from the seventh or preceding one cut down, this last having been "wounded to death by a sword". But this *"deadly wound was healed"* by the sprouting up of an eighth in its place. It was a new seventh in place of the old seventh; so that the last head visible on the beast, though *visibly the seventh*, was in point of chronological succession the *eighth*. It was on this *new seventh* head, or in other words, the *eighth* head that the ten horns appear with the ten diadems on them.

"is of the seven",—Not *one* of the seven, but *out* of them, i. e., their result and succession. (A.) It is not therefore that "his fate is that of the seven", i. e., he must fall, go to ruin (Hen. Gebh.); nor that he is *one* of the seven, in the sense of Nero coming back (D. St. Ew. Vol. Hil.), which is incompatible with the words of the text and unjustified in a simple exegetical respect.

Fausset has well expressed what seems to be the right interpretation of these words. He says, "The eighth is a new power or person proceeding *out of* the seven, and at the same time embodying all the god-opposed features of the previous seven concentrated and consummated, the eight being the embodiment of all the seven." He proceeds from the totality of the seven, says Lange.

Milligan says, "The preposition 'of' is to be understood in its common acceptance in John's writings, as denoting origin, identity of nature: as Primasius puts it, 'the beast is the essence, the concentrated expression of the seven, the embodiment of their spirit'."

THE REVELATION OF JOHN

"goeth into perdition",—"He does not fall like the other seven, but is destroyed by the Lord in person, going to his own perdition." (F. A. Weid.) It means being cast into the lake of fire and brimstone.

Ver. 12. The angel now turns from the heads of the beast to the horns.

"And the ten horns are ten kings",—i. e., kingdoms regarded as summed up in their kings. (A. F. El. Bar. Hen. Mil. Sim. Gab. Weid.) These ten kingdoms represent *the ultimate kingdoms of this world which will wage war against Christ*. "These correspond", says Gaebelein, "to the ten toes of Nebuchadnezzar's image and the ten horns of Daniel's fourth beast."

Alford and Fausset say they are the ten European kingdoms which are to grow out of the fourth great kingdom of Daniel 7.23, and "in the precise number and form here indicated, they have not," says Alford. "yet arisen, and what changes in Europe may bring them into the required number and form is not for us to say." "They are not therefore," says Fausset, "kingdoms that arose in the overthrow of Rome, but *are to arise* out of the last state of the fourth kingdom under the eighth head."

Daniel says, "The fourth beast shall be a fourth kingdom upon the earth (the Roman empire of John's time); and as for the ten horns, out of this kingdom shall ten kings arise; and another shall arise after them, and he shall be diverse from the former and he shall put down three kings."

For the ten Romano-Gothic kingdoms extant A. D. 532 to which Elliott refers the ten horns see page 672. Elliott calls attention to the fact that while the number has varied slightly from time to time, now one less, and now one or two more, still the number ten will be found to have been maintained from time to time as that of the Western Rome or Papal kingdoms from the date mentioned on down to the present time. He also calls attention to the fact that these Romano-Gothic kingdoms did in the sixth century appropriate to themselves the Roman diademic badge of sovereignty.

Many take the number *"ten"* symbolically as representing completeness, and referring to all the antichristian powers of the earth which were to arise after the sixth head or Roman empire had been broken up. (Hen. Mil.)

Others, like Simcox, who take the same view of the kingdoms, say the number is exactly ten, but that we cannot as yet point them out exactly. Fausset and Alford and those agreeing with their interpretation also take the number as literally ten. It seems that there is no sufficient reason why it should not be so taken.

"have received no kingdom as yet",—i. e., in John's time, for that was still the period of the sixth kingdom. (Mil. Bar. Weid.)

"authority as kings",—i. e., have the authority usually exercised by kings. They will receive this authority about the time that Antichrist's manifestation draws near.

"with the beast",—It is implied that they reserve their kingly rights in their alliance with the beast (F. A.); "with the aid or cooperation of the beast" (St.). They depend upon the beast for their authority,

"exercise their authority in connection with the beast and under his influence" (Bar.); "receive authority as associates and aids of the beast". (Dus.)

Fausset says it implies that they will be contemporaneous with the beast in its last or eighth form, although not until the latter part of his reign does the Antichrist associate these ten kings wih him.

"one hour",—This is by all taken schematically or symbolically for a brief while. "The end will be very near when the ten horns appear." (Sim.) This, says Lange, is "the specific antichristian evening of the world which preceded the Parousia." Except for some preconceived opinion no one would ever think of taking these words otherwise than here explained.

Fausset says, "It is a definite time of short duration, during which the Devil is come down to the inhabiters of the earth and of the sea, having great wrath, because he knows that his time is short. It is probably the last three and one-half years." With Fausset agree all Futurists who conceive the period in question to be that after the Rapture of the Church has taken place, at which time the "war in heaven" occurred and Satan was cast down.

Ver. 13. "one mind",—i. e., view, interest, consent. They have a common cause and a common theory and are united in one and the same purpose.

Ver. 14. "war with the Lamb",—i. e., in concert with the beast, described in Chap. 19.19. This will not be, says Fausset, until after they have executed judgment on the harlot, as set forth in verses 15 and 16.

"they that are with him",—i. e., the saints who shall accompany Him when He comes.

Ver. 15. (See Isa. 8.7 for a similar figure.) It is here, says Alford, an infamous parody of Jehovah who sitteth upon the flood. (Psa. 29.10.) The waters seem to signify the sum total of the inhabitants of the earth, for the great city Babylon "shall reign over the kings of the earth". (Dus. Weid.)

Ver. 16. "these shall hate the harlot",—The harlot is ruined in a manner least expected. The next verse shows that God is the moving cause of this ruin, but the immediate occasion is not revealed; it is simply stated that they shall hate the harlot and annihilate all her glory. This verse is an anticipation of the theme of the next chapter.

"desolate and naked",—Her former lovers shall desert her and she shall be stripped of her adornments.

"eat her flesh",—A symbolic expression meaning to confiscate her possessions.

"burn her with fire",—The legal punishment of abominable fornication. Elliott very strangely conceives of the burning of the harlot by the ten horns as referring to a state of existence previous to that pictured in the chapter before us and explains it of the spoiling and burning of imperial Rome by the ten Gothic powers in the fifth and sixth centuries.

Ver. 17. "to do his mind",—i. e., to accomplish his purpose, whilst they think only of doing their own purpose. The word "his" refers to

God (F. A. L. Hen. Vul. Weid.), and not to the *beast* (D. B. Dus. Lud. Vol.).

"should be accomplished",—i. e., in the destruction of the harlot.

Ver. 18.   Showing that the harlot, the great city and Babylon the great are one.

Recurring now to the question of *who the great harlot is,* we must come to some decision as between Heathen Rome, Papal Rome and the Apostate Church, as set forth under verse 1 of this chapter.

First.   Pagan Rome. (Dus. Hen.)   But against it are the following arguments:

- (a) John would not have dared to so speak of Rome in either the days of Nero or Domitian, as cherishing an antichristian thirst for the blood of the saints. (L.)
- (b) Pagan Rome was never turned upon and treated by any world-powers as is set forth by verse 16.
- (c) Chap. 18.2 describes a devastation such as never took place with regard to Rome as a heathen city. (A. Sim.)
- (d) Chap. 17.2 is unsuitable to Pagan Rome because she ruled all the world and there were practically no independent kings for her to commit fornication with. She ruled with crushing sway rather than enticed with blandishments. (L. A. Sim.)
- (e) Chap. 18.11,19 is unsuitable to Pagan Rome because she never was a great commercial city, and she did not cease to purchase even after her pagan condition came to an end. (Mil.)
- (f) Chap. 18.19 is fatal to the Pagan Rome theory because Babylon the great is to be in existence when the last plagues are poured out.
- (g) It is with great difficulty that Chap. 18.24 is applied to Pagan Rome because it is hardly true in her case. The words of this verse are apparently founded on Matt. 23.35.
- (h) Simcox says this view supposes that the beast in its final form is controlled by the metropolis of the Roman empire (Chap. 17.3), but this *is* so far from being the case that the Roman pagan empire is fallen before the woman comes on the stage, it having disappeared as completely as the other world-powers that ruled before it.

Verses 9 (if the mountains are taken literally), 15, and 18 may seem in a way to favor Pagan Rome, but the arguments against this view are decidedly preponderant.

Second.   Papal Rome. (A. El. Bar. Wor. Gab. Glas.)   The old Protestant view. Alford argues for this view from the fact that eighteen times out of the twenty-one mentions of harlotry in the Bible, the reference is to the Church or the apostate people of God; and Simcox says the three exceptions may be more apparent than real. (See Isa. 1.21; Jer. 2.20; 3.1; Ezek. 16 and 23; Micah 1.7.)

Milligan argues also that the harlot is so distinctly contrasted with the woman of Chap. 12 and with the bride of Chap. 21 that it seems there is a much closer resemblance between them than that which exists between a woman and a city.

Simcox objects with great fervor to the application of this image to Papal Rome. He says John's first epistle Chap. 4.2,3 shows distinctly that it cannot be her. The spirit of the theology of the Roman Catholic Church is on the whole of God, and certainly is *not* the spirit of Antichrist.

Third. The apostate Church of the future. (F. Pet. Sim. Hahn. Moor.) Says Fausset, "It cannot be Pagan Rome, but if *a particular seat* of error be meant it may find its reference in Papal Rome, but I incline to think that the judgment of Chap. 18.2 and the spiritual fornication of Chap. 18.3, though finding perhaps their culmination in Papal Rome, are not to be restricted to it, but comprise the whole apostate Church, Roman, Greek and even Protestant, so far as it has been seduced from its first love to Christ, the heavenly Bridegroom, and given its affections to worldly pomp and idols." In favor of this view are the following:

(a) All the arguments for Papal Rome given above apply with equal and even greater force to the Apostate Church in general.

(b) Antichristianity rises only in corrupt Christianity, and any other reference misapprehends this fact; though this argument, while militating against the idea of Pagan Rome, applies with equal force to Papal Rome.

(c) This view alone recognizes the broad scope of the aschatological vision.

CHAPTER EIGHTEEN

1 After these things I saw another angel coming down out of heaven, having great authority; and the earth was lightened with his glory. 2 And he cried with a mighty voice, saying, Fallen, fallen is Babylon the great, and is become a habitation of demons, and a [1]hold of every unclean spirit, and a [1]hold of every unclean and hateful bird. 3 For [2]by [3]the wine of the wrath of her fornication all the nations are fallen; and the kings of the earth committed fornication with her, and the merchants of the earth waxed rich by the power of her [4]wantonness.

4 And I heard another voice from heaven, saying, Come forth, my people, out of her, that ye have no fellowship with her sins, and that ye receive not of her plagues: 5 for her sins [5]have reached even unto heaven, and God hath remembered her iniquities. 6 Render unto her even as she rendered, and double *unto her* the double according to her works; in the cup which she mingled, mingle unto her double. 7 How much soever she glorified herself, and waxed [6]wanton, so much give her of torment and mourning: for she saith in her heart, I sit a queen, and am no widow, and shall in nowise see mourning.

8 Therefore in one day shall her plagues come, death, and mourning, and famine; and she shall be utterly burned with fire; for strong is [7]the Lord God who judged her.

[1]Or, *prison*
[2]Some authorities read *of the wine . . . have drunk*
[3]Some authorities omit *the wine of*
[4]Or, *luxury*

[5]Or, *clave together*
[6]Or, *luxurious*
[7]Some ancient authorities omit *the Lord*

Vers. 1-8.   GOD'S PEOPLE WARNED TO COME OUT OF BABYLON.

As in Chap. 14.8, so here in verses 1-3 we have a proleptic announcement of the destruction of Babylon as having already taken place.

"The chapter relates," says Elliott, "to the probable progress of events in *the fast coming future.*"

Ver. 1. *"another angel"*,—This doubtless refers to another angel besides the one who had just showed John the mystery of the woman and the beast in Chap. 17 (St. Dus. Bar. Weid.), or, joining the words to the following *"coming down"*, it may mean besides the one that last came down (B.). It does not therefore mean Christ (Ca. Hen.), nor the Holy Spirit (V. Coc.), and of course not Luther (Nicolai).

"having great authority",—i. e., possibly as the executor of the judgment he announced (E. Weid.), although there is in the expression a strong intimation that he was an angel of the higher rank or order. (St. Bar. Weid.)

"the earth was lightened with his glory",—The visible sign of his great plentitude of power and authority just mentioned; the glory of the Lord accompanied him.

Elliott thinks that this together with the fact that the angel cried with a *"mighty"* voice, thus reaching throughout the whole earth, indicates that just prior to the event prophesied "there will be a diffusion of great religious light". Vitringa is of the same opinion, while Daubuz infers that not only will the idolaters of the corrupt Church be enlightened and converted by the fall of Babylon, but that this event will be followed by a conversion more general. All this is, however, mere inference, and that without the merest warrant.

Ver. 2. *"he cried with a mighty voice"*,—So that his message resounds throughout the whole earth, as far as the dominion of the city that has incurred the judgment extends. This is the only place where the word *"mighty"* is used with *"voice"*, the usual word being "great". Milligan thinks the thought is not that all men might hear the voice, although this is true, but that it is to strike all with awe and terror.

"habitation of demons",—The stately city shall be entirely desolate. (Isa. 13.22; 34.14.)

"a hold",—A place of detention, a prison house. (A. F. St. Hen. Sim.) It is a figurative description of entire desolation; beasts and birds of prey dwelling in the deserted ruins and demons making their abode there. So great will be the desolation of Babylon the Great after it has been destroyed by the Antichrist and his allied kings. John uses the very words of Isaiah in describing this destruction. (Isa. 21.9.)

Scofield says here, "Babylon, 'confusion', is repeatedly used by the prophets in a symbolic sense. Two 'Babylons' are to be distinguished in the Revelation: ecclesiastical Babylon, which is apostate Christendom, headed up under the Papacy; and political Babylon, which is the beast's confederate empire, the last form of Gentile world-dominion. Ecclesiastical Babylon is 'the great whore' (Rev. 17.1), and is destroyed by political Babylon (Rev. 17.15-18), that the beast may be the only object of worship (II Thess. 2.3,4; Rev. 13.15). The power of political Babylon is destroyed by the return of the Lord in glory. The notion of a literal Babylon to be rebuilt on the site of ancient Babylon is in conflict with Isa. 13.18-22. But the language of Rev. 18 (e. g., verses 10, 16, 18) seems beyond question to identify 'Babylon', the 'city' of luxury and traffic, with 'Babylon' the ecclesiastical center, viz. Rome. The very kings who hate ecclesiastical Babylon deplore the destruction of commercial Babylon."

Ver. 3. *"For"*, etc.,—The guilt of sin is here declared to be the foundation of the judgment. (See Chap. 17.2.)

"by the power of her wantonness",—The word *"wantonness"* means insolence, pride, revel, riot, luxury, and the thought is that of insolence and voluptuousness breaking out into boastful vauntings of pride and dissolute revelry. "Wanton luxury" is really a good translation for it. Of course the views here taken are colored by the general view of the expositor.

Those referring Babylon to Pagan Rome (V. Dus. Gro. And. et al.) explain the expression of the wantonness exercised with respect to the vast resources of the state. It must be remembered, however, that the outside kingdoms did *not* get rich off of Rome, but vice versa.

Fausset rightly says the reference is not to earthly merchandise, but to spiritual wares, to indulgences, idolatries, superstitions, worldly compromises wherewith the harlot, the apostate Church, has made merchandise out of men. He says it may and doubtless does apply to Rome papal, but it applies to the Protestant Church as well, i. e., the whole apostate Church.

Ver. 4. *"another voice from heaven"*,—Not the voice of the Church triumphant speaking to the Church of God on earth (L.); nor is it the voice of God or Christ (B. Hen.), which would not accord with the length or the descriptive tone of the lamentation, the discourse extending to verse 20; this together with the fact that from verse 9 the grievance of another is presented is not appropriate for the mouth of God or Christ. It is doubtless an angel speaking in the name of Christ.

"Come forth, my people, out of her",—Saints of God even to the last are found mingling with the great city. (See Jer. 51.6,9,45, whence the words are taken.)

"have no fellowship with her sins",—To thus have fellowship with her sins means to incur the guilt of her sins, and hence the plagues, if received, would be deserved. It would be impossible to remain in her without guilt.

Sadler says, "This of course will not come as an audible voice from heaven, but it will be a secret, yet universal intimation to all that are in the mystical Babylon, that they are to leave her society and her fellowship."

"The period," says Williams, "of this command in the Apocalypse appears to be on the great rising of the Antichrist above all; and on the destruction apparently of the outward, visible frame and form of Christianity, which is to precede the end."

Ver. 5. *"her sins"*,—Not the cry of her sins (D.), but her sins being heaped up, as it were, reach even unto heaven.

"The Babel-tower of sin is a tower which man builds in pride, and when its top reaches to heaven, then it is suddenly thrown down." (Wor.)

Ver. 6. The one speaking in God's name now turns to those who are to execute God's wrath. Not to angels (St.), but rather to Antichrist and his allied kings. (Mil. Weid.)

"double unto her the double",—(See Isa. 40.2 and Jer. 50.15,29).

680

"in the cup",—She is to receive a double portion of the wine of the wrath of God. (See Chap. 14.8,10; 17.4.)

Ver. 7. Proud security transformed into deepest sorrow.

"queen",— (See Isa. 47.7).

"no widow",—i. e., because the world-power is my husband and supporter. (See Chap. 17.5; Isa. 17.8.)

"shall in no wise see mourning",—i. e., not know it by experience.

Ver. 8. *"Therefore"*,—i. e., on account of her pride, her luxury and her boasting.

"in one day",—i. e., in one great catastrophe, without succession through a contracted period.

"death",—That which makes her a widow.

"mourning",—That which she said she would never experience.

"famine",—This she is to have instead of luxury and abundance.

"and she shall be utterly burned with fire",—The punishment of a fornicatress according to the Old Testament law. (Lev. 21.9, etc.; see Chap. 17.6.) It is here the emblem of thorough destruction.

9 And the kings of the earth, who committed fornication and lived [1]wantonly with her, shall weep and wail over her, when they look upon the smoke of her burning, 10 standing afar off for the fear of her torment, saying, Woe, woe, the great city, Babylon, the strong city! for in one hour is thy judgment come. 11 And the merchants of the earth weep and mourn over her, for no man buyeth their [2]merchandise anymore; 12 [2]merchandise of gold, and silver, and precious stone and pearls, and fine linen, and purple, and silk, and scarlet; and all thyine wood, and every vessel of ivory, and every vessel made of most precious wood and of brass, and iron, and marble; 13 and cinnamon, and [3]spice, and incense, and ointment, and frankincense, and wine, and oil, and fine flour, and wheat, and cattle, and sheep; and *merchandise* of horses and chariots and [4]slaves; and [5]souls of men. 14 And the fruits which thy soul lusted after are gone from thee, and all things that were dainty and sumptuous are perished from thee, and *men* shall find them no more at all. 15 The merchants of these things, who were made rich by her, shall stand afar off for the fear of her torment, weeping and mourning; 16 saying, Woe, woe, the great city, she that was arrayed in fine linen and purple and scarlet, and [6]decked with gold and precious stone and pearl! 17 for in one hour so great riches is made desolate. And every shipmaster, and every one that saileth any whither, and mariners, and as many as [7]gain their living by sea, stood afar off, 18 and cried out as they looked upon the smoke of her burning, saying, What *city* is like the great city? 19 And they cast dust on their heads, and cried, weeping and mourning, saying, Woe, woe, the great city, wherein all that had their ships in the sea were made rich by reason of her costliness! for in one hour she is made desolate.

[1]Or, *luxuriously*
[2]Or, *cargo*
[3]Gr. *amomum*
[4]Gr. *bodies*. Gen. 36.6 (Sept.)
[5]Or, *lives*
[6]Gr. *gilded*
[7]Gr. *work the sea*

Vers. 9-19. THE EARTHLY LAMENTATION OVER THE DESOLATION OF BABYLON.

Ver. 9. At this point three distinct classes of persons are introduced to us, uttering their lamentations over the fall of Babylon; kings, merchants and sailors, their lamentations being of a selfish nature of course.

"the kings of the earth",—Who bore a more or less immediately active part in her destruction.

"weep and wail",—"The deed of the wicked," says Milligan, "even when effecting the purposes of God, bring no joy to themselves."

"the smoke of her burning",—Dusterdieck adheres to an actual burning and says that the kings, dreading the burning, stand at a distance according to verse 10; whereas Alford contends that this verse is an actual objection to the literal understanding of the prophecy in its details. "It can hardly be imagined", he says, "that the kings should bodily stand and look as described, seeing that no combination of events contemplated in the prophecy has brought them together as yet."

Fausset of course refers the expression to a mystical burning of the Apostate Church, as a figure of total and irretrievable desolation.

Barnes, who refers it to the fall of Papal Rome, must of course also take it figuratively.

Elliott thinks that this destruction, which he refers to Rome, the mystic Babylon, comprehending not the mere *city* of Rome, but at least Papal Ecclesiastical Rome, is to be effected by the agency of an earthquake and a volcanic fire the smoke of which it is said in Chap. 19.3, *"goeth up forever and ever"*. This, he says, could not well be if it was a mere burning by human agency, and if by human agency, "whence all the terror and standing afar off of the kings, merchants, and shipmasters", he asks.

Vitringa and Daubuz refer the catastrophe to the fire with which the ten kings are represented in Chap. 17 as burning the harlot, but Elliott's objections just registered, if valid, would apply equally here; and besides, says Elliott, "how could the kings well have been her burners now, when in fact they were her mourners?"

Ver. 10. *"standing afar off for the fear"*,—i. e., because of their own fear. They seem to be afraid that the destruction might reach them. (L. F. Dus. Sim. Weid.)

Fausset says, "God's judgments inspire fear even in the worldly, but it is of short duration, for the kings and great men soon attach themselves to the beast in its last and worst shape, as open Antichrist, claiming all that the harlot had claimed in blasphemous pretentions and more, and so making up to them for the loss of the harlot."

"great city . . . strong city",—Making still more forcible the impression of its destruction.

Ver. 11. The lament of the merchants. Many think that the description in this verse and the following goes hard with the mystical or spiritual interpretation and that it favors the literal one.

Alford, however, says the difficulty is not confined to its own interpretation, i. e., Papal Rome, but extends to Pagan Rome in the literal sense, because Rome never was a commercial center, much less a market for the things mentioned. Thus also Fausset.

Craven, who holds the view that by Babylon the city of Rome is meant, says the difficulties suggested by Alford are imaginary rather than real. He says that John doubtless had Rome in mind as symbolizing the Apostate Church, and that the description does fit Rome of the time of John. And what Rome was in the past, the center of all commerce by sea and by land, it may again become in the future.

Fausset, of course, says that all the merchandise is spiritual; Craven says that to Rome actual and Rome symbolical the description of these verses is applicable.

Alford frankly acknowledges that he must leave the difficulty unsolved. But Barnes, who holds the same view as Alford, seems perhaps best to resolve the difficulty, and what he says as respects Papal Rome one may as easily and as properly say of the Apostate Church in general. He says, "It is not necessary to suppose that all this would be literally true or characteristic of Papal Rome. All this is symbolical, designed to exhibit the Papacy under the image of a great city, with what was customary in such a city, or with what most naturally presented itself to the imagination of John as found in such a city. The enumeration of the articles of merchandise seems to have been inserted for the purpose of following out the representation of what is usually found in such a city, and to show the desolation that would occur when the traffic was suspended. So in regard to the traffic in slaves (verse 13), it is no more necessary to suppose the Papacy would be engaged in the traffic of slaves than in the traffic of cinnamon, or fine flour, or sheep or horses."

Vers. 12,13. These, says Dusterdieck, give a view of the previous necessities of the luxurious city.

Ver. 13. *"slaves; and souls of men"*,—(Ezek. 27.13) Dusterdieck perhaps rightly remarks that the *"souls of men"* refer to slaves in general, while the word *"slaves"* (literally, bodies) refer to slaves belonging to the horses and chariots. (Thus also B. St. Ew. Hen. Sim. Weid.) By some the word *"slaves"* is translated "grooms". (St. Sim.) However, Lange well says, that the second expression is indicative of an augmentation, the extreme consequence of slave-holding.

Fausset says that apostate Christendom enslaves both body and soul, and that the selling of indulgences is but a sample of the latter.

Weidner says, "Many commentators interpret the contents of verses 12 and 13 spiritually and refer these things to the Papacy, but Sadler correctly remarks, 'Not one of these commodities can be connected particularly with any ecclesiastical state of things. It is impossible, as regards the greater part of them, to interpret them spiritually'."

Ver. 14. A direct address to the city, not perhaps by John himself (St.), nor by the merchantmen in their lamentation (Weid.), nor perhaps by the angel of verse 1, but the rather by the angel of verse 4. It breaks the narrative which is resumed again in the next verse. It is a species of composition which greatly heightens the energy of the discourse. Alford, who seems to think of the merchantmen as speaking, says the passage need not occasion any difficulty, as it takes up the weeping and mourning of verse 11 as if the *"their"* had been *"our"*, which is not unnatural in rhapsodical passages.

Ver. 15. *"these things"*,—Those mentioned in verses 12 and 13, which have been summed up in verse 14 under things dainty and sumptuous. (A. B. Dus.)

Ver. 19. *"cast dust on their heads"*,—A sign of their great mourning.

"costliness",—i. e., treasures; the abstract being put for the concrete. The writer, says Stuart, means to designate the splendor and magnificence of building, furniture, dress, etc., which made a great demand for articles imported by sea from foreign lands. The Babylon of the future will thus become the source of great wealth to all sea-merchants on account of the extravagance and luxury which mark her inhabitants.

20 Rejoice over her thou heaven, and ye saints, and ye apostles, and ye prophets; for God hath judged your judgment on her.

21 And [1]a strong angel took up a stone as it were a great millstone and cast it into the sea, saying, Thus with a mighty fall shall Babylon, the great city, be cast down, and shall be found no more at all. 22 And the voice of harpers and minstrels and flute-players and trumpeters shall be heard no more at all in thee; and no craftsman, [2]of what-soever craft, shall be found any more at all in thee; and the voice of a mill shall be heard no more at all in thee; 23 and the light of a lamp shall shine no more at all in thee; and the voice of the bridegroom and of the bride shall be heard no more at all in thee: for thy merchants were the princes of the earth; for with thy sorcery were all the nations deceived. 24 And in her was found the blood of prophets and of saints, and of all that have been slain upon the earth.

[1]Gr. *one*
[2]Some ancient authorities omit *of whatsoever craft*

Vers. 20-24. THE HEAVENLY REJOICING OVER THE DESOLATION OF BABYLON.

Ver. 20. *"Rejoice over her, thou heaven"*,—We cannot tell whether these words are John's (Zu.), or those of the angel of verse 1, or those of the voice of verse 4. The last reference is perhaps the better. (St. Sim. Dus.)

"thou heaven",—i. e., those who dwell in heaven.

"saints, apostles and prophets",—These are regarded as being in heaven. (L. A. St. Bar. Sim. Hen.) Hengstenberg says *"saints"* are the genus of which apostles and prophets are the most eminent species included in it. Dusterdieck, on the other hand, thinks these are referred to as being on earth, and so he makes a distinction in this verse as between heaven and earth.

"judged your judgment",—"Hath exacted from her that judgment of vengeance which is due to you." (A.)

Ver. 21. *"a strong angel"*,—The strength of the angel is emphasized by what he did.

"cast it into the sea",—This is a symbolical act presenting in a most vivid manner both the suddenness and the completeness of the destruction of Babylon.

"found no more",—i. e., as the magnificent city it had been (L.), but would continue as a desolate ruin for a memorial. (L.)

Ver. 22. In this verse, says Weidner, emphasis is laid upon the fact that three kinds of the activities of life have ceased—the life of pleasure, the life of business and domestic life. For the imagery see Jer. 25.10 and Ezek. 26.13, the first referring to Jerusalem and the second to Tyre.

Ver. 23. What a contrast to the city of God in Chap 22!

Ver. 24. Says Weidner, "The future Babylon, the great world-city of the last days, will be the central power from which all the persecutions of the saints will arise, especially in the earlier part of Antichrist's reign, before Babylon is destroyed by him and his allied kings."

CHAPTER NINETEEN

1 After these things I heard as it were a great voice of a great multitude in heaven, saying,

Hallelujah; Salvation, and glory, and power, belong to our God: 2 for true and righteous are his judgments; for he hath judged the great harlot, her that corrupted the earth with her fornication, and he hath avenged the blood of his [1]servants at her hand.

3 And a second time they [2]say, Hallelujah. And her smoke goeth up [3]for ever and ever. 4 And the four and twenty elders and the four living creatures fell down and worshipped God that sitteth on the throne, saying, Amen; Hallelujah. 5 And a voice came forth from the throne, saying,

Give praise to our God, all ye his [1]servants, ye that fear him, the small and the great.

6 And I heard as it were the voice of a great multitude, and as the voice of many waters, and as the voice of mighty thunders, saying,

Hallelujah; for the Lord our God, the Almighty, reigneth.

[1]Gr. *bondservants*
[2]Gr. *have said*
[3]Gr. *unto the ages of the ages*

Vers. 1-6. THE FOURFOLD HALLELUJAH OF THE HEAVENLY MULTITUDE.

The fall of Babylon is now assumed to have taken place and in this chapter the overthrow is celebrated in heaven by·a song of triumph.

Ver. 1. *"great multitude"*,—Not necessarily those mentioned in Chap. 18.20 (B. Hen.), nor the glorified martyrs only (Ew. Gab.), but those who dwell in heaven, "the united hosts of heaven," says Stuart. Others (A. L. F.) say the glorified Church, but inasmuch as the elders (representing the glorified Church) give the response in verse 4, it may be better here to think, as Weidner does, of the heavenly host of angels standing around about the throne and about the elders and about the four living creatures. (See Chap. 7.11.)

"Hallelujah",—Elliott calls attention to the fact that the word here used (Hallelujah) is for the first time *Hebrew,* and therefore with others (V. Br. Dau. Bic.) thinks that the Jews are to have a prominent part in this song. He says that "the Jews will probably just at, or after this catastrophe, be converted and join, and perhaps take the lead in, the earthly Church's song of praise on the occasion." Elliott further says, "I infer that down to the time figured by this chorus (i. e., after the destruction of mystical Babylon) no translation of living saints, or resurrection of the saints departed, will have taken place." But this is mere conjecture, and Alford rightly says that the Hebrew form passed with the Psalter into the Christian Church and is quite natural here.

Ver. 2. This is an answer to the prayer of Chap. 6.10. Alford says, "The vengeance is considered as a penalty exacted, forced out of the reluctant hand."

"true",—i. e., just,—in the way of retribution.

Ver. 3. *"her smoke"*,—i. e., the smoke of Babylon, the smoke of her burning.

"forever and ever",—Unto the ages of the ages. Says Lange, "This

far surpasses modern sentimentalities."

Wordsworth says, "Another proof that the destruction of mystical Babylon will be final and that therefore Babylon cannot be heathen Rome." While this refers to the temporal destruction of the mystical Babylon, as seen in the last chapter, it implies that those upon whom the judgment falls shall suffer everlasting punishment.

Ver. 4. Confirmation of the praise by the elders and the four living creatures. The last act related of them.

Ver. 5. "a voice",—Bengel says it belonged to the four living creatures, while others (D. Zu.) say it belonged to one of them. It is useless to conjecture whose, although it is hardly Christ's (Ew. St. Hen.), who never spoke thus of "our God". Dusterdieck thinks because of the expression "our God" the voice belonged to the elders.

Ver. 6. "reigneth",—i. e., hath taken to Himself a Kingdom. Christ is considered prophetically as already reigning, for His Advent in glory is to follow so soon after the fall of Babylon. The tense of the verb in the Greek is past, but our English past tenses are wholly inadequate to reproduce the Greek ones and we must therefore in English translate in the present tense, "reigneth"; or we might translate "did take the kingdom".

7 Let us rejoice and be exceeding glad, and let us give the glory unto him: for the marriage of the Lamb is come, and his wife hath made herself ready. 8 And it was given unto her that she should array herself in fine linen, bright and pure: for the fine linen is the righteous acts of the saints.
9 And he saith unto me, Write, Blessed are they that are bidden to the marriage supper of the Lamb. And he saith unto me, These are true words of God. 10 And I fell down before his feet to ¹worship him. And he saith unto me, See thou do it not: I am a fellow-servant with thee and with thy brethren that hold the testimony of Jesus: ¹worship God: for the testimony of Jesus is the spirit of prophecy.
¹See marginal note on Chap. 13.12

Vers. 7-10. THE MARRIAGE OF THE LAMB.

Ver. 7. "rejoice and be glad",—Not alone because Babylon has fallen, but as the rest of the verse indicates because of the prospects and privileges of the Church,—the marriage of the Lamb.

"the marriage of the Lamb is come",—This is introduced here proleptically referring either to the far away future or to the immediate future, that is, to the time after the Millennium or to the time before the Millennium. Fausset, with others (A. Zu. Dus. Hen. Weid.), takes the first view and says, "The full and final consummation is at Chap. 21.2-9, but before this there must be the overthrow of the beast at the Lord's coming, the binding of Satan, the Millennium reign, the loosing of Satan, his final overthrow and the general judgment. The elect Church is transfigured soon after the destruction of the harlot, is transfigured at the Lord's coming and joins with Him in His triumph over the beast."

Weidner says, "In its prophetic aspect it is assumed that the time of the marriage of the Lamb is come, though it has not yet occurred in the vision, and will not happen until after the events foretold in Chap. 20.14."

Hengstenberg says, "This is not the marriage supper, the marriage feast, as Vitringa falsely infers from verse 9, but the marriage itself. Here it *'is come'*, is already at the door, but it is only in Chap. 21.2 that the new Jerusalem comes into view, prepared and adorned as a bride for her husband. We are here, therefore, already beyond the victory of the ten kings, beyond the thousand years, beyond the last victory over Gog and Magog."

On the other hand many maintain that the proleptical reference under consideration is to the immediate future, and that this marriage of the Lamb takes place at the beginning of the Millennial reign, and that Chap. 21.2,9,10, does not refer to this marriage but to a new and later manifestation of the bride. (L. Sco. Mor. Gab. Glas. Crav.)

Lange says the above views are very contracted, and that even in the parables of our Lord His Parousia is designated as the beginning of the marriage. The marriage and the marriage supper, he says, though distinct in themselves, coincide in point of time.

Craven says, "The bride is the whole body of the saints (the quick and the dead, at the first resurrection) at the Second Advent, and the marriage is of this body with a personally present Christ in glory and government; and the vision of Chap. 21.1 and 2 refers not to the marriage but to a new manifestation of the bride."

According to this view the marriage consists in the union of Christ with the saints, the quick and the dead of the first resurrection, in the glory and government of the Millennial Kingdom.

We are inclined to agree with the teaching of these latter authorities as to this matter. Certainly *"is come"* refers to something present or proleptically *soon to come*, and as Craven says, it cannot be supposed that a space of one thousand years is grasped by such an expression.

Zundel says that both expressions, the *"marriage"* and the *"marriage supper"*, are alike in meaning and designate not the future marriage itself, but the *"preliminary* festival of the Messiah's marriage", i. e., the one thousand years' reign.

"his wife hath made herself ready",—i. e., arrayed herself in a becoming manner as seen in the next verse.

Ver. 8. It is difficult to decide here whether these words are a part of the song or an explanation given by the angel or by John, but they are probably the words of the Seer himself as would appear from the fact that the nature of the linen is explained, and likewise because the expression, *"And it was given unto her"*, is the same form which recurs so often throughout the vision, from Chap. 6.2 onwards.

"given unto her",—Her garments were given unto her by Christ Himself. In a sense she, through the Holy Spirit, made herself ready, but in the fullest sense, as Fausset says, it is not she but her Lord who by giving Himself for her, presents her to Himself a glorious Church, not having spot, but holy and without blemish, and sanctifies her, naturally vile and without beauty, and puts His own comeliness upon her, which thus becomes her.

"bright and pure",—"The brilliant glory of a virtuous life and spotless purity from sin."

"righteous acts of the saints",—The reference here is doubtless to the righteous deeds of the saints themselves (D. A. L. Eb. Ph. Dus. Kli. Sim.

Gab. Gebh. Weid. R-V.). It is plural, and the literal translation is "the righteousnesses". Milligan says, "John had no fear of saying that the redeemed shall be presented before God in righteous acts of their own. He could not think of them except as at once justified and sanctified in Jesus." Says Dusterdieck, "A delicate allusion to the grace given by God, as the cause and source of the "righteousnesses" peculiar to the saints is contained in the expression, *'And it was given unto her'*."

This very expression, however, *"it was given unto her,"* furnishes some ground for the other view, namely that it is the imputed righteousness of Christ that is here meant rather than the saints' own righteousness. (F. St. Ew. Bar. Bez. Sco. Gerh.)

Stuart points with much force to Phil. 3.9 in answer to the statement of Lange, namely, that Christ's righteousness is not a thing reserved for the last times, being something received at the time of regeneration.

However, this contention of Lange's together with the comparison of what is really its parallel, Chap. 14.4, and the fact of the plural form "righteousnesses" seems to favor the view first given.

Ver. 9. *"And he saith"*,—i. e., not the *"strong angel"* of Chap. 18.21 (Mil.), not an angel constantly attending him (Ew. Eb.), but the angel of Chap. 17.1. (A. B. D. Dus. Hen. Sim. Weid.)

"the marriage supper",—It might be well here to quote the words of Glasgow for what they are worth in themselves and in any possible bearing they may have on the order of events in this portion of the Apocalypse. He says, "In every instance of the word 'marriage' (gamos) in the New Testament it means the festivities, which were sometimes a considerable period after the actual covenant or bond of marriage. The wedding day was rather the day when the bride was taken to the home of her husband's house, than what we should designate the day of marriage, that is, after the marriage itself had really taken place. (See Fairbairn, Dictionary of the Bible.) By His incarnation Jesus becomes the Bridegroom and His Church became the bride. And if it be necessary to distinguish *'wife'* from *'bride'*, let it be observed that *'wife'* (gune) is the word employed in the text of verse 7, and not *'bride'* (numphe) as in Chap. 21.2. The same festive occasion which in verse 7 is called the *'marriage'* is here, in verse 9, called the *'marriage supper'*, which shows that not the marriage ceremony, but the joyous festivities are meant."

Milligan says, "After the marriage will come the marriage supper, the fullness of blessing to be enjoyed by the redeemed. It may be a question whether we are to distinguish between the bride herself and those who appear to be spoken of as guests at the marriage supper. But the analogy of Scripture, and especially of such passages as Matt. 22.2; 26.29, lead to the conclusion that no such distinction can be drawn. Those who are faithful to the Lord are at once the Lamb's bride and the Lamb's guests."

Lange says, "The Church in its unitous form is the Bride; in its individual members it consists of guests." (Sim. Weid.)

"These are true words of God",—The reference is perhaps to all this angel has said from Chap. 17.1 onward. (Fausset refers it to all the previous revelations.) They are the very truth of God and so shall veritably come to pass. (A. B. Eb. Bl. Ew. Dus.)

The more proper meaning of *"true"* is "genuine", though this need not be pressed here. Being the genuine, the veritable words of God, they shall come to pass; but this is equally the thought from the use of the word *"true"*, which sense is the usual one throughout the Apocalypse. The reference seems not so much to the truth of the contents, but to the reality of their being the words of God, being which they are of course true.

Ver. 10. *"to worship him"*,—This was doubtless out of an overweening reverence for the one who had imparted to him such great things. Simcox says that from the last words John thought the speaker was God Himself who was present in the angel, as in the Old Testament, and that John meant to worship God in the Angel. Stuart says John lost consciousness of what he was doing, believing that Christ Himself was veiled in the form of the angel.

Fausset says, "John intending to worship the angel here, as in Chap. 22.8, is the involuntary impulse of adoring joy at so blessed a prospect as that portrayed by the angel. It exemplifies the corrupt tendencies of our fallen nature that even John, an Apostle, should all but have fallen into 'voluntary humility and worshipping of angels' which Paul warns us against."

Some (A. L. Dus.) say that John probably thought the angel who was speaking to him was the Lord Himself; but Chap. 17.1 would seem to contradict this sufficiently. Hengstenberg takes it as an act of humility on John's part and commends him for it. Others (V. B. Gro.) recognize in it only an excessive token of gratitude. Lange says that the action must be regarded as entirely a procedure taking place within the vision, and not therefore as a subject for moral criticism. Dusterdieck says at first (Chap. 17.1) John had a proper estimate of the angel, but that the last words of verse 9 made him suppose the Lord Himself had spoken to him. The view either of Fausset or of Dusterdieck may be acceptable, but as between the two we the rather prefer the latter.

"thy fellow servant",—i. e., serves the same Lord.

"thy brethren that hold the testimony of Jesus",—An expression referring to all believers.

"for the testimony", etc.,—Not the words of John explaining what the angel had just said (Dus.), but of the angel himself in explanation. (F. A. L. V. D. Bar. Sim.)

"of Jesus",—i. e., respecting Jesus (F. A. L. V. D.), and not "proceeding from Jesus" (Dus.).

"the spirit of prophecy",—What the angel says is in substance, "Thou and I and our brethren are all witnesses of Jesus, i. e., we bear testimony respecting Jesus, and this is the spirit of prophecy, i. e., the result of the Spirit of prophecy working in us." (A. F.)

11 And I saw the heaven opened; and behold, a white horse, and he that sat thereon called Faithful and True: and in righteousness he doth judge and make war. 12 And his eyes *are* a flame of fire, and upon his head *are* many diadems; and he hath a name written which no one knoweth but he himself. 13 And he *is* arrayed in a garment ¹sprinkled with blood: and his name is called The Word of God. 14 And the armies which are in heaven followed him upon white horses, clothed in fine linen, white *and* pure. 15 And out of

¹Some ancient authorities read *dipped in*

his mouth proceedeth a sharp sword, that with it he should smite the nations: and he shall rule them with a rod of iron: and he treadeth the ²winepress of the fierceness of the wrath of God, the Almighty. 16 And he hath on his garment and on his thigh a name written, KING OF KINGS, AND LORD OF. LORDS.

²Gr. *winepress of the wine of fierceness*

Vers. 11-16. THE VISION OF THE SECOND COMING OF CHRIST IN GLORY.

Ver. 11. *"And I saw the heaven opened"*,—In Chap. 17.3 John in spirit was carried to the earth. (B.)

"a white horse and he that sat thereon",—It is certain that the rider of this white horse is none other than Christ, whatever may be the case in Chap. 6.2.

Many (F. A. L. St. Mil. Bar. Hen. Dus.) claim that the horse and rider in this chapter is the same as in Chap. 6.2, much of this verse being verbatim, as they say, with the passage there, and the very construction of the participles being the same. Still others (Pet. Gab. Sco. Weid. Moor.) say they are different.

Says Scofield, "The vision is of the departure from heaven of Christ and the saints and angels preparatory to the catastrophe in which Gentile world-power, headed up in the beast, is smitten by the 'stone cut out without hands' (Dan. 2.34,35). It is at this coming of Christ in glory that He will deliver the Jewish remnant besieged by the Gentile world-powers under the beast and false prophet. This battle is the first event in 'the day of Jehovah', and is the fulfillment of the smiting-stone prophecy of Daniel."

"Faithful and True",—(See Chap. 3.14). *"Faithful,"* because his promises to His believers have always been and are now again in largest possible measure fulfilled. *"True"*, because by His triumphant going forth He proves Himself to be the Messiah announced from olden time. Fausset says we must distinguish between this coming, His Parousia (Matt. 24.27, 29,37,39) and the end or final judgment (Matt. 25.31; I Cor. 15.23).

Ver. 12. *"his eyes are a flame of fire"*,—Verbatim with Chap. 6.4.

"many diadems",—Not the crowns of the ten kings, because having the crowns signifies that he has already conquered them (Zu.); because in fact He is just going forth to conquer them. Nor is it as representing the dominion of Christ over all, both in heaven and earth (And.). It is, no doubt, because He is King of kings. (F. A. L. D. H. Bl. St. Ew. Dus. Hen. Vol. Lud. Bar. Sim.)

"written",—Probably on His forehead (A. Ew. Hen. Dus. Bl.), rather than on His vesture (Ca.), or on His diadem (Ei.).

"a name",—To conjecture definite names, unless it be that of verse 13 is useless and a violation of the very context. It is either the name mentioned in verse 13, or a name visible to John, but which was to him inscrutable (D. B. Eb. Hen. Gro. Dus.). The latter is the more likely inasmuch as the name was known to none but the Lord. Those who so take it (V.) say the *"no one knoweth"* refers to the mystery hidden in that name rather than to the name itself. It is perhaps the new and glorious name of Chap. 3.12, whose meaning will perhaps be disclosed

to believers in the day of their complete union with Him, perhaps at the marriage feast of the Lamb.

Ver. 13.   (See Isa. 63.1-6.)   The reference here is to the blood of his enemies, after the manner of the victor. (F. A. B. D. Zu. St. Dus. Hen. Sim. Bar. Mil. Weid.)   The prophetic description of Isa. 63.1-6 finds fulfillment in these words.

"The Word of God",—Used only by John,—a strong argument in favor of his authorship.   It indicates His incommunicable Godhead, joined to His manhood which He shall then manifest in glory, as Fausset says. It is, as Lange says, his theological name and marks His divine nature alone.

Ver. 14.   *"the armies which are in heaven"*,—Not the angels only (D. Bl. Hen. Lud.), but the glorified saints as well, and pre-eminently so, inasmuch as the vesture of the hosts is described as *"white and pure"*. (A. F. L. St. Dus. Bar. Sim. Mil.)

Mackintosh says, "These armies are not angels, but saints; for we do not read of angels being clothed in fine linen, which is expressly declared in this very chapter (verse 8) to be 'the righteousness of the saints'."

"white and pure",—i. e., symbolizing the purity and holiness of the heavenly armies.

This mighty host has no armor and most expositors take it that the saints are mere spectators of His victory and are there to participate in the joy of His triumph and not to engage in the work of blood, their garments indeed not being sprinkled with blood as are the garments of their Lord. (Mil. Sim. Bar. Weid.)

Ver. 15.   *"a sharp sword"*,—i. e., the Word of God in its judging power, its avenging power. (See on Chap. 1.16.)

"he treadeth the winepress",—Dusterdieck says the idea is that from the winepress the wine of God's wrath flows which is to be given to His enemies to drink.   We prefer, however, the thought that the winepress is the wrath of God and the wine flowing from it is the blood of His enemies, i. e., His enemies would be crushed before Him, as grapes are crushed under the feet of him who treads the winepress. (St. Hen. Bar.)

Ver. 16.   *"on His garment and on His thigh"*,—Some (A. F. Sim. Weid.) think it is at the place where in an equestrian figure the robe drops from the thigh, and so the name is *partly* on the vesture and partly on the thigh.

Others (B. Bar.) think it was written both on the garment and on the thigh so that when the bloody garment is laid aside or is open and flowing so as to expose the limb of the rider, the name would be conspicuous.

Many (D. Su. Dus. Mil. Vol.) take the *"and"* in an explanatory way, i. e., on his vesture, that part of it covering his thigh.   It is impossible to determine but perhaps this last view is the more correct, the part referred to being doubtless his girdle holding the tucked up vesture of one advancing to battle.

17 And I saw [1]an angel standing in the sun; and he cried with a loud voice, saying to all the birds that fly in mid heaven, Come and be gathered together unto the great supper of God; 18 that ye may eat the flesh of kings, and the flesh of [2]captains, and the flesh of mighty men, and the flesh of horses and of them that sin thereon, and the flesh of all men, both free and bond, and small and great.

19 And I saw the beast, and the kings of the earth, and their armies, gathered together to make war against him that sat upon the horse, and against his army. 20 And the beast was taken, and with him the false prophet that wrought the signs in his sight, wherewith he deceived them that had received the mark of the beast and them that [3]worshipped his image: they two were cast alive into the lake of fire that burneth with brimstone: 21 and the rest were killed with the sword of him that sat upon the horse, even the sword which came forth out of his mouth: and all the birds were filled with their flesh.

[1]Gr. one
[2]Or, military tribunes; Gr. chiliarchs
[3]See marginal note on Chap. 13.12

Vers. 17-21.   THE BATTLE OF ARMAGEDDON.

Ver. 17.   "an angel standing in the sun",—A place of brightness and glory becoming such a herald of so great a victory, and the standpoint from which he can best call the birds flying in mid-heaven.

"Come", etc.,—A close reproduction of Ezek. 39.17.   The whole description shows how great and universal the slaughter is to be and how relentless the judgment.

Says Dennett, "The flower of Europe in men and arms will be gathered together, and in anticipation of their dreadful fate this angelic summons resounds, throughout the heavens."

"the great supper of God",—It is "great" because of the number of victims slain; it is "of God" because He ordained it and gives it.   It is in antithesis to the marriage supper of the Lamb.

Ver. 19.   "gathered together",—At Armageddon, as under the sixth vial, for the conflict already proclaimed in Chap. 16.14.   (F. A. Dus. Bar. Sco. Gab. Sim. Mil. Weid.)

"his army",—The singular is chosen to show the unity of Christ's forces in contrast with the rent body of his enemies where the plural is used. (L. A. B. Dus. Hen.)

"gathered together to make war",—Says Scofield, "The day of Jehovah (called also 'that day' and 'the great day') is that lengthened period of time beginning with the return of the Lord in glory, and ending with the purgation of the heavens and the earth by fire preparatory to the new heavens and the new earth (II Pet. 3.13; Rev. 21.1).   The order of events seems to be: (1) The return of the Lord in glory (Matt. 24.29,30); (2) the destruction of the beast and his host, 'the kings of the earth and their armies', and the false prophet, which is the 'great and terrible' aspect of the day (Rev. 19.11-21); (3) the judgment of the nations (Zech. 14.1-9; Matt. 25.31-46); (4) the thousand years, i. e., the kingdom-age (Rev. 20.4-6); (5) the Satanic revolt and its end (Rev. 20.7-10); (6) the second resurrection and final judgment (Rev. 20.11-15); and (7) the 'day of God', earth purged by fire (II Pet. 3.10-13)."

Ver. 20.   "the beast was taken",—"This beast," says Scofield, "is the 'little horn' of Dan. 7.24-26, and 'desolator' of Dan. 9.27; the 'abomination of desolation' of Matt. 24.15; the 'man of sin' of II Thess. 2.4-8;

earth's last and most awful tyrant, Satan's fell instrument of wrath and hatred against God and the saints. He is, perhaps, identical with the rider on the white horse of Rev. 6.2, who begins by the peaceful conquest of three of the ten kingdoms into which the former Roman empire will then be divided, but who soon establishes the ecclesiastical and governmental tyranny dscribed in Dan. 7.9,11; Rev. 13. To him Satan gives the power which he offered to Christ (Matt. 4.8,9; Rev. 13.4)."

"the false prophet that wrought the signs",—This shows the false prophet to be the same as the second beast.

"alive",—This heightens the idea of the terror and awfulness of their punishment.

Hengstenberg says, "The term *'alive'*, without bodily death, confirms the idea that the beast and the false prophet are not human individuals at all, but purely ideal forms. A human individual cannot enter hell alive." If this be so, it might be in order to ask Hengstenberg that if the beast and false prophet are merely ideal forms or emblems of mere powers, what then can be the meaning of the emblematic trait of such ideal forms and emblems of powers being cast *alive* into hell.

"into the lake of fire", etc.,—The Gehenna, or Hell, properly so-called. (Matt. 5.22.) We are told later that Satan and Death and Hades are cast into this same place. This is the second death.

Ver. 21. *"the rest"*,—i. e., all the followers of Antichrist, not the whole remaining human race. (L. F. Bar. Weid.)

"killed by the sword which came out of his mouth",—Weidner suggests that they may have been stricken down by the word of Christ as were Ananias and Sapphira. A simple word from the mouth of Christ suffices to destroy the whole army in an instant. (D. L. Bar. Sim.) "A magnificent description, indeed, of his power," says Stuart.

CHAPTER TWENTY

1 And I saw an angel coming down out of heaven, having the key of the abyss and a great chain [1]in his hand. 2 And he laid hold on the dragon, the old serpent, which is the Devil and Satan, and bound him for a thousand years, 3 and cast him into the abyss, and shut *it*, and sealed *it* over him, that he should deceive the nations no more, until the thousand years should be finished: after this he must be loosed for a little time.

[1]Gr. *upon*

Vers. 1-3. SATAN BOUND FOR ONE THOUSAND YEARS.

Ver. 1. *"an angel coming down out of heaven"*,—Not Christ (V. Ca. Aug. And. Hen.), nor the Holy Spirit (Coc.), but merely as the text says, *"an angel"*. (A. Dus. Weid.)

"the abyss",—Not identical with the lake of Chap. 19.20, but the abode of the devil and his angels prior to the Devil being cast into the lake.

Ver. 2. The various names express the character of the Devil and show how necessary it is to bind him.

"bound him",—"This refers to Satan's complete banishment from earth, so that while sin is still to exist in individuals, it is no longer to be

a power forming a fellowship, and thus making a kingdom of sin and Satan."

"a thousand years",—(See remarks under verse 4).

Ver. 3. *"the nations"*,—It is clearly implied here that after the destruction of Antichrist in Chap. 19.21, there will remain nations on earth who doubtless did not take part in that conflict.

What nations are these? They seem to be mentioned again in verse 8. Bleek says they are the heathen nations still remaining on the earth, and who remain there during the thousand years, but at the most extreme ends of the earth, so that the citizens of the Millennial kingdom do not come in contact with them. (Kl.)

Alford has the same idea except that during the Millennium they are "the quiet and willing subjects of the kingdom" who are again seduced by Satan at the end of the 1000 years.

Klieforth says they are different from those intended by the expression, "whole inhabited world", which latter refers to the civilized nations, while the nations of our verse refer to the barbarous people living far out at the four corners of the globe. There is certainly no sufficient ground for this last view. Perhaps the view of Bleek covers the ground best, although a combination of the first two views might better still answer the question. Dusterdieck makes them simply the heathen.

"must be loosed for a little time",—i. e., according to the necessity of God's purpose.

4 And I saw thrones, and they sat upon them, and judgment was given unto them: and *I saw* the souls of them that had been beheaded for the testimony of Jesus, and for the word of God, and such as [1]worshipped not the beast, neither his image, and received not the mark upon their forehead and upon their hand; and they lived, and reigned with Christ a thousand years. 5 The rest of the dead lived not until the thousand years should be finished. This is the first resurrection. 6 Blessed and holy is he that hath part in the first resurrection: over these the second death hath no [2]power; but they shall be priests of God and of Christ, and shall reign with him [3]a thousand years.

[1]See marginal note on Chap. 13.12
[2]Or, *authority*
[3]Some ancient authorities read *the*

Vers. 4-6. THE FIRST RESURRECTION AND THE ONE THOUSAND YEAR REIGN OF THE SAINTS.

Ver. 4. That the binding of Satan and the events of this verse are still future there can be no doubt. Weidner says, "If any one thing is clear, it is this, that the power of Satan has as yet not been bound." He further says, "There is every reason to maintain that this chapter follows the preceding one in chronological order, and that there is no recapitulation here."

"Indeed," says Dusterdieck, "every exposition must utterly fail which in verses 1-10 maintains a recapitulation."

"thrones",—Many (D. Ew. Bl. Dus. Hen. Hei.) think these are merely seats for judgment, as the following words show and as the prefigurement of Dan. 7.9,22 indicates. But the idea of reigning would appear to be the prominent one of the context here, and not only here, but in Daniel as well as in other Scriptures on which this passage seems to be founded, and many authorities (L. Ei. Zu. Mil.), we believe, take these

thrones rightly as places of exalted dignity, that is, thrones of kings, the function of judgment belonging to them.

"and they sat upon them",—If those sitting upon these thrones are to reign with Christ, then Christ Himself must have been sitting upon one of them as the center and the source of their authority.

But who are the other occupants of these thrones?

1. God Himself and Christ with His holy angels. (St. Gro.)
   But the statement that judgment was *given* unto them forbids this.

2. The twenty-four Elders. (D. Dus. Hen.)
   But John always seems to mention the twenty-four Elders when he has them in view.

3. The martyrs and those who had not worshipped the beast, as mentioned in this verse. (Ei. Eb. Bez. Bar.)
   But the special mention of these does not necessarily imply, nor would it seem from the generally admitted parallel passages (Chap. 11.17,18 and Dan. 7.18) that they were the only enthroned ones.

4. The twelve Apostles as in Matt. 19.28, and the saints in general, Old Testament and New, as in I Cor. 6.2,3. (F. A. L. B. El. Zu. Ew. Sim. Mil. Tor. Sco. Mor. Gab. Pet. Weid. Gebh. Moor.)

View 4 is by all means to be preferred.

"and judgment was given unto them",—Milligan says the word used for judgment does not mean the act of judging, but the result of the judgment, and that this fact together with the word *"given"* shows that they themselves were the ones affected by the judgment, that is, that they were judged worthy and did not therefore have to come into the judgment (John 5.24). He says the righteous are not to be seated with Christ as assessors in judgment because there were none before them at this moment to be judged.

But the word *"judgment"* is by no means to be confined in its meaning to that asserted by Milligan and furthermore it is assuredly the teaching of Scripture that those who are to sit on these thrones are to exercise a judicial rule of some kind. (F. Hen. Weid.)

The reference here is more properly to "the right of judging" (Sim.), "judgment exercised" (Dus.), "power of pronouncing judgment" (Bar.).

To whom then shall their judgment as rendered refer? Certainly not to the judgment of verses 1-3 and Chaps. 19,20,21 (Eb.), since, as Lange says, in those passages the sentence of judgment was decided by war, and we would hardly expect Antichrist and Satan to be sentenced through a trial by jury.

1. Many (St. Dus. Hen.) say the persons upon whom this judgment is to pass are the martyrs and those who had not rendered homage to the beast, as specified in the next part of the verse, and the sentence is that they are "to live and reign with Christ a thousand years", that is, they were to have part in the first Resurrection.

But this view under discussion is, according to Alford, warranted neither by the context nor any other part of Scripture, and is contradicted by John 5.24.

2. Others (El. Sim. Gab. Pet. Weid. Moor.) say the reference can only be to a judicial rule over the nations of the earth during the 1000 years, the nature of which we cannot explain.

3. Lange combines the two views and says, "The decision to be rendered is concerning those who are still living (who were not in the antichristian army) as to whether their lives shall be preserved throughout the 1000 years; and concerning those who were beheaded and those who refused, homage to the beast, as to how far they were worthy of being called to the first resurrection."

While Dusterdieck and Stuart advocate the same view as to who are the parties judged they each of them have their own view as to who the judges are, Dusterdieck referring them to the twenty-four elders, and Stuart to God, Christ and His angels.

Taking up this view of Stuart's once more; he claims that if the martyrs, etc., are made the judges, we have the difficulty of having them take their places upon the thrones *before* they "*lived*", i. e., were resurrected. But the *order* of the transactions may not be absolutely determined by the words of the text; but only the *facts* of the case, the writer combining all of these in a single sentence, grouping things related and not narrating them after the strict order of succession. These are practically Stuart's own words, but instead of resting the case thus, he resolves the difficulty in another way. He says God and Christ must be included among the judges. We do not see why God must be conceived of as one of the judges, but on this view Stuart is confronted with the difficulty found in the sentence, "*And judgment was given unto them*". He asks, "who could commit judgment to them?" To relieve this situation he brings in the angels, and then thinks of John having these angels in mind in the use of the expression, "*given unto them*".

Now this interpretation is possible, but hardly probable. It is quite true that the cooperation of angels, in some important sense, on great occasions, is not foreign to the Bible. But where in Scripture are the angels represented as judging? Besides I Cor. 6.3 says the Christians "shall judge angels". II Tim. 2.12 says that saints "shall sit down with the Redeemer upon His throne". Matt. 19.28 says the Apostles "shall sit on thrones and judge the twelve tribes of Israel".

So far as the view of Dusterdieck is concerned, it is sufficient to inquire as to the propriety of having ordinary saints, or the twenty-four elders, who represent the Church, sit in judgment on the martyrs as to whether they were worthy of the first resurrection. It would seemingly be more appropriate to reverse the case.

There is no other safe way to interpret this passage than in keeping with Scripture representations elsewhere, and the view that takes the sitters upon the thrones as saints in general, including the martyrs, and as exercising a rule over the nations, the nature of which we are not to conjecture, is perhaps the best that can be advanced. In this case the martyrs and those who had not bowed to the beast are set forward as worthy of special mention.

Where are these thrones?

We are inclined to think of them as in heaven where the martyrs and the glorified saints, throughout the Apocalypse and Scriptures in general, are represented as being with Christ. Fausset's objection, however, that "earth is not yet transfigured and cannot therefore be the meet locality for the transfigured Church" is hardly to the point, for while it may be true, and doubtless is, that the transfiguration of earth spoken of in the following chapter refers to the condition of things at the close of the Millennium and of all time, namely, at the beginning of eternity, yet if there is to be in any sense a glorification of earth during the Millennium, the beginning of this glorification must follow immediately after the close of Chap. 19 and therefore be coincident with the vision of Chap. 20 with which we are now dealing.

But so far as our exegesis has led us we see no reason to take issue with Stuart when he says that there is no intimation anywhere that Christ comes from heaven and takes up his abode upon the earth, nor must we overlook the difficulty of conceiving of a material earth fitted up as the abode of spiritual bodies, or the physical association of those with spiritual bodies with those of material bodies even on a glorified earth.

"them that had been beheaded",—Referring to decapitation by the axe, the old Roman method of execution (literally, "struck with an axe"), and used here as a symbol of any and every kind of martyrdom.

"for the testimony of Jesus",—i. e., because of their testimony concerning Him, referring both to those who preached the Christian doctrine and to those who believed it.

"for the word of God",—An expression somewhat wider in extent than the former one, embracing all the doctrines of true religion.

"and such as worshipped not the beast",—Is this a mere relative clause referring to *"the souls of them that had been beheaded"*, or does it designate a different or additional class of Christians, who had suffered in various ways but had not been actually martyred? Plainly the latter. (St. Dus. Pet. Gab. Weid.)

"souls",—This word has caused some to deny to the following word *"lived"* the idea of a literal resurrection of the body.

Barnes says, "If he saw the souls of the martyrs, not the bodies, this would seem to exclude the notion of a literal resurrection and of a literal reign of the saints with Christ during the Millennium. The word used here is fatal to this notion. There is here not the slightest intimation of the resurrection of the body, and John did not mean to teach the doctrine of any such resurrection occurring at this time." (Brown, Whitby, Faber.)

Alford on the other hand says, "As regards the text itself, no legitimate treatment of it will extort what is known as the spiritual interpretation now in fashion. If in a passage where two resurrections are mentioned, where certain souls lived at the first, and the rest of the dead lived only at the end of a specified period after the first,—if in such a passage the first resurrection may be understood to mean *spiritual* rising with Christ, while the second means literal rising from the grave; then there is an end to all significance in language, and Scripture is wiped out as a definite testimony to anything. If the first resurrection is spiritual, then so is the second, which I suppose none will be hardy enough to maintain; but if the second is literal, then so is the first, which in common with the whole primitive Church and many of the best modern expositors, I do maintain and receive as an article of faith and hope." Dean Alford has here without doubt the weight of scholarship with him. (F. El. St. Lud. Mil. Sim. Pet. Gab. Bla. Sco. Mor. Tor. Mack. Weid. Crav. Moor.)

We are convinced that if the argument for a non-literal resurrection had to depend alone upon the meaning of the word "souls", it would have a scant and unsubstantial ground upon which to rest.

Milligan is doubtless right in saying that the analogy of Chap. 6.9 makes it clear that they were no more than souls which John says he saw, and that at the time to which John refers they had not yet been clothed with their resurrection bodies.

Fausset also is quite clear here. He says, "The word 'souls' expresses their disembodied state as John saw them at first in Chap. 6.9; and the expression 'they lived' implies their coming to life in the body again so as to be visible. It accords with Paul's expression, 'they that are Christ's at His coming'. While 'souls' is doubtless used here in the sense of disembodied spirits when first seen by John, the word is also used in general for 'persons' and even for 'dead bodies'."

Various reasons are given by others for taking the resurrection here mentioned in a spiritual sense, i. e., the soul as raised *now* by vivifying faith from the death of sin, i. e., regeneration; and while these reasons are not altogether without force, they are hardly sufficient to overthrow the more normal intrepretation of Alford and the many others who agree with him.

"*and they lived*",—Milligan says, "By every rule of interpretation this word must be understood in the same sense here as in the following clause, where it is applied to '*the rest of the dead*'."

Stuart handles this question quite thoroughly, as follows:

(a) It cannot mean simply "to live"; for thus it would imply that the *soul* had been dead; whereas the Apocalypse and all Scripture teaches that the soul continues to exist after the death of the body. The word therefore cannot mean merely to recover a psychological existence which was lost.

(b) It cannot mean to live spiritually, in opposition to being dead in trespasses and sins, for all the saints and martyrs possess such a life from the moment of their regeneration.

(c) It cannot mean to become immortal; for this they always were.

(d) It cannot mean merely to become happy at the beginning of the Millennium, for those who die in the Lord are made happy immediately. There would seem to remain therefore only one meaning which can consistently be given to the word, namely, that they are now restored to life, such life as implies the revivification of the body—a union of the soul with a spiritual body.

Those who take the opposite view find here only a prophecy of a resuscitation of the martyr spirit at the beginning of the Millennium; the "raising up of increased zeal and holiness; the revival in the Church of the spirit and energy of the martyrs of old."

"*reigned with Christ*",—Seiss says, "This thousand years' reign of the saints is specifically preceded by a description of the coming forth from the opened heavens of the Lord of lords and King of kings, accompanied by the glorified saints, to judge and to make war (Chap. 19.11-21), to crush out the antichristian beasts and their armies, to bind Satan, and to tread 'the winepress of the fierceness and wrath of Almighty God'. Whatever then this judgeship, regency and dominion of the saints may be, the record places it after the Second Advent and not before it."

Here again all that Barnes can see in these words is, "They were exalted in their principles and in their personal happiness in heaven, *as if* they occupied the throne with Him and shared in its honors and triumphs."

"a thousand years",—The equivalent of this expression in the Latin language is the word Millennium, at the very mention of which word we are at once confronted with a number of varying views as to what it means and what relation it holds to the Parousia of our Lord. These views fall into four general classes:

I. *No-Millennium.*

The expression is to be taken in a symbolical sense without reference to any time period whatsoever. (Kl. Dus. Mil. Naylor, Heagle.) There is to be no Millennium whatsoever. The Old Testament prophecies of the time when swords shall be beaten into plowshares and the wolf shall dwell with the lamb and the lion eat straw like an ox are only figurative expressions of the peace that was to come to humanity as a result of Christ's first coming as the Saviour of the world (Naylor), or describe in a figurative way the full blessing and glory of the world to come (Heagle). The first resurrection is a spiritual one from the death of sin into life in Christ, and when Christ comes again the general resurrection of all dead will take place, at which time Christ will judge both them and the living, and usher in the eternal world. The Millennium being thus disposed of, *Christ may return at any moment* when time will end and eternity will begin.

These one thousand years, according to Milligan, are to be taken "simply as an exalted symbol of the glory of the redeemed at the particular moment referred to by the Seer." The expression, he says, denotes completeness, thoroughness, and the reign of one thousand years refers to the completeness of the blessedness when Christ's people shall shine forth in the glory they have received from Him. As referred to Satan the one thousand years represent the *completeness* of his overthrow, and as referred to the saints they represent their confirmation in happiness as above noted. "They complete the picture of that glorious condition in which believers have all along really been, but which only now reaches its highest point and is revealed as well as possessed."

Klieforth finds in the expression only the idea that the Lord's victory is absolute, i. e., complete. Dusterdieck calls it merely an ideal description, a poetical picture in a long series of special acts, of what according to the real prophecy of Scripture falls upon *one* day of the coming of the Lord.

Fausset says, "As *seven* mystically implies universality, so a *thousand* implies perfection, whether in good or evil. *Thousand* symbolizes that the world is perfectly leavened and pervaded by the Divine; since *thousand* is *ten*, the number of the world, raised to the *third* power, *three* being the number of God."

Lange says, "The one thousand years are a symbolic number denoting the aeon of transition."

It is hard, however, to think that these are legitimate interpretations of John's words, and seems rather to be a somewhat gratuitous way of avoiding seeming exegetical difficulties. The interpretation of the various Scriptures involved, both those which have gone before and those which are to follow, will show how unreliable are the grounds upon which this whole unsubstantial theory rests. Besides to so take the expression is a radical departure from the method of interpretation applied to other designations of time in the Apocalypse which are referred to in a numerical way.

Stuart is well worth quoting here. He says, "The great question whether this is to be taken literally or symbolically, is one that must be settled by the analogy of the book in regard to specific periods. We have seen that the famous period of three and one-half years—forty-two months—twelve hundred and sixty days—is to be understood, in all probability, in its literal sense, not indeed with rigid arithmetical exactness, but as designating at least a period of moderate extent. Here, then, assuming a similar usage with respect to numbers, we may suppose that the thousand years may be taken in their ordinary sense, or at least for a very long period. The latter idea is sufficient; and the general tone of the book may justify such a mode of interpretation."

This leaves us to deal with the expression as a designation of time, and as such it may be taken either (1) as an expression denoting literally one thousand years, or (2) as a symbolical expression for a long but indefinite period of time, or (3) as a symbolical expression for 365,000 years, according to the year-day theory, a day standing for a year. The expression may, of course, be taken in either of the last two ways, but as long as there is no good reason for rejecting the literal interpretation ("When the literal sense will stand, that furthest from the letter is the worst"), and no difficulties are resolved by accepting either of the other explanations, it would seem best to adhere to the literal meaning of one thousand years or a period of about that length. (E. A. El. Gab. Pet. Sim. Sco. Mor. Tor. Weid. Mack. Moor.)

Accepting then the time element in the expression we have next to consider as to what period in the world's history the time indicated refers, and this introduces us to the second general theory.

II. *Past-Millennium.*

A Millennium which began in the fourth century with the reign of Constantine the Great, and ended with the assault made upon Christendom, in the fourteenth century, by the Ottoman Turks. This view was especially advocated by Grotius and Hammond, and while it has had some advocates in recent times it never has been taken seriously by critics in general. Much, if not all, of what is said of criticism of other views might be said here, our purpose being served by the mere mention of the theory.

III. *Present-Millennium.*

A Millennium reaching from the first to the second coming of Christ, and in which, of course, we are now living. This is the old Augustinian or *spiritual* theory, and that usually accepted by Catholic theologians. The resurrection mentioned is a spiritual one, from the death of sin to spiritual life in Christ. The Devil is the "strong man armed", who according to Christ's own saying was bound and expelled from the hearts of

His disciples, and so their reign over him made to begin. The resurrection mentioned is one which will go on wherever the Gospel is preached, and this will continue until Christ's Second Coming at the end of time to destroy the Antichrist, the one thousand years being the world's sixth chiliad, the length of which is to be determined only by the end of time, when the final judgment takes place and eternity begins. (Wor.)

But there are serious objections to this view.

1. The place in the book where the vision is found is unsuitable to it. It cannot be a recapitulation. It describes a condition of the Church *after* the reign of the beast in Chap. 13 and *after* the great struggle with the Antichrist in Chap. 19.
2. The blessed reign is ascribed to all who have been faithful unto death, and if the period intended is the present reign of the Church many of the saints will not reign throughout this time because they have been already a long time dead. Those who died in the early times of the Christian dispensation have missed the most of it.
3. Surely Satan cannot be spoken of as bound now. If so, it will be a sorry world indeed when he is loosed.
4. Making the first resurrection spiritual and the second one literal is not at all according to the principles of sound exegesis.

It might be said in passing that Augustine tells us he was induced to forsake the pre-millennial view of the early Fathers because some perverted the doctrine to carnal views. A strange reason indeed!

IV. *Future-Millennium.*

There remains, therefore, only the explanation which takes the expression as a statement of *a Millennium which is still in the future,* a period of one thousand years preferably, as we have seen, although even with this view it may be taken as an indefinite period of time. Here again we have two widely diverse views as to the relation in time of this one thousand years to the Second Coming of Christ.

A. The *Post-Millennial,* or Whitbyian view, teaching that Christ's Second Coming takes place *after* the Millennium. This view was first fully propounded by Whitby and explains the first resurrection as a resurrection of the cause, spirit, doctrine, principles and character of the Christian martyrs and saints departed, which, after the evil of the world has been largely overthrown, will usher in a thousand years of paradisical blessedness. At this point comes division of opinion. Vitringa and others regard the implied second resurrection as that of the literal dead, small and great, who shall appear before the judgment of the great white throne; while Whitby, Brown and others explain it as the uprising (the living again) of antichristian principles at the end of the Millennium in the persons and confederacy of Gog and Magog. The *New Jerusalem* Whitby and Vitringa explain as the blessedness of the earthly Church during this Millennium; while Brown and Faber explain it as including the whole company of saints in heaven after the Millennium. (H.)

The objections which have been brought to bear against this view, so far as the immediate text and context is concerned, and with this only we have here to do, are as follows:

1. The *"souls"* beheld by the Seer were of those who had been *beheaded*. This fixes their death as a literal one. So, too, then must the resurrection have been a literal one, for it is a rule that must never be overlooked that the resurrection must be of a corresponding nature with the death out of which it is a revival of life.

2. The first resurrection is contrasted with the second at the end of the one thousand years. These dead even Vitringa and many others of the Postmillennial School admit to be the literal dead. The expression, *"the rest of the dead"*, connects these with those first mentioned; the rest of anything is a part of what was the whole. If, therefore, *"the rest of the dead"* refers to those literally dead, then must those of the first resurrection have been also literally dead people.

3. It is now conceded by practically all scientific scholarship that the result of the Seventh Trumpet refers to that which is symbolized in this chapter. Even Drs. Whitby and Brown are agreed as to this. At the sounding of this trumpet it is said that the time has come for *"the dead to be judged"*—literal dead, of course, and if these dead, *"the rest of the dead"*, refer to those literally so, then those of the first resurrection must have likewise been literally dead.

4. The Greek word for *"they lived"* (ἔζησαν) is in the New Testament always applied to man in his complete condition of body and spirit united, and is never applied to the *"soul"* as a disembodied entity.

5. The Greek word used for *"resurrection"* (ἀνάστασις) always signifies in the New Testament, with perhaps a single exception, corporeal resurrection. It is used some forty-two times.

6. Whitby, Brown and others contend that the *"rest of the dead"* refers to the dead antichristian cause and faction slain in Chap. 19 by Him who sat on the white horse and revived in the person and through the instrumentality, inspired by Satan, of Gog and Magog. But if the first resurrection refers to the revival of Christian doctrine, cause and spirit, as these authorities hold, then we are forced to think of the Christian cause and the antichristian cause as being dead at the same time.

7. If there is such a thing as a dead Christian cause to be revived is it not strange that it is nowhere symbolized in the Apocalypse?

B. *The pre-millennial* view teaching that Christ's Second Coming takes place before the Millennium. This view, which is that of the earliest Fathers of the Church, explains the first resurrection to be literally that of departed martyrs and saints which takes place at the Second Coming of Christ before the Millennium, during which Millennium Satan's power is to be restricted and the government of the earth is to be administered by Christ and His risen saints, until at length, the Millennium having ended, and Satan again gone forth to deceive the nations, the final consummation will follow, which consists in the antichristian hosts of Gog and Magog being destroyed by fire from heaven, the resurrection and judgment of the wicked, the Devil and his servants cast into the lake of fire, and the Millennial reign of the saints being extended into one of eternal duration.

A number of arguments have been brought against this view in general. But again, we are concerned only with those that have to do with the text or context before us, and these are as follows:

1. It is said that John saw only what is described as the *"souls"* of certain saints, which fact excludes the notion of a literal resurrection. (See Barnes on page 697.) But this does not indicate that they were still disembodied spirits or souls anymore than I Pet. 3.20 indicates that the eight souls (Ψυχάs—same word) mentioned there are to be taken in this sense, or that the *"dead"* whom John saw in the twelfth verse of our chapter *"standing before God"* were still at the very time of their standing before God, *dead men*.

2. It is said that only martyrs and those *"who had not worshipped the beast"* were seen sitting upon the thrones. But this does not necessarily imply that they were the only enthroned ones. Certainly Christ, though unmentioned, must be supposed to have appeared in this self-same vision, since the enthroned ones are spoken of as *reigning with Christ*, and may not the vision have been equally inclusive of others though not receiving special mention which for some reason was given to the martyrs and saints under consideration.

3. It is said that *"the rest of the dead"* did not live *till* the thousand years were finished and that therefore they lived again *immediately* after the Millennium, and consequently they could not have been raised just before the final judgment, as the Premillennial view teaches, because this would leave no room for the *"little space"* of the Devil's loosing. But surely this objection rests, as Elliott says, "upon a quite mistaken assumption of the requirements of the preposition *till"*.

Further objections, as drawn from other Scriptures, have been registered against this view. Alford and Barnes, indeed, have twelve arguments against it, while David Brown contents himself with nine, but these arguments do not, however, seem to us formidable, while the exegetical difficulties which arise on any other view are seemingly quite insuperable.

Ver. 5. *"The rest of the dead"*,—The rest of the pious dead, says Barnes, inasmuch as only the martyrs and those who had not worshipped the beast take part in the first resurrection and the reigning (St. Dus.), and are therefore included exclusively in the first resurrection. For his depleted idea of what this first resurrection means see under verse 4, page 697. Gebhardt says the first resurrection is that of the martyrs and all the saints of this dispensation who had died, and that the second resurrection is of the wicked dead and the saints of the Old Testament. By others *"the rest of the dead"* is taken to mean the wicked dead only, including of course those who die during the Millennium, although nothing is said in the text of this latter class. (F. A. El. Mil. Pet. Gab. Sim. Sco. Mor. Tor. Moor.)

"This is the first resurrection",—Referring to those who were to reign with Christ during the one thousand years.

Ver. 6. *"Blessed and holy"*,—All saints are blessed and holy, but here the words are used in an emphatic sense, the resurrection being the precursor of a higher degree of blessedness and an eternal and complete consecration of God. It is possible that the word *"holy"* has a special reference to the priestly dignity and character coming forth then in complete glory.

"the second death",—The casting into the lake of fire and brimstone which is to take place at the final judgment. (See verse 14.)

"priests of God and of Christ",—A strong proof of Christ's coequal Diety. (See Chaps. 1.6 and 5.10.) They shall be near to God and Christ and most honorably employed in their service.

7 And when the thousand years are finished, Satan shall be loosed out of his prison, 8 and shall come forth to deceive the nations which are in the four corners of the earth, Gog and Magog, to gather them together to the war: the number of whom is as the sand of the sea. 9 And they went up over the breadth of the earth, and compassed the camp of the saints about, and the beloved city: and fire came down ¹out of heaven, and devoured them. 10 And the devil that deceived them was cast into the lake of fire and brimstone, where are also the beast and the false prophet; and they shall be tormented day and night ²for ever and ever.

¹Some ancient authorities insert *from God*
²Gr. *unto the ages of the ages*

Vers. 7-10. THE LOOSING AND THE DOOM OF SATAN.

Ver. 7. Says Weidner, "In the providence of God, Satan is once more permitted to turn his demoniacal power against the Church, that the glory of God may be manifested in his irrecoverable overthrow. The reign of the saints does not cease and it is highly probable that this final struggle will be as brief as it is fierce." Stuart seems to think that the reign of the saints will be somewhat interrupted, and commence again in full glory and power after the overthrow of Satan with his great army of Gog and Magog.

Ver. 8. *"nations which are in the four corners of the earth"*,— These are the nations which were left on the earth when the one thousand years began, heathen nations who had not, of course, been in the antichristian army, all of which was destroyed. The question now arises whether these nations had become subject to the kingdom during the Millennium and then apostatized when seduced by Satan (F. Bar. Hen.), or whether they were heathen nations in the far corners of the earth which had never come into close contact with the Gospel, if at all. (A. L. V. D. Ew. St.)

Stuart advocates the latter view, declaring them to be nations who live beyond the boundaries of the Millennial empire. Says he, "Not an intimation is given that they become apostates from the former profession of Christianity, or that Christianity had ever spread among them. If this were not so, how comes it that Satan finds no access to men anywhere except in the four corners of the earth?"

Lange argues for the second view from the fact that Satan *"goes out"* to deceive the nations and that these nations *"go up"* on the breadth of the

704

earth. The fact also that the word for *"nations"* is the usual one for the heathen nations argues in its favor.

The only objection with any force against this view is that it limits the Millennial kingdom of Christ and His saints to only a portion of the earth, the same not being world-wide.

Gaebelein says that many during the Millennium will yield a feigned obedience, submitting perhaps to the divine government through fear, while sin is in their hearts and they long for the time when they can throw off the restraint.

It is perhaps a combination of these last two views that ought to be accepted, and this will appear the more acceptable when it is remembered that the expression *"the four corners of the earth"* may, as Hengstenberg affirms, be taken to mean not only the dwellers at the remotest corners of the earth but all between those corners and the central point from which the distance is calculated and may be equivalent to the expression in the following verse, *"the breadth of the earth"*. (See Judges 20.1,2; I Sam. 14.38; Isa. 19.3; 11.12.) It would then mean that Satan went everywhere seducing the people and gathering his army.

Satan was, of course, loosed according to God's divine method of testing, just as he was allowed to enter the first Paradise.

"Gog and Magog",—(See Ezek. 38 and 39, the final and complete fulfillment of which seems to be here referred to). Magog was the son of Japheth (Gen. 10.2), who with his brothers represented the northern and north-eastern nations. Gog seems to have been their prince. (Ezek. 38.2.)

Josephus says Magog denoted the Scythians, and Hitzig says John chose the expression on account of the Scythians being the most remote people. Winer says Magog seems to be a collective name denoting the sum of the peoples situated in Media and the Caucasian mountains concerning whom a vague report had reached the Jews. They are, of course, used here in a mystical or symbolical sense as representing the final adversaries of Christ led on by Satan in person.

"to the war",—i. e., the last great war foretold by prophecy.

"as the sand of the sea",—The usual Biblical expression for an innumerable multitude.

Ver. 9. *"went up"*,—Dusterdieck says, "A common expression for a military expedition, the place of attack usually being an elevated position, and here especially appropriate because of Jerusalem's elevated position, the approaching of which from any quarter of the earth, is in the idiom of Scriptures called "going up". It may, however, be taken, together with *"over the breadth of the earth"* (meaning Palestine) in accordance with the Old Testament conception (Zech. 12.7,8), as the image of an invading army overspreading all the land.

"encompassed the camp of the saints",—The saints are represented as encamped about their beloved city to stand in its defense against the enemies of God.

"the beloved city",—Says Dusterdieck, "That the *'beloved city'* is the earthly Jerusalem,—not the new Jerusalem of Chap. 21.1,—is acknowledged with substantial unanimity."

Many (V. B. Kl. Aug. And. Hen. Bar.) take the city as a symbolic expression for the Church, but this would seem to be an ordinary eluding of the context. Barnes says, "all that is necessarily implied is that there will be a state of hostility to the Church of Christ which would be well illustrated by such a comparison with an invading host of barbarians".

"fire came down",—(See II Kings 1.10,12,14; Ezek. 38.22; 39.6). To be taken literally or symbolically according to one's method of interpretation.

Ver. 10. *"forever and ever"*,—As strong an expression for absolute endlessness as Biblical language affords.

> 11 And I saw a great white throne, and him that sat upon it, from whose face the earth and the heaven fled away; and there was found no place for them. 12 And I saw the dead, the great and the small, standing before the throne; and books were opened: and another book was opened, which is *the book* of life: and the dead were judged out of the things which were written in the books, according to their works. 13 And the sea gave up the dead that were in it; and death and Hades gave up the dead that were in them: and they were judged every man according to their works. 14 And death and Hades were cast into the lake of fire. This is the second death, *even* the lake of fire. 15 And if any was not found written in the book of life, he was cast into the lake of fire.

Vers. 11-15. THE LAST JUDGMENT; THE DOOM OF THE UNBELIEVING.

Ver. 11. *"a great white throne"*,—It is *"white"* as symbolical of the holiness and purity of its occupant and the judgment to be administered, and *"great"*, not so much in comparison with the throne of verse 4 (Sim.), as in correspondence with the great Being who sits upon it, although by these descriptions this throne is distinguished from those in verse 4. It is probably, though not absolutely, the same throne as in Chap. 4.2, upon which the Occupant now sits as a Judge.

"Him that sat on it",—This is by many referred to God, the Father (A. D. Zu. Dus. Hen. Sim. Weid.), but it would seem best to refer it to Christ, seeing here God in Christ as His Revealer. (F. B. L. Ew. St. Ei. Gab. Bar. Mil.) The analogy of Christian doctrine throughout the Word, as well as Rev. 21.5-8 seems to substantiate this interpretation. (See John 5.22,27.)

"the earth and the heaven fled away",—This is elsewhere represented as their consumption by fire, says Alford (II Peter 3.10-12). It would seem from this that the final conflagration precedes the final general judgment, as Fausset says, although this conception is not necessarily imperative by reason of the order of the language used here. The reference in any case is to the passing away of the present corruptible state and the changing to a state glorious and incorruptible. Even the natural creation shrinks back with awe and seeks to hide itself.

Ver. 12. *"the dead"*,—i. e., the rest of the dead, as in verse 5. Alford says, "That this judgment refers to the wicked dead alone there can be no doubt from a plain exegesis of the word *"dead"* and from the context. All the righteous who had been resurrected and caught up before the Millennium as well as those who had died during the Millennium and those who were alive at the close of the Millennium will be there also, not, however, to be judged (John 5.24), but to have their judgment confirmed. We must *all* appear, etc."

Fausset says the number will consist of the wicked who have died from Adam to the Millennium and the wicked who have died during the Millennium and the righteous who have died during the Millennium. The living believers, he says, are not especially mentioned, as they, just before the destruction of the ungodly, or after it (having been preserved from the judgment of fire which destroyed all the living wicked), shall probably be first transfigured and caught up with the saints transfigured at the first resurrection. Some think, however, that all believers dying during the Millennium will be immediately glorified, given their resurrection bodies as were those in the first resurrection. But whether this be so or whether their bodies are to await the final resurrection, it would seem, contrary to Fausset, no more appropriate for them to be judged than for any other class of believers. They will doubtless be glorified, given resurrection bodies either immediately upon their death or at the time just preceding the final judgment and escape the judgment just as all other believers, except in the sense mentioned a moment ago.

Our reasons for confining this judgment to the wicked dead only, the living wicked having been destroyed, are as follows:

1. The word *"dead"* as used by John is used of the wicked only. (See verse 5 and Chap. 11.18.)
2. The assurance of John 5.24 that the believer shall not come into judgment.
3. The judgment takes place according to what is written in *"the books"*, and the books are expressly distinguished from the *"book of life"*.

"books . . . and another book",—Hengstenberg says a name cannot be written in both books. When erased from the books by the blood of Christ, the name is then written in the other book.

Dusterdieck says, "According to the works which stand indicated in the books, the names are or are not found in the Book of Life." The question naturally arises then: What use for the Book of Life at all, since the record of the books decides the matter?

Alford says that both bear record independently of one another; the books by their records and the book by the inscription or otherwise of the name, the books being as it were vouchers for the Book of Life. Thus also the majority (F. L. St. Dus. Bar. Sim.). Many others (Mil. Pet. Gab. Weid.) agree with Hengstenberg and we are inclined to believe that a plain and natural exegesis of the text favors this view. Note in addition to the above three reasons, that it is only the *"dead"* who are judged, i. e., the wicked who are raised from their graves at that time, and they are judged out of the *"books"*, which, as Hengstenberg says, are books of guilt, condemnation and death.

The reason why the books relating to the wicked are more than one, while there is but one Book of Life, is that names only are recorded in the latter, while both names and works are recorded in the former, or it may be also because there are few that are saved in comparison with the many who are lost.

Ver. 13. The reference is to the fact that all the dead, both unburied (in the sea) and buried, rose again.

"death and Hades",—These appear personified as demoniacal powers exercising sway over wicked men. This is not only proven by Chap. 6.8,

but by the fact that they are both in the next verse cast into the lake of fire; another proof that the souls they were called upon to give up were the souls of the wicked, i. e., that it was a resurrection especially of the wicked dead that is referred to here.

Says Dusterdieck, "Since verse 5 is understood as applying to all believers, this is only the resurrection of those who are to be delivered to the second death."

"according to their works",—The constant teaching of Scripture. (See Rom. 2.6; II Cor. 5.10; Matt. 16.27.)

Hengstenberg takes *"sea"* in a figurative sense, maintaining that the reference is to those who have perished in the battles of the nations. Milligan also takes the figurative view and refers it to the tossed and troubled evil world. Not only are these views unnatural, but there is no good reason at all for not taking the word in its literal sense, as the vast majority do.

Ver. 14. The second death is the being cast into the lake of fire, the intensified death, the coming of the wicked in their risen bodies to eternal perdition. This explains Chaps. 2.11 and 20.6.

Ver. 15. Says Milligan, "Here, then, is the purpose and the only one for which the book of life is spoken of as used at the judgment before us. It was searched to see if any man's name was *not* written in it."

CHAPTER TWENTY-ONE

1 And I saw a new heaven and a new earth; for the first heaven and the first earth are passed away; and the sea is no more. 2 And I saw ¹the holy city, new Jerusalem, coming down out of heaven from God, made ready as a bride adorned for her husband. 3 And I heard a great voice out of the throne saying, Behold, the tabernacle of God is with men, and he shall ²dwell with them, and they shall be his peoples, and God himself shall be with them, ³*and be* their God: 4 and he shall wipe away every tear from their eyes; and death shall be no more; neither shall there be mourning, nor crying, nor pain, any more: the first things are passed away. 5 And he that sitteth on the throne said, Behold, I make all things new. And he saith, ⁴Write: for these words are faithful and true. 6 And he said unto me, They are come to pass. I am the Alpha and the Omega, the beginning and the end. I will give unto him that is athirst of the fountain of the water of life freely. 7 He that overcometh shall inherit these things; and I will be his God, and he shall be my son. 8 But for the fearful, and unbelieving, and abominable, and murderers, and fornicators, and sorcerers, and idolaters, and all liars, their part *shall be* in the lake that burneth with fire and brimstone; which is the second death.

¹Or, *the holy city Jerusalem coming down new out of heaven*
²Gr. *tabernacle*
³Some ancient authorities omit, and be *their God*
⁴Or, *Write, These words are faithful and true*

Vers. 1-8. The New Heaven and the New Earth.

"We now come," says Gaebelein, "to the revelation concerning the final and eternal state of the earth." Says Weidner, "The final judgment has taken place, as well as the final consummation of all things. What follows in these last two chapters refers to the eternal kingdom of God in the new heavens and earth. The purified and renewed earth has become the abode of glorified humanity and the tabernacle of God is with man." (Mor.) It would seem as though we must take these things literally because there is no other way to take them.

Ver. 1. Now Isa. 65.17 and 66.22 have received their fulfillment.

"a new heaven and a new earth",—The first creation had passed away by being changed, and a renovated and purified creation had taken its place.

"passed away",—The annihilation of the old creation is by no means here necessarily implied, but only, as Alford says, "its passing away as to its outward and recognizable form and its renewal to a fresh and more glorious one."

Though not here stated, it is evident that the method of this renewal and purification is that described in II Pet. 3.13.

"the sea is no more",—Inasmuch as the sea is a constituent part of the old creation, we see no reason why the meaning of this passage should not be that the sea passed away just as did the earth and the heaven and that a new sea accompanied the new earth and the new heaven. Many (F. A. Be. Bar. Sad. Aug. Gab. Weid.) take the removal of the sea in an absolutely literal sense. Bede says it is dried up by the universal conflagration, as Alford and Weidner seem also to imply. Sadler says that three-fourths of the earth's surface is to be no longer barren and uninhabitable. Andreas says navigation is no longer necessary.

Others (Mil. Sim. Wor. Hen. et al.) take the word symbolically. It is the sea of peoples, the wicked restless world, and the turbulent state of nations shall cease.

Ver. 2. *"the holy city, new Jerusalem"*,—The new earth must have a new metropolis. (See Gal. 4.26; Heb. 12.22 and Heb. 11.10.) The name of the material city stands for the community formed by its inhabitants, says Alford. It is the glorified Church coming down out of heaven upon the renewed earth.

"made ready as a bride",—Says Lange, "The new Jerusalem as the sum of perfected individuals is the City of God, the Holy City, and in its unity it is the Bride of Christ." (See Chap. 19.7,8.)

Ver. 3. *"a great voice"*,—Not perhaps the voice of God Himself, but of one of the presence-angels as in Chap. 16.17 and Chap. 19.5.

"the tabernacle of God",—i. e., the place where God dwells. An allusion to the tabernacle of the wilderness where God dwelt symbolically.

"is with men",—They, as it were, pitch their tents around His. Thus the ancient promises are fulfilled. (Exodus 29.45; Lev. 26.11; Ezek. 37.27.)

"they shall be his peoples",—In the Old Testament it is *"people"*; here the many peoples of redeemed humanity are substituted for the single elect nation; the world is substituted for Israel.

Ver. 4. *"wipe away every tear"*,—i. e., gently like a mother from the face of her child. It means, of course, that He will so constitute things that no more tears will be shed.

"death shall be no more",—Sin being no more, its results also disappear. Morgan says, "Some regard the promise that death shall cease, as applying to the Millennium; whereas the old prophets tell us that in that period the sinner shall be accursed and the child shall die. But in this city of God, on this renewed earth, the great ultimate place of the kingdom

of Christ after the thousand years, there shall be no death, pain, nor curse because there is no sin. No temptation to sin shall ever be allowed to assault the dwellers in that home of the future, as verse 27 clearly foretells." (See Chap. 20.14.)

"neither shall there be mourning",—i. e., because of death.

"nor crying",—i. e., because of violence and oppression.

"nor pain",—i. e., grievance or misery in general.

"first things are passed away",—The trials just mentioned belonged to the *"first things"*, to the old earth, and the old earth has passed away. The reference is to the whole order of things which existed in the first creation, especially the evils of this present age.

Ver. 5. *"he that sitteth on the throne"*,—We would perhaps think here of God (A. L. Sw. Sim. Sad. Mil. Dus. Hen. Gab. Weid.) rather than Christ (St. Ew. Bar.). Simcox aptly remarks that the reference is rather to the eternal throne of Chap. 4.2 than to the judgment throne of Chap. 20.11, so far as the two can be distinguished.

"make all things new",—i. e., an order of things to correspond with the new creation. The former state of things when sin and death reigned will be changed and the change will extend of course to everything.

"And he saith",—Many make this an interlogue on the part of the angel of Chap. 19.9. (A. B. Sw. Zu. Hen. Dus.) They call attention to the fact that the second *"said"* of verse 5 is a different verb from the first *"said"* of this same verse, and also from the third *"said"* of verse 6. This and the nature of the command they think argue in favor of a change of speaker, and so they refer the second *"said"* to the angel. This is a possible construction, and yet we find ourselves asking, Why should an angelic speech interrupt the voice of God from the throne, or an angel corroborate the language of God Himself?

"words faithful and true",—The same sense as in Chap. 19.9, i. e., they may be relied upon with entire confidence.

Swete says, "These great sayings which concern the future of humanity and the world must be seen to rest upon a secure basis. Men need to be assured that they are not only worthy of confidence, but answer to realities which in due time will enter into the experience of life, though for the present they cannot be fully realized or adequately expressed."

Ver. 6. *"he said unto me"*,—i. e., the one sitting on the throne, which is the throne of "God and the Lamb". It makes little if any difference whether we think of God or of Christ here speaking. Some (L. Sim. Dus. Mil.) refer the speaker to God, while Barnes and Stuart think of Christ, the latter calling attention to the fact that the promises are such as Christ was wont to make.

"They are come to pass",—The same expression as in Chap. 16.17. Lange refers this to the *"words"* just mentioned in the sense of their highest realization. (Sw. Mil.)

Simcox thinks the reference is to the *"all things"* just mentioned, and similarly Alford and others (Dus. Sad. Weid.), by whom it is taken as the perishing of the old creation and the bringing in of the new. In the ultimate all these views amount to one and the same thing.

"the Alpha and the Omega",—The reference is here perhaps to the eternal Father as in Chap. 1.8, by whom the old was and the new shall be. (D. A. L. Sw. Sim.)

"the beginning and the end",—The beginning from whom all things created sprung and the end to whose glory they all converge.

"fountain",—Oriental thrones usually have a fountain of cool water springing up, and from this John doubtless draws his picture.

"freely",—Not abundantly, but *"gratis"*, as the Greek implies.

"I will give unto him that is athirst",—The meaning is not that He would do this in the future, the words being spoken to those who had already drunk of the living water, but the words as well as those of the next two verses are written for the encouragement and warning of believers yet in this life. "Added," says Fausset, "lest any should despair of attaining to this exceeding weight of glory."

Ver. 7. *"He that overcometh"*,— (See Chap. 2.7,11,17).

"these things",—i. e., the fulfillment of all these promises, the glories of the New Jerusalem, the new creation with its immunities from sorrow and death, the fullness and freeness of the water of life, the dwelling with God and the consciousness of the filial relation spoken of in this verse.

Ver. 8. *"the fearful"*,—i. e., as contrasted with the overcomer. Many refer these to the cowards in Christ's army, the apostates, those mentioned in Heb. 10.38. (B. A. D. St. Ew. Hen. Dus. Mil.)

"abominable",—Referring not alone to idol worship, but to the foul and abominable sins committed in the licentious rites practiced in idol-worship. (See Chap. 17.4 and Romans 1.)

9 And there came one of the seven angels who had the seven bowls, who were laden with the seven last plagues; and he spake with me, saying, Come hither, I will show thee the bride, the wife of the Lamb. 10 And he carried me away in the Spirit to a mountain great and high, and showed me the holy city Jerusalem, coming down out of heaven from God, 11 having the glory of God: her [1]light was like unto a stone most precious, as it were a jasper stone, clear as crystal: 12 having a wall great and high; having twelve [2]gates, and at the [2]gates twelve angels; and names written thereon, which are *the names* of the twelve tribes of the children of Israel: 13 on the east were three [2]gates; and on the north three [2]gates; and on the south three [2]gates; and on the west three [2]gates. 14 And the wall of the city had twelve foundations, and on them twelve names of the twelve apostles of the Lamb. 15 And he that spake with me had for a measure a golden reed to measure the city, and the [2]gates thereof, and the wall thereof. 16 And the city lieth foursquare, and the length thereof is as great as the breadth: and he measured the city with the reed, twelve thousand furlongs: the length and the breadth and the height thereof are equal. 17 And he measured the wall thereof, a hundred and forty and four cubics, *according to* the measure of a man, that is, of an angel. 18 And the building of the wall thereof was jasper: and the city was pure gold, like unto pure glass. 19 The foundations of the wall of the city were adorned with all manner of precious stones. The first foundation was jasper; the second, [3]sapphire; the third, chalcedony; the fourth, emerald; 20 the fifth, sardonyx; the sixth, sardius; the seventh, chrysolite; the eighth, beryl; the ninth, topaz; the tenth, chrysoprase; the eleventh, [4]jacinth; the twelfth, amethyst. 21 And the twelve [2]gates were twelve pearls; each one of the several [2]gates was of one pearl: and the street of the city was pure gold, [5]as it were transparent glass. 22 And I saw no [6]temple therein: for the Lord God the Almighty, and the

[1]Gr. *luminary*
[2]Gr. *portals*

[3]Or, *lapis lazuli*
[4]Or, *sapphire*
[5]Or, *transparent as glass*
[6]Or, *sanctuary*

Lamb, are the [6]temple thereof. 23 And the city hath no need of the sun, neither of the moon, to shine upon it: for the glory of God did lighten it, [7]and the lamp thereof *is* the Lamb. 24 And the nations shall walk [8]amidst the light thereof: and the kings of the earth bring their glory into it. 25 And the [2]gates thereof shall in no wise be shut by day [*] (for there shall be no night there): 26 and they shall bring the glory and the honor of the nations into it: 27 and there shall in no wise enter into it anything [9]unclean, or he that [10]maketh an abomination and a lie: but only they that are written in the Lamb's book of life.

[7]Or, *and the lamb, the lamp thereof*
[8]Or, *by*
[9]Gr. *common*
[10]Or, *doeth*

Vers. 9-27. THE BRIDE OF THE LAMB; THE NEW JERUSALEM COMING DOWN OUT OF HEAVEN.

Ver. 9.   One of these angels had shown John the great harlot in Chap. 17.   Note the contrast of the bride here with the harlot there, which is maintained throughout these opening verses.

Ver. 10.   *"in the Spirit"*,—(See Chap. 17.3).

"mountain great and high",—Compare the parallel vision in Ezek. 40.1,2.   While the city is descending from heaven to earth, John is carried away to the mountain that he might have a nearer and fuller view of the vision already communicated to him in verse 2.   It is not said and probably is not meant to be inferred that the city itself descends upon a mountain.   "Any attempt to spiritualize the description of this city," says Campbell Morgan, "is out of harmony with the whole proper prophetic treatment of the book of Revelation.   We may no more discuss this than the resurrected body of Jesus, which was palpable to the touch of Thomas, yet was spiritual enough to stand in the midst of His Disciples without the opening of doors."

Ver. 11.   *"the glory of God"*,—Not merely a divine and celestial brightness, but the glorious presence of God Himself, the Shekinah abiding in her.   The splendor which surrounds the presence of God, the "light inaccessible and full of radiance" cuts off all need of sun or moon.

"her light",—The effect of the divine glory shining in her.

"jasper stone",—Perhaps the diamond, as what we know of jasper is opaque and not clear as crystal; nor is it one of the most precious stones, unless reference is made to some particular crystalizing jasper selected for its beauty, splendor and diaphanous nature.

Ver. 12.   *"a wall great and high"*,—As may be seen in verse 17.   A type of the absolute security of the heavenly city.

"twelve gates",—Corresponding to the twelve tribes of Israel, and denoting also, as Stuart says, free and easy access.   (See Ezekiel 48.30.)

"twelve angels",—Stationed there to set forth the divine and eternal security of the city, and to preserve the image of a well-ordered city.   It is not that they are stationed there as "guards" (St. Ew.) because the New Jerusalem is no longer menaced by enemies.   The case does not call for speculation.   Angels are described as "ministering spirits sent forth to minister to them who are heirs of salvation", and as Craven says, "veritable angels ministering at the gates of that glorious abode would add to its glory, and might perform other offices which in our present condition it is impossible for us to conceive."

"twelve tribes of the children of Israel",—Spiritual Israel of course is here symbolized by the names of the actual tribes of Israel, the whole people of God being in the mind of the Seer. (A. L. F. Sw. St. Dus. Bar. Mil. Weid.)

Ver. 13. The gates stand open on all sides, says Swete, and so represent the catholicity and universality of the new Society.

Ver. 14. *"twelve foundations"*,—Probably each portion of the wall between the gates, each section thus representing one vast foundation stone. (A. D. Sw. Dus. Sad. Sim. Weid.) Lee thinks of twelve layers, one on top of the other, and each layer or course running clear around the city. This magnifies the splendor a bit and is adopted by Stuart.

"on them twelve names of the twelve apostles",—Because they by their doctrine founded the Church and in this respect it rests upon them as an immovable foundation. The Apostles were the first leading and most important instruments in building up the Church of Christ and erecting His spiritual temple, and they are here honored as the founders.

Ver. 15. (See Ephesians, where, however, the ruling idea is a different one.) The measuring shows that the discourse is of something real, and that the city is not to be resolved into mere thought and imagination.

Ver. 16. It is impossible to decide whether the entire circumference of the city is 12,000 furlongs (F. A. L. V. St. Sad.), or that each side was 12,000 furlongs in measurement (B. Sw. Zu. Hen. Dus. Sim. Mil. Weid.), but it would seem that the latter is the plainer meaning of the text. Literally interpreted this would mean that the city is about 1500 miles in breadth and length and height. That the city is one vast cube is typical of its perfect nature, setting forth the love of God, as Williams says, "Infinite and perfect on every side".

Swete is assuredly correct when he says, "Such dimensions defy imagination and are permissible only in the language of symbolism." And so Stuart, "Everything shows that a literal exegesis in such a case as the present, excepting merely so far as to get a proper idea of the grandeur and the congruity of the image, is entirely out of the question."

Alford says the height of the city may include the hill on which the city is built; but there is no evidence that the city is built on a hill, and besides the highest mountain in the world is little more than five miles high.

Sadler agrees with De Wette in seeing a certain looseness in the use of the word *"equal"*, and in thinking that while the length and breadth are equal to each other, the height is *equal* all around and is only 144 cubits, as stated in the next verse. But the account given is that of a vision and inasmuch as the description must be taken symbolically there is no need to attempt to reduce the enormous dimensions given here, as no reduction could bring them within the bounds of verisimilitude, and no effort in that direction is required. "The stupendous height, length and breadth being exactly alike imply its faultless symmetry, transcending in glory all our most glowing conceptions. The city being measured implies the entire consecration of every part, all things being brought up to the most exact standard of God's holy requirements." (F.)

Ver. 17. *"measured the wall"*,—The wall seems to be introduced rather for the purpose of completing the idea of a city. Some (Mil. Will. Weid.) think the measurement of the wall refers to its thickness, but we see no reason to depart from the natural inference of the text; the length of the wall is, of course, identical with the length and breadth of the city, and this measurement would therefore naturally be of the height of the wall. (F. L. St. Bar. Dus. Sim.) The wall is but 216 feet high, less than the height of the walls of Babylon. Lange reminds us of the fact that the wall being so much less than the height of the city should occasion no difficulty inasmuch as all is to be taken symbolically. The glory of the city is not thus obscured. The unnatural and grotesque difference between the height of the city and of the wall is that which had led many to think of the thickness of the wall being intended by its measurement.

"the measure of a man, that is of an angel",—Not that "the measure of a glorified man is like that of an angel" (Eb.), nor that in this matter of measure men and angels use the same standard (A.), but that the measure of the angel (who makes his measurement for men) is like the measure of men (Dus. Hen.), which is really the same as the explanation of De Wette, Stuart and Sadler, namely, that the angel adopted a human standard of measurement.

Ver. 18. *"the building of the wall"*,—i. e., the superstructure built upon the foundation.

"jasper",—(See verse 11).

"pure gold, like unto clear glass",—The most precious metal known, but in this case transfigured and glorified.

Ver. 19. *"foundations"*,—(See verse 14).

"adorned",—Not that they are merely beautified with precious stones, but as the following description shows, that the foundations themselves consisted of these stones.

Vers. 20,21, together with verse 19, describe the city, as Dusterdieck says, "with the greatest glory whereof human fantasy is capable".

Ver. 22. *"no temple therein"*,—The temple was the place where God dwelt, but here all is temple. As Alford says, "The inhabitants need no place of worship, the object of all worship being present; they need no place of sacrifice, the great sacrifice Himself being there." There is no conflict here with Chaps. 3.12 and 7.15, for there the language is figurative and means they shall dwell in the divine presence and behold His glory. But in the New Jerusalem God and the Lamb are everywhere and so the whole place is to the worshippers what the temple of old was to him who visited it, and they shall see his face (Chap. 22.4), no veil between Him and them—no inner sanctuary to be approached but once a year.

Ver. 23. God and the Lamb, being everywhere and always surrounded with a light that is full of glory, give a radiance far exceeding that of the sun and moon. There is no occasion to individualize the members of the sentence, making the glory of God to be the sun and that of the Lamb to be the moon. (See verse 11 and Isa. 60.9.)

Ver. 24. (See also verse 26, and Chap. 22.2.) There are several views as to the meaning of these verses:

I. Simcox, Stuart and others think that these expressions are only a part of the imagery, the conception of John being modeled by the representations of the Old Testament prophets, and the New Jerusalem is conceived, as in Isa. 45.14; 49.23; 60.10,11, as an imperial city receiving the tribute of the world, simply because that was the form of world-wide sovereignty recognized and understood in the prophets' times.

II. Fausset, Lange, Milligan, Weidner and many others think the reference is to the nations and kings who lived on this earth before the renovation and before the judgment on Satan and his army, and who were believers at that time, and now are pictured as walking in the midst of the light of the Holy City and bringing their glory and honor into it. In verse 27 it is said distinctly that none shall enter the city save those whose names are written in the Lamb's Book of Life, and therefore the names of these nations and kings must have been written in these books.

Says Fausset, "The kings of the earth, who once had regard only for their own glory, having been converted, now in the new Jerusalem do bring their glory into it to lay it down at the feet of their Lord and their God."

Dusterdieck says, "In the tone and the language of the ancient prophets, John describes the people who are to find entrance into the future city, and here the Gentiles are expressly designated as those who, according to the ancient prophecies, are to find admission into the city. The Gentiles, just as the Jews, receive full citizenship in the new Jerusalem, and in like manner partake of the blessed glory of that holy place."

III. Others, again, conceive of these nations and kings as those who will still be living on this renewed earth outside of the city and in whom there still remains original sin. "They are," says Sadler, "outsiders, and yet friendly, evidently holy in a certain sense and fearing God"; while Craven asks, "May it not be that the great truth is adumbrated in this revelation that even after the new creation the human race is to be continued under the government of the glorified Church, and ever propagating a holy seed such as would have been begotten had Adam never sinned?"

Alford says, "Among the mysteries of this new heaven and new earth this is set forth to us; that besides the glorified Church there shall still be dwelling on the redeemed earth, nations organized under kings and saved by means of influences of the heavenly city."

But we ask:

(a) If the whole earth is purified and renewed by fire and there is a new earth, *"wherein dwelleth righteousness"*, how are we to conceive of people unclean in any respect dwelling in it, who shall in no wise enter into the city?

(b) How did these nations survive the judgment and the passing away of the old earth and the old heaven, or, if they did not exist prior to that time, where did they come from? They could not be the offspring of those in the city, for these neither marry nor are given in marriage.

715

IV. Gaebelein and Elliott refer the whole section (Chap. 21.9-7 to Chap. 22.5) to the period of the Millennium. Gaebelein says, "We have followed from Chap. 19.1 events which are chronological, but with the ninth verse of Chap. 21 we are brought back once more to the Millennial state. The coming down mentioned in verse 10 precedes the one mentioned in verses 2-3 by a thousand years, the chronological order at verse 9 being interrupted. The coming down mentioned in verses 2-3 is undoubtedly *to* the new earth, but here in verse 10 the holy city comes down to be *over*, still above, the earth. The holy city of verse 10 will be seen by the inhabitants suspended in the heavens, and human eyes will look up to behold the flashes of glory never ceasing. It is from this city of verse 10 that Christ and His saints shall reign during the Millennium, and the twelve Apostles judge the twelve tribes of Israel (Matt. 19.28). No doubt there will be communication between this Holy City, the heavenly New Jerusalem, and the earthly Jerusalem."

This last view, if it can be substantiated, does furnish the easier explanation of the nations that *"shall walk by its light"*, and of the kings of the earth who shall *"bring their glory and honor unto it"* (Gaebelein reads "unto" in place of *"into"* of the Revised Version), for these are the saved nations of the Millennial times, who not only walk in its eternal and undiminished light, but bring their glory and honor unto it, i. e., bow in homage in its hallowed presence.

Elliott defends, in general, this view at great length. He says:

1. In Chap. 19 the twenty-four elders gave in glad shout the announcement of two things, (a) the beginning of Christ's reign, and (b) the presentation of the bride. The first of these is immediately seen in Chap. 20.4, but where is the second unless it be this new Jerusalem of Chap. 21 coming down out of heaven as a bride adorned for her husband? Surely there cannot be one thousand years between the bride's preparing and her presentation.

   But may not the marriage of the Lamb and the bride have taken place in Chap. 19 at the Rapture, and this coming down of the bride in Chap. 21 be a new manifestation of the bride?

2. There are kings on the earth who bring glory into the holy city and men in need of healing, and therefore the reference must be to Millennial times.

   But may not the answer to this be found in general view number II, and also in the fact that the word *"healing"* may be translated *"health"*. (See explanation of this word under Chap. 22.2.)

3. It was a Vial angel who showed the vision to John and therefore it must have followed right after the Vial judgments and so during the Millennium, while the fact that John fell at the feet of the angel in each instance indicates that the reference must have been to the same thing.

   But these conclusions by no means necessarily follow.

4. Dan. 7.18 dates the saints' everlasting reign from the fall of the Antichrist, and the everlasting reign of Rev. 22.5 ought to be co-temporaneous with it and not begin one thousand years later.

But there need be no discrepancy here. The reign of the saints beginning with the beginning of the Millennium is everlasting, but at the close of the Millennium when earth has been transfigured and eternity has begun there certainly can be nothing contradictory in saying that the saints shall continue to reign or reign forever and ever.

5. Paul says that creation's deliverance from bondage is at the manifestation (the Rapture) of the sons of God, and this is without doubt at the beginning of the Millennium, and therefore the new earth and new heaven of Chap. 21.1 cannot be at the end of the Millennium.

   This is one of Elliott's strongest arguments, and the only reply is that given by a number of scholars, namely, that there was a partial glorification of heaven and earth at the beginning of the Millennium and a fuller and complete one at the close.

6. Isaiah's new heaven and new earth commence at the restoration of the Jews at the opening of the Millennium, and John's being the same, must begin at the same time.

   But are these two necessarily the same? Gaebelein puts Isaiah's on earth and John's above the earth, both beginning at the same time, but Isaiah's ending in one thousand years and John's continuing *"forever and ever"*.

   Keil argues against the restoration of the Jews, and makes the reference both of Isaiah and John pertain to the same thing beginning after the Millennium and continuing through eternity. Even if Jewish restoration be admitted may not Isaiah's prediction have been realized during the Millennium and John's begun upon afterward, upon an earth wholly transformed and fitted for the abiding place of the eternal city, which he calls the New Jerusalem?

   Elliott accordingly says the throne upon which Christ sits during the Millennial reign is the Great White Throne and this judgment lasts a thousand years, the books being opened before Him, as stated both in Daniel and Revelation. The Judgment continues right on through the Millennium, there being two great and special acts connected with it, one at the beginning and the other at the close, the Seventh Trumpet at the beginning of the Millennium being the time when the dead were judged.

It must now be noted that there is a big difference between the view of Gaebelein and that of Elliott. Elliott refers the Holy City, the New Jerusalem of Chap. 21, both of verses 1,2 and verse 10, to the earthly Millennium while Gaebelein refers the Holy City of verse 10 to the New Jerusalem above the earth, and that of verses 1,2 to the same New Jerusalem coming on down at the close of the Millennium.

As against the views of both these authorities it may be said that Chap. 20.11 plainly affirms that the old earth and heaven that was fled away from the face of Him that sat on the Great White Throne, and then in the next chapter, following chronologically, John *"saw a new heaven and a new earth; for the first heaven and the first earth are passed away"*, and to this new earth John saw the holy city, the New Jerusalem, descend. This ought to settle the New Jerusalem here mentioned as post-millennial.

Furthermore, so far as Elliott's view is concerned, the fourth verse of the twenty-first chapter distinctly says of this New Jerusalem that *"death shall be no more"*, whereas it is an undisputed fact that death does continue throughout the period of the Millennium.

To the views of both these authorities there can be only one answer, and it is given well by Weidner, "This Holy City which John saw coming down from God out of heaven (Chap. 21.10) is the same city which is referred to in Chap. 21.1,2, and belongs to the new heaven and new earth there mentioned. The final consummation has taken place, and on this renewed earth there shall be no other inhabitants save the glorified saints, which compose the Holy City Jerusalem, even the bride, the wife of the Lamb (verse 9). Any other interpretation is contrary to the whole context, and belongs to the crudities of exegesis."

Our own conviction is that the second (II) general view given is the much to be preferred one.

Alford remarks, "It follows then that these nations and these kings are written in the Book of Life; and so perhaps some light may be thrown on one of the darkest mysteries of redemption. There may be—I say it with diffidence—those who have been saved by Christ without ever forming a part of His visible organized Church." But this, says Fausset, is "a rash speculation above what is written, and entirely uncalled for by the text."

Ver. 25. *"not shut by day"*,—i. e., never, seeing it is always day, for there shall be no night there.

Ver. 27. Blunt says, "This verse may be said to be retrospective, referring to the times preceding the last judgment, since all evil was then destroyed." It does not mean that such persons, at the time to which the vision refers, were living outside the Holy City and could not enter in because they were unclean.

"The smallest part of the meaning of this verse," says Morgan, "is that which lies on its surface. It *does* teach that no unclean person and no liar shall be able to pass into the ctiy; but it teaches vastly more. How came the mystery of sin into Eden? He who worketh abomination made a lie and tainted the brightness of the garden; and the stream of evil outworked into all human history. But into this fair city, Christ's all-glorious bride, the earthly dwelling place of a heavenly people, shall no unclean thing come. No temptation to sin shall ever be allowed to assault the dwellers in this home of the future. This truth reveals a Divine purpose more glorious than even the blessedness of the Millennium."

CHAPTER TWENTY-TWO

1 And he showed me a river of water of life, bright as crystal, proceeding out of the throne of God and of [1]the Lamb, 2 in the midst of the street thereof. And on this side of the river and on that was [2]the tree of life, bearing twelve [3]manner of fruits, yielding its fruit every month: and the leaves of the tree were for the healing of the nations. 3 And there shall be [4]no curse any more: and

[1]Or, *the Lamb. In the midst of the street thereof, and on either side of the river, was the tree of life &c.*

[2]Or, *a tree*
[3]Or, *crops of fruit*
[4]Or, *no more anything accursed*

the throne of God and of the Lamb shall be therein: and his [6]servants shall serve him; 4 and they shall see his face; and his name *shall be* on their foreheads. 5 And there shall be night no

[6]Gr. *bondservants*

more; and they need no light of lamp, neither light of sun; for the Lord God shall give them light; and they shall reign [6]for ever and ever.

[6]Gr. *unto the ages of the ages*

Vers. 1-5. THE RIVER AND THE TREE OF LIFE IN THE NEW JERUSALEM.

These verses are a continuation and a completion of the description of the glory prepared for believers in the New Jerusalem.

Ver. 1. *"river of water of life"*,—The description depends, as no doubt does Ezek. 27.1-12, upon the prototype Gen. 2.10. Stuart thinks John had in his mind only the passage in Ezekiel, while Barnes thinks he drew his picture from Genesis. But why not believe that both these rivers were in the mind of John as he gave us this description.

Of course, the expression is symbolical. The waters are those of peace and spiritual life; those drinking of these waters are immortal and will never die.

This symbol has often, and with no little propriety, been interpreted of the Holy Ghost, of whom water is one of the most frequent Scriptural emblems. (Li. Ca. Ger. Blunt.) These authorities call attention to the fact that the Holy Spirit proceeds from the Son, no less than from the Father, just as the waters here proceed from the throne of the Father and the Son, God and the Lamb, this throne being one and the same. (See Chap. 3.21.)

"proceeding out of the throne",—The idea is strictly in accordance with oriental imagery. Here is symbolized the uninterrupted continuance of life derived by the saints ever fresh from God who is the fountain-source of all grace.

"the throne of God and the Lamb",—Dusterdieck says it is the Lamb's no less than God's because only through the mediation of the Lamb is the participation of believers in the eternal life of God made possible.

Ver. 2. The punctuation of the Authorized Version is much to be preferred to that of the Revised Version. If the words *"in the midst"* belonged to verse 1 they would more naturally have been placed before the word *"shewed"* than after the word *"Lamb"*. Again, the words *"on either side of"* are adverbial rather than prepositional. The better reading is that of the margin of the Revised Version, "In the midst of the street thereof, and on either side of the river, was the tree of life . . ."

Stuart and Barnes think of the river running through the city, with a street running parallel on each side of the river and then the trees planted on either side of the river between the river and the street. It is better, however, to think with others (A. Dus. Sei. Weid.) of the river flowing through the broad street, a row of trees being on either bank, the tree (without the article, and therefore best taken collectively) being therefore manifold but of course all of one and the same kind. It was certainly not as Durham thinks, namely, that the tree was in the midst of the river, extending its branches to both banks.

719

"twelve manner of fruits",—It is not clear whether twelve kinds of fruit are intended, signifying, as Ebrard says, "the ever new enjoyments of the blessed" (A-V. R-V. A. F. Eb. Ew. Sad.), or whether twelve crops of fruit are intended (L. St. Mil. Sim. Bar. Dus. Weid.). We prefer the latter of the two interpretations; in fact it is almost demanded by the third clause of the verse, *"yielding her fruit every month"*. The general idea of the passage is, as Milligan says, rather that of continuous nourishment than of variety of blessings.

Two questions present themselves: What is the fruit for? and, What are the leaves for? The last question is answered by the text, but to the first question no explanation is offered. The fruits, many aver, are for the sustenance of the glorified bodies of the saints. (St. Sw. Dus. Sad. Mil. Weid.) "In eternity, the continually growing fruits of the tree of life serve the blessed for food." (Dus.)

"According to all analogy of God's dealings, the various forms of life have to be sustained by nourishment, and here God provides the water of life as well as the tree of life to sustain the eternal life of His people." (Sad.)

"leaves of the tree for the healing of the nations",—(See Chap. 21.24,26).

1. Alford thinks here of "nations outside" and "dwelling on the renewed earth, organized under kings and saved by the influences of the heavenly city". (Thus also D. Bl. Ew. Eb. Zu. St.)

2. Fausset takes severe exception to Alford's view and says, "The *'nations'* mentioned are those which have long before, viz., in the Millennium, become the Lord's and His Christ's. The leaves shall be the health-giving preventive securing the redeemed against, not healing them of, sickness."

Similar to this is the view of Milligan, who says, "It is impossible to think that the nations here spoken of have yet to be converted. They have already entered the New Jerusalem, and that they are healed can signify no more than this, that they are kept in constant soundness of health by what is there administered to them."

This view of Fausset, which is no doubt correct, is adopted by the majority (Dus. Sim. Bar. Mil. Weid.). The reference, says Weidner, is to "the converted Gentiles who are among the glorified saints".

Says Morgan, "On the authority of a Greek scholar of repute we may substitute the word *health* for *healing*. Healing pre-supposes disease, while health does not. In the perfect kingdom, where sin is cast out, the nations can have no need of healing. This and the previous descriptions, as well as verses 3, 4 and 5, which follow, are passing glimpses of the glory of a kingdom on earth, *beyond* the Millennium, the Great White Throne, and the final casting out of evil. This is a picture of the fullness of the times when all things shall be subdued to the sway of Jesus."

Bengel holds that the reference is to the conversion of the heathen to whom in this life the Gospel had not been preached (!) while Hengstenberg thinks it refers to the conversion of the heathen of the present age (!). Gaebelein makes this to be still a part of the Millennium scene, which closes with verse 5 of this chapter.

Dusterd.eck well remarks, "The expression, 'for the healing of the nations,' is as little to be pressed, in the sense that a still present sickness of the heathen were pre-supposed, as it is to be inferred that the tears which God will wipe away from the blessed (see Chap. 21.4) are the signs of pains still endured in the eternal city."

Ver. 3. *"no curse any more"*,—The word *"curse"* is perhaps meant as a translation of that rendered *"utter destruction"* in Zech. 14.11, of which this verse is doubtless a reminiscence. It means literally "no more an accursed thing"; for every evil has been judged and received its merited punishment, and there is therefore nothing upon which the curse of Almighty God can or needs to rest. (See Chap. 21.4.)

"his servants shall serve him",—In ministration and holy service they shall perform their priestly functions forever in His presence. (See Chap. 7.15 and Chap. 21.3.)

Ver. 4. *"they shall see his face"*,—They shall be admitted to His immediate presence, an honor seldom granted to private individuals by earthly sovereigns. This is the reward of the pure in heart. (Matt. 5.8.)

"his name on their foreheads",—Herein is conveyed the idea of entire consecration to the service of God; they belong absolutely to Him. (See Chaps. 14.1; 7.1-8; 2.17.)

Ver. 5. *"And there shall be night no more"*,—A repetition of Chap. 21.25 stated there to indicate that the gates of the city shall be continually open so that the redeemed can enter in continually with their gifts in order to magnify their King; stated here to show that having entered they shall suffer no interruption in their joyful service, and shall need no nightly rest to recruit their weary frame for the service of the following day, says Milligan.

"they shall reign forever and ever",—In a higher sense than during the Millennium. (A. D. St. Wei.) (See Chap. 3.21.)

Sadler asks, "Over whom shall they reign?" and then answers, "Perhaps over countless worlds which God created, and will create."

With this verse the Apocalypse proper closes and the Epilogue begins.

6 And he said unto me, These words are faithful and true: and the Lord, the God of the spirits of the prophets, sent his angel to show unto his [1]servants the things which must shortly come to pass. 7 And behold, I come quickly. Blessed is he that keepeth the words of the prophecy of this book. 8 And I John am he that heard and saw these things. And when I heard and saw, I fell down to [2]worship before the feet of the angel that showed me these things. 9 And he saith unto me, See thou do it not: I am a fellow-servant with thee and with thy brethren the prophets, and with them that keep the words of this book: [2]worship God.

10 And he saith unto me, Seal not up the words of the prophecy of this book; for the time is at hand. 11 He that is unrighteous, let him do unrighteousness [3]still: and he that is filthy, let him be made filthy [3]still: and he that is righteous, let him do righteousness [3]still: and he that is holy, let him be made holy [3]still. 12 Behold, I come quickly; and my [4]reward is with me, to render to each man according as his work is. 13 I am the Alpha and the Omega, the first and the last, the beginning and the end. 14 Blessed are they that wash their robes, that they may have [5]the right to come to the tree of life, and may enter in by the [6]gates into the city.

[1]Gr. *bondservants*
[2]See marginal note on Chap. 13.12
[3]Or, *yet more*
[4]Or, *wages*
[5]Or, *the authority over.* Comp. Chap. 6.8
[6]Gr. *portals*

15 Without are the dogs, and the sorcerers, and the fornicators, and the murderers, and the idolaters, and every one that loveth and [7]maketh a lie.

16 I Jesus have sent mine angel to testify unto you these things [8]for the churches. I am the root and the offspring of David, the bright, the morning star.

17 [9]And the Spirit and the bride say, Come. And he that heareth, let him say, Come. And he that is athirst, let him come: he that will, let him take the water of life freely.

[7]Or, *doeth*. Comp. Chap. 21.27
[8]Gr. *over*
[9]Or, *Both*

18 I testify unto every man that heareth the words of the prophecy of this book, If any man shall add [10]unto them, God shall add [10]unto him the plagues which are written in this book:

19 and if any man shall take away from the words of the book of this prophecy, God shall take away his part from the tree of life, and out of the holy city, [11]which are written in this book.

20 He who testifieth these things saith, Yea: I come quickly. Amen: come, Lord Jesus.

21 The grace of the Lord Jesus [12]be [13]with the saints. Amen.

[10]Gr. *upon*
[11]Or, even from *the things which are written*
[12]Some ancient authorities add *Christ*
[13]Two ancient authorities read *with all*

Vers. 6-21. FINAL TESTIMONY, INVITATION, WARNING, PROMISE AND BENEDICTION.

Ver. 6. *"And he said unto me"*,—Who is speaking here? The angel of Chap. 1.1 (L. Eb. St. Mil. Weid.), or the angel of Chap. 21.9 (D. Bl. Vol. Bar. Dus. and the majority), or *"he that sitteth on the throne"* as in Chap. 21.5, or Christ, as in verse 16. The second view, the angel of Chap. 21.9, is perhaps the right one.

"these words",—i. e., the whole book. (L. Mil. Dus. Bar. Weid.)

"faithful and true",—The absolute certainty that the testimony John had received is trustworthy and true, and could be fully relied upon.

"the spirits of the prophets",—Are we to understand the spirits of the prophets themselves (A. F. St. Dus.), or the Spirit of God by which the prophets were inspired (D. Mil.)? The latter view is doubtless the correct one. By *"spirits"* is meant, of course, the spirit of each prophet, which God by His Holy Spirit inspires and directs.

"his servants",—i. e., believers in general, by the instrumentality of John through the visions as interpreted by the angels.

"shortly come to pass",—(See Chap. 1.1).

Ver. 7. *"I come quickly"*,—Words spoken no doubt in corroboration of the *"shortly come to pass"* of the previous verse, and spoken by the angel in the name of the coming Christ. (A. Sw. St. Dus. Bar. Weid.) Milligan thinks that Christ Himself speaks.

"keepeth the word of the prophecy of this book",—The word *"keepeth"* may mean "to remember", "to keep in the mind" (St.), or it may mean "to obey" (Mil.). The latter idea is, no doubt, the main one, although in it the former must be included. Stuart supports this view from the fact that the record is mainly prediction and precepts to be obeyed, and says the blessings to be derived from this storing of the mind with the saying of this book are those which arise from the promises and encouragement which are contained in the book. The book referred to is not the whole Bible (Sad.), but the now all but completed roll lying on the Seer's knee.

Ver. 8. *"fell down to worship"*,—Ebrard is entirely wrong in thinking that John is here merely recapitulating what had taken place in Chap. 19.10. Auberlen says that rapturous emotion, gratitude and adoration at the prospect of the future glory of the Church transported John out of himself so that he all but fell into an unjustifiable act.

Fausset says it is not likely that John when having been once reproved for his intention of worshipping an angel would fall a second time into the same error; but the explanation given of this passage by Fausset is rather weak and cannot be accepted. He says in the former instance John fell down at the feet of the angel to worship *him*, but that here he fell down at the angel's feet to worship, that is to worship God. It is better with others (St. Bar. Dus.) to think that the words, "*I come quickly*", which he had just heard might easily have given rise in John's mind to the suspicion that the one speaking was Christ Himself, although perhaps Milligan is right, when he says, "We need not wonder that John should do it again. Such had been the glory of the revelation that a mistake of this kind might easily be made more than once." If the angel speaking here was the same as the one in Chap. 21.9, it looks like John would have known he was not the Christ.

Ver. 9. (See notes on Chap. 19.10 where almost the identical words are found.)

Ver. 10. The book is not to be sealed up because it is to be put to immediate use, the time being at hand. Unlike the book of Daniel (Dan. 10.4), which was to be sealed because the time was for many days, it is to be diffused, read and explained.

"*the time is at hand*",—There is not a moment to be lost, the Lord is at hand. Let all who believe prepare themselves for His coming.

Ver. 11. (See Ezek. 3.27). "The punishment of sin is sin and the reward of holiness is holiness," says Fausset.

Alford has well commented on this verse, "The saying has solemn irony of it (compare Matt. 26.45), the idea being that the time is so short that there is hardly any room for any change, but down in its depths the lesson conveyed is, 'Change while yet there is time'."

Ver. 12. Jesus is now plainly speaking in His own name. It is entirely out of keeping with the claims that are made to regard the speaker as the angel, as a few have done. If the angel should be regarded as the speaker, he must of course be considered as speaking, not in his own, but in the name of Jesus. But all interpreters of note, regard the speaker as Jesus Himself.

"*according as his work is*",—It is faith alone that saves us, but we are rewarded according to our works.

Ver. 13. (See notes on Chaps. 1.8,17 and 21.6). These are plainly the words of Christ. (L. F. Sw. St. Sad. Bar. Sim. Weid.) Dusterdieck thinks God is the speaker, or rather seems to be in verse 13, because those expressions were used of God elsewhere; he also thinks that Christ is the speaker of verse 12, or rather seems to be. Because this seems to be the case, he says it will not do to represent the angel as speaking first in the name of Christ and then in the name of God, and to think of Christ and God themselves as actually speaking introduces too many changes in the speakers; therefore Dusterdieck thinks that John himself speaks these words of verses 12 and 13, "after the manner of the ancient prophets, and thus in two compendious Divine declarations fixes the fundamental thoughts of this entire prophecy". Dusterdieck says it is true that these words were in other places spoken by God Himself; but this is no reason why Christ cannot use the same declaration of Himself. (See Rom. 11.36 and Col. 1.16.)

Ver. 14.   "wash their robes",—This reading must be preferred to that of the Authorized Version, "keep his (God's) commandments". All whose sins are forgiven and whose names are therefore written in the Book of Life, have a right to enter into the city and eat of the tree of life.

Ver. 15.   Dusterdieck, Benson and some others take the words in the sense of a command. "Out with the dogs," etc. But this not only destroys the clearness of the antithesis which the region of the lost presents to Paradise, but furthermore, the dogs, etc., have already been cast out.

"dogs',—The dog was unclean and therefore odious to the Jews, and is used in this sense as representing impure, filthy persons.

Ver. 16.   Jesus attests the good faith of His angel messenger, referring now perhaps to the angel of Chap. 1.1. (St. Bar. Weid.)

"unto you",—Some (Hen. and Dus.) refer this to the prophets, but it is more likely that it is to be taken in the sense of the "servants of God" as in verse 6, ministers and people in the seven Churches, representative churches, and through you, to testify to all Christians of all places. (F. L.)

"for the churches",—Not the seven churches only, but the Christian churches throughout the world. The Authorized Version reads "in the churches". But the preposition, and the more important and proper meaning is "for the churches", on "in reference to the churches", on "on account of the churches". (St. Zu. Bar. Dus. Hen. Weid.)

"A book for the congregation; not a book merely for the few and for a select circle, is this book of prophecy," says Ludhardt.

"the root",—Not the root in the sense that David sprang from him, as a tree does from a root, but in the sense that he was the "root-shoot" of David, or that He Himself sprang from David, as a sprout starts up from a decayed and fallen tree. The meaning is that He was the true Messianic progeny of David foretold in Scriptures, i. e., the product of the root.

"the offspring",—Plainly stating what the other word set forth in a figure of speech. He is the root and the offspring, the beginning and the end of the whole economy associated with the Davidic family.

"the bright, the morning star",—(See Chap. 2.28, where the meaning is quite akin to this, this being an interpretation of that.)   He brings in the everlasting day. He is the star that never sets.

Ver. 17.   By some this verse is taken as a reply to Christ's previous words, spoken by the Seer in the name of the Holy Spirit and the bride, the Church. (A. D. Eb. Hen. Dus.) This is perhaps the case, as it would be unusual to find Jesus thus addressing Himself, "Come, Lord Jesus", for this, the word "come" in this instance really means.

Lange, on the other hand, refers the whole verse to John as the speaker, remarking that John utters his own "Come, Lord Jesus" in verse 20, while the latter part of our verse seems to demand the Lord Christ as the speaker.

Barnes makes the speaker throughout the entire verse to be Christ and avoids the difficulty mentioned above by making the word *"come"* mean an invitation to the Gospel throughout the entire verse.

Milligan thinks of the Church speaking in the first clause, of John speaking in the second clause, and of Christ speaking in the last two clauses. But such an interchange of speakers in a single verse can hardly be appreciated.

"the Spirit",—The Holy Spirit who inspires the prophets and dwells in the Church, the bride herself.

"he that heareth",—This may be taken as hearing the cry of the Spirit and the bride (A. Sad.), or as hearing the contents of this book wherever it is read (St. Sw.), which latter is perhaps the better idea.

Milligan says that "these words must be taken in the same sense as the similar words in Chap. 21.6. The thirst is of one who has already been refreshed for deeper, fuller draughts. The persons referred to are believers within the city, within the reach of the water of life." Lange, however, we think, is nearer the truth when he says, "It is the last full evangelic tone in the New Testament." It is the invitation given for the last time to the weary and heavy laden to come and drink of the water of salvation.

Ver. 18. *"every one that heareth"*,—i. e., those reading the book or present where it is read. It was thus designed to be read aloud in the churches.

It is not said who the speaker is here but the majority of the commentators (B. St. Mil. Wor. Dus. Bar. Weid.) refer him to John himself.

Swete says, "It is not uncommon for writers to protect their works by adding a solemn abjuration to the scribes to correct the copies carefully, and in no case to mutilate or interpolate the original. If the solemn warning of the present verse was intended in this sense, it has signally failed, for in no other book of the New Testament is the text so uncertain as in Revelation. It is, however, no error of judgment that is condemned, nor merely intellectual fault, but the deliberate falsification or misinterpretation."

Says Wordsworth, "Here is a prophetic protest against the spurious Revelations forged by false teachers in the name of the Apostles." Stuart says, "The practice of tampering with books of such a nature must have been somewhat frequent in the region where the Apocalypse was published; otherwise there would be something not perfectly natural in the severity of the interdict before us."

Simcox says, "The curse denounced is on those who interpolate false doctrines in the prophecy, or who neglect essential ones; not on transcribers who might unadvisedly interpolate or omit something from the text. The curse, if understood in the latter sense, has been remarkably ineffective, for the common text of this book is more corrupt, and the true text oftener doubtful, than in any other part of the New Testament."

Some (V. Bl.) say the threat is directed against careless transcribers, while others (D. Ew.) say it is against oral inaccuracies of repetition, and

Dusterdieck and Alford agree with Swete in referring it to deliberate falsification. Hengstenberg says it is against anything that affects the actual kernel of the book.

Fausset has remarked, "As in the beginning of this book (Chap. 1.3) a blessing was promised to the devout, obedient student of it, so now at its close a curse is denounced against those who add to or take from it."

Sadler thinks that by *"book"* the whole New Testament was meant. But when John wrote there was as yet no united whole New Testament, and he could not therefore have had this in mind, and the reference is to be immediately referred to this book of Revelation.

Ver. 19. Says Alford, "This is at least an awful warning both to those who add to it by irrelevant and trifling interpretations."

Ver. 20. Christ is the speaker in the first part of the verse and John in the last. The Lord Jesus answers, as it were, the cry of the Spirit and the bride and him that heareth. They had bidden Him come (verse 17), and here He replies that He is coming quickly. Christ Himself here bears testimony, that is, vouches for the truth of what John had disclosed.

Ver. 21. The following benediction' is the usual form of benediction in the epistles of the New Testament, and it no doubt has special reference to the blessings disclosed and promised in the book before us. With the benediction of grace the Apocalypse opens and with the same benediction it closes.

For those who desire the satisfaction of knowing what authorities uphold the various interpretations, a list of those consulted and quoted in the preceding pages is here appended. The economy of space makes necessary the use of abbreviations.

A.	Alford	Cra.	Cramer
Ab.	Aben Ezra	Crav.	Craven
Aba.	Abarbenel	Cre.	Cremer
Af.	Africanus	Cum.	Cumming
Al.	Alexander	Cun.	Cuninghame
Alc.	Alcasar	Cy.	Cyril
Am.	Ambrose	Cyp.	Cyprian
Amm.	Ammon		
An.	Angus	D.	De Wette
And.	Andreas	Da.	Davidson
Aq.	Aquila	Dat.	Dathe
Ar.	Aretius	Dau.	Daubuz
Are.	Aretas	Del.	Delitzsch
Au.	Auberlen	Den.	Dennett
Aug.	Augustine	Der.	Dererer
Augu.	Augusti	Di.	Didymus
		Die.	Dietlein
B.	Bengel	Din.	Dindorf
Ba.	Baumgarten	Do.	Doderlein
Bah.	Bahr	Dod.	Dods
Bal.	Balduin	Dodd.	Doddridge
Bar.	Barnes	Dor.	Dorner
Bark.	Barkeyus	Dr.	Driedo
Bau.	Bauer	Dre.	Dreschler
Baud.	Baudissen	Dri.	Driver
Baum.	Baumlein	Dru.	Drusius
Be.	Bede	Dus.	Dusterdieck
Bec.	Beckhaus	Dw.	Dwight
Ben.	Benson		
Ber.	Bertholdt	E.	Ellicott
Bert.	Bertheau	Ea.	Eadie
Bes.	Besser	Eb.	Ebrard
Bez.	Beza	Ec.	Eckerman
Bi.	Birks	Ed.	Edwards
Bic.	Bickersteth	Ei.	Eichorn
Bil.	Bilroth	El.	Elliott
Bis.	Bisping	Els.	Elsner
Bl.	Bleek	Em.	Emmerling
Bla.	Blackstone	Ep.	Episcopius
Blo.	Bloomfield	Eph.	Ephrem
Bo.	Bochart	Er.	Erdman, W. J.
Boe.	Boehme	Era	Eramus
Bol.	Bolten	Erd.	Erdman, Chas. R.
Bon.	Bonnet	Ern.	Ernesti
Bor.	Borneman	Es	Estius
Bos.	Bossuet	Eu.	Eusebius
Bou.	Bouman	Eut.	Euthymius
Boy.	Boyd	Ev.	Evans
Br.	Brightman	Ew.	Ewald
Bra.	Braune		
Bre.	Brentius	F.	Fausset
Bred.	Bredencamp	Fa.	Farrar
Bret.	Bretschneider	Fai.	Fairbairn
Bro.	Brown (David)	Fi.	Fischer
Brou.	Broughton	Fl.	Flatt
Bru.	Bruckner	Fle.	Fleck
Bu.	Buddeus	Fo.	Forsyth
Bul.	Bullinger	For.	Forerius
Bun.	Bunsen	Fr.	Fronmuller
Bur.	Burger	Fra.	Franc
		Fri.	Fritzsche
C.	Calvin	Fro.	Fromann
Ca.	Calovius	From.	Fromond
Cal.	Calmet	Fu.	Fuller
Cali.	Calixtus	Fue.	Fuerst
Cap.	Cappellus		
Car.	Carpzovius	G.	Godet
Carp.	Carpenter	Gab.	Gaebelein
Cas.	Caspari	Gar	Gartner
Cast.	Castalio	Gau.	Gaussen
Ch.	Chambers	Geb.	Gebser
Cha.	Chaldee	Gebh.	Gebhardt
Chal.	Chalmers	Gei.	Geier
Che.	Cheyne	Geo.	Georgii
Chr.	Chrysostom	Ger.	Gerlach
Chri.	Christiani	Gerh.	Gerhard
Cl.	Clark	Ges.	Gesenius
Cla.	Clarius	Gi.	Gill
Cle.	Clericus	Gl.	Gloag
Co.	Cowles	Gla.	Glasgow
Coc.	Cocceius	Glo.	Gloecken
Con.	Conybeare	Gloe.	Gloeckler
Cor.	Corrodi	Goe.	Goeschel
Cora.	Coray	Gor.	Gordon, A. J.
Cr.	Credner	Gr.	Greene

Gra.	Gray
Gri.	Griesbach
Gro.	Grotius
Gui.	Guinness
H.	Hodge
Ha.	Hackett
Hah.	Hahn
Ham.	Hammond
Har.	Harless
Hart.	Hartman
Has.	Hasse
Hav.	Havernick
He.	Henderson
Heb.	Hebart
Heg.	Hegel
Hei.	Heinrichs
Hein.	Heinrici
Hel.	Helmst
Hen.	Hengstenberg
Hend.	Hendewerk
Heng.	Hengle
Hens.	Hensler
Her.	Herder
Hes.	Hesychius
Heu.	Heubner
Heum.	Heumann
Hey.	Heydenreich
Hi.	Hilary
Hil.	Hilgenfeld
Hila.	Hilarianus
Hit.	Hitzig
Ho	Horsley
Hoe.	Hoelemann
Hof.	Hofman
Hol.	Holzhausen
Hols.	Holsten
Holt.	Holtzman
Hor.	Horneius
Hot.	Hottinger
How.	Howson
Hu.	Huther
Hun.	Hunnius
Hus.	Huschke
Ire.	Irenaeus
It.	Itala
J.	Jacobus
Ja.	Jahn
Jac.	Jachmann
Jam.	Jamieson
Jan.	Jansen
Jar.	Jarchi
Jer.	Jerome
Jo.	Joachin
Jow.	Jowett
Ju.	Junius
Jus.	Justin
K.	Keil
Ka.	Kamphausen
Kae.	Kaeuffer
Ke.	Keim
Kel.	Kellogg
Ken.	Kendrick
Ki.	Kirkpatrick
Kim.	Kimchi
Kl.	Klieforth
Kle.	Kleinert
Klee.	Klee
Kli.	Kling
Klo.	Klostermann
Klu.	Kluge
Kn.	Knobel
Kna.	Knapp
Ko.	Kostlin
Koc.	Koch
Koe.	Koehler
Kol.	Kollner
Kop.	Koppe
Kos.	Koster
Kr.	Kranichfeld
Kra.	Krauss
Kre.	Krebs

727

Ku. .... Kuenen
Kui. .... Kuinoel
Kur. .... Kurtz
Ky. .... Kypke

L. .... Lange
La. .... Lagarde
Lac. .... Lachmann
Lact. .... Lactantius
Lam. .... Lampe
Lap. .... Lapide
Lau. .... Laurentius
Le. .... Lechler
Len. .... Lengerke
Ley. .... Leyser
Li. .... Lightfoot
Lil. .... Lillie
Lim. .... Limborch
Lin. .... Lindsay
Lo. .... Lowth
Lor. .... Lorinus
Lu. .... Lunneman
Luc. .... Lucke
Lud. .... Ludhardt
Lum. .... Lumby
Lut. .... Luther
Lutt. .... Lutterbach
Luz. .... Luzzatto
Ly. .... Lyra

M. .... Meyer
Ma. .... Maurer
Mac. .... Macknight
Mack. .... Mackintosh
Mai. .... Maier
Mal. .... Malondatus
Mar. .... Marck
Marc. .... Marckius
Mat. .... Matthies
Mau. .... Maurice
May. .... Mayer
Mc. .... McFadden
McC. .... McCurdy
Me. .... Mede
Mei. .... Meier
Mel. .... Melancthon
Men. .... Menken
Mi. .... Michaelis
Mil. .... Milligan
Mo. .... Moule
Mol. .... Moll
Mold. .... Moldenhauer
Moo. .... Moore
Moor. .... Moorehead
Mor. .... Morgan
Mos. .... Mosheim
Mu. .... Murphy
Mue. .... Muenster
Mul. .... Muller
Mus. .... Musculus
My. .... Myberg

N. .... Newton, Isaac
Na. .... Nagelsbach
Ne. .... Newcome
Nea. .... Neander
Neu. .... Neuman
New .... Newton, Bishop
Ni. .... Nitzsch
Nie. .... Nielsen
No. .... Nowack
Noe. .... Noesselt
Noy. .... Noyes

O. .... Olshausen
Oe. .... Oecolampadius
Oec. .... Oecumenius
Of. .... Offerhaus
Ol. .... Olearius
Oo. .... Oosterzee
Or. .... Orelli
Ori. .... Origen
Ort. .... Ortenburg
Os. .... Osiander
Ow. .... Owen

P. .... Perowne
Pa. .... Packard
Pau. .... Paulus
Pe. .... Peshito
Pei. .... Peirce
Pel. .... Pelagius
Pelt .... Pelt
Pet. .... Petingill
Peta. .... Petavius
Pf. .... Pfaff
Pfl. .... Pfleiderer
Ph. .... Philippi
Pho. .... Photius
Pi. .... Piscator
Pl. .... Plummer
Pli. .... Plitt
Plu. .... Plumptre
Po. .... Polanus
Poo. .... Poole
Por. .... Porphry
Pot. .... Pott
Pre. .... Pressel
Pri. .... Prideaux
Prim. .... Primasius
Pu. .... Pusey

R. .... Riddle
Ram. .... Rambonnet
Ramb. .... Rambach
Re. .... Reinbeck
Red. .... Redepenning
Rei. .... Reinke
Reic. .... Reiche
Reu. .... Reuss
Ri. .... Rickli
Rie. .... Riehm
Rig. .... Riggenbach
Rin. .... Rinck
Ro. .... Rohling
Rob. .... Robinson
Roe. .... Roesch
Ros. .... Rosenmuller
Ru. .... Rueckert
Rup. .... Rupert
Ry. .... Ryle

S. .... Stier
Sa. .... Sander
Sad. .... Sadler
Sal. .... Salmond
Salm. .... Salmeron
Say. .... Sayce
Sca. .... Scaliger
Sch. .... Schmoller
Scha. .... Schaff
Schau. .... Schaubach
Sche. .... Schegg
Schen. .... Schenkle
Schi. .... Schimidius
Schl. .... Schleusner
Schlei. .... Schleiermacher
Schli. .... Schlichting
Schm. .... Schmid
Schn. .... Schneckenburger
Scho. .... Schottgen
Schot. .... Schott
Schr. .... Schroeder
Schu. .... Schultz
Schw. .... Schweizer
Sco. .... Scofield
Se. .... Secker
Sem. .... Semler
Sep. .... Septuagint
Sey. .... Seyffarth
Sim. .... Simcox
Sm. .... Smith, G. Adam
So. .... Socinus
Som. .... Sommelius
Sp. .... Spener
Spa. .... Spanheim
St. .... Stuart
Sta. .... Starke
Stae. .... Staehelin
Stan. .... Stanley
Ste. .... Steudel
Stei. .... Steinhofer

Steig. .... Steiger
Stein. .... Steinmeyer
Steinf. .... Steinfass
Sten. .... Stengel
Sto. .... Storr
Str. .... Strong
Stra. .... Strauss
Strac. .... Strachey
Stu. .... Studer
Sw. .... Swete
Syr. .... Syriac

Tar. .... Targum
Ter. .... Tertullian
The. .... Theodoret
Then. .... Thenius
Theo. .... Theophylact
Thi. .... Thiersch
Thie. .... Thiele
Tho. .... Tholuck
Ti. .... Tischendorf
Til. .... Tillotson
To. .... Toletus
Tor. .... Torrey
Tr. .... Trench
Tre. .... Treggeles
Trem. .... Tremellius
Tur. .... Turretin
Ty. .... Tychsen

U. .... Uri
Um. .... Umbreit
Us. .... Usteri

V. .... Vitringa
Va. .... Vatka
Val. .... Valla
Van. .... VanDyke
Vat. .... Vatablus
Van. .... Vaughan
Vel. .... Velthusen
Vic. .... Victorinus
Vin. .... Vincent
Vo. .... Volck
Vog. .... Vogel
Vol. .... Volkmar
Vor. .... Vorstius
Vul. .... Vulgate

W. .... Westcott
W-W. Webster and Wilkinson
We. .... Weizel
Wei. .... Weiss
Weid. .... Weidner
Weis. .... Weisenbach
Wet. .... Wetstein
Wh. .... Whitby
Whe. .... Whedon
Wi. .... Wiesinger
Wic. .... Wichelhaus
Wie. .... Wiesler
Wil. .... Willett
Will. .... Williams
Win. .... Winer
Winz. .... Winzer
Wit. .... Witsius
Witt. .... Wittich
Wo. .... Wolfendale
Woe. .... Woerner
Wol. .... Wolf
Wor. .... Wordsworth
Wr. .... Wright
Wu. .... Wunsche

Za. .... Zachariae
Zah. .... Zahn
Zan. .... Zanchius
Ze. .... Zeis
Zeg. .... Zeger
Zel. .... Zeltner
Zig. .... Zigabemus
Zo. .... Zoeckler
Zu. .... Zundel
Zue. .... Zuellig
Zw. .... Zwingli